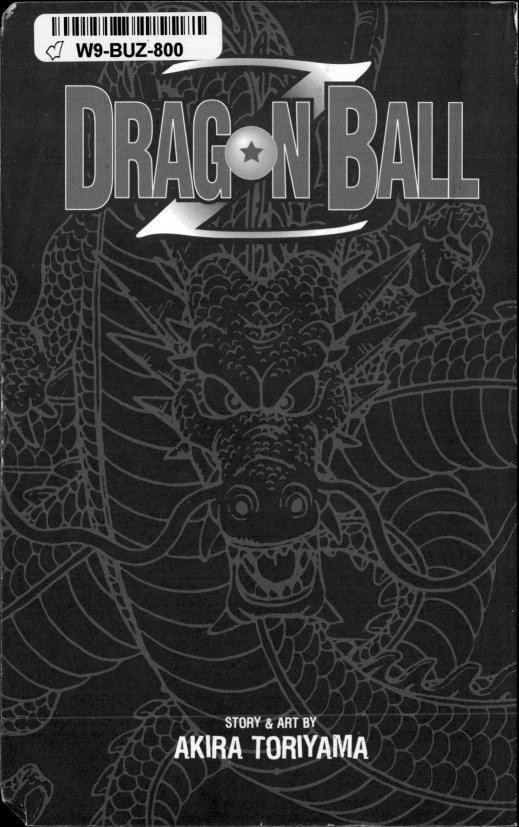

DRAGON BALL Z

STORY & ART BY

AKIRA TORIYAMA

Dragon Ball Z
Volume 9
VIZBIG Edition

STORY AND ART BY
AKIRA TORIYAMA

Translation **Lillian Olsen**
Touch-up Art & Lettering **Wayne Truman, Eric Erbes, HudsonYards**
Shonen Jump Series Design **Sean Lee**
VIZBIG Edition Design **Frances O. Liddell**
Shonen Jump Series Editor **Jason Thompson**
VIZBIG Edition Editor **Daniel Gillespie**

Printed in China

Published by VIZ Media, LLC
P.O. Box 77010
San Francisco, CA 94107

11
First printing, October 2010
Eleventh printing, December 2022

VIZ
MEDIA
www.viz.com

大 VIZBIG
EDITION

VOLUME 25
LAST HERO STANDING!

VOLUME 26
FAREWELL,
DRAGON WORLD!

STORY & ART BY
AKIRA TORIYAMA

SHONEN JUMP MANGA . VIZBIG EDITION

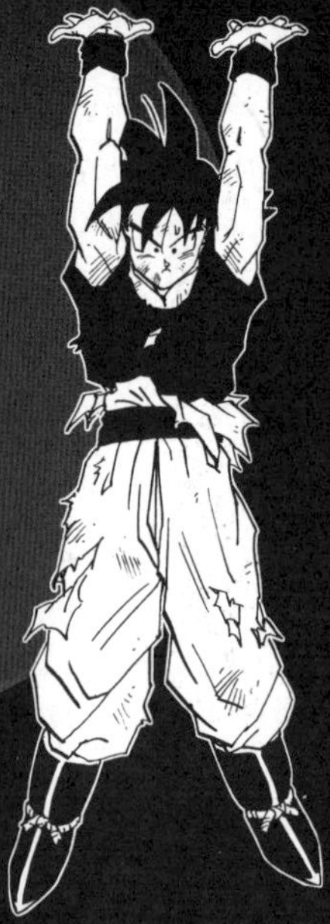

CONTENTS

VOLUME 26
FAREWELL, DRAGON WORLD!

CAST OF CHARACTERS

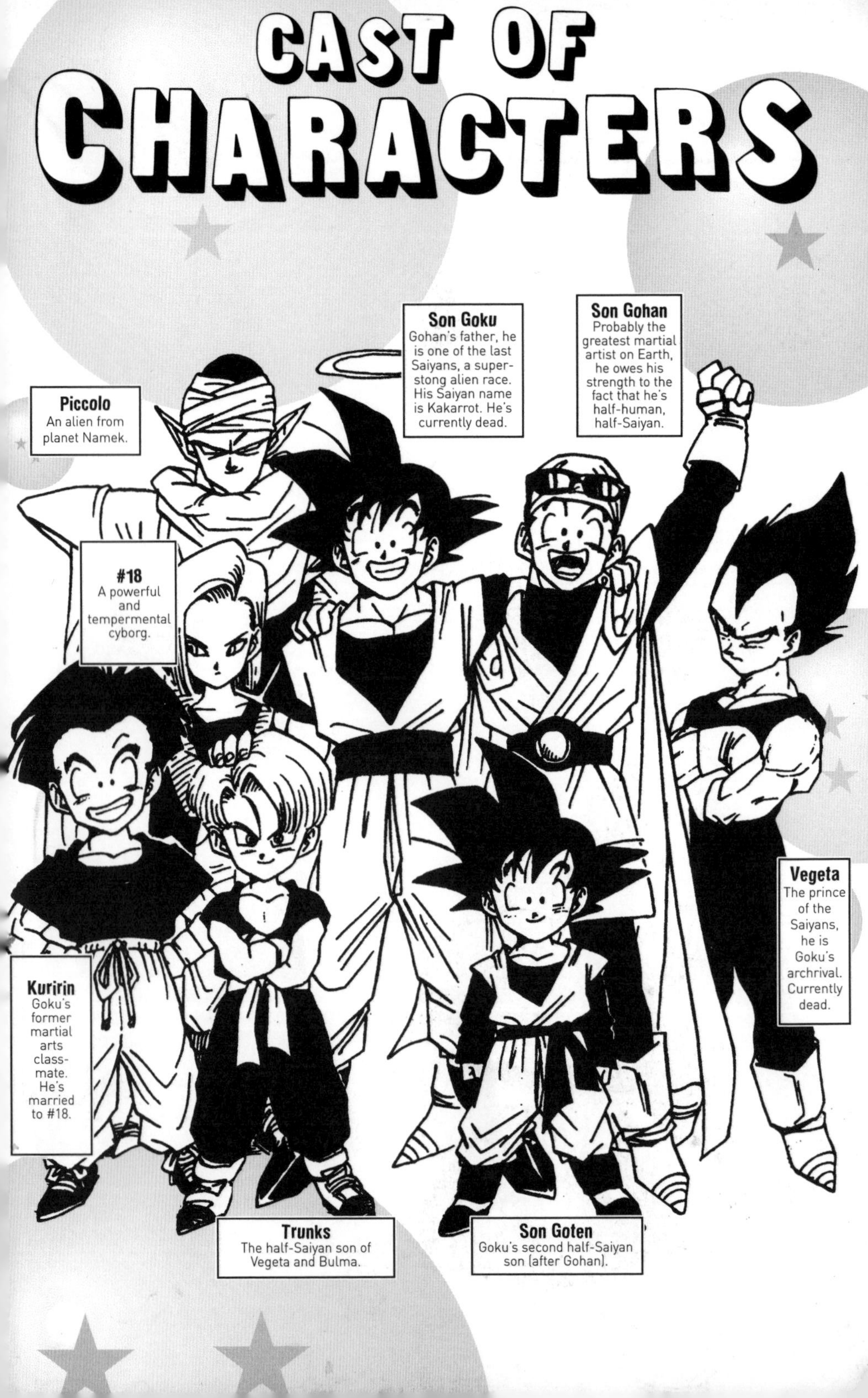

Son Goku
Gohan's father, he is one of the last Saiyans, a super-stong alien race. His Saiyan name is Kakarrot. He's currently dead.

Son Gohan
Probably the greatest martial artist on Earth, he owes his strength to the fact that he's half-human, half-Saiyan.

Piccolo
An alien from planet Namek.

#18
A powerful and tempermental cyborg.

Vegeta
The prince of the Saiyans, he is Goku's archrival. Currently dead.

Kuririn
Goku's former martial arts classmate. He's married to #18.

Trunks
The half-Saiyan son of Vegeta and Bulma.

Son Goten
Goku's second half-Saiyan son (after Gohan).

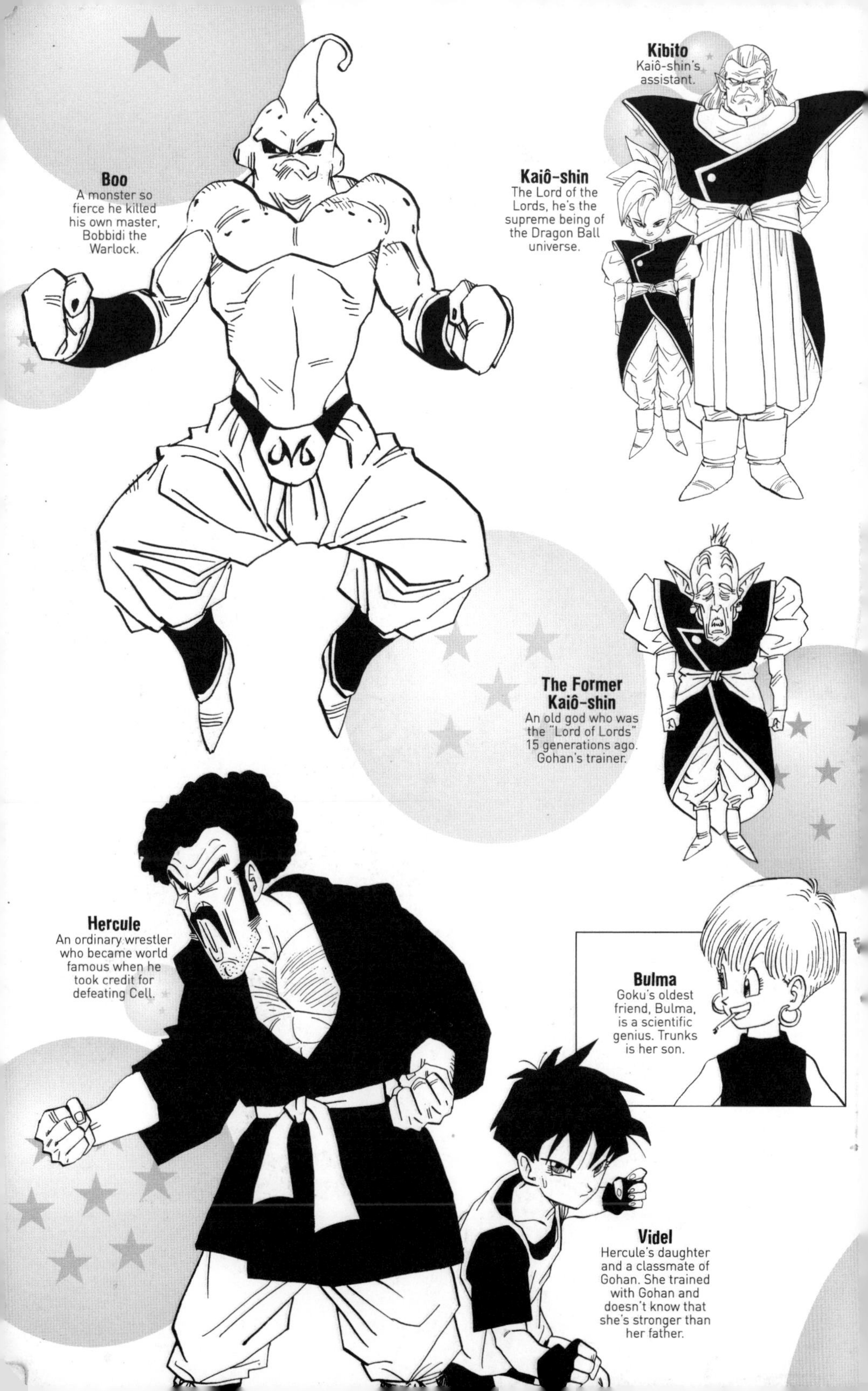
Kibito
Kaiô-shin's assistant.
Kaiô-shin
The Lord of the Lords, he's the supreme being of the Dragon Ball universe.
Boo
A monster so fierce he killed his own master, Bobbidi the Warlock.
The Former Kaiô-shin
An old god who was the "Lord of Lords" 15 generations ago. Gohan's trainer.
Bulma
Goku's oldest friend, Bulma, is a scientific genius. Trunks is her son.
Hercule
An ordinary wrestler who became world famous when he took credit for defeating Cell.
Videl
Hercule's daughter and a classmate of Gohan. She trained with Gohan and doesn't know that she's stronger than her father.

DragonBallZ

VOLUME 25

LAST HERO STANDING!

DBZ:292 · The New, Terrible Boo

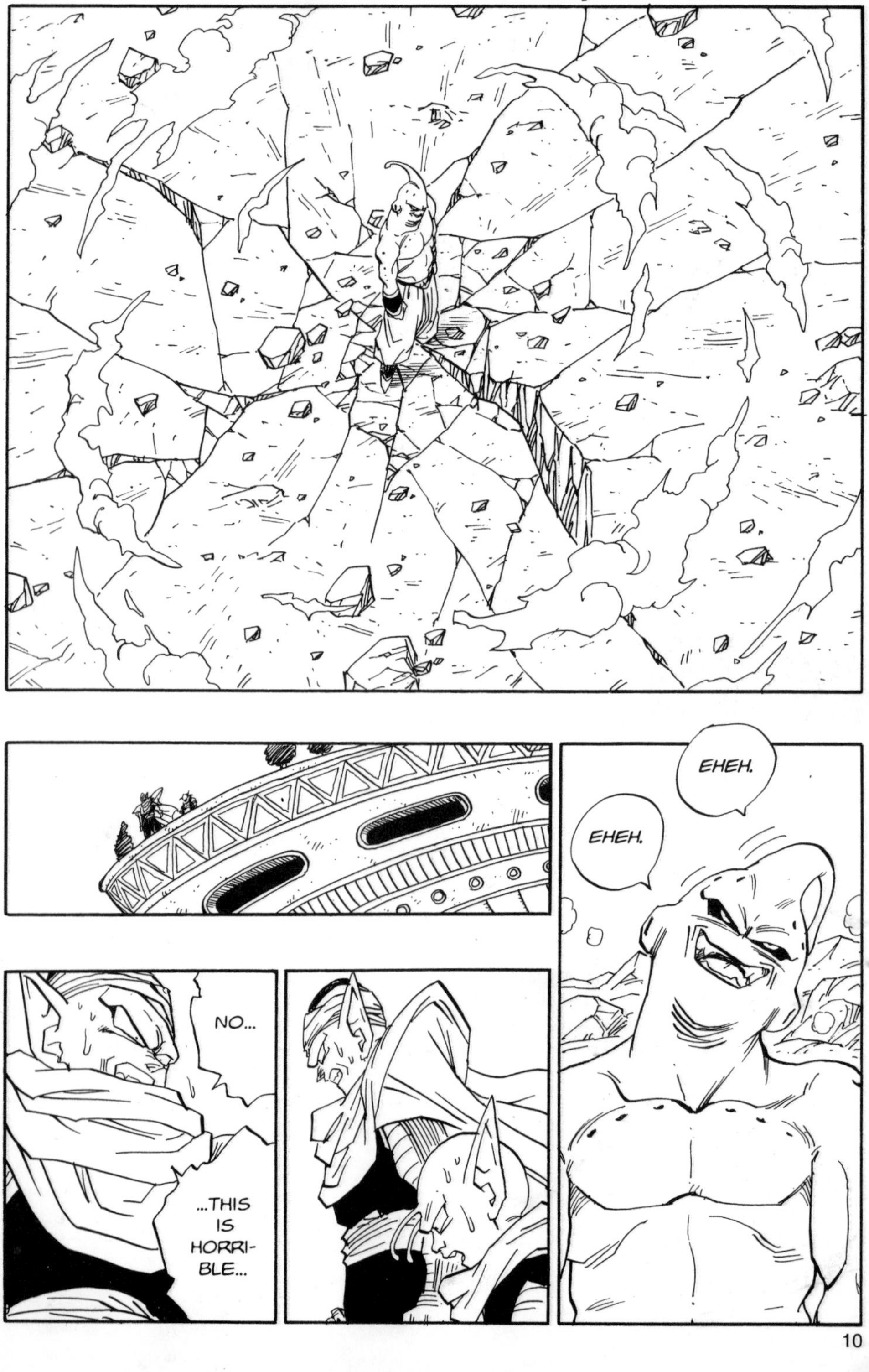

EHEH.
EHEH.
NO...
...THIS IS HORRIBLE...

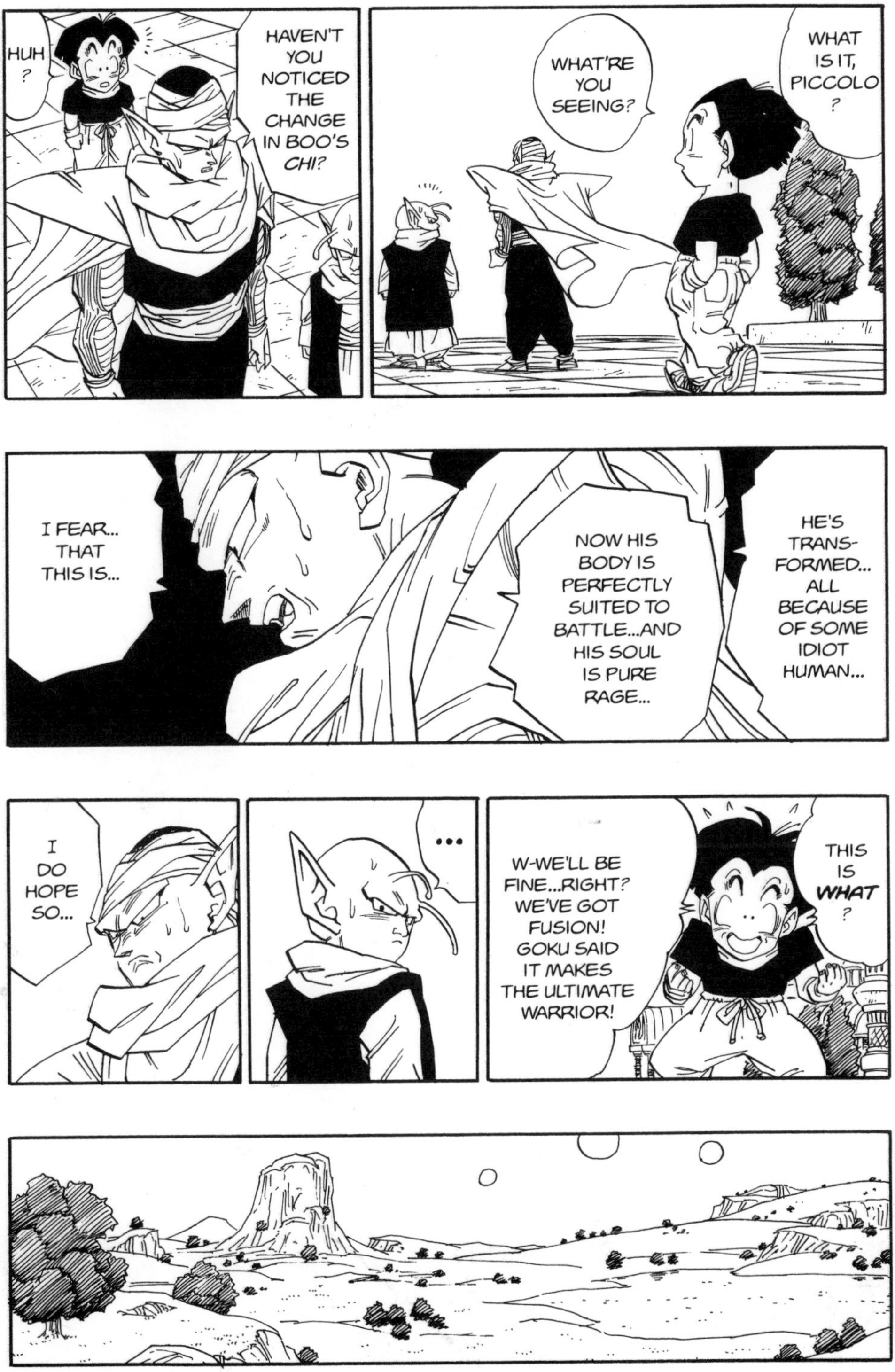
WHAT IS IT, PICCOLO?
WHAT'RE YOU SEEING?
HAVEN'T YOU NOTICED THE CHANGE IN BOO'S *CHI*?
HUH?
HE'S TRANSFORMED... ALL BECAUSE OF SOME IDIOT HUMAN...
NOW HIS BODY IS PERFECTLY SUITED TO BATTLE...AND HIS SOUL IS PURE RAGE...
I FEAR... THAT THIS IS...
THIS IS ***WHAT***?
W-WE'LL BE FINE...RIGHT? WE'VE GOT FUSION! GOKU SAID IT MAKES THE ULTIMATE WARRIOR!
...
I DO HOPE SO...

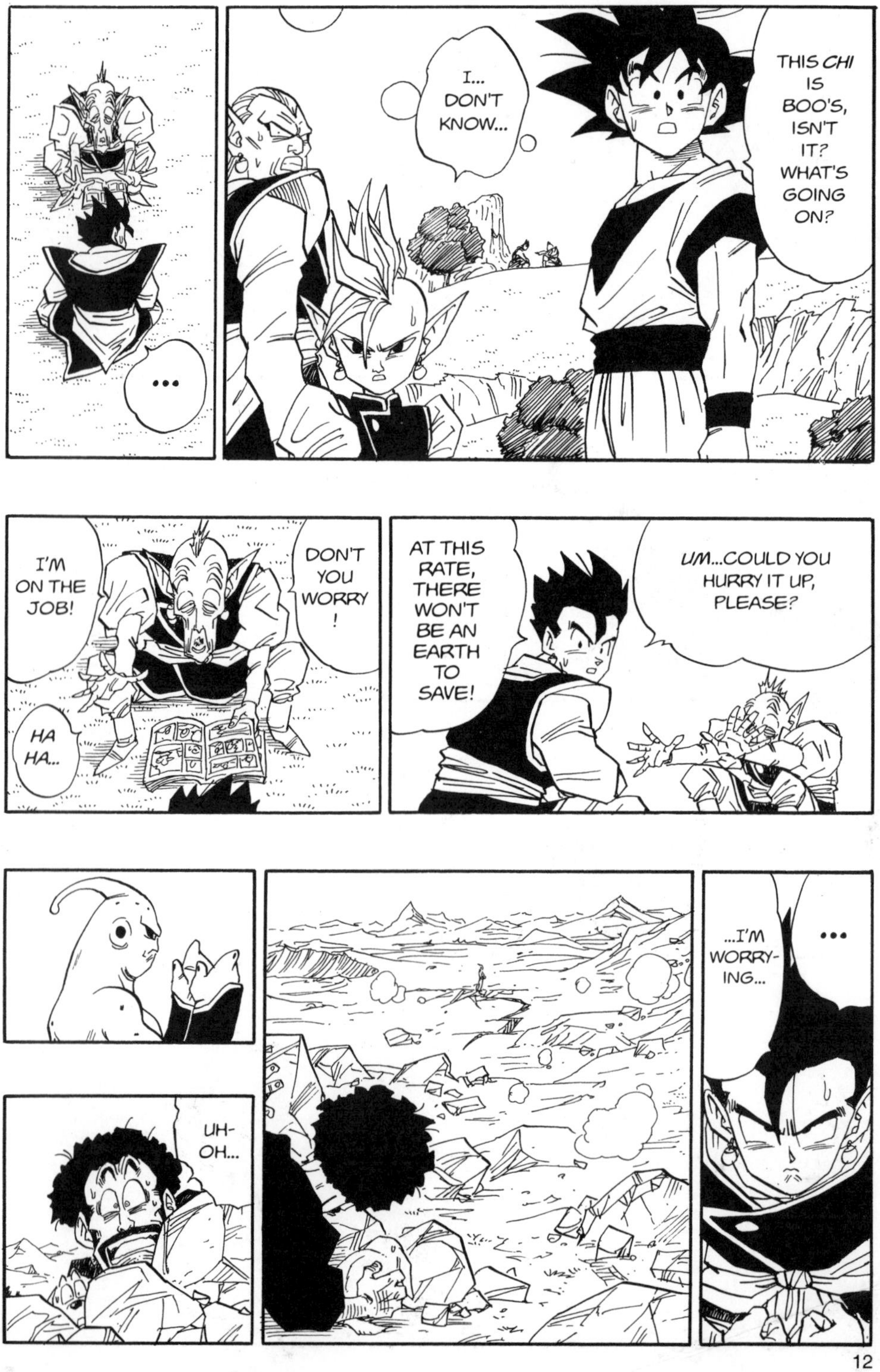
THIS *CHI* IS BOO'S, ISN'T IT? WHAT'S GOING ON?
I... DON'T KNOW...
...
UM...COULD YOU HURRY IT UP, PLEASE?
AT THIS RATE, THERE WON'T BE AN EARTH TO SAVE!
DON'T YOU WORRY!
I'M ON THE JOB!
HA HA...
...
...I'M WORRY-ING...
UH-OH...

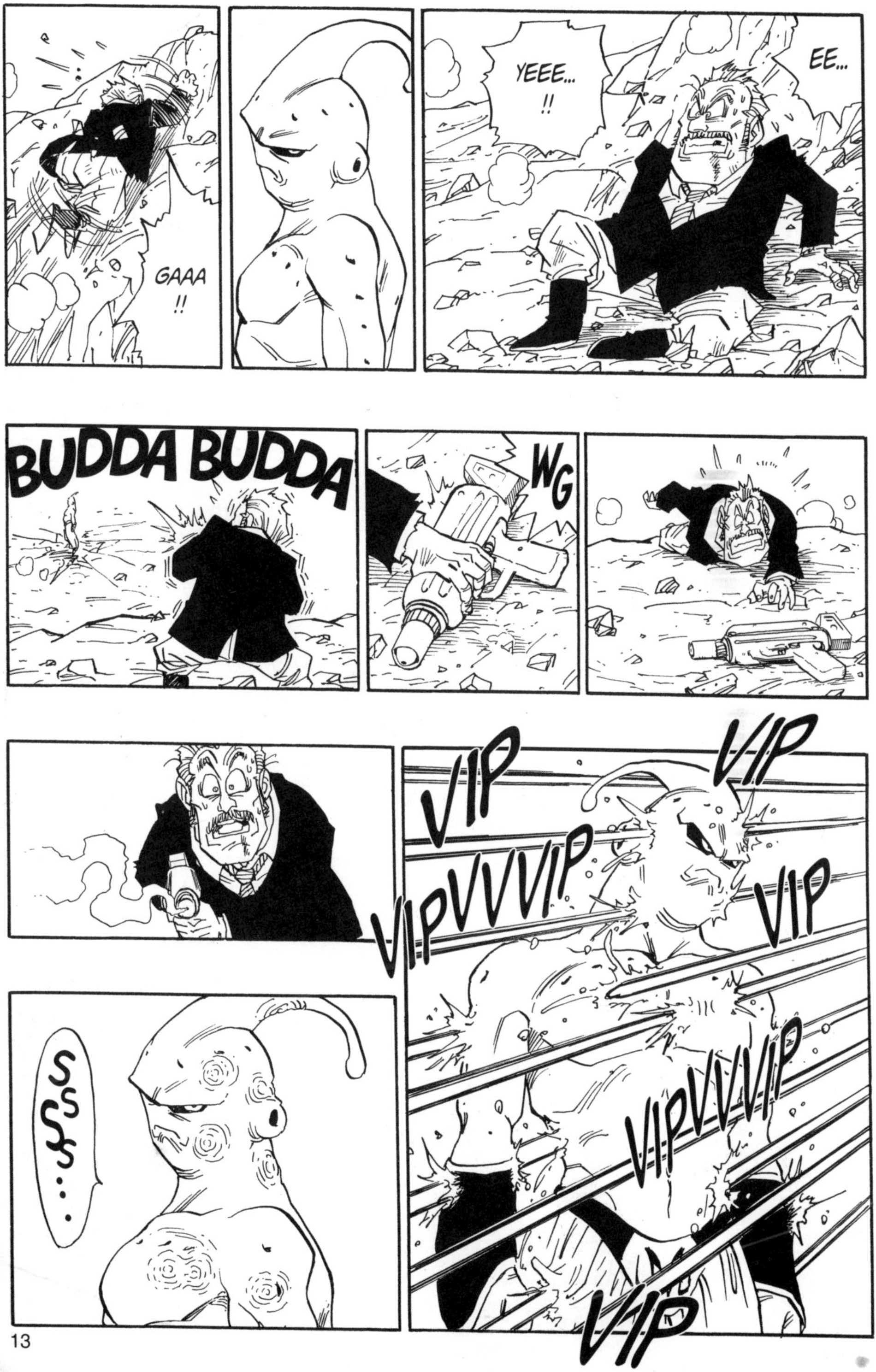
EE...
YEEE... !!
GAAA !!
WG
BUDDA BUDDA
VIP
VIP
VIPVVVIP
VIP
VIPVVVIP
VIP
SSSS...

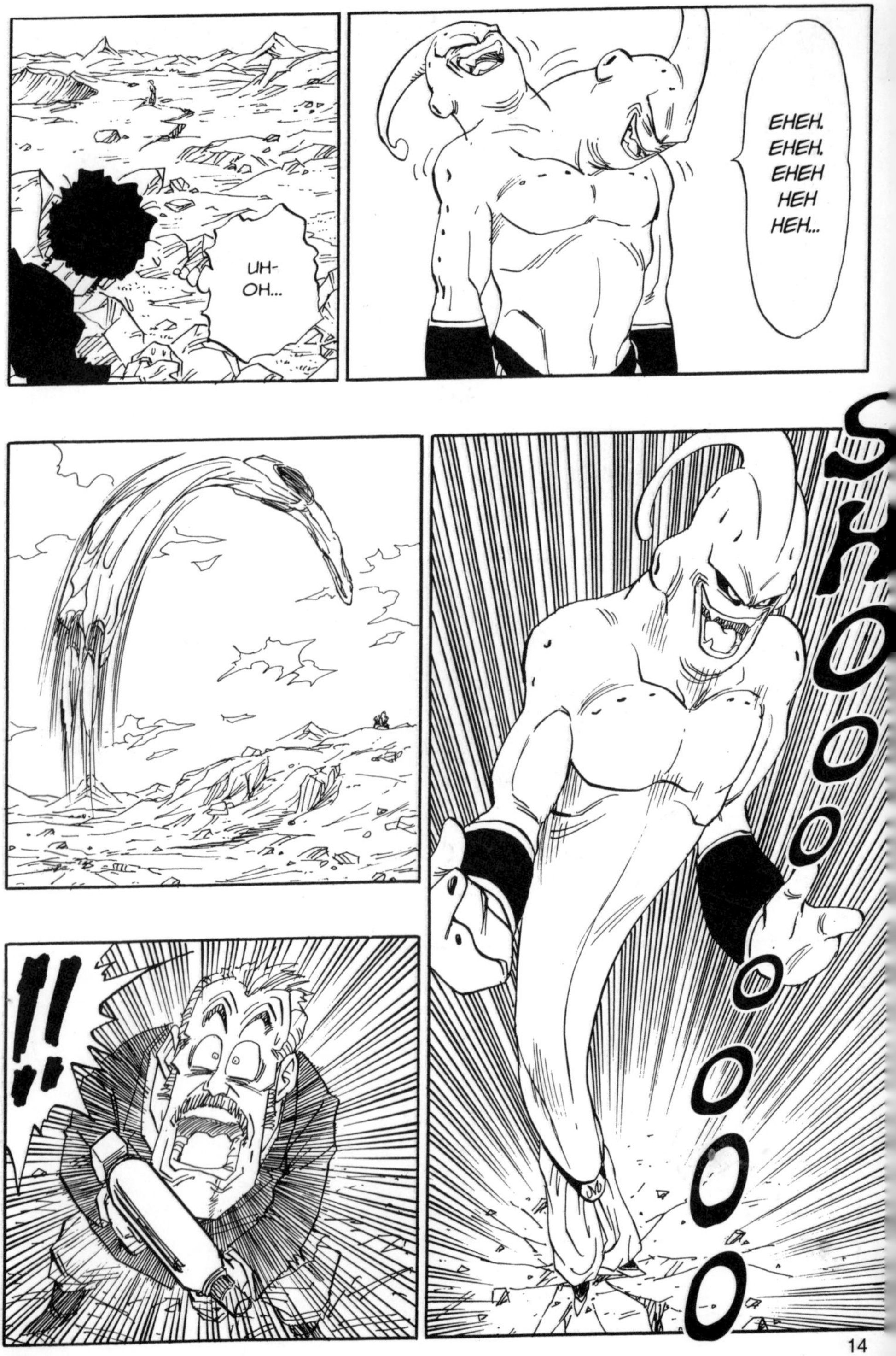

EHEH. EHEH. EHEH HEH HEH...
UH- OH...
SHOOOOOOOOOO
!!

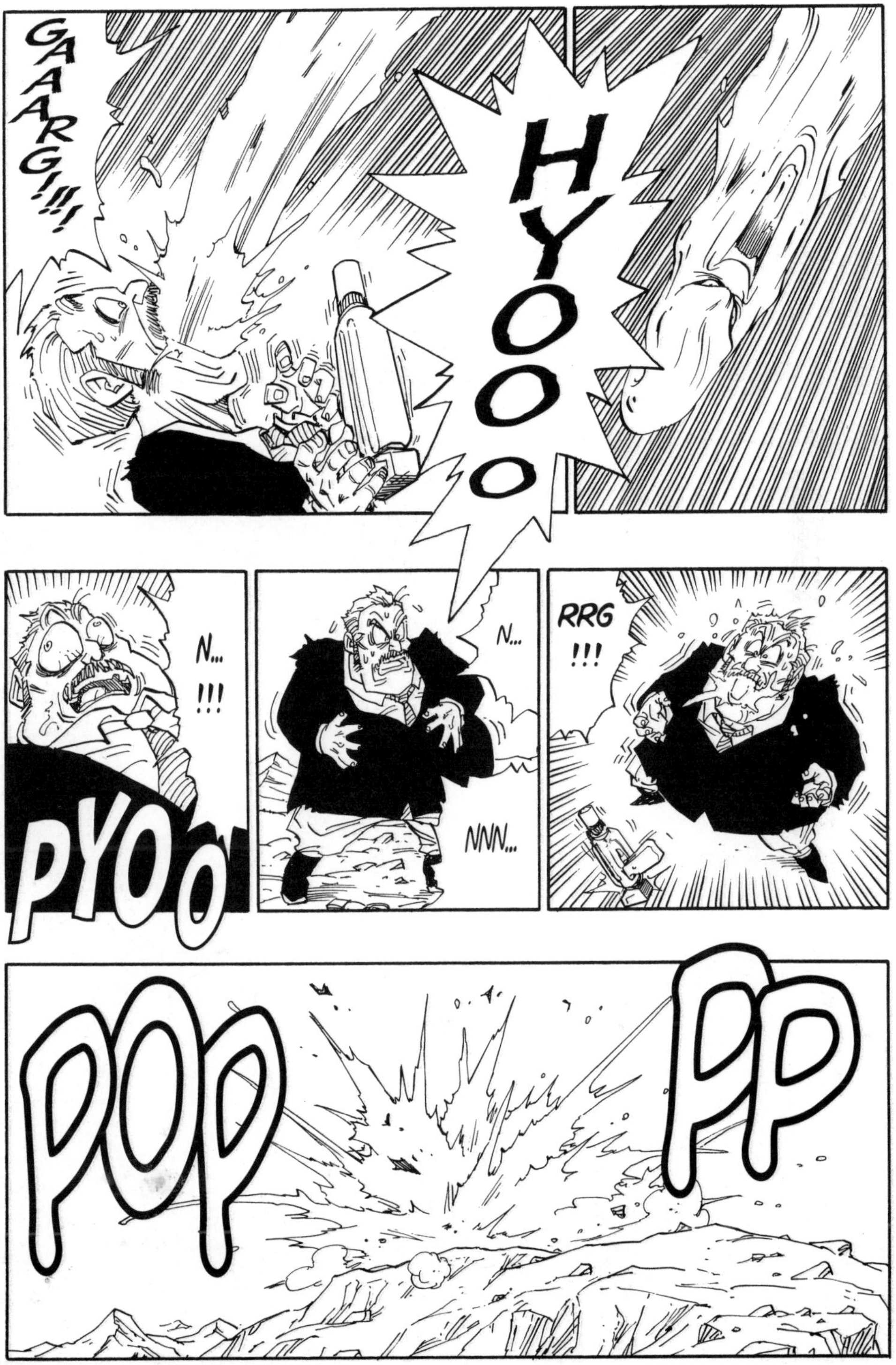
HYOOOO
GAAARG!!!!
RRG !!!
N...
NNN...
N... !!!
PYOO
POP PP

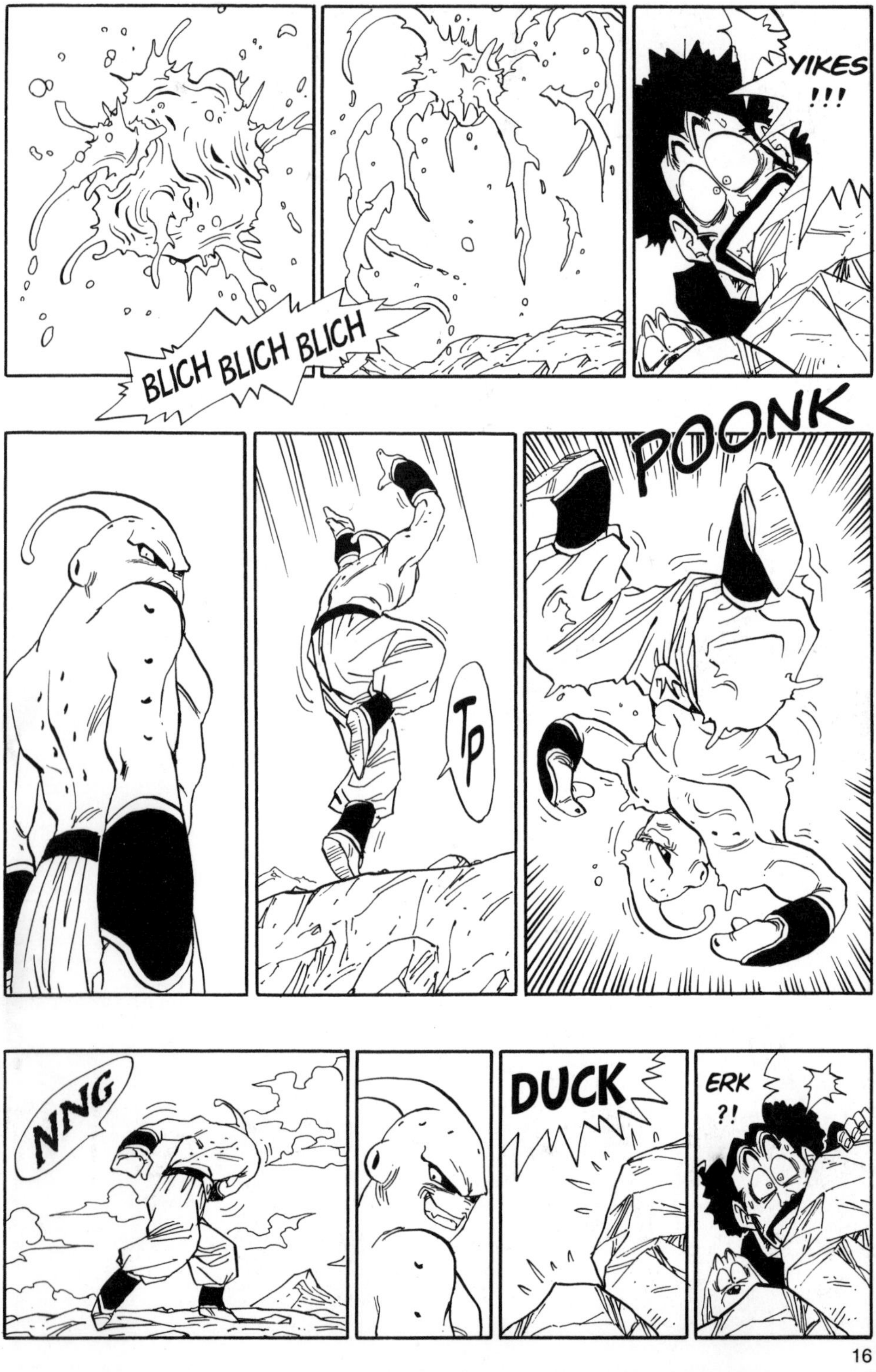
YIKES !!!
BLICH BLICH BLICH
POONK
TP
ERK ?!
DUCK
NNG

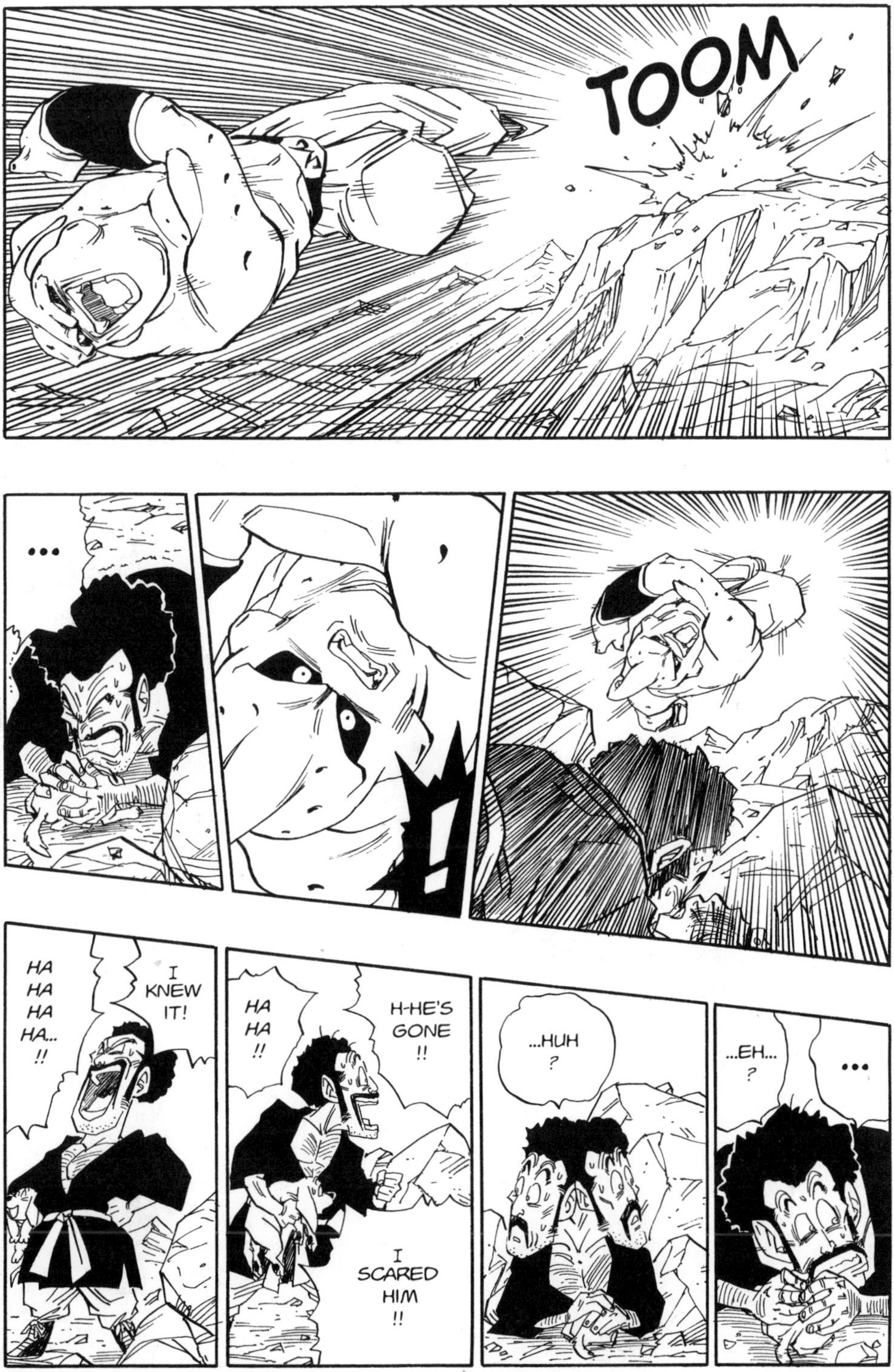
TOOM
!
...
...
...EH...?
...HUH?
H-HE'S GONE!!
HA HA!!
I SCARED HIM!!
I KNEW IT!
HA HA HA HA...!!

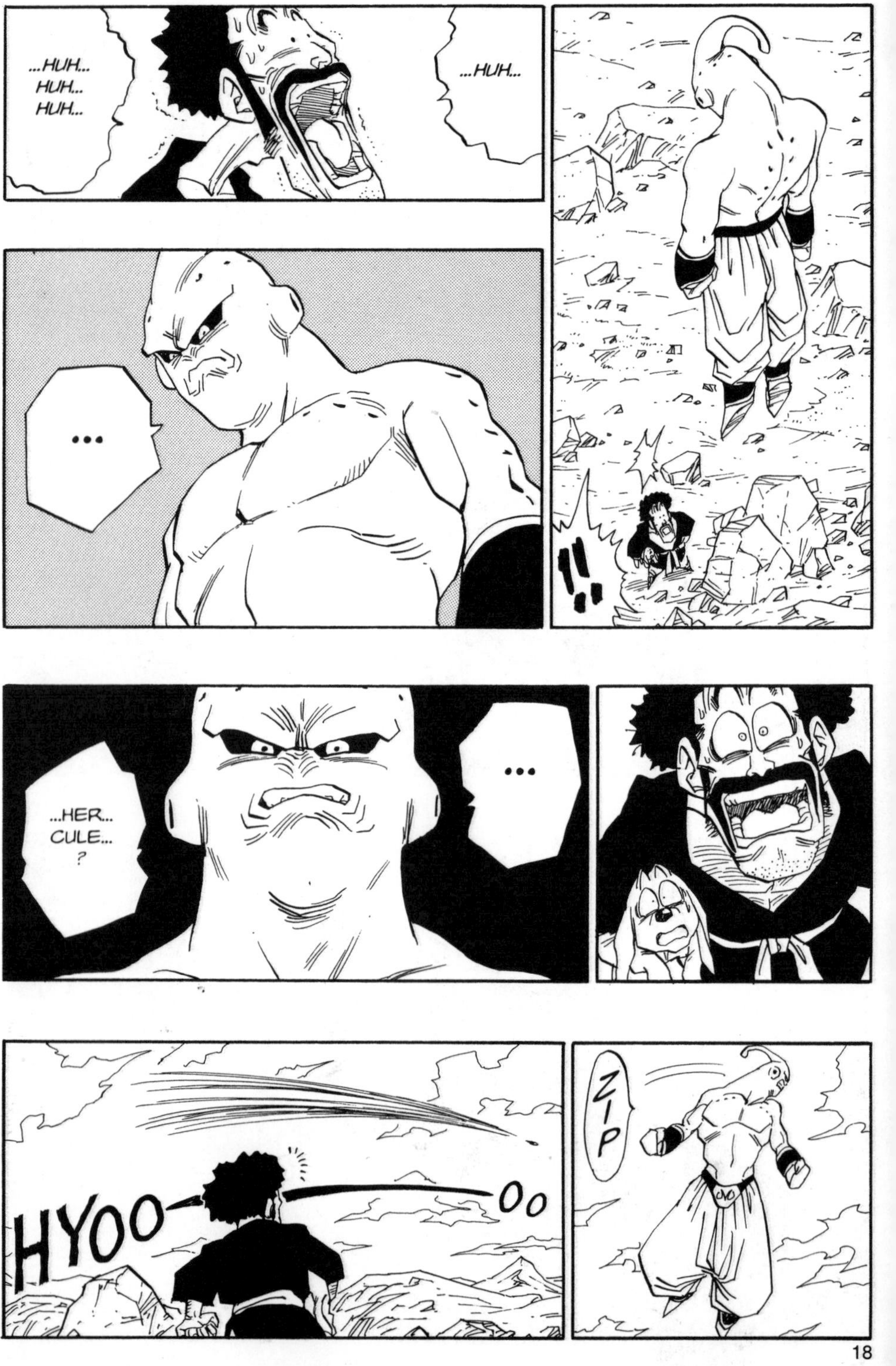
!!
...HUH...
...HUH... HUH... HUH...
...
...
...HER... CULE... ?
ZIP
HYOO—OO

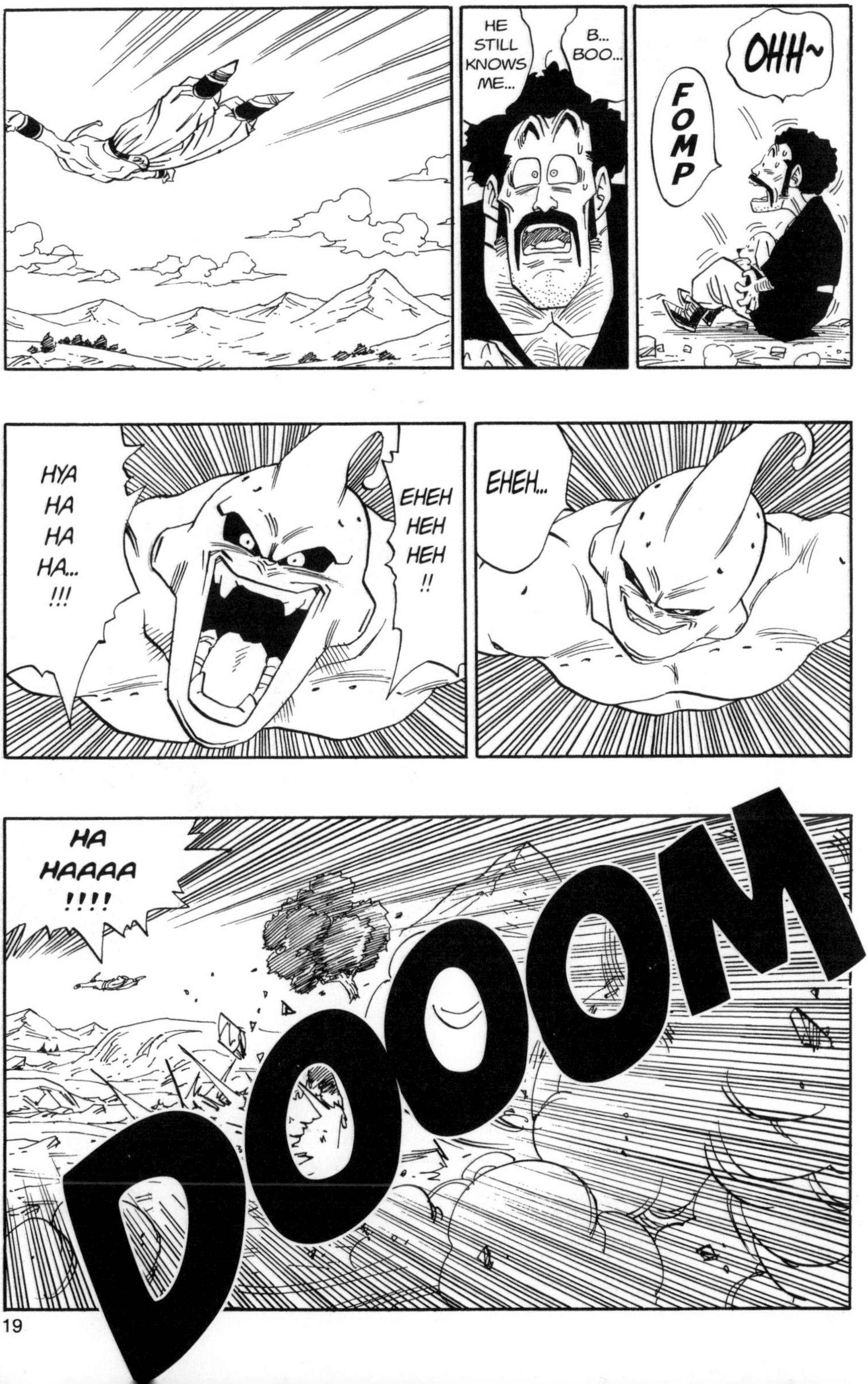
OHH~
FOMP
B... BOO...
HE STILL KNOWS ME...
EHEH...
EHEH HEH HEH !!
HYA HA HA HA... !!!
HA HAAAA !!!!
DOOOOM

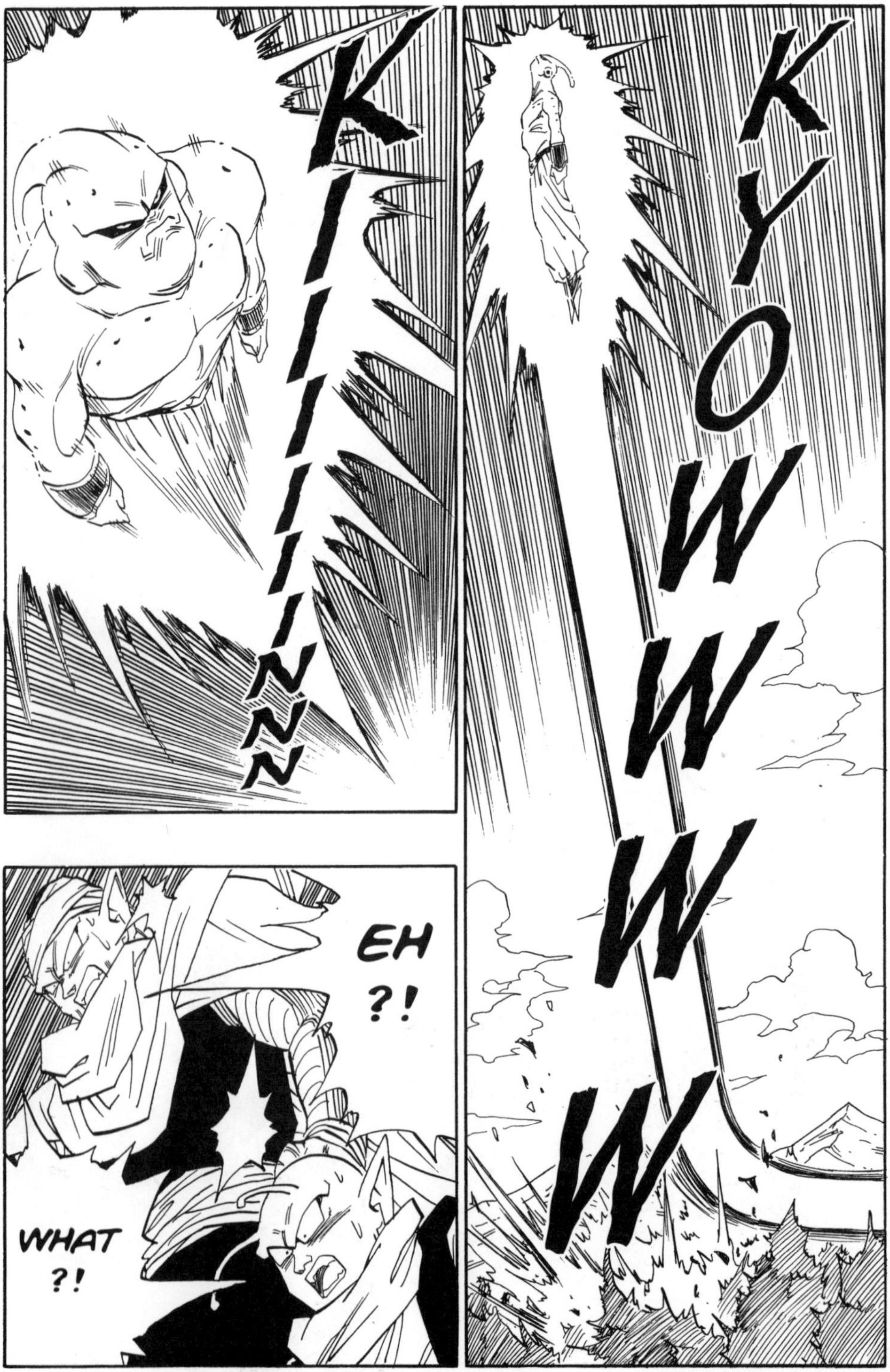
KYOWWWWW
KIIIIIIIIINNN
EH ?!
WHAT ?!

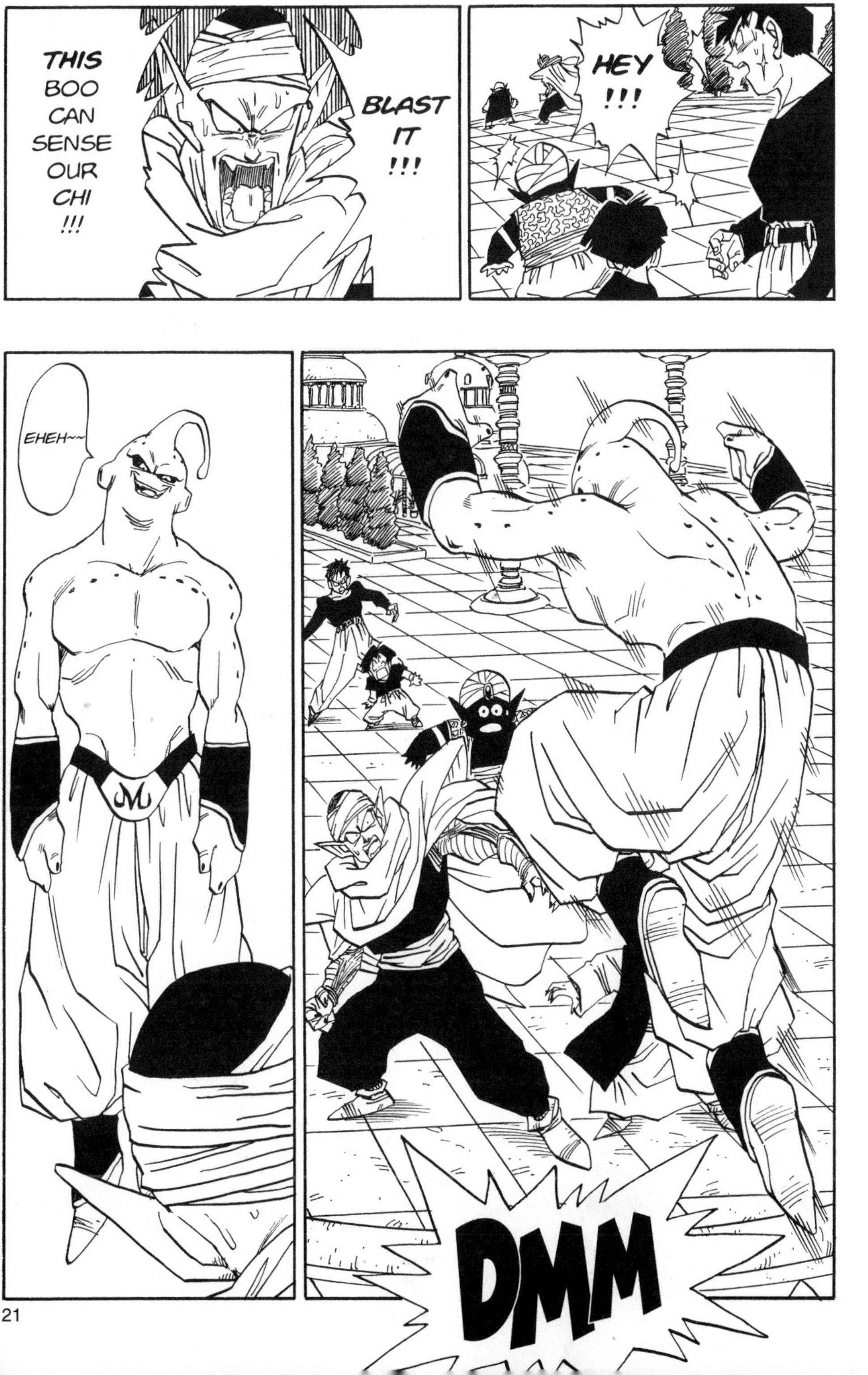
HEY !!!
BLAST IT !!!
THIS BOO CAN SENSE OUR CHI !!!
DMM
EHEH~~

DRAGON BALL ドラゴンボール

DBZ:293 · Humanity's End

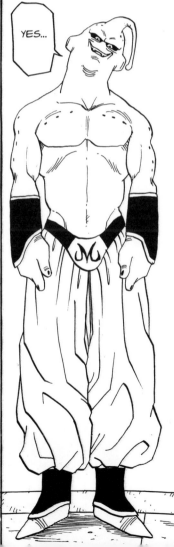

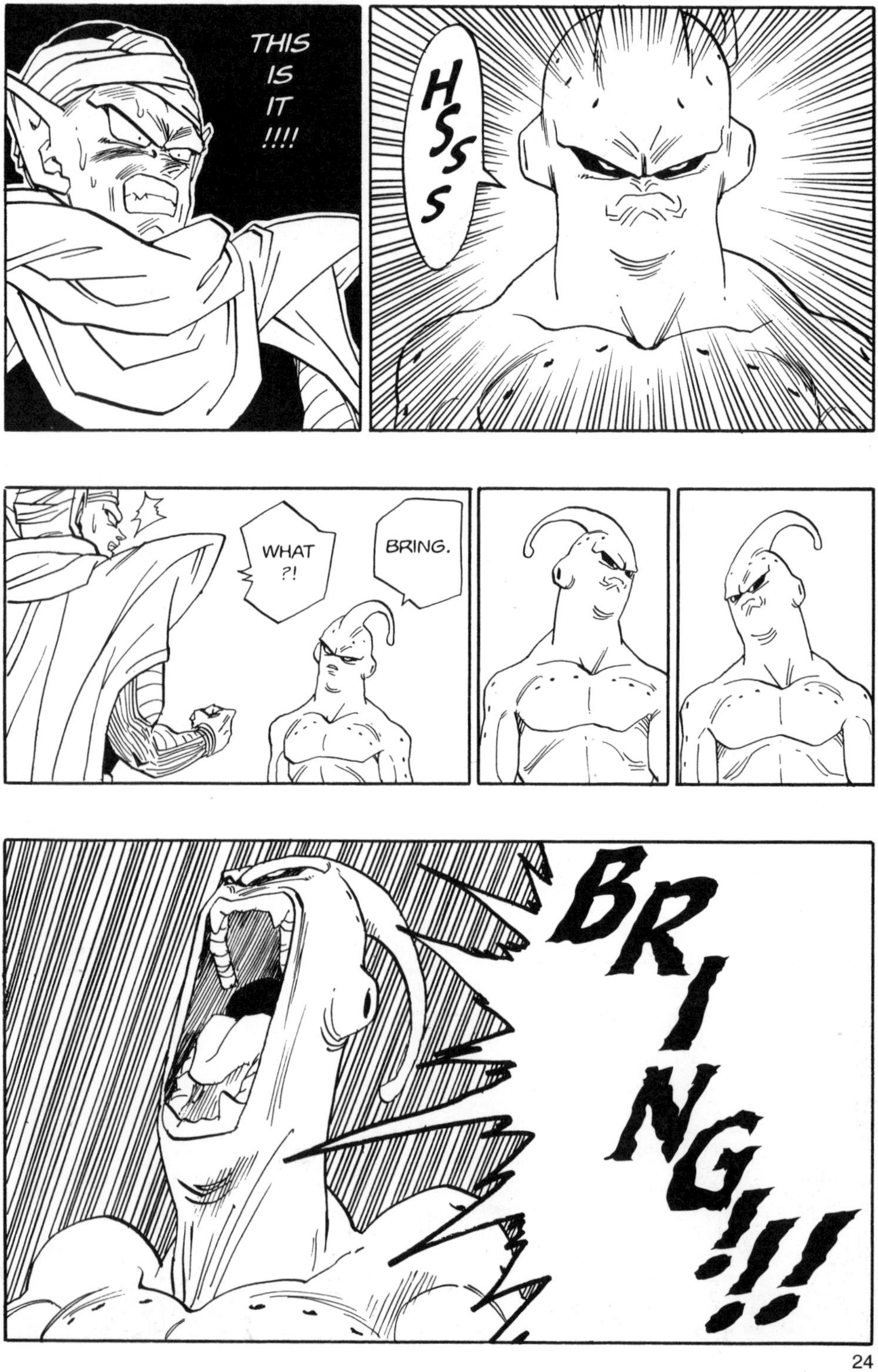
HSSS
THIS IS IT!!!!
BRING.
WHAT ?!
BRING!!!!

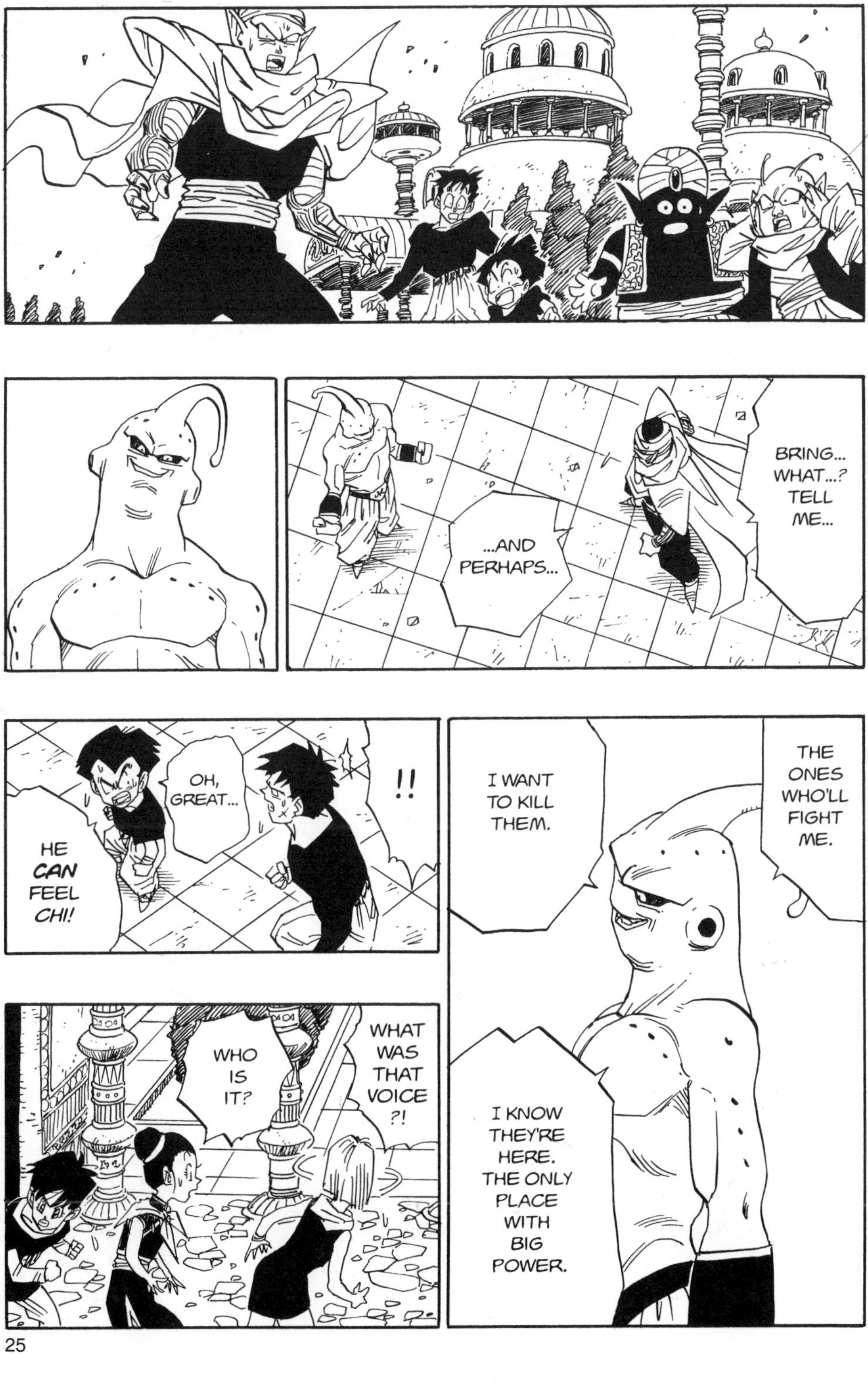
BRING... WHAT...? TELL ME...
...AND PERHAPS...
THE ONES WHO'LL FIGHT ME.
I WANT TO KILL THEM.
I KNOW THEY'RE HERE. THE ONLY PLACE WITH BIG POWER.
!!
OH, GREAT...
HE **CAN** FEEL CHI!
WHAT WAS THAT VOICE?!
WHO IS IT?

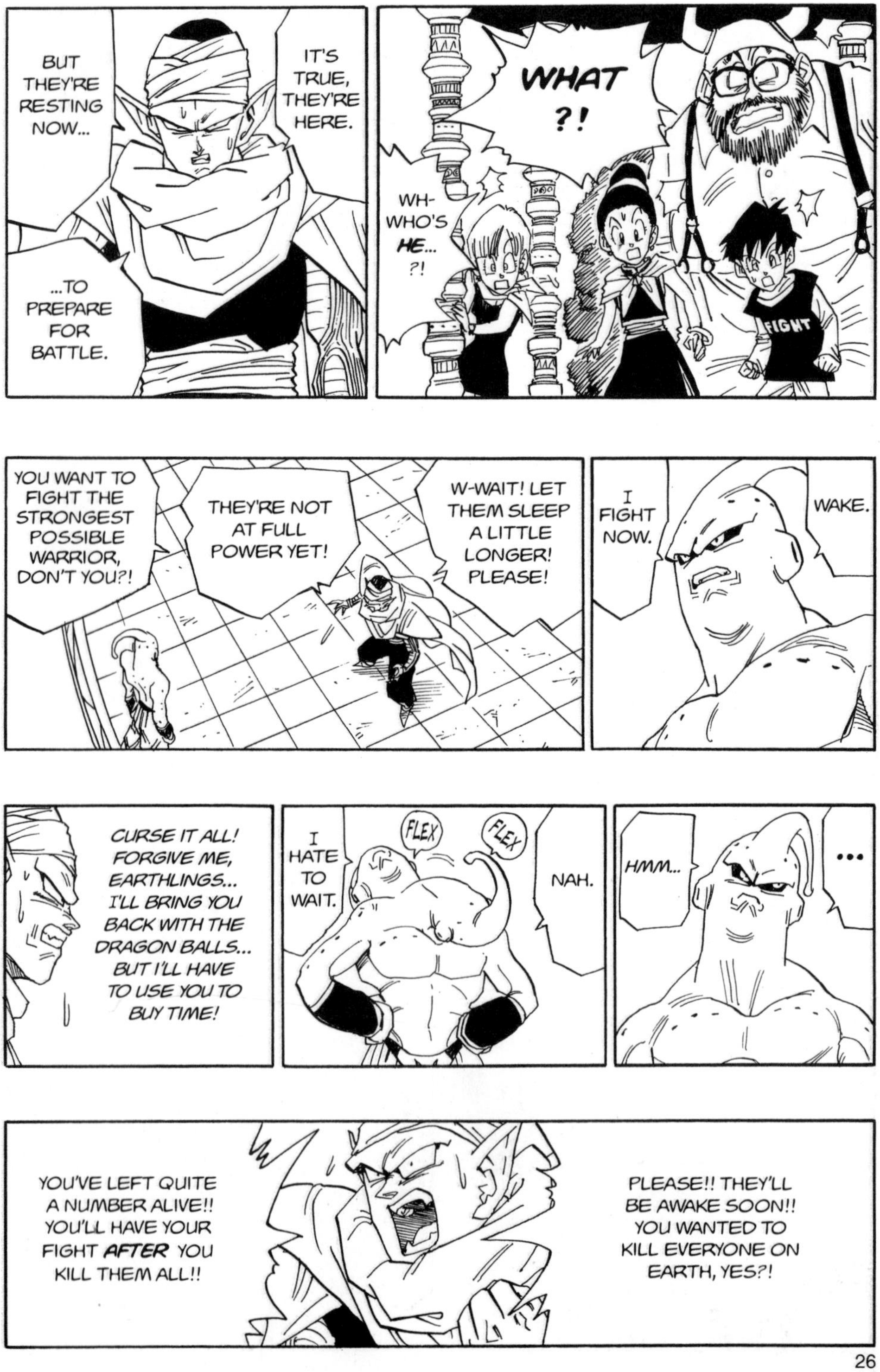
WHAT ?!
WH-WHO'S HE...?!
IT'S TRUE, THEY'RE HERE.
BUT THEY'RE RESTING NOW...
...TO PREPARE FOR BATTLE.
WAKE.
I FIGHT NOW.
W-WAIT! LET THEM SLEEP A LITTLE LONGER! PLEASE!
THEY'RE NOT AT FULL POWER YET!
YOU WANT TO FIGHT THE STRONGEST POSSIBLE WARRIOR, DON'T YOU?!
...
HMM...
NAH.
FLEX
FLEX
I HATE TO WAIT.
CURSE IT ALL! FORGIVE ME, EARTHLINGS... I'LL BRING YOU BACK WITH THE DRAGON BALLS... BUT I'LL HAVE TO USE YOU TO BUY TIME!
PLEASE!! THEY'LL BE AWAKE SOON!! YOU WANTED TO KILL EVERYONE ON EARTH, YES?!
YOU'VE LEFT QUITE A NUMBER ALIVE!! YOU'LL HAVE YOUR FIGHT AFTER YOU KILL THEM ALL!!

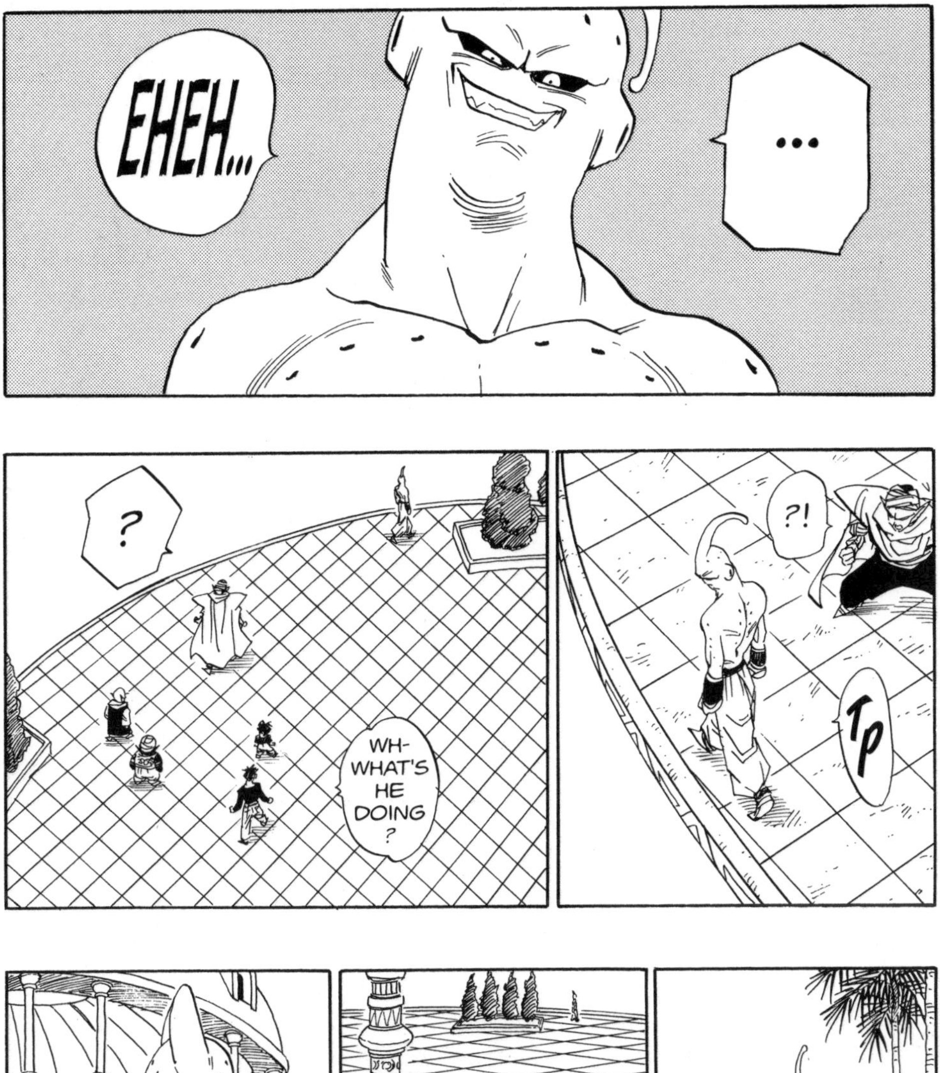
...
EHEH...
?!
TP
?
WH-WHAT'S HE DOING?
WHY'S HE WALKING AROUND?!

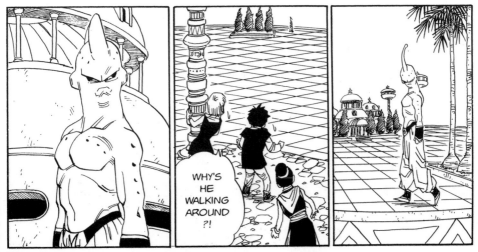

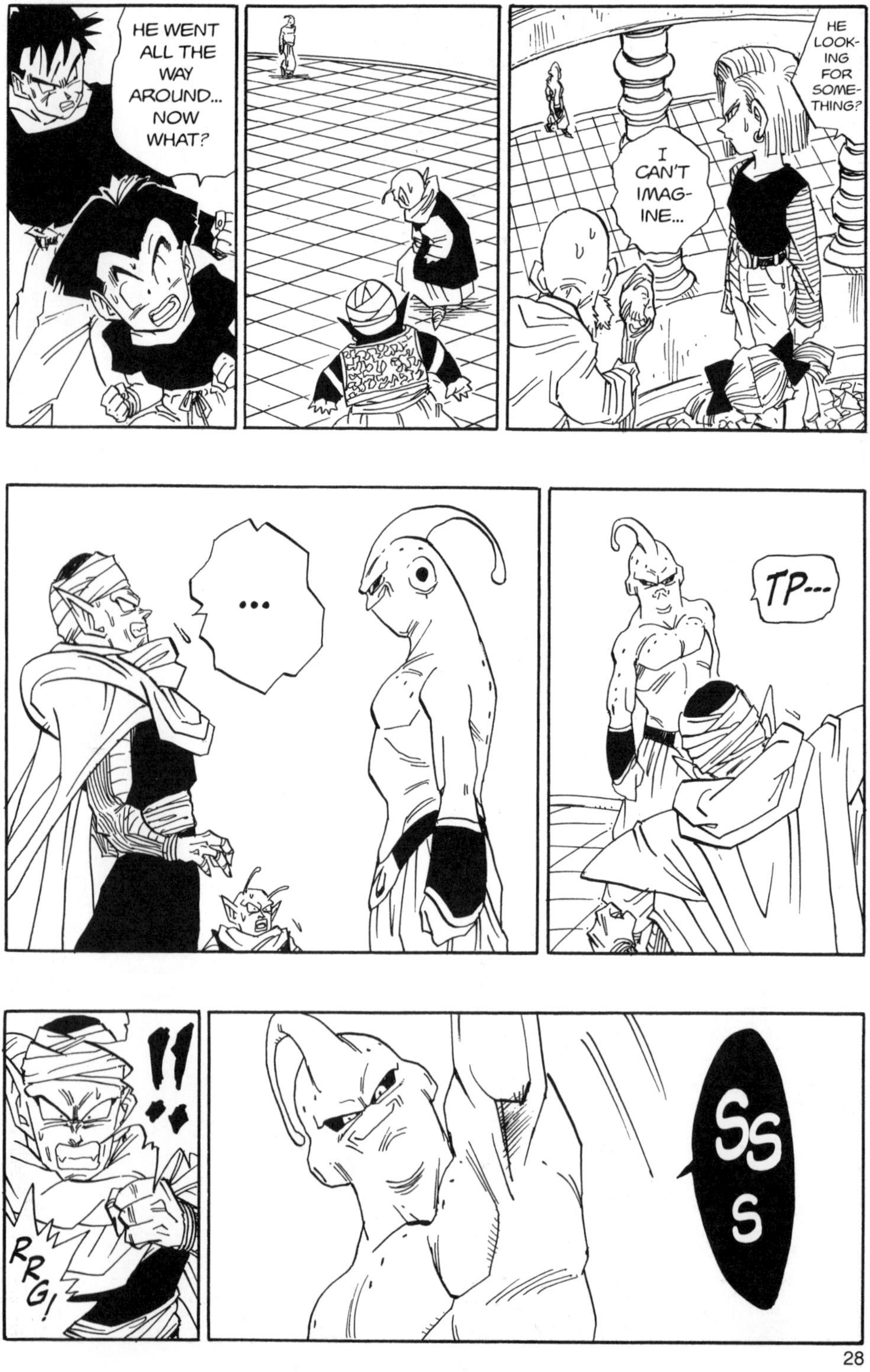
HE LOOKING FOR SOMETHING?
I CAN'T IMAGINE...
HE WENT ALL THE WAY AROUND... NOW WHAT?
TP...
...
Ss s
!!
RRG!

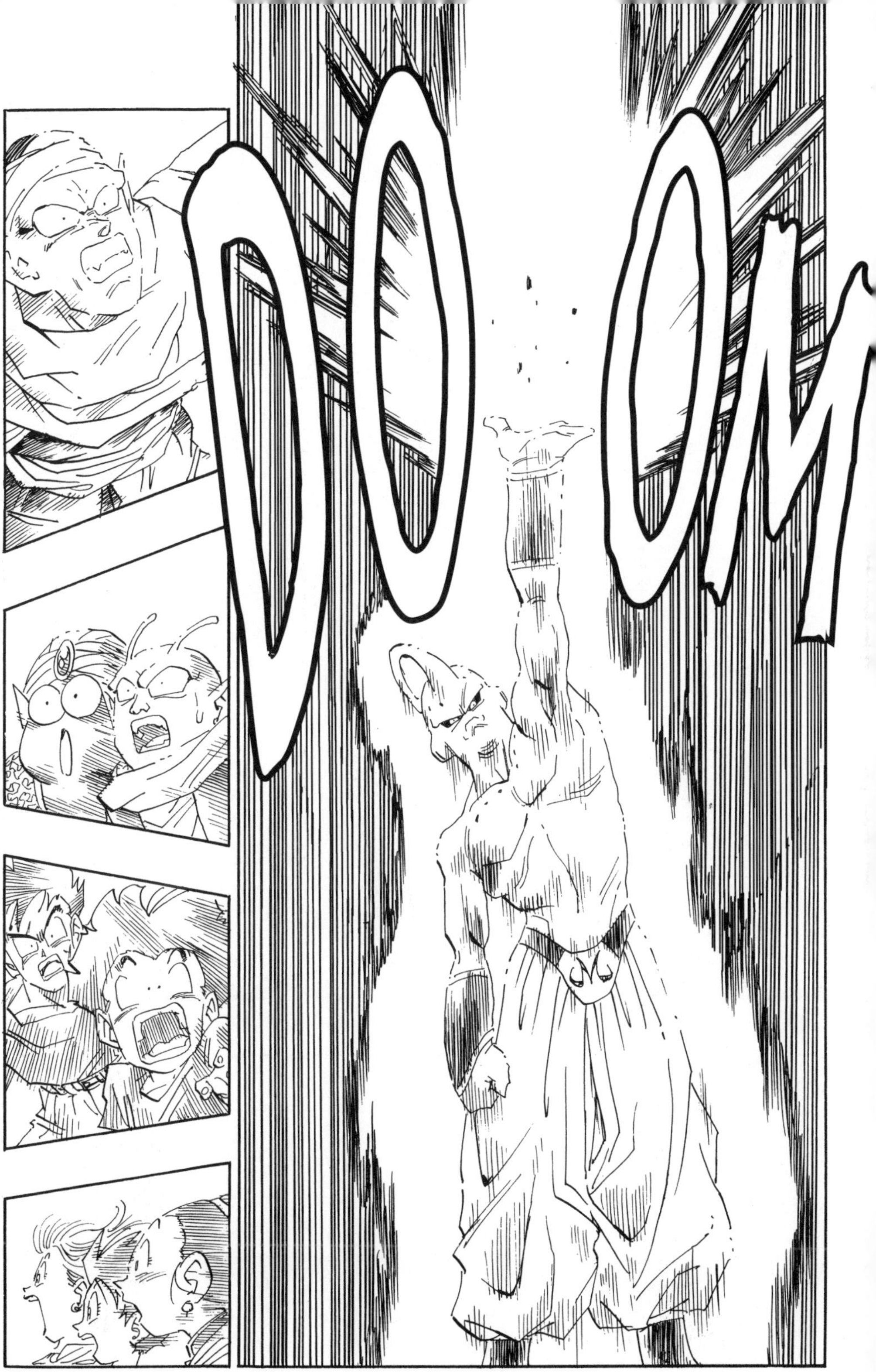
DOOOM

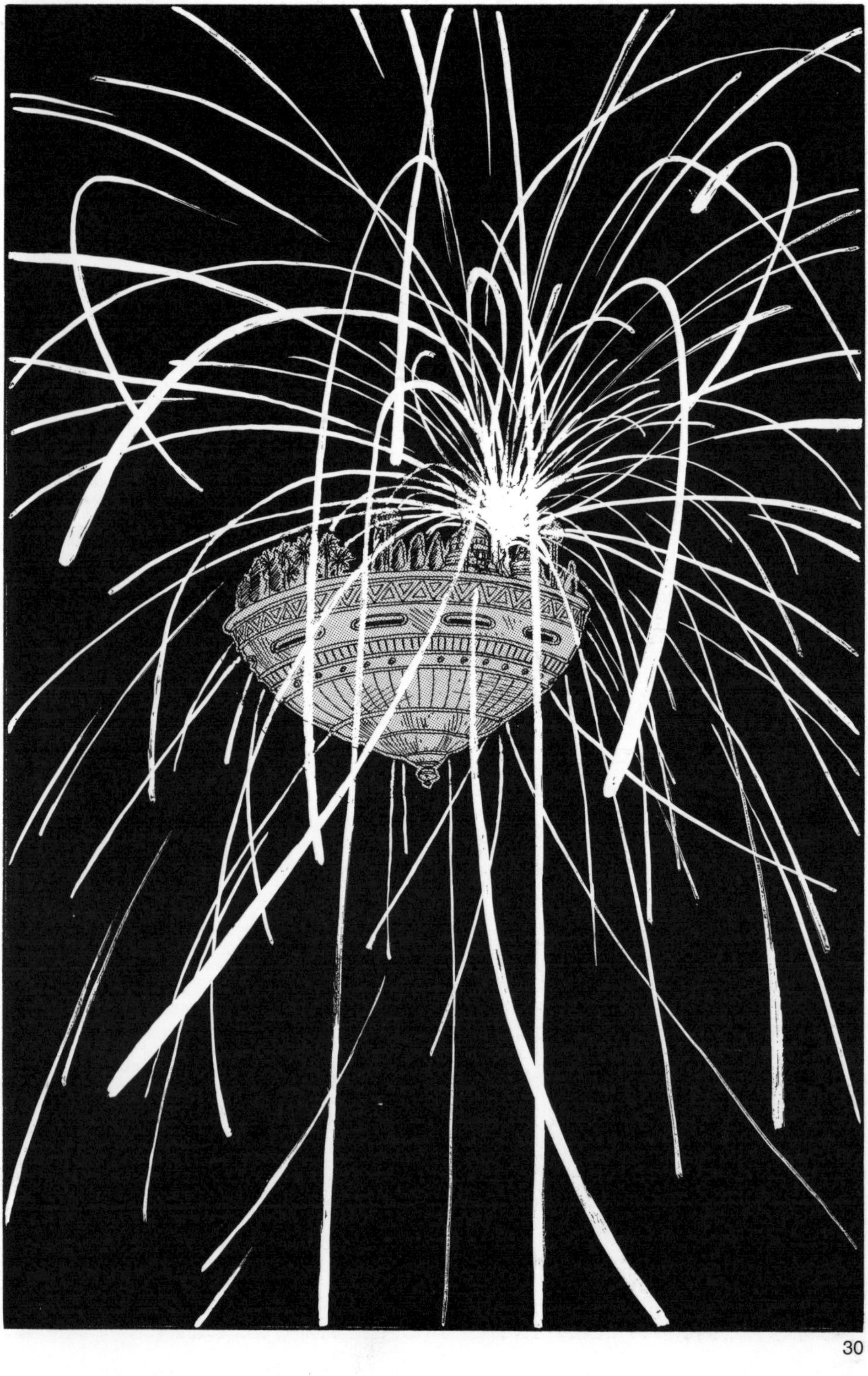

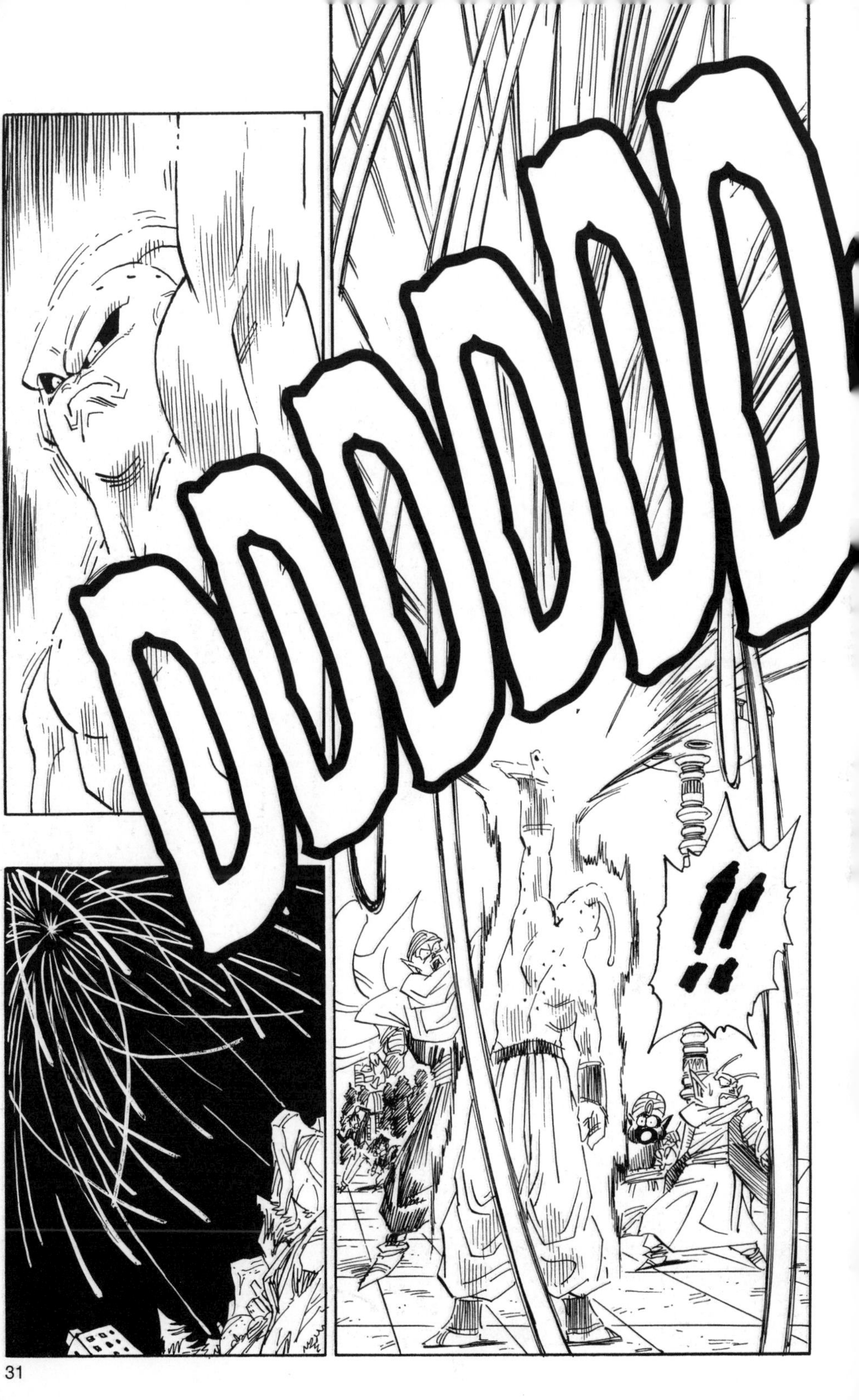
DDDDDD
!!

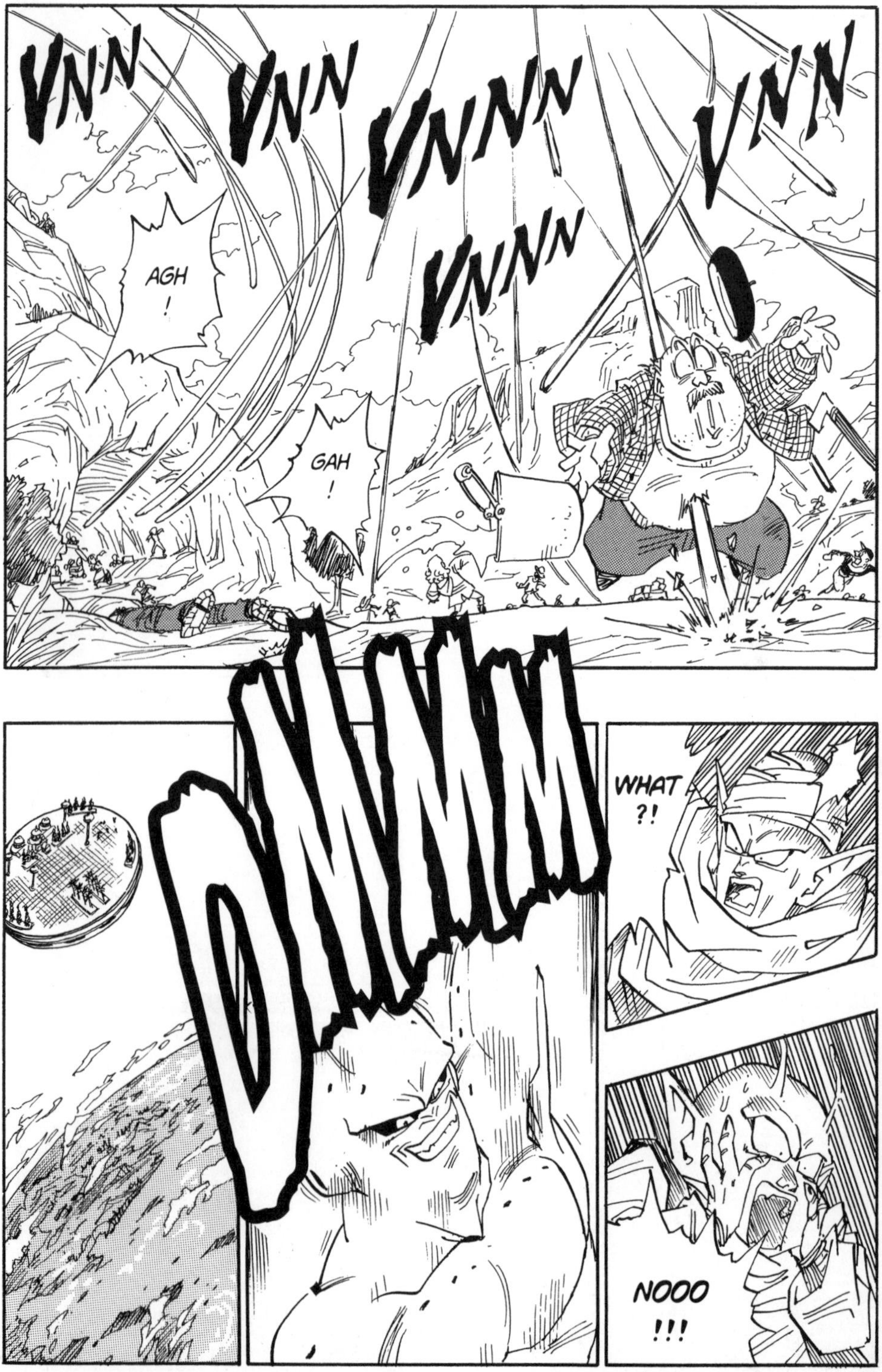
VNN
VNNN
VNNN
VNN
VNN
AGH!
GAH!
WHAT?!
NOOO!!!
DMMMM

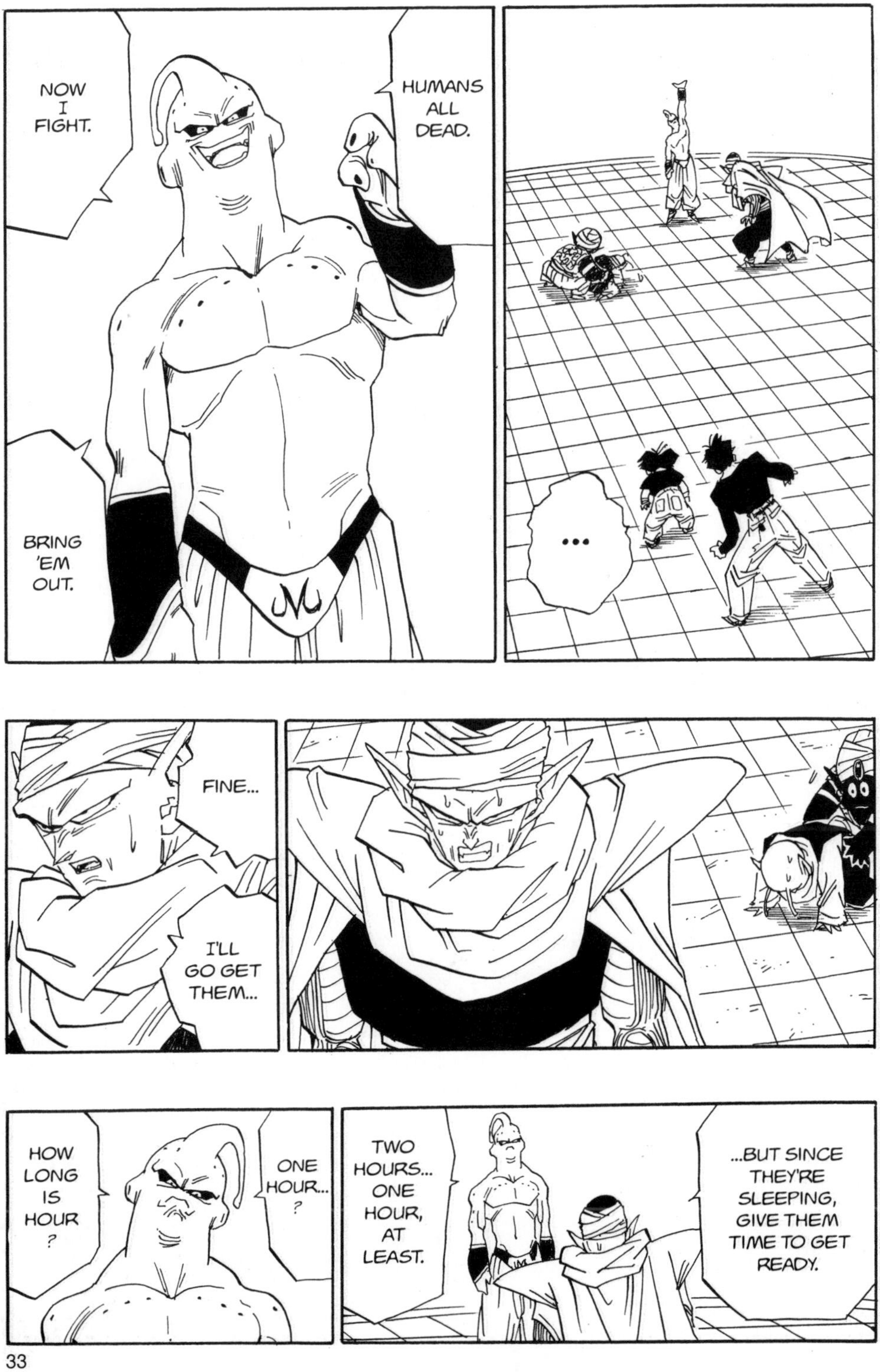
...
HUMANS ALL DEAD.
NOW I FIGHT.
BRING 'EM OUT.
FINE...
I'LL GO GET THEM...
TWO HOURS... ONE HOUR, AT LEAST.
...BUT SINCE THEY'RE SLEEPING, GIVE THEM TIME TO GET READY.
ONE HOUR... ?
HOW LONG IS HOUR ?

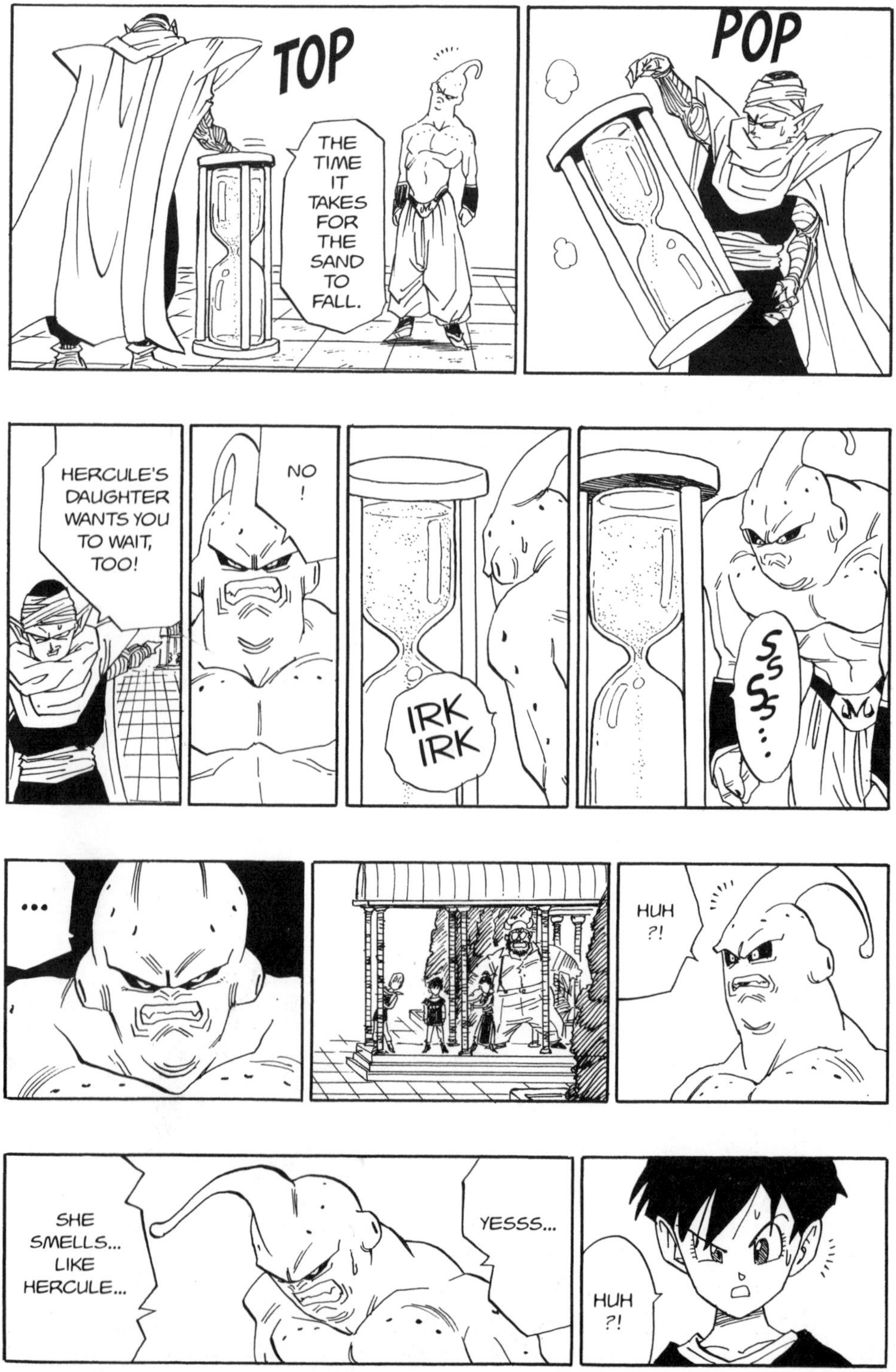
POP
TOP
THE TIME IT TAKES FOR THE SAND TO FALL.
SSSS...
IRK IRK
NO!
HERCULE'S DAUGHTER WANTS YOU TO WAIT, TOO!
HUH ?!
...
HUH ?!
YESSS...
SHE SMELLS... LIKE HERCULE...

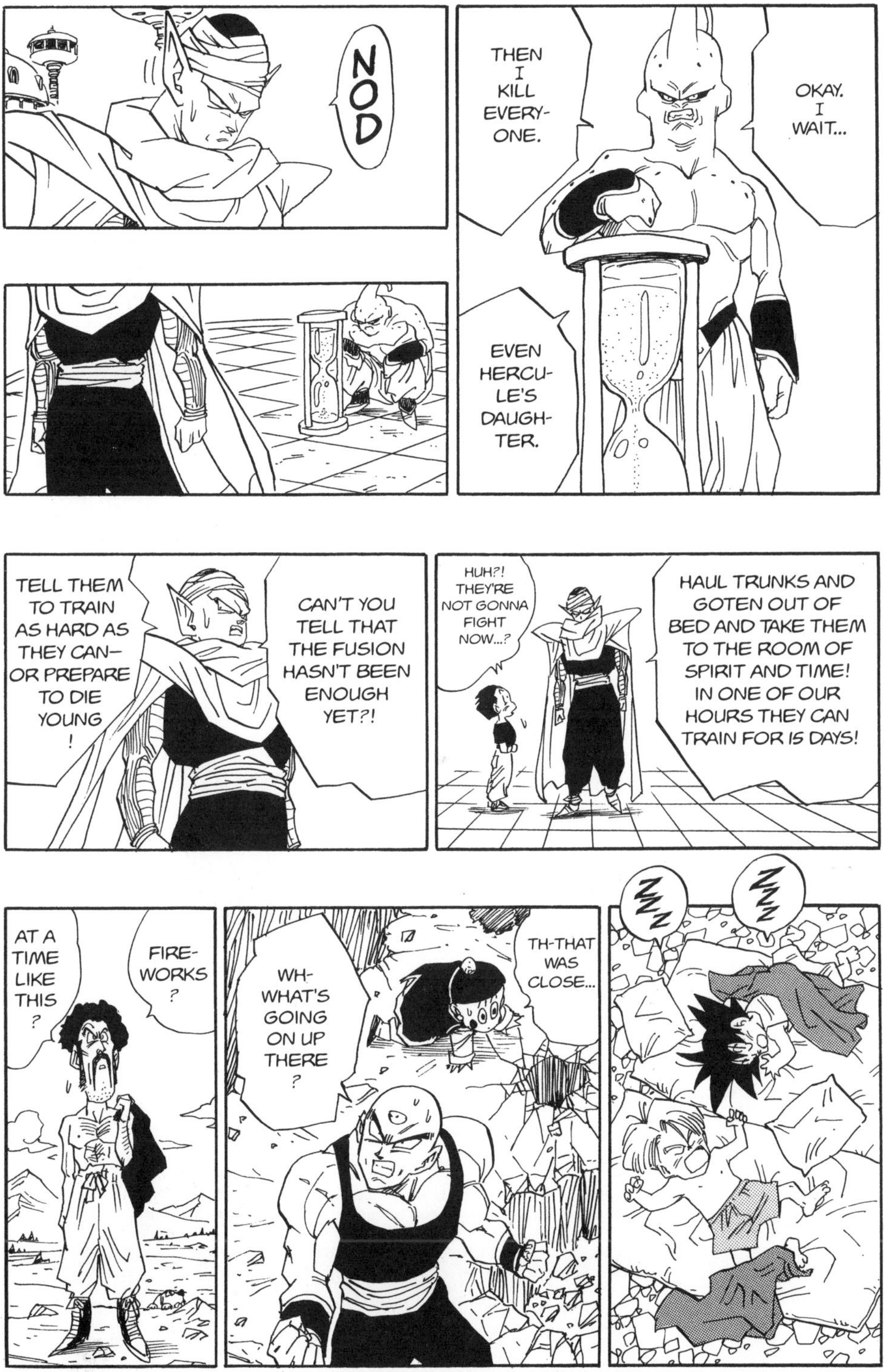
OKAY. I WAIT...
THEN I KILL EVERY-ONE.
EVEN HERCULE'S DAUGHTER.
NOD
HAUL TRUNKS AND GOTEN OUT OF BED AND TAKE THEM TO THE ROOM OF SPIRIT AND TIME! IN ONE OF OUR HOURS THEY CAN TRAIN FOR 15 DAYS!
HUH?! THEY'RE NOT GONNA FIGHT NOW...?
CAN'T YOU TELL THAT THE FUSION HASN'T BEEN ENOUGH YET?!
TELL THEM TO TRAIN AS HARD AS THEY CAN— OR PREPARE TO DIE YOUNG!
ZZZ
ZZZ
TH-THAT WAS CLOSE...
WH-WHAT'S GOING ON UP THERE?
FIRE-WORKS?
AT A TIME LIKE THIS?

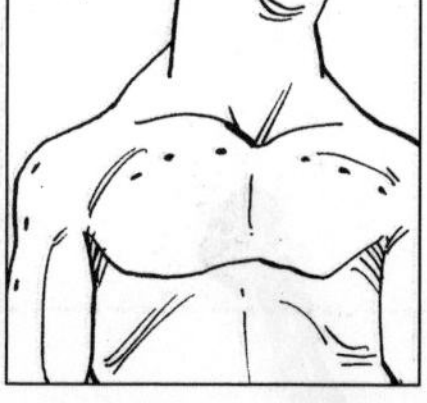

DRAGON BALL ドラゴンボール

DBZ:294 • Return to the Room of Spirit and Time

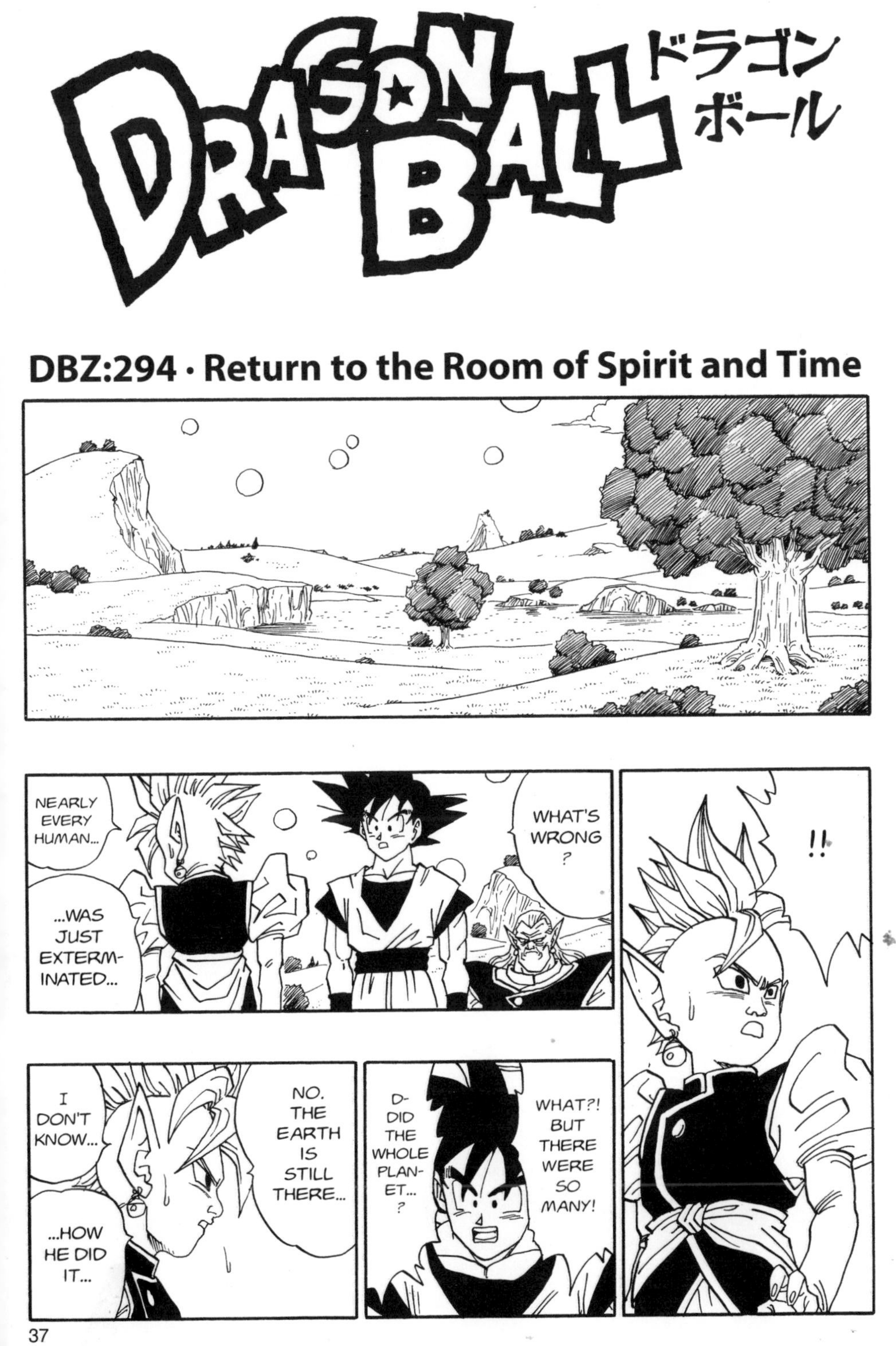
!!
WHAT'S WRONG?
NEARLY EVERY HUMAN...
...WAS JUST EXTERMINATED...
WHAT?! BUT THERE WERE SO MANY!
D-DID THE WHOLE PLANET...?
NO. THE EARTH IS STILL THERE...
I DON'T KNOW...
...HOW HE DID IT...

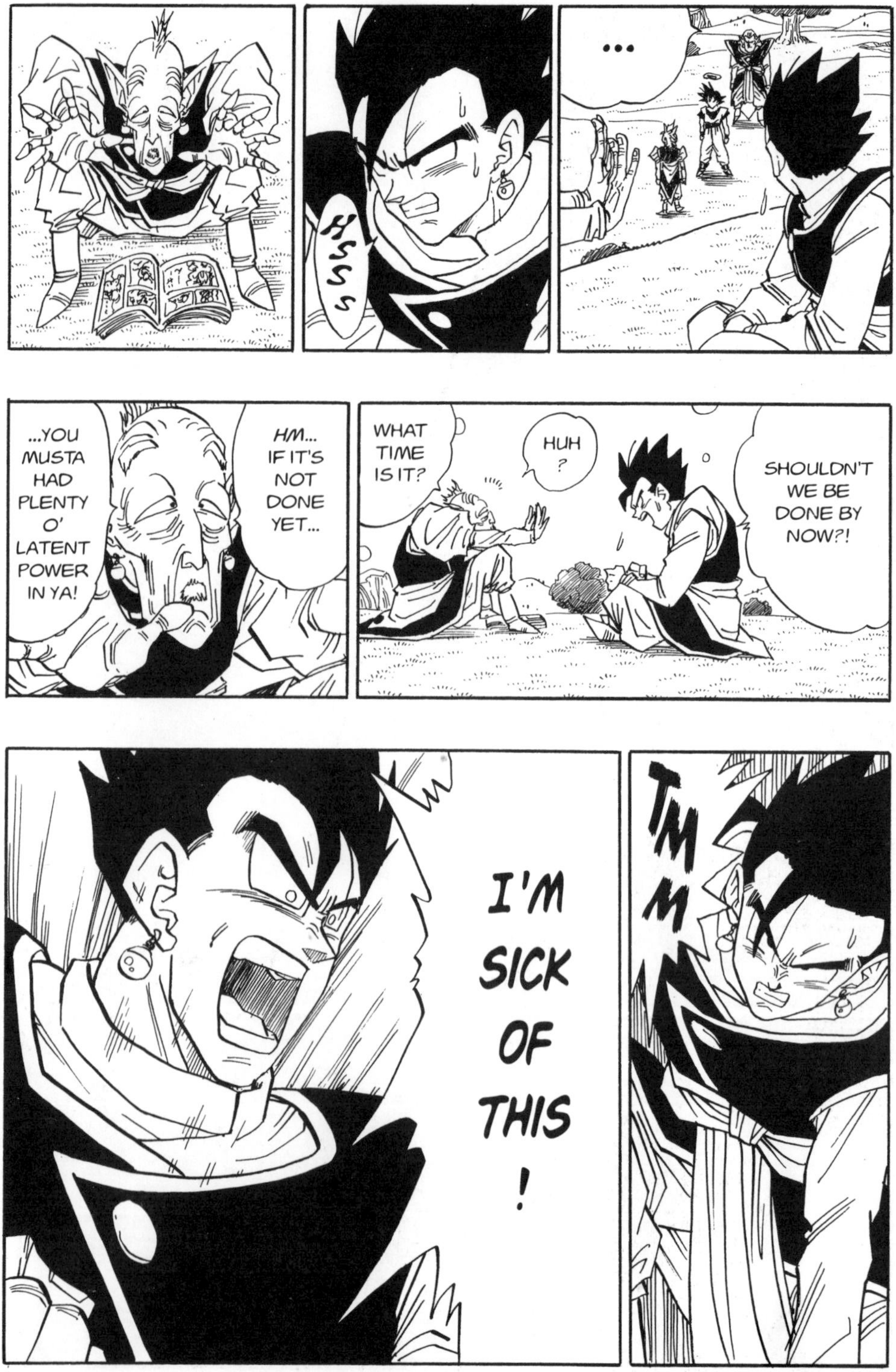
...
HSSS
SHOULDN'T WE BE DONE BY NOW?!
HUH ?
WHAT TIME IS IT?
HM... IF IT'S NOT DONE YET...
...YOU MUSTA HAD PLENTY O' LATENT POWER IN YA!
TMM
I'M SICK OF THIS !

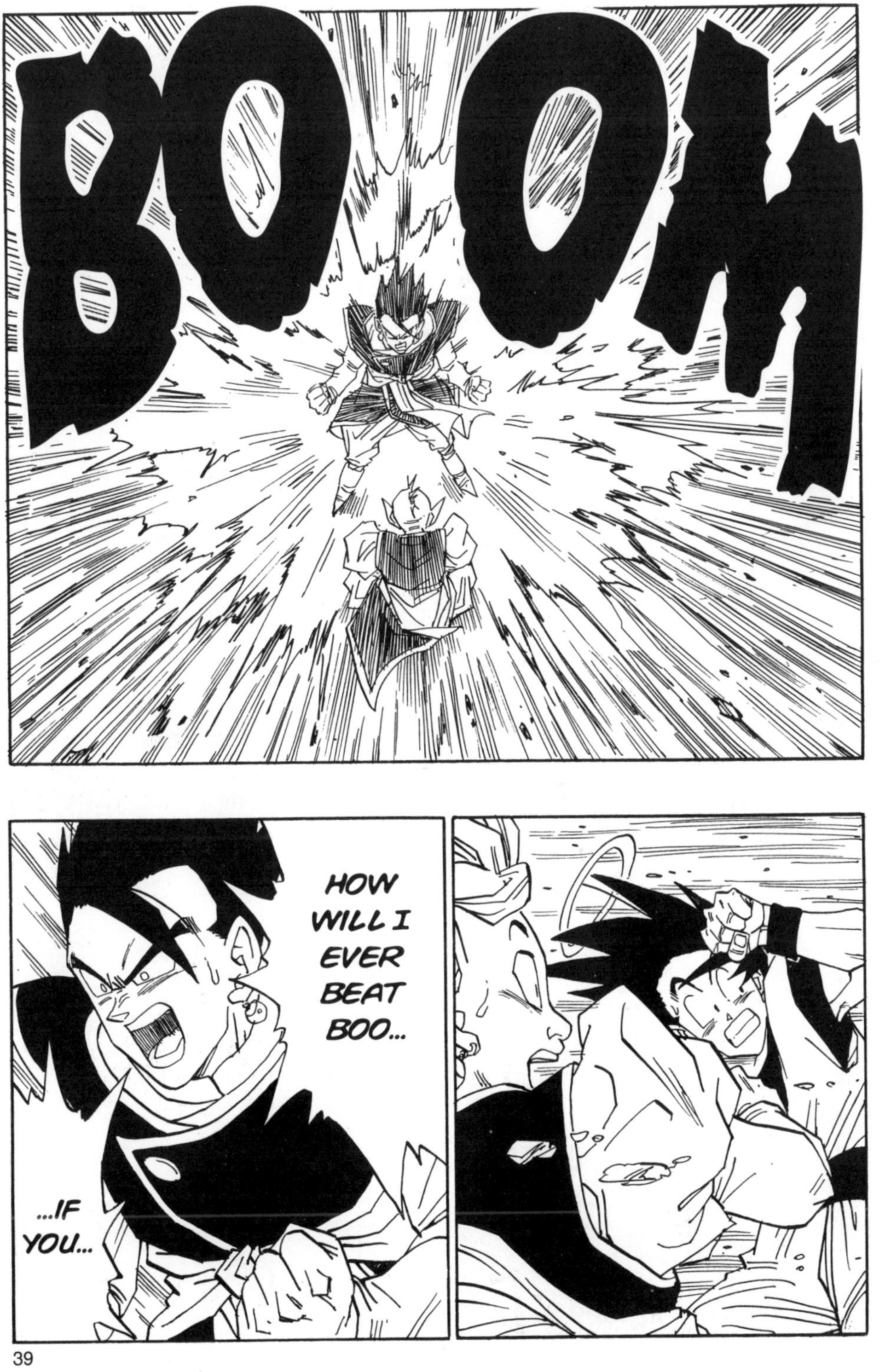
BOOM
HOW WILL I EVER BEAT BOO...
...IF YOU...

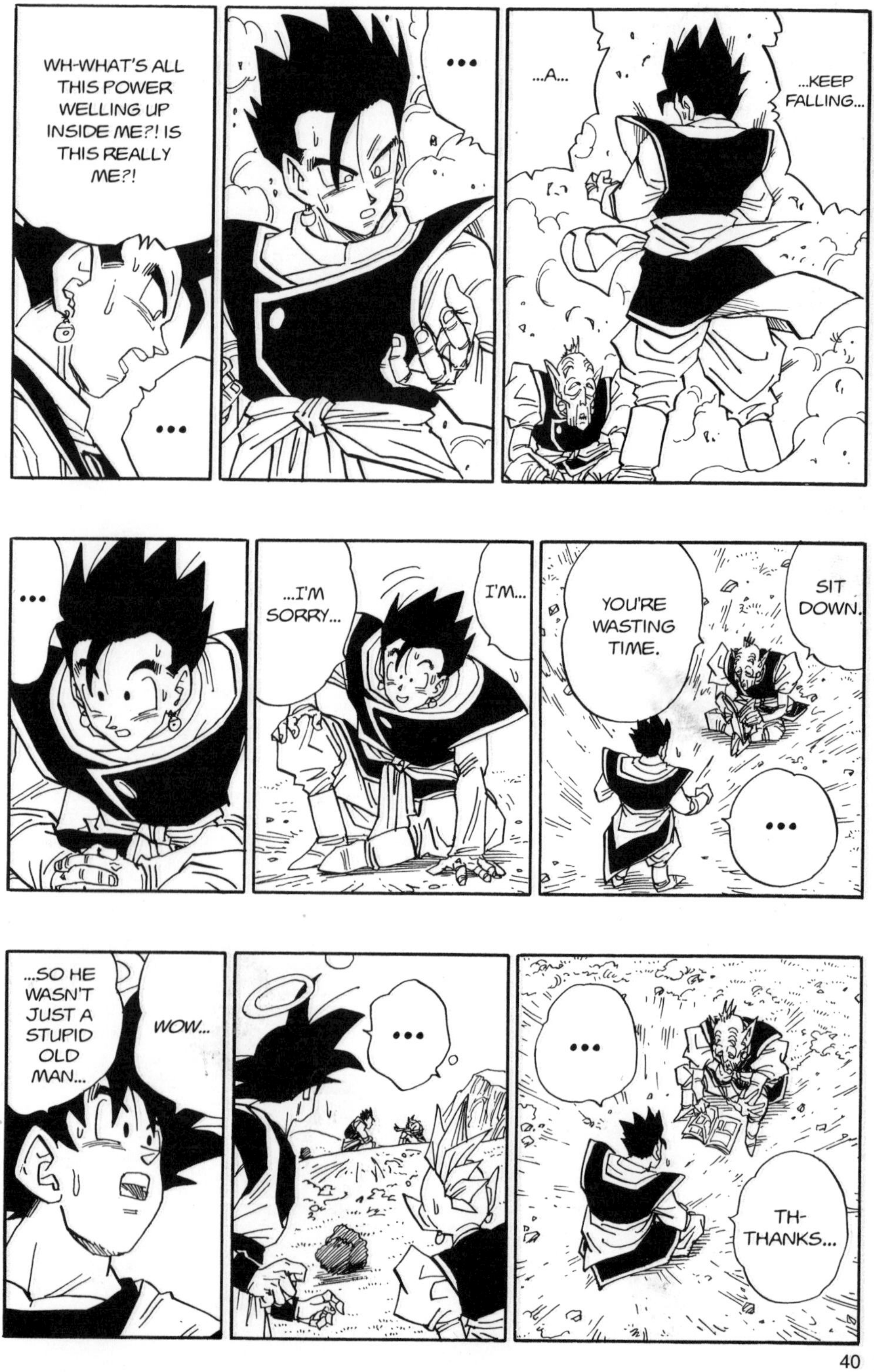
...KEEP FALLING...
...A...
...
WH-WHAT'S ALL THIS POWER WELLING UP INSIDE ME?! IS THIS REALLY ME?!
...
SIT DOWN.
YOU'RE WASTING TIME.
...
I'M...
...I'M SORRY...
...
...
TH-THANKS...
...
WOW...
...SO HE WASN'T JUST A STUPID OLD MAN...

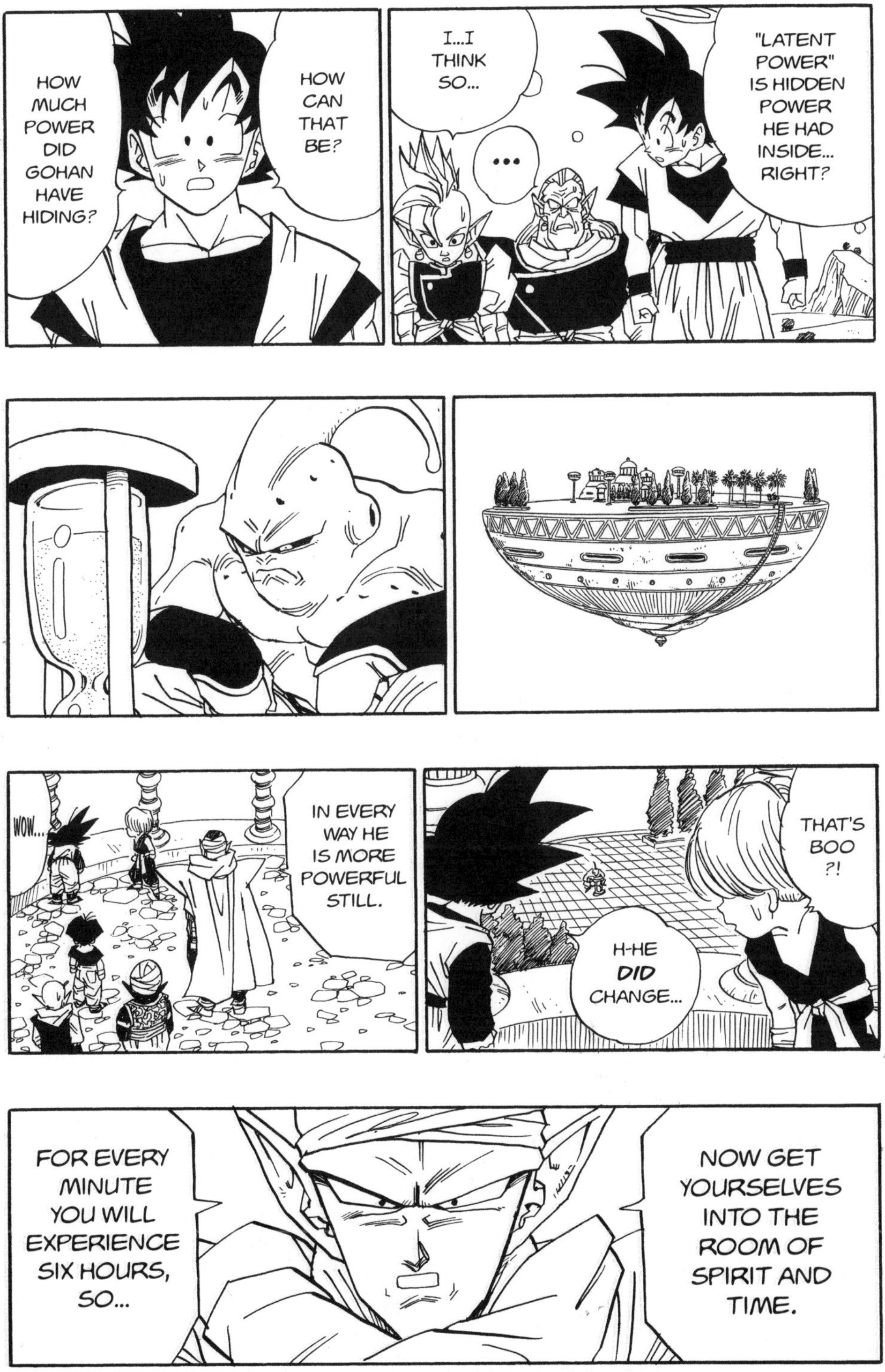
"LATENT POWER" IS HIDDEN POWER HE HAD INSIDE... RIGHT?
I...I THINK SO...
...
HOW CAN THAT BE?
HOW MUCH POWER DID GOHAN HAVE HIDING?
THAT'S BOO ?!
H-HE DID CHANGE...
IN EVERY WAY HE IS MORE POWERFUL STILL.
WOW...
NOW GET YOURSELVES INTO THE ROOM OF SPIRIT AND TIME.
FOR EVERY MINUTE YOU WILL EXPERIENCE SIX HOURS, SO...

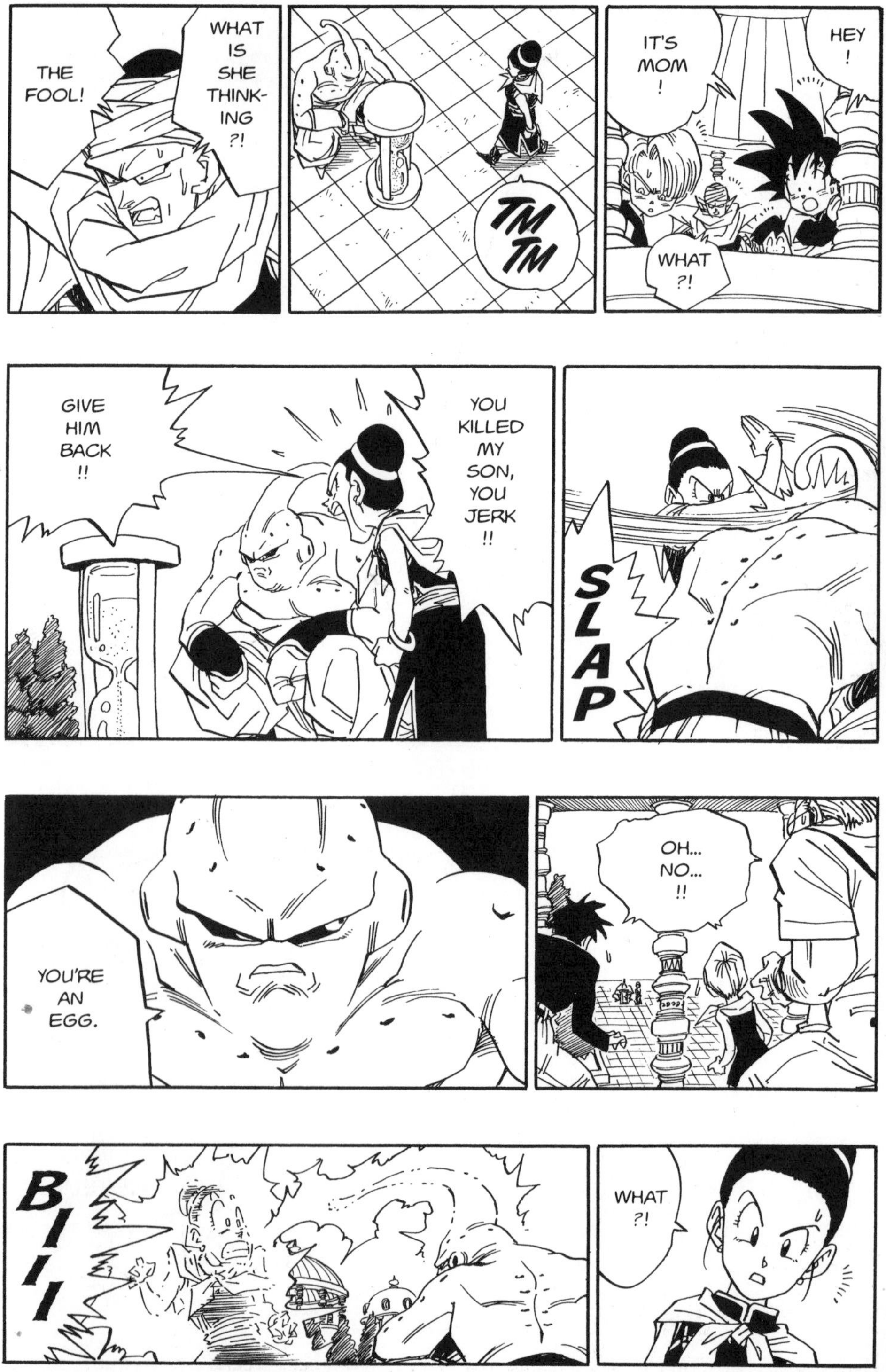
HEY!
IT'S MOM!
WHAT?!
TM TM
WHAT IS SHE THINKING?!
THE FOOL!
SLAP
YOU KILLED MY SON, YOU JERK!!
GIVE HIM BACK!!
OH... NO...!!
YOU'RE AN EGG.
WHAT?!
BIII

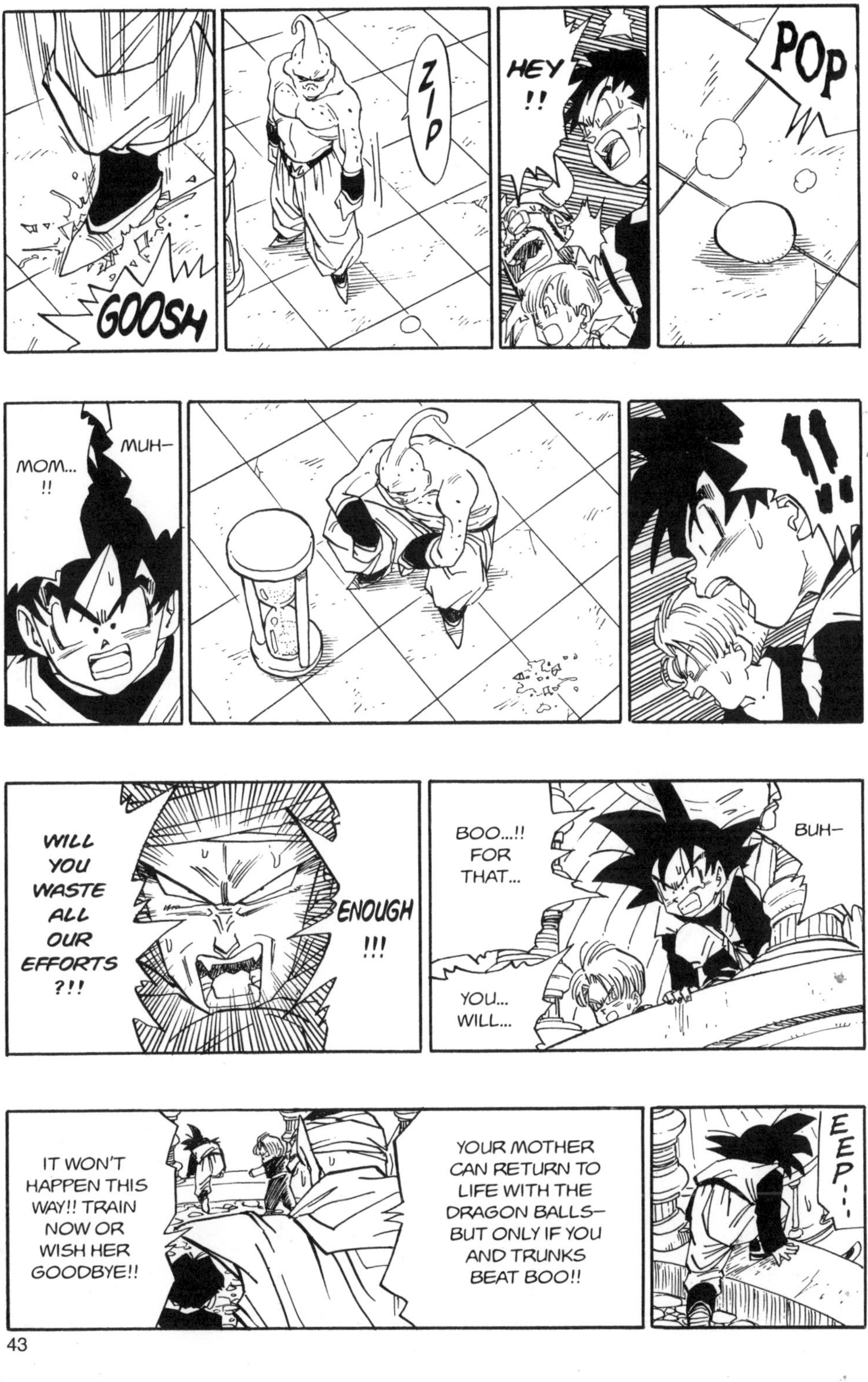
POP
HEY !!
ZIP
GOOSH
!!
MUH-
MOM... !!
BUH-
BOO...!! FOR THAT...
YOU... WILL...
ENOUGH !!!
WILL YOU WASTE ALL OUR EFFORTS ?!!
EEP...
YOUR MOTHER CAN RETURN TO LIFE WITH THE DRAGON BALLS— BUT ONLY IF YOU AND TRUNKS BEAT BOO!!
IT WON'T HAPPEN THIS WAY!! TRAIN NOW OR WISH HER GOODBYE!!

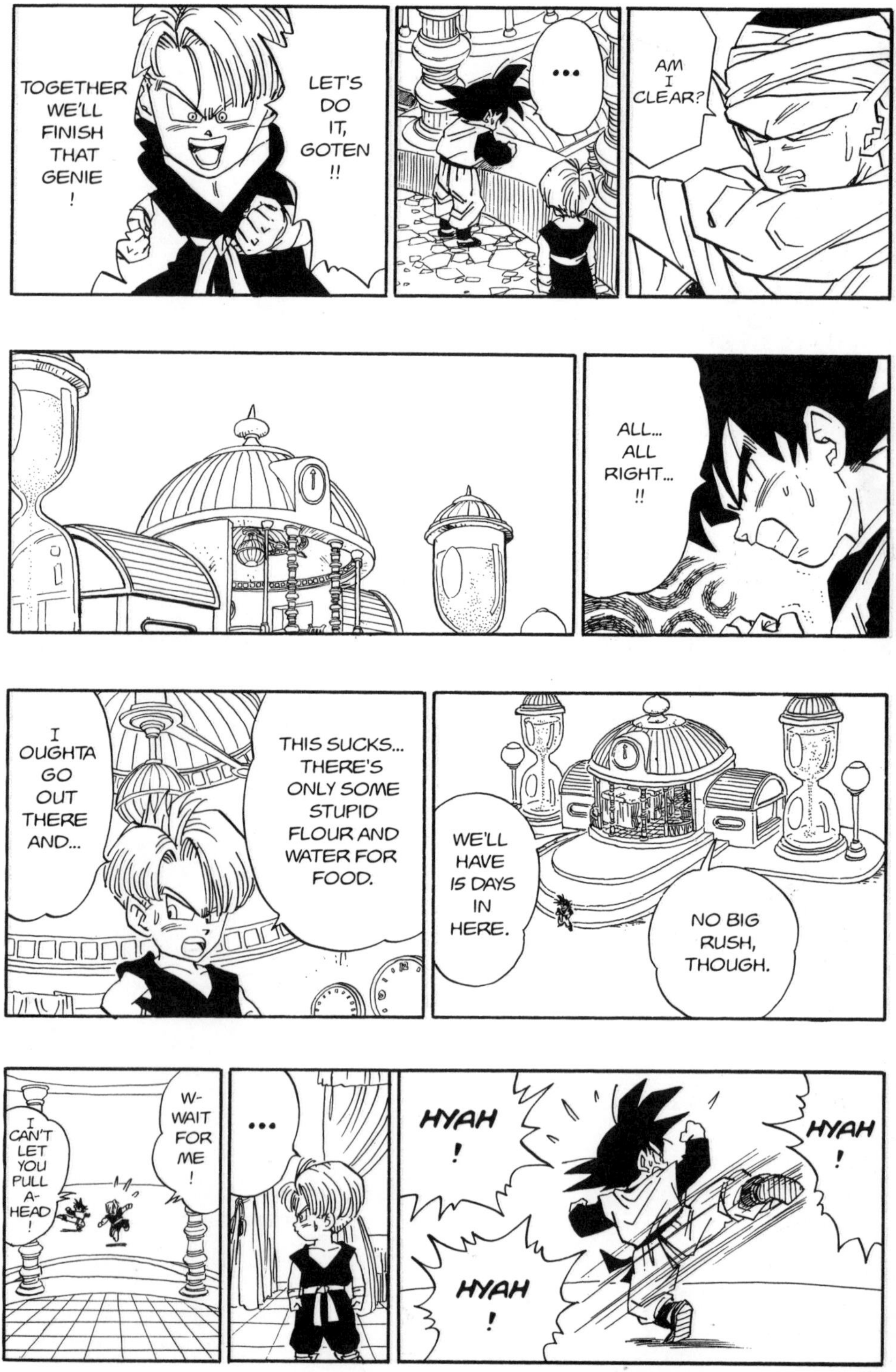
AM I CLEAR?
...
LET'S DO IT, GOTEN!!
TOGETHER WE'LL FINISH THAT GENIE!
ALL... ALL RIGHT...!!
WE'LL HAVE 15 DAYS IN HERE.
NO BIG RUSH, THOUGH.
THIS SUCKS... THERE'S ONLY SOME STUPID FLOUR AND WATER FOR FOOD.
I OUGHTA GO OUT THERE AND...
HYAH!
HYAH!
HYAH!
...
W-WAIT FOR ME!
I CAN'T LET YOU PULL A-HEAD!

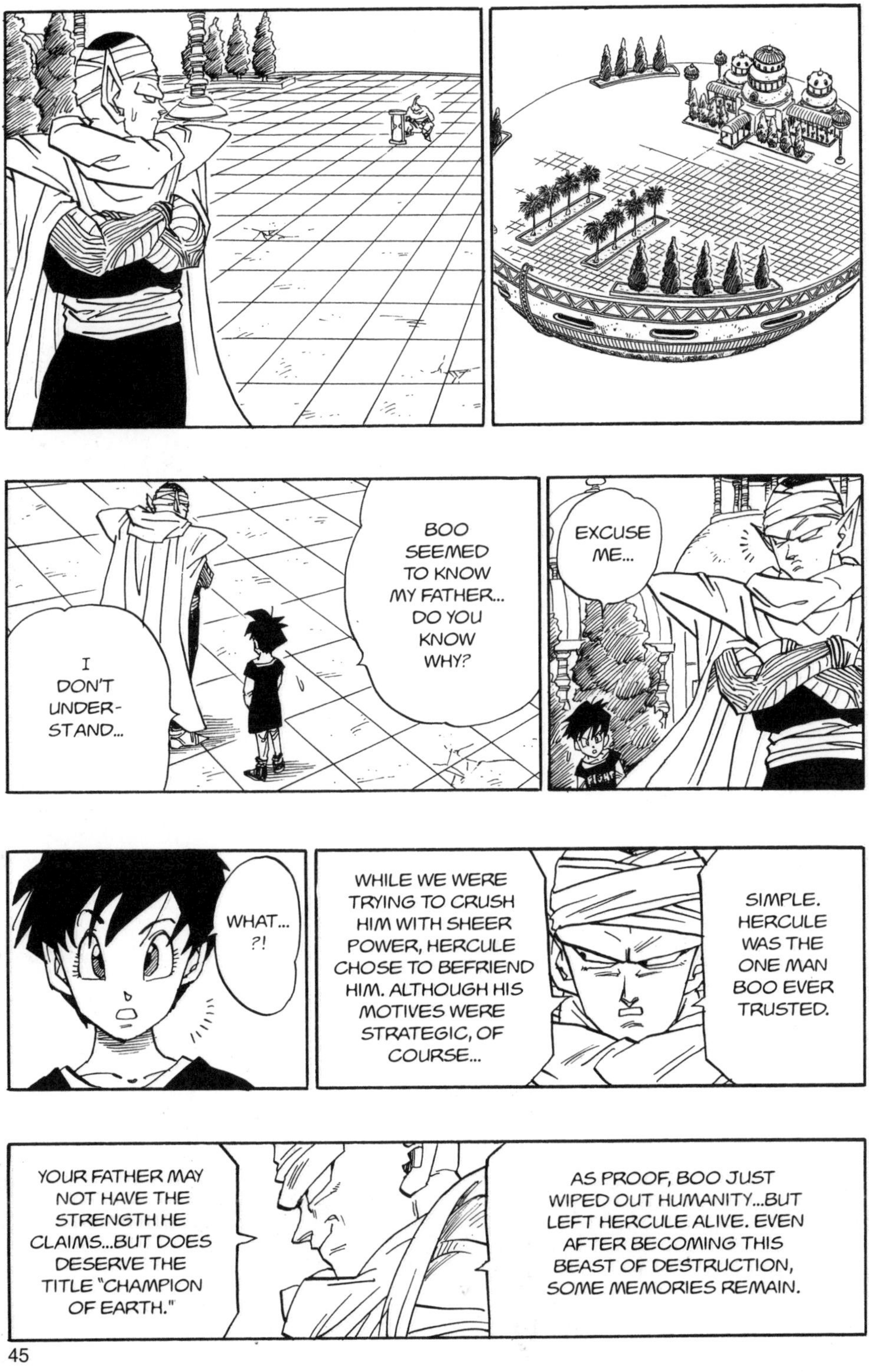
EXCUSE ME...
BOO SEEMED TO KNOW MY FATHER... DO YOU KNOW WHY?
I DON'T UNDER-STAND...
SIMPLE. HERCULE WAS THE ONE MAN BOO EVER TRUSTED.
WHILE WE WERE TRYING TO CRUSH HIM WITH SHEER POWER, HERCULE CHOSE TO BEFRIEND HIM. ALTHOUGH HIS MOTIVES WERE STRATEGIC, OF COURSE...
WHAT... ?!
AS PROOF, BOO JUST WIPED OUT HUMANITY...BUT LEFT HERCULE ALIVE. EVEN AFTER BECOMING THIS BEAST OF DESTRUCTION, SOME MEMORIES REMAIN.
YOUR FATHER MAY NOT HAVE THE STRENGTH HE CLAIMS...BUT DOES DESERVE THE TITLE "CHAMPION OF EARTH."

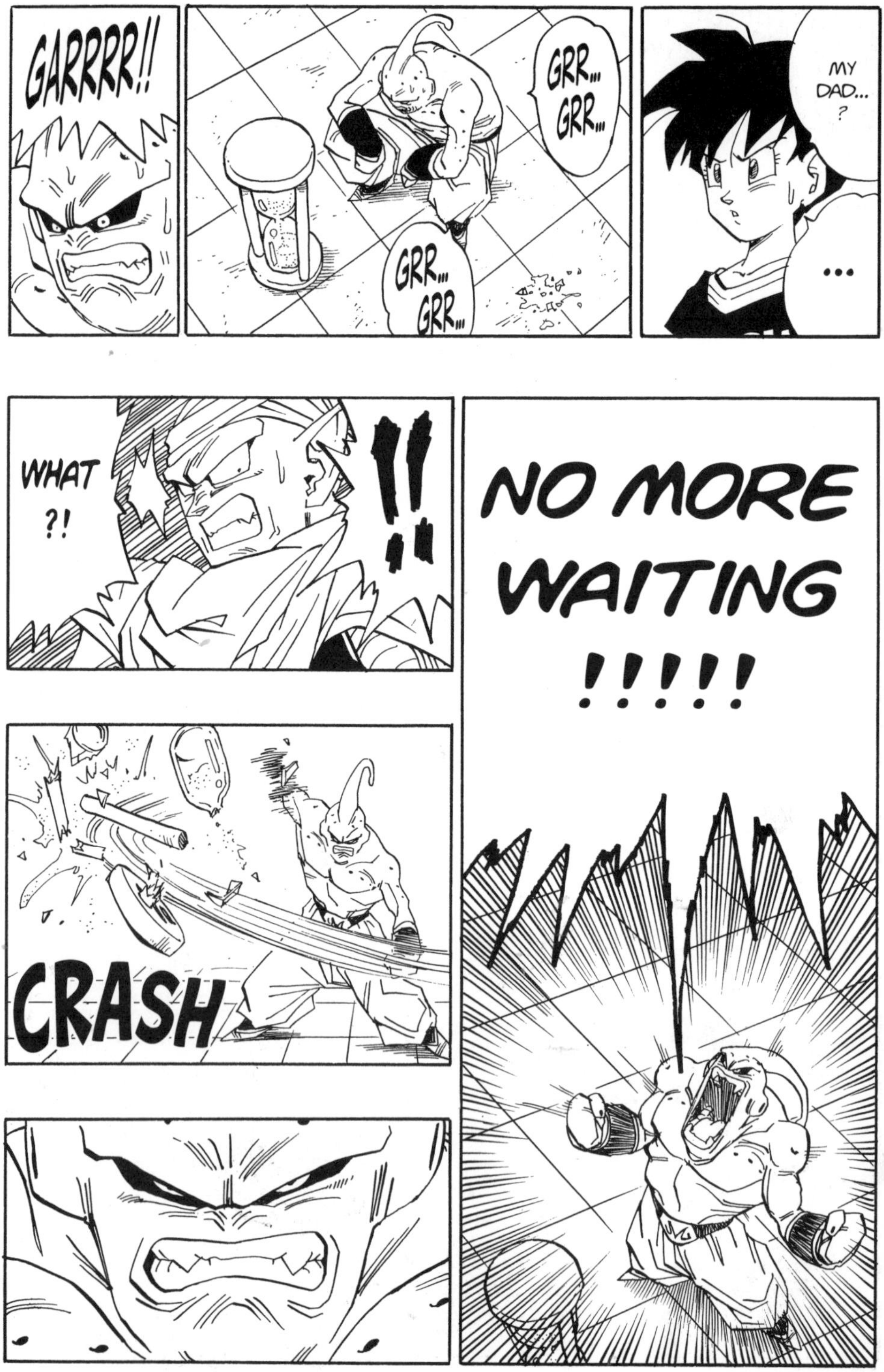
MY DAD...?
...
GRR... GRR...
GRR... GRR...
GARRRR!!
NO MORE WAITING!!!!!
WHAT?!
!!
CRASH

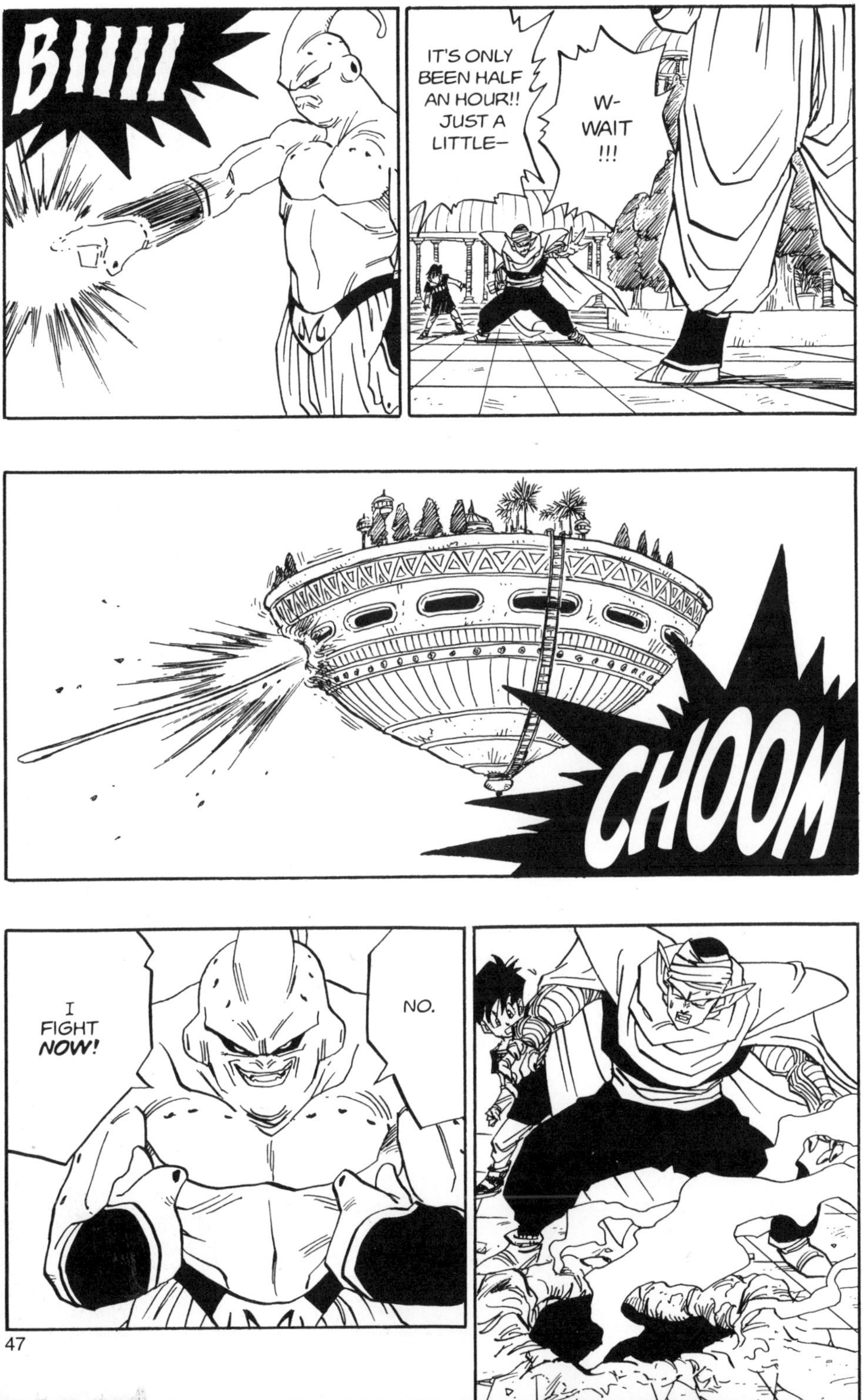
W- WAIT !!!
IT'S ONLY BEEN HALF AN HOUR!! JUST A LITTLE—
BIIII
CHOOM
NO.
I FIGHT ***NOW!***

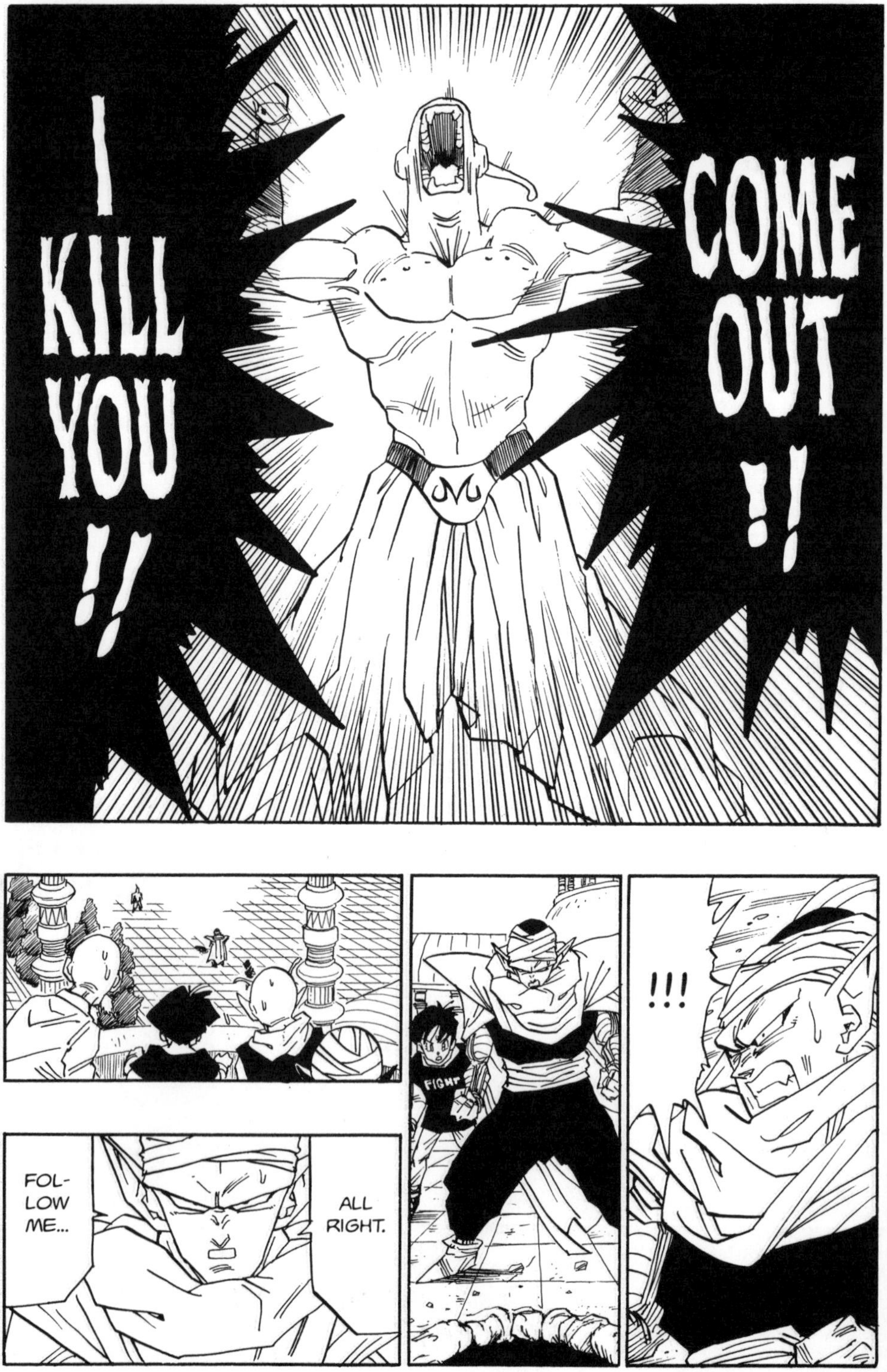
COME OUT!!
I KILL YOU!!
!!!
ALL RIGHT.
FOL-LOW ME...

THIS WAY...

EHEH...

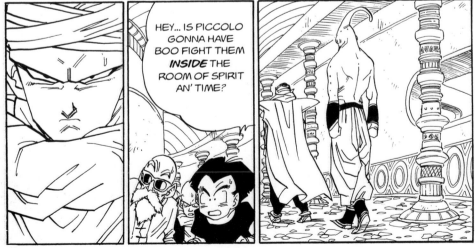

HEY... IS PICCOLO GONNA HAVE BOO FIGHT THEM *INSIDE* THE ROOM OF SPIRIT AN' TIME?

DBZ:295 • The Confidence of Gotenks!!

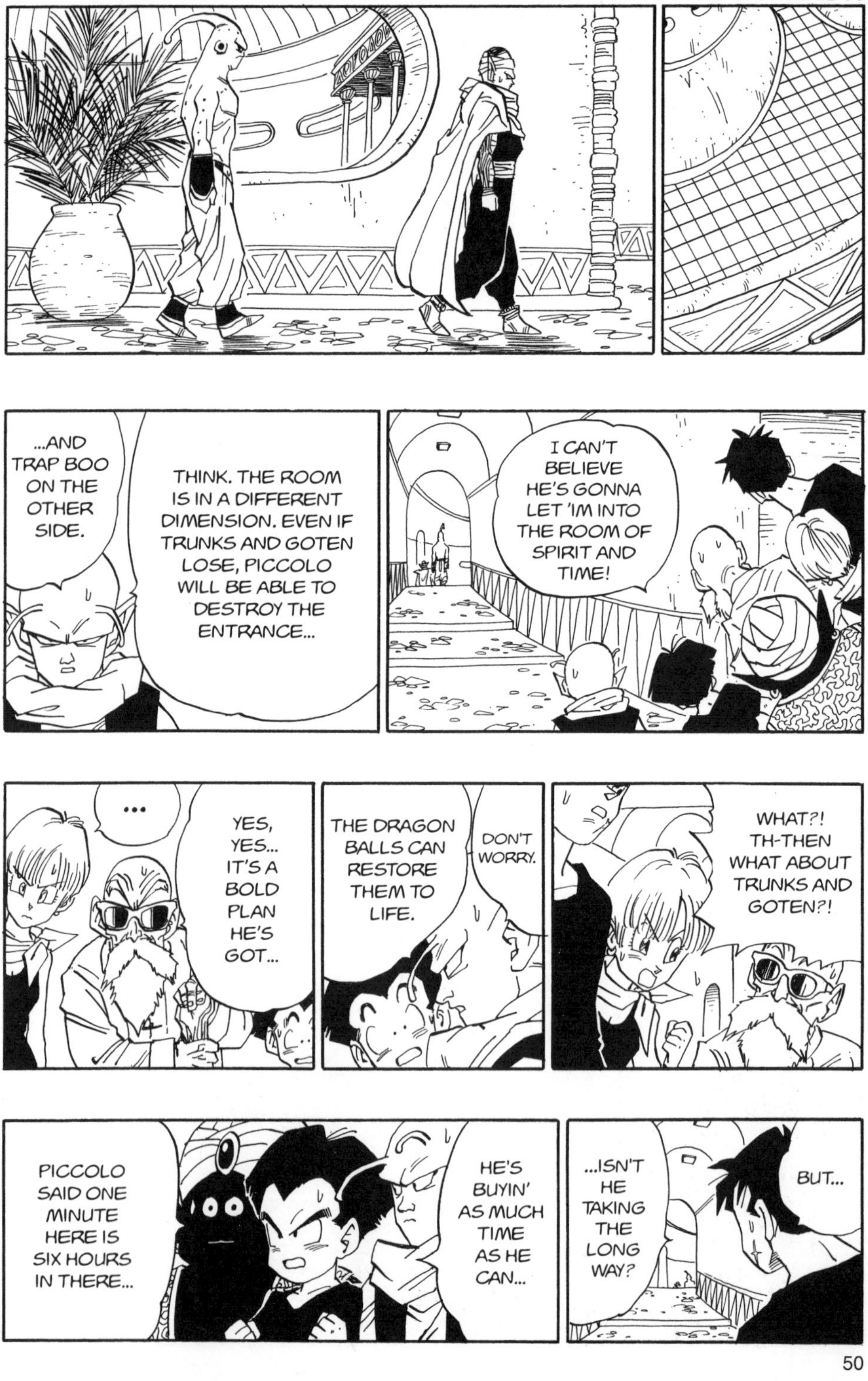

I CAN'T BELIEVE HE'S GONNA LET 'IM INTO THE ROOM OF SPIRIT AND TIME!
THINK. THE ROOM IS IN A DIFFERENT DIMENSION. EVEN IF TRUNKS AND GOTEN LOSE, PICCOLO WILL BE ABLE TO DESTROY THE ENTRANCE...
...AND TRAP BOO ON THE OTHER SIDE.
WHAT?! TH-THEN WHAT ABOUT TRUNKS AND GOTEN?!
DON'T WORRY.
THE DRAGON BALLS CAN RESTORE THEM TO LIFE.
YES, YES... IT'S A BOLD PLAN HE'S GOT...
...
BUT...
...ISN'T HE TAKING THE LONG WAY?
HE'S BUYIN' AS MUCH TIME AS HE CAN...
PICCOLO SAID ONE MINUTE HERE IS SIX HOURS IN THERE...

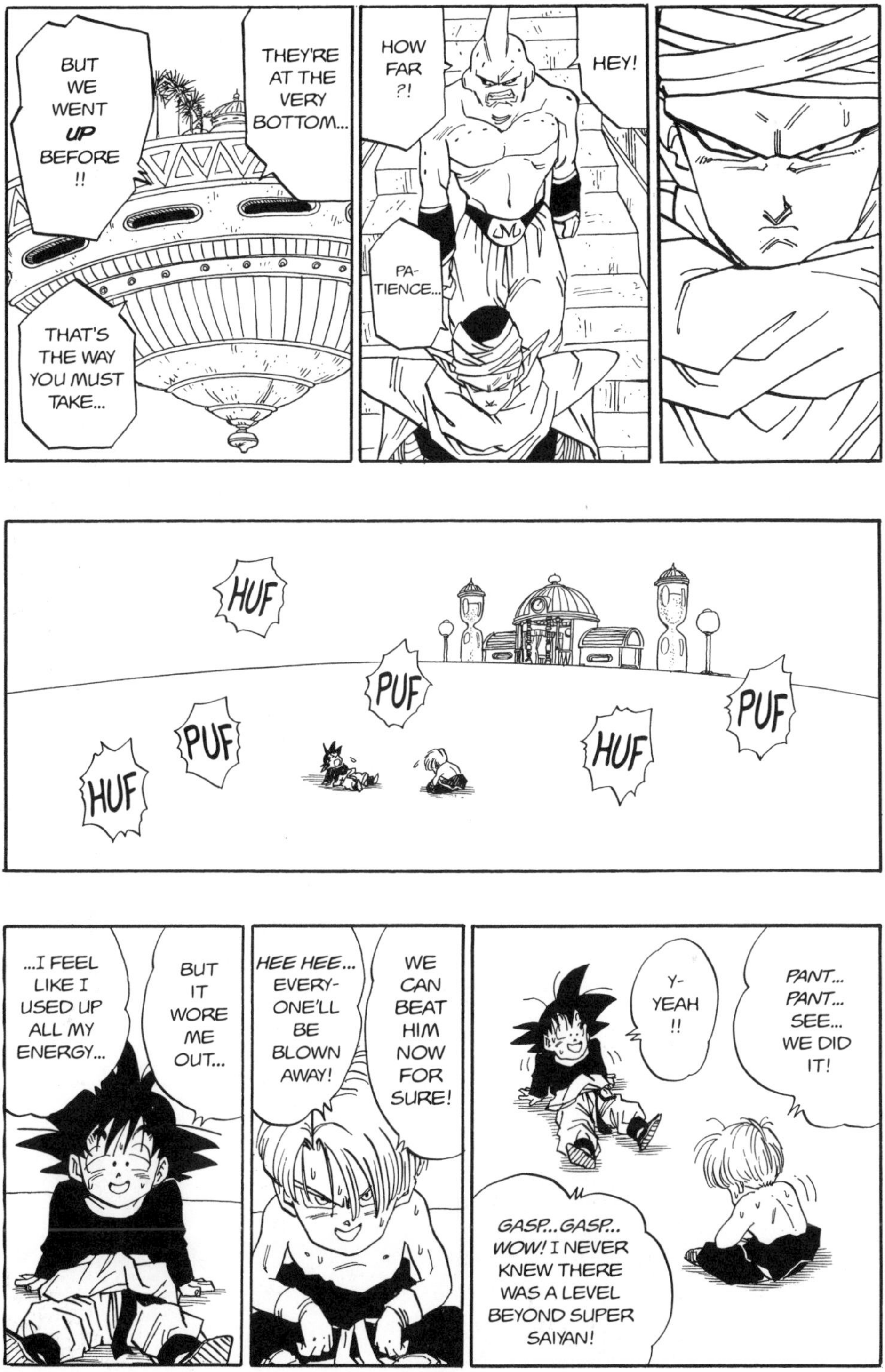
HEY!
HOW FAR ?!
PA-TIENCE...
THEY'RE AT THE VERY BOTTOM...
BUT WE WENT UP BEFORE !!
THAT'S THE WAY YOU MUST TAKE...
PUF
HUF
PUF
HUF
PUF
HUF
PANT... PANT... SEE... WE DID IT!
Y-YEAH !!
GASP... GASP... WOW! I NEVER KNEW THERE WAS A LEVEL BEYOND SUPER SAIYAN!
WE CAN BEAT HIM NOW FOR SURE!
HEE HEE... EVERY-ONE'LL BE BLOWN AWAY!
BUT IT WORE ME OUT...
...I FEEL LIKE I USED UP ALL MY ENERGY...

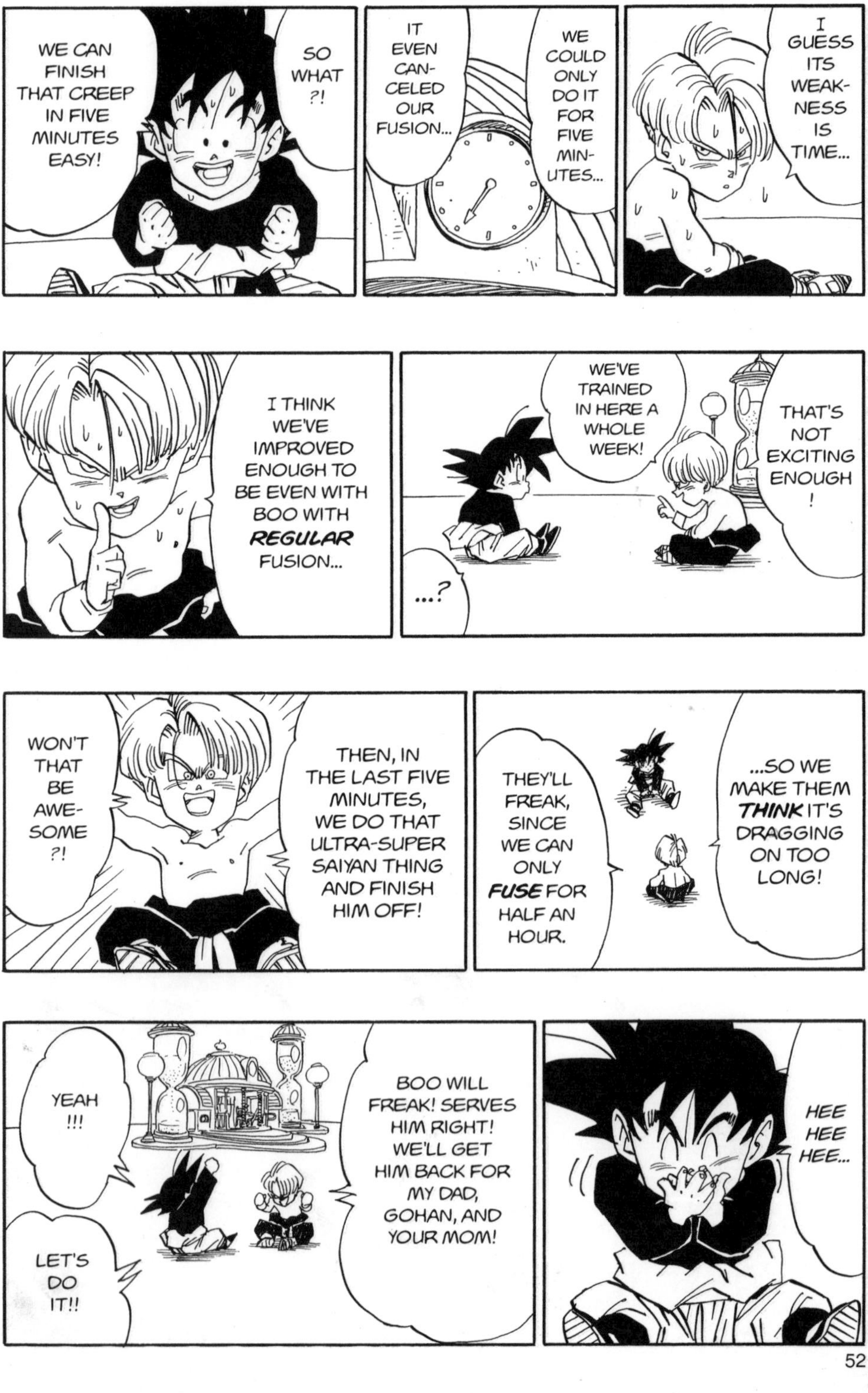
I GUESS ITS WEAKNESS IS TIME...
WE COULD ONLY DO IT FOR FIVE MINUTES...
IT EVEN CANCELED OUR FUSION...
SO WHAT?!
WE CAN FINISH THAT CREEP IN FIVE MINUTES EASY!
THAT'S NOT EXCITING ENOUGH!
WE'VE TRAINED IN HERE A WHOLE WEEK!
...?
I THINK WE'VE IMPROVED ENOUGH TO BE EVEN WITH BOO WITH ***REGULAR*** FUSION...
...SO WE MAKE THEM ***THINK*** IT'S DRAGGING ON TOO LONG!
THEY'LL FREAK, SINCE WE CAN ONLY ***FUSE*** FOR HALF AN HOUR.
THEN, IN THE LAST FIVE MINUTES, WE DO THAT ULTRA-SUPER SAIYAN THING AND FINISH HIM OFF!
WON'T THAT BE AWESOME?!
HEE HEE HEE...
BOO WILL FREAK! SERVES HIM RIGHT! WE'LL GET HIM BACK FOR MY DAD, GOHAN, AND YOUR MOM!
YEAH!!!
LET'S DO IT!!

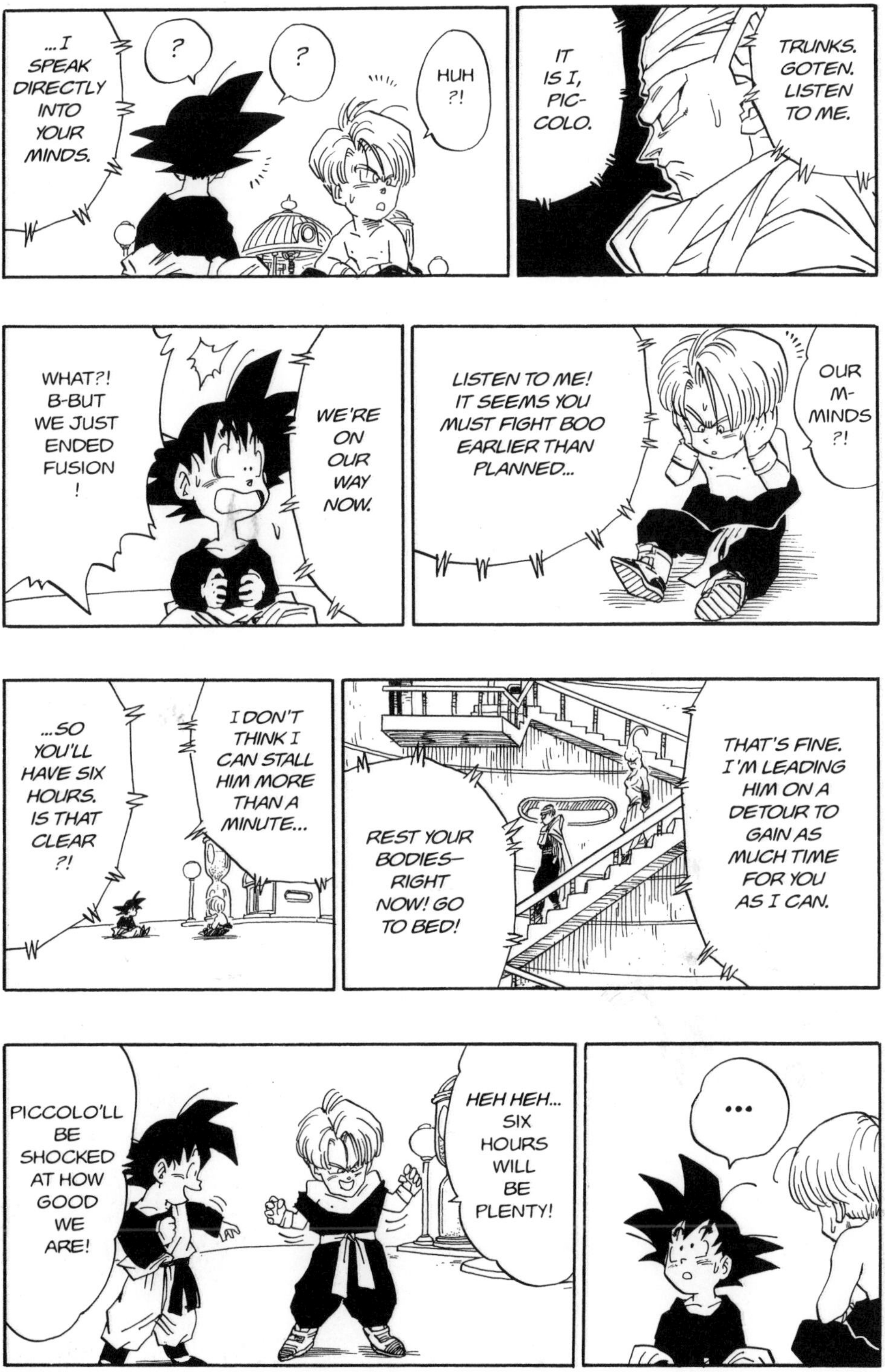
TRUNKS. GOTEN. LISTEN TO ME.
IT IS I, PICCOLO.
HUH ?!
?
?
...I SPEAK DIRECTLY INTO YOUR MINDS.
OUR M-MINDS ?!
LISTEN TO ME! IT SEEMS YOU MUST FIGHT BOO EARLIER THAN PLANNED...
WE'RE ON OUR WAY NOW.
WHAT?! B-BUT WE JUST ENDED FUSION !
THAT'S FINE. I'M LEADING HIM ON A DETOUR TO GAIN AS MUCH TIME FOR YOU AS I CAN.
REST YOUR BODIES—RIGHT NOW! GO TO BED!
I DON'T THINK I CAN STALL HIM MORE THAN A MINUTE...
...SO YOU'LL HAVE SIX HOURS. IS THAT CLEAR ?!
...
HEH HEH... SIX HOURS WILL BE PLENTY!
PICCOLO'LL BE SHOCKED AT HOW GOOD WE ARE!

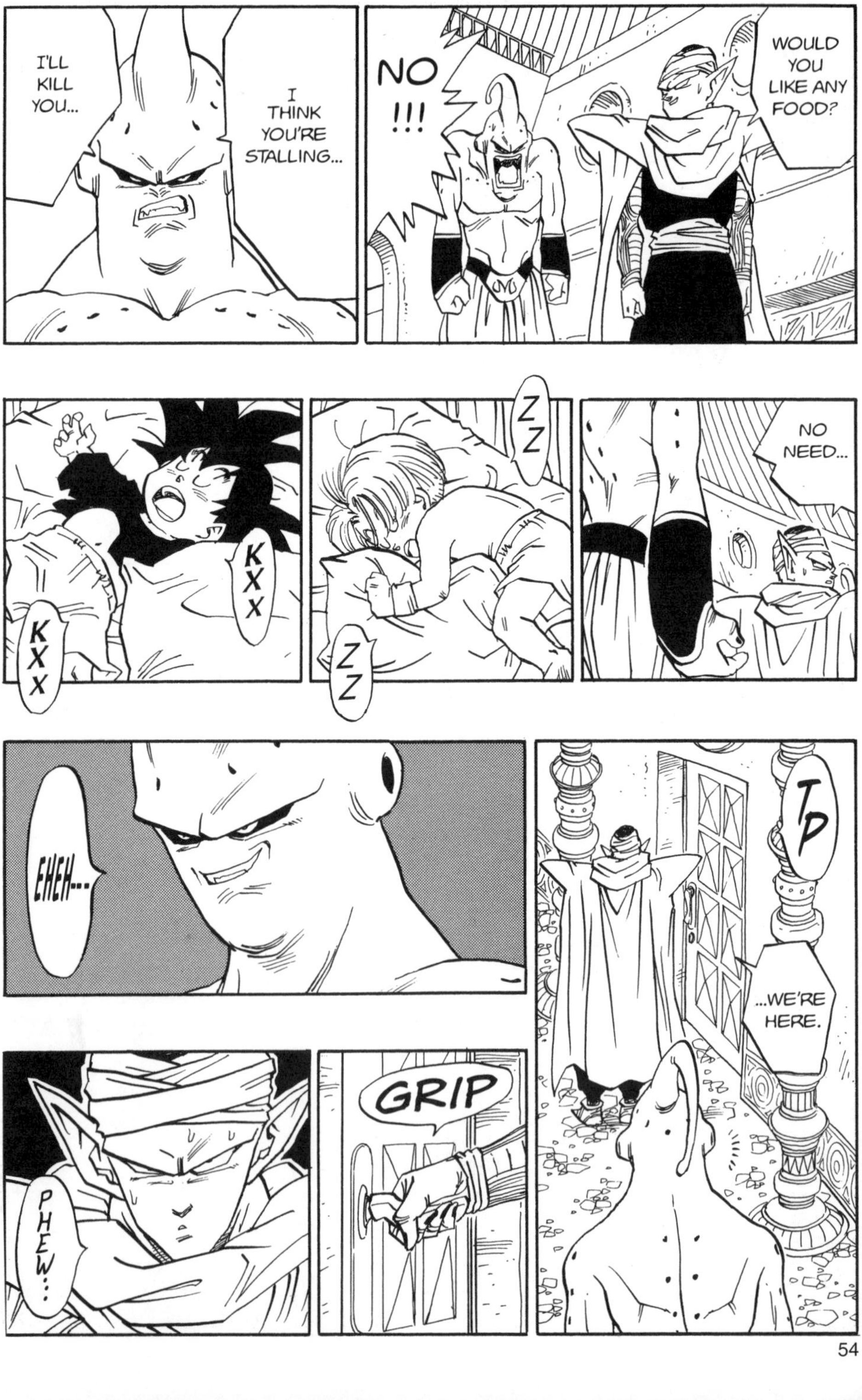
WOULD YOU LIKE ANY FOOD?
NO !!!
I THINK YOU'RE STALLING...
I'LL KILL YOU...
NO NEED...
ZZ
ZZ
KXX
KXX
TP
...WE'RE HERE.
EHEH...
GRIP
PHEW...

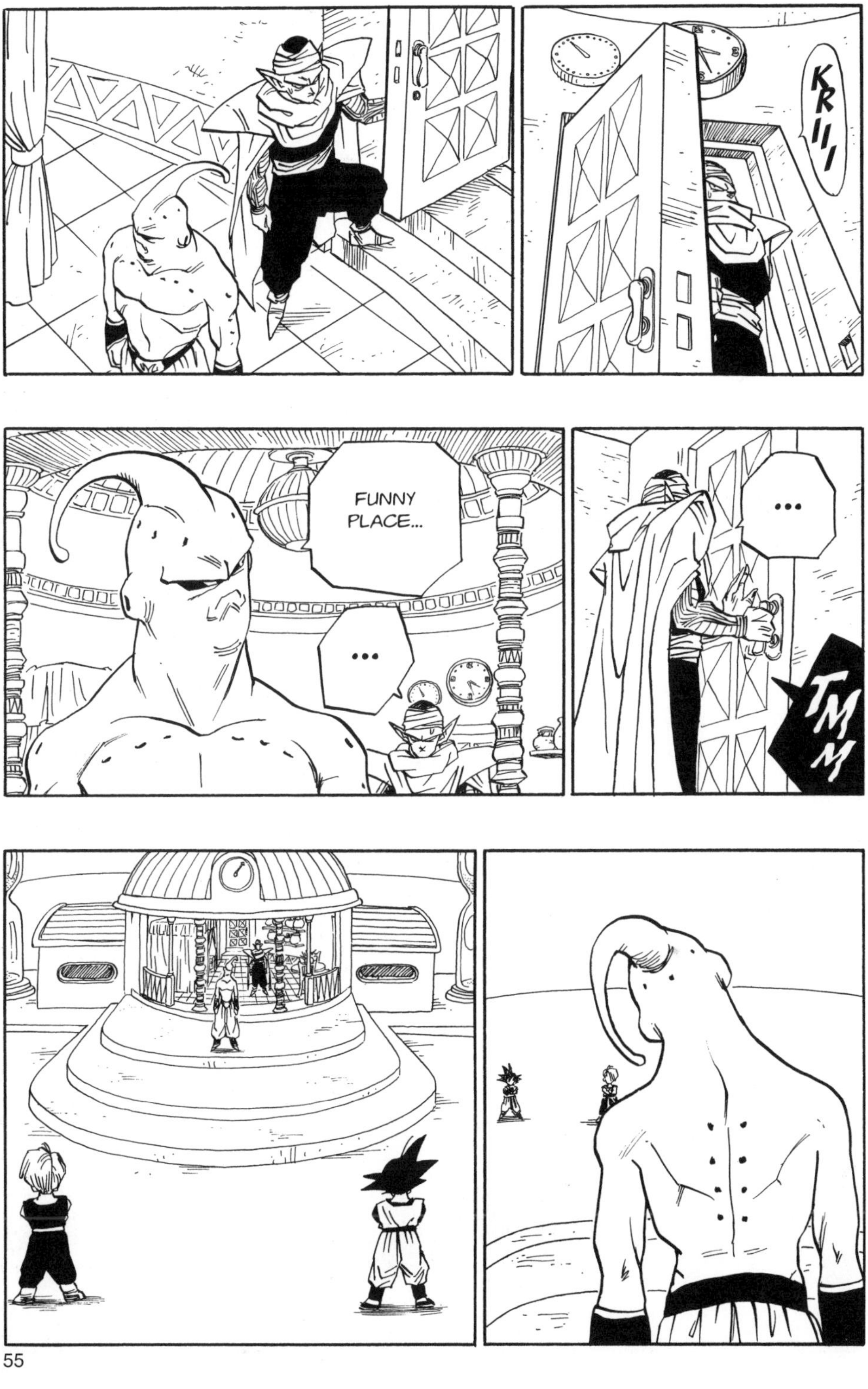
KRIIII
...
TMM
FUNNY PLACE...
...

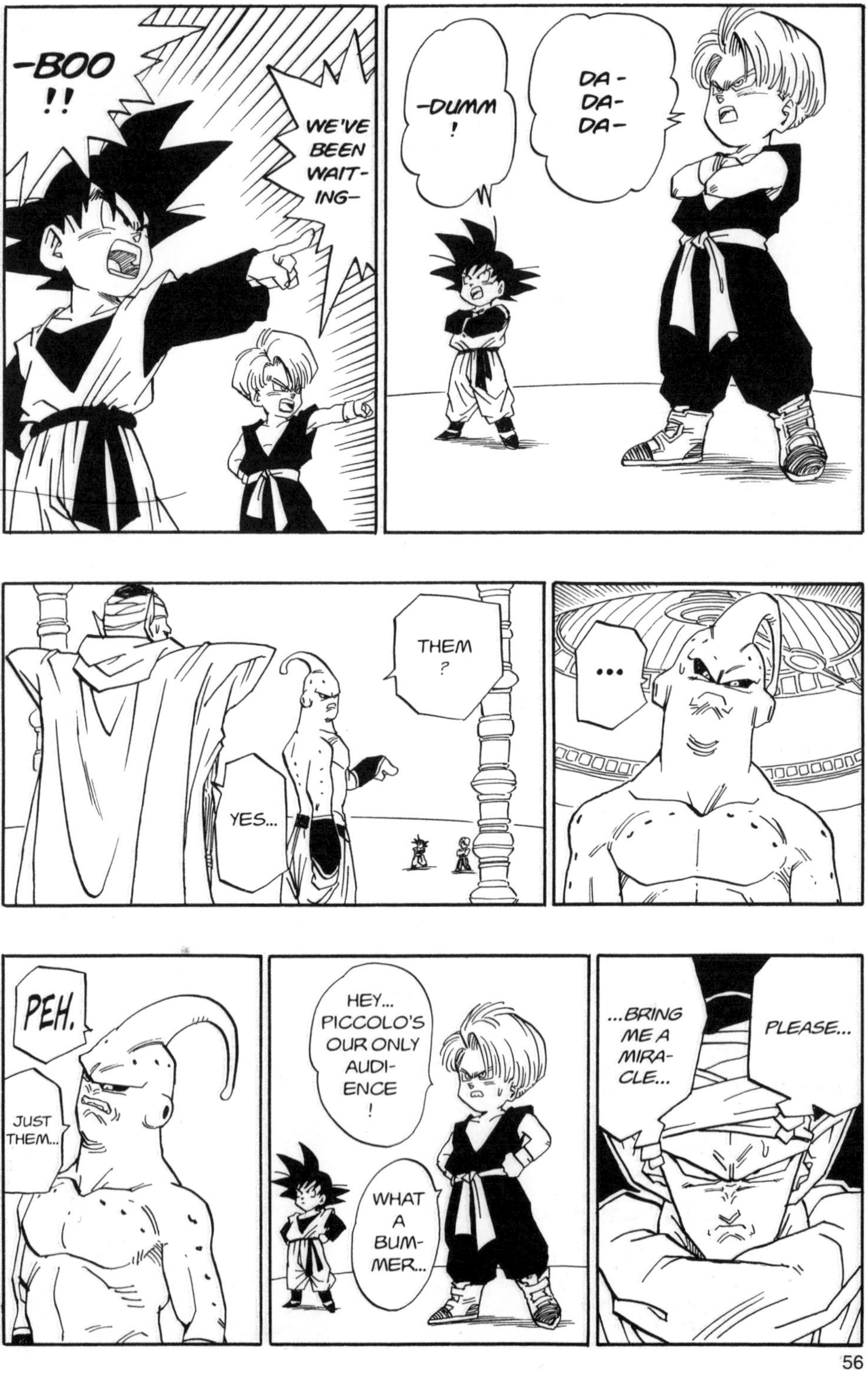
DA-DA-DA-
-DUMM!
WE'VE BEEN WAITING-
-BOO!!
...
THEM?
YES...
PLEASE...
...BRING ME A MIRACLE...
HEY... PICCOLO'S OUR ONLY AUDIENCE!
WHAT A BUMMER...
PEH.
JUST THEM...

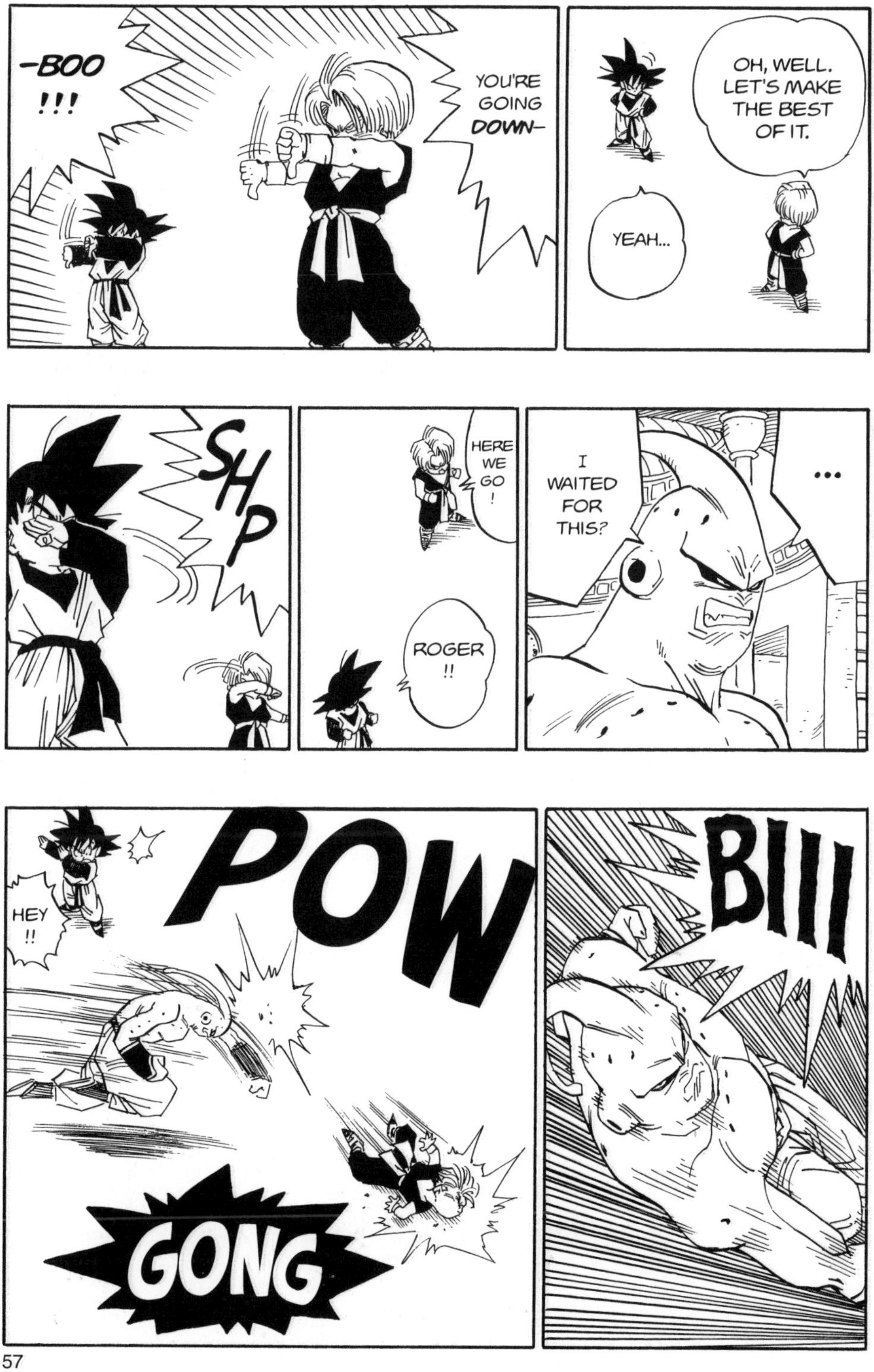
OH, WELL. LET'S MAKE THE BEST OF IT.
YEAH...
YOU'RE GOING DOWN-
-BOO !!!
...
I WAITED FOR THIS?
HERE WE GO !
ROGER !!
SHP
BIII
POW
HEY !!
GONG

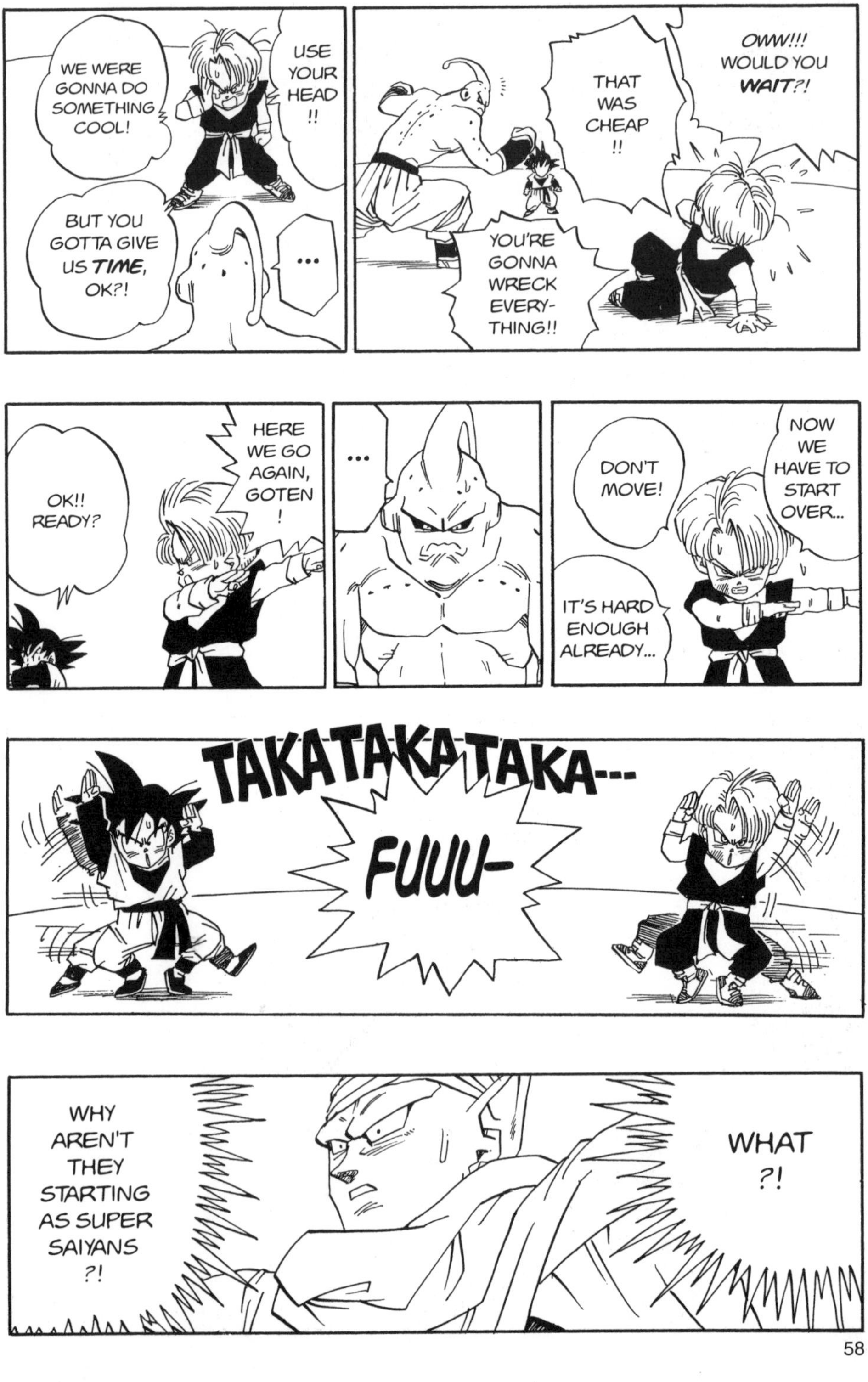
OWW!!! WOULD YOU WAIT?!
THAT WAS CHEAP!!
YOU'RE GONNA WRECK EVERY-THING!!
USE YOUR HEAD!!
WE WERE GONNA DO SOMETHING COOL!
BUT YOU GOTTA GIVE US TIME, OK?!
...
NOW WE HAVE TO START OVER...
DON'T MOVE!
IT'S HARD ENOUGH ALREADY...
...
HERE WE GO AGAIN, GOTEN!
OK!! READY?
TAKATAKATAKATAKA...
FUUU-
WHAT?!
WHY AREN'T THEY STARTING AS SUPER SAIYANS?!

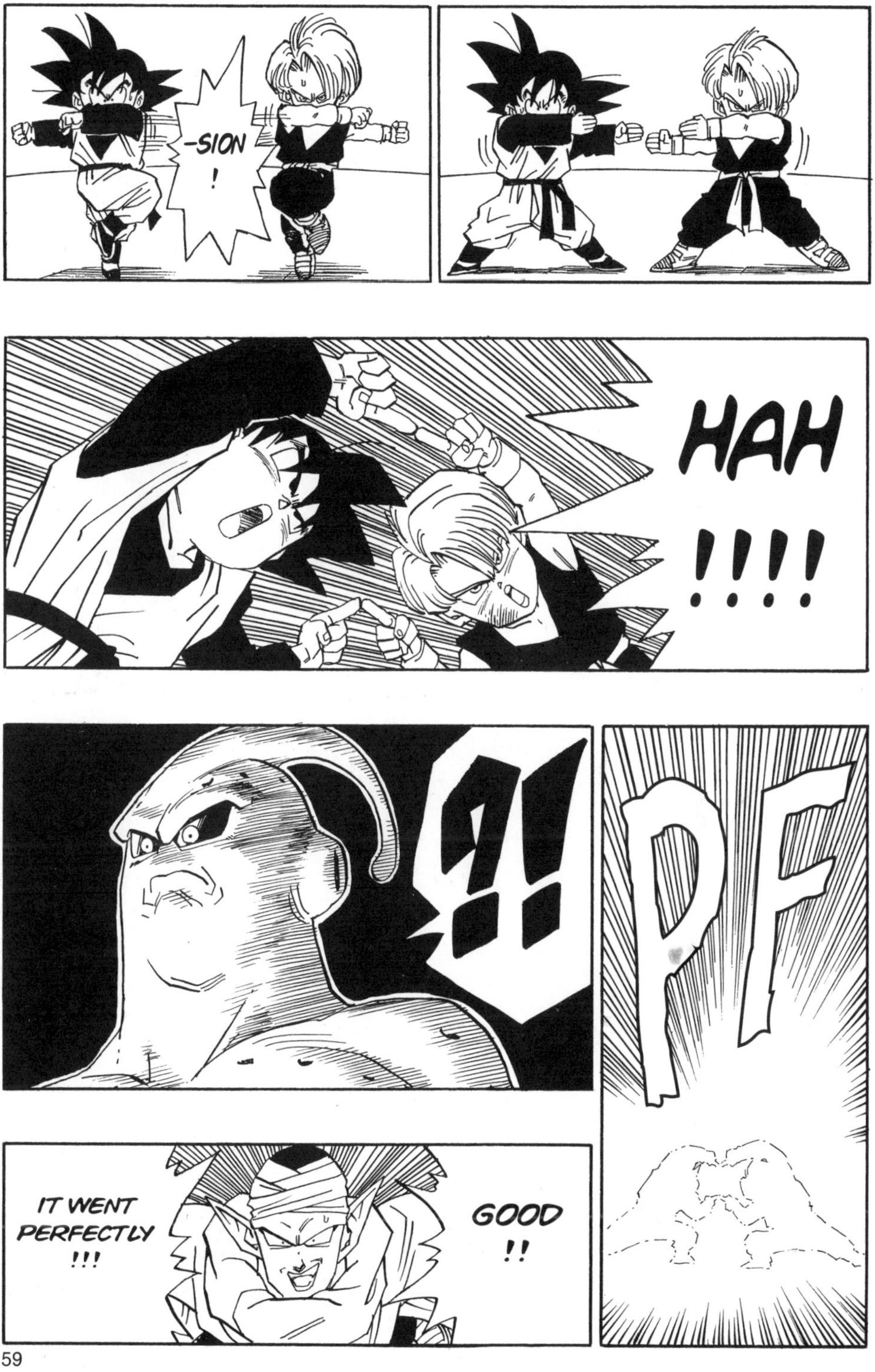
-SION
!
HAH
!!!!
PF
?!!
GOOD
!!
IT WENT
PERFECTLY
!!!

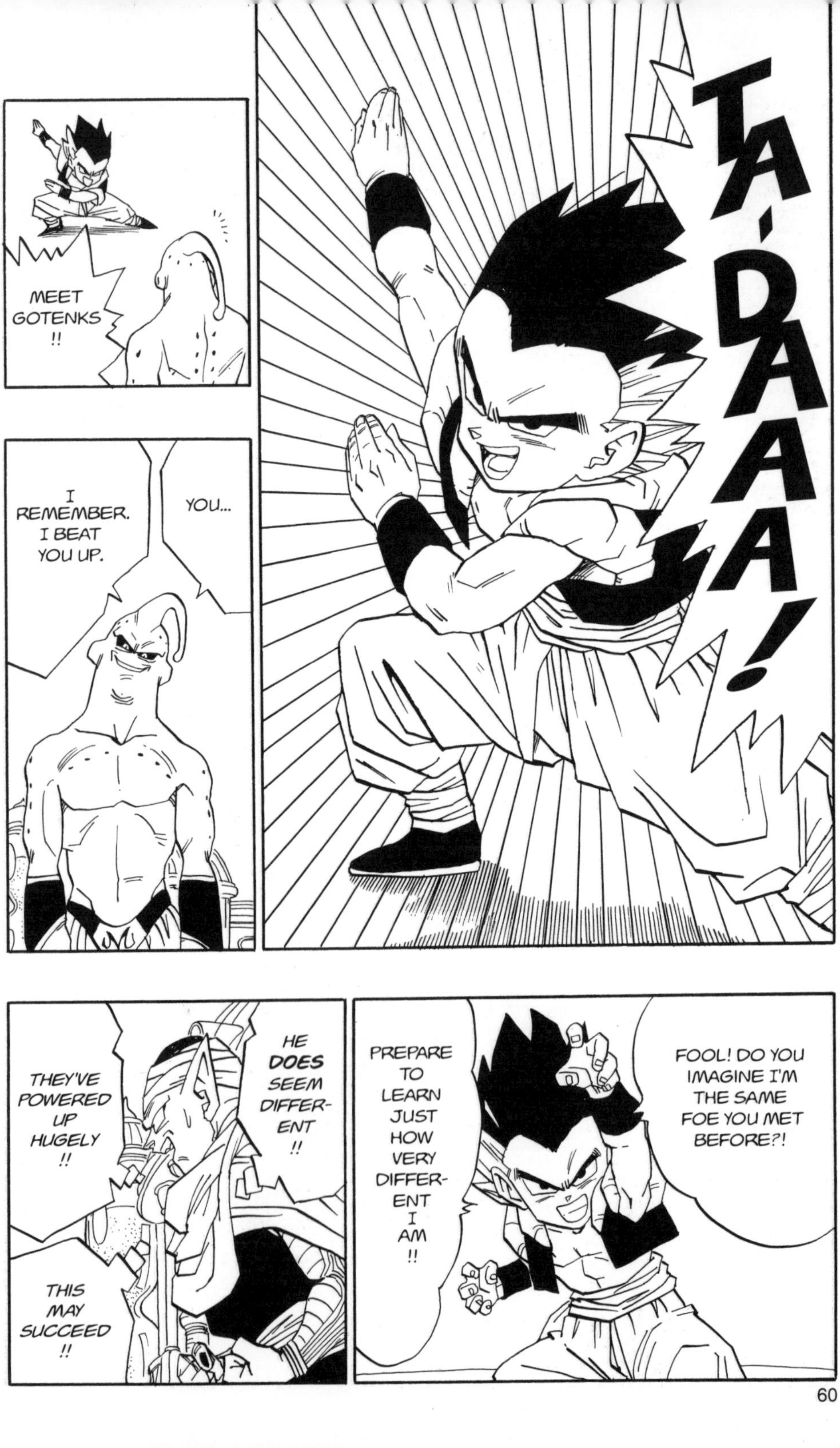
TA-DAAAA!
MEET GOTENKS !!
YOU...
I REMEMBER. I BEAT YOU UP.
FOOL! DO YOU IMAGINE I'M THE SAME FOE YOU MET BEFORE?!
PREPARE TO LEARN JUST HOW VERY DIFFER-ENT I AM !!
HE **DOES** SEEM DIFFER-ENT !!
THEY'VE POWERED UP HUGELY !!
THIS MAY SUCCEED !!

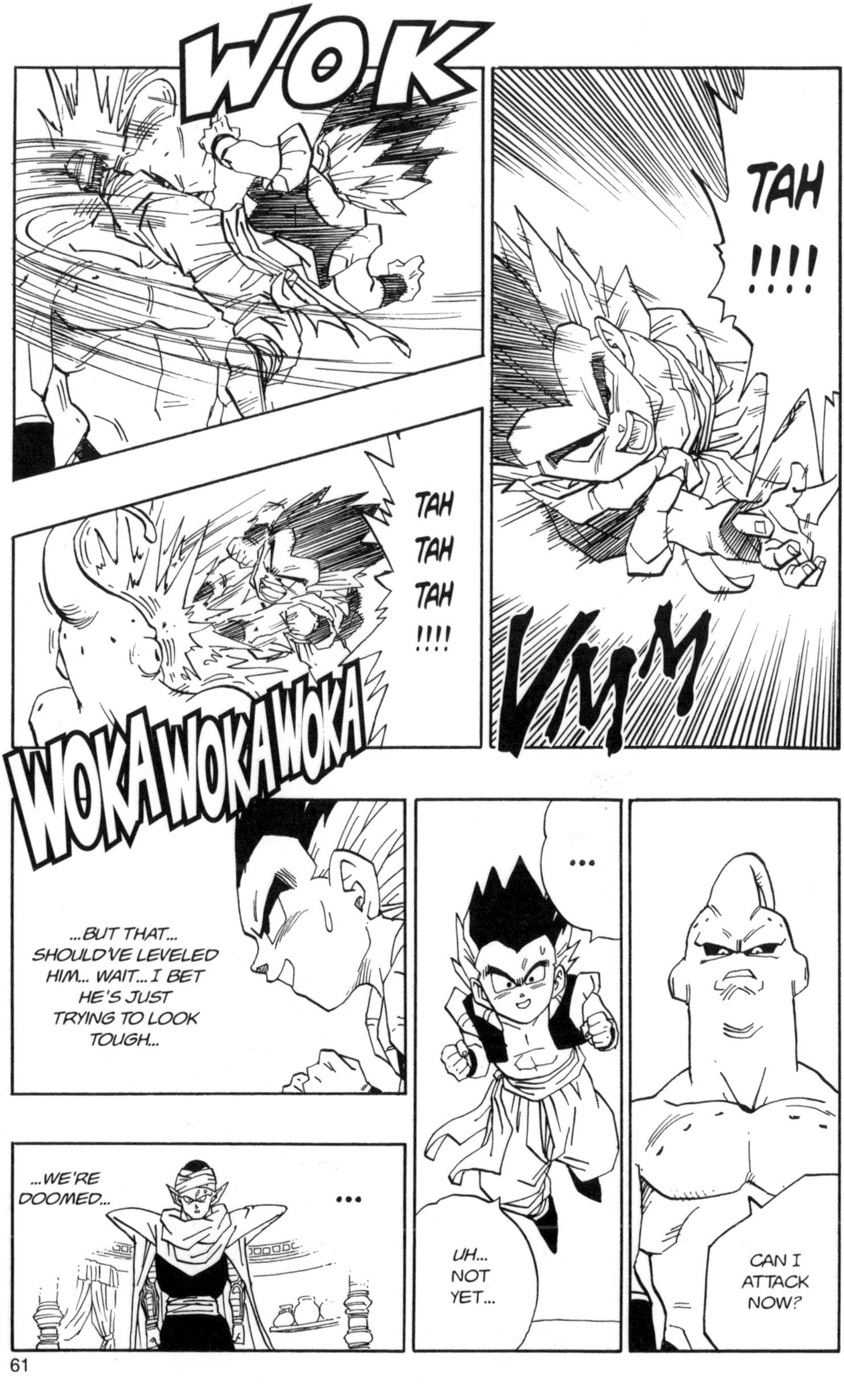
TAH !!!!
VMM
WOK
TAH TAH TAH !!!!
WOKAWOKAWOKA
CAN I ATTACK NOW?
...
UH... NOT YET...
...BUT THAT... SHOULD'VE LEVELED HIM... WAIT... I BET HE'S JUST TRYING TO LOOK TOUGH...
...WE'RE DOOMED...
...

DRAGON BALL ドラゴンボール

DBZ:296 · The *Extreme* Confidence of Gotenks!!

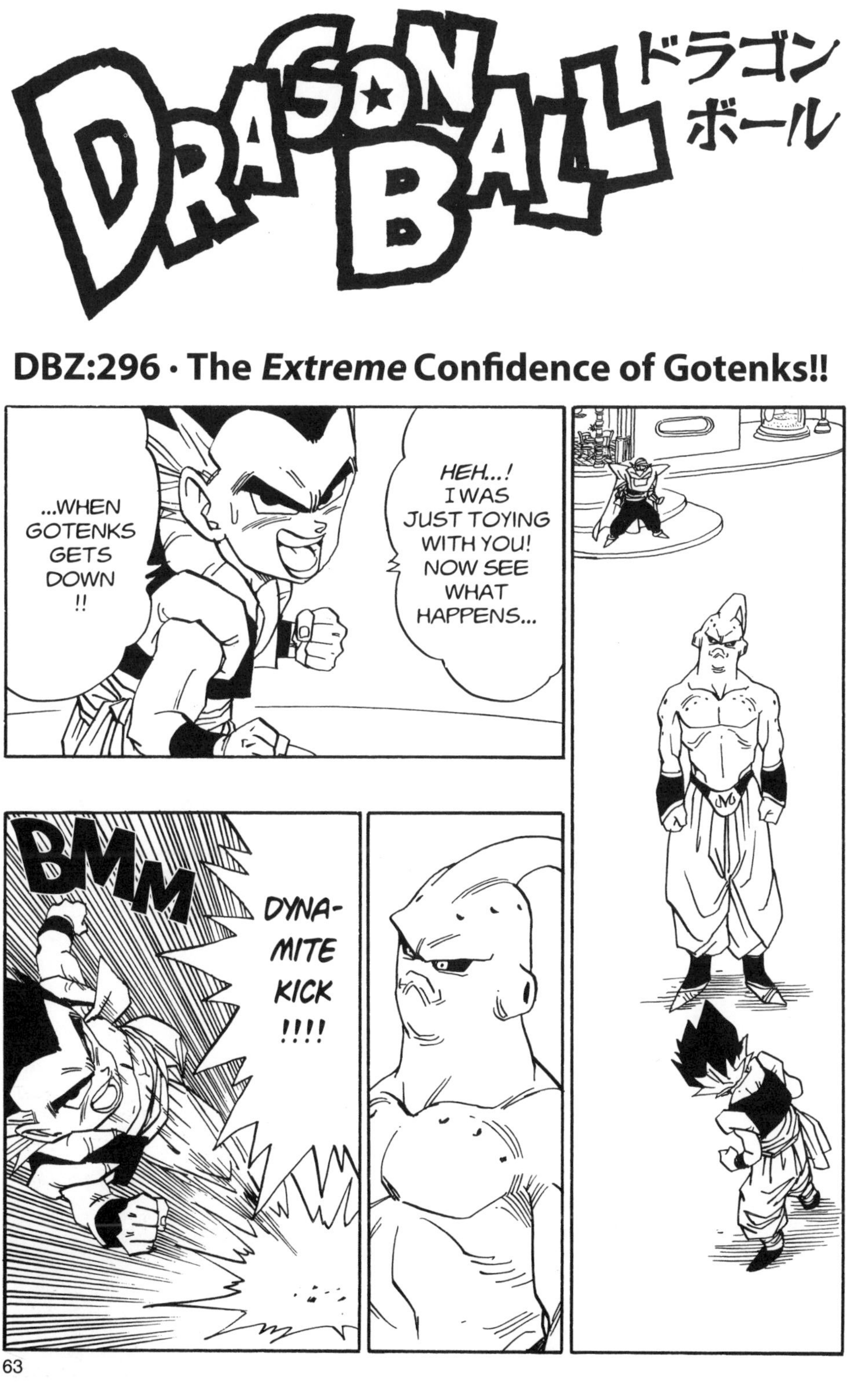
HEH...! I WAS JUST TOYING WITH YOU! NOW SEE WHAT HAPPENS...
...WHEN GOTENKS GETS DOWN !!
DYNA-MITE KICK !!!!
BMM

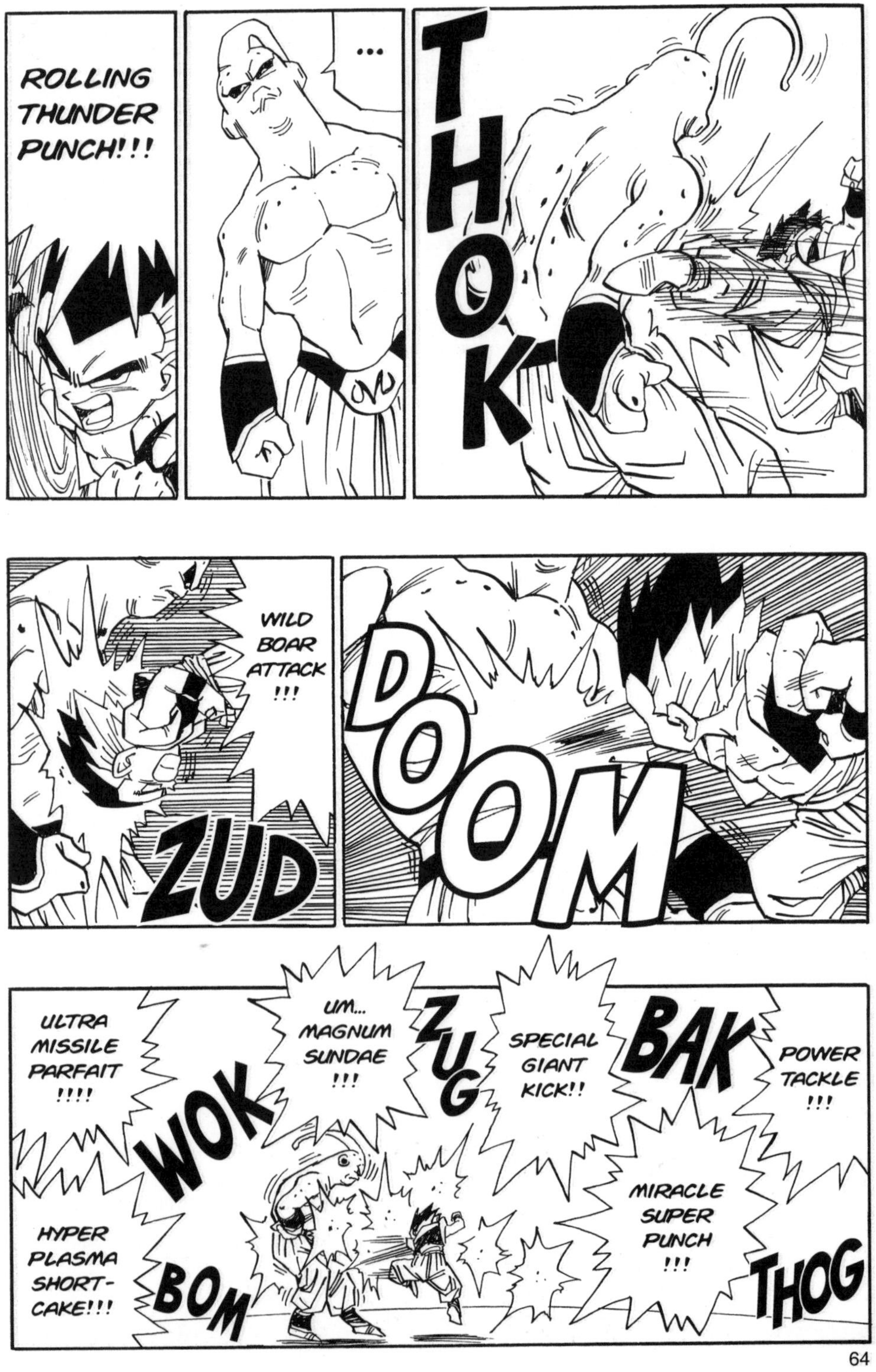
THOK
...
ROLLING THUNDER PUNCH!!!
DOOM
WILD BOAR ATTACK !!!
ZUD
POWER TACKLE !!!
BAK
SPECIAL GIANT KICK!!
ZUG
UM... MAGNUM SUNDAE !!!
ULTRA MISSILE PARFAIT !!!!
WOK
MIRACLE SUPER PUNCH !!!
THOG
HYPER PLASMA SHORT-CAKE!!!
BOM

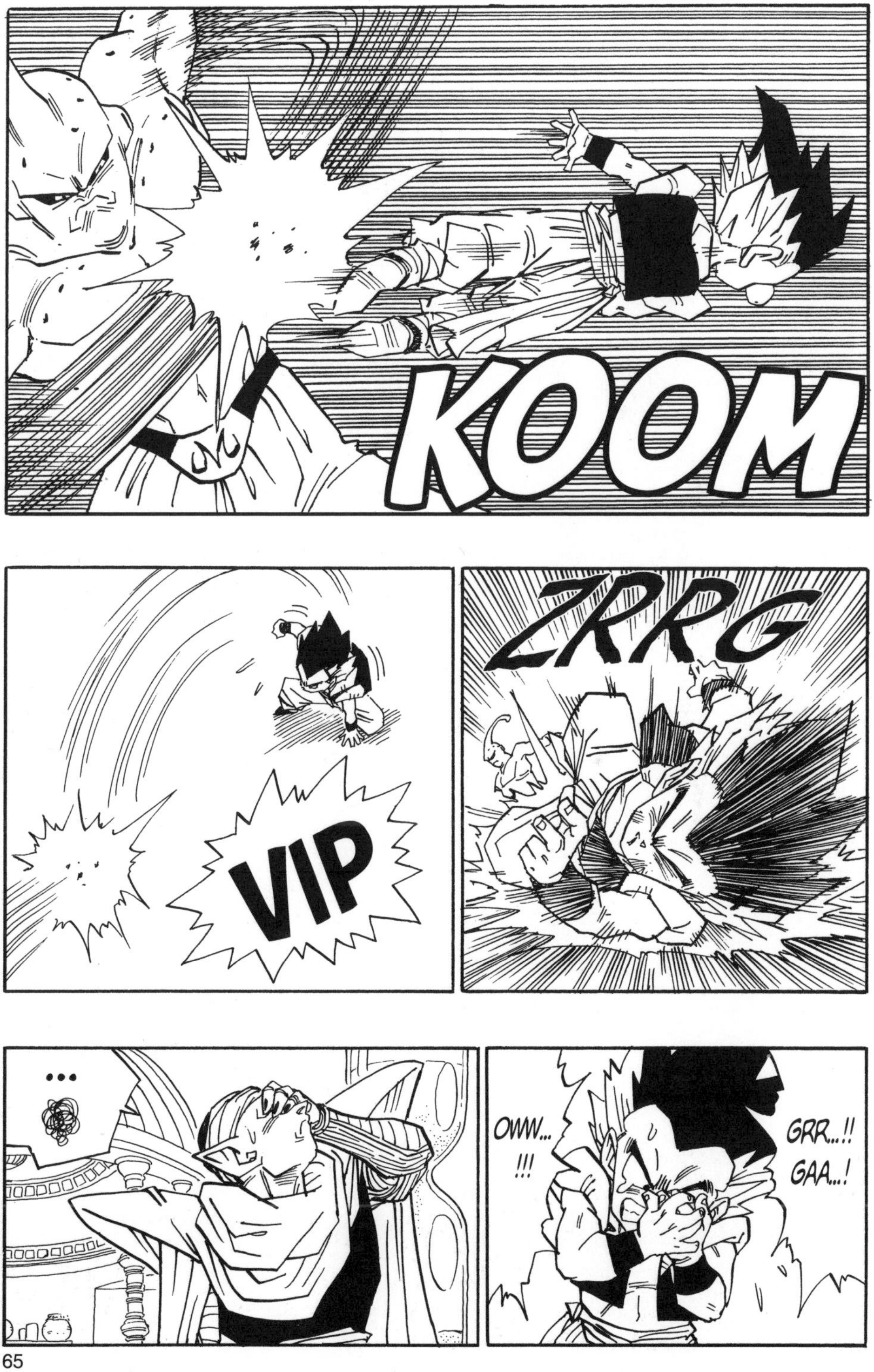
KOOM
ZRRG
VIP
GRR...!! GAA...!
OWW... !!!
...

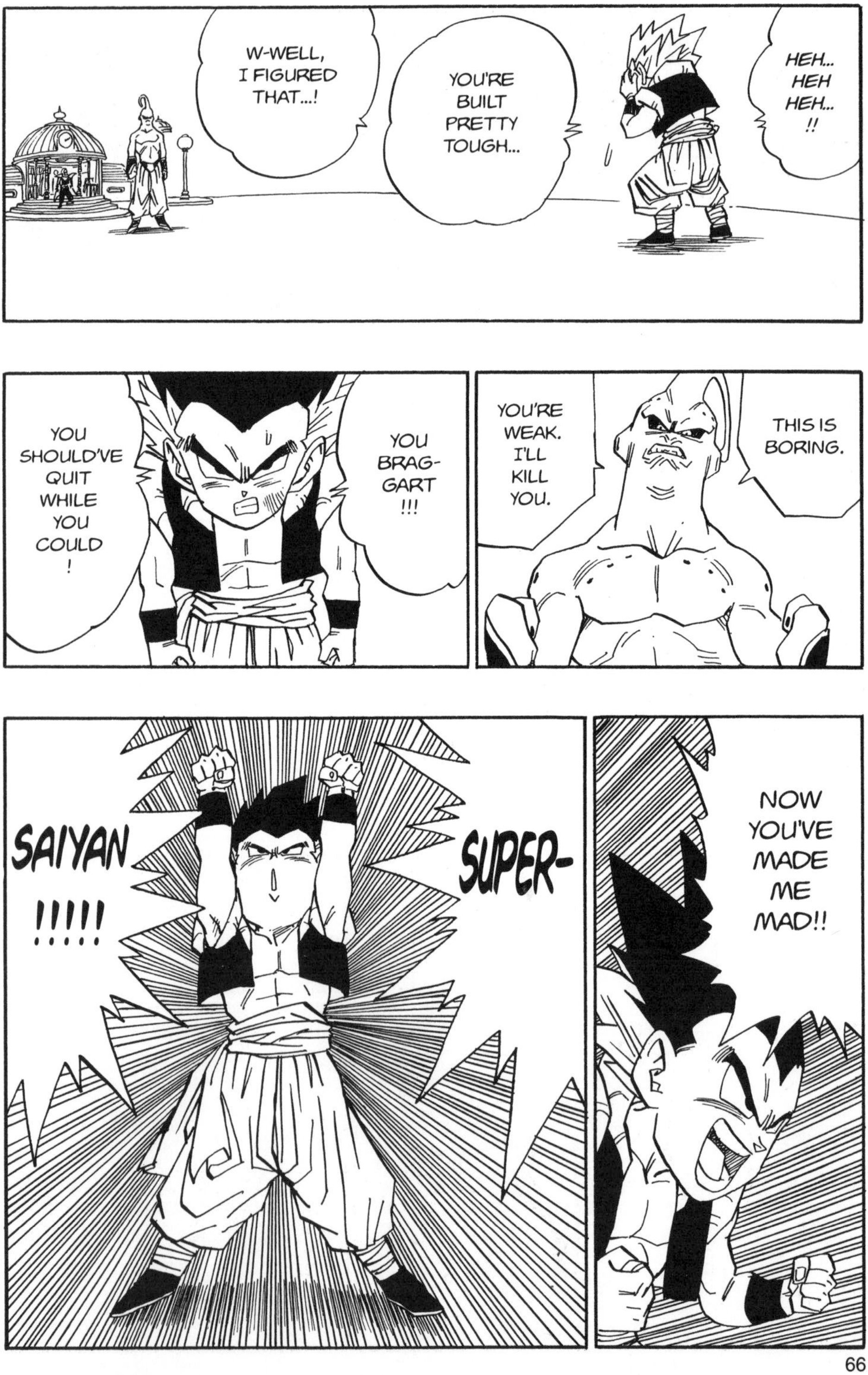
HEH... HEH HEH... !!
YOU'RE BUILT PRETTY TOUGH...
W-WELL, I FIGURED THAT...!
THIS IS BORING.
YOU'RE WEAK. I'LL KILL YOU.
YOU BRAG-GART!!!
YOU SHOULD'VE QUIT WHILE YOU COULD!
NOW YOU'VE MADE ME MAD!!
SUPER-
SAIYAN!!!!!

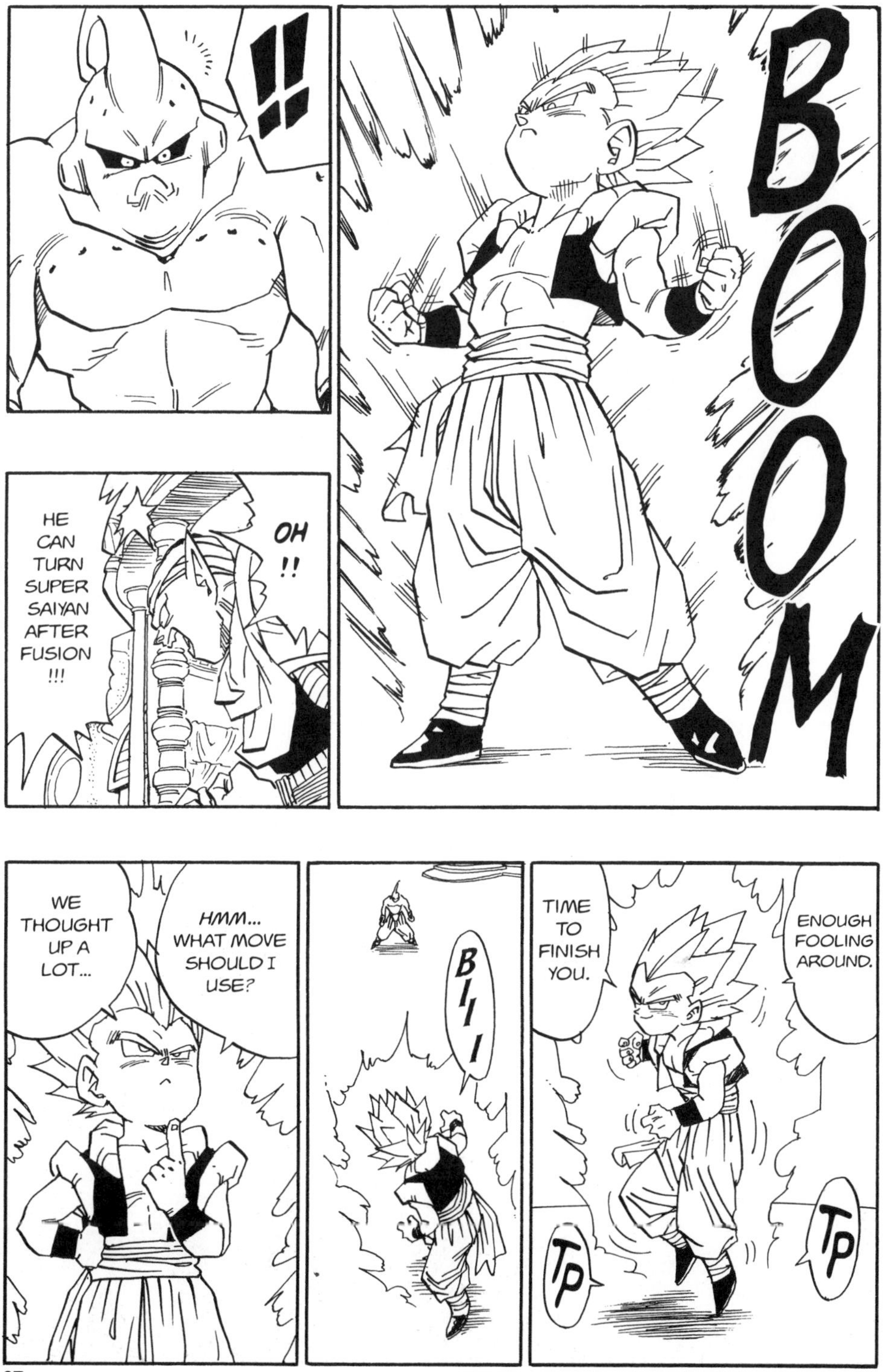
BOOOM
!!
OH!!
HE CAN TURN SUPER SAIYAN AFTER FUSION!!!
ENOUGH FOOLING AROUND.
TIME TO FINISH YOU.
TP
TP
BIII
HMM... WHAT MOVE SHOULD I USE?
WE THOUGHT UP A LOT...

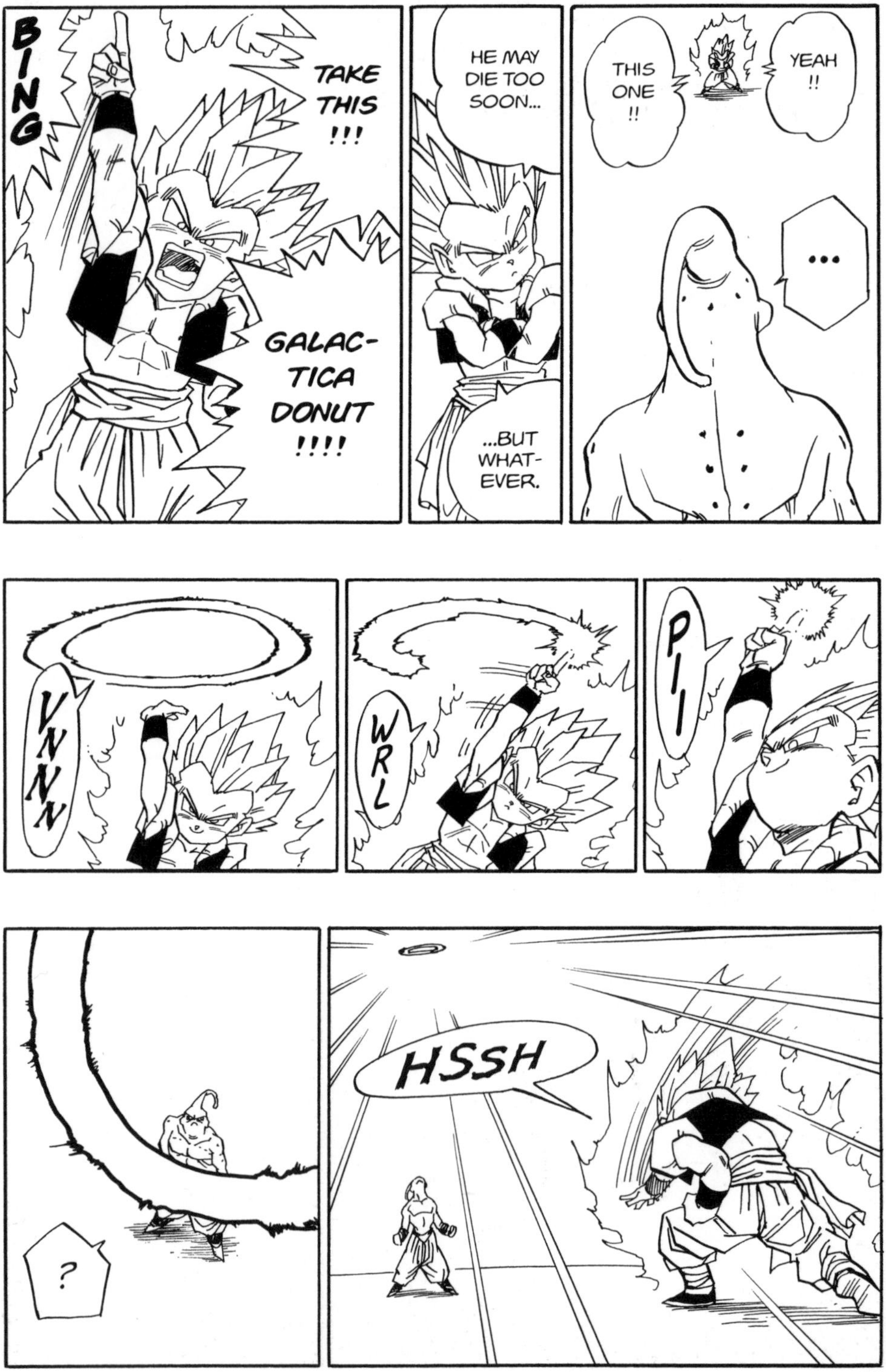
YEAH !!
THIS ONE !!
...
HE MAY DIE TOO SOON...
...BUT WHAT-EVER.
TAKE THIS !!!
BING
GALAC-TICA DONUT !!!!
PI
WRL
VNNN
HSSH
?

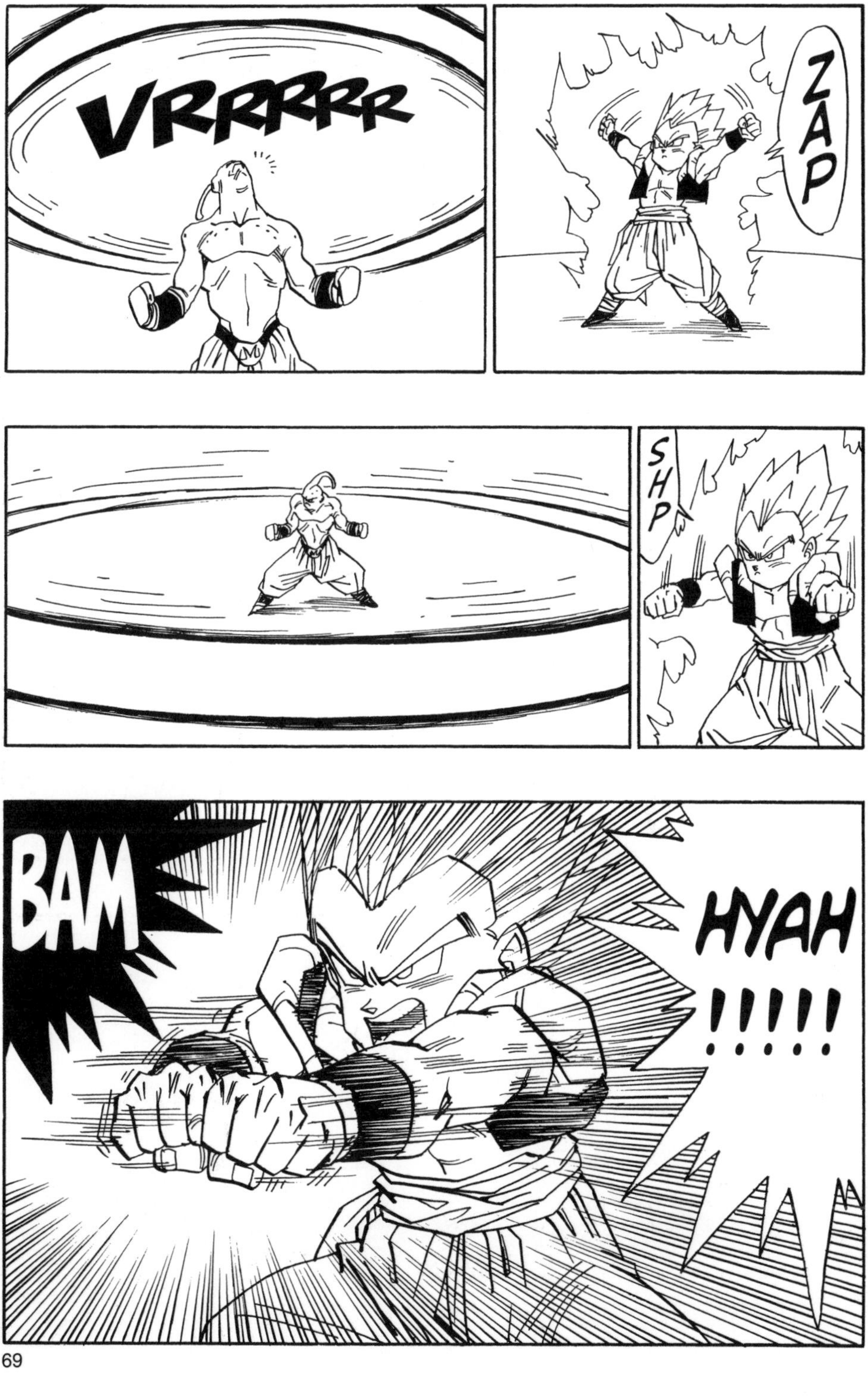
ZAP
VRRRRR
SHP
HYAH!!!!!
BAM

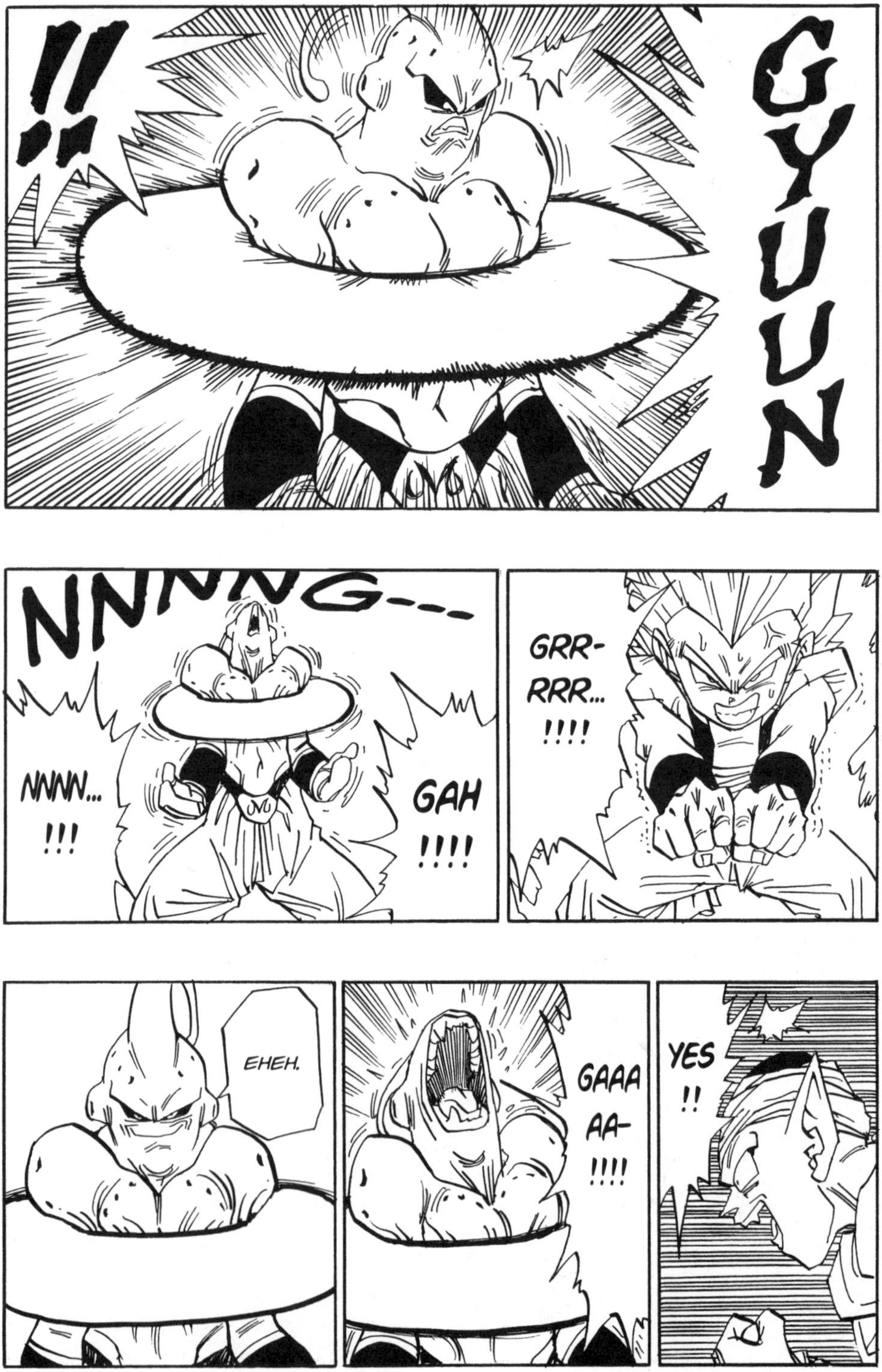
GYUUN
!!
GRR-RRR... !!!!
NNNNG---
GAH !!!!
NNNN... !!!
YES !!
GAAAAA- !!!!
EHEH.

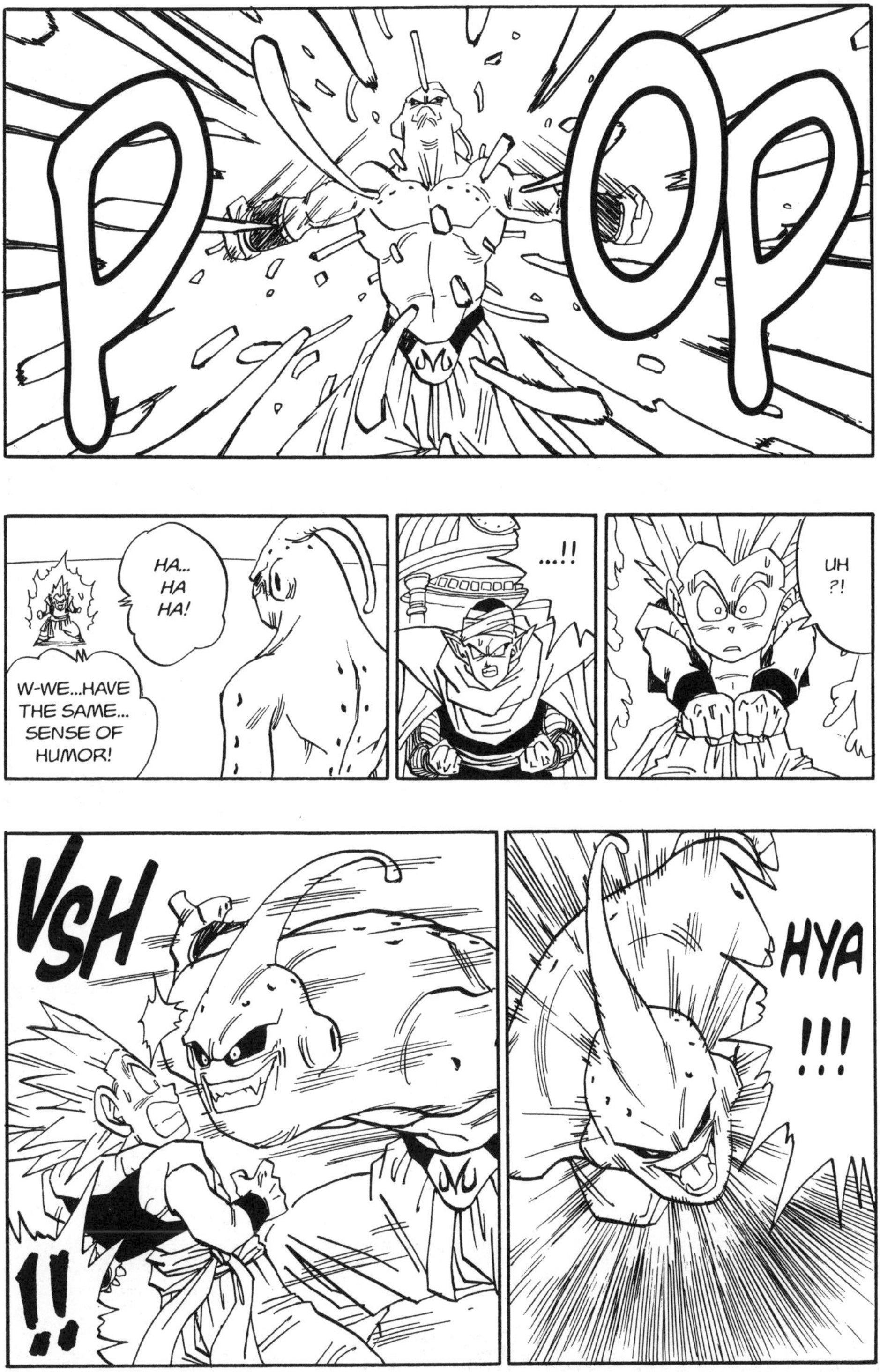
POP
UH ?!
...!!
HA... HA HA!
W-WE...HAVE THE SAME... SENSE OF HUMOR!
HYA !!!
VSH
!!

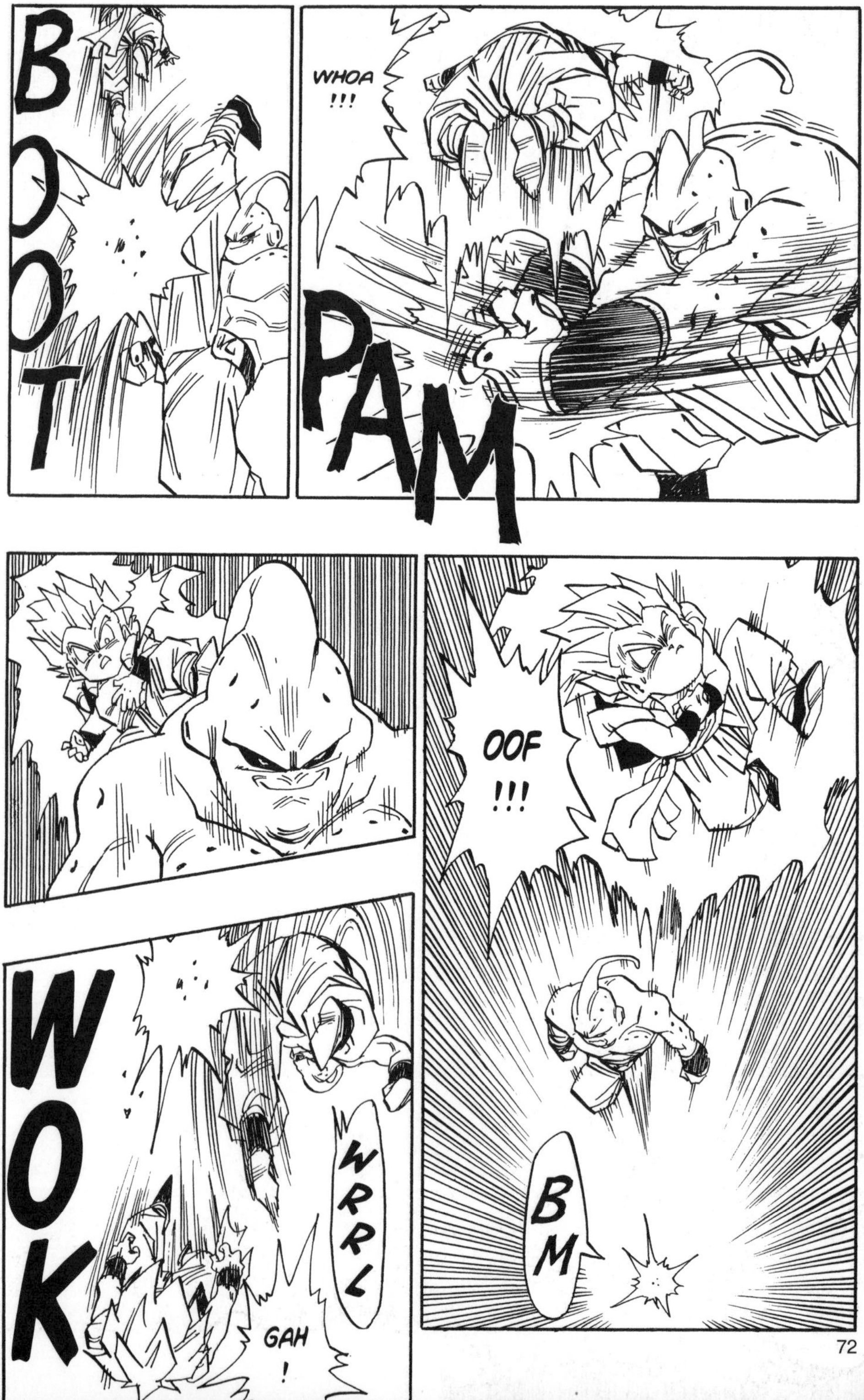
WHOA !!!
PAM
BOOT
OOF !!!
BM
WOK
WRRL
GAH !

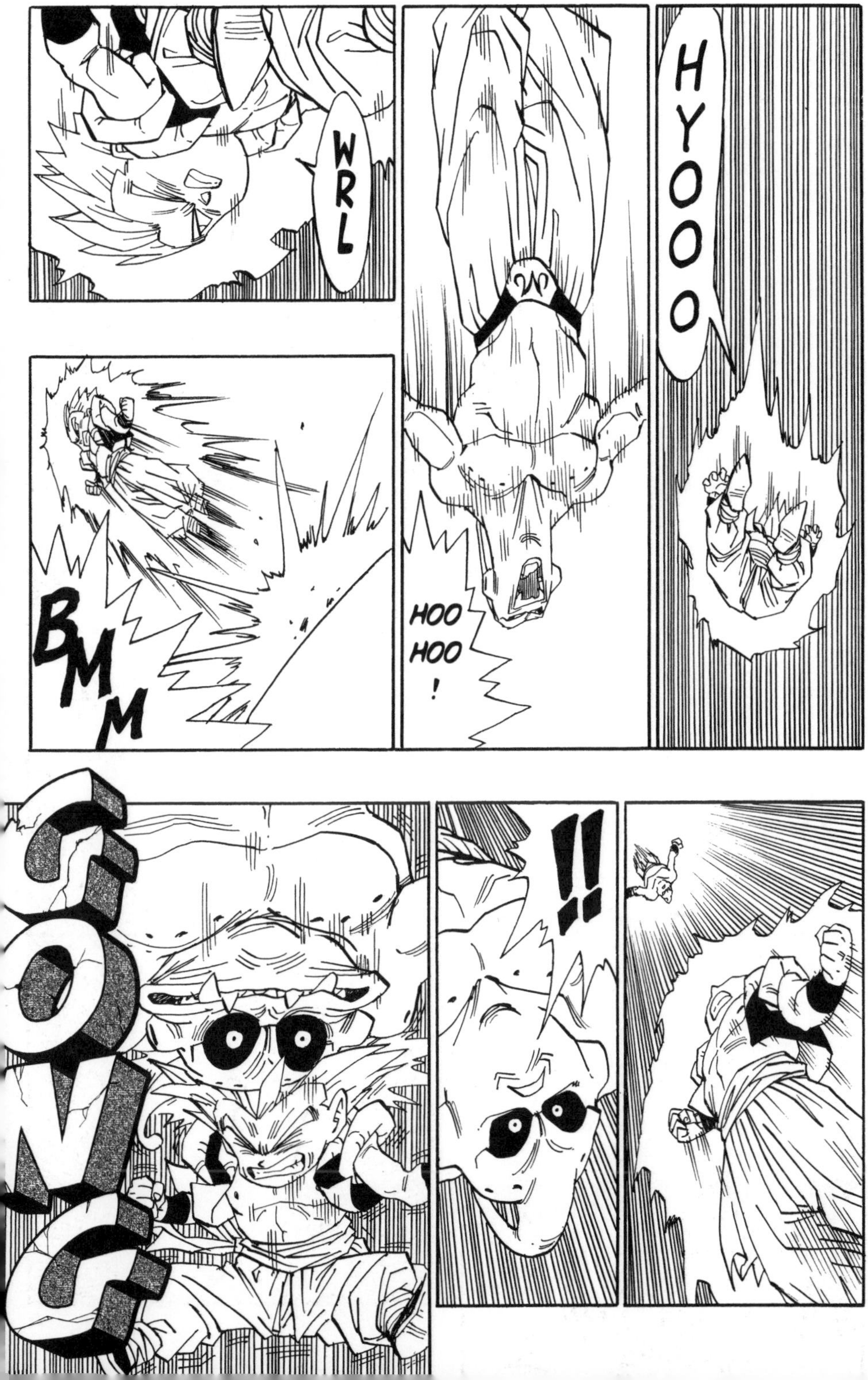
HYOOO
HOO HOO!
WRL
BMM
!!
GONG

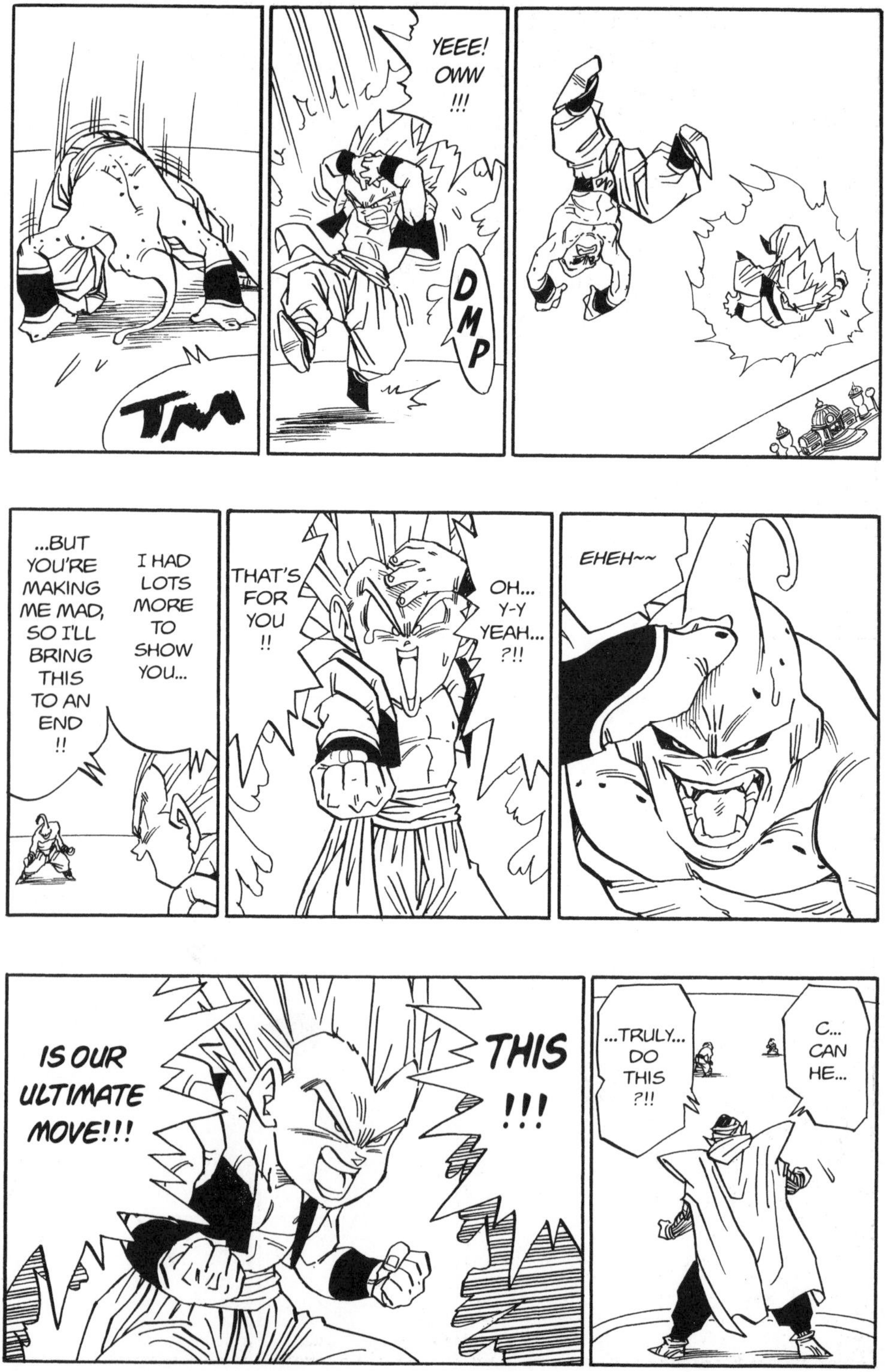
YEEE! OWW!!!
DMP
TM
EHEH~~
OH... Y-Y YEAH...?!!
THAT'S FOR YOU!!
I HAD LOTS MORE TO SHOW YOU...
...BUT YOU'RE MAKING ME MAD, SO I'LL BRING THIS TO AN END!!
C... CAN HE...
...TRULY... DO THIS?!!
THIS!!!
IS OUR ULTIMATE MOVE!!!

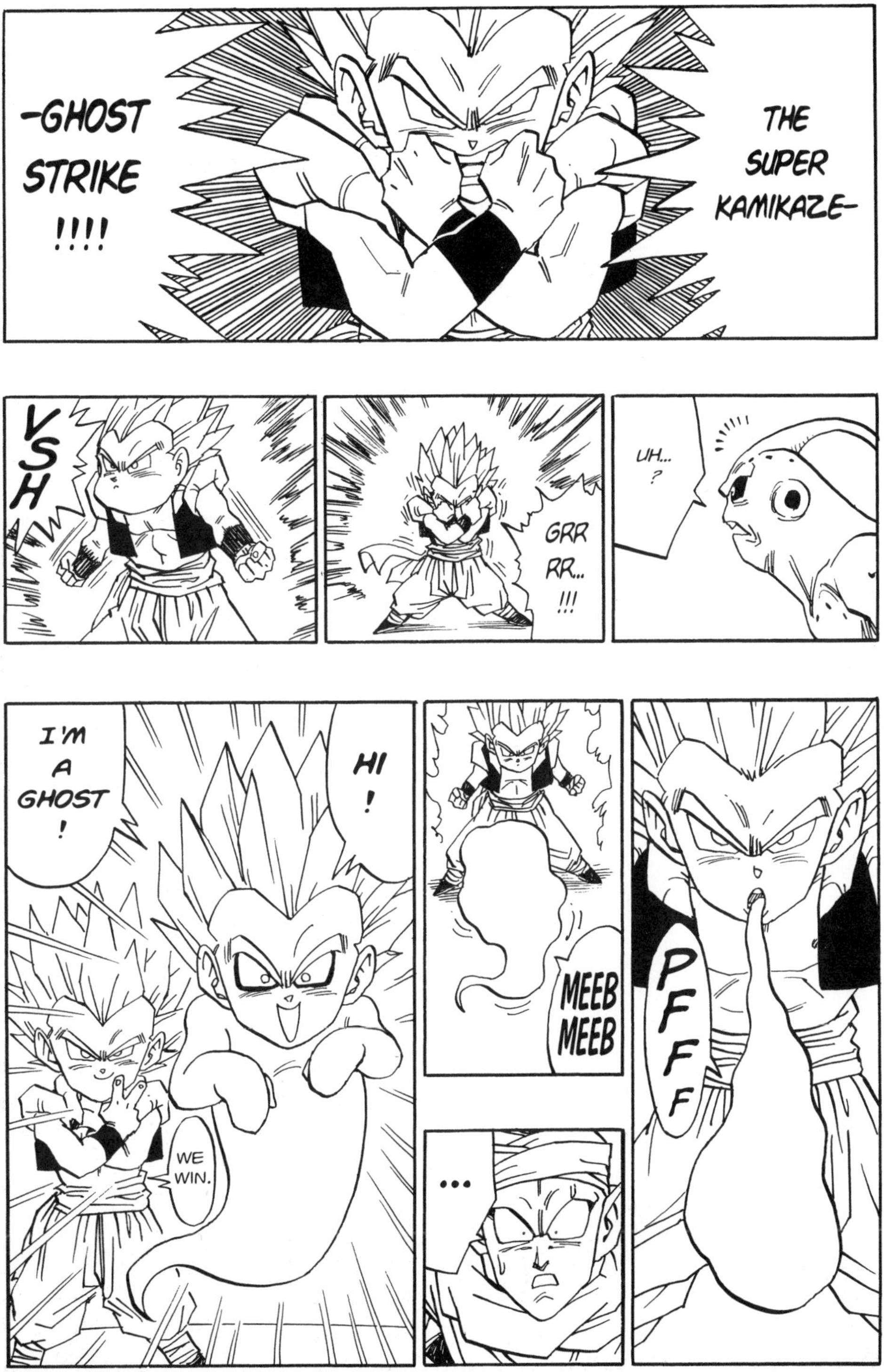
THE SUPER KAMIKAZE-
-GHOST STRIKE !!!!
UH... ?
GRR RR... !!!
VSH
PFFF
MEEB MEEB
...
HI !
I'M A GHOST !
WE WIN.

DRAGON BALL ドラゴンボール

DBZ:297 • The Kamikaze Ghost!

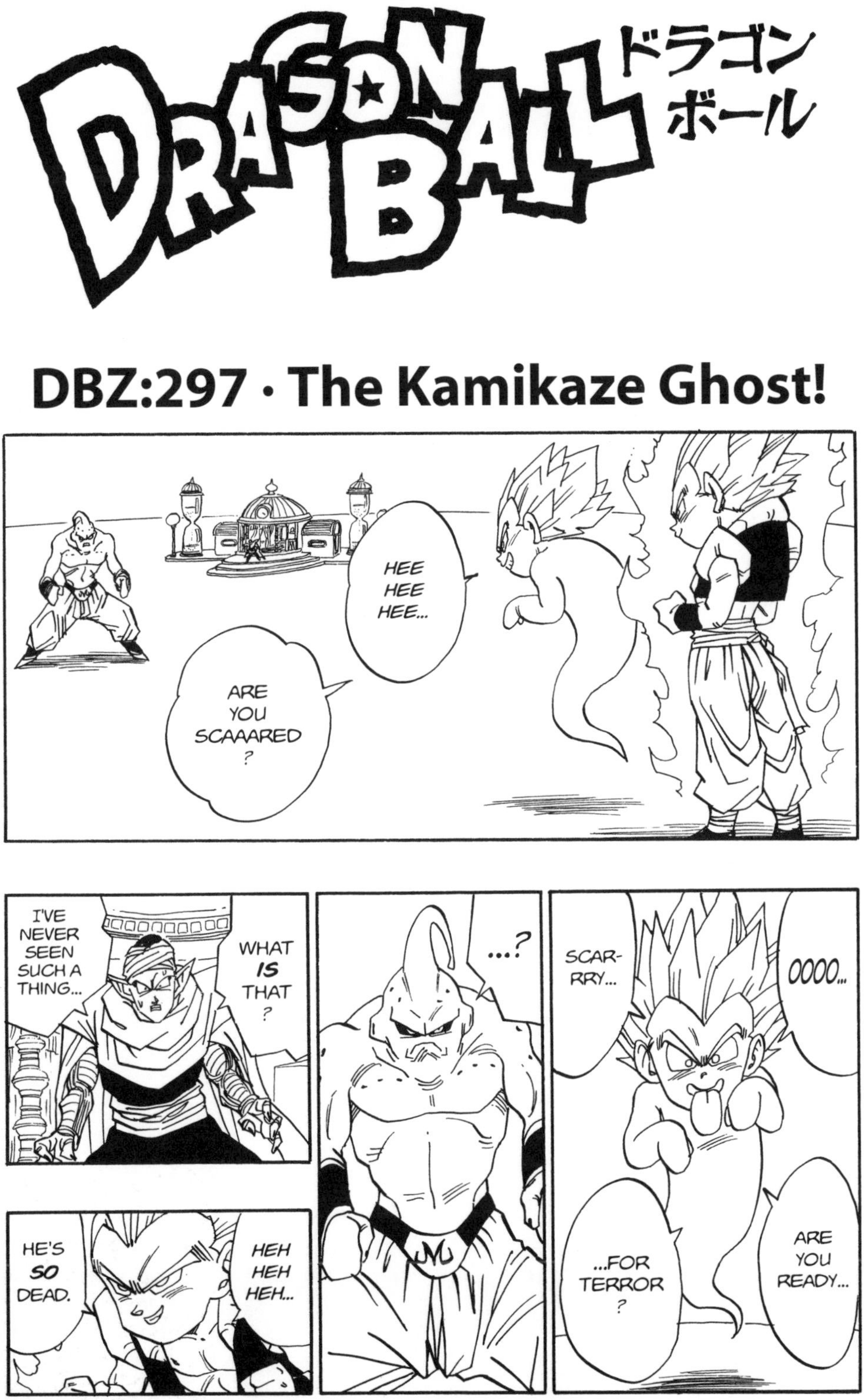
HEE HEE HEE...
ARE YOU SCAAARED?
OOOO...
SCAR-RRY...
ARE YOU READY...
...FOR TERROR?
...?
WHAT *IS* THAT?
I'VE NEVER SEEN SUCH A THING...
HEH HEH HEH...
HE'S *SO* DEAD.

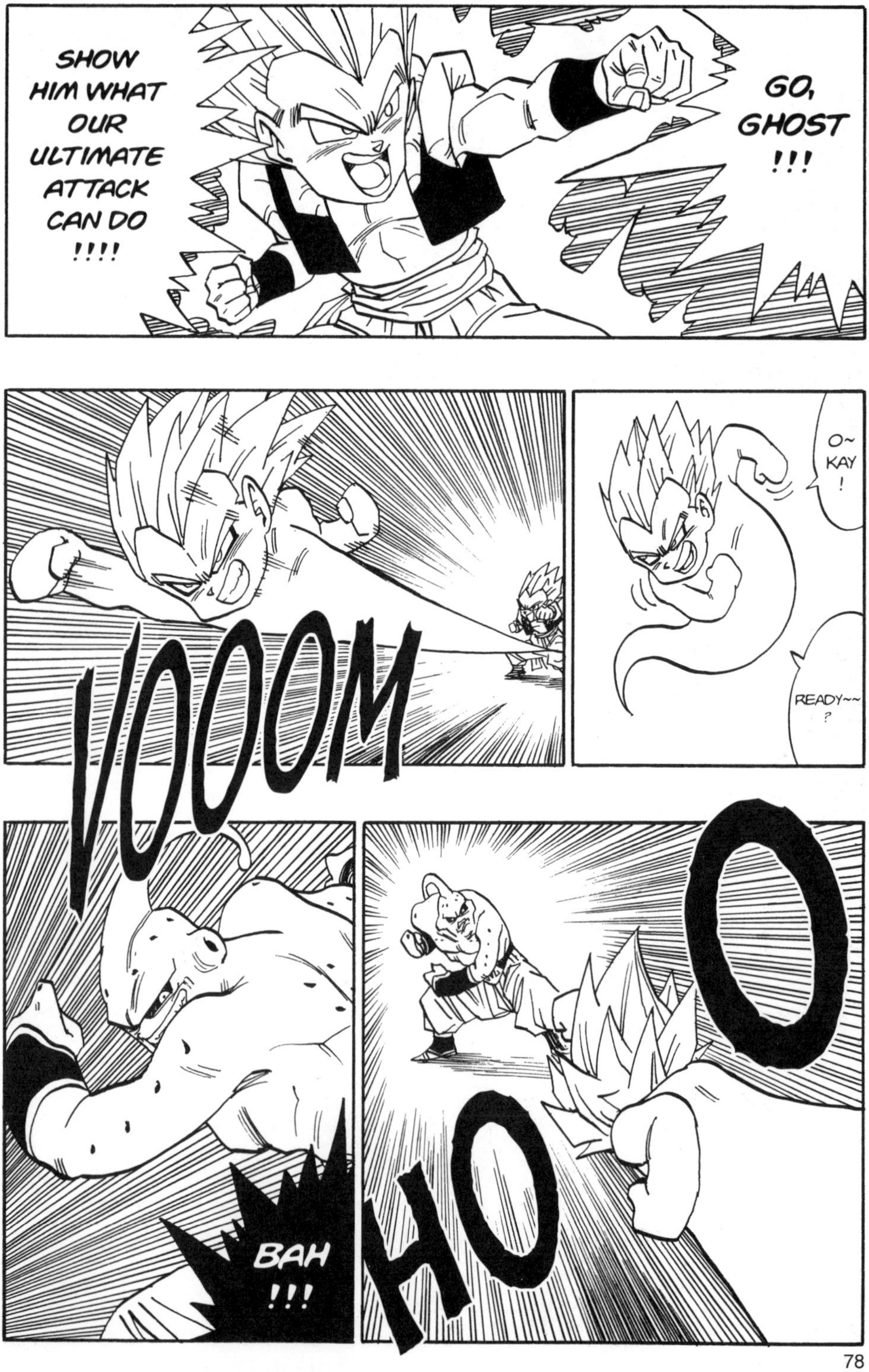
GO, GHOST!!!
SHOW HIM WHAT OUR ULTIMATE ATTACK CAN DO!!!!
O~ KAY!
READY~~?
VOOOM
HOOO
BAH!!!

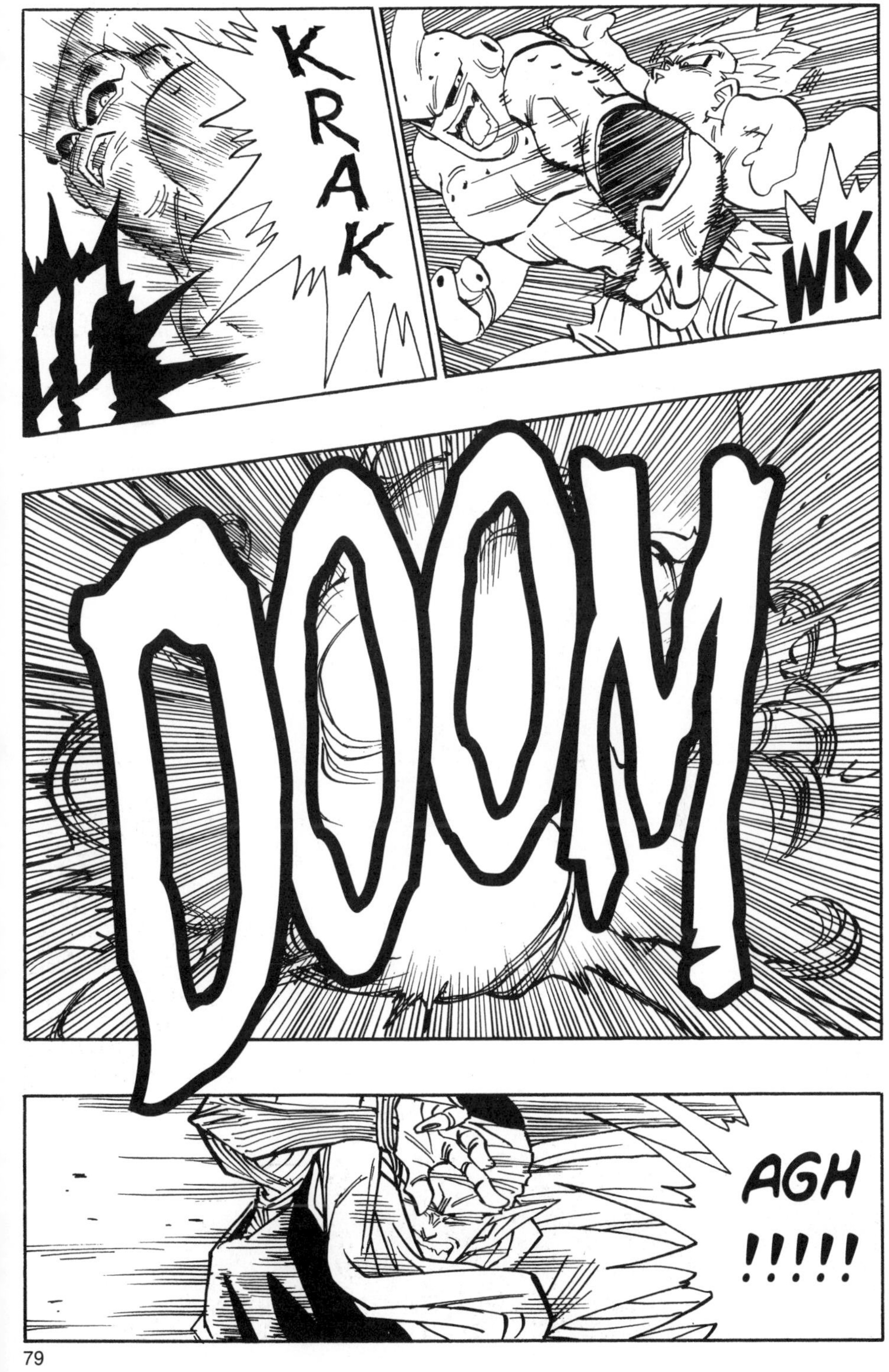
WK
KRAK
DOOM
AGH !!!!!

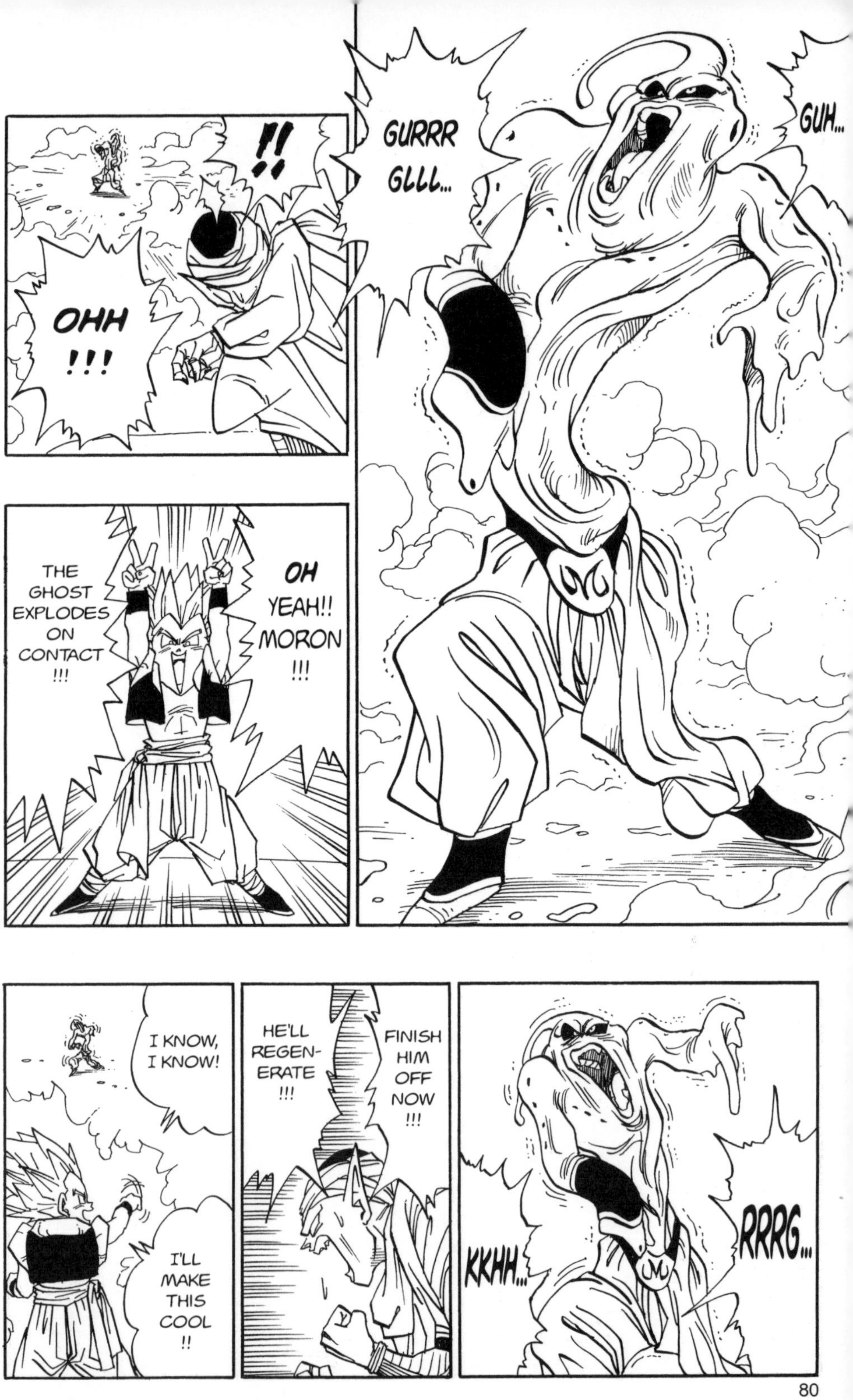
GUH...
GURRR GLLL...
!!
OHH!!!
OH YEAH!! MORON!!!
THE GHOST EXPLODES ON CONTACT!!!
RRRG...
KKHH...
FINISH HIM OFF NOW!!!
HE'LL REGENERATE!!!
I KNOW, I KNOW!
I'LL MAKE THIS COOL!!

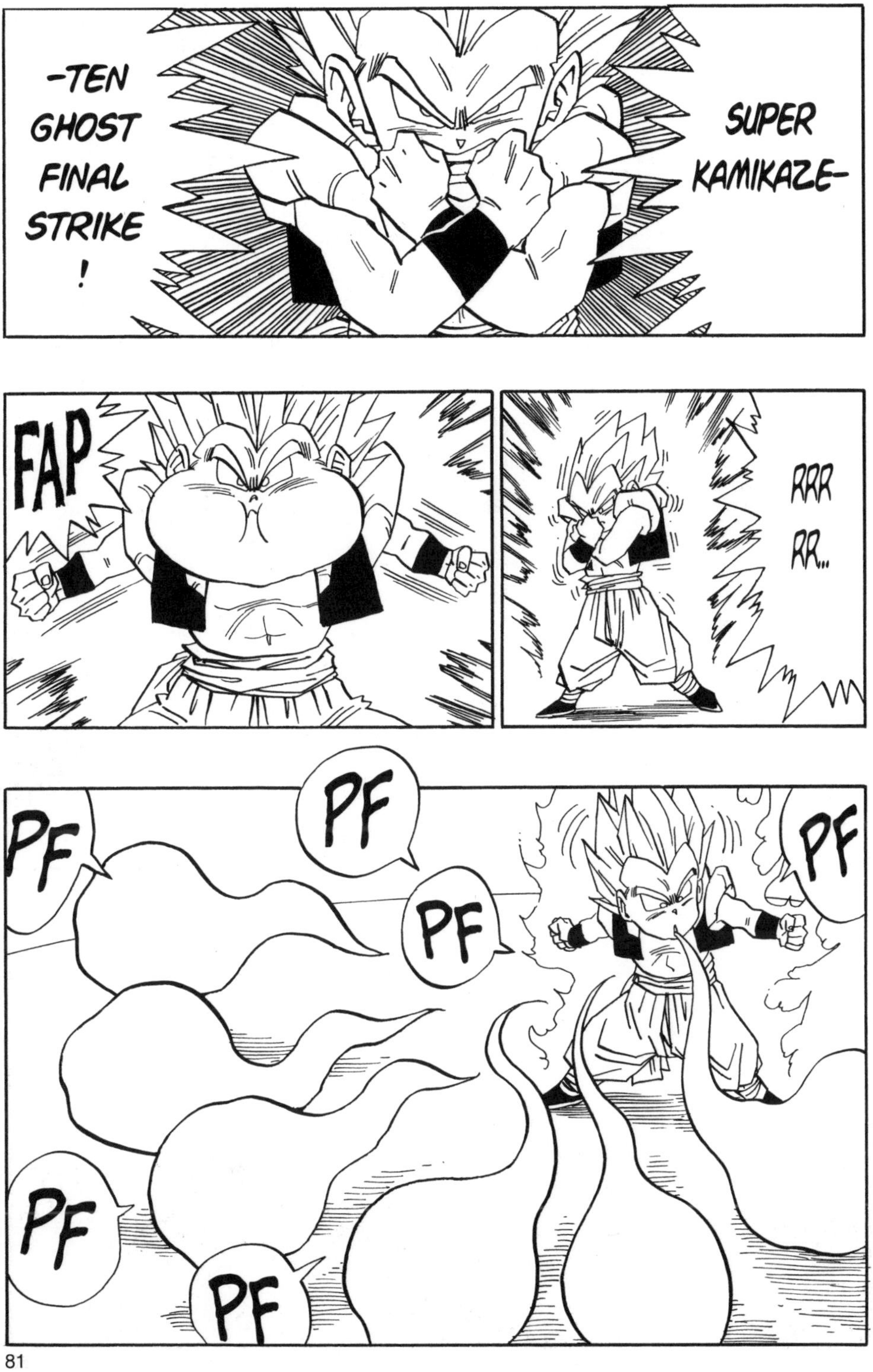
SUPER KAMIKAZE-
-TEN GHOST FINAL STRIKE !
RRR RR...
FAP
PF
PF
PF
PF
PF
PF

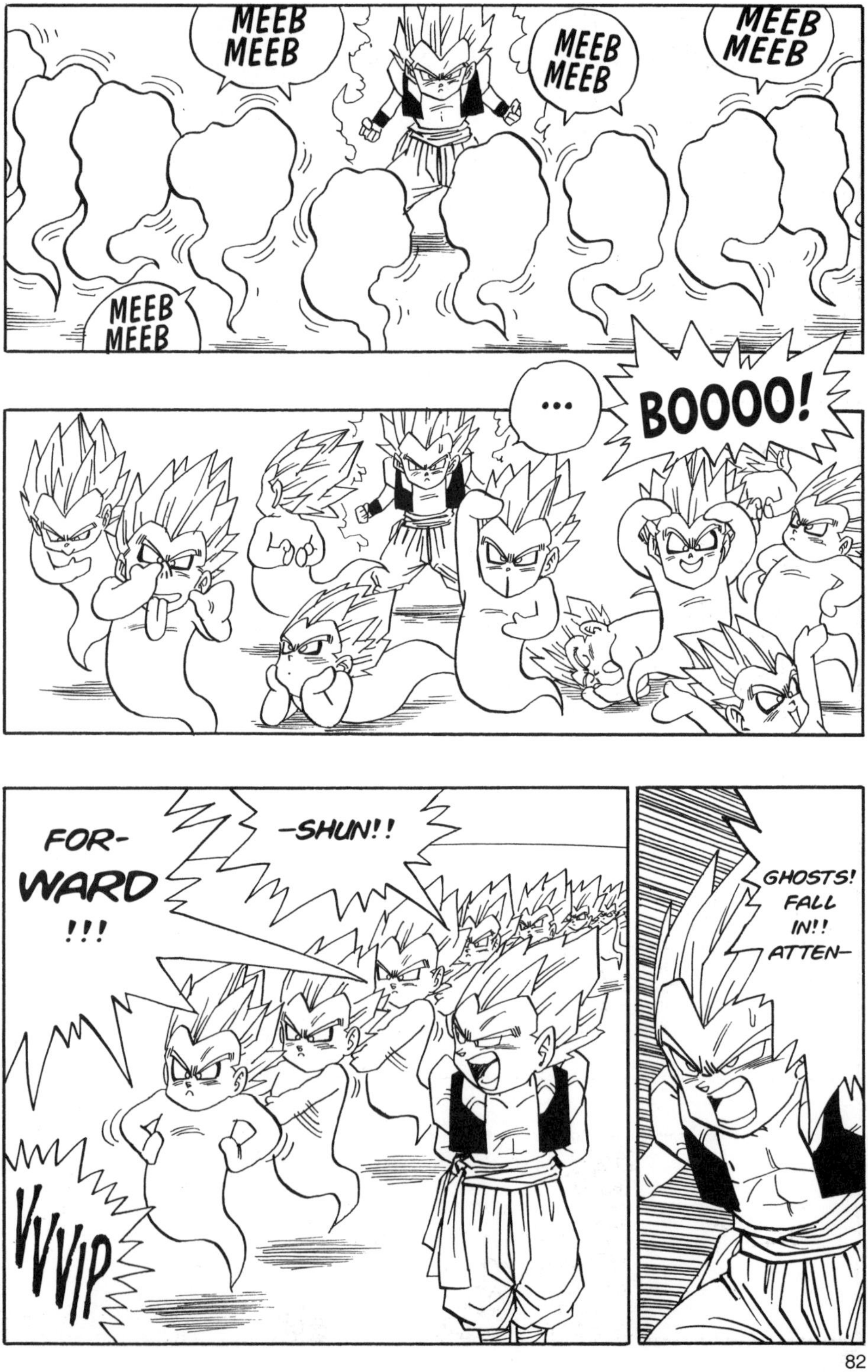
MEEB MEEB
MEEB MEEB
MEEB MEEB
MEEB MEEB
BOOOO!
...
GHOSTS! FALL IN!! ATTEN-
-SHUN!!
FOR-WARD!!!
VVVIP

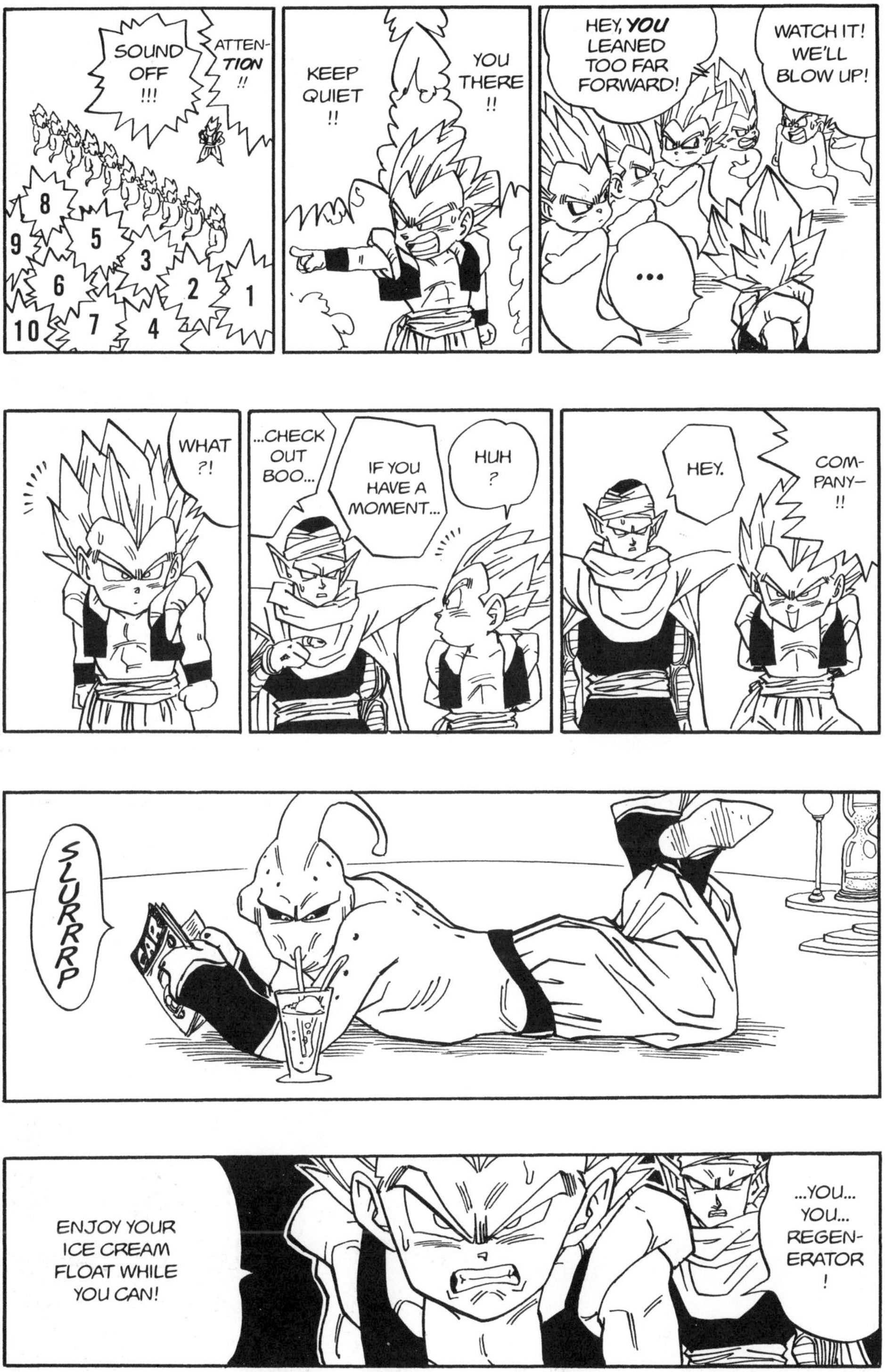
WATCH IT! WE'LL BLOW UP!
HEY, ***YOU*** LEANED TOO FAR FORWARD!
...
YOU THERE !!
KEEP QUIET !!
ATTEN-***TION*** !!
SOUND OFF !!!
1
2
3
4
5
6
7
8
9
10
COM-PANY— !!
HEY.
HUH ?
IF YOU HAVE A MOMENT...
...CHECK OUT BOO...
WHAT ?!
SLURRRP
...YOU... YOU... REGEN-ERATOR !
ENJOY YOUR ICE CREAM FLOAT WHILE YOU CAN!

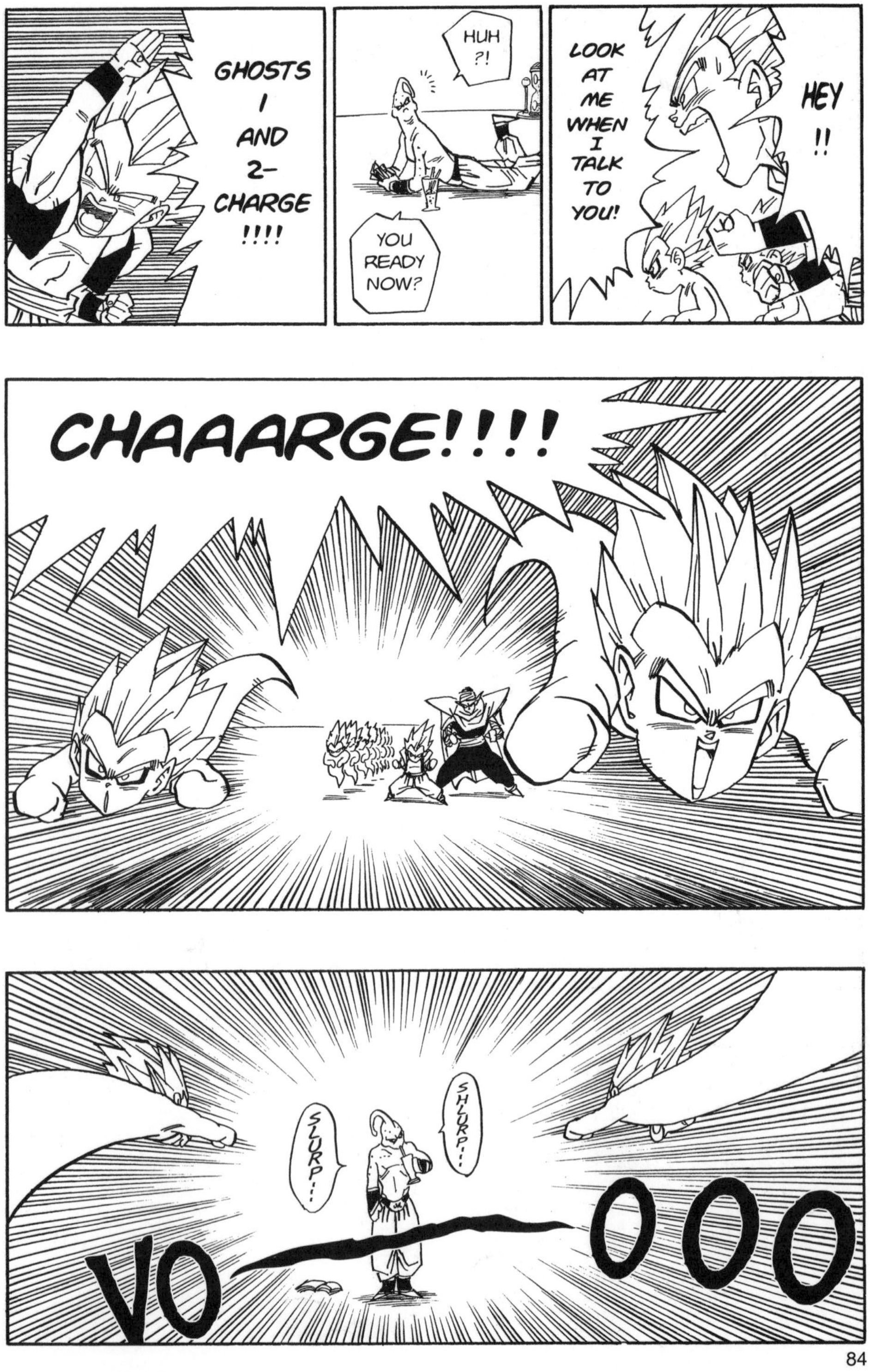
HEY !!
LOOK AT ME WHEN I TALK TO YOU!
HUH ?!
YOU READY NOW?
GHOSTS 1 AND 2— CHARGE !!!!
CHAAARGE!!!!
SHLURP!!
SLURP!!
VO—OOO

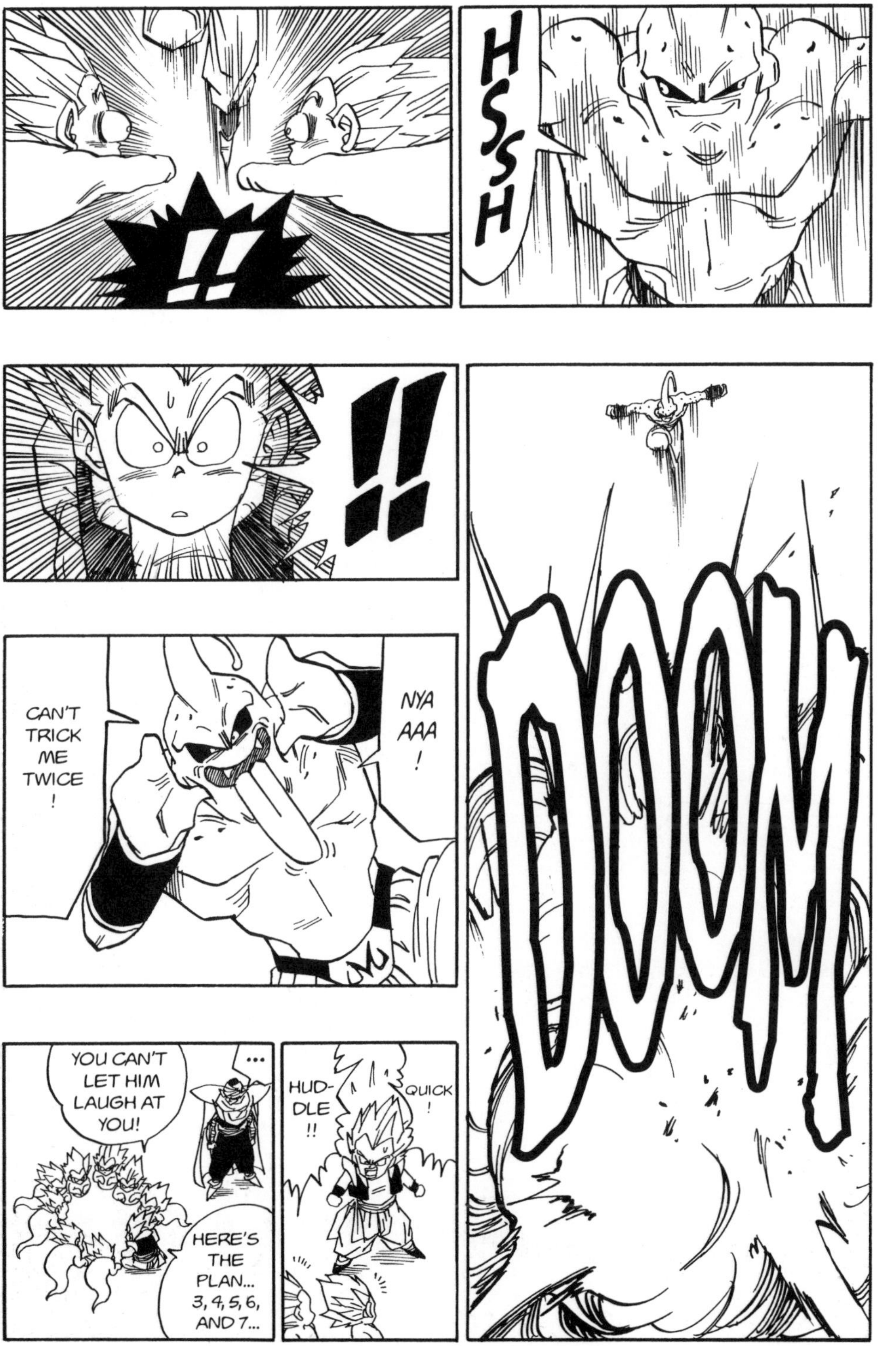
HSSH
!!
DOOM
!!
NYA AAA!
CAN'T TRICK ME TWICE!
QUICK!
HUD-DLE!!
...
YOU CAN'T LET HIM LAUGH AT YOU!
HERE'S THE PLAN... 3, 4, 5, 6, AND 7...

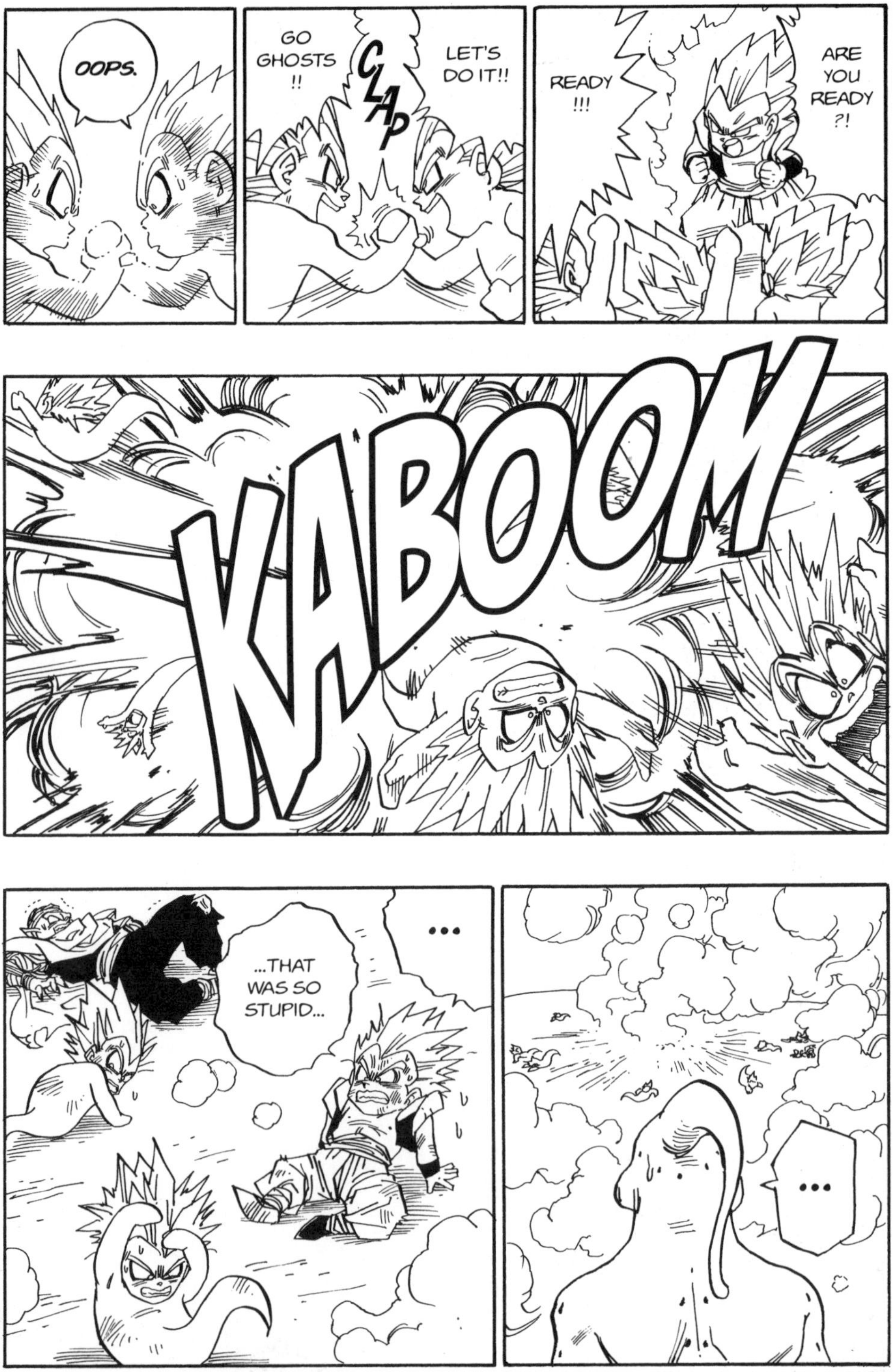

ARE YOU READY ?!
READY !!!
LET'S DO IT!!
CLAP
GO GHOSTS !!
OOPS.
KABOOM
...
...
...THAT WAS SO STUPID...

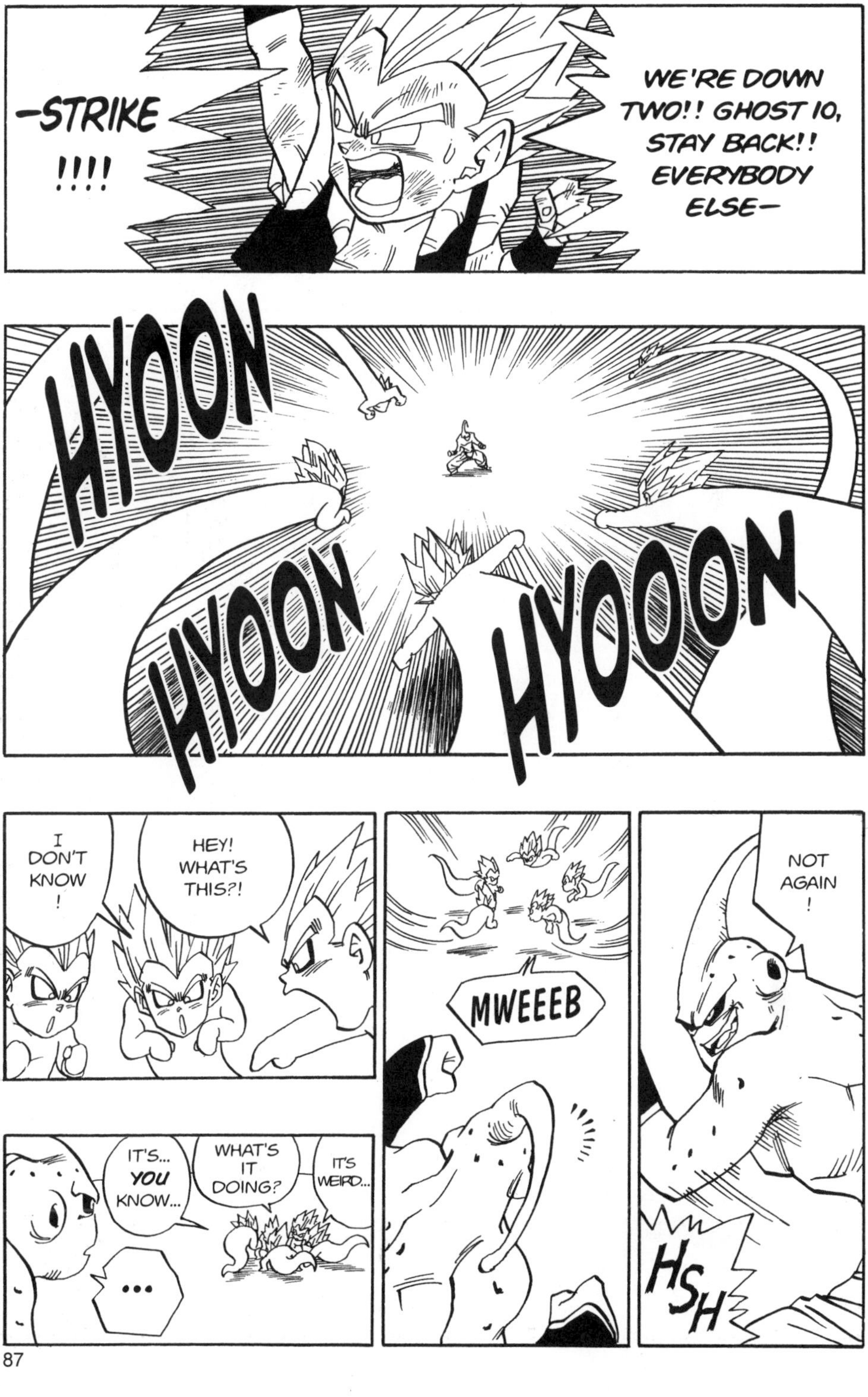
WE'RE DOWN TWO!! GHOST 10, STAY BACK!! EVERYBODY ELSE—
—STRIKE !!!!
HYOOON
HYOON
HYOON
NOT AGAIN!
HSH
MWEEEB
HEY! WHAT'S THIS?!
I DON'T KNOW!
IT'S WEIRD...
WHAT'S IT DOING?
IT'S... YOU KNOW...
...

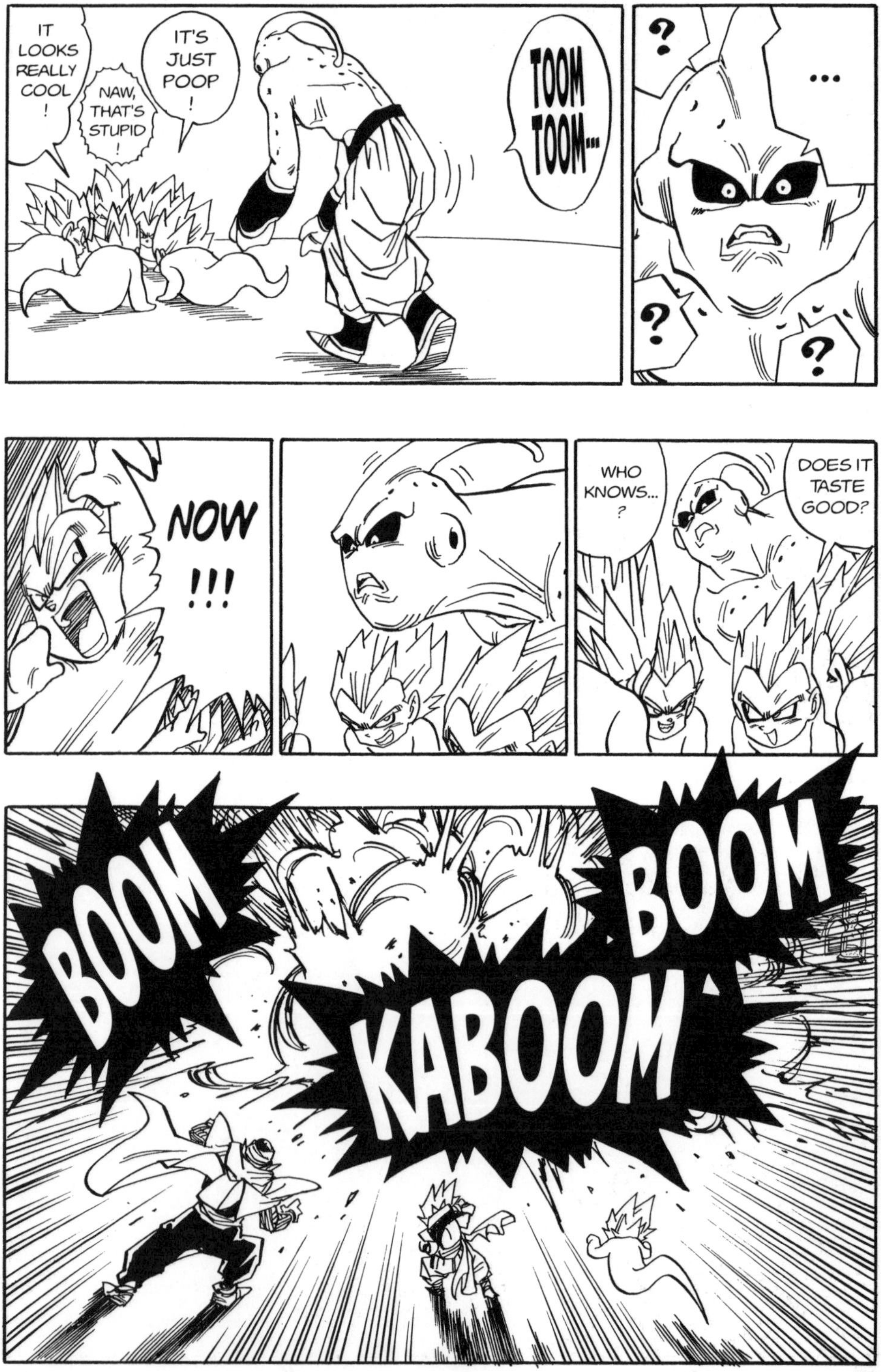
?
...
?
?
TOOM TOOM...
IT'S JUST POOP!
NAW, THAT'S STUPID!
IT LOOKS REALLY COOL!
DOES IT TASTE GOOD?
WHO KNOWS...?
NOW!!!
BOOM
BOOM
KABOOM

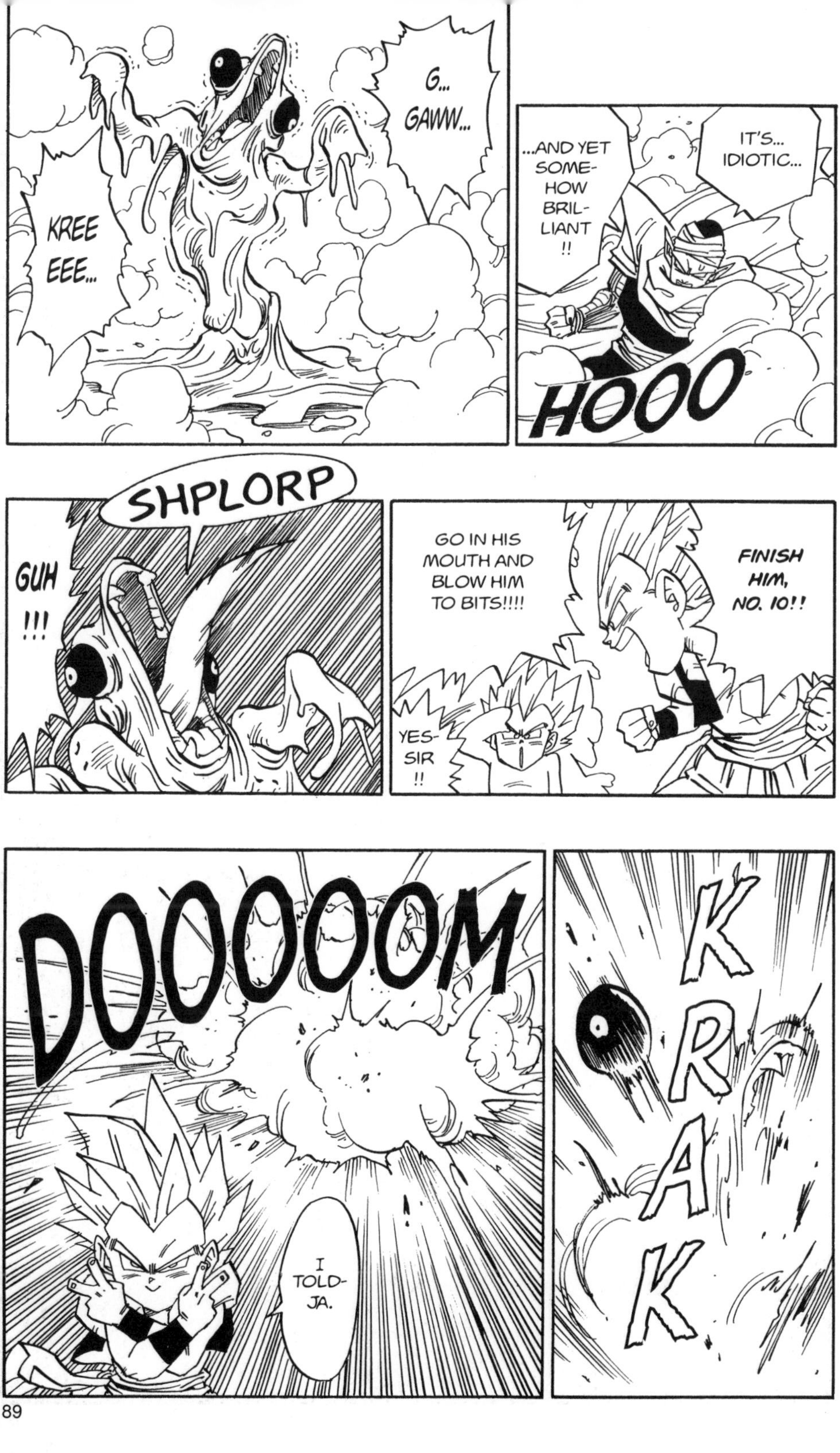
IT'S... IDIOTIC...
...AND YET SOME-HOW BRIL-LIANT !!
HOOO
G... GAWW...
KREE EEE...
FINISH HIM, NO. 10!!
GO IN HIS MOUTH AND BLOW HIM TO BITS!!!!
YES-SIR !!
SHPLORP
GUH !!!
KRAK
DOOOOOM
I TOLD-JA.

DRAGON BALL ドラゴンボール

DBZ:298 • The Door Closes

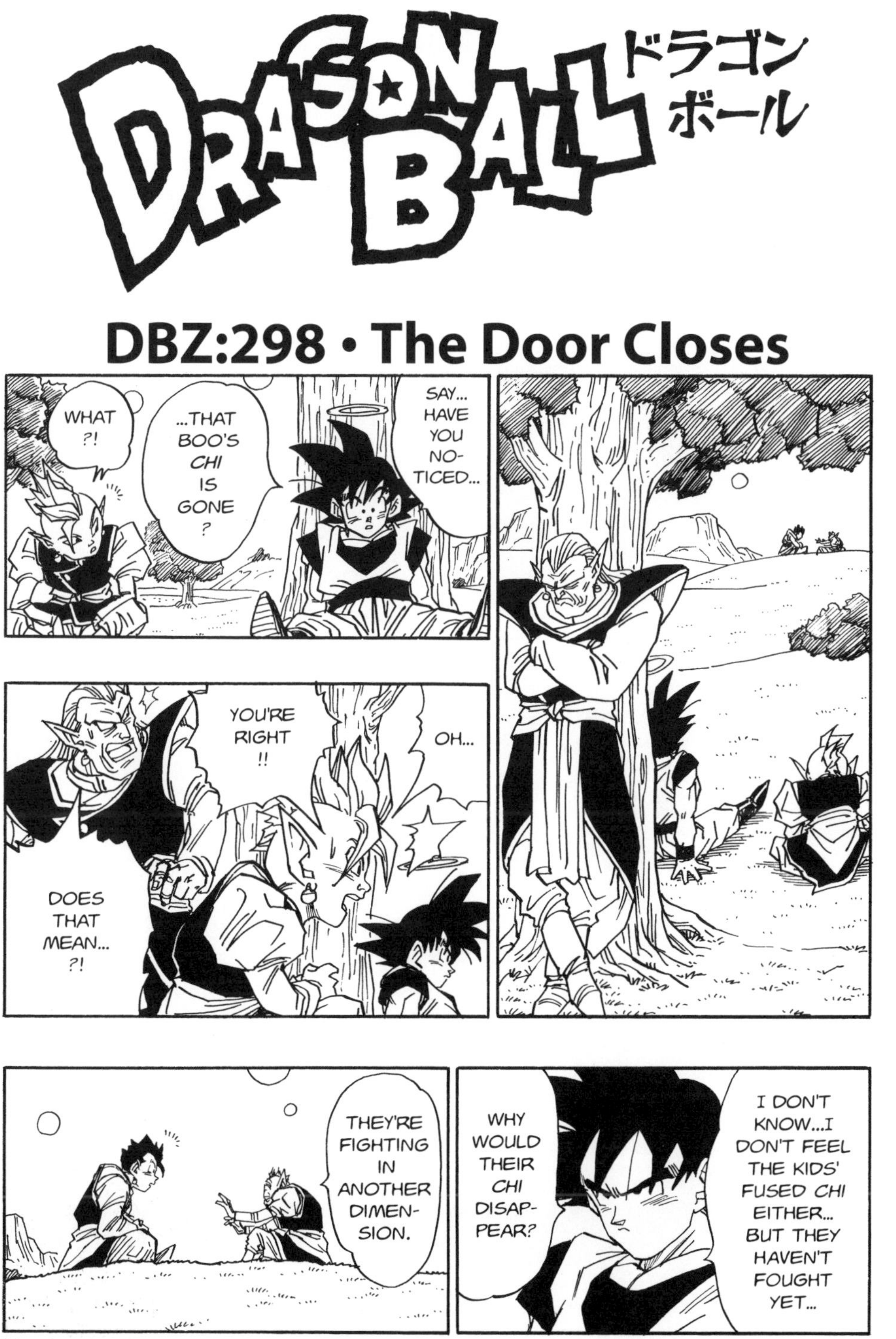
SAY... HAVE YOU NOTICED...
...THAT BOO'S CHI IS GONE?
WHAT?!
OH...
YOU'RE RIGHT!!
DOES THAT MEAN...?!
I DON'T KNOW...I DON'T FEEL THE KIDS' FUSED CHI EITHER... BUT THEY HAVEN'T FOUGHT YET...
WHY WOULD THEIR CHI DISAPPEAR?
THEY'RE FIGHTING IN ANOTHER DIMENSION.

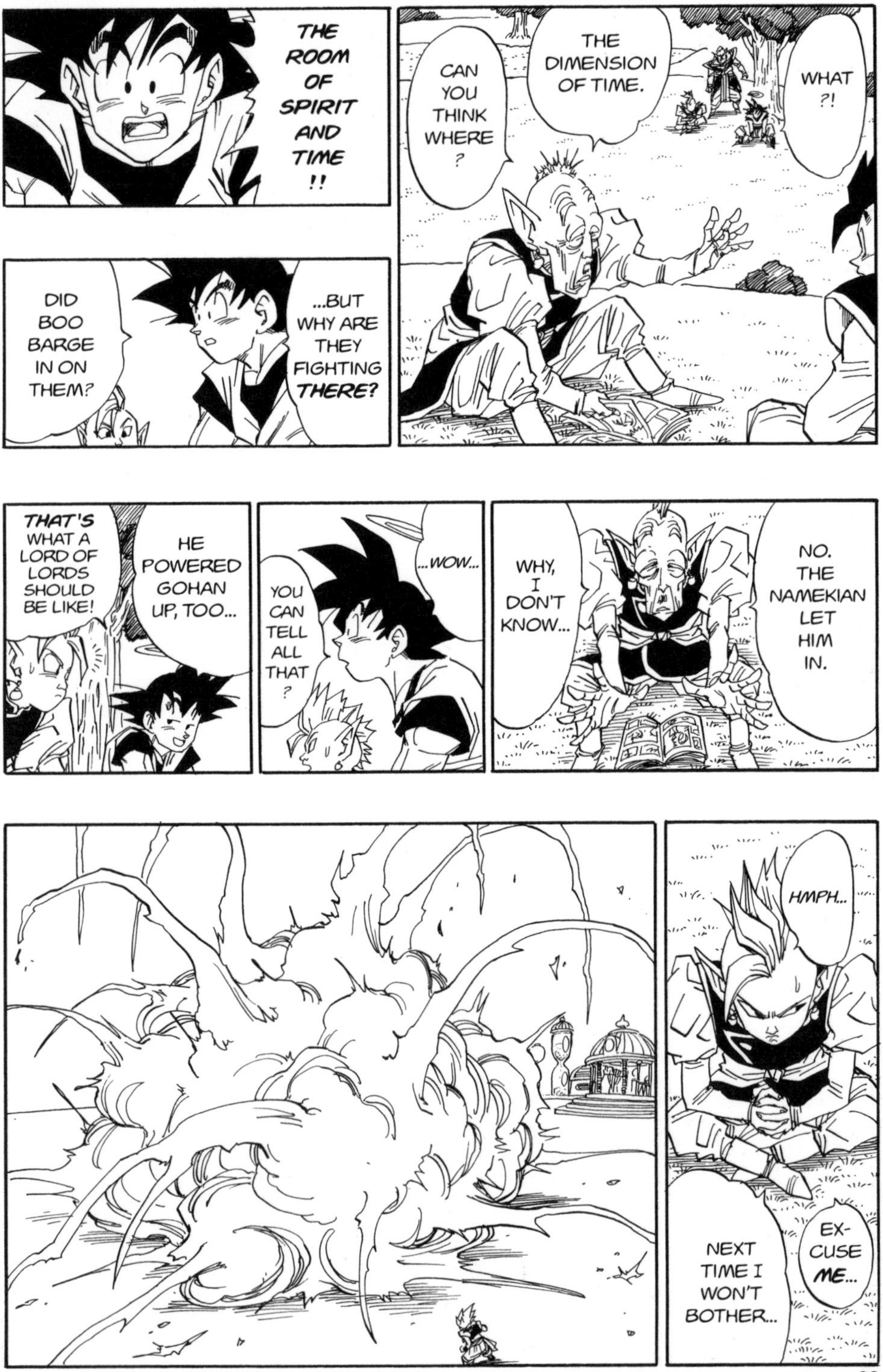
WHAT ?!
THE DIMENSION OF TIME.
CAN YOU THINK WHERE ?
THE ROOM OF SPIRIT AND TIME !!
...BUT WHY ARE THEY FIGHTING THERE?
DID BOO BARGE IN ON THEM?
NO. THE NAMEKIAN LET HIM IN.
WHY, I DON'T KNOW...
...WOW...
YOU CAN TELL ALL THAT ?
HE POWERED GOHAN UP, TOO...
THAT'S WHAT A LORD OF LORDS SHOULD BE LIKE!
HMPH...
EX-CUSE ME...
NEXT TIME I WON'T BOTHER...

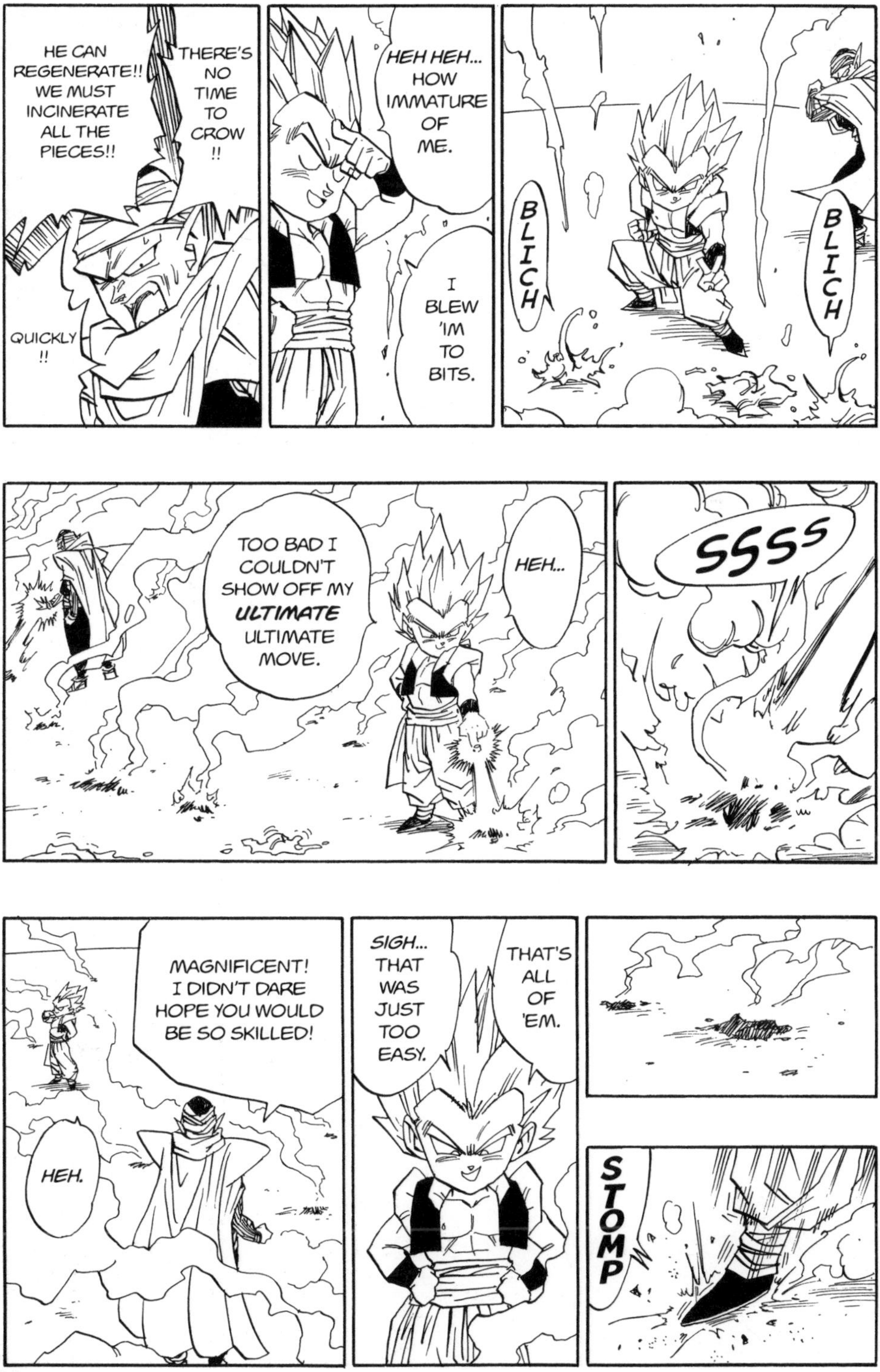
BLICH
BLICH
HEH HEH... HOW IMMATURE OF ME.
I BLEW 'IM TO BITS.
THERE'S NO TIME TO CROW!!
HE CAN REGENERATE!! WE MUST INCINERATE ALL THE PIECES!!
QUICKLY!!
SSSS
HEH...
TOO BAD I COULDN'T SHOW OFF MY ULTIMATE ULTIMATE MOVE.
STOMP
THAT'S ALL OF 'EM.
SIGH... THAT WAS JUST TOO EASY.
MAGNIFICENT! I DIDN'T DARE HOPE YOU WOULD BE SO SKILLED!
HEH.

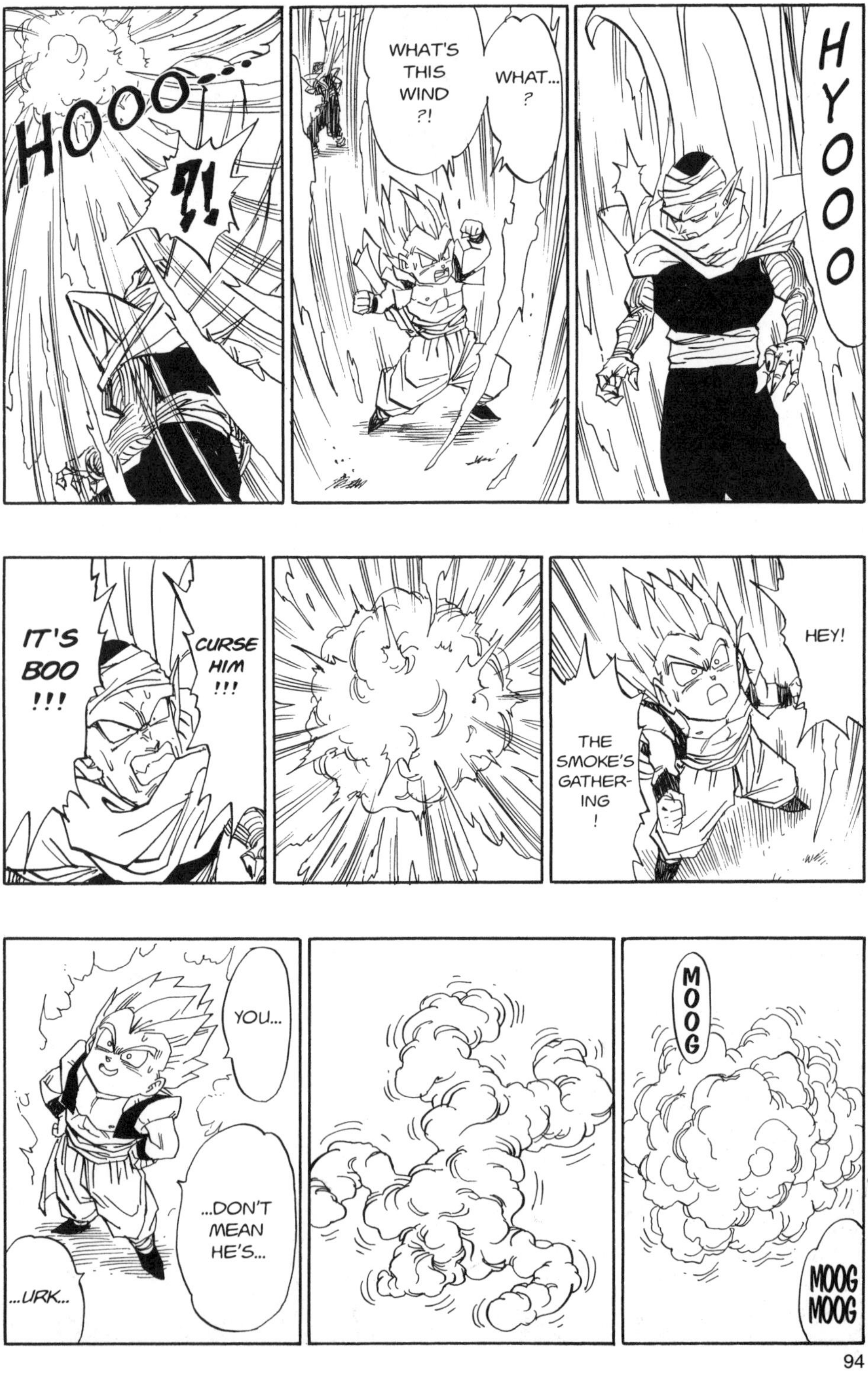
HYOOO
WHAT... ?
WHAT'S THIS WIND ?!
HOOO.....
?!
HEY!
THE SMOKE'S GATHER-ING !
CURSE HIM !!!
IT'S BOO !!!
MOOG
MOOG MOOG
YOU...
...DON'T MEAN HE'S...
...URK...

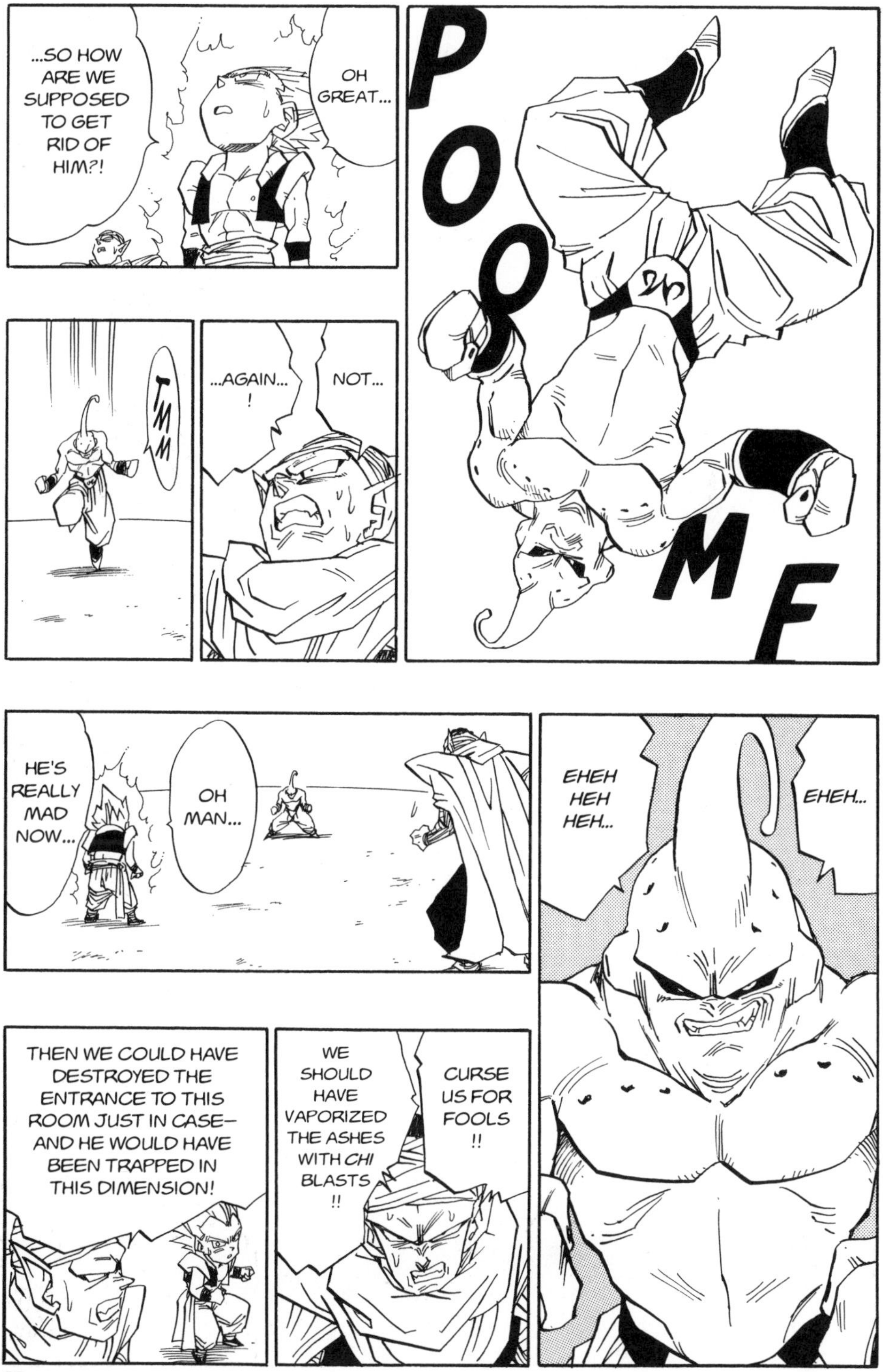
POOOMF
OH GREAT...
...SO HOW ARE WE SUPPOSED TO GET RID OF HIM?!
NOT...
...AGAIN...!
TMM
EHEH...
EHEH HEH HEH...
OH MAN...
HE'S REALLY MAD NOW...
CURSE US FOR FOOLS!!
WE SHOULD HAVE VAPORIZED THE ASHES WITH CHI BLASTS!!
THEN WE COULD HAVE DESTROYED THE ENTRANCE TO THIS ROOM JUST IN CASE— AND HE WOULD HAVE BEEN TRAPPED IN THIS DIMENSION!

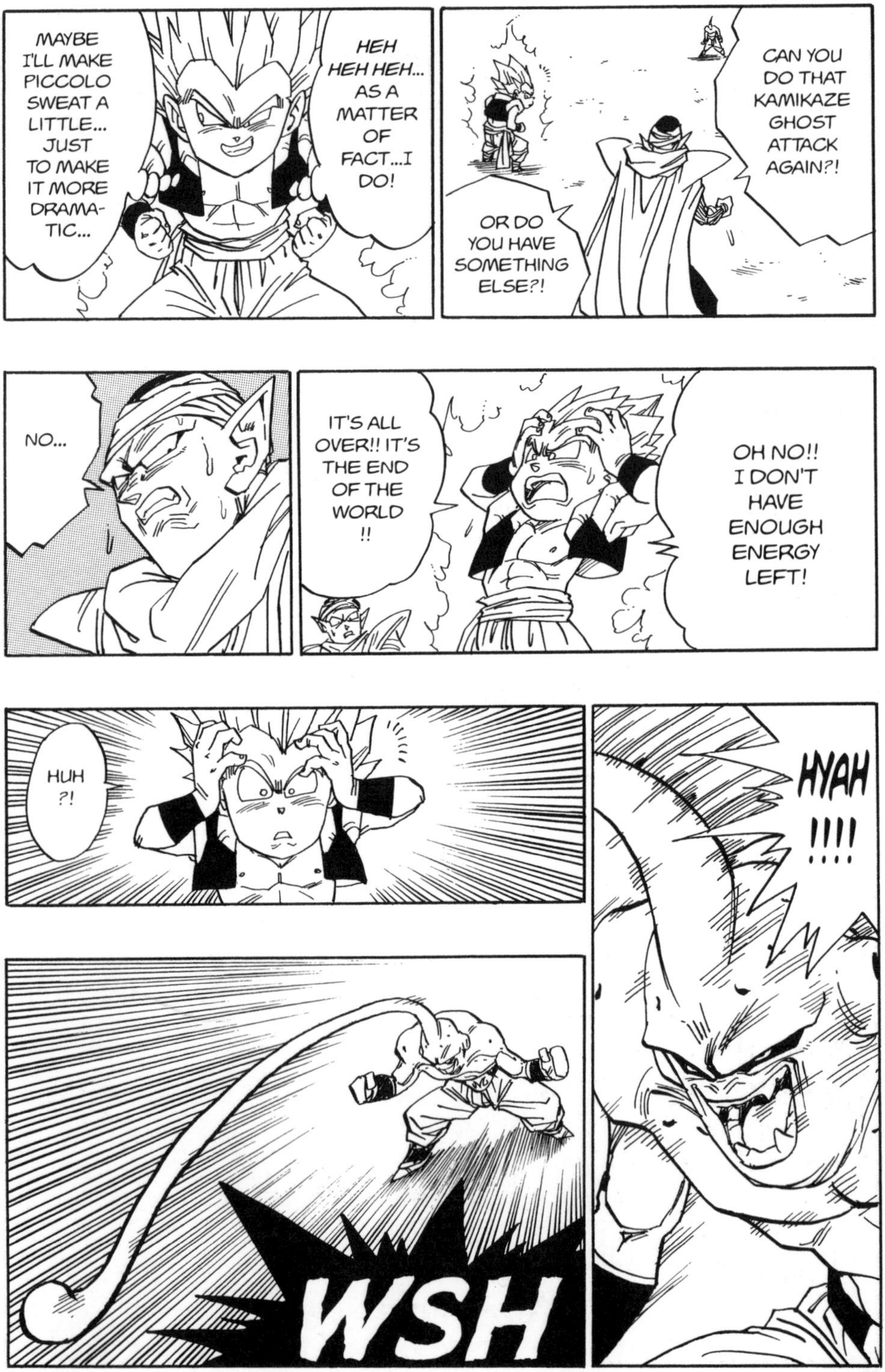
CAN YOU DO THAT KAMIKAZE GHOST ATTACK AGAIN?!
OR DO YOU HAVE SOMETHING ELSE?!
HEH HEH HEH... AS A MATTER OF FACT...I DO!
MAYBE I'LL MAKE PICCOLO SWEAT A LITTLE... JUST TO MAKE IT MORE DRAMATIC...
OH NO!! I DON'T HAVE ENOUGH ENERGY LEFT!
IT'S ALL OVER!! IT'S THE END OF THE WORLD!!
NO...
HYAH!!!!
HUH?!
WSH

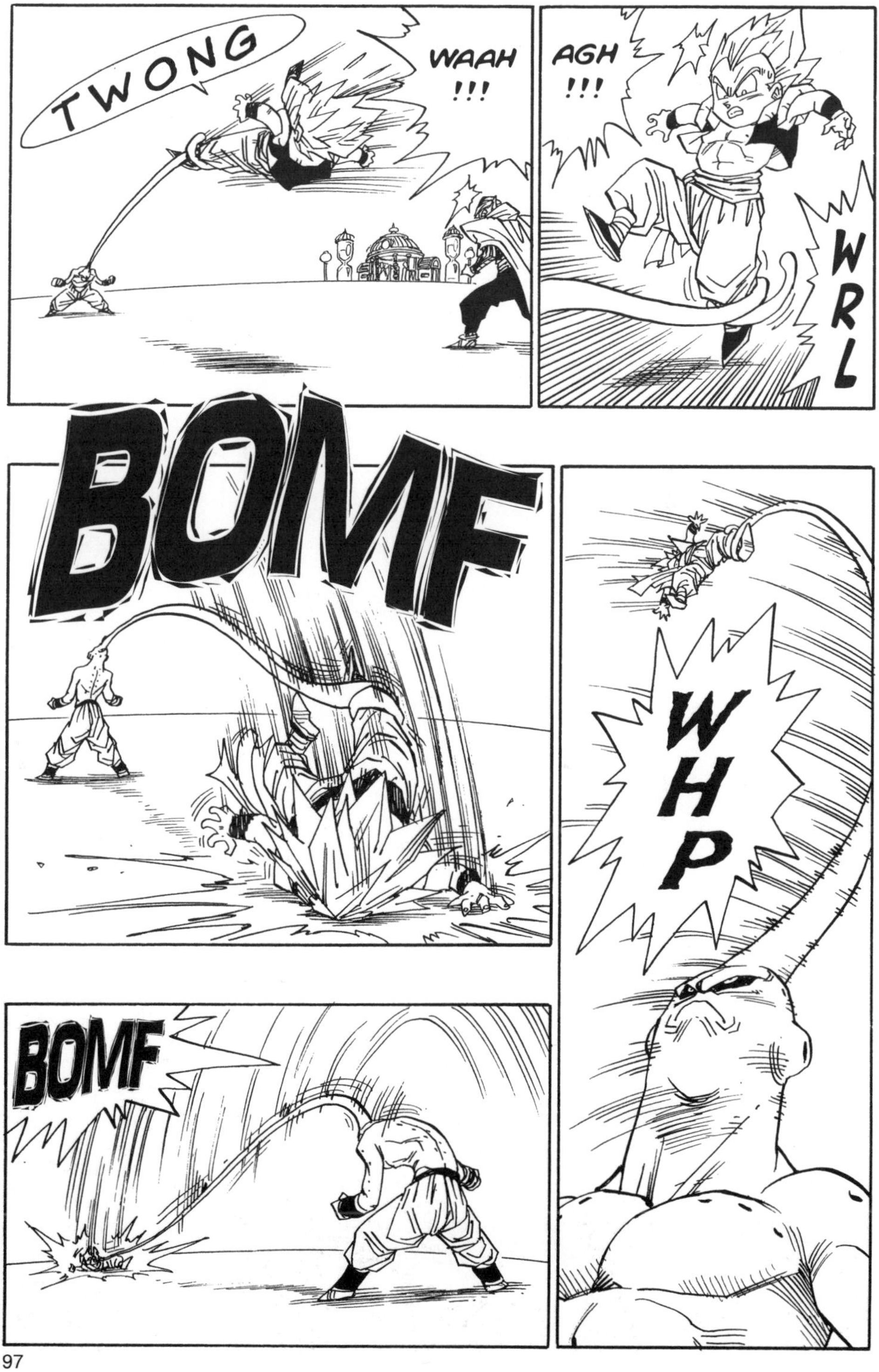
AGH !!!
WRL
TWONG
WAAH !!!
WHP
BOMF
BOMF

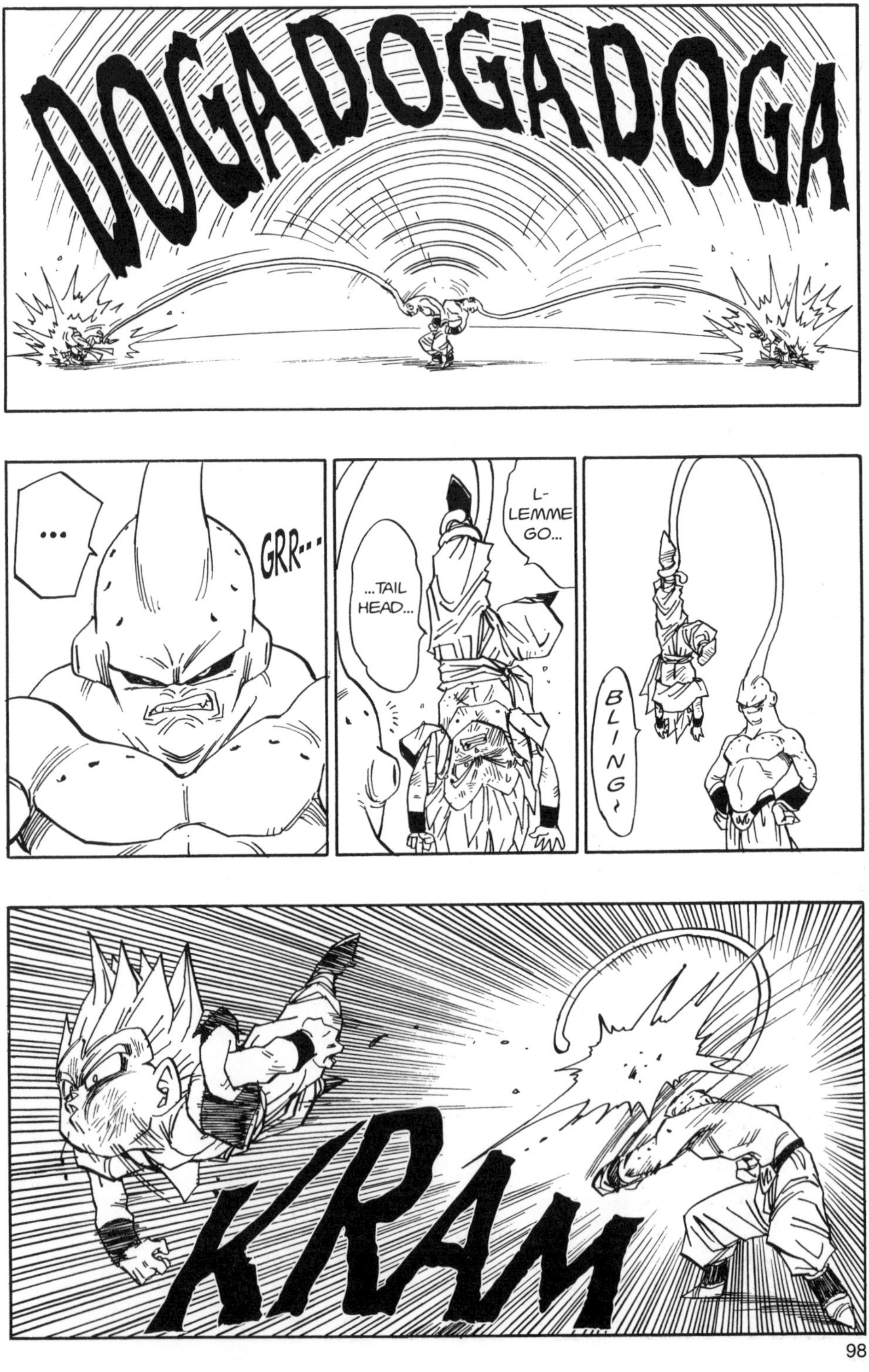
DOGADOGADOGA
BLING
L-LEMME GO...
...TAIL HEAD...
GRR...
...
KRAM

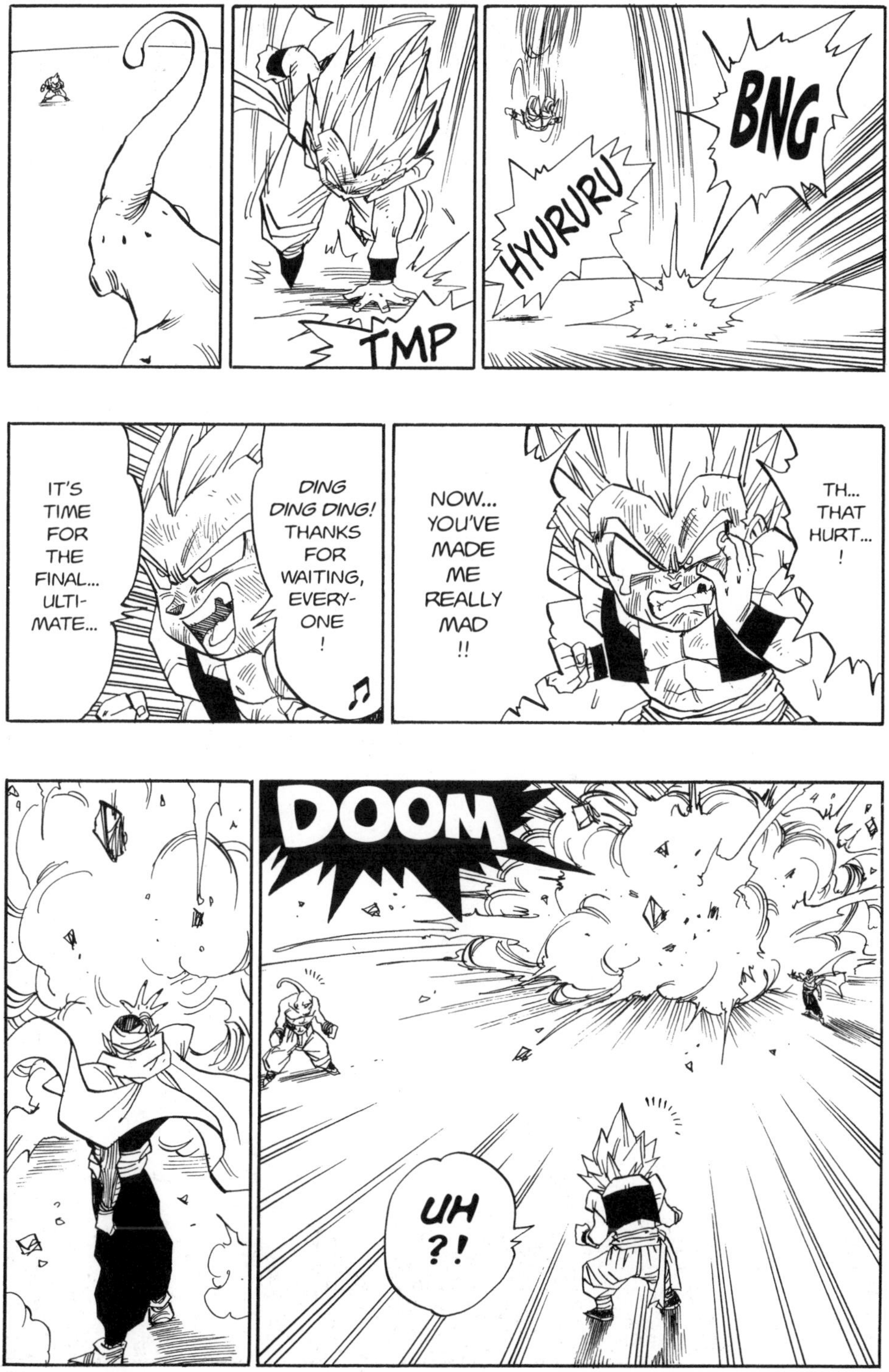
BNG
HYURURU
TMP
TH... THAT HURT...!
NOW... YOU'VE MADE ME REALLY MAD!!
DING DING DING! THANKS FOR WAITING, EVERYONE! ♪
IT'S TIME FOR THE FINAL... ULTIMATE...
DOOM
UH?!

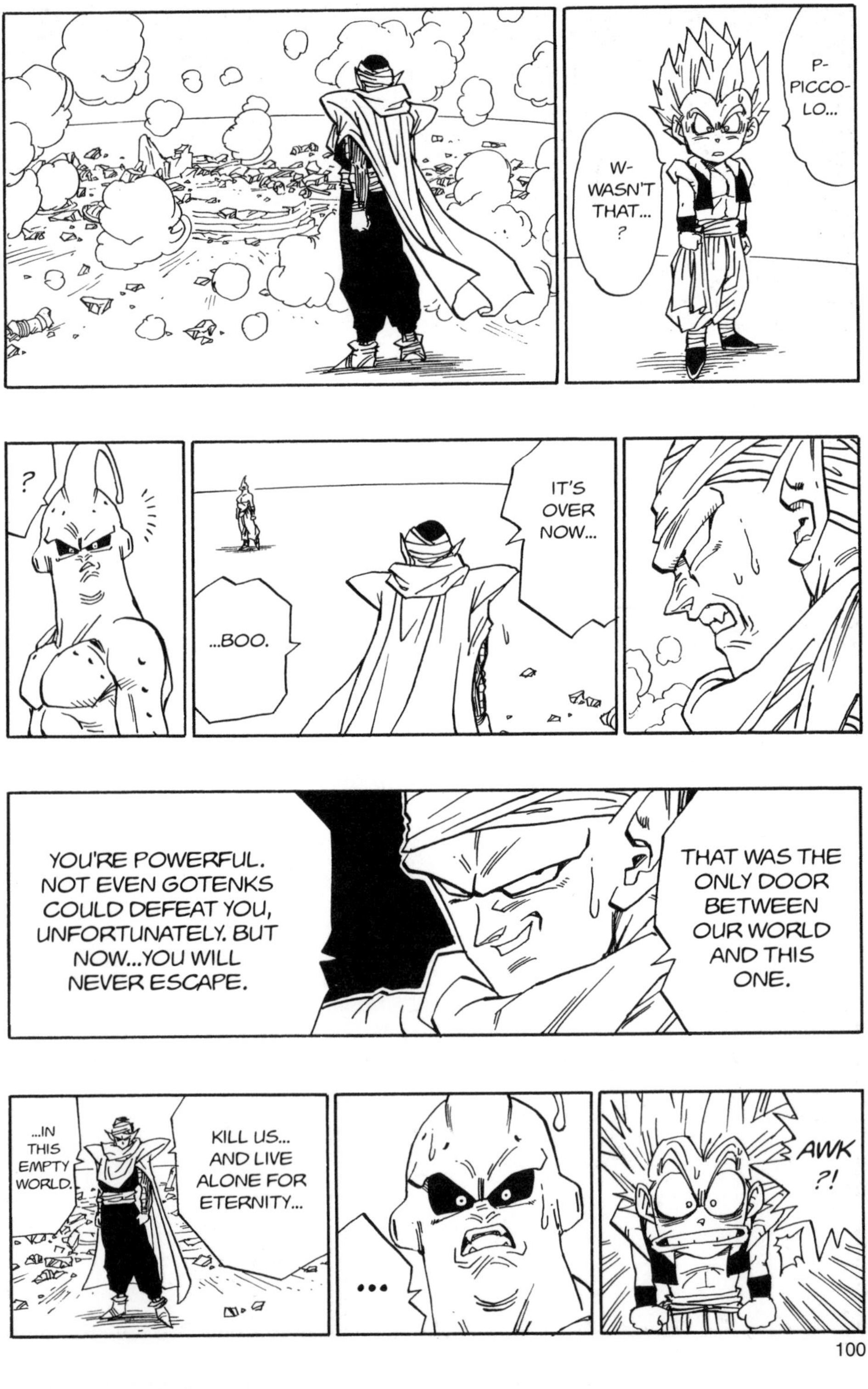
P-PICCO-LO...
W-WASN'T THAT...?
IT'S OVER NOW...
...BOO.
?
THAT WAS THE ONLY DOOR BETWEEN OUR WORLD AND THIS ONE.
YOU'RE POWERFUL. NOT EVEN GOTENKS COULD DEFEAT YOU, UNFORTUNATELY. BUT NOW...YOU WILL NEVER ESCAPE.
AWK ?!
...
KILL US... AND LIVE ALONE FOR ETERNITY...
...IN THIS EMPTY WORLD.

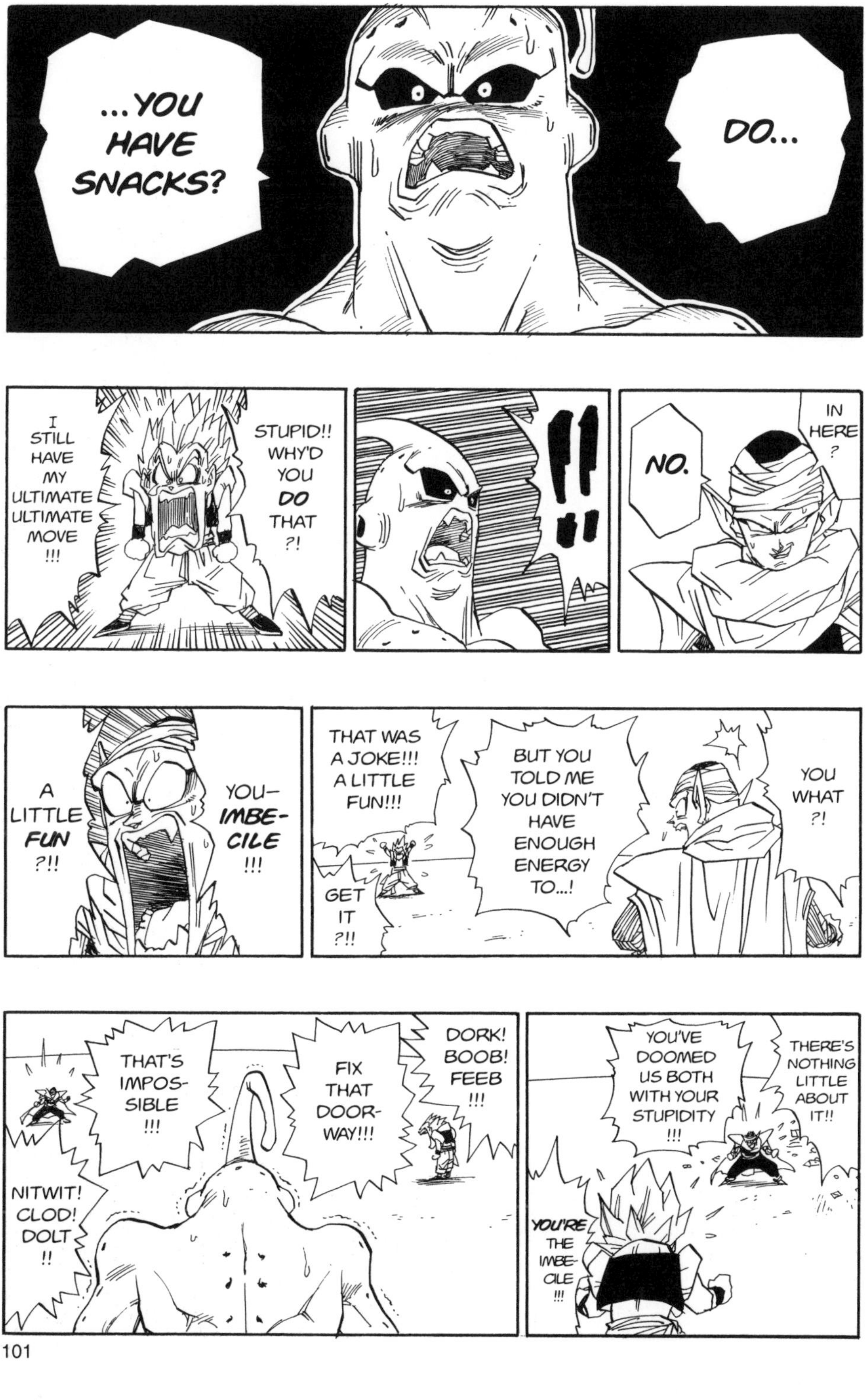

DO...
...YOU HAVE SNACKS?
IN HERE?
NO.
!!
STUPID!! WHY'D YOU DO THAT?!
I STILL HAVE MY ULTIMATE ULTIMATE MOVE!!!
YOU WHAT?!
BUT YOU TOLD ME YOU DIDN'T HAVE ENOUGH ENERGY TO...!
THAT WAS A JOKE!!! A LITTLE FUN!!!
GET IT?!!
YOU— IMBECILE!!!
A LITTLE FUN?!!
THERE'S NOTHING LITTLE ABOUT IT!!
YOU'VE DOOMED US BOTH WITH YOUR STUPIDITY!!!
YOU'RE THE IMBECILE!!!
DORK! BOOB! FEEB!!!
FIX THAT DOORWAY!!!
THAT'S IMPOSSIBLE!!!
NITWIT! CLOD! DOLT!!

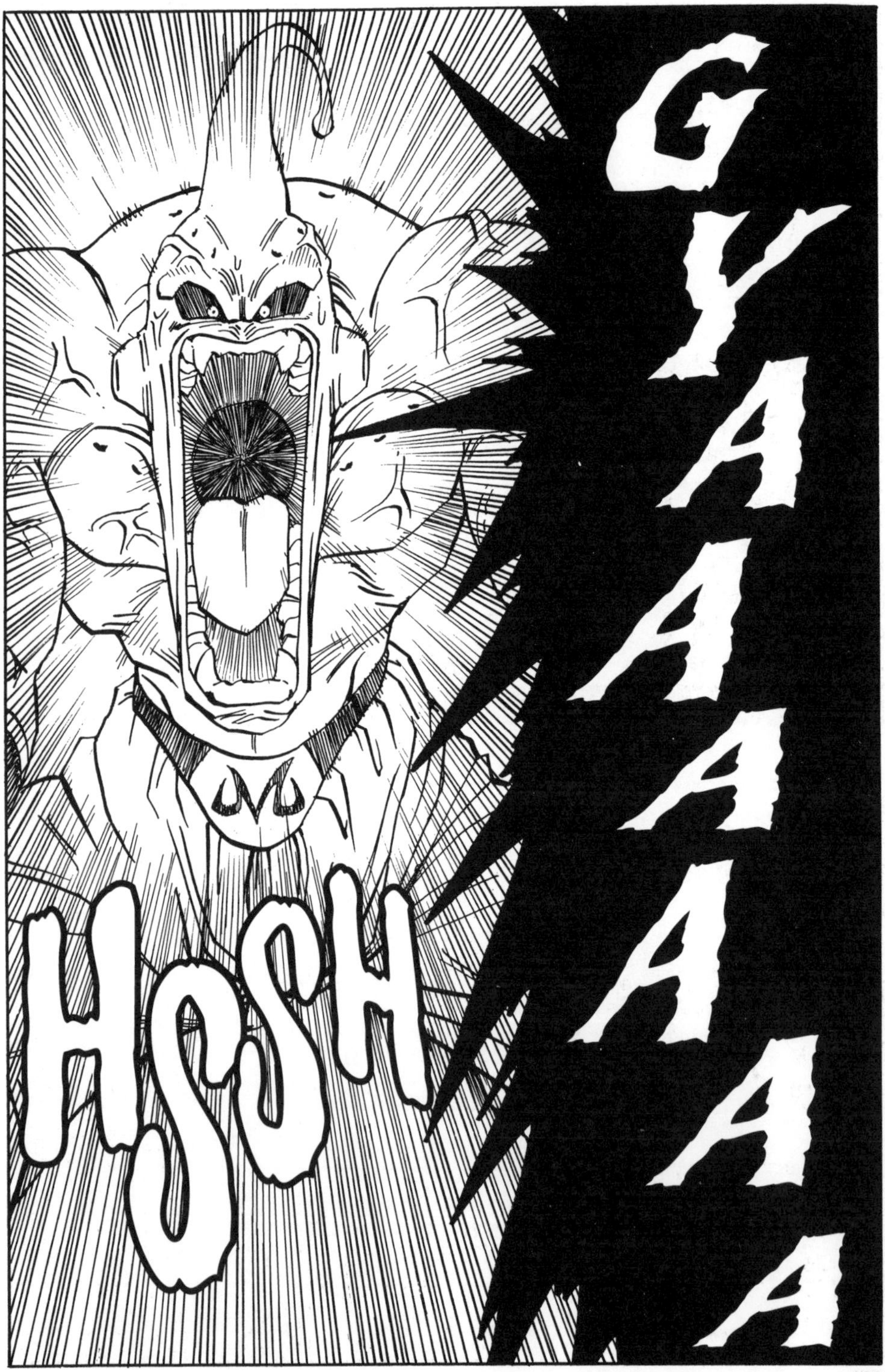
GIYAAAAAAAA
HSSH

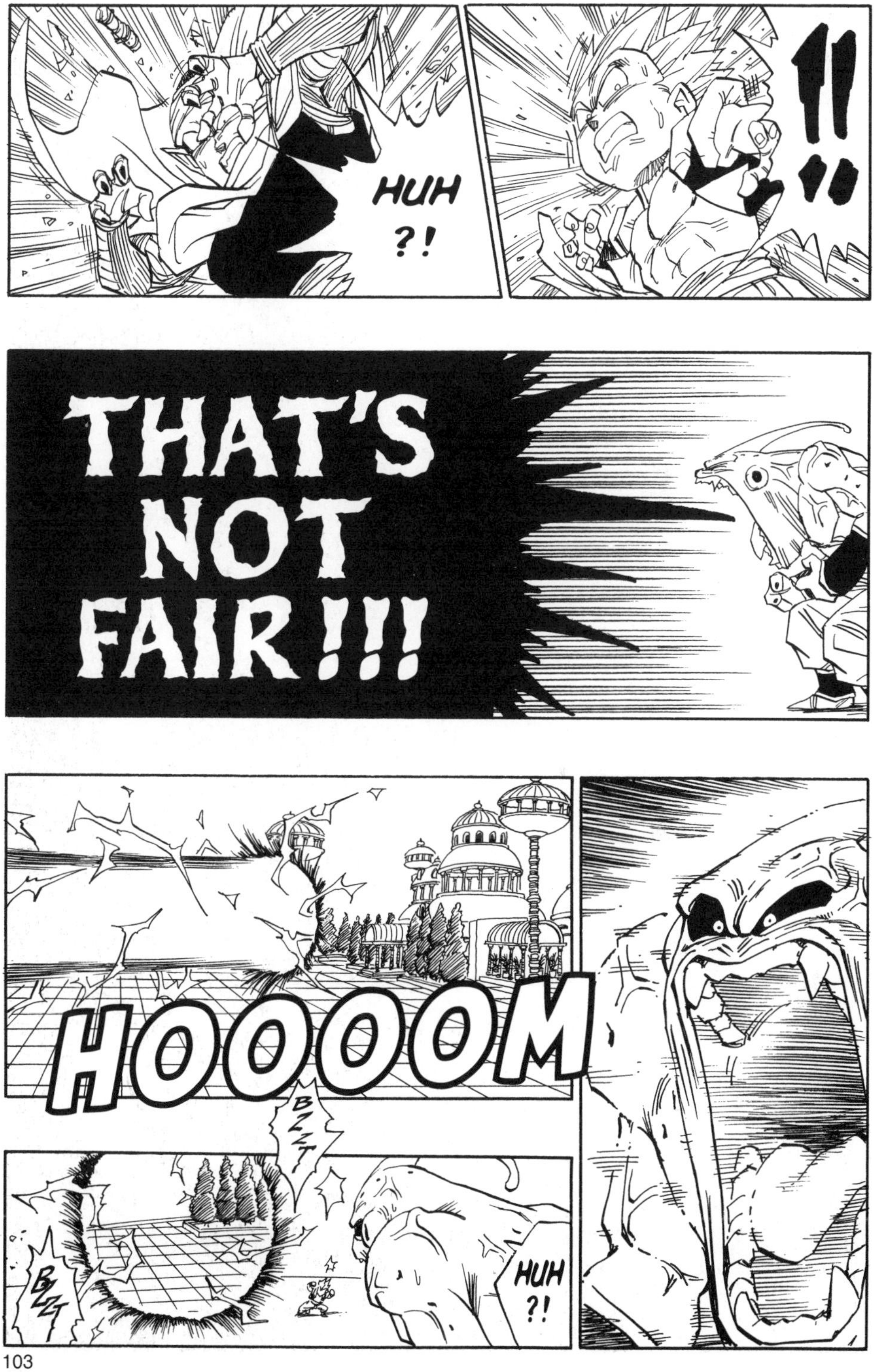
!!
!!
HUH ?!
THAT'S NOT FAIR!!!
HOOOOM
BZZT
HUH ?!
BZZT

DBZ:299 • Escape from the Time Dimension

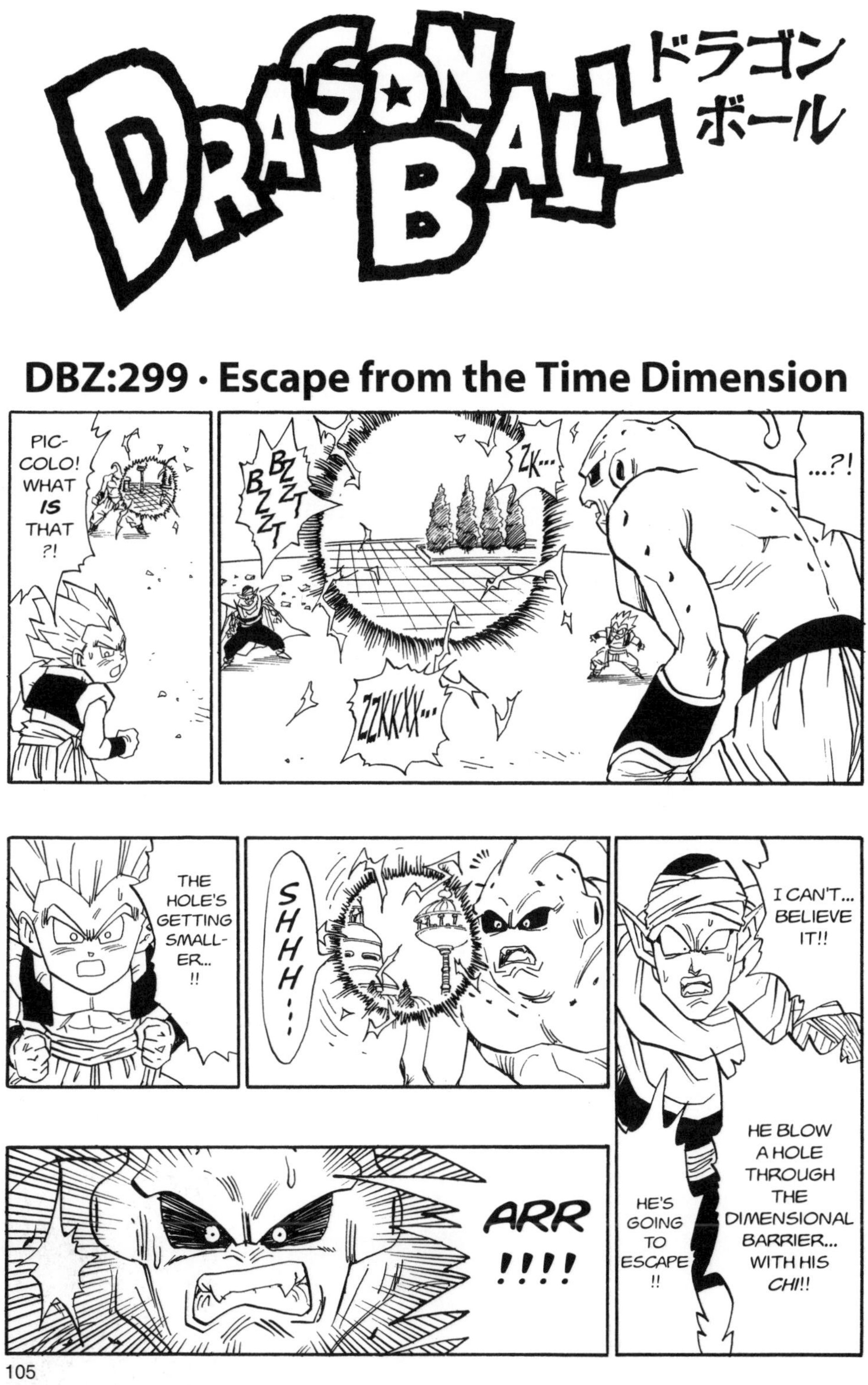
BZZZT BZZZT
ZK...
...?!
ZZKKXX...
PIC-COLO! WHAT *IS* THAT?!
I CAN'T... BELIEVE IT!!
HE BLOW A HOLE THROUGH THE DIMENSIONAL BARRIER... WITH HIS *CHI*!!
HE'S GOING TO ESCAPE!!
SHHH...
THE HOLE'S GETTING SMALLER...!!
ARR!!!!

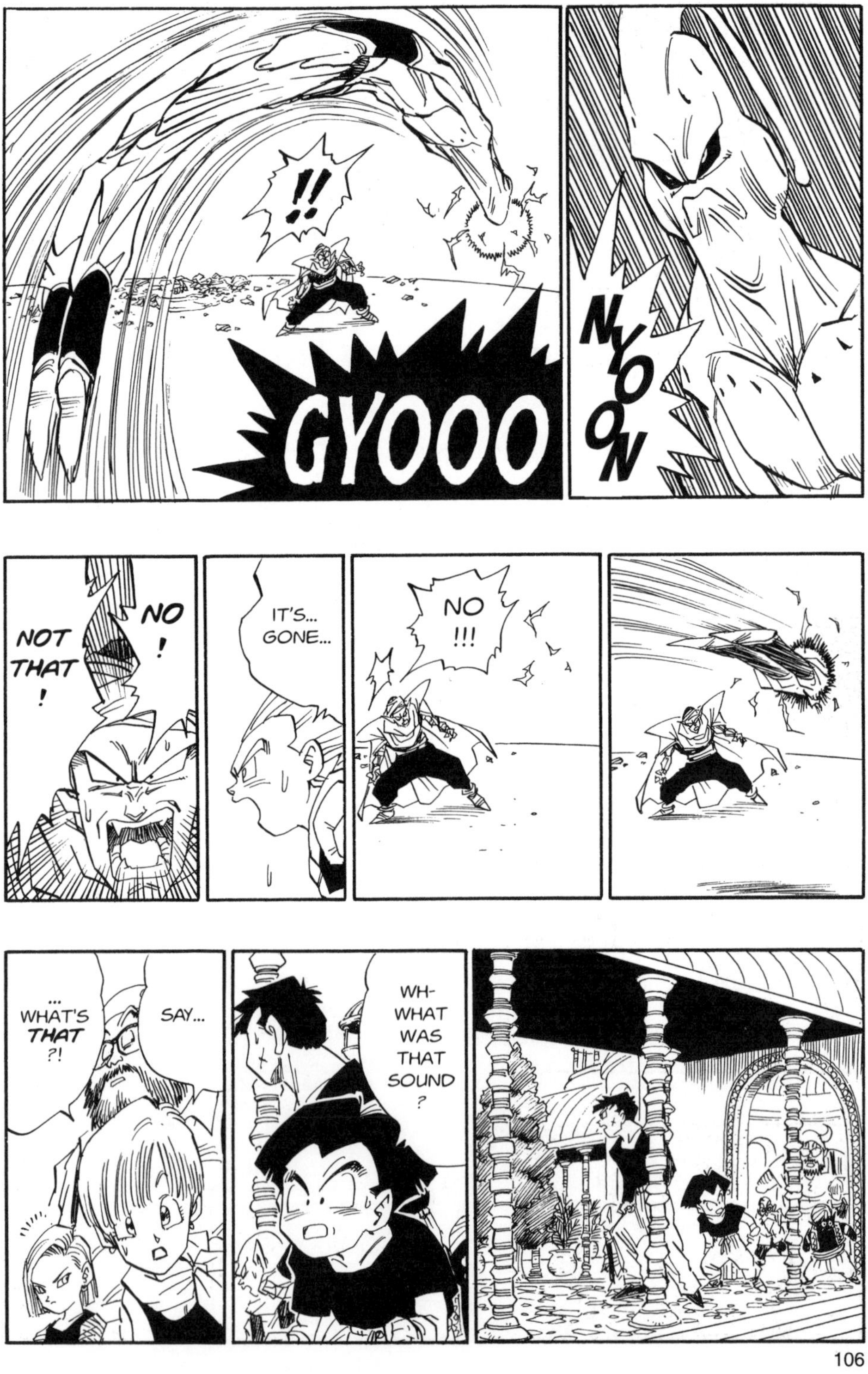
NYOON
!!
GYOOO
NO !!!
IT'S... GONE...
NO !
NOT THAT !
WH-WHAT WAS THAT SOUND ?
SAY...
...WHAT'S THAT ?!

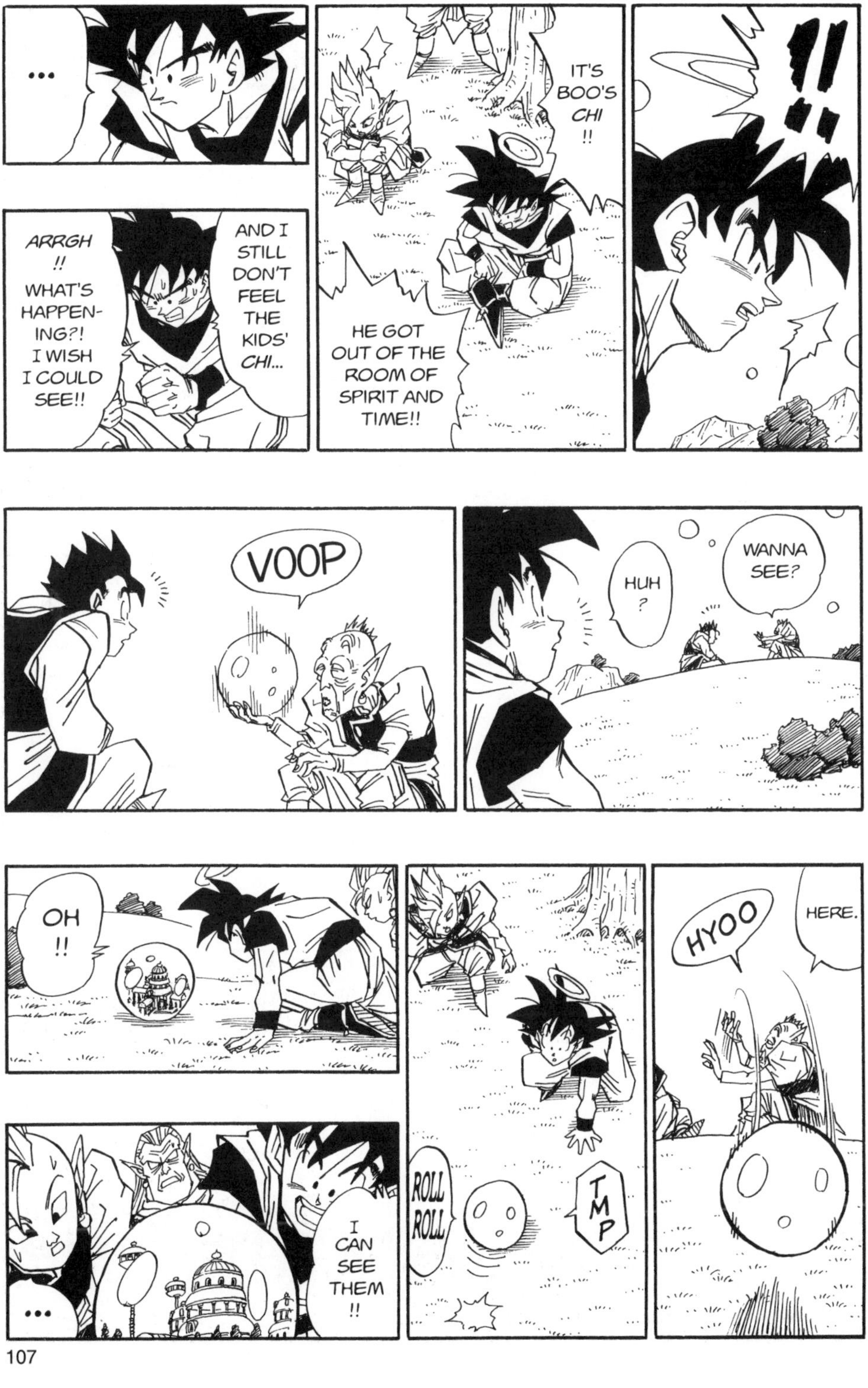
!!
IT'S BOO'S CHI !!
HE GOT OUT OF THE ROOM OF SPIRIT AND TIME!!
...
AND I STILL DON'T FEEL THE KIDS' CHI...
ARRGH!! WHAT'S HAPPEN-ING?! I WISH I COULD SEE!!
WANNA SEE?
HUH?
VOOP
HERE.
HYOO
TMP
ROLL ROLL
OH!!
I CAN SEE THEM!!
...

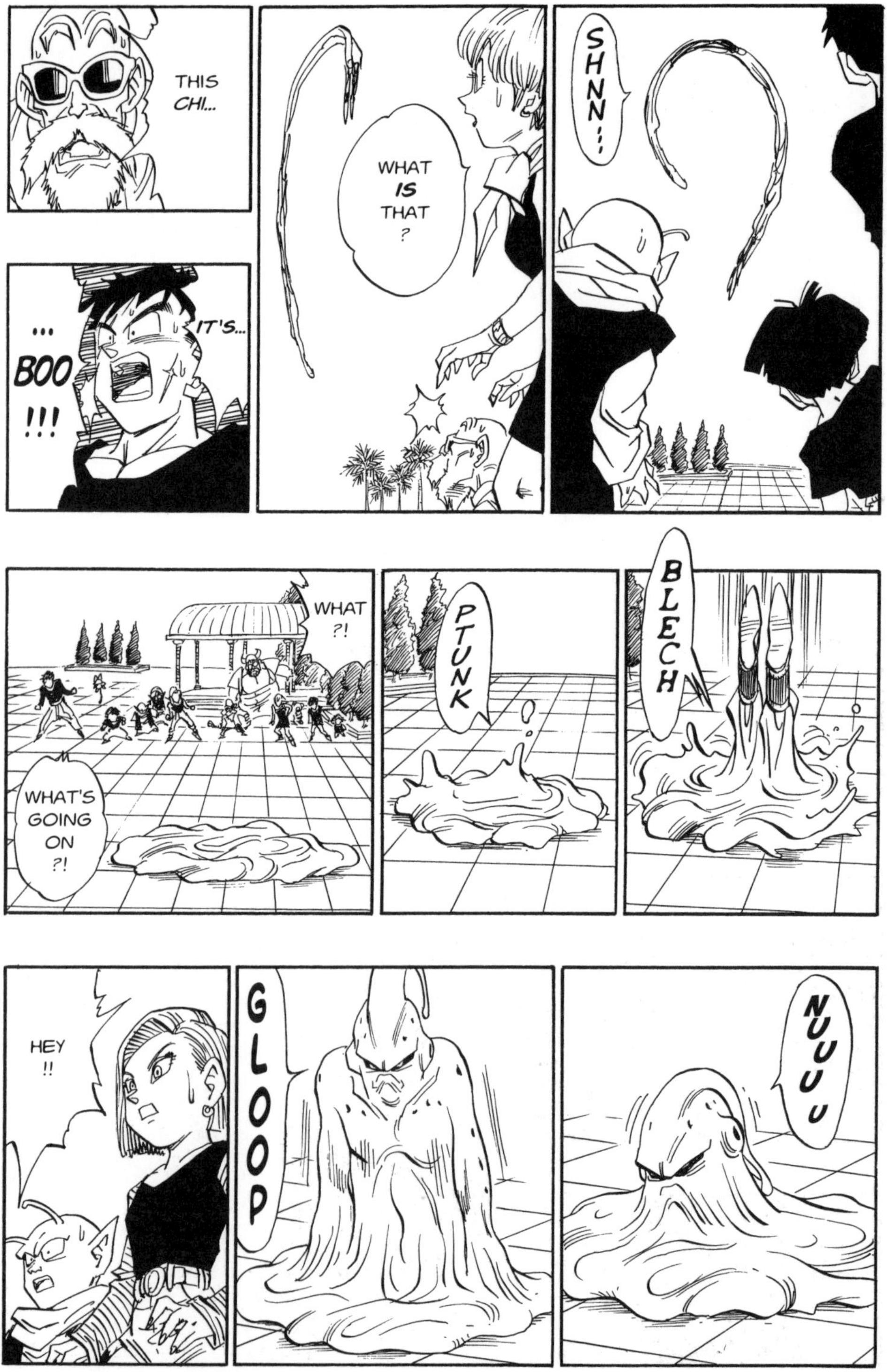
SHNN...
WHAT IS THAT ?
THIS CHI...
IT'S...
... BOO !!!
BLECH
PTUNK
WHAT ?!
WHAT'S GOING ON ?!
NUUUU
GLOOP
HEY !!

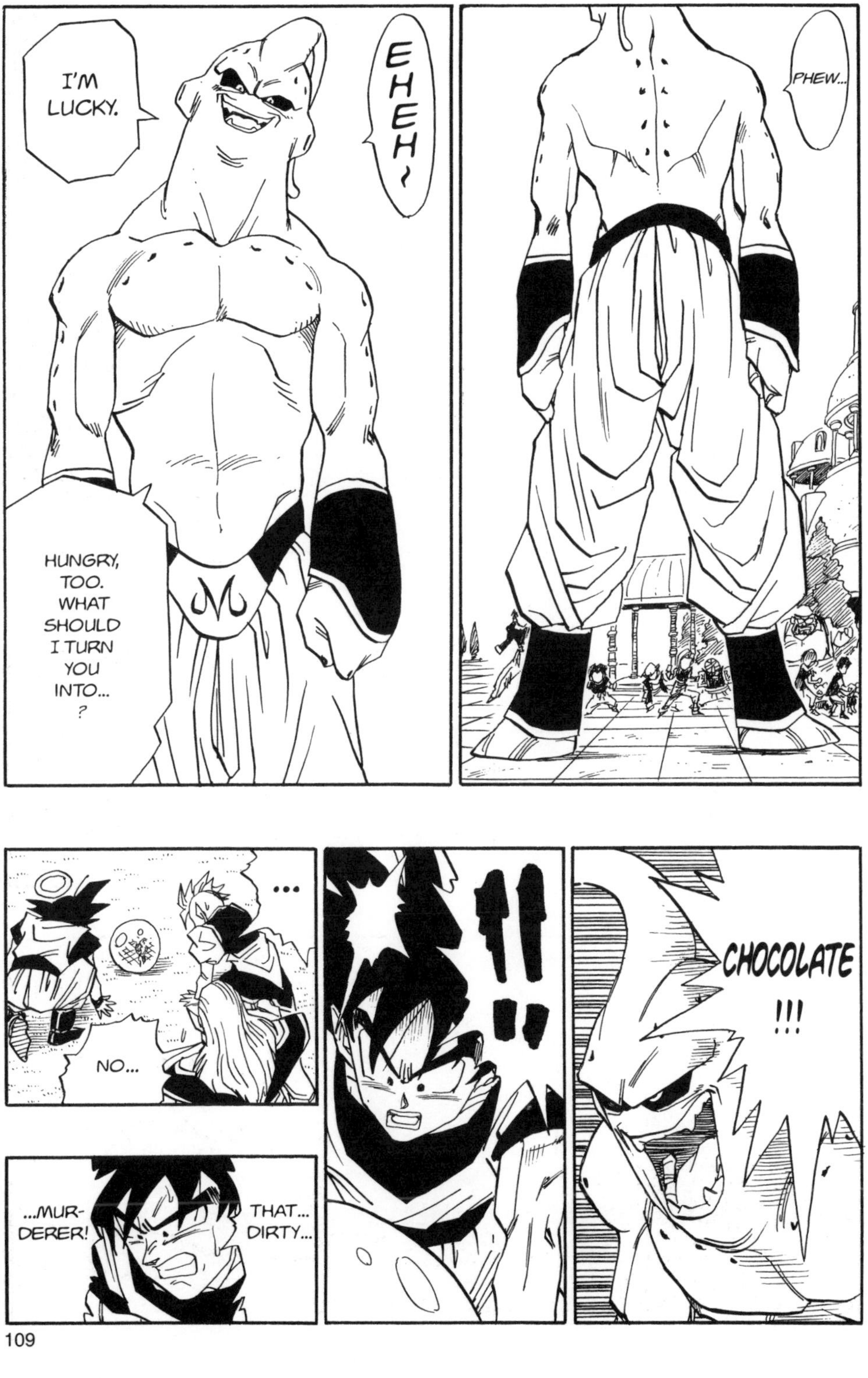
PHEW...
EHEH~
I'M LUCKY.
HUNGRY, TOO. WHAT SHOULD I TURN YOU INTO...?
CHOCOLATE !!!
!!
!!
...
NO...
THAT... DIRTY...
...MUR-DERER!

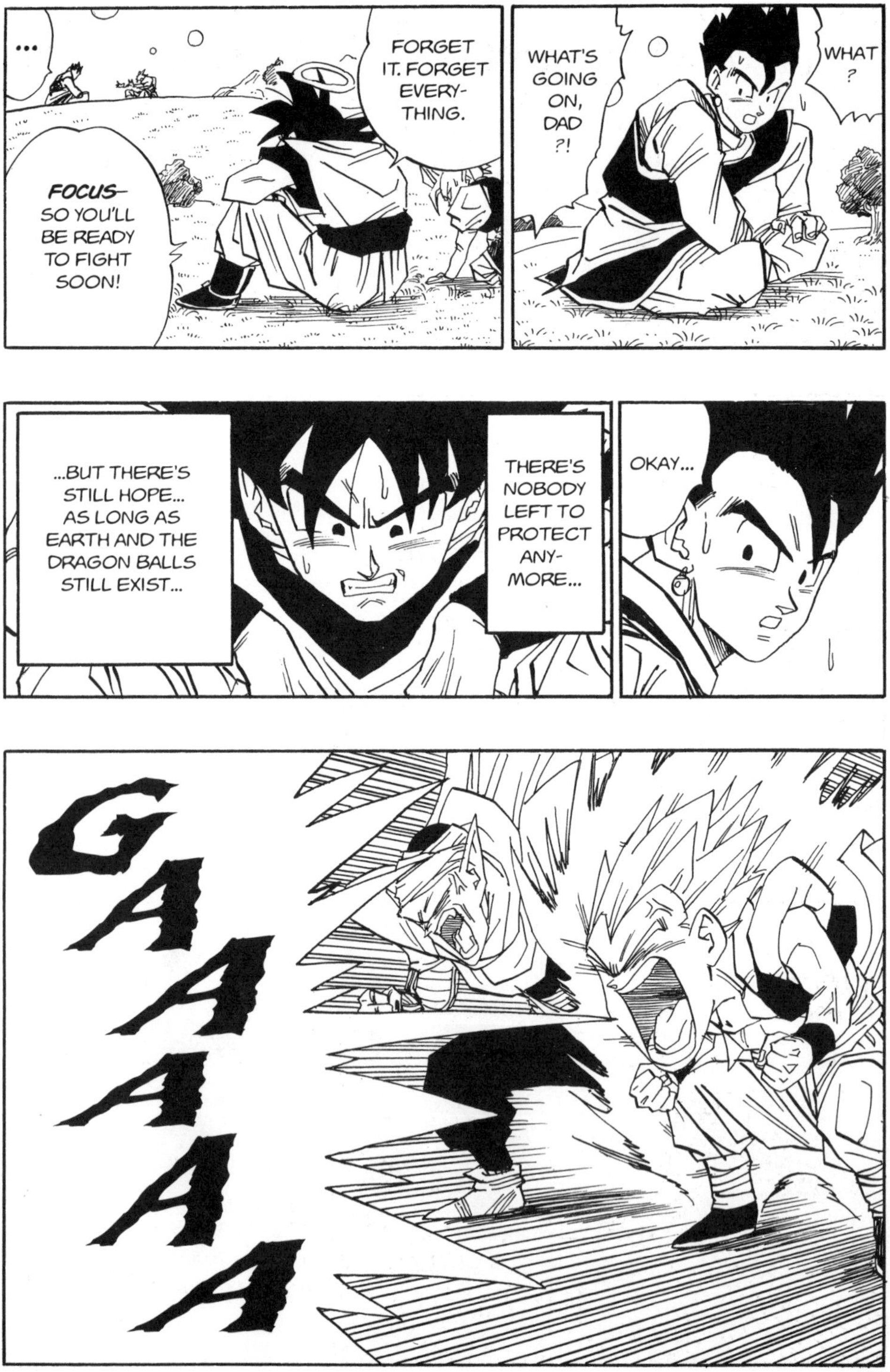
WHAT ?
WHAT'S GOING ON, DAD ?!
FORGET IT. FORGET EVERY-THING.
...
FOCUS— SO YOU'LL BE READY TO FIGHT SOON!
OKAY...
THERE'S NOBODY LEFT TO PROTECT ANY-MORE...
...BUT THERE'S STILL HOPE... AS LONG AS EARTH AND THE DRAGON BALLS STILL EXIST...
GAAAAAA

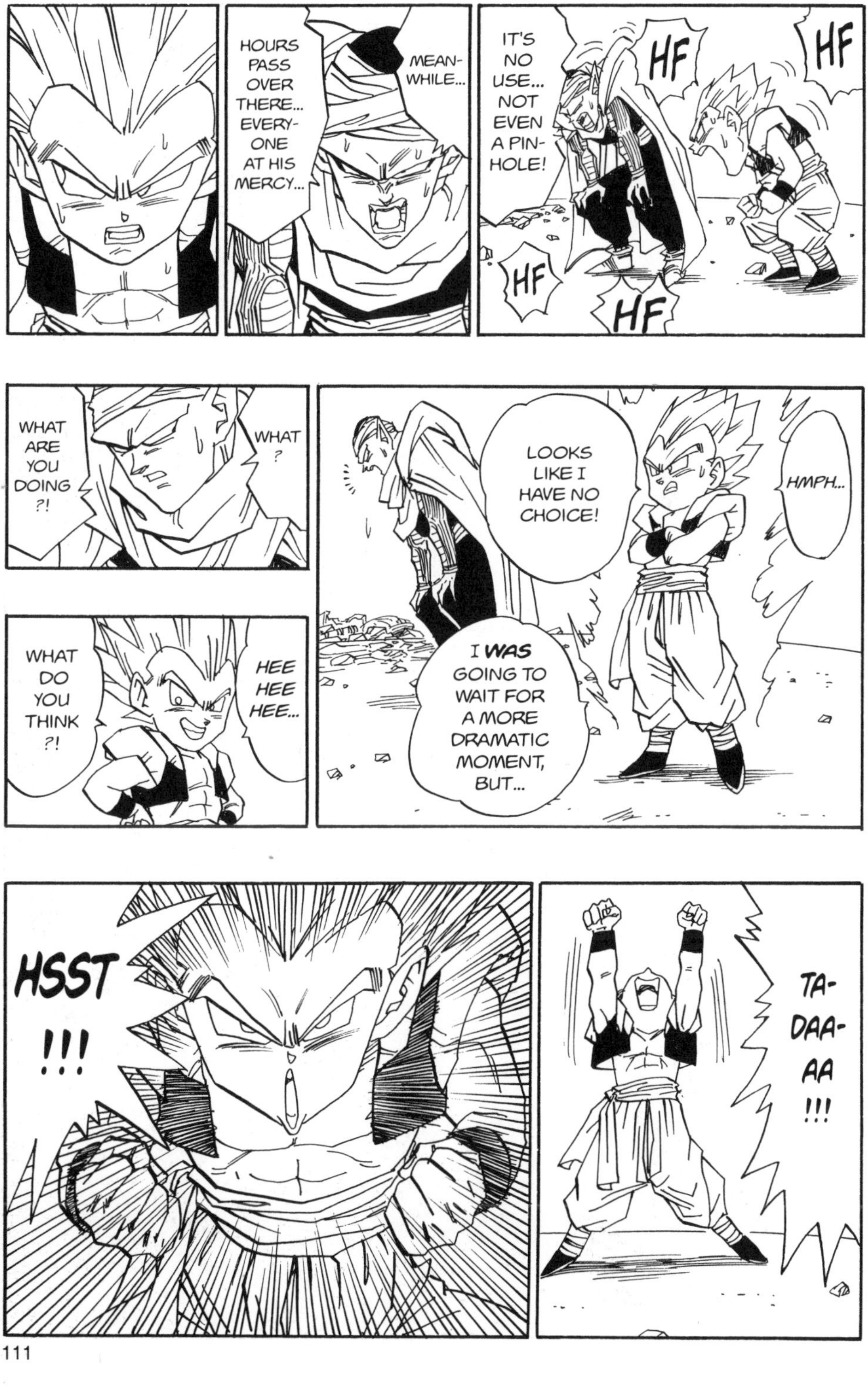
IT'S NO USE... NOT EVEN A PIN-HOLE!
HF
HF
HF
HF
MEAN-WHILE...
HOURS PASS OVER THERE... EVERY-ONE AT HIS MERCY...
HMPH...
LOOKS LIKE I HAVE NO CHOICE!
I **WAS** GOING TO WAIT FOR A MORE DRAMATIC MOMENT, BUT...
WHAT?
WHAT ARE YOU DOING?!
HEE HEE HEE...
WHAT DO YOU THINK?!
TA-DAA-AA!!!
HSST!!!

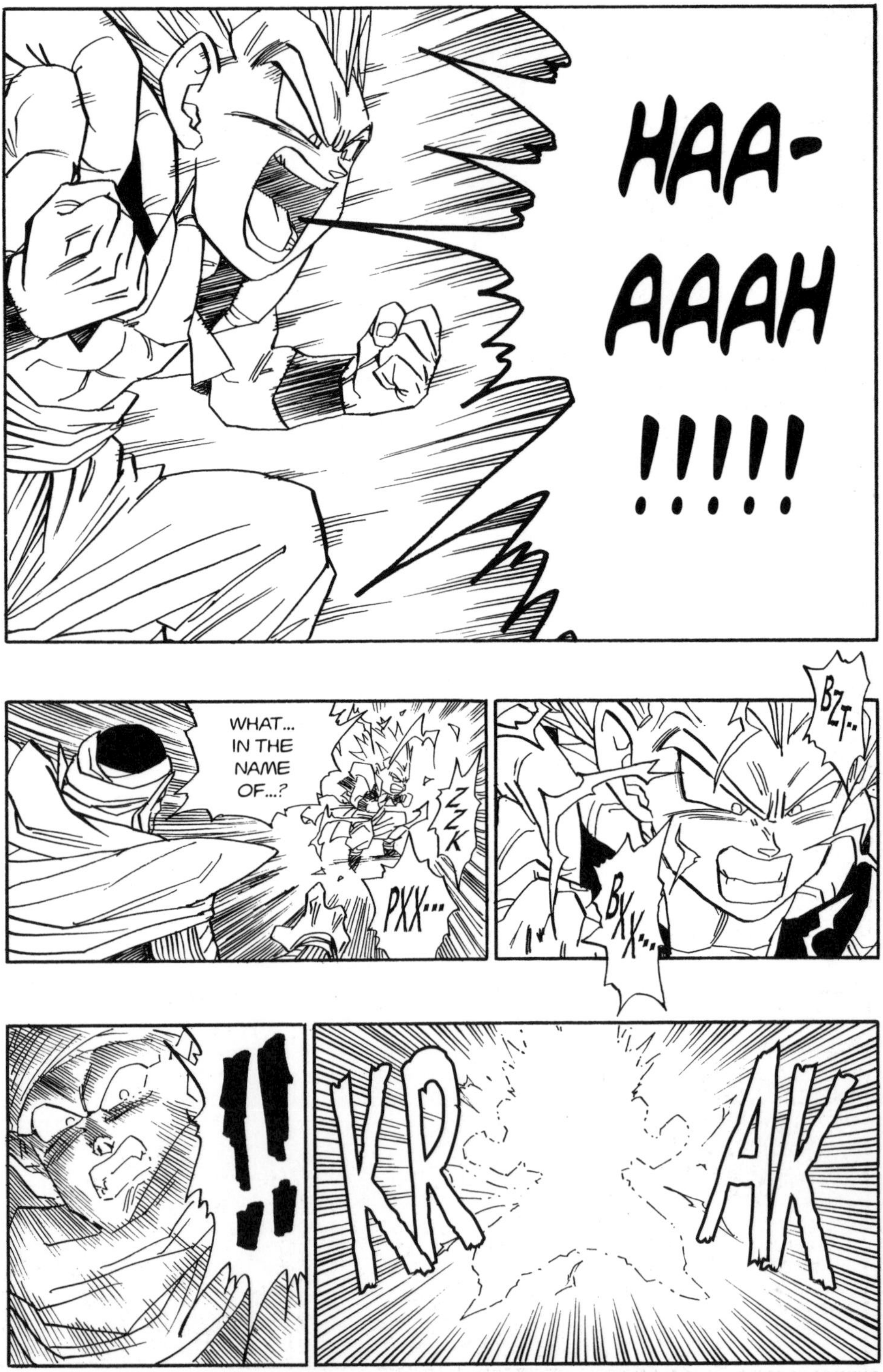
HAA-AAAH!!!!!
BZT..
BXX...
WHAT... IN THE NAME OF...?
ZZK
PXX...
KR AK
!!

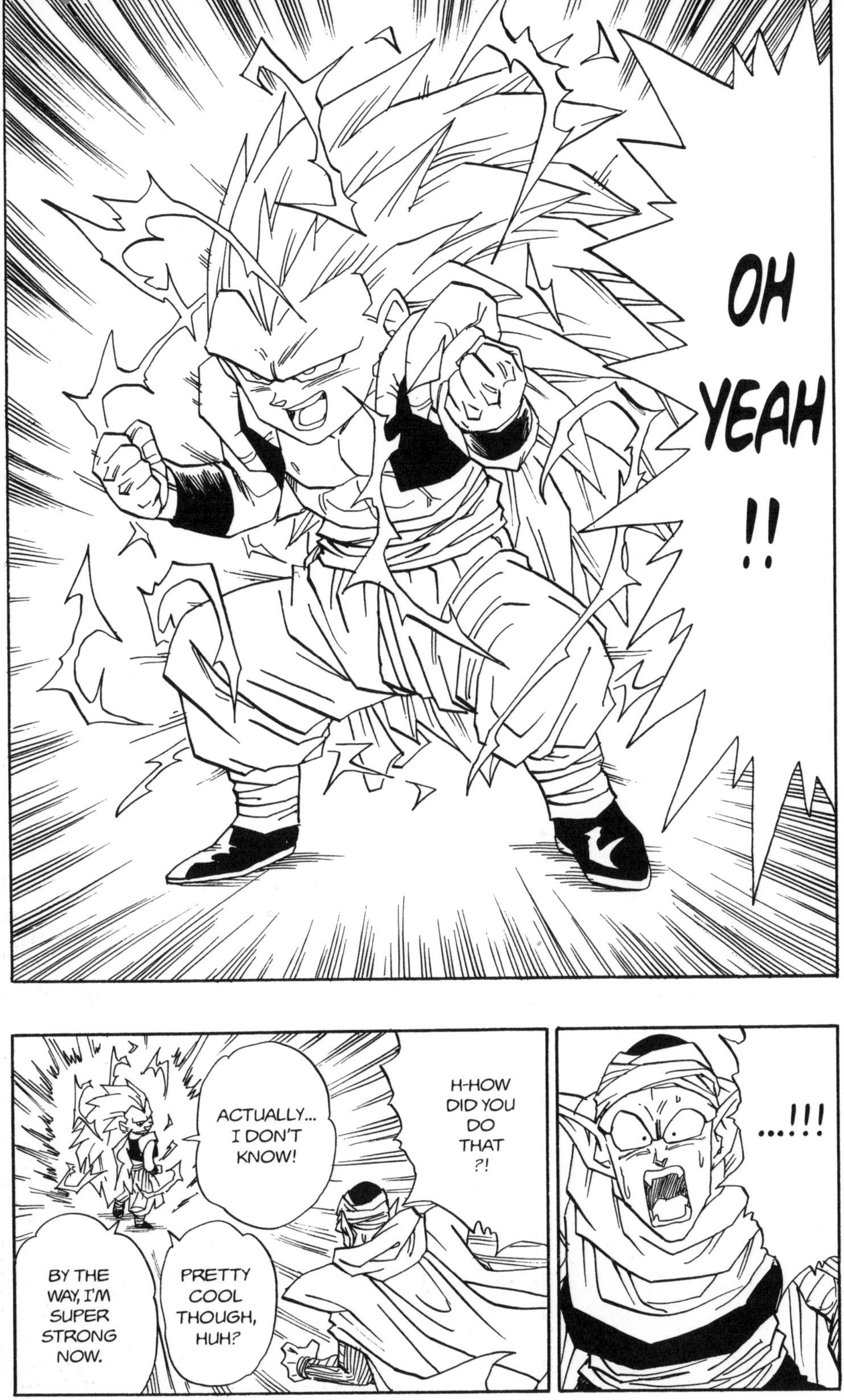
OH YEAH !!
...!!!
H-HOW DID YOU DO THAT ?!
ACTUALLY... I DON'T KNOW!
PRETTY COOL THOUGH, HUH?
BY THE WAY, I'M SUPER STRONG NOW.

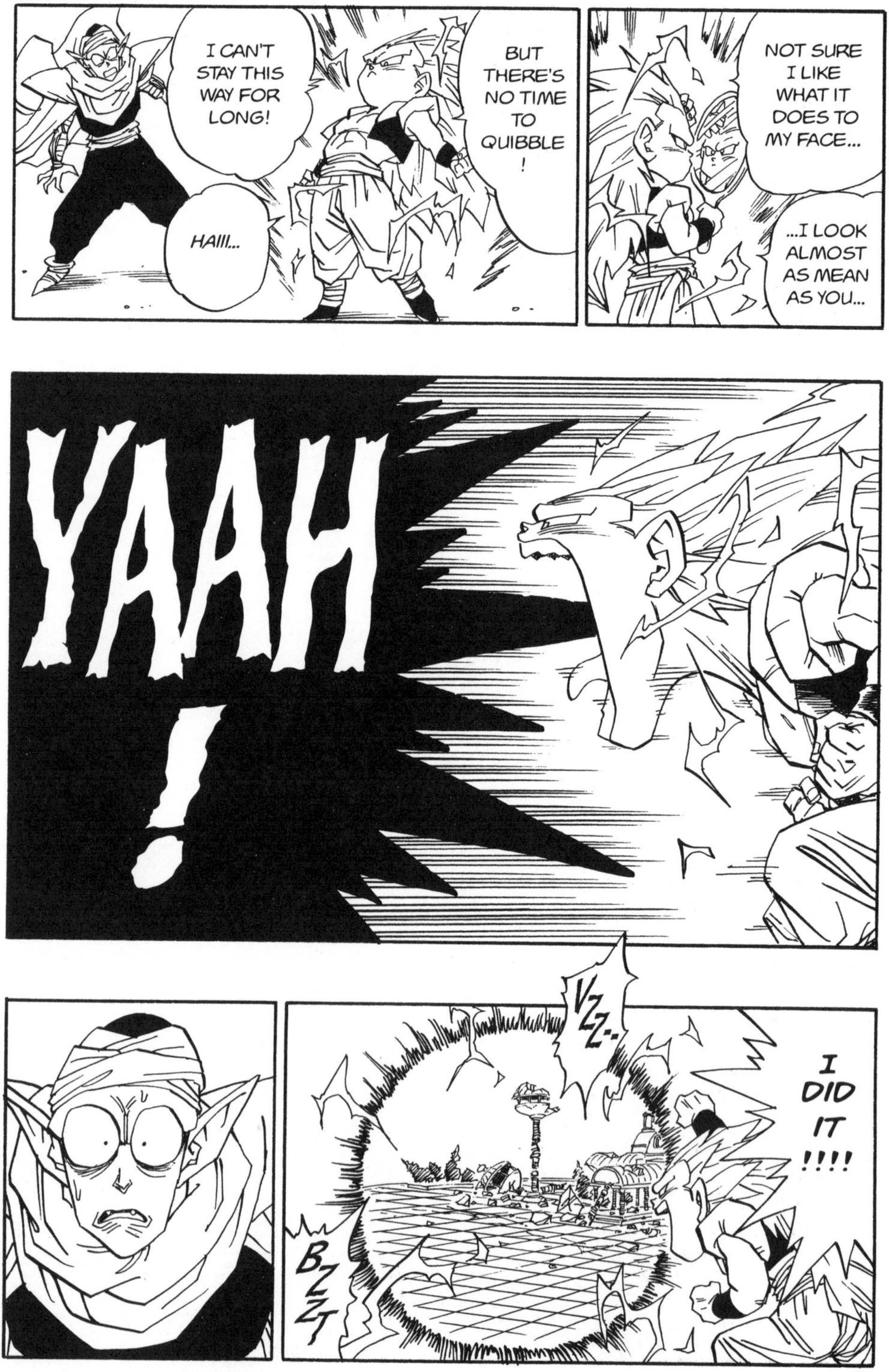
NOT SURE I LIKE WHAT IT DOES TO MY FACE...
...I LOOK ALMOST AS MEAN AS YOU...
BUT THERE'S NO TIME TO QUIBBLE!
I CAN'T STAY THIS WAY FOR LONG!
HAIII...
YAAH!
I DID IT!!!!
VZZ..
BZZT

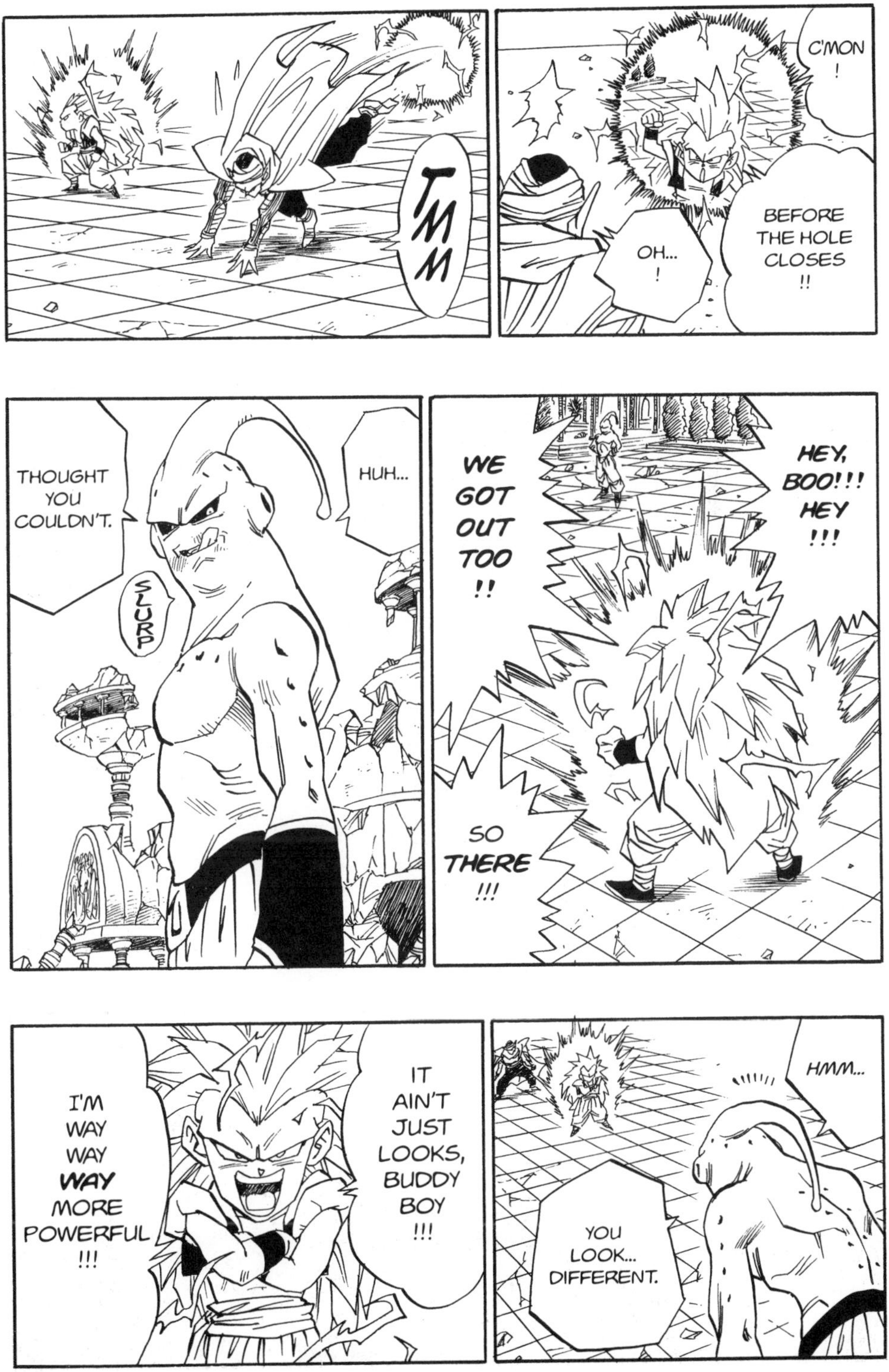
C'MON!
BEFORE THE HOLE CLOSES!!
OH...!
TMM
HEY, BOO!!! HEY!!!
WE GOT OUT TOO!!
SO THERE!!!
HUH...
THOUGHT YOU COULDN'T.
SLURP
HMM...
YOU LOOK... DIFFERENT.
IT AIN'T JUST LOOKS, BUDDY BOY!!!
I'M WAY WAY WAY MORE POWERFUL!!!

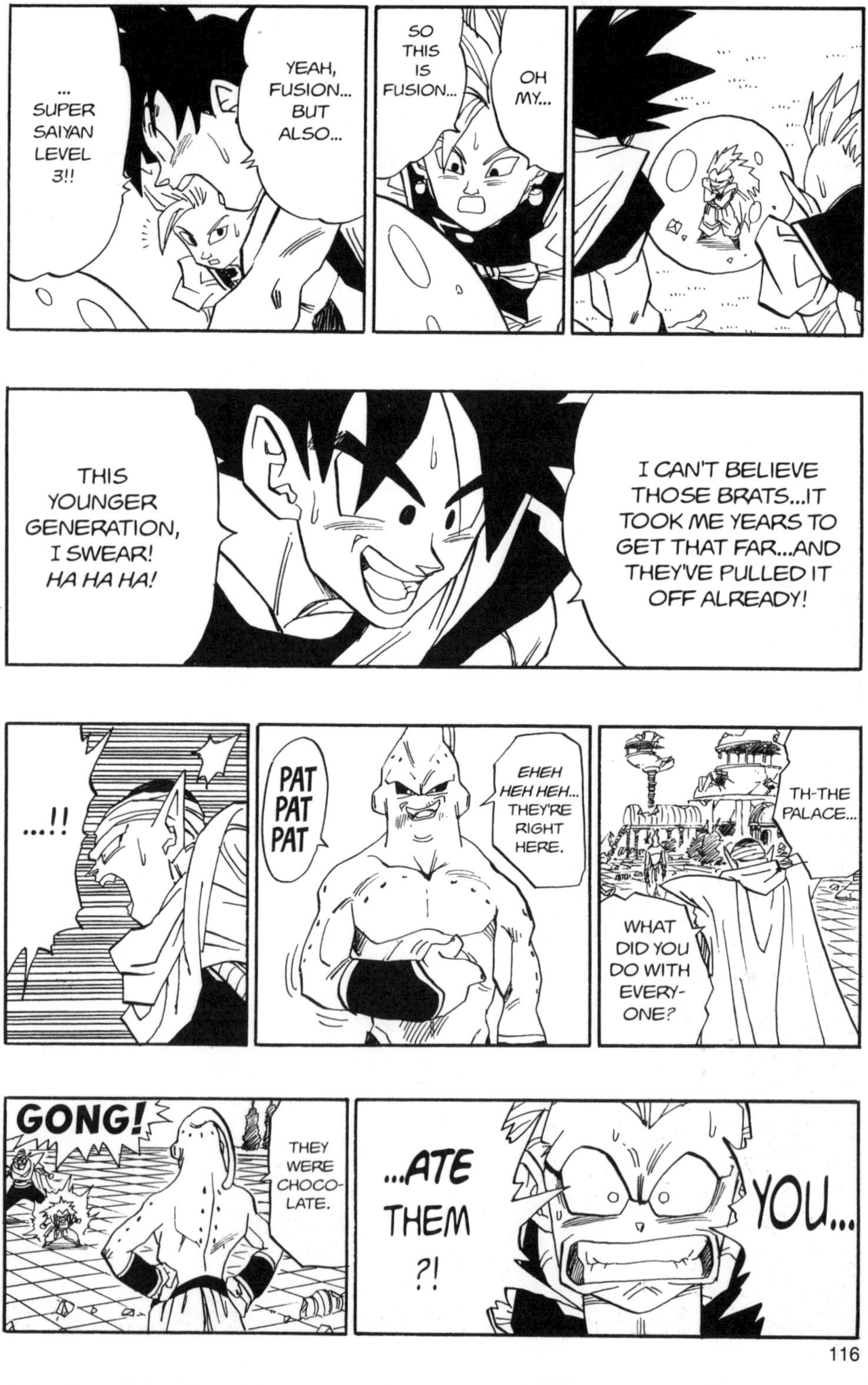
OH MY...
SO THIS IS FUSION...
YEAH, FUSION... BUT ALSO...
... SUPER SAIYAN LEVEL 3!!
I CAN'T BELIEVE THOSE BRATS...IT TOOK ME YEARS TO GET THAT FAR...AND THEY'VE PULLED IT OFF ALREADY!
THIS YOUNGER GENERATION, I SWEAR! *HA HA HA!*
TH-THE PALACE...
WHAT DID YOU DO WITH EVERY-ONE?
EHEH HEH HEH... THEY'RE RIGHT HERE.
PAT PAT PAT
...!!
YOU...
...ATE THEM ?!
THEY WERE CHOCO-LATE.
GONG!

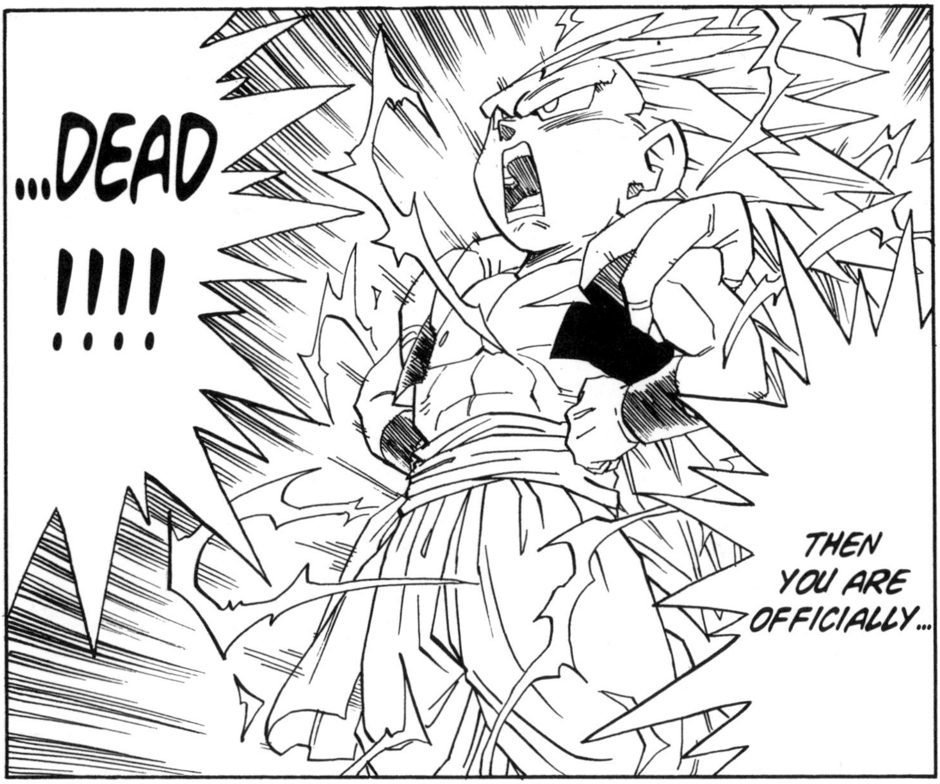
THEN YOU ARE OFFICIALLY...
...DEAD !!!!

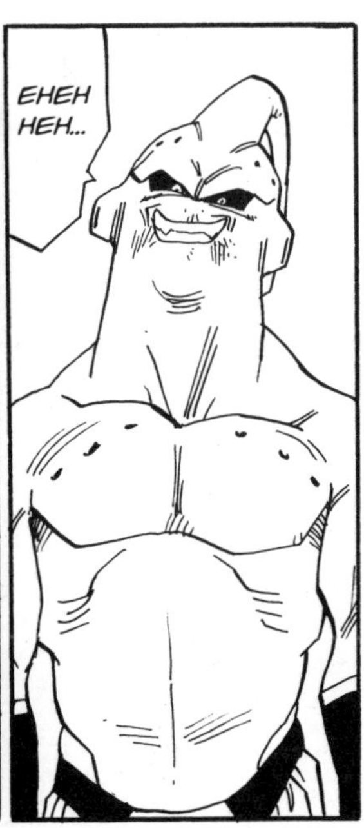
EHEH HEH...

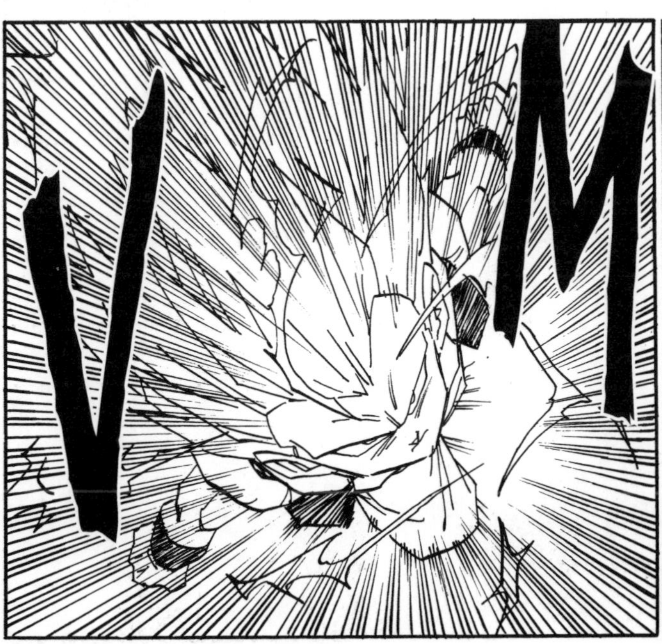
VM

DBZ:300 • Super Gotenks!

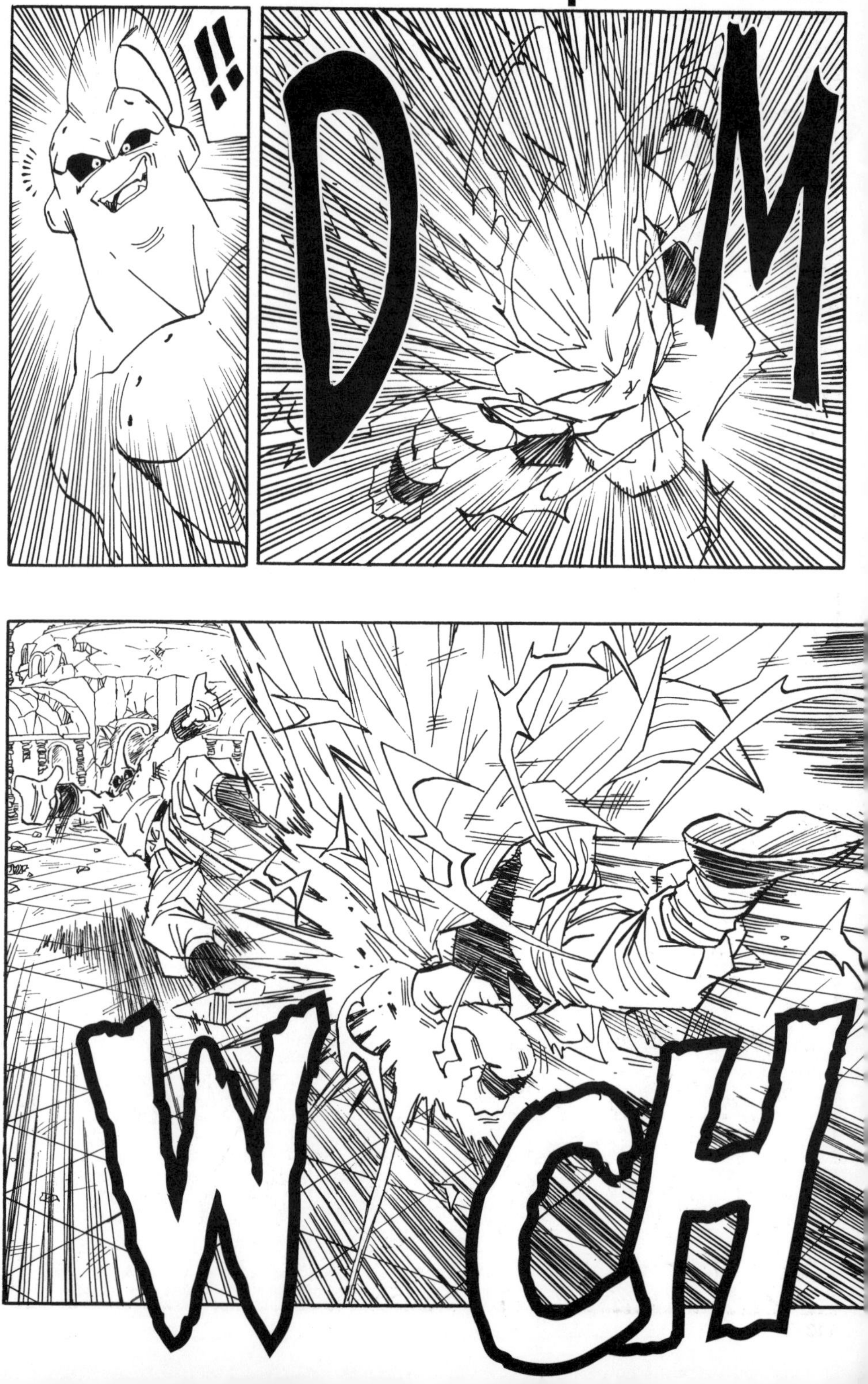
D M
!!
W CH

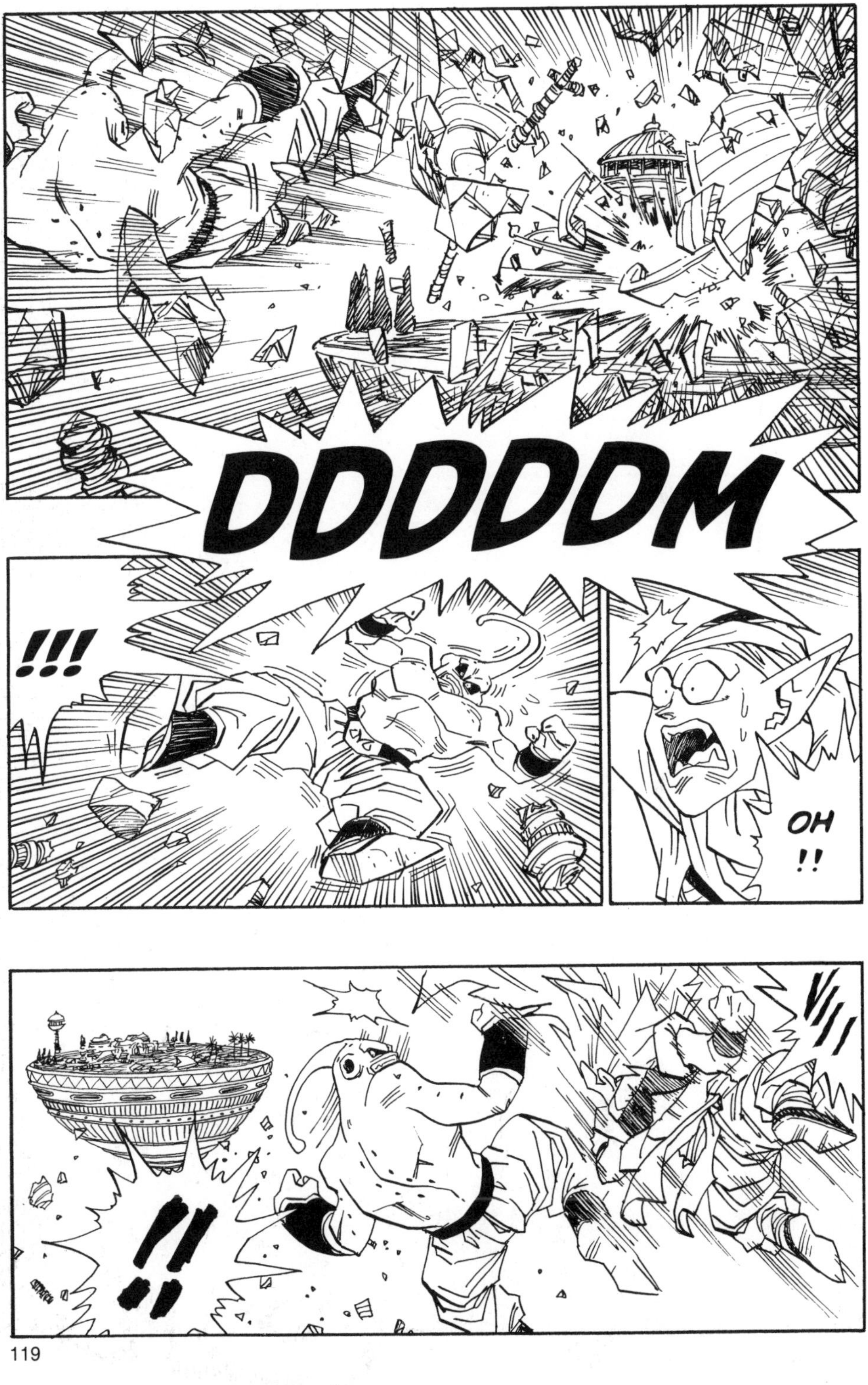
DDDDDM
OH !!
!!!
!!

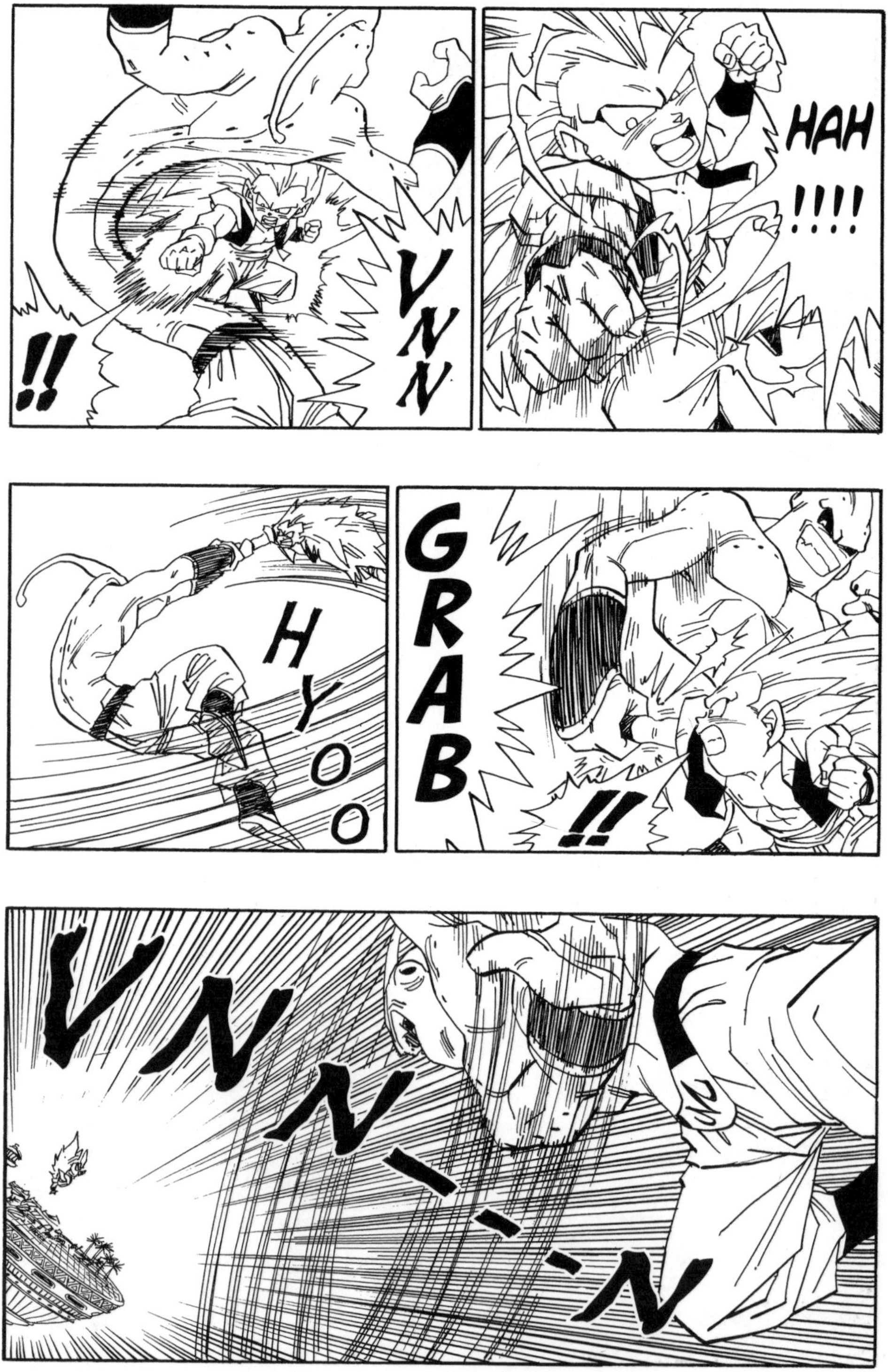
HAH !!!!
VNN
!!
GRAB
!!
HYOO
VNN---N

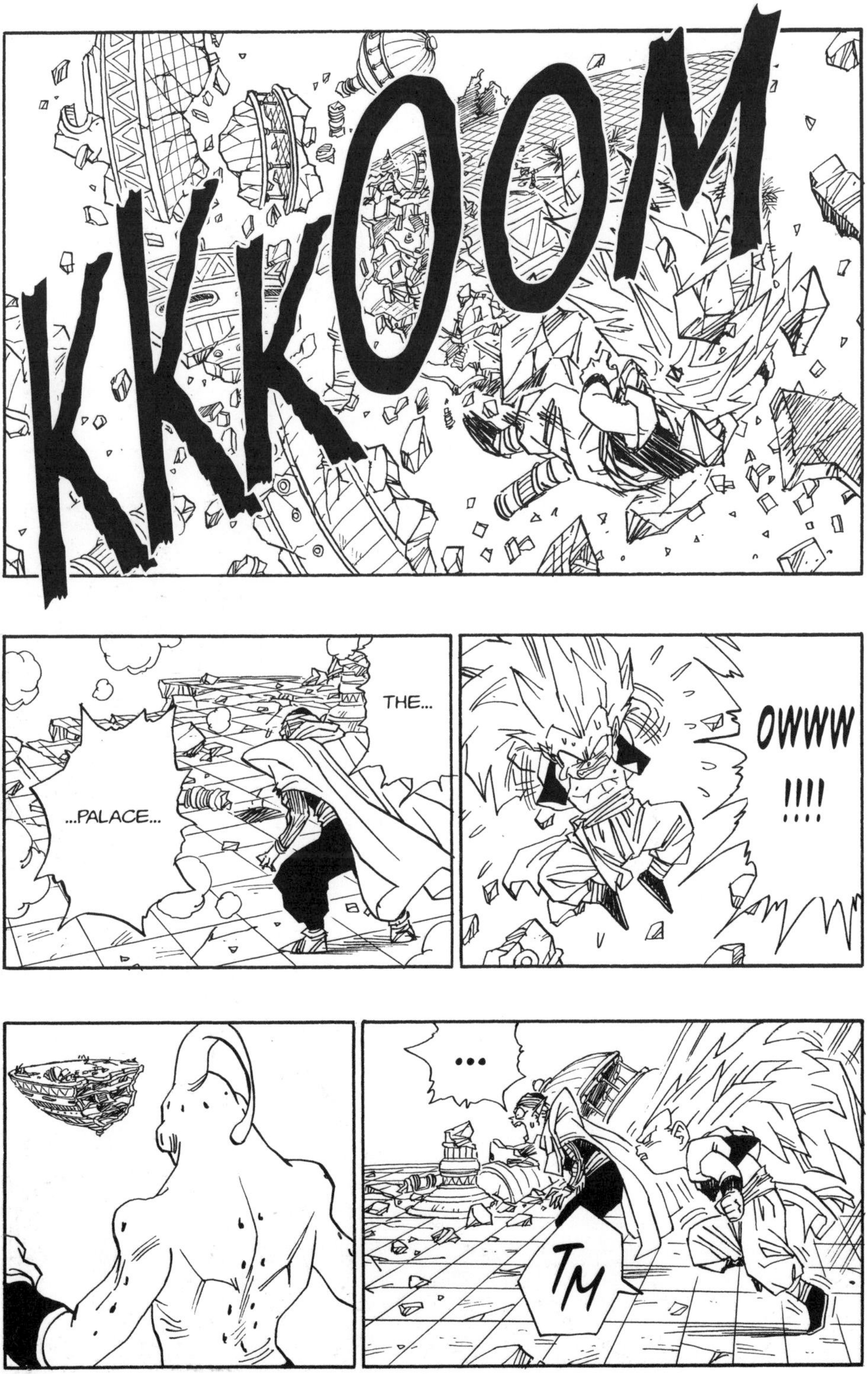
KKKOOM
OWWW !!!!
THE...
...PALACE...
...
TM

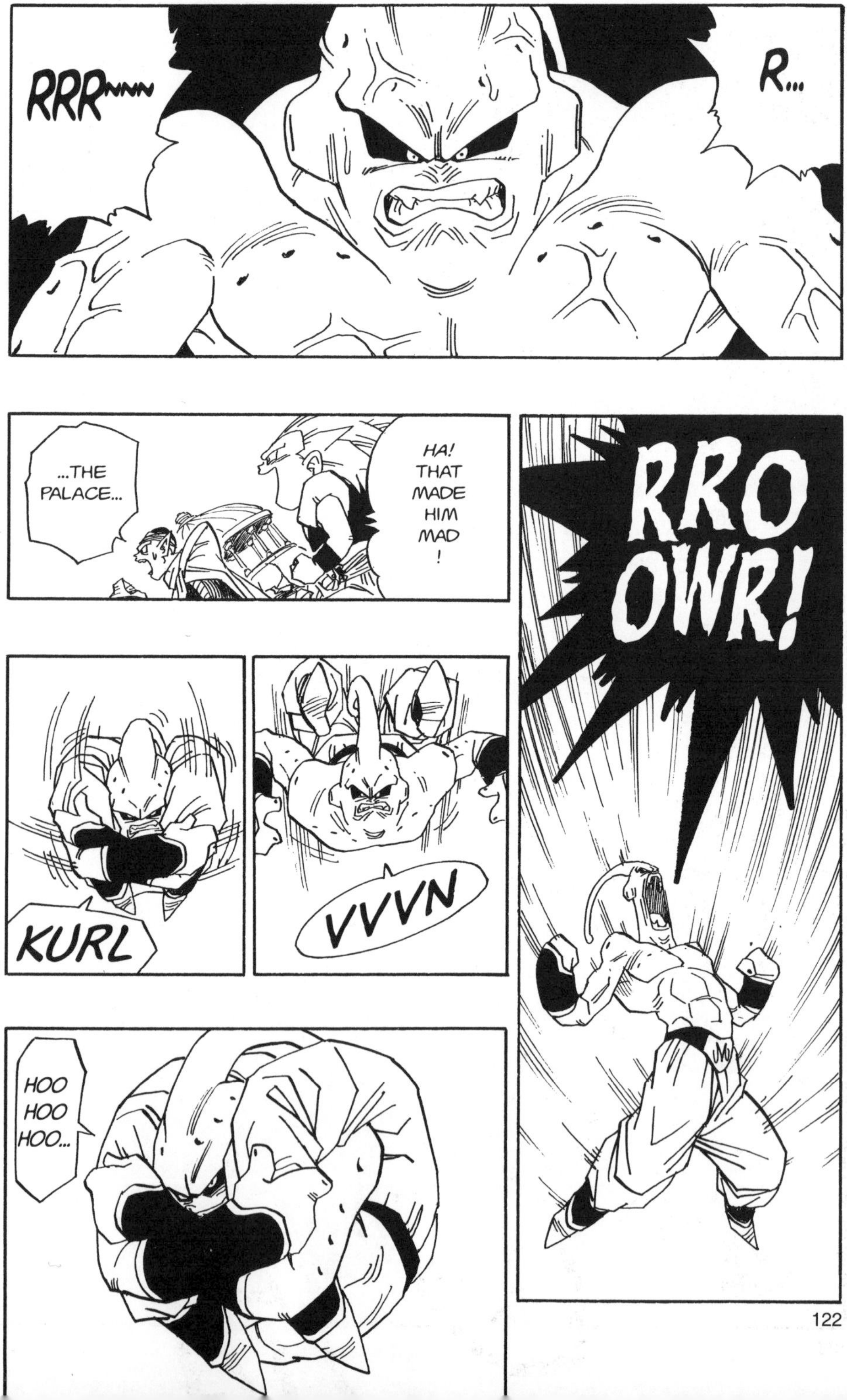
R...
RRRnnnn
RRO OWR!
HA! THAT MADE HIM MAD!
...THE PALACE...
VVVN
KURL
HOO HOO HOO...

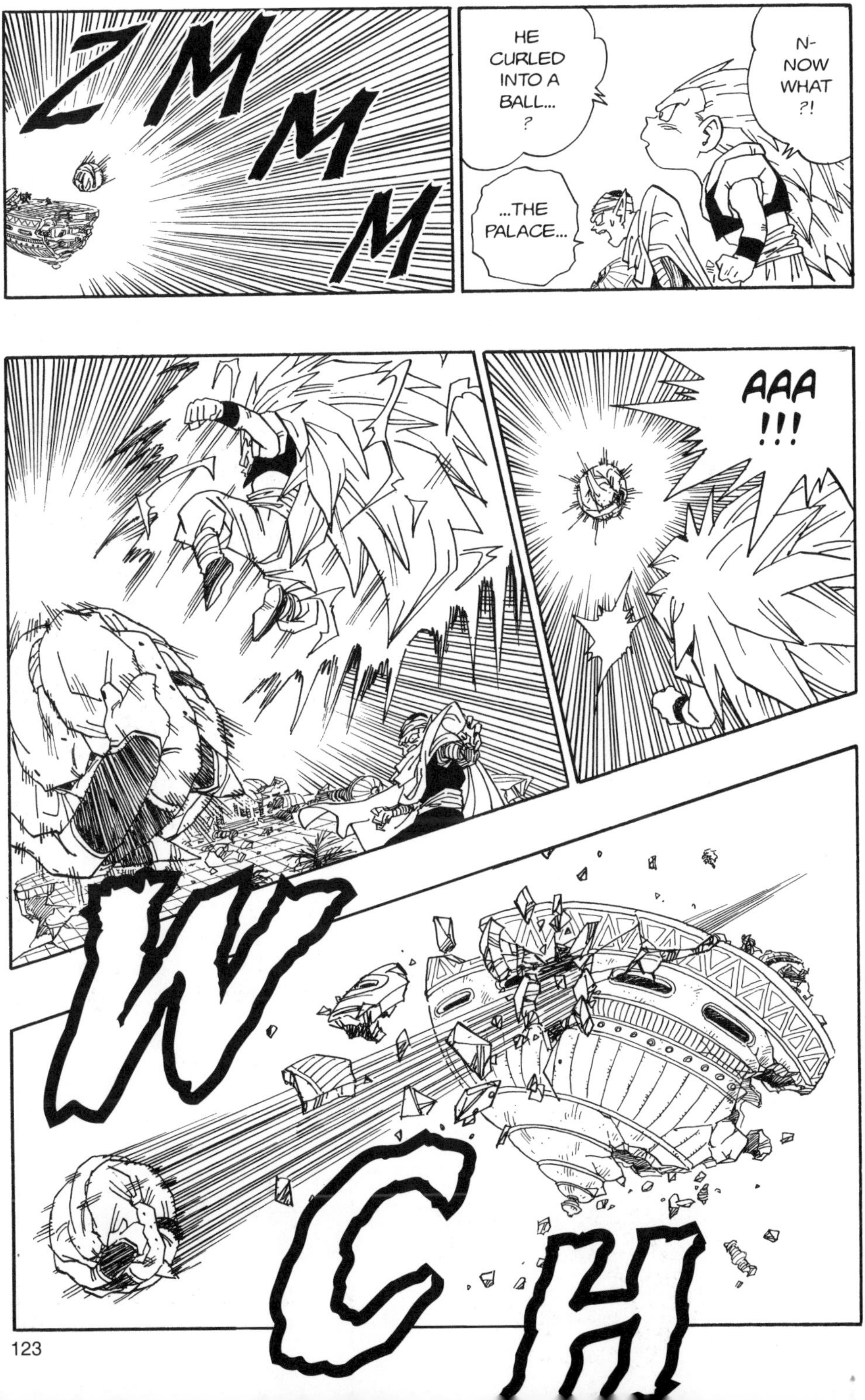
N- NOW WHAT ?!
HE CURLED INTO A BALL... ?
...THE PALACE...
ZMMMM
AAA !!!
WNCH

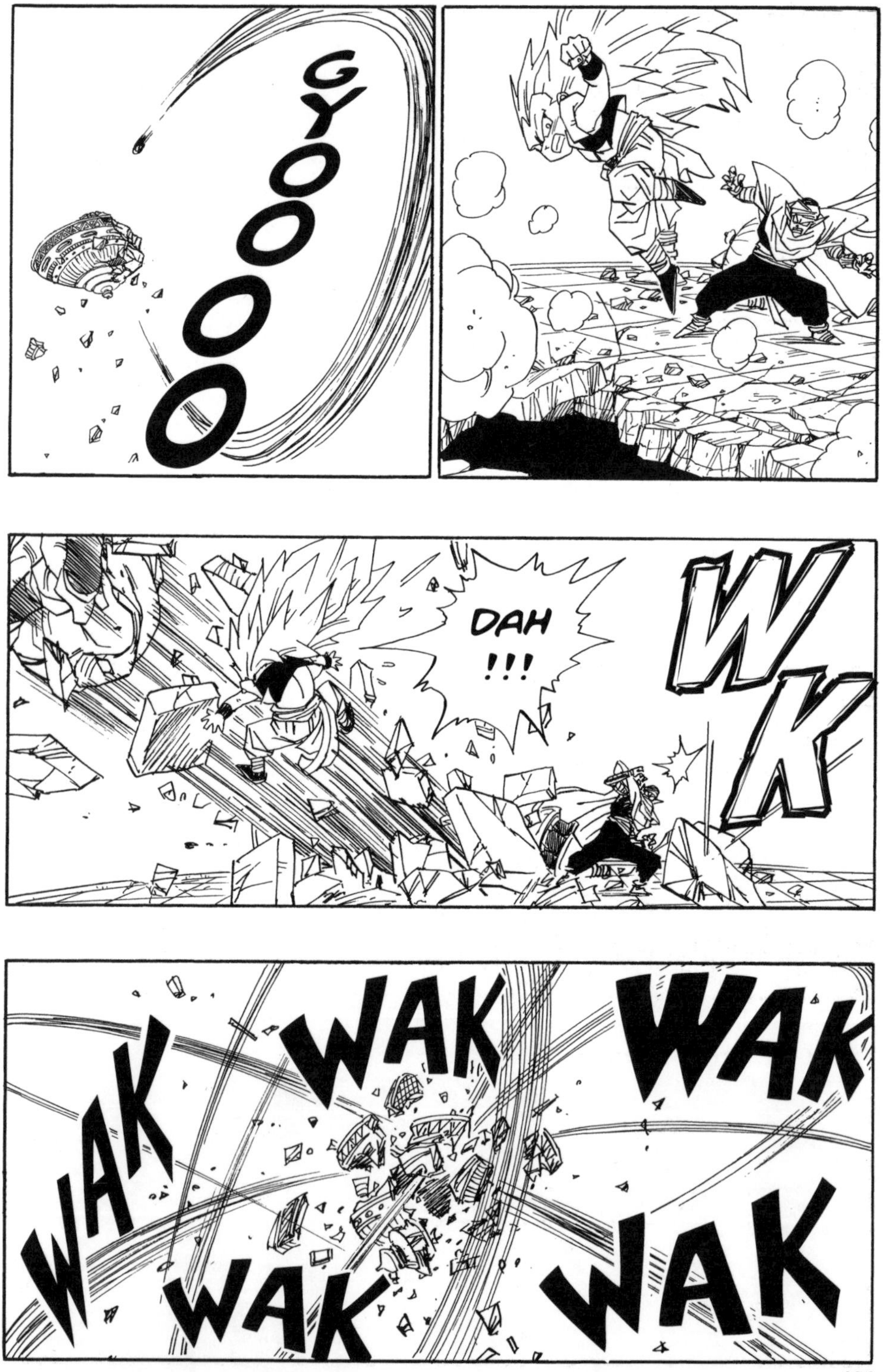
GYOOOOO
WK
DAH!!!
WAK
WAK
WAK
WAK
WAK
WAK

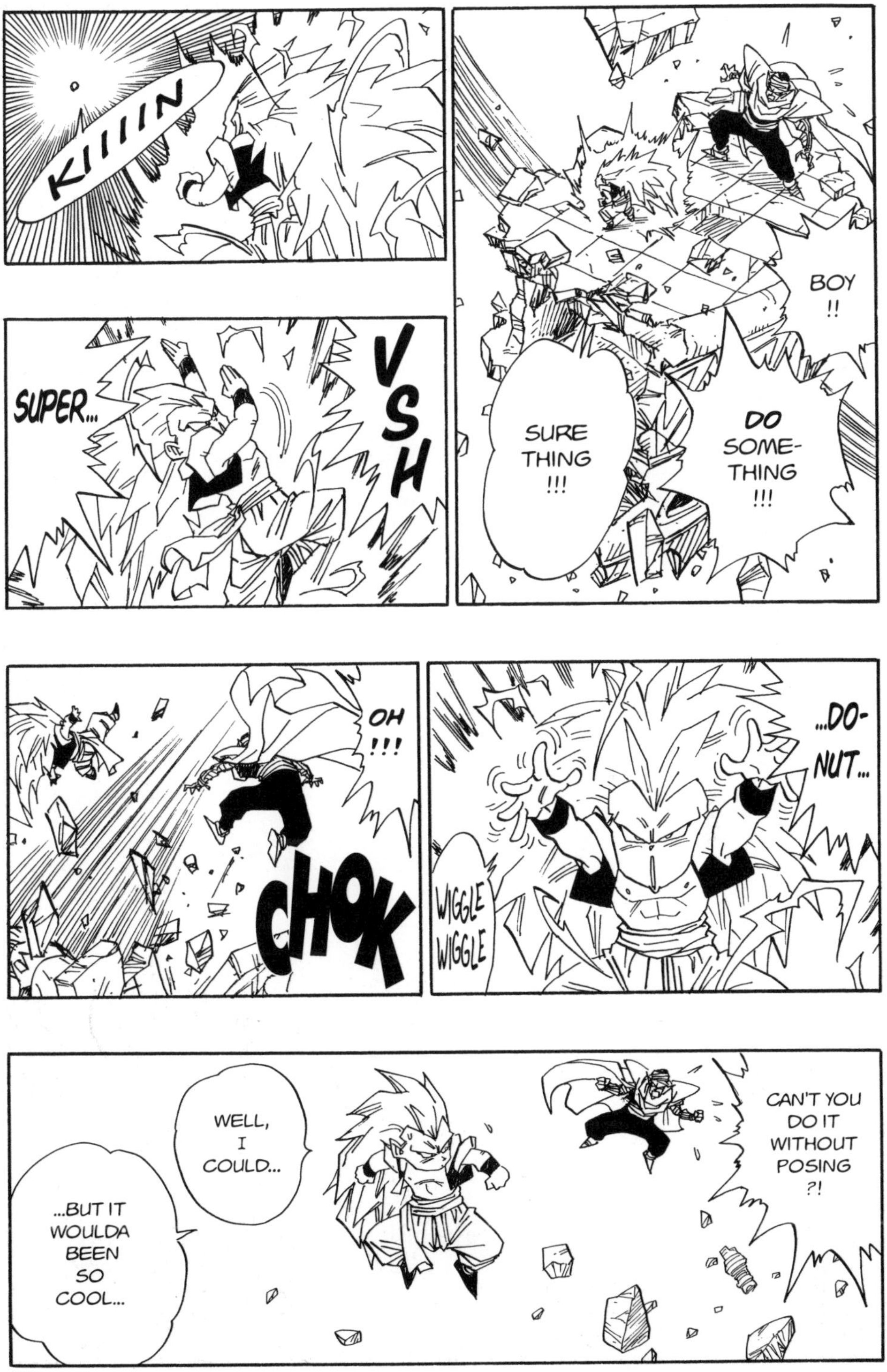
BOY !!
DO SOMETHING !!!
SURE THING !!!
KIIIIN
VSH
SUPER...
...DO-NUT...
WIGGLE WIGGLE
OH !!!
CHOK
CAN'T YOU DO IT WITHOUT POSING ?!
WELL, I COULD...
...BUT IT WOULDA BEEN SO COOL...

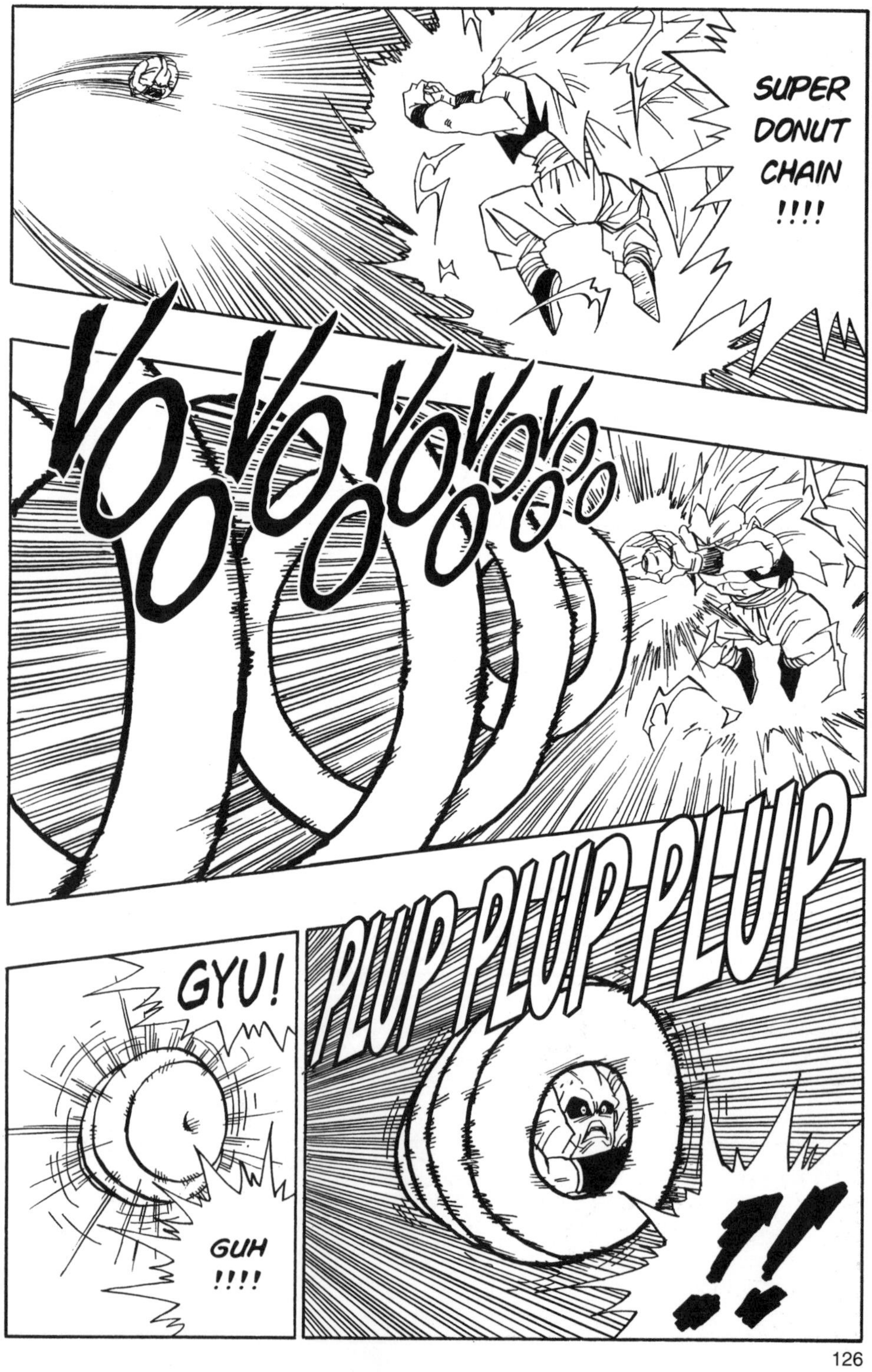
SUPER DONUT CHAIN !!!!
VoVoVoVoVoVo
PLUP PLUP PLUP
!!
GYU!
GUH !!!!

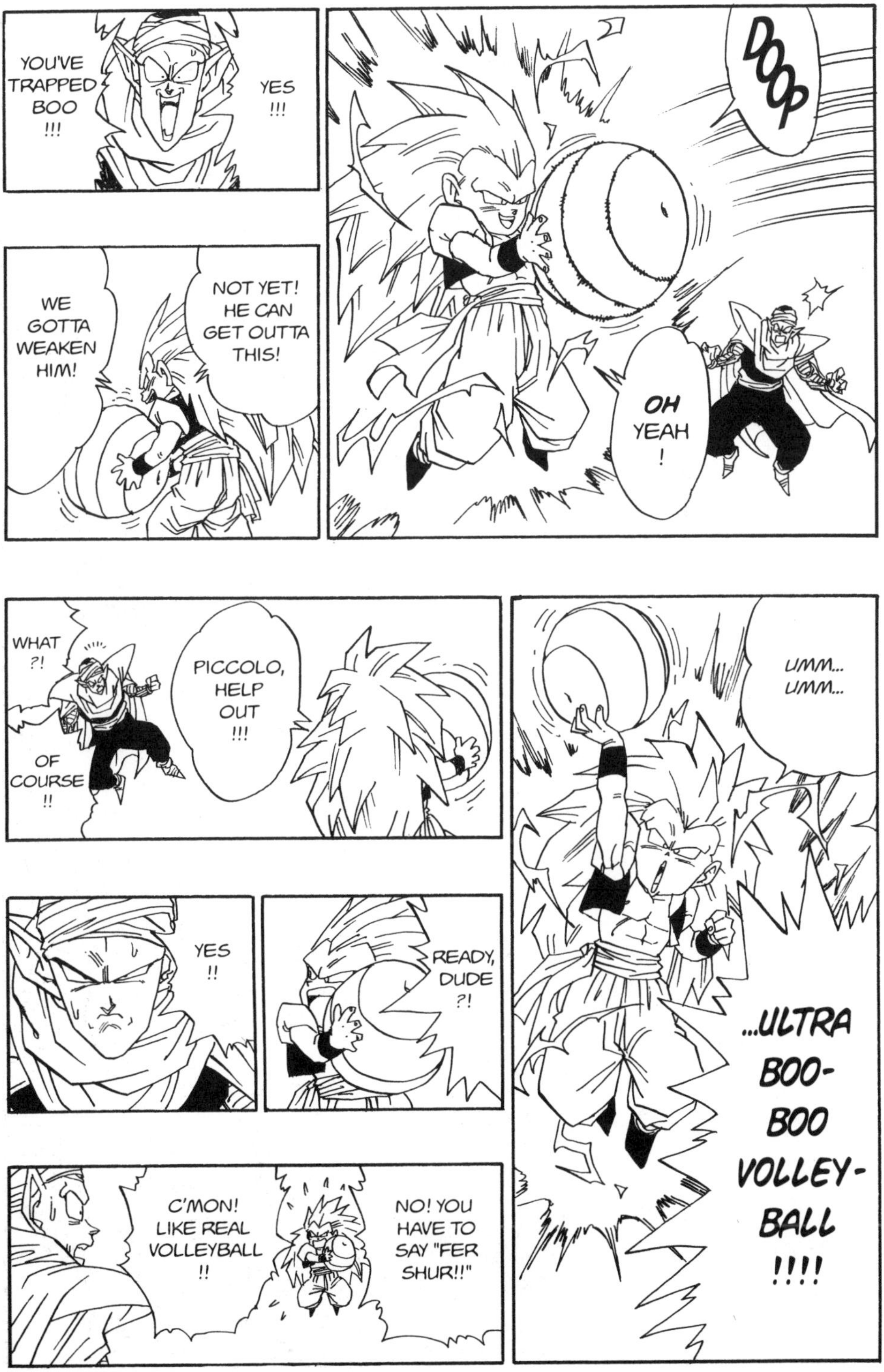
DOOP
OH YEAH!
YES!!!
YOU'VE TRAPPED BOO!!!
NOT YET! HE CAN GET OUTTA THIS!
WE GOTTA WEAKEN HIM!
UMM... UMM...
...ULTRA BOO-BOO VOLLEY-BALL!!!!
PICCOLO, HELP OUT!!!
WHAT?!
OF COURSE!!
READY, DUDE?!
YES!!
NO! YOU HAVE TO SAY "FER SHUR!!"
C'MON! LIKE REAL VOLLEYBALL!!

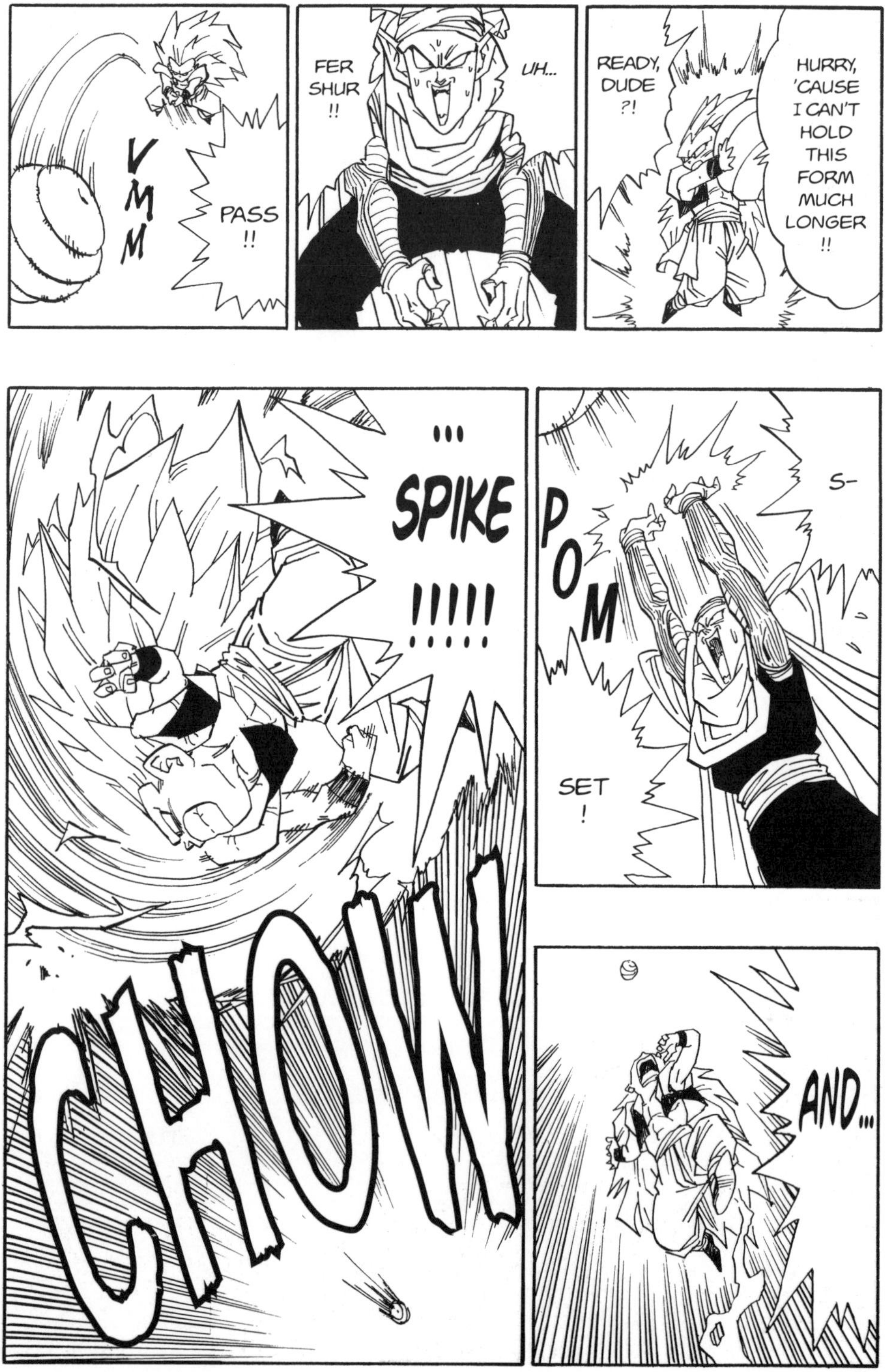
HURRY, 'CAUSE I CAN'T HOLD THIS FORM MUCH LONGER!!
READY, DUDE?!
UH...
FER SHUR!!
PASS!!
VMM
S-
POM
SET!
AND...
...
SPIKE!!!!!!
CHOW

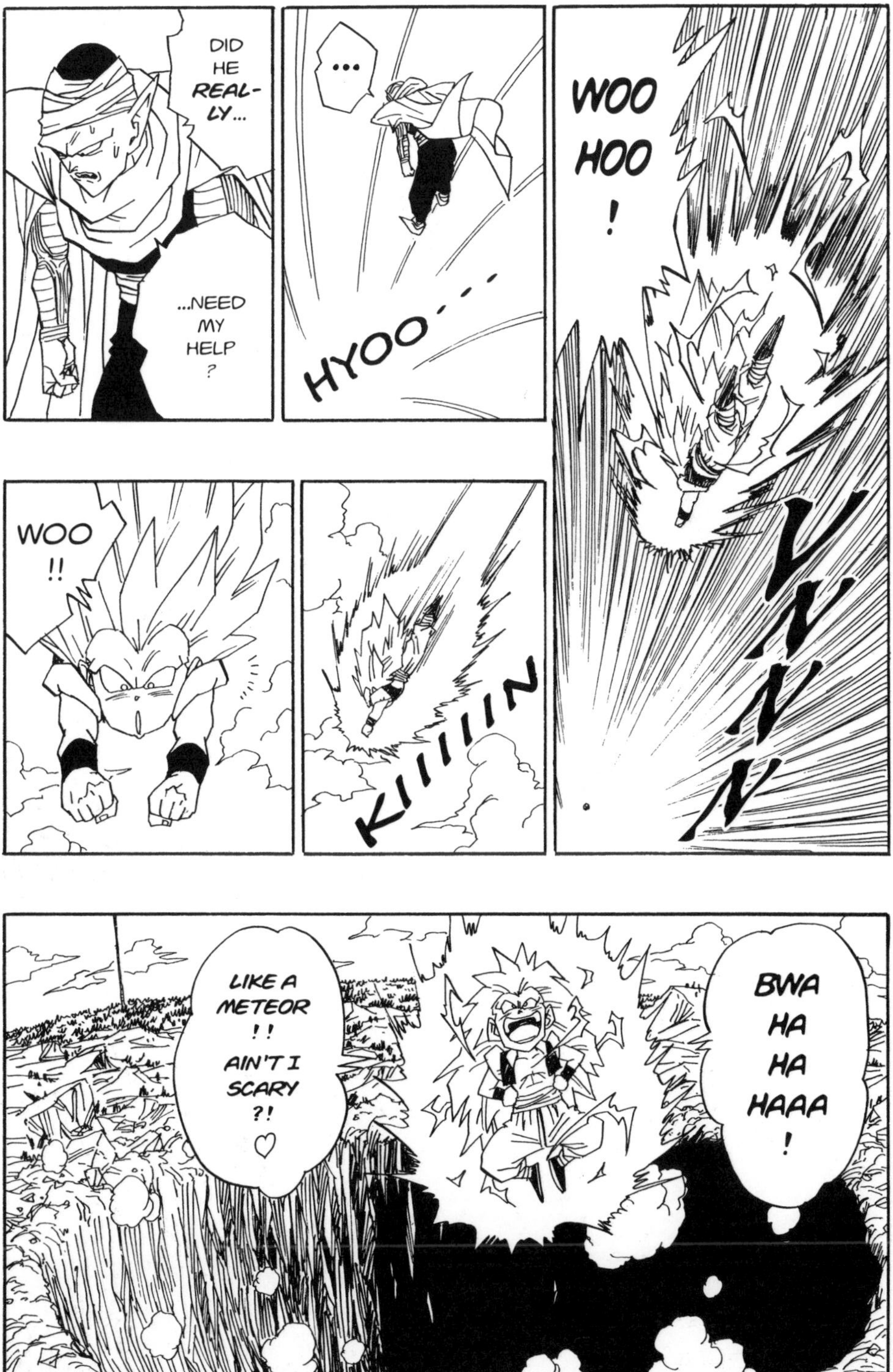
WOO HOO!
VNNN
HYOO...
...
DID HE REALLY...
...NEED MY HELP?
KIIIIIN
WOO!!
BWA HA HA HAAA!
LIKE A METEOR!! AIN'T I SCARY?! ♡

DRAGON BALL ドラゴンボール

DBZ:301 · Super Fusion Unleashed!!

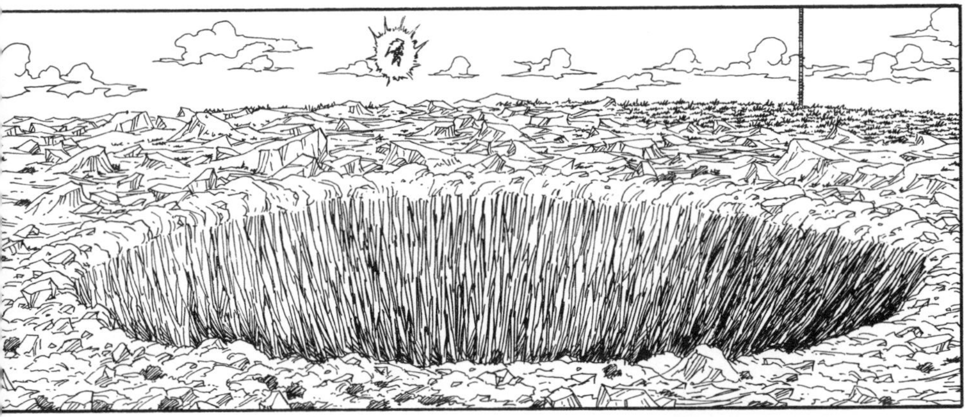

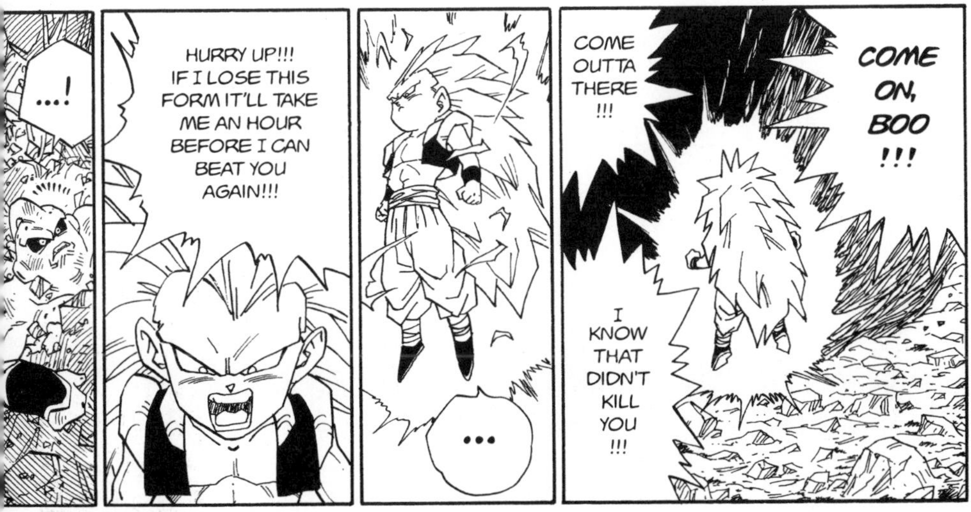
COME ON, BOO!!!
COME OUTTA THERE!!!
I KNOW THAT DIDN'T KILL YOU!!!
...
HURRY UP!!! IF I LOSE THIS FORM IT'LL TAKE ME AN HOUR BEFORE I CAN BEAT YOU AGAIN!!!
...!

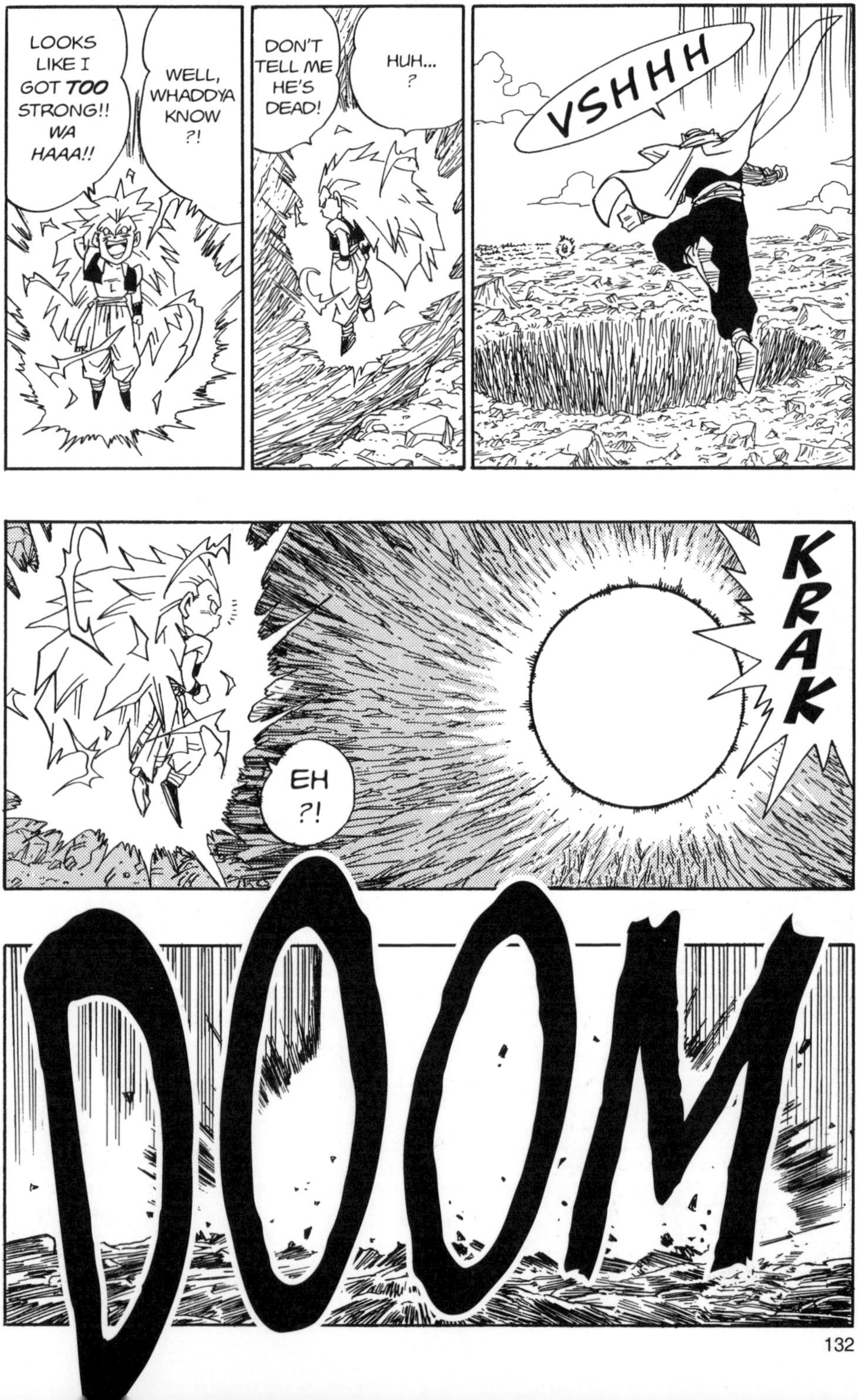
VSHHH
HUH... ?
DON'T TELL ME HE'S DEAD!
WELL, WHADDYA KNOW ?!
LOOKS LIKE I GOT **TOO** STRONG!! *WA HAAA!!*
KRAK
EH ?!
DOOM

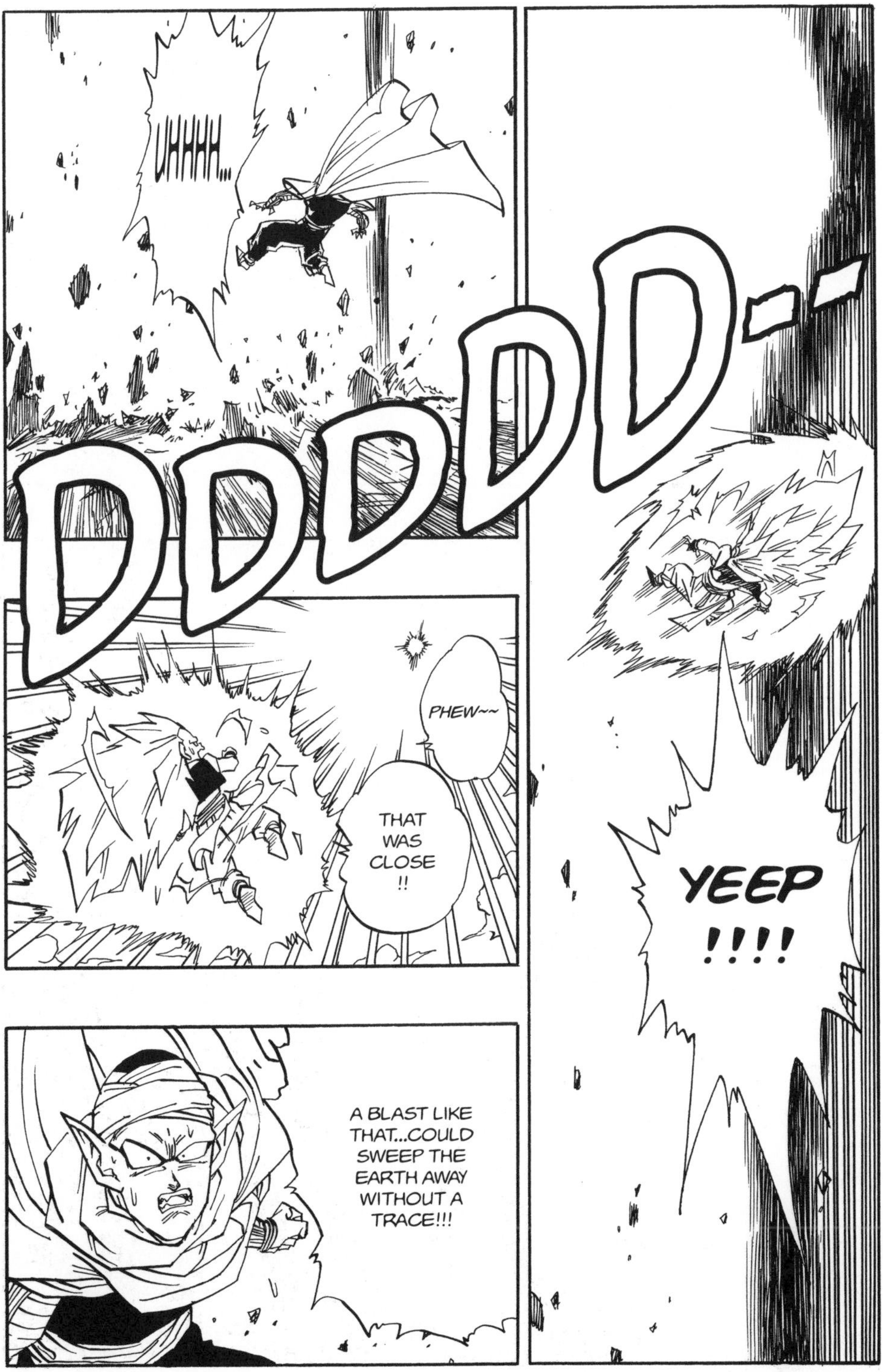
DDDDDD--
YEEP!!!!
UHHHH...
PHEW~~
THAT WAS CLOSE!!
A BLAST LIKE THAT...COULD SWEEP THE EARTH AWAY WITHOUT A TRACE!!!

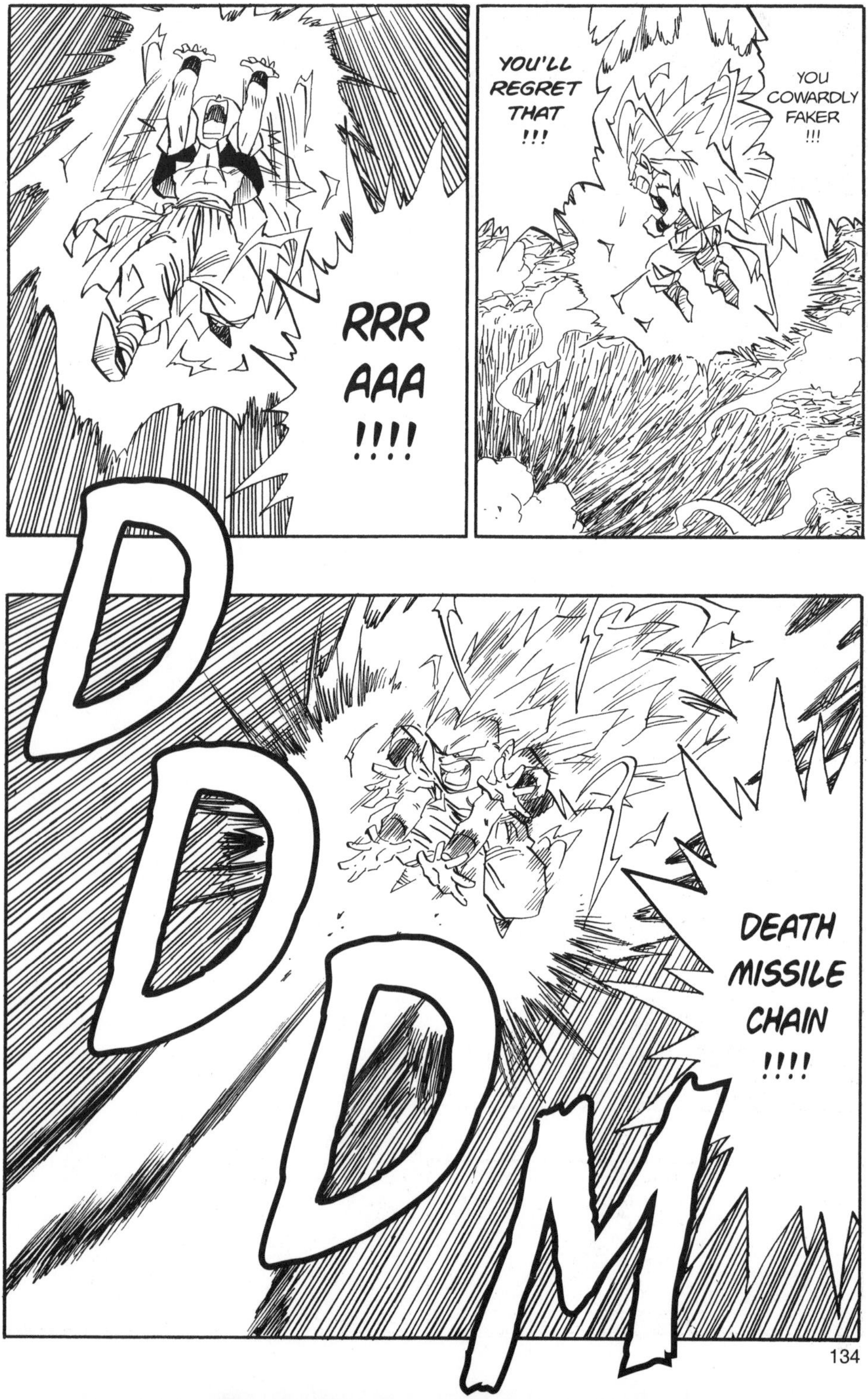
YOU COWARDLY FAKER !!!
YOU'LL REGRET THAT !!!
RRR AAA !!!!
DEATH MISSILE CHAIN !!!!
DDDM

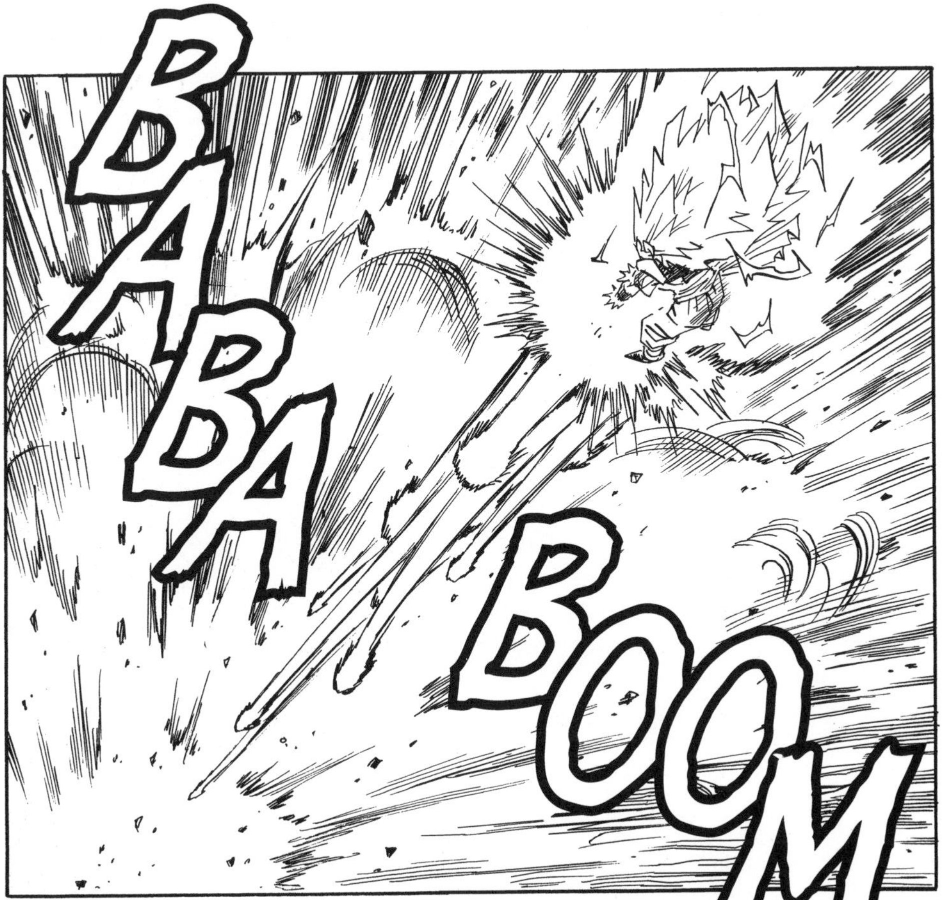
BABABA
BOOM
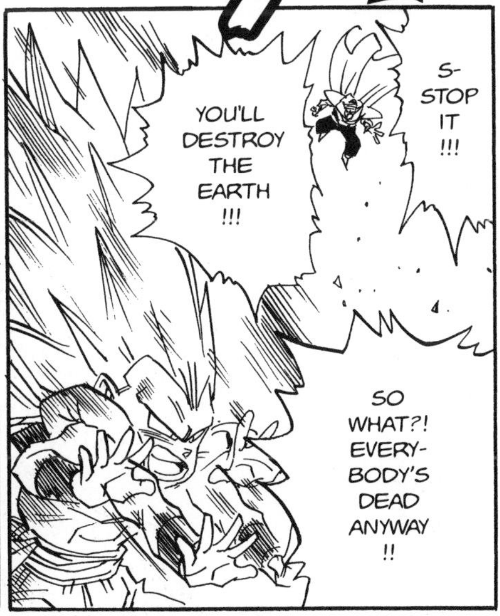
S-STOP IT!!!
YOU'LL DESTROY THE EARTH!!!
SO WHAT?! EVERYBODY'S DEAD ANYWAY!!
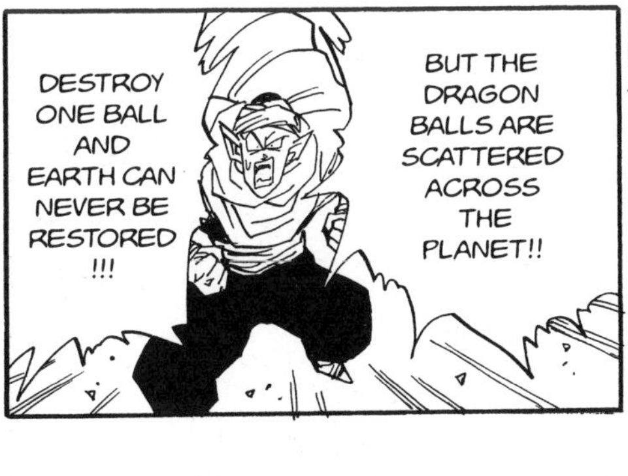
BUT THE DRAGON BALLS ARE SCATTERED ACROSS THE PLANET!!
DESTROY ONE BALL AND EARTH CAN NEVER BE RESTORED!!!
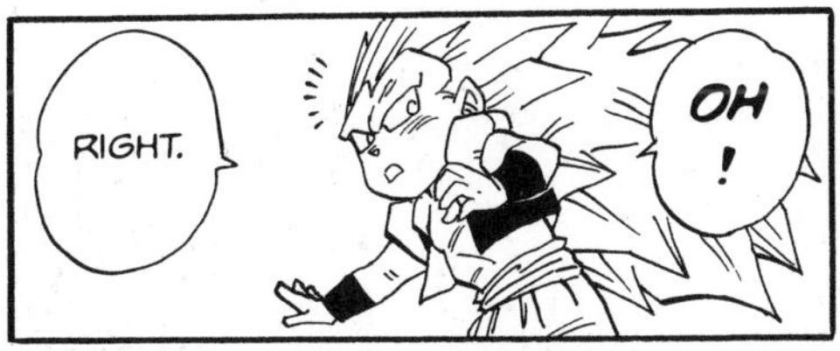
OH!
RIGHT.

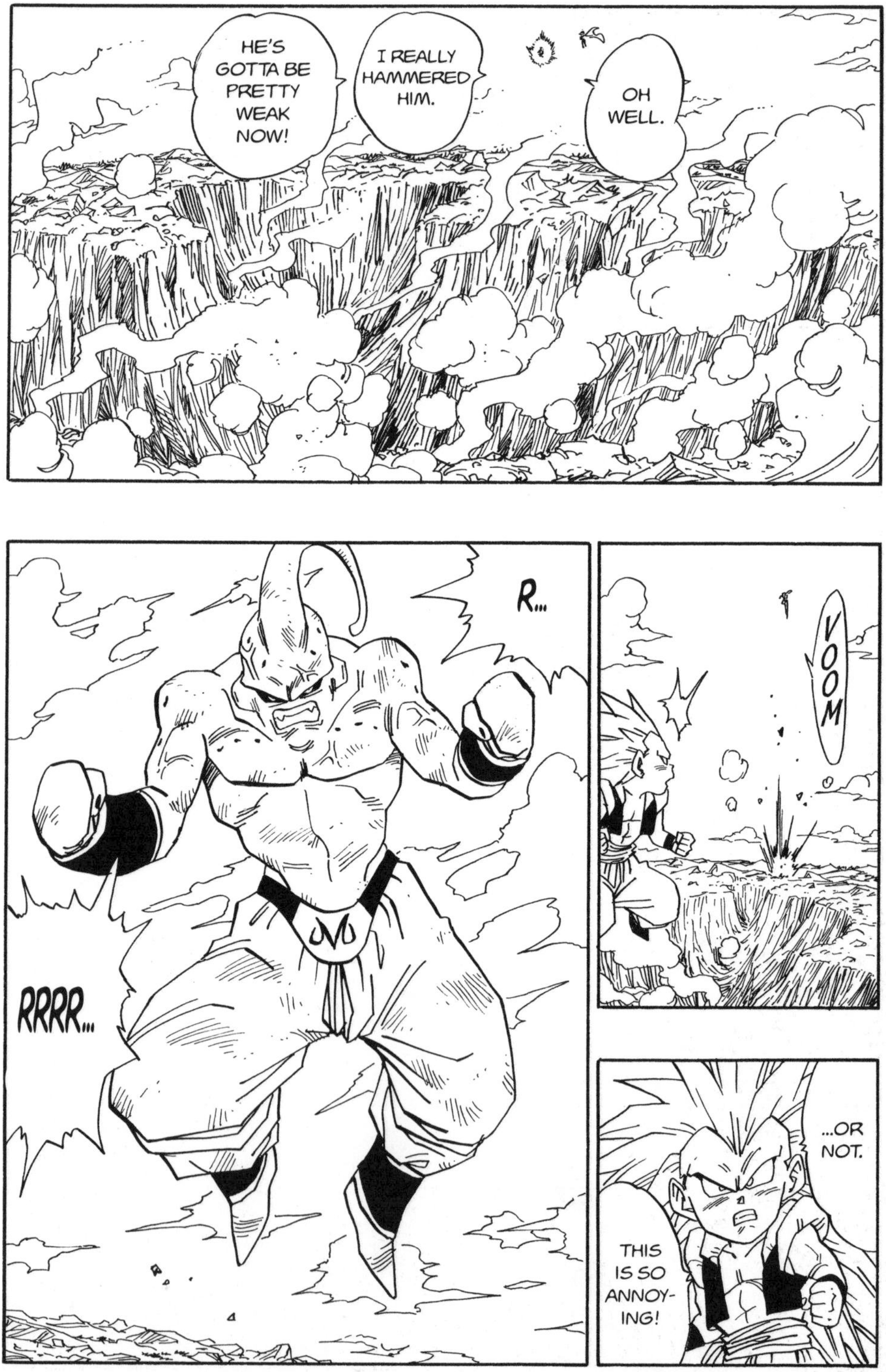
OH WELL.
I REALLY HAMMERED HIM.
HE'S GOTTA BE PRETTY WEAK NOW!
VOOM
...OR NOT.
THIS IS SO ANNOY-ING!
R...
RRRR...

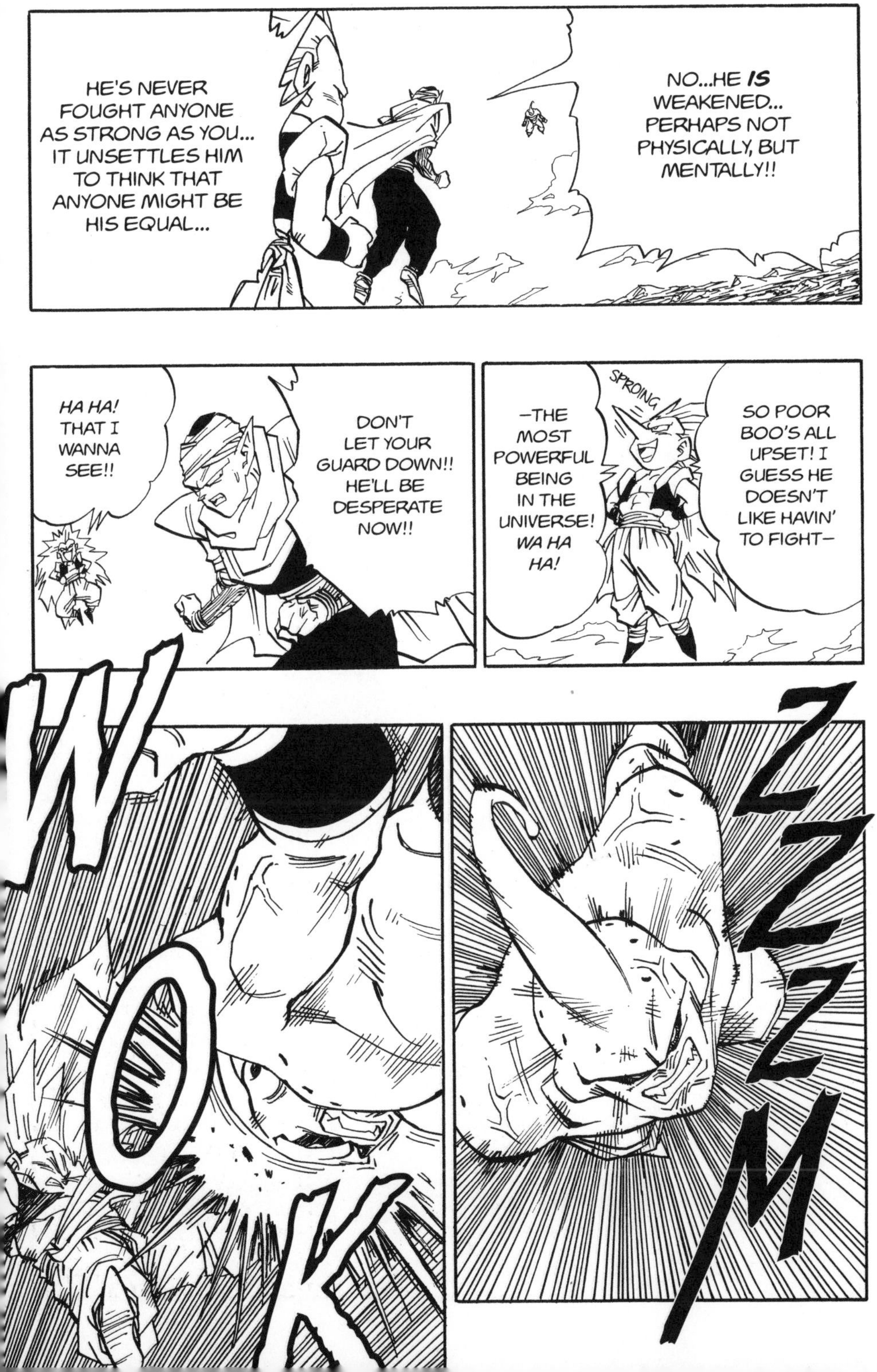
NO...HE **IS** WEAKENED... PERHAPS NOT PHYSICALLY, BUT MENTALLY!!
HE'S NEVER FOUGHT ANYONE AS STRONG AS YOU... IT UNSETTLES HIM TO THINK THAT ANYONE MIGHT BE HIS EQUAL...
SO POOR BOO'S ALL UPSET! I GUESS HE DOESN'T LIKE HAVIN' TO FIGHT—
SPROING
—THE MOST POWERFUL BEING IN THE UNIVERSE! *WA HA HA!*
DON'T LET YOUR GUARD DOWN!! HE'LL BE DESPERATE NOW!!
HA HA! THAT I WANNA SEE!!
ZZZZM
WOK

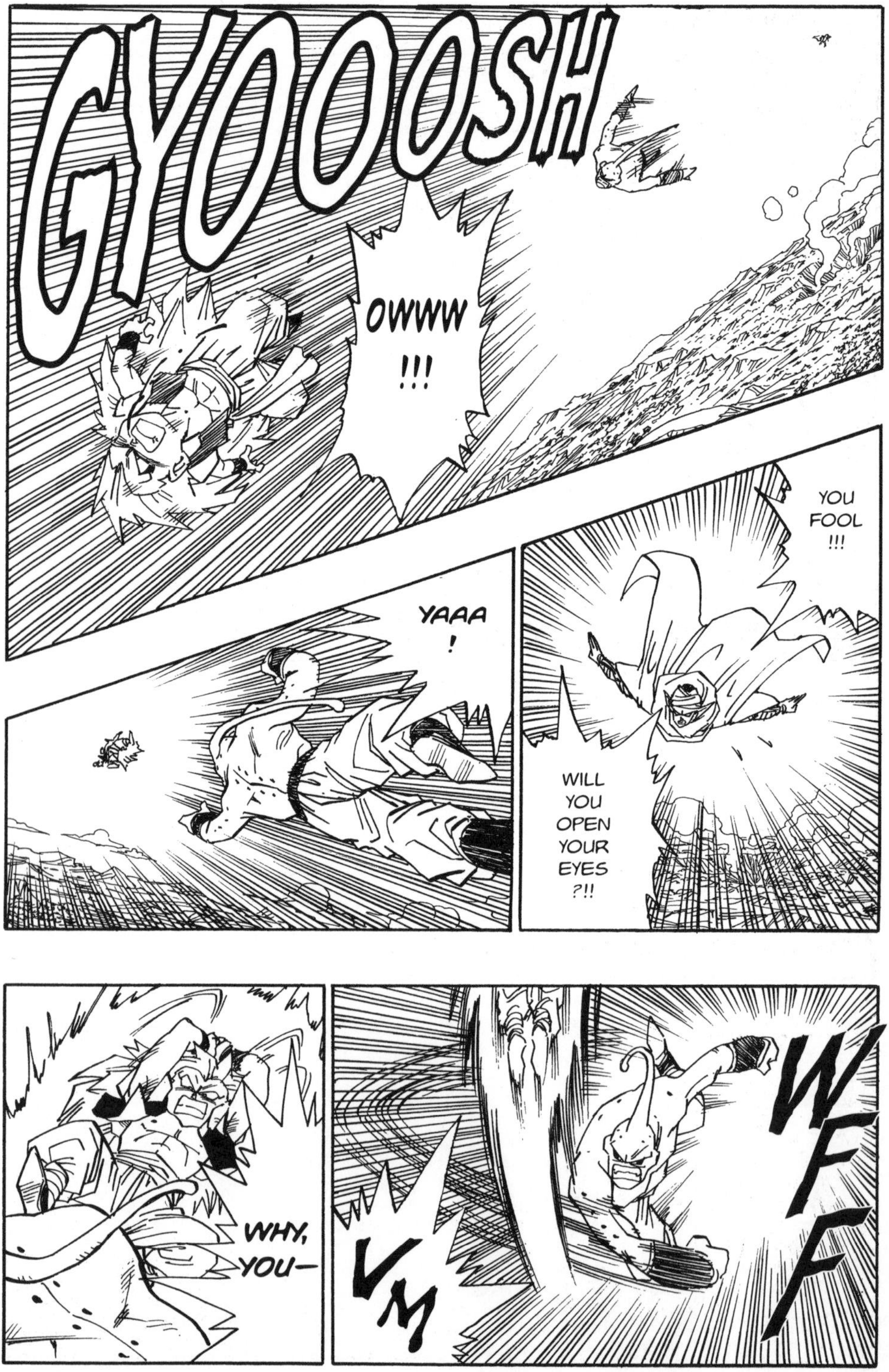
GYOOOSH
OWWW!!!
YOU FOOL!!!
WILL YOU OPEN YOUR EYES?!!
YAAA!
VM
WFF
WHY, YOU—

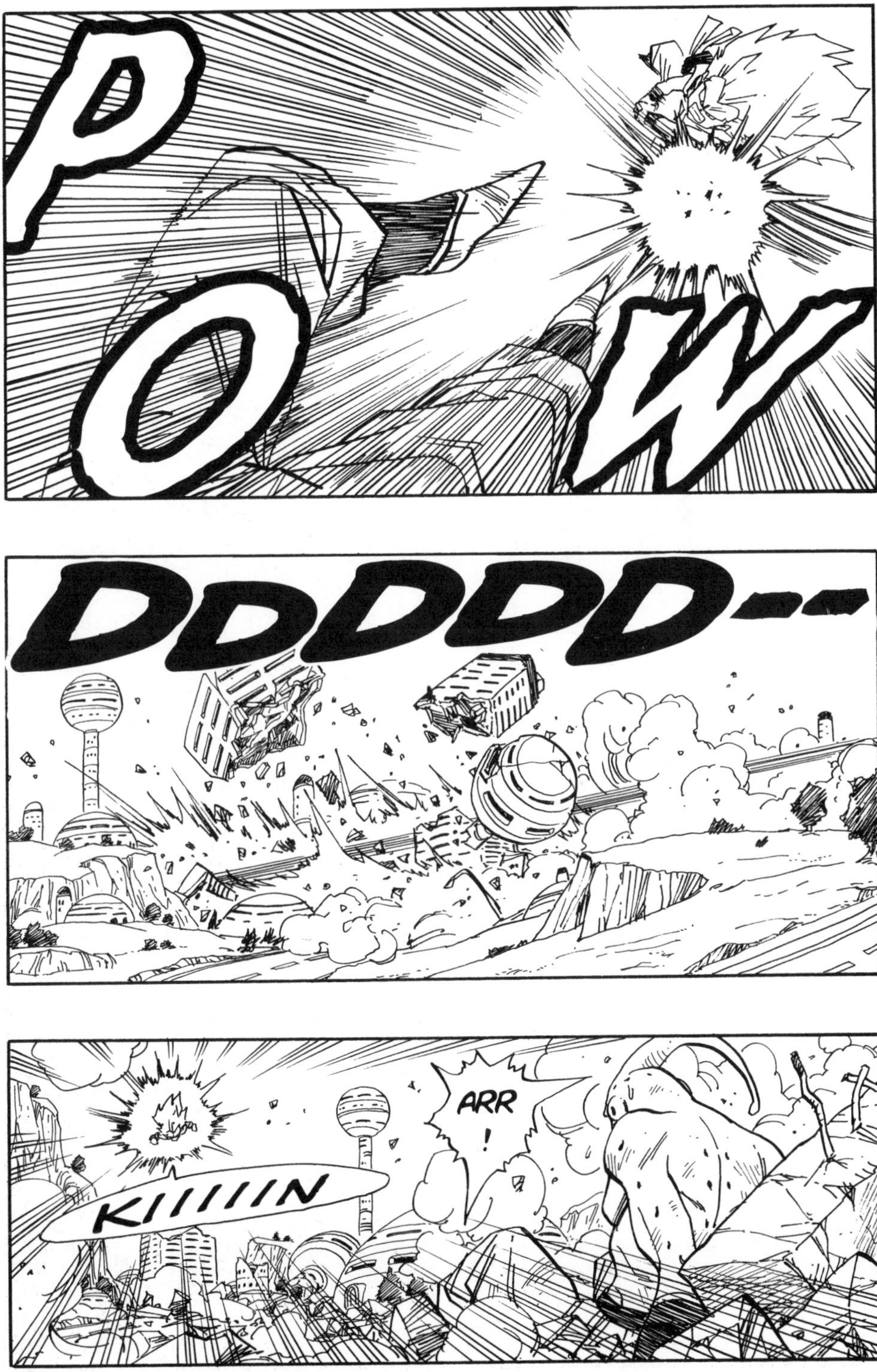
POW
DDDDD--
ARR
!
KIIIIIN

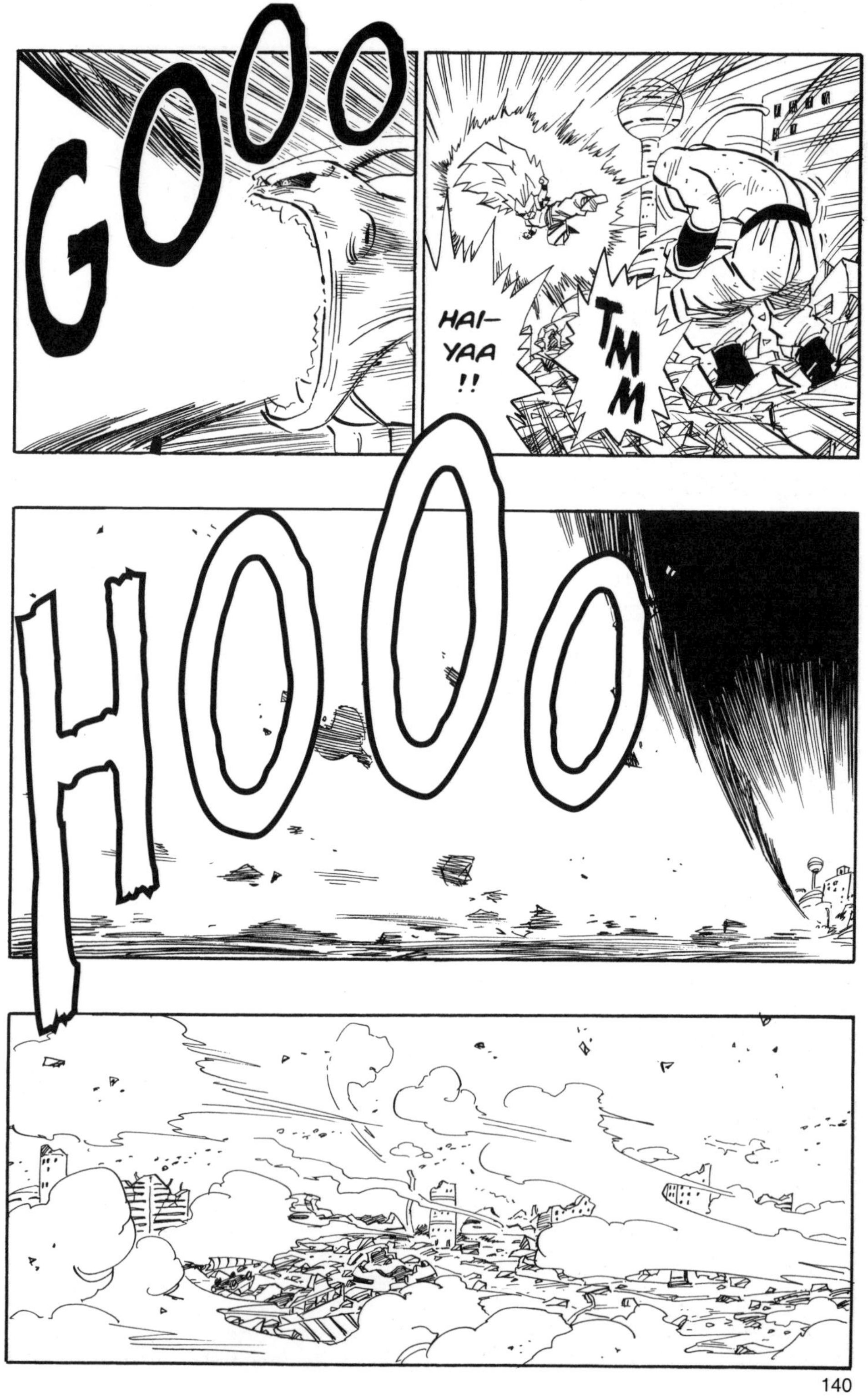
HAI-YAA!!
TMM
GOOO
HOOO

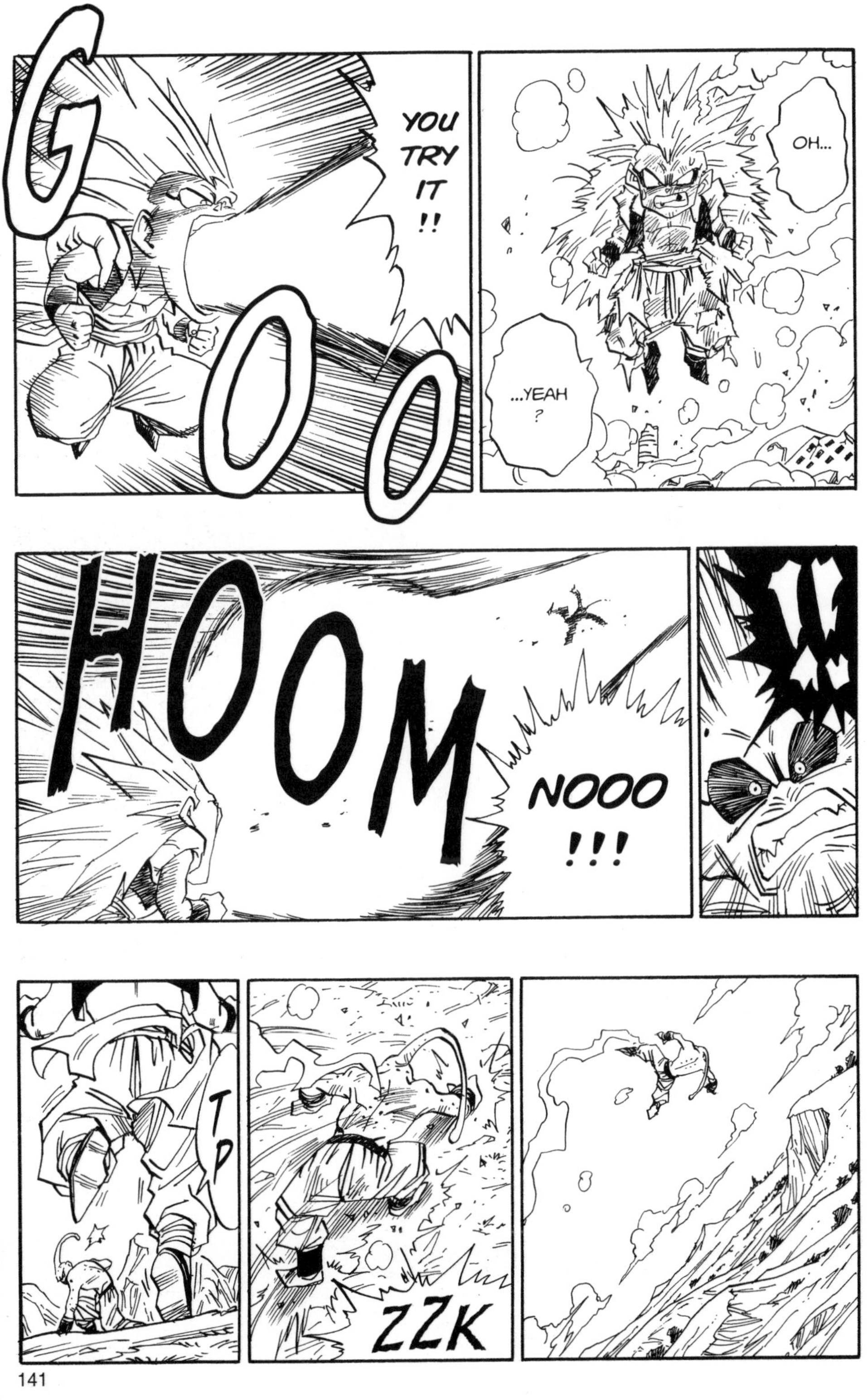
OH...
...YEAH ?
GOOO
YOU TRY IT !!
!!
HOOM
NOOO !!!
ZZK
TP

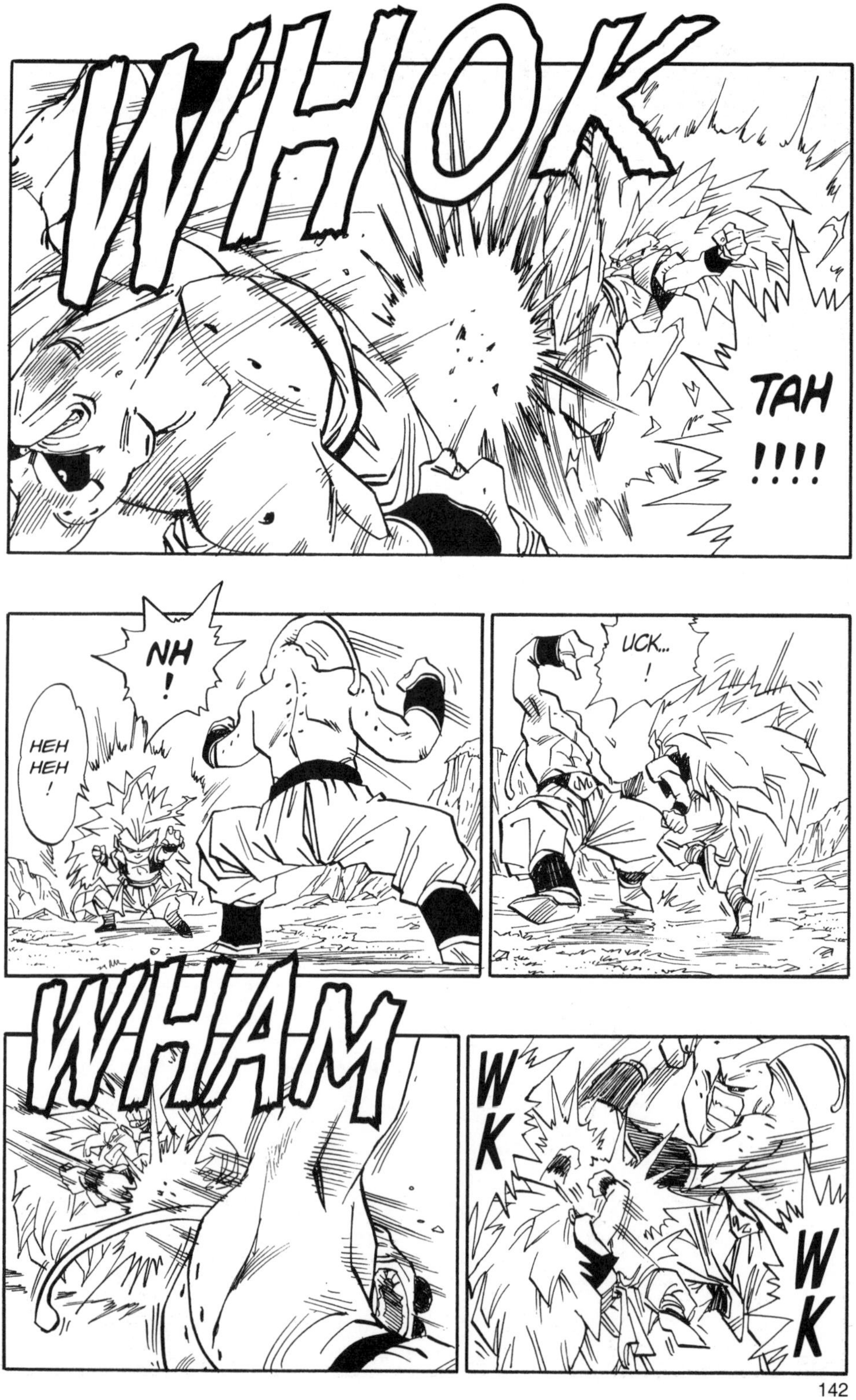
WHOK
TAH !!!!
UCK... !
NH !
HEH HEH !
WK
WK
WHAM

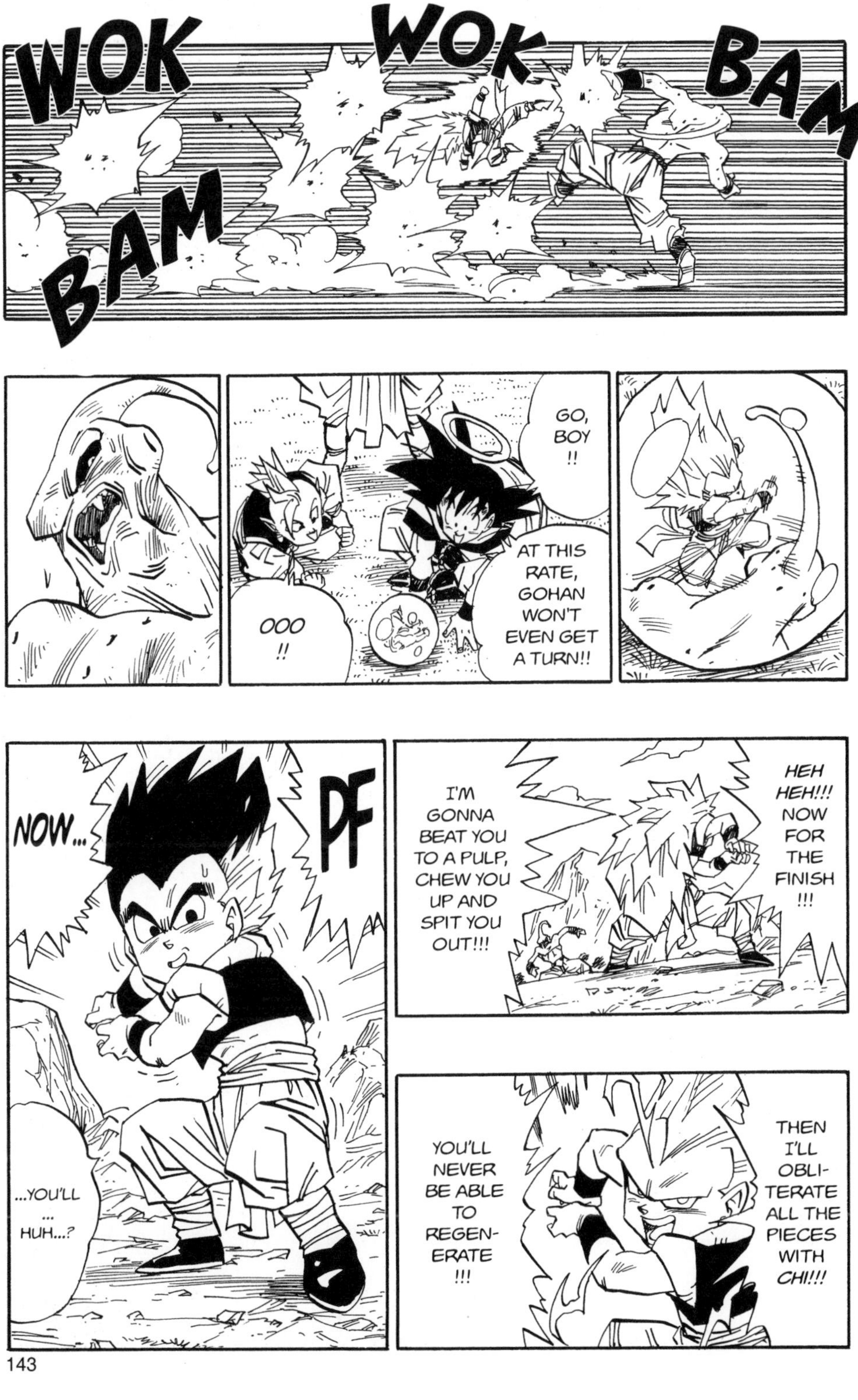
BAM
WOK
WOK
BAM
GO, BOY!!
AT THIS RATE, GOHAN WON'T EVEN GET A TURN!!
OOO!!
HEH HEH!!! NOW FOR THE FINISH!!!
I'M GONNA BEAT YOU TO A PULP, CHEW YOU UP AND SPIT YOU OUT!!!
THEN I'LL OBLITERATE ALL THE PIECES WITH CHI!!!
YOU'LL NEVER BE ABLE TO REGENERATE!!!
PF
NOW...
...YOU'LL ... HUH...?

DRAGON BALL ドラゴンボール

DBZ:302 • Deep Trouble!!

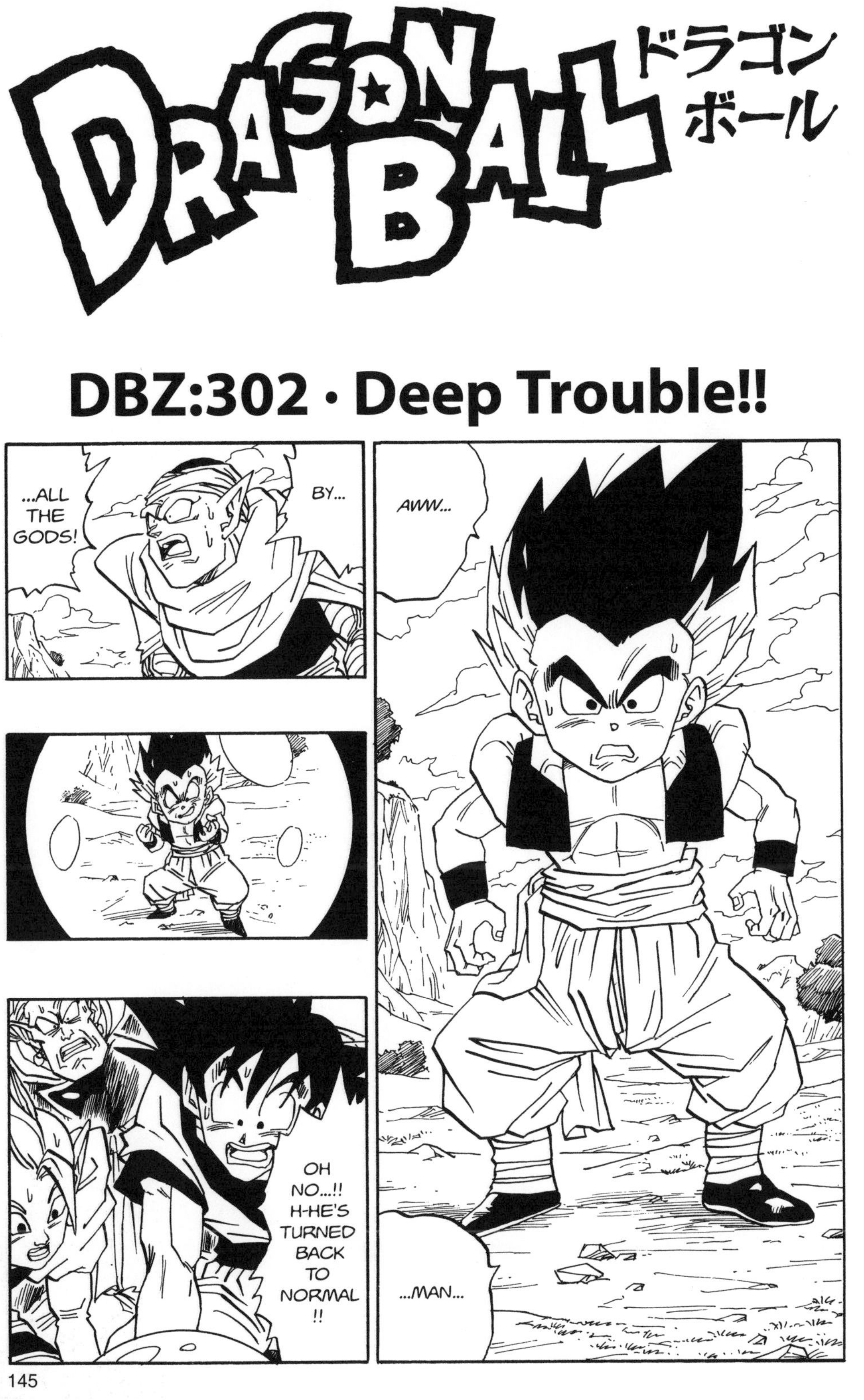
AWW...
...MAN...
BY...
...ALL THE GODS!
OH NO...!! H-HE'S TURNED BACK TO NORMAL!!

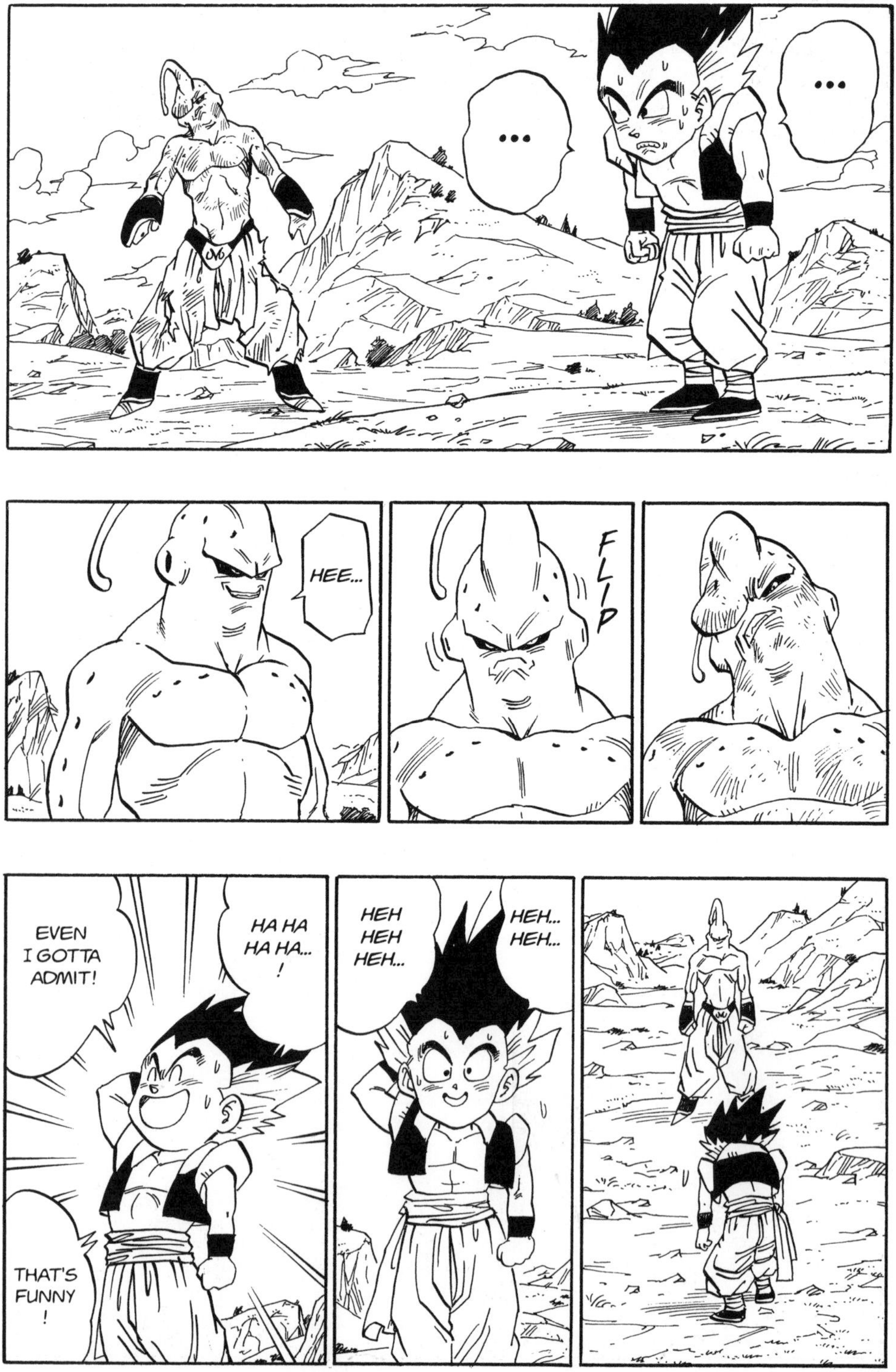
...
...
FLIP
HEE...
HEH... HEH...
HEH HEH HEH...
HA HA HA HA...!
EVEN I GOTTA ADMIT!
THAT'S FUNNY!

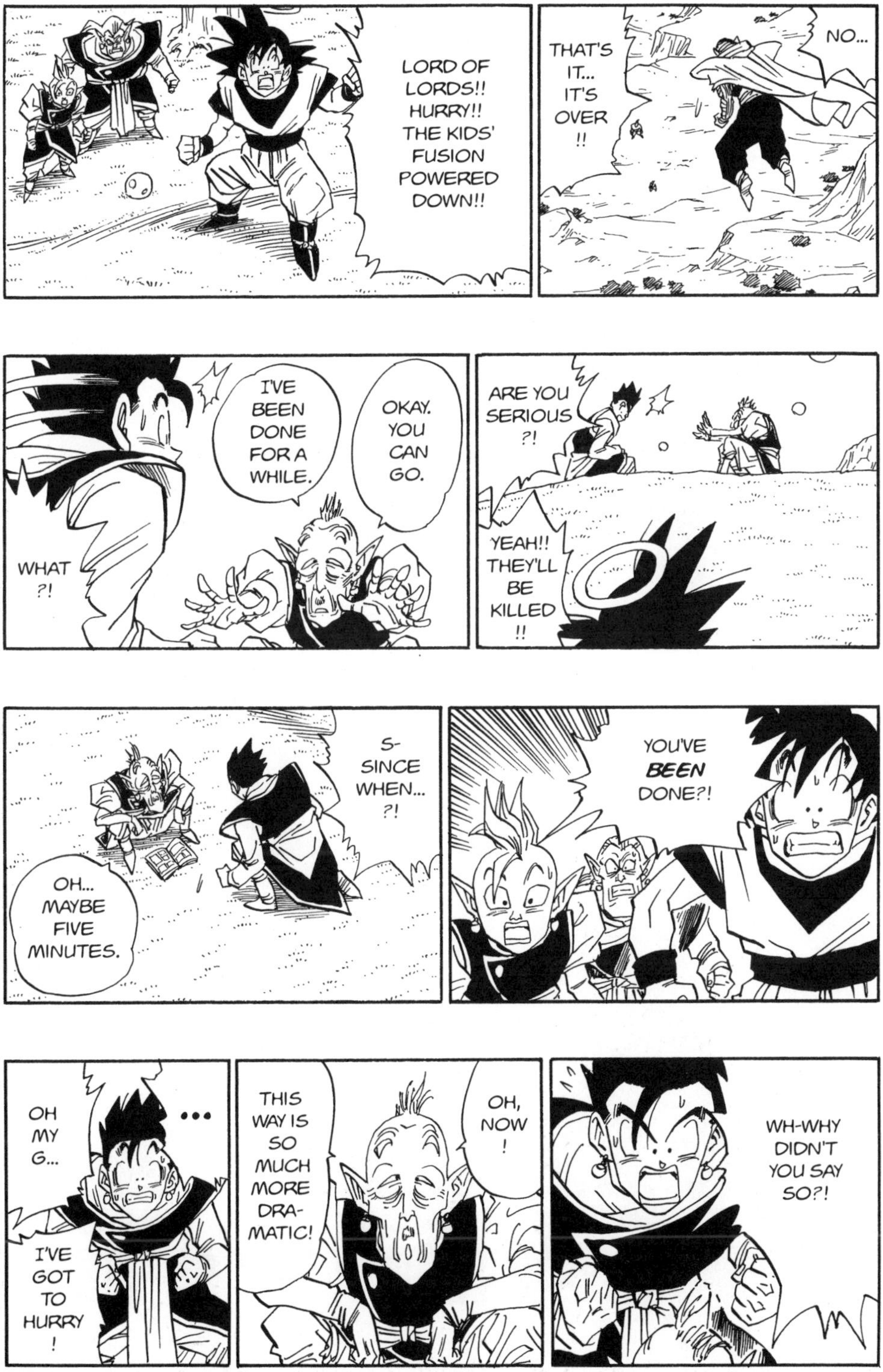
NO...
THAT'S IT... IT'S OVER !!
LORD OF LORDS!! HURRY!! THE KIDS' FUSION POWERED DOWN!!
ARE YOU SERIOUS ?!
YEAH!! THEY'LL BE KILLED !!
OKAY. YOU CAN GO.
I'VE BEEN DONE FOR A WHILE.
WHAT ?!
YOU'VE **BEEN** DONE?!
S-SINCE WHEN... ?!
OH... MAYBE FIVE MINUTES.
WH-WHY DIDN'T YOU SAY SO?!
OH, NOW !
THIS WAY IS SO MUCH MORE DRA-MATIC!
...
OH MY G...
I'VE GOT TO HURRY !

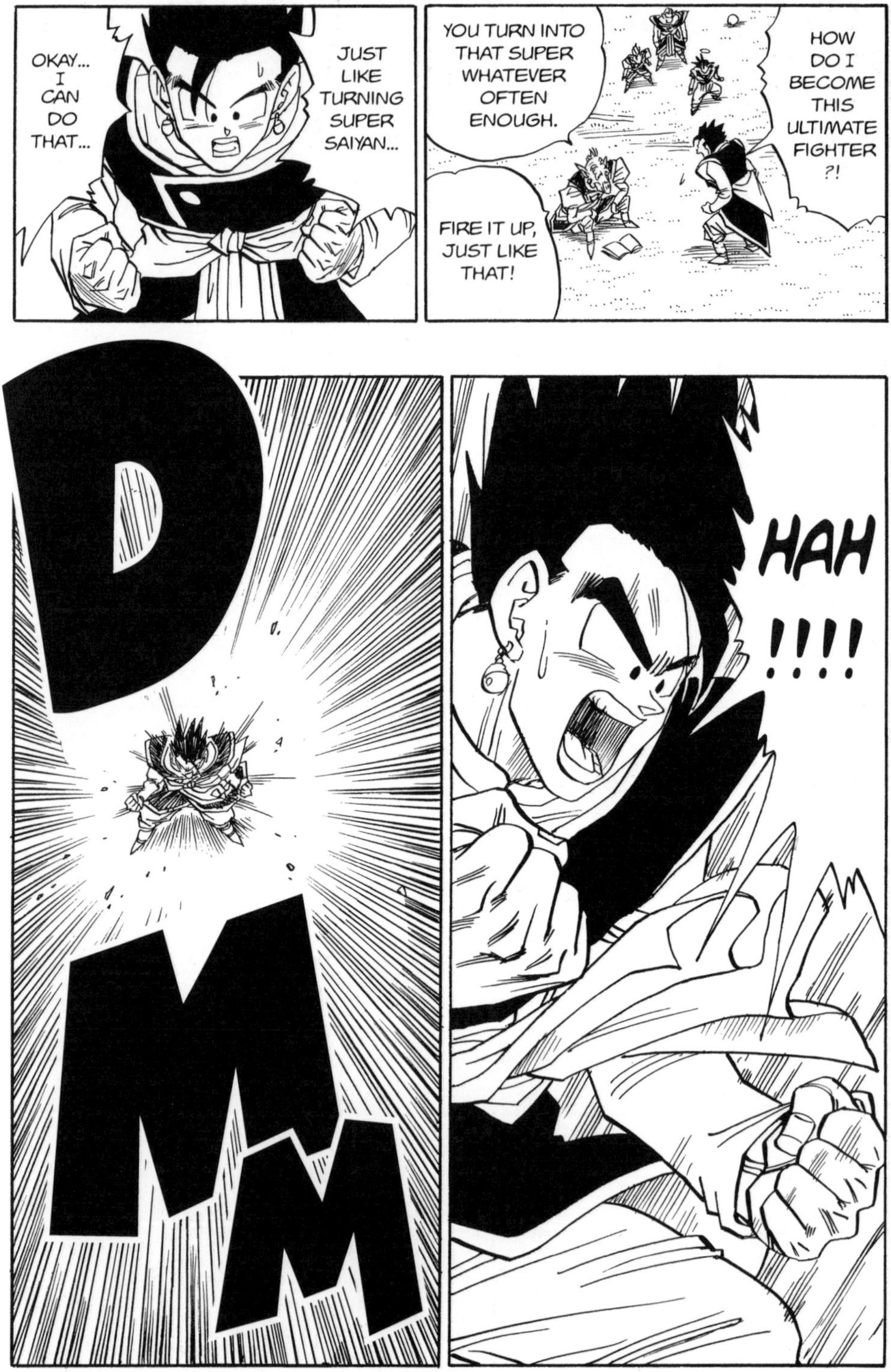
HOW DO I BECOME THIS ULTIMATE FIGHTER ?!
YOU TURN INTO THAT SUPER WHATEVER OFTEN ENOUGH.
FIRE IT UP, JUST LIKE THAT!
JUST LIKE TURNING SUPER SAIYAN...
OKAY... I CAN DO THAT...
HAH !!!!
DMM

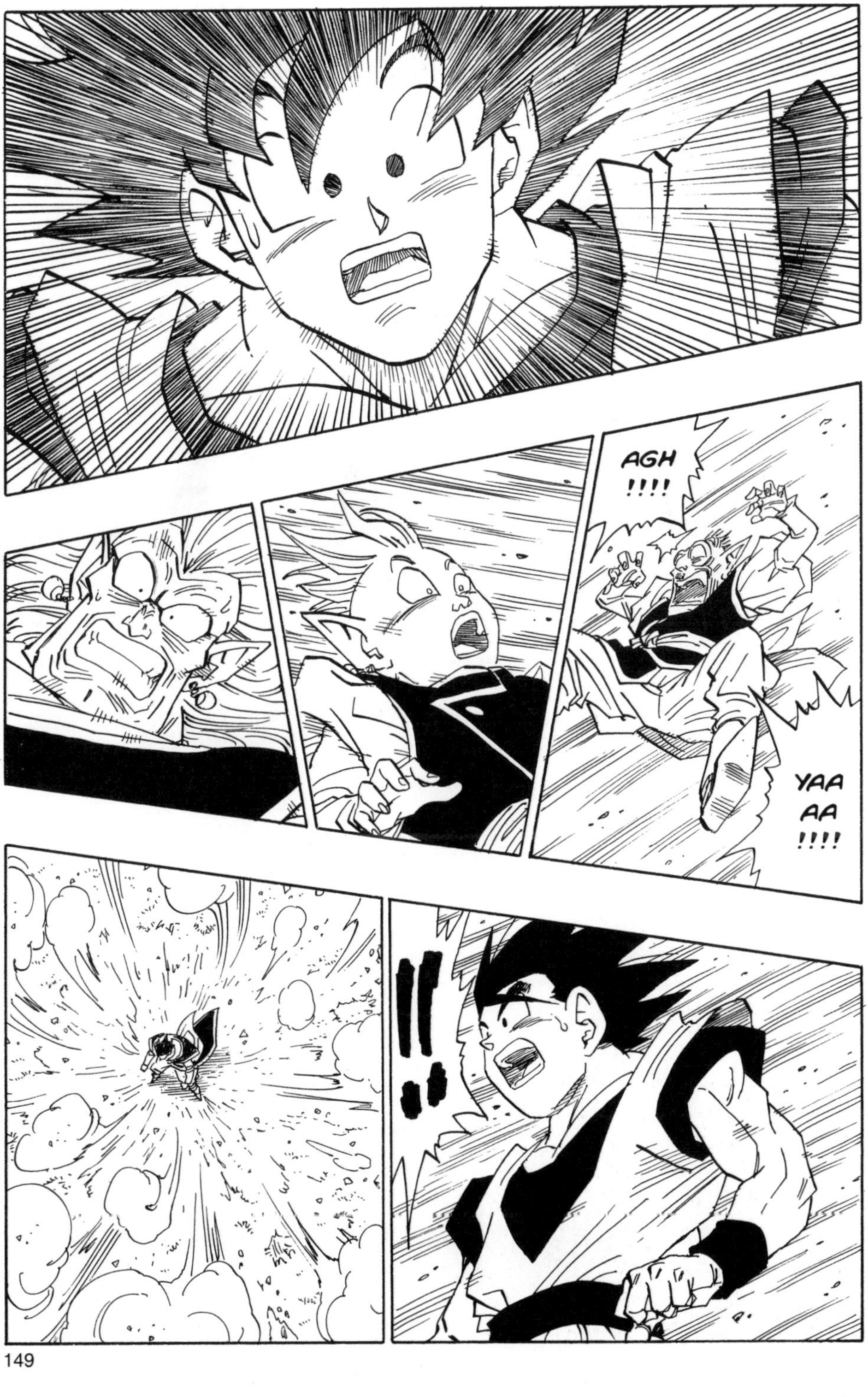
AGH !!!!
YAA AA !!!!
!!

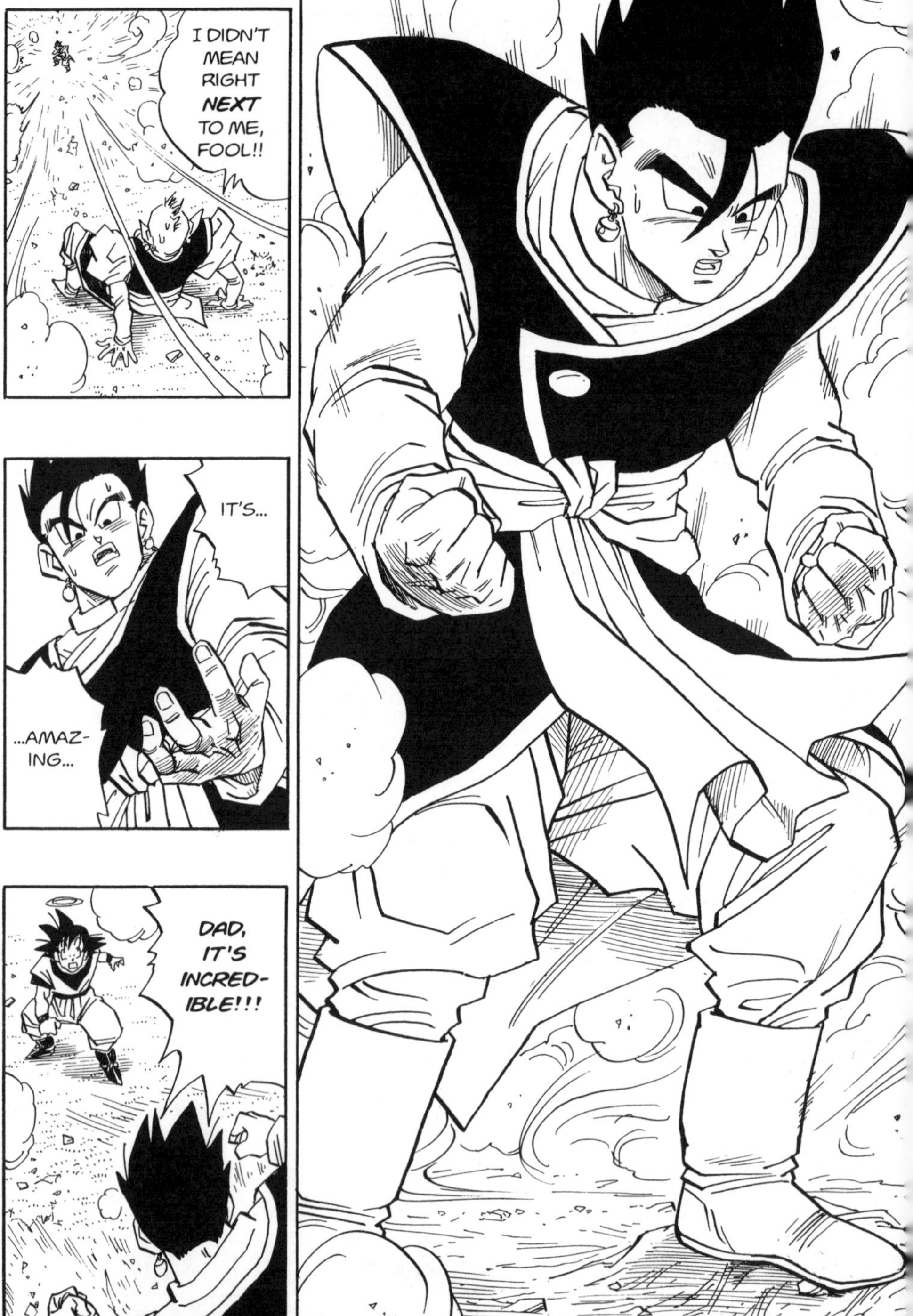
I DIDN'T MEAN RIGHT NEXT TO ME, FOOL!!
IT'S...
...AMAZ-ING...
DAD, IT'S INCRED-IBLE!!!

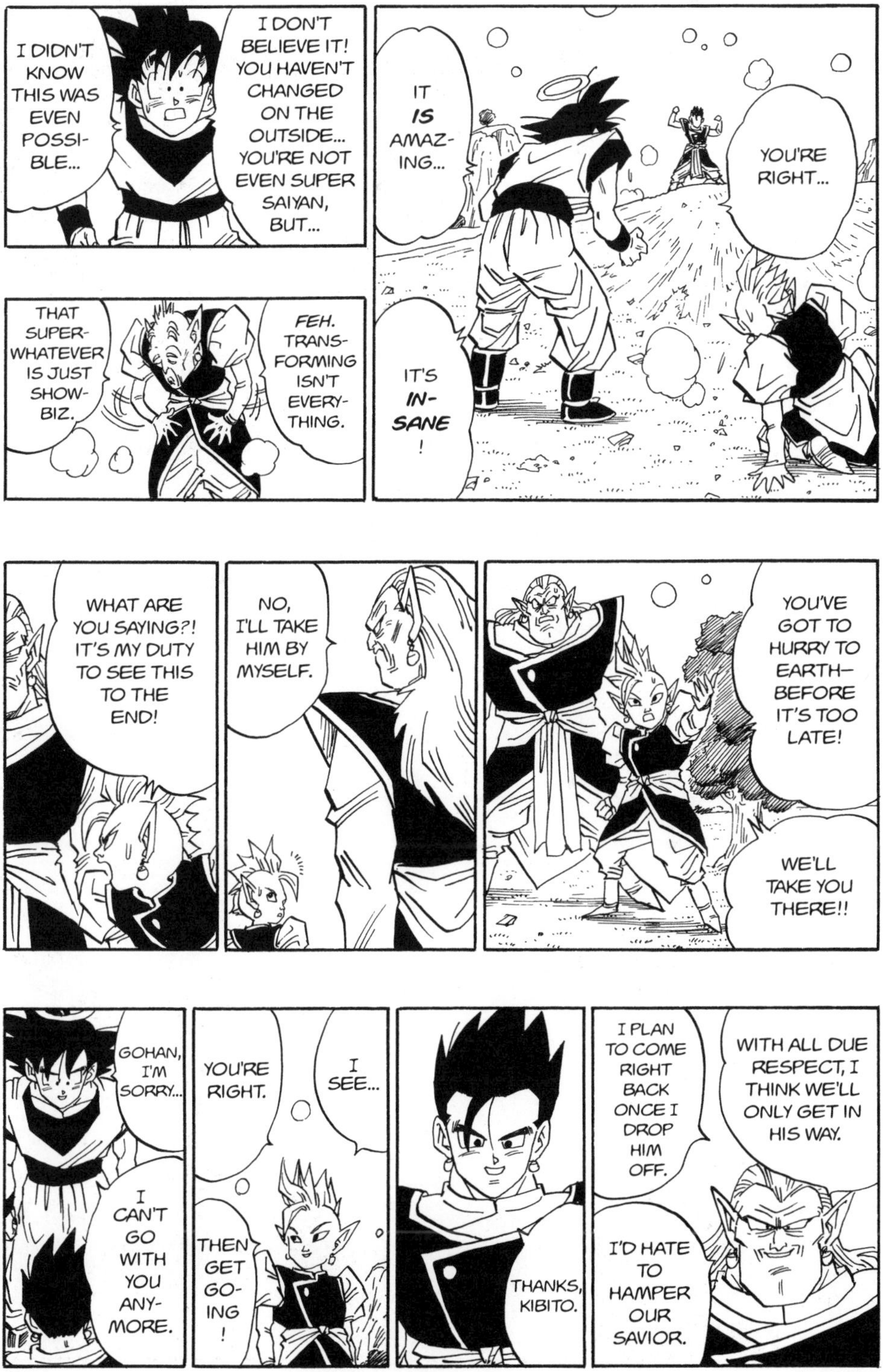
YOU'RE RIGHT...
IT IS AMAZING...
IT'S INSANE!
I DON'T BELIEVE IT! YOU HAVEN'T CHANGED ON THE OUTSIDE... YOU'RE NOT EVEN SUPER SAIYAN, BUT...
I DIDN'T KNOW THIS WAS EVEN POSSIBLE...
FEH. TRANSFORMING ISN'T EVERYTHING.
THAT SUPER-WHATEVER IS JUST SHOWBIZ.
YOU'VE GOT TO HURRY TO EARTH—BEFORE IT'S TOO LATE!
WE'LL TAKE YOU THERE!!
NO, I'LL TAKE HIM BY MYSELF.
WHAT ARE YOU SAYING?! IT'S MY DUTY TO SEE THIS TO THE END!
WITH ALL DUE RESPECT, I THINK WE'LL ONLY GET IN HIS WAY.
I PLAN TO COME RIGHT BACK ONCE I DROP HIM OFF.
I'D HATE TO HAMPER OUR SAVIOR.
THANKS, KIBITO.
I SEE...
YOU'RE RIGHT.
THEN GET GOING!
GOHAN, I'M SORRY...
I CAN'T GO WITH YOU ANYMORE.

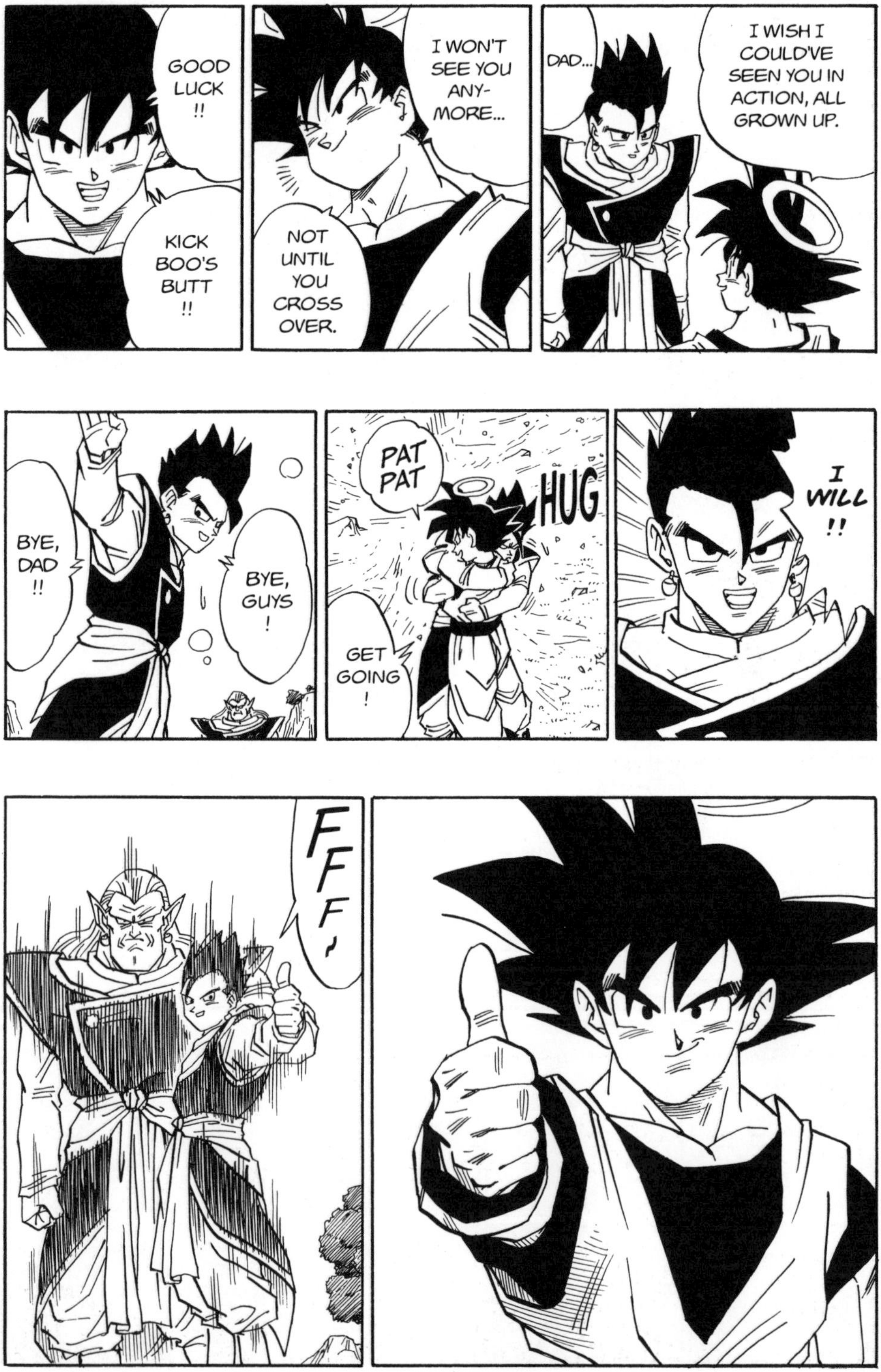
I WISH I COULD'VE SEEN YOU IN ACTION, ALL GROWN UP.
DAD...
I WON'T SEE YOU ANY-MORE...
NOT UNTIL YOU CROSS OVER.
GOOD LUCK!!
KICK BOO'S BUTT!!
I WILL!!
HUG
PAT PAT
GET GOING!
BYE, GUYS!
BYE, DAD!!
FFF,

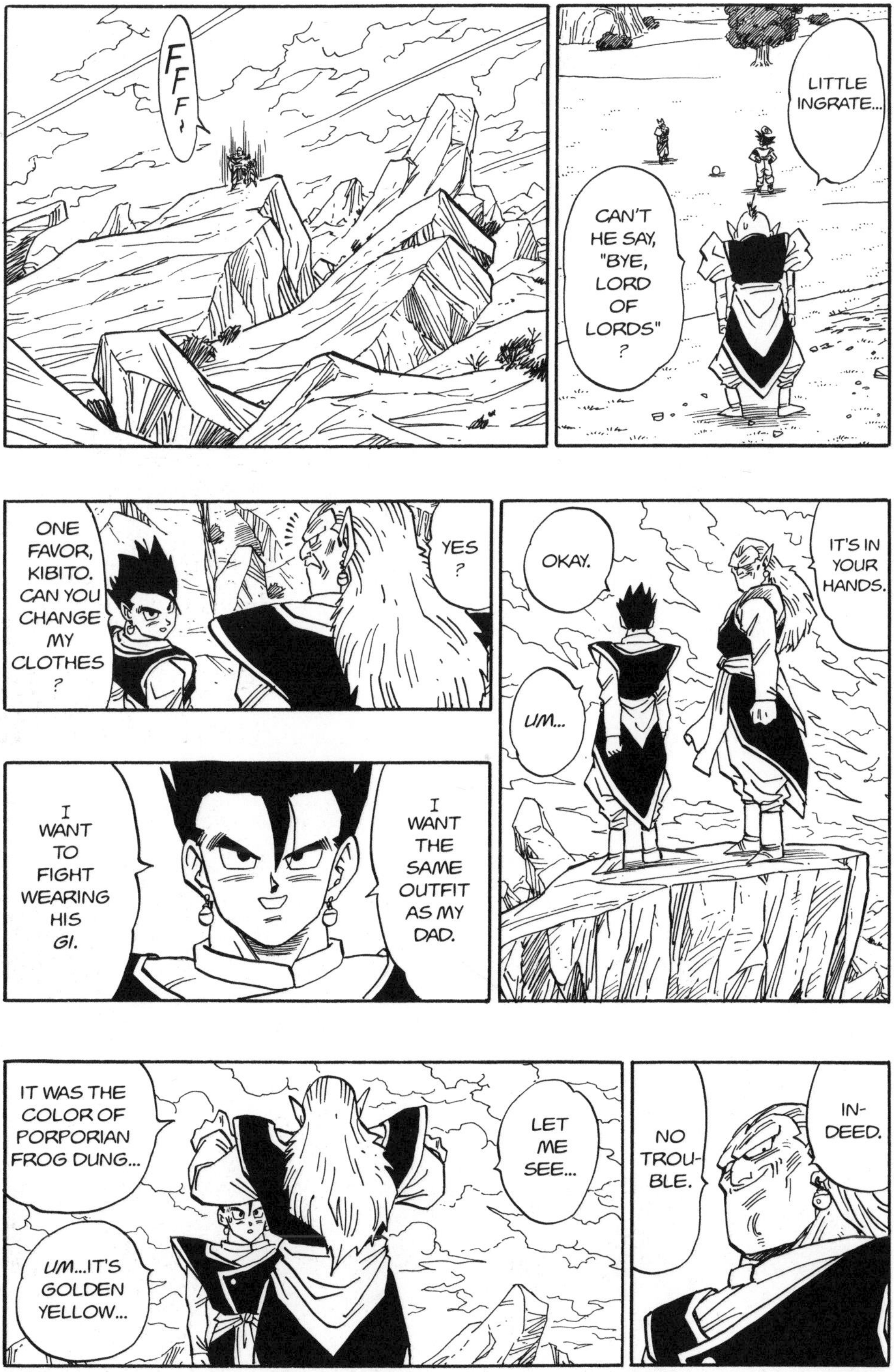
LITTLE INGRATE...
CAN'T HE SAY, "BYE, LORD OF LORDS"?
FFF...
IT'S IN YOUR HANDS.
OKAY.
UM...
YES?
ONE FAVOR, KIBITO. CAN YOU CHANGE MY CLOTHES?
I WANT THE SAME OUTFIT AS MY DAD.
I WANT TO FIGHT WEARING HIS GI.
INDEED.
NO TROUBLE.
LET ME SEE...
IT WAS THE COLOR OF PORPORIAN FROG DUNG...
UM...IT'S GOLDEN YELLOW...

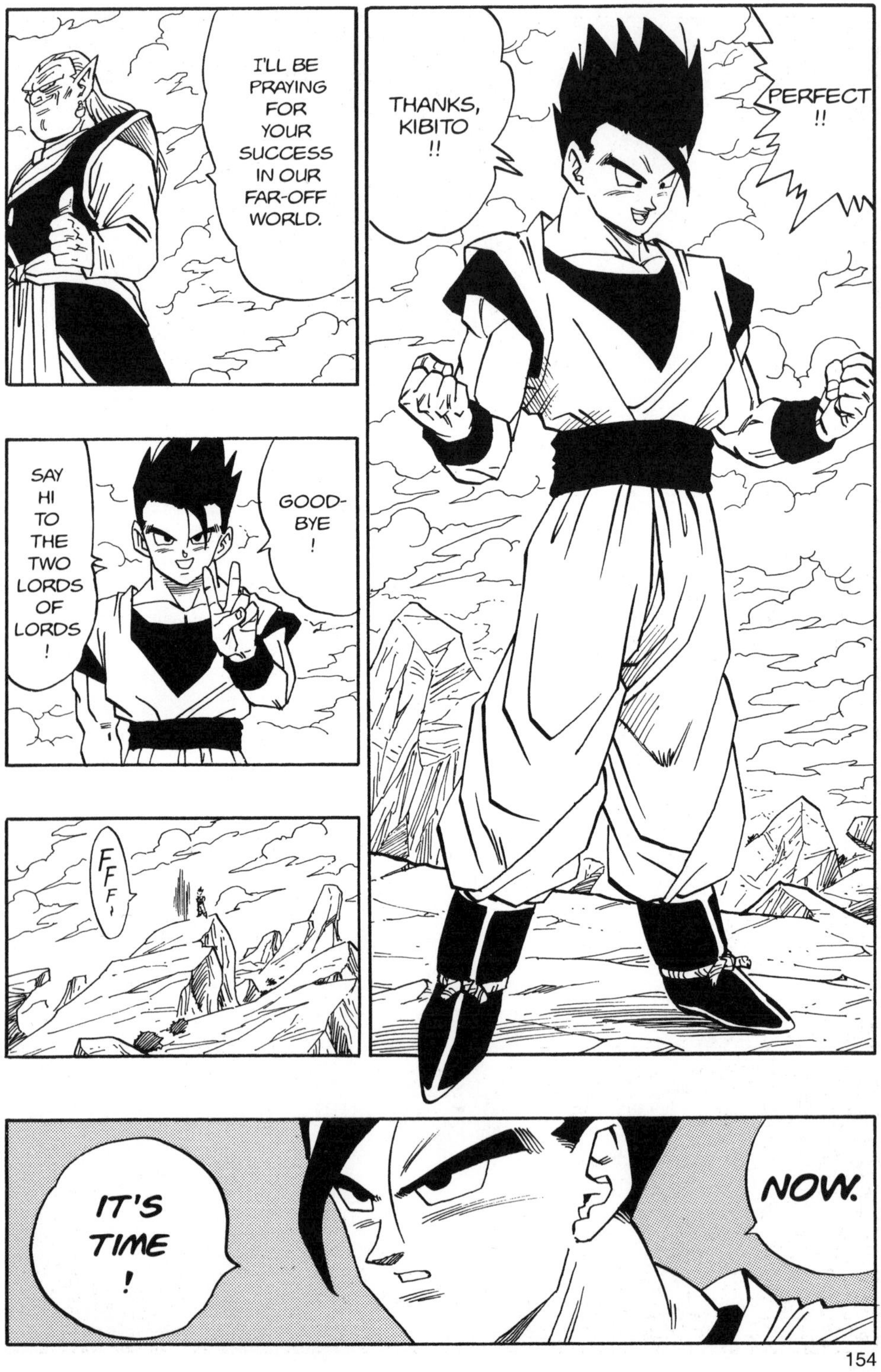
PERFECT !!
THANKS, KIBITO !!
I'LL BE PRAYING FOR YOUR SUCCESS IN OUR FAR-OFF WORLD.
GOOD-BYE !
SAY HI TO THE TWO LORDS OF LORDS !
FFF
NOW.
IT'S TIME !

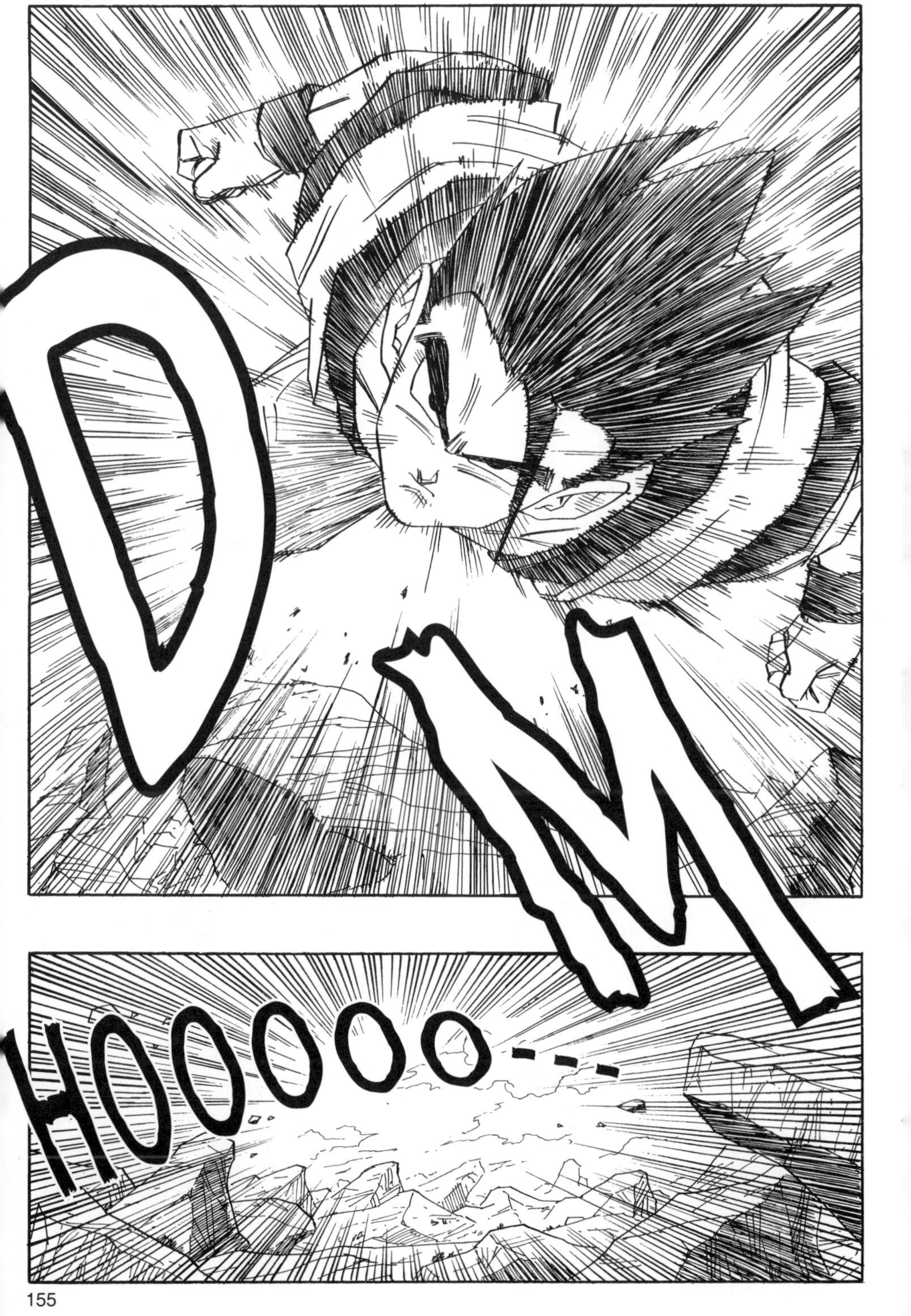
DOM
HOOOOO...

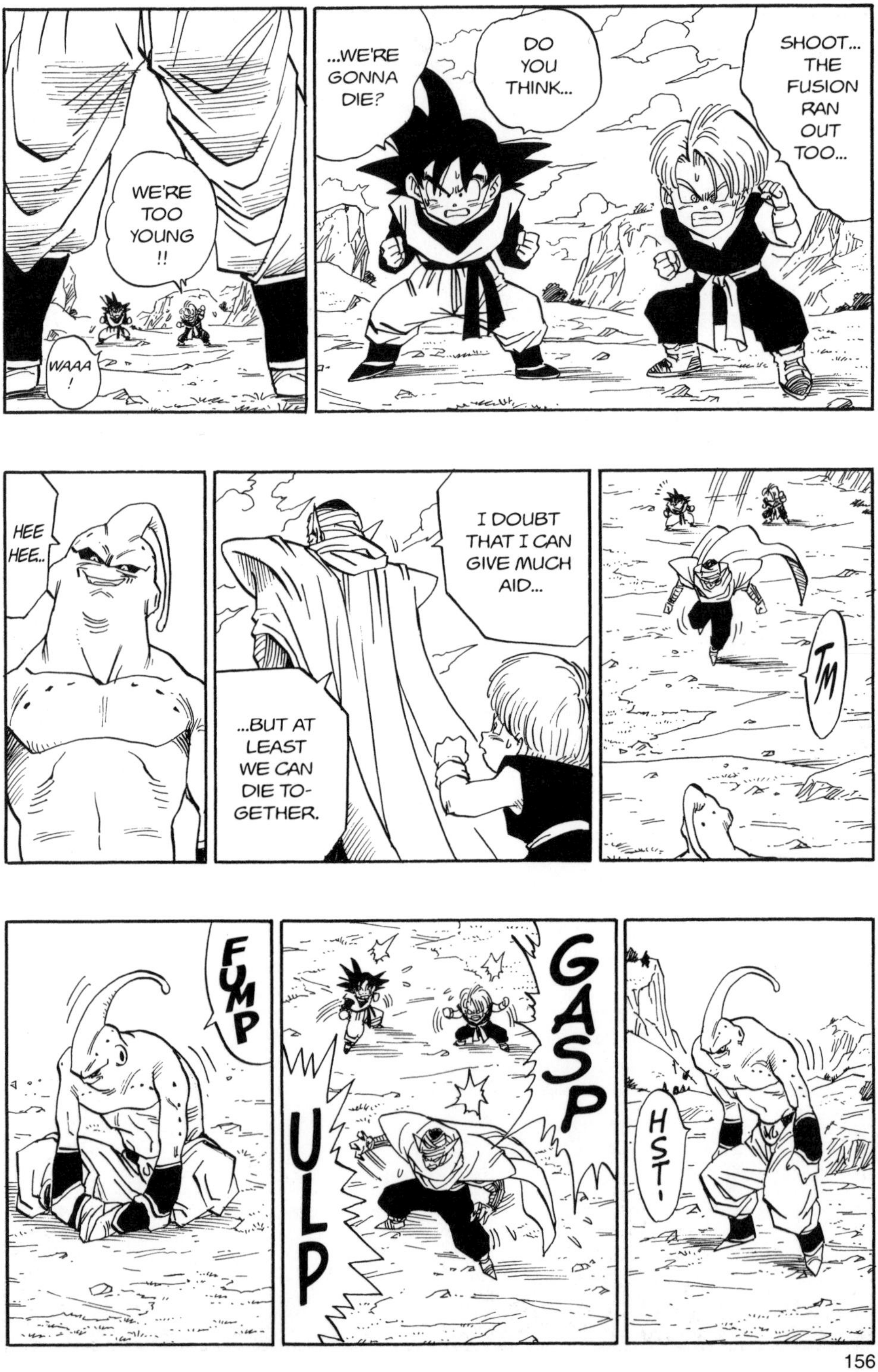
SHOOT... THE FUSION RAN OUT TOO...
DO YOU THINK...
...WE'RE GONNA DIE?
WE'RE TOO YOUNG !!
WAAA !
TM
I DOUBT THAT I CAN GIVE MUCH AID...
...BUT AT LEAST WE CAN DIE TO-GETHER.
HEE HEE..
HST!
GASP
ULP
FUMP

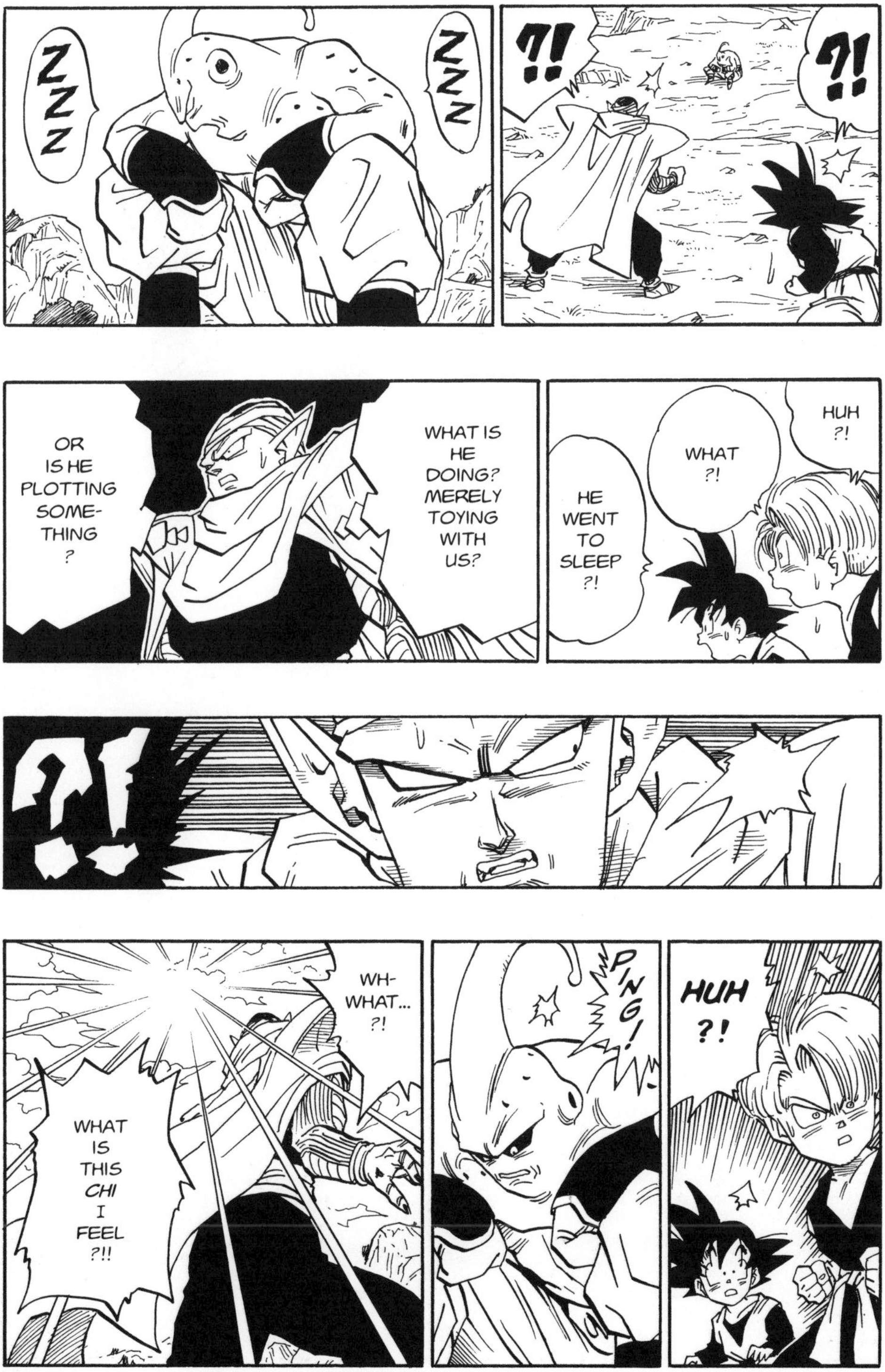
?!
?!
ZZZ
ZZZ
HUH ?!
WHAT ?!
HE WENT TO SLEEP ?!
WHAT IS HE DOING? MERELY TOYING WITH US?
OR IS HE PLOTTING SOME-THING ?
?!
HUH ?!
PING!
WH-WHAT... ?!
WHAT IS THIS *CHI* I FEEL ?!!

DBZ:303 • Gohan's Counterattack!

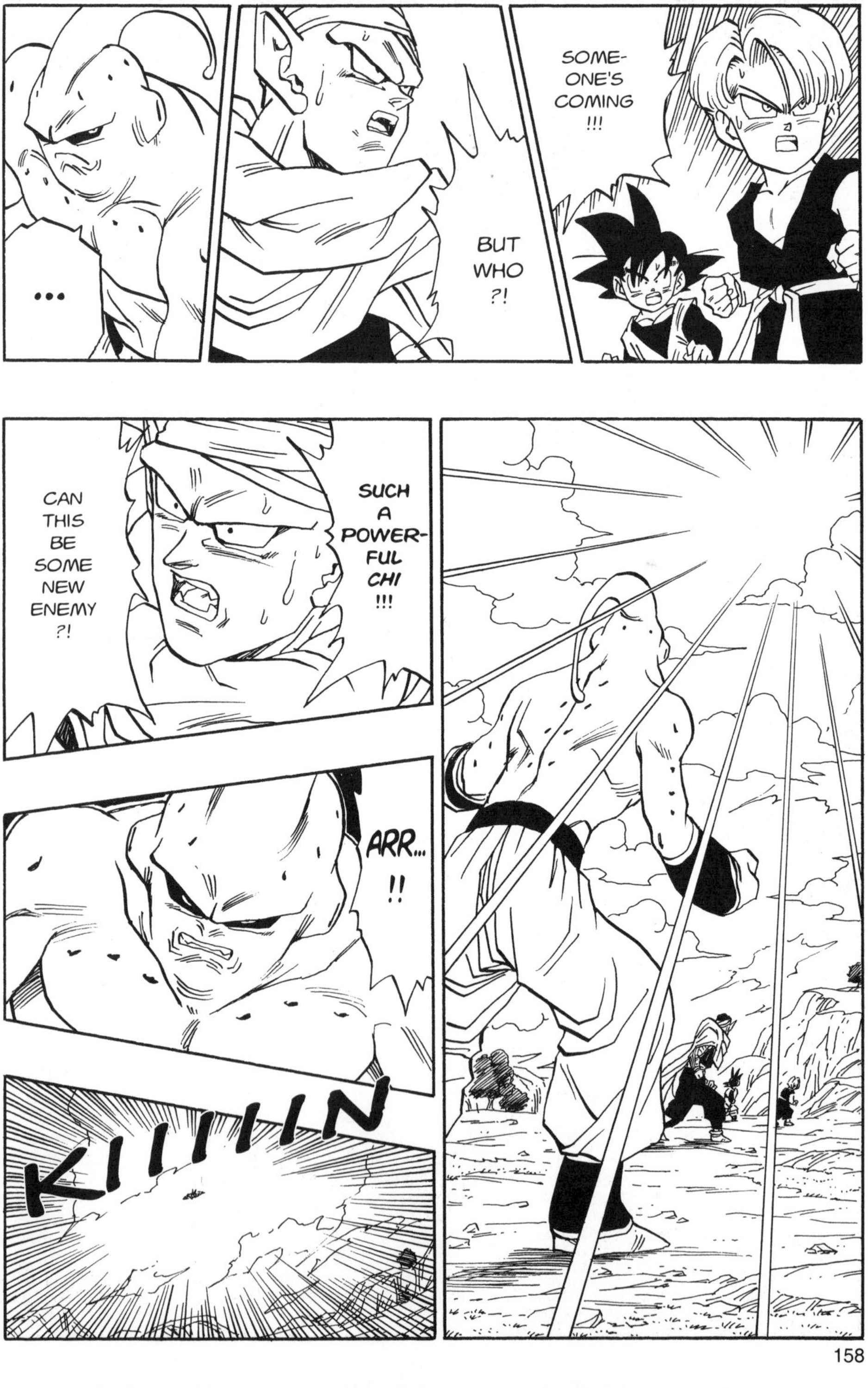
SOME-ONE'S COMING !!!
BUT WHO ?!
...
SUCH A POWER-FUL CHI !!!
CAN THIS BE SOME NEW ENEMY ?!
ARR... !!
KIIIIIN

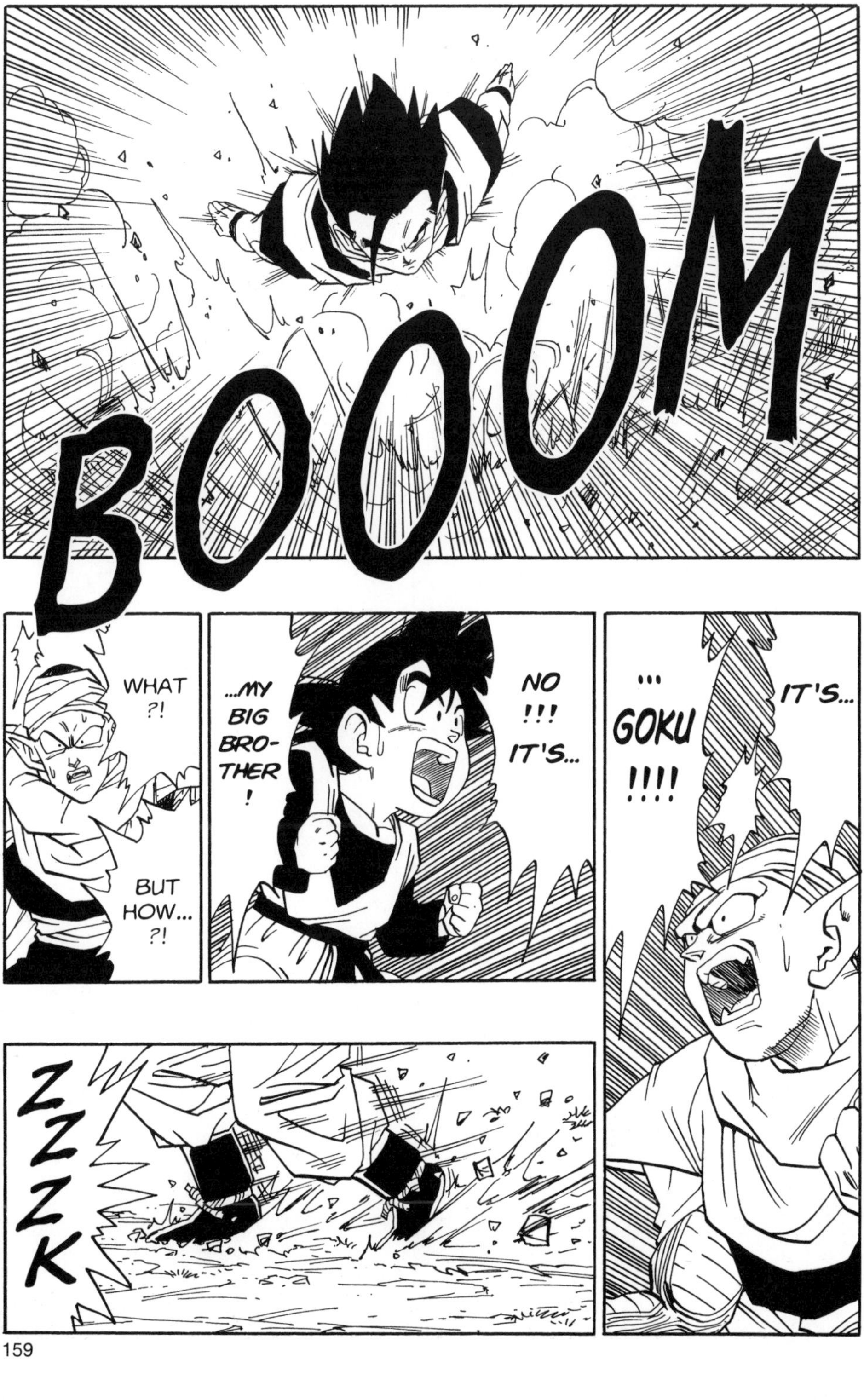
BOOOM
IT'S...
... GOKU !!!!
NO !!! IT'S...
...MY BIG BRO-THER !
WHAT ?!
BUT HOW... ?!
ZZZK

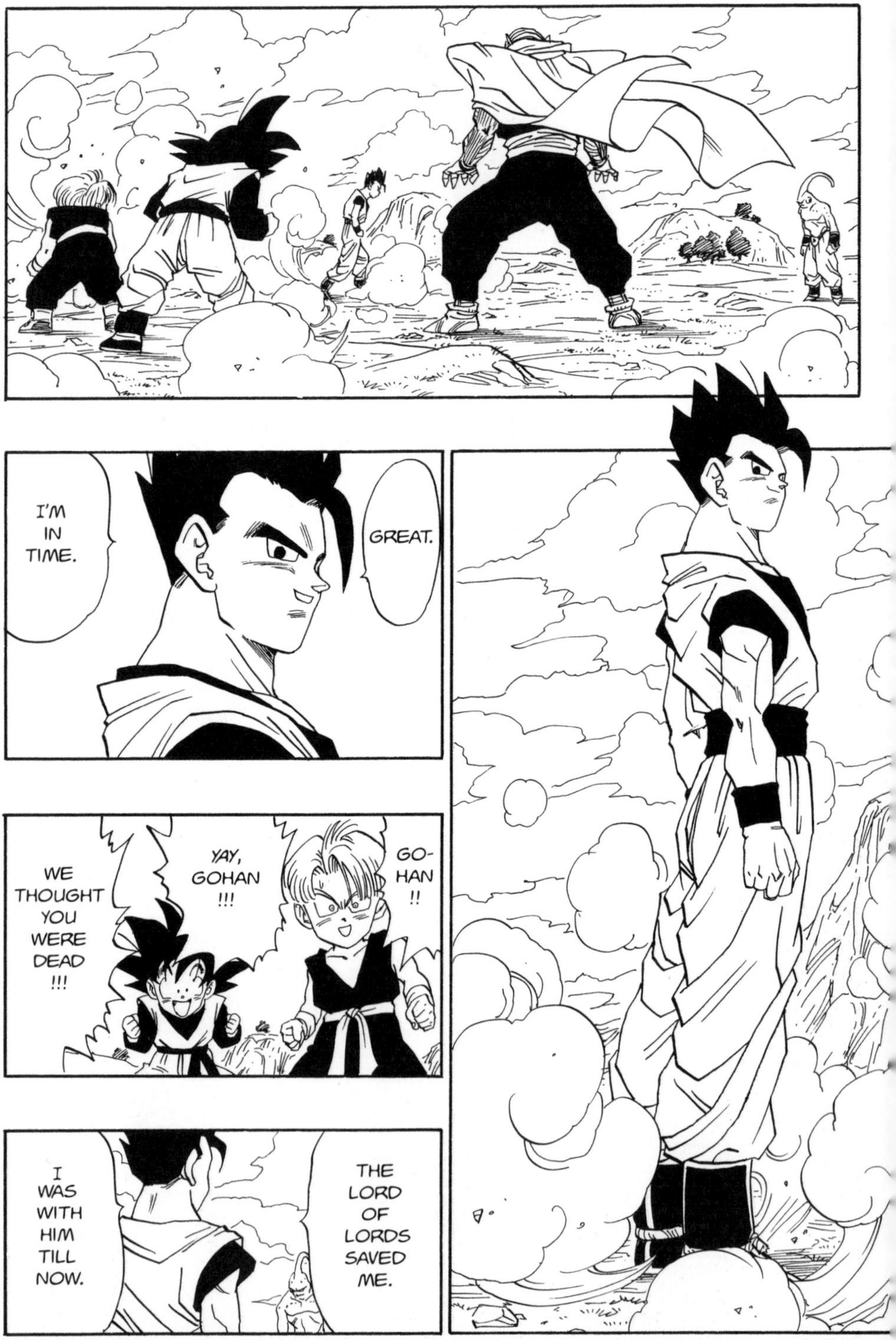
GREAT.
I'M IN TIME.
GO-HAN !!
YAY, GOHAN !!!
WE THOUGHT YOU WERE DEAD !!!
THE LORD OF LORDS SAVED ME.
I WAS WITH HIM TILL NOW.

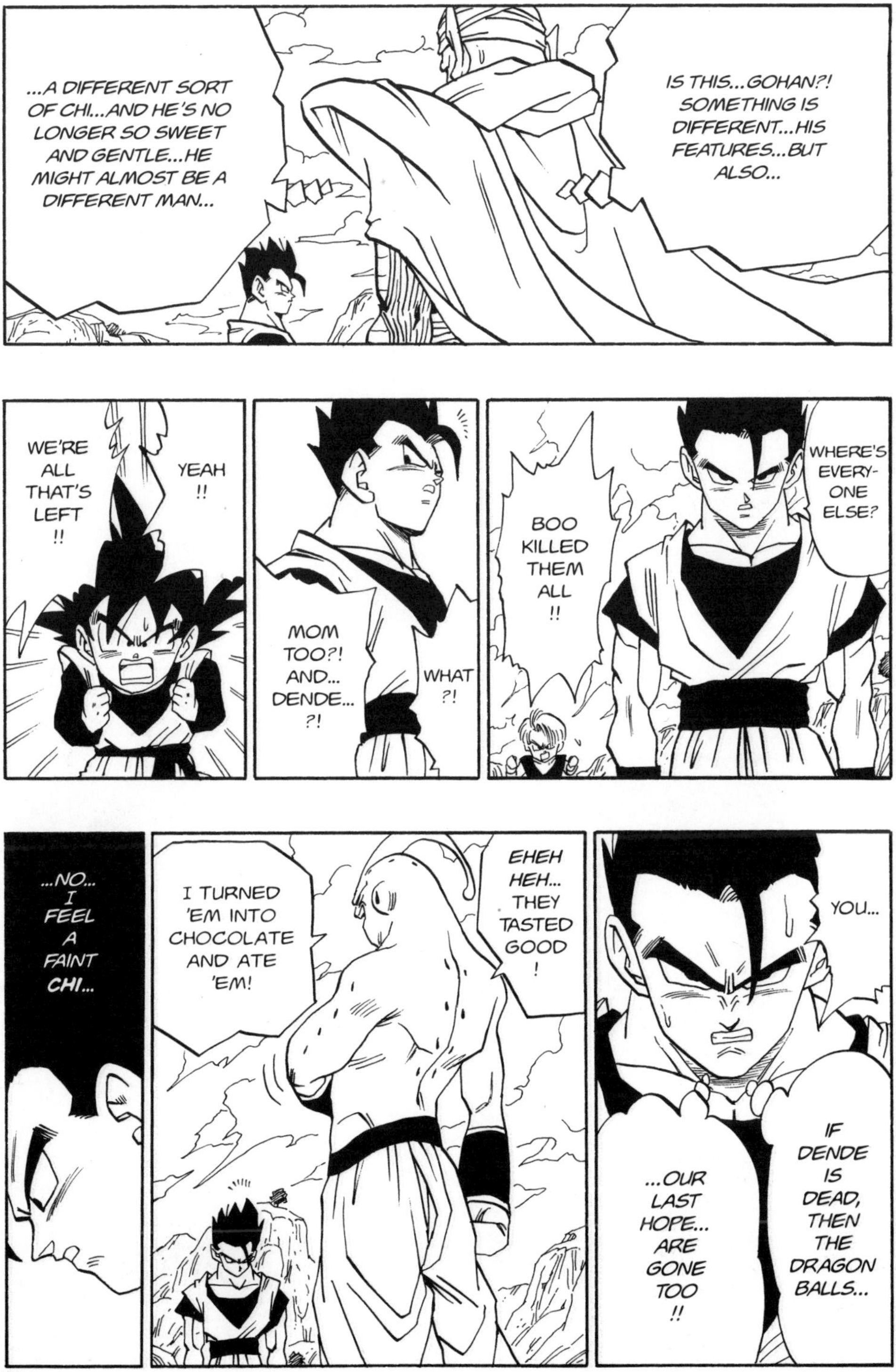
IS THIS...GOHAN?! SOMETHING IS DIFFERENT...HIS FEATURES...BUT ALSO...
...A DIFFERENT SORT OF CHI...AND HE'S NO LONGER SO SWEET AND GENTLE...HE MIGHT ALMOST BE A DIFFERENT MAN...
WHERE'S EVERY-ONE ELSE?
BOO KILLED THEM ALL!!
WHAT?!
MOM TOO?! AND... DENDE...?!
YEAH!!
WE'RE ALL THAT'S LEFT!!
YOU...
IF DENDE IS DEAD, THEN THE DRAGON BALLS...
...OUR LAST HOPE... ARE GONE TOO!!
EHEH HEH... THEY TASTED GOOD!
I TURNED 'EM INTO CHOCOLATE AND ATE 'EM!
...NO... I FEEL A FAINT CHI...

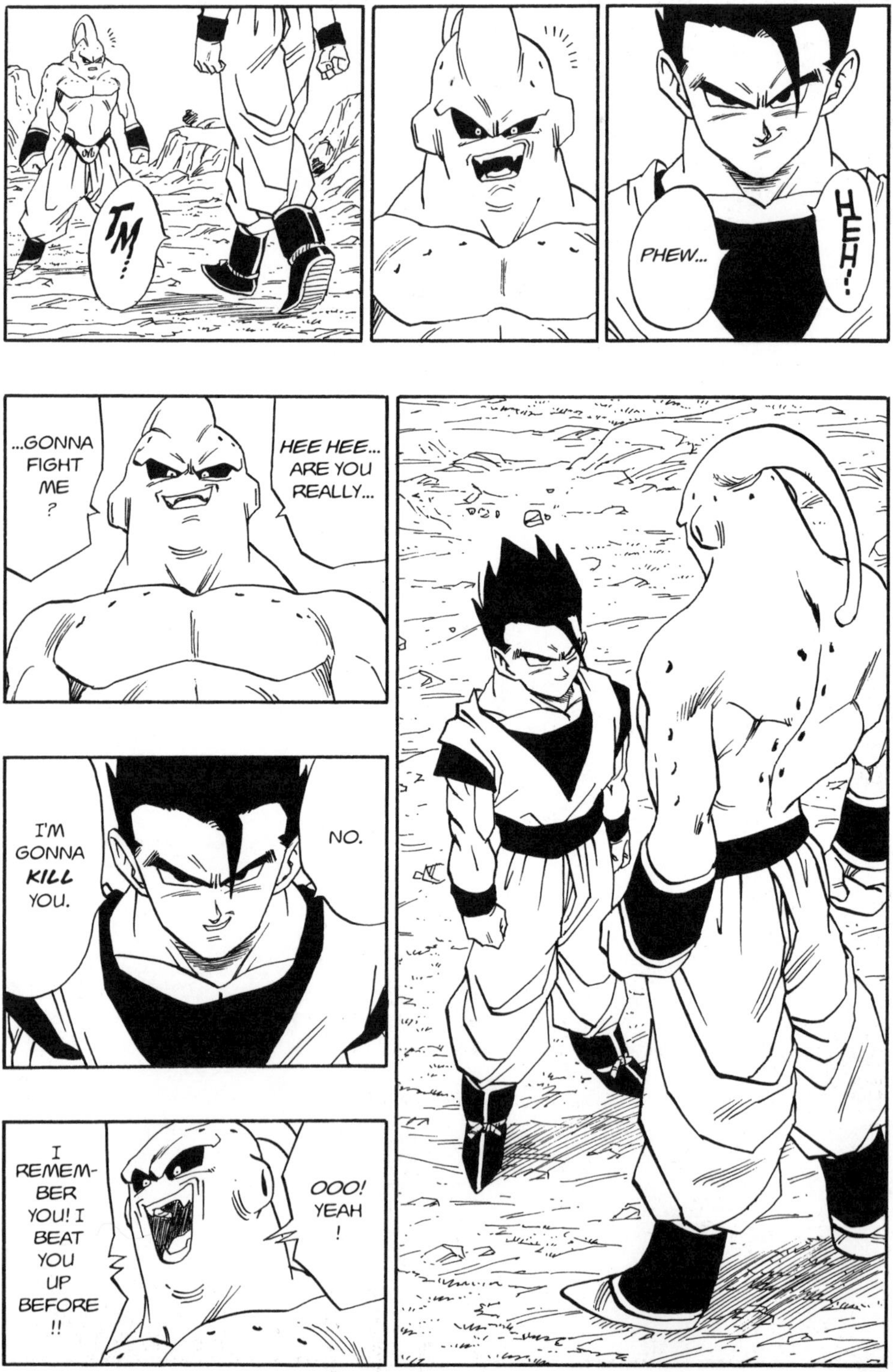
HEH!!
PHEW...
TM...
HEE HEE... ARE YOU REALLY...
...GONNA FIGHT ME ?
NO.
I'M GONNA **KILL** YOU.
OOO! YEAH !
I REMEMBER YOU! I BEAT YOU UP BEFORE !!

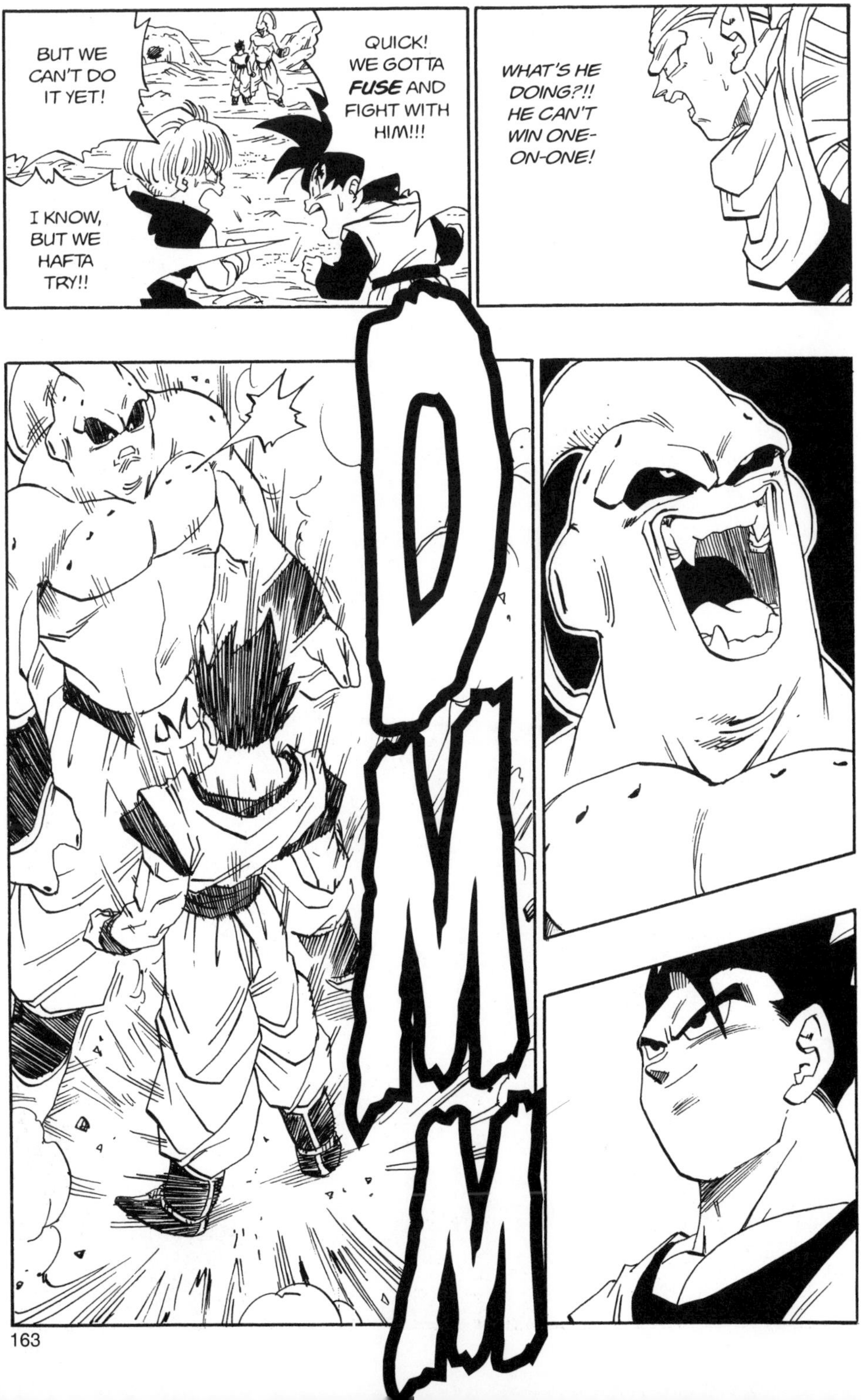
WHAT'S HE DOING?!! HE CAN'T WIN ONE-ON-ONE!
QUICK! WE GOTTA FUSE AND FIGHT WITH HIM!!!
BUT WE CAN'T DO IT YET!
I KNOW, BUT WE HAFTA TRY!!
DMM

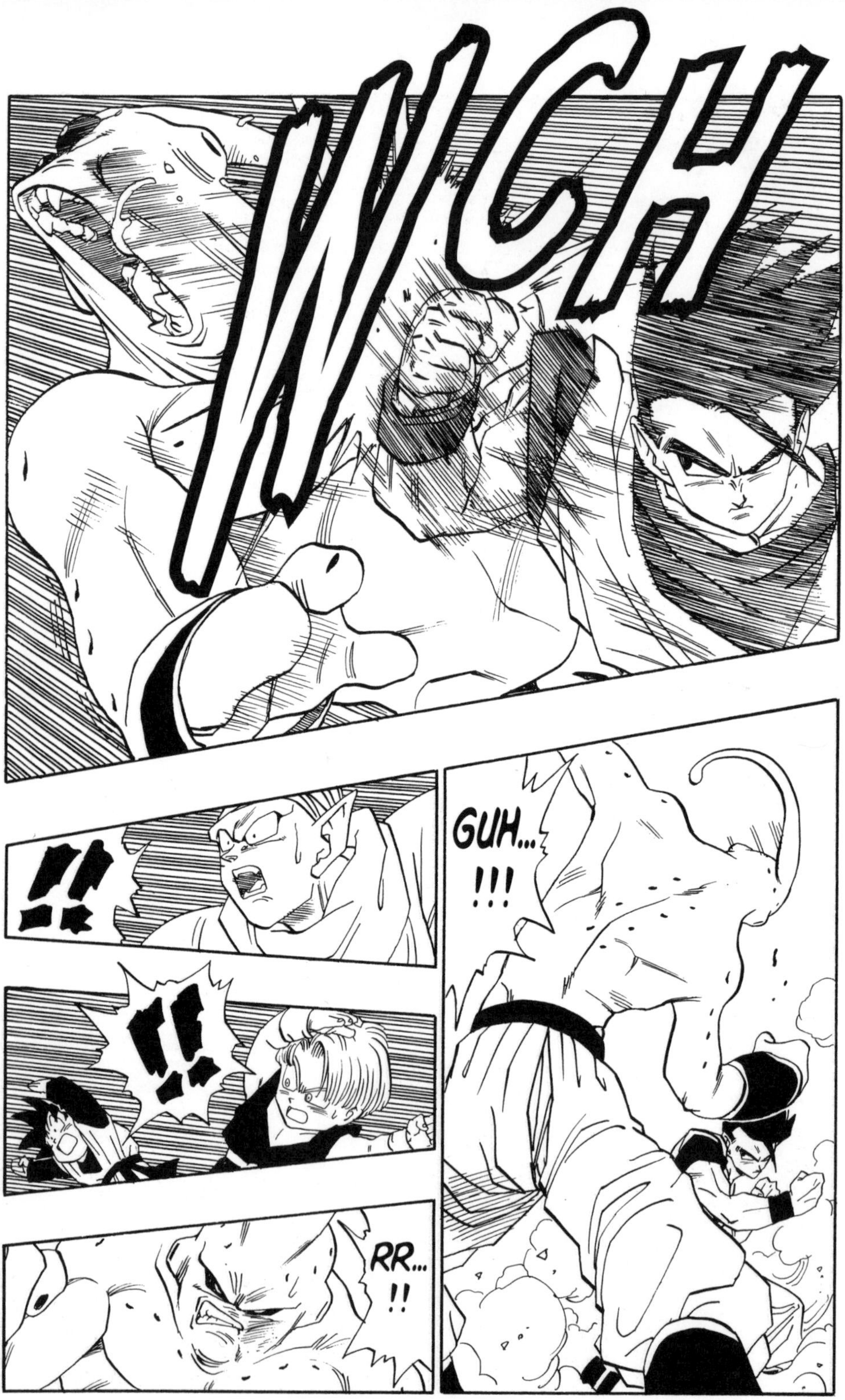
WCH
GUH... !!!
!!
!!
RR... !!

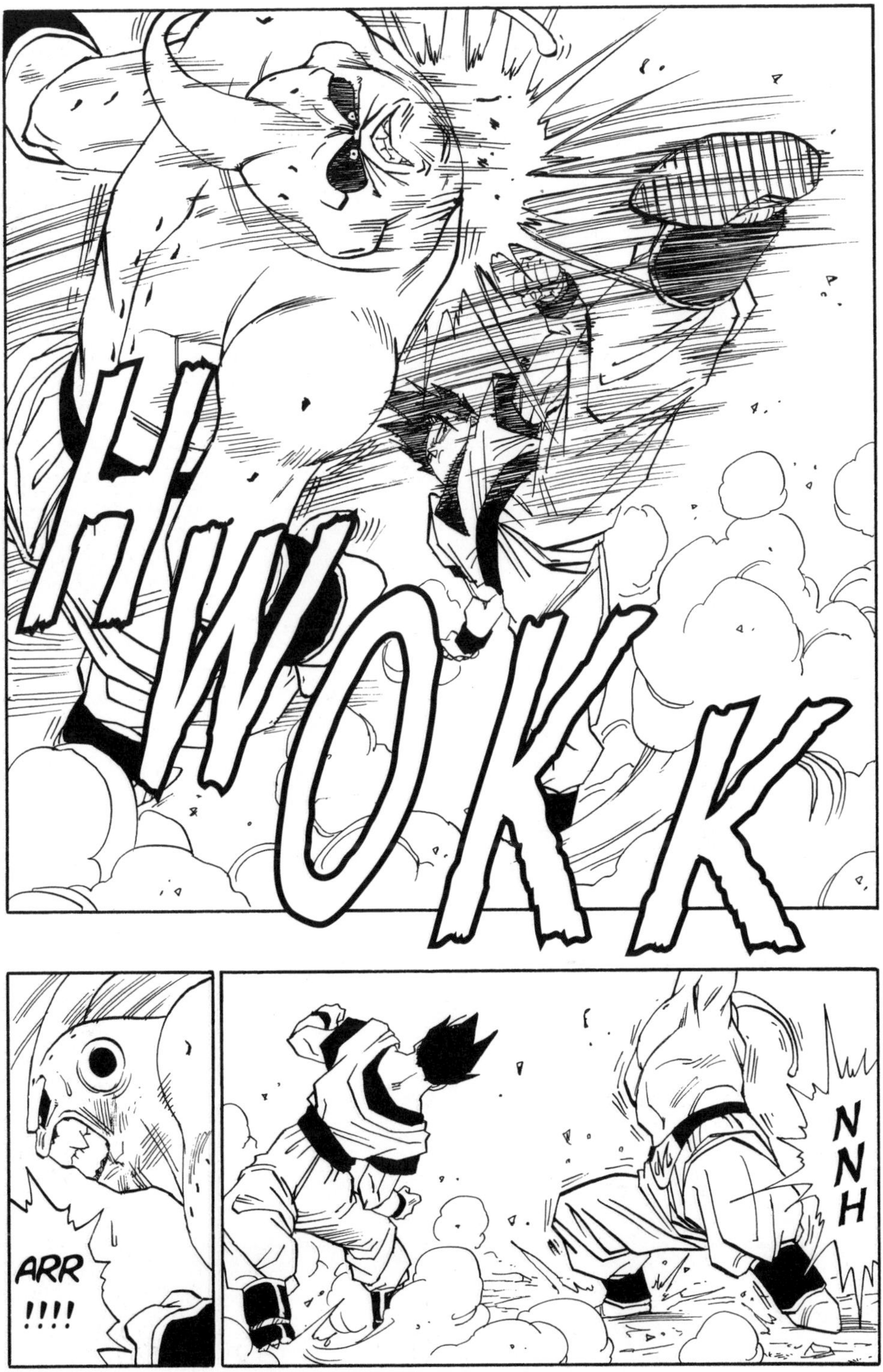
HWOKK
NNH
ARR !!!!

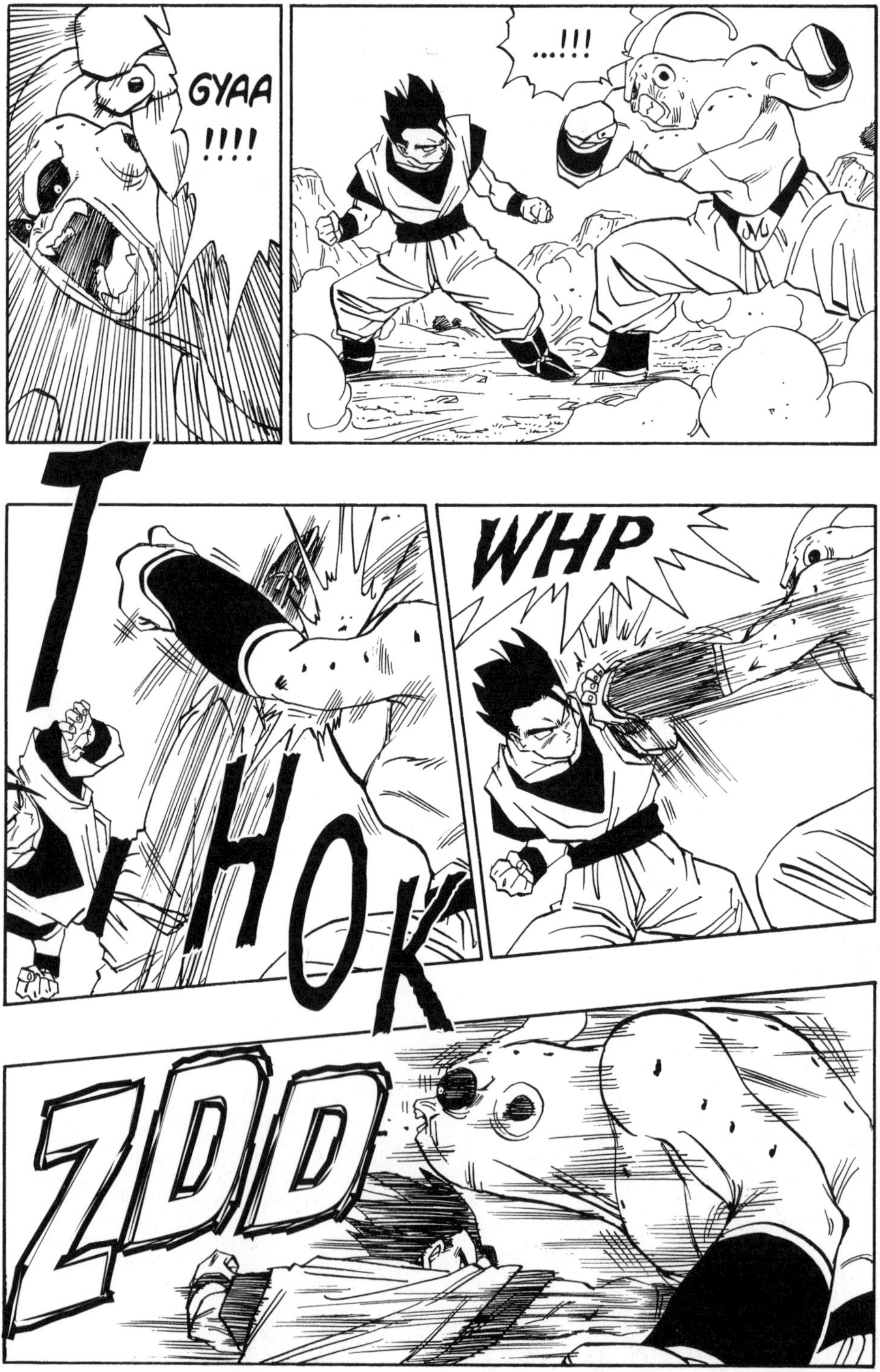
...!!!
GYAA !!!!
WHP
THOK
ZDD

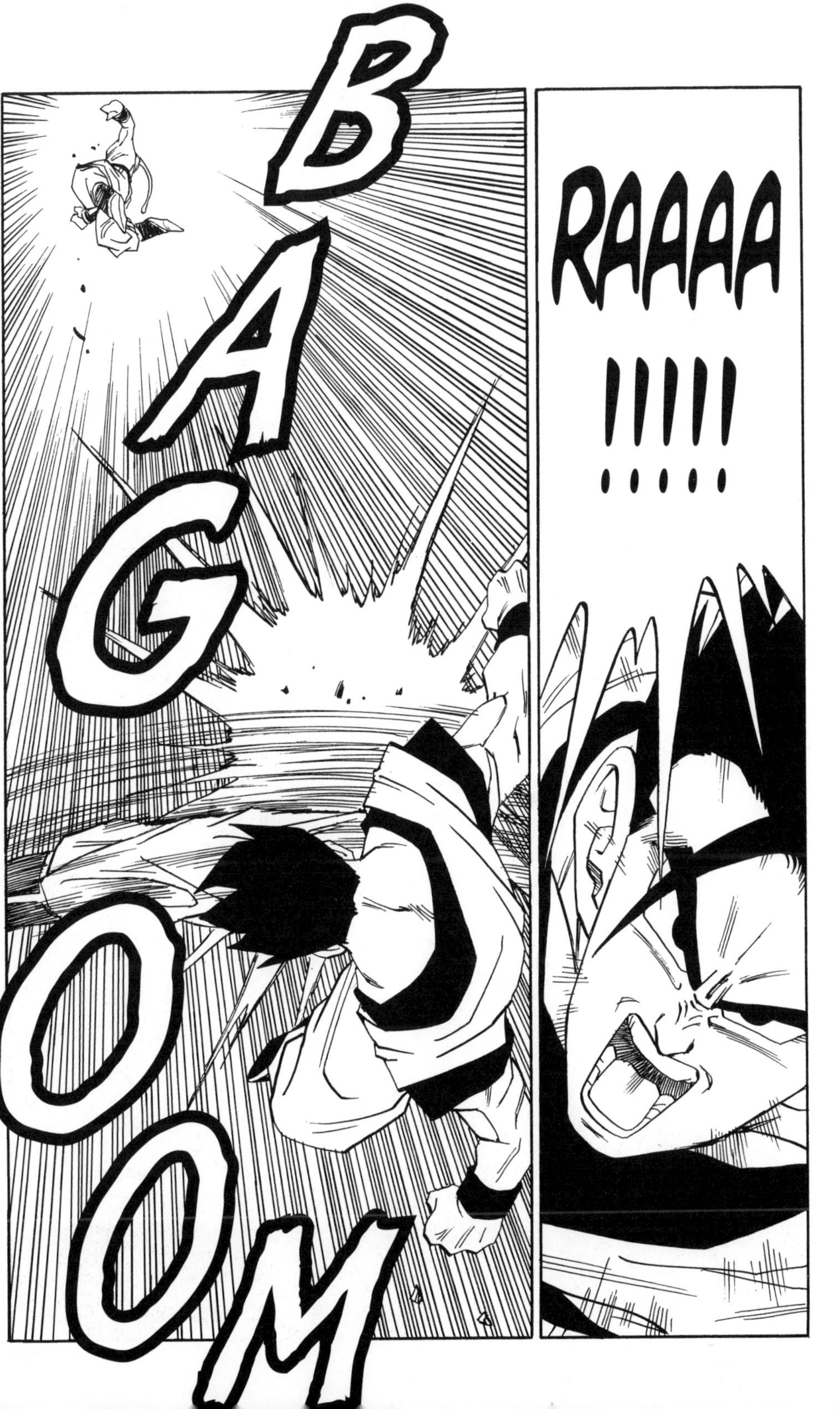
RAAAA!!!!!
BAGOOM

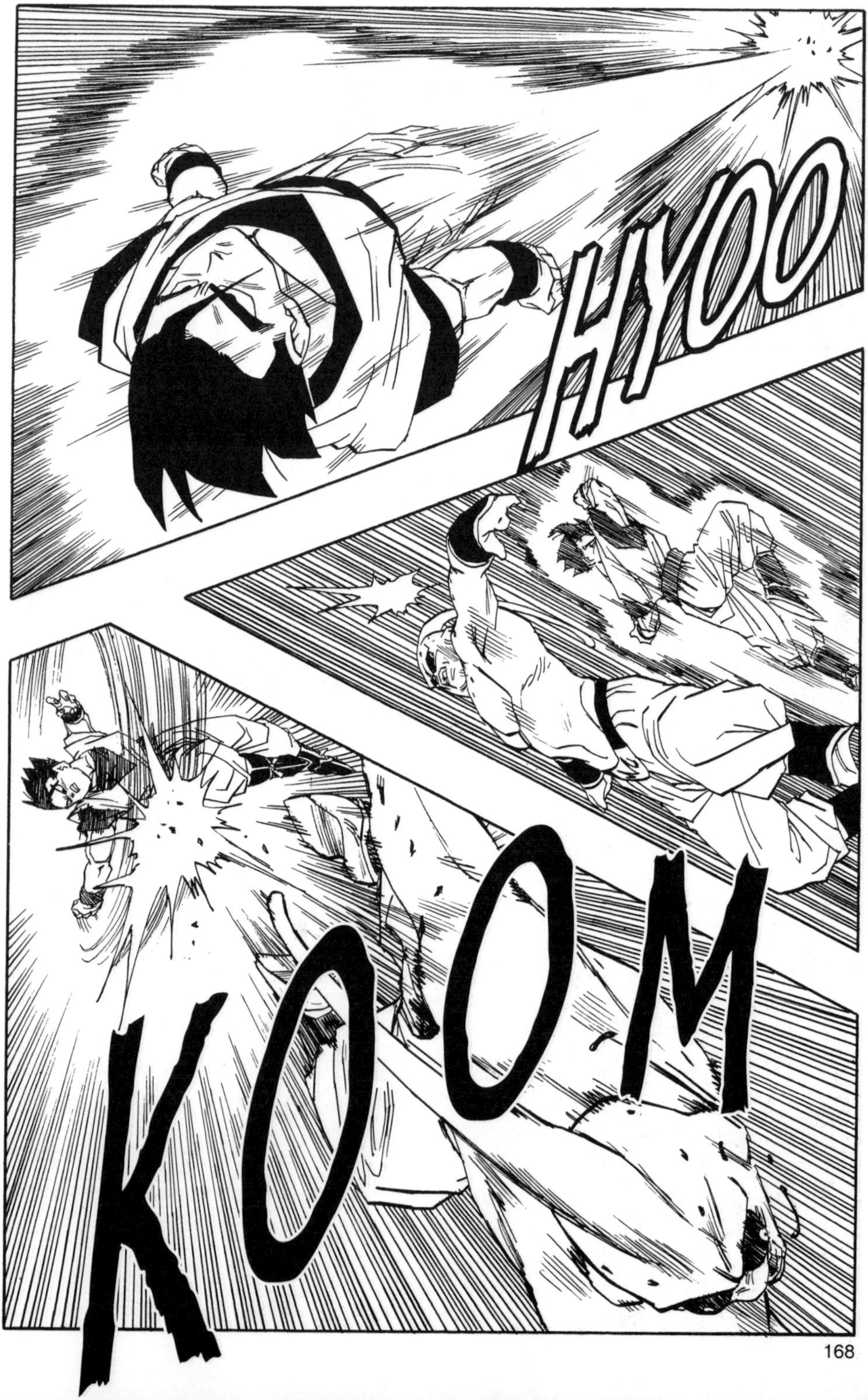
HYOO
KOOM

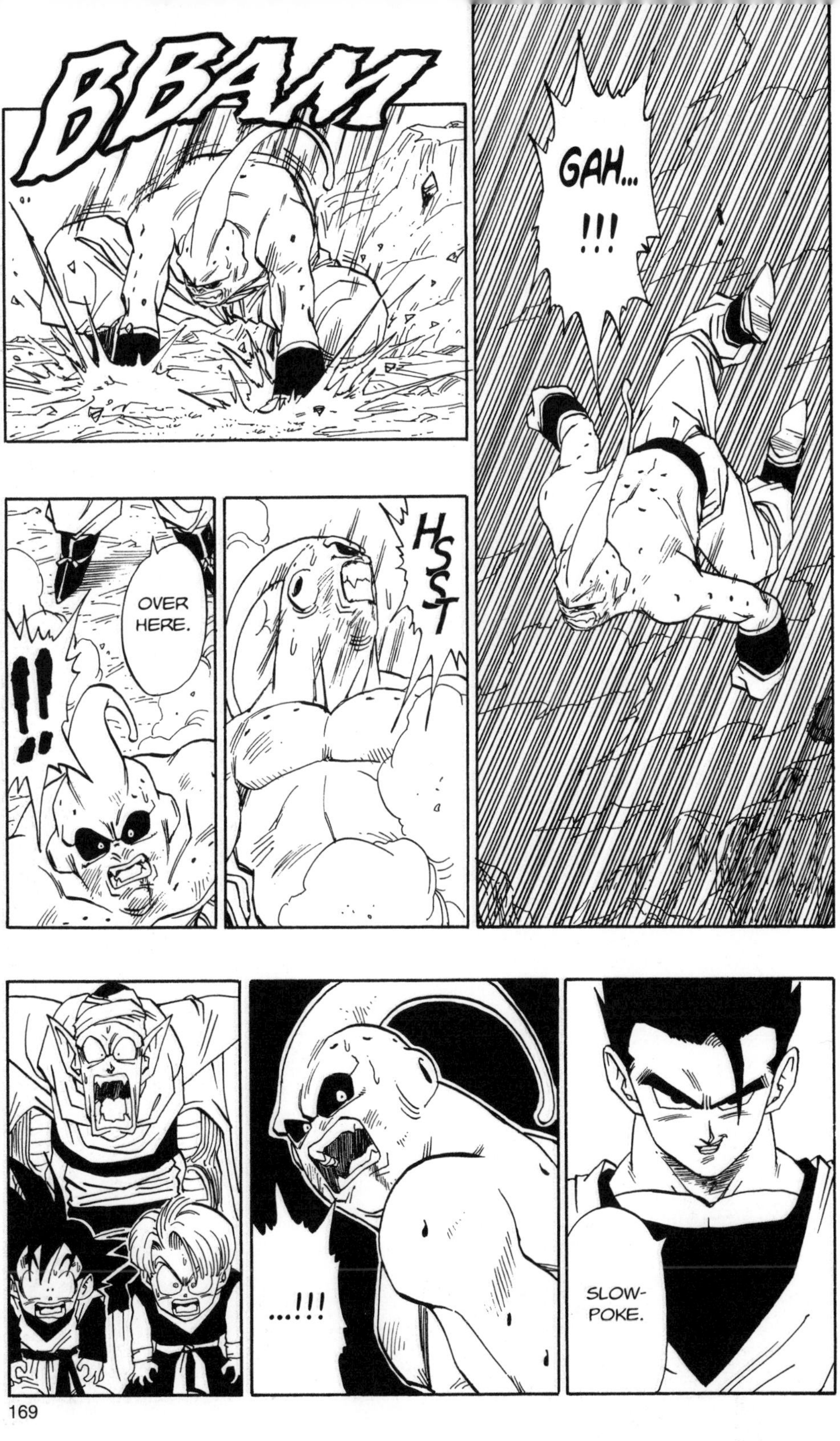
GAH...
!!!
BBAM
HSST
OVER HERE.
!!
SLOW-POKE.
...!!!

DRAGON BALL ドラゴンボール

DBZ:304 • What's Boo Doing?!

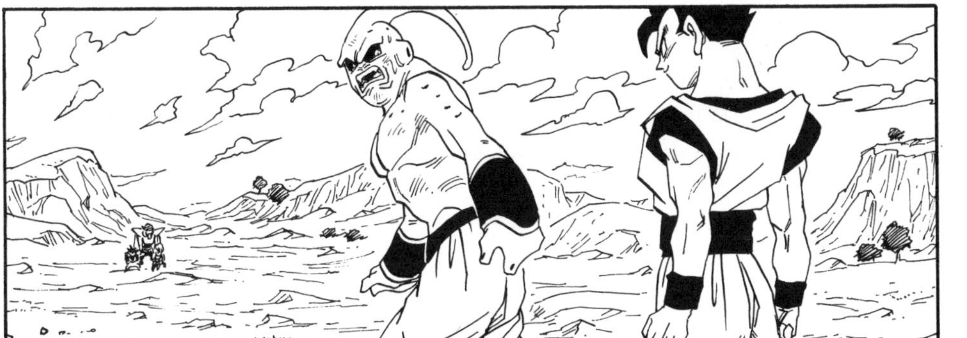

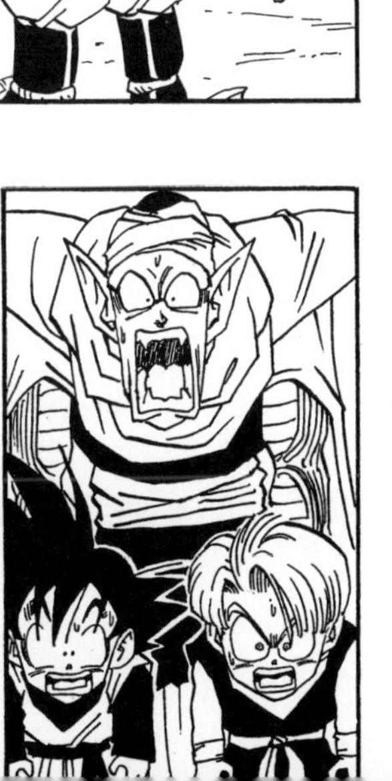

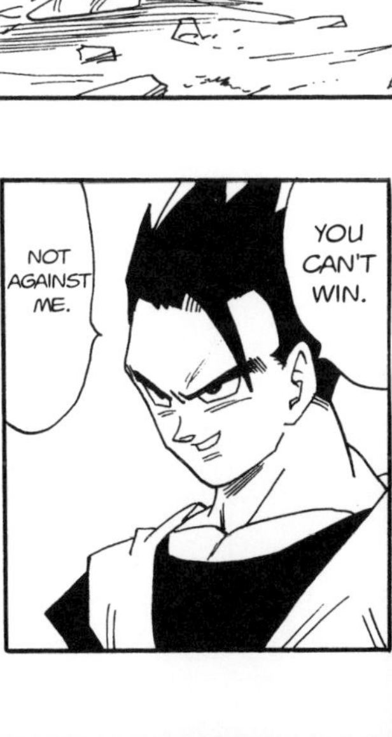
YOU CAN'T WIN.
NOT AGAINST ME.

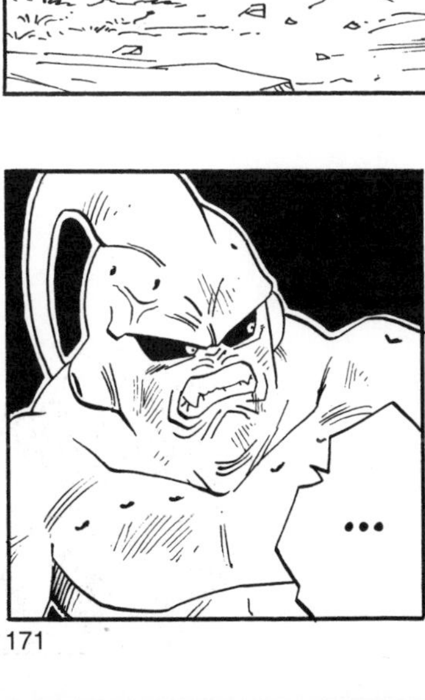
...

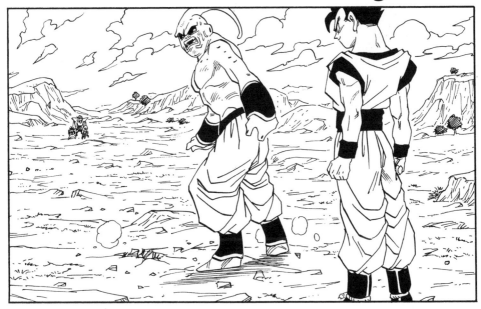

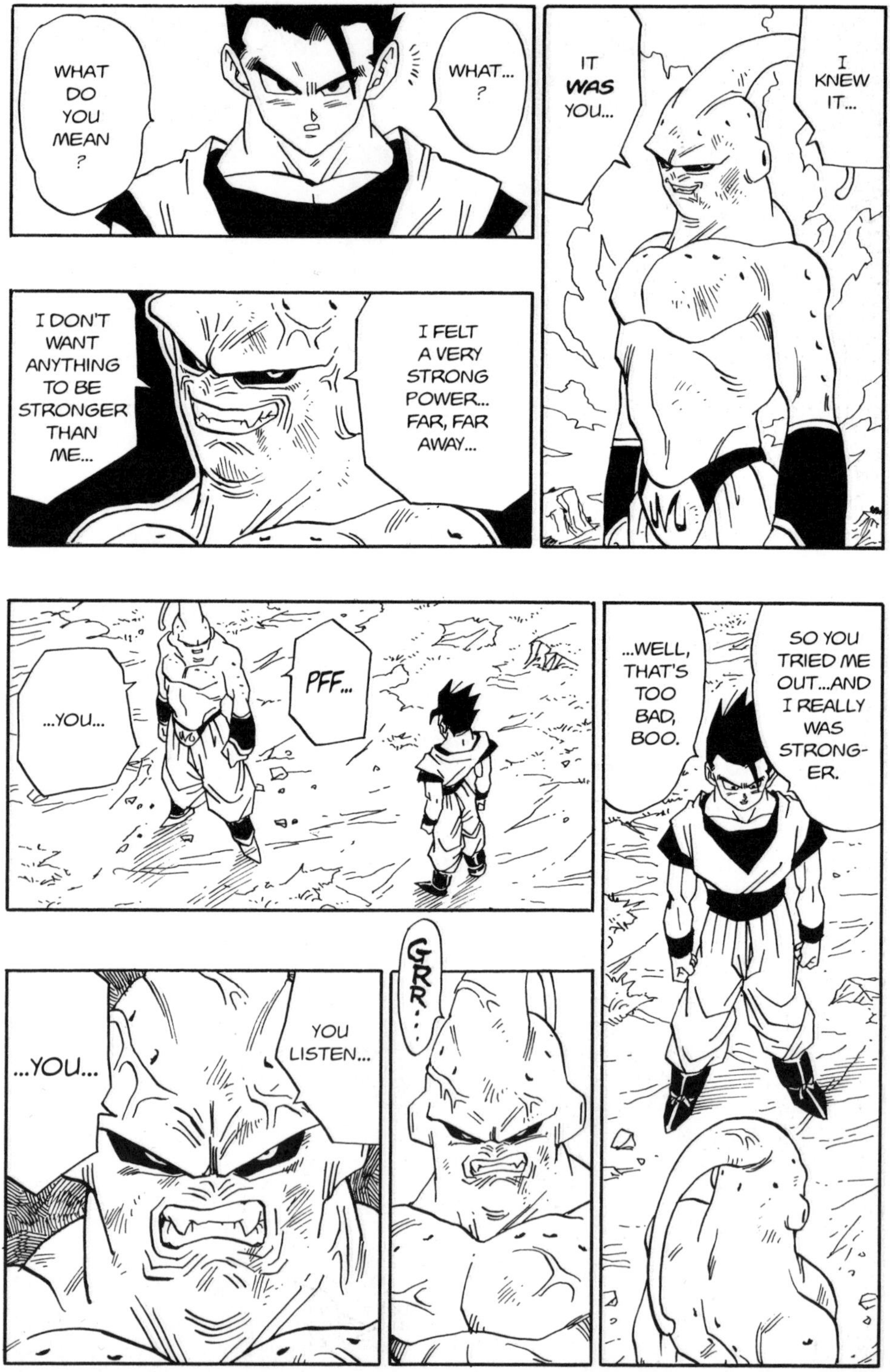
I KNEW IT...
IT WAS YOU...
WHAT... ?
WHAT DO YOU MEAN ?
I FELT A VERY STRONG POWER... FAR, FAR AWAY...
I DON'T WANT ANYTHING TO BE STRONGER THAN ME...
SO YOU TRIED ME OUT...AND I REALLY WAS STRONGER.
...WELL, THAT'S TOO BAD, BOO.
PFF...
...YOU...
GRR...
YOU LISTEN...
...YOU...

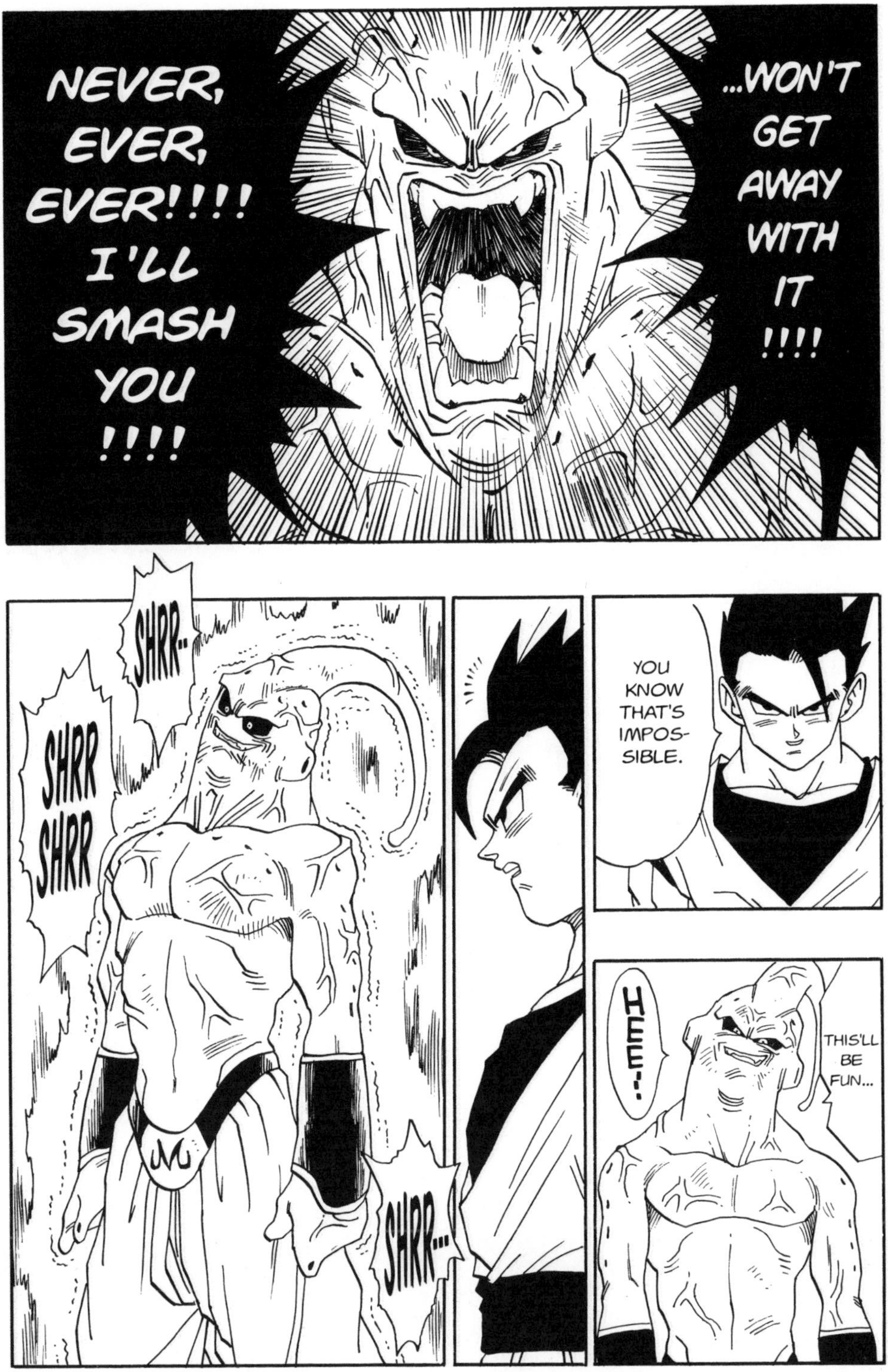
...WON'T GET AWAY WITH IT!!!!
NEVER, EVER, EVER!!!! I'LL SMASH YOU!!!!
YOU KNOW THAT'S IMPOS-SIBLE.
HEEE...
THIS'LL BE FUN...
SHRR..
SHRR SHRR
SHRR...

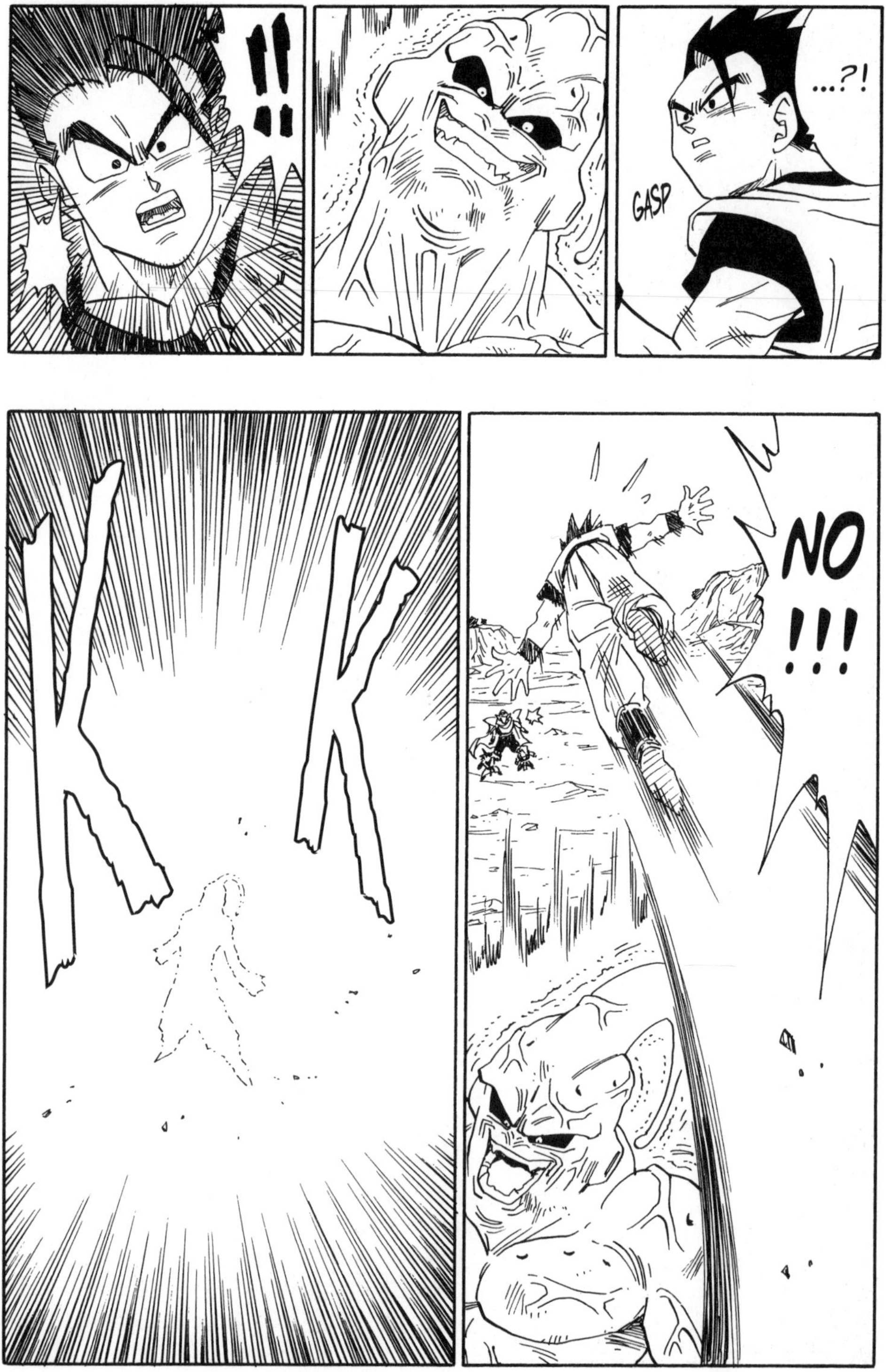
...?!
GASP
!!
NO!!!
K K

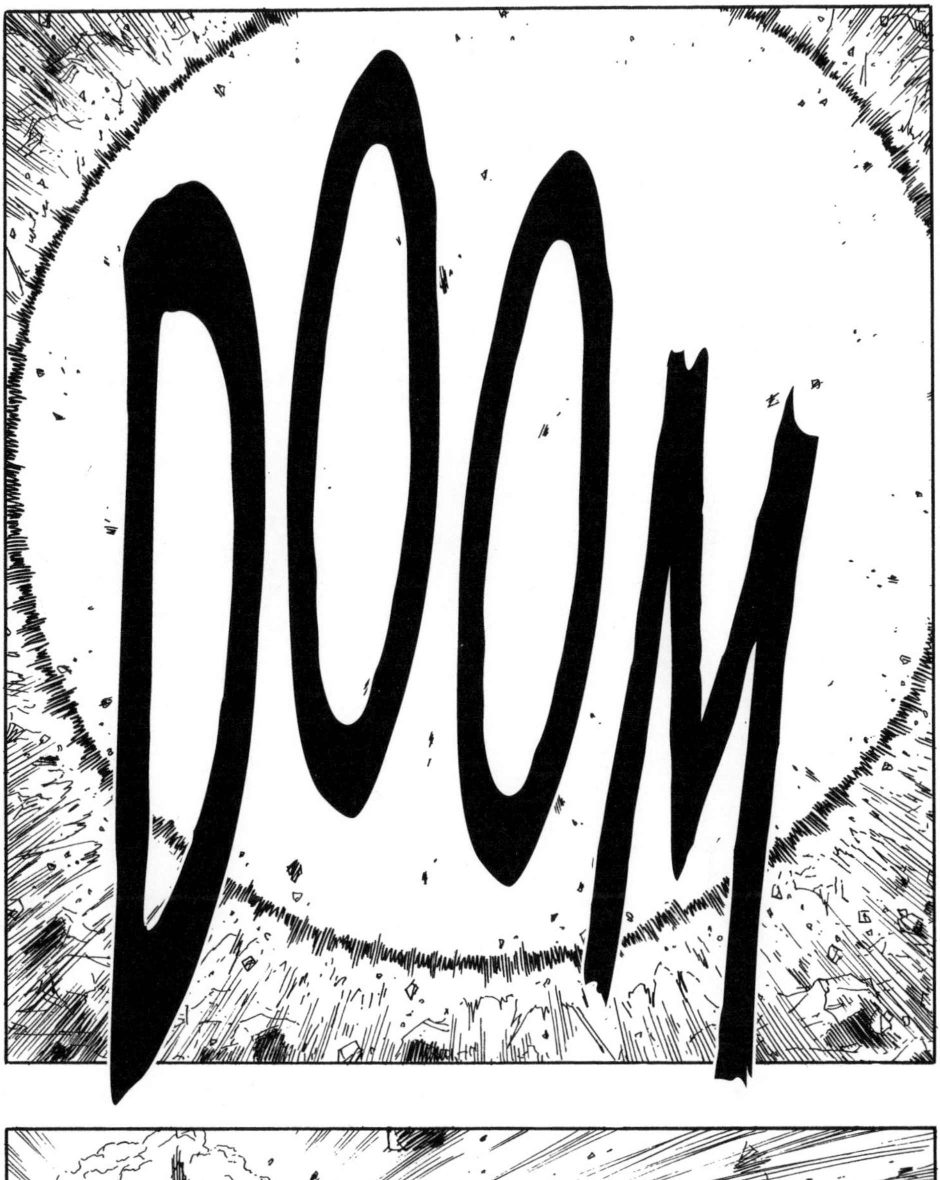
DOOM
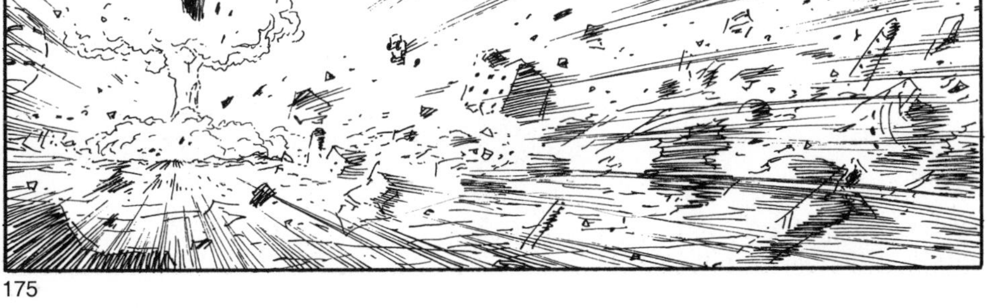

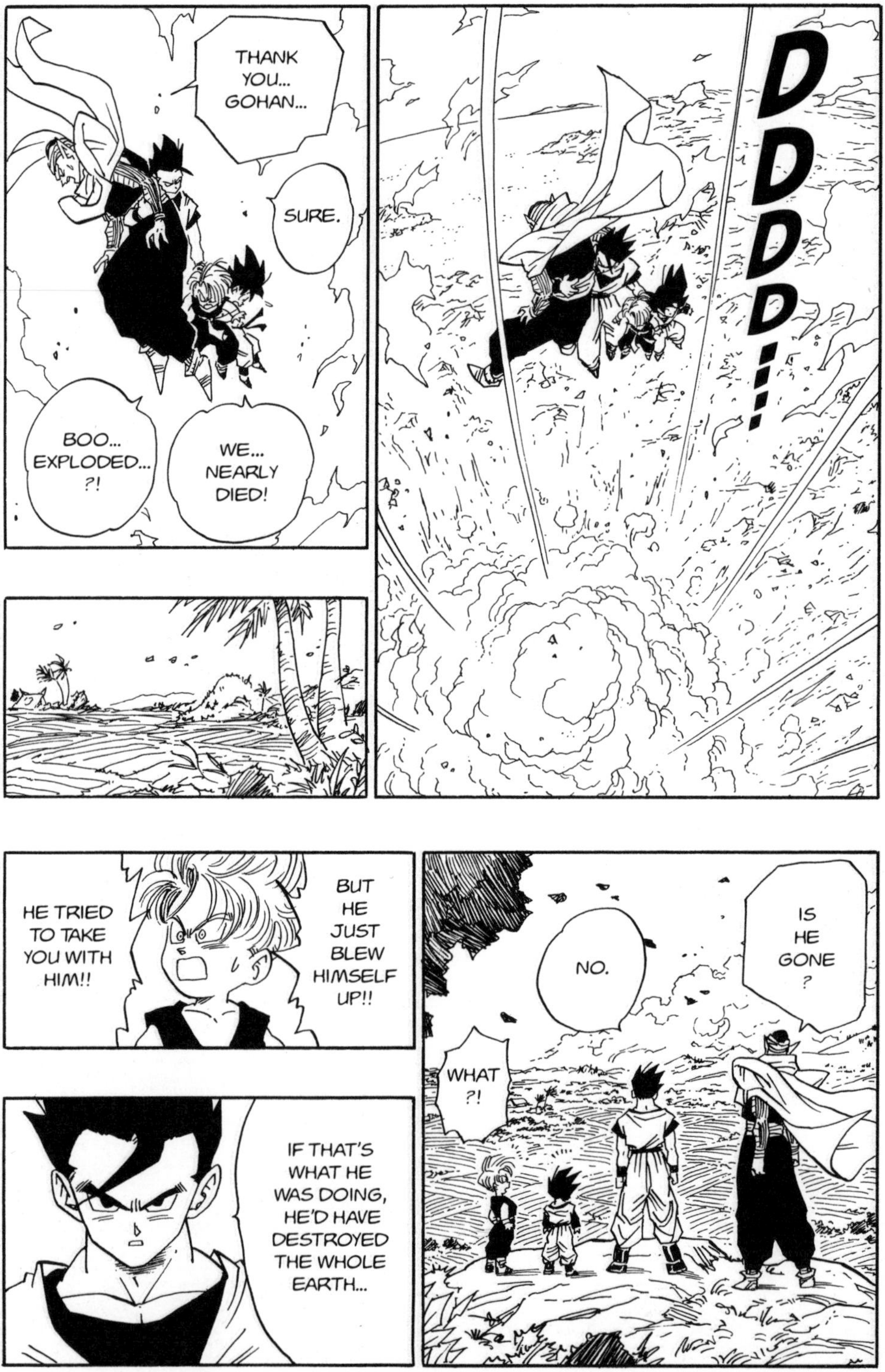
DDDD!!!!
THANK YOU... GOHAN...
SURE.
WE... NEARLY DIED!
BOO... EXPLODED...?!
IS HE GONE?
NO.
WHAT?!
BUT HE JUST BLEW HIMSELF UP!!
HE TRIED TO TAKE YOU WITH HIM!!
IF THAT'S WHAT HE WAS DOING, HE'D HAVE DESTROYED THE WHOLE EARTH...

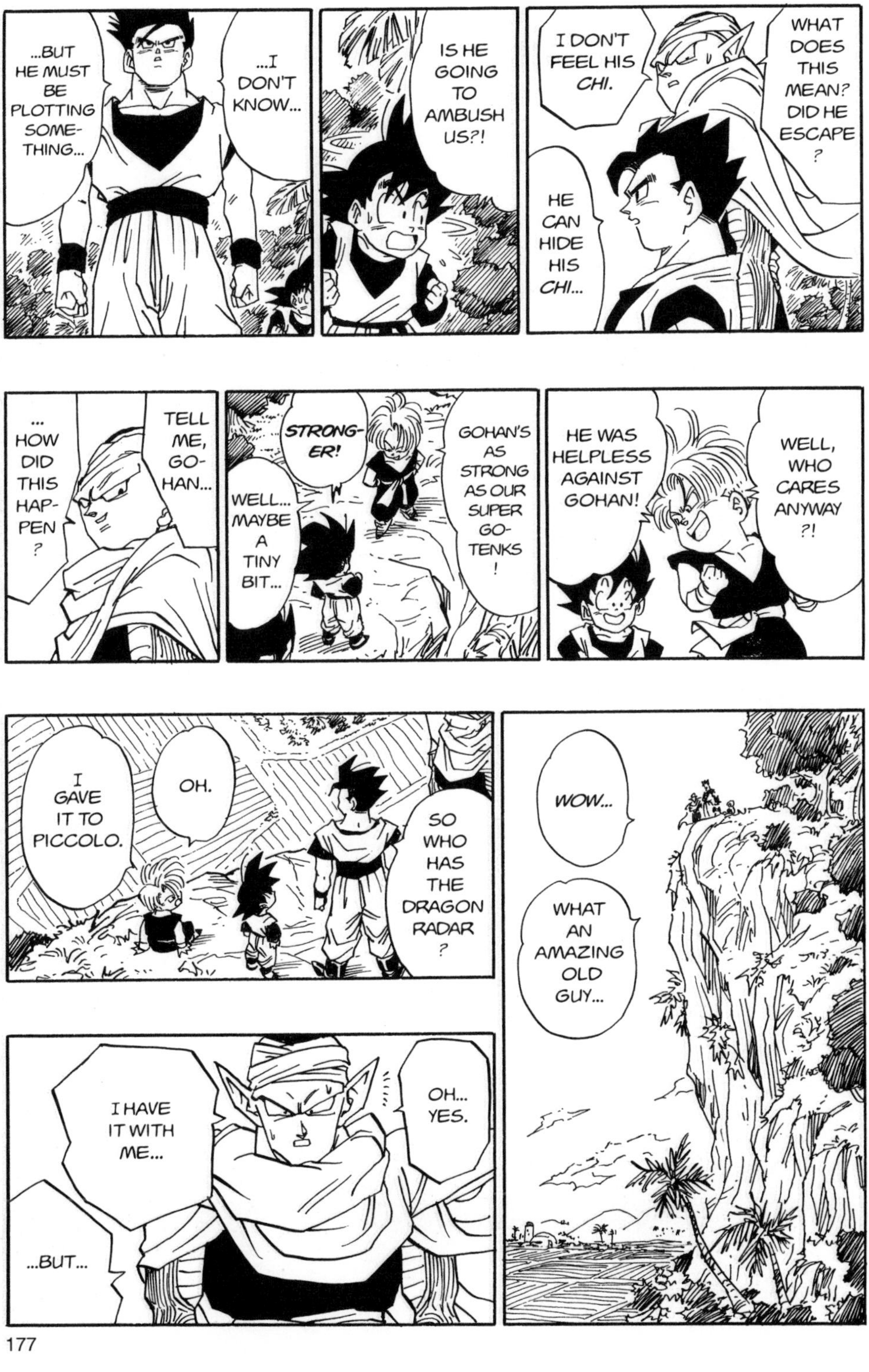
WHAT DOES THIS MEAN? DID HE ESCAPE?
I DON'T FEEL HIS *CHI*.
HE CAN HIDE HIS *CHI*...
IS HE GOING TO AMBUSH US?!
...I DON'T KNOW...
...BUT HE MUST BE PLOTTING SOMETHING...
WELL, WHO CARES ANYWAY?!
HE WAS HELPLESS AGAINST GOHAN!
GOHAN'S AS STRONG AS OUR SUPER GOTENKS!
STRONGER!
WELL... MAYBE A TINY BIT...
TELL ME, GOHAN...
...HOW DID THIS HAPPEN?
WOW...
WHAT AN AMAZING OLD GUY...
SO WHO HAS THE DRAGON RADAR?
OH.
I GAVE IT TO PICCOLO.
OH... YES.
I HAVE IT WITH ME...
...BUT...

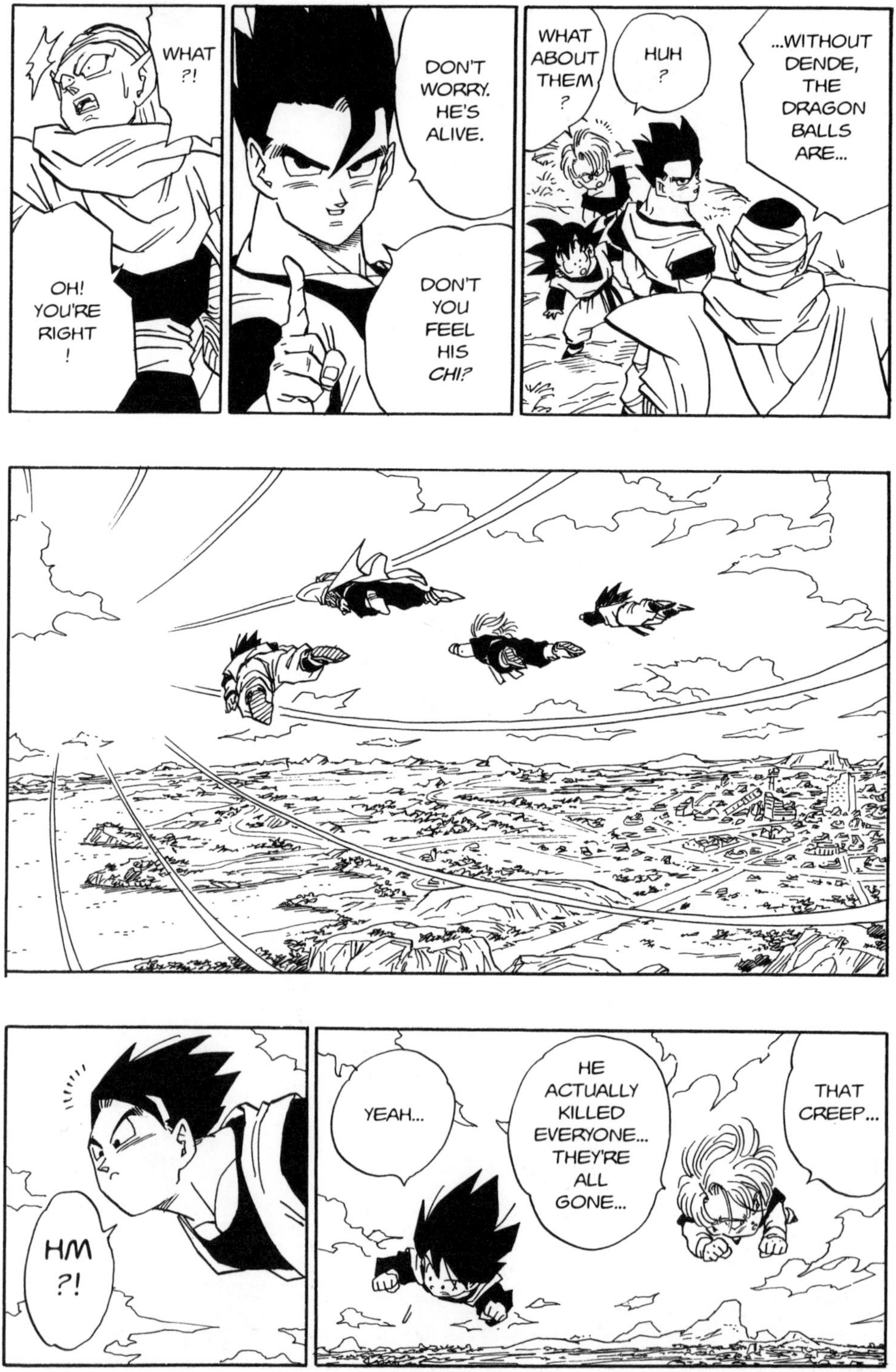
...WITHOUT DENDE, THE DRAGON BALLS ARE...
HUH?
WHAT ABOUT THEM?
DON'T WORRY. HE'S ALIVE.
DON'T YOU FEEL HIS *CHI*?
WHAT?!
OH! YOU'RE RIGHT!
THAT CREEP...
HE ACTUALLY KILLED EVERYONE... THEY'RE ALL GONE...
YEAH...
HM?!

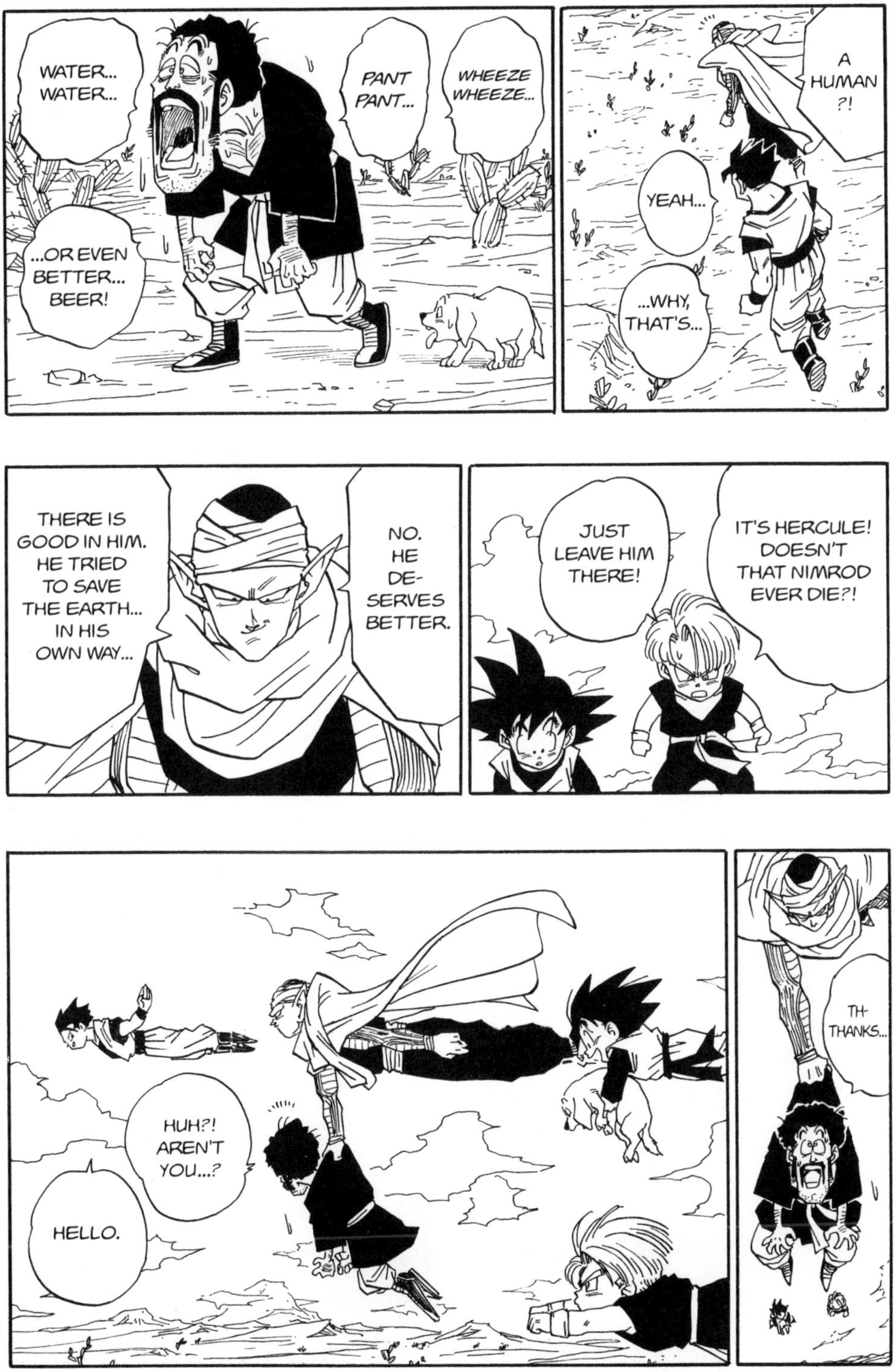
A HUMAN ?!
YEAH...
...WHY, THAT'S...
WHEEZE WHEEZE...
PANT PANT...
WATER... WATER...
...OR EVEN BETTER... BEER!
IT'S HERCULE! DOESN'T THAT NIMROD EVER DIE?!
JUST LEAVE HIM THERE!
NO. HE DE-SERVES BETTER.
THERE IS GOOD IN HIM. HE TRIED TO SAVE THE EARTH... IN HIS OWN WAY...
TH- THANKS...
HUH?! AREN'T YOU...?
HELLO.

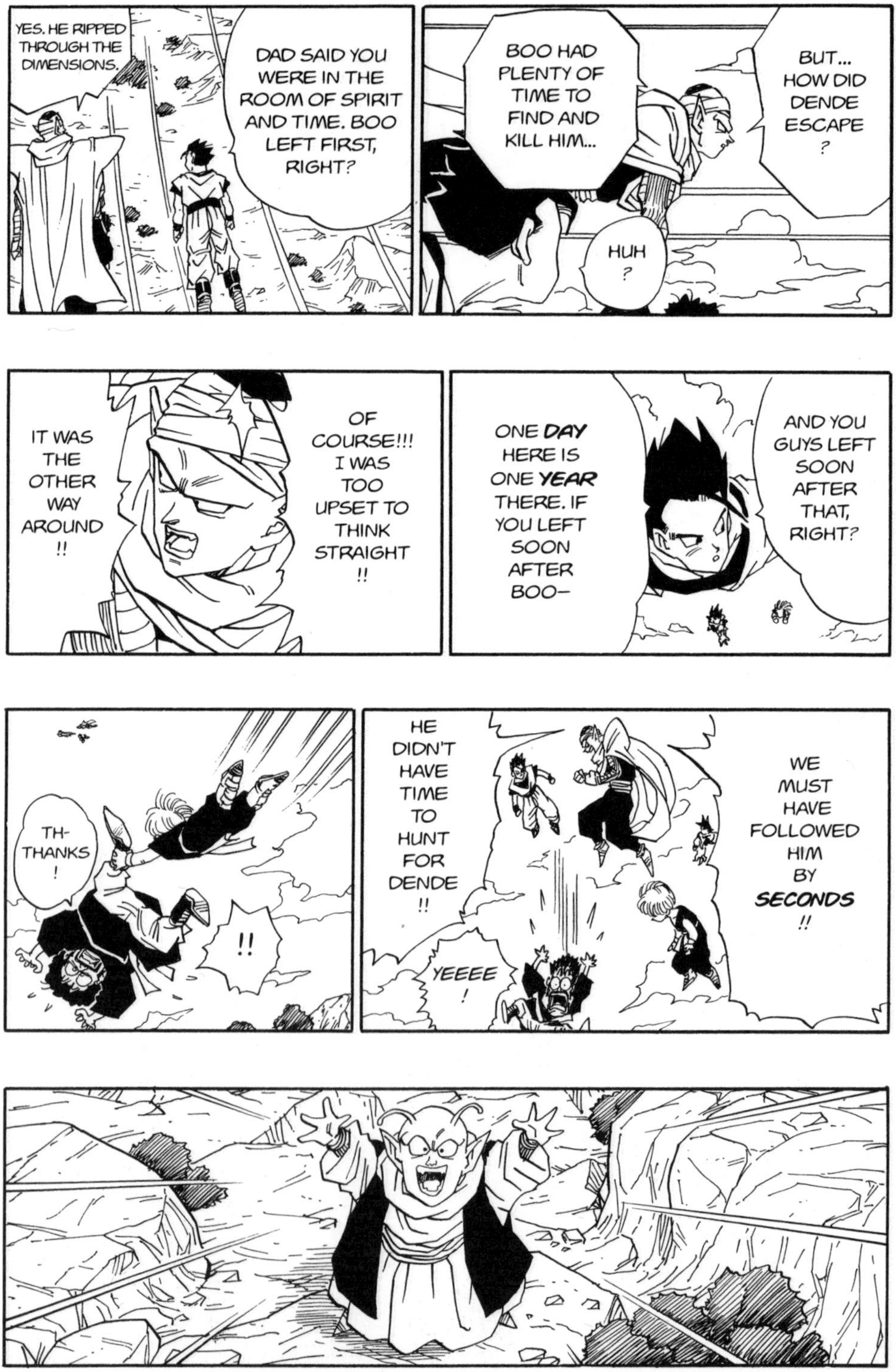
BUT... HOW DID DENDE ESCAPE?
BOO HAD PLENTY OF TIME TO FIND AND KILL HIM...
HUH?
DAD SAID YOU WERE IN THE ROOM OF SPIRIT AND TIME. BOO LEFT FIRST, RIGHT?
YES. HE RIPPED THROUGH THE DIMENSIONS.
AND YOU GUYS LEFT SOON AFTER THAT, RIGHT?
ONE **DAY** HERE IS ONE **YEAR** THERE. IF YOU LEFT SOON AFTER BOO—
OF COURSE!!! I WAS TOO UPSET TO THINK STRAIGHT!!
IT WAS THE OTHER WAY AROUND!!
WE MUST HAVE FOLLOWED HIM BY **SECONDS**!!
HE DIDN'T HAVE TIME TO HUNT FOR DENDE!!
YEEEE!
!!
TH-THANKS!

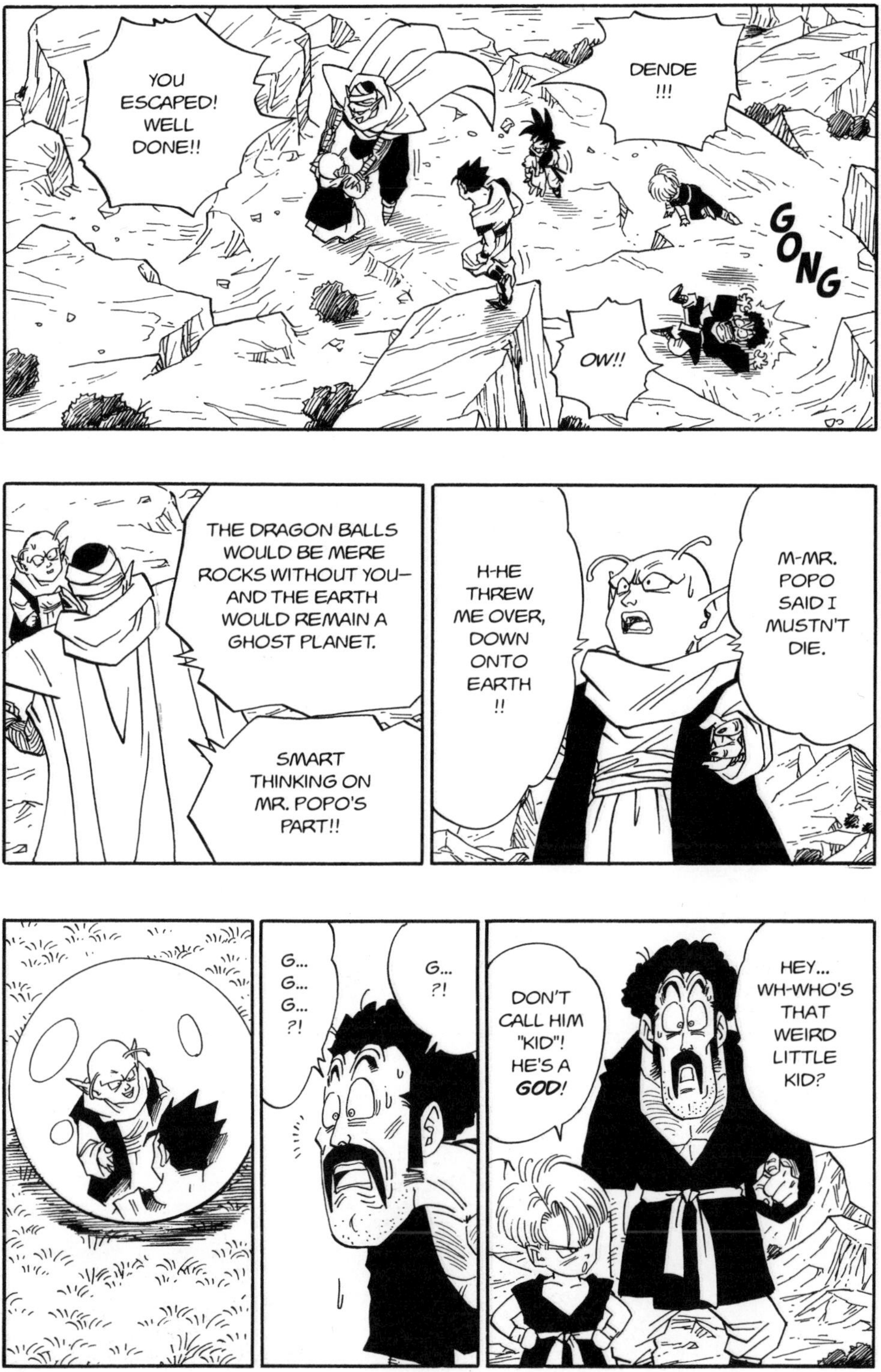
DENDE !!!
YOU ESCAPED! WELL DONE!!
GONG
OW!!
M-MR. POPO SAID I MUSTN'T DIE.
H-HE THREW ME OVER, DOWN ONTO EARTH !!
THE DRAGON BALLS WOULD BE MERE ROCKS WITHOUT YOU— AND THE EARTH WOULD REMAIN A GHOST PLANET.
SMART THINKING ON MR. POPO'S PART!!
HEY... WH-WHO'S THAT WEIRD LITTLE KID?
DON'T CALL HIM "KID"! HE'S A **GOD**!
G... ?!
G... G... G... ?!

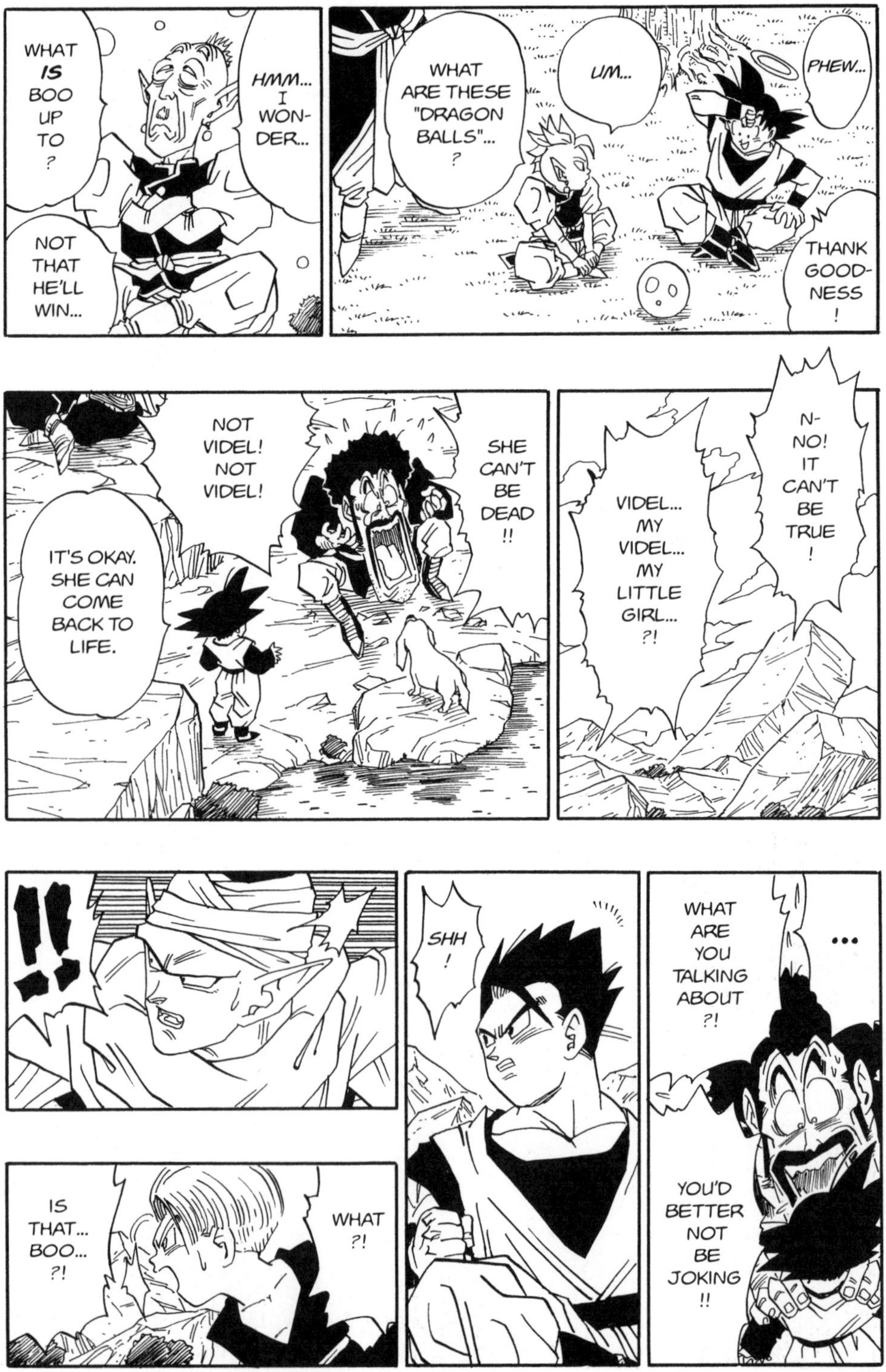
PHEW...
THANK GOODNESS!
UM...
WHAT ARE THESE "DRAGON BALLS"...?
HMM... I WONDER...
WHAT IS BOO UP TO?
NOT THAT HE'LL WIN...
N-NO! IT CAN'T BE TRUE!
VIDEL... MY VIDEL... MY LITTLE GIRL...?!
SHE CAN'T BE DEAD!!
NOT VIDEL! NOT VIDEL!
IT'S OKAY. SHE CAN COME BACK TO LIFE.
...
WHAT ARE YOU TALKING ABOUT?!
YOU'D BETTER NOT BE JOKING!!
SHH!
!!
WHAT?!
IS THAT... BOO...?!

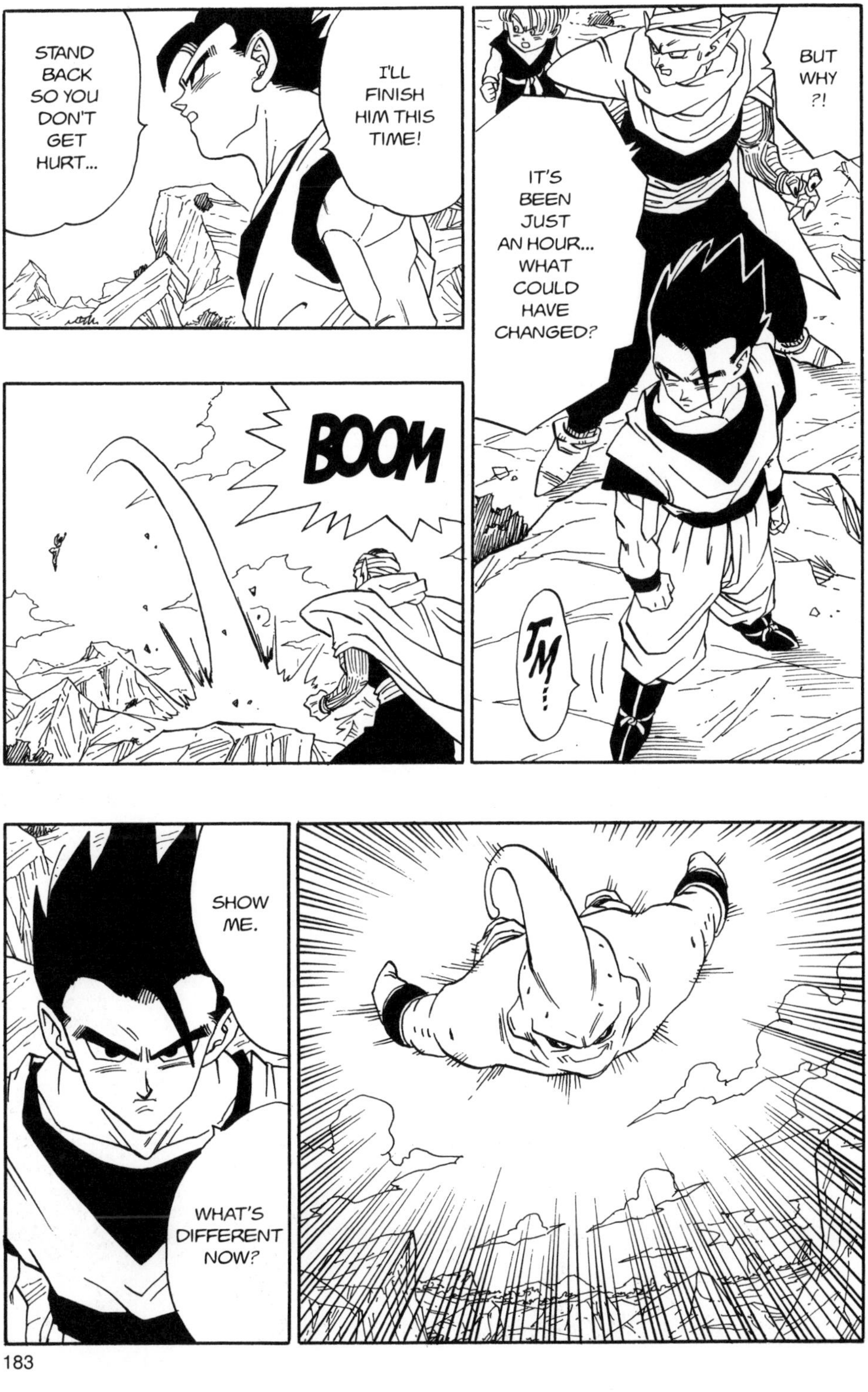
BUT WHY ?!
IT'S BEEN JUST AN HOUR... WHAT COULD HAVE CHANGED?
TM!
I'LL FINISH HIM THIS TIME!
STAND BACK SO YOU DON'T GET HURT...
BOOM
SHOW ME.
WHAT'S DIFFERENT NOW?

DBZ:305 • Ambush!

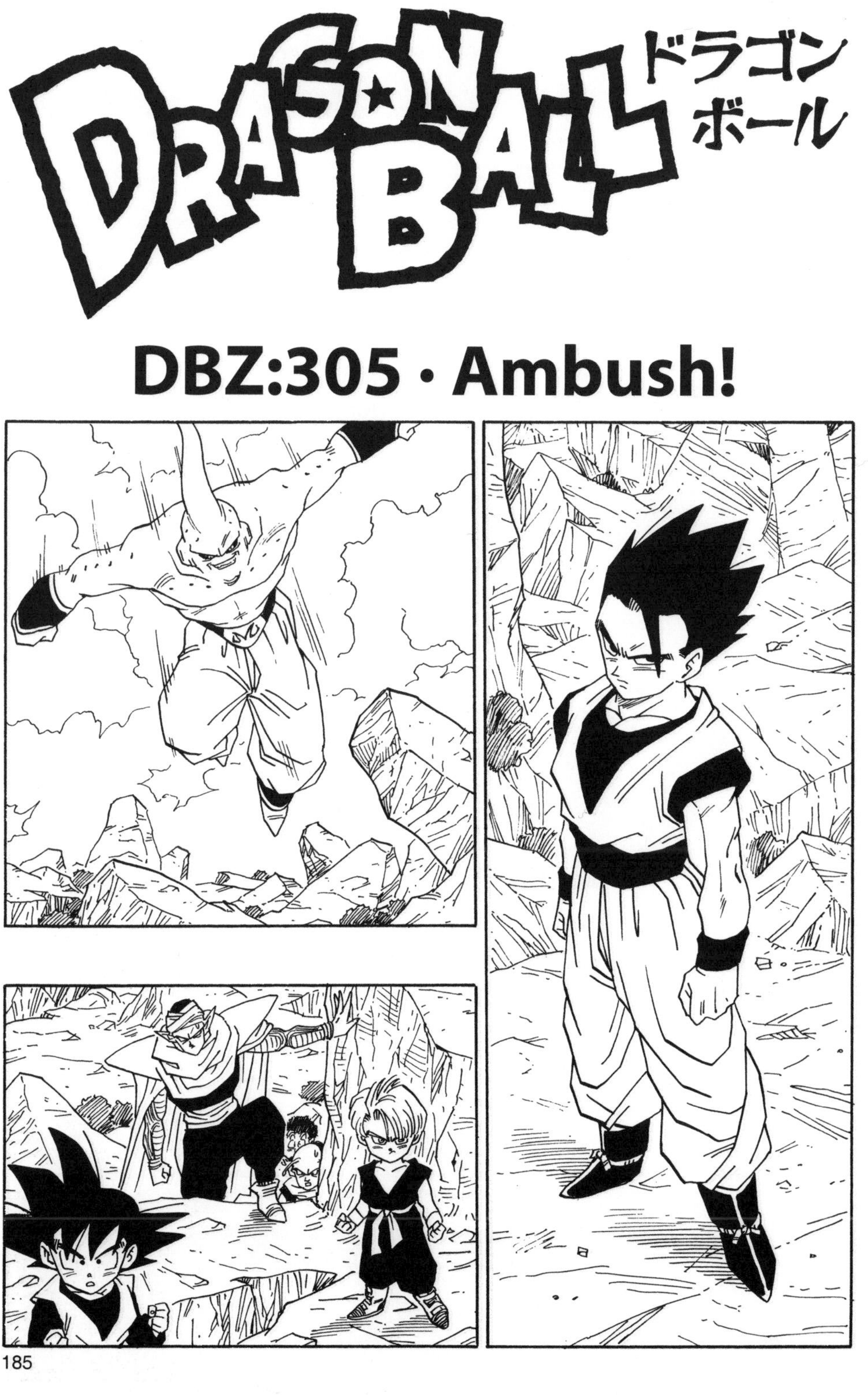

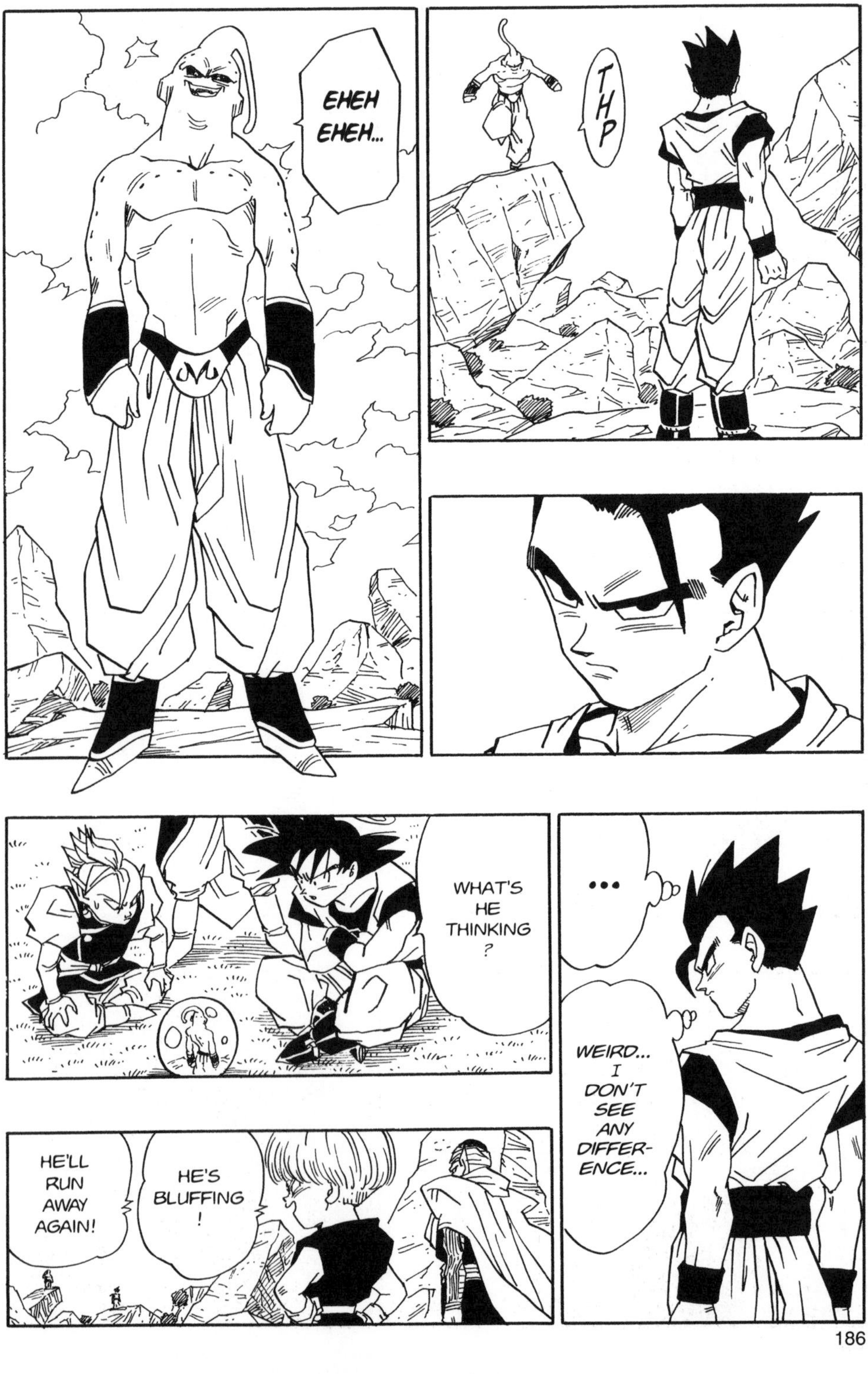
THP
EHEH EHEH...
...
WEIRD... I DON'T SEE ANY DIFFERENCE...
WHAT'S HE THINKING?
HE'S BLUFFING!
HE'LL RUN AWAY AGAIN!

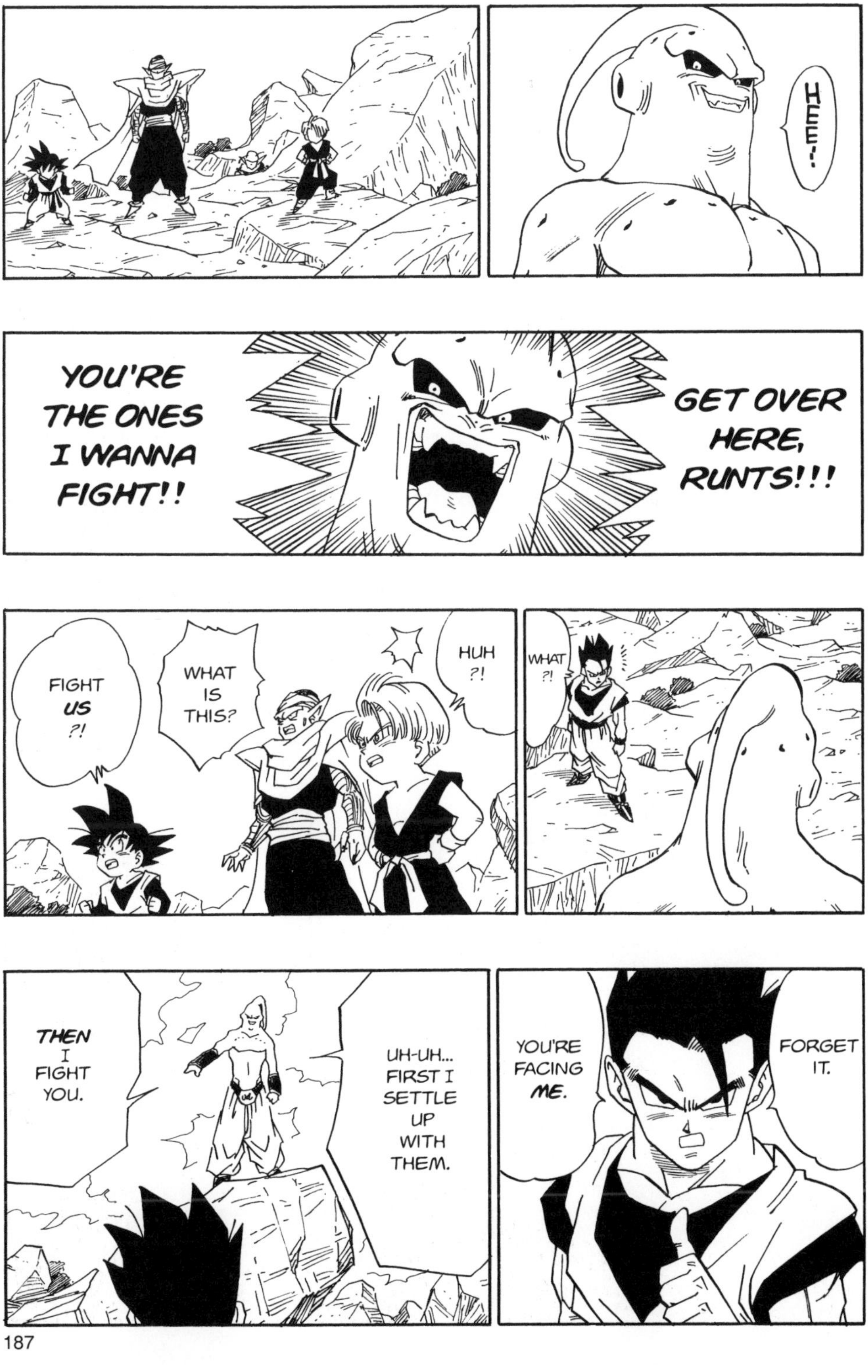
HEE!!
GET OVER HERE, RUNTS!!!
YOU'RE THE ONES I WANNA FIGHT!!
WHAT ?!
HUH ?!
WHAT IS THIS?
FIGHT US ?!
FORGET IT.
YOU'RE FACING ME.
UH-UH... FIRST I SETTLE UP WITH THEM.
THEN I FIGHT YOU.

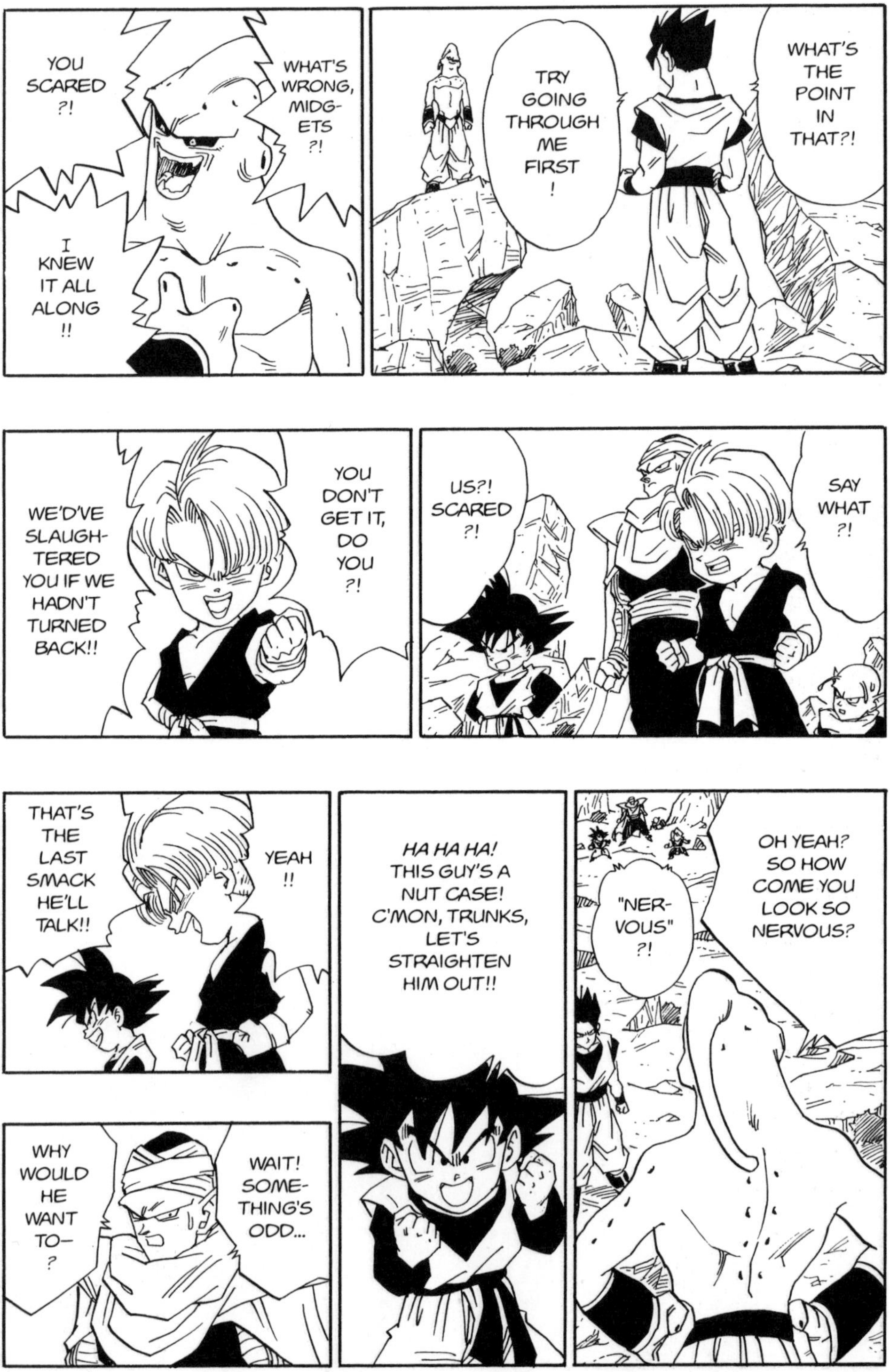
WHAT'S THE POINT IN THAT?!
TRY GOING THROUGH ME FIRST!
WHAT'S WRONG, MIDGETS?!
YOU SCARED?!
I KNEW IT ALL ALONG!!
SAY WHAT?!
US?! SCARED?!
YOU DON'T GET IT, DO YOU?!
WE'D'VE SLAUGHTERED YOU IF WE HADN'T TURNED BACK!!
OH YEAH? SO HOW COME YOU LOOK SO NERVOUS?
"NERVOUS"?!
HA HA HA! THIS GUY'S A NUT CASE! C'MON, TRUNKS, LET'S STRAIGHTEN HIM OUT!!
YEAH!!
THAT'S THE LAST SMACK HE'LL TALK!!
WAIT! SOMETHING'S ODD...
WHY WOULD HE WANT TO–?

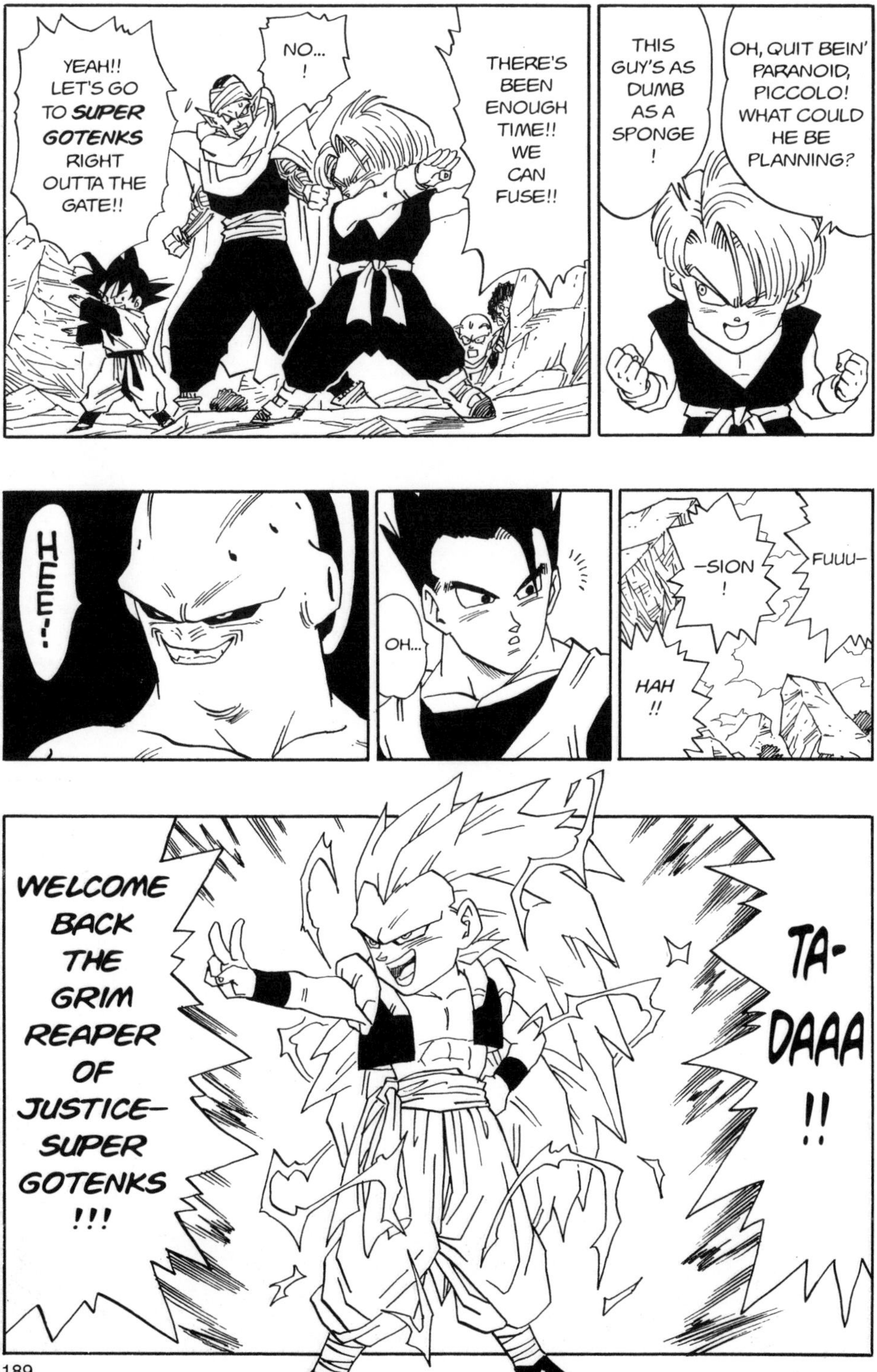
OH, QUIT BEIN' PARANOID, PICCOLO! WHAT COULD HE BE PLANNING?
THIS GUY'S AS DUMB AS A SPONGE!
THERE'S BEEN ENOUGH TIME!! WE CAN FUSE!!
NO...!
YEAH!! LET'S GO TO SUPER GOTENKS RIGHT OUTTA THE GATE!!
FUUU-
-SION!
HAH!!
OH...
HEE!!
TA-DAAA!!
WELCOME BACK THE GRIM REAPER OF JUSTICE—SUPER GOTENKS!!!

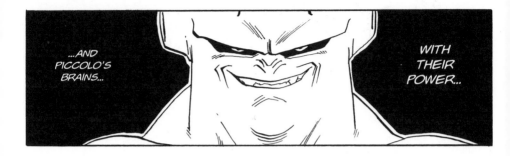

WITH THEIR POWER...
...AND PICCOLO'S BRAINS...
WAIT!
FOOLS!!
BM
TP
BLP...
ZLUP...
LET ME HANDLE THIS!
JUST TAKE A SEAT AND WATCH, GOHAN!
OKAY, BUT...
...BE CAREFUL.
ZUU---

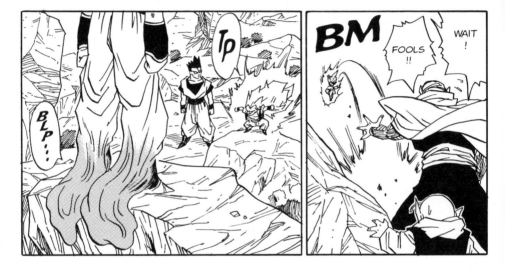

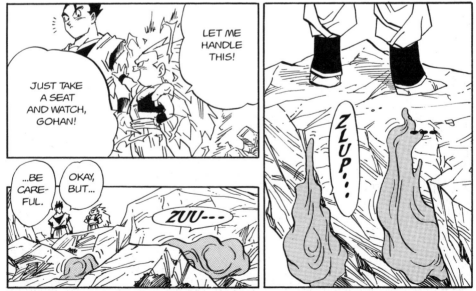

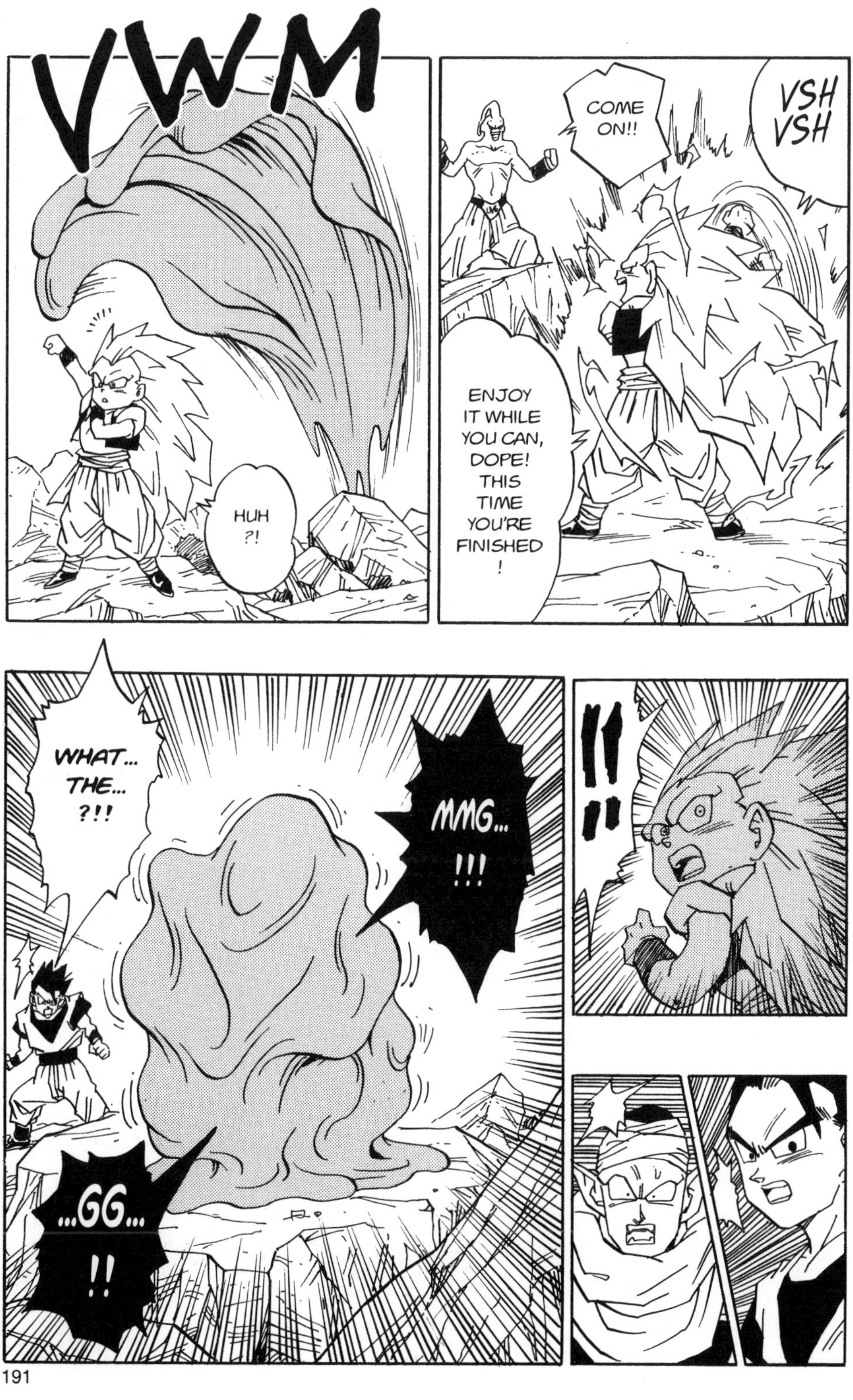
VSH VSH
COME ON!!
ENJOY IT WHILE YOU CAN, DOPE! THIS TIME YOU'RE FINISHED!
VWM
HUH ?!
!!
MMG... !!!
WHAT... THE... ?!!
...GG... !!

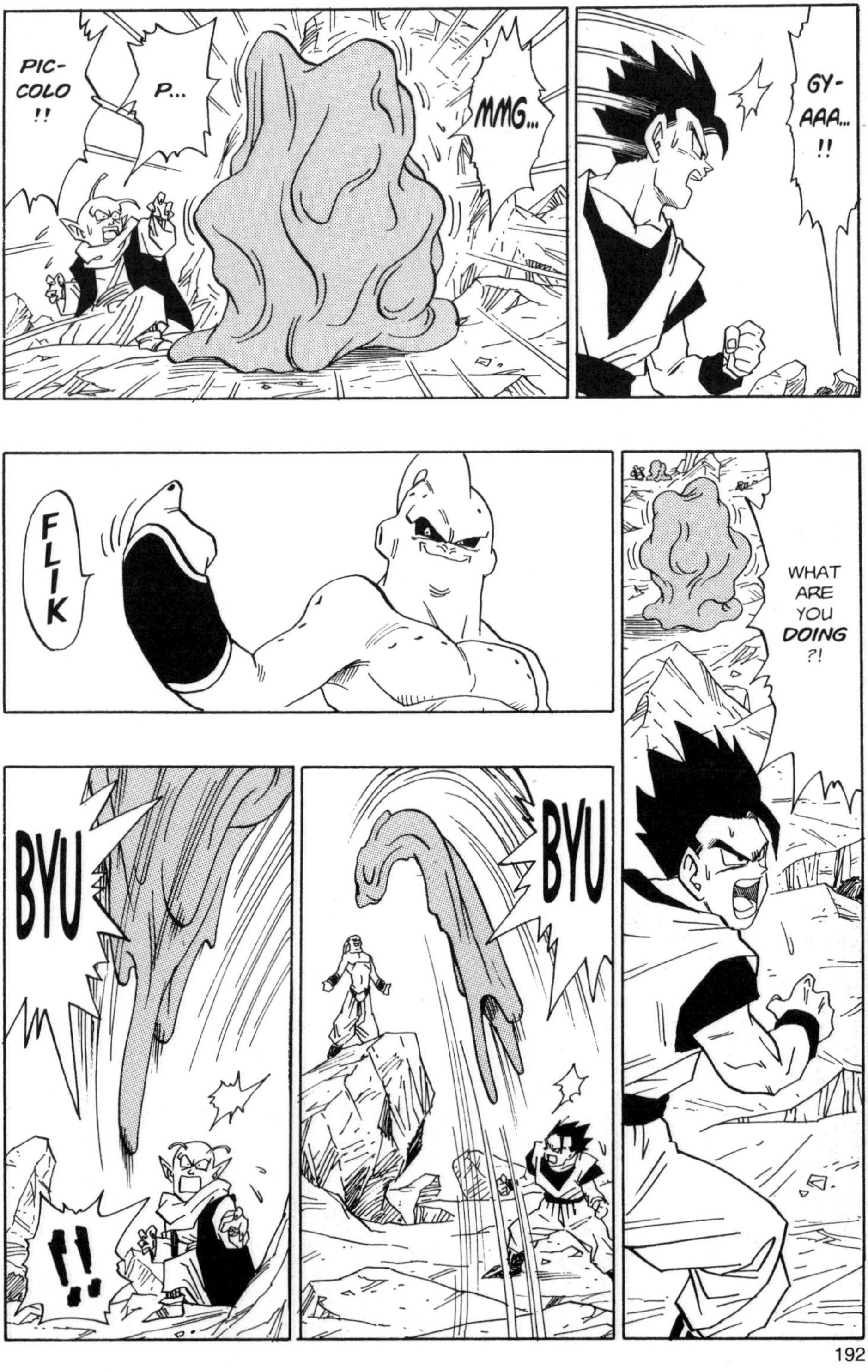
GY-AAA...!!
MMG...
P...
PIC-COLO!!
WHAT ARE YOU **DOING** ?!
FLIK
BYU
BYU
!!

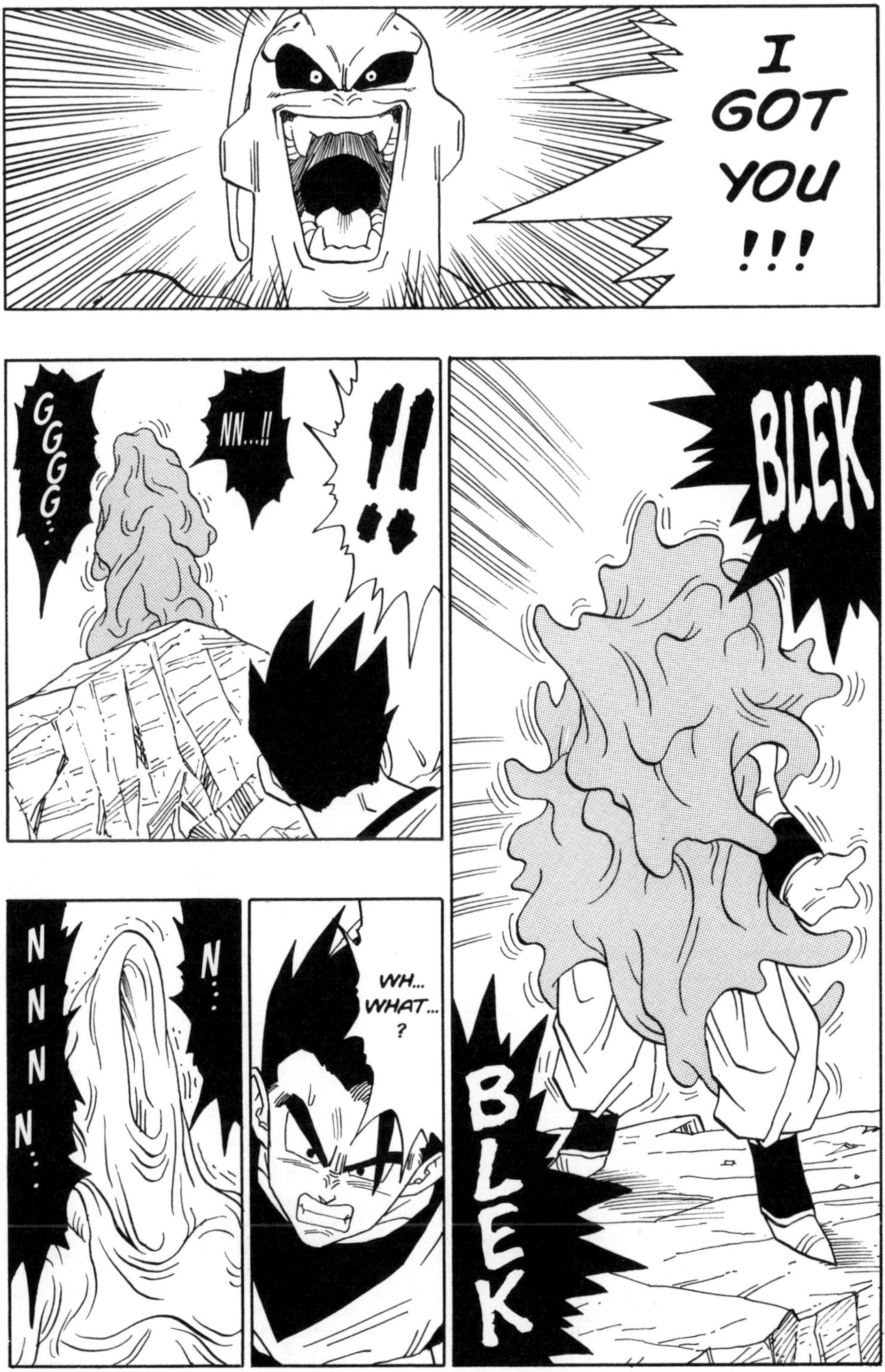
I GOT YOU !!!
BLEK
BLEK
NN...!!
GGGG...
!!
WH... WHAT... ?
N...
NNNN...

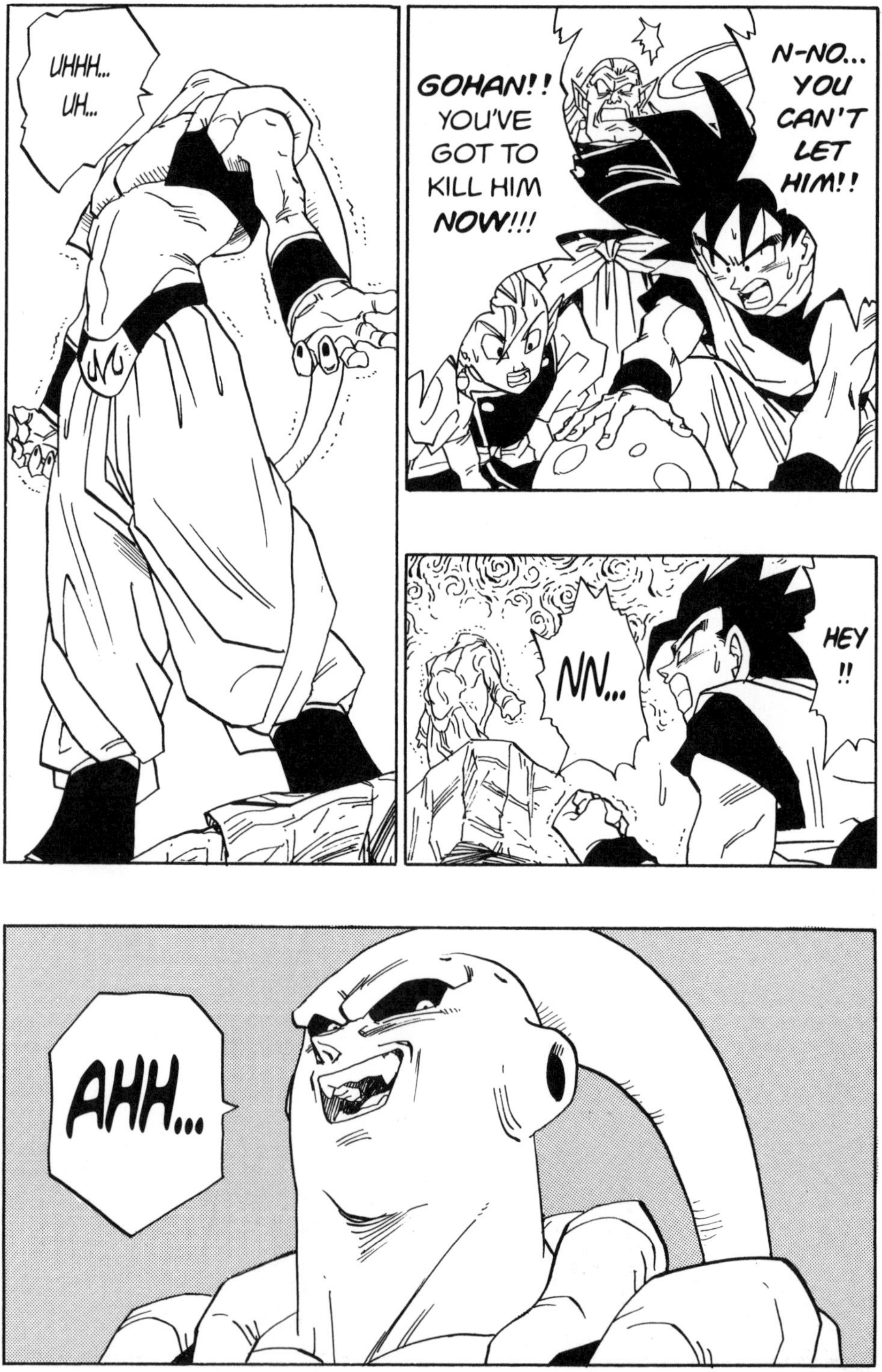
N-NO... YOU CAN'T LET HIM!!
GOHAN!! YOU'VE GOT TO KILL HIM NOW!!!
HEY !!
NN...
UHHH... UH...
AHH...

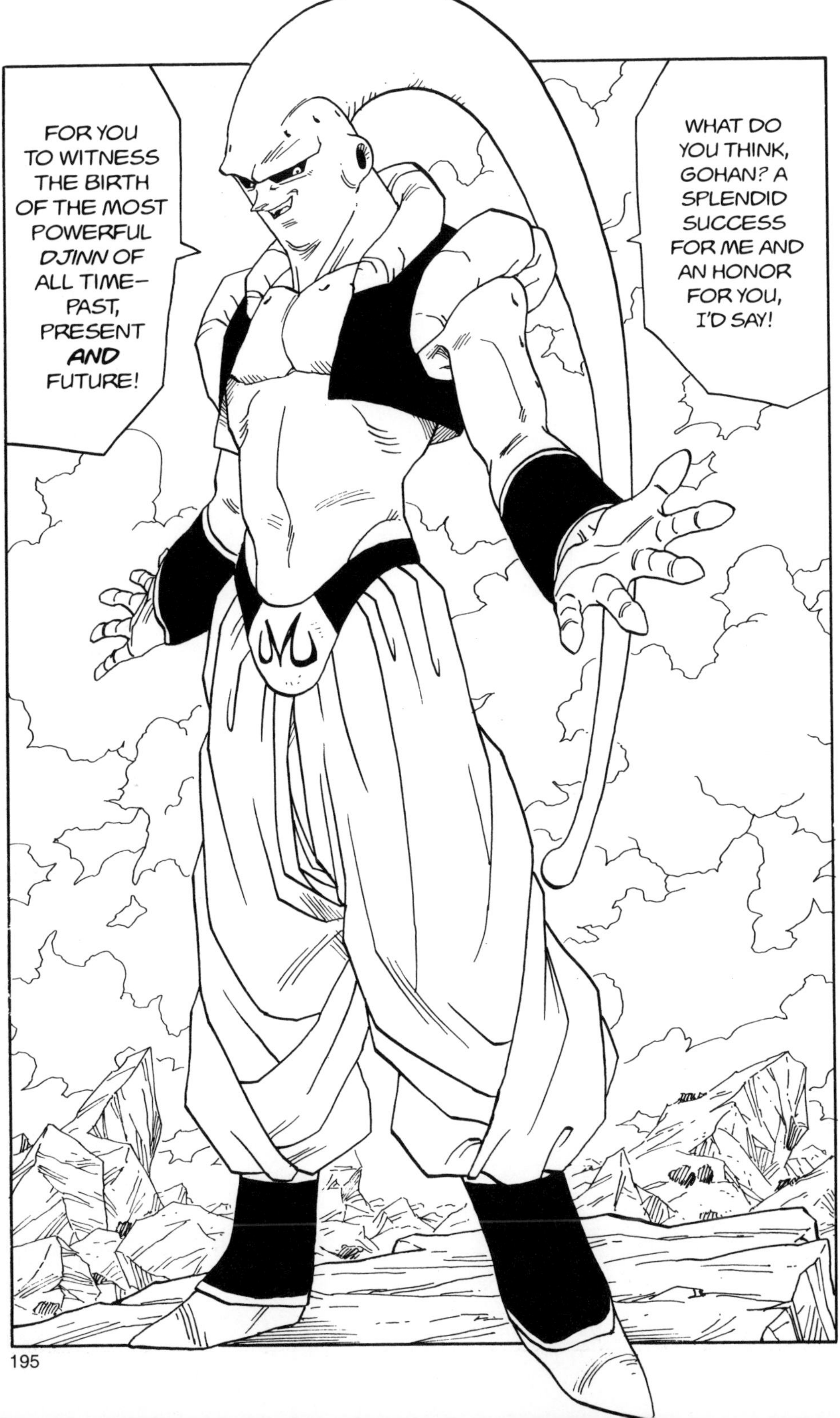
WHAT DO YOU THINK, GOHAN? A SPLENDID SUCCESS FOR ME AND AN HONOR FOR YOU, I'D SAY!
FOR YOU TO WITNESS THE BIRTH OF THE MOST POWERFUL DJINN OF ALL TIME– PAST, PRESENT **AND** FUTURE!

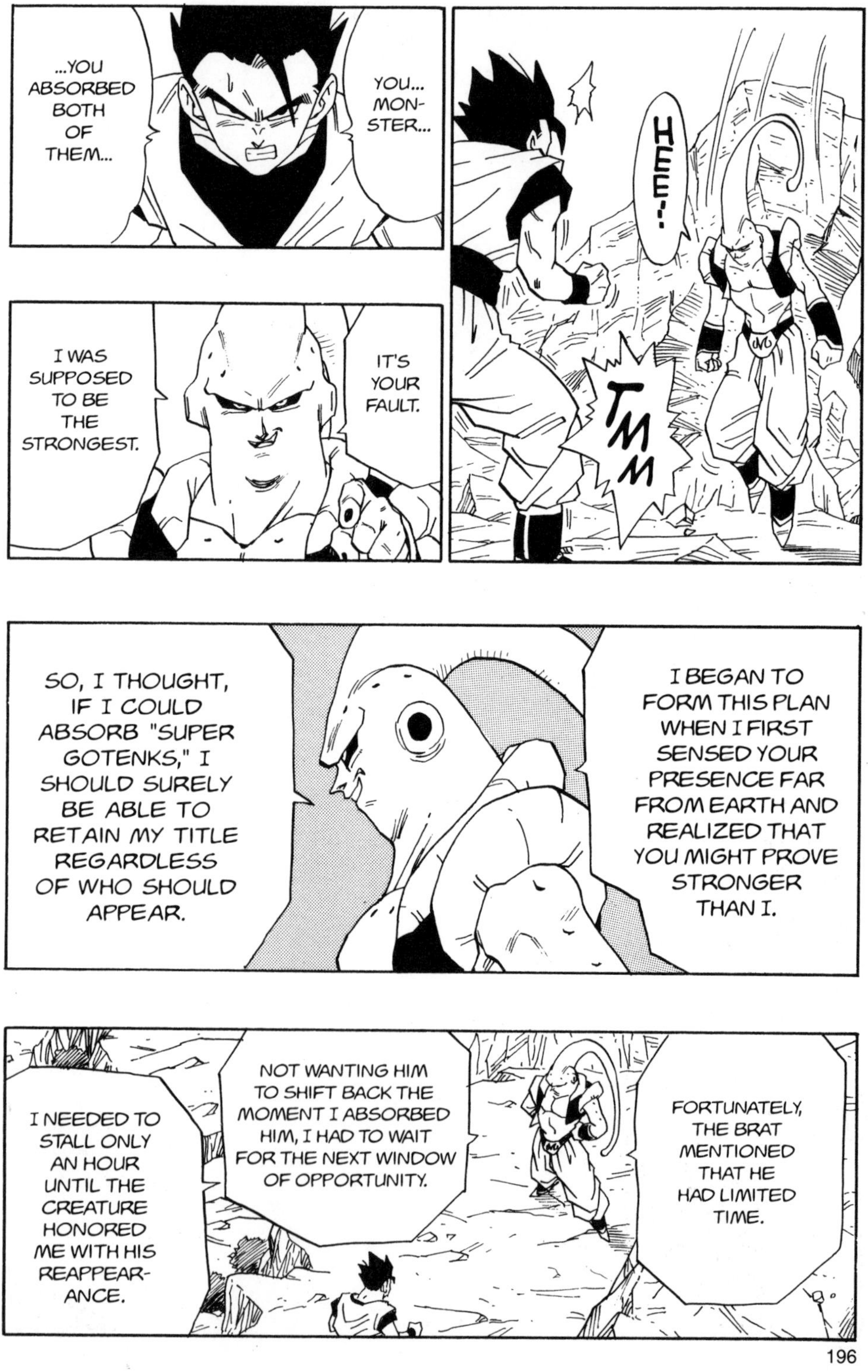
HEE!!
TMM
YOU... MON-STER...
...YOU ABSORBED BOTH OF THEM...
IT'S YOUR FAULT.
I WAS SUPPOSED TO BE THE STRONGEST.
I BEGAN TO FORM THIS PLAN WHEN I FIRST SENSED YOUR PRESENCE FAR FROM EARTH AND REALIZED THAT YOU MIGHT PROVE STRONGER THAN I.
SO, I THOUGHT, IF I COULD ABSORB "SUPER GOTENKS," I SHOULD SURELY BE ABLE TO RETAIN MY TITLE REGARDLESS OF WHO SHOULD APPEAR.
FORTUNATELY, THE BRAT MENTIONED THAT HE HAD LIMITED TIME.
NOT WANTING HIM TO SHIFT BACK THE MOMENT I ABSORBED HIM, I HAD TO WAIT FOR THE NEXT WINDOW OF OPPORTUNITY.
I NEEDED TO STALL ONLY AN HOUR UNTIL THE CREATURE HONORED ME WITH HIS REAPPEAR-ANCE.

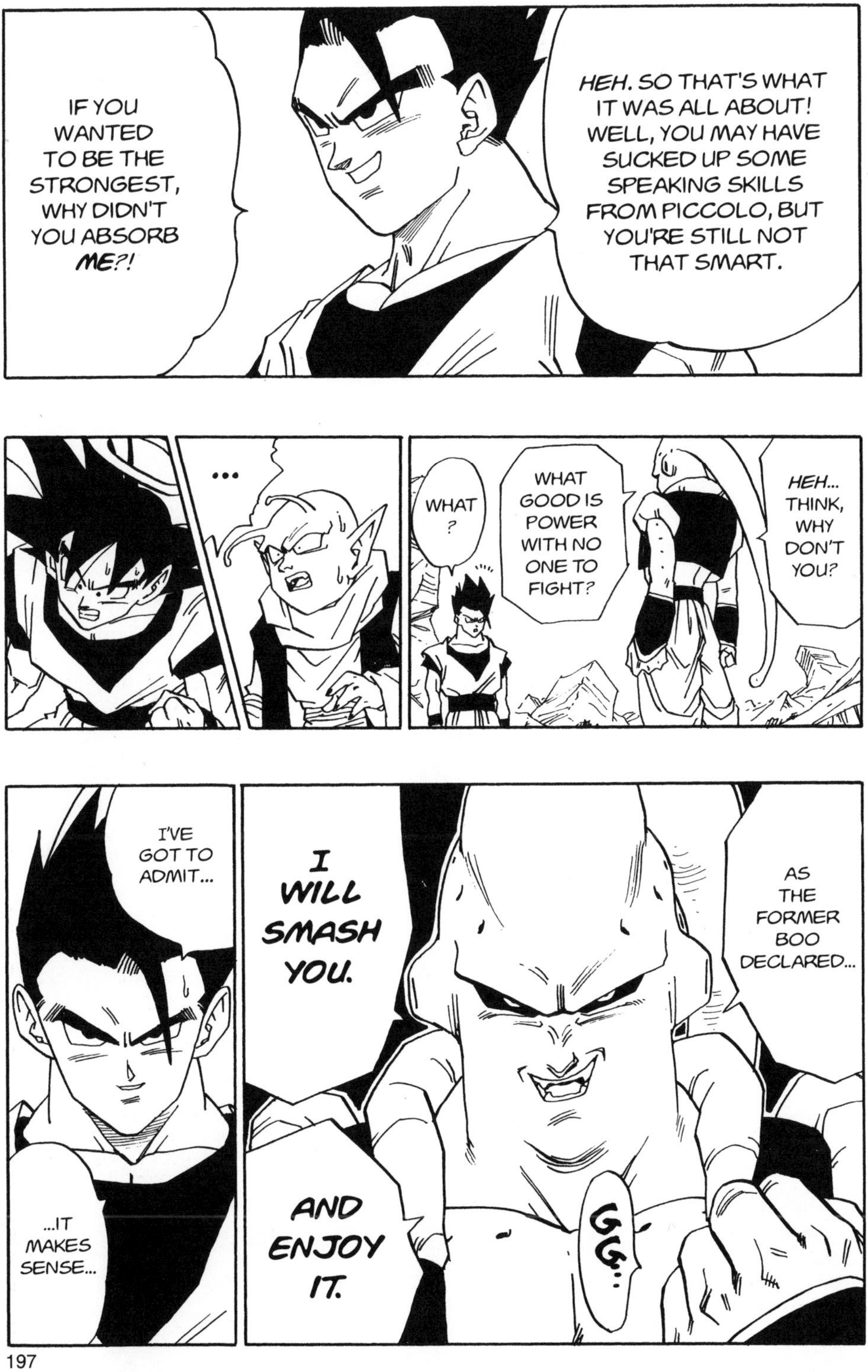
HEH. SO THAT'S WHAT IT WAS ALL ABOUT! WELL, YOU MAY HAVE SUCKED UP SOME SPEAKING SKILLS FROM PICCOLO, BUT YOU'RE STILL NOT THAT SMART.
IF YOU WANTED TO BE THE STRONGEST, WHY DIDN'T YOU ABSORB ME?!
HEH... THINK, WHY DON'T YOU?
WHAT GOOD IS POWER WITH NO ONE TO FIGHT?
WHAT?
...
AS THE FORMER BOO DECLARED...
I WILL SMASH YOU.
AND ENJOY IT.
GG..
I'VE GOT TO ADMIT...
...IT MAKES SENSE...

DRAGON BALL ドラゴンボール

DBZ:306 • A Turn of the Tables

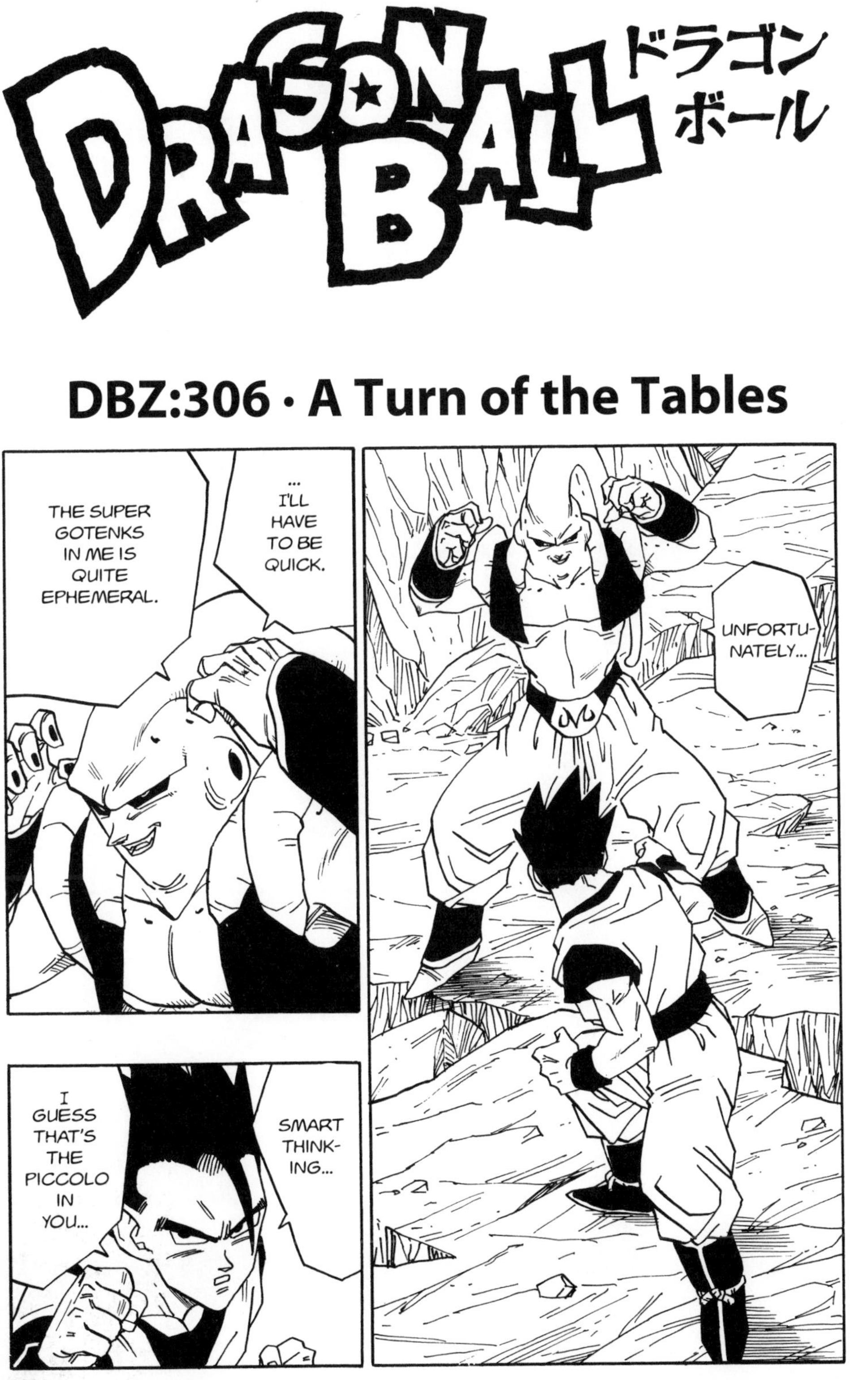
UNFORTU-NATELY...
... I'LL HAVE TO BE QUICK.
THE SUPER GOTENKS IN ME IS QUITE EPHEMERAL.
SMART THINK-ING...
I GUESS THAT'S THE PICCOLO IN YOU...

SHAH!!!!!
WHK
!!
UNH!!!
WHK
RRR...!!
VNN--

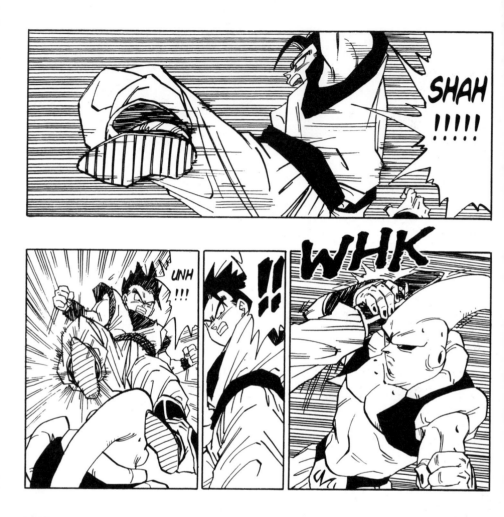

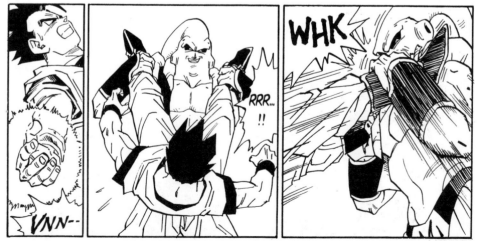

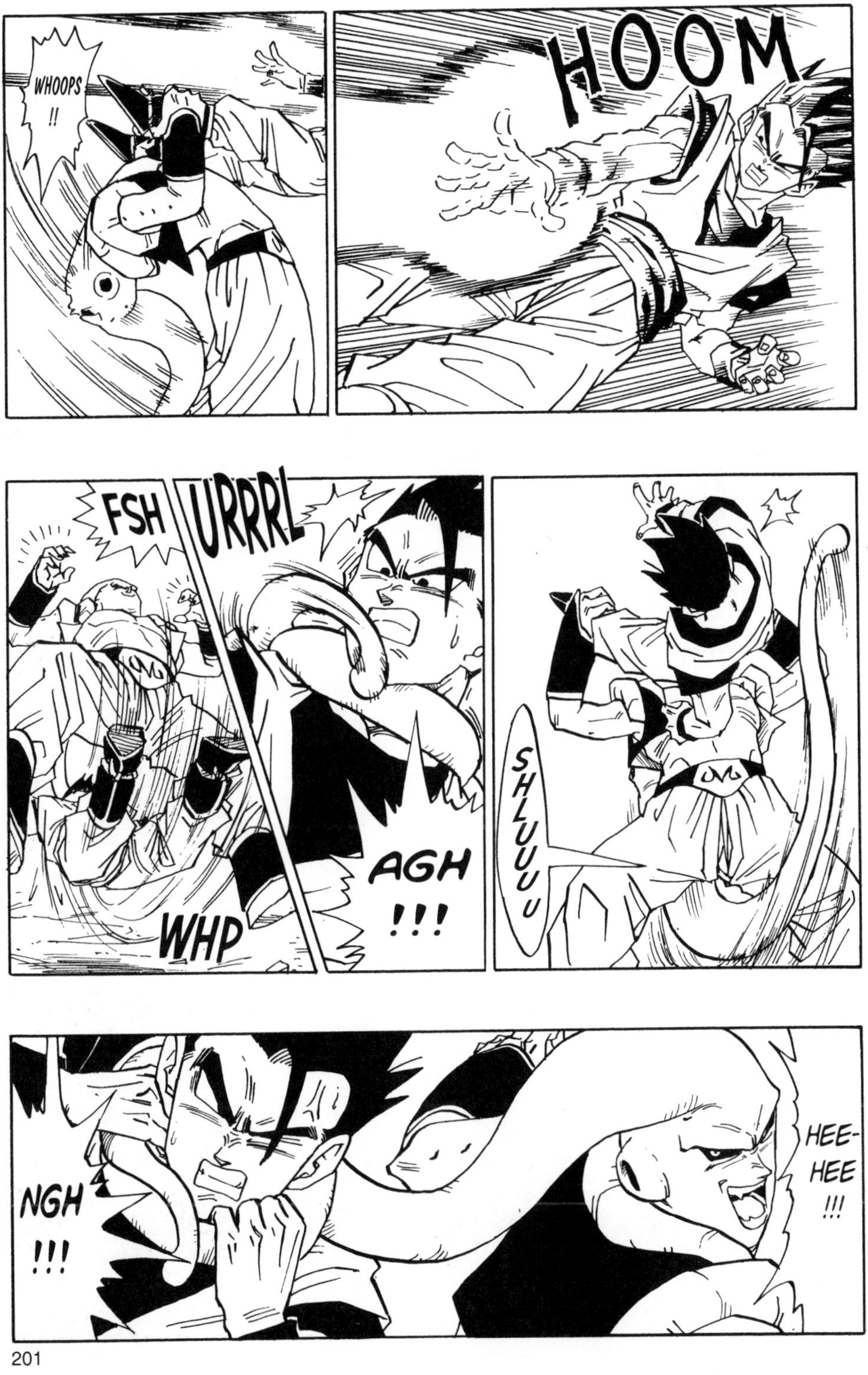

HOOM
WHOOPS !!
SHLUUUU
URRRL
AGH !!!
FSH
WHP
HEE-HEE !!!
NGH !!!

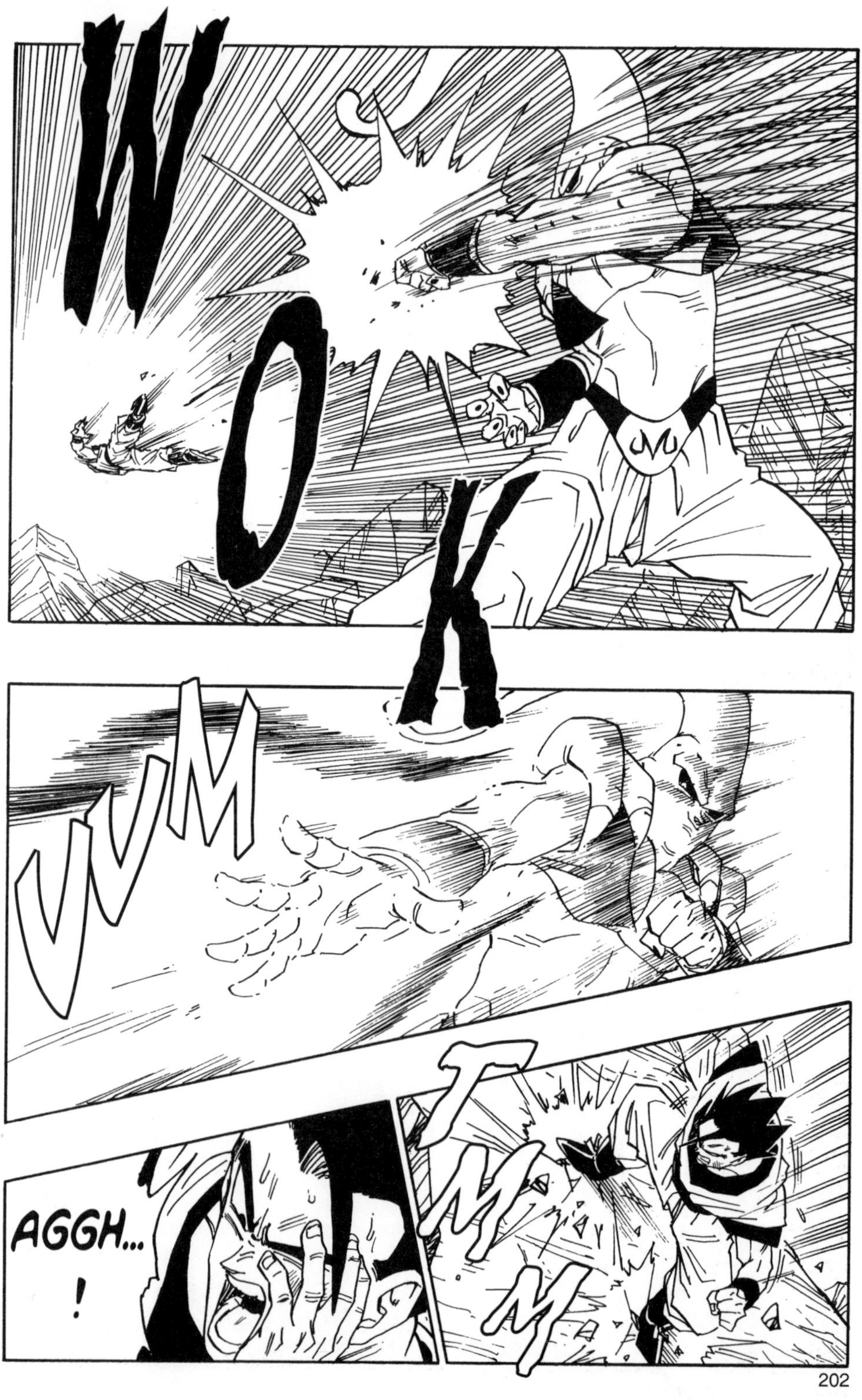
WOK
VUM
TMM
AGGH...
!

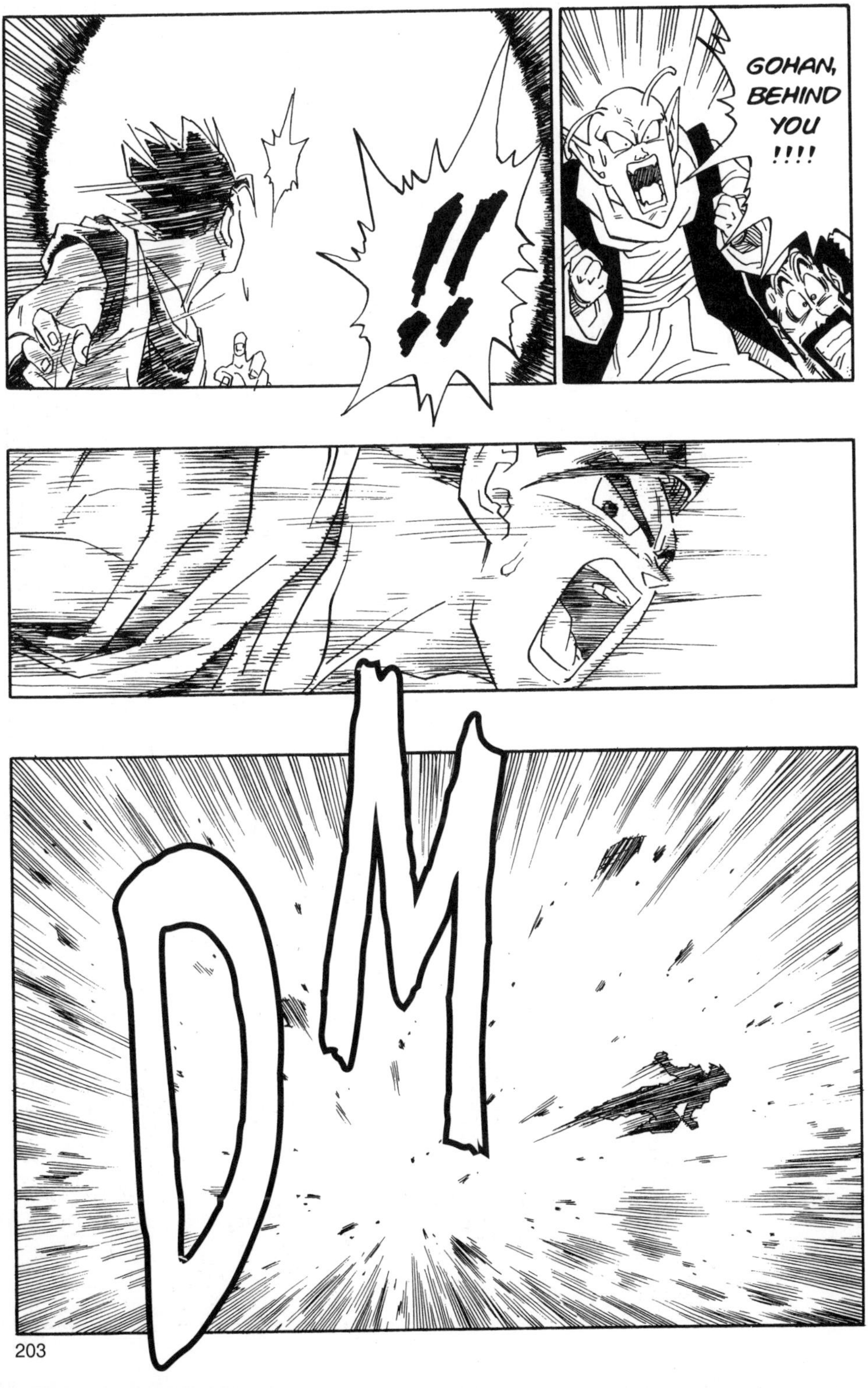
GOHAN, BEHIND YOU !!!!
!!
DM

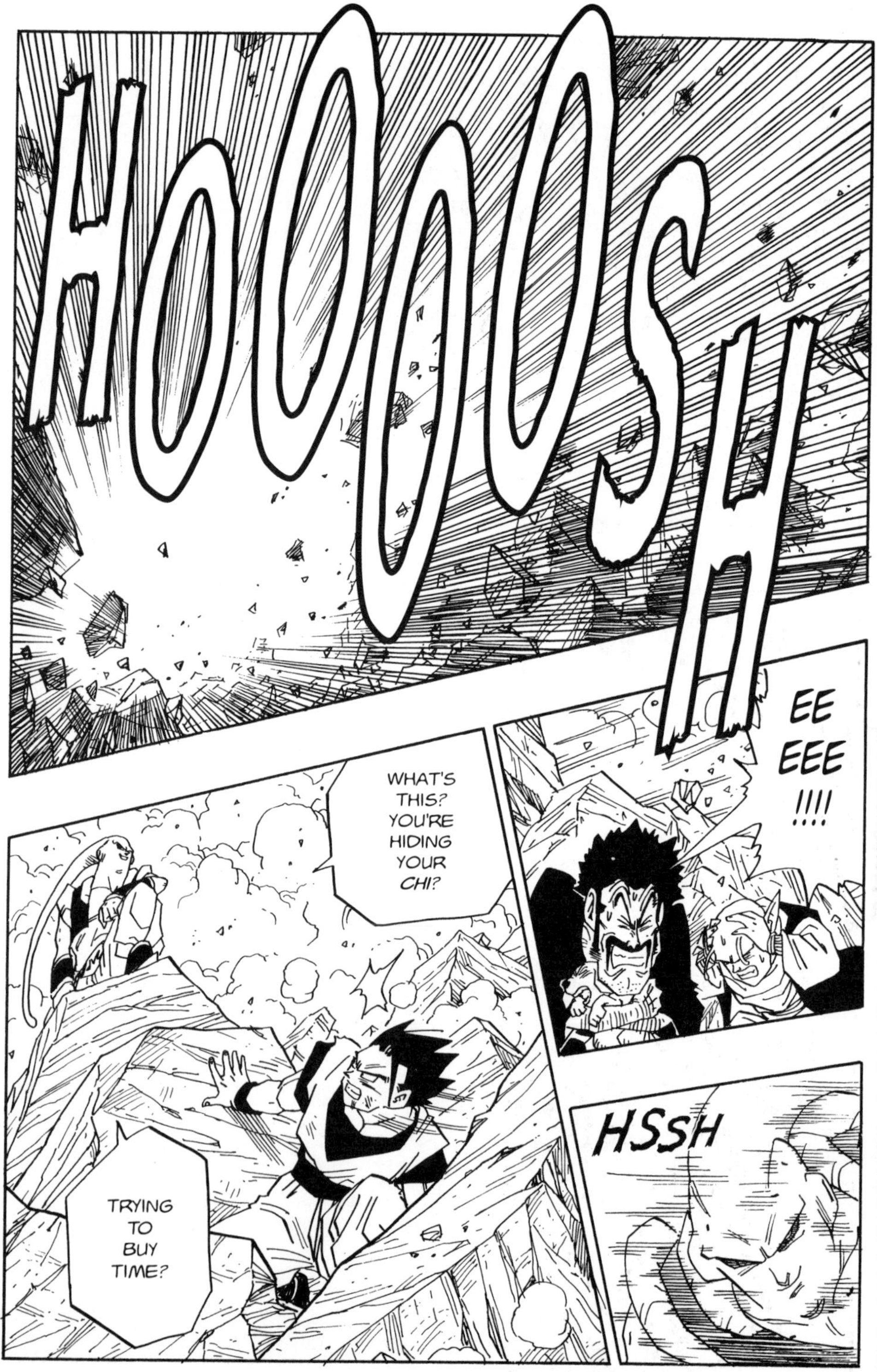
HOOOOSH
EE EEE !!!!
HSSH
WHAT'S THIS? YOU'RE HIDING YOUR CHI?
TRYING TO BUY TIME?

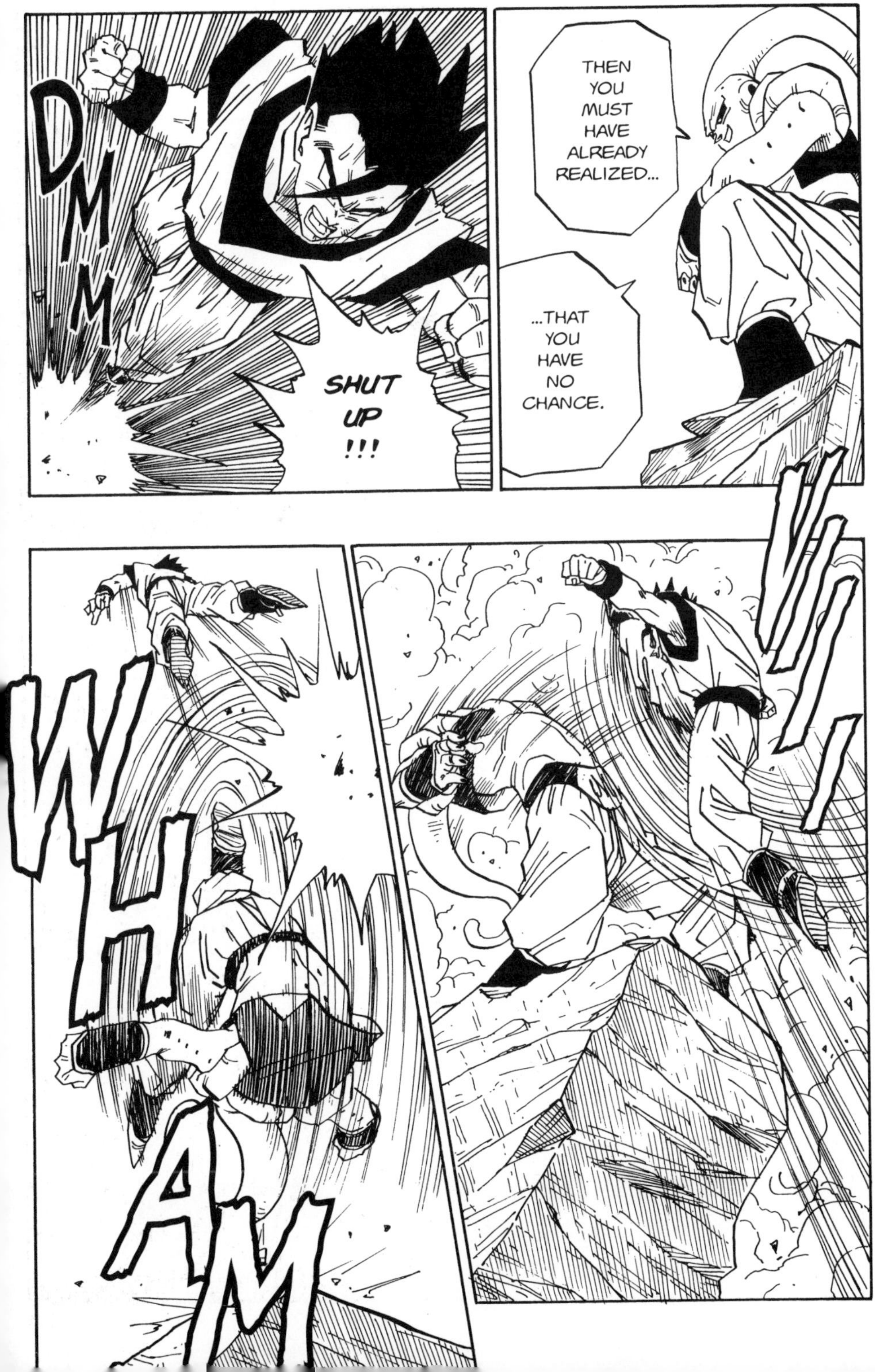
THEN YOU MUST HAVE ALREADY REALIZED...
...THAT YOU HAVE NO CHANCE.
DMMM
SHUT UP!!!
WHAM

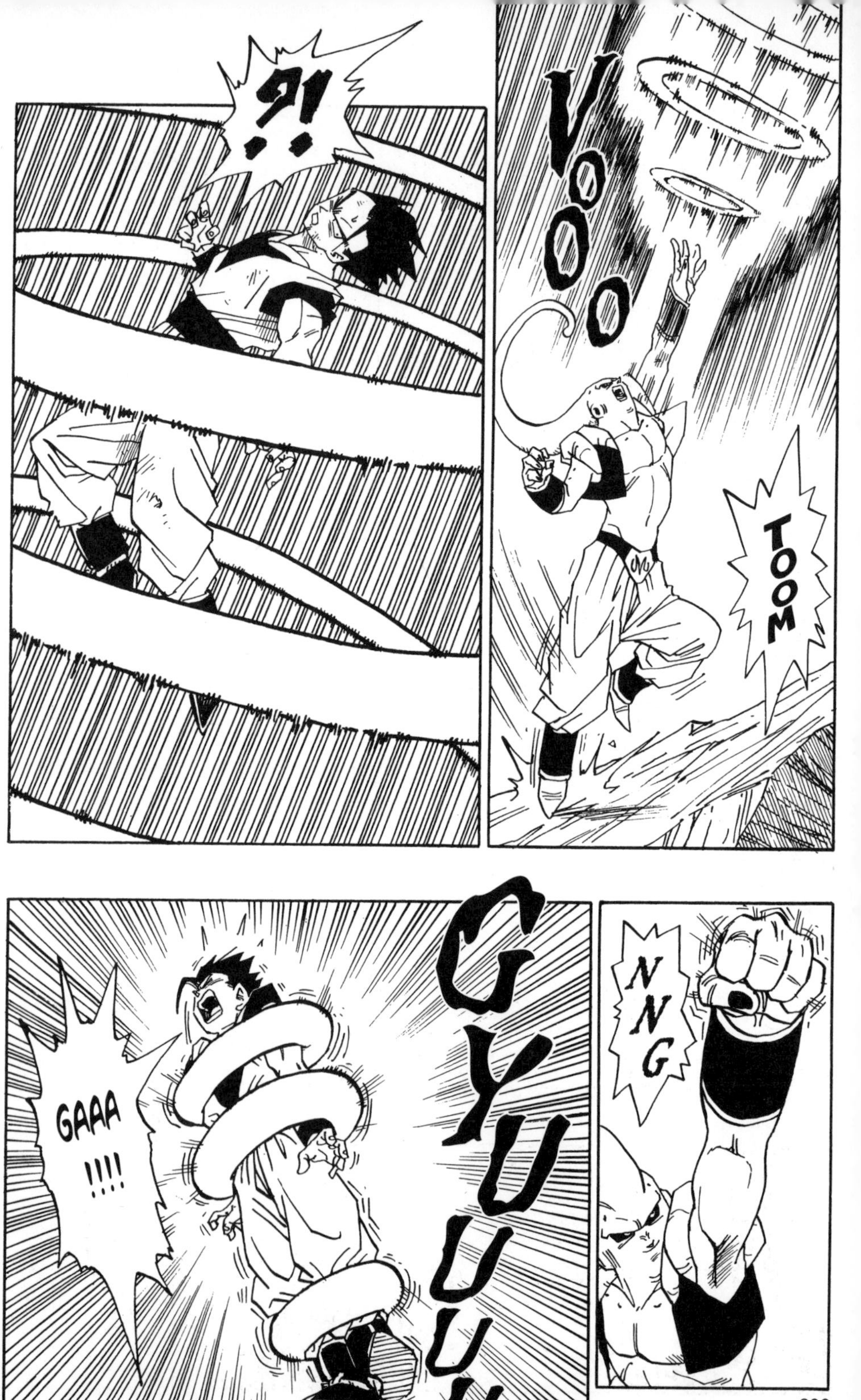
VOOOO
TOOM
?!
NNG
GYUUUU
GAAA !!!!

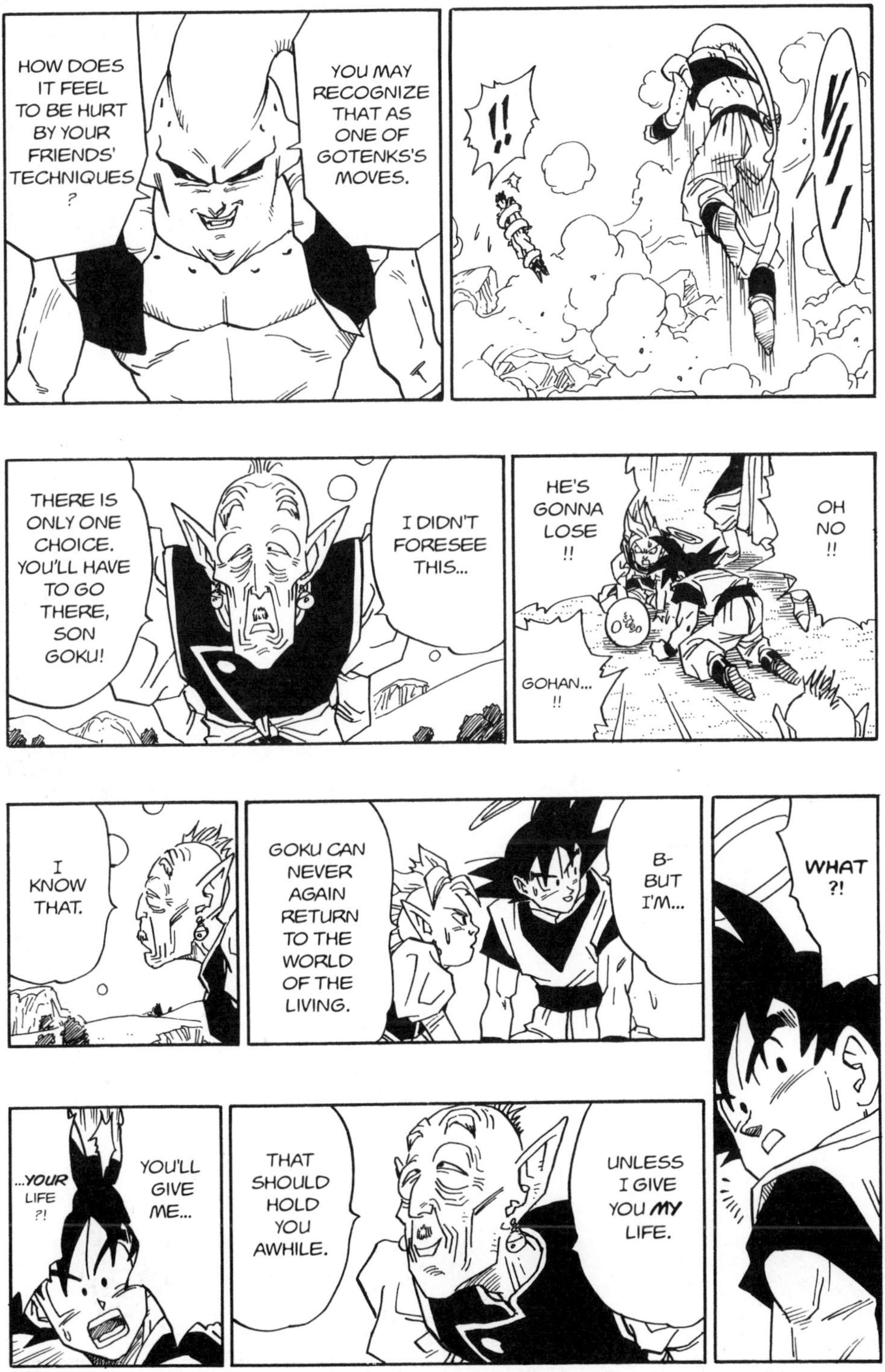

!!
YOU MAY RECOGNIZE THAT AS ONE OF GOTENKS'S MOVES.
HOW DOES IT FEEL TO BE HURT BY YOUR FRIENDS' TECHNIQUES ?
OH NO !!
HE'S GONNA LOSE !!
GOHAN... !!
I DIDN'T FORESEE THIS...
THERE IS ONLY ONE CHOICE. YOU'LL HAVE TO GO THERE, SON GOKU!
WHAT ?!
B- BUT I'M...
GOKU CAN NEVER AGAIN RETURN TO THE WORLD OF THE LIVING.
I KNOW THAT.
UNLESS I GIVE YOU ***MY*** LIFE.
THAT SHOULD HOLD YOU AWHILE.
YOU'LL GIVE ME...
...***YOUR*** LIFE ?!

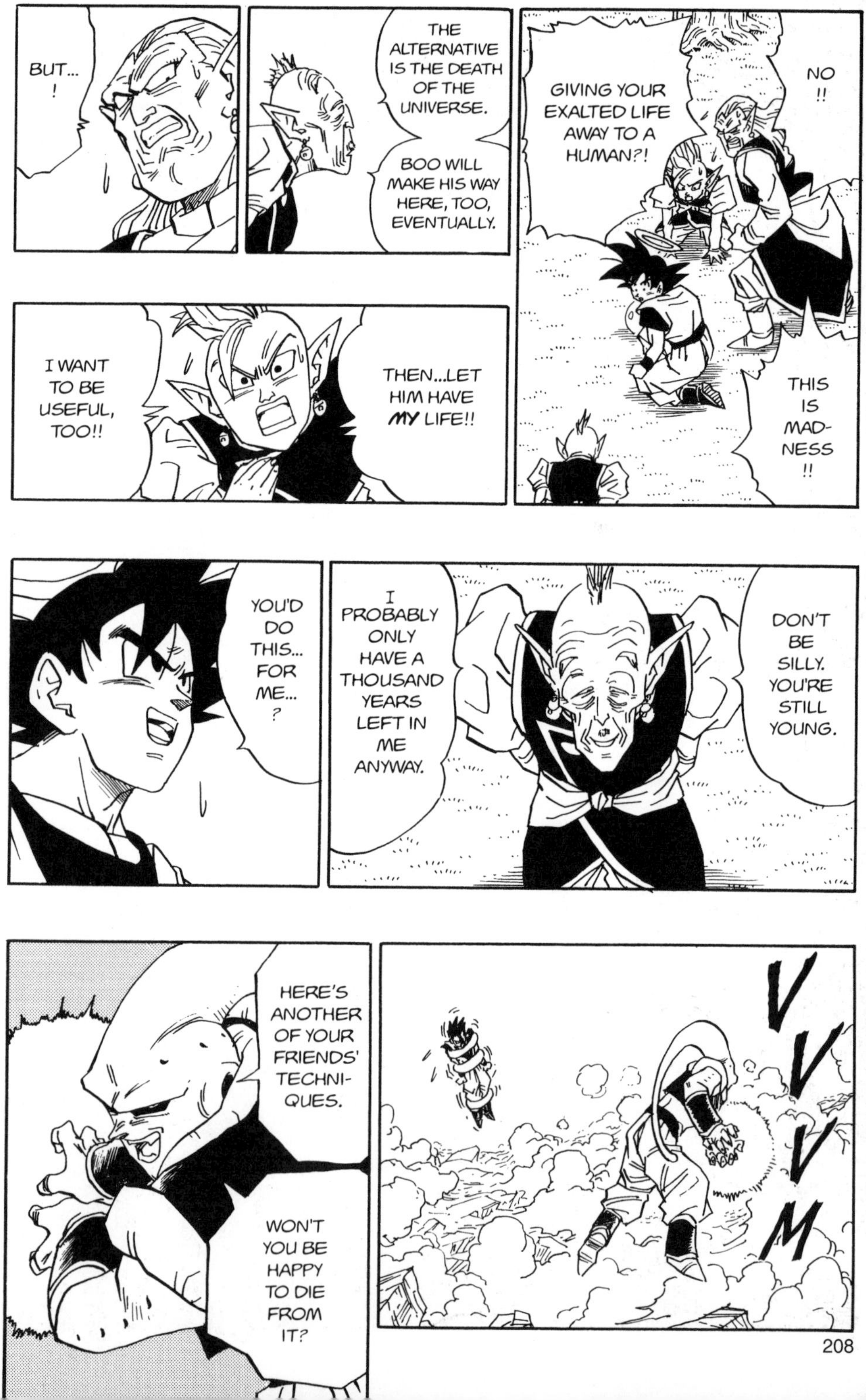
NO!!
GIVING YOUR EXALTED LIFE AWAY TO A HUMAN?!
THIS IS MADNESS!!
THE ALTERNATIVE IS THE DEATH OF THE UNIVERSE.
BOO WILL MAKE HIS WAY HERE, TOO, EVENTUALLY.
BUT...!
THEN...LET HIM HAVE MY LIFE!!
I WANT TO BE USEFUL, TOO!!
DON'T BE SILLY. YOU'RE STILL YOUNG.
I PROBABLY ONLY HAVE A THOUSAND YEARS LEFT IN ME ANYWAY.
YOU'D DO THIS... FOR ME...?
VVVM
HERE'S ANOTHER OF YOUR FRIENDS' TECHNIQUES.
WON'T YOU BE HAPPY TO DIE FROM IT?

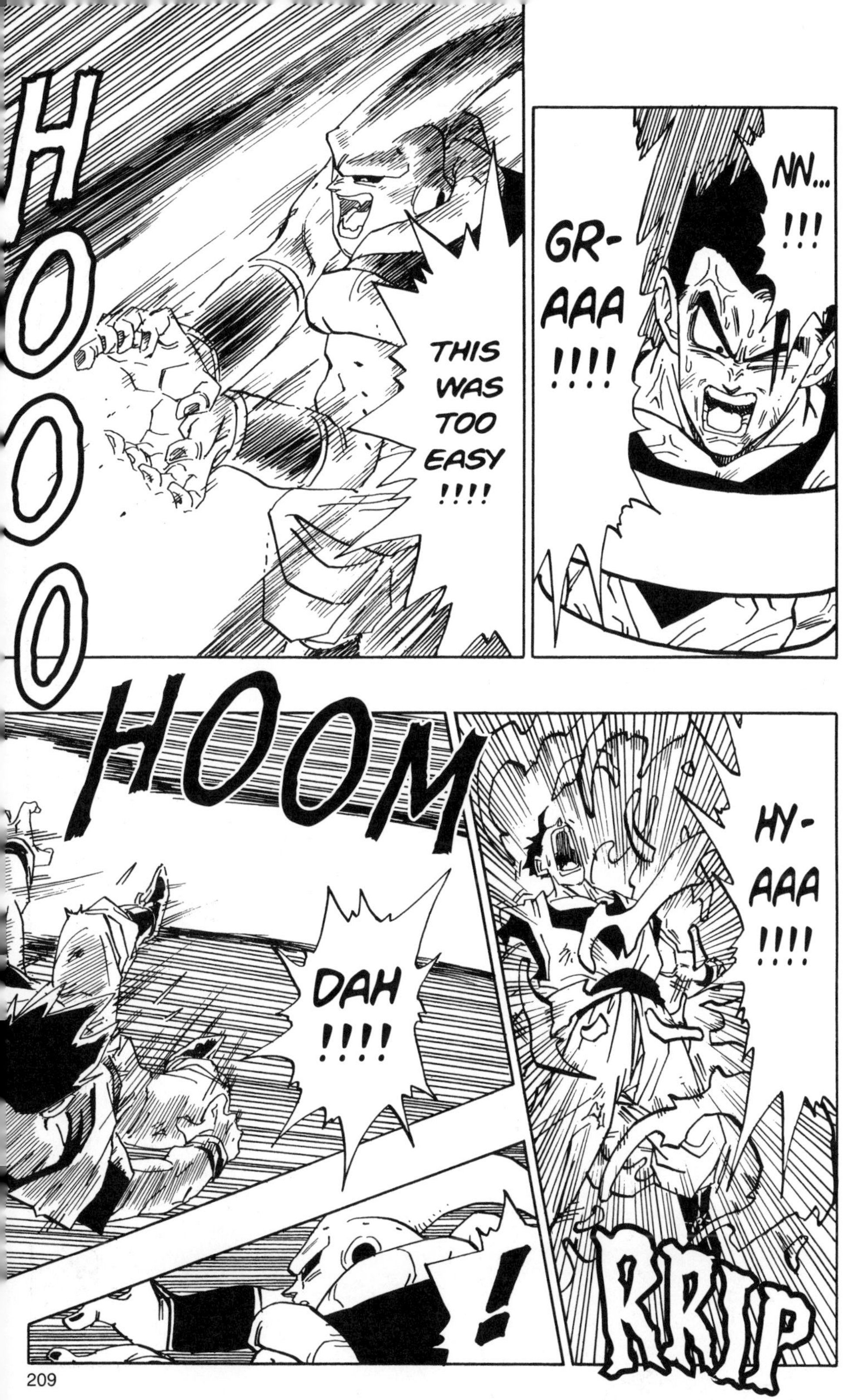
NN... !!!
GR-AAA !!!!
THIS WAS TOO EASY !!!!
HOOOO
HY-AAA !!!!
RRIP
HOOOM
DAH !!!!
!

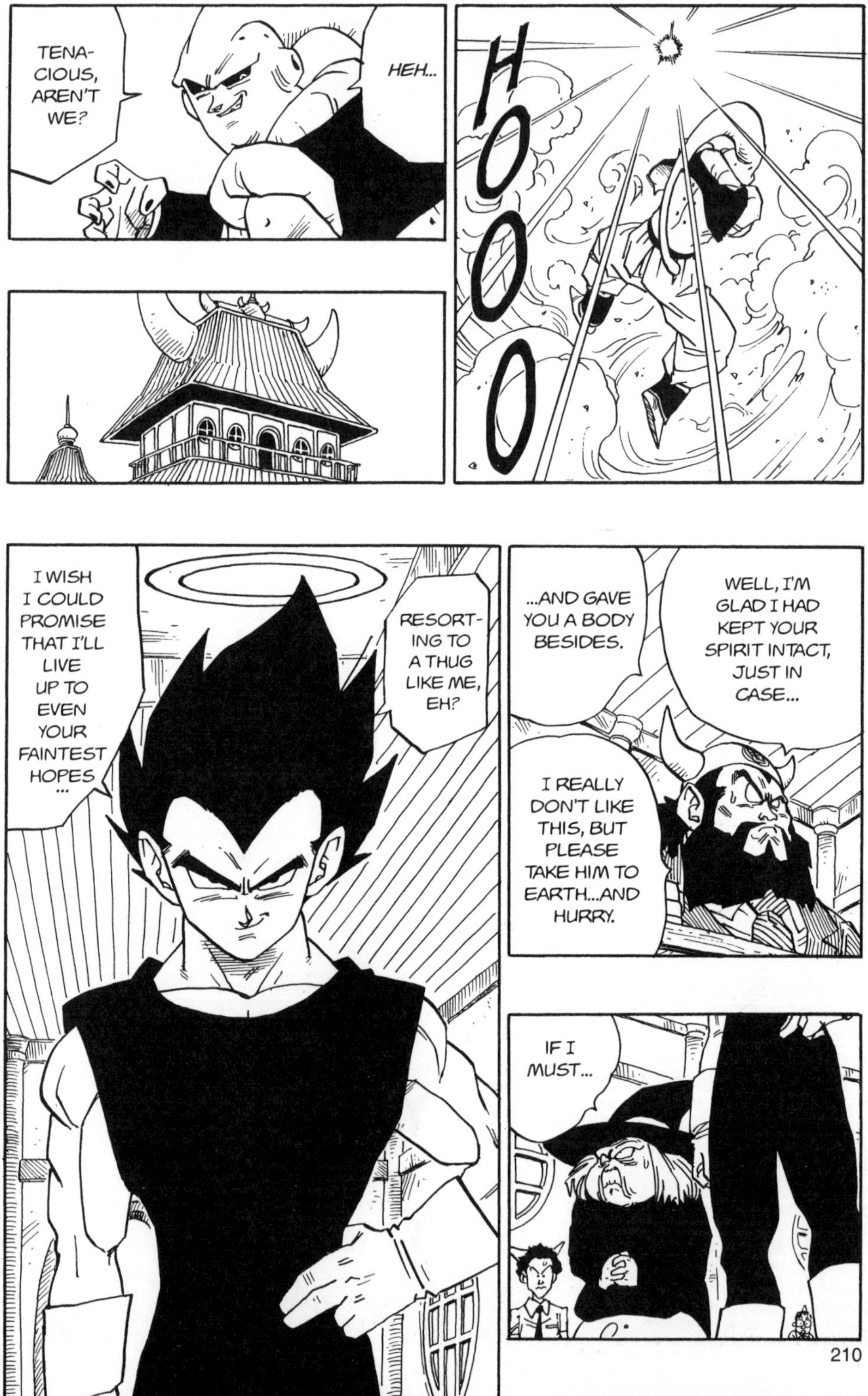
HOOOO
HEH...
TENACIOUS, AREN'T WE?
WELL, I'M GLAD I HAD KEPT YOUR SPIRIT INTACT, JUST IN CASE...
...AND GAVE YOU A BODY BESIDES.
I REALLY DON'T LIKE THIS, BUT PLEASE TAKE HIM TO EARTH...AND HURRY.
IF I MUST...
RESORTING TO A THUG LIKE ME, EH?
I WISH I COULD PROMISE THAT I'LL LIVE UP TO EVEN YOUR FAINTEST HOPES...

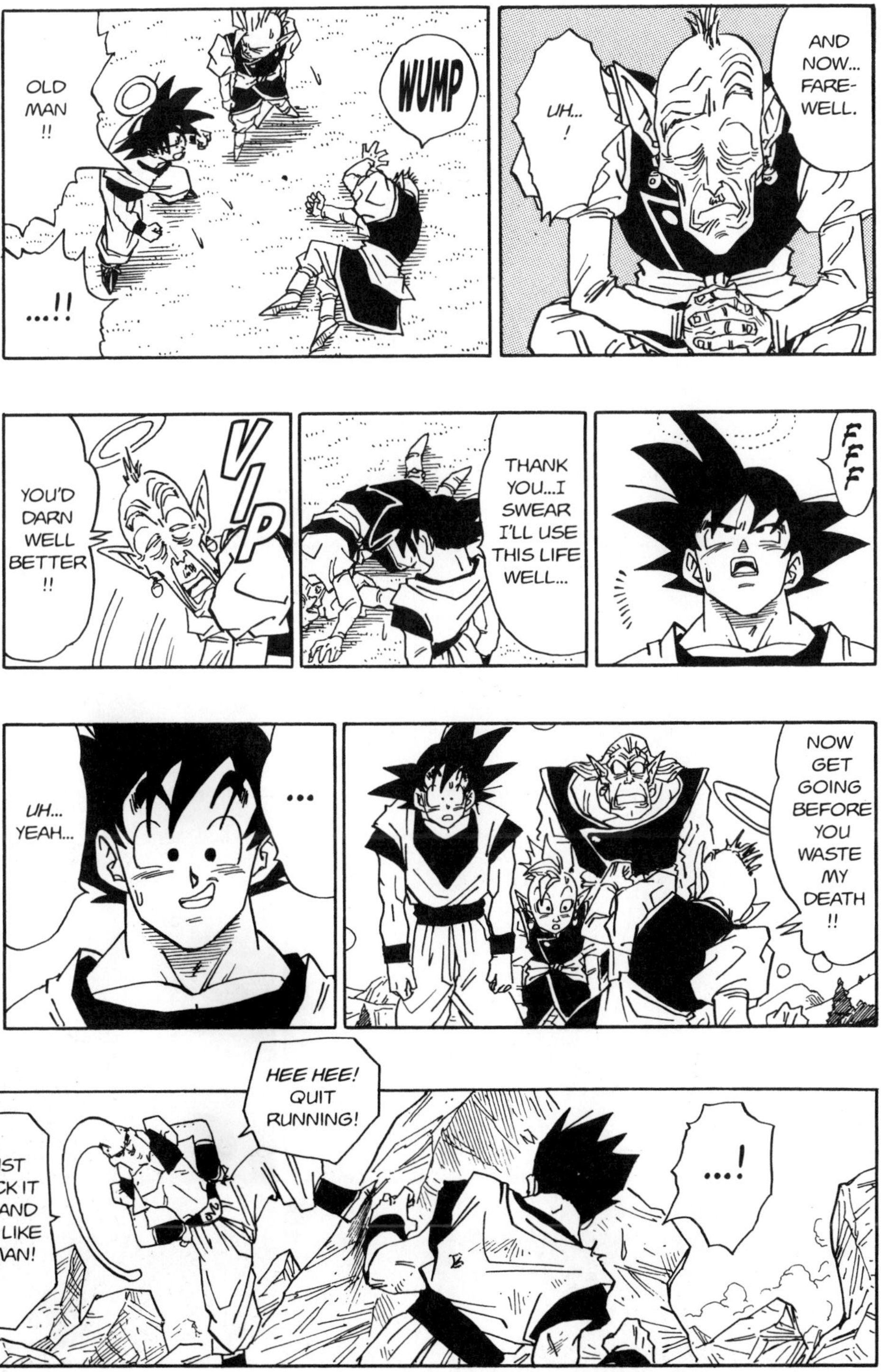
AND NOW... FARE-WELL.
UH... !
WUMP
OLD MAN !!
...!!
FFF
THANK YOU...I SWEAR I'LL USE THIS LIFE WELL...
VIP
YOU'D DARN WELL BETTER !!
NOW GET GOING BEFORE YOU WASTE MY DEATH !!
...
UH... YEAH...
...!
HEE HEE! QUIT RUNNING!
JUST SUCK IT UP AND DIE LIKE A MAN!

DBZ:307 • Enter a Savior?!

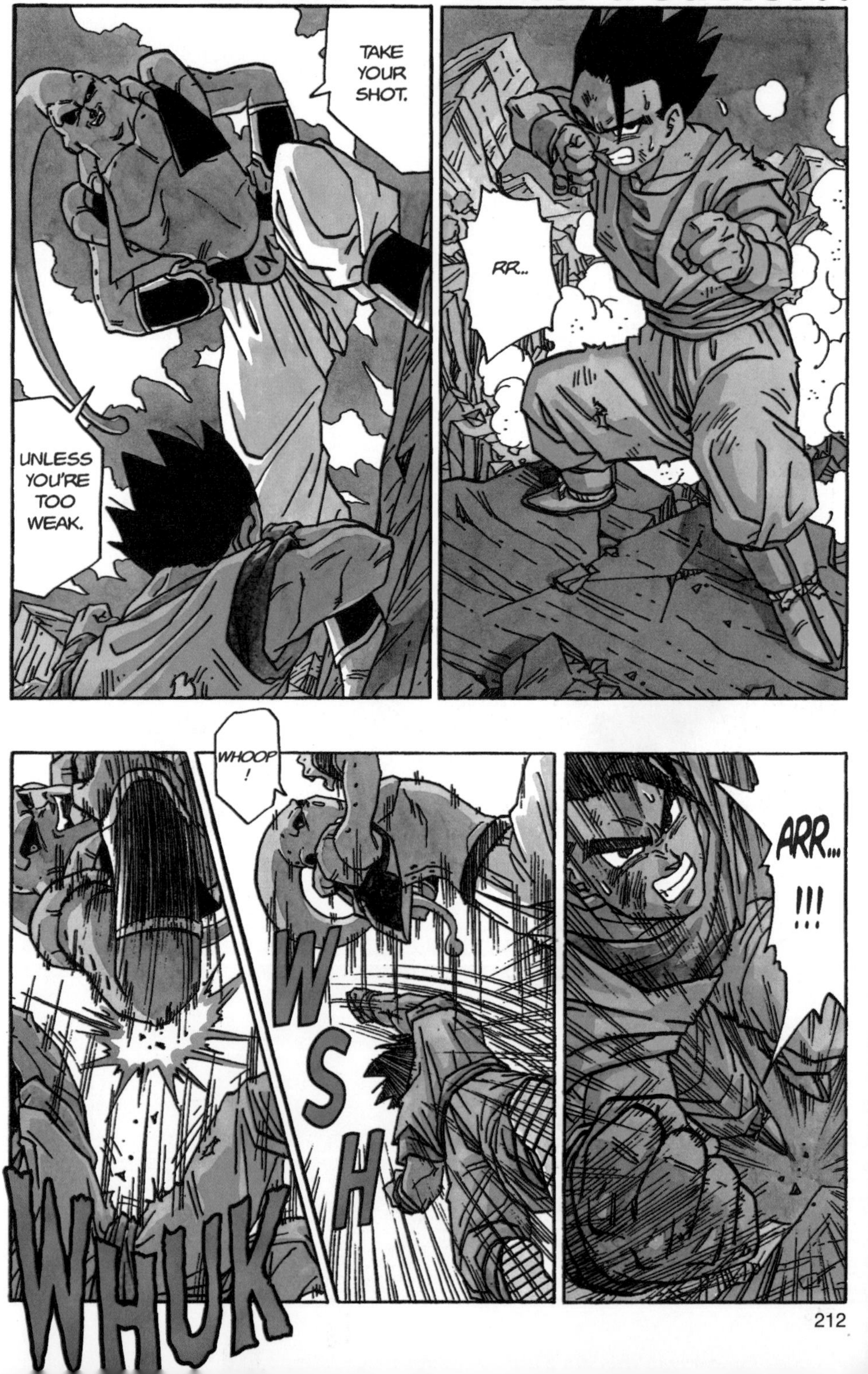
RR...
TAKE YOUR SHOT.
UNLESS YOU'RE TOO WEAK.
ARR... !!!
WHOOP!
WSH
WHUK

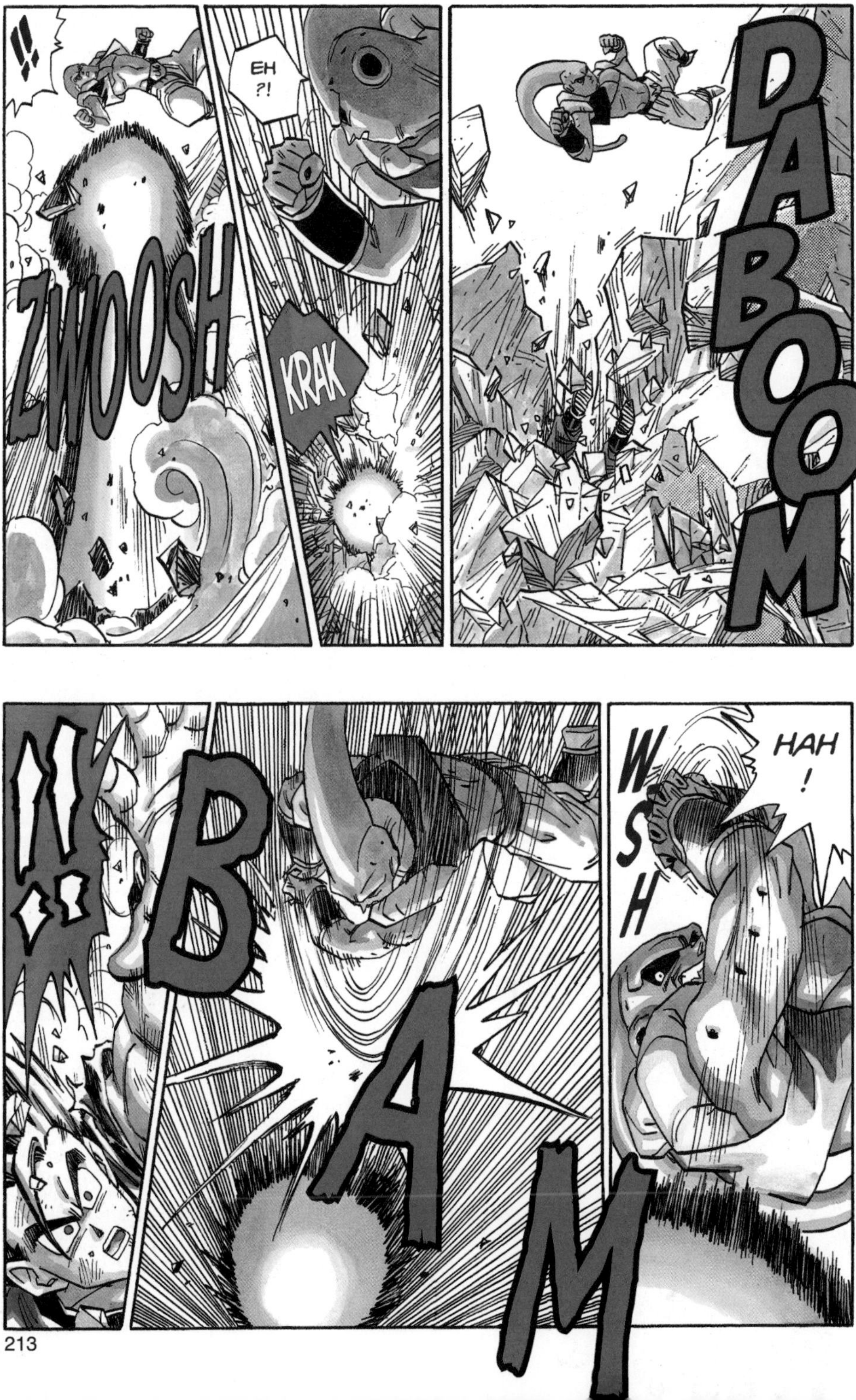
DABOOM
EH ?!
KRAK
!!
ZWOOSH
HAH !
WSH
BAM
!!

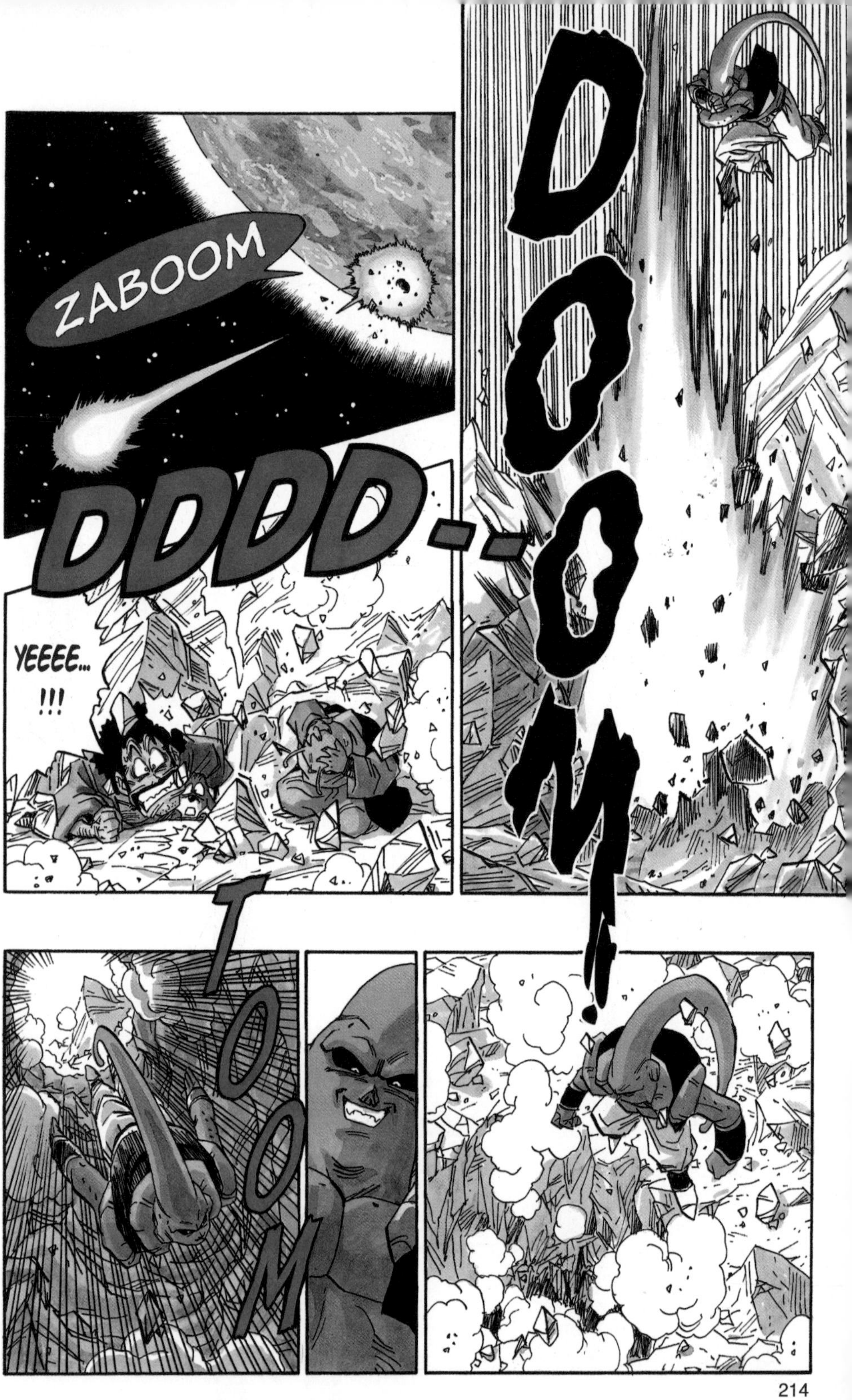
DOOOM!
ZABOOM
DDDD...
YEEEE... !!!
TOOOM

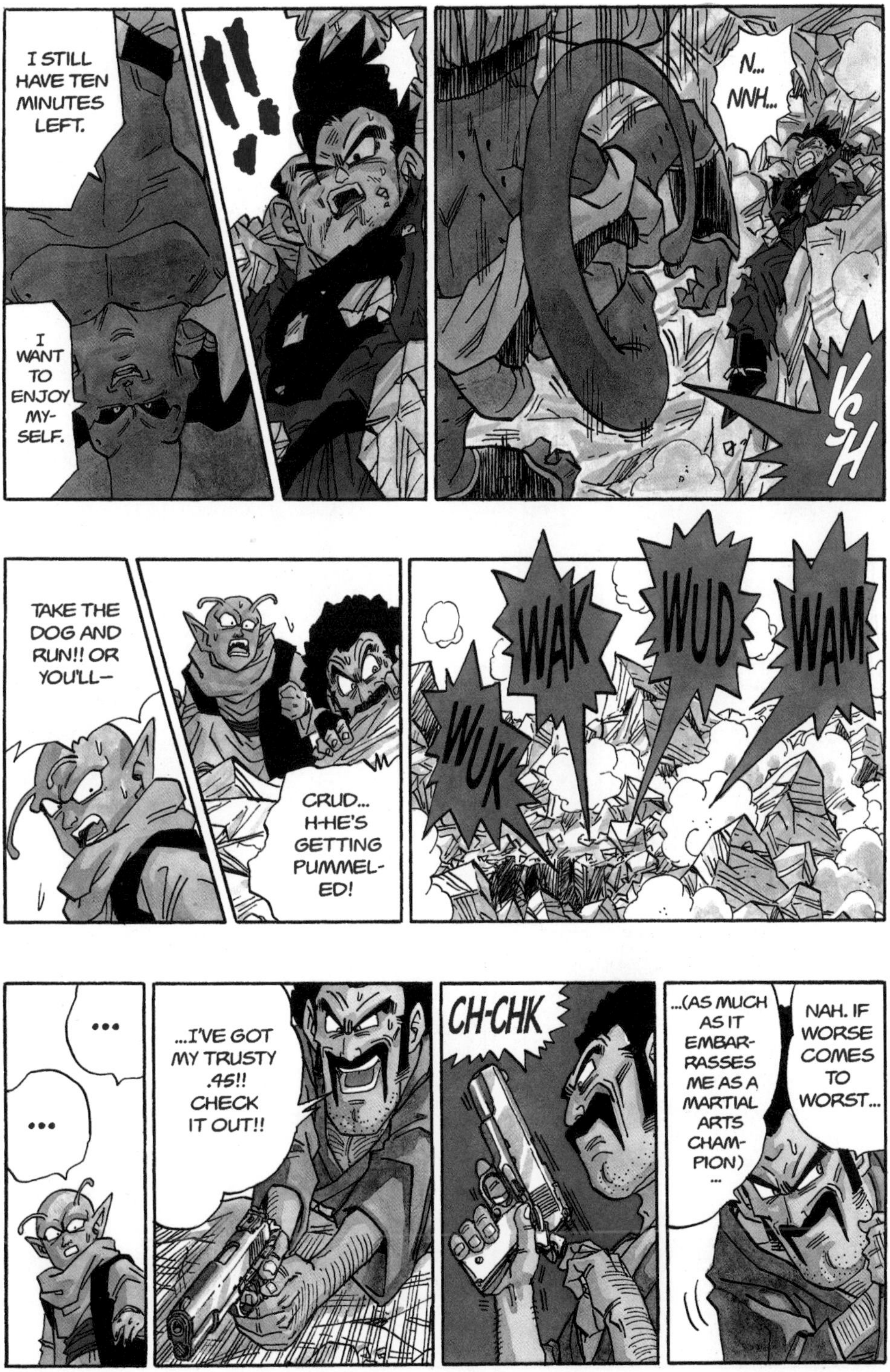
N... NNH...
VCH
!!
I STILL HAVE TEN MINUTES LEFT.
I WANT TO ENJOY MYSELF.
WAM
WUD
WAK
WUK
CRUD... H-HE'S GETTING PUMMELED!
TAKE THE DOG AND RUN!! OR YOU'LL—
NAH. IF WORSE COMES TO WORST...
...(AS MUCH AS IT EMBARRASSES ME AS A MARTIAL ARTS CHAMPION)...
CH-CHK
...I'VE GOT MY TRUSTY .45!! CHECK IT OUT!!
...
...

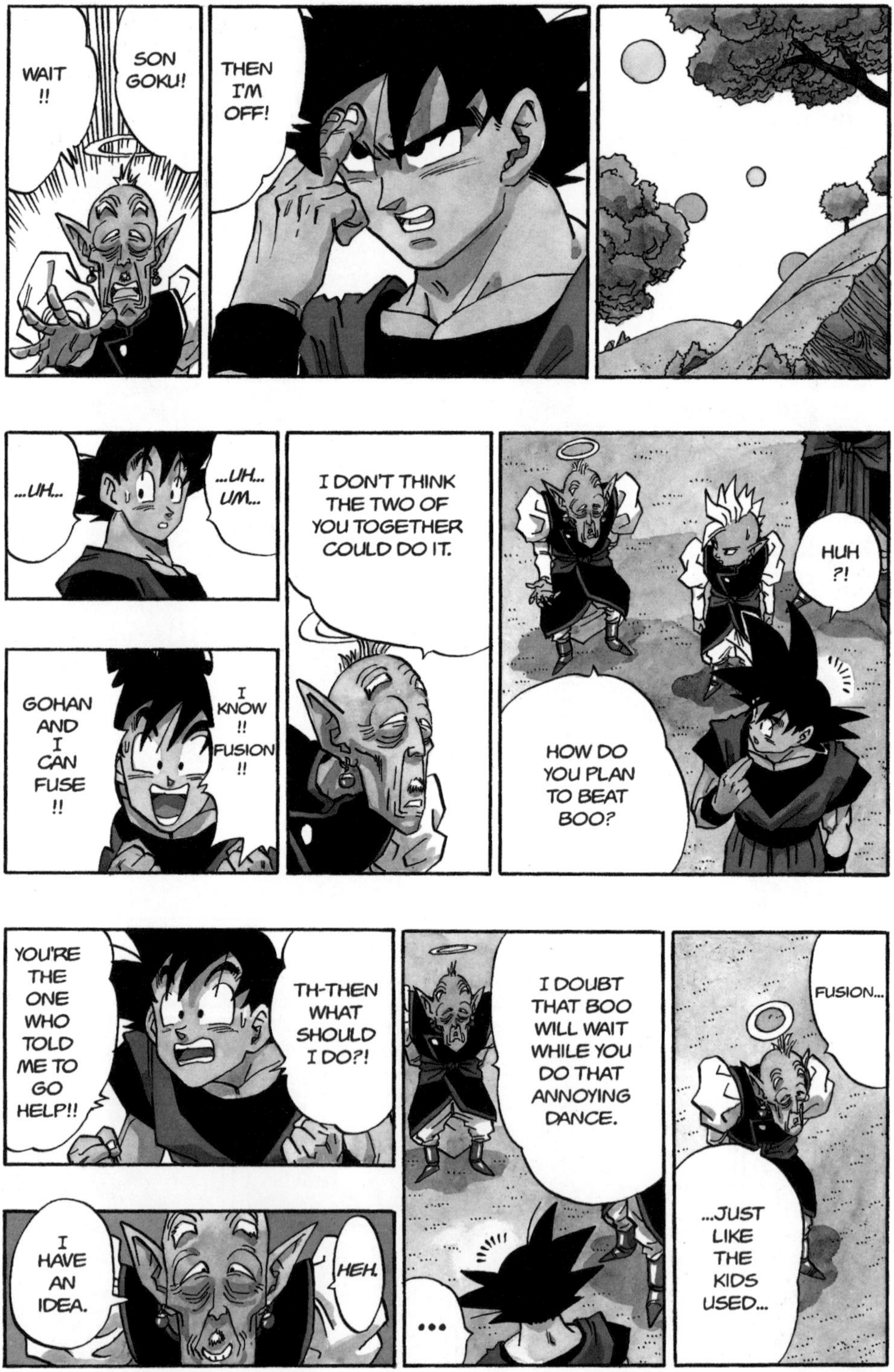
THEN I'M OFF!
SON GOKU!
WAIT !!
HUH ?!
HOW DO YOU PLAN TO BEAT BOO?
I KNOW !! FUSION !!
GOHAN AND I CAN FUSE !!
I DON'T THINK THE TWO OF YOU TOGETHER COULD DO IT.
...UH... UM...
...UH...
FUSION...
...JUST LIKE THE KIDS USED...
...
I DOUBT THAT BOO WILL WAIT WHILE YOU DO THAT ANNOYING DANCE.
TH-THEN WHAT SHOULD I DO?!
YOU'RE THE ONE WHO TOLD ME TO GO HELP!!
HEH.
I HAVE AN IDEA.

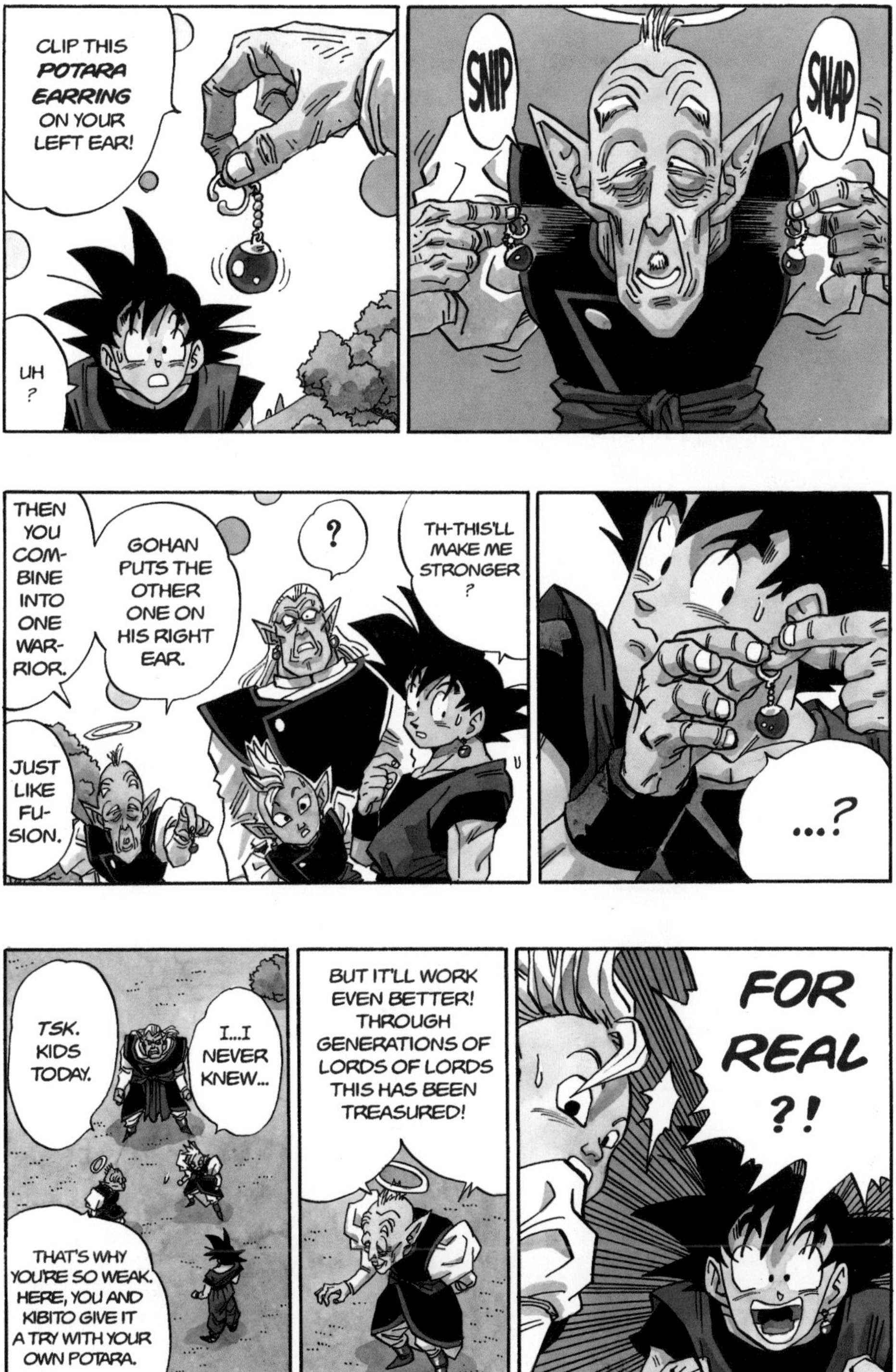
SNIP
SNAP
CLIP THIS *POTARA EARRING* ON YOUR LEFT EAR!
UH ?
...?
?
TH-THIS'LL MAKE ME STRONGER ?
GOHAN PUTS THE OTHER ONE ON HIS RIGHT EAR.
THEN YOU COMBINE INTO ONE WARRIOR.
JUST LIKE FUSION.
FOR REAL ?!
BUT IT'LL WORK EVEN BETTER! THROUGH GENERATIONS OF LORDS OF LORDS THIS HAS BEEN TREASURED!
I...I NEVER KNEW...
TSK. KIDS TODAY.
THAT'S WHY YOU'RE SO WEAK. HERE, YOU AND KIBITO GIVE IT A TRY WITH YOUR OWN POTARA.

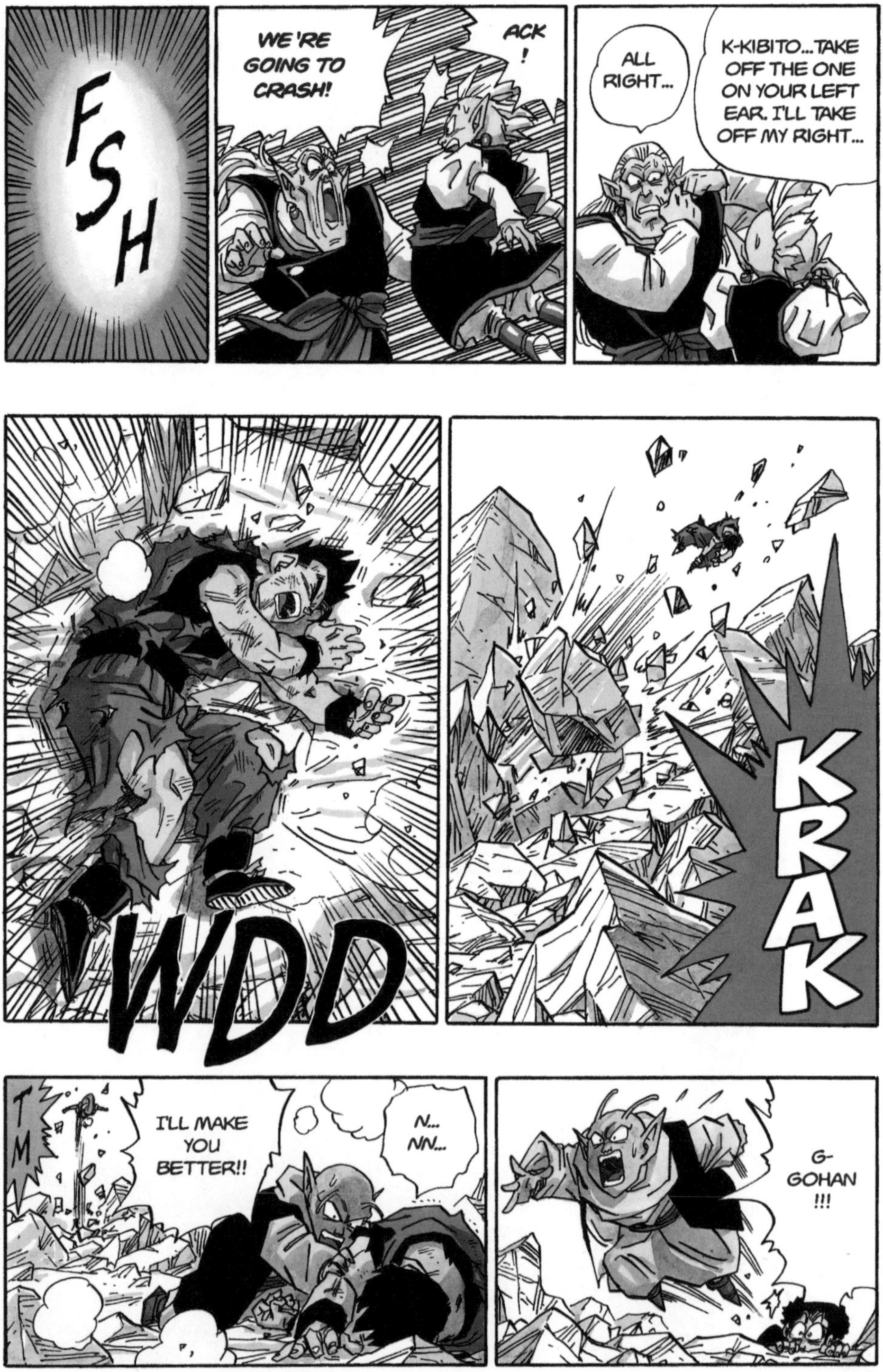
K-KIBITO...TAKE OFF THE ONE ON YOUR LEFT EAR. I'LL TAKE OFF MY RIGHT...
ALL RIGHT...
ACK!
WE'RE GOING TO CRASH!
FSH
KRAK
WDD
G-GOHAN!!!
N... NN...
I'LL MAKE YOU BETTER!!
TM

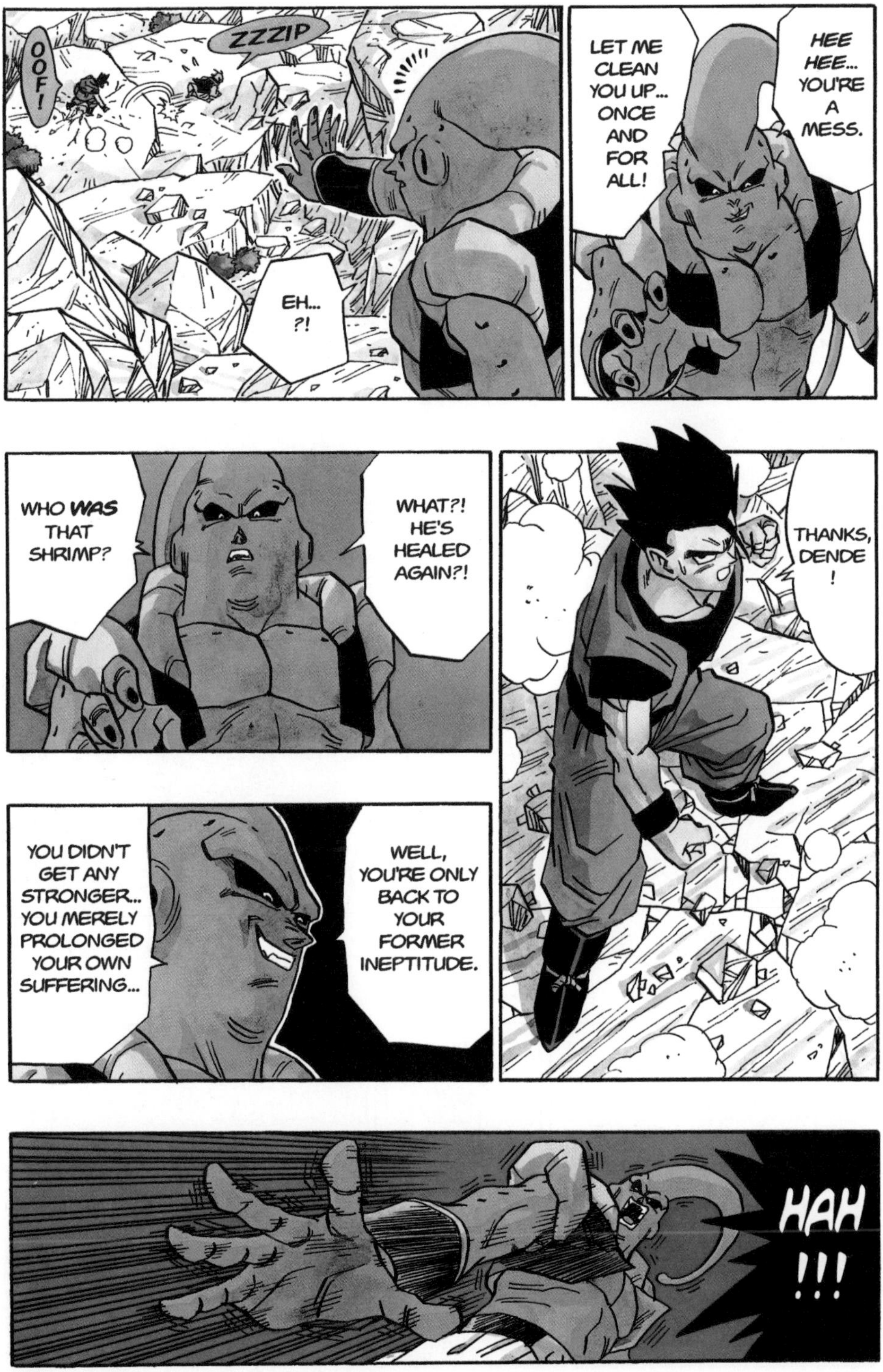
HEE HEE... YOU'RE A MESS.
LET ME CLEAN YOU UP... ONCE AND FOR ALL!
ZZZIP
OOF!
EH... ?!
THANKS, DENDE!
WHAT?! HE'S HEALED AGAIN?!
WHO *WAS* THAT SHRIMP?
WELL, YOU'RE ONLY BACK TO YOUR FORMER INEPTITUDE.
YOU DIDN'T GET ANY STRONGER... YOU MERELY PROLONGED YOUR OWN SUFFERING...
HAH!!!

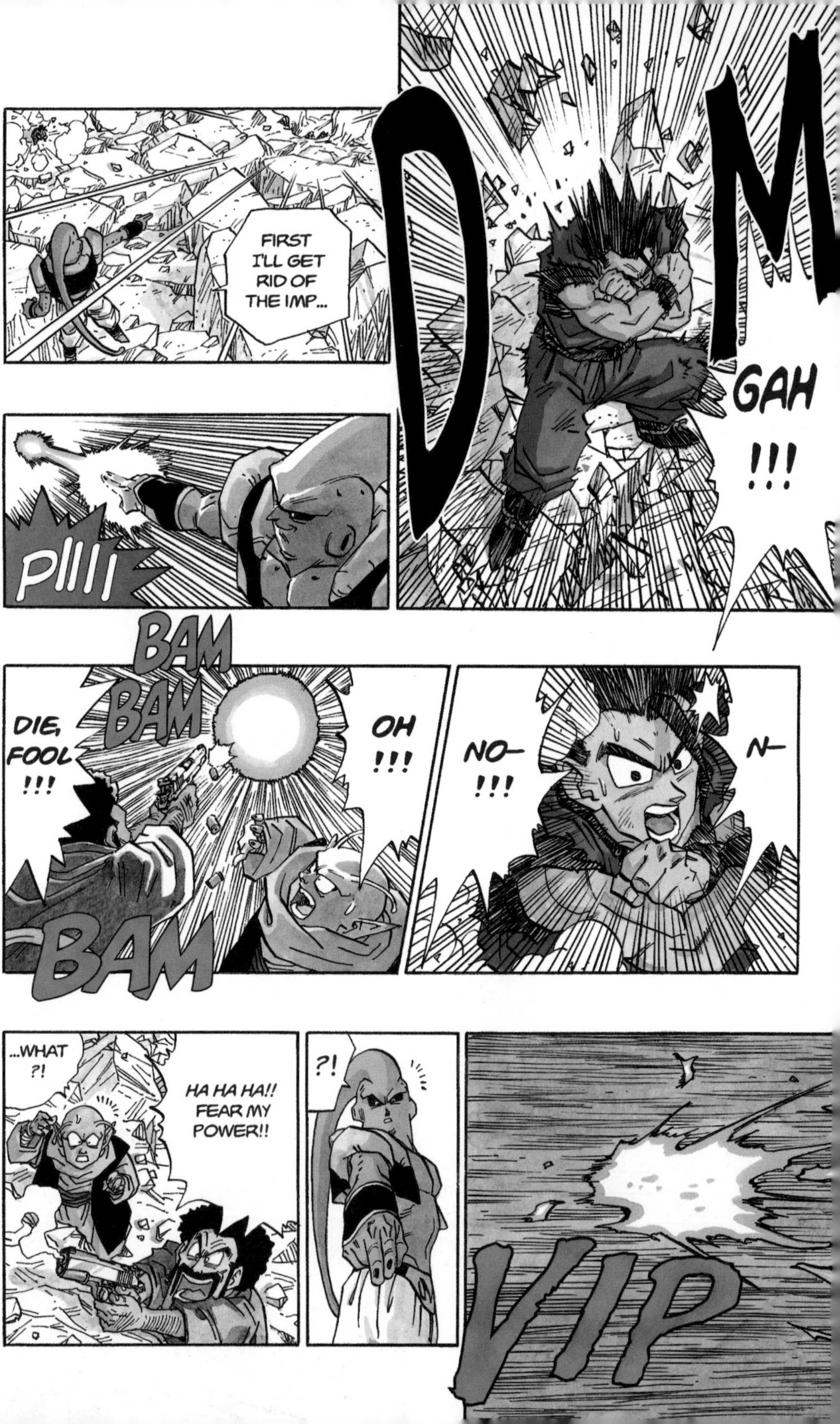

DM
GAH !!!
FIRST I'LL GET RID OF THE IMP...
PIIII
N—
NO— !!!
OH !!!
BAM BAM
DIE, FOOL !!!
BAM
VIP
?!
HA HA HA!! FEAR MY POWER!!
...WHAT ?!

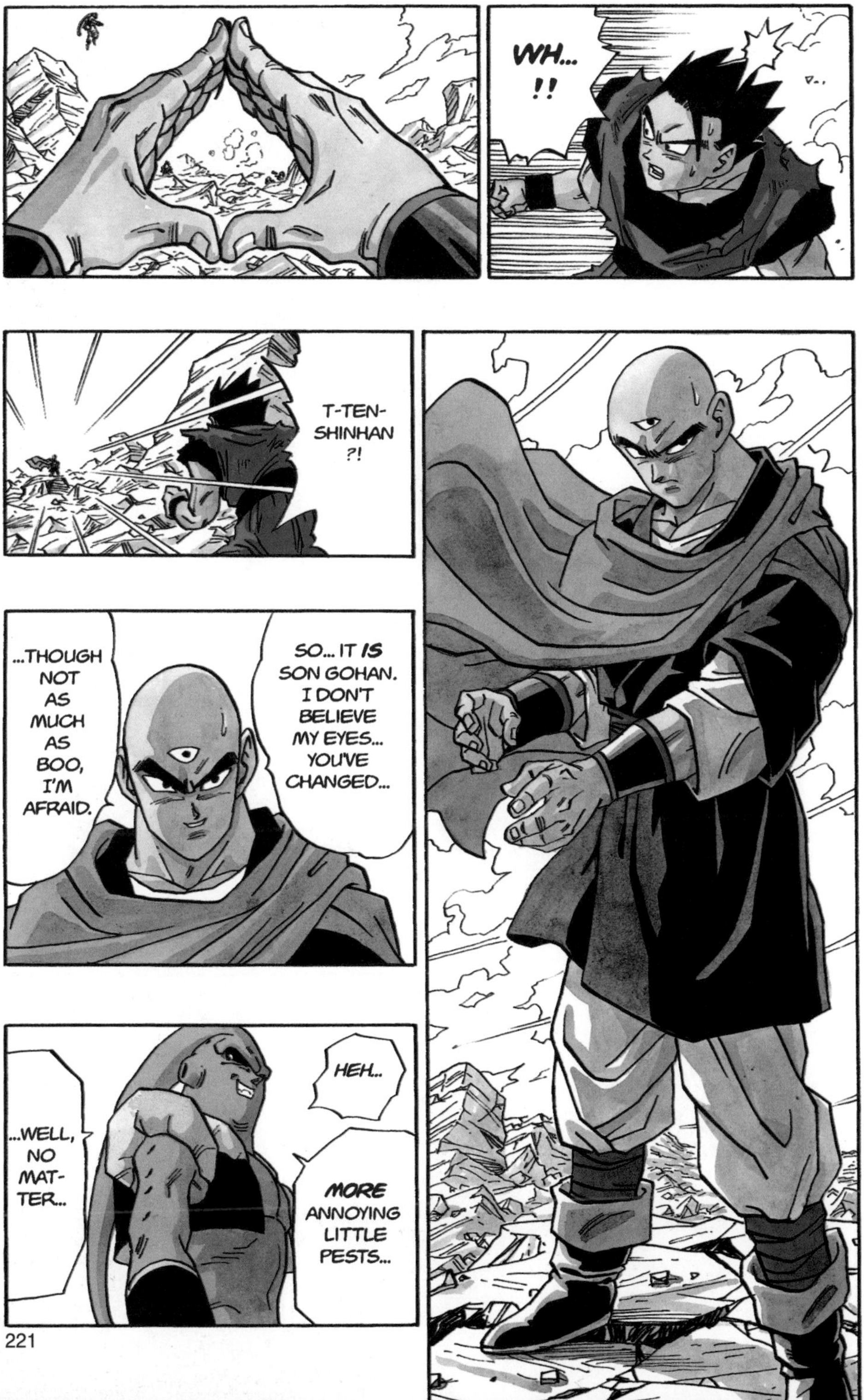
WH... !!
T-TEN-SHINHAN?!
SO... IT *IS* SON GOHAN. I DON'T BELIEVE MY EYES... YOU'VE CHANGED...
...THOUGH NOT AS MUCH AS BOO, I'M AFRAID.
HEH...
MORE ANNOYING LITTLE PESTS...
...WELL, NO MATTER...

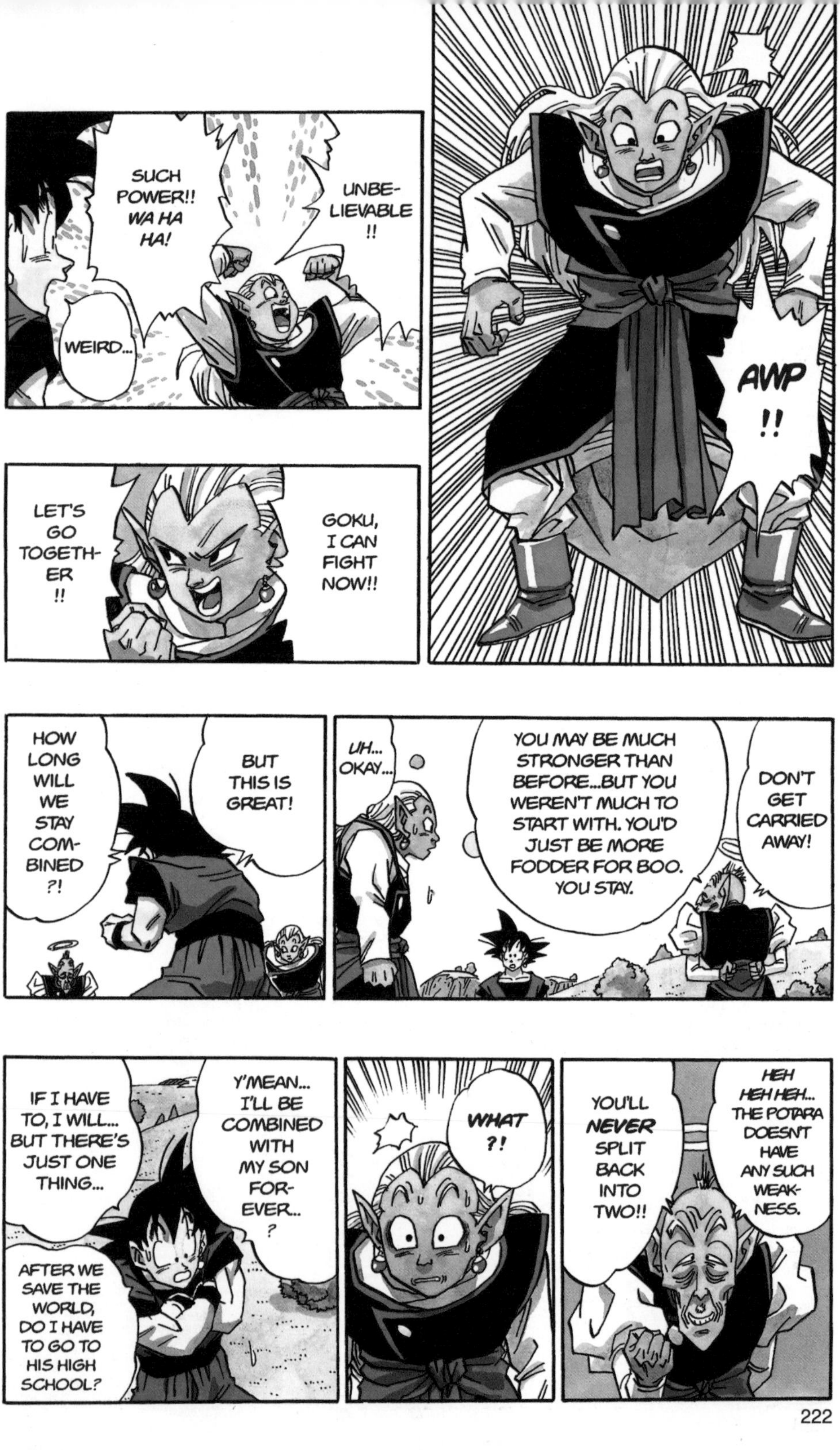
AWP !!
UNBE-LIEVABLE !!
SUCH POWER!! WA HA HA!
WEIRD...
GOKU, I CAN FIGHT NOW!!
LET'S GO TOGETH-ER !!
DON'T GET CARRIED AWAY!
YOU MAY BE MUCH STRONGER THAN BEFORE...BUT YOU WEREN'T MUCH TO START WITH. YOU'D JUST BE MORE FODDER FOR BOO. YOU STAY.
UH... OKAY...
BUT THIS IS GREAT!
HOW LONG WILL WE STAY COM-BINED ?!
HEH HEH HEH... THE POTARA DOESN'T HAVE ANY SUCH WEAK-NESS.
YOU'LL NEVER SPLIT BACK INTO TWO!!
WHAT ?!
Y'MEAN... I'LL BE COMBINED WITH MY SON FOR-EVER.. ?
IF I HAVE TO, I WILL... BUT THERE'S JUST ONE THING...
AFTER WE SAVE THE WORLD, DO I HAVE TO GO TO HIS HIGH SCHOOL?

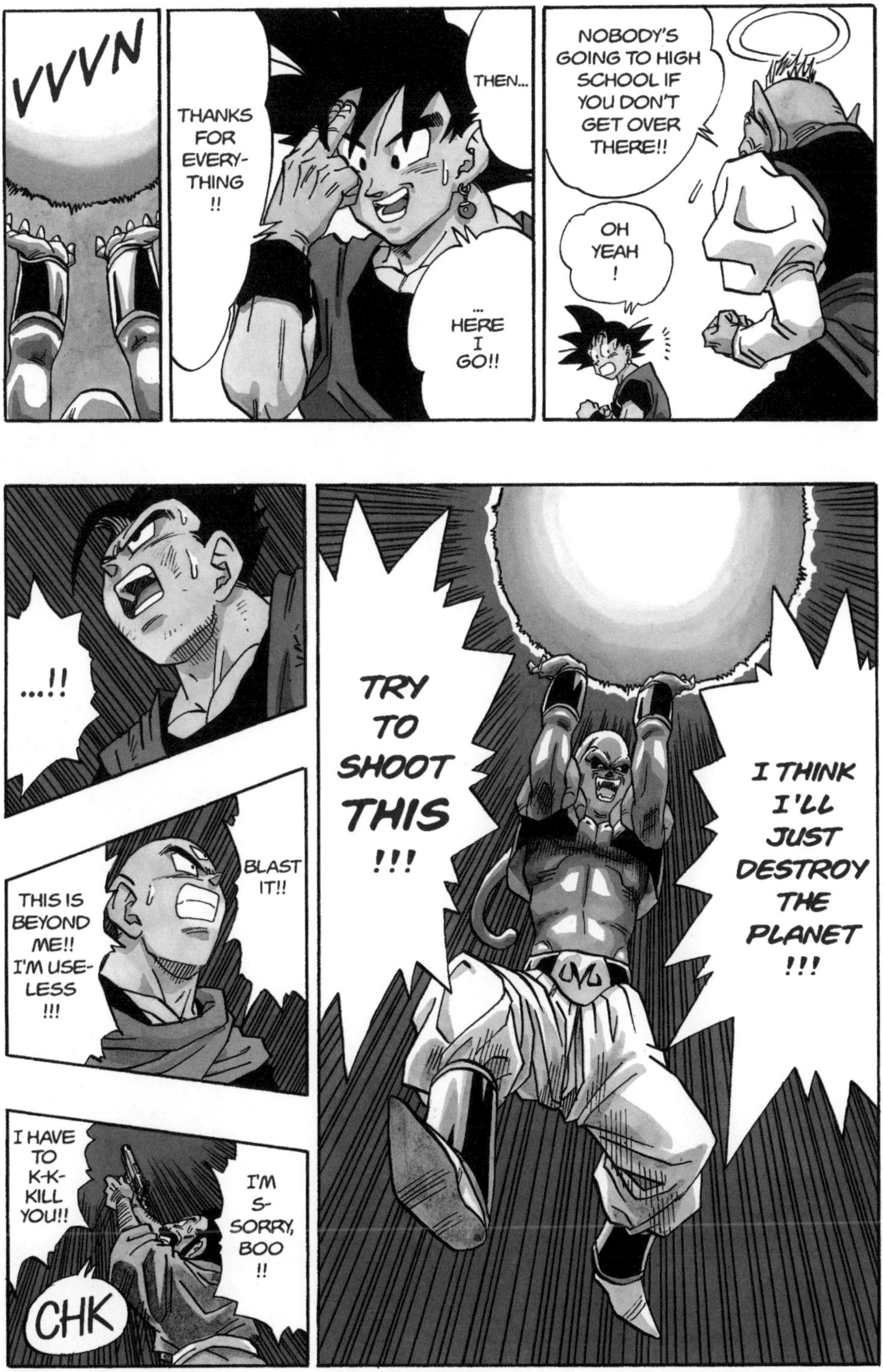
NOBODY'S GOING TO HIGH SCHOOL IF YOU DON'T GET OVER THERE!!
OH YEAH !
THEN...
THANKS FOR EVERY-THING !!
... HERE I GO!!
VVVN
I THINK I'LL JUST DESTROY THE PLANET !!!
TRY TO SHOOT THIS !!!
...!!
BLAST IT!!
THIS IS BEYOND ME!! I'M USE-LESS !!!
I'M S-SORRY, BOO !!
I HAVE TO K-K-KILL YOU!!
CHK

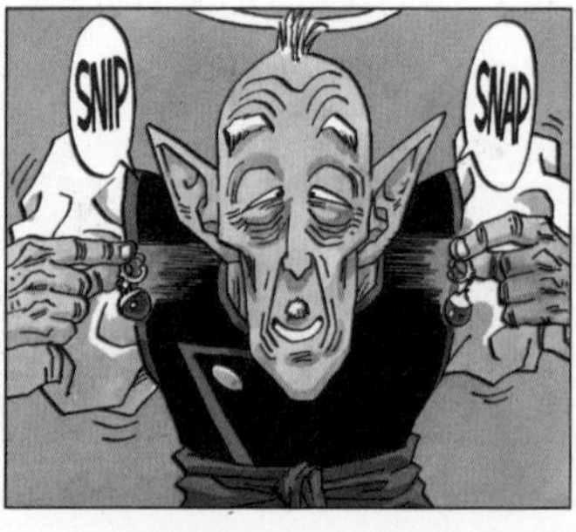
SNIP
SNAP

DBZ:308 • Will the Potara Prevail?!

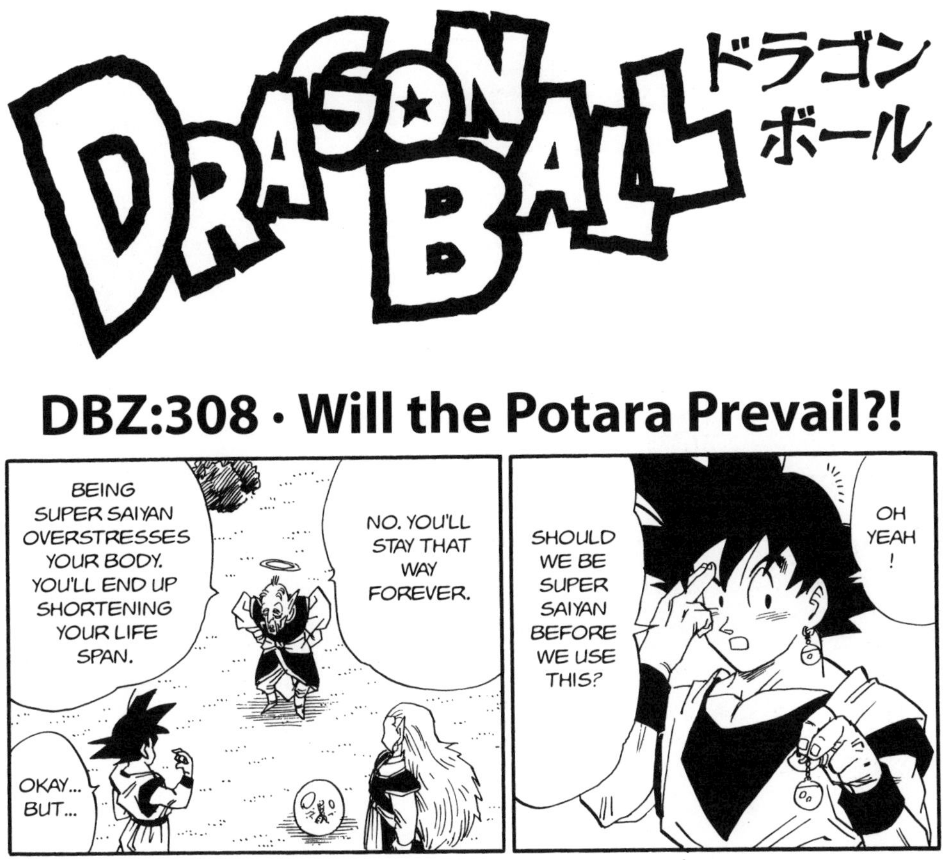
OH YEAH!
SHOULD WE BE SUPER SAIYAN BEFORE WE USE THIS?
NO. YOU'LL STAY THAT WAY FOREVER.
BEING SUPER SAIYAN OVERSTRESSES YOUR BODY. YOU'LL END UP SHORTENING YOUR LIFE SPAN.
OKAY... BUT...

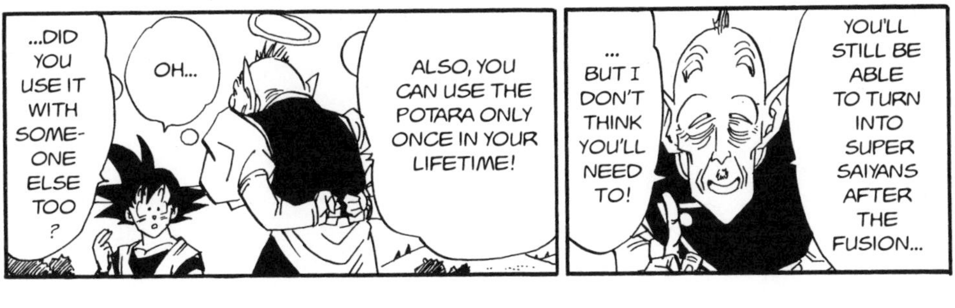
YOU'LL STILL BE ABLE TO TURN INTO SUPER SAIYANS AFTER THE FUSION...
... BUT I DON'T THINK YOU'LL NEED TO!
ALSO, YOU CAN USE THE POTARA ONLY ONCE IN YOUR LIFETIME!
OH...
...DID YOU USE IT WITH SOMEONE ELSE TOO?

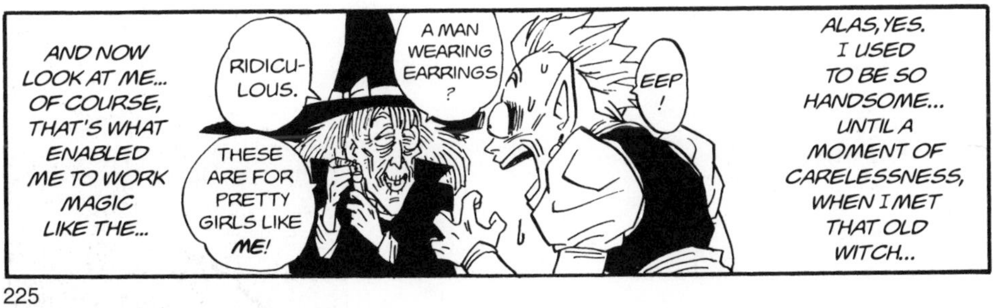
ALAS, YES. I USED TO BE SO HANDSOME... UNTIL A MOMENT OF CARELESSNESS, WHEN I MET THAT OLD WITCH...
EEP!
A MAN WEARING EARRINGS?
RIDICULOUS.
THESE ARE FOR PRETTY GIRLS LIKE ME!
AND NOW LOOK AT ME... OF COURSE, THAT'S WHAT ENABLED ME TO WORK MAGIC LIKE THE...

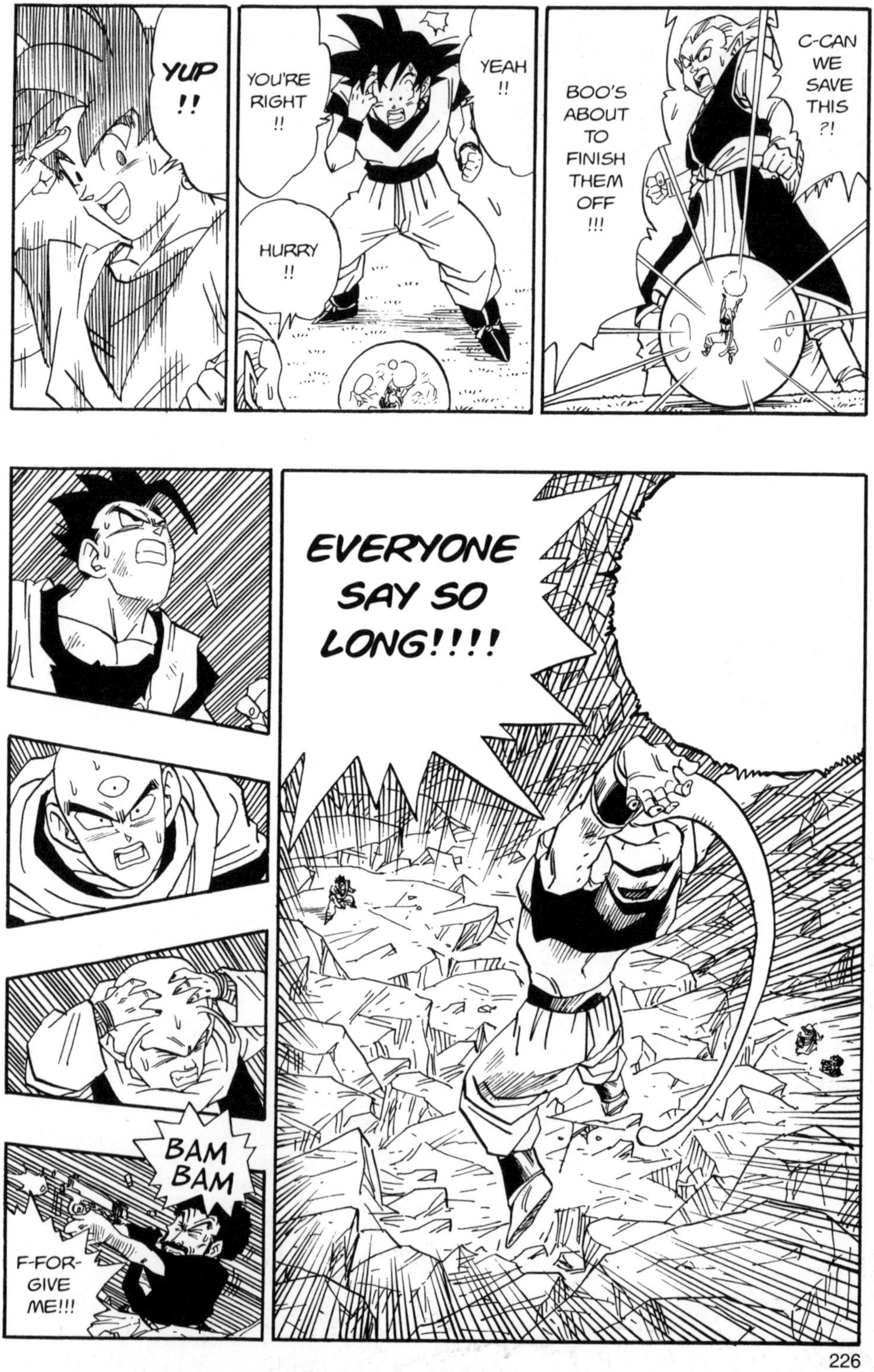
C-CAN WE SAVE THIS ?!
BOO'S ABOUT TO FINISH THEM OFF !!!
YEAH !!
YOU'RE RIGHT !!
HURRY !!
YUP !!
EVERYONE SAY SO LONG!!!!
BAM BAM
F-FOR-GIVE ME!!!

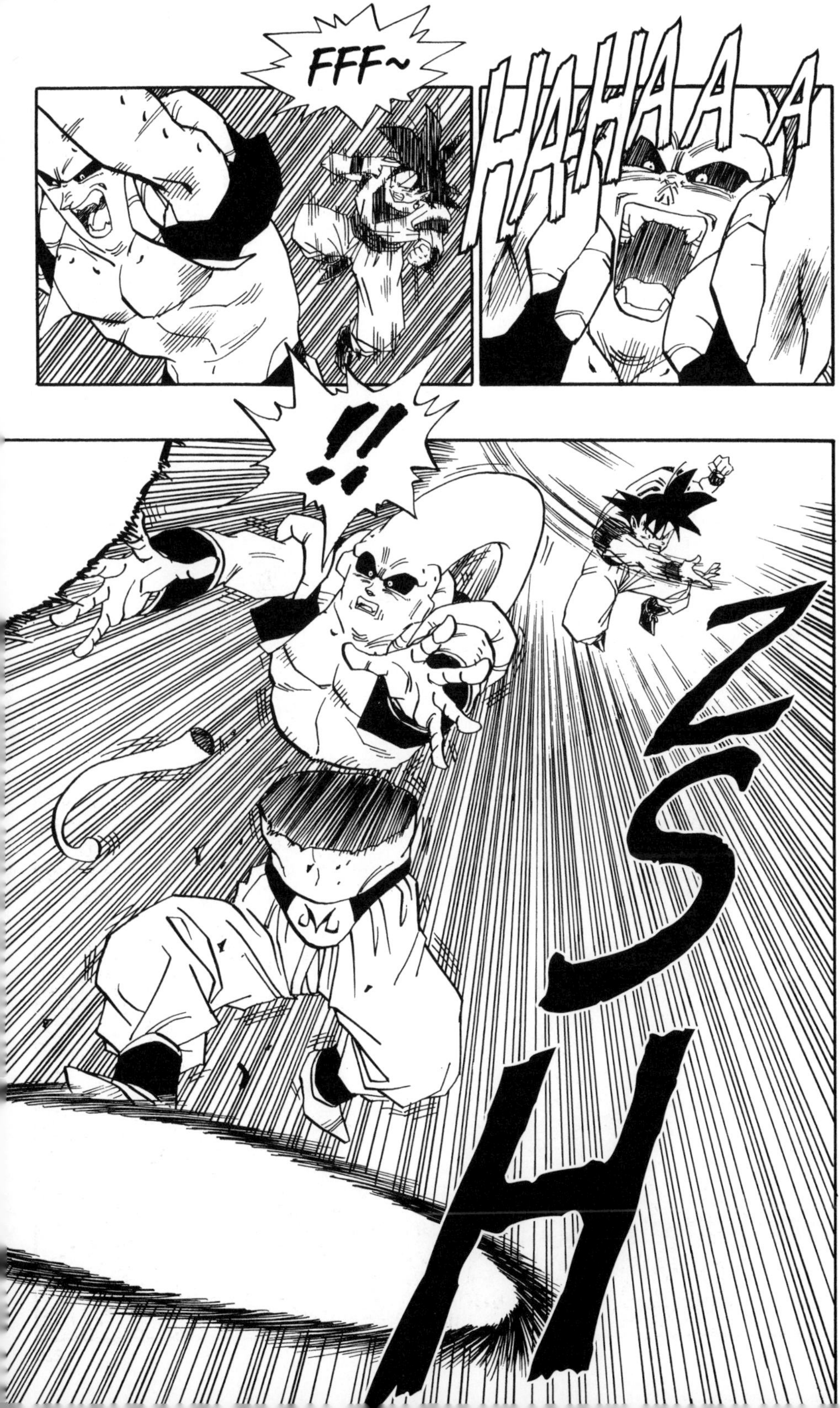
HAHAA A
FFF~
!!
ZSH

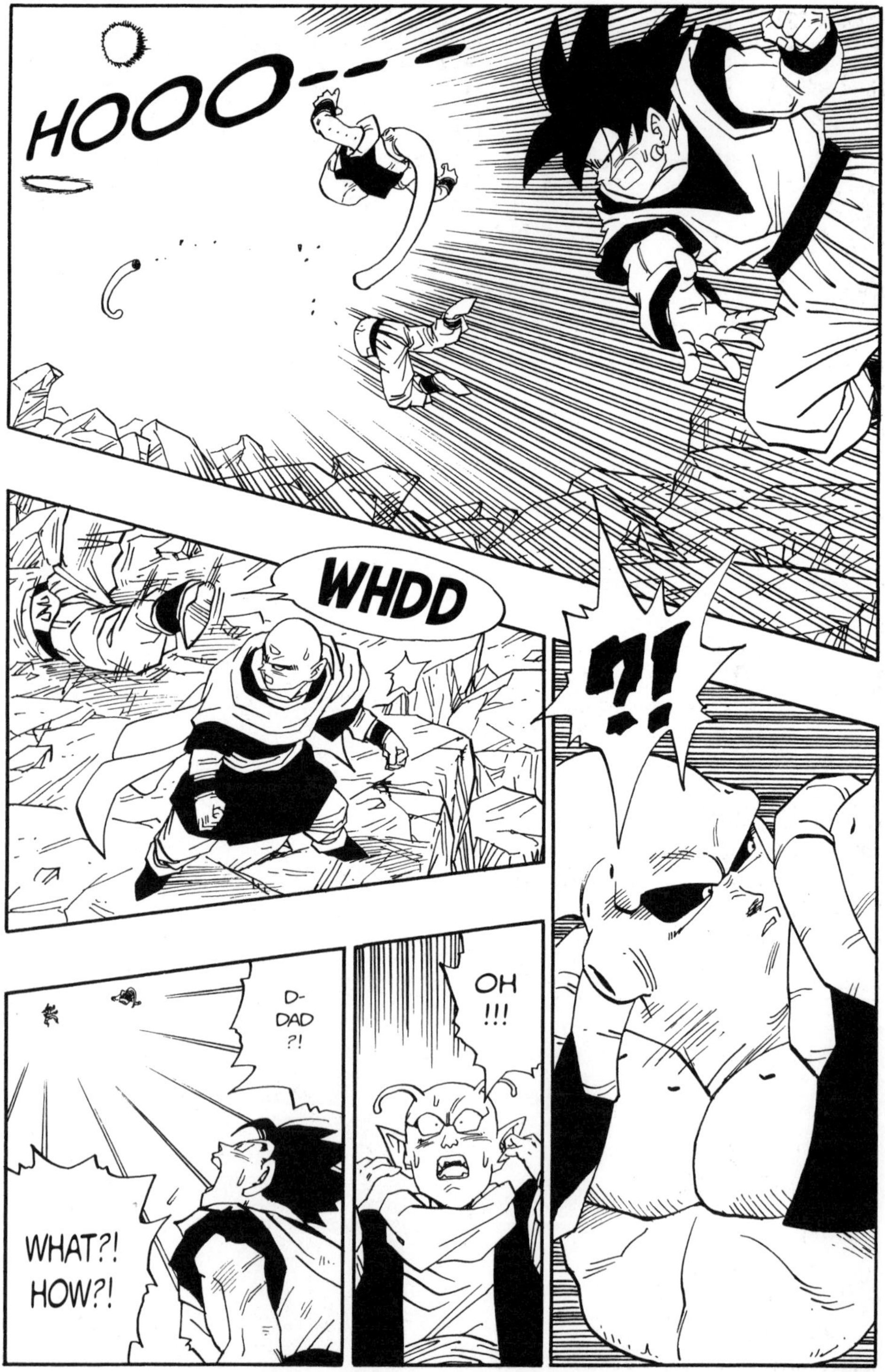
HOOO----
?!
WHDD
OH !!!
D-DAD ?!
WHAT?! HOW?!

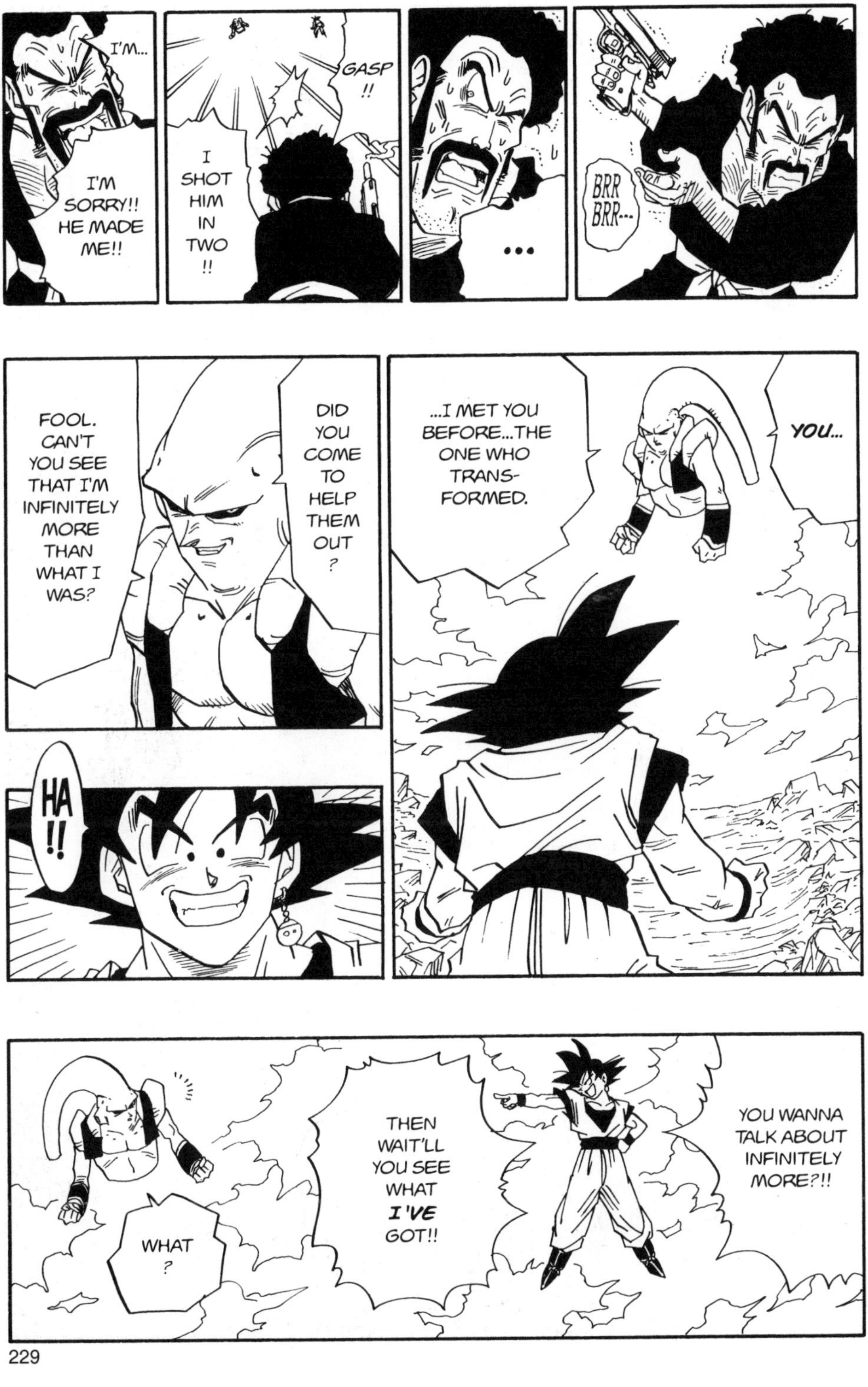
BRR BRR...
...
GASP!!
I SHOT HIM IN TWO!!
I'M...
I'M SORRY!! HE MADE ME!!
YOU...
...I MET YOU BEFORE...THE ONE WHO TRANS-FORMED.
DID YOU COME TO HELP THEM OUT?
FOOL. CAN'T YOU SEE THAT I'M INFINITELY MORE THAN WHAT I WAS?
HA!!
YOU WANNA TALK ABOUT INFINITELY MORE?!!
THEN WAIT'LL YOU SEE WHAT *I'VE* GOT!!
WHAT?

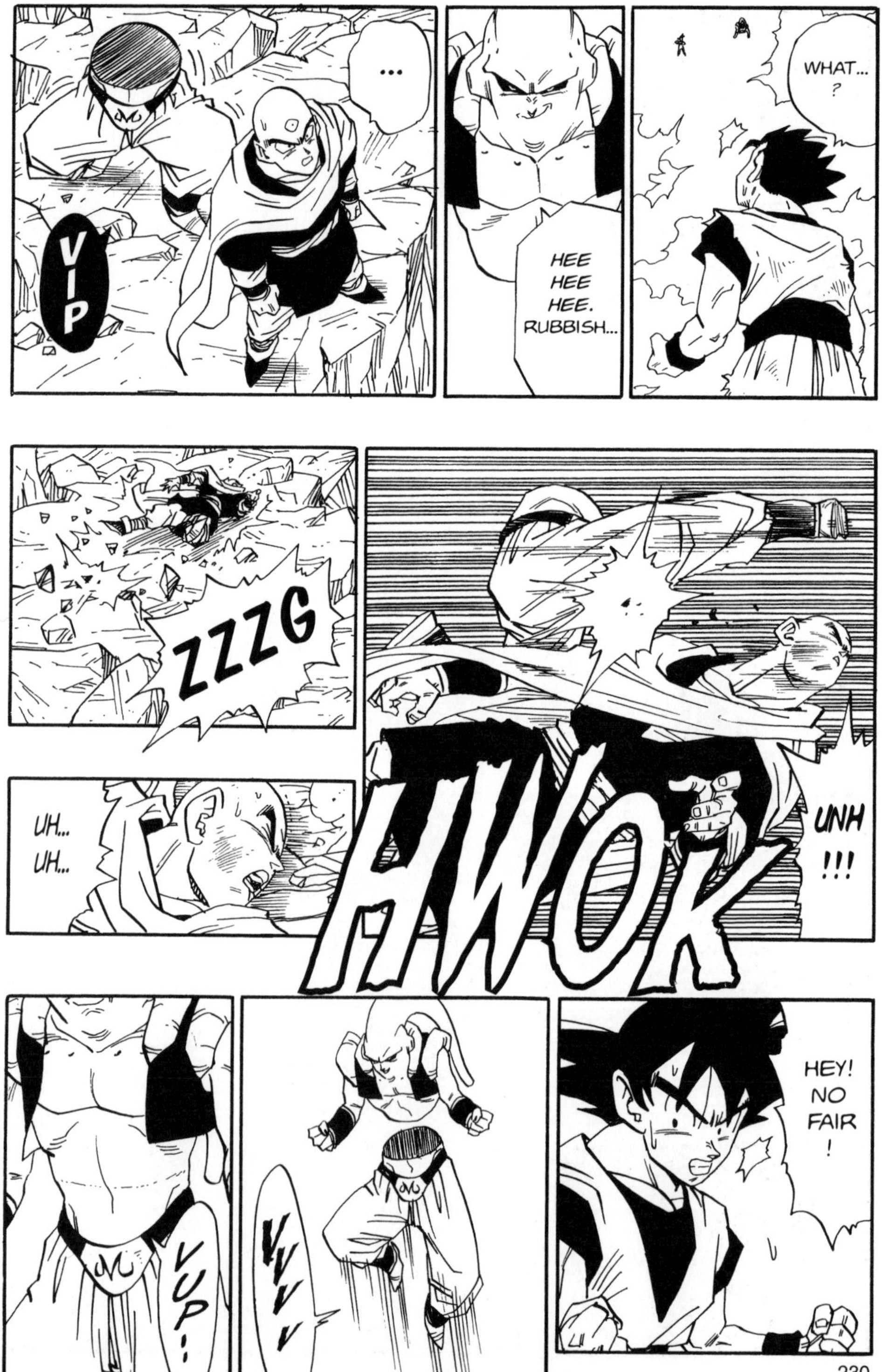
WHAT... ?
HEE HEE HEE. RUBBISH...
...
VIP
UNH !!!
HWOK
ZZZG
UH... UH...
HEY! NO FAIR !
VUP!

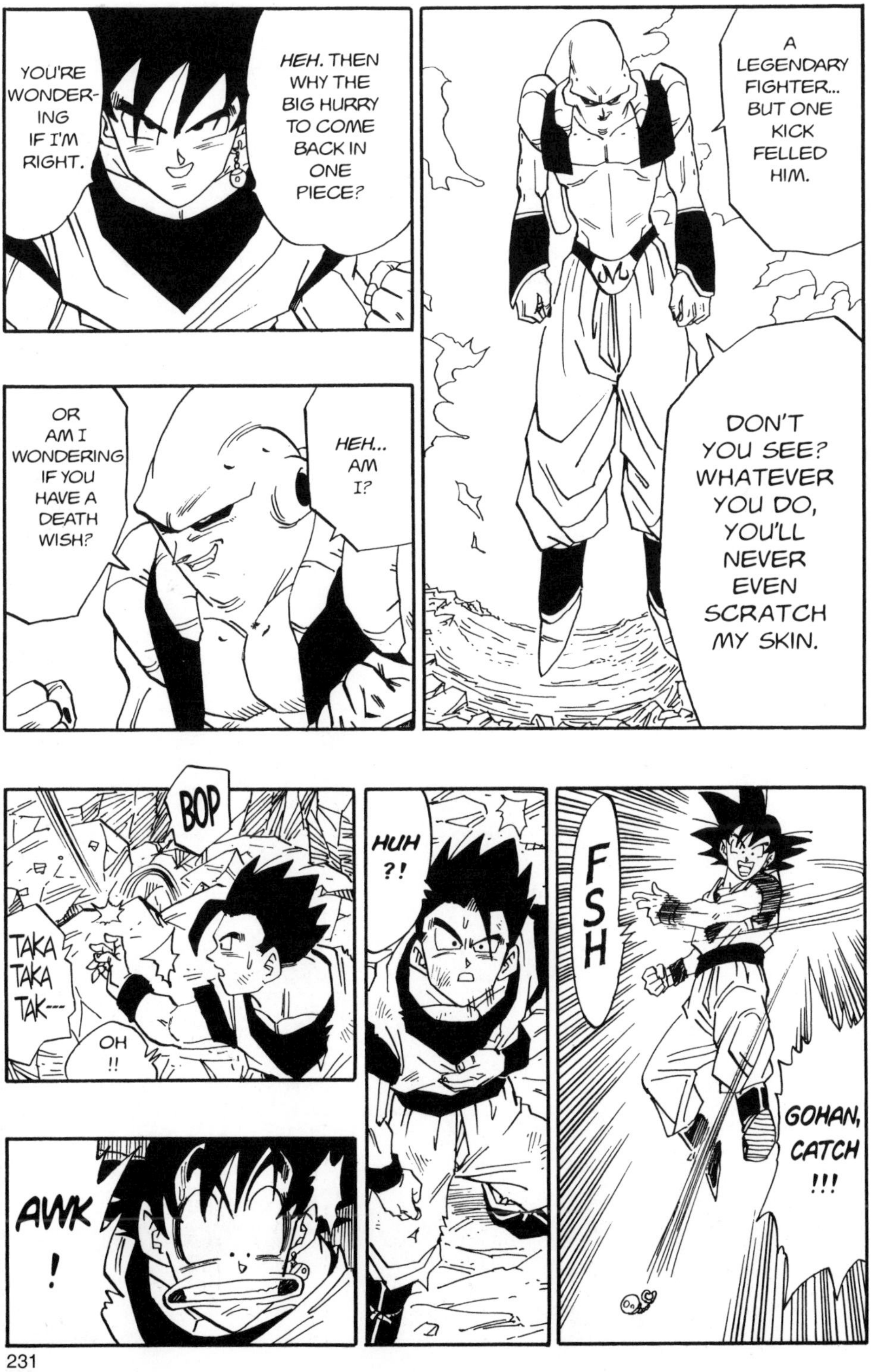
A LEGENDARY FIGHTER... BUT ONE KICK FELLED HIM.
DON'T YOU SEE? WHATEVER YOU DO, YOU'LL NEVER EVEN SCRATCH MY SKIN.
HEH. THEN WHY THE BIG HURRY TO COME BACK IN ONE PIECE?
YOU'RE WONDER-ING IF I'M RIGHT.
HEH... AM I?
OR AM I WONDERING IF YOU HAVE A DEATH WISH?
FSH
GOHAN, CATCH!!!
HUH?!
BOP
TAKA TAKA TAK---
OH !!
AWK!

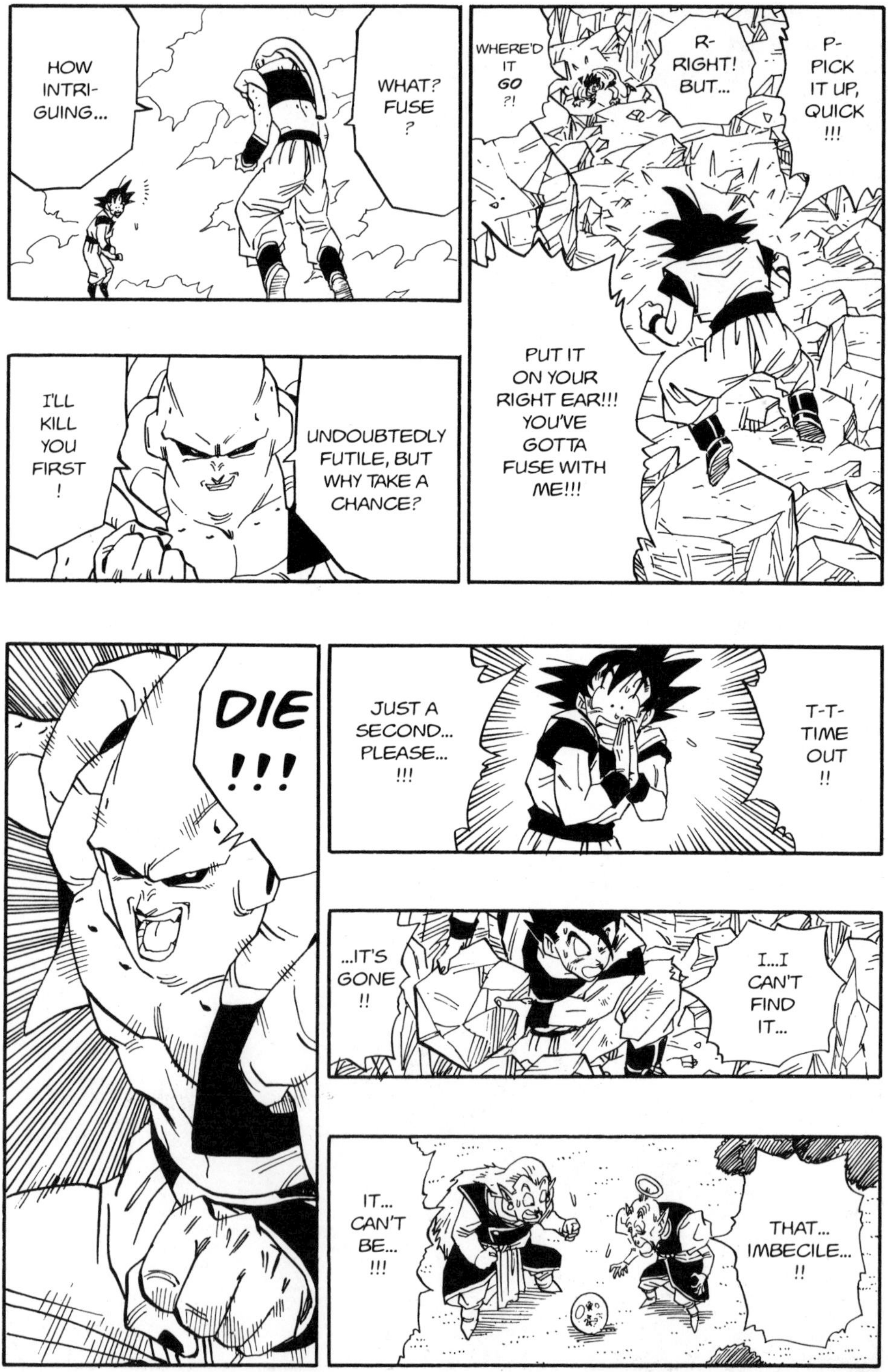
P-PICK IT UP, QUICK!!!
R-RIGHT! BUT...
WHERE'D IT GO?!
PUT IT ON YOUR RIGHT EAR!!! YOU'VE GOTTA FUSE WITH ME!!!
WHAT? FUSE?
HOW INTRIGUING...
UNDOUBTEDLY FUTILE, BUT WHY TAKE A CHANCE?
I'LL KILL YOU FIRST!
T-T-TIME OUT!!
JUST A SECOND... PLEASE...!!!
I...I CAN'T FIND IT...
...IT'S GONE!!
THAT... IMBECILE...!!
IT... CAN'T BE...!!!
DIE!!!

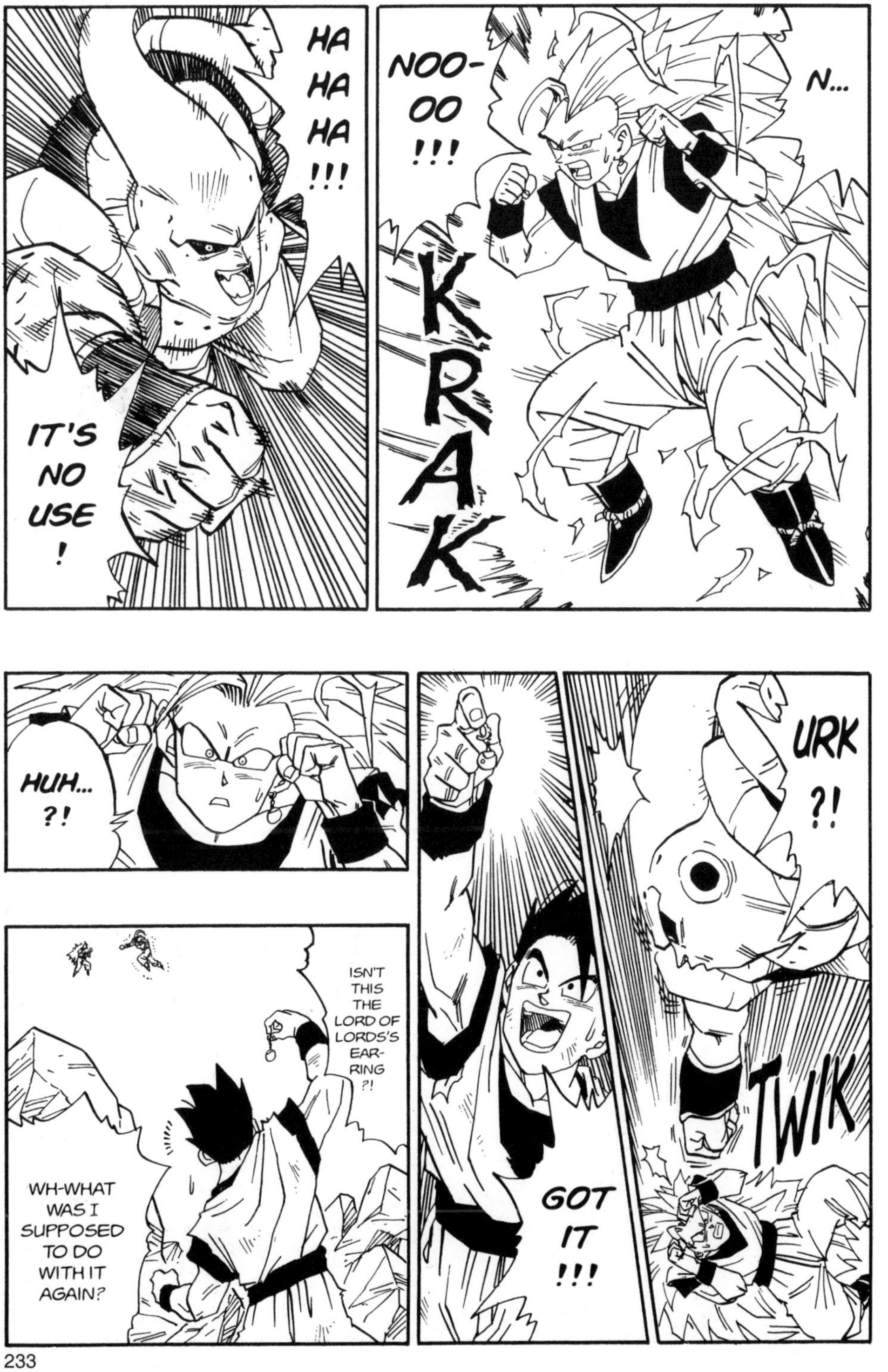
N...
NOO-OO!!!
KRAK
HA HA HA!!!
IT'S NO USE!
URK ?!
TWIK
GOT IT!!!
HUH... ?!
ISN'T THIS THE LORD OF LORDS'S EAR-RING ?!
WH-WHAT WAS I SUPPOSED TO DO WITH IT AGAIN?

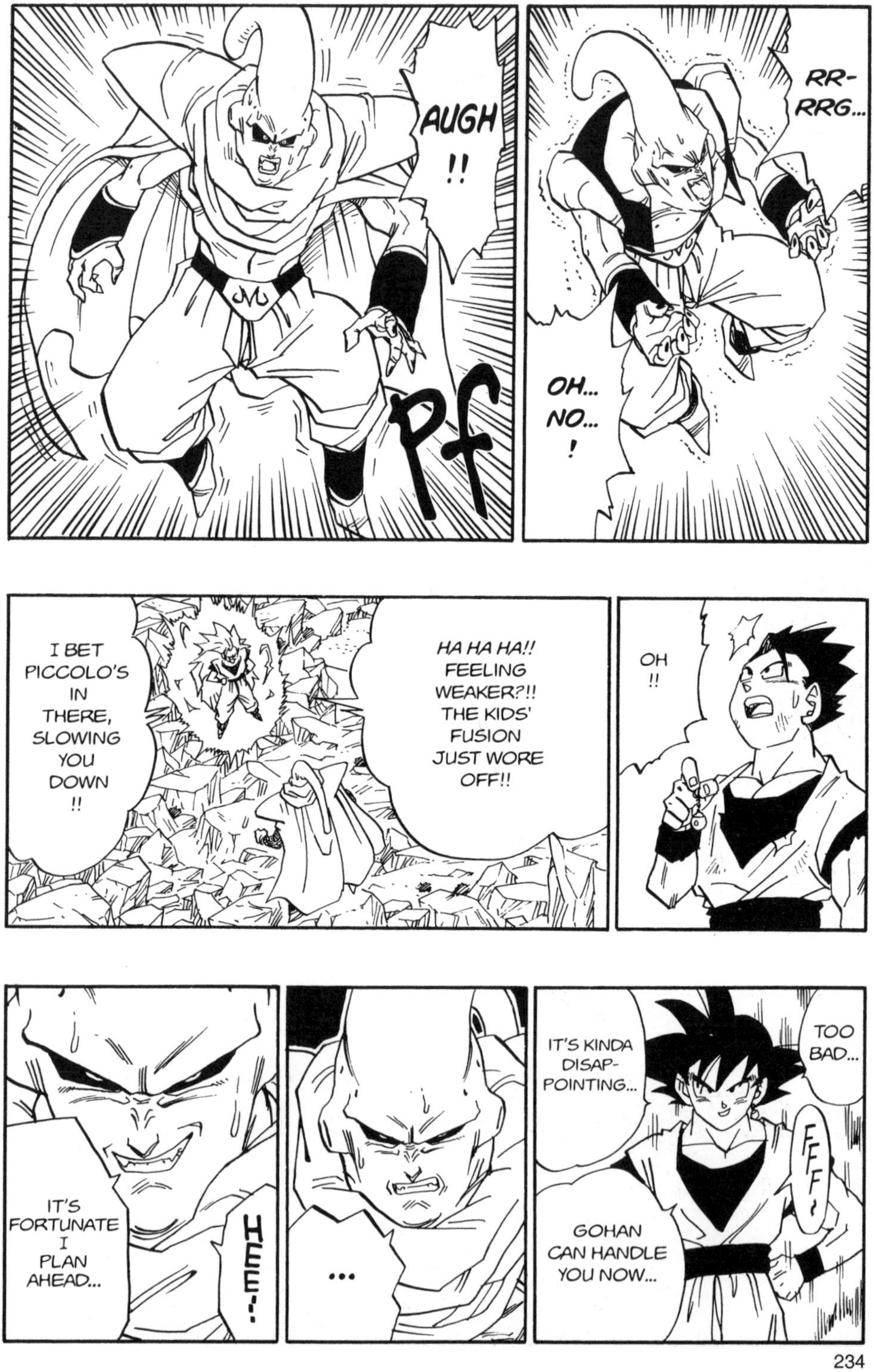
RR-RRG...
OH... NO...!
AUGH!!
Pf
OH!!
HA HA HA!! FEELING WEAKER?!! THE KIDS' FUSION JUST WORE OFF!!
I BET PICCOLO'S IN THERE, SLOWING YOU DOWN!!
TOO BAD...
IT'S KINDA DISAP-POINTING...
FFF
GOHAN CAN HANDLE YOU NOW...
...
HEEE!!
IT'S FORTUNATE I PLAN AHEAD...

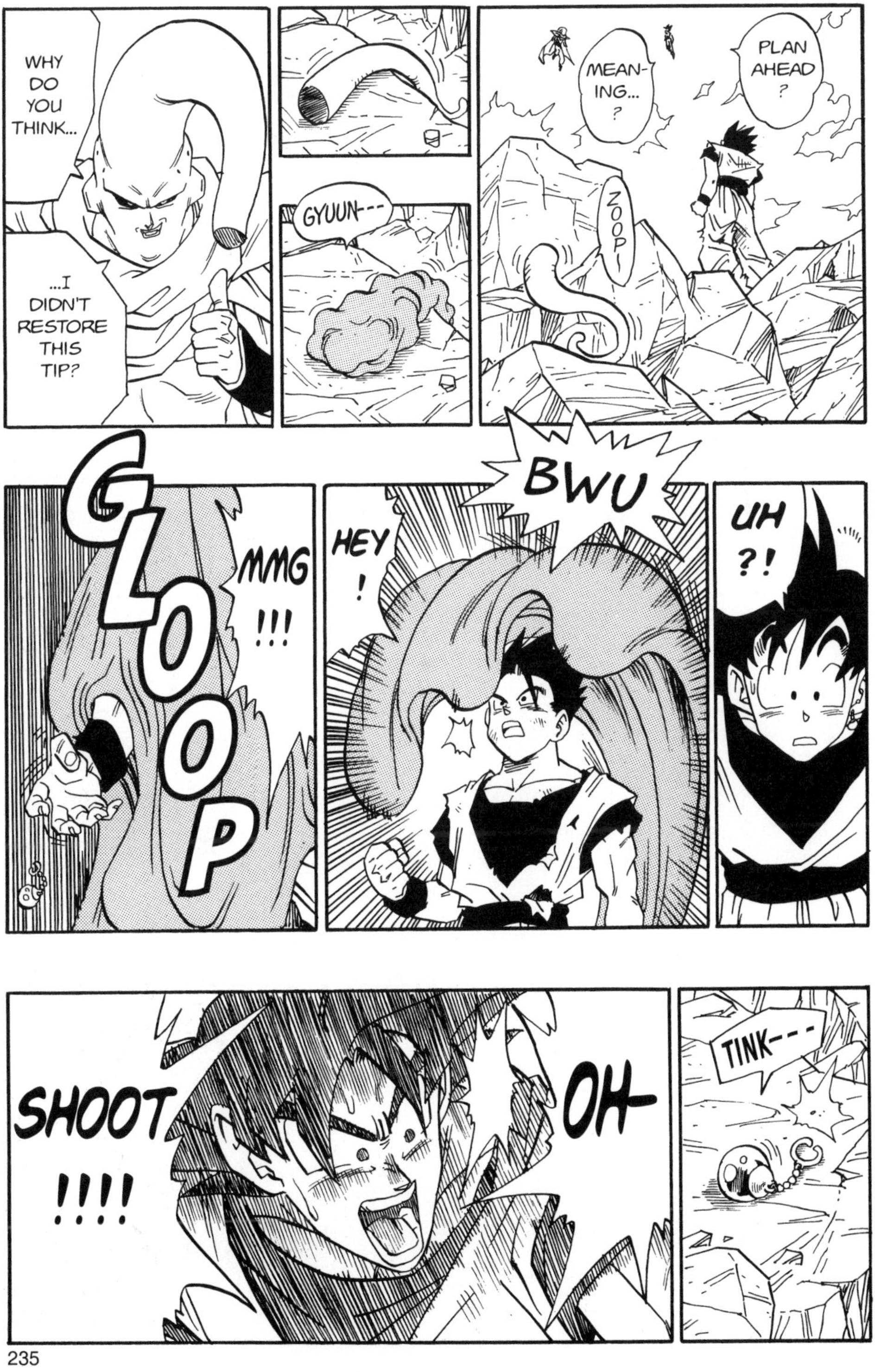
PLAN AHEAD ?
MEANING... ?
ZOOP
GYUUN---
WHY DO YOU THINK...
...I DIDN'T RESTORE THIS TIP?
UH ?!
BWU
HEY !
MMG !!!
GLOOP
TINK---
OH-
SHOOT !!!!

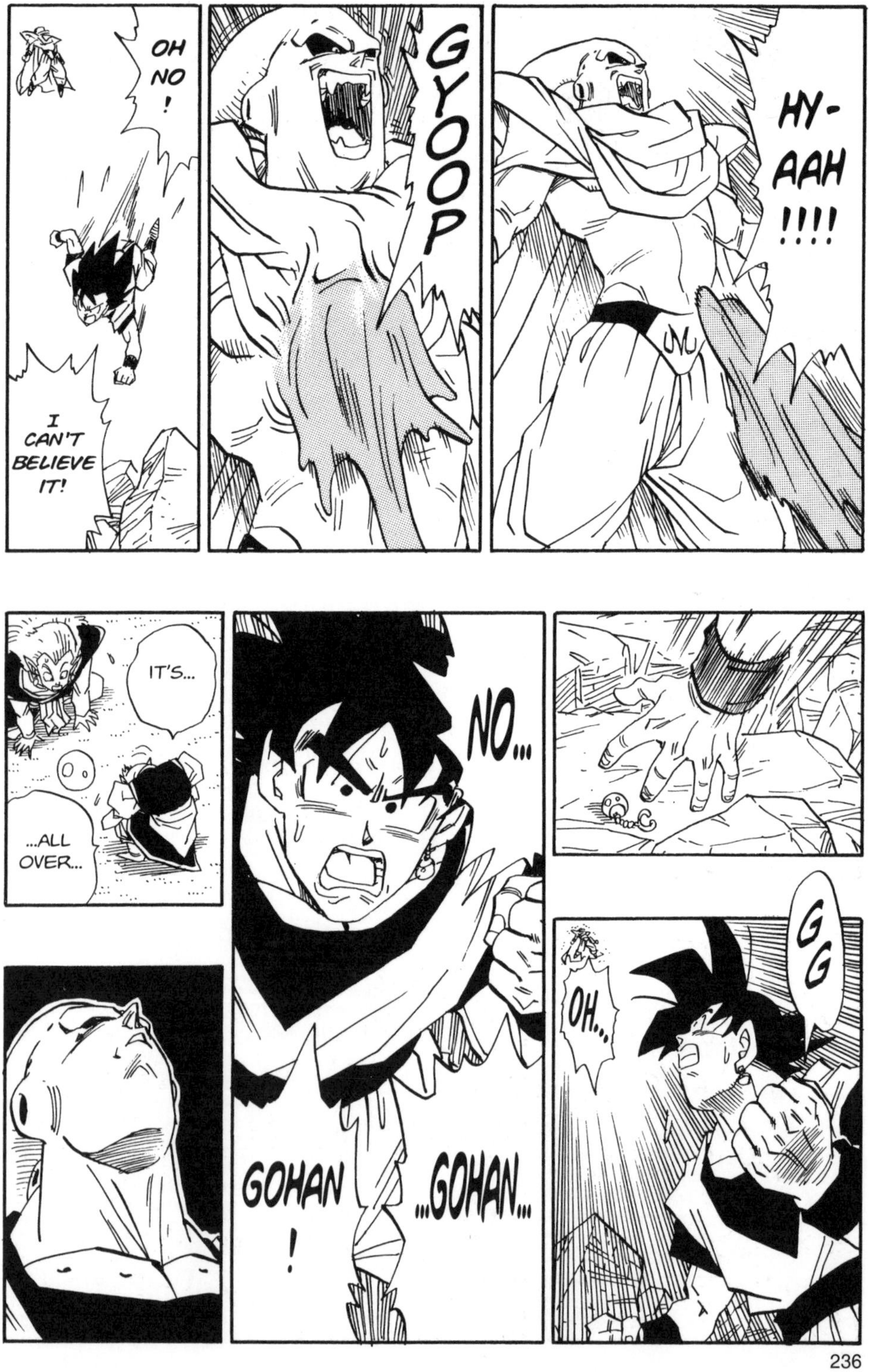

HY-AAH!!!!
GYOOP
OH NO!
I CAN'T BELIEVE IT!
GG
OH...
NO...
...GOHAN...
GOHAN!
IT'S...
...ALL OVER...

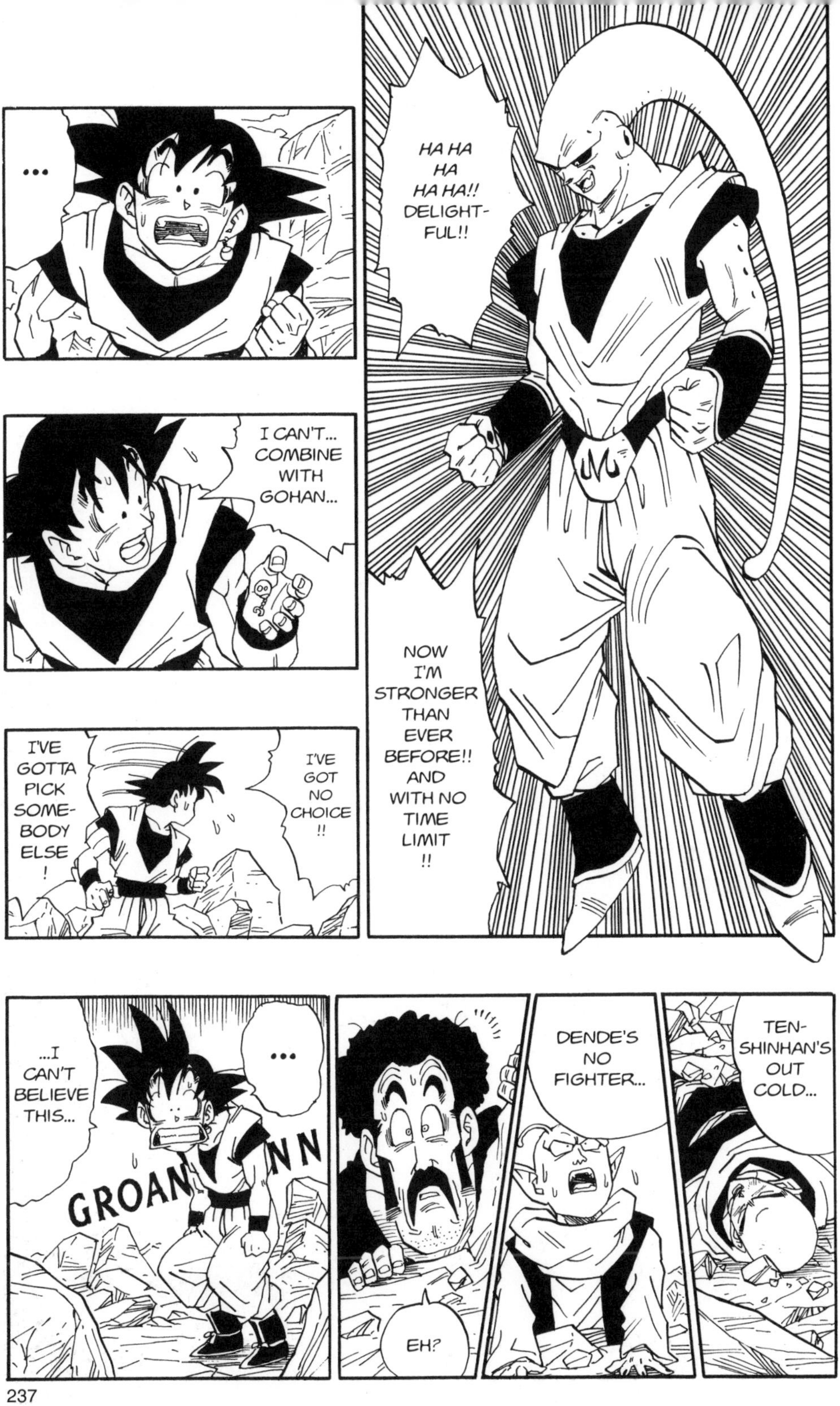
HA HA HA HA HA!! DELIGHTFUL!!
NOW I'M STRONGER THAN EVER BEFORE!! AND WITH NO TIME LIMIT!!
...
I CAN'T... COMBINE WITH GOHAN...
I'VE GOT NO CHOICE!!
I'VE GOTTA PICK SOMEBODY ELSE!
TEN-SHINHAN'S OUT COLD...
DENDE'S NO FIGHTER...
EH?
...
...I CAN'T BELIEVE THIS...
GROANNN

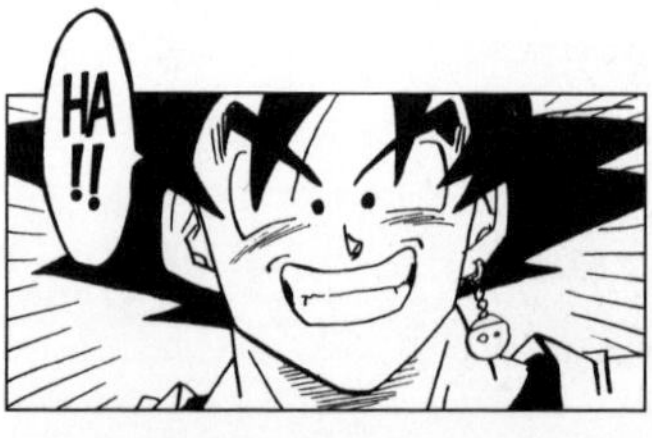
HA !!

DragonBallZ

VOLUME 26

FAREWELL, DRAGON WORLD!

DRAGON BALL ドラゴンボール

DBZ:309 • The Ultimate Combination!!

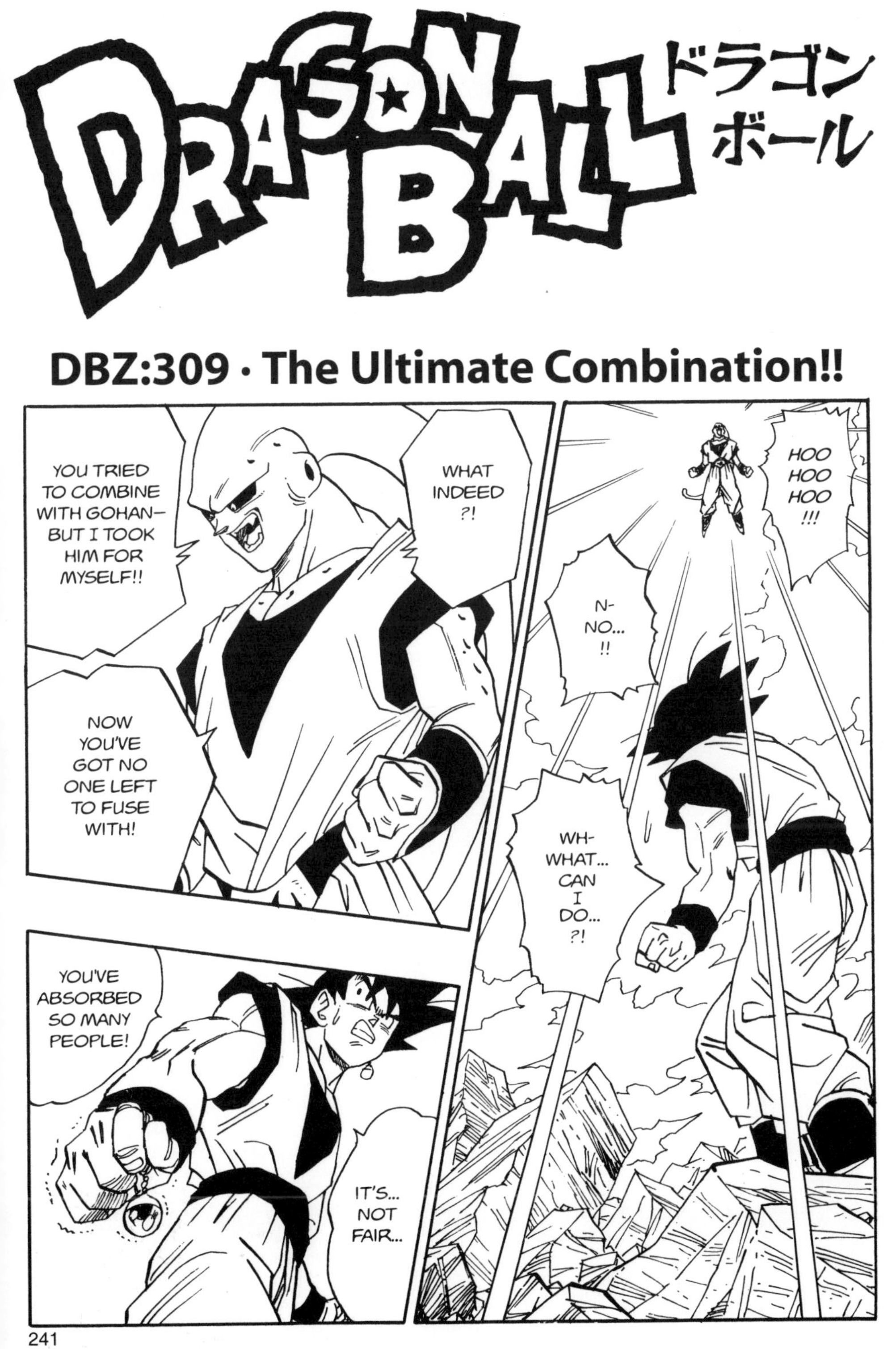
HOO HOO HOO!!!
N-NO...!!
WH-WHAT... CAN I DO...?!
WHAT INDEED?!
YOU TRIED TO COMBINE WITH GOHAN—BUT I TOOK HIM FOR MYSELF!!
NOW YOU'VE GOT NO ONE LEFT TO FUSE WITH!
YOU'VE ABSORBED SO MANY PEOPLE!
IT'S... NOT FAIR...

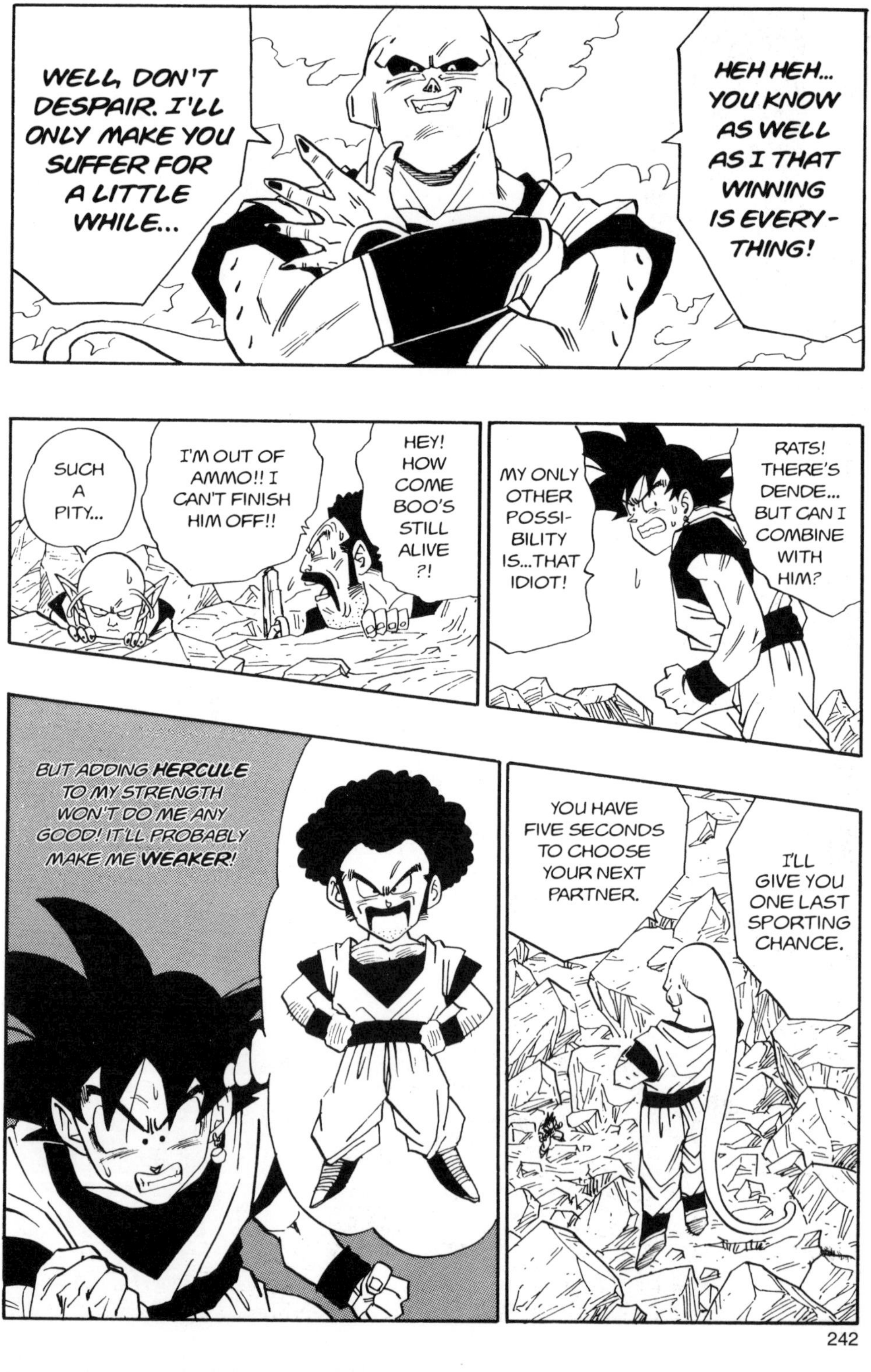
HEH HEH... YOU KNOW AS WELL AS I THAT WINNING IS EVERYTHING!
WELL, DON'T DESPAIR. I'LL ONLY MAKE YOU SUFFER FOR A LITTLE WHILE...
RATS! THERE'S DENDE... BUT CAN I COMBINE WITH HIM?
MY ONLY OTHER POSSIBILITY IS...THAT IDIOT!
HEY! HOW COME BOO'S STILL ALIVE?!
I'M OUT OF AMMO!! I CAN'T FINISH HIM OFF!!
SUCH A PITY...
I'LL GIVE YOU ONE LAST SPORTING CHANCE.
YOU HAVE FIVE SECONDS TO CHOOSE YOUR NEXT PARTNER.
BUT ADDING HERCULE TO MY STRENGTH WON'T DO ME ANY GOOD! IT'LL PROBABLY MAKE ME WEAKER!

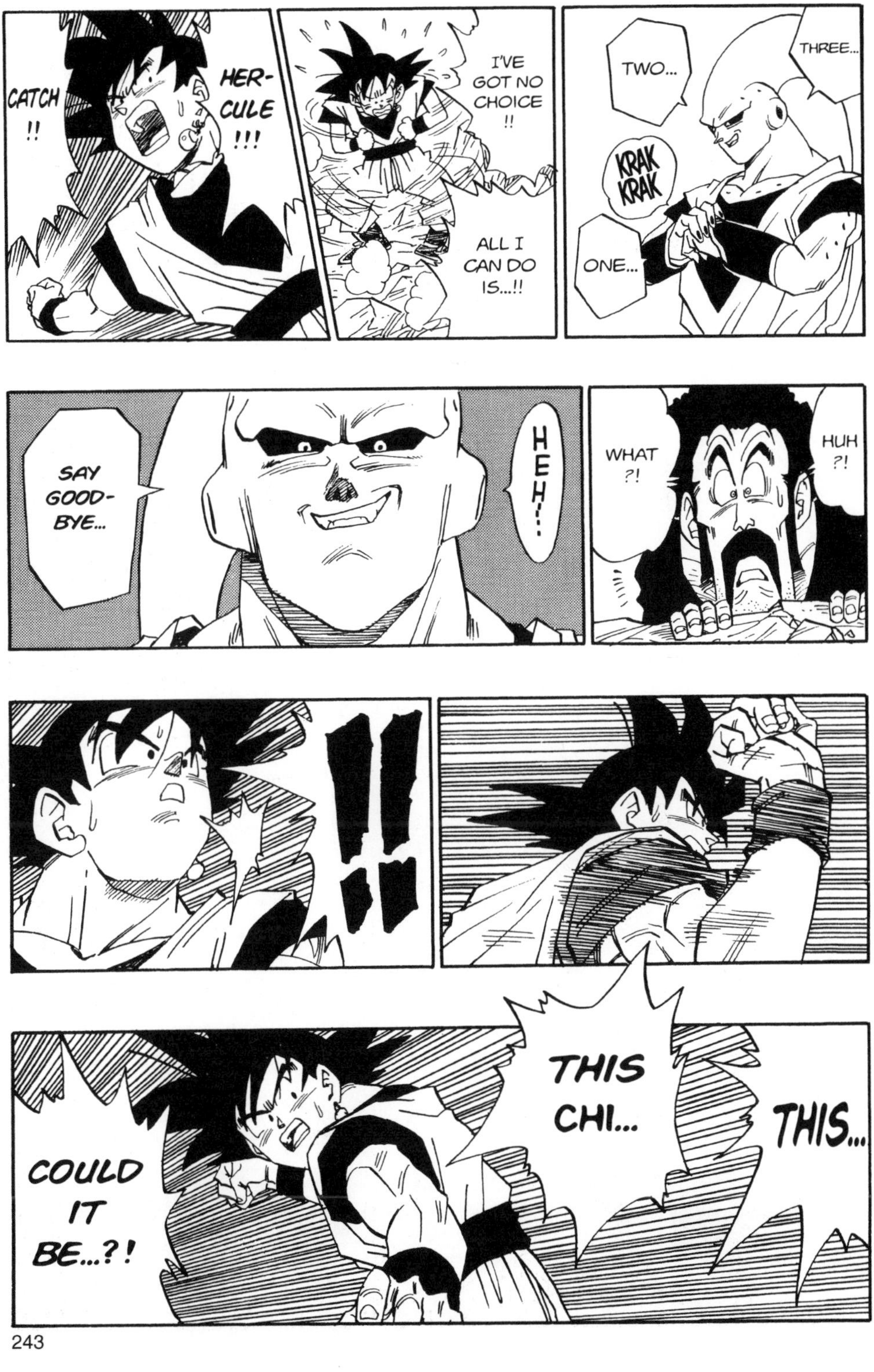
THREE...
TWO...
KRAK KRAK
ONE...
I'VE GOT NO CHOICE!!
ALL I CAN DO IS...!!
HER-CULE!!!
CATCH!!
HUH?!
WHAT?!
HEH!..
SAY GOOD-BYE...
!!
THIS...
THIS CHI...
COULD IT BE...?!

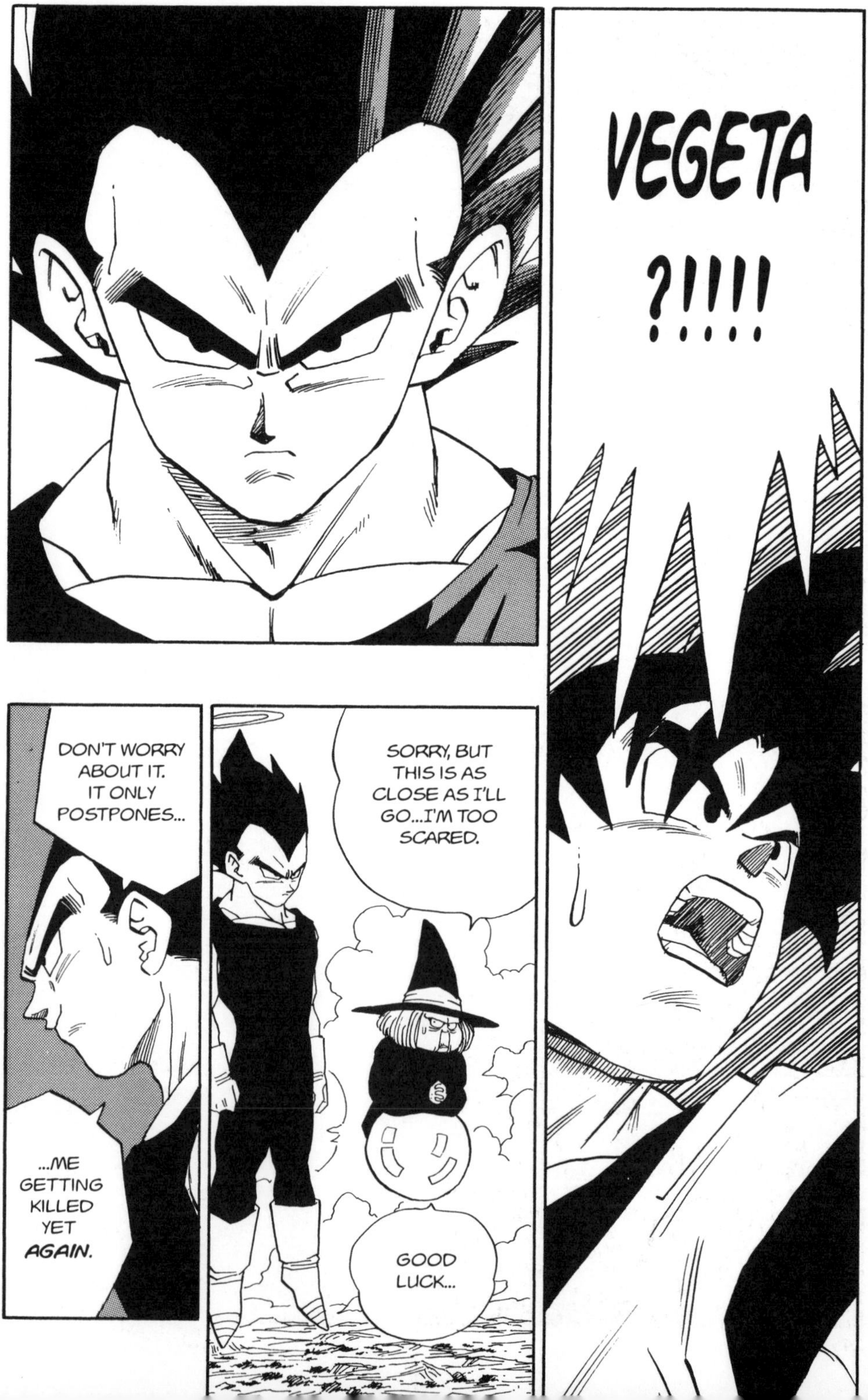
VEGETA ?!!!!!
SORRY, BUT THIS IS AS CLOSE AS I'LL GO...I'M TOO SCARED.
GOOD LUCK...
DON'T WORRY ABOUT IT. IT ONLY POSTPONES...
...ME GETTING KILLED YET ***AGAIN.***

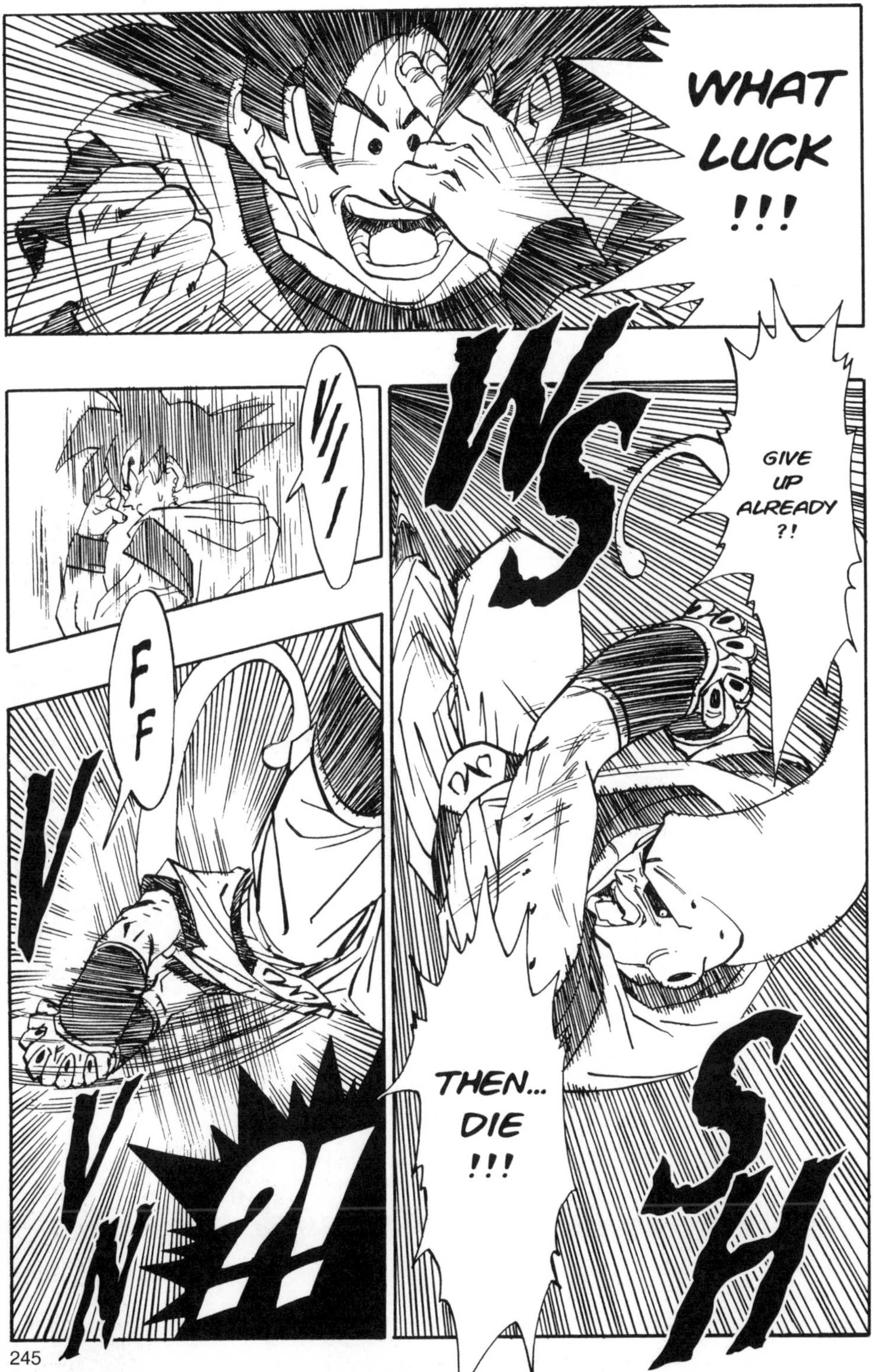
WHAT LUCK !!!
WS
GIVE UP ALREADY ?!
THEN... DIE !!!
SH
FF
V
VN
?!

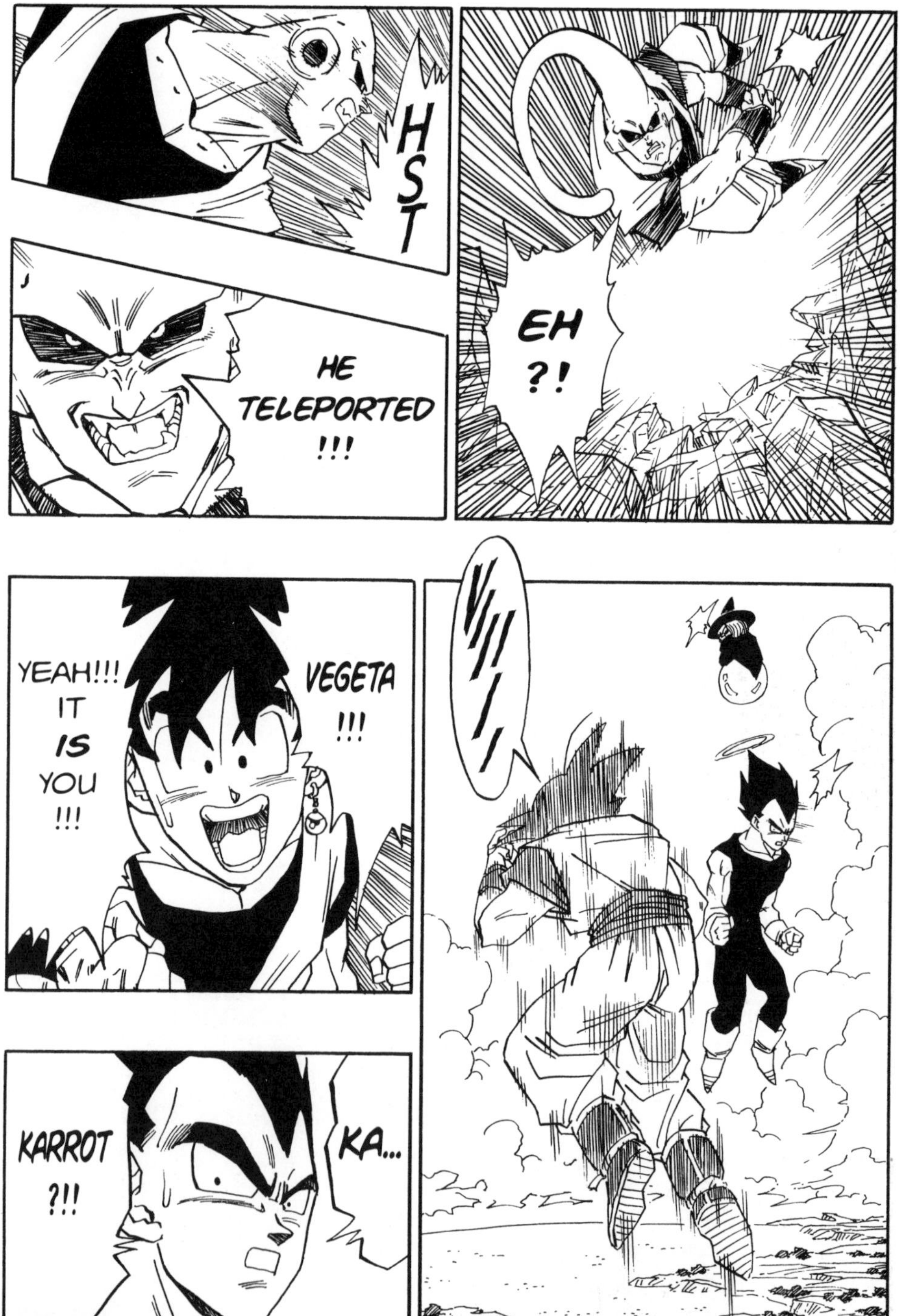
EH ?!
HST
HE TELEPORTED !!!
VEGETA !!!
YEAH!!! IT *IS* YOU !!!
KA...
KARROT ?!!

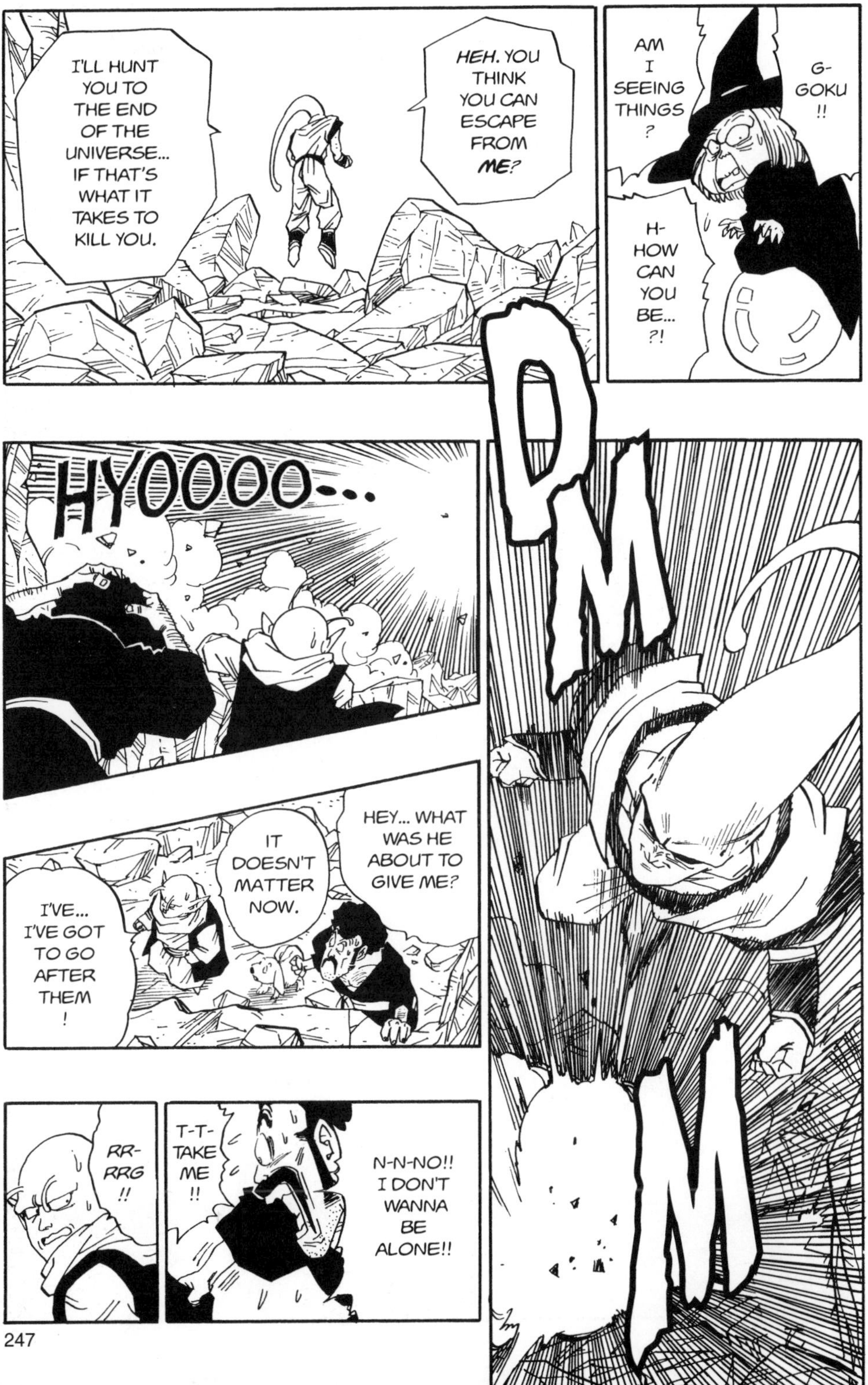
G-GOKU!!
AM I SEEING THINGS?
H-HOW CAN YOU BE...?!
HEH. YOU THINK YOU CAN ESCAPE FROM *ME?*
I'LL HUNT YOU TO THE END OF THE UNIVERSE... IF THAT'S WHAT IT TAKES TO KILL YOU.
DMM
HYOOOO...
HEY... WHAT WAS HE ABOUT TO GIVE ME?
IT DOESN'T MATTER NOW.
I'VE... I'VE GOT TO GO AFTER THEM!
N-N-NO!! I DON'T WANNA BE ALONE!!
T-T-TAKE ME!!
RR-RRG!!

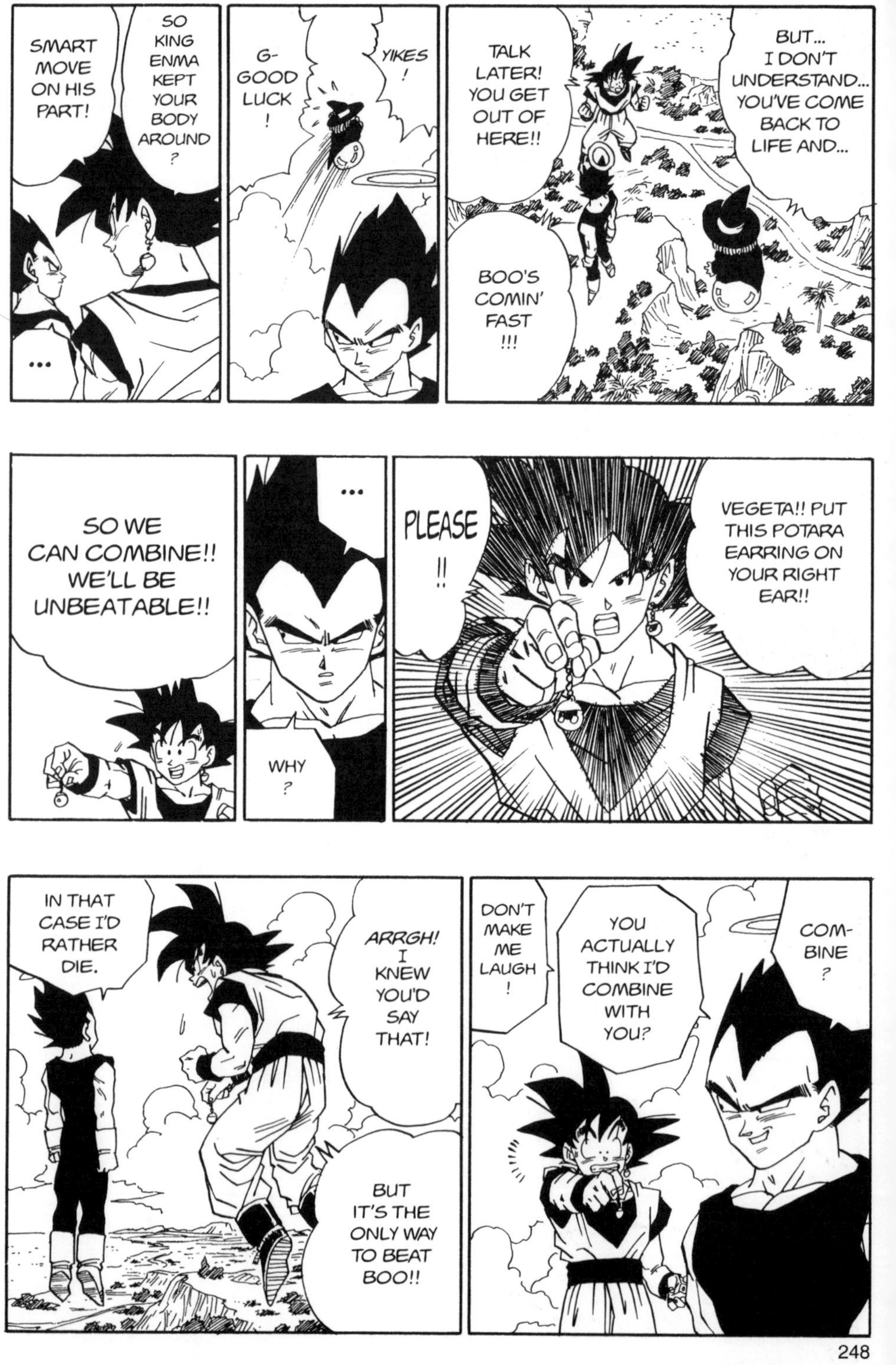
BUT... I DON'T UNDERSTAND... YOU'VE COME BACK TO LIFE AND...
TALK LATER! YOU GET OUT OF HERE!!
BOO'S COMIN' FAST !!!
YIKES!
G-GOOD LUCK!
SO KING ENMA KEPT YOUR BODY AROUND?
SMART MOVE ON HIS PART!
...
VEGETA!! PUT THIS POTARA EARRING ON YOUR RIGHT EAR!!
PLEASE!!
...
WHY?
SO WE CAN COMBINE!! WE'LL BE UNBEATABLE!!
COMBINE?
YOU ACTUALLY THINK I'D COMBINE WITH YOU?
DON'T MAKE ME LAUGH!
ARRGH! I KNEW YOU'D SAY THAT!
BUT IT'S THE ONLY WAY TO BEAT BOO!!
IN THAT CASE I'D RATHER DIE.

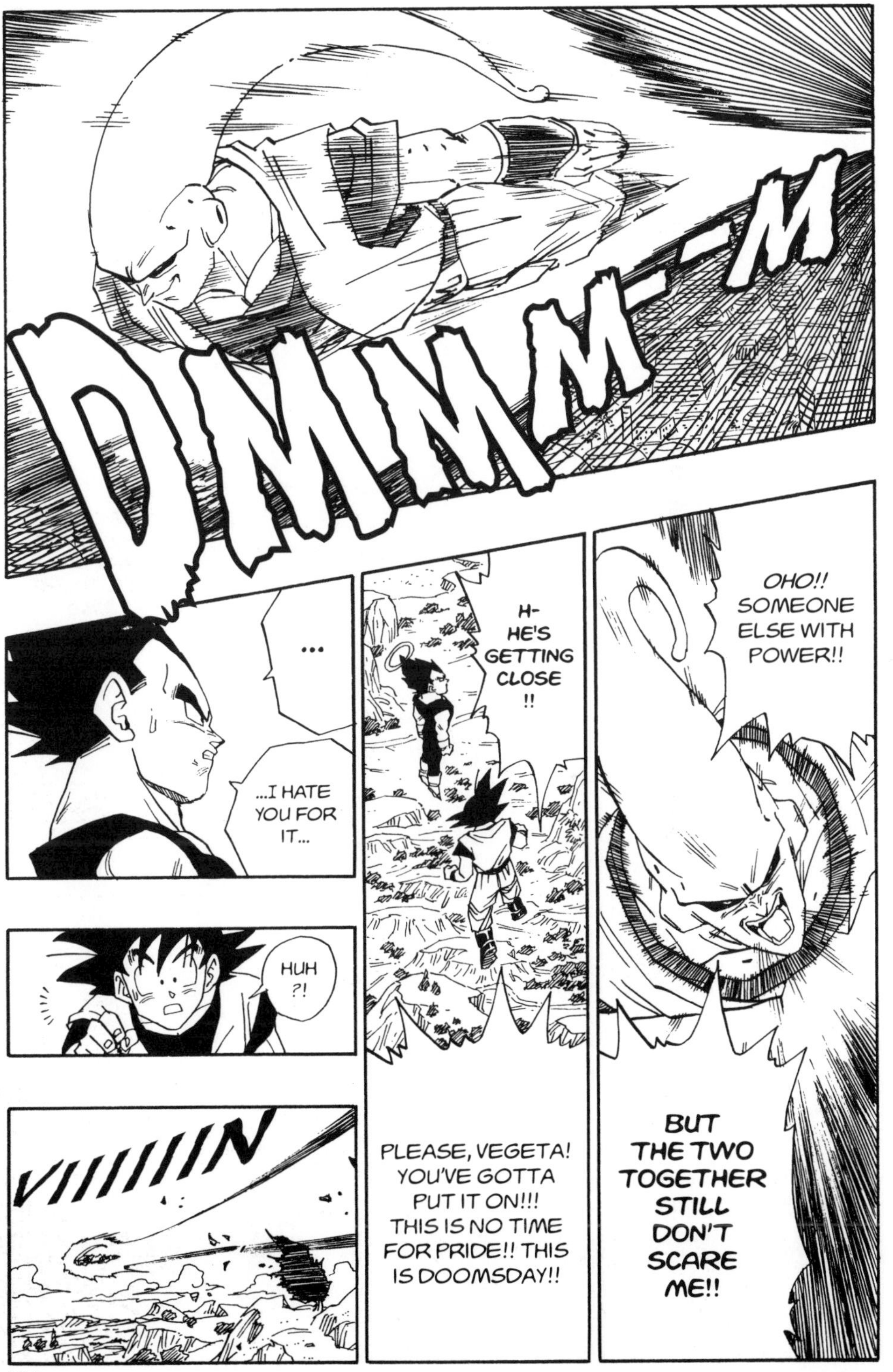
DMMMM--M
OHO!! SOMEONE ELSE WITH POWER!!
BUT THE TWO TOGETHER STILL DON'T SCARE ME!!
H-HE'S GETTING CLOSE!!
PLEASE, VEGETA! YOU'VE GOTTA PUT IT ON!!! THIS IS NO TIME FOR PRIDE!! THIS IS DOOMSDAY!!
...
...I HATE YOU FOR IT...
HUH?!
VIIIIIIN

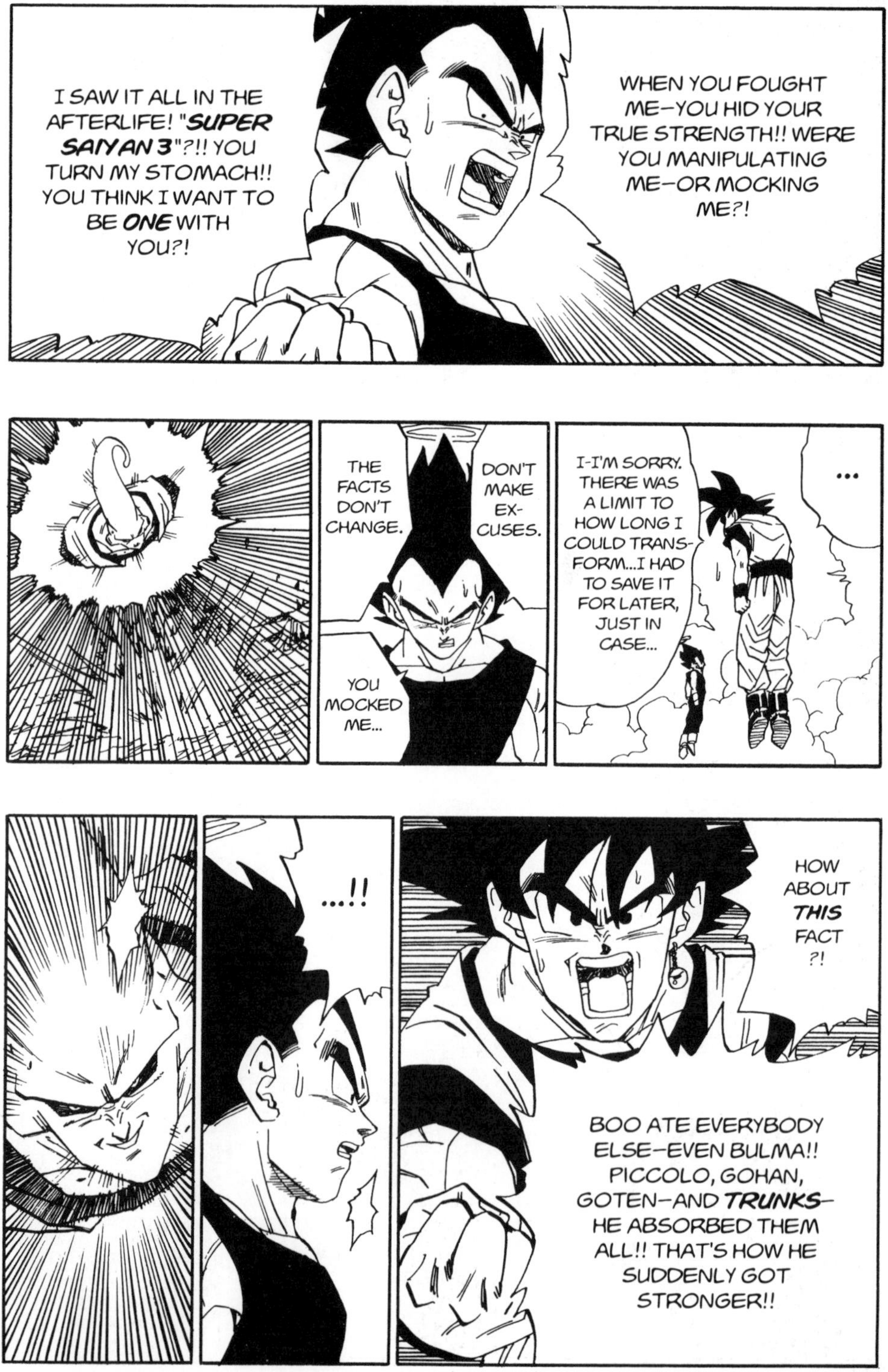
WHEN YOU FOUGHT ME—YOU HID YOUR TRUE STRENGTH!! WERE YOU MANIPULATING ME—OR MOCKING ME?!
I SAW IT ALL IN THE AFTERLIFE! "SUPER SAIYAN 3"?!! YOU TURN MY STOMACH!! YOU THINK I WANT TO BE ONE WITH YOU?!
...
I-I'M SORRY. THERE WAS A LIMIT TO HOW LONG I COULD TRANSFORM...I HAD TO SAVE IT FOR LATER, JUST IN CASE...
DON'T MAKE EXCUSES.
THE FACTS DON'T CHANGE.
YOU MOCKED ME...
HOW ABOUT THIS FACT?!
BOO ATE EVERYBODY ELSE—EVEN BULMA!! PICCOLO, GOHAN, GOTEN—AND TRUNKS—HE ABSORBED THEM ALL!! THAT'S HOW HE SUDDENLY GOT STRONGER!!
...!!

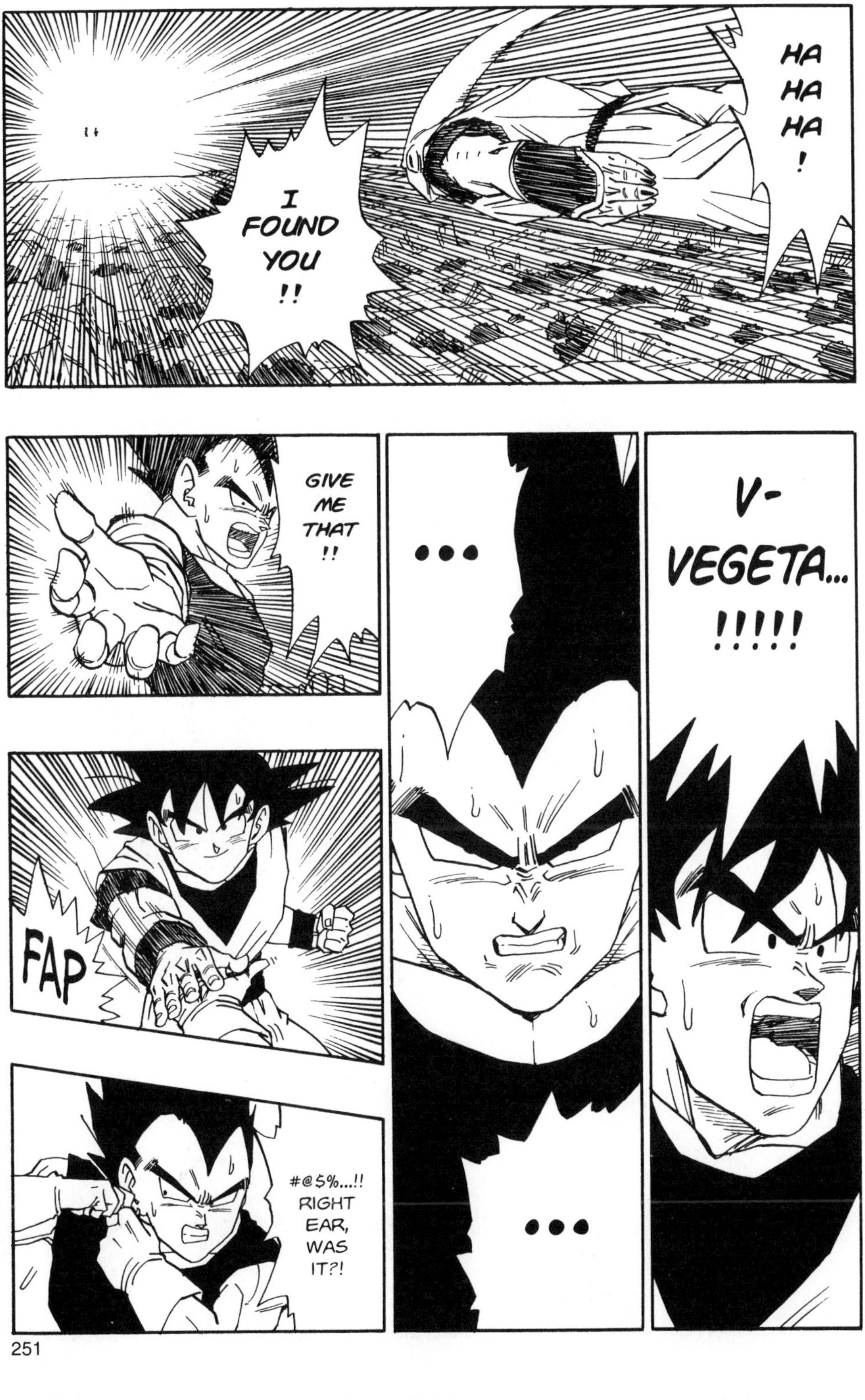

HA HA HA!
I FOUND YOU!!
V-VEGETA...!!!!!
...
...
GIVE ME THAT!!
FAP
#@$%...!! RIGHT EAR, WAS IT?!

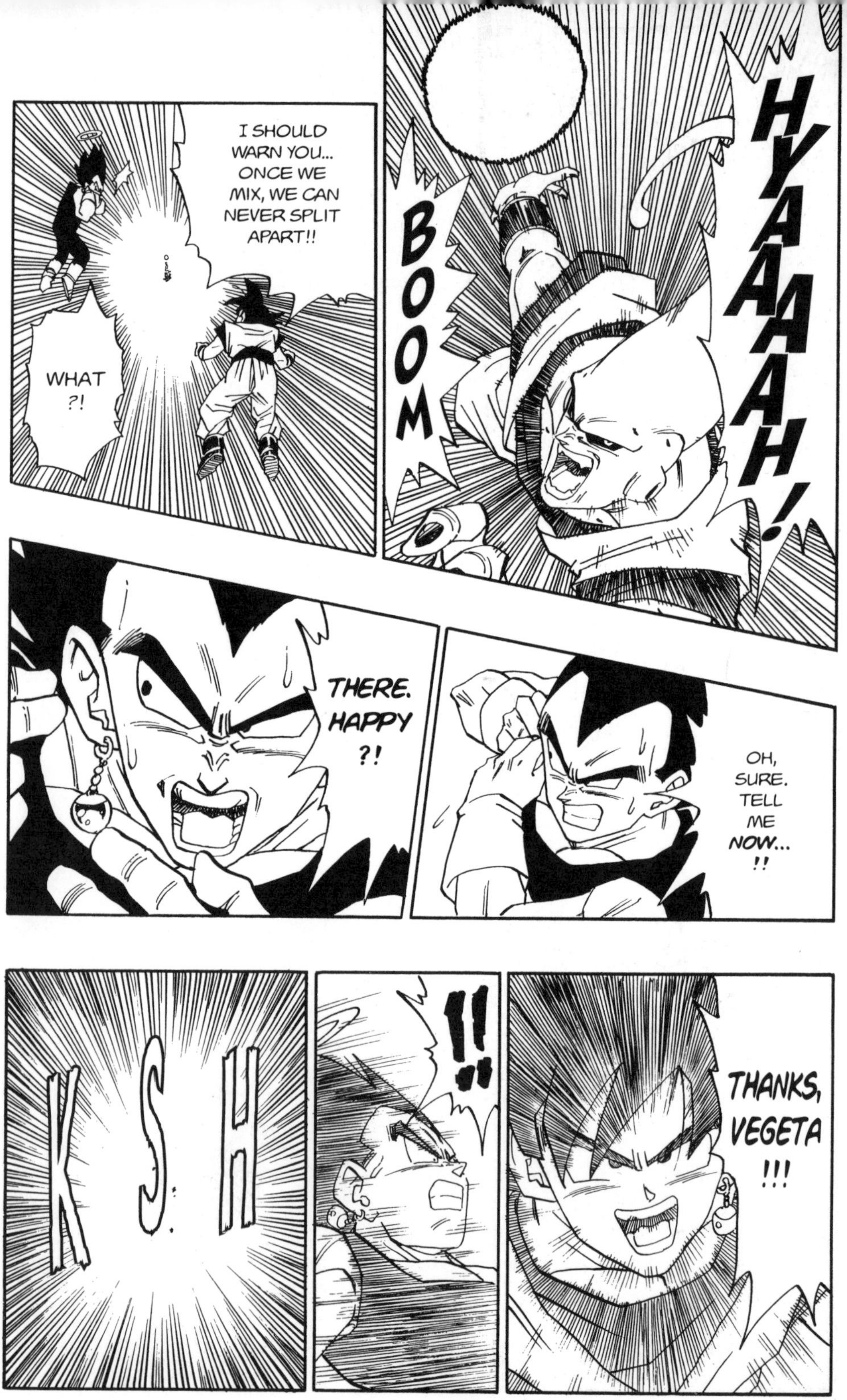

HYAAAAH!
BOOM
I SHOULD WARN YOU... ONCE WE MIX, WE CAN NEVER SPLIT APART!!
WHAT ?!
OH, SURE. TELL ME NOW... !!
THERE. HAPPY ?!
THANKS, VEGETA !!!
!!
KSH

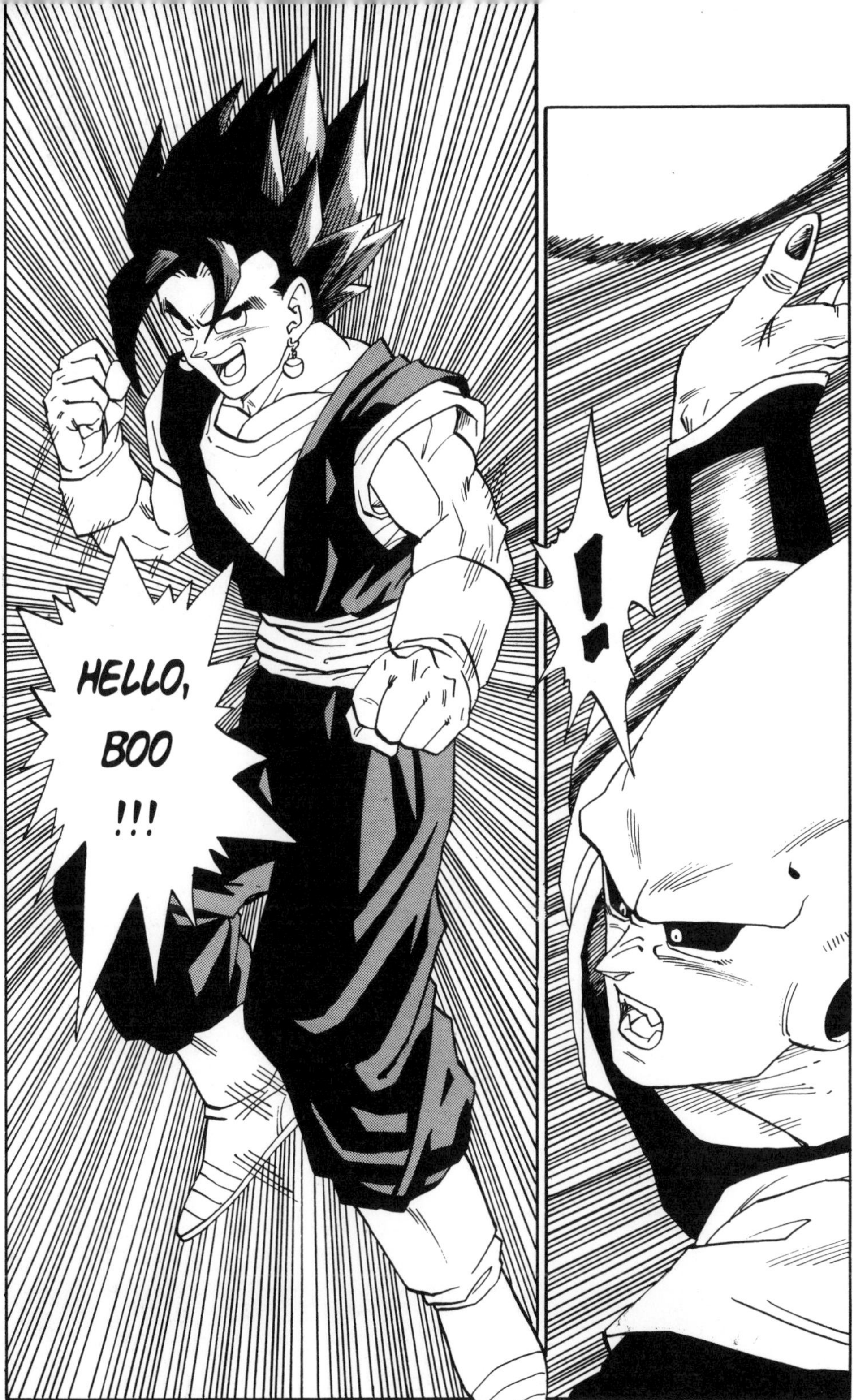
!!
HELLO, BOO!!!

DRAGON BALL ドラゴンボール

DBZ:310 · The Ultimate Fighter

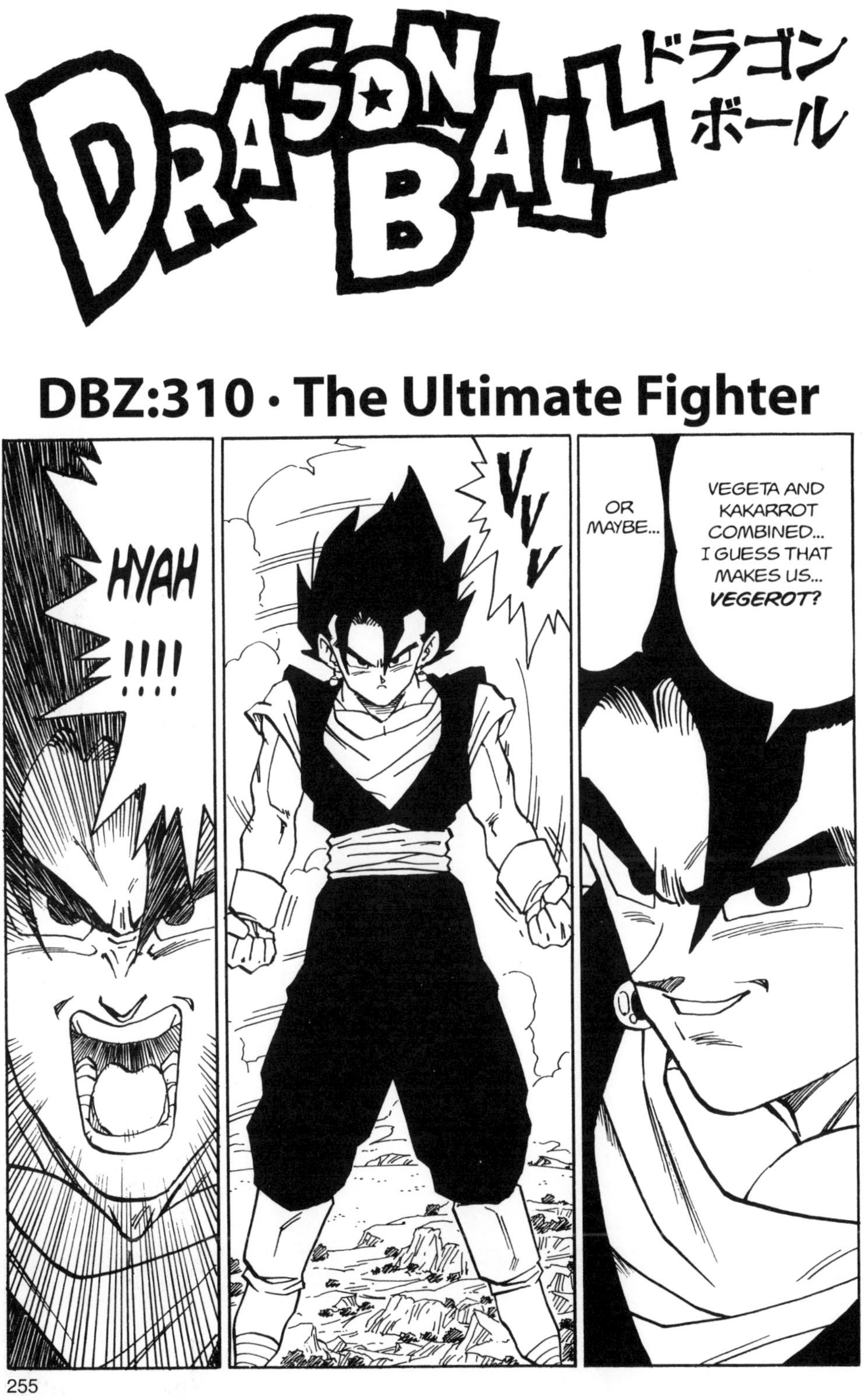

VEGETA AND KAKARROT COMBINED... I GUESS THAT MAKES US... ***VEGEROT?***
OR MAYBE...
VVV
HYAH !!!!

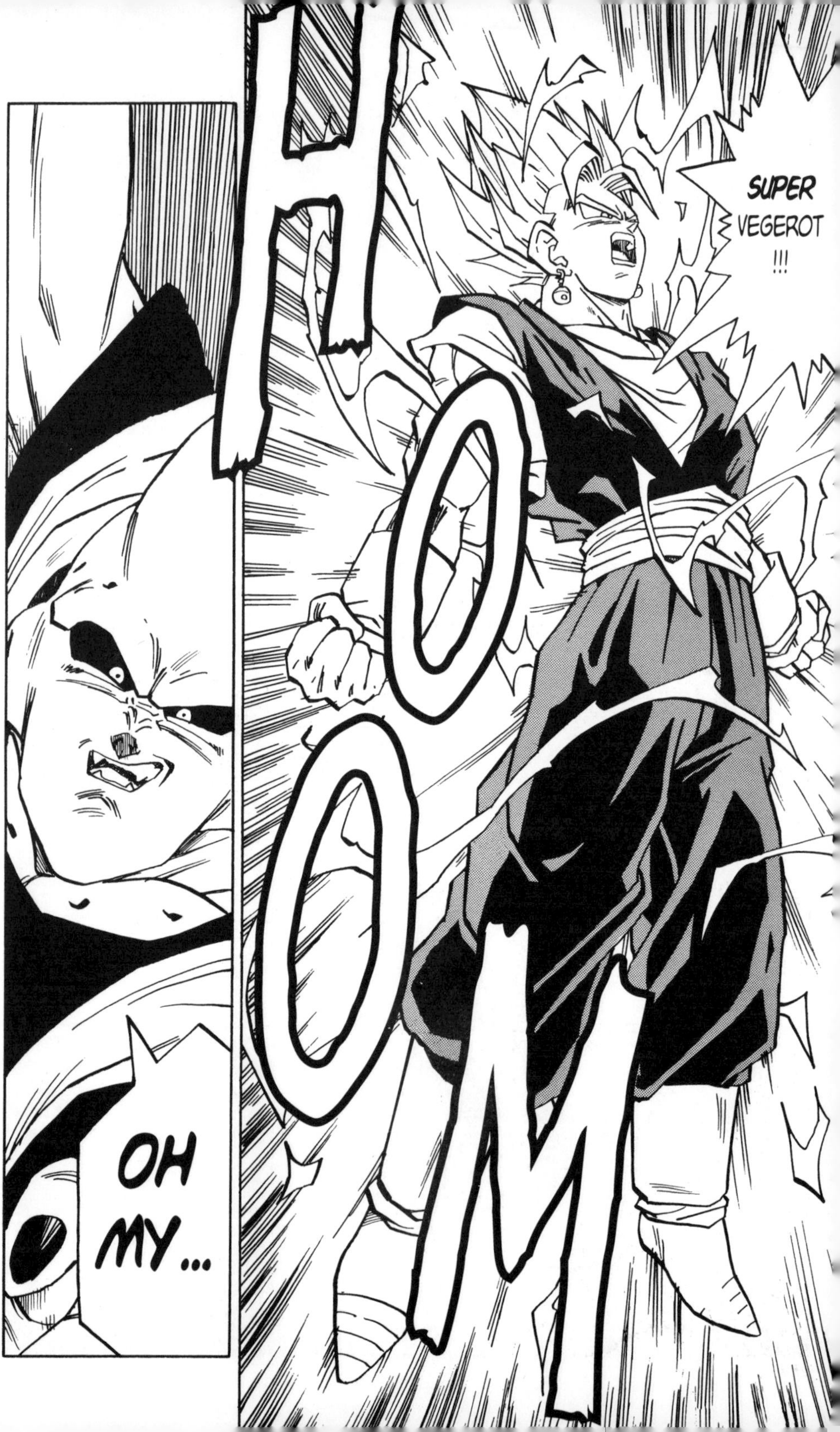
SUPER VEGEROT !!!
HOOM
OH MY...

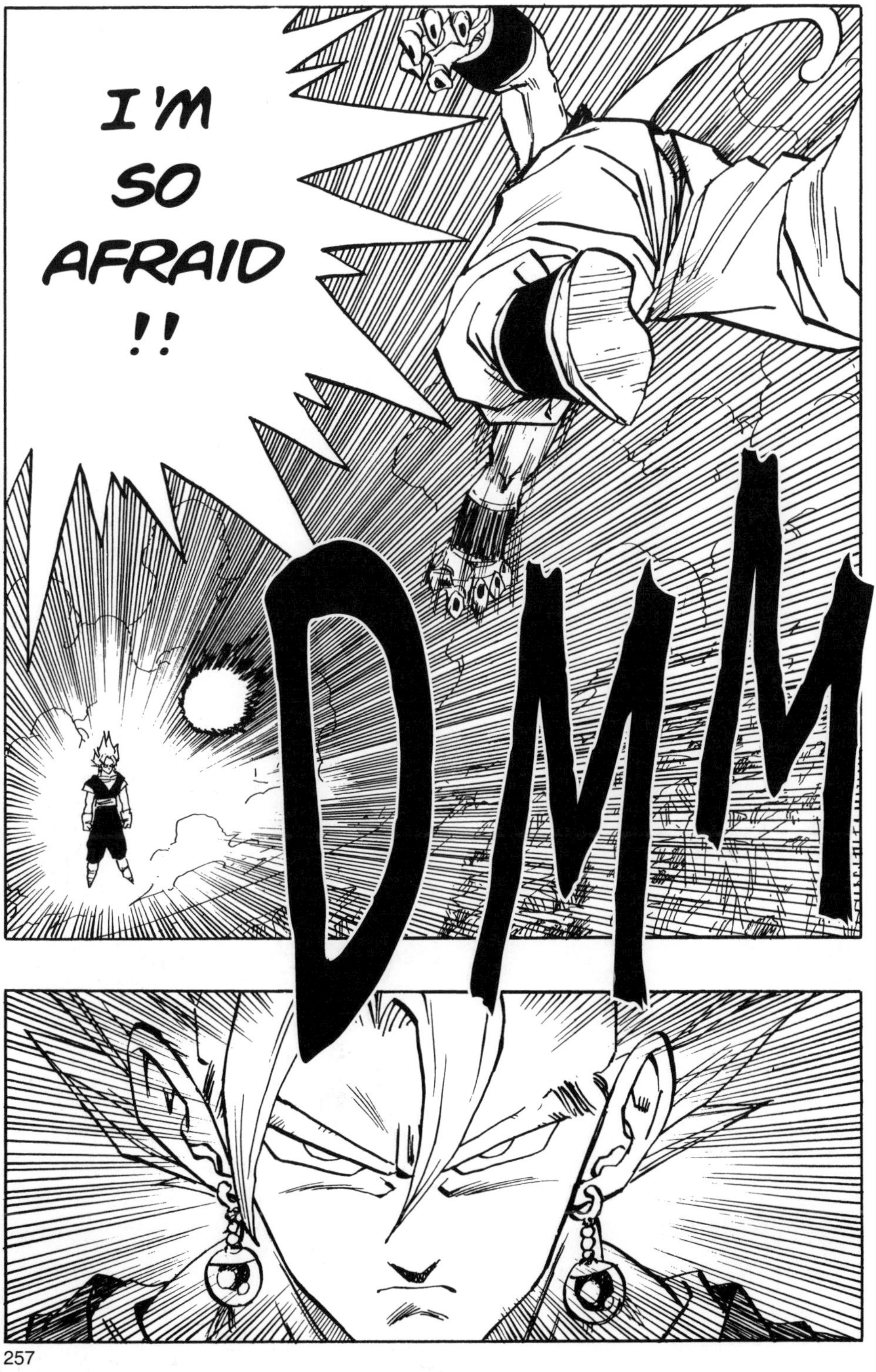
I'M SO AFRAID !!
DMM

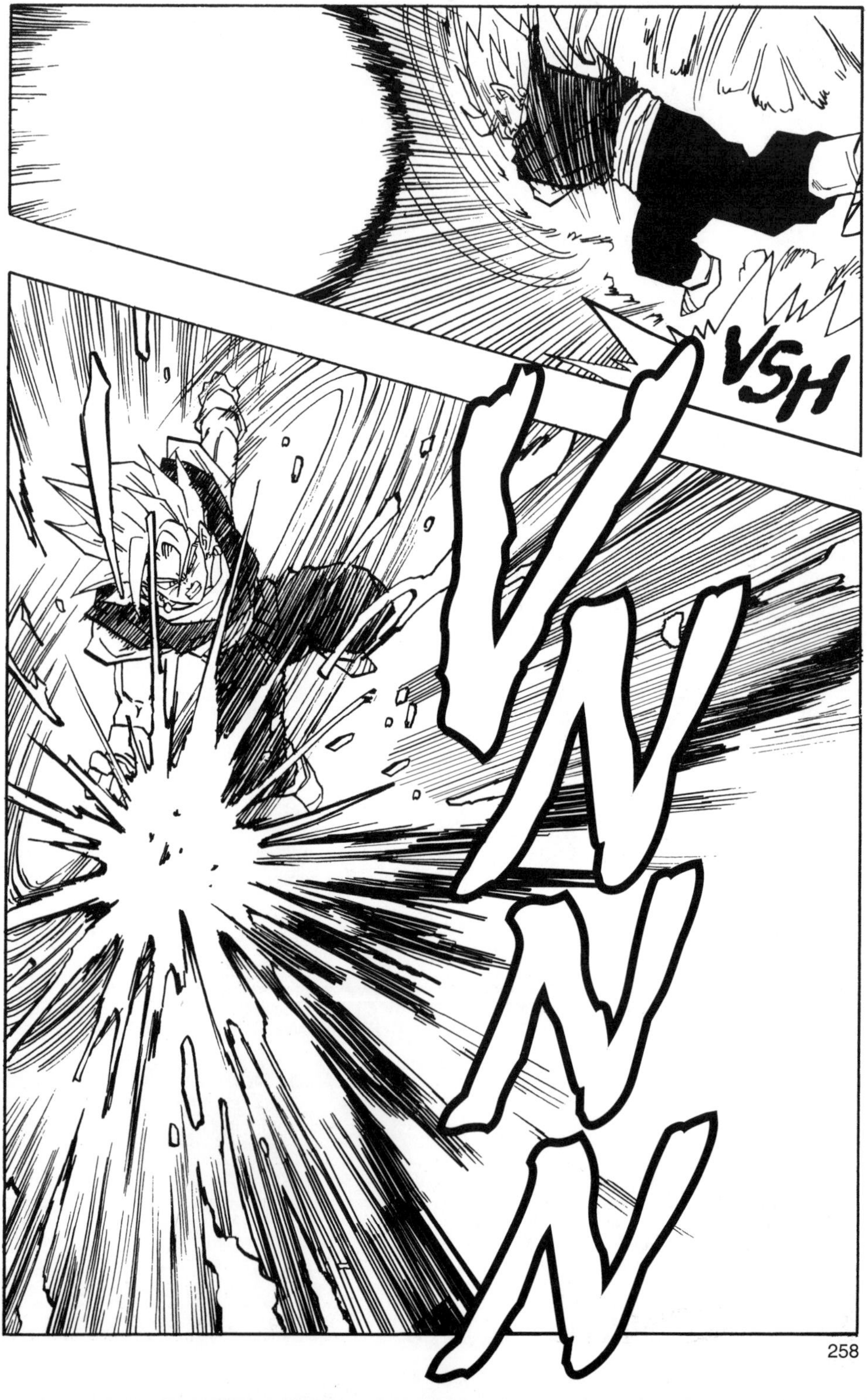
VSH
VNNN

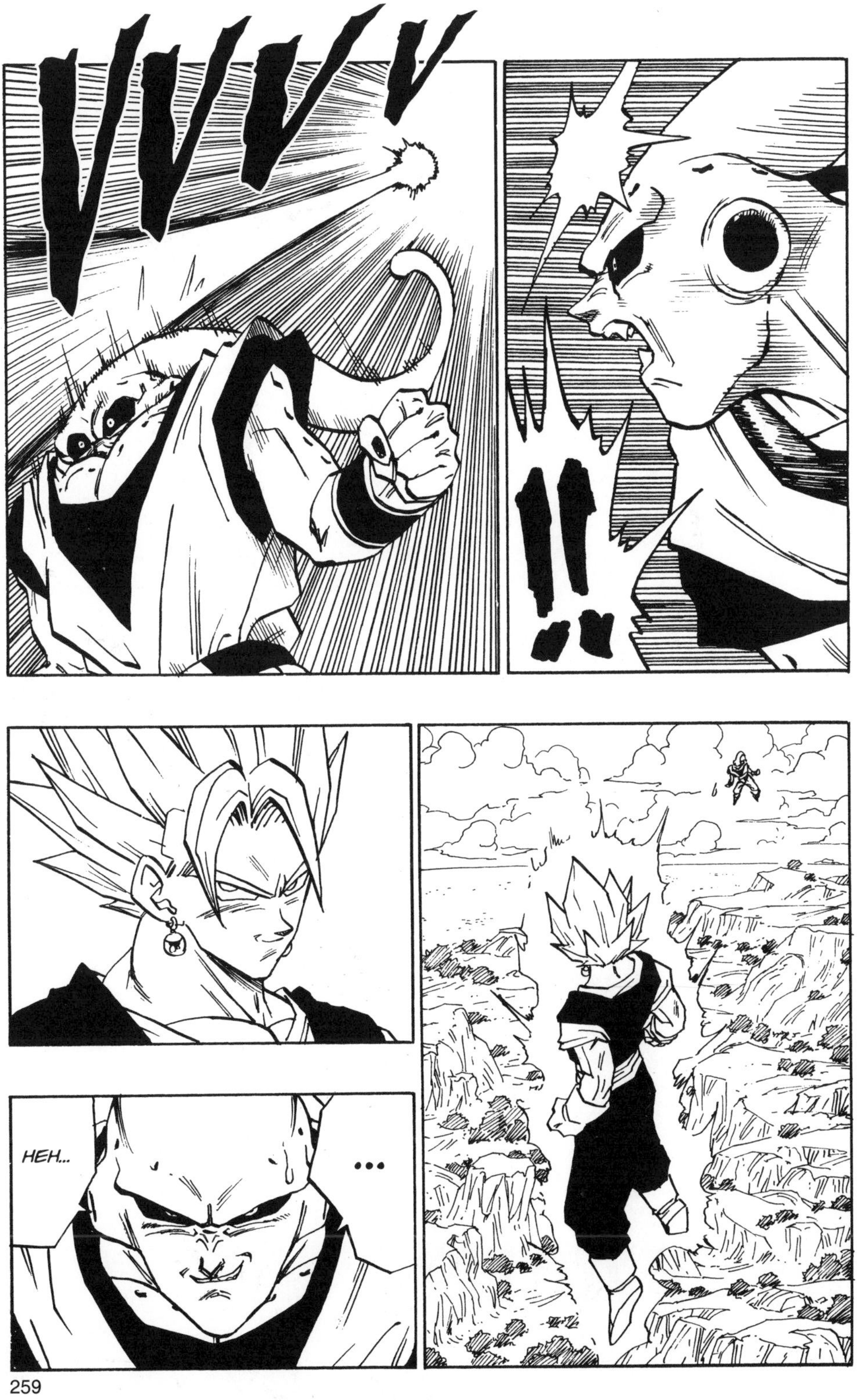
!!
VVVV
...
HEH...

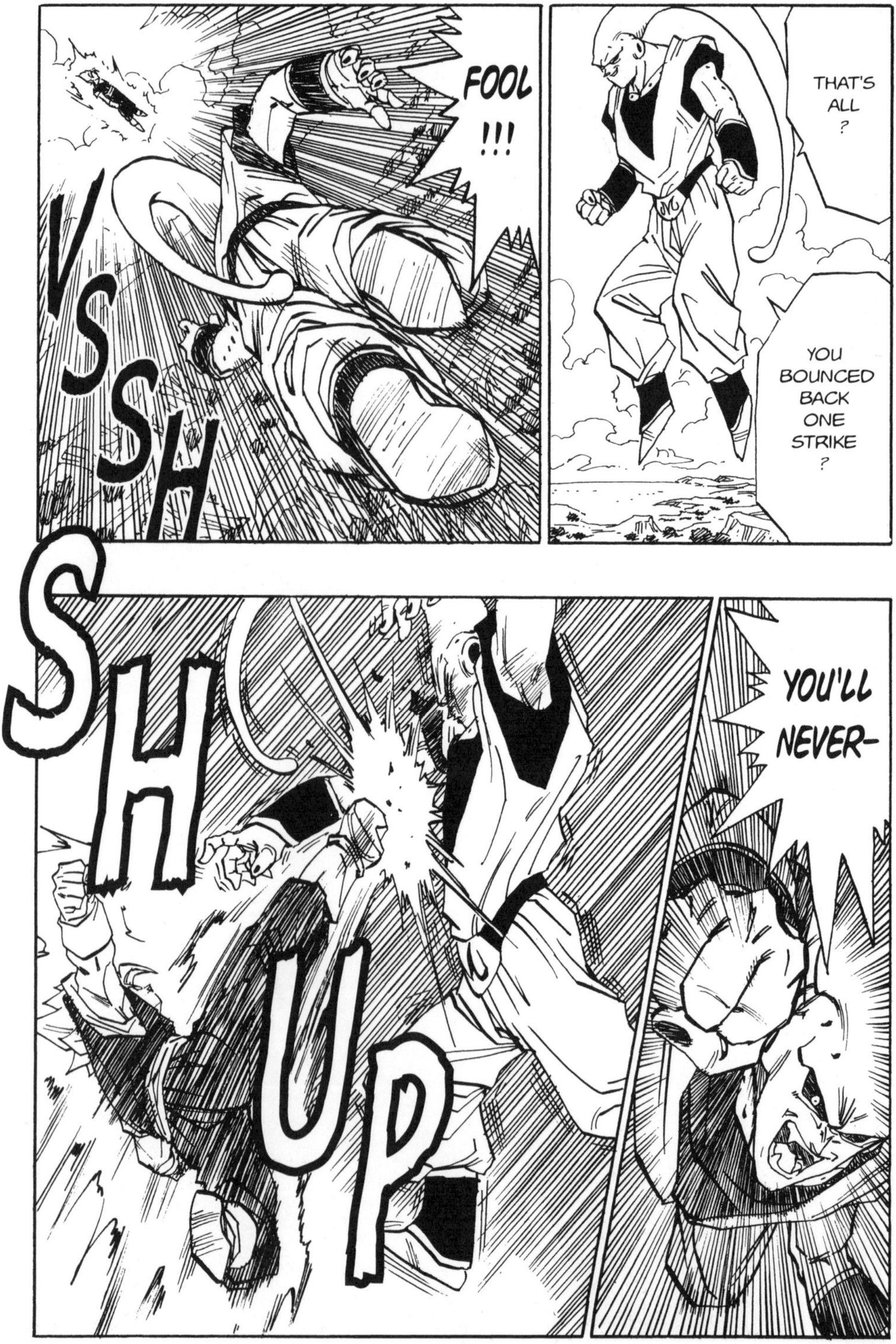
THAT'S ALL ?
YOU BOUNCED BACK ONE STRIKE ?
FOOL !!!
VSSH
YOU'LL NEVER-
SHUP

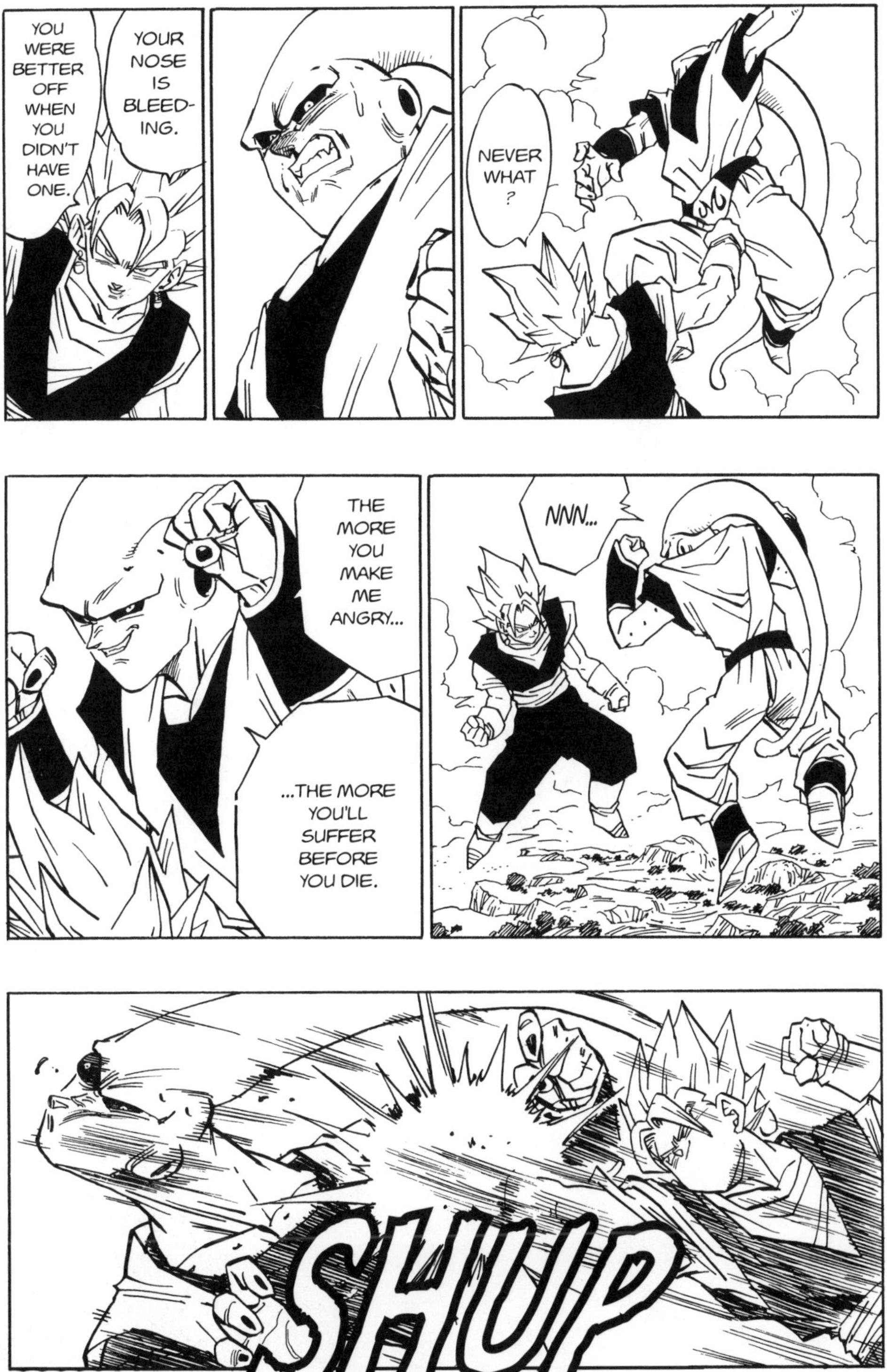
NEVER WHAT ?
YOUR NOSE IS BLEED-ING.
YOU WERE BETTER OFF WHEN YOU DIDN'T HAVE ONE.
NNN...
THE MORE YOU MAKE ME ANGRY...
...THE MORE YOU'LL SUFFER BEFORE YOU DIE.
SHUIP

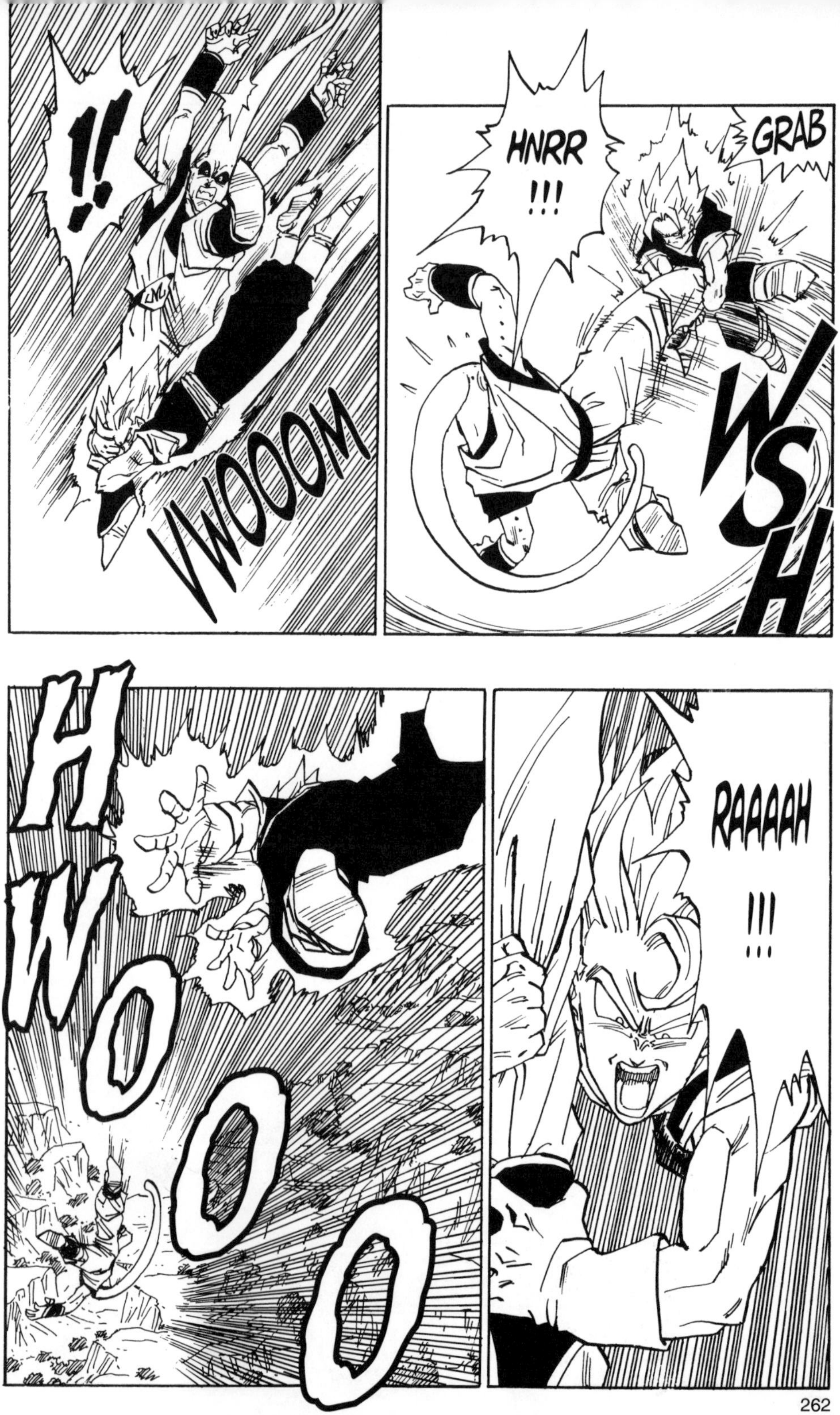
HNRR !!!
GRAB
WSH
!!
VWOOOM
RAAAAH !!!
HWOOOO

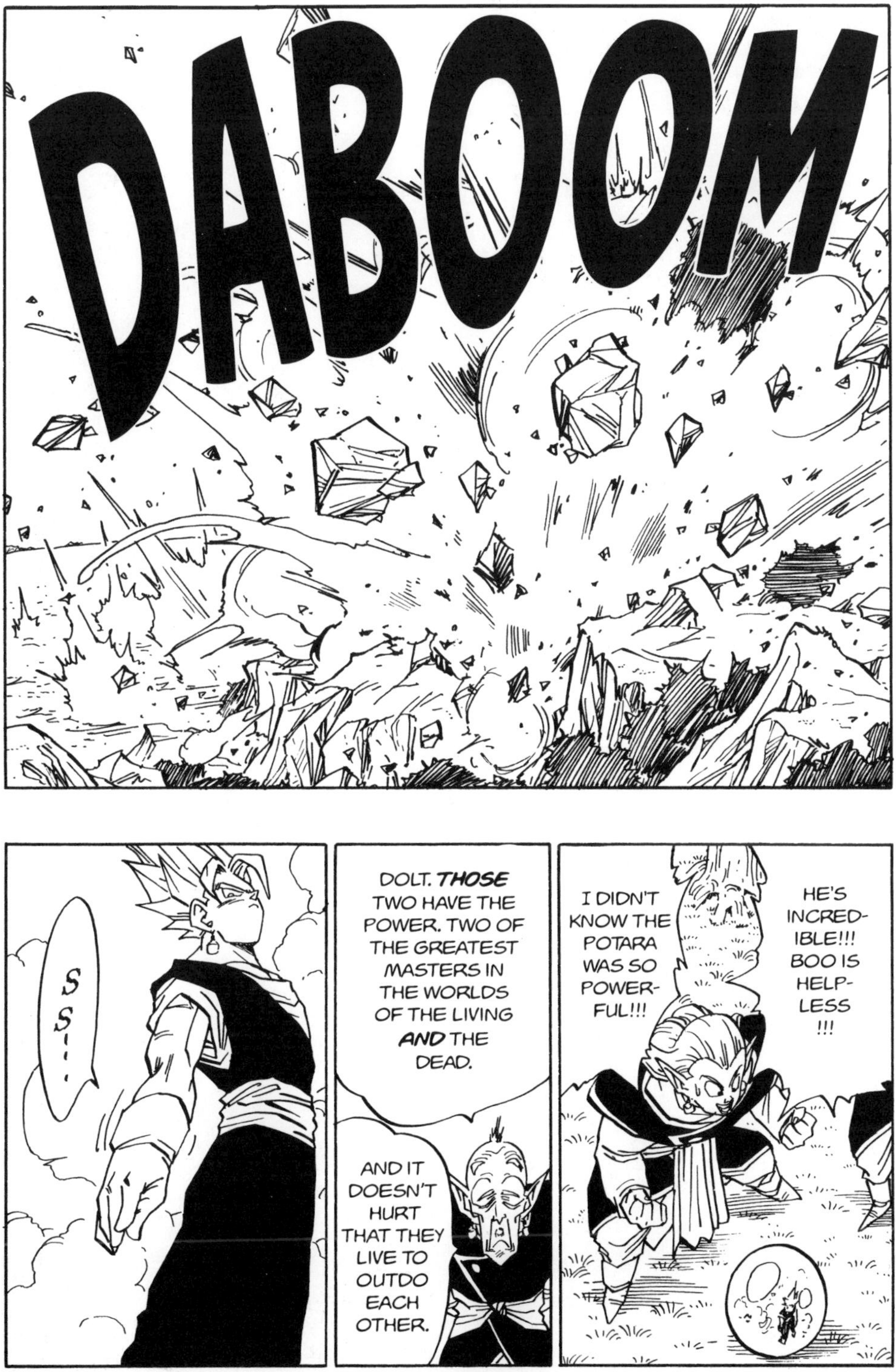
DABOOM
HE'S INCREDIBLE!!! BOO IS HELPLESS!!!
I DIDN'T KNOW THE POTARA WAS SO POWERFUL!!!
DOLT. *THOSE* TWO HAVE THE POWER. TWO OF THE GREATEST MASTERS IN THE WORLDS OF THE LIVING *AND* THE DEAD.
AND IT DOESN'T HURT THAT THEY LIVE TO OUTDO EACH OTHER.
SS...

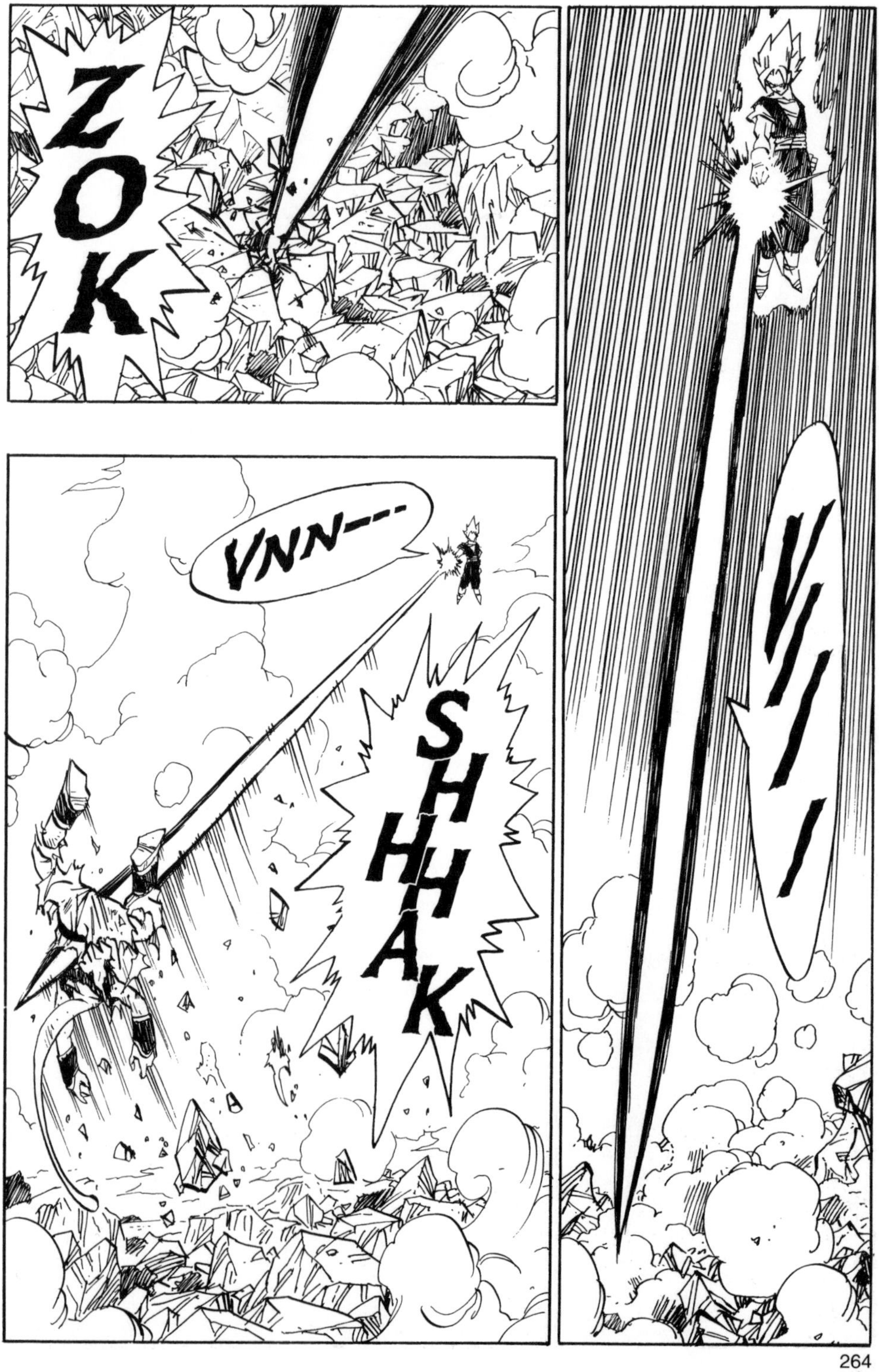
V---
ZOK
VNN---
SHHHAK

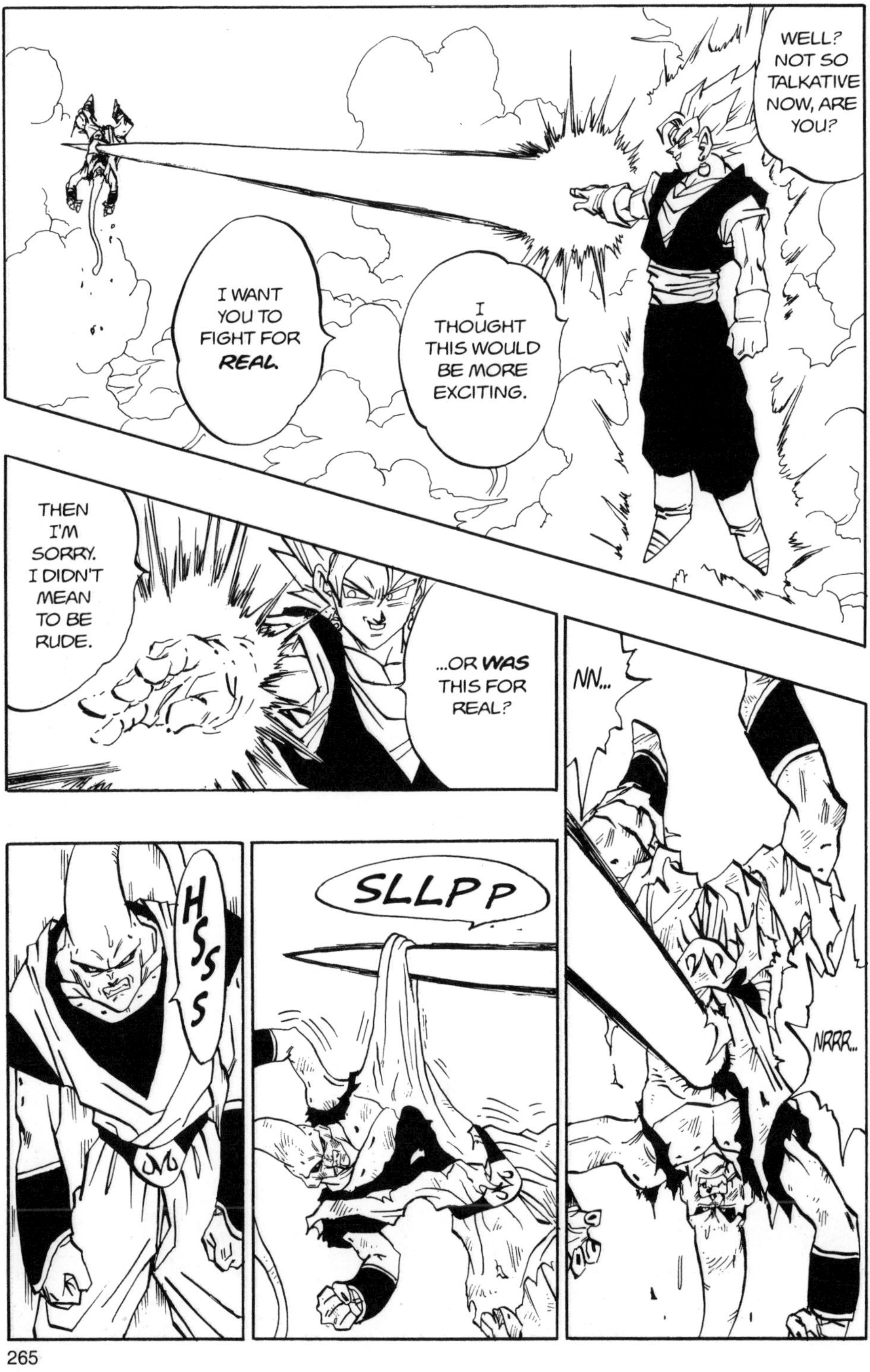
WELL? NOT SO TALKATIVE NOW, ARE YOU?
I THOUGHT THIS WOULD BE MORE EXCITING.
I WANT YOU TO FIGHT FOR **REAL.**
THEN I'M SORRY. I DIDN'T MEAN TO BE RUDE.
...OR **WAS** THIS FOR REAL?
NN...
NRRR...
SLLPP
HSSS

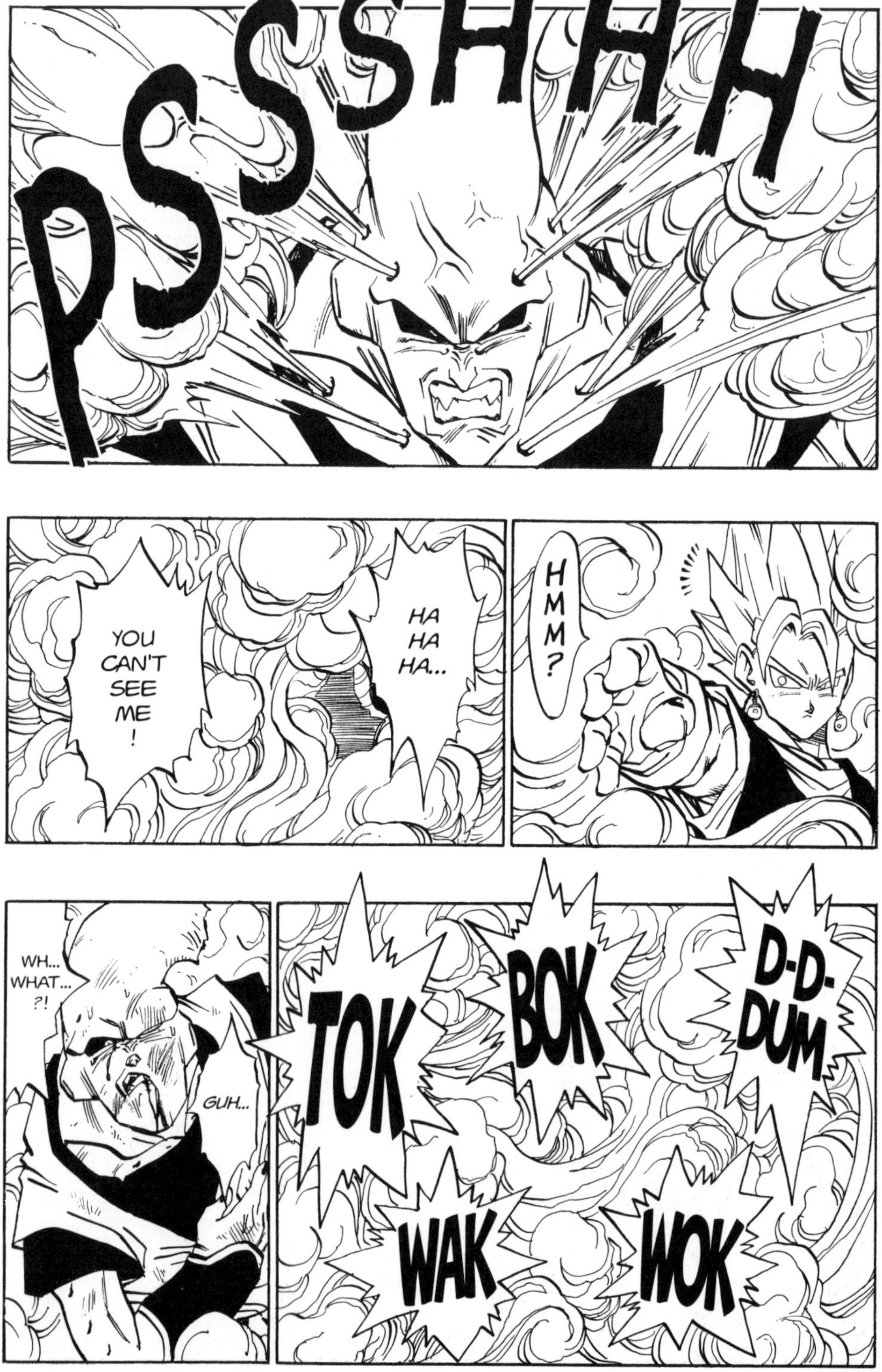
PSSSHHH
HMMM?
HA HA HA...
YOU CAN'T SEE ME!
D-D-DUM
BOK
TOK
WOK
WAK
WH... WHAT...?!
GUH...

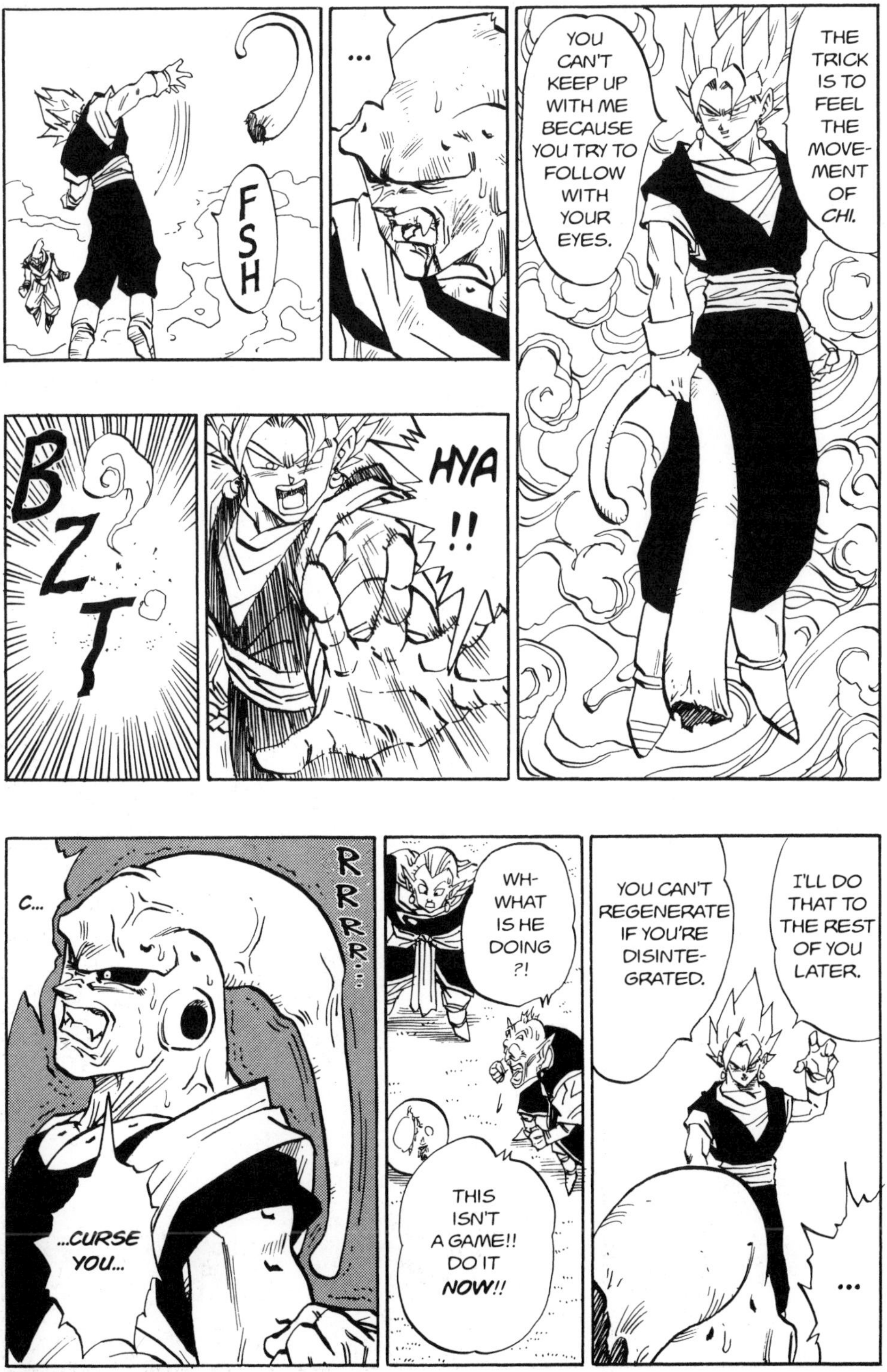
THE TRICK IS TO FEEL THE MOVEMENT OF CHI.
YOU CAN'T KEEP UP WITH ME BECAUSE YOU TRY TO FOLLOW WITH YOUR EYES.
...
FSH
HYA!!
BZZT
I'LL DO THAT TO THE REST OF YOU LATER.
YOU CAN'T REGENERATE IF YOU'RE DISINTEGRATED.
...
WH-WHAT IS HE DOING?!
THIS ISN'T A GAME!! DO IT NOW!!
RRRR...
C...
...CURSE YOU...

DRAGON BALL ドラゴンボール

DBZ:311 • Vegerot's Game

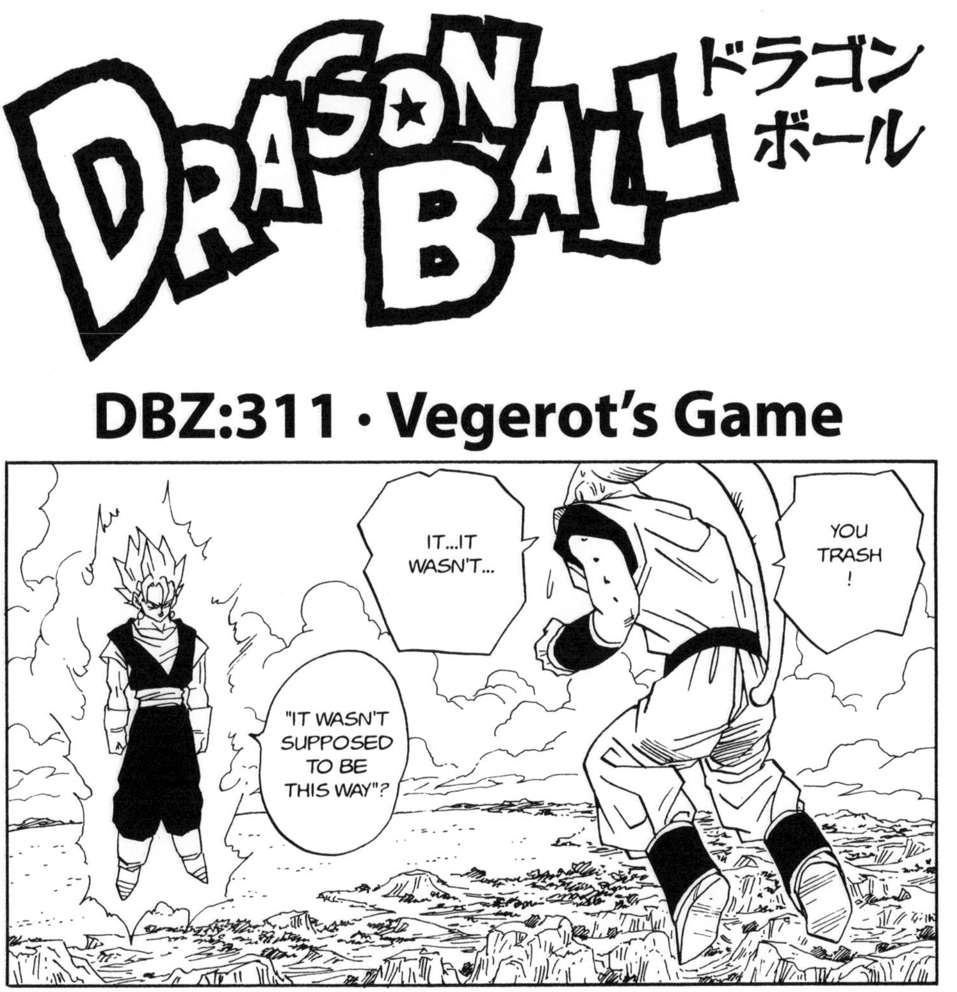
YOU TRASH!
IT...IT WASN'T...
"IT WASN'T SUPPOSED TO BE THIS WAY"?

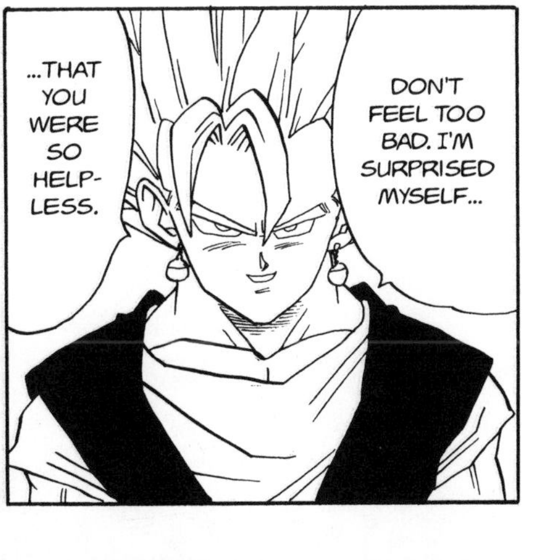
DON'T FEEL TOO BAD. I'M SURPRISED MYSELF...
...THAT YOU WERE SO HELP-LESS.

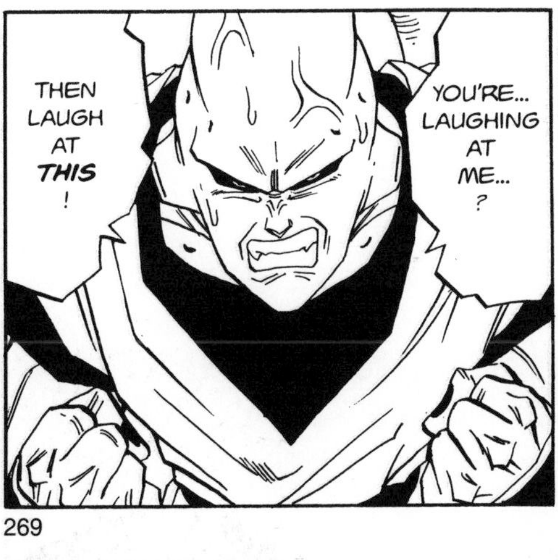
YOU'RE... LAUGHING AT ME...?
THEN LAUGH AT *THIS*!

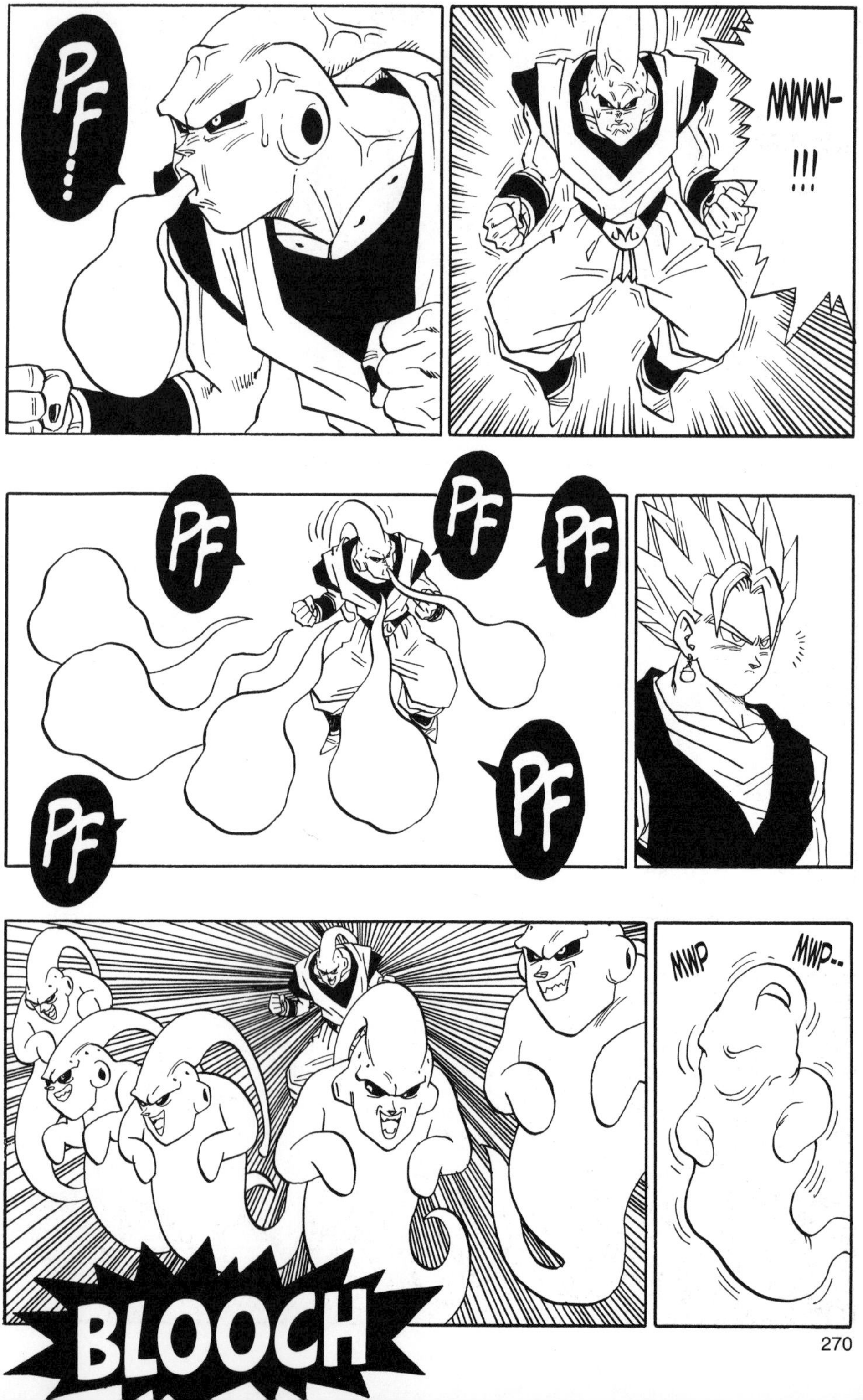
NNNNN-
!!!
PF...
PF
PF
PF
PF
PF
MWP
MWP..
BLOOCH

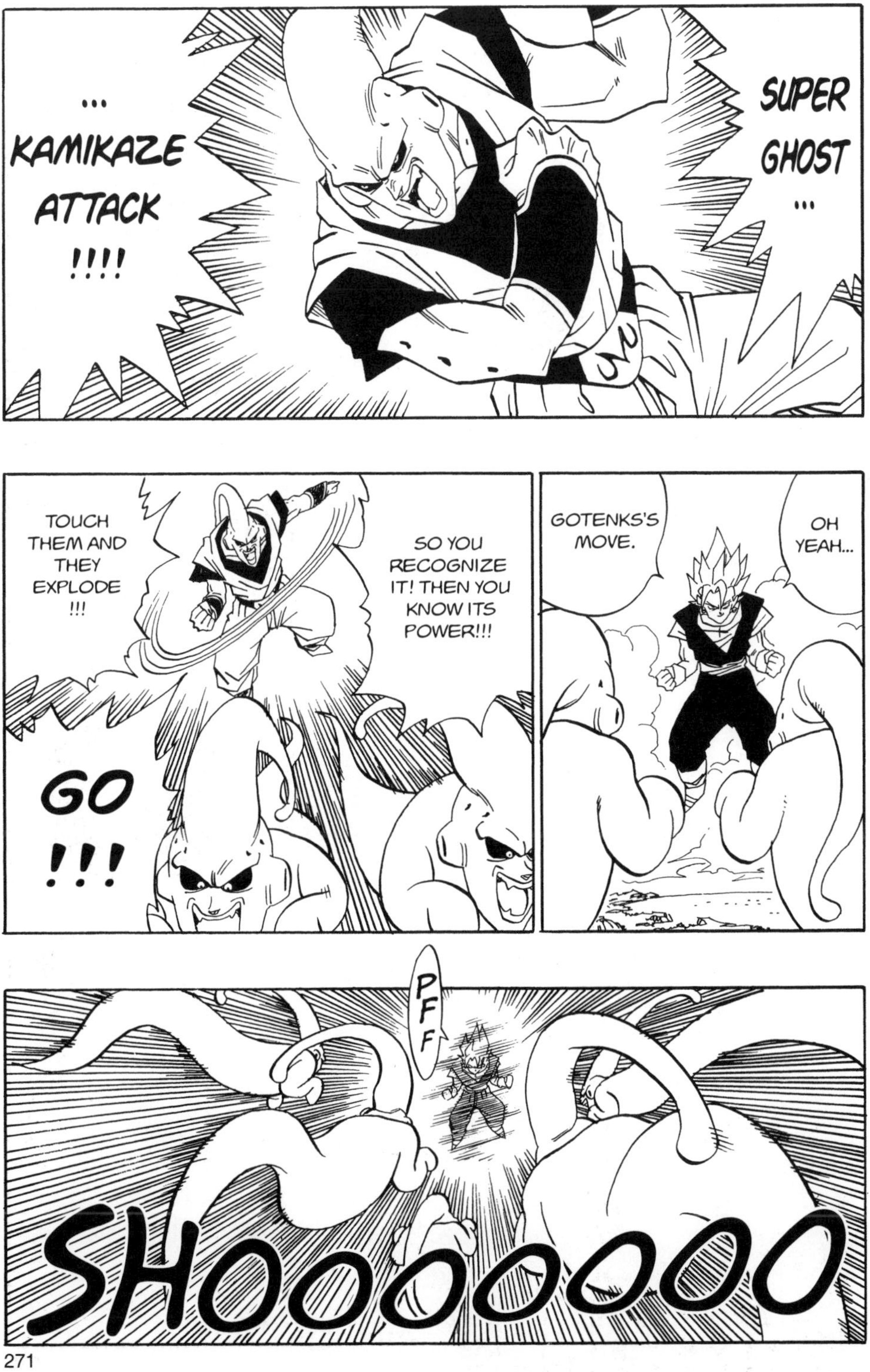
SUPER GHOST...
...KAMIKAZE ATTACK!!!!
OH YEAH...
GOTENKS'S MOVE.
SO YOU RECOGNIZE IT! THEN YOU KNOW ITS POWER!!!
TOUCH THEM AND THEY EXPLODE!!!
GO!!!
PFF
SHOOOOOOOO

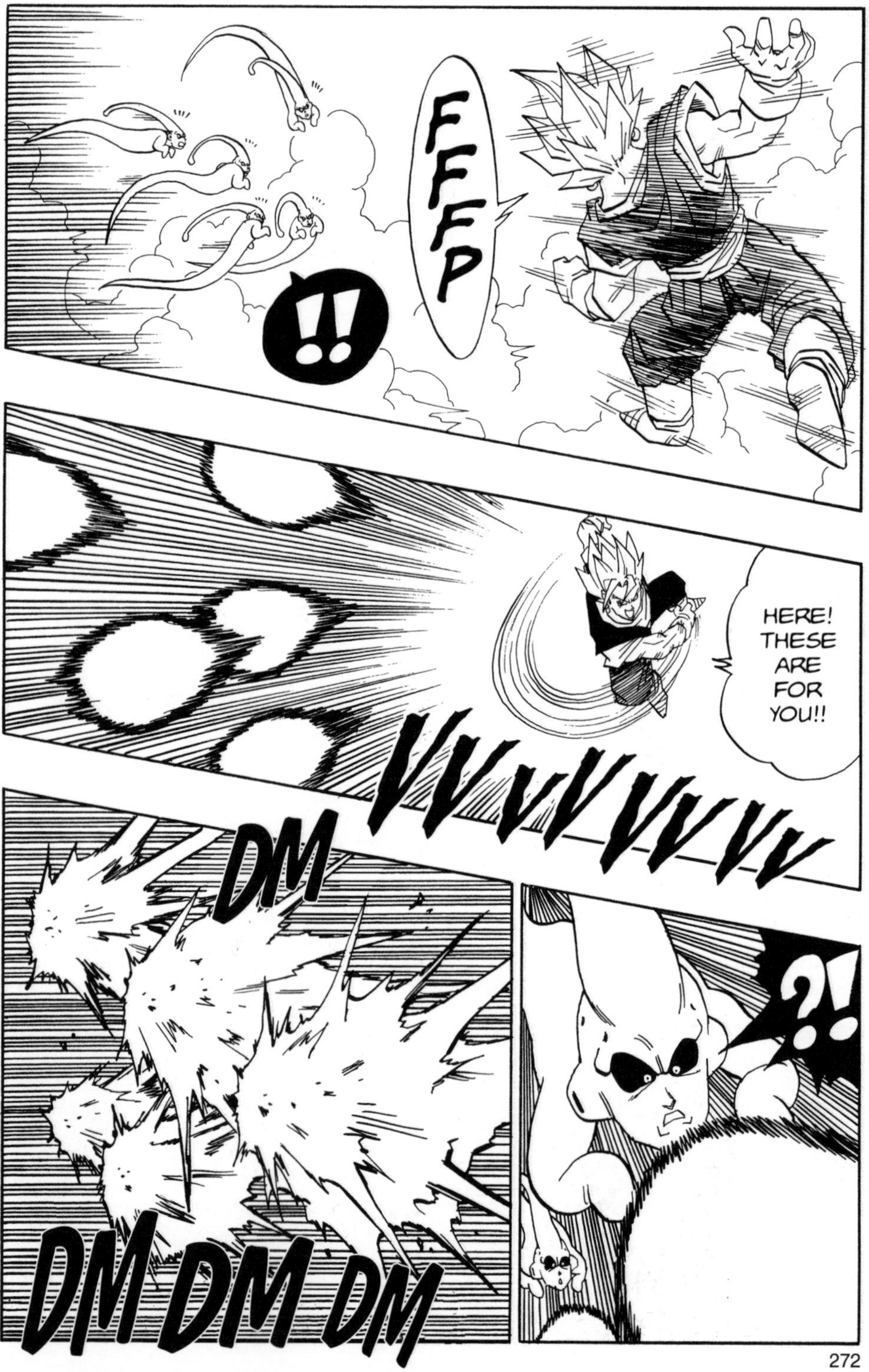

FFFP
!!
HERE! THESE ARE FOR YOU!!
VVVVVVVVVVV
?!
DM
DM DM DM

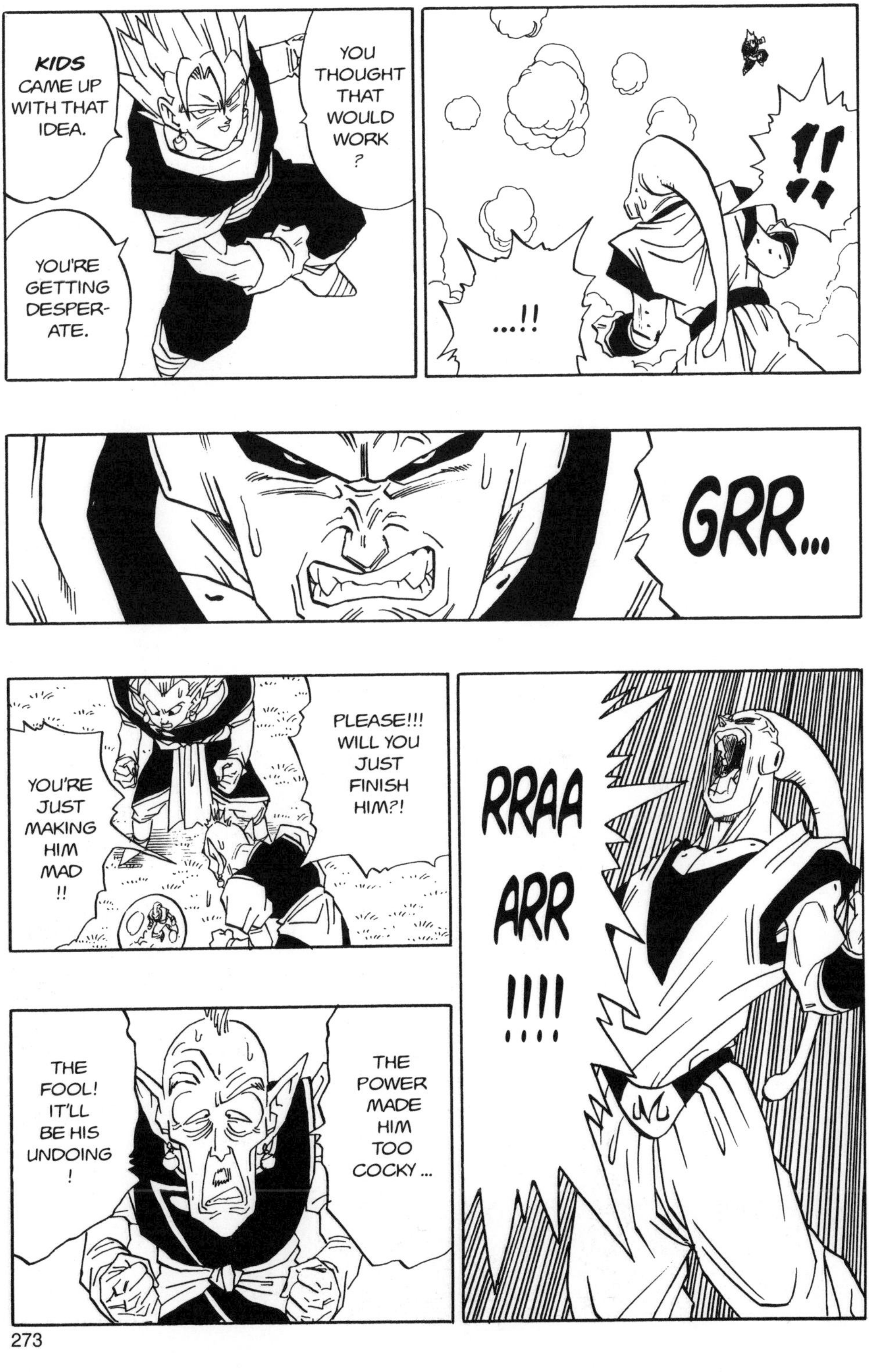
!!
...!!
YOU THOUGHT THAT WOULD WORK?
KIDS CAME UP WITH THAT IDEA.
YOU'RE GETTING DESPERATE.
GRR...
RRAAARR!!!!
PLEASE!!! WILL YOU JUST FINISH HIM?!
YOU'RE JUST MAKING HIM MAD!!
THE POWER MADE HIM TOO COCKY...
THE FOOL! IT'LL BE HIS UNDOING!

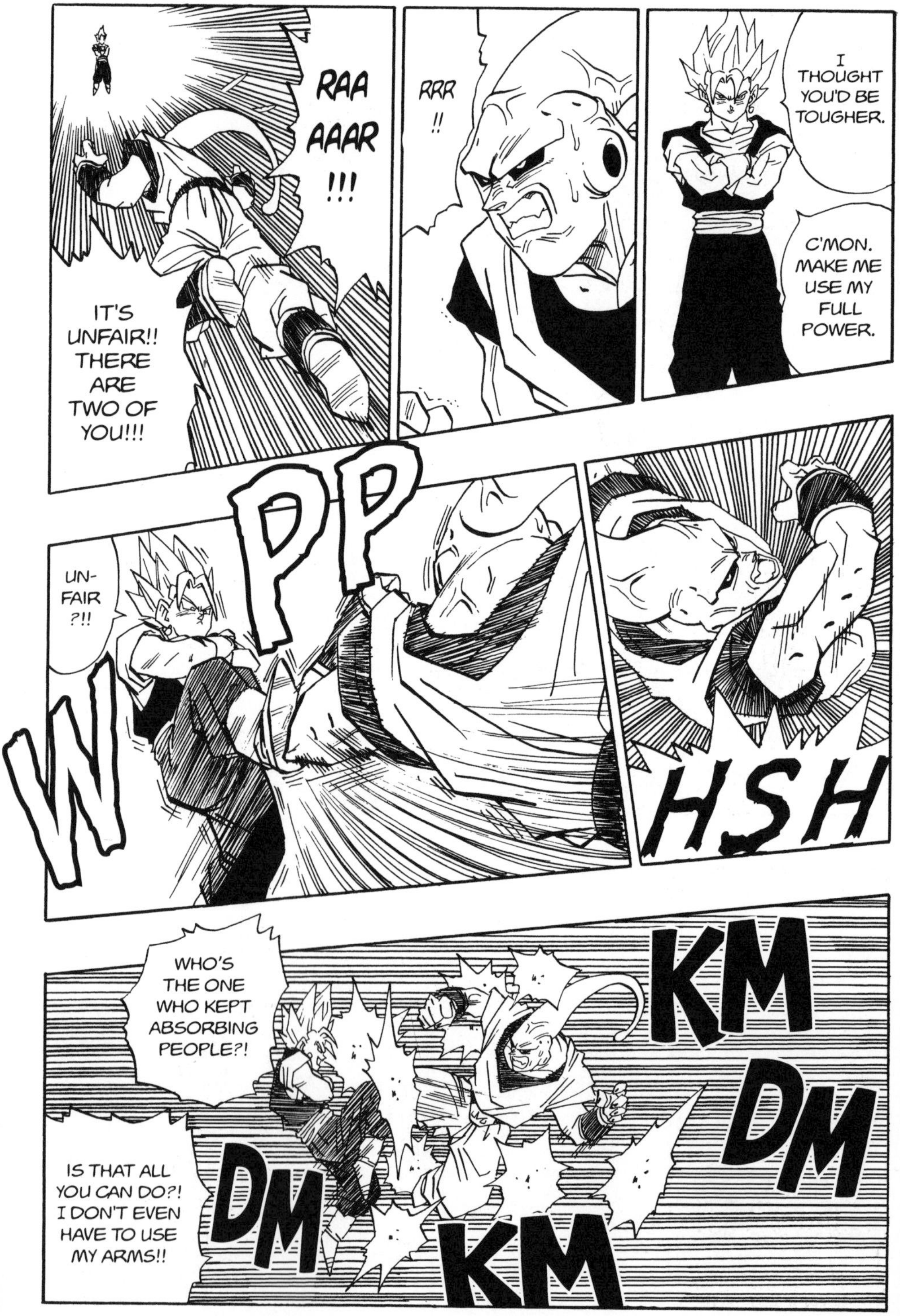
I THOUGHT YOU'D BE TOUGHER.
C'MON. MAKE ME USE MY FULL POWER.
RRR!!
RAAAAAR!!!
IT'S UNFAIR!! THERE ARE TWO OF YOU!!!
HSH
WPP
UN-FAIR?!!
KM
DM
WHO'S THE ONE WHO KEPT ABSORBING PEOPLE?!
DM
KM
IS THAT ALL YOU CAN DO?! I DON'T EVEN HAVE TO USE MY ARMS!!

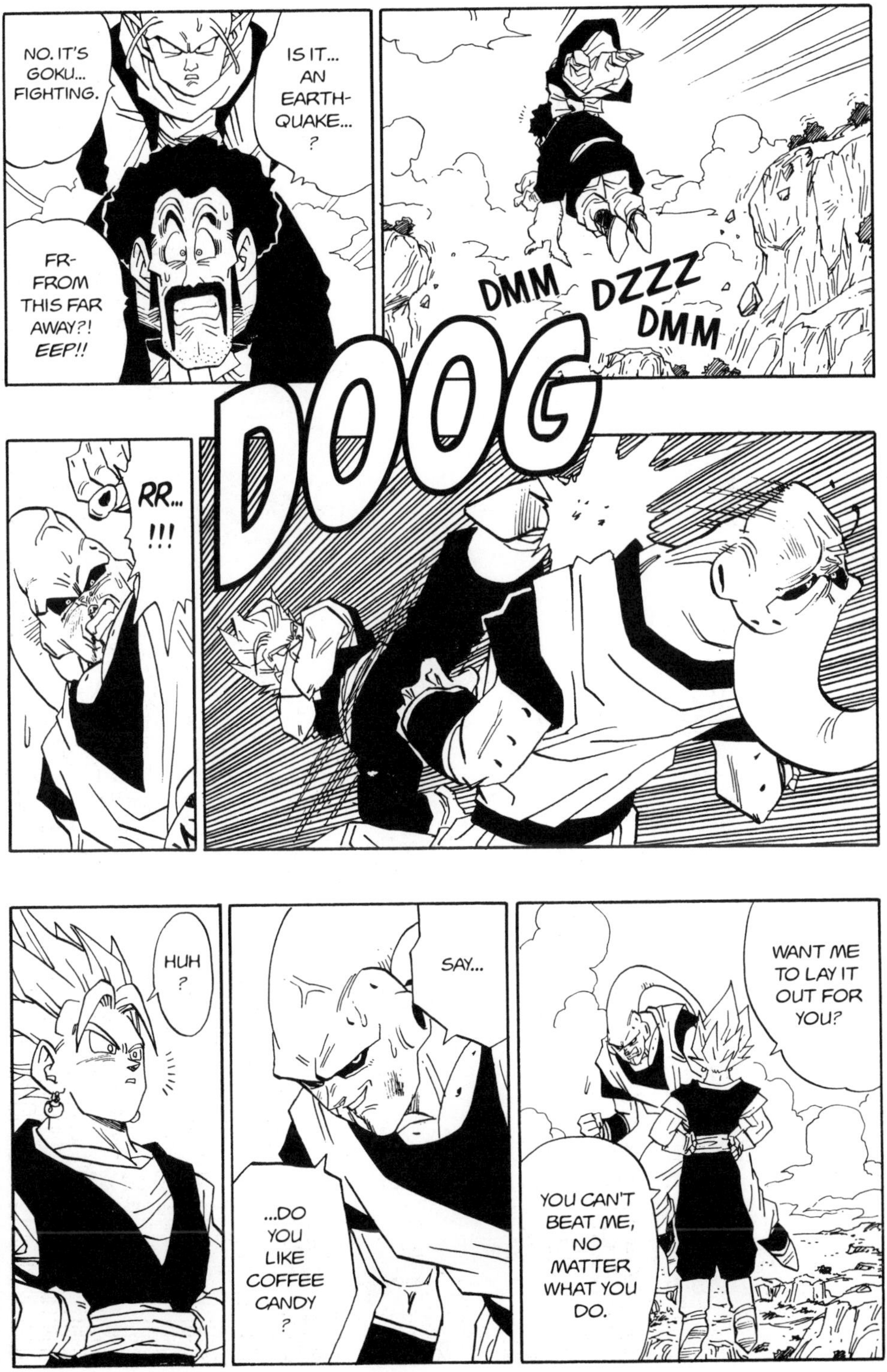
DZZZ
DMM
DMM
IS IT... AN EARTHQUAKE...?
NO. IT'S GOKU... FIGHTING.
FR- FROM THIS FAR AWAY?! EEP!!
DOOG
RR... !!!
WANT ME TO LAY IT OUT FOR YOU?
YOU CAN'T BEAT ME, NO MATTER WHAT YOU DO.
SAY...
...DO YOU LIKE COFFEE CANDY?
HUH?

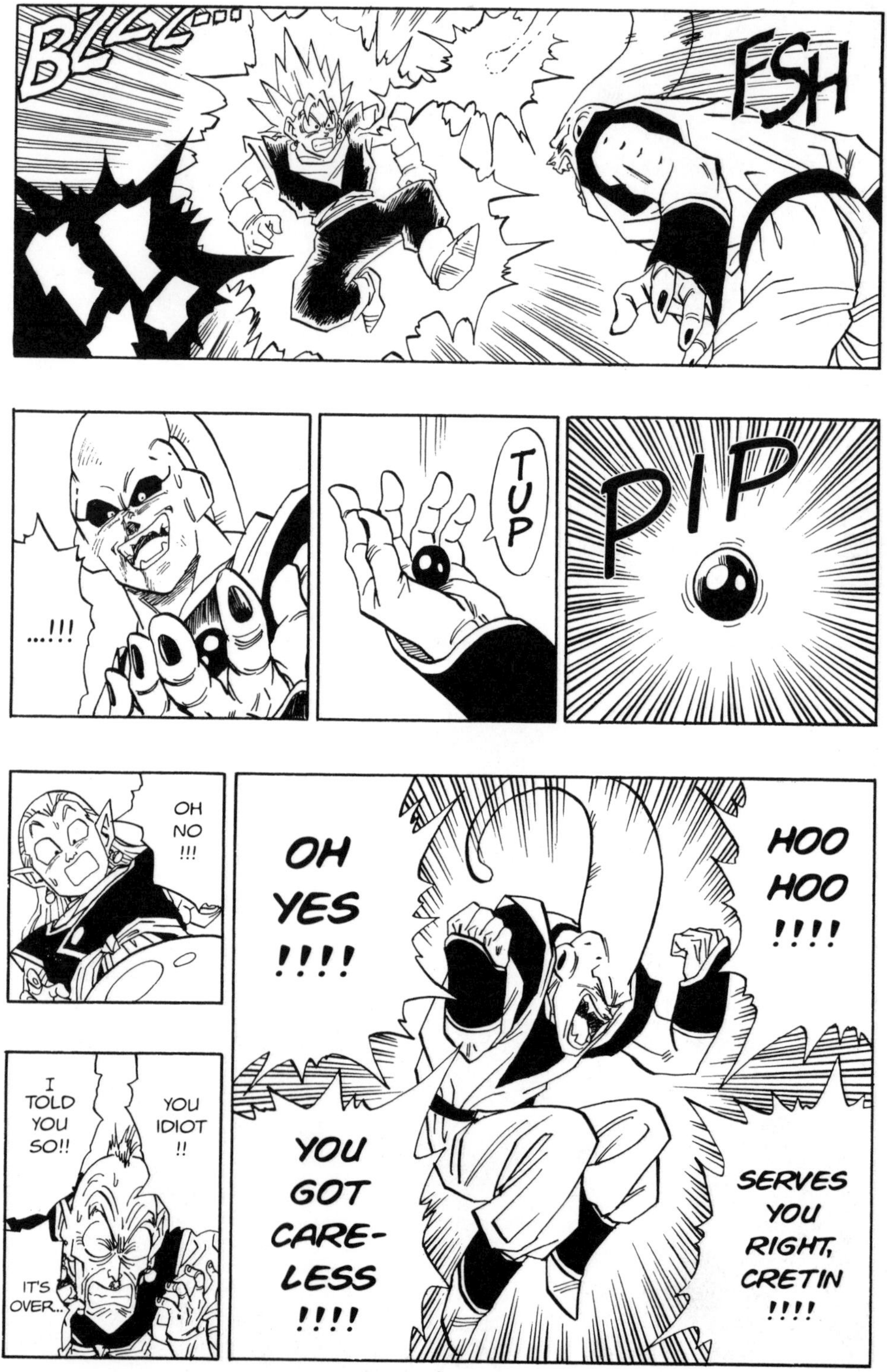
FSH
BZZZ...
PIP
TUP
...!!!
HOO HOO !!!!
OH YES !!!!
SERVES YOU RIGHT, CRETIN !!!!
YOU GOT CARE-LESS !!!!
OH NO !!!
YOU IDIOT !!
I TOLD YOU SO!!
IT'S OVER...

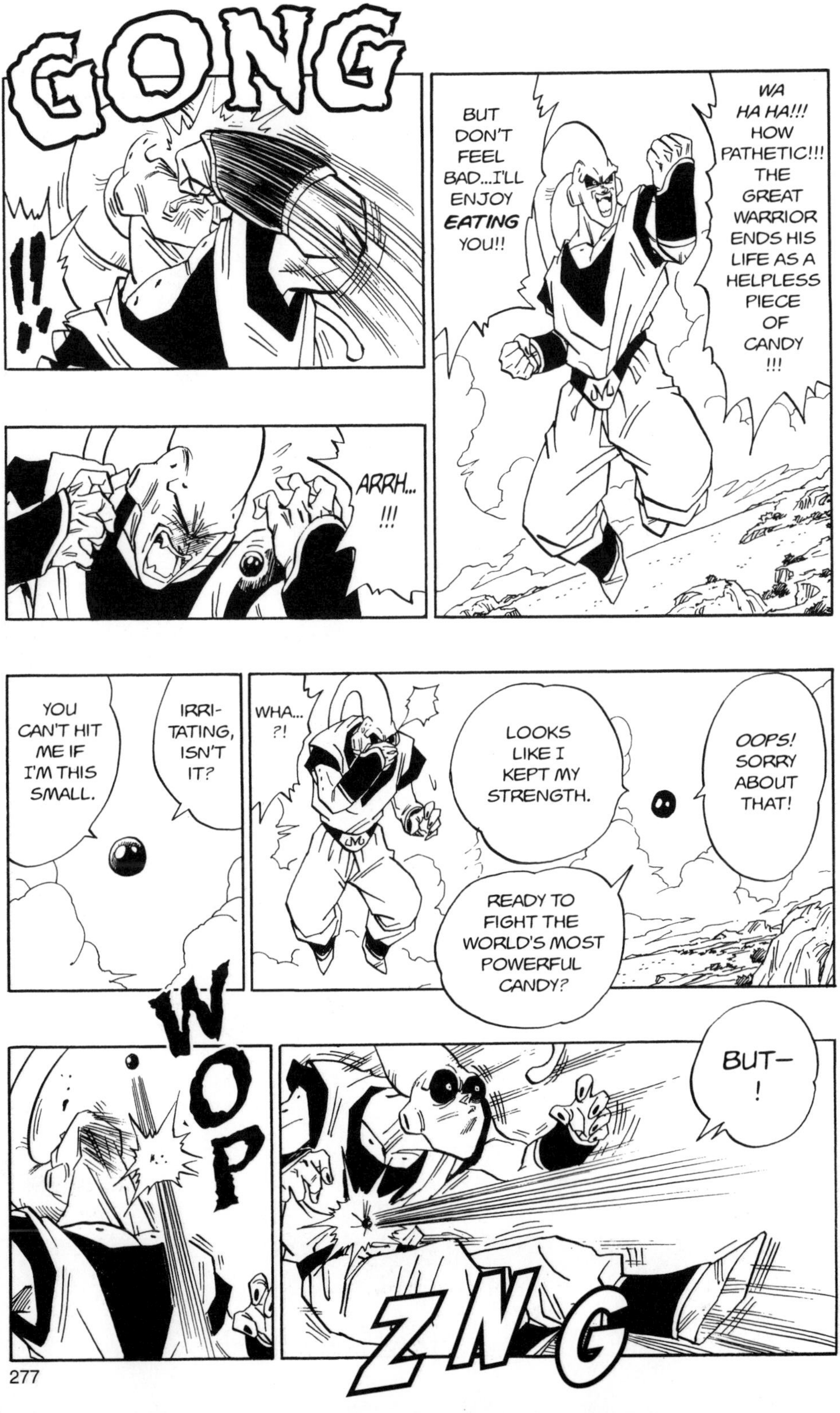
WA HA HA!!! HOW PATHETIC!!! THE GREAT WARRIOR ENDS HIS LIFE AS A HELPLESS PIECE OF CANDY !!!
BUT DON'T FEEL BAD...I'LL ENJOY *EATING* YOU!!
GONG
!!
ARRH... !!!
OOPS! SORRY ABOUT THAT!
LOOKS LIKE I KEPT MY STRENGTH.
WHA... ?!
READY TO FIGHT THE WORLD'S MOST POWERFUL CANDY?
IRRI-TATING, ISN'T IT?
YOU CAN'T HIT ME IF I'M THIS SMALL.
BUT— !
ZNG
WOP

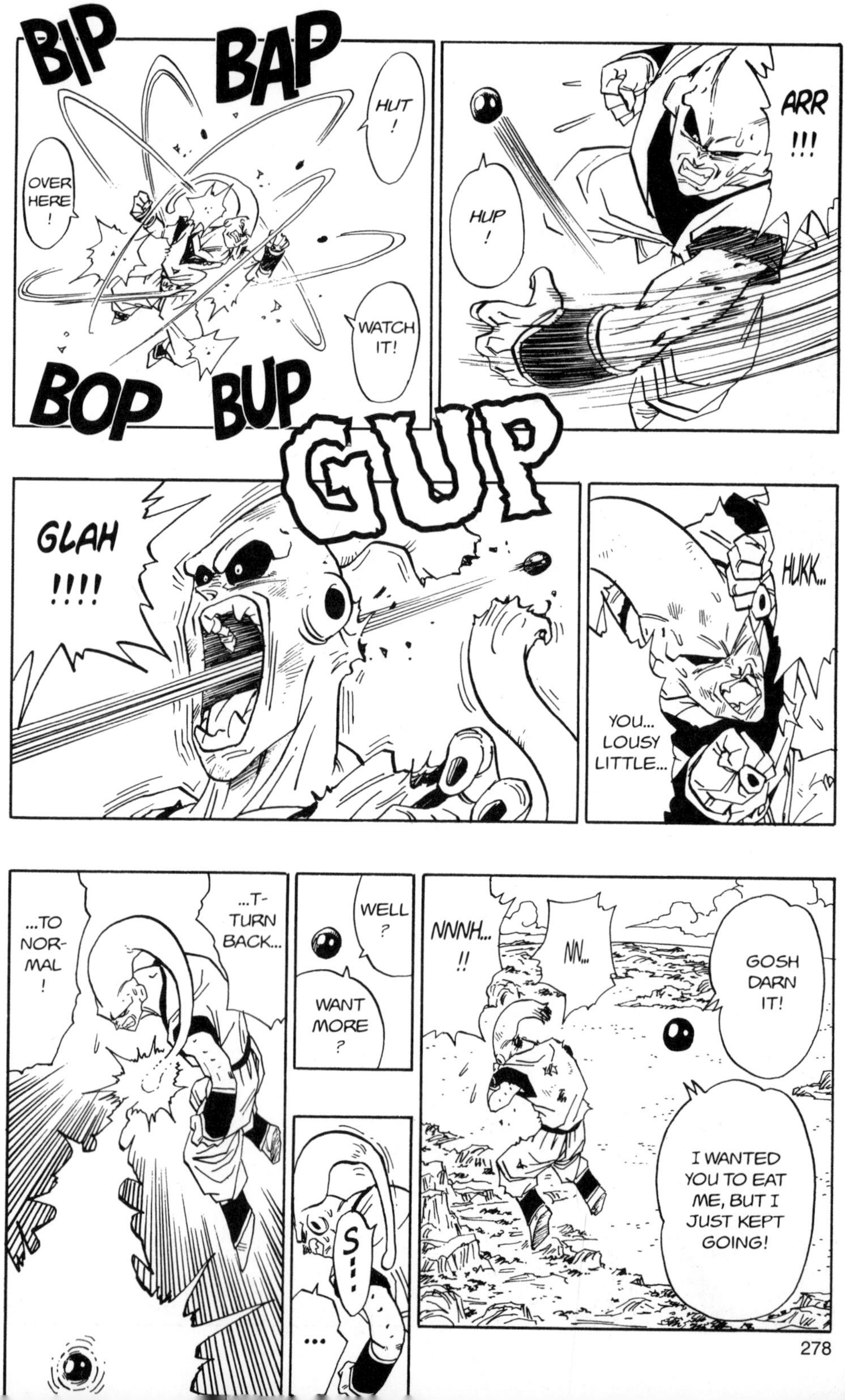
ARR!!!
HUP!
HUT!
BAP
BIP
OVER HERE!
WATCH IT!
BUP
BOP
HUKK...
YOU... LOUSY LITTLE...
GUP
GLAH!!!!
GOSH DARN IT!
I WANTED YOU TO EAT ME, BUT I JUST KEPT GOING!
NN...
NNNH...!!
WELL?
WANT MORE?
S...!
...
...T-TURN BACK...
...TO NORMAL!

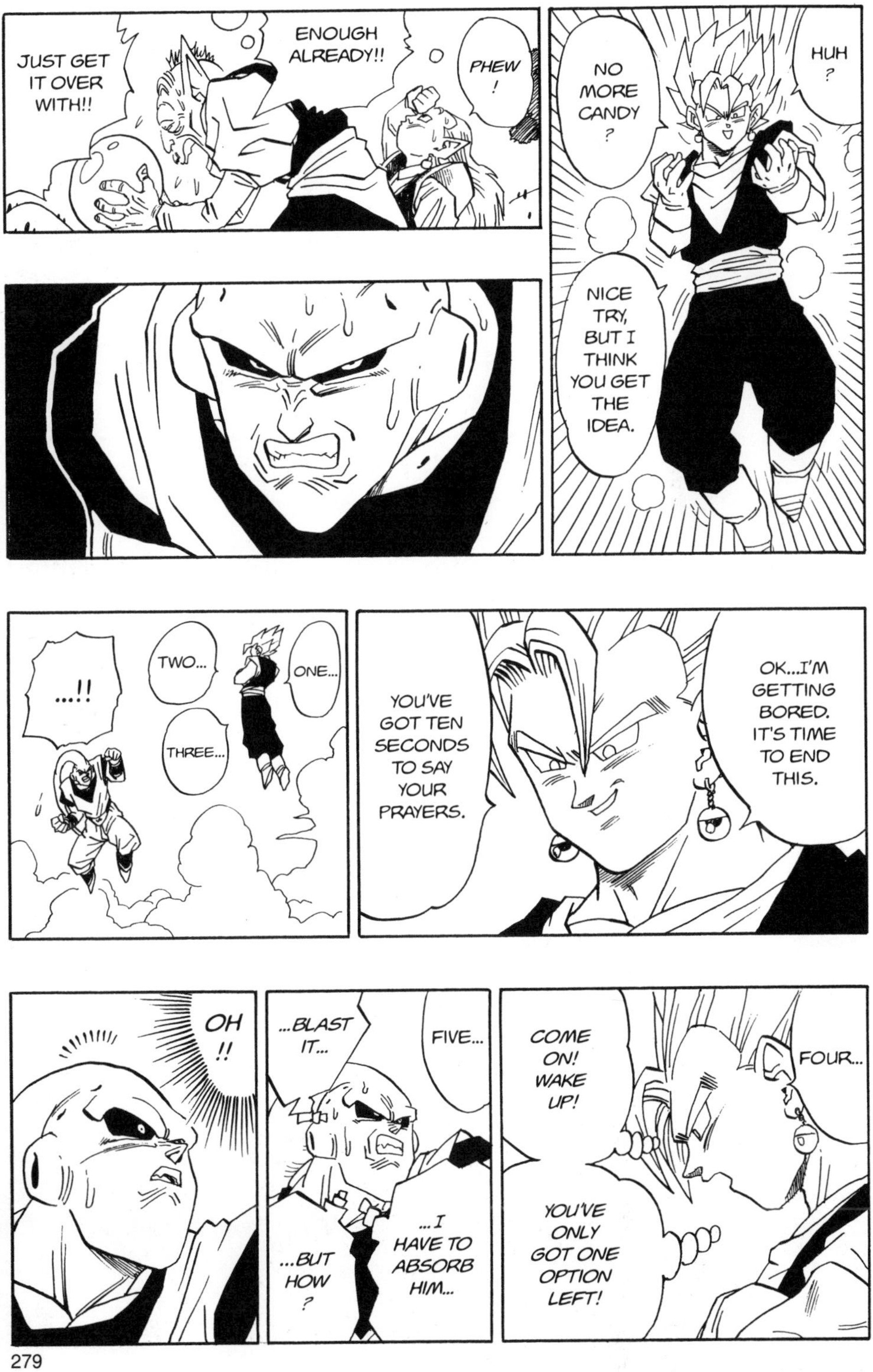
HUH?
NO MORE CANDY?
NICE TRY, BUT I THINK YOU GET THE IDEA.
PHEW!
ENOUGH ALREADY!!
JUST GET IT OVER WITH!!
OK...I'M GETTING BORED. IT'S TIME TO END THIS.
YOU'VE GOT TEN SECONDS TO SAY YOUR PRAYERS.
ONE...
TWO...
THREE...
...!!
FOUR...
COME ON! WAKE UP!
YOU'VE ONLY GOT ONE OPTION LEFT!
FIVE...
...BLAST IT...
...I HAVE TO ABSORB HIM...
...BUT HOW?
OH!!

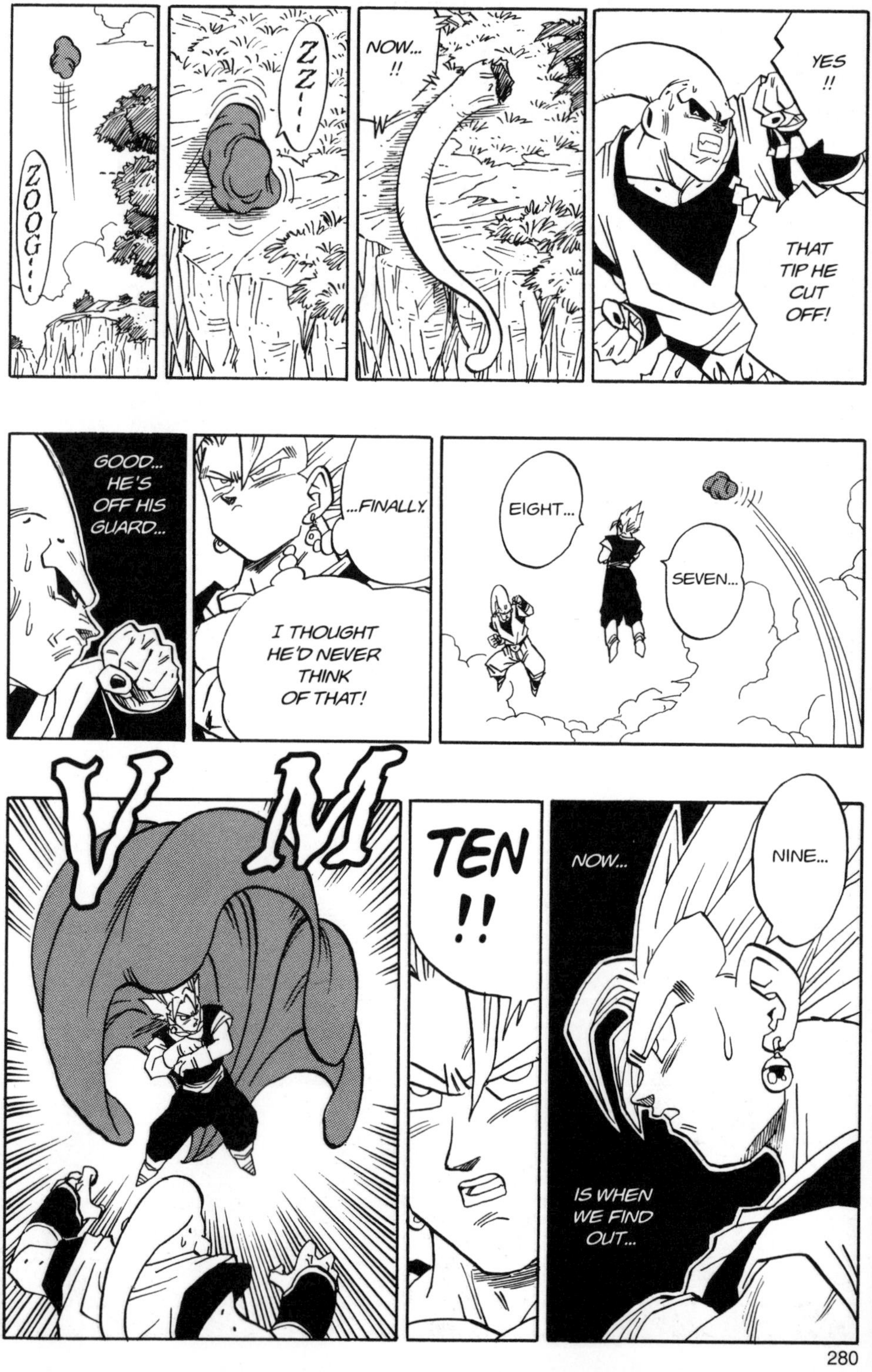
YES !!
THAT TIP HE CUT OFF!
NOW... !!
ZZ...
ZOOG...
SEVEN...
EIGHT...
...FINALLY.
I THOUGHT HE'D NEVER THINK OF THAT!
GOOD... HE'S OFF HIS GUARD...
NINE...
NOW...
IS WHEN WE FIND OUT...
TEN !!
V M

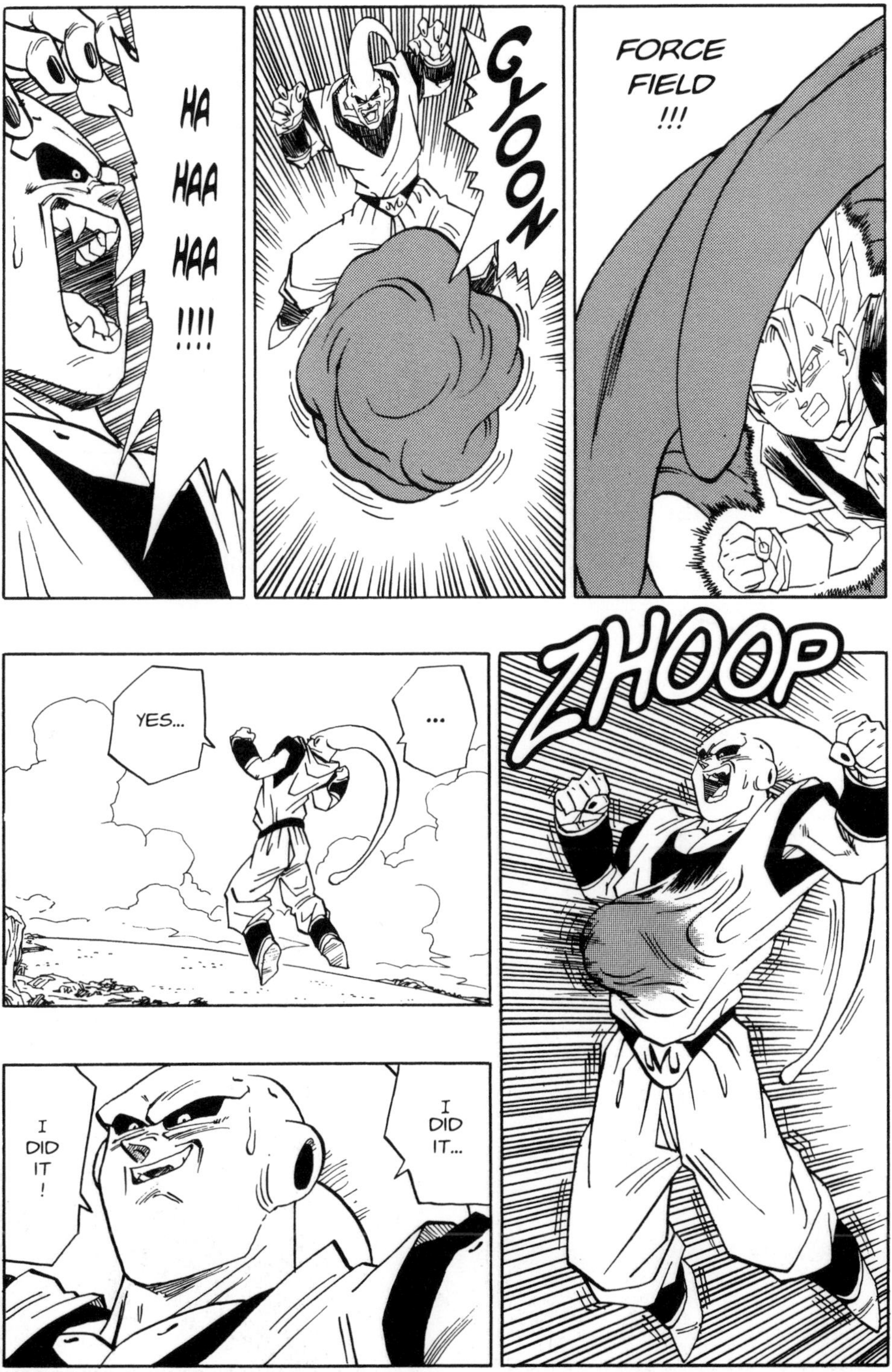
FORCE FIELD !!!
GYOON
HA HAA HAA !!!!
ZHOOP
...
YES...
I DID IT...
I DID IT !

DRAGON BALL ドラゴンボール

DBZ:312 • Two Inside Boo

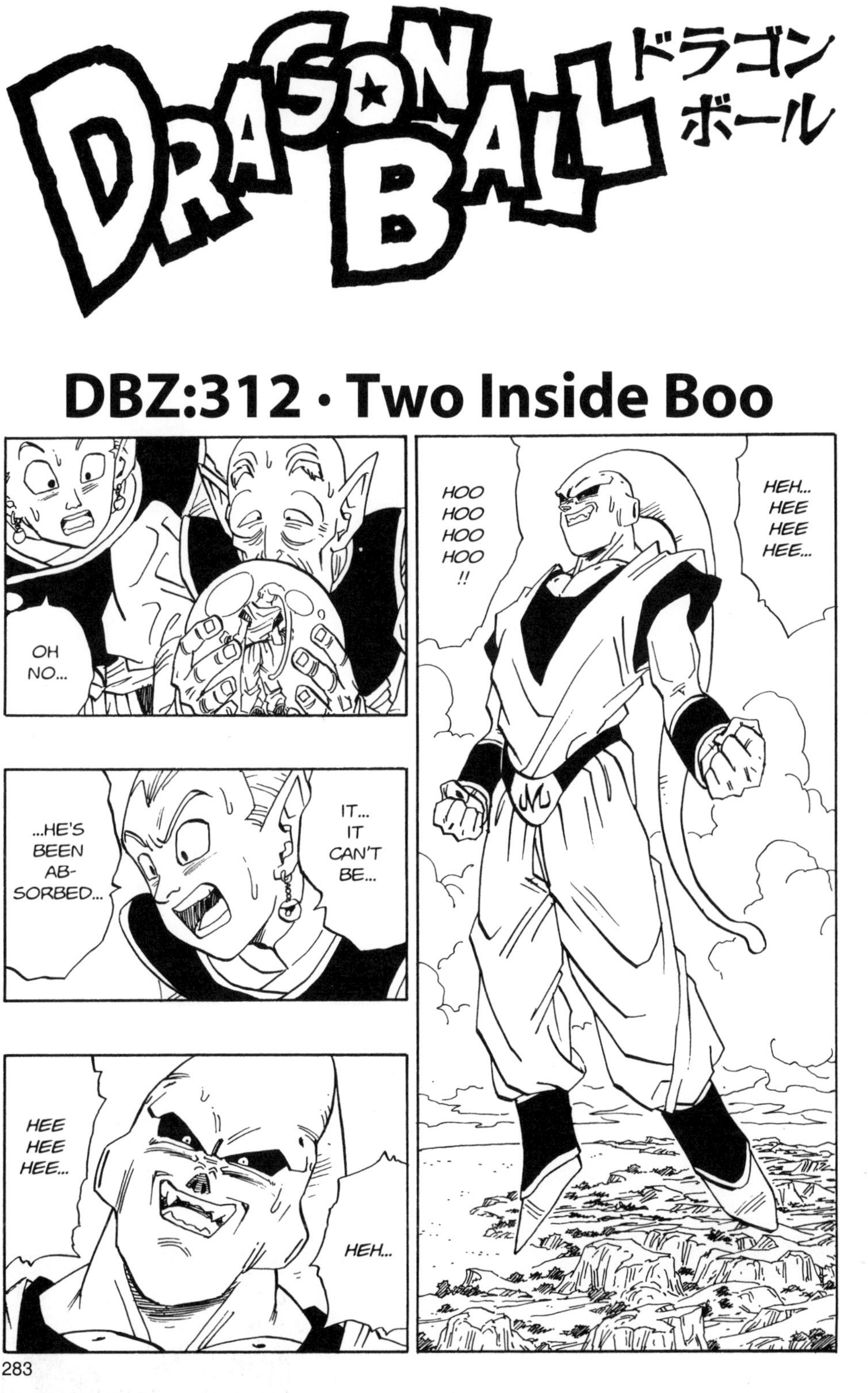

HEH... HEE HEE HEE...
HOO HOO HOO HOO !!
OH NO...
IT... IT CAN'T BE...
...HE'S BEEN AB-SORBED...
HEE HEE HEE...
HEH...

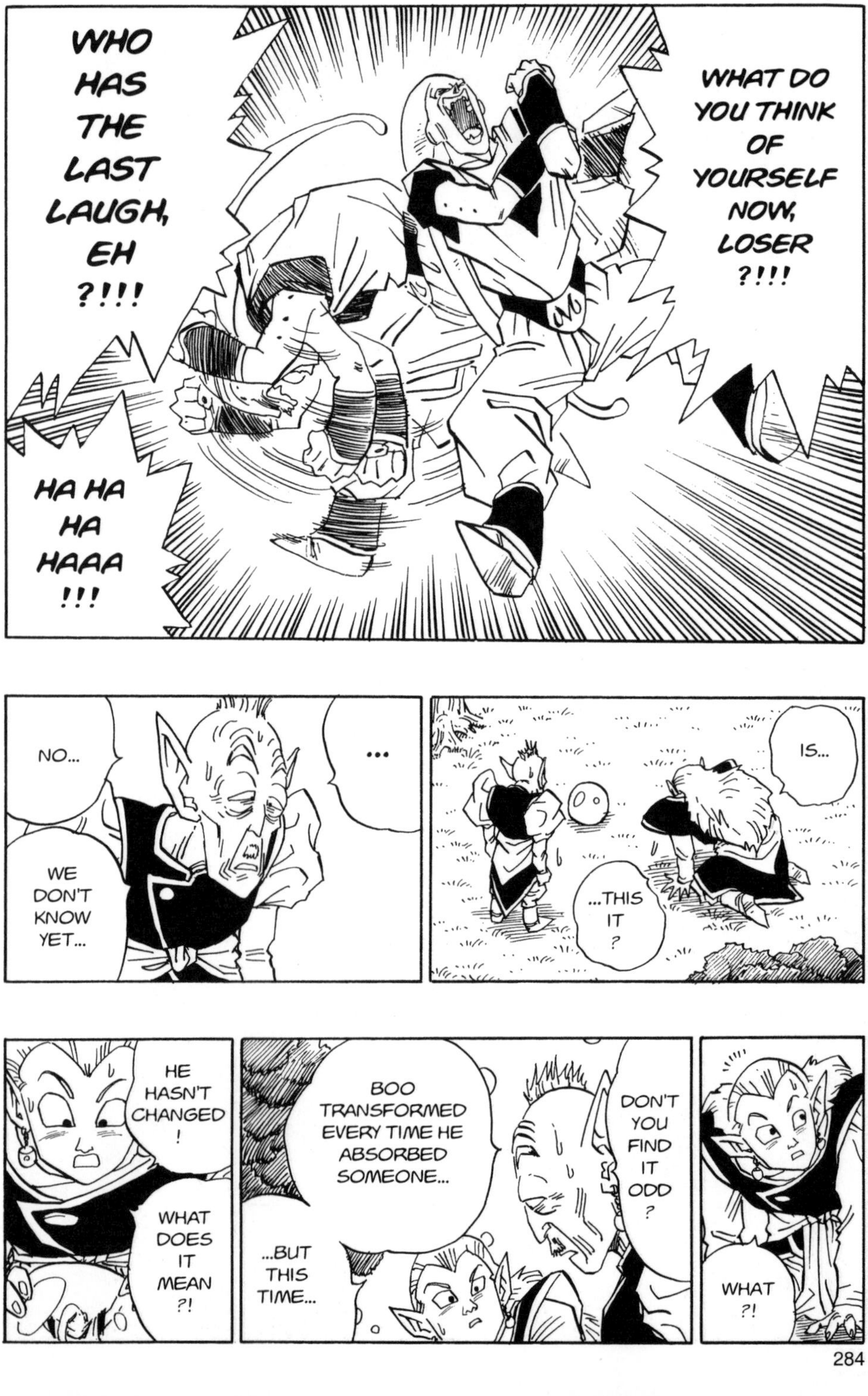
WHAT DO YOU THINK OF YOURSELF NOW, LOSER ?!!!
WHO HAS THE LAST LAUGH, EH ?!!!
HA HA HA HAAA !!!
IS...
...THIS IT ?
...
NO...
WE DON'T KNOW YET...
WHAT ?!
DON'T YOU FIND IT ODD ?
BOO TRANSFORMED EVERY TIME HE ABSORBED SOMEONE...
...BUT THIS TIME...
HE HASN'T CHANGED !
WHAT DOES IT MEAN ?!

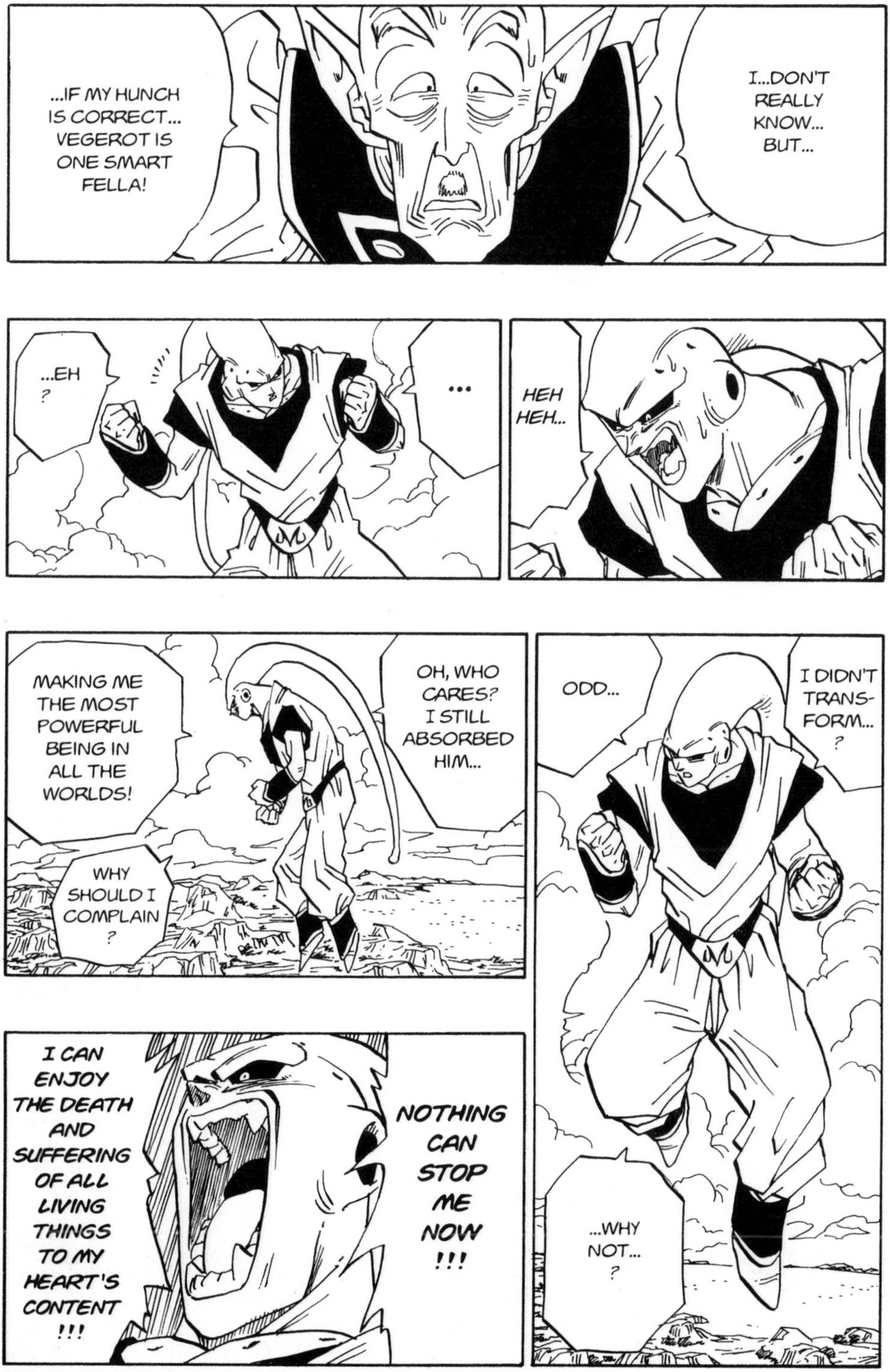
I...DON'T REALLY KNOW... BUT...
...IF MY HUNCH IS CORRECT... VEGEROT IS ONE SMART FELLA!
HEH HEH...
...
...EH?
I DIDN'T TRANSFORM...?
ODD...
...WHY NOT...?
OH, WHO CARES? I STILL ABSORBED HIM...
MAKING ME THE MOST POWERFUL BEING IN ALL THE WORLDS!
WHY SHOULD I COMPLAIN?
NOTHING CAN STOP ME NOW!!!
I CAN ENJOY THE DEATH AND SUFFERING OF ALL LIVING THINGS TO MY HEART'S CONTENT!!!

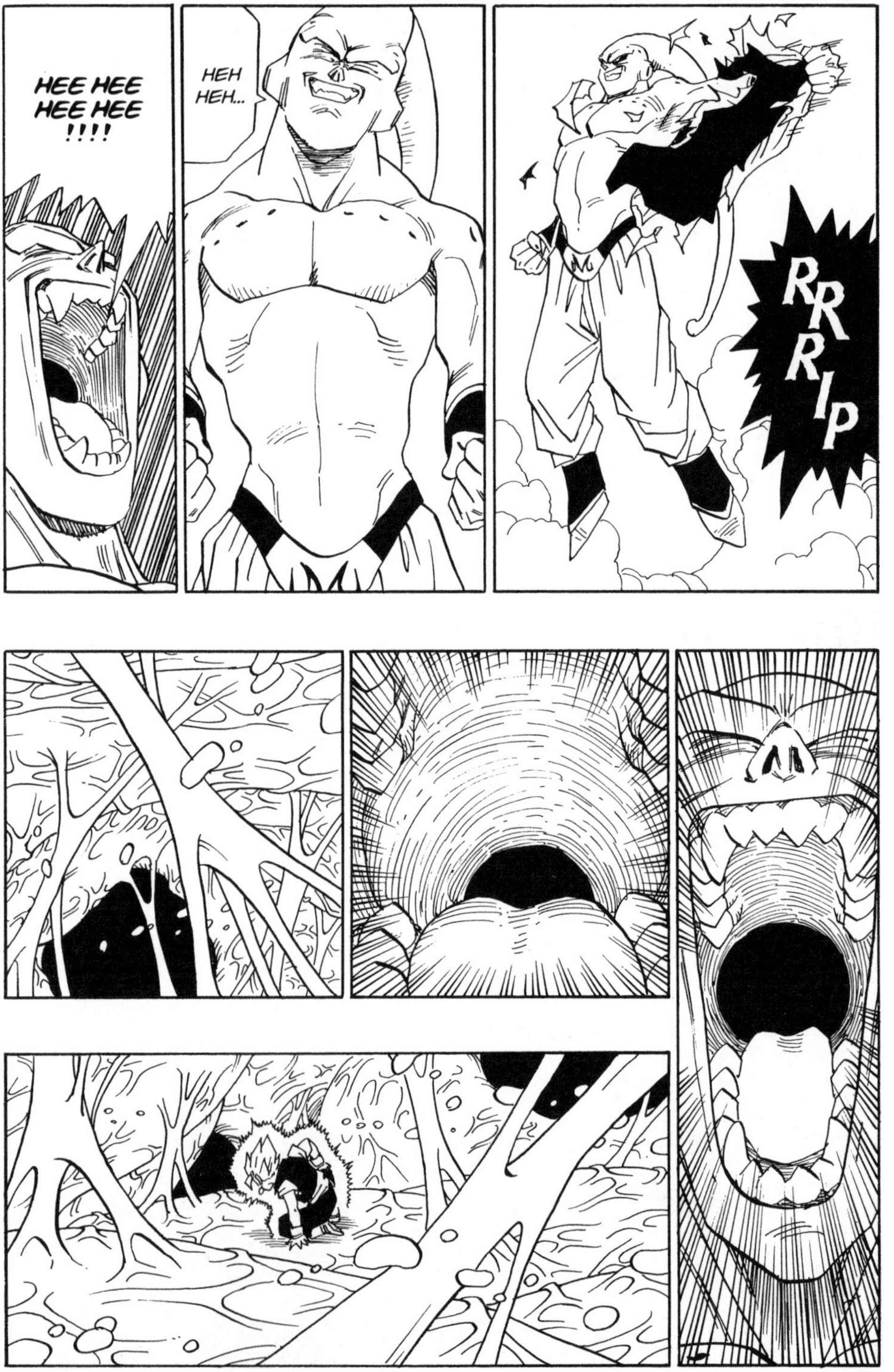
HEE HEE
HEE HEE
!!!!
HEH
HEH...
RRRIP

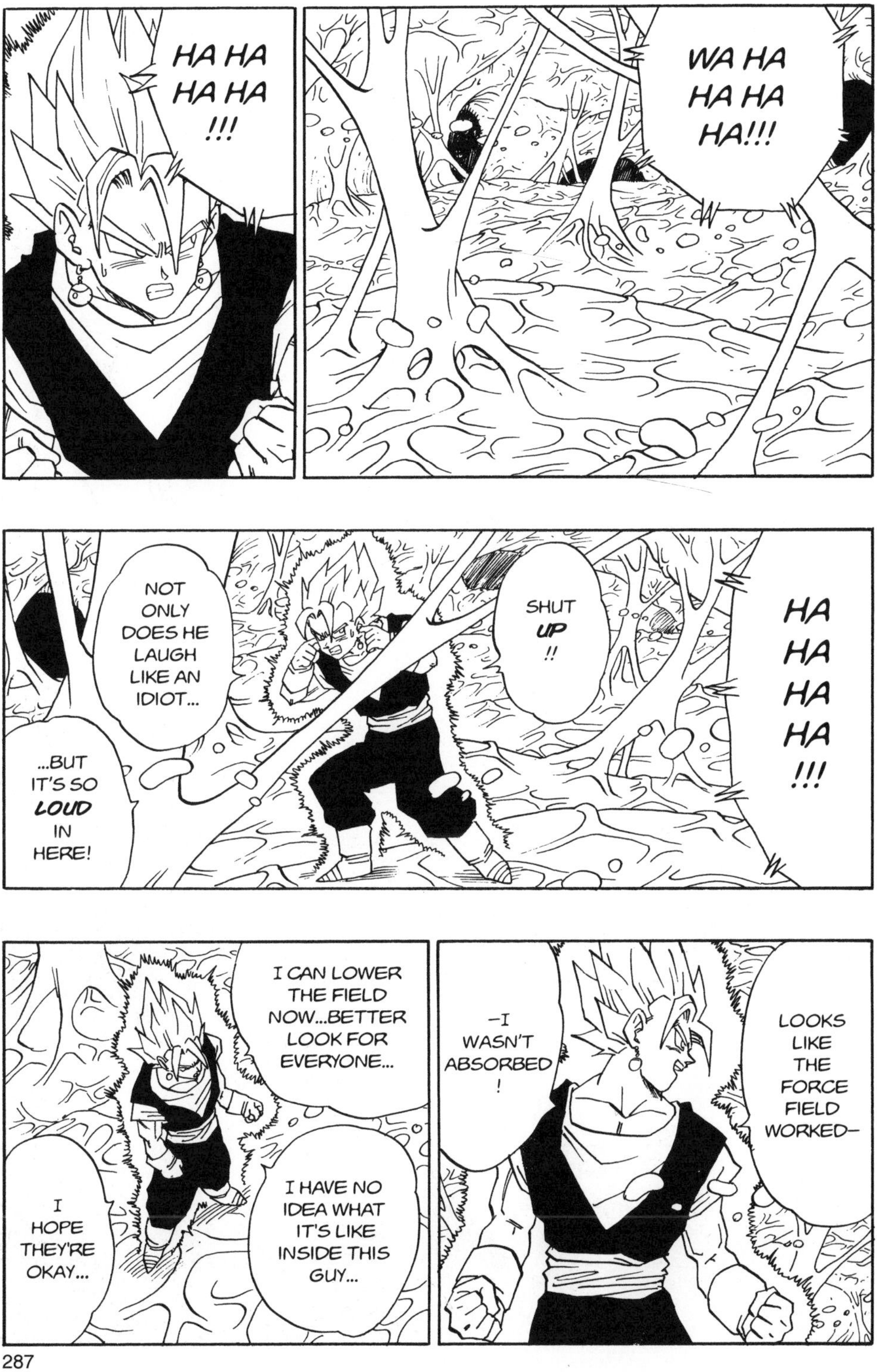
WA HA HA HA HA!!!
HA HA HA HA!!!
HA HA HA HA!!!
SHUT UP!!
NOT ONLY DOES HE LAUGH LIKE AN IDIOT...
...BUT IT'S SO LOUD IN HERE!
LOOKS LIKE THE FORCE FIELD WORKED—
—I WASN'T ABSORBED!
I CAN LOWER THE FIELD NOW...BETTER LOOK FOR EVERYONE...
I HAVE NO IDEA WHAT IT'S LIKE INSIDE THIS GUY...
I HOPE THEY'RE OKAY...

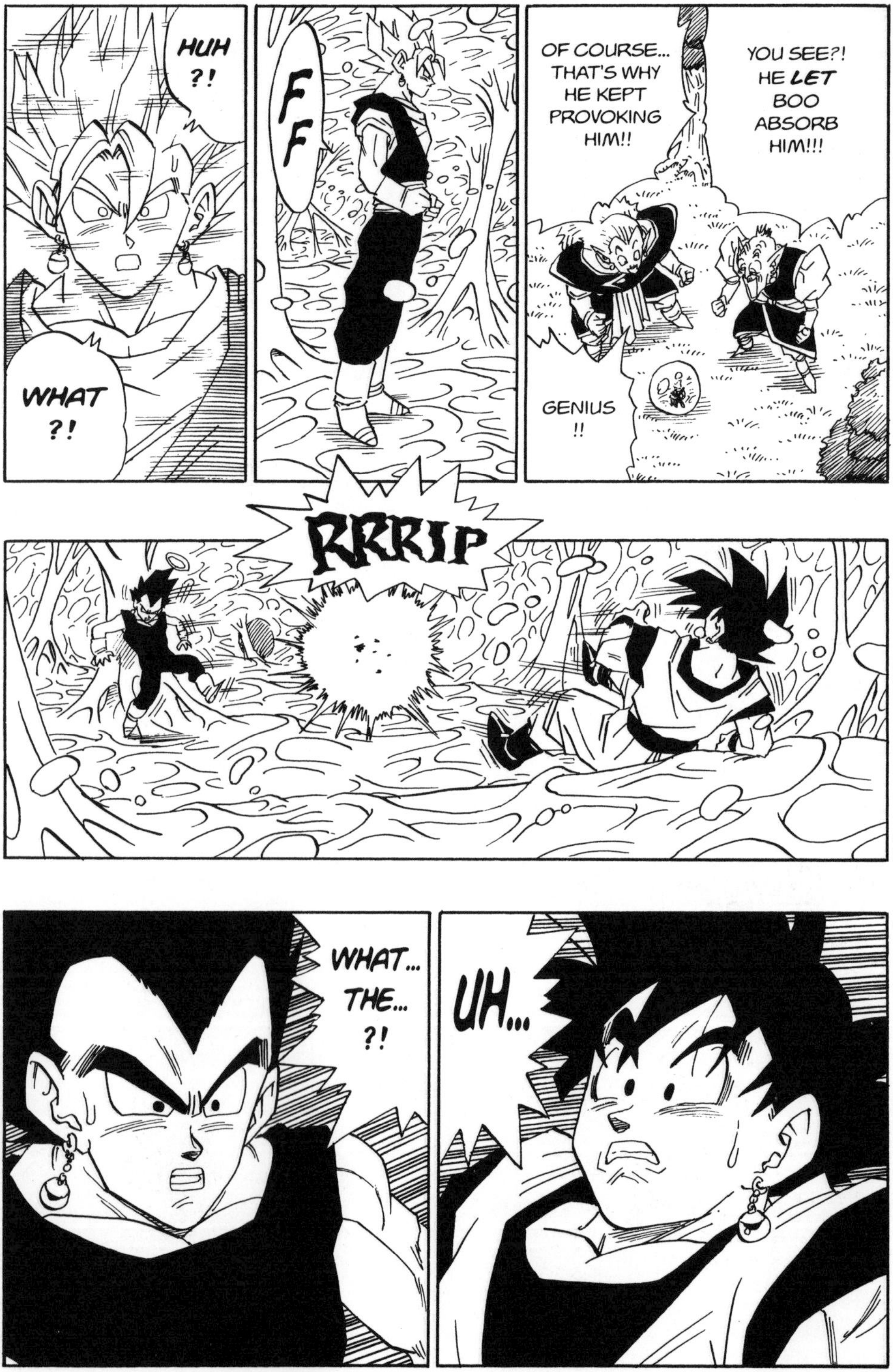
YOU SEE?! HE LET BOO ABSORB HIM!!!
OF COURSE... THAT'S WHY HE KEPT PROVOKING HIM!!
GENIUS !!
FF
HUH ?!
WHAT ?!
RRRIP
UH...
WHAT... THE... ?!

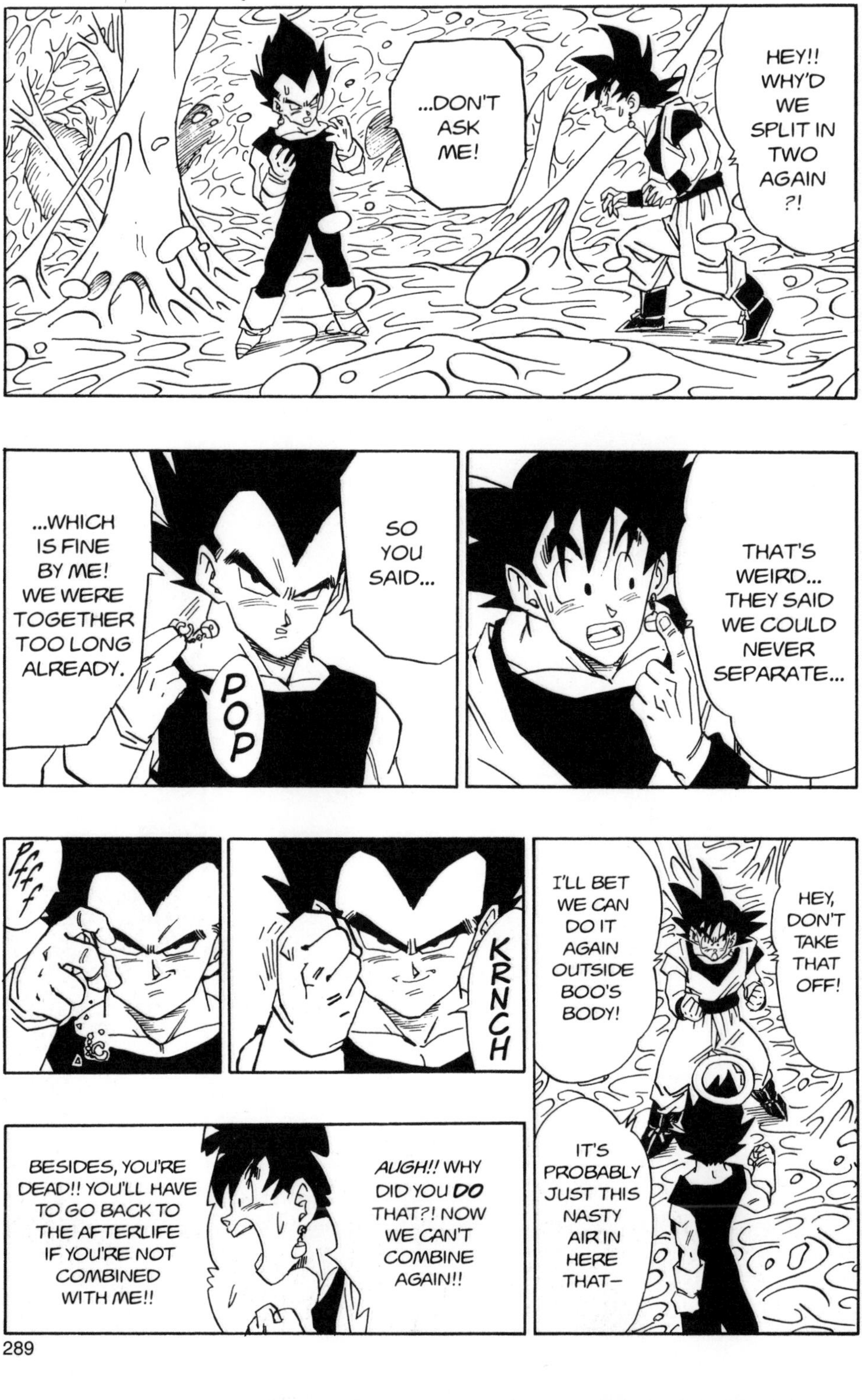
HEY!! WHY'D WE SPLIT IN TWO AGAIN?!
...DON'T ASK ME!
THAT'S WEIRD... THEY SAID WE COULD NEVER SEPARATE...
SO YOU SAID...
...WHICH IS FINE BY ME! WE WERE TOGETHER TOO LONG ALREADY.
POP
HEY, DON'T TAKE THAT OFF!
I'LL BET WE CAN DO IT AGAIN OUTSIDE BOO'S BODY!
IT'S PROBABLY JUST THIS NASTY AIR IN HERE THAT—
KRNCH
Pfff
AUGH!! WHY DID YOU **DO** THAT?! NOW WE CAN'T COMBINE AGAIN!!
BESIDES, YOU'RE DEAD!! YOU'LL HAVE TO GO BACK TO THE AFTERLIFE IF YOU'RE NOT COMBINED WITH ME!!

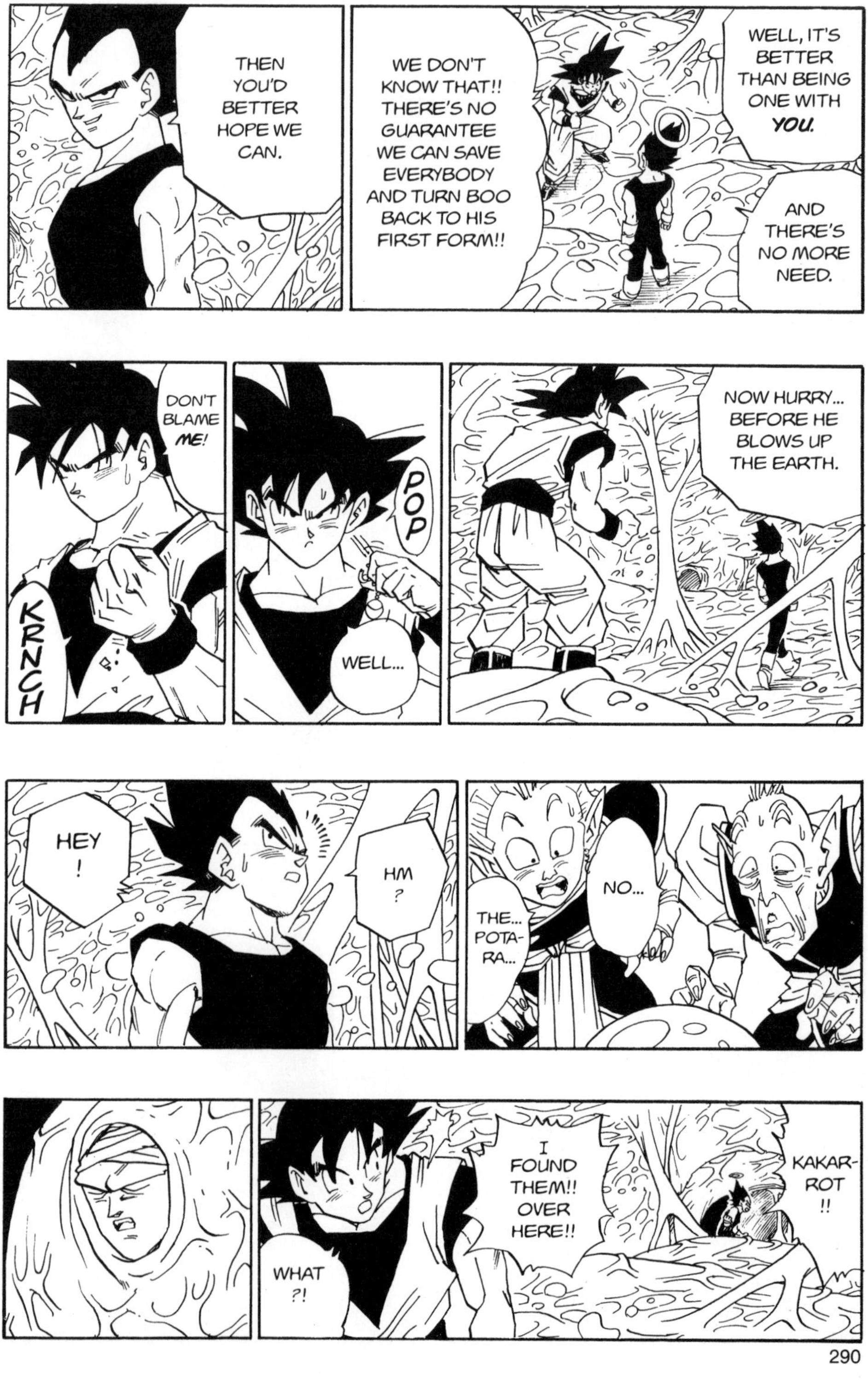
WELL, IT'S BETTER THAN BEING ONE WITH *YOU.*
AND THERE'S NO MORE NEED.
WE DON'T KNOW THAT!! THERE'S NO GUARANTEE WE CAN SAVE EVERYBODY AND TURN BOO BACK TO HIS FIRST FORM!!
THEN YOU'D BETTER HOPE WE CAN.
NOW HURRY... BEFORE HE BLOWS UP THE EARTH.
POP
WELL...
DON'T BLAME *ME!*
KRNCH
NO...
THE... POTA-RA...
HM ?
HEY !
KAKAR-ROT !!
I FOUND THEM!! OVER HERE!!
WHAT ?!

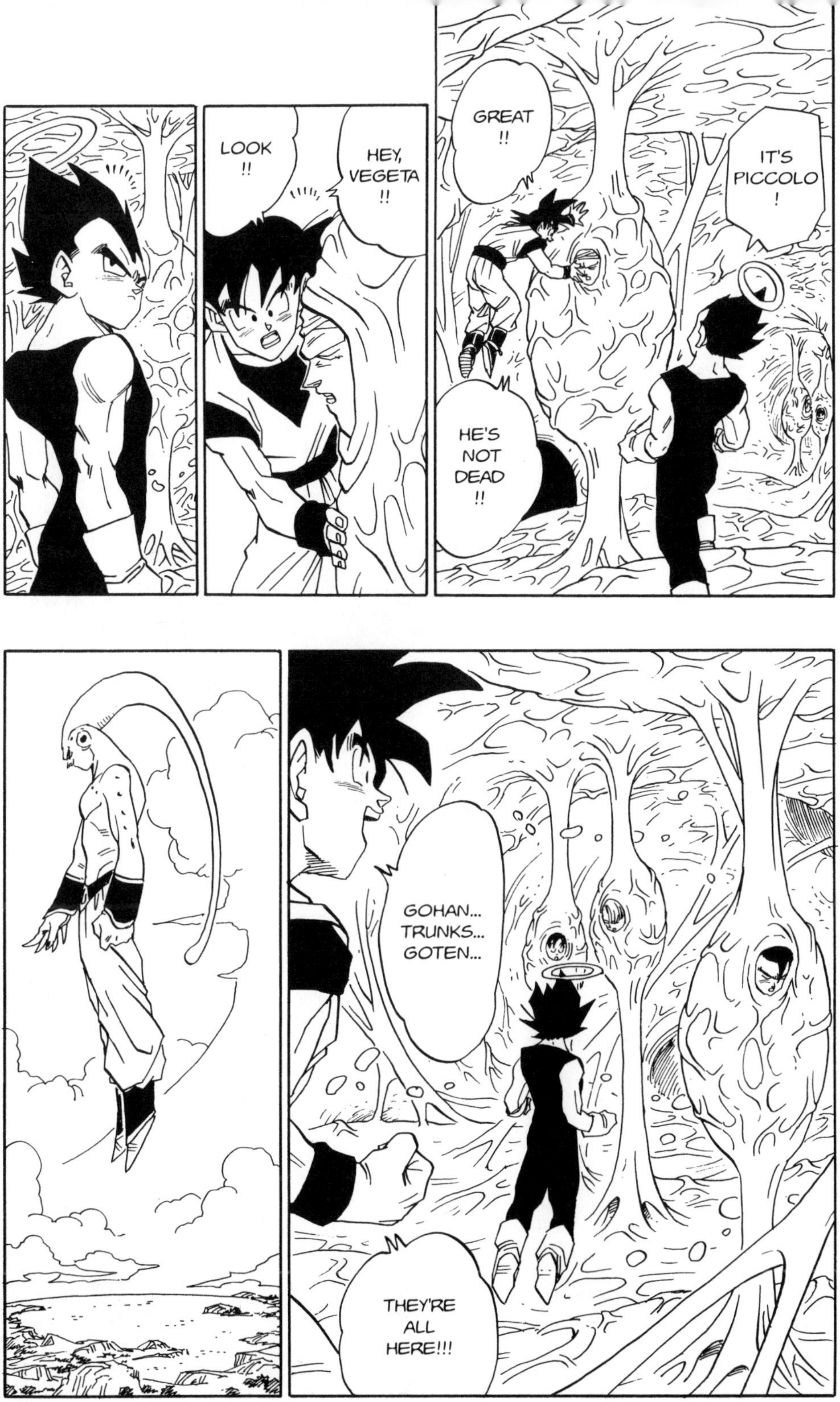
IT'S PICCOLO!
GREAT!!
HE'S NOT DEAD!!
HEY, VEGETA!!
LOOK!!
GOHAN... TRUNKS... GOTEN...
THEY'RE ALL HERE!!!

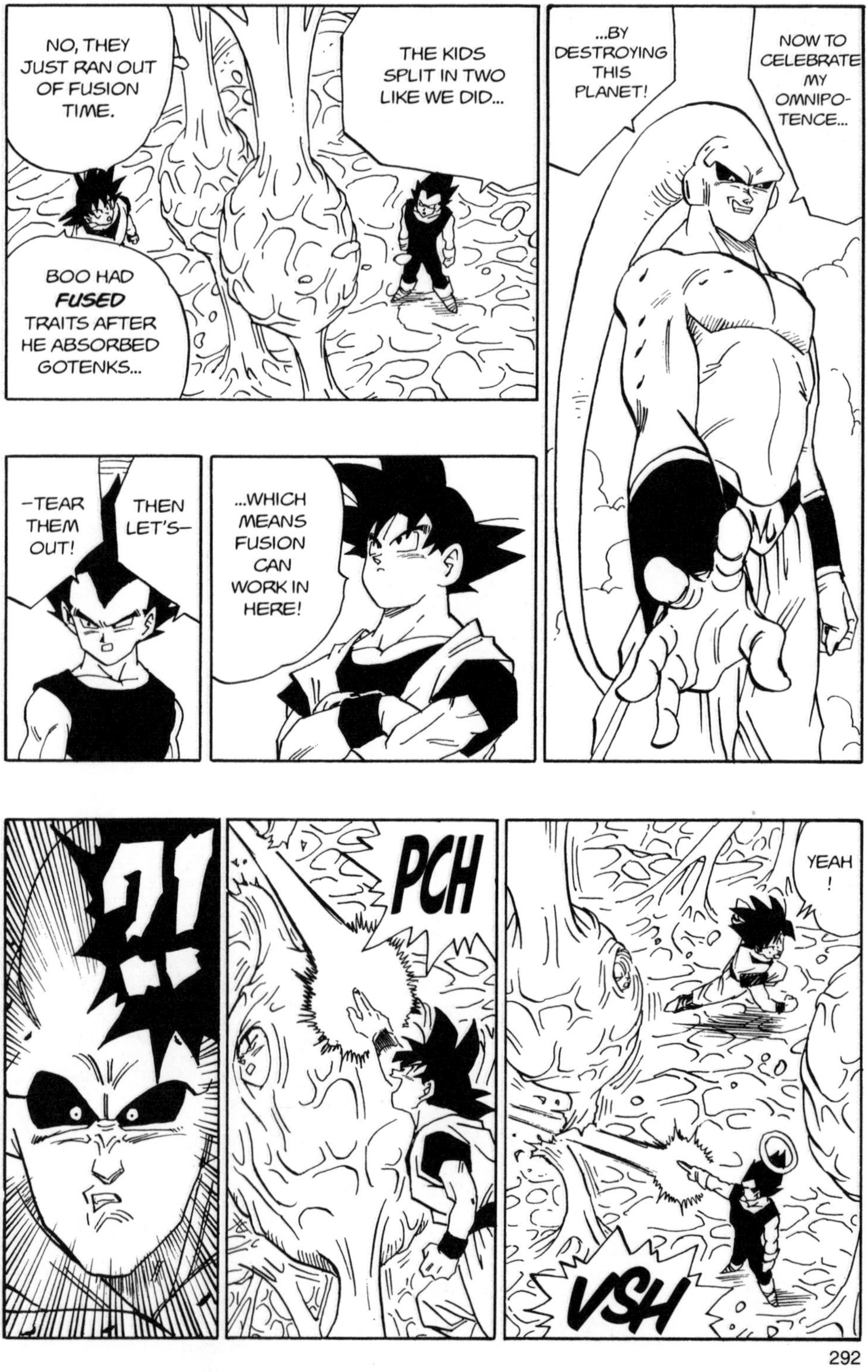
NOW TO CELEBRATE MY OMNIPOTENCE...
...BY DESTROYING THIS PLANET!
THE KIDS SPLIT IN TWO LIKE WE DID...
NO, THEY JUST RAN OUT OF FUSION TIME.
BOO HAD **FUSED** TRAITS AFTER HE ABSORBED GOTENKS...
...WHICH MEANS FUSION CAN WORK IN HERE!
THEN LET'S—
—TEAR THEM OUT!
YEAH !
VSH
PCH
?!

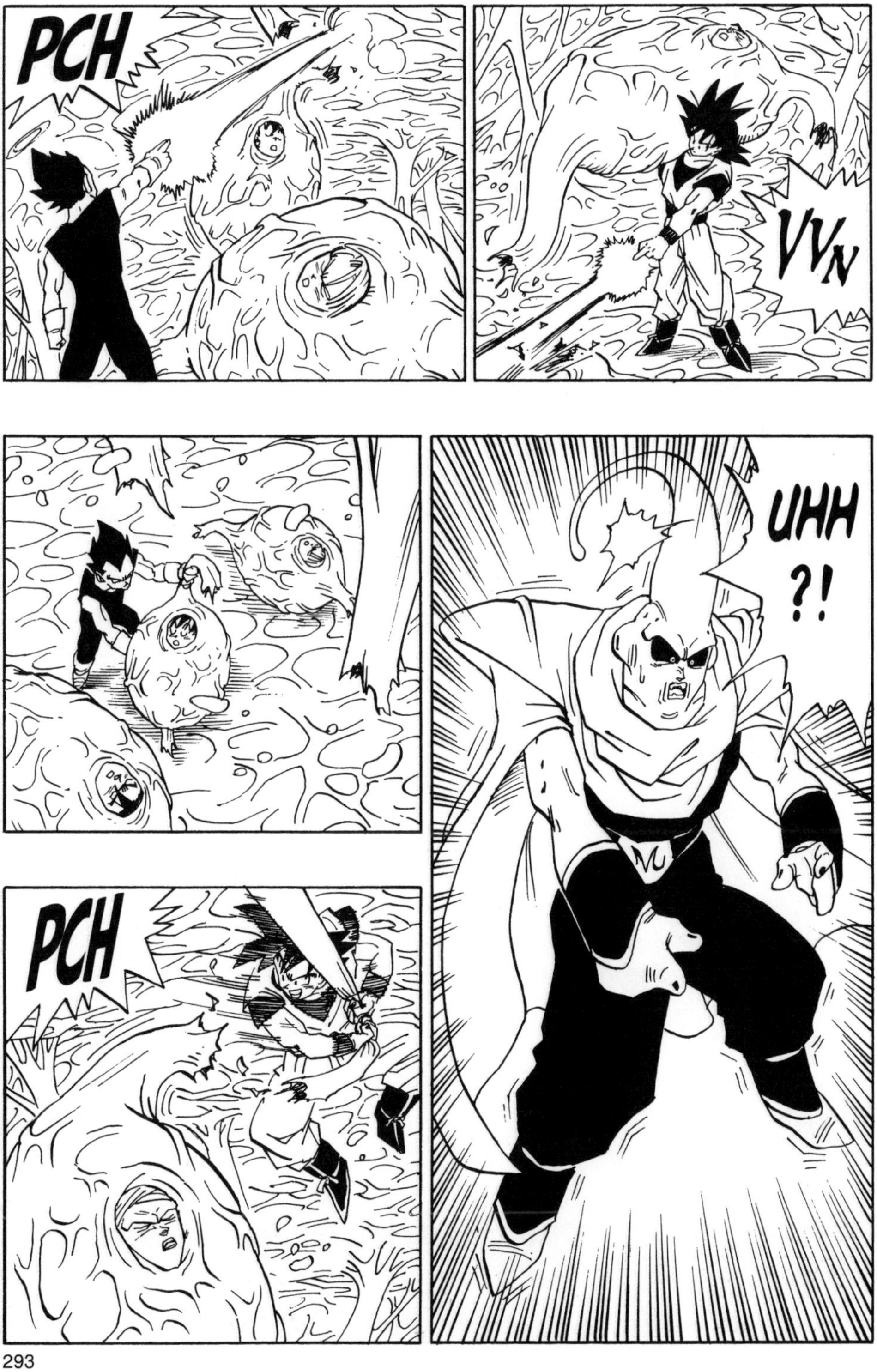
VVN
PCH
UHH ?!
PCH

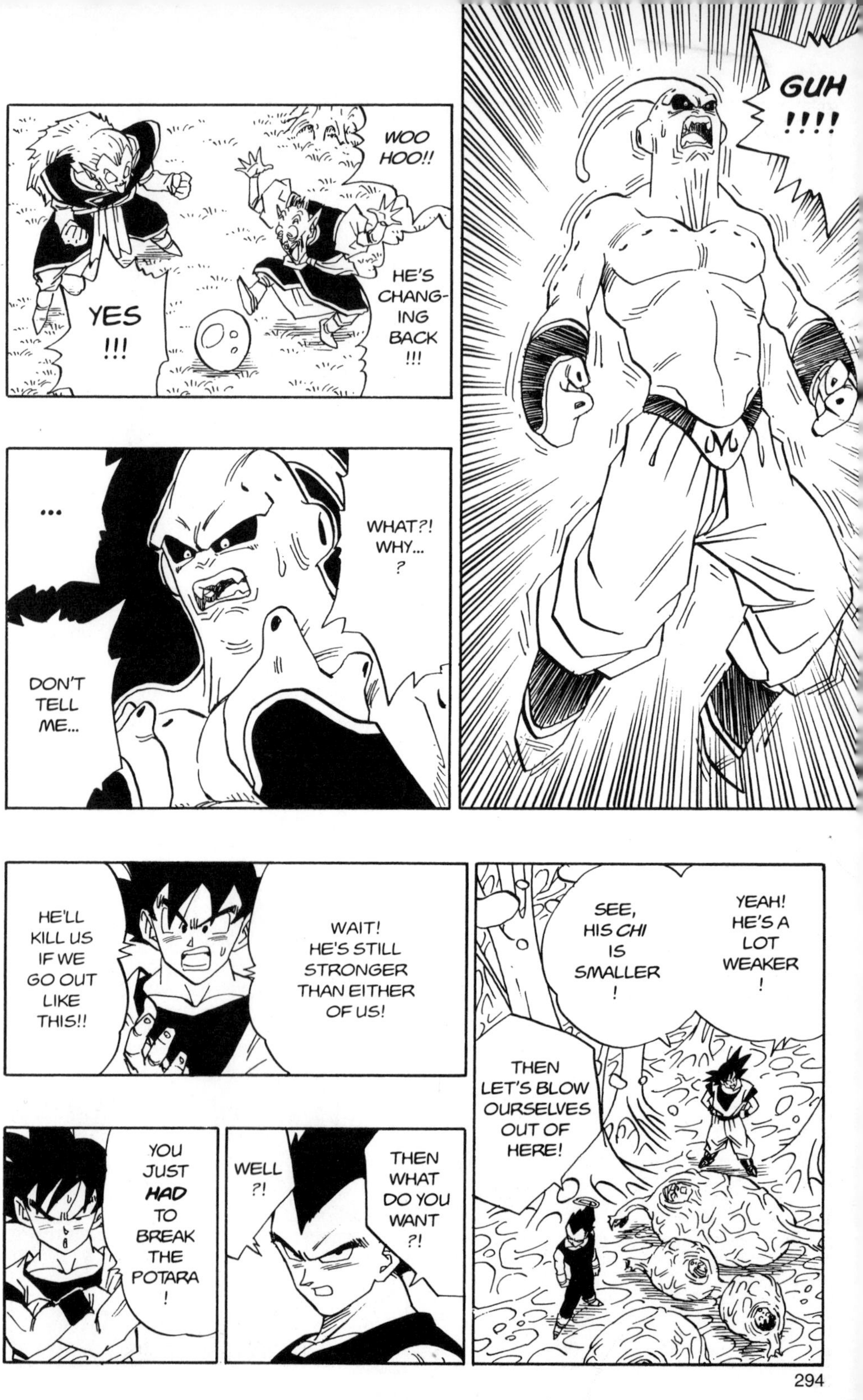
GUH !!!!
WOO HOO!!
HE'S CHANGING BACK !!!
YES !!!
WHAT?! WHY... ?
...
DON'T TELL ME...
YEAH! HE'S A LOT WEAKER !
SEE, HIS CHI IS SMALLER !
THEN LET'S BLOW OURSELVES OUT OF HERE!
WAIT! HE'S STILL STRONGER THAN EITHER OF US!
HE'LL KILL US IF WE GO OUT LIKE THIS!!
THEN WHAT DO YOU WANT ?!
WELL ?!
YOU JUST HAD TO BREAK THE POTARA !

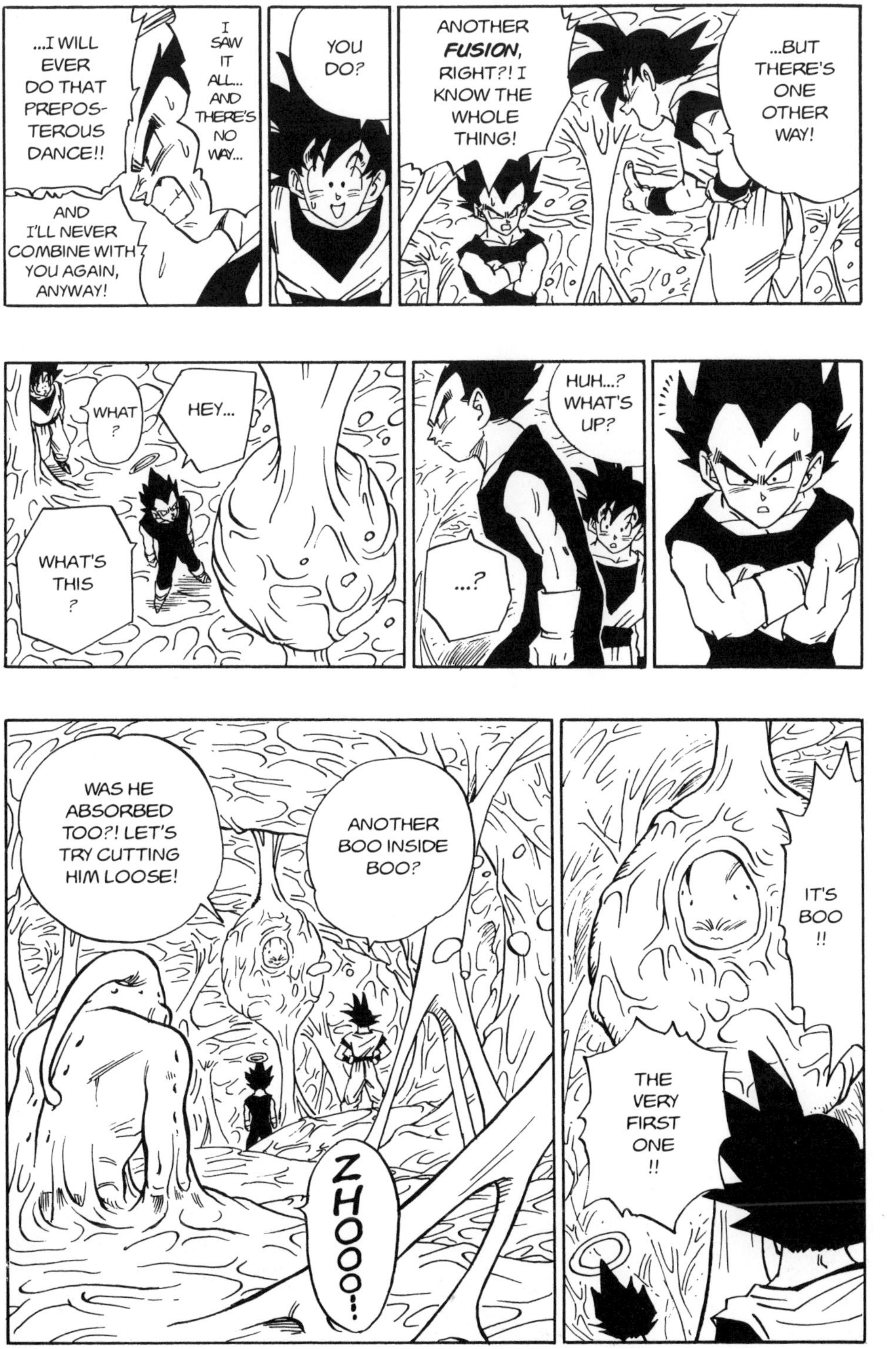
...BUT THERE'S ONE OTHER WAY!
ANOTHER FUSION, RIGHT?! I KNOW THE WHOLE THING!
YOU DO?
I SAW IT ALL... AND THERE'S NO WAY...
...I WILL EVER DO THAT PREPOSTEROUS DANCE!!
AND I'LL NEVER COMBINE WITH YOU AGAIN, ANYWAY!
HUH...? WHAT'S UP?
...?
HEY...
WHAT ?
WHAT'S THIS ?
IT'S BOO !!
THE VERY FIRST ONE !!
ANOTHER BOO INSIDE BOO?
WAS HE ABSORBED TOO?! LET'S TRY CUTTING HIM LOOSE!
ZHOOO!!

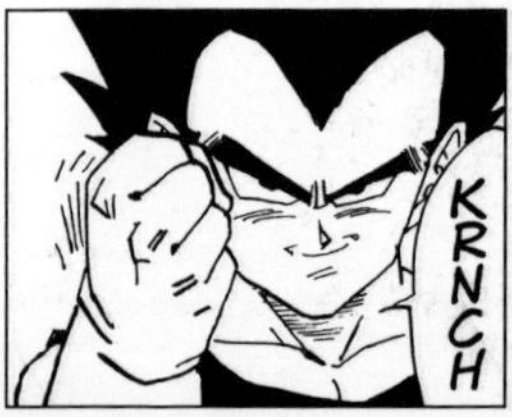
KRNCH

DRAGON BALL ドラゴンボール

DBZ:313 • Boos Inside Boo

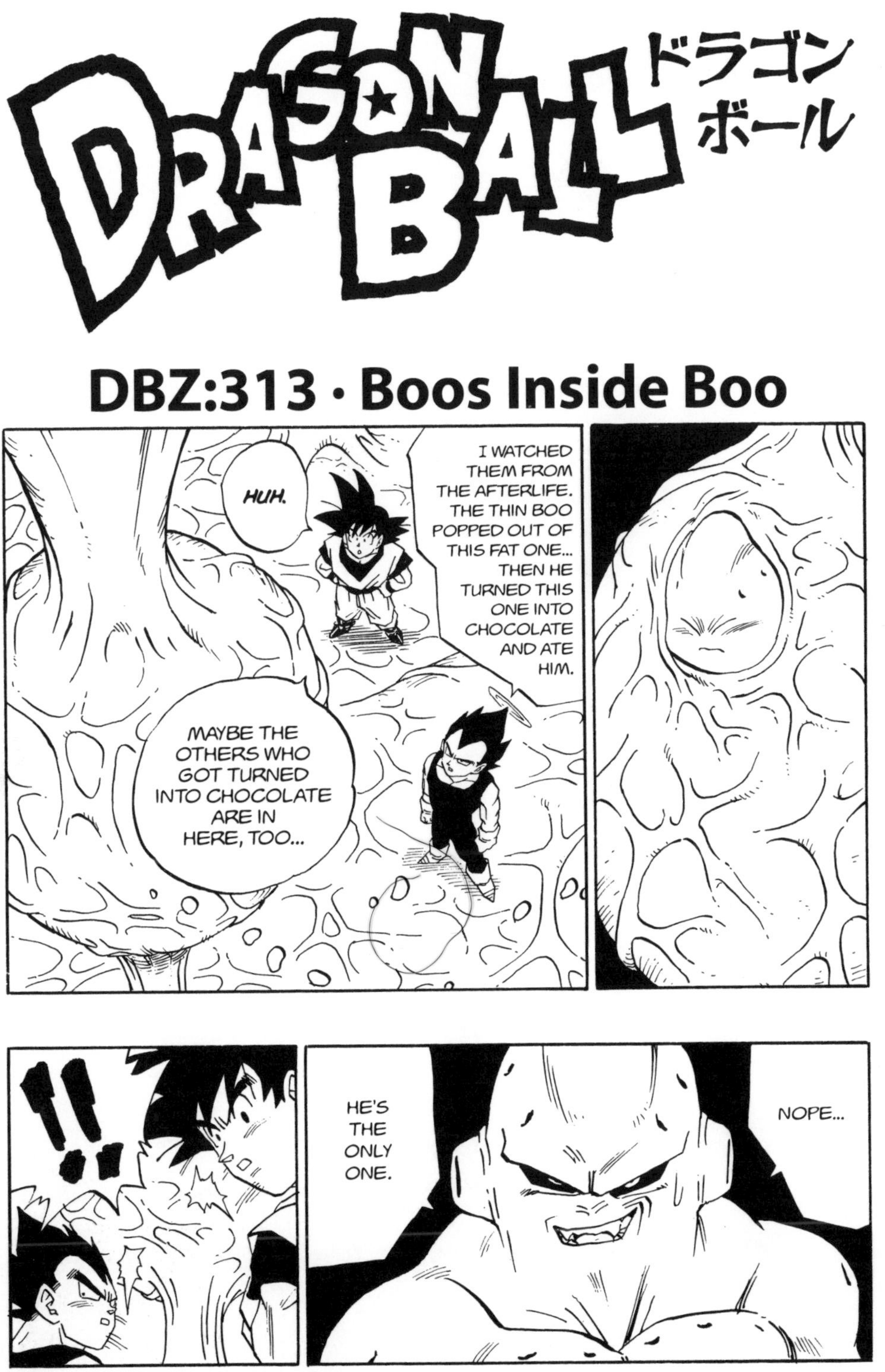
I WATCHED THEM FROM THE AFTERLIFE. THE THIN BOO POPPED OUT OF THIS FAT ONE... THEN HE TURNED THIS ONE INTO CHOCOLATE AND ATE HIM.
HUH.
MAYBE THE OTHERS WHO GOT TURNED INTO CHOCOLATE ARE IN HERE, TOO...
NOPE...
HE'S THE ONLY ONE.
!!

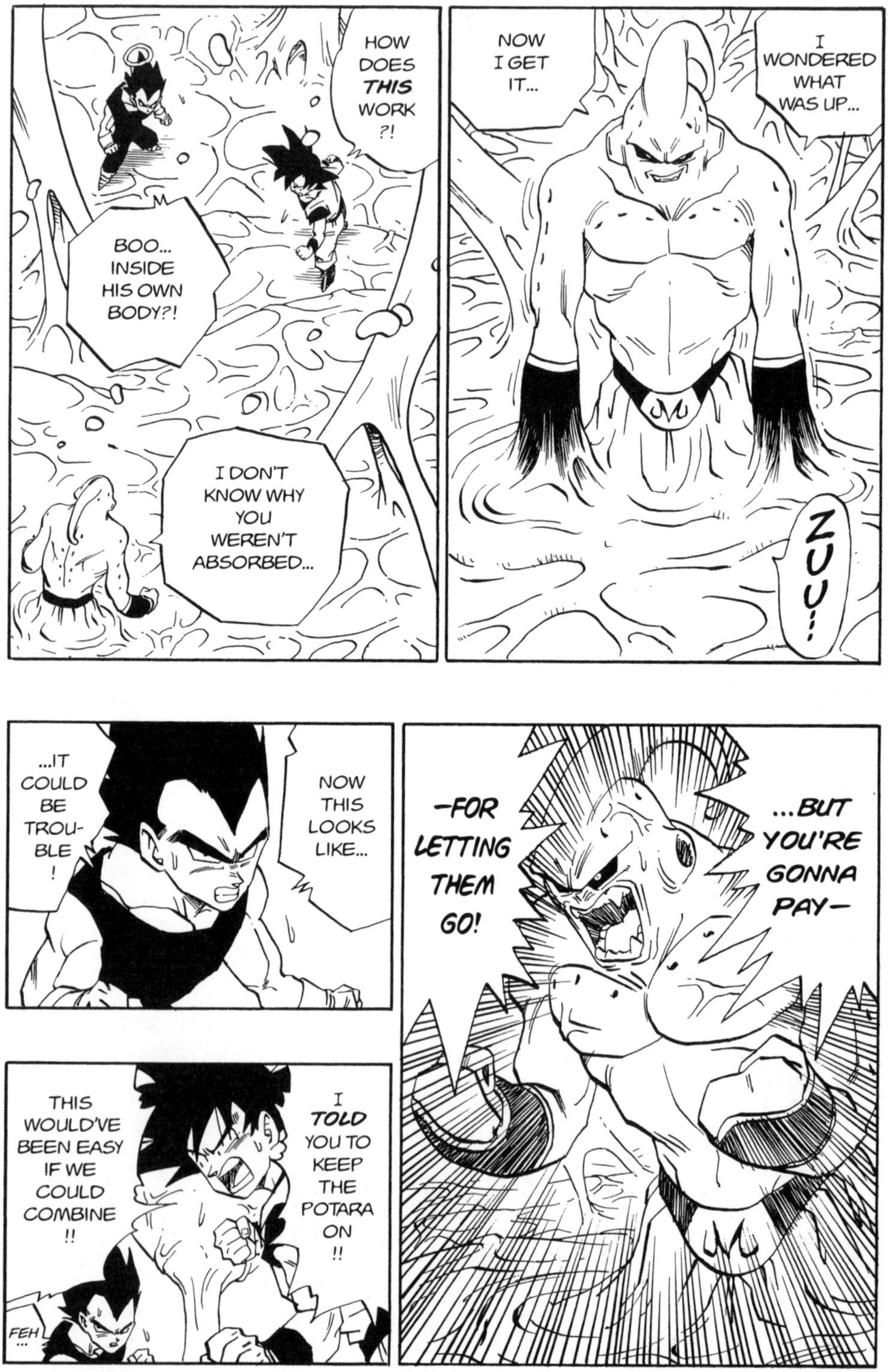
I WONDERED WHAT WAS UP...
NOW I GET IT...
ZUUU!!
HOW DOES THIS WORK?!
BOO... INSIDE HIS OWN BODY?!
I DON'T KNOW WHY YOU WEREN'T ABSORBED...
...BUT YOU'RE GONNA PAY—
—FOR LETTING THEM GO!
NOW THIS LOOKS LIKE...
...IT COULD BE TROUBLE!
I TOLD YOU TO KEEP THE POTARA ON!!
THIS WOULD'VE BEEN EASY IF WE COULD COMBINE!!
FEH...

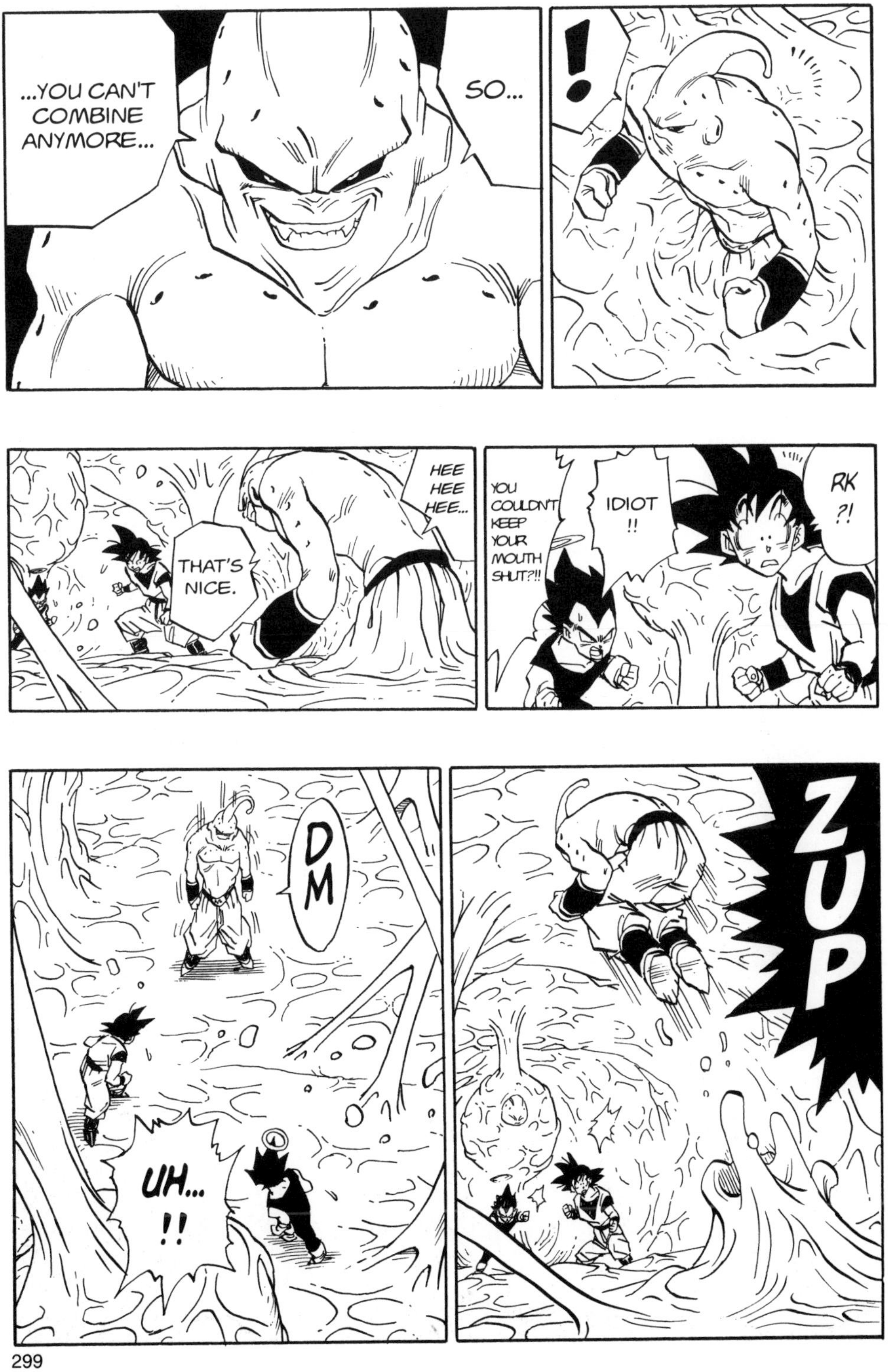
!
SO...
...YOU CAN'T COMBINE ANYMORE...
RK ?!
IDIOT !!
YOU COULDN'T KEEP YOUR MOUTH SHUT?!!
HEE HEE HEE...
THAT'S NICE.
ZUP
DM
UH... !!

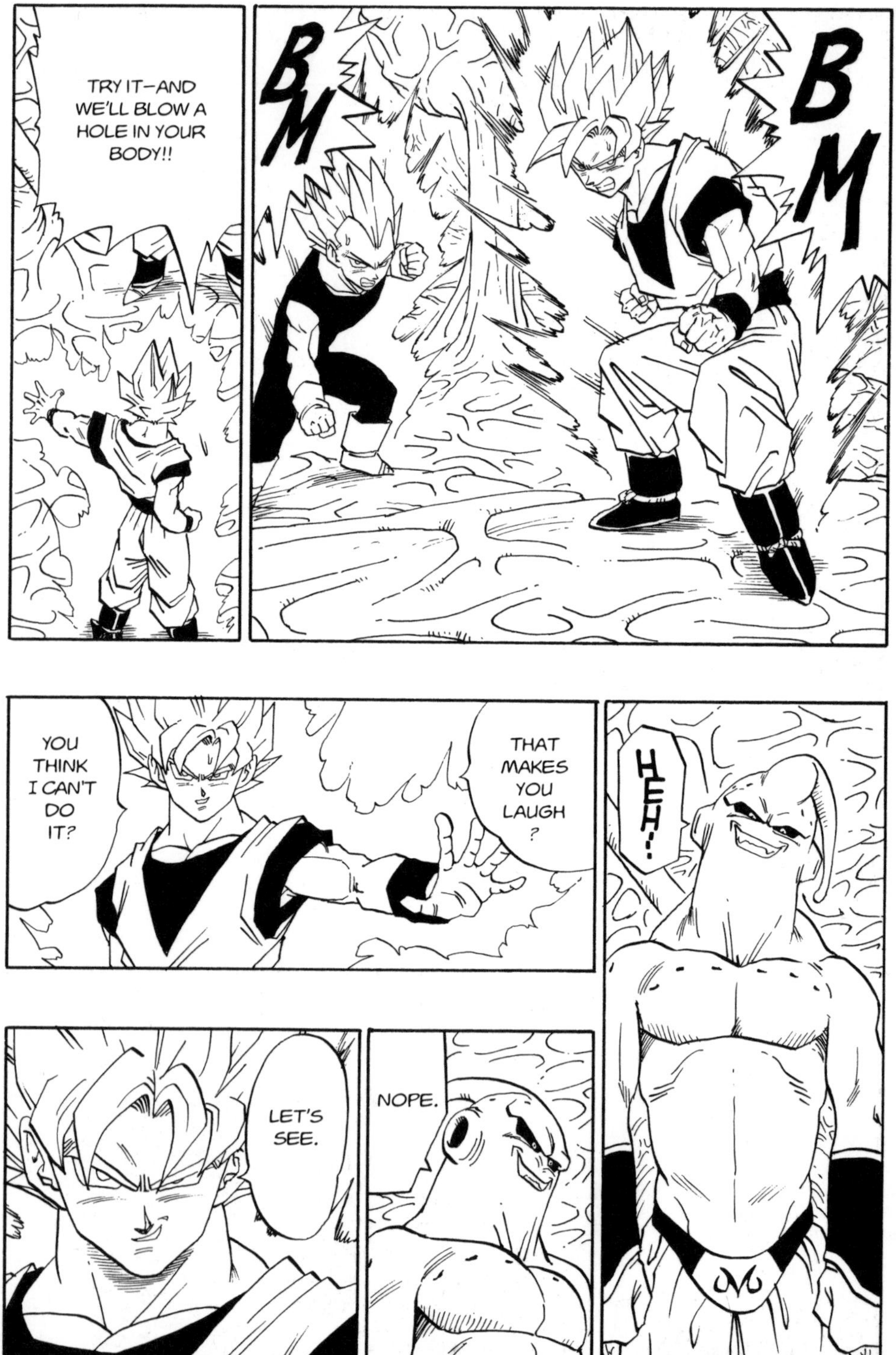
BM
BM
TRY IT—AND WE'LL BLOW A HOLE IN YOUR BODY!!
HEH!!
THAT MAKES YOU LAUGH?
YOU THINK I CAN'T DO IT?
NOPE.
LET'S SEE.

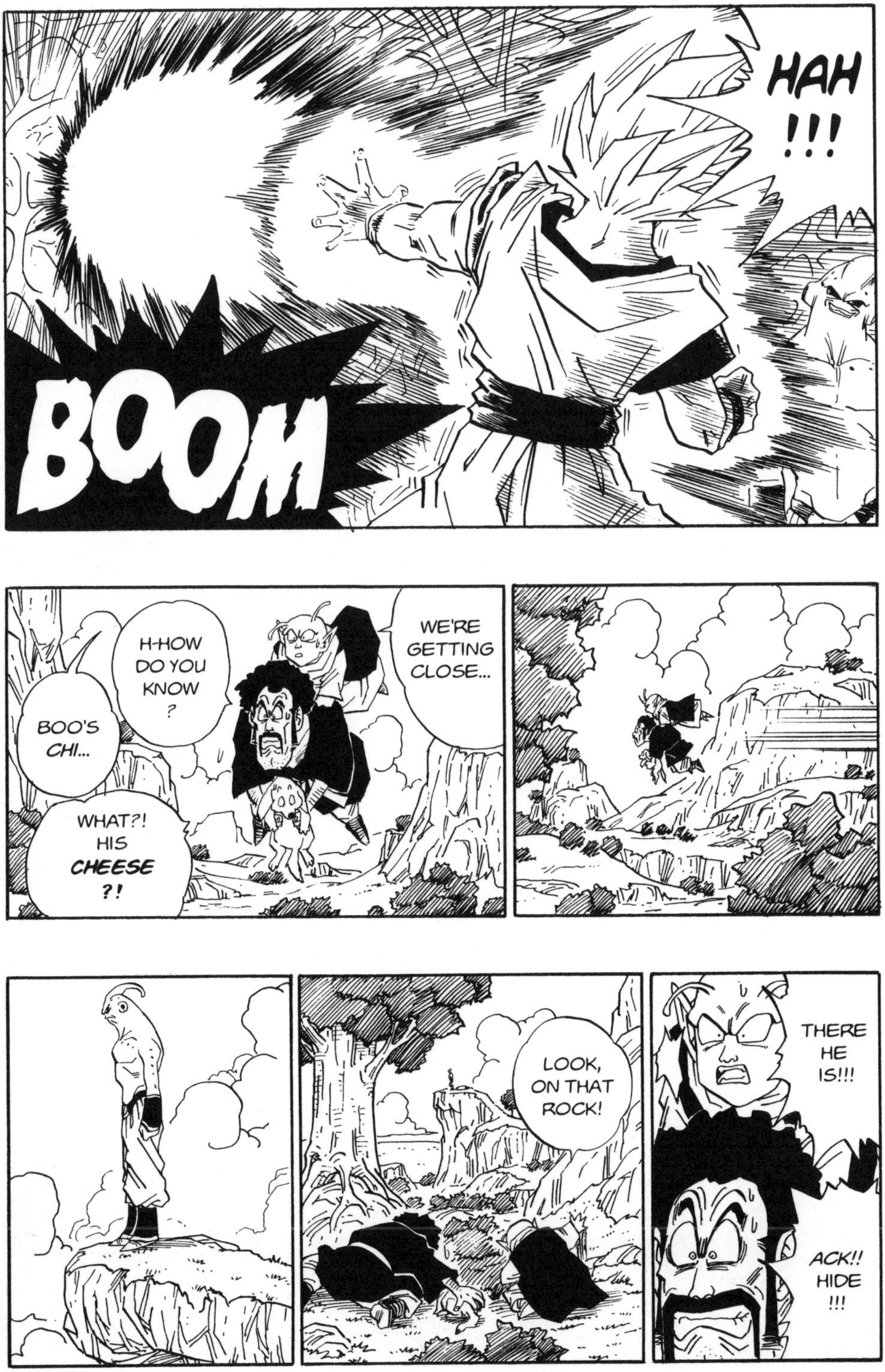
HAH!!!
BOOM
WE'RE GETTING CLOSE...
H-HOW DO YOU KNOW?
BOO'S CHI...
WHAT?! HIS **CHEESE**?!
THERE HE IS!!!
ACK!! HIDE!!!
LOOK, ON THAT ROCK!

BUT...WHY ISN'T HE MOVING...?
OH!
HE'S... HE'S TURNED BACK...!!
...
IT DIDN'T WORK?!
I JUST FELT A LITTLE PRICK.
LIKE BEING BITTEN BY A FLEA.
...
SO WE HAVE TO BEAT YOU FIRST?
YOU CAN'T DO IT.
YOU'RE GONNA DIE.
YOU THINK SO?
I WONDER...

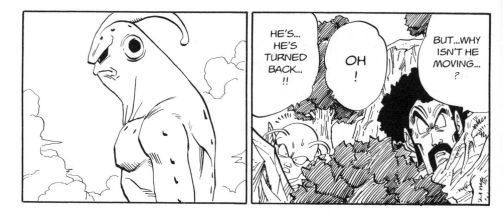

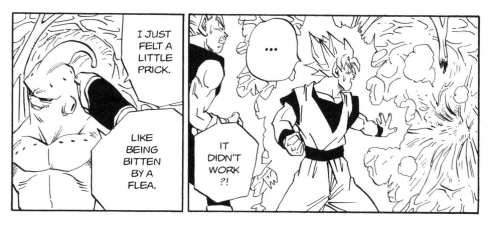

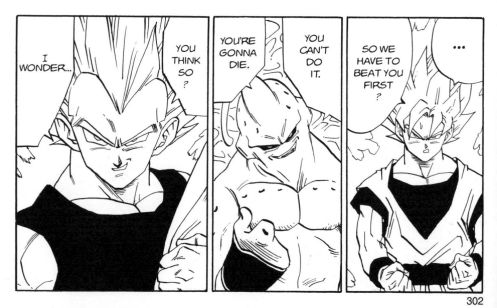

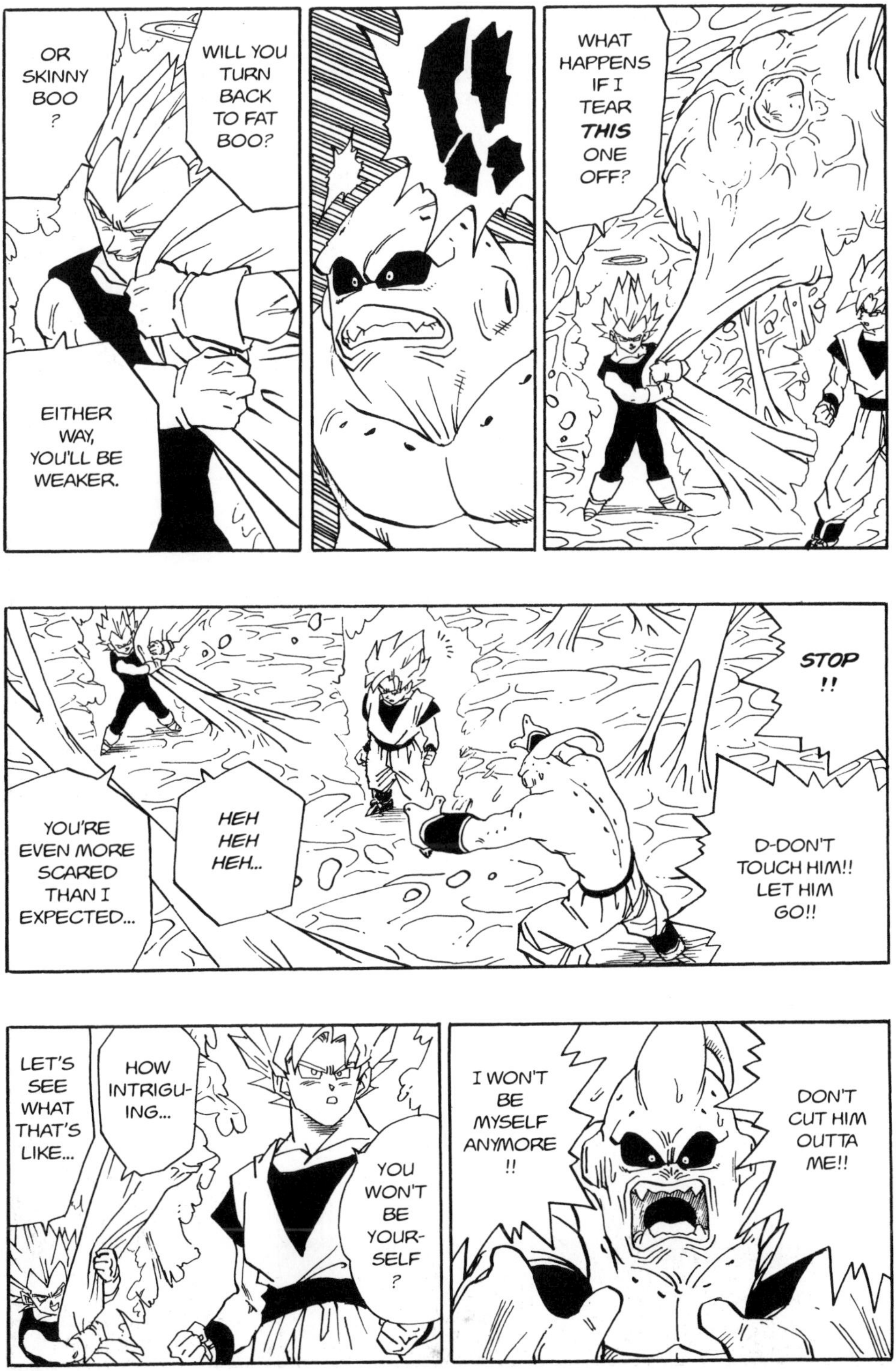
WHAT HAPPENS IF I TEAR **THIS** ONE OFF?
WILL YOU TURN BACK TO FAT BOO?
OR SKINNY BOO?
EITHER WAY, YOU'LL BE WEAKER.
STOP!!
D-DON'T TOUCH HIM!! LET HIM GO!!
HEH HEH HEH...
YOU'RE EVEN MORE SCARED THAN I EXPECTED...
DON'T CUT HIM OUTTA ME!!
I WON'T BE MYSELF ANYMORE!!
YOU WON'T BE YOURSELF?
HOW INTRIGUING...
LET'S SEE WHAT THAT'S LIKE...

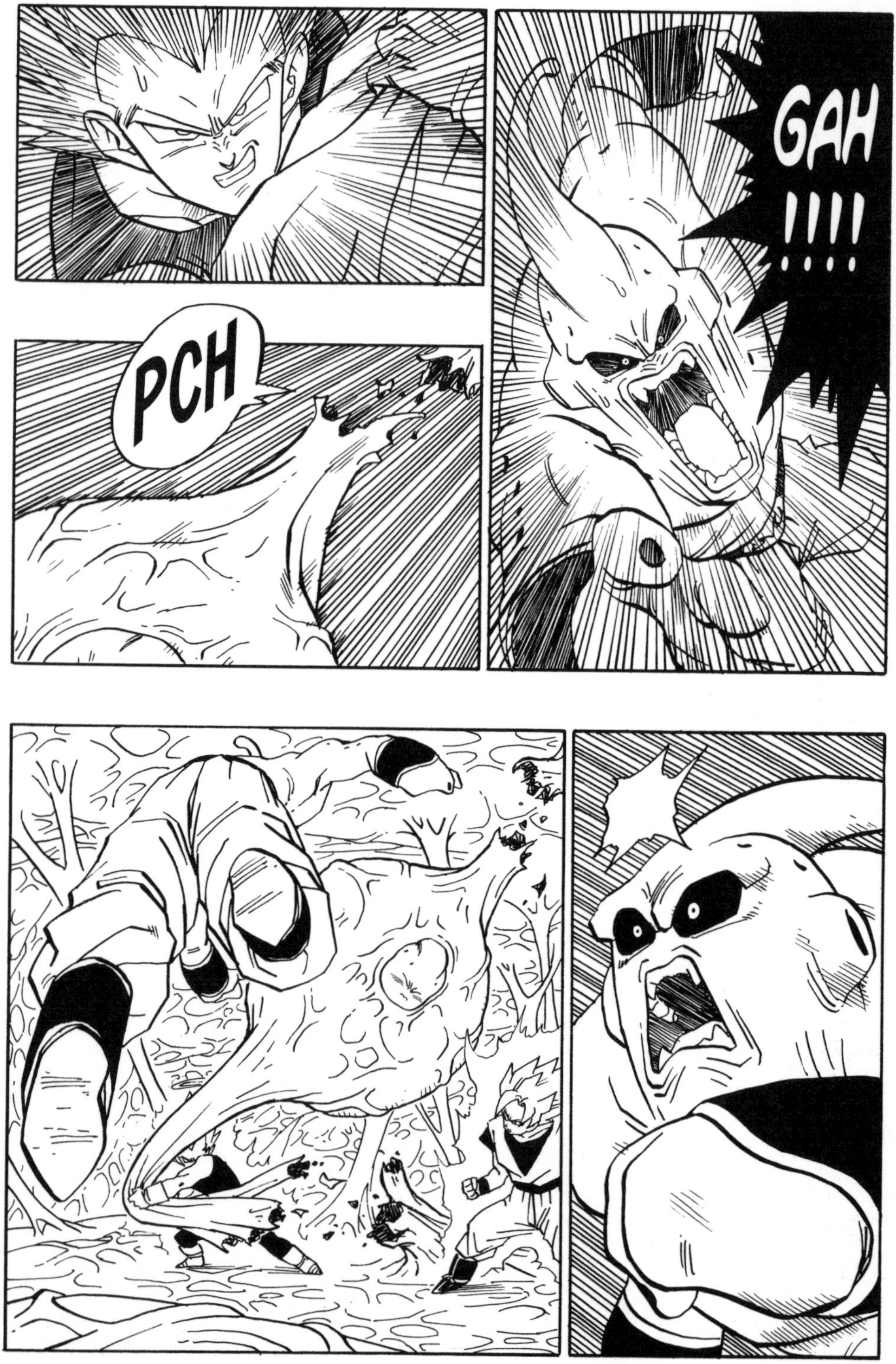
GAH!!!!
PCH

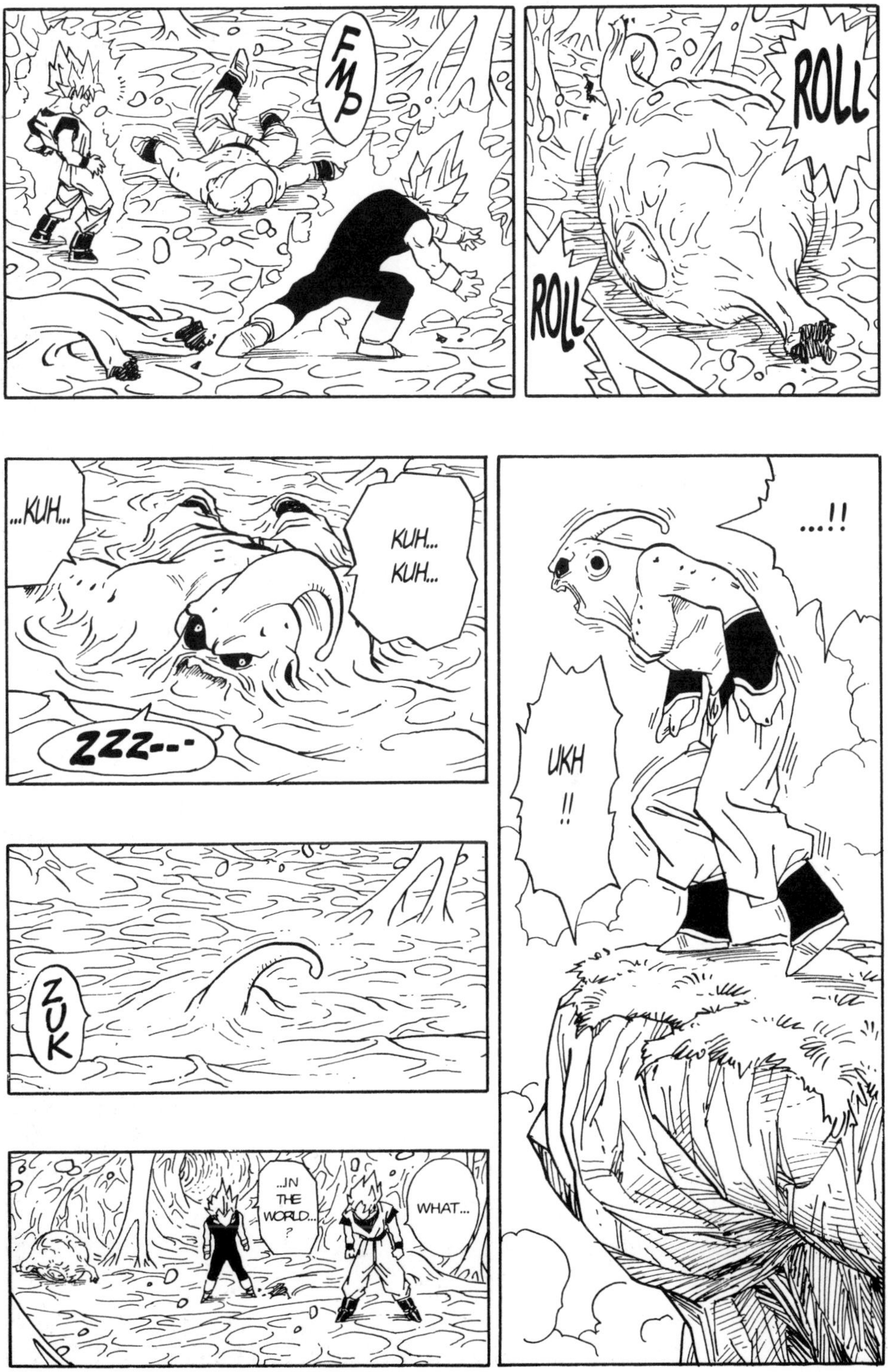
ROLL
ROLL
FMP
...!!
UKH !!
KUH... KUH...
...KUH...
ZZZ---
ZUK
WHAT...
...IN THE WORLD... ?

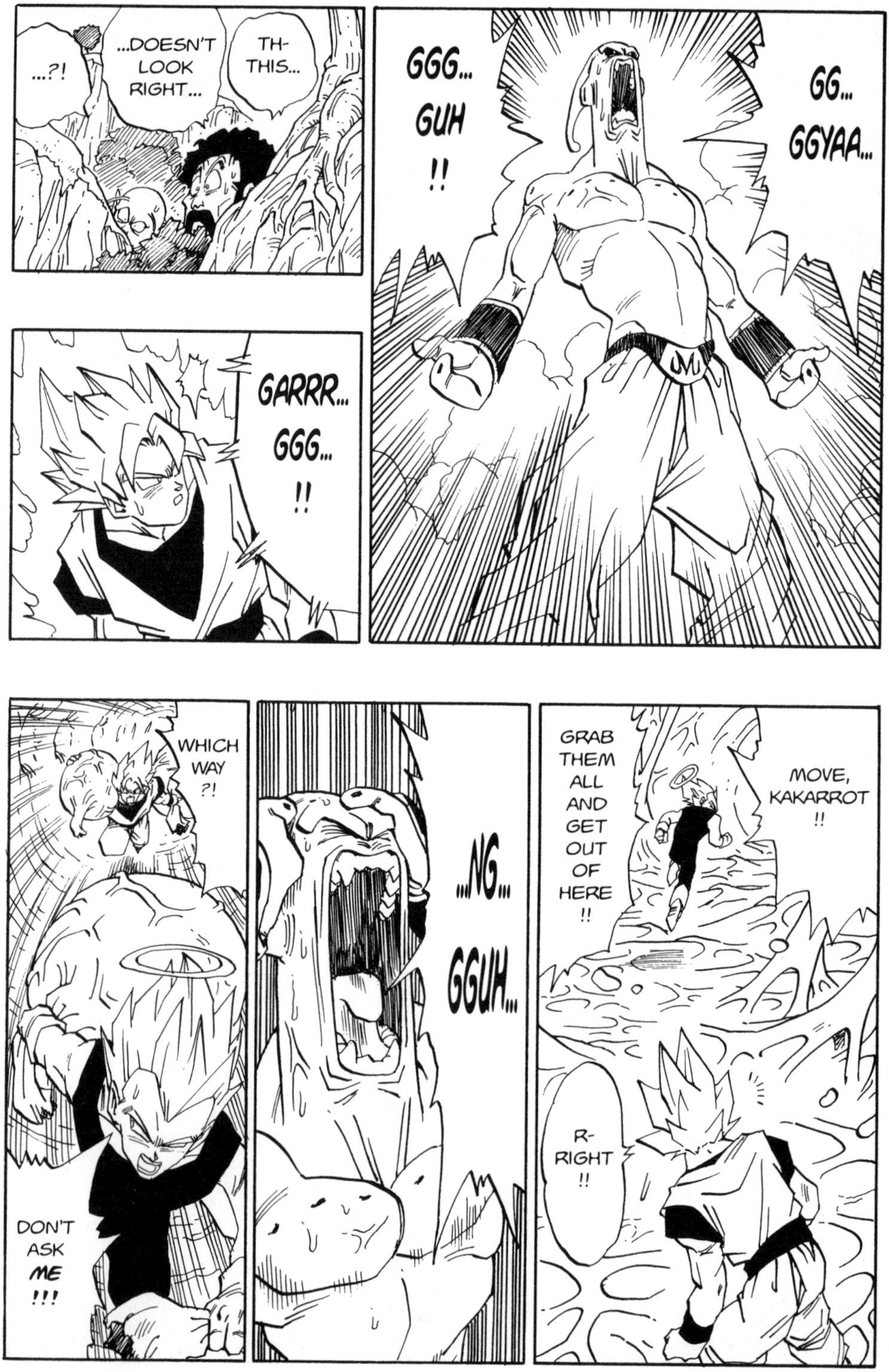
GG... GGYAA...
GGG... GUH !!
TH- THIS...
...DOESN'T LOOK RIGHT...
...?!
GARRR... GGG... !!
MOVE, KAKARROT !!
GRAB THEM ALL AND GET OUT OF HERE !!
R- RIGHT !!
...NG... GGUH...
WHICH WAY ?!
DON'T ASK ME !!!

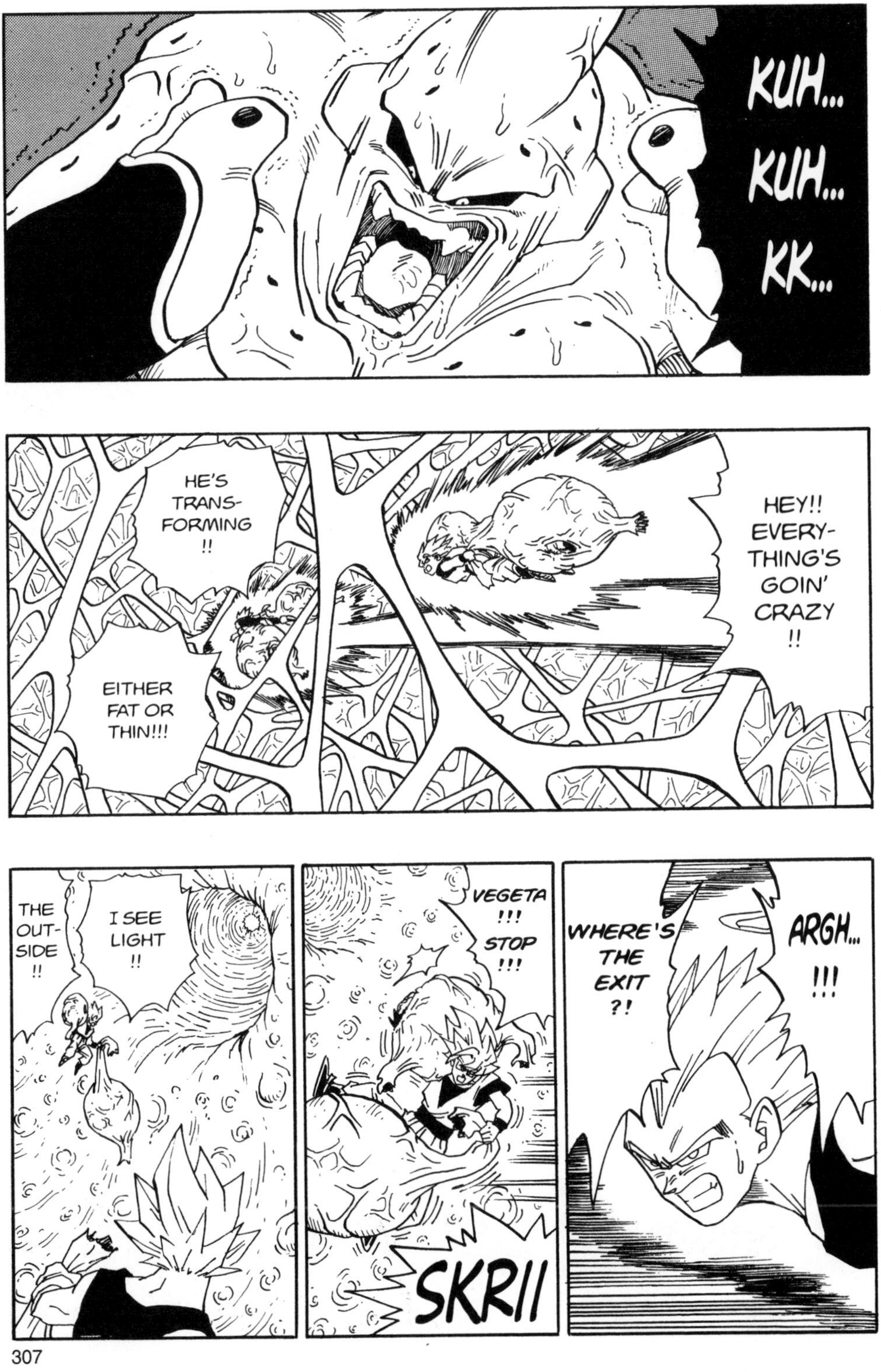
KUH... KUH... KK...
HEY!! EVERY-THING'S GOIN' CRAZY!!
HE'S TRANS-FORMING!!
EITHER FAT OR THIN!!!
ARGH... !!!
WHERE'S THE EXIT?!
VEGETA!!!
STOP!!!
SKRII
I SEE LIGHT!!
THE OUT-SIDE!!

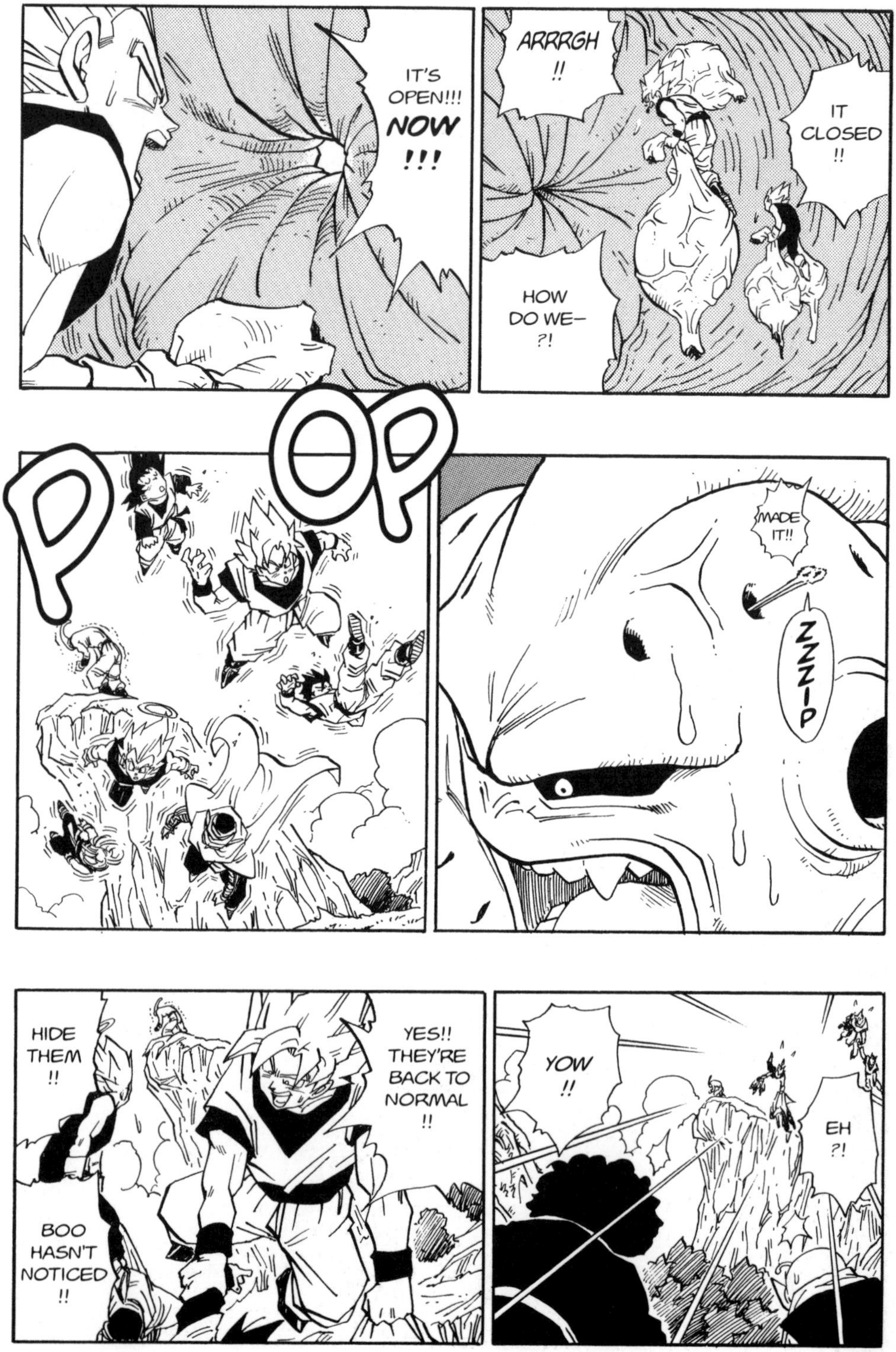
ARRRGH!!
IT CLOSED!!
HOW DO WE—?!
IT'S OPEN!!! NOW!!!
MADE IT!!
ZZZIP
POP
YOW!!
EH?!
YES!! THEY'RE BACK TO NORMAL!!
HIDE THEM!!
BOO HASN'T NOTICED!!

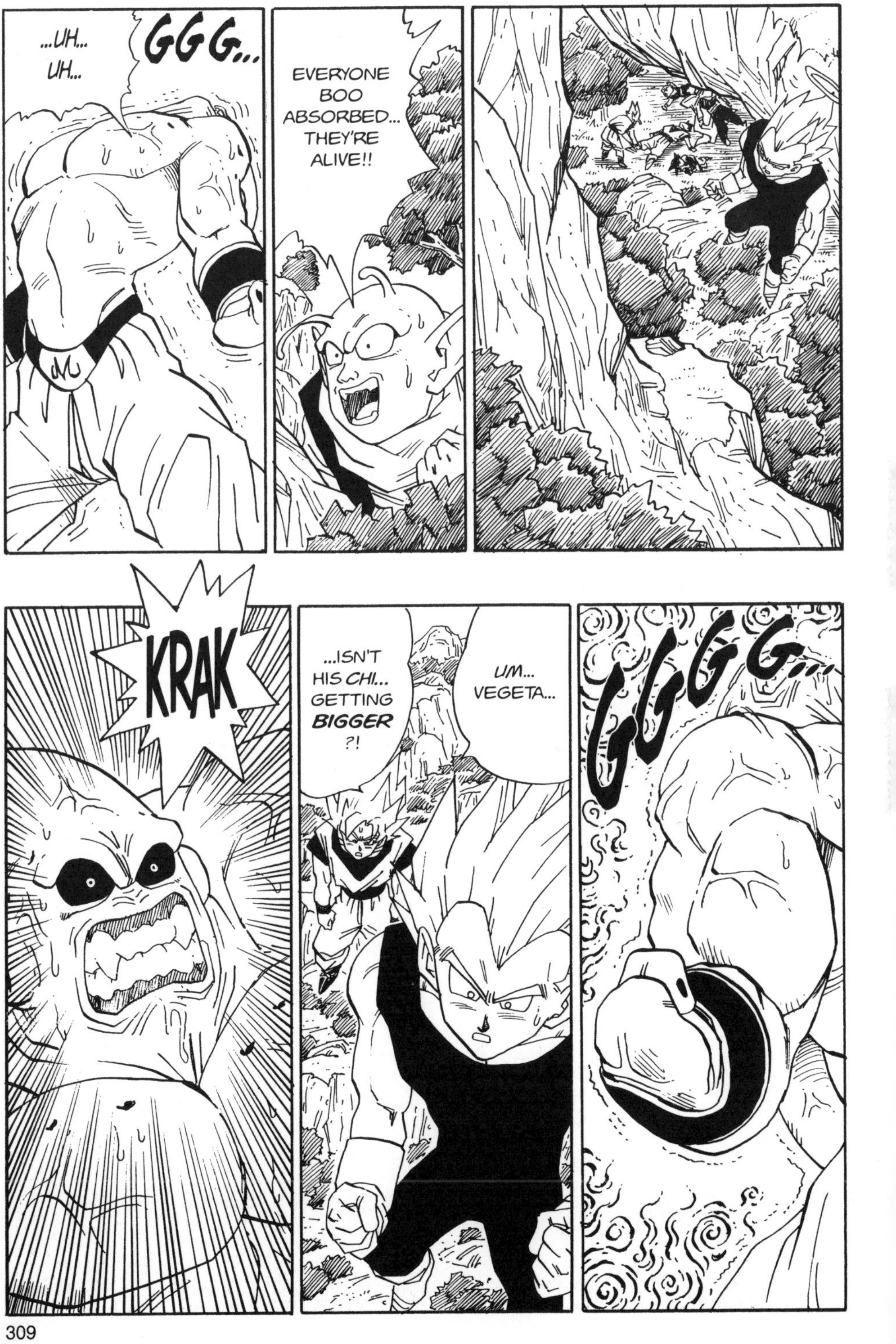
EVERYONE BOO ABSORBED... THEY'RE ALIVE!!
GGG...
...UH... UH...
GGGG...
UM... VEGETA...
...ISN'T HIS CHI... GETTING BIGGER ?!
KRAK

DRAGON BALL ドラゴンボール

DBZ:314 • The Boo of Pure Evil

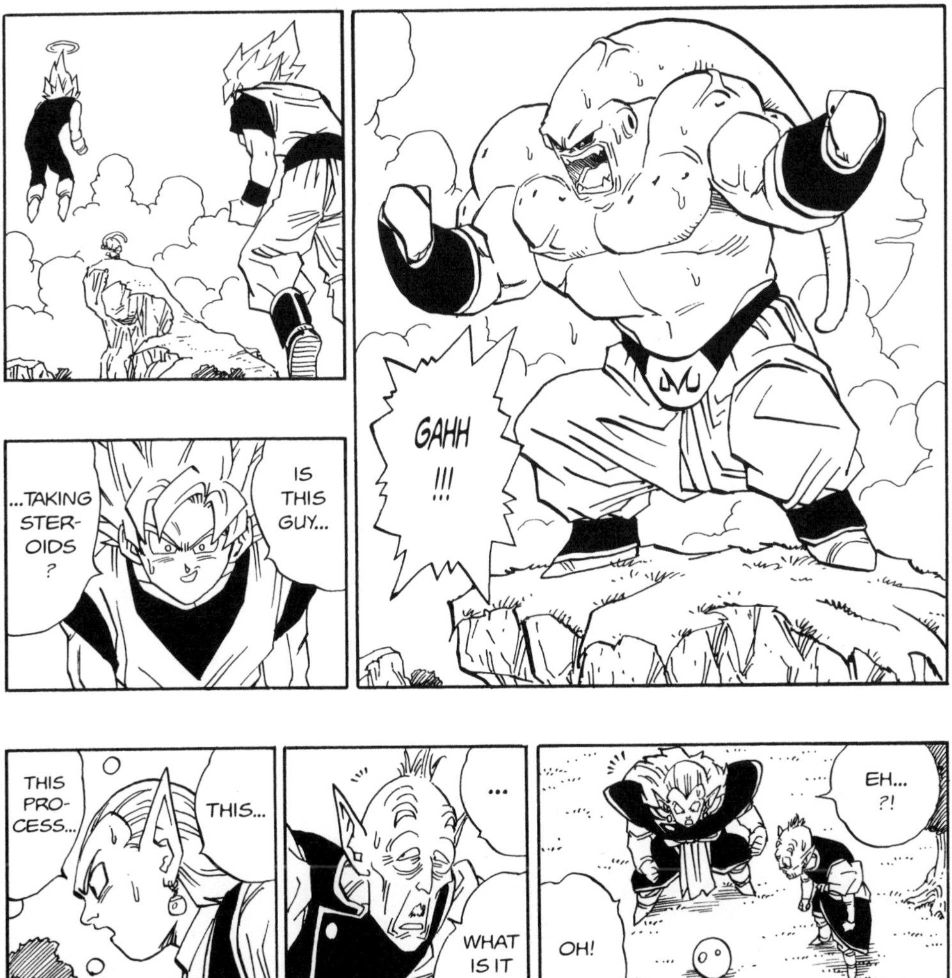
GAHH !!!
IS THIS GUY...
...TAKING STEROIDS ?
EH... ?!
OH!
...
WHAT IS IT ?
THIS...
THIS PROCESS...

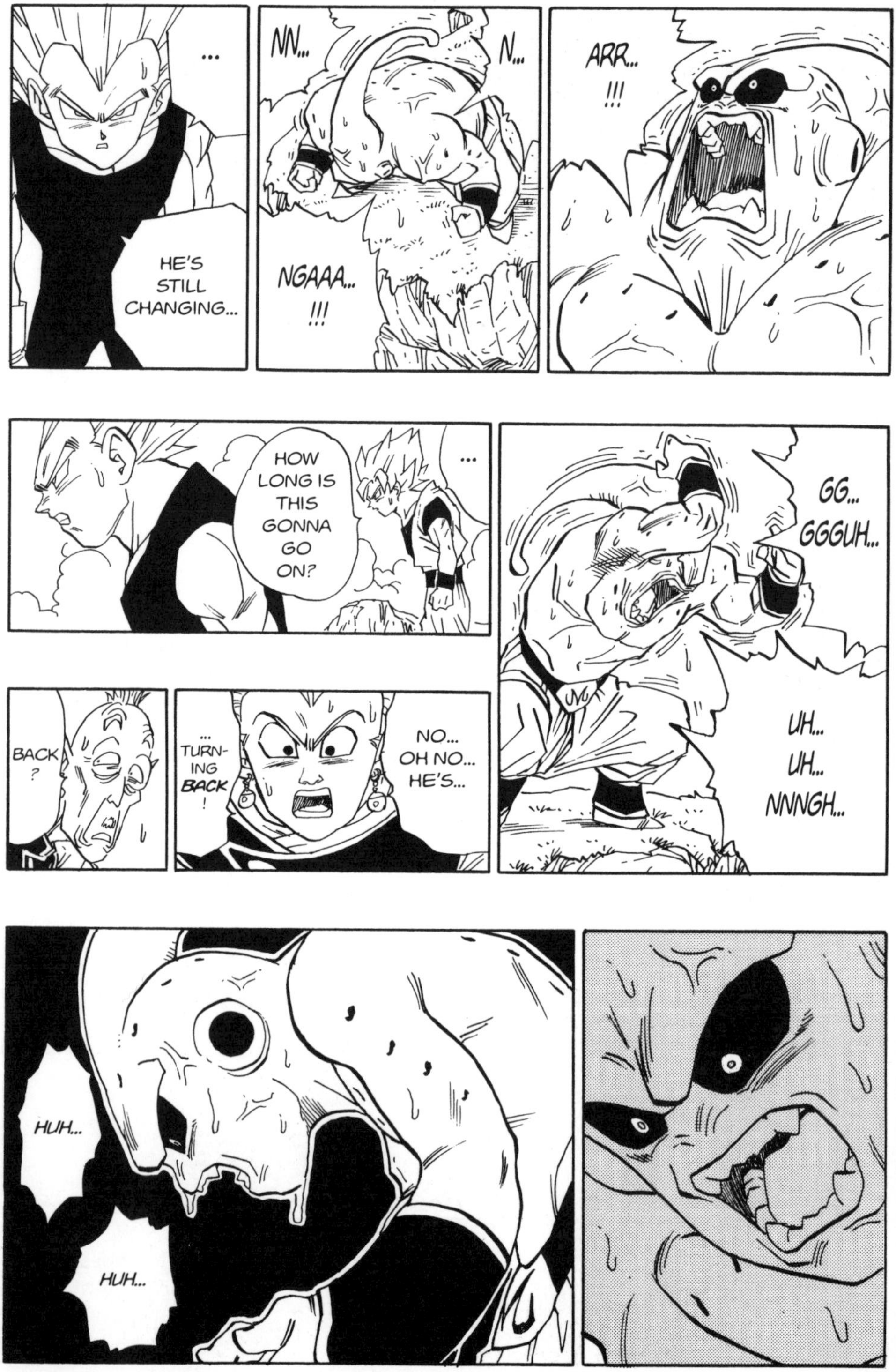
ARR... !!!
N...
NN...
NGAAA... !!!
...
HE'S STILL CHANGING...
GG... GGGUH...
UH... UH... NNNGH...
...
HOW LONG IS THIS GONNA GO ON?
NO... OH NO... HE'S...
... TURNING BACK!
BACK?
HUH...
HUH...

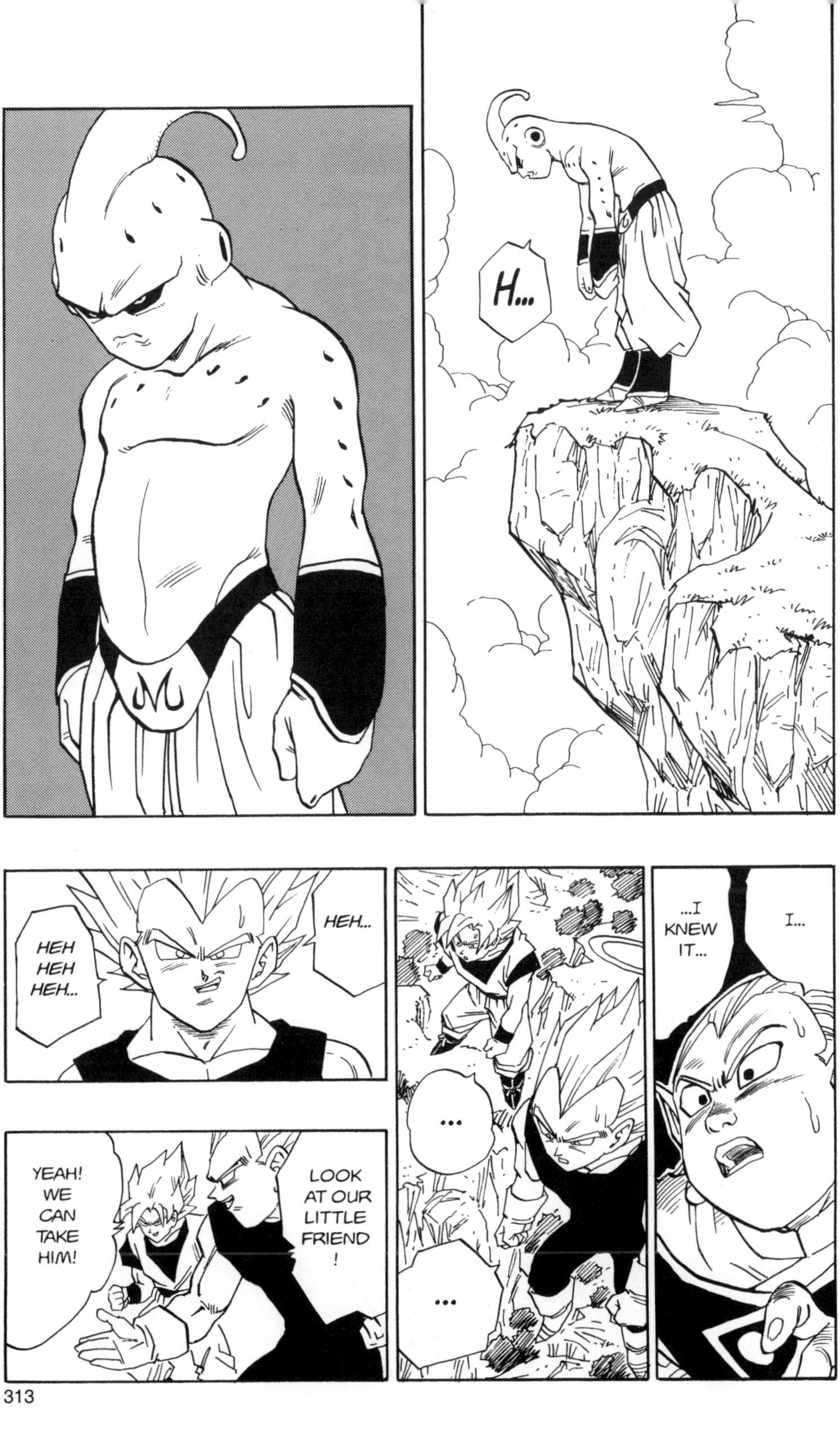
H...
I...
...I KNEW IT...
...
...
HEH...
HEH HEH HEH...
LOOK AT OUR LITTLE FRIEND!
YEAH! WE CAN TAKE HIM!

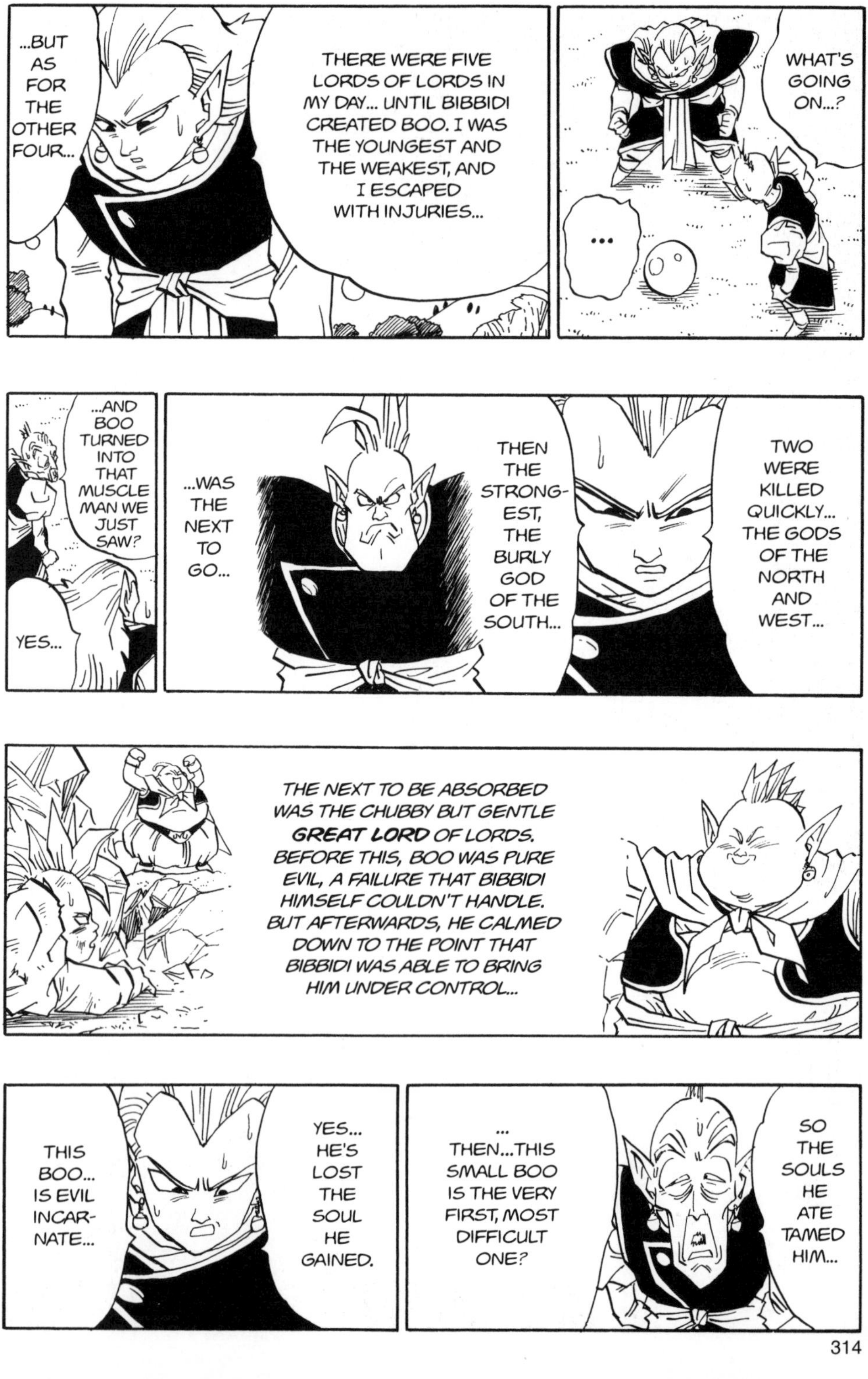
WHAT'S GOING ON...?
...
THERE WERE FIVE LORDS OF LORDS IN MY DAY... UNTIL BIBBIDI CREATED BOO. I WAS THE YOUNGEST AND THE WEAKEST, AND I ESCAPED WITH INJURIES...
...BUT AS FOR THE OTHER FOUR...
TWO WERE KILLED QUICKLY... THE GODS OF THE NORTH AND WEST...
THEN THE STRONG-EST, THE BURLY GOD OF THE SOUTH...
...WAS THE NEXT TO GO...
...AND BOO TURNED INTO THAT MUSCLE MAN WE JUST SAW?
YES...
THE NEXT TO BE ABSORBED WAS THE CHUBBY BUT GENTLE **GREAT LORD** OF LORDS. BEFORE THIS, BOO WAS PURE EVIL, A FAILURE THAT BIBBIDI HIMSELF COULDN'T HANDLE. BUT AFTERWARDS, HE CALMED DOWN TO THE POINT THAT BIBBIDI WAS ABLE TO BRING HIM UNDER CONTROL...
SO THE SOULS HE ATE TAMED HIM...
... THEN...THIS SMALL BOO IS THE VERY FIRST, MOST DIFFICULT ONE?
YES... HE'S LOST THE SOUL HE GAINED.
THIS BOO... IS EVIL INCARNATE...

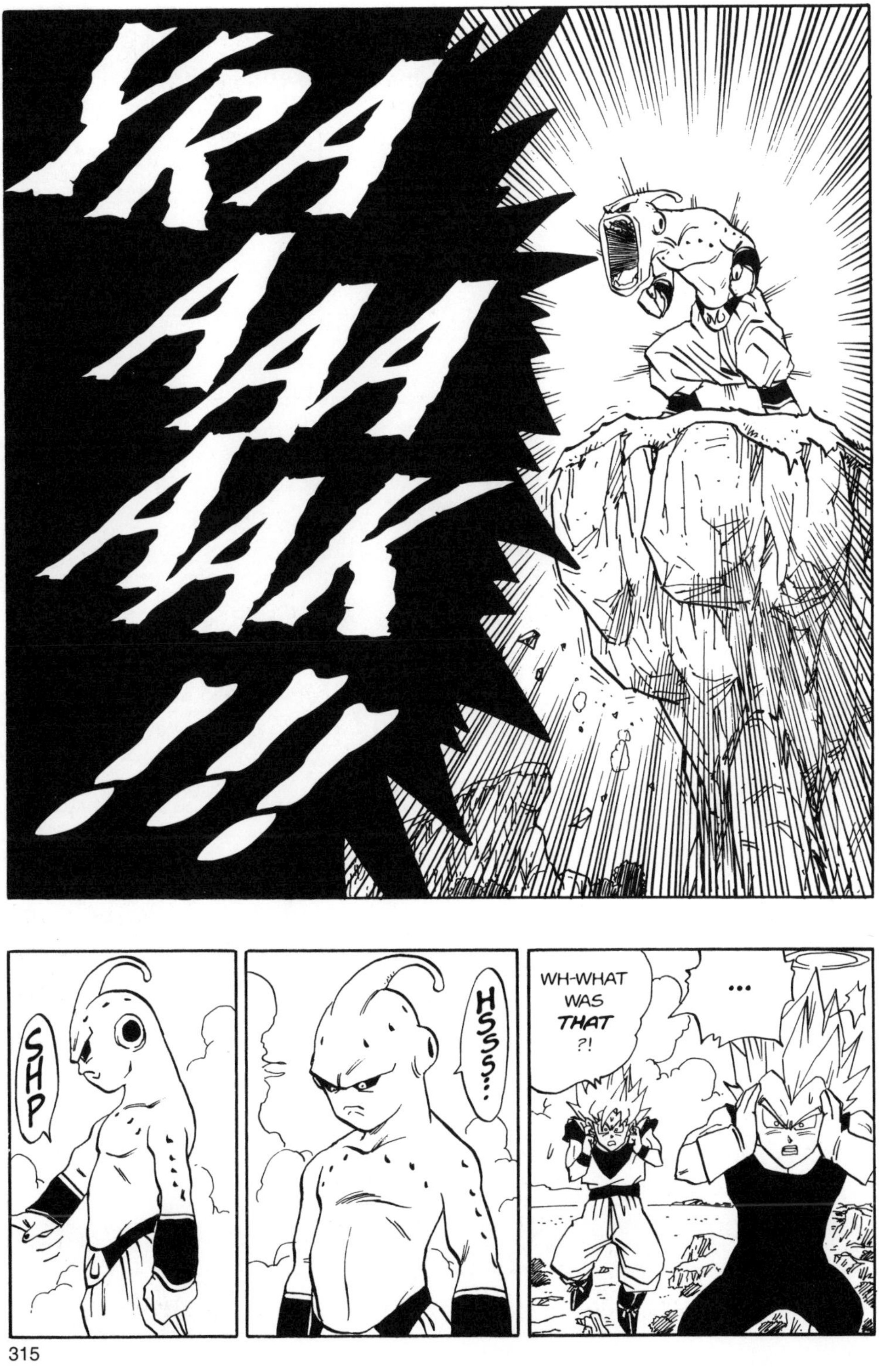
YRAAAAAAK!!!
...
WH-WHAT WAS THAT ?!
HSSS...
SHP

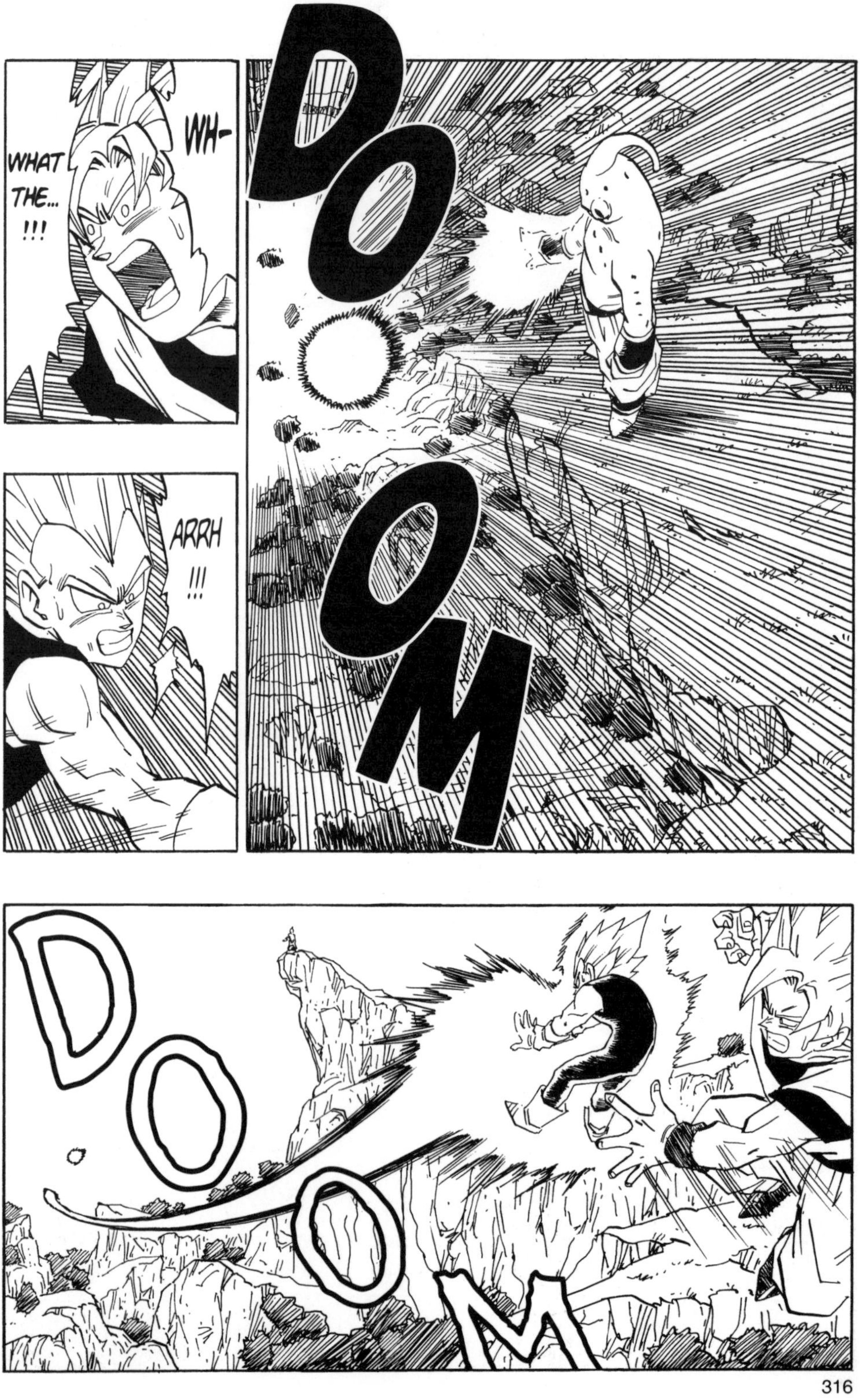
DOOM
WH-
WHAT THE... !!!
ARRH !!!
DOOOM

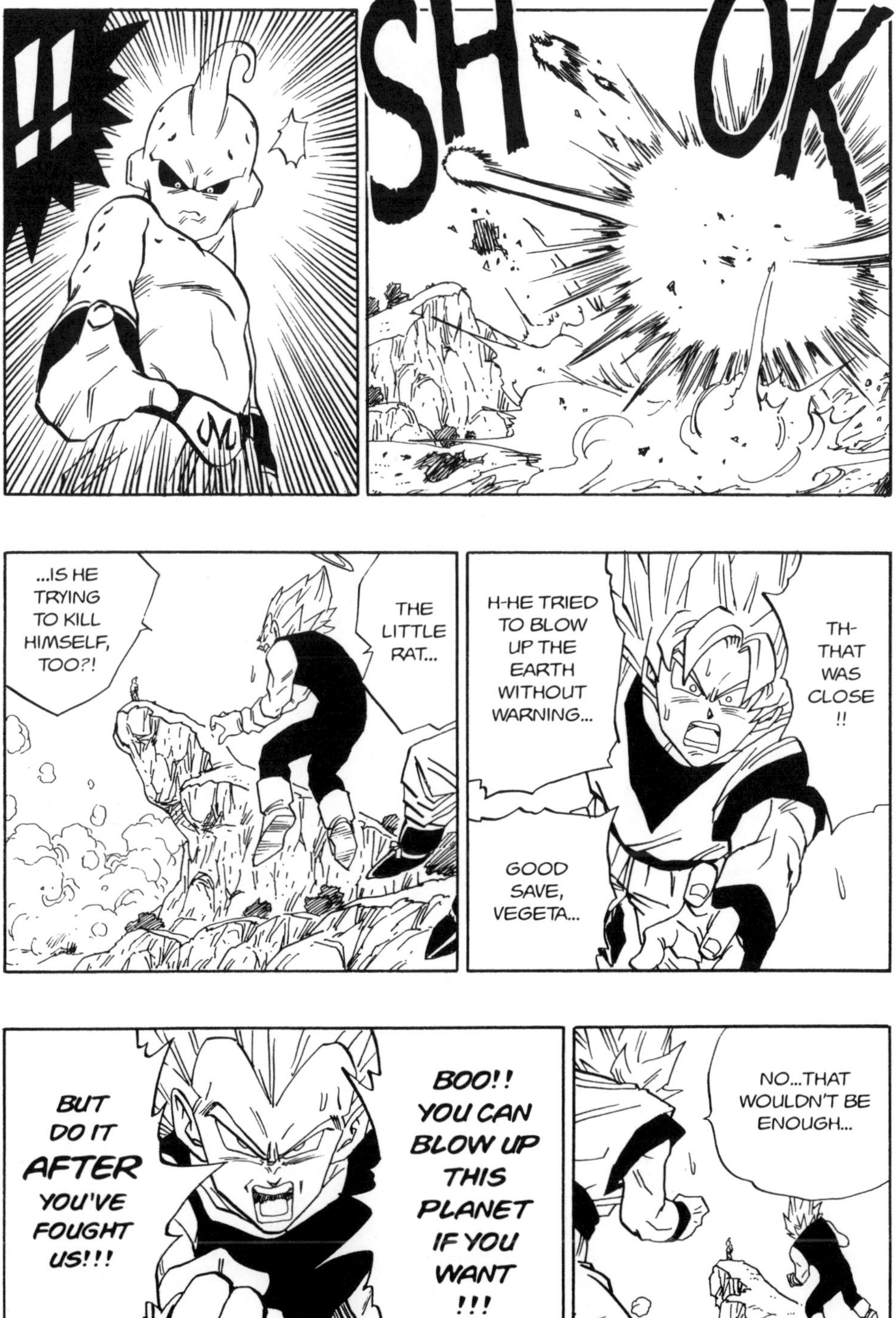
SHOOK
!!
TH-THAT WAS CLOSE!!
H-HE TRIED TO BLOW UP THE EARTH WITHOUT WARNING...
GOOD SAVE, VEGETA...
THE LITTLE RAT...
...IS HE TRYING TO KILL HIMSELF, TOO?!
NO...THAT WOULDN'T BE ENOUGH...
BOO!! YOU CAN BLOW UP THIS PLANET IF YOU WANT!!!
BUT DO IT AFTER YOU'VE FOUGHT US!!!

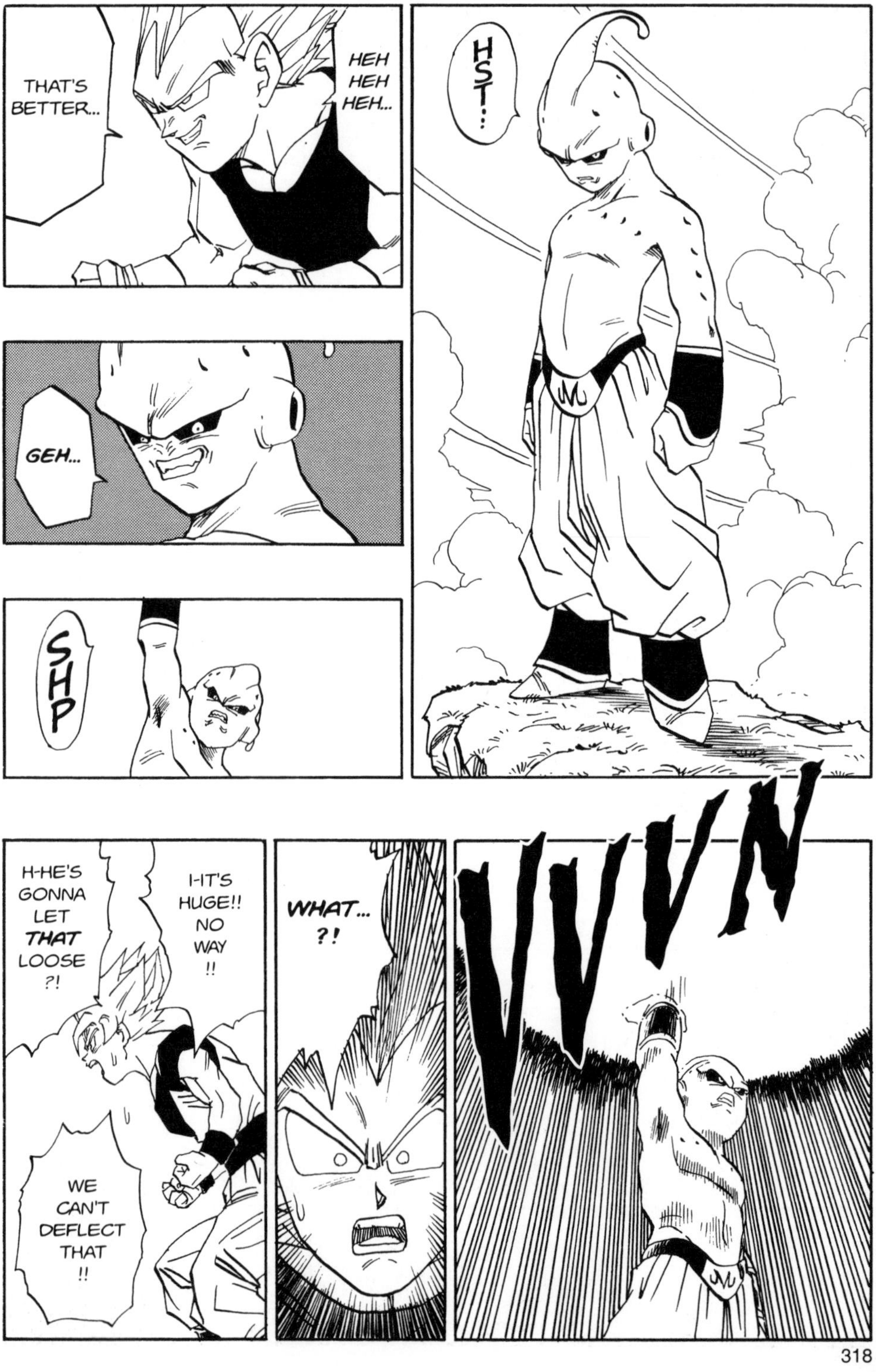
HST...
HEH HEH HEH...
THAT'S BETTER...
GEH...
SHP
VVVN
WHAT...?!
I-IT'S HUGE!! NO WAY!!
H-HE'S GONNA LET THAT LOOSE?!
WE CAN'T DEFLECT THAT!!

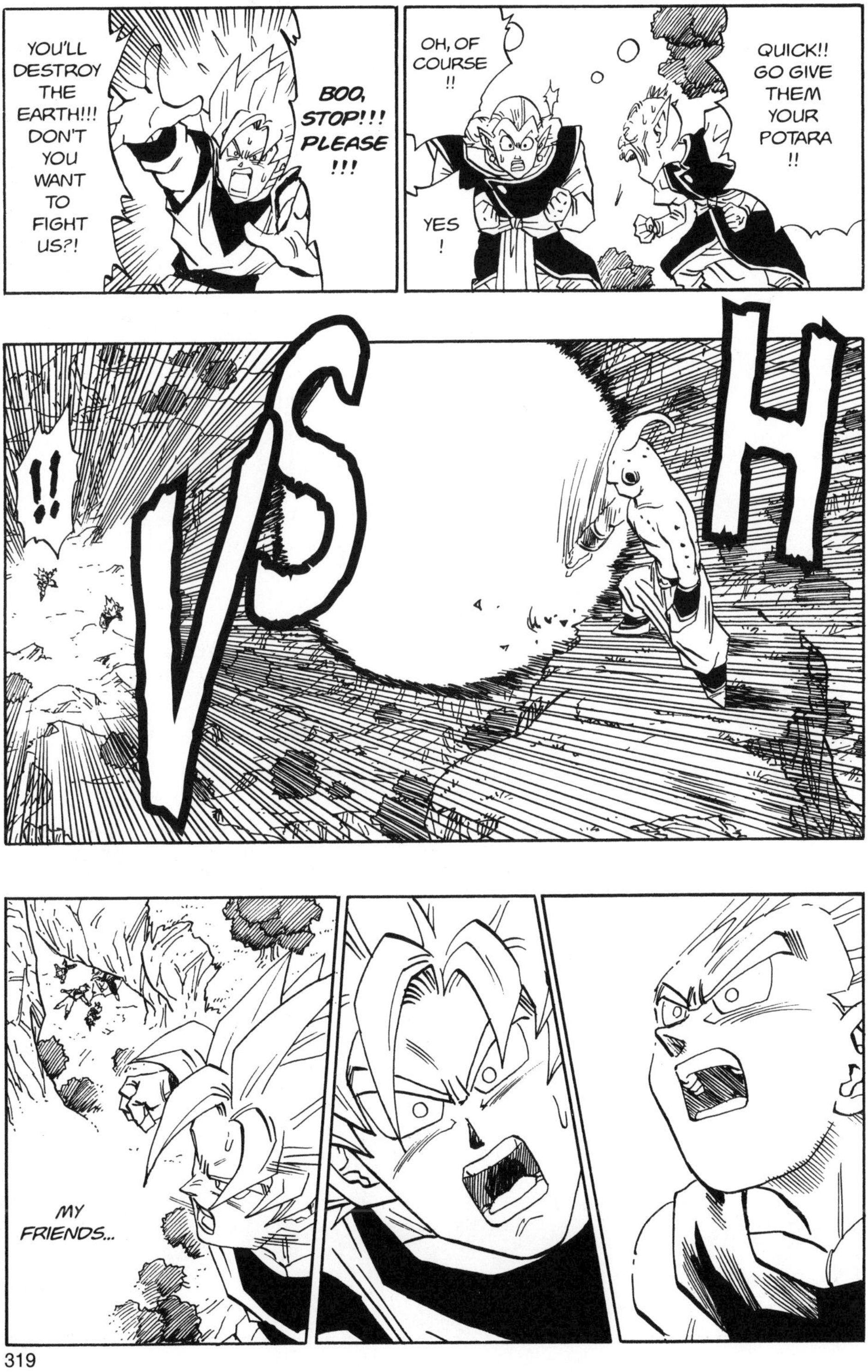
QUICK!! GO GIVE THEM YOUR POTARA!!
OH, OF COURSE!!
YES!
BOO, STOP!!! PLEASE!!!
YOU'LL DESTROY THE EARTH!!! DON'T YOU WANT TO FIGHT US?!
VSH
!!
MY FRIENDS...

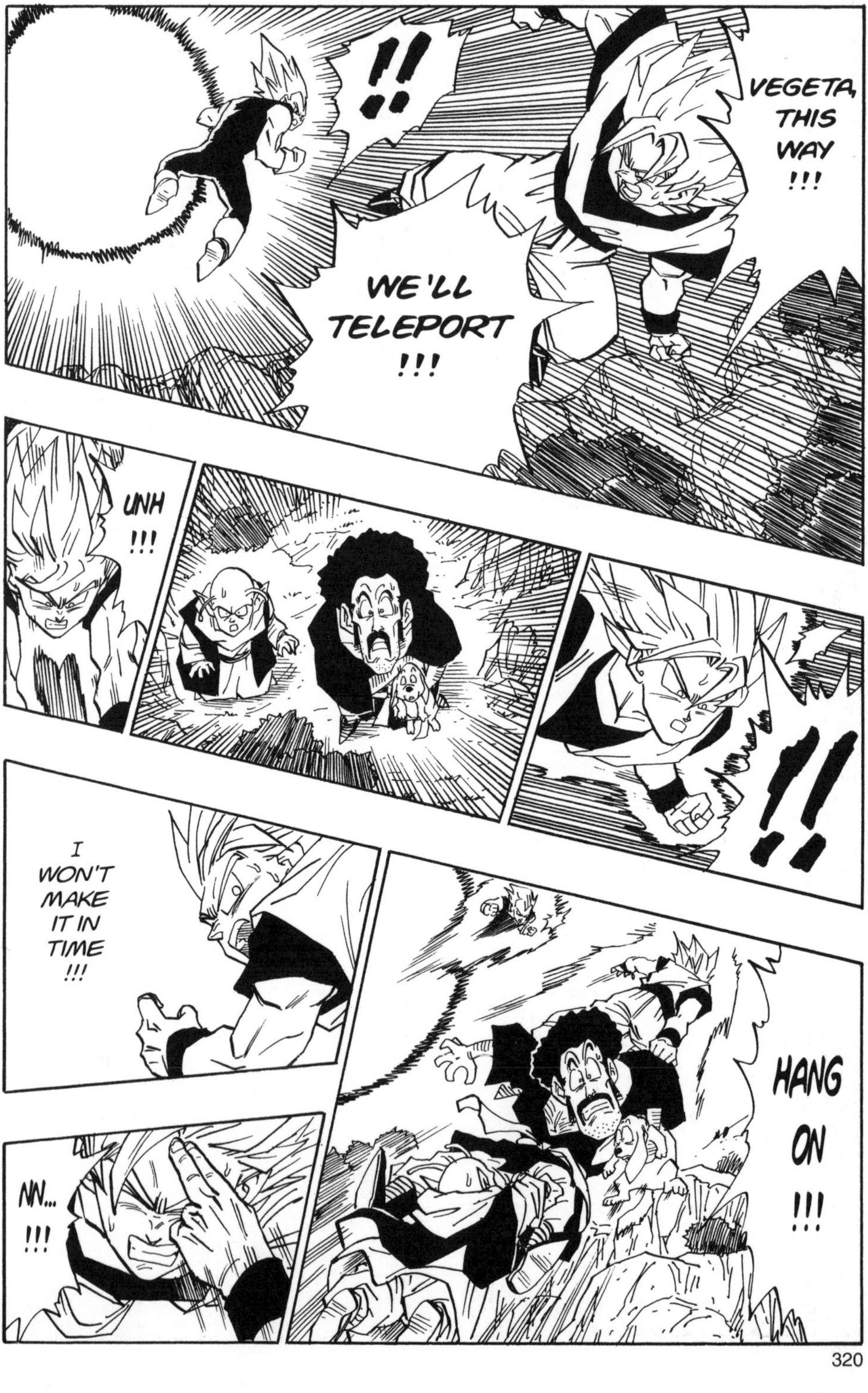
VEGETA, THIS WAY !!!
!!
WE'LL TELEPORT !!!
!!
UNH !!!
HANG ON !!!
I WON'T MAKE IT IN TIME !!!
NN... !!!

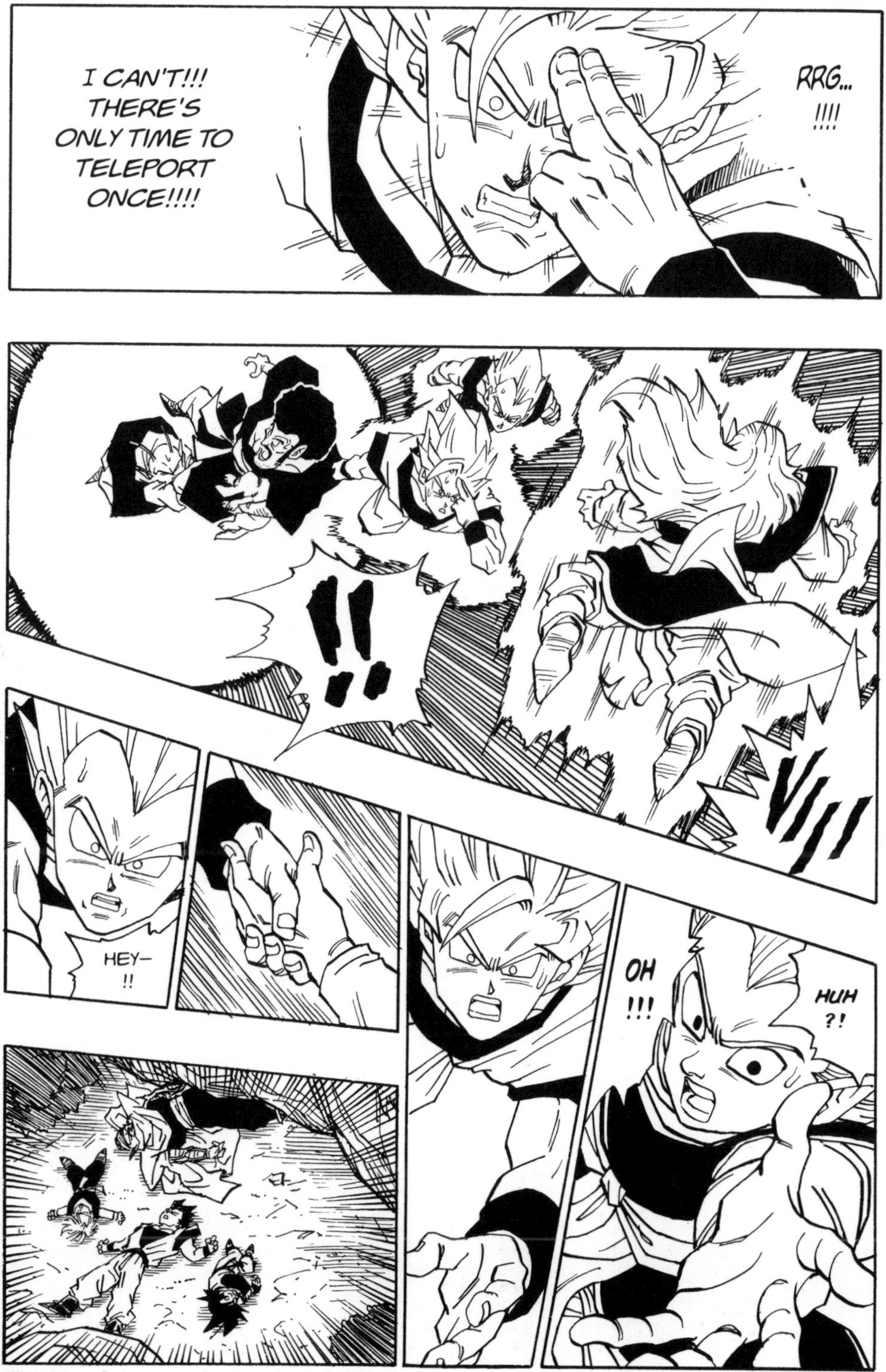
RRG... !!!!
I CAN'T!!! THERE'S ONLY TIME TO TELEPORT ONCE!!!!
!!
HUH ?!
OH !!!
HEY— !!

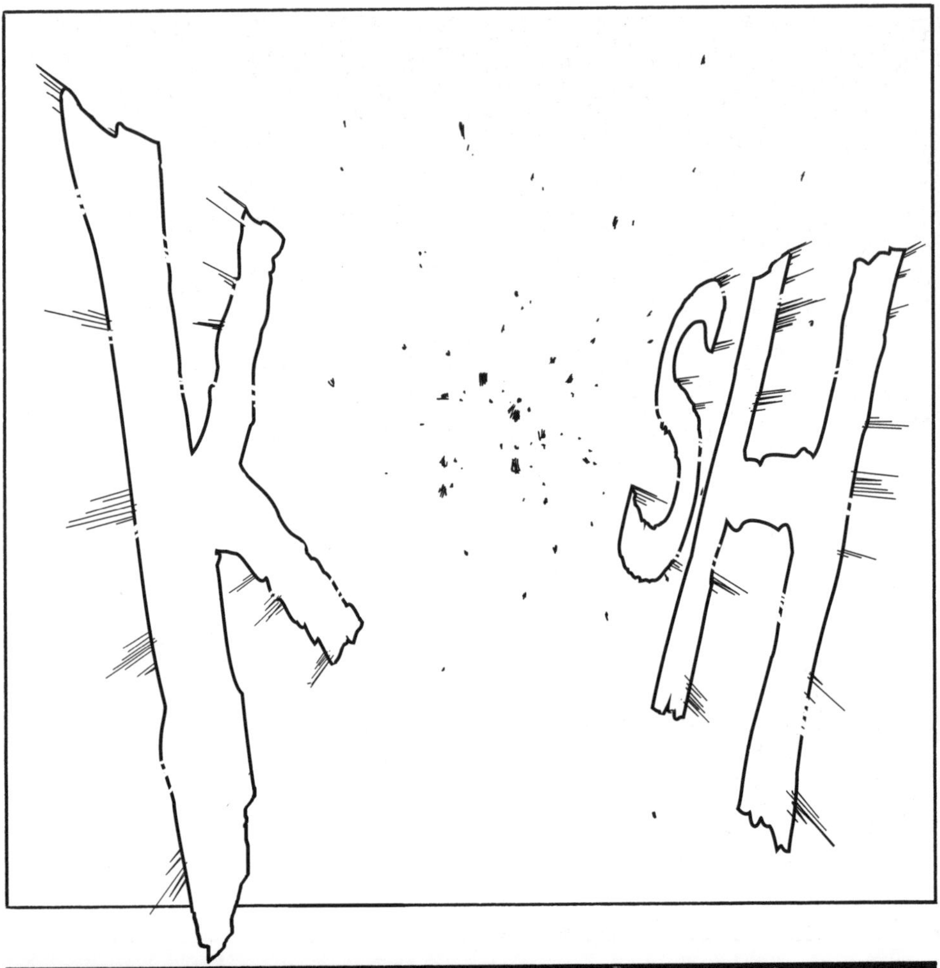
KSH

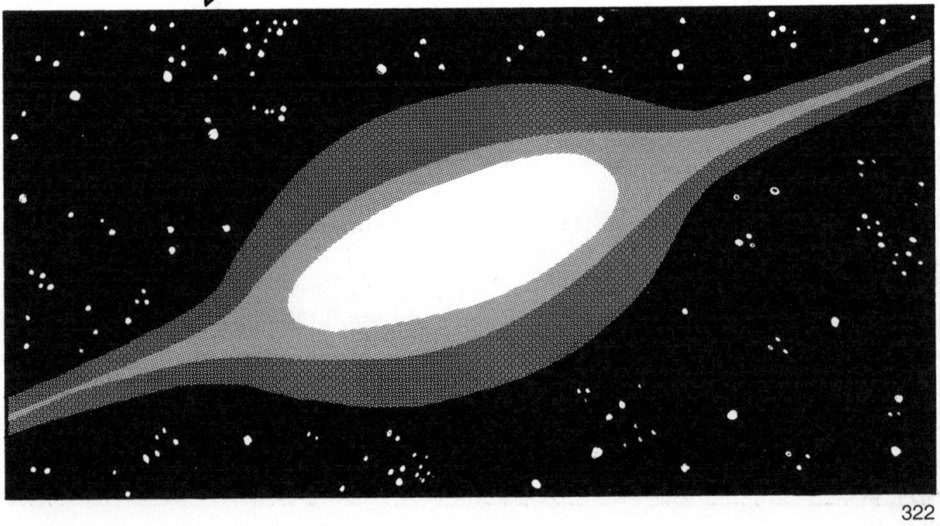

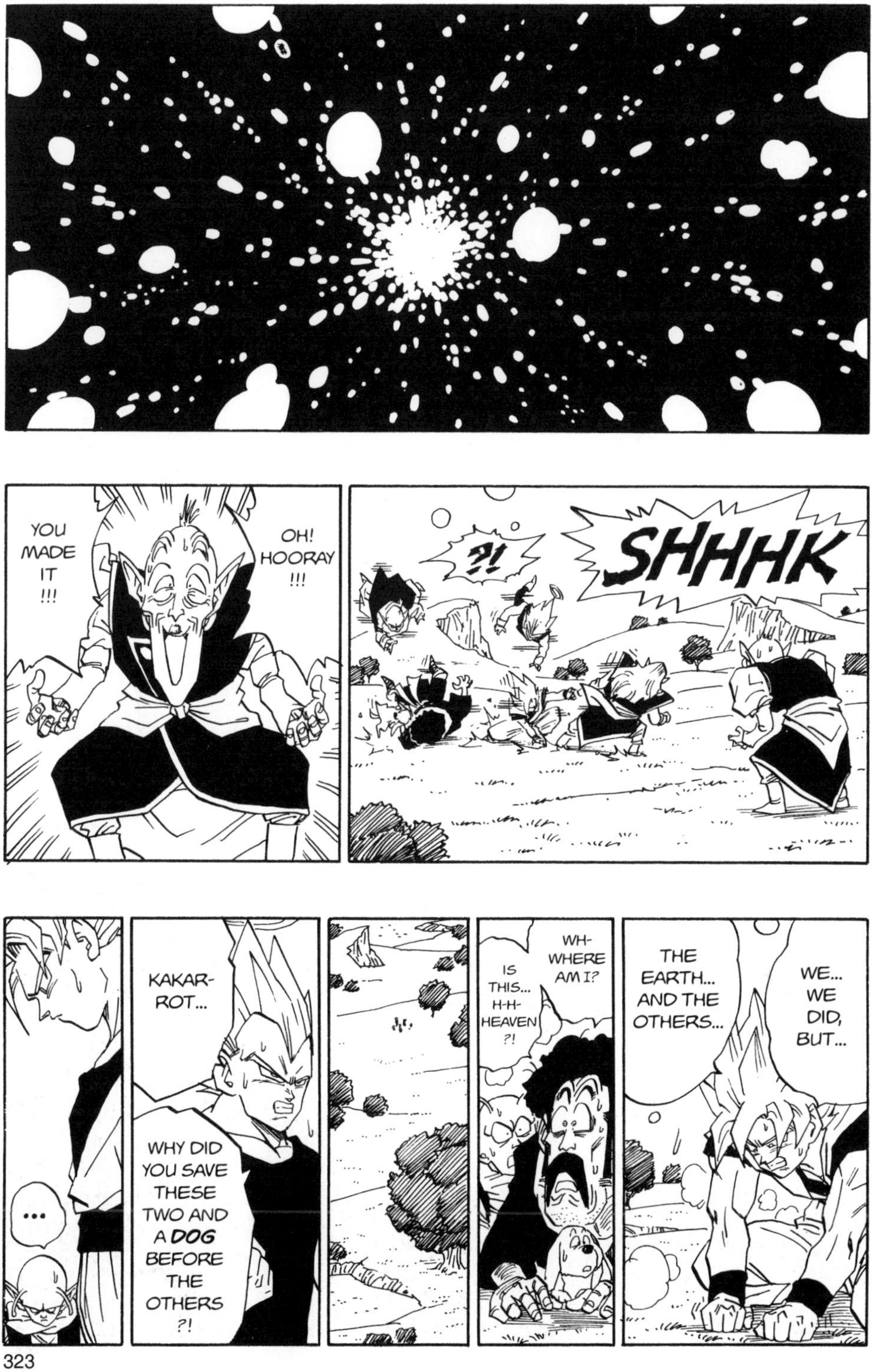

SHHHK
?!
OH! HOORAY !!!
YOU MADE IT !!!
WE... WE DID, BUT...
THE EARTH... AND THE OTHERS...
WH- WHERE AM I?
IS THIS... H-H-HEAVEN ?!
KAKAR-ROT...
WHY DID YOU SAVE THESE TWO AND A **DOG** BEFORE THE OTHERS ?!
...

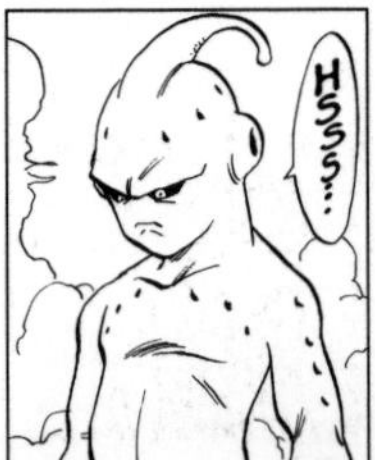
HSSSS...

DRAGON BALL ドラゴンボール

DBZ:315 • Battle for the Universe

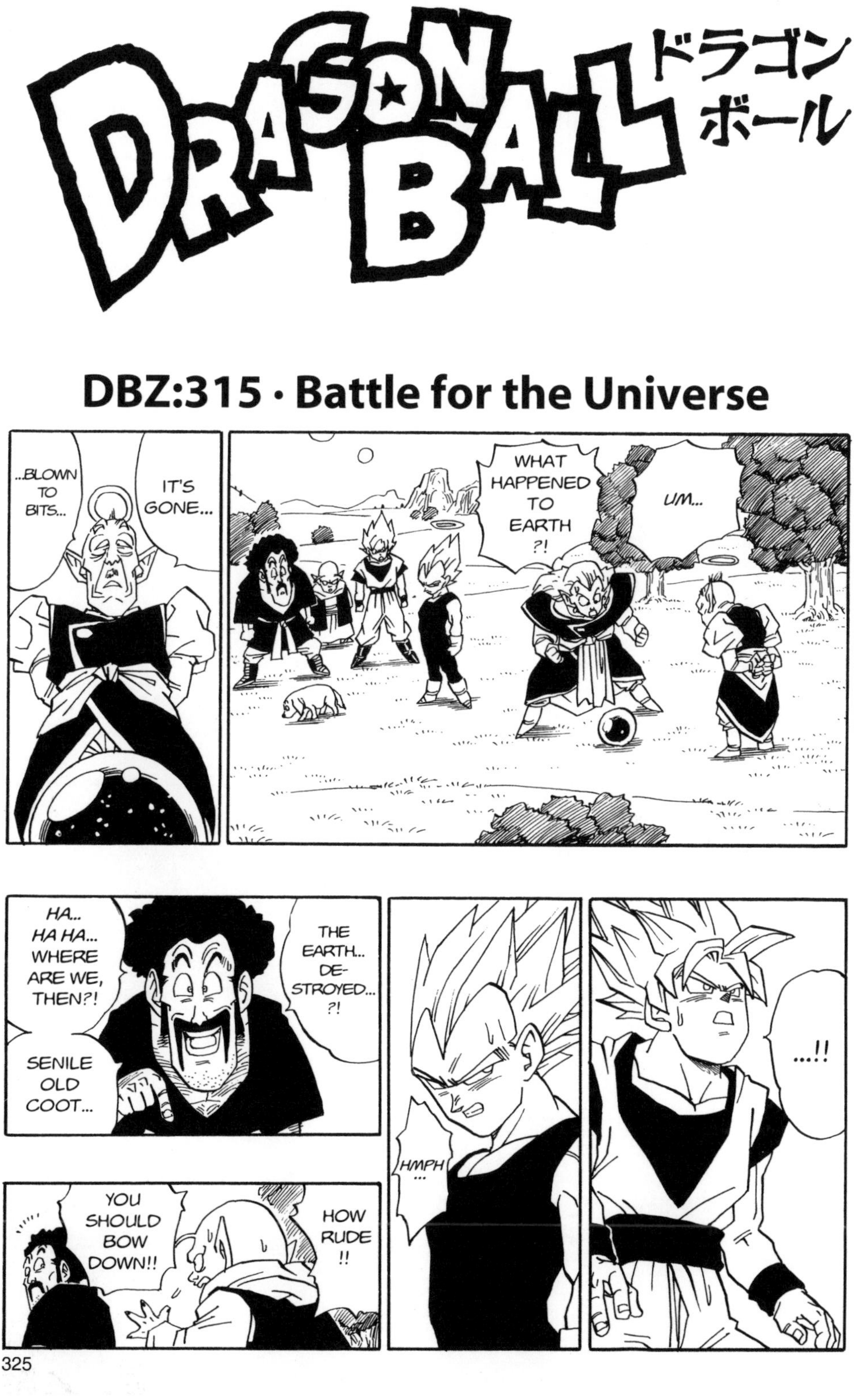

UM...
WHAT HAPPENED TO EARTH ?!
IT'S GONE...
...BLOWN TO BITS...
...!!
HMPH ...
THE EARTH... DE-STROYED... ?!
HA... HA HA... WHERE ARE WE, THEN?!
SENILE OLD COOT...
HOW RUDE !!
YOU SHOULD BOW DOWN!!

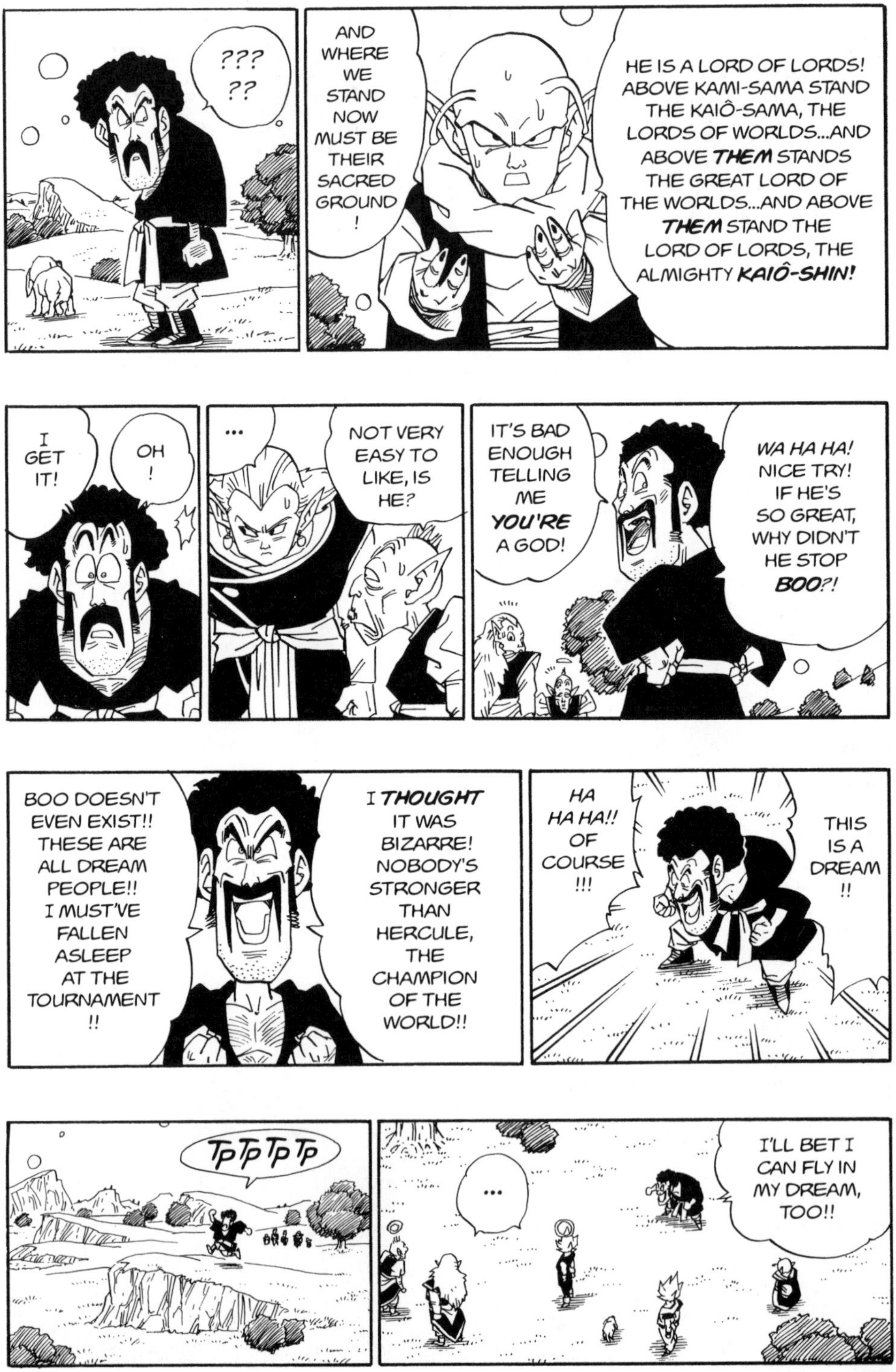
HE IS A LORD OF LORDS! ABOVE KAMI-SAMA STAND THE KAIÔ-SAMA, THE LORDS OF WORLDS...AND ABOVE ***THEM*** STANDS THE GREAT LORD OF THE WORLDS...AND ABOVE ***THEM*** STAND THE LORD OF LORDS, THE ALMIGHTY ***KAIÔ-SHIN!***
AND WHERE WE STAND NOW MUST BE THEIR SACRED GROUND !
??? ??
WA HA HA! NICE TRY! IF HE'S SO GREAT, WHY DIDN'T HE STOP ***BOO****?!*
IT'S BAD ENOUGH TELLING ME ***YOU'RE*** A GOD!
NOT VERY EASY TO LIKE, IS HE?
...
OH !
I GET IT!
THIS IS A DREAM !!
HA HA HA!! OF COURSE !!!
I ***THOUGHT*** IT WAS BIZARRE! NOBODY'S STRONGER THAN HERCULE, THE CHAMPION OF THE WORLD!!
BOO DOESN'T EVEN EXIST!! THESE ARE ALL DREAM PEOPLE!! I MUST'VE FALLEN ASLEEP AT THE TOURNAMENT !!
I'LL BET I CAN FLY IN MY DREAM, TOO!!
...
TpTpTpTp

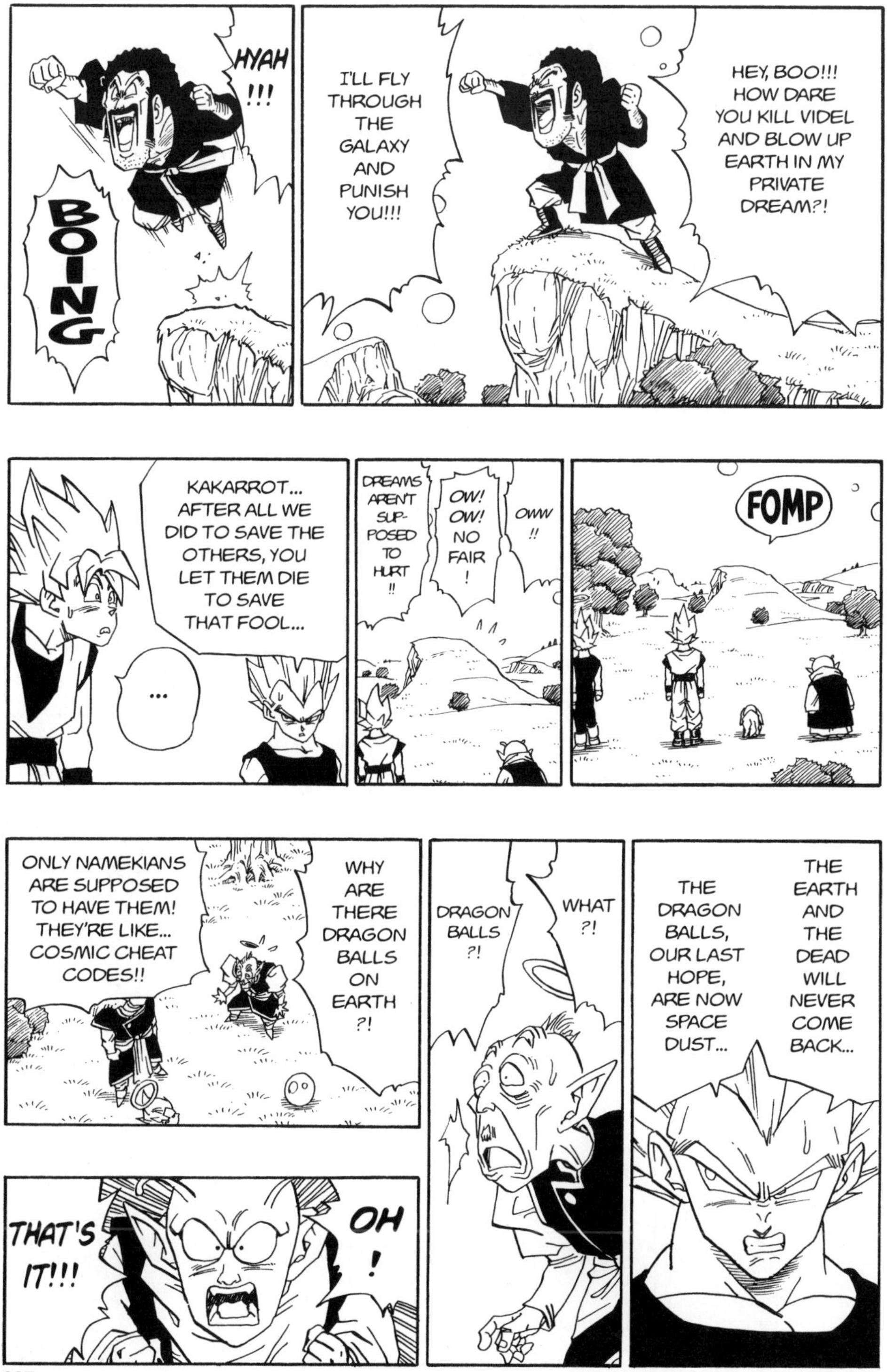
HEY, BOO!!! HOW DARE YOU KILL VIDEL AND BLOW UP EARTH IN MY PRIVATE DREAM?!
I'LL FLY THROUGH THE GALAXY AND PUNISH YOU!!!
HYAH!!!
BOING
FOMP
OWW!!
OW! OW! NO FAIR!
DREAMS AREN'T SUP-POSED TO HURT!!
KAKARROT... AFTER ALL WE DID TO SAVE THE OTHERS, YOU LET THEM DIE TO SAVE THAT FOOL...
...
THE EARTH AND THE DEAD WILL NEVER COME BACK...
THE DRAGON BALLS, OUR LAST HOPE, ARE NOW SPACE DUST...
WHAT?!
DRAGON BALLS?!
WHY ARE THERE DRAGON BALLS ON EARTH?!
ONLY NAMEKIANS ARE SUPPOSED TO HAVE THEM! THEY'RE LIKE... COSMIC CHEAT CODES!!
OH!
THAT'S IT!!!

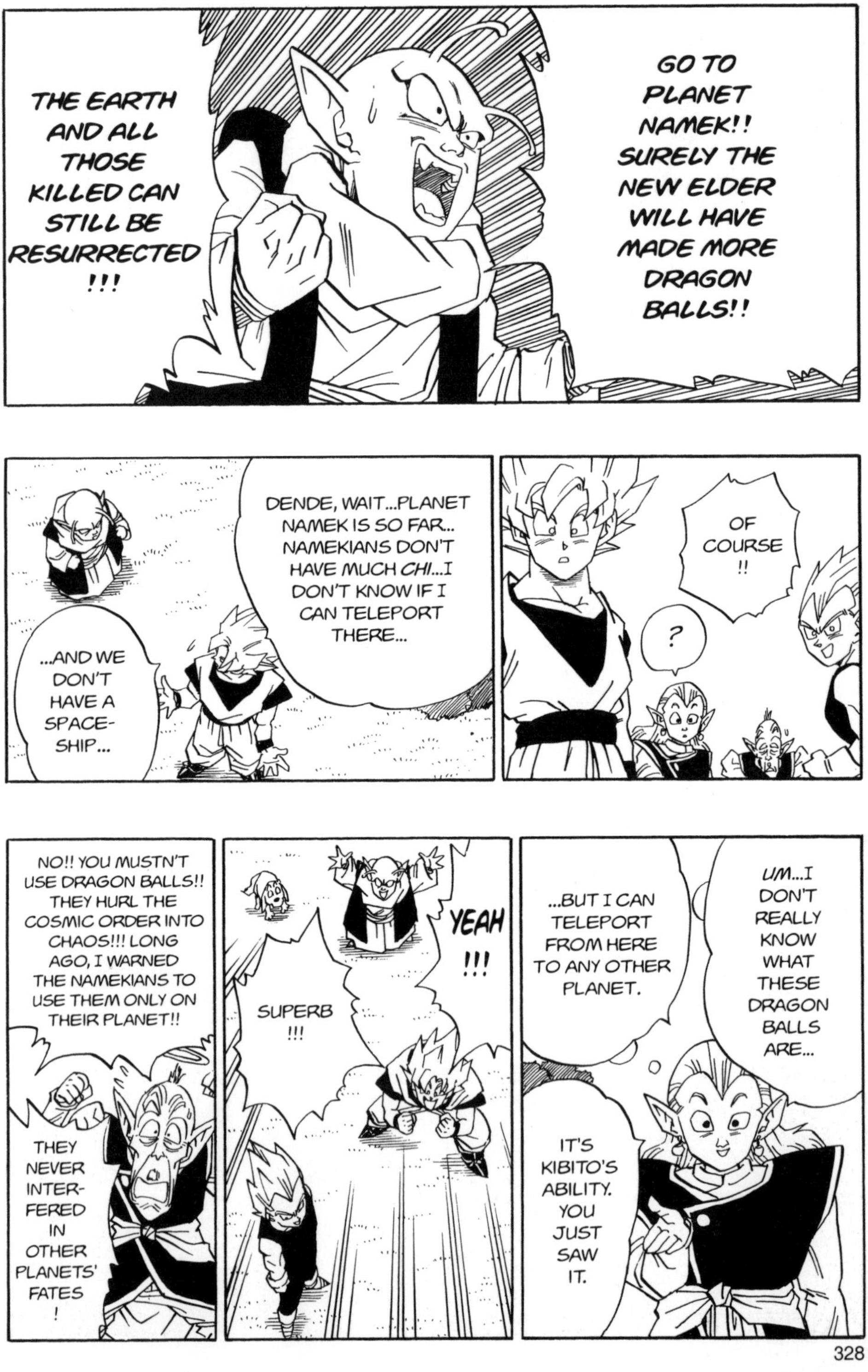
GO TO PLANET NAMEK!! SURELY THE NEW ELDER WILL HAVE MADE MORE DRAGON BALLS!!
THE EARTH AND ALL THOSE KILLED CAN STILL BE RESURRECTED!!!
OF COURSE !!
?
DENDE, WAIT...PLANET NAMEK IS SO FAR... NAMEKIANS DON'T HAVE MUCH *CHI*...I DON'T KNOW IF I CAN TELEPORT THERE...
...AND WE DON'T HAVE A SPACE-SHIP...
UM...I DON'T REALLY KNOW WHAT THESE DRAGON BALLS ARE...
...BUT I CAN TELEPORT FROM HERE TO ANY OTHER PLANET.
IT'S KIBITO'S ABILITY. YOU JUST SAW IT.
YEAH !!!
SUPERB !!!
NO!! YOU MUSTN'T USE DRAGON BALLS!! THEY HURL THE COSMIC ORDER INTO CHAOS!!! LONG AGO, I WARNED THE NAMEKIANS TO USE THEM ONLY ON THEIR PLANET!!
THEY NEVER INTER-FERED IN OTHER PLANETS' FATES !

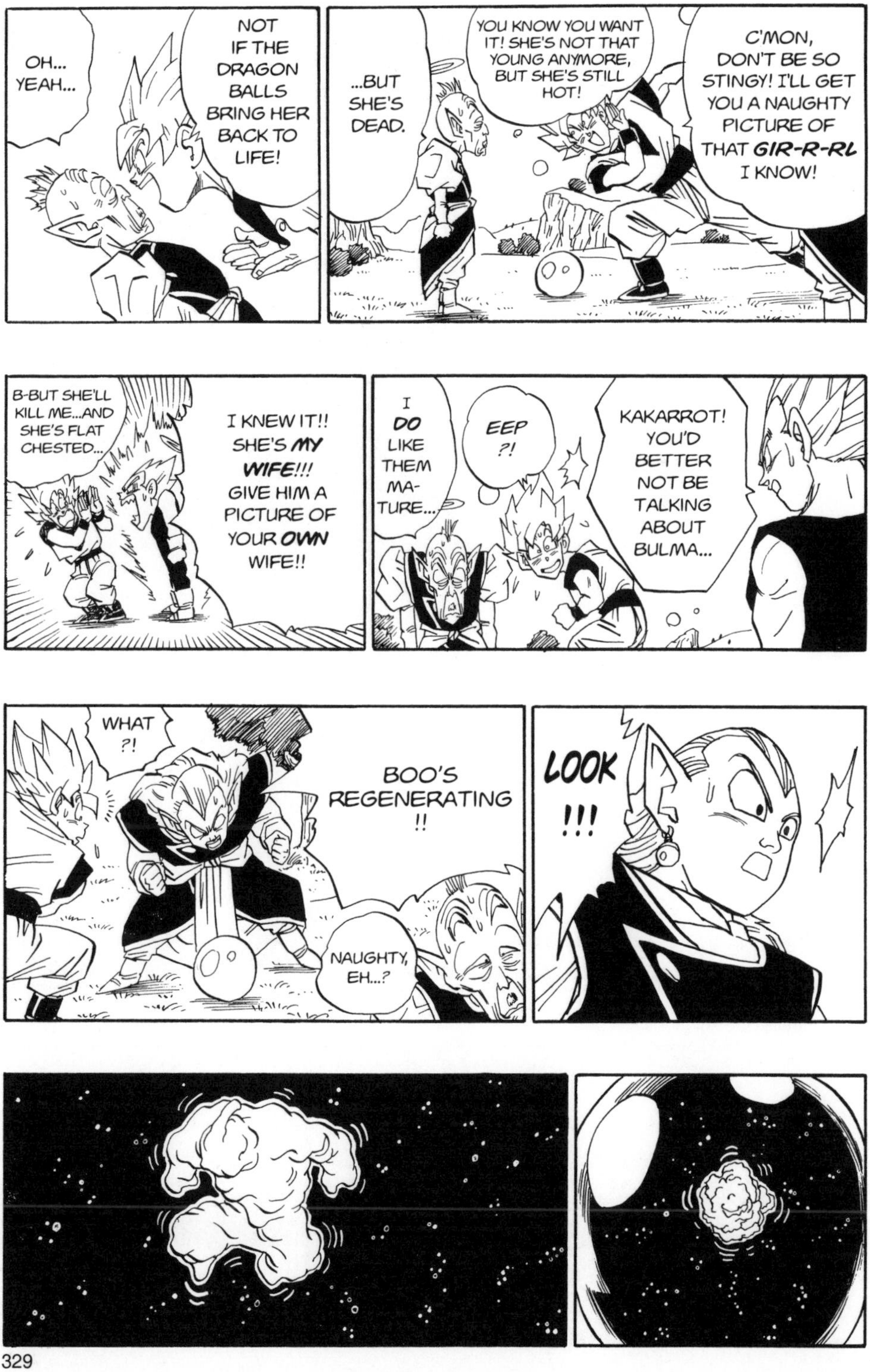
C'MON, DON'T BE SO STINGY! I'LL GET YOU A NAUGHTY PICTURE OF THAT **GIR-R-RL** I KNOW!
YOU KNOW YOU WANT IT! SHE'S NOT THAT YOUNG ANYMORE, BUT SHE'S STILL HOT!
...BUT SHE'S DEAD.
NOT IF THE DRAGON BALLS BRING HER BACK TO LIFE!
OH... YEAH...
KAKARROT! YOU'D BETTER NOT BE TALKING ABOUT BULMA...
EEP ?!
I ***DO*** LIKE THEM MA-TURE...
I KNEW IT!! SHE'S ***MY WIFE***!!! GIVE HIM A PICTURE OF YOUR ***OWN*** WIFE!!
B-BUT SHE'LL KILL ME...AND SHE'S FLAT CHESTED...
LOOK !!!
BOO'S REGENERATING !!
WHAT ?!
NAUGHTY, EH...?

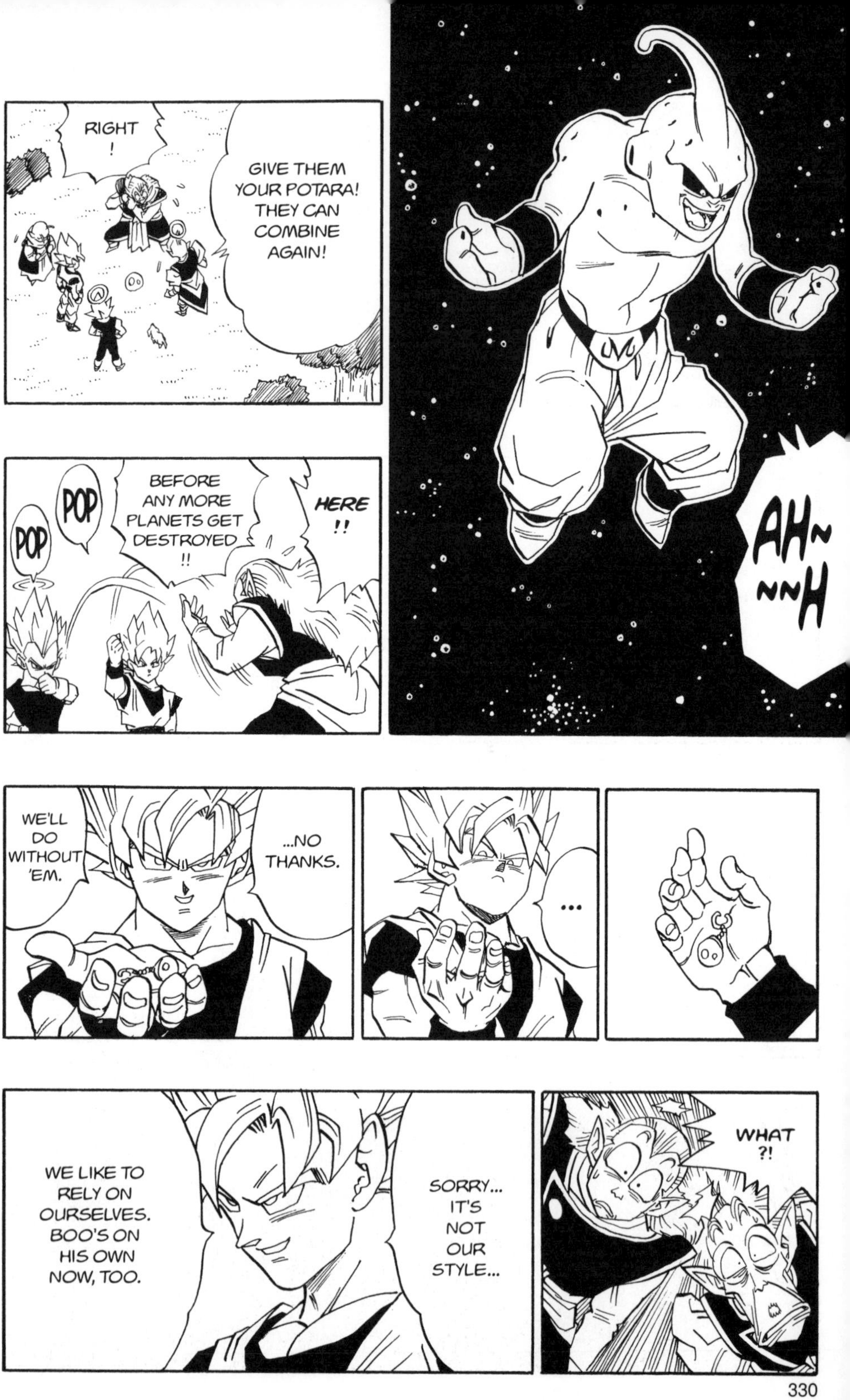
AH~ ~~H
GIVE THEM YOUR POTARA! THEY CAN COMBINE AGAIN!
RIGHT !
HERE !!
BEFORE ANY MORE PLANETS GET DESTROYED !!
POP
POP
...
...NO THANKS.
WE'LL DO WITHOUT 'EM.
WHAT ?!
SORRY... IT'S NOT OUR STYLE...
WE LIKE TO RELY ON OURSELVES. BOO'S ON HIS OWN NOW, TOO.

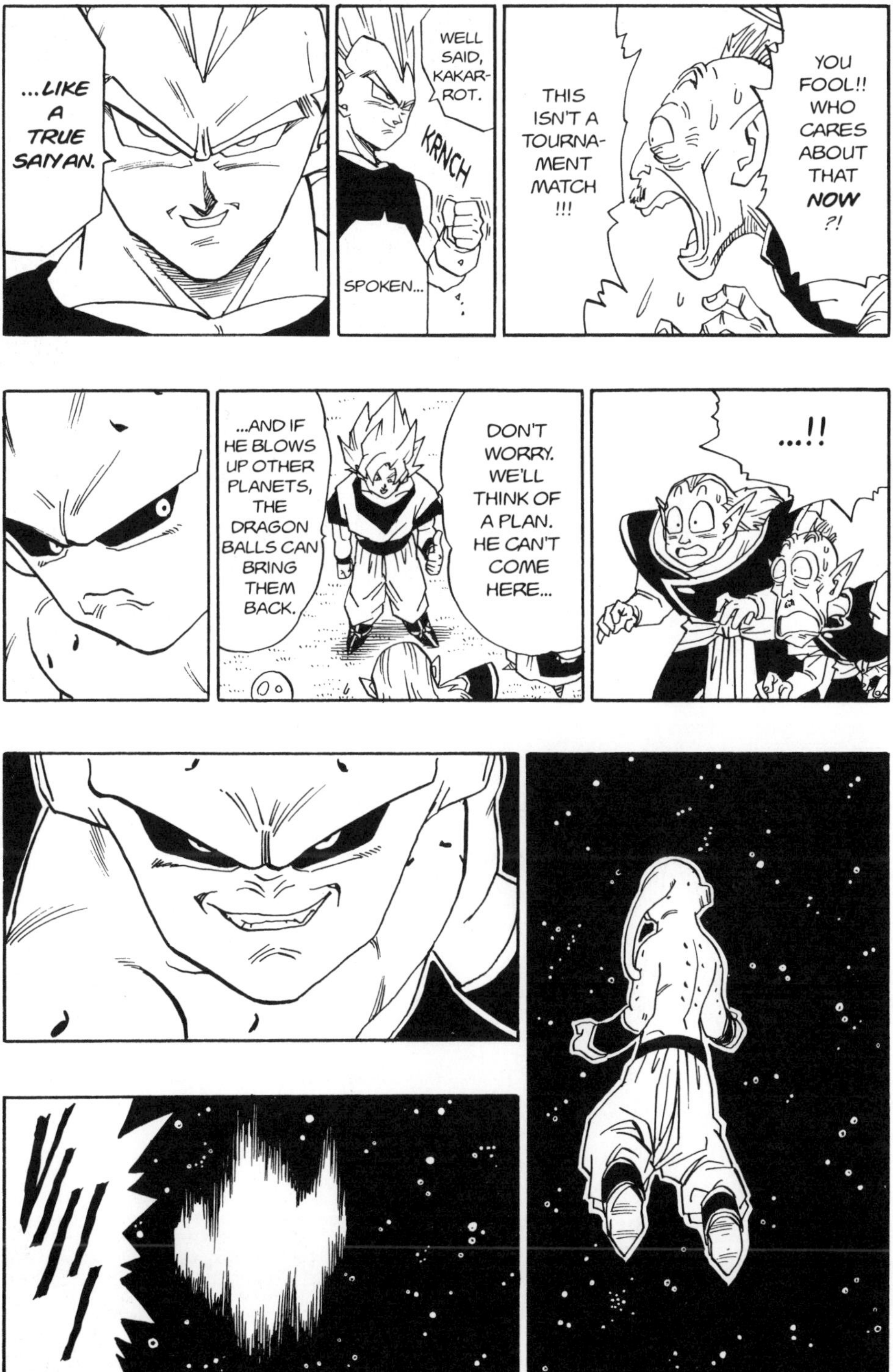

YOU FOOL!! WHO CARES ABOUT THAT NOW?!
THIS ISN'T A TOURNAMENT MATCH!!!
WELL SAID, KAKARROT.
KRNCH
SPOKEN...
...LIKE A TRUE SAIYAN.
...!!
DON'T WORRY. WE'LL THINK OF A PLAN. HE CAN'T COME HERE...
...AND IF HE BLOWS UP OTHER PLANETS, THE DRAGON BALLS CAN BRING THEM BACK.

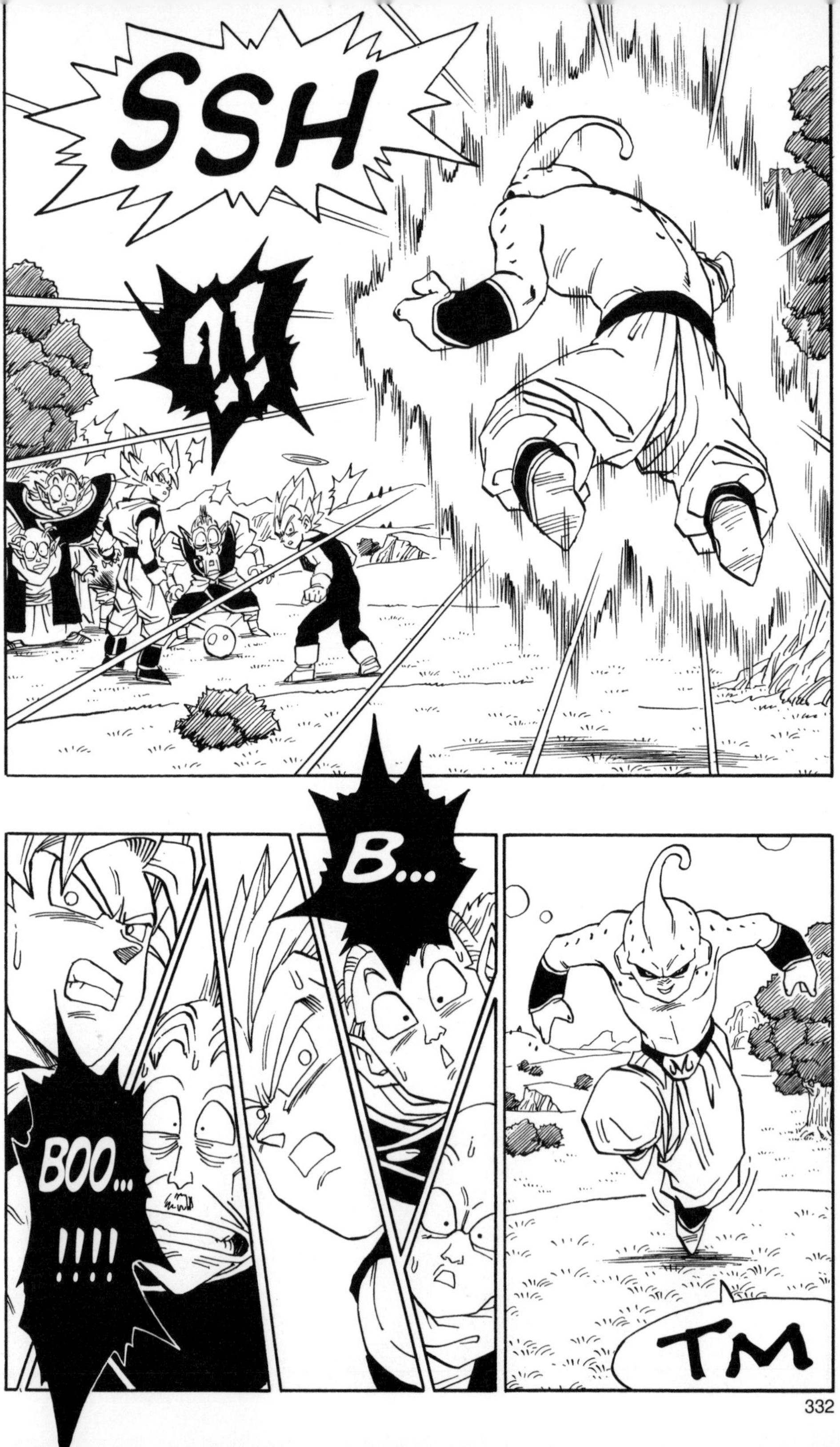
SSH
!!
TM
B...
BOO... !!!!!

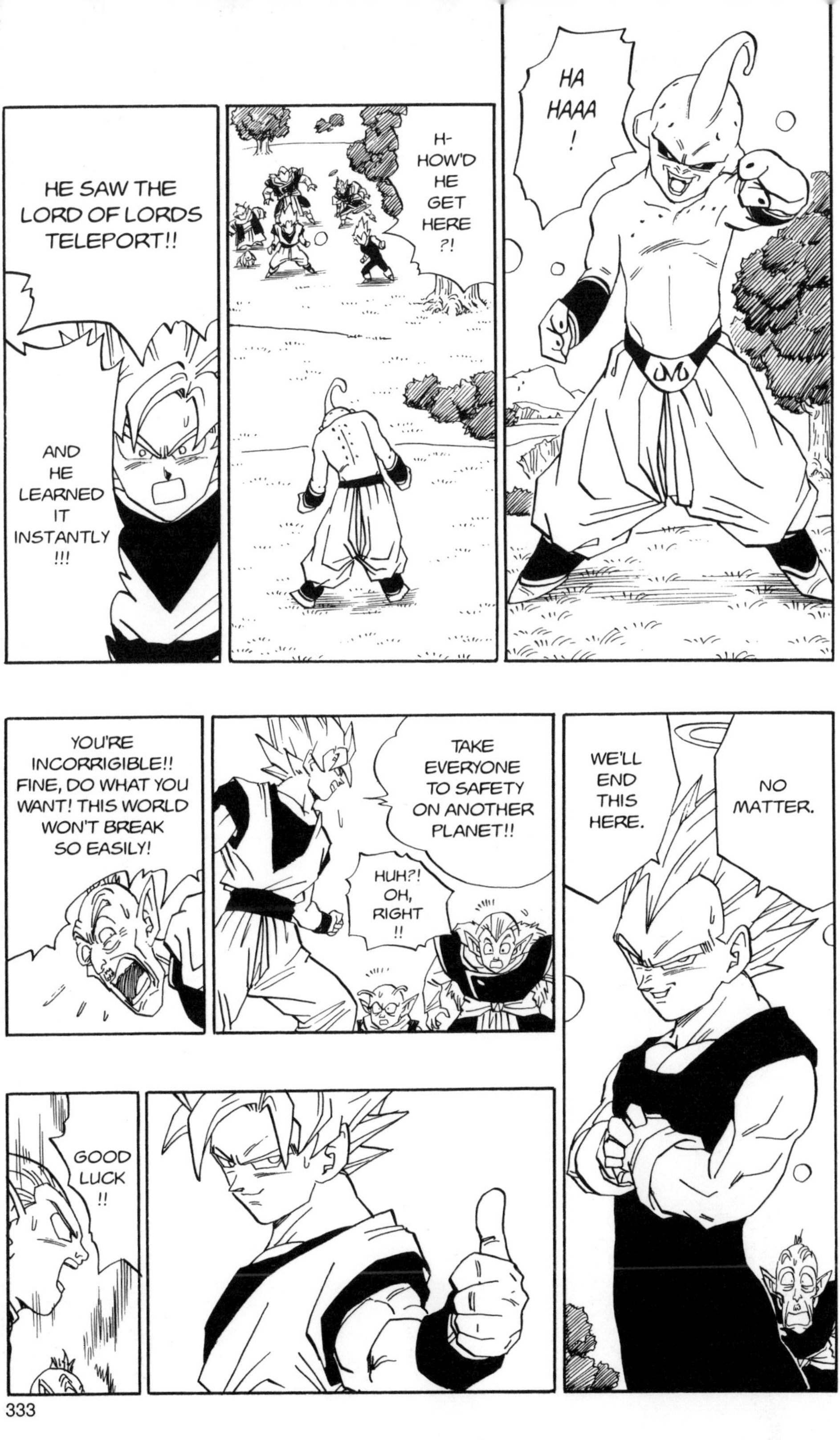
HA HAAA !
H- HOW'D HE GET HERE ?!
HE SAW THE LORD OF LORDS TELEPORT!!
AND HE LEARNED IT INSTANTLY !!!
NO MATTER.
WE'LL END THIS HERE.
TAKE EVERYONE TO SAFETY ON ANOTHER PLANET!!
HUH?! OH, RIGHT !!
YOU'RE INCORRIGIBLE!! FINE, DO WHAT YOU WANT! THIS WORLD WON'T BREAK SO EASILY!
GOOD LUCK !!

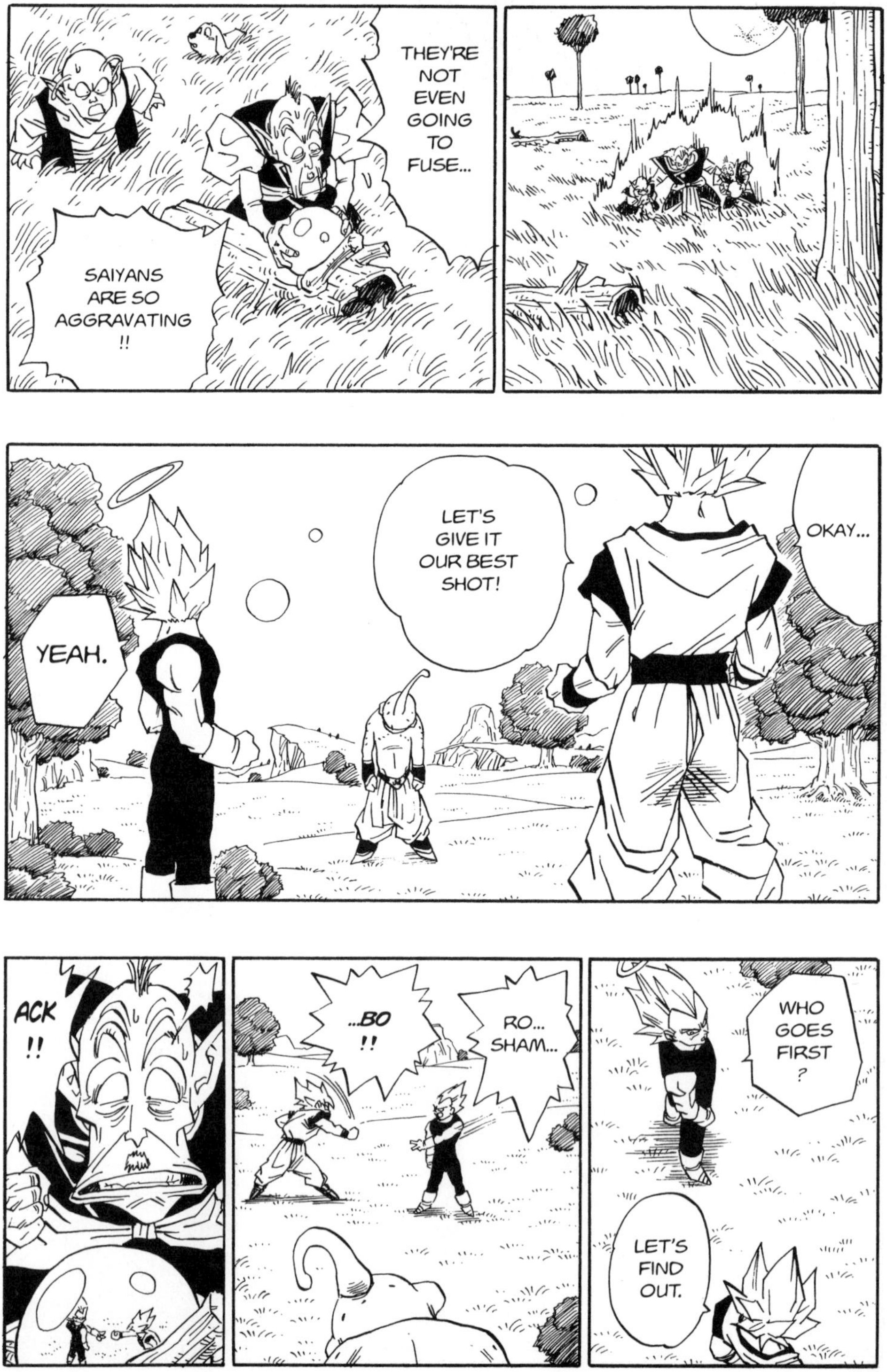
THEY'RE NOT EVEN GOING TO FUSE...
SAIYANS ARE SO AGGRAVATING !!
OKAY...
LET'S GIVE IT OUR BEST SHOT!
YEAH.
WHO GOES FIRST ?
LET'S FIND OUT.
RO... SHAM...
...BO !!
ACK !!

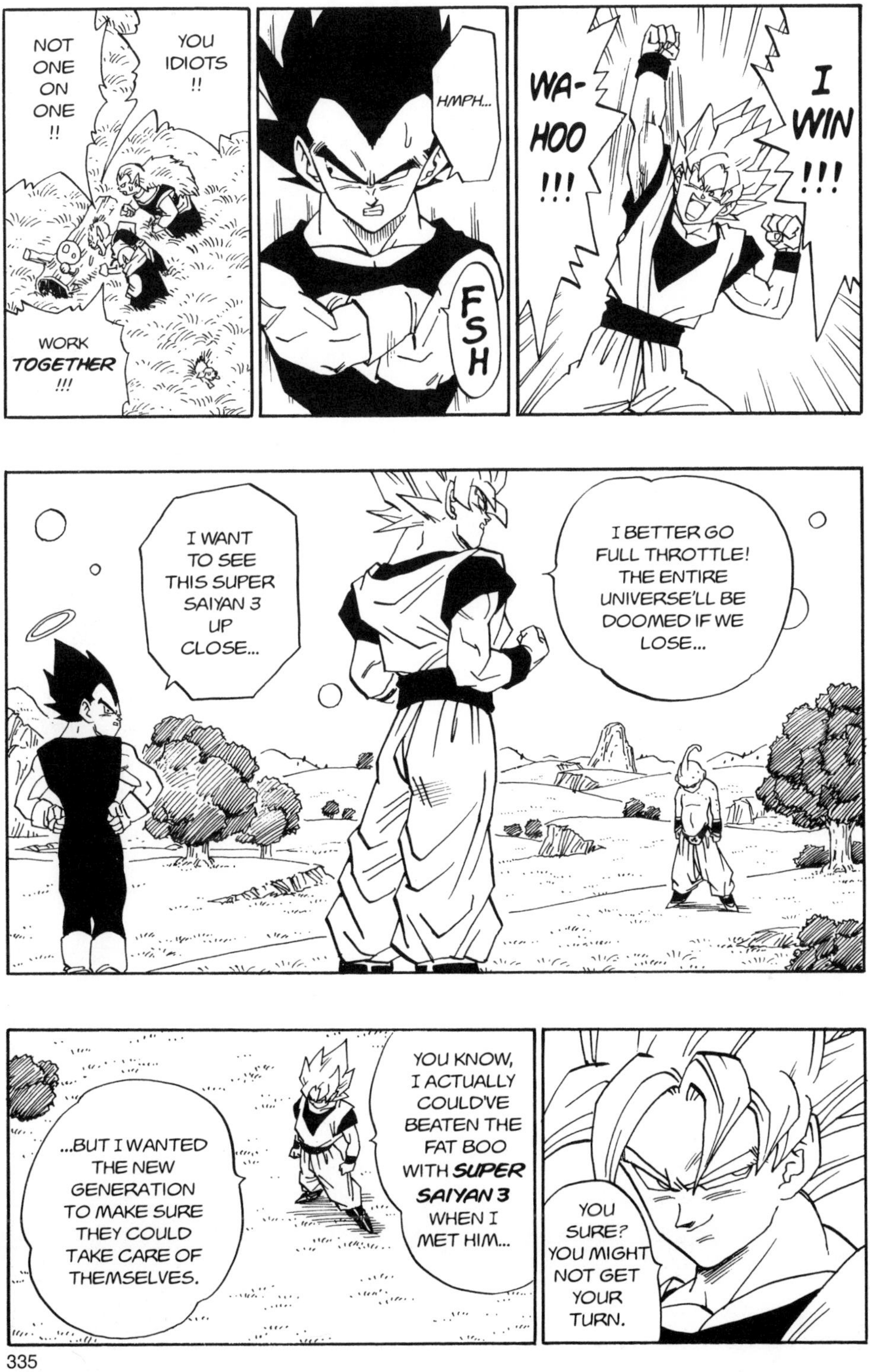
I WIN!!!
WA-HOO!!!
HMPH...
FSH
YOU IDIOTS!!
NOT ONE ON ONE!!
WORK **TOGETHER**!!!
I BETTER GO FULL THROTTLE! THE ENTIRE UNIVERSE'LL BE DOOMED IF WE LOSE...
I WANT TO SEE THIS SUPER SAIYAN 3 UP CLOSE...
YOU SURE? YOU MIGHT NOT GET YOUR TURN.
YOU KNOW, I ACTUALLY COULD'VE BEATEN THE FAT BOO WITH **SUPER SAIYAN 3** WHEN I MET HIM...
...BUT I WANTED THE NEW GENERATION TO MAKE SURE THEY COULD TAKE CARE OF THEMSELVES.

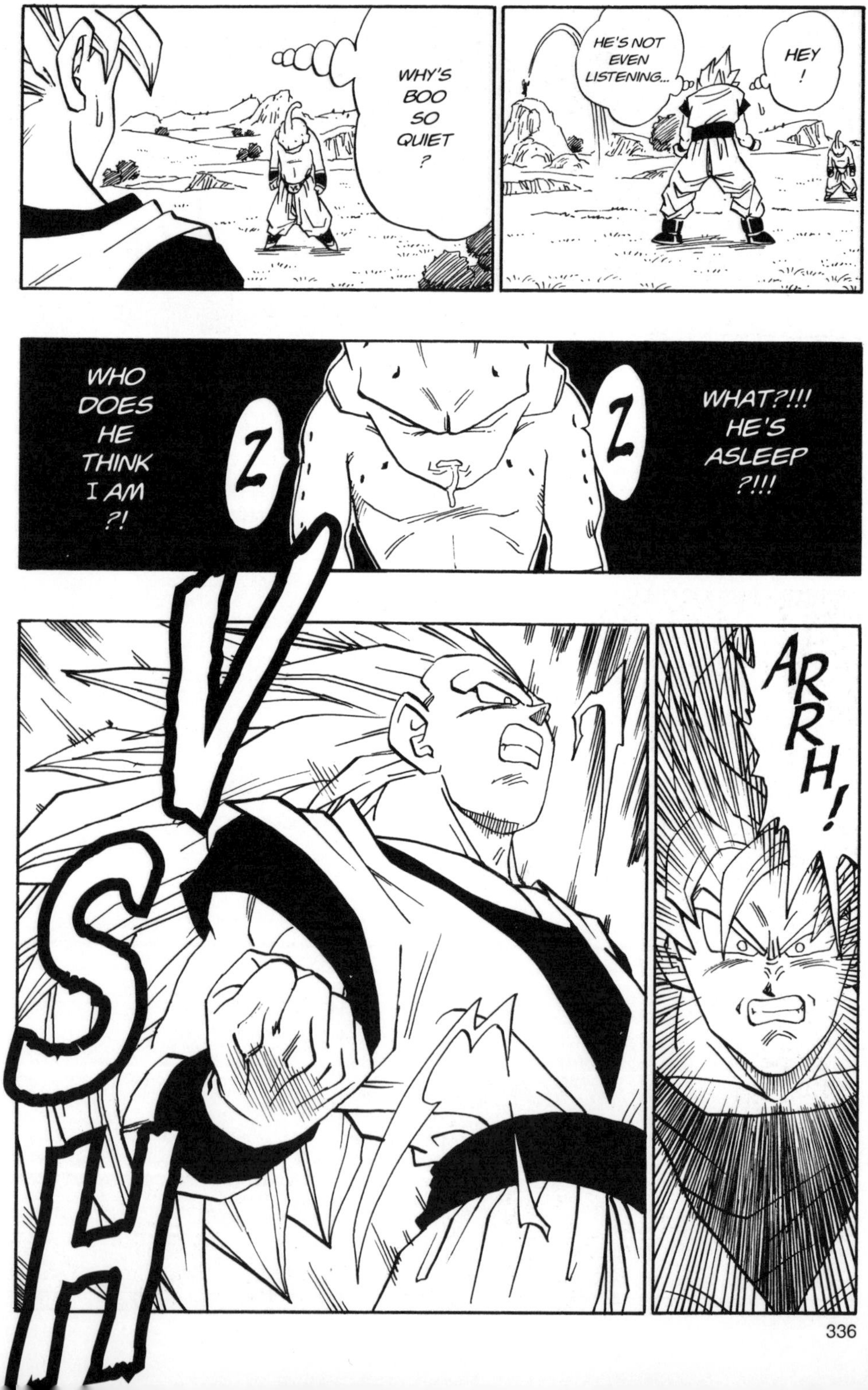
HEY!
HE'S NOT EVEN LISTENING...
WHY'S BOO SO QUIET?
WHAT?!!! HE'S ASLEEP?!!!
Z
Z
WHO DOES HE THINK I AM?!
ARRH!
VSHH

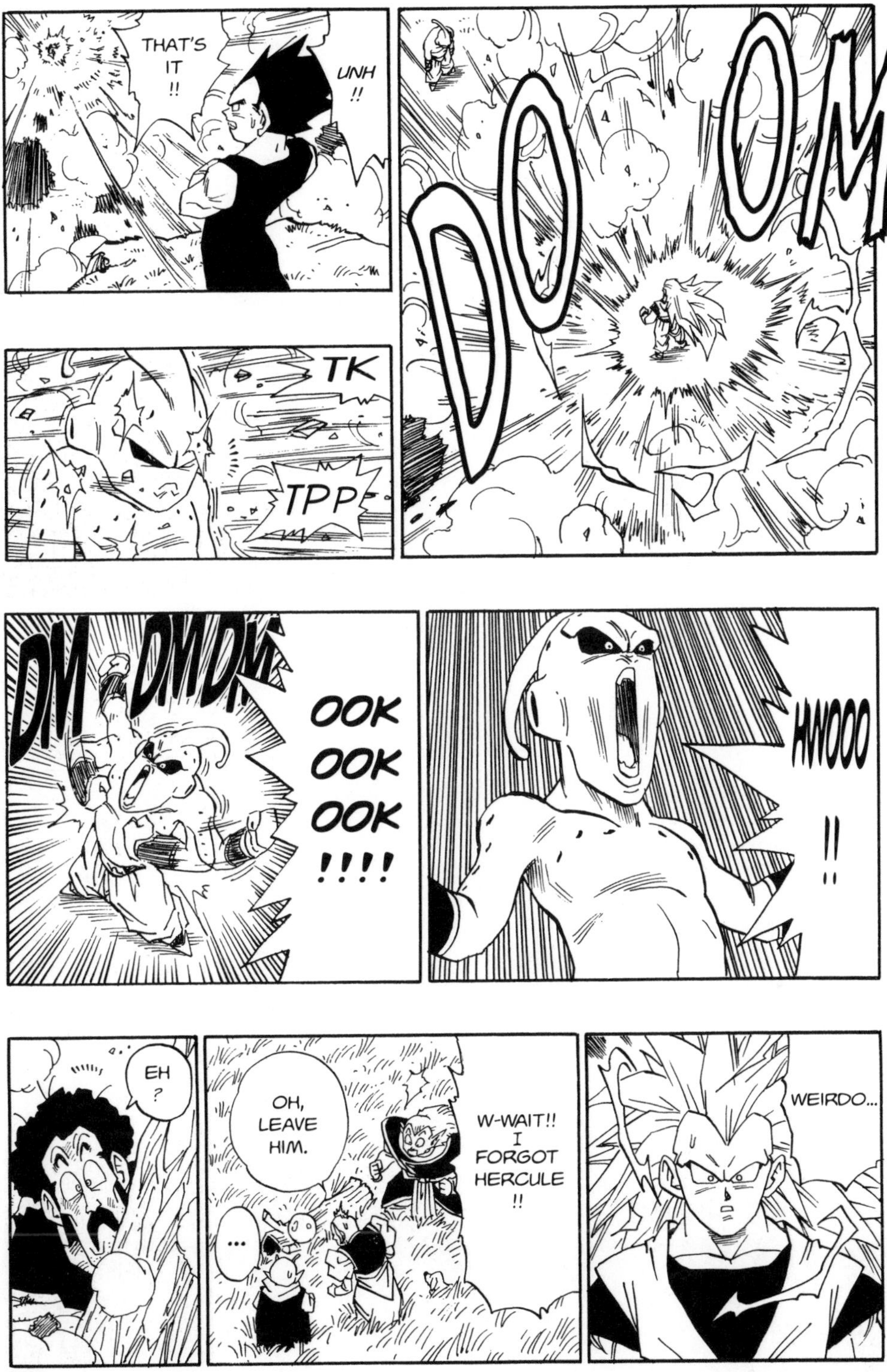
DOOM
THAT'S IT!!
UNH!!
TK
TPP
HWOOO!!
DM DMDM
OOK OOK OOK!!!!
WEIRDO...
W-WAIT!! I FORGOT HERCULE!!
OH, LEAVE HIM.
...
EH?

DRAGON BALL ドラゴンボール

DBZ:316 • Vegeta and Kakarrot

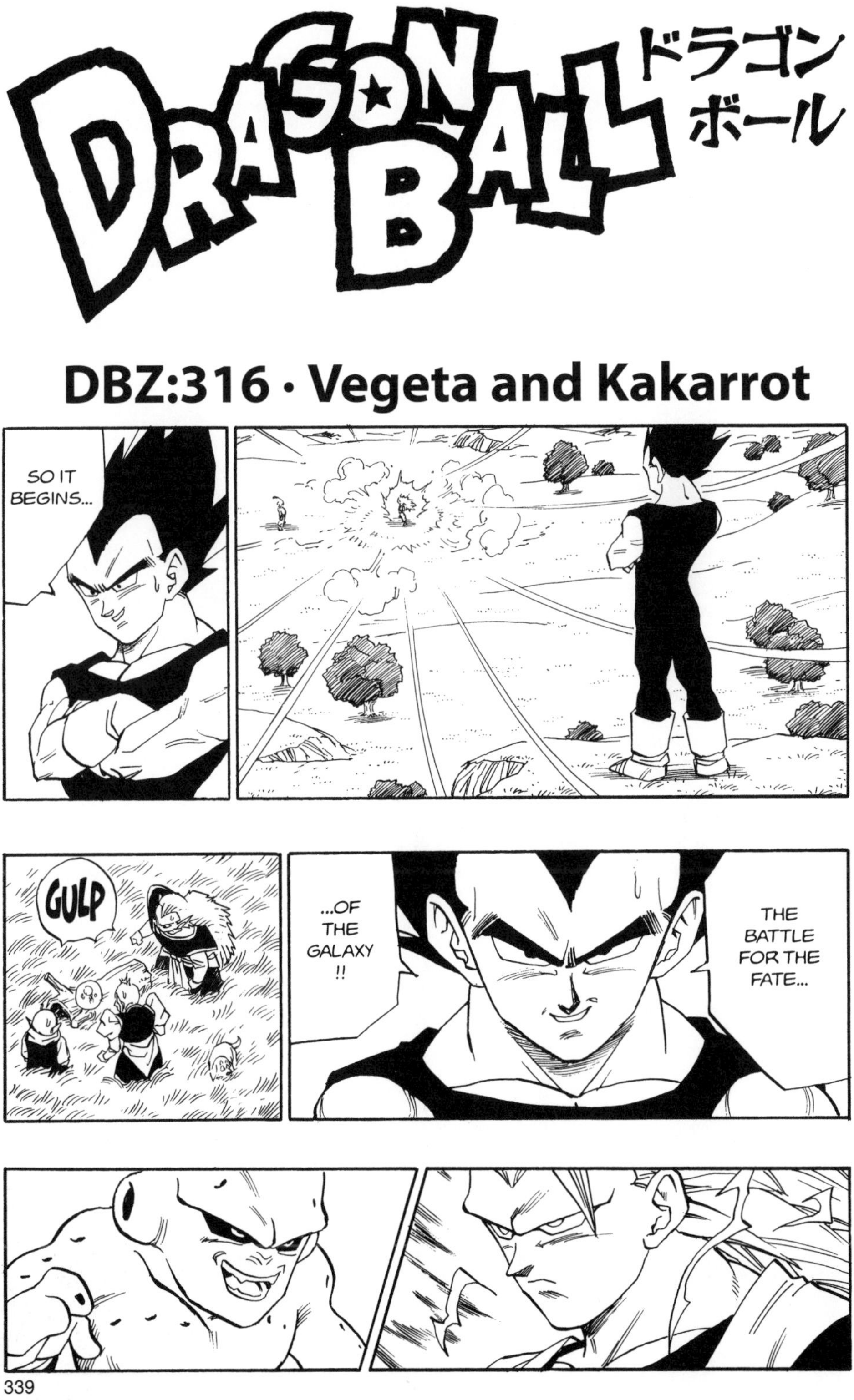
SO IT BEGINS...
THE BATTLE FOR THE FATE...
...OF THE GALAXY !!
GULP

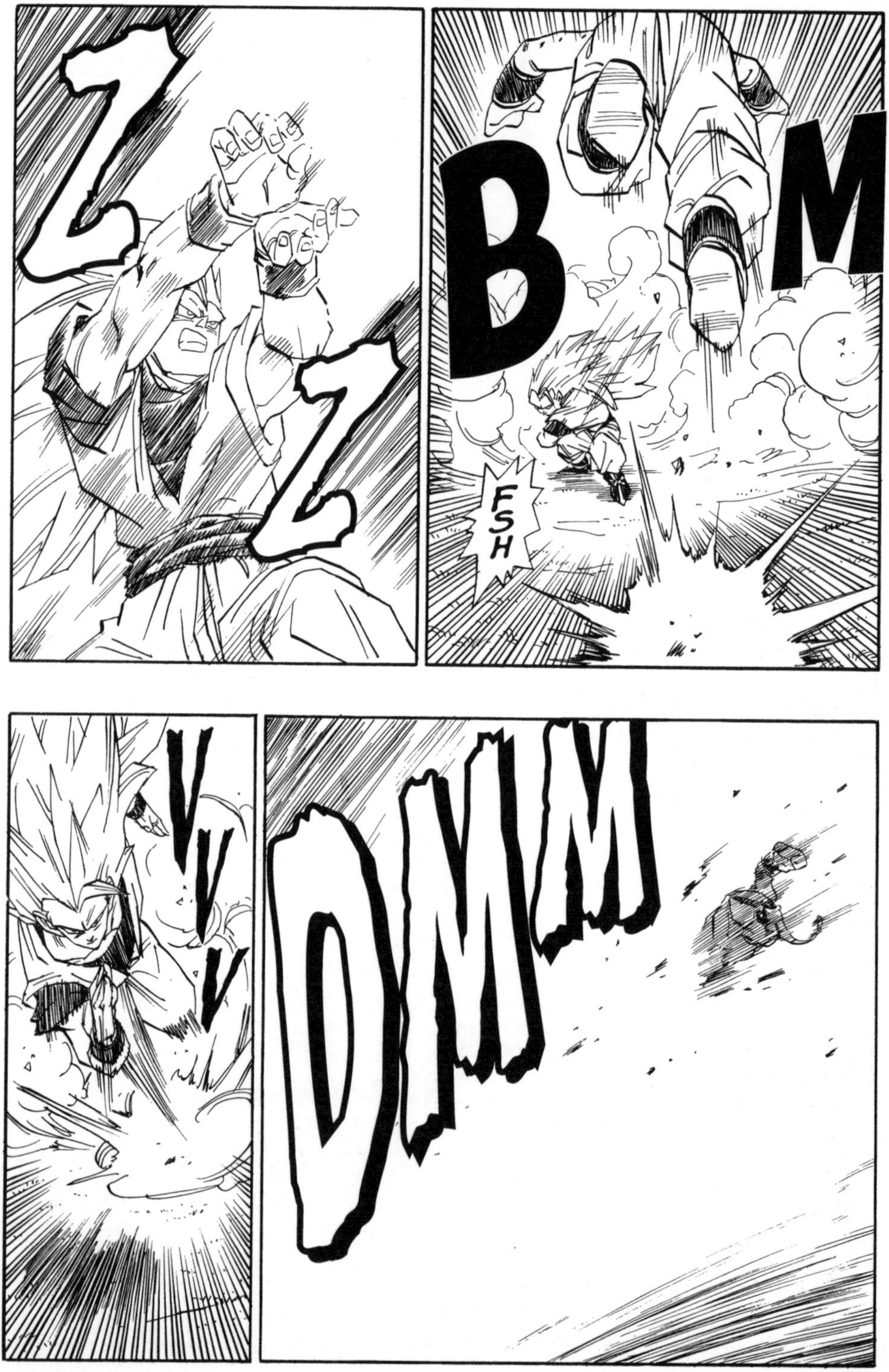

B M
FSH
Z Z
D M M M
V V V

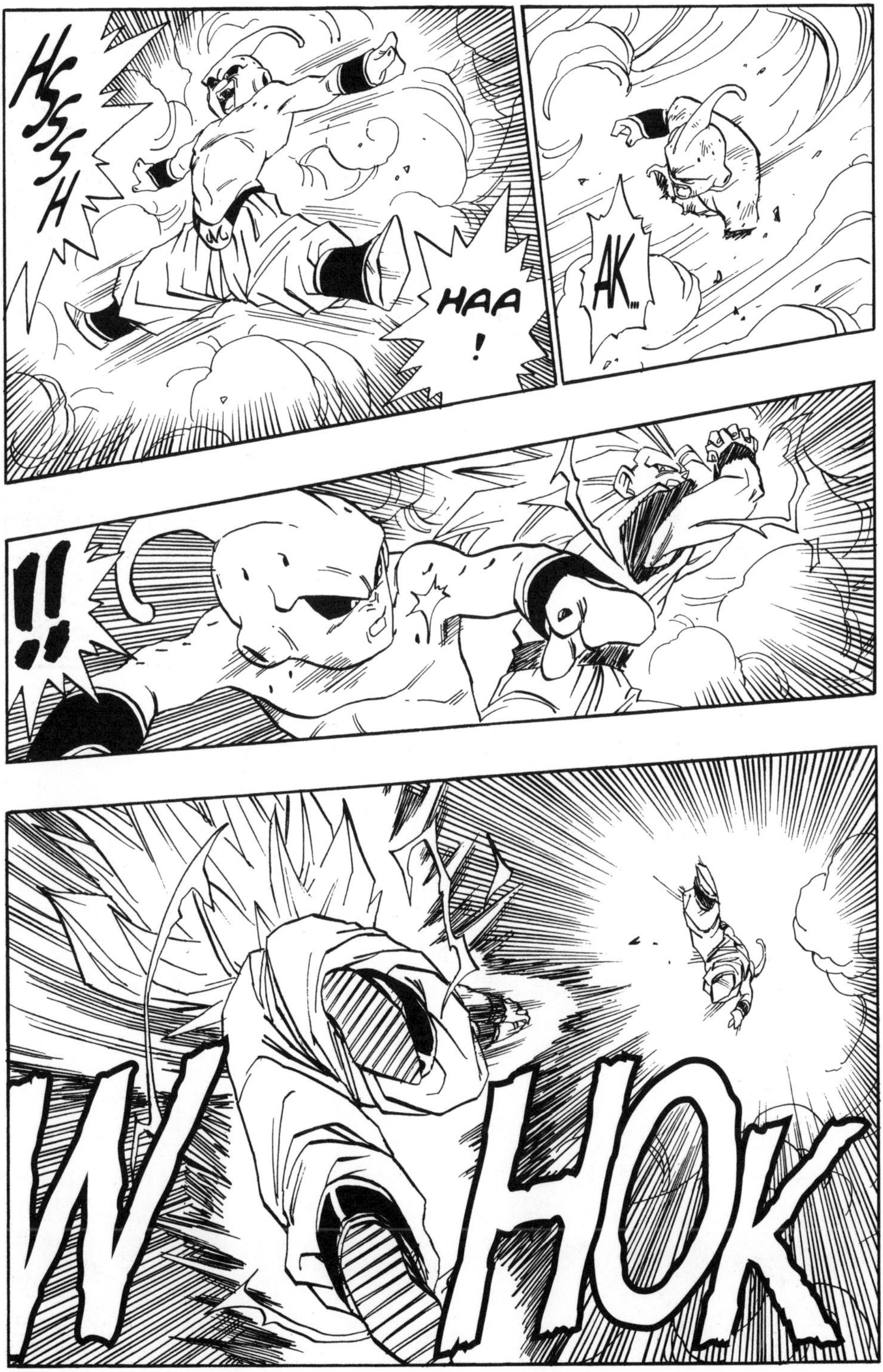
AK...
HAA!
HSSSH
!!
WHOK

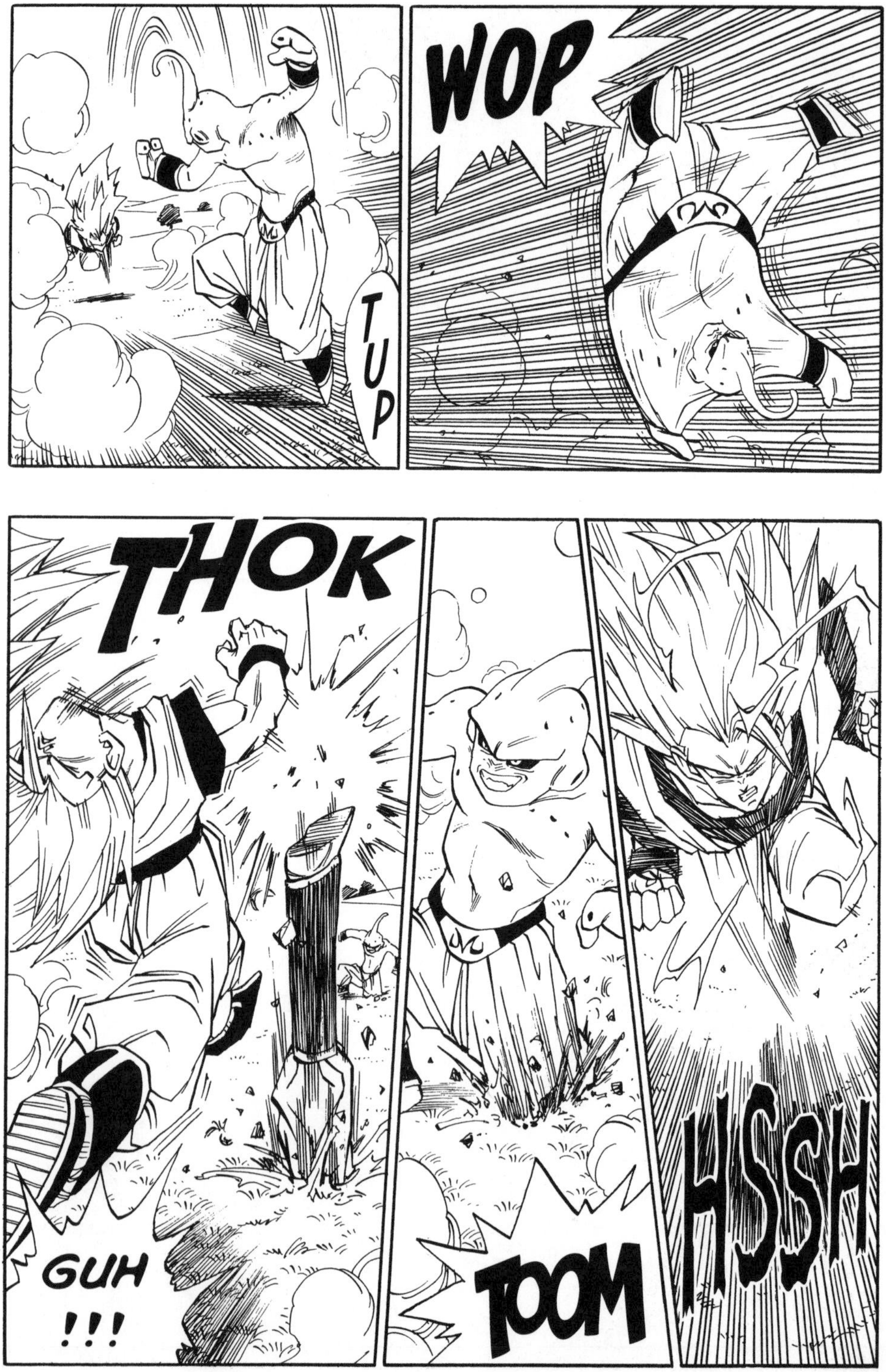
WOP
TUP
HISSH
TOOM
THOK
GUH !!!

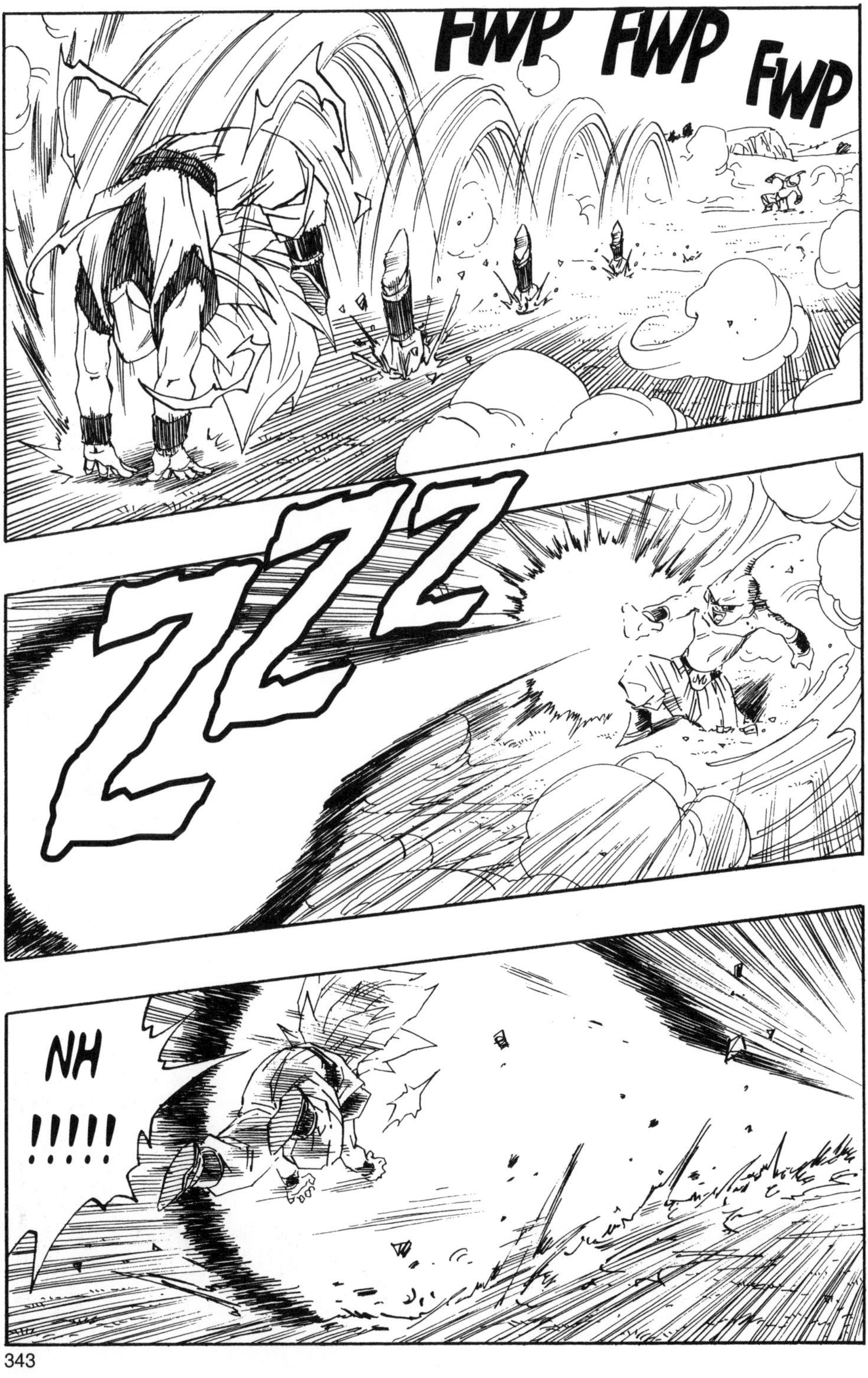
FWP FWP FWP
ZZZ
NH
!!!!!

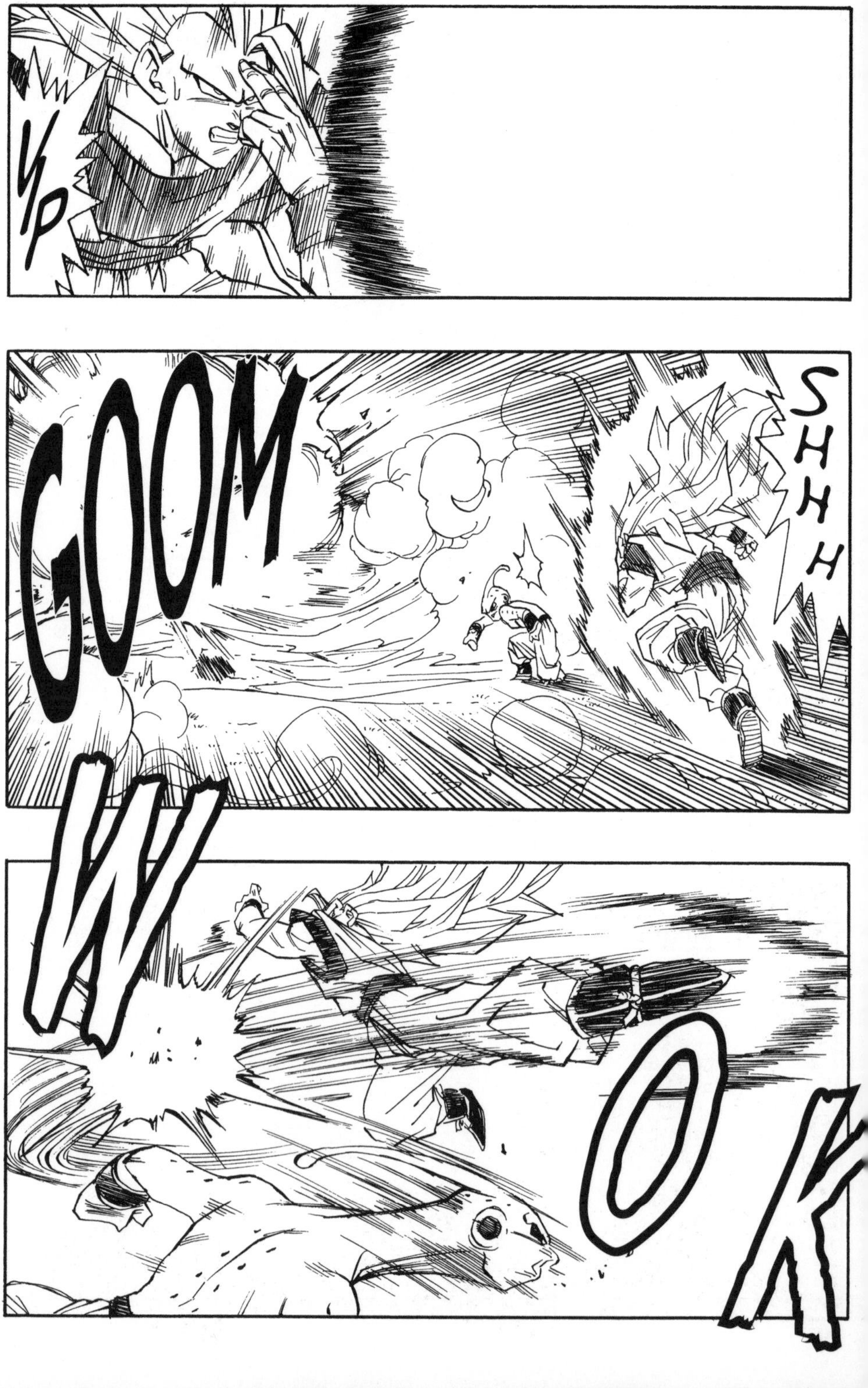
YIP
SHHH
GOOM
WOK

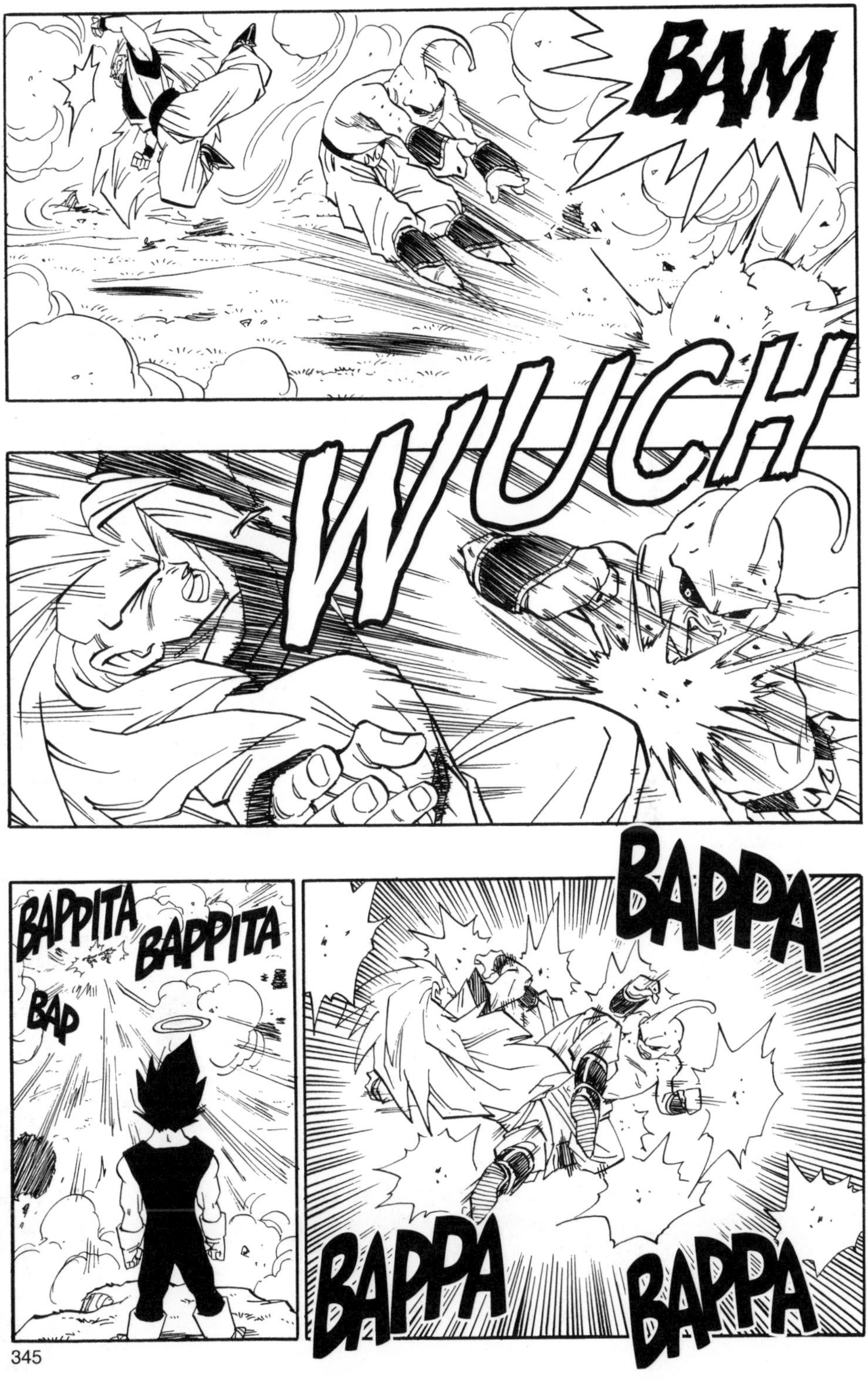
BAM
WUCH
BAPPA
BAPPA
BAPPA
BAPPITA
BAPPITA
BAP

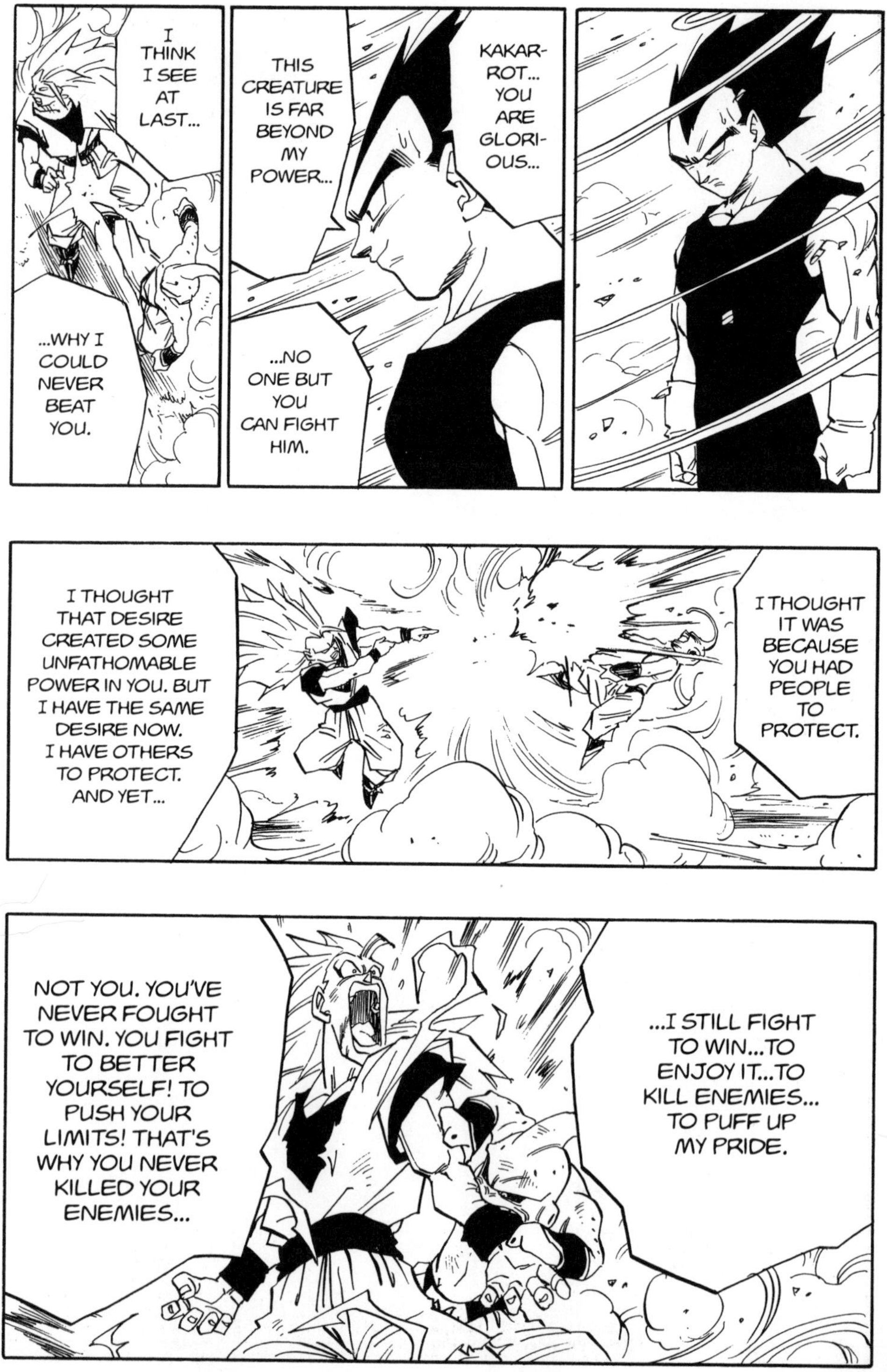
KAKAR-ROT... YOU ARE GLORI-OUS...
THIS CREATURE IS FAR BEYOND MY POWER...
...NO ONE BUT YOU CAN FIGHT HIM.
I THINK I SEE AT LAST...
...WHY I COULD NEVER BEAT YOU.
I THOUGHT IT WAS BECAUSE YOU HAD PEOPLE TO PROTECT.
I THOUGHT THAT DESIRE CREATED SOME UNFATHOMABLE POWER IN YOU. BUT I HAVE THE SAME DESIRE NOW. I HAVE OTHERS TO PROTECT. AND YET...
...I STILL FIGHT TO WIN...TO ENJOY IT...TO KILL ENEMIES... TO PUFF UP MY PRIDE.
NOT YOU. YOU'VE NEVER FOUGHT TO WIN. YOU FIGHT TO BETTER YOURSELF! TO PUSH YOUR LIMITS! THAT'S WHY YOU NEVER KILLED YOUR ENEMIES...

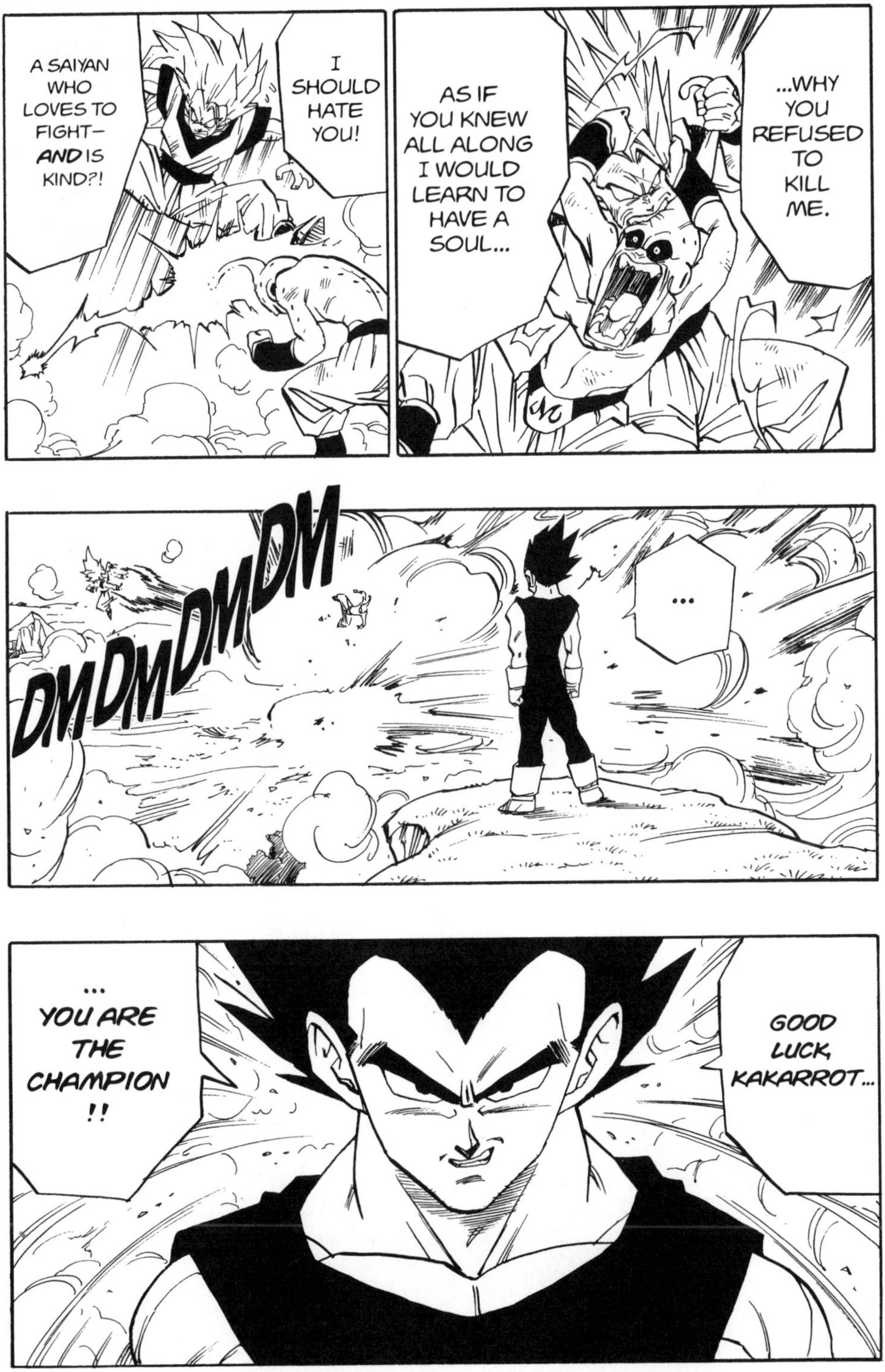
...WHY YOU REFUSED TO KILL ME.
AS IF YOU KNEW ALL ALONG I WOULD LEARN TO HAVE A SOUL...
I SHOULD HATE YOU!
A SAIYAN WHO LOVES TO FIGHT— AND IS KIND?!
...
DMDMDMDM
GOOD LUCK, KAKARROT...
... YOU ARE THE CHAMPION!!

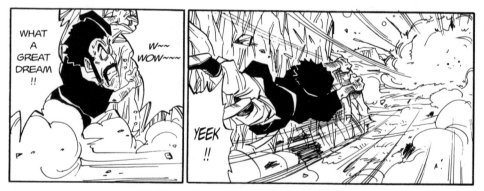

WHAT A GREAT DREAM !!

W~~ WOW~~~

YEEK !!

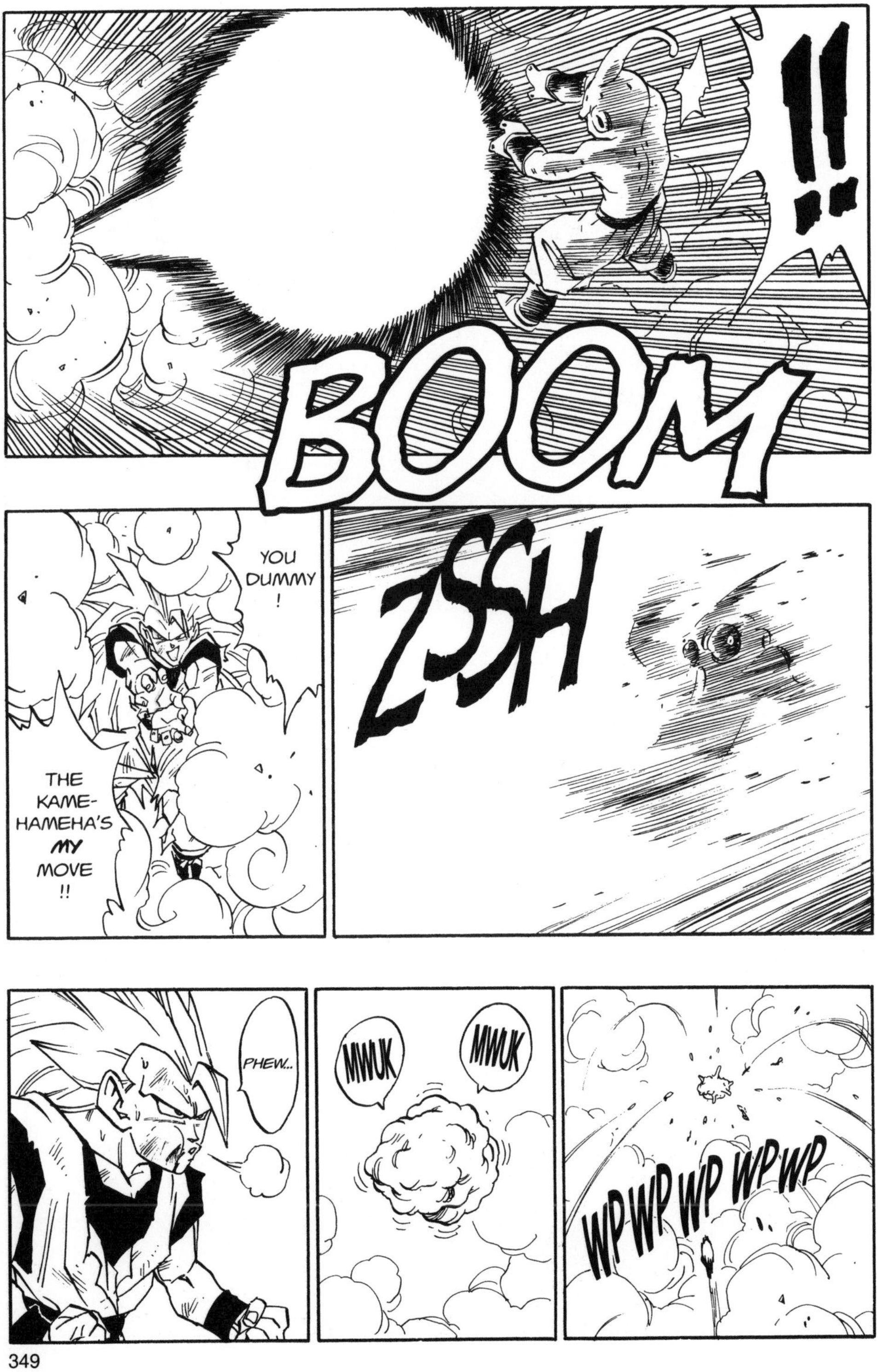
!!
BOOM
ZSSH
YOU DUMMY !
THE KAME-HAMEHA'S *MY* MOVE !!
WP WP WP WP WP
MWUK
MWUK
PHEW...

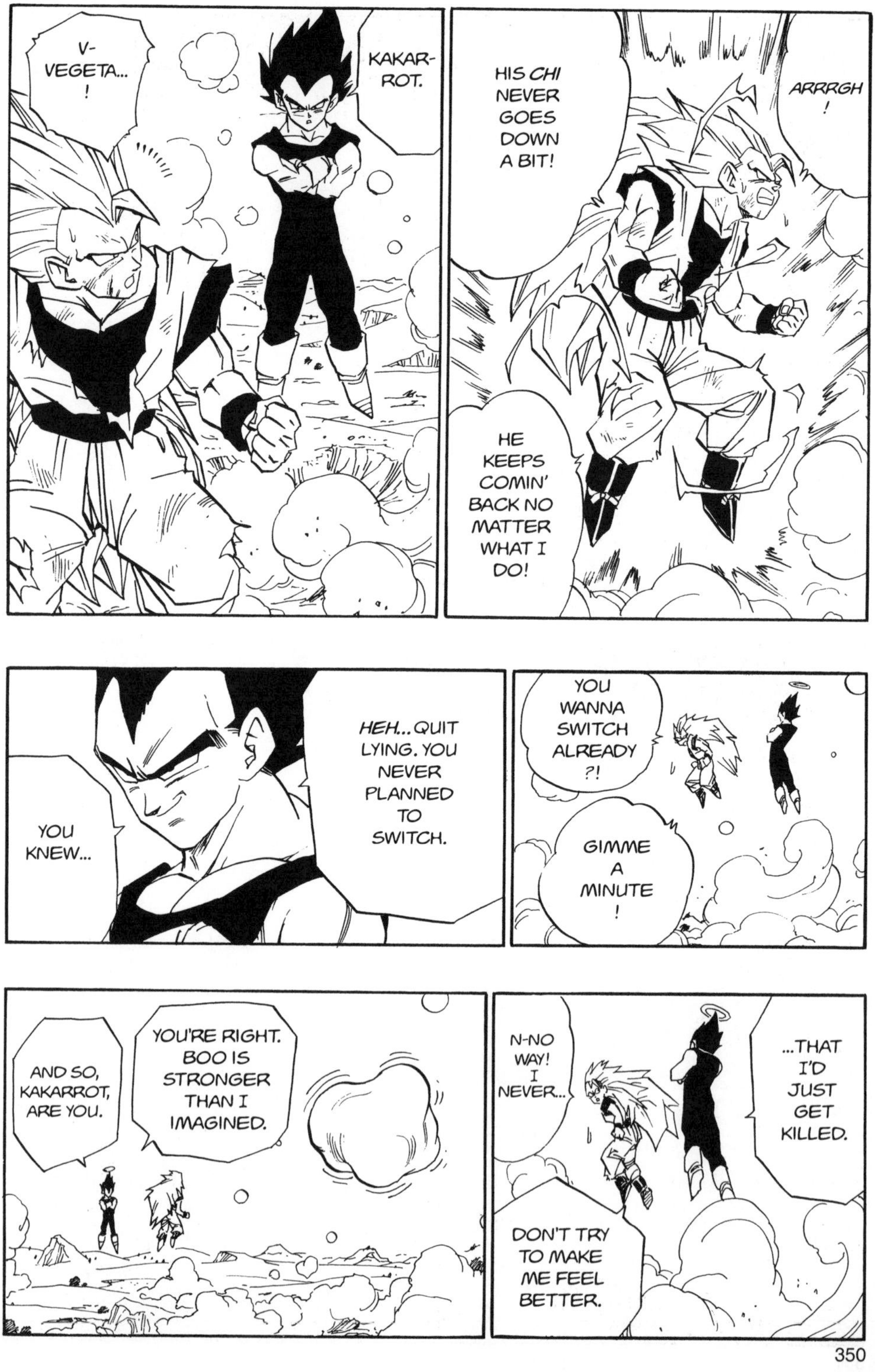
ARRRGH!
HIS *CHI* NEVER GOES DOWN A BIT!
HE KEEPS COMIN' BACK NO MATTER WHAT I DO!
KAKARROT.
V-VEGETA...!
YOU WANNA SWITCH ALREADY?!
GIMME A MINUTE!
HEH... QUIT LYING. YOU NEVER PLANNED TO SWITCH.
YOU KNEW...
...THAT I'D JUST GET KILLED.
N-NO WAY! I NEVER...
DON'T TRY TO MAKE ME FEEL BETTER.
YOU'RE RIGHT. BOO IS STRONGER THAN I IMAGINED.
AND SO, KAKARROT, ARE YOU.

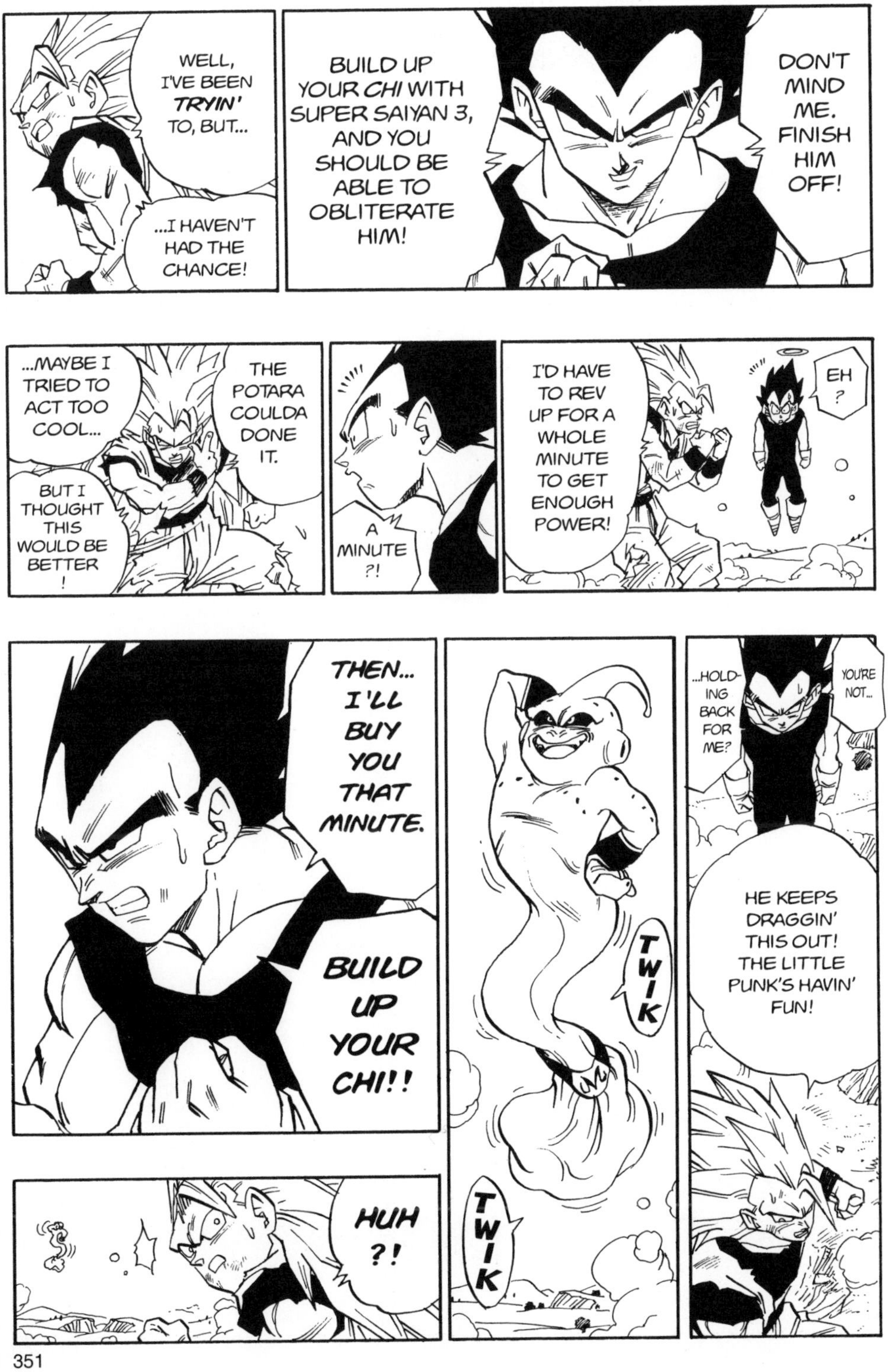
DON'T MIND ME. FINISH HIM OFF!
BUILD UP YOUR *CHI* WITH SUPER SAIYAN 3, AND YOU SHOULD BE ABLE TO OBLITERATE HIM!
WELL, I'VE BEEN ***TRYIN'*** TO, BUT...
...I HAVEN'T HAD THE CHANCE!
EH?
I'D HAVE TO REV UP FOR A WHOLE MINUTE TO GET ENOUGH POWER!
A MINUTE?!
THE POTARA COULDA DONE IT.
...MAYBE I TRIED TO ACT TOO COOL...
BUT I THOUGHT THIS WOULD BE BETTER!
YOU'RE NOT...
...HOLDING BACK FOR ME?
HE KEEPS DRAGGIN' THIS OUT! THE LITTLE PUNK'S HAVIN' FUN!
TWIK
TWIK
THEN... I'LL BUY YOU THAT MINUTE.
BUILD UP YOUR CHI!!
HUH?!

DRAGON BALL ドラゴンボール

DBZ:317 • Vegeta Puts His Life on the Line!

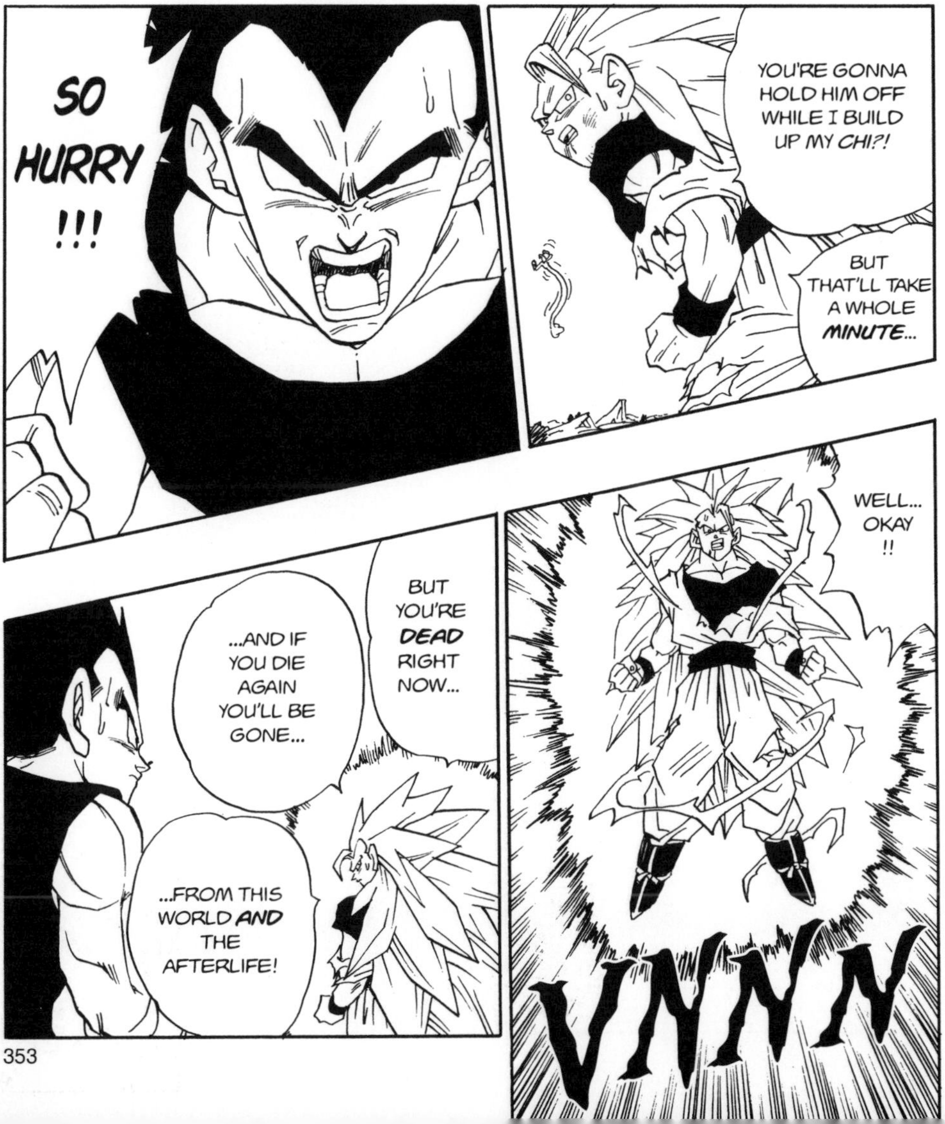
YOU'RE GONNA HOLD HIM OFF WHILE I BUILD UP MY *CHI*?!
BUT THAT'LL TAKE A WHOLE ***MINUTE***...
SO HURRY !!!
WELL... OKAY !!
VNNN
BUT YOU'RE ***DEAD*** RIGHT NOW...
...AND IF YOU DIE AGAIN YOU'LL BE GONE...
...FROM THIS WORLD ***AND*** THE AFTERLIFE!

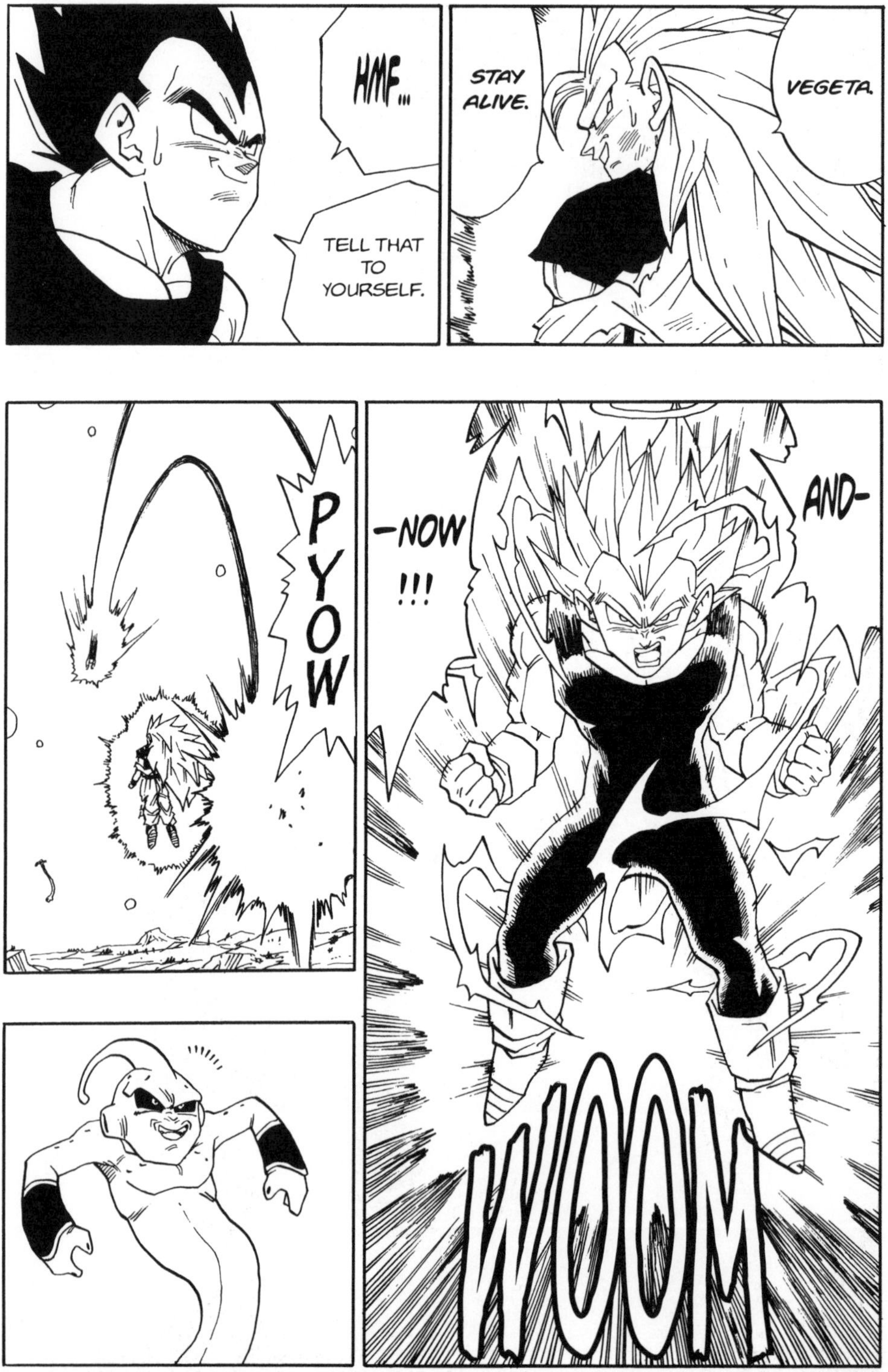
VEGETA.
STAY ALIVE.
HMF...
TELL THAT TO YOURSELF.
AND-
-NOW !!!
WOOM
PYOW

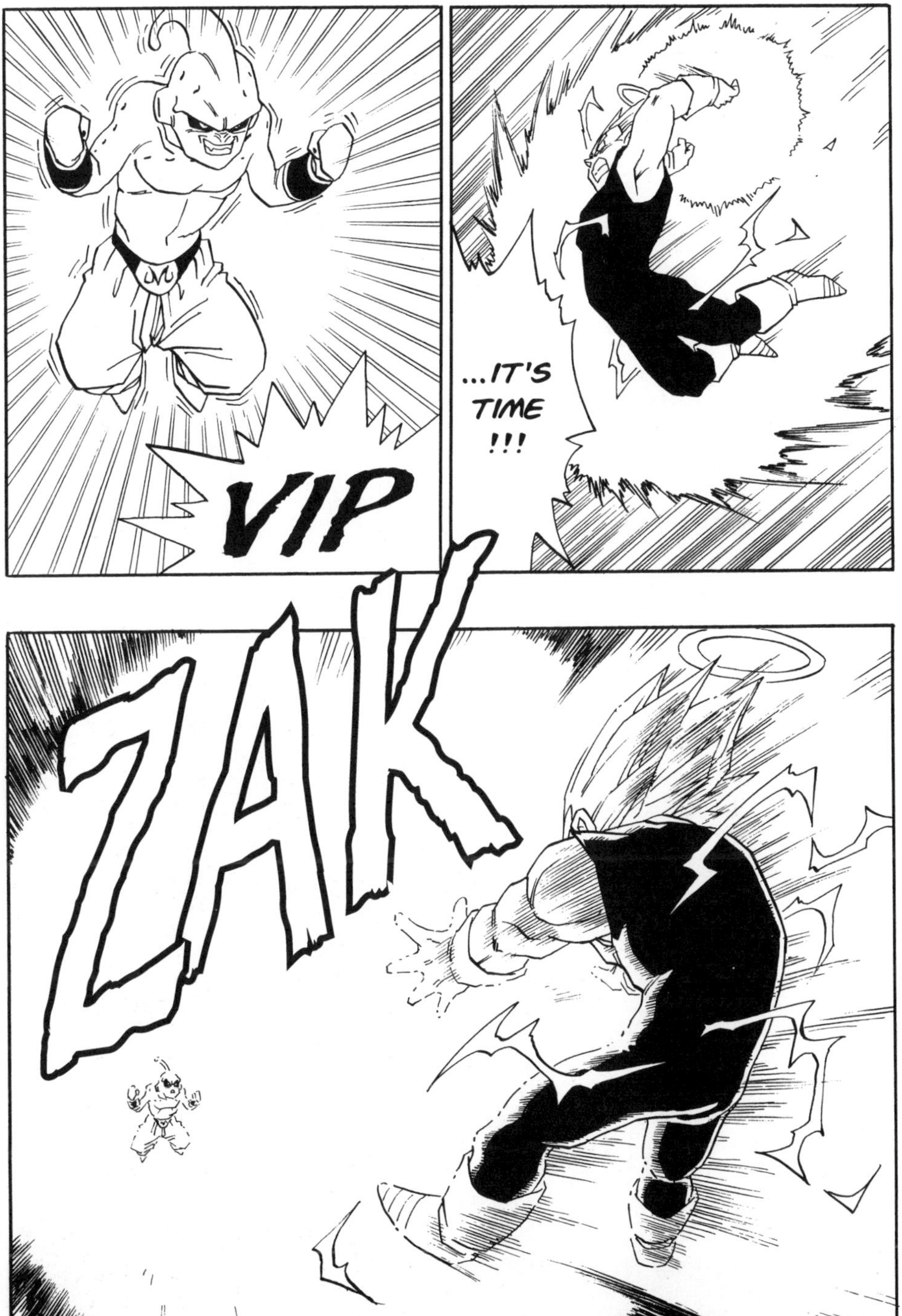
...IT'S TIME !!!
VIP
ZAK

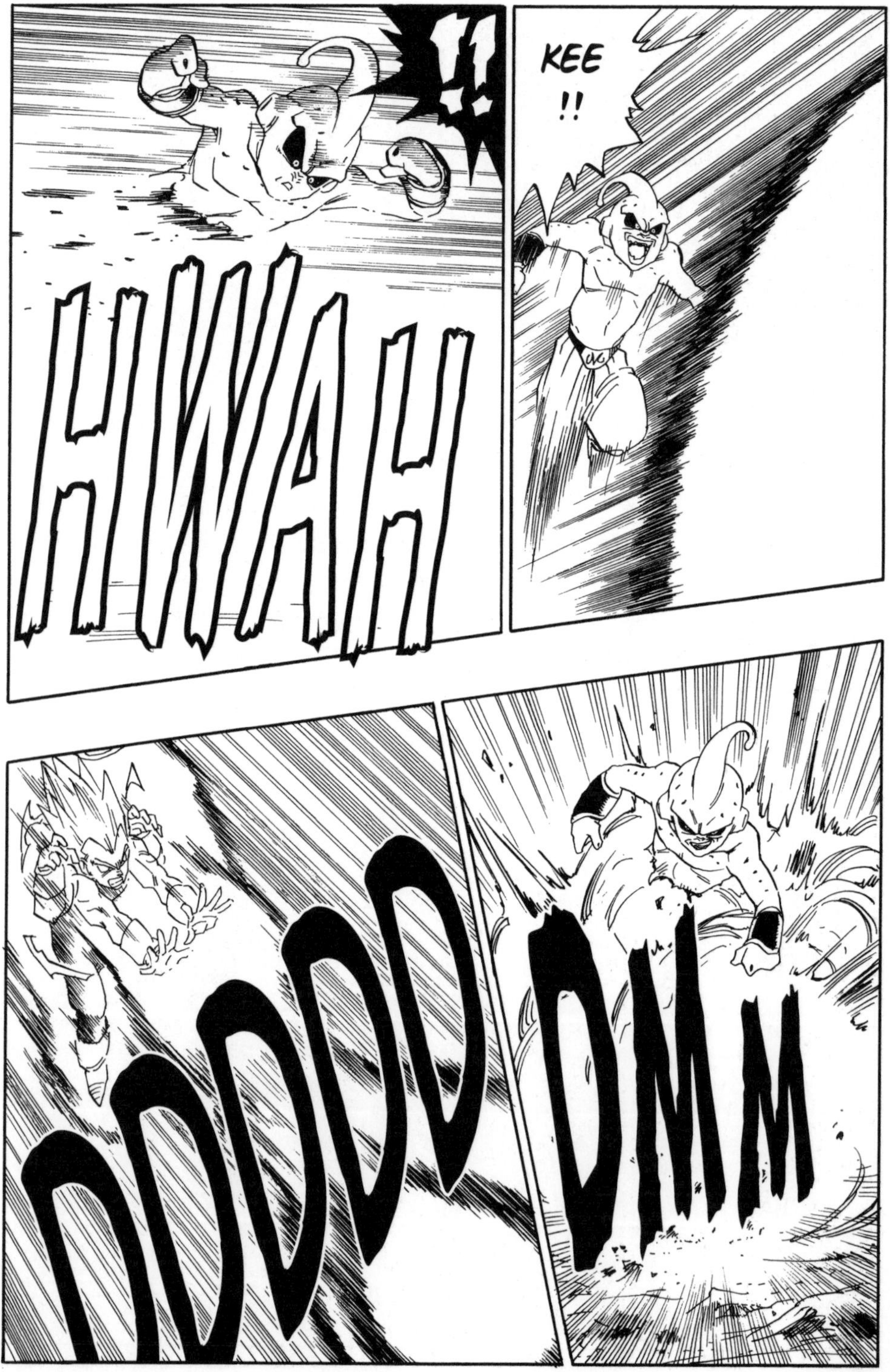
KEE !!
!!
HWAH
DDDDDDMM

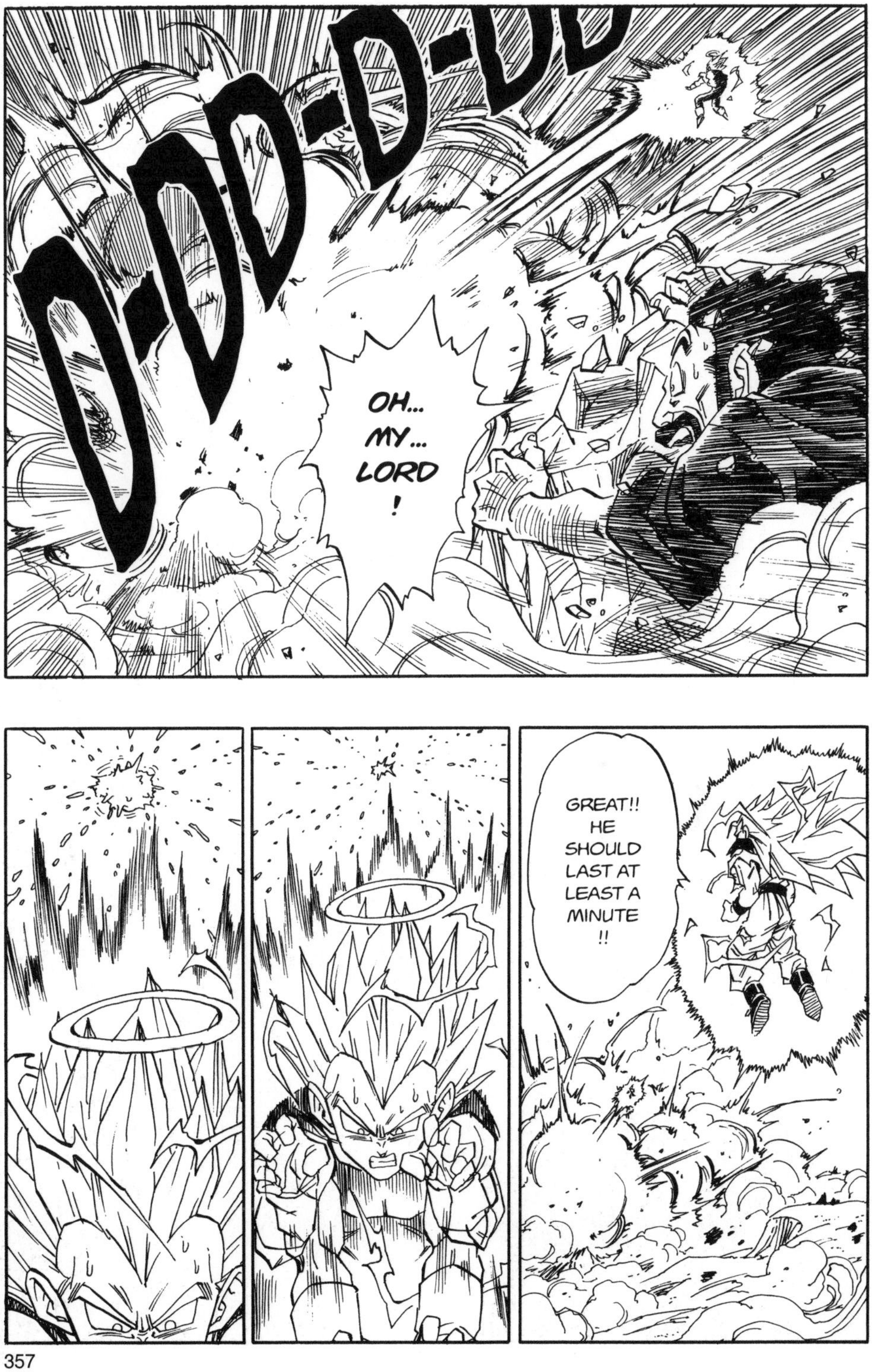
D-DD-D-DD
OH... MY... LORD!
GREAT!! HE SHOULD LAST AT LEAST A MINUTE!!

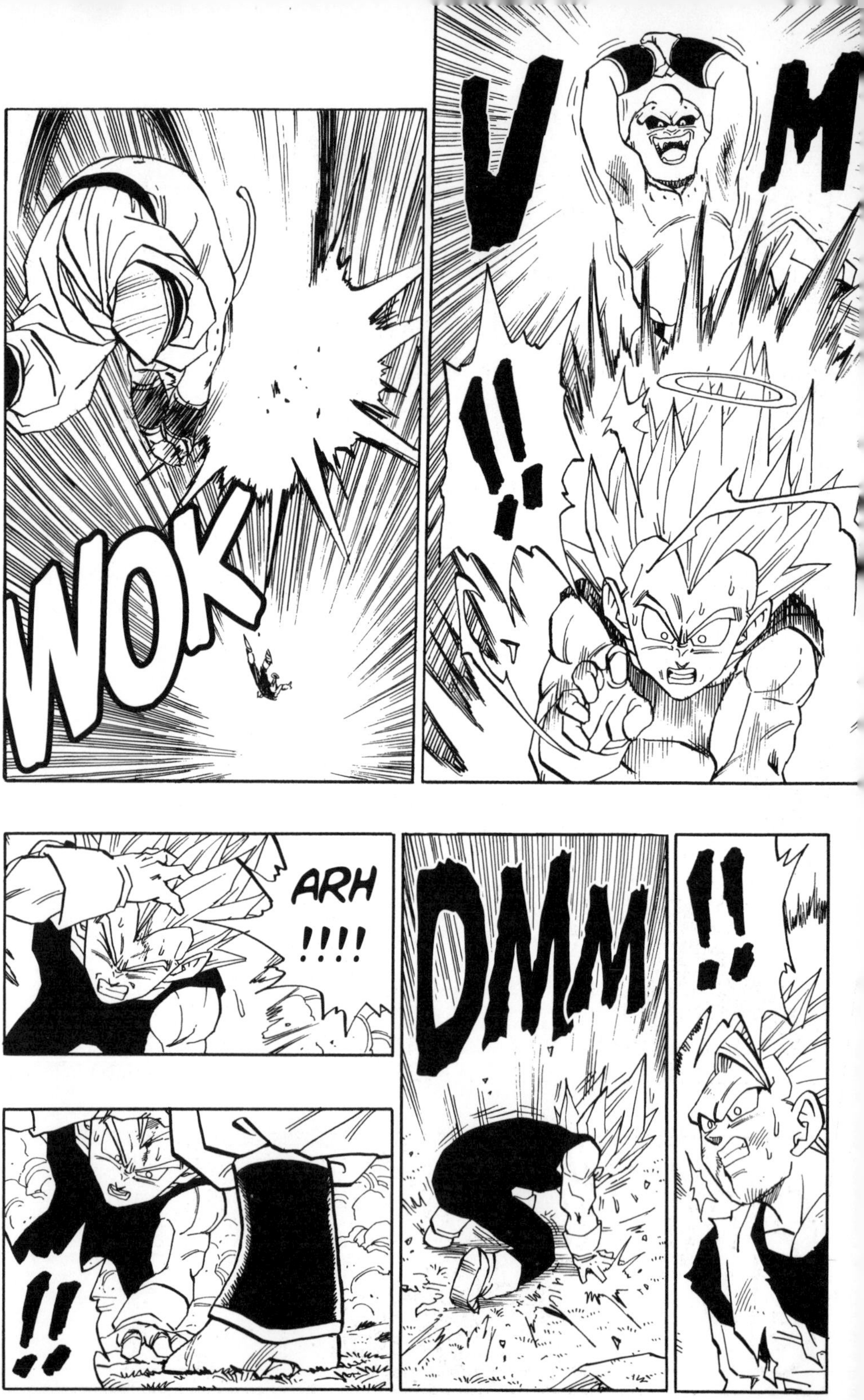
VM
!!
WOK
!!
DMM
ARH
!!!!
!!

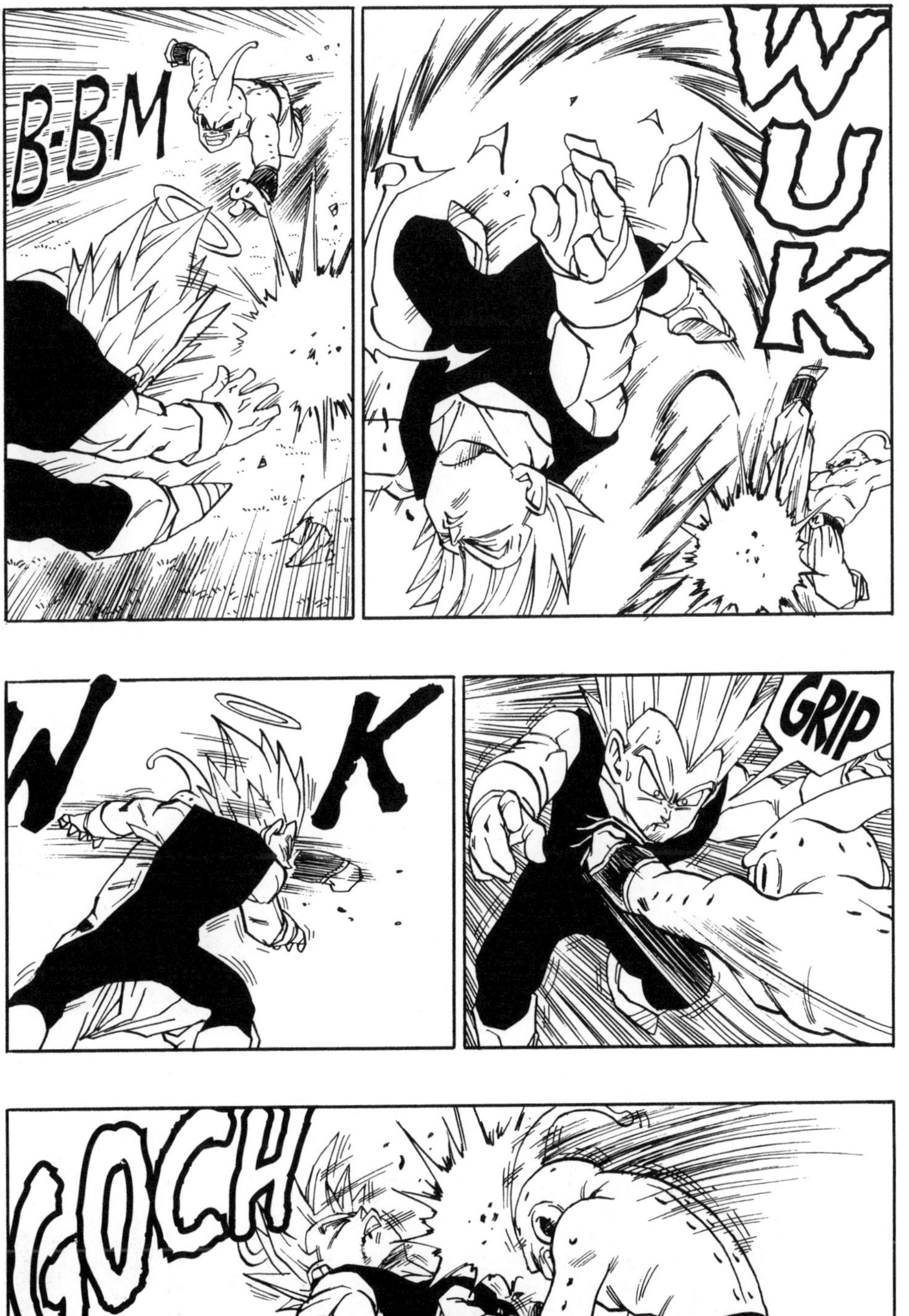
WUK
B-BM
GRIP
W K
GOCH

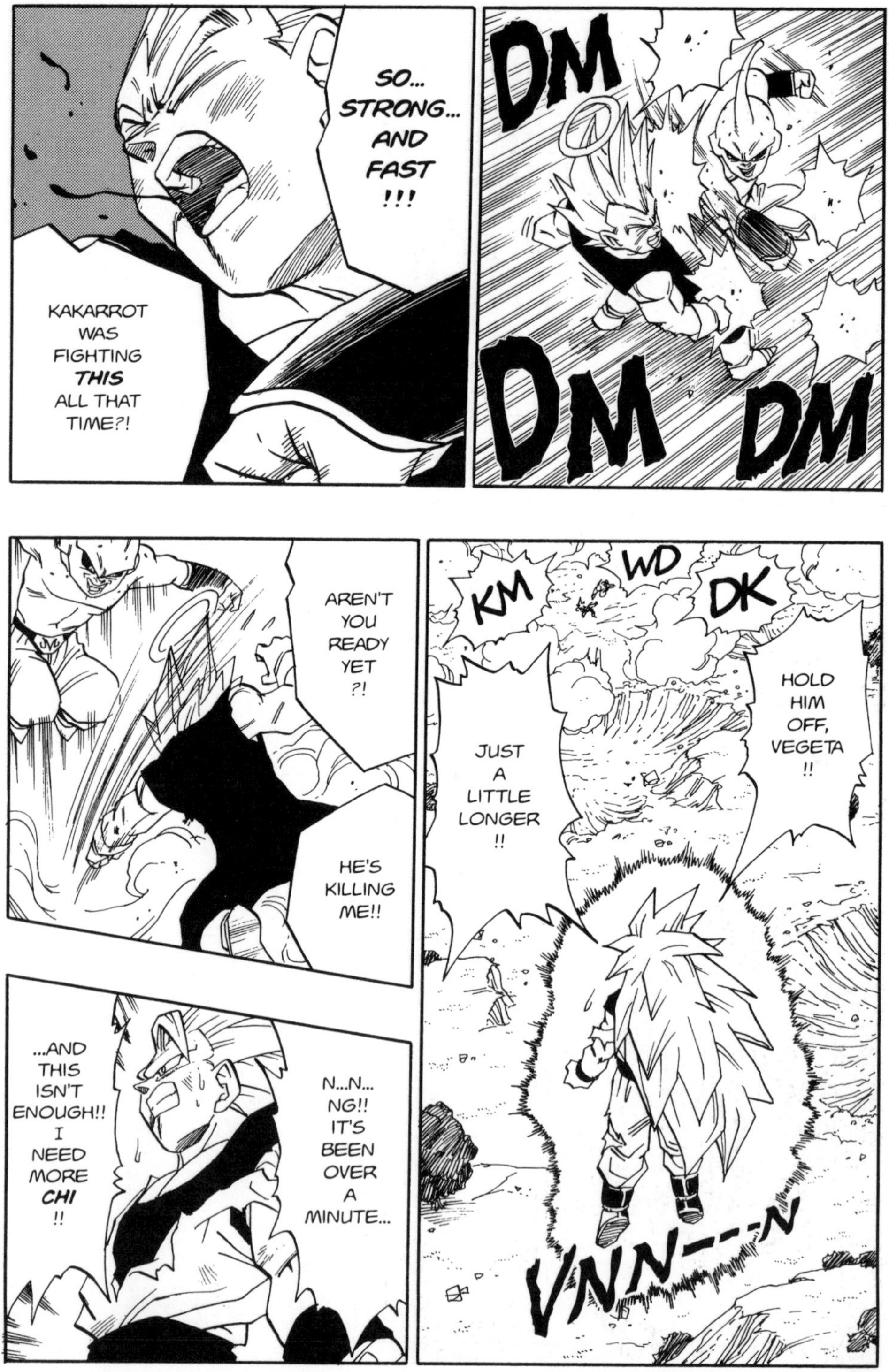
DM
DM DM
SO... STRONG... AND FAST!!!
KAKARROT WAS FIGHTING ***THIS*** ALL THAT TIME?!
DK
WD
KM
HOLD HIM OFF, VEGETA!!
JUST A LITTLE LONGER!!
VNN---N
AREN'T YOU READY YET?!
HE'S KILLING ME!!
N...N... NG!! IT'S BEEN OVER A MINUTE...
...AND THIS ISN'T ENOUGH!! I NEED MORE ***CHI***!!

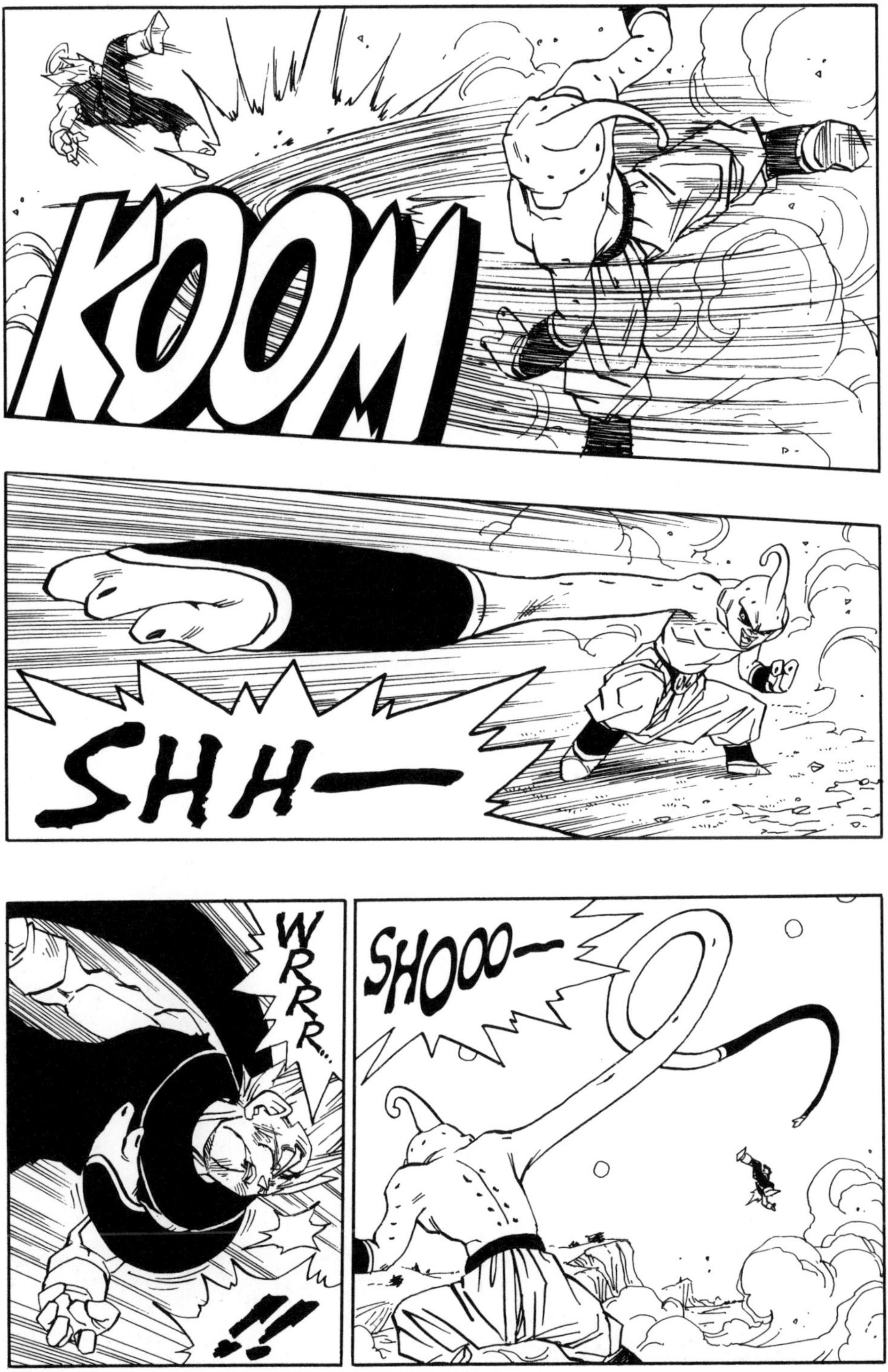
KOOM
SHH—
SHOOO—
WRRRR...
!!

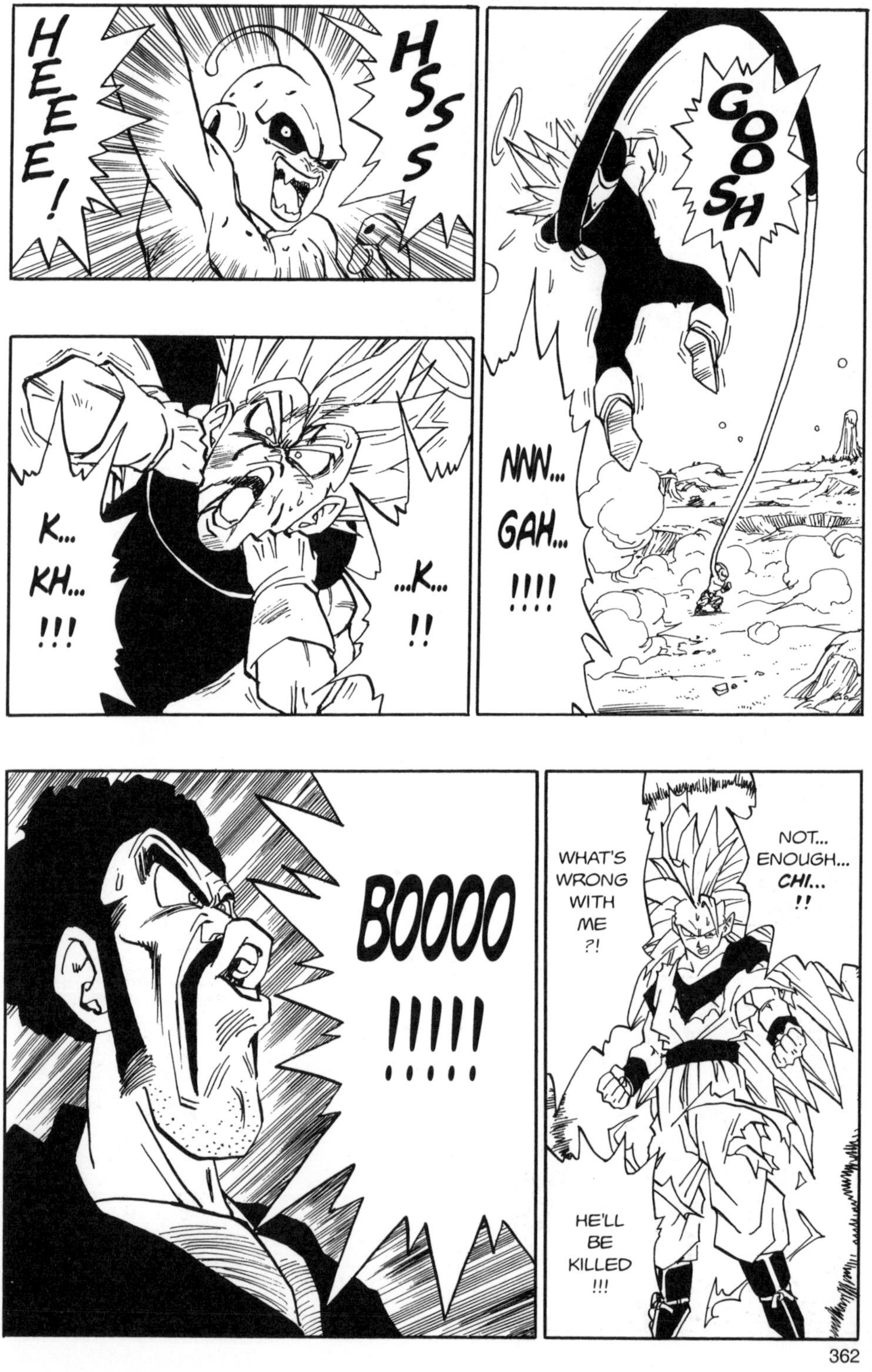
GOOOSH
NNN... GAH... !!!!
HSSS
HEEEE!
...K... !!
K... KH... !!!
NOT... ENOUGH... CHI... !!
WHAT'S WRONG WITH ME ?!
HE'LL BE KILLED !!!
BOOOO !!!!!

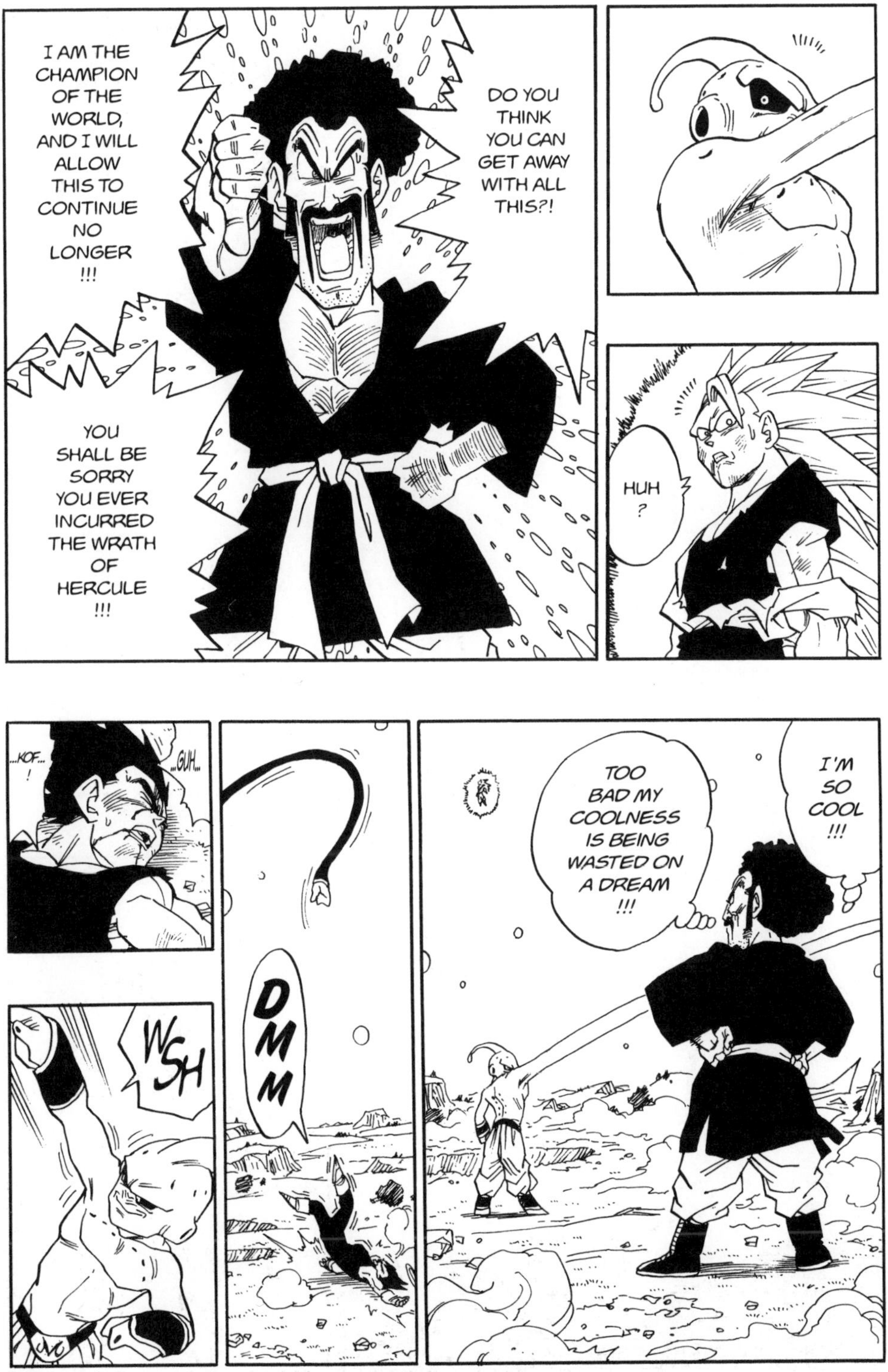
I AM THE CHAMPION OF THE WORLD, AND I WILL ALLOW THIS TO CONTINUE NO LONGER !!!
DO YOU THINK YOU CAN GET AWAY WITH ALL THIS?!
YOU SHALL BE SORRY YOU EVER INCURRED THE WRATH OF HERCULE !!!
HUH ?
...KOF... !
...GUH...
WSH
DMM
TOO BAD MY COOLNESS IS BEING WASTED ON A DREAM !!!
I'M SO COOL !!!

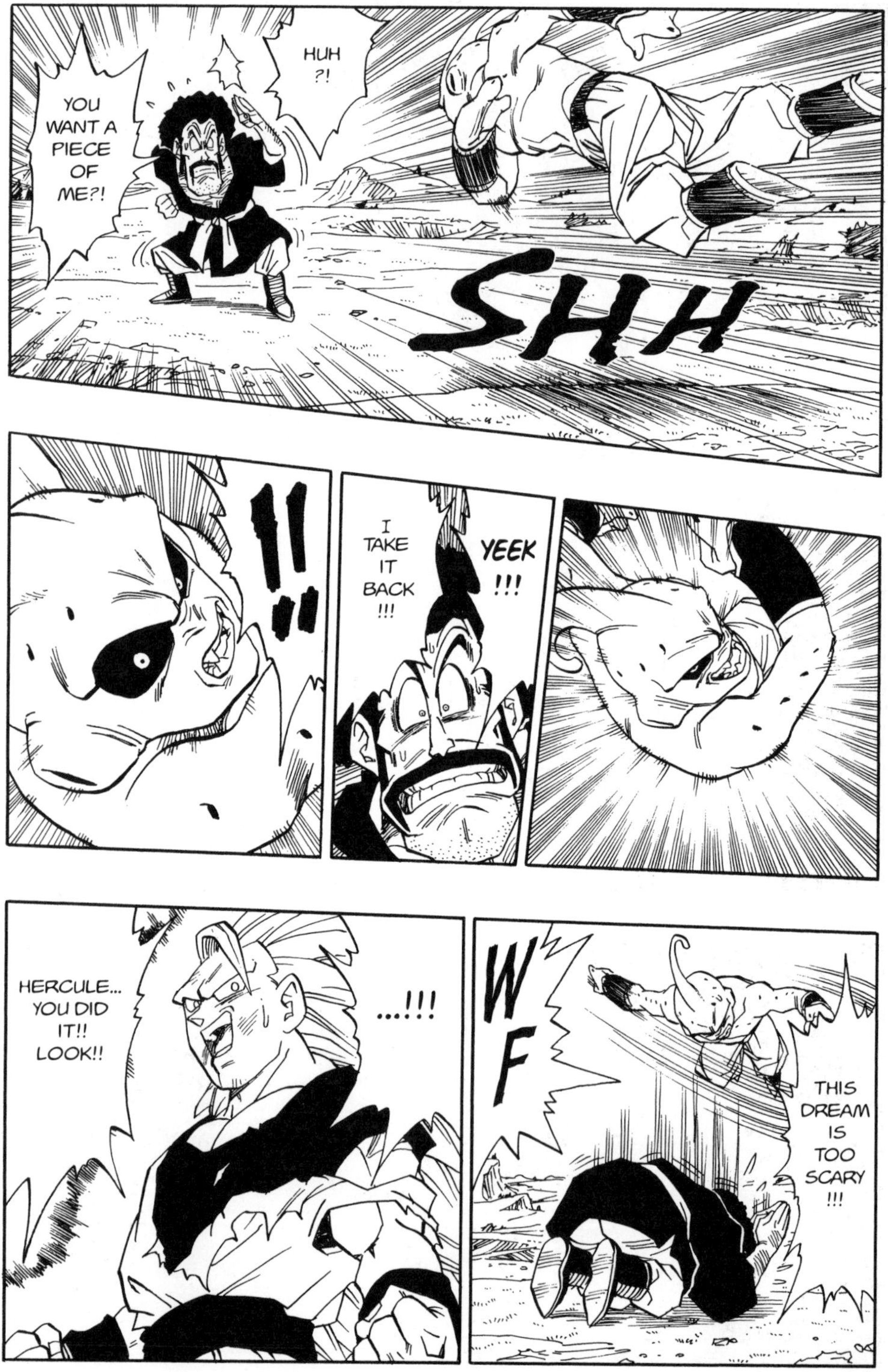
HUH ?!
YOU WANT A PIECE OF ME?!
SHH
YEEK !!!
I TAKE IT BACK !!!
!!
THIS DREAM IS TOO SCARY !!!
WF
...!!!
HERCULE... YOU DID IT!! LOOK!!

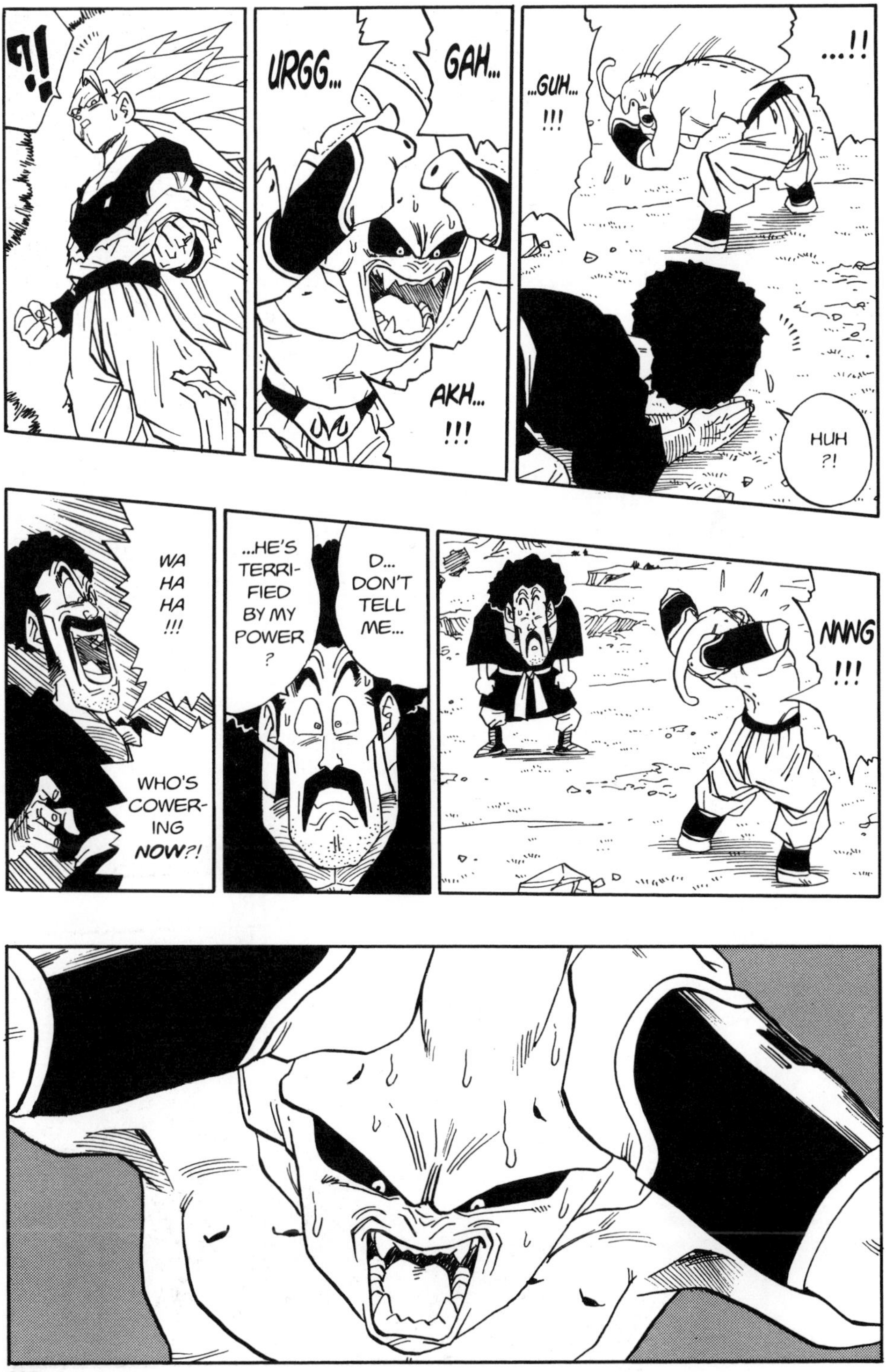
...!!
...GUH... !!!
HUH ?!
GAH...
URGG...
AKH... !!!
?!
NNNG !!!
D... DON'T TELL ME...
...HE'S TERRI-FIED BY MY POWER ?
WA HA HA !!!
WHO'S COWER-ING NOW?!

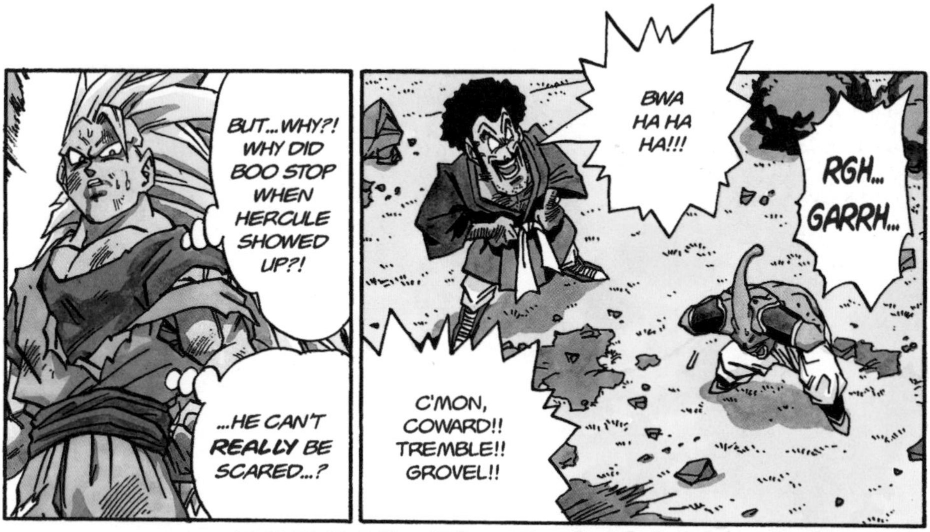
BWA HA HA HA!!!
RGH... GARRH...
C'MON, COWARD!! TREMBLE!! GROVEL!!
BUT...WHY?! WHY DID BOO STOP WHEN HERCULE SHOWED UP?!
...HE CAN'T REALLY BE SCARED...?

DBZ:318 • The End of Super Saiyan 3

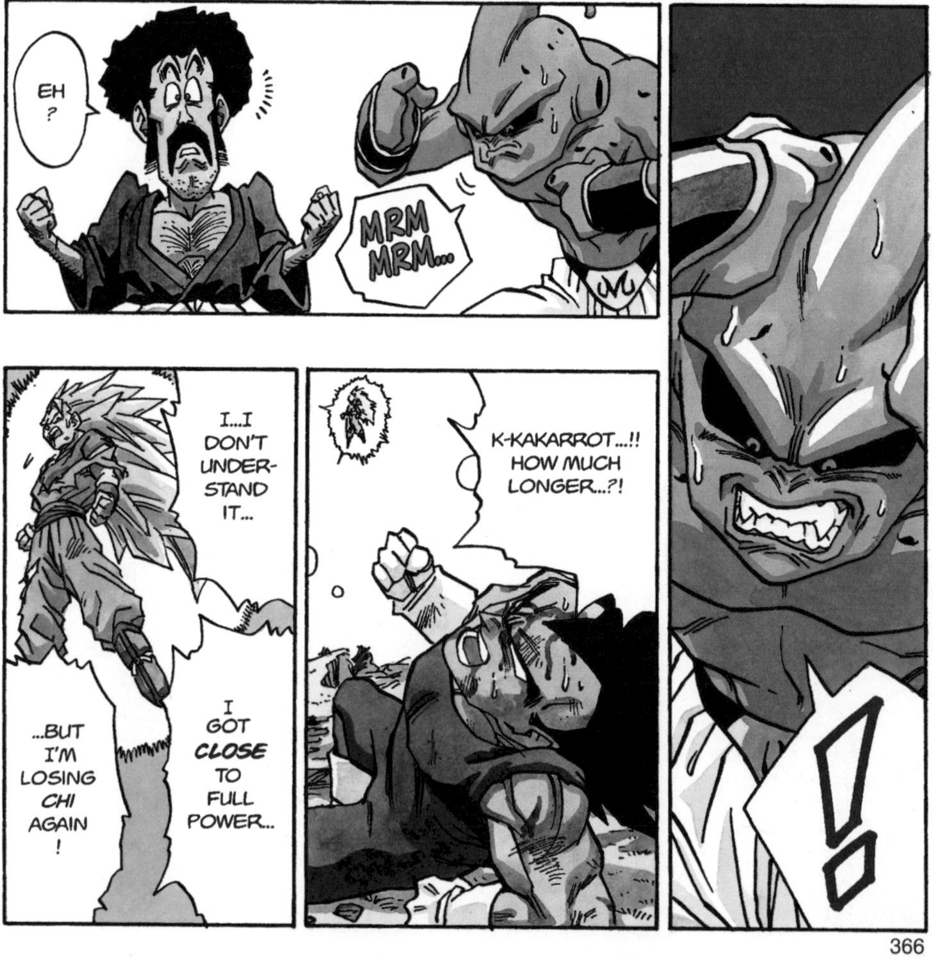
!
MRM MRM...
EH ?
K-KAKARROT...!! HOW MUCH LONGER...?!
I...I DON'T UNDER-STAND IT...
I GOT CLOSE TO FULL POWER...
...BUT I'M LOSING CHI AGAIN !

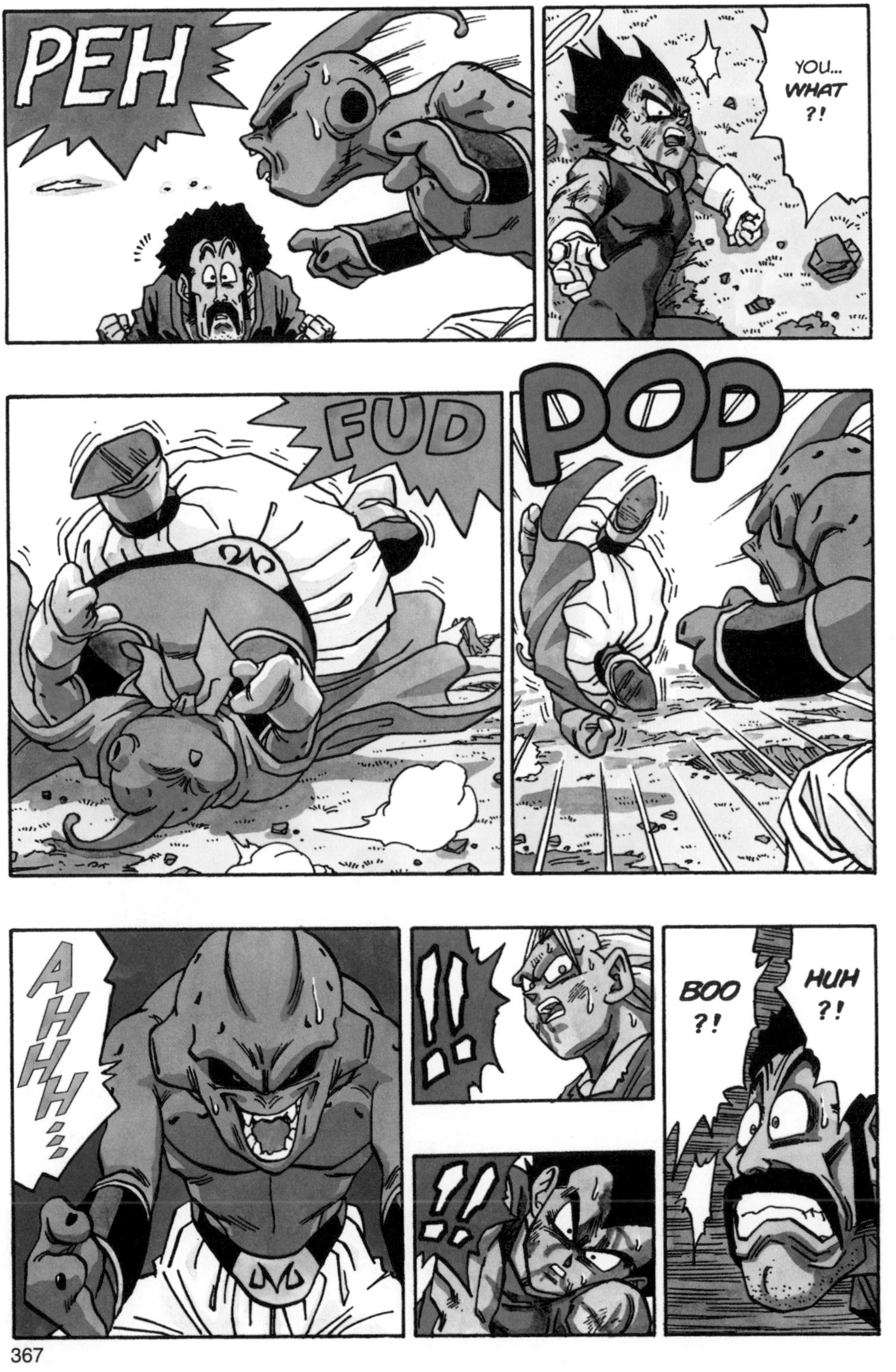
YOU... WHAT ?!
PEH
POP
FUD
HUH ?!
BOO ?!
!!
!!
AHHHH...

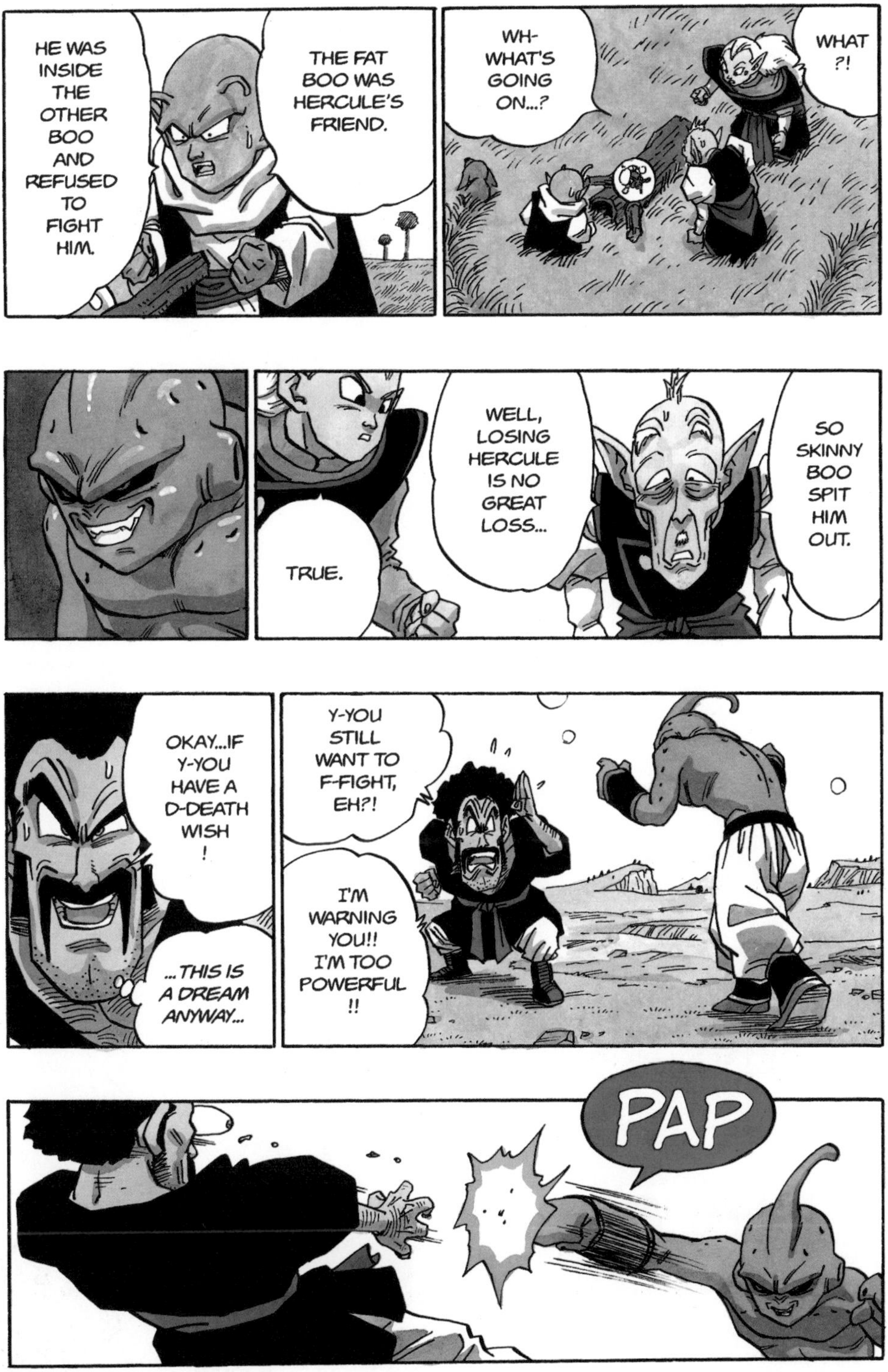
WHAT ?!
WH- WHAT'S GOING ON...?
THE FAT BOO WAS HERCULE'S FRIEND.
HE WAS INSIDE THE OTHER BOO AND REFUSED TO FIGHT HIM.
SO SKINNY BOO SPIT HIM OUT.
WELL, LOSING HERCULE IS NO GREAT LOSS...
TRUE.
Y-YOU STILL WANT TO F-FIGHT, EH?!
I'M WARNING YOU!! I'M TOO POWERFUL !!
OKAY...IF Y-YOU HAVE A D-DEATH WISH !
...THIS IS A DREAM ANYWAY...
PAP

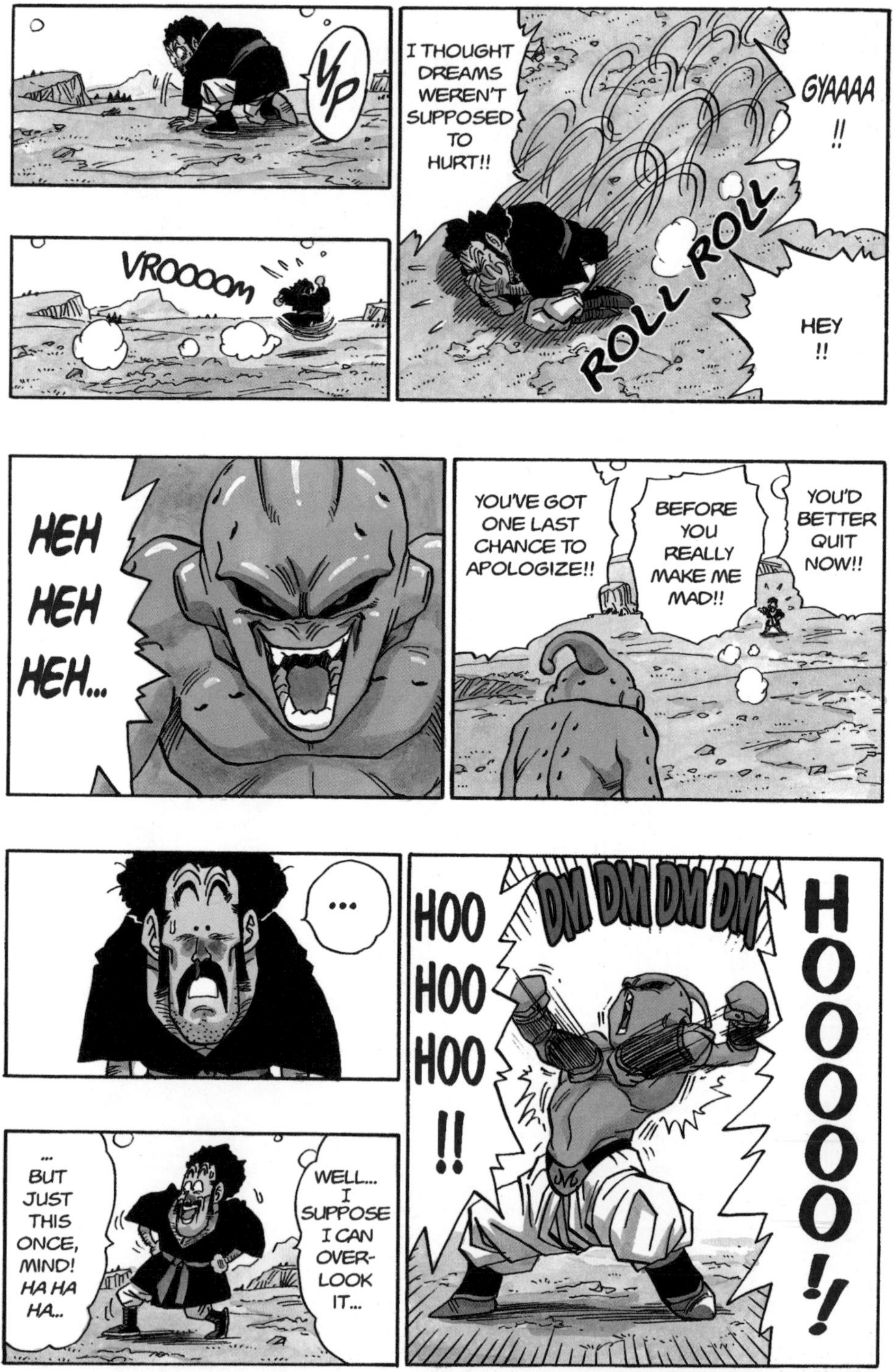
GYAAAA!!
I THOUGHT DREAMS WEREN'T SUPPOSED TO HURT!!
ROLL ROLL
HEY!!
YIP
VROOOOM
YOU'D BETTER QUIT NOW!!
BEFORE YOU REALLY MAKE ME MAD!!
YOU'VE GOT ONE LAST CHANCE TO APOLOGIZE!!
HEH HEH HEH...
HOOOOOO!!
DM DM DM DM
HOO HOO HOO HOO!!
...
WELL... I SUPPOSE I CAN OVER-LOOK IT...
... BUT JUST THIS ONCE, MIND! HA HA HA...

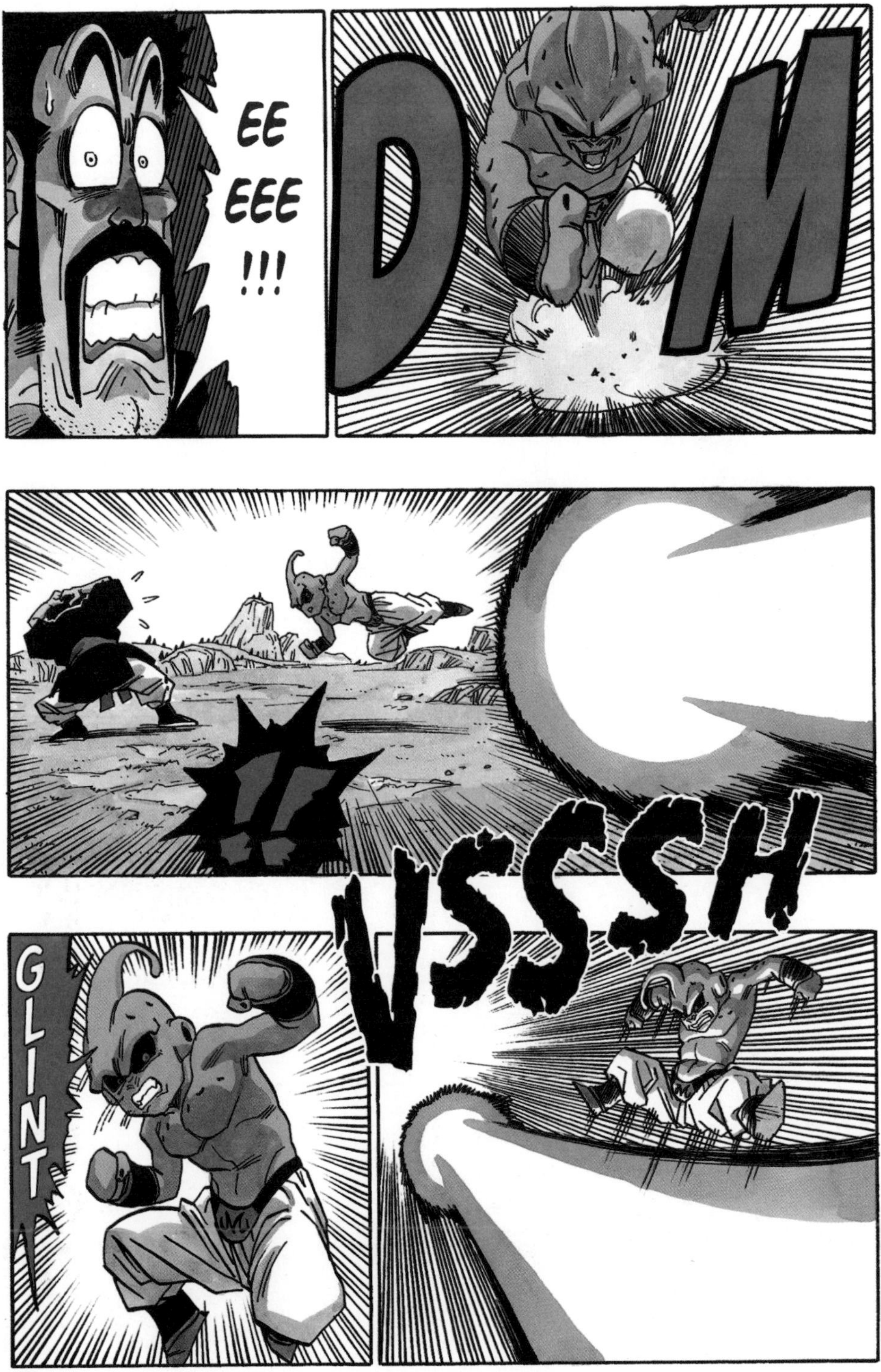
D M
EE EEE !!!
VSSSH
GLINT

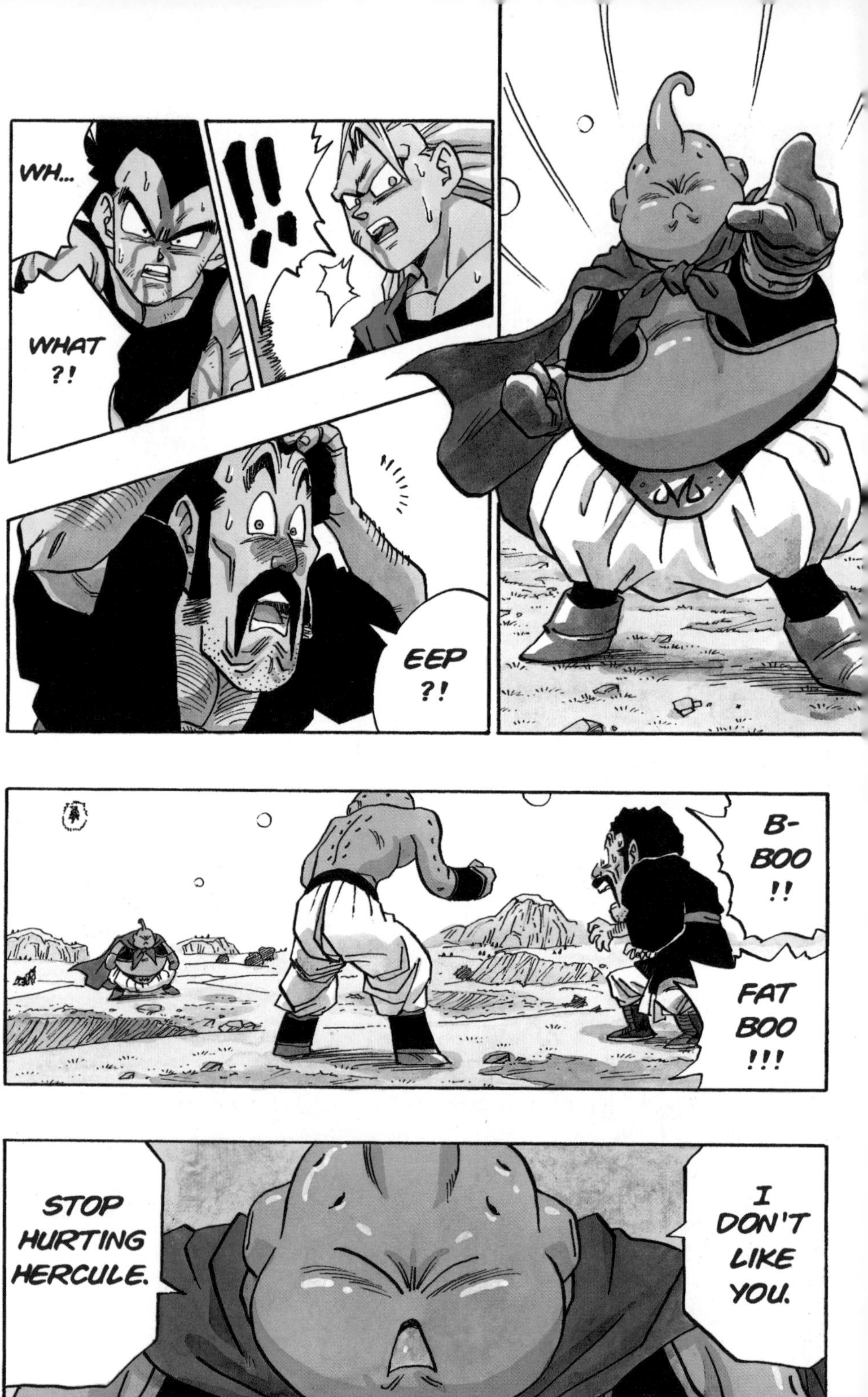
!!
WH... WHAT ?!
EEP ?!
B-BOO !!
FAT BOO !!!
I DON'T LIKE YOU.
STOP HURTING HERCULE.

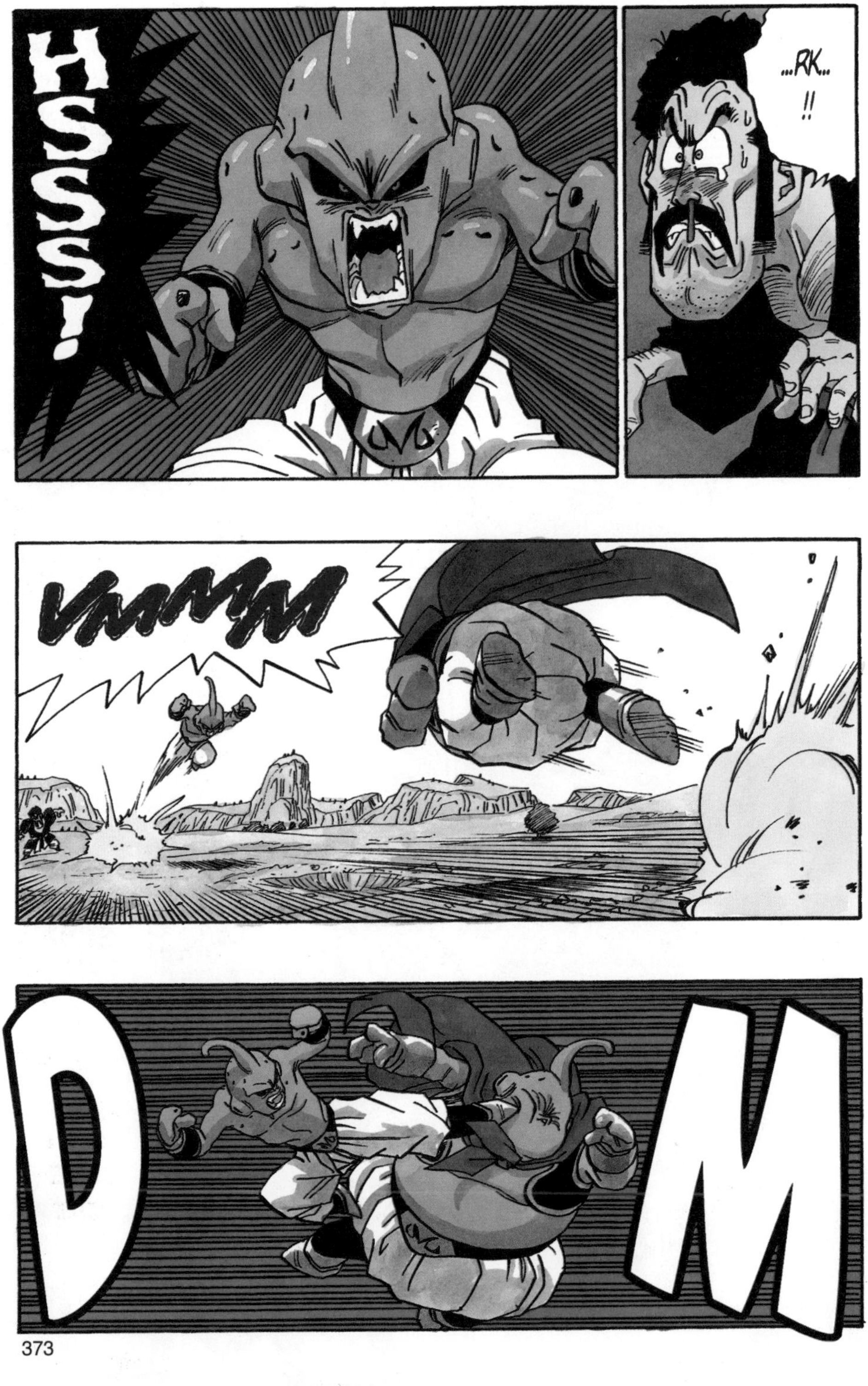
...RK...
!!
HSSS!
VMMM
D M

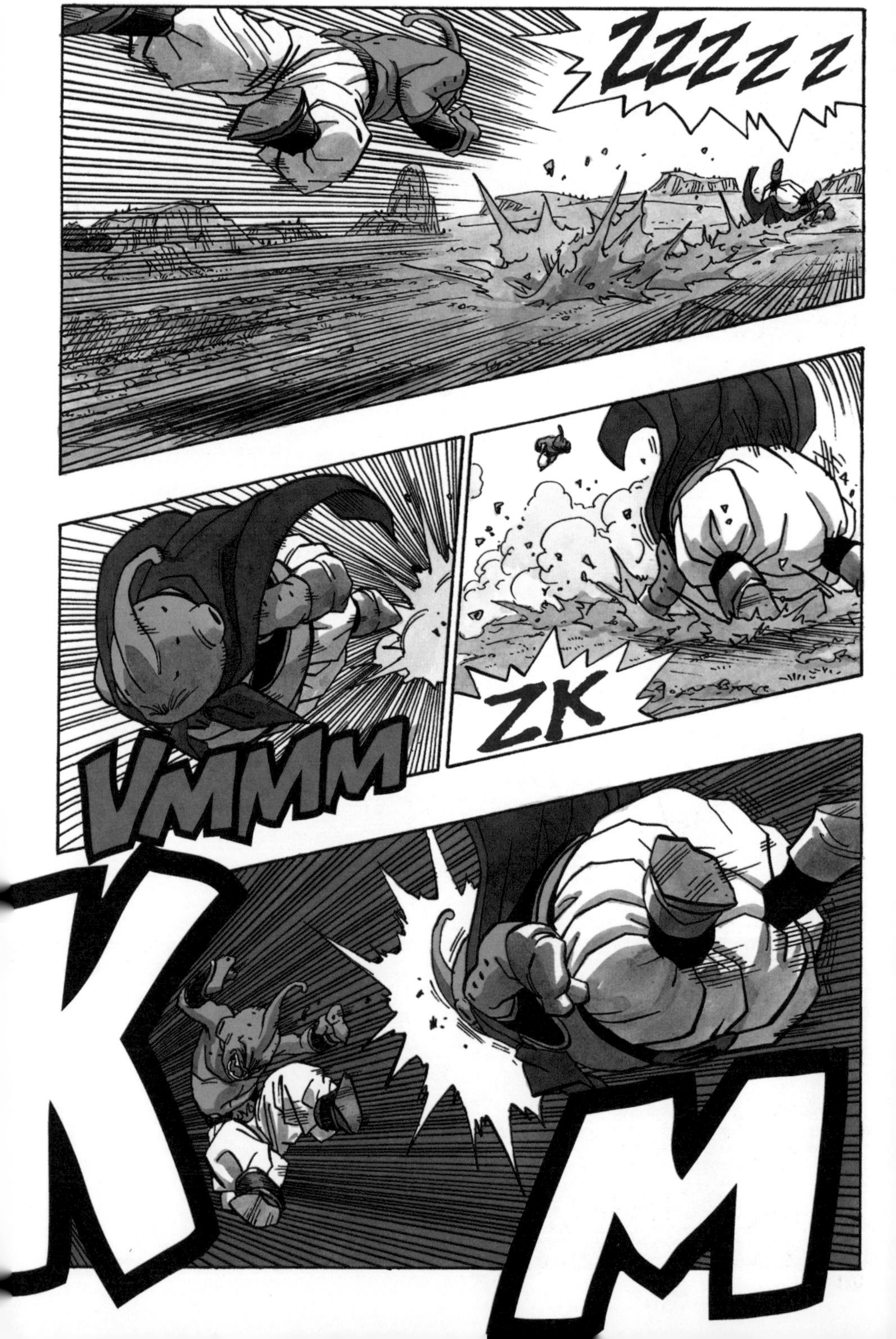
ZZZZZZ
ZK
VMMM
KM

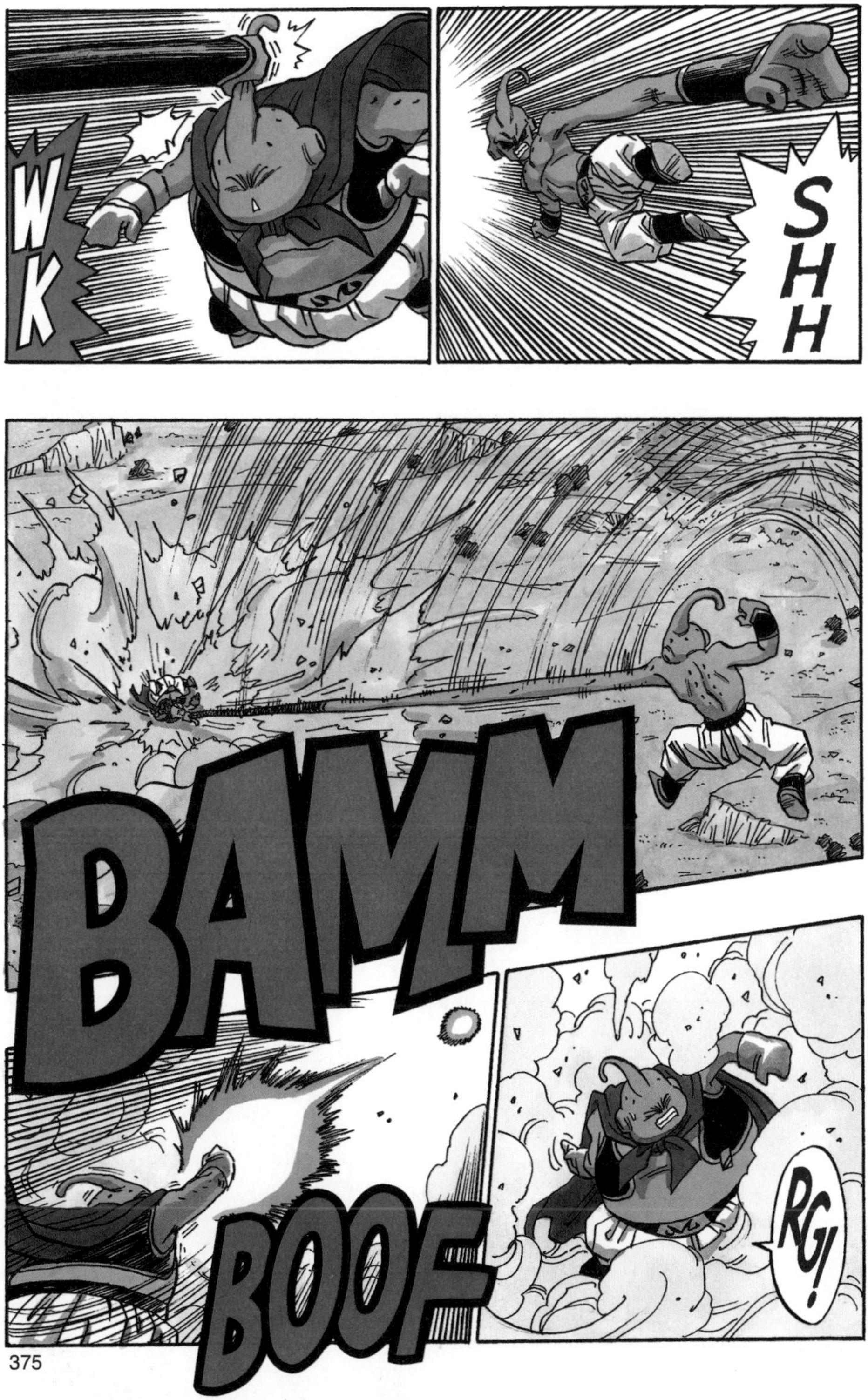
SHH
WK
BAMM
RG!
BOOF

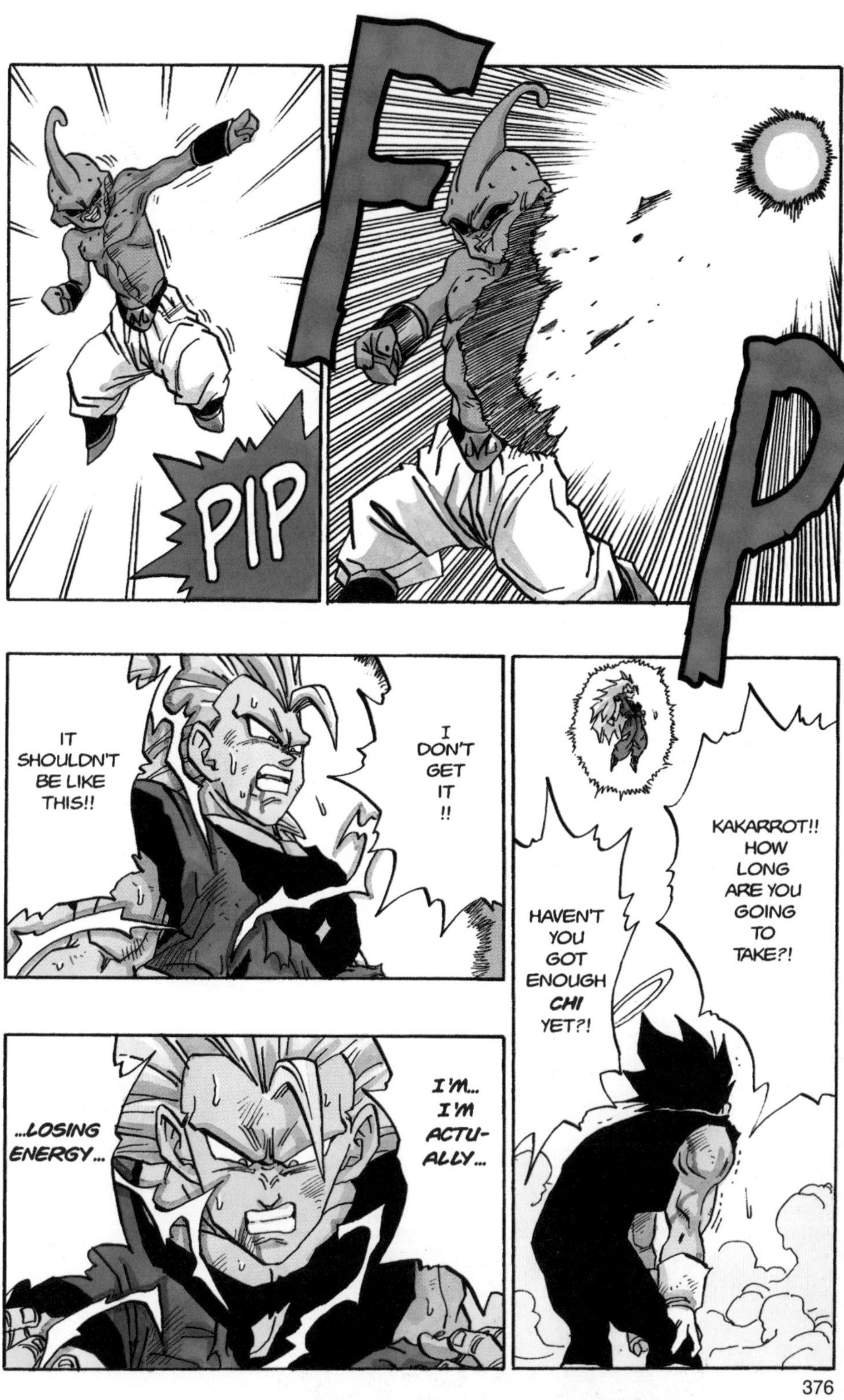
FP
PIP
KAKARROT!! HOW LONG ARE YOU GOING TO TAKE?!
HAVEN'T YOU GOT ENOUGH *CHI* YET?!
I DON'T GET IT !!
IT SHOULDN'T BE LIKE THIS!!
I'M... I'M ACTUALLY...
...LOSING ENERGY...

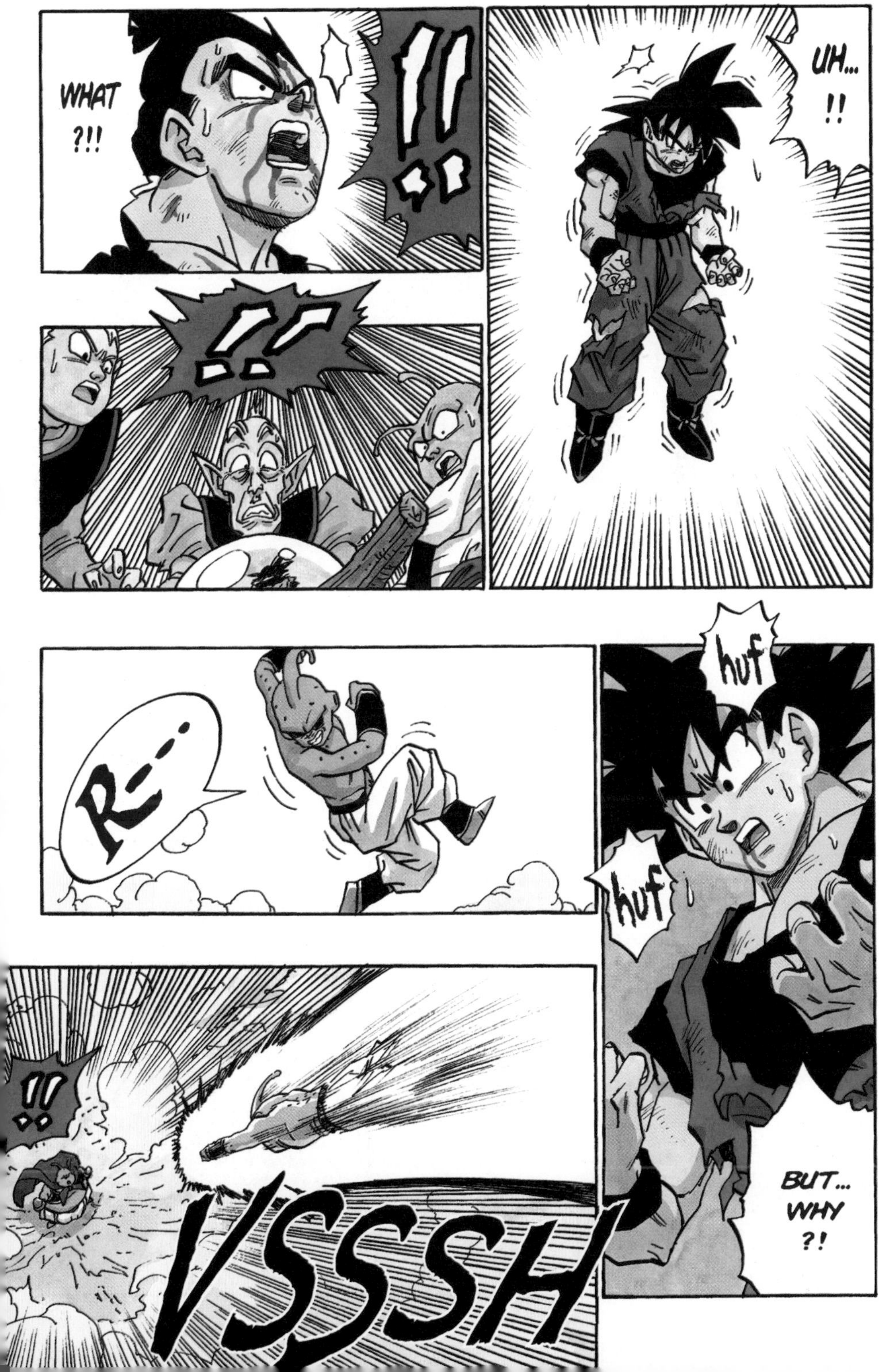
UH...
!!
WHAT
?!!
!!
!?
huf
huf
BUT...
WHY
?!
R-...
!!
VSSSH

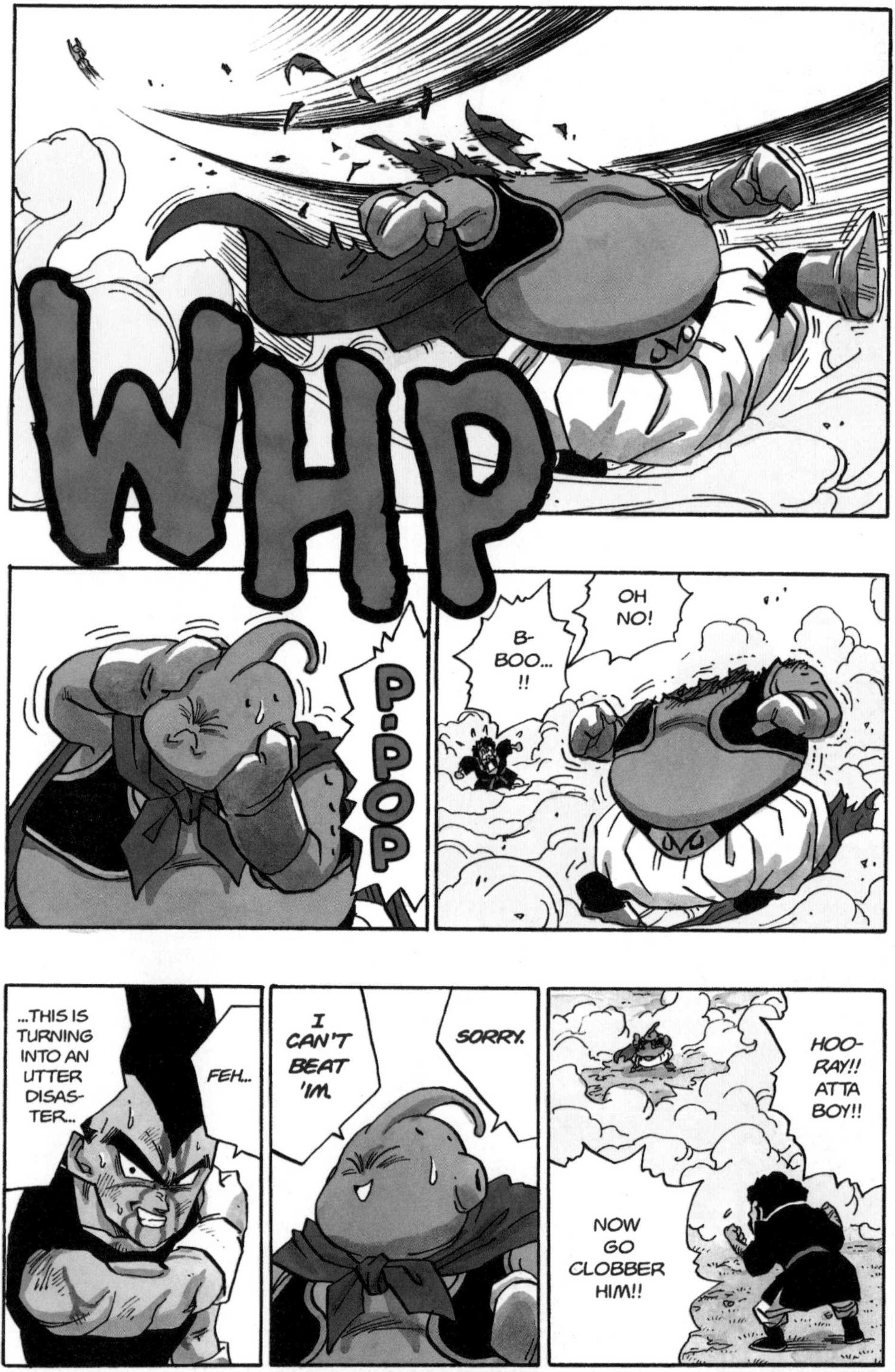
WHP
OH NO!
B-BOO...!!
P-POP
HOO-RAY!! ATTA BOY!!
NOW GO CLOBBER HIM!!
SORRY.
I CAN'T BEAT 'IM.
FEH...
...THIS IS TURNING INTO AN UTTER DISASTER...

DRAGON BALL ドラゴンボール

DBZ:319 • Vegeta's Plan

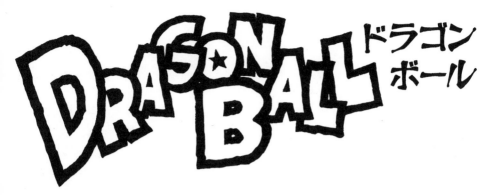

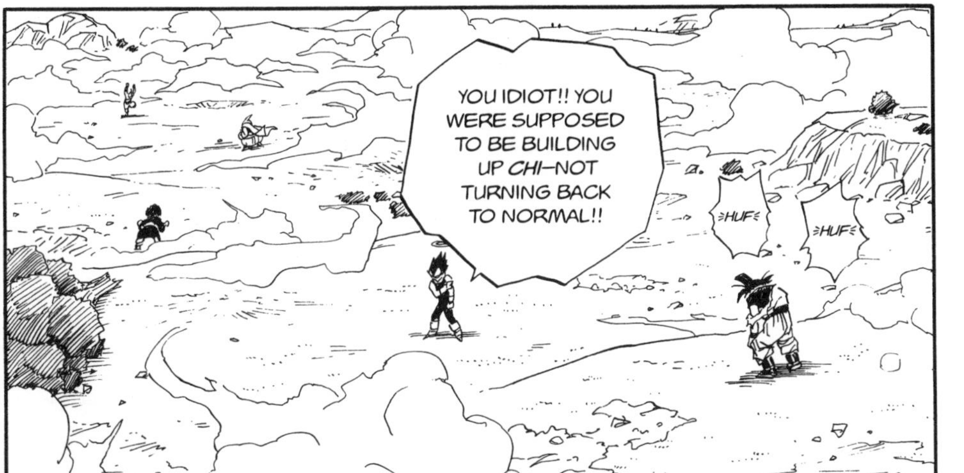
YOU IDIOT!! YOU WERE SUPPOSED TO BE BUILDING UP *CHI*—NOT TURNING BACK TO NORMAL!!
HUF
HUF

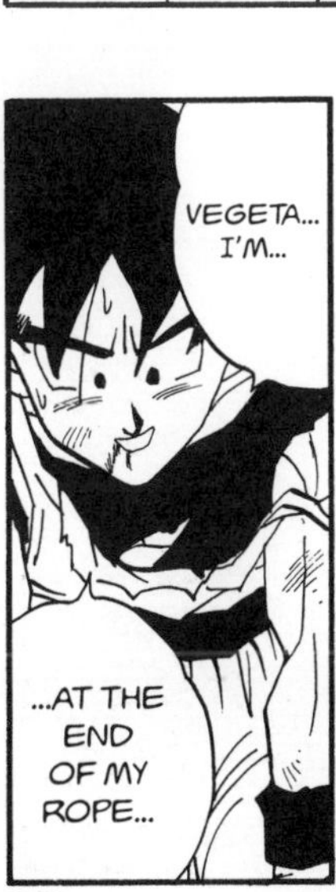
VEGETA... I'M...
...AT THE END OF MY ROPE...

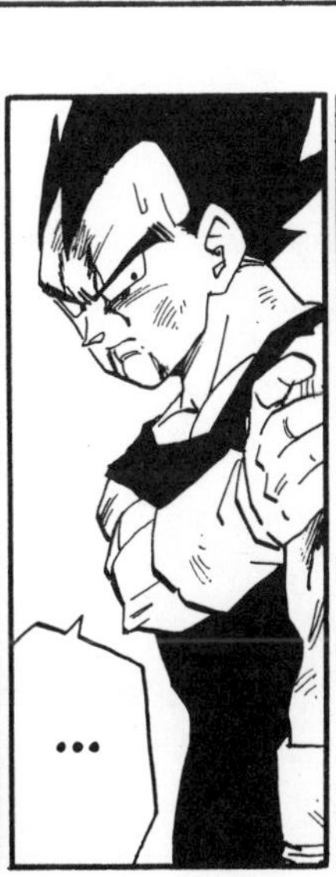
...

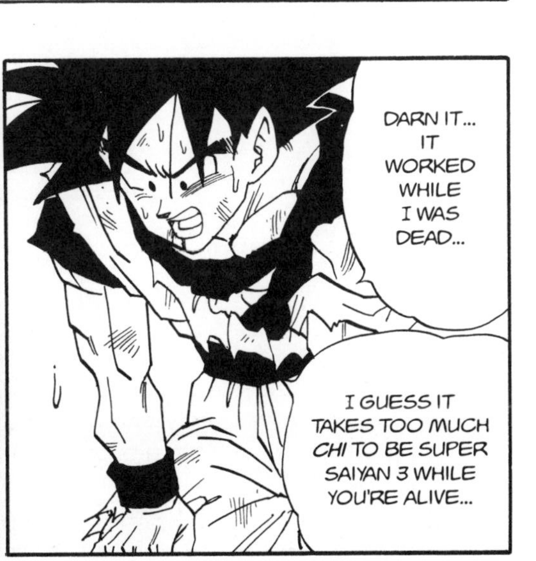
DARN IT... IT WORKED WHILE I WAS DEAD...
I GUESS IT TAKES TOO MUCH *CHI* TO BE SUPER SAIYAN 3 WHILE YOU'RE ALIVE...

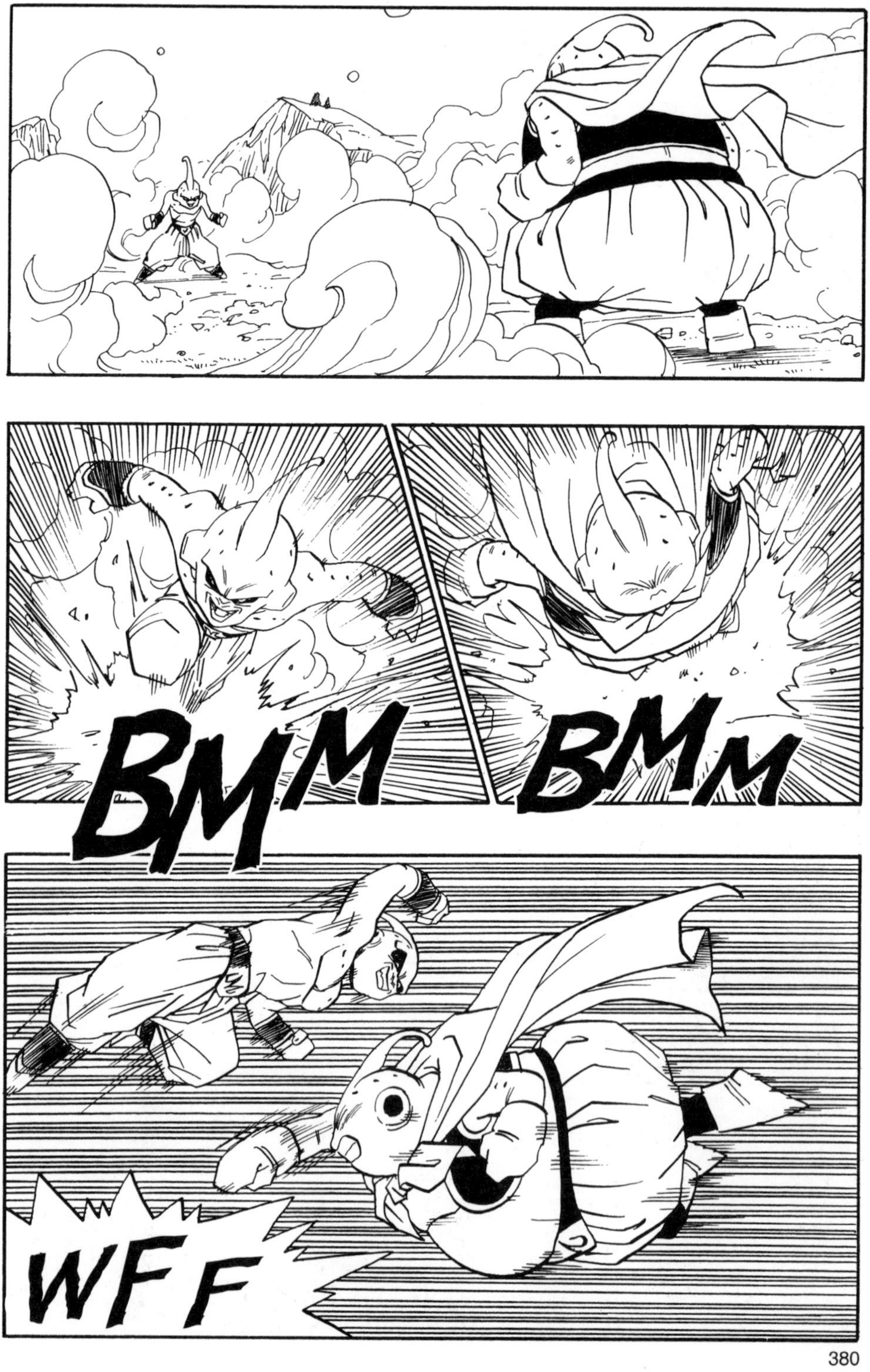
BMM
BMM
WFF

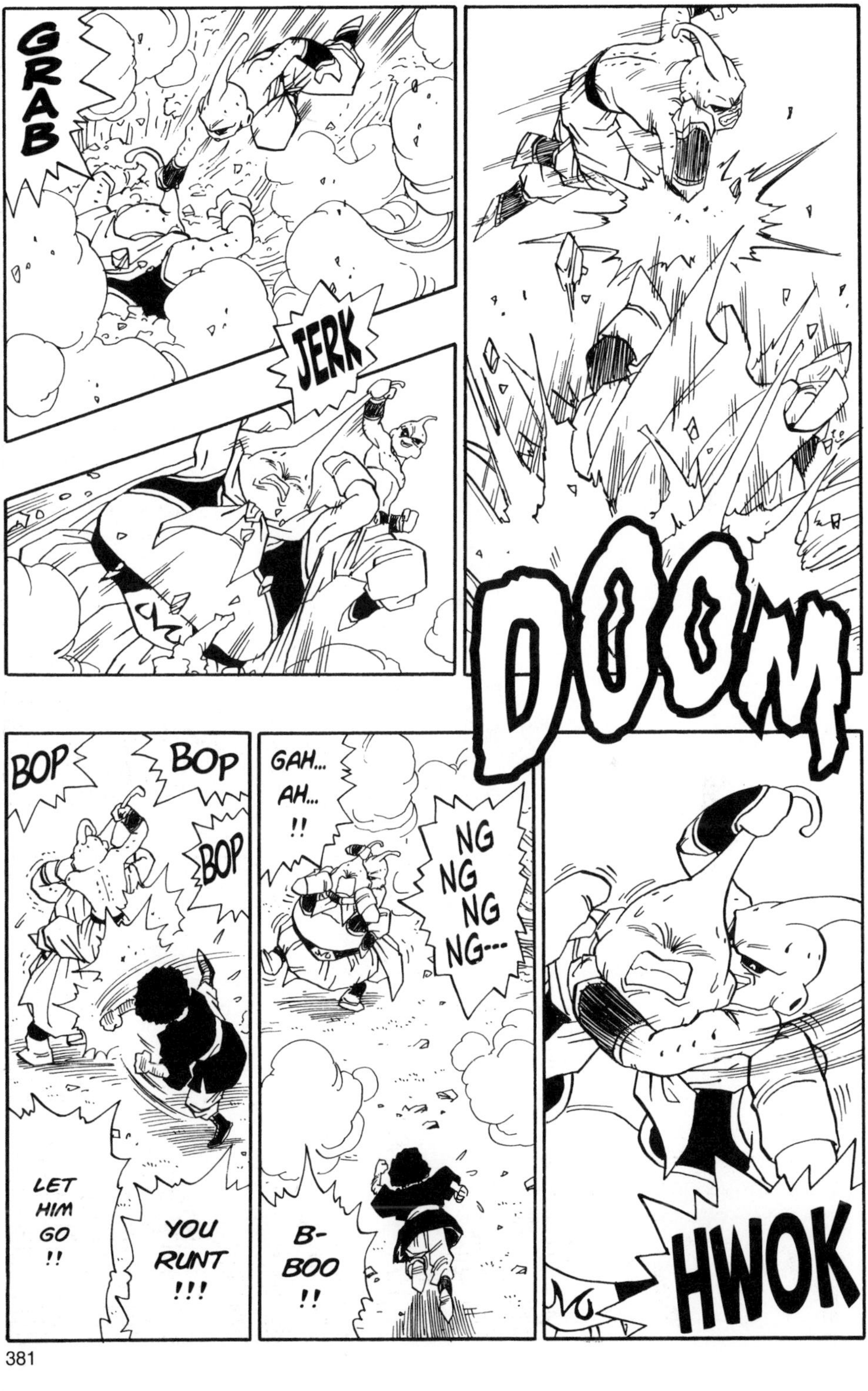
DOOM
GRAB
JERK
HWOK
GAH... AH... !!
NG NG NG NG...
B- BOO !!
BOP
BOP
BOP
LET HIM GO !!
YOU RUNT !!!

FWAP
!!
EE-YOW !!
ERP?!
ZLOOP
WAM
CHOCOLATE !!
BZZZ
BOING
!!

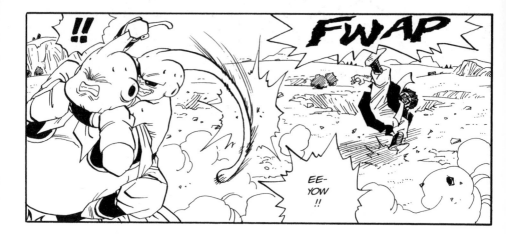

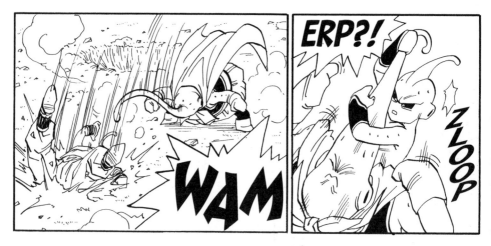

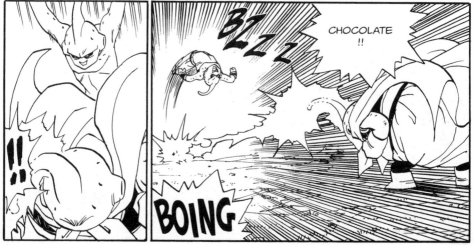

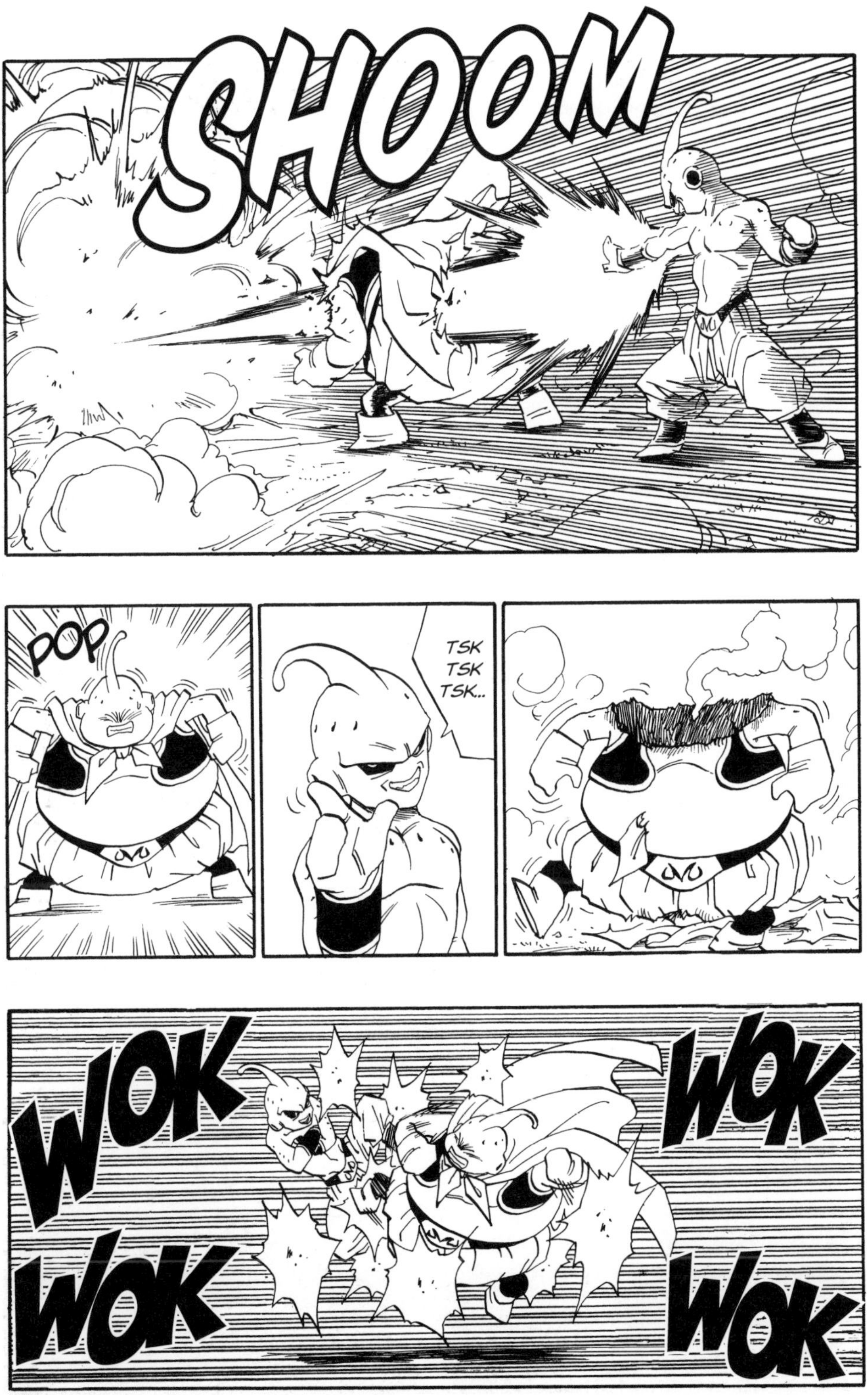
SHOOM
TSK TSK TSK...
POP
WOK
WOK
WOK
WOK

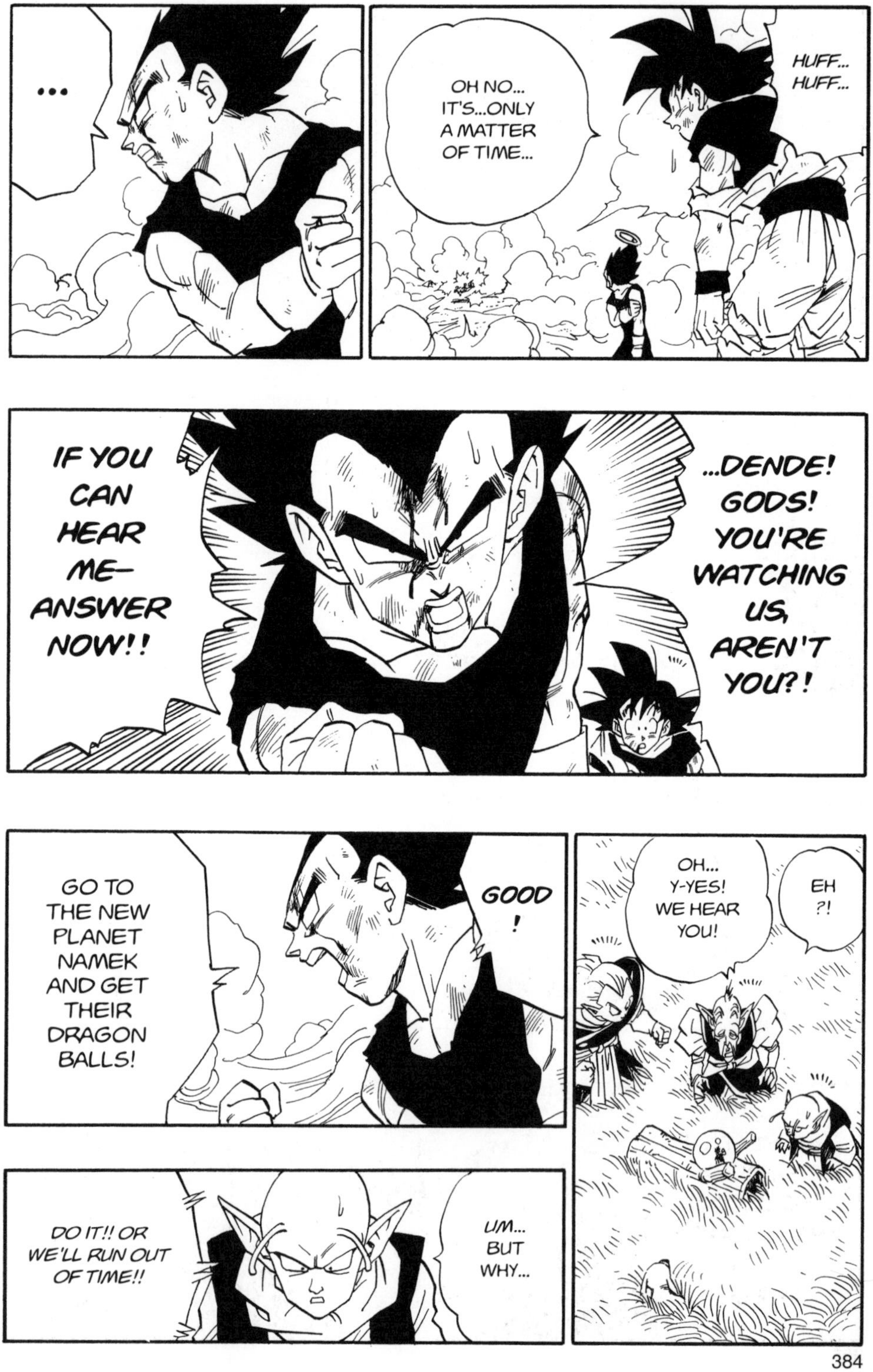
HUFF... HUFF...
OH NO... IT'S...ONLY A MATTER OF TIME...
...
...DENDE! GODS! YOU'RE WATCHING US, AREN'T YOU?!
IF YOU CAN HEAR ME— ANSWER NOW!!
EH ?!
OH... Y-YES! WE HEAR YOU!
GOOD!
GO TO THE NEW PLANET NAMEK AND GET THEIR DRAGON BALLS!
UM... BUT WHY...
DO IT!! OR WE'LL RUN OUT OF TIME!!

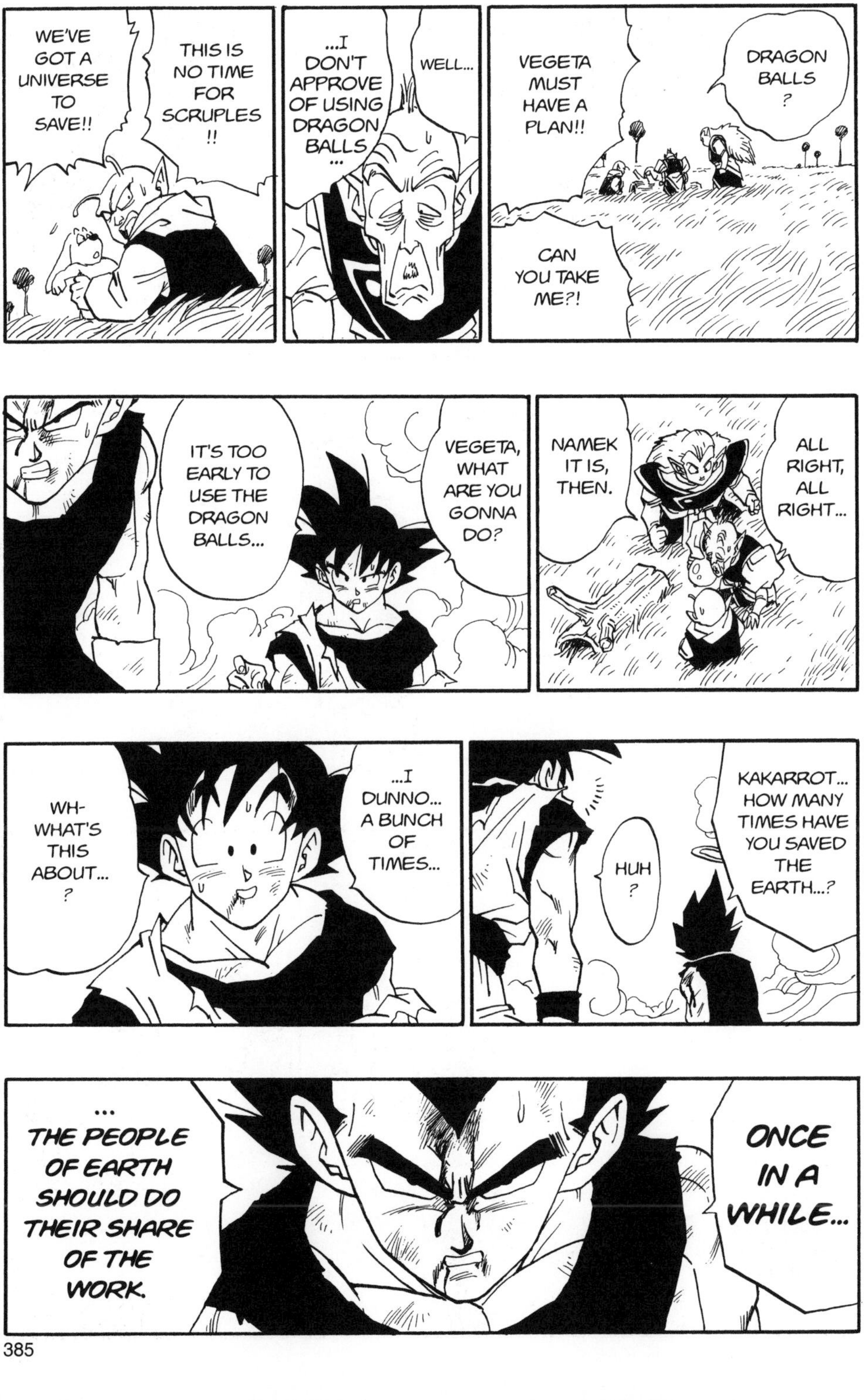
DRAGON BALLS?
VEGETA MUST HAVE A PLAN!!
CAN YOU TAKE ME?!
WELL...
...I DON'T APPROVE OF USING DRAGON BALLS...
THIS IS NO TIME FOR SCRUPLES!!
WE'VE GOT A UNIVERSE TO SAVE!!
ALL RIGHT, ALL RIGHT...
NAMEK IT IS, THEN.
VEGETA, WHAT ARE YOU GONNA DO?
IT'S TOO EARLY TO USE THE DRAGON BALLS...
KAKARROT... HOW MANY TIMES HAVE YOU SAVED THE EARTH...?
HUH?
...I DUNNO... A BUNCH OF TIMES...
WH-WHAT'S THIS ABOUT...?
ONCE IN A WHILE...
... THE PEOPLE OF EARTH SHOULD DO THEIR SHARE OF THE WORK.

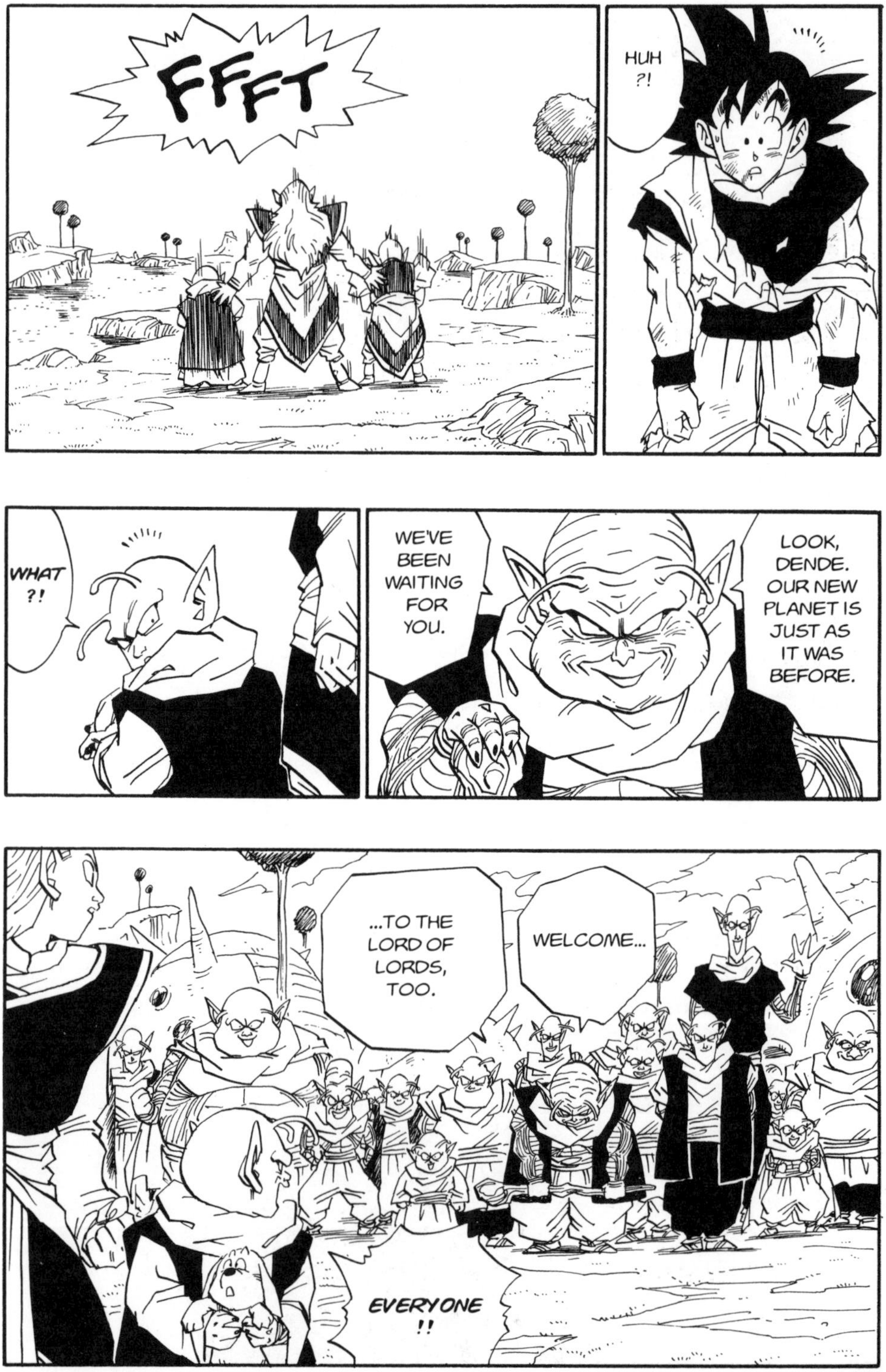
HUH ?!
FFFT
LOOK, DENDE. OUR NEW PLANET IS JUST AS IT WAS BEFORE.
WE'VE BEEN WAITING FOR YOU.
WHAT ?!
WELCOME...
...TO THE LORD OF LORDS, TOO.
EVERYONE !!

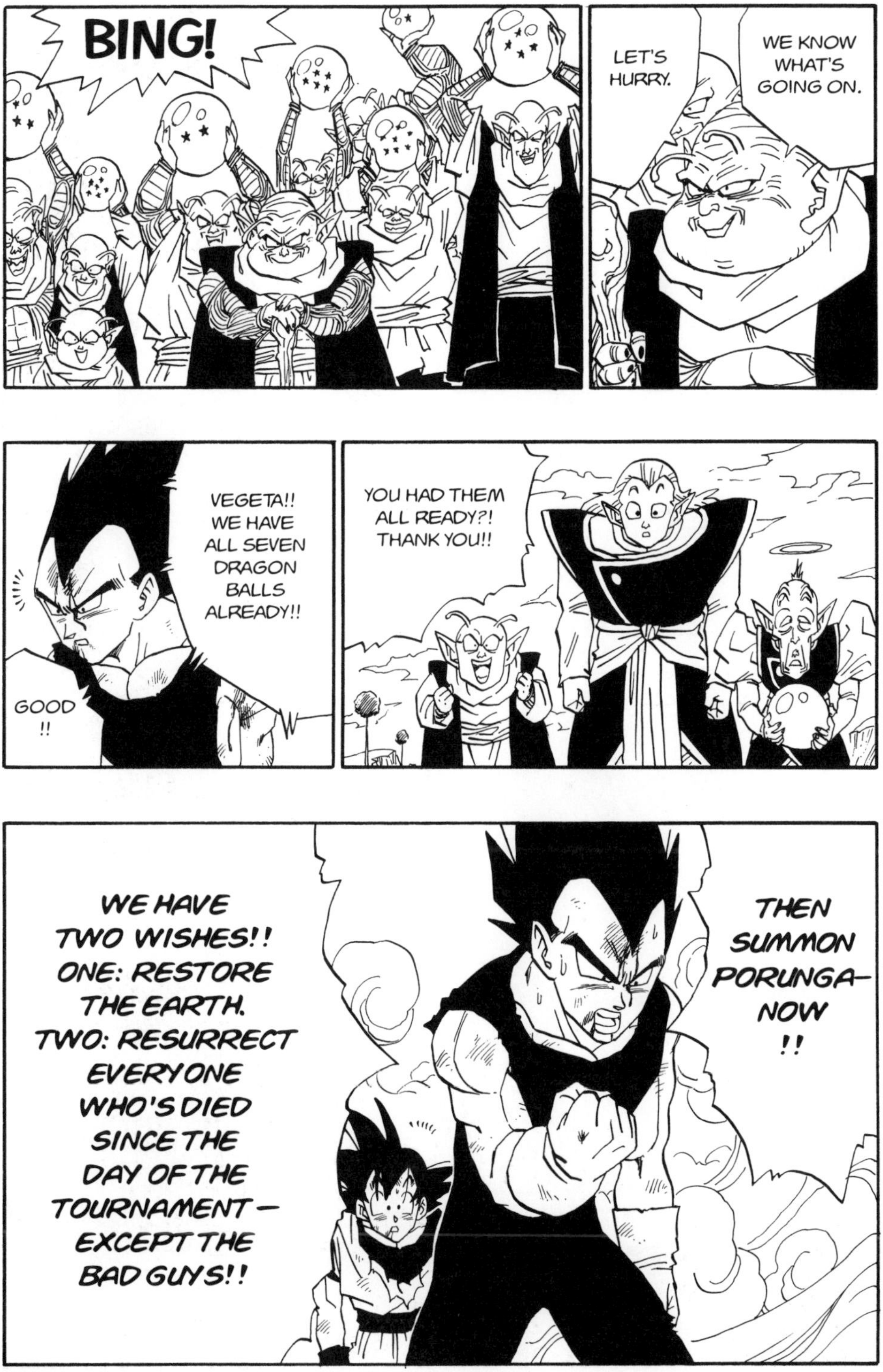
WE KNOW WHAT'S GOING ON.
LET'S HURRY.
BING!
YOU HAD THEM ALL READY?! THANK YOU!!
VEGETA!! WE HAVE ALL SEVEN DRAGON BALLS ALREADY!!
GOOD!!
THEN SUMMON PORUNGA-NOW!!
WE HAVE TWO WISHES!! ONE: RESTORE THE EARTH. TWO: RESURRECT EVERYONE WHO'S DIED SINCE THE DAY OF THE TOURNAMENT—EXCEPT THE BAD GUYS!!

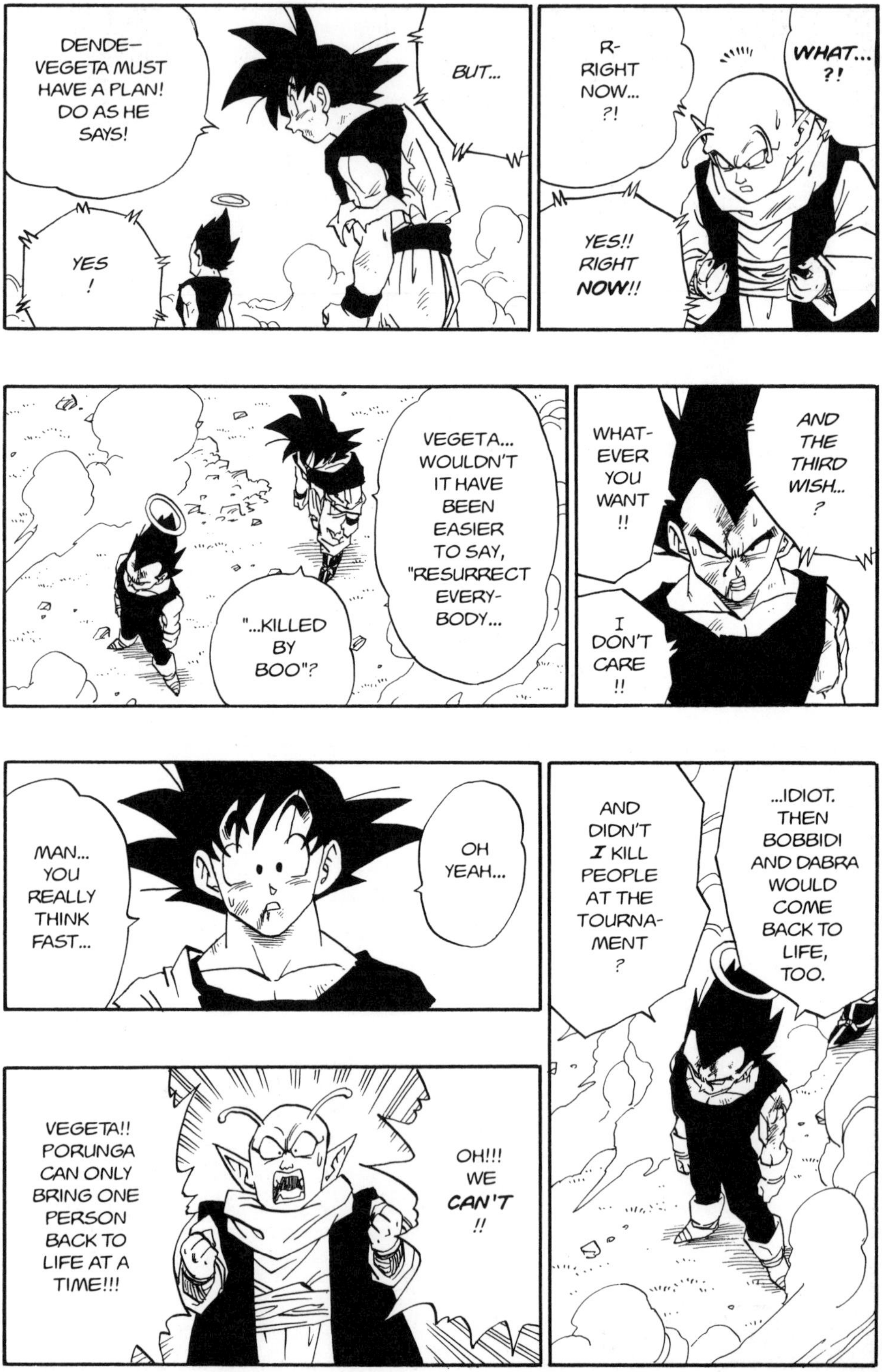
WHAT... ?!
R-RIGHT NOW... ?!
YES!! RIGHT NOW!!
BUT...
DENDE— VEGETA MUST HAVE A PLAN! DO AS HE SAYS!
YES!
AND THE THIRD WISH... ?
WHAT-EVER YOU WANT!!
I DON'T CARE!!
VEGETA... WOULDN'T IT HAVE BEEN EASIER TO SAY, "RESURRECT EVERY-BODY...
"...KILLED BY BOO"?
...IDIOT. THEN BOBBIDI AND DABRA WOULD COME BACK TO LIFE, TOO.
AND DIDN'T I KILL PEOPLE AT THE TOURNA-MENT ?
OH YEAH...
MAN... YOU REALLY THINK FAST...
OH!!! WE CAN'T!!
VEGETA!! PORUNGA CAN ONLY BRING ONE PERSON BACK TO LIFE AT A TIME!!!

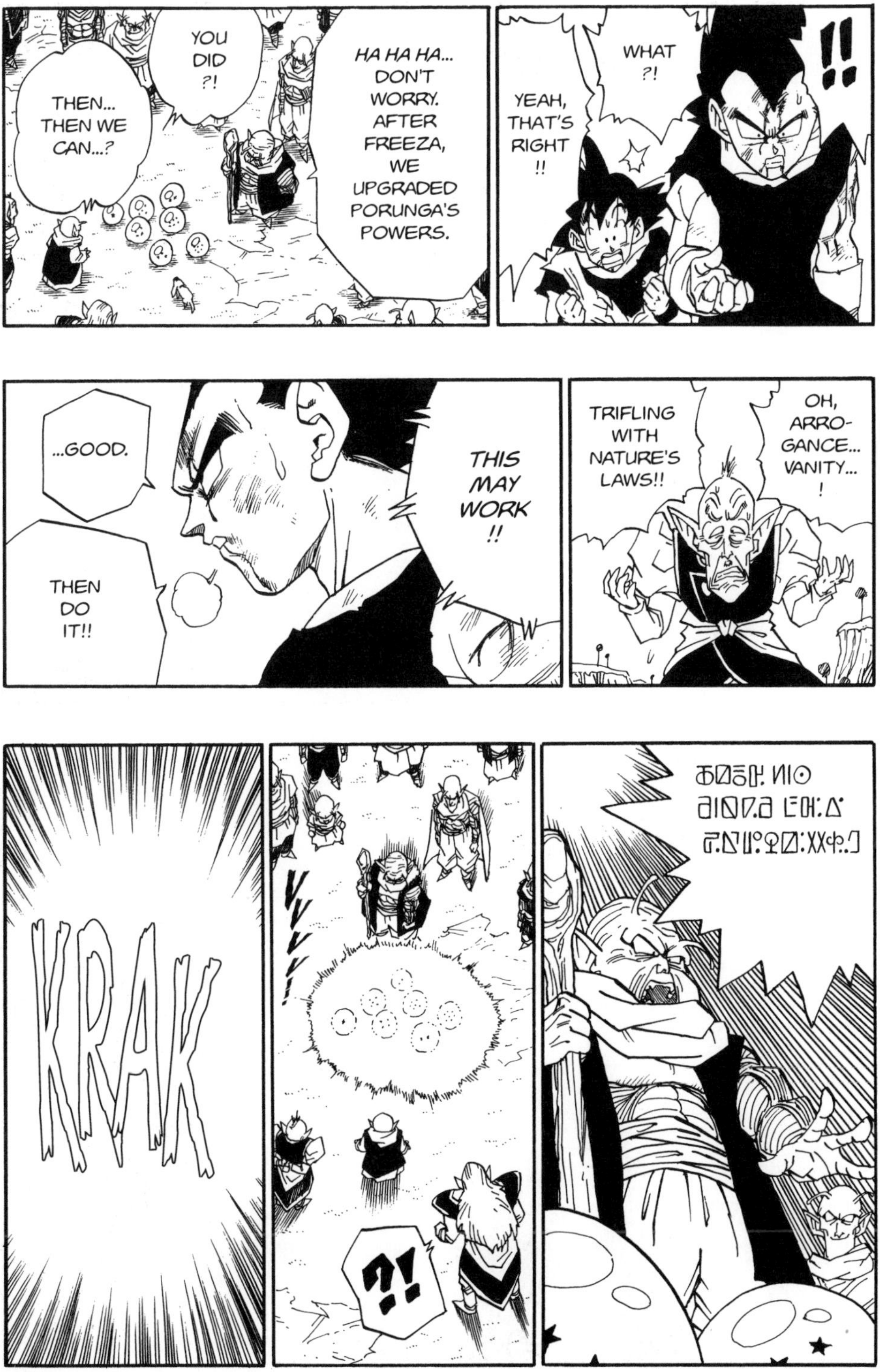
!!
WHAT ?!
YEAH, THAT'S RIGHT !!
HA HA HA... DON'T WORRY. AFTER FREEZA, WE UPGRADED PORUNGA'S POWERS.
YOU DID ?!
THEN... THEN WE CAN...?
OH, ARRO- GANCE... VANITY... !
TRIFLING WITH NATURE'S LAWS!!
THIS MAY WORK !!
...GOOD.
THEN DO IT!!
?!
KRAK

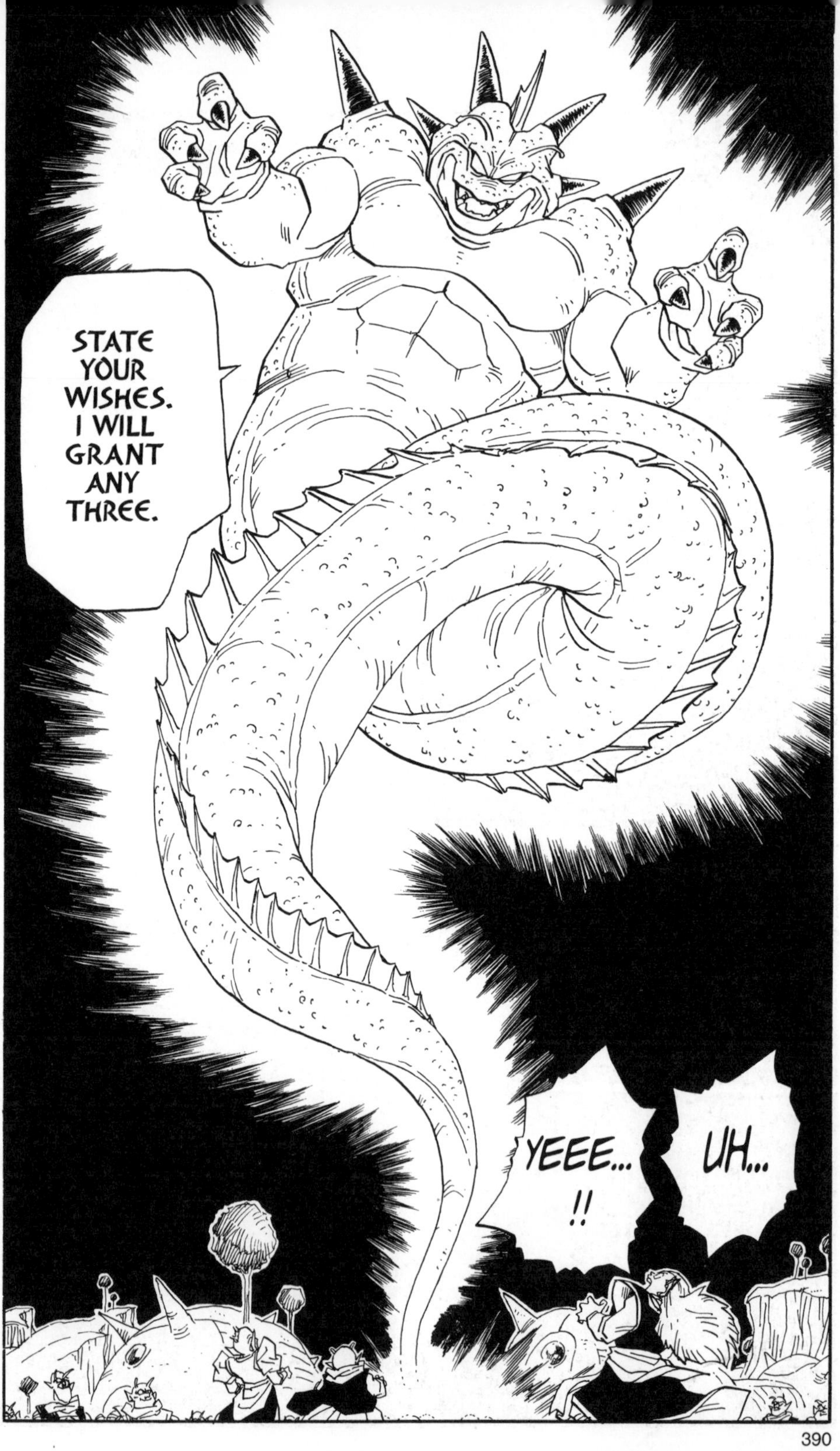
STATE YOUR WISHES. I WILL GRANT ANY THREE.
UH...
YEEE... !!

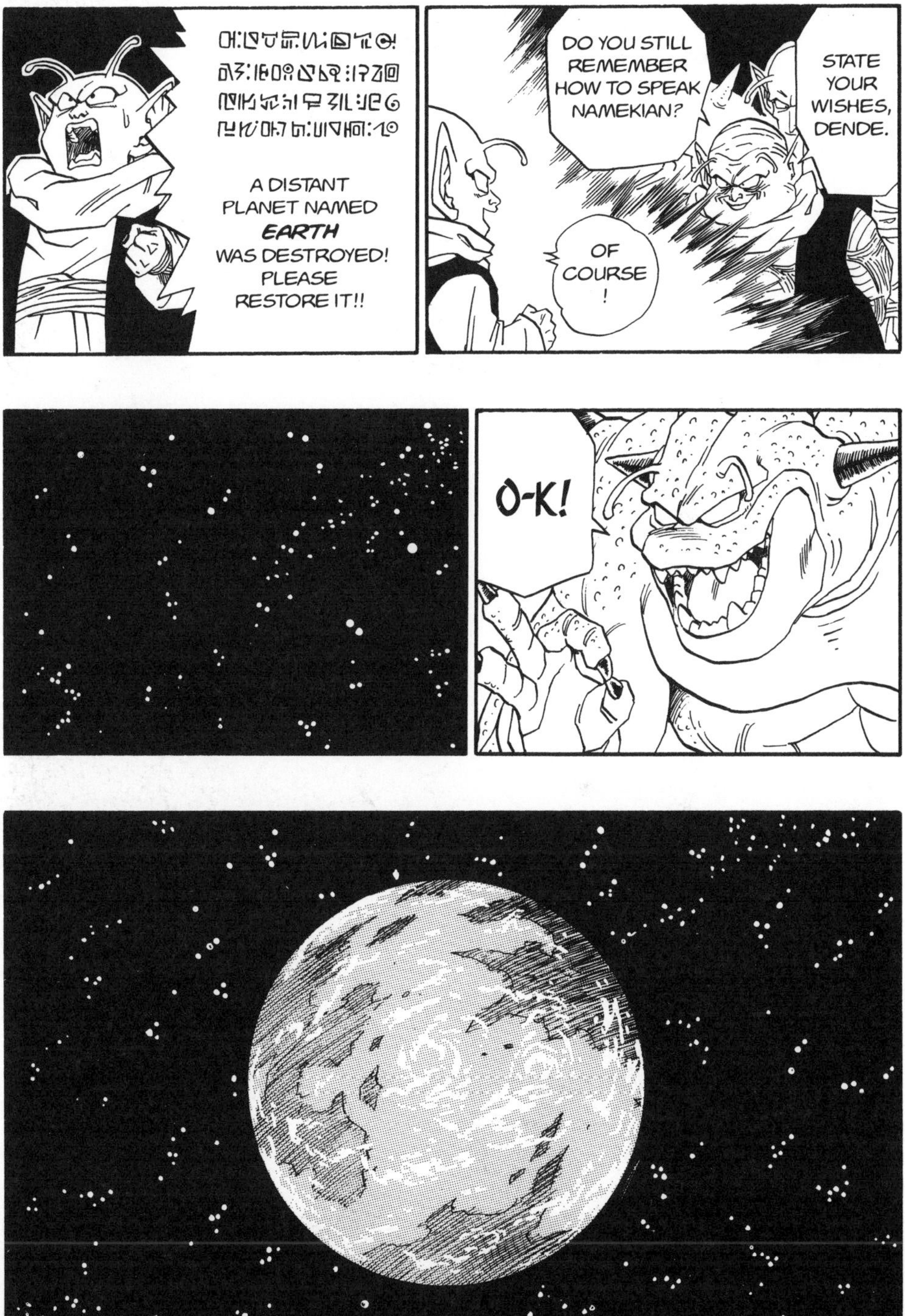
STATE YOUR WISHES, DENDE.
DO YOU STILL REMEMBER HOW TO SPEAK NAMEKIAN?
OF COURSE!
A DISTANT PLANET NAMED EARTH WAS DESTROYED! PLEASE RESTORE IT!!
O-K!

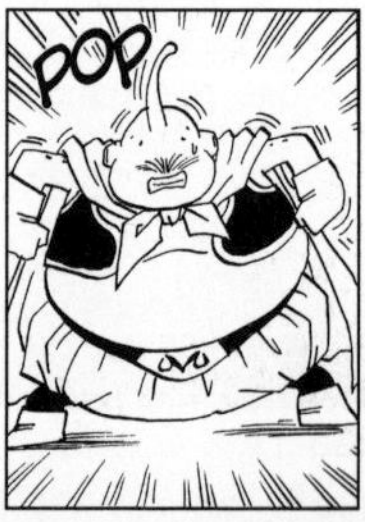
POP

DRAGON BALL ドラゴンボール

DBZ:320 • A Message to Earth

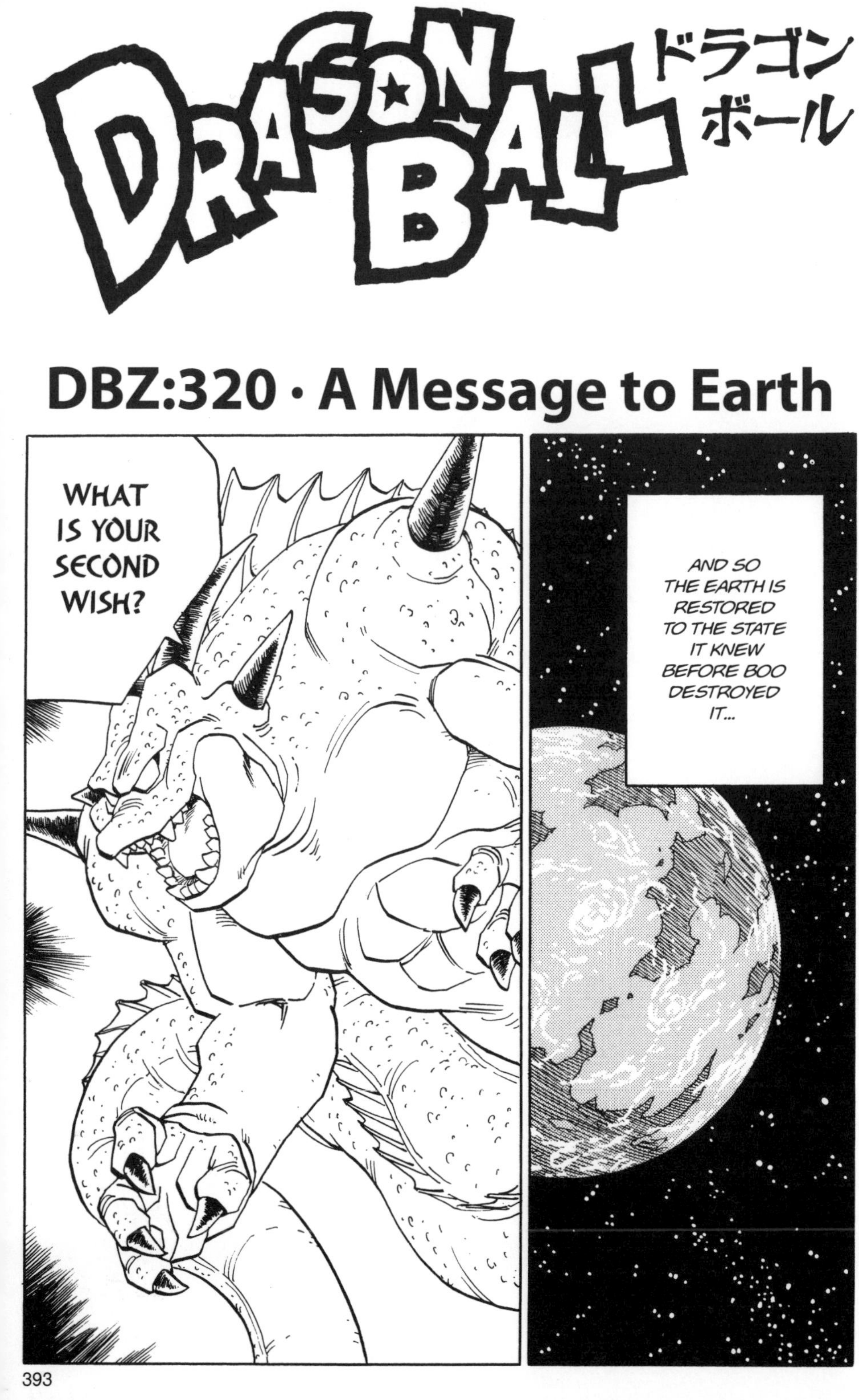
AND SO THE EARTH IS RESTORED TO THE STATE IT KNEW BEFORE BOO DESTROYED IT...
WHAT IS YOUR SECOND WISH?

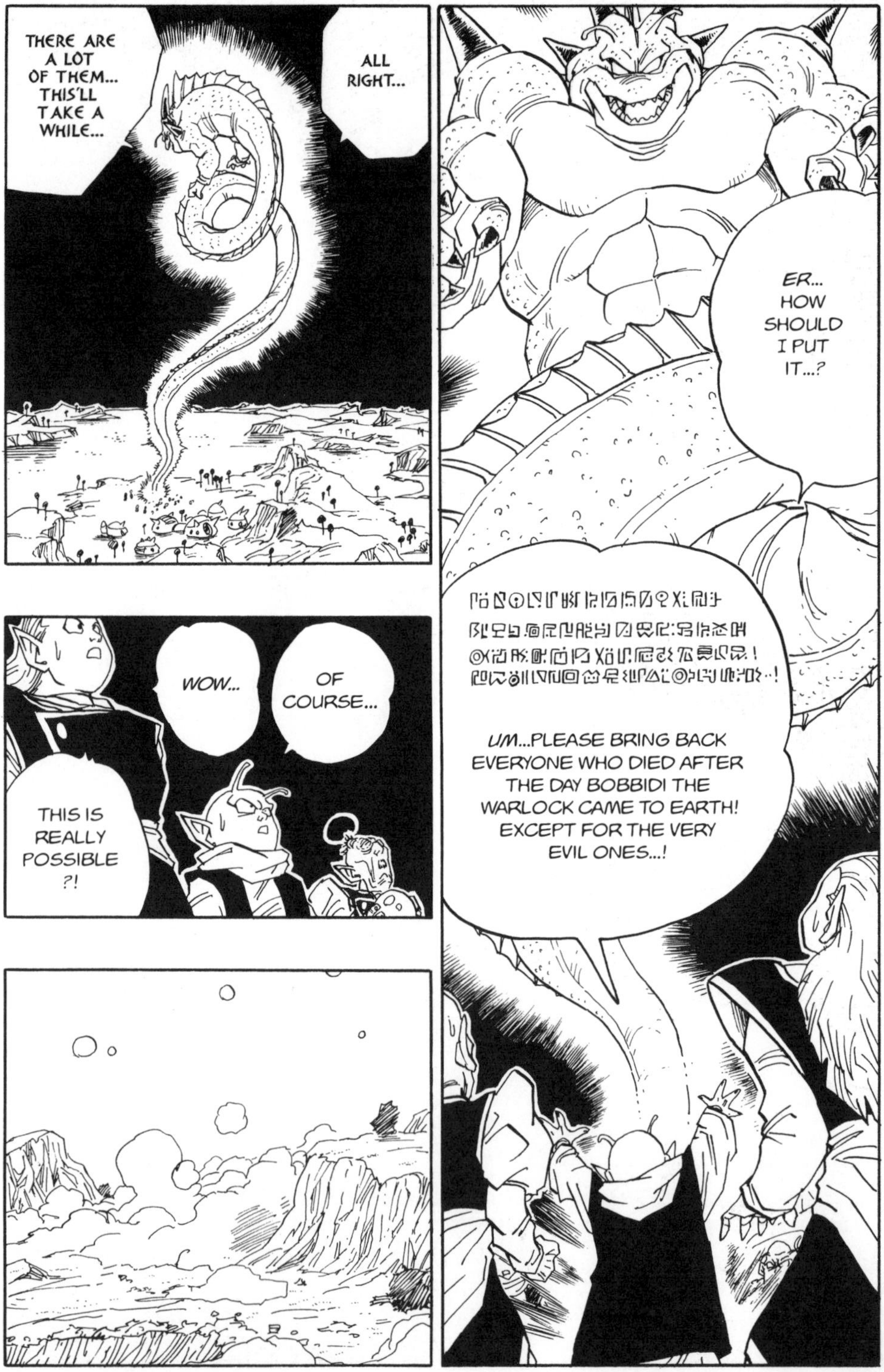
ER... HOW SHOULD I PUT IT...?
UM...PLEASE BRING BACK EVERYONE WHO DIED AFTER THE DAY BOBBIDI THE WARLOCK CAME TO EARTH! EXCEPT FOR THE VERY EVIL ONES...!
ALL RIGHT...
THERE ARE A LOT OF THEM... THIS'LL TAKE A WHILE...
OF COURSE...
WOW...
THIS IS REALLY POSSIBLE ?!

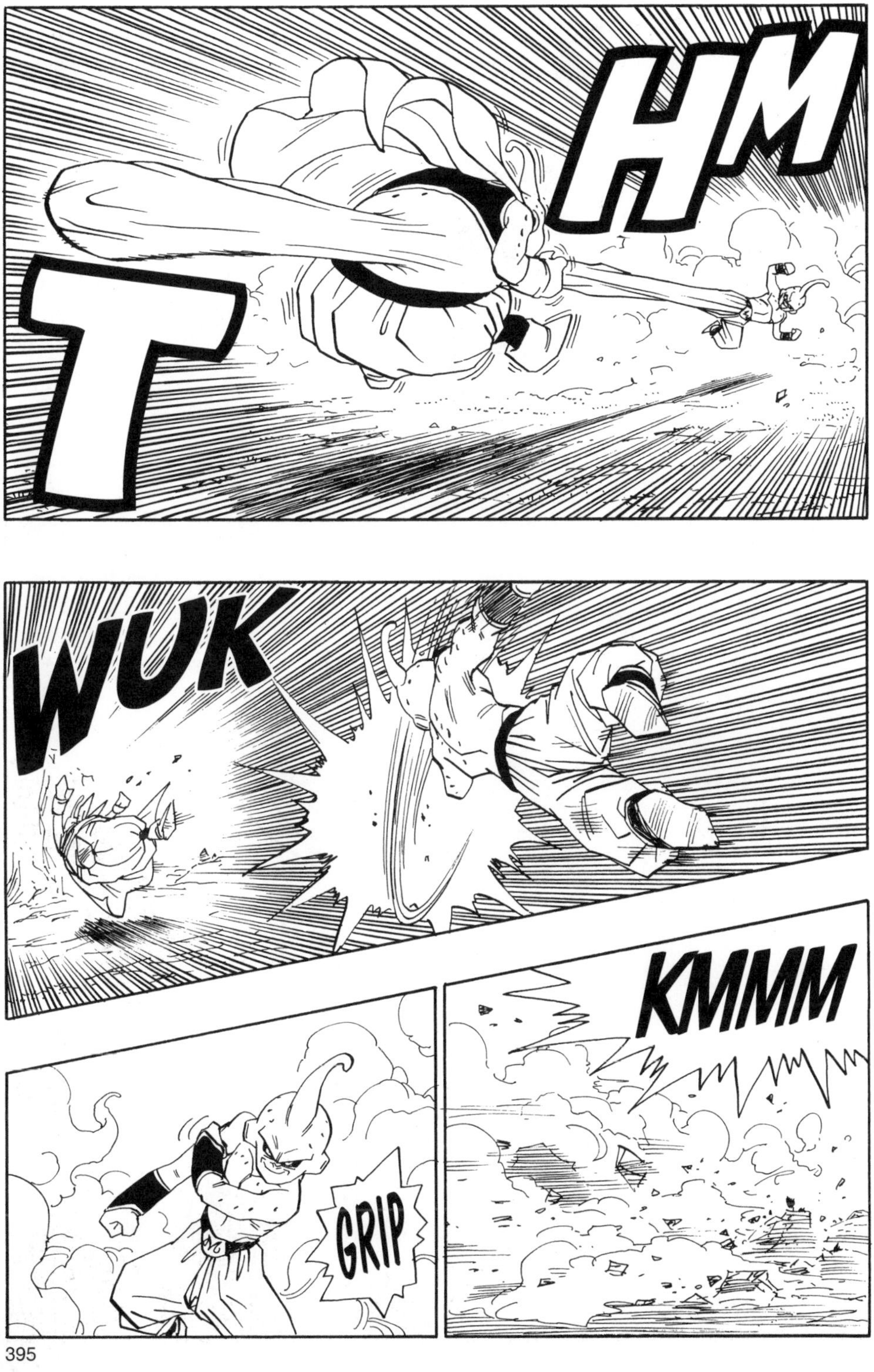
HM
T
WUK
KMMM
GRIP

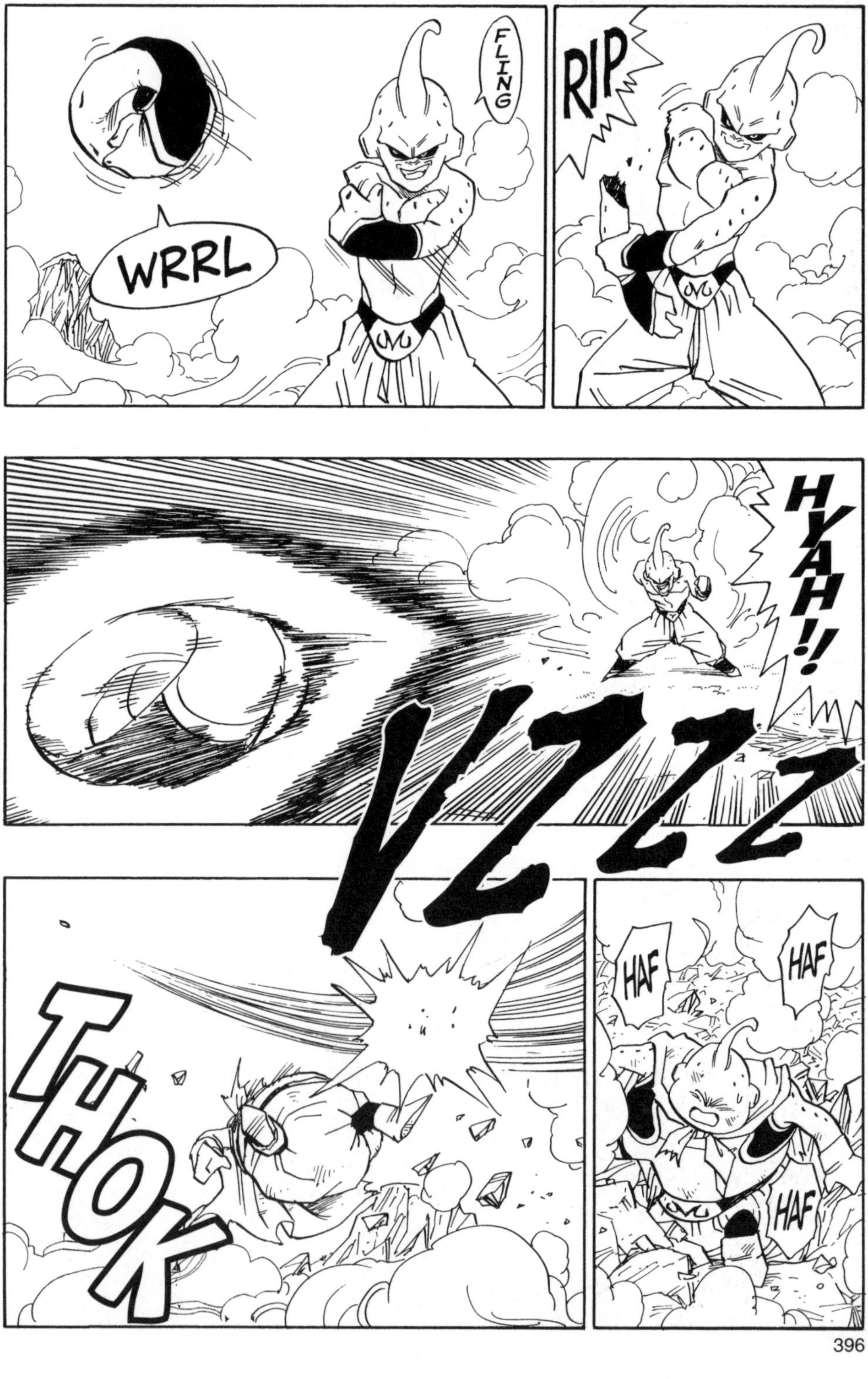
RIP
FLING
WRRL
HYAH!!
VZZZ
HAF
HAF
HAF
THOK

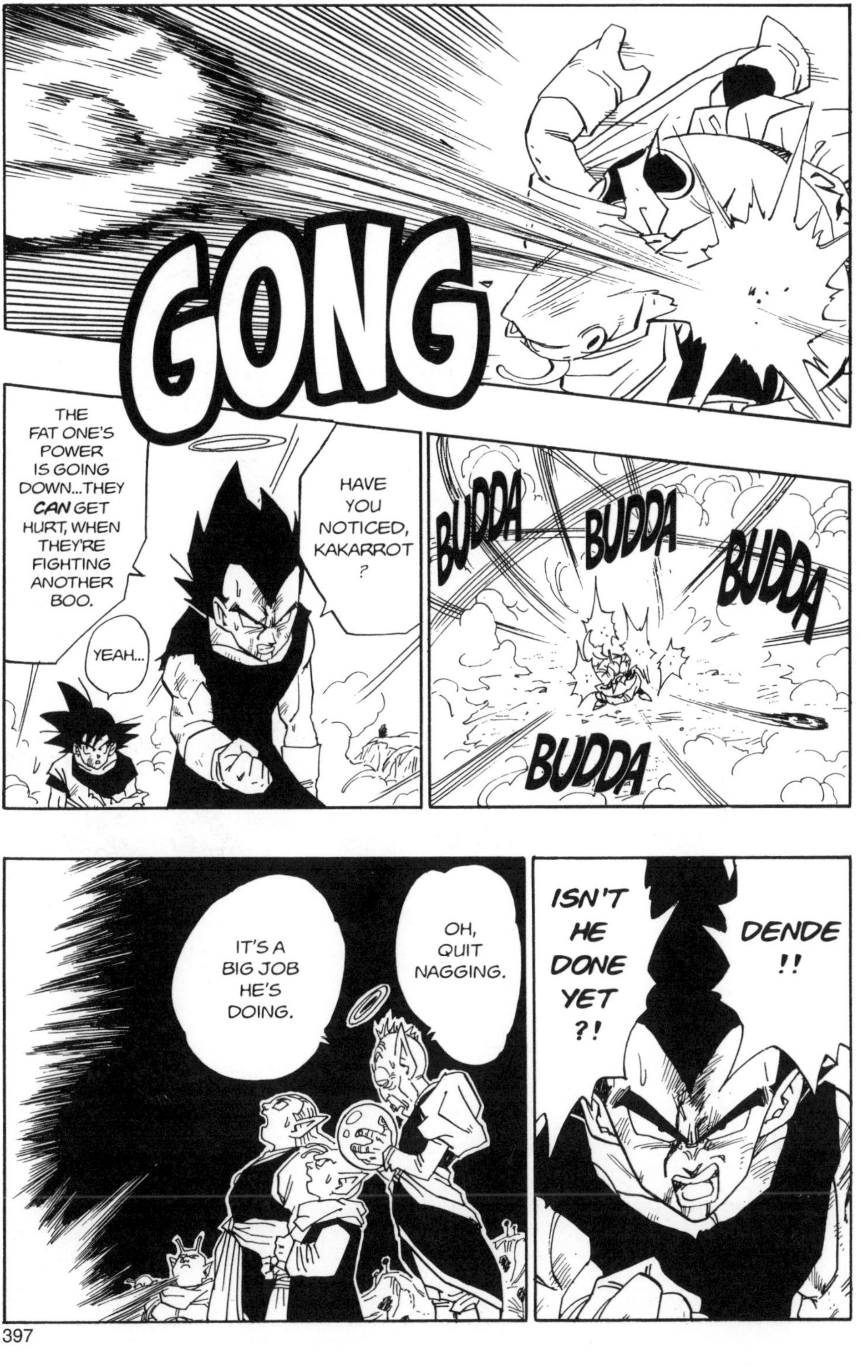
GONG
BUDDA
BUDDA
BUDDA
BUDDA
HAVE YOU NOTICED, KAKARROT?
THE FAT ONE'S POWER IS GOING DOWN...THEY *CAN* GET HURT, WHEN THEY'RE FIGHTING ANOTHER BOO.
YEAH...
DENDE!!
ISN'T HE DONE YET?!
OH, QUIT NAGGING.
IT'S A BIG JOB HE'S DOING.

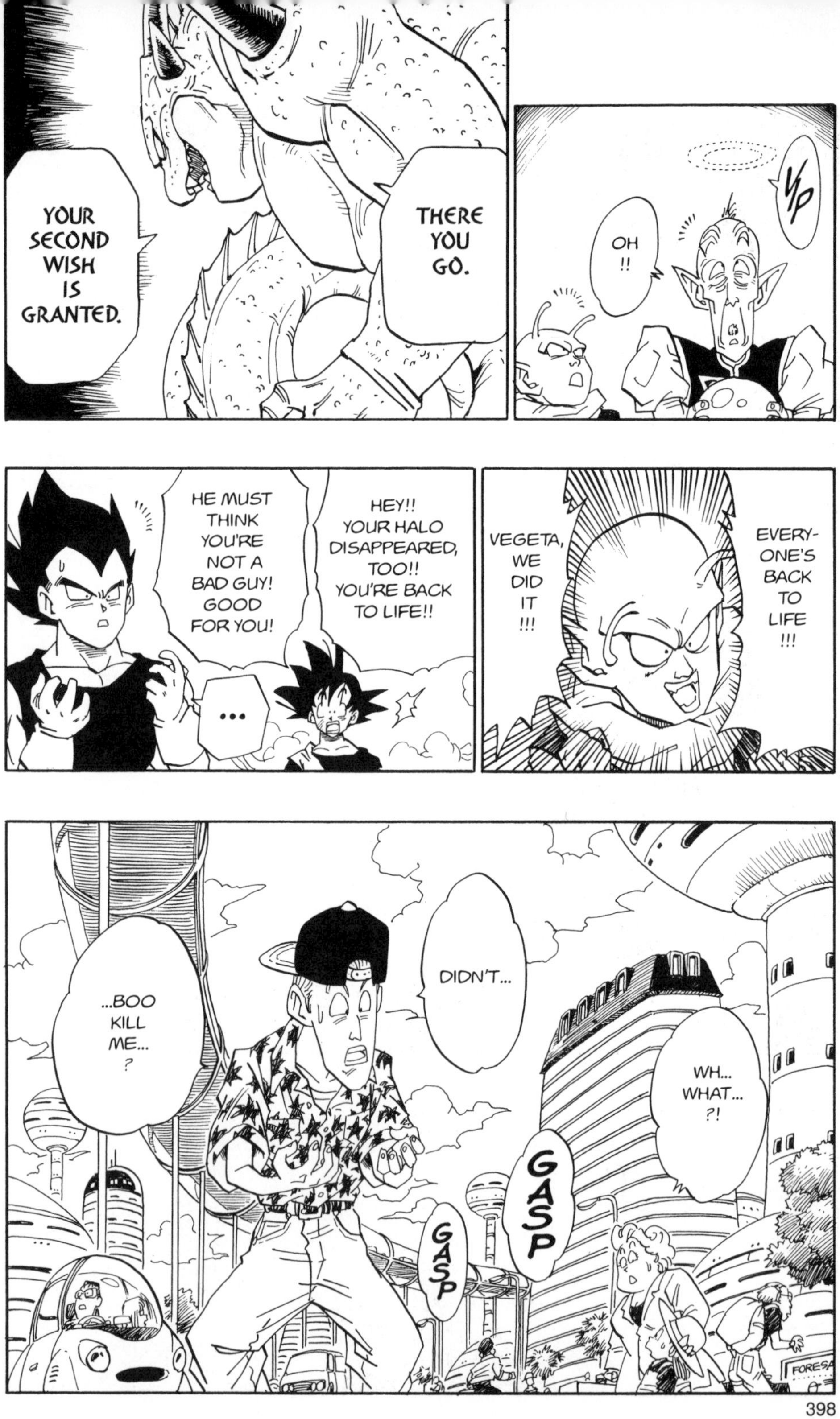
OH !!
THERE YOU GO.
YOUR SECOND WISH IS GRANTED.
EVERY-ONE'S BACK TO LIFE !!!
VEGETA, WE DID IT !!!
HEY!! YOUR HALO DISAPPEARED, TOO!! YOU'RE BACK TO LIFE!!
HE MUST THINK YOU'RE NOT A BAD GUY! GOOD FOR YOU!
...
WH... WHAT... ?!
GASP
GASP
DIDN'T...
...BOO KILL ME... ?

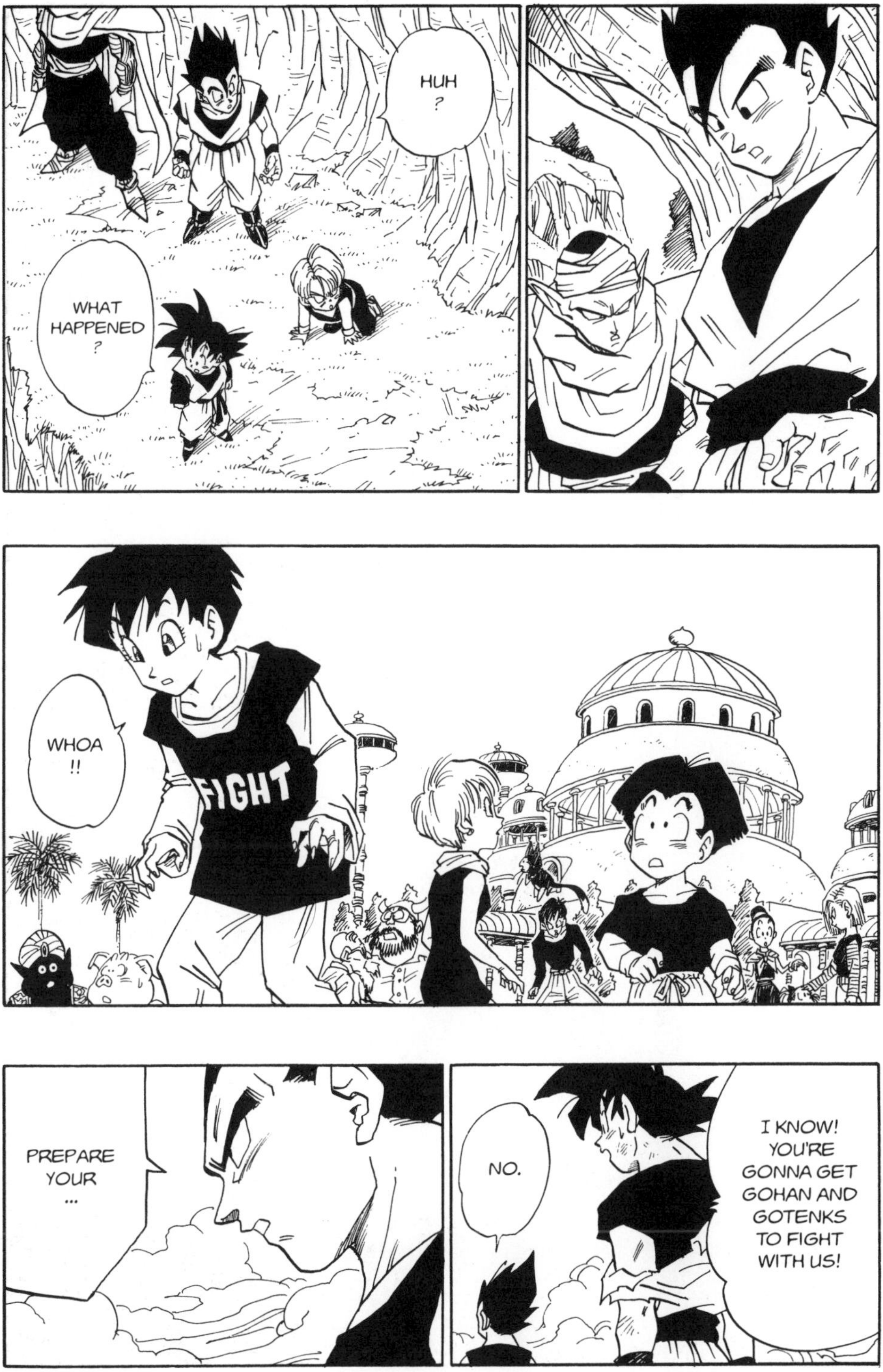
HUH ?
WHAT HAPPENED ?
WHOA !!
I KNOW! YOU'RE GONNA GET GOHAN AND GOTENKS TO FIGHT WITH US!
NO.
PREPARE YOUR ...

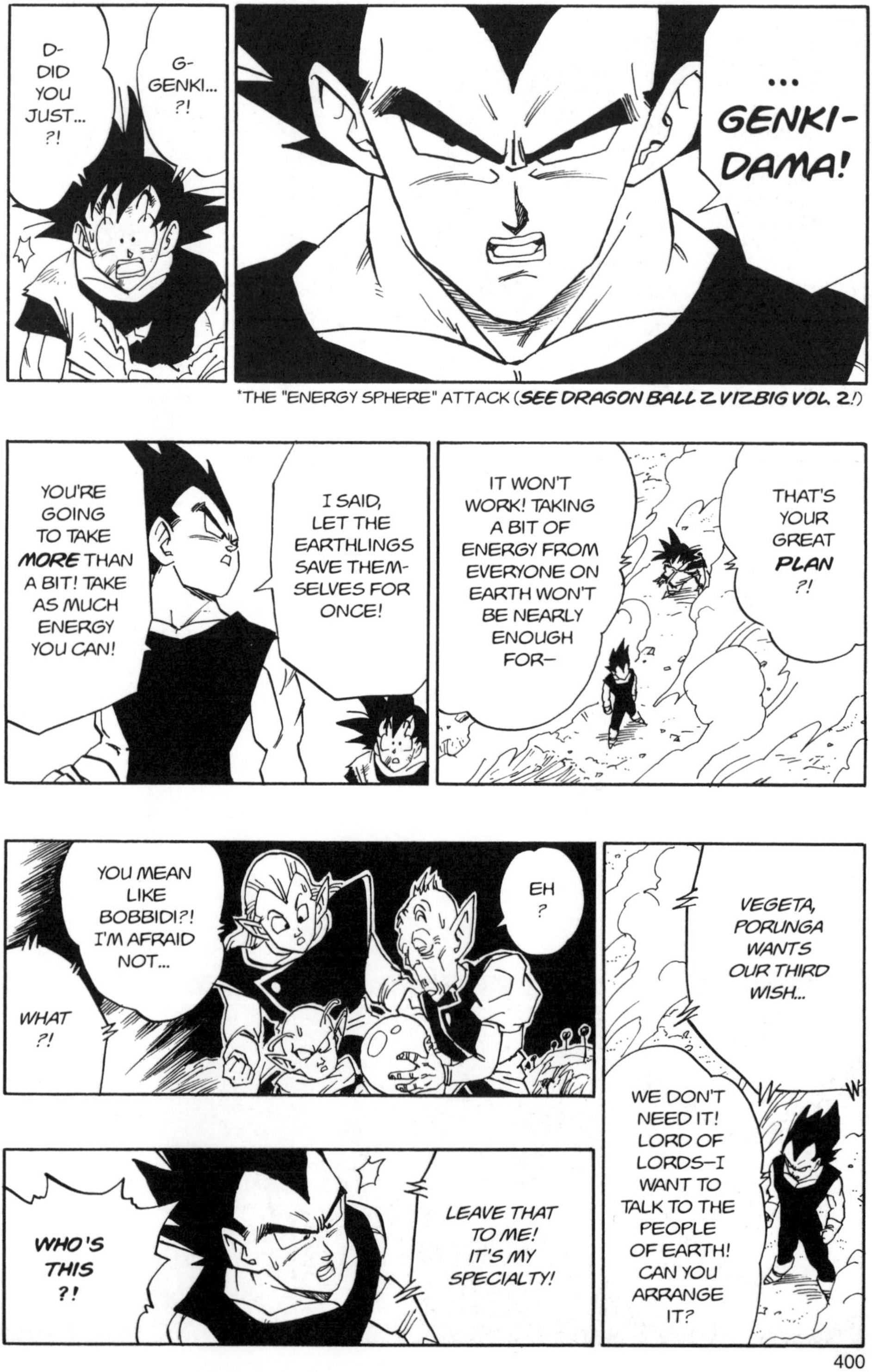
...GENKI-DAMA!
G-GENKI...?!
D-DID YOU JUST...?!
THAT'S YOUR GREAT PLAN ?!
IT WON'T WORK! TAKING A BIT OF ENERGY FROM EVERYONE ON EARTH WON'T BE NEARLY ENOUGH FOR–
I SAID, LET THE EARTHLINGS SAVE THEMSELVES FOR ONCE!
YOU'RE GOING TO TAKE MORE THAN A BIT! TAKE AS MUCH ENERGY YOU CAN!
VEGETA, PORUNGA WANTS OUR THIRD WISH...
WE DON'T NEED IT! LORD OF LORDS—I WANT TO TALK TO THE PEOPLE OF EARTH! CAN YOU ARRANGE IT?
EH ?
YOU MEAN LIKE BOBBIDI?! I'M AFRAID NOT...
WHAT ?!
LEAVE THAT TO ME! IT'S MY SPECIALTY!
WHO'S THIS ?!

*THE "ENERGY SPHERE" ATTACK (**SEE DRAGON BALL Z VIZBIG VOL. 2!**)

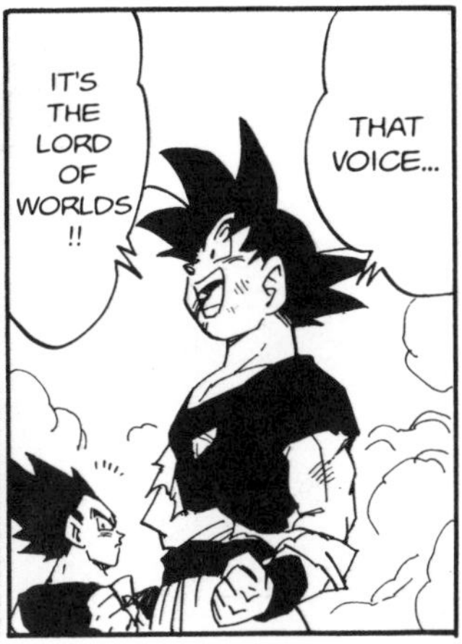
THAT VOICE...
IT'S THE LORD OF WORLDS!!

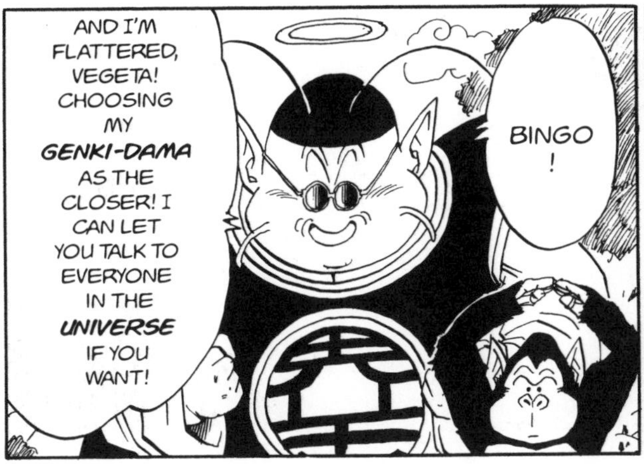
BINGO!
AND I'M FLATTERED, VEGETA! CHOOSING MY ***GENKI-DAMA*** AS THE CLOSER! I CAN LET YOU TALK TO EVERYONE IN THE ***UNIVERSE*** IF YOU WANT!

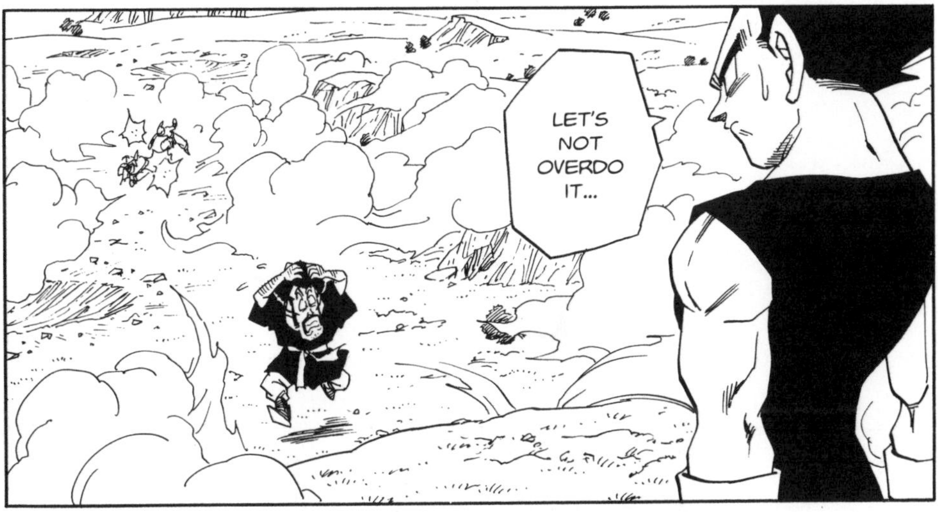
LET'S NOT OVERDO IT...

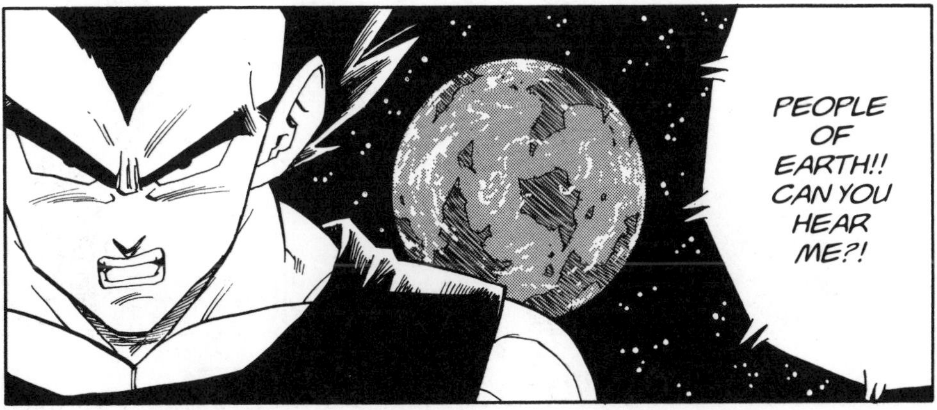
PEOPLE OF EARTH!! CAN YOU HEAR ME?!

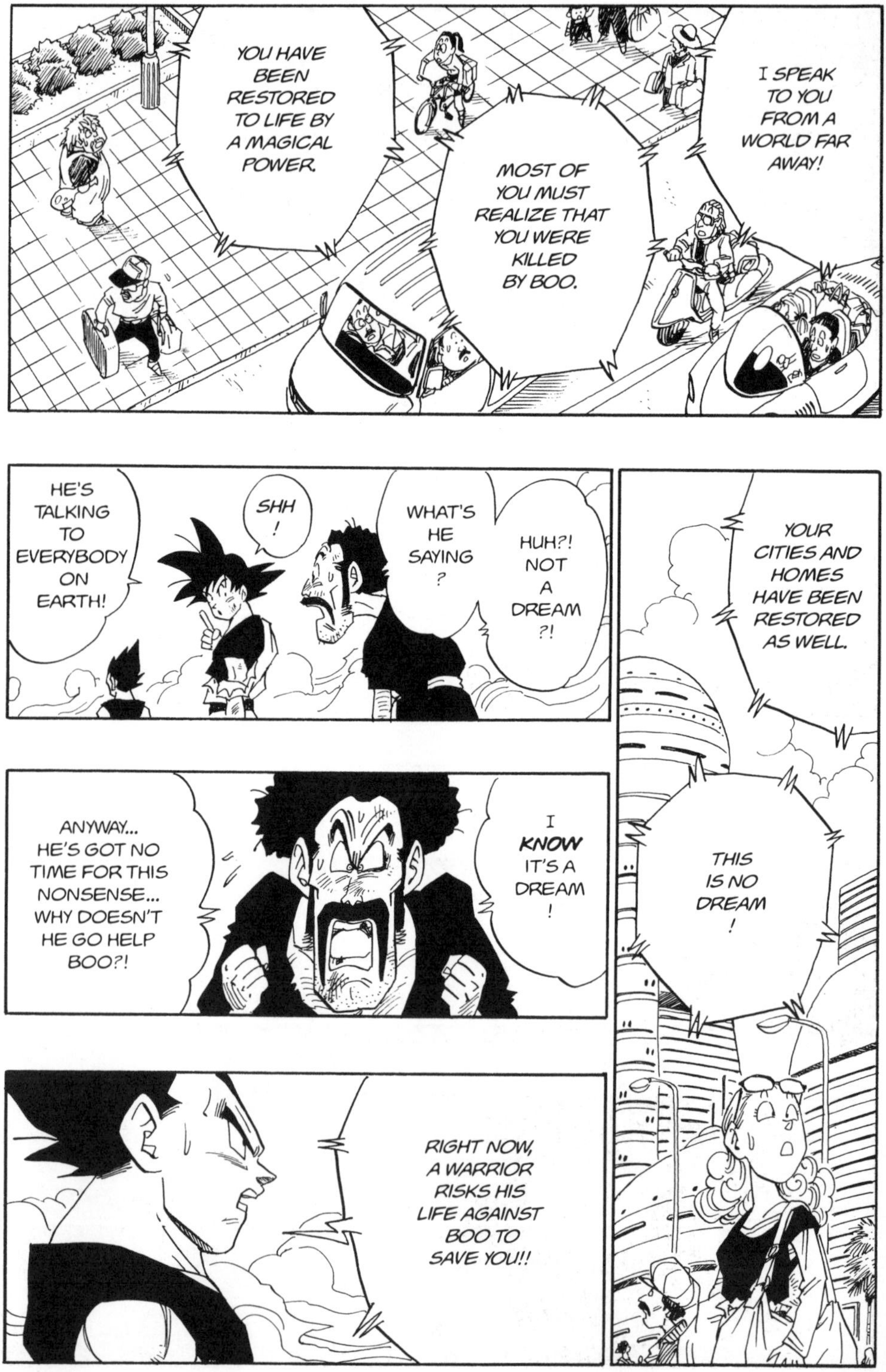
I SPEAK TO YOU FROM A WORLD FAR AWAY!
MOST OF YOU MUST REALIZE THAT YOU WERE KILLED BY BOO.
YOU HAVE BEEN RESTORED TO LIFE BY A MAGICAL POWER.
YOUR CITIES AND HOMES HAVE BEEN RESTORED AS WELL.
THIS IS NO DREAM!
HUH?! NOT A DREAM?!
WHAT'S HE SAYING?
SHH!
HE'S TALKING TO EVERYBODY ON EARTH!
I **KNOW** IT'S A DREAM!
ANYWAY... HE'S GOT NO TIME FOR THIS NONSENSE... WHY DOESN'T HE GO HELP BOO?!
RIGHT NOW, A WARRIOR RISKS HIS LIFE AGAINST BOO TO SAVE YOU!!

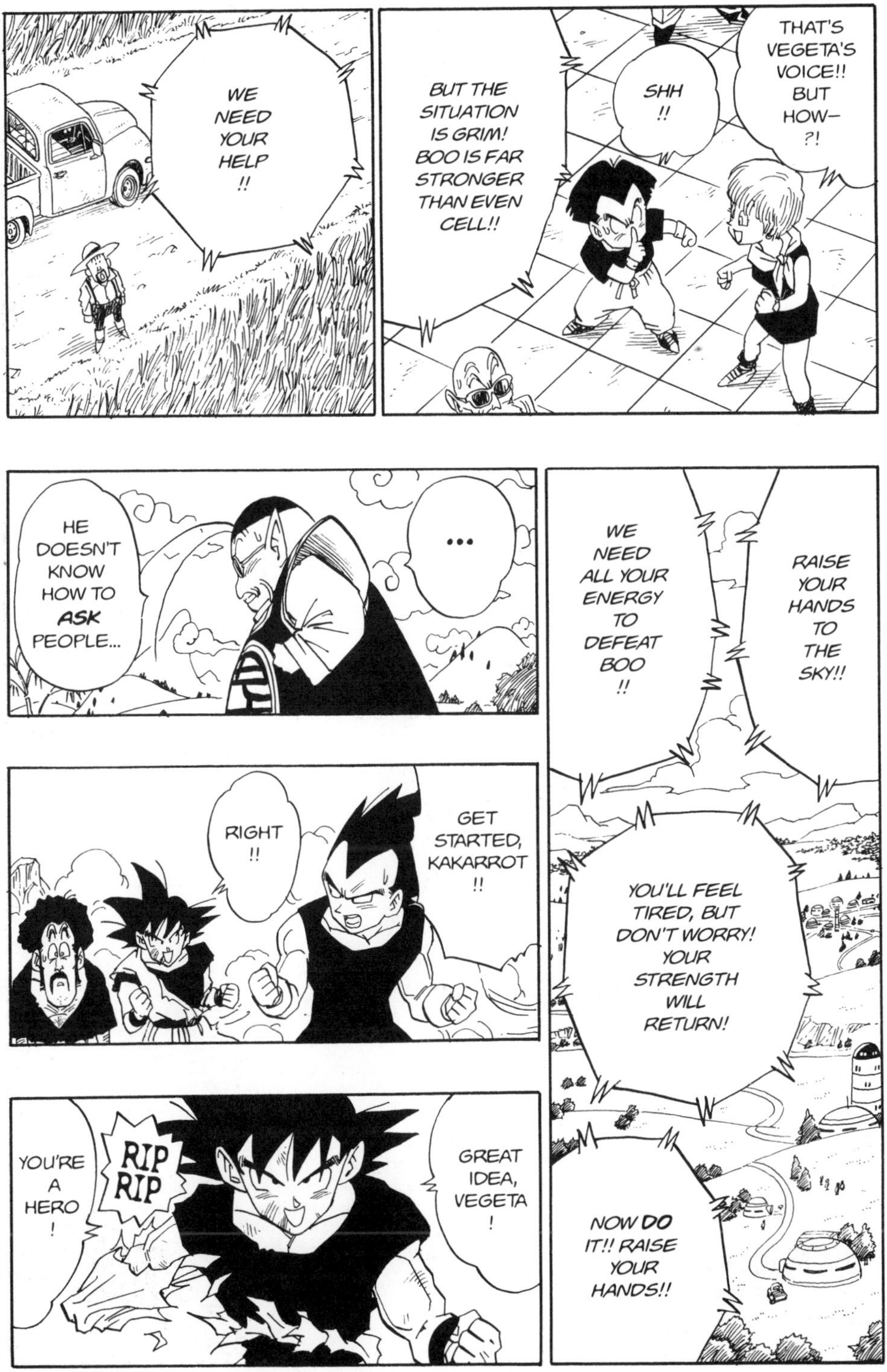
THAT'S VEGETA'S VOICE!! BUT HOW—?!
SHH!!
BUT THE SITUATION IS GRIM! BOO IS FAR STRONGER THAN EVEN CELL!!
WE NEED YOUR HELP!!
RAISE YOUR HANDS TO THE SKY!!
WE NEED ALL YOUR ENERGY TO DEFEAT BOO!!
YOU'LL FEEL TIRED, BUT DON'T WORRY! YOUR STRENGTH WILL RETURN!
NOW **DO** IT!! RAISE YOUR HANDS!!
...
HE DOESN'T KNOW HOW TO **ASK** PEOPLE...
GET STARTED, KAKARROT!!
RIGHT!!
GREAT IDEA, VEGETA!
RIP RIP
YOU'RE A HERO!

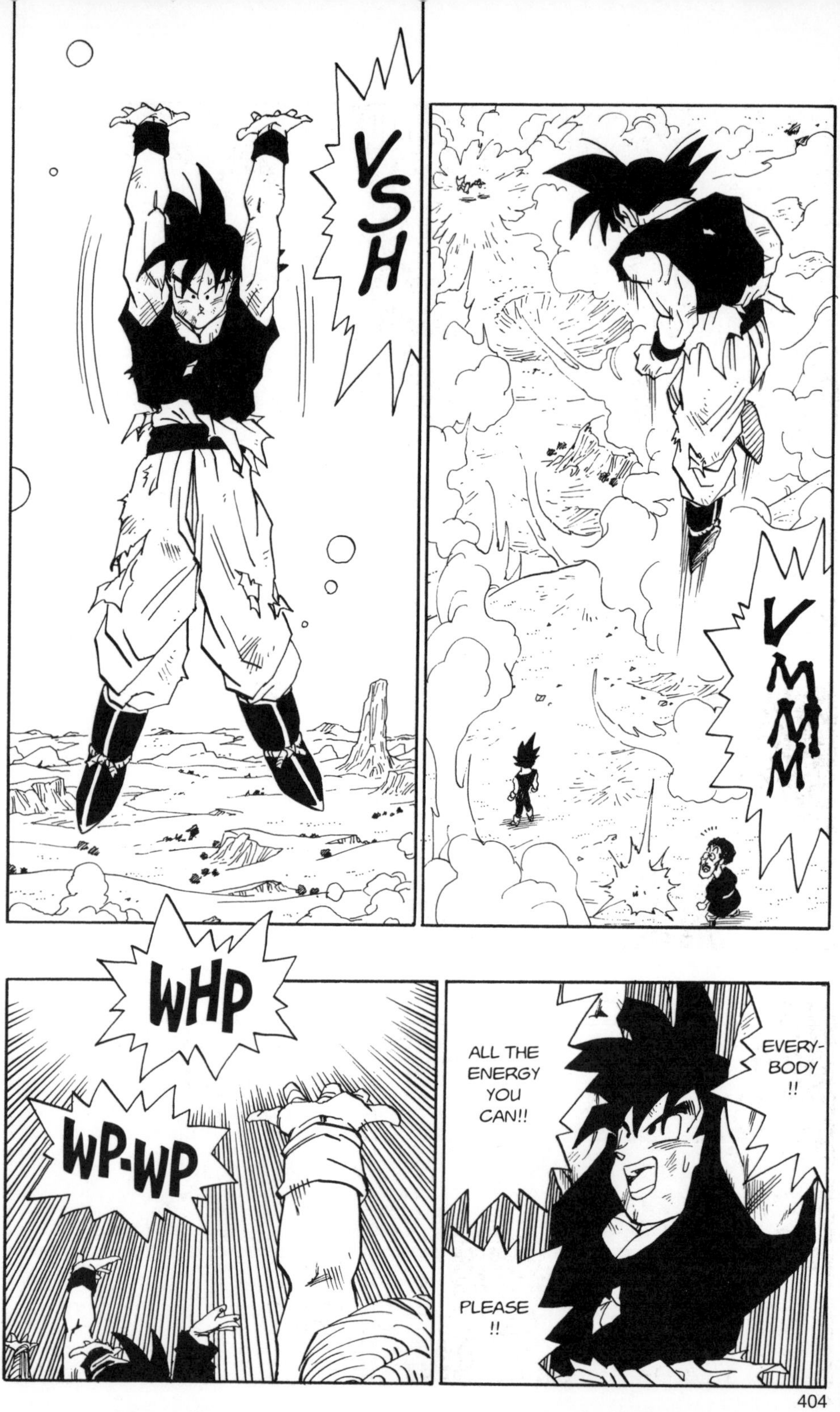
VMMM
VSH
EVERY-BODY!!
ALL THE ENERGY YOU CAN!!
PLEASE!!
WHP
WP-WP

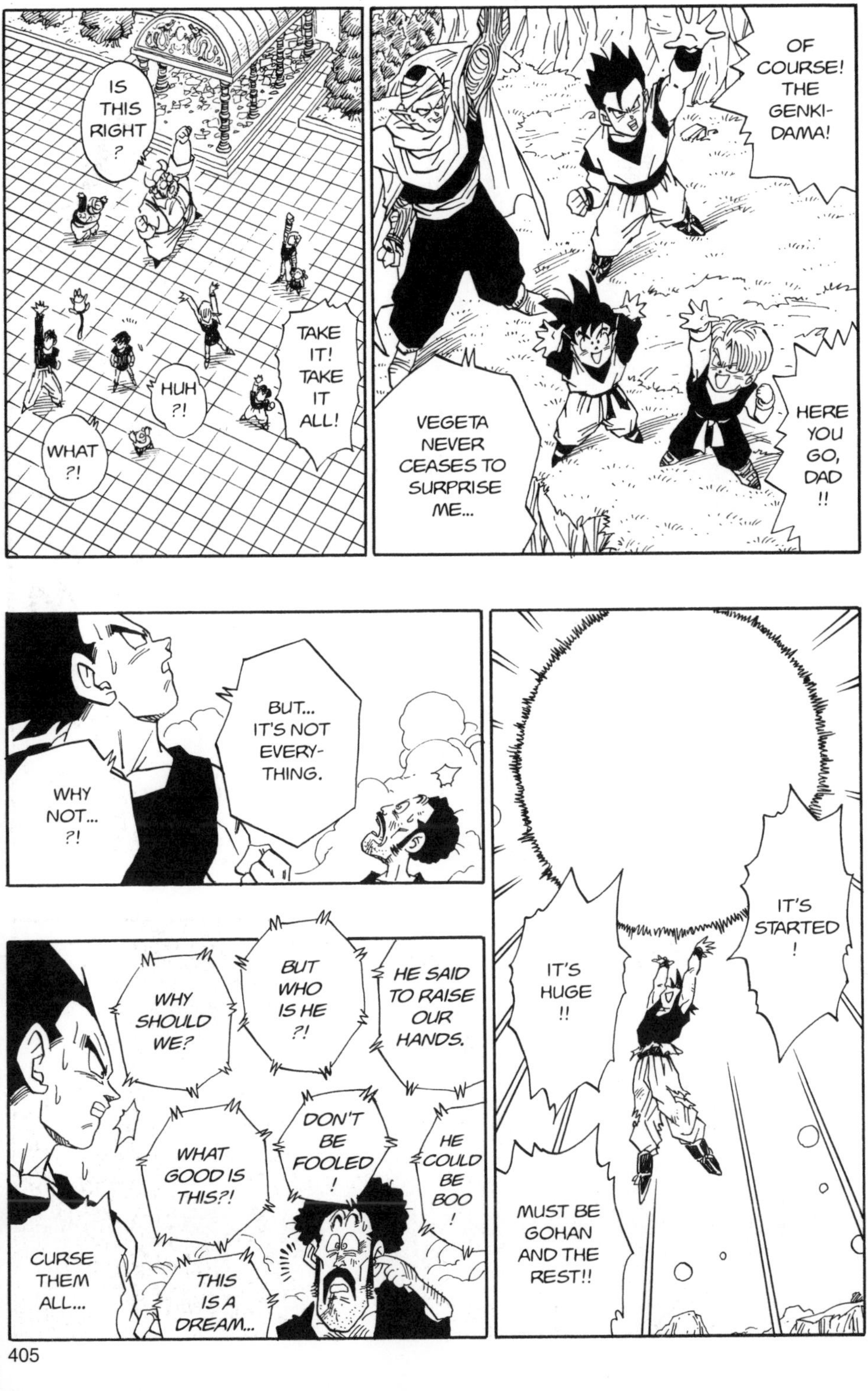
OF COURSE! THE GENKI-DAMA!
HERE YOU GO, DAD!!
VEGETA NEVER CEASES TO SURPRISE ME...
IS THIS RIGHT?
TAKE IT! TAKE IT ALL!
HUH?!
WHAT?!
IT'S STARTED!
IT'S HUGE!!
MUST BE GOHAN AND THE REST!!
BUT... IT'S NOT EVERYTHING.
WHY NOT...?!
HE SAID TO RAISE OUR HANDS.
BUT WHO IS HE?!
WHY SHOULD WE?
HE COULD BE BOO!
DON'T BE FOOLED!
WHAT GOOD IS THIS?!
THIS IS A DREAM...
CURSE THEM ALL...

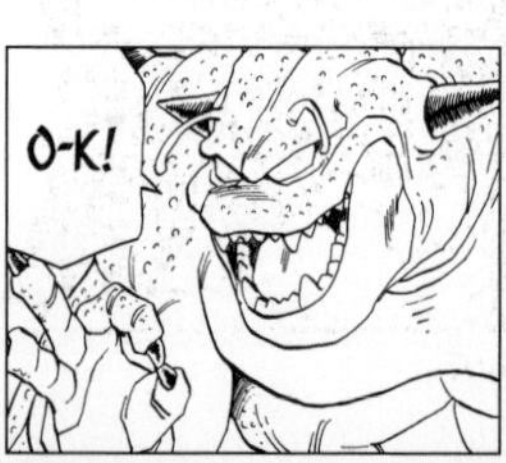
O-K!

DRAGON BALL ドラゴンボール

DBZ:321 • Just Not Enough

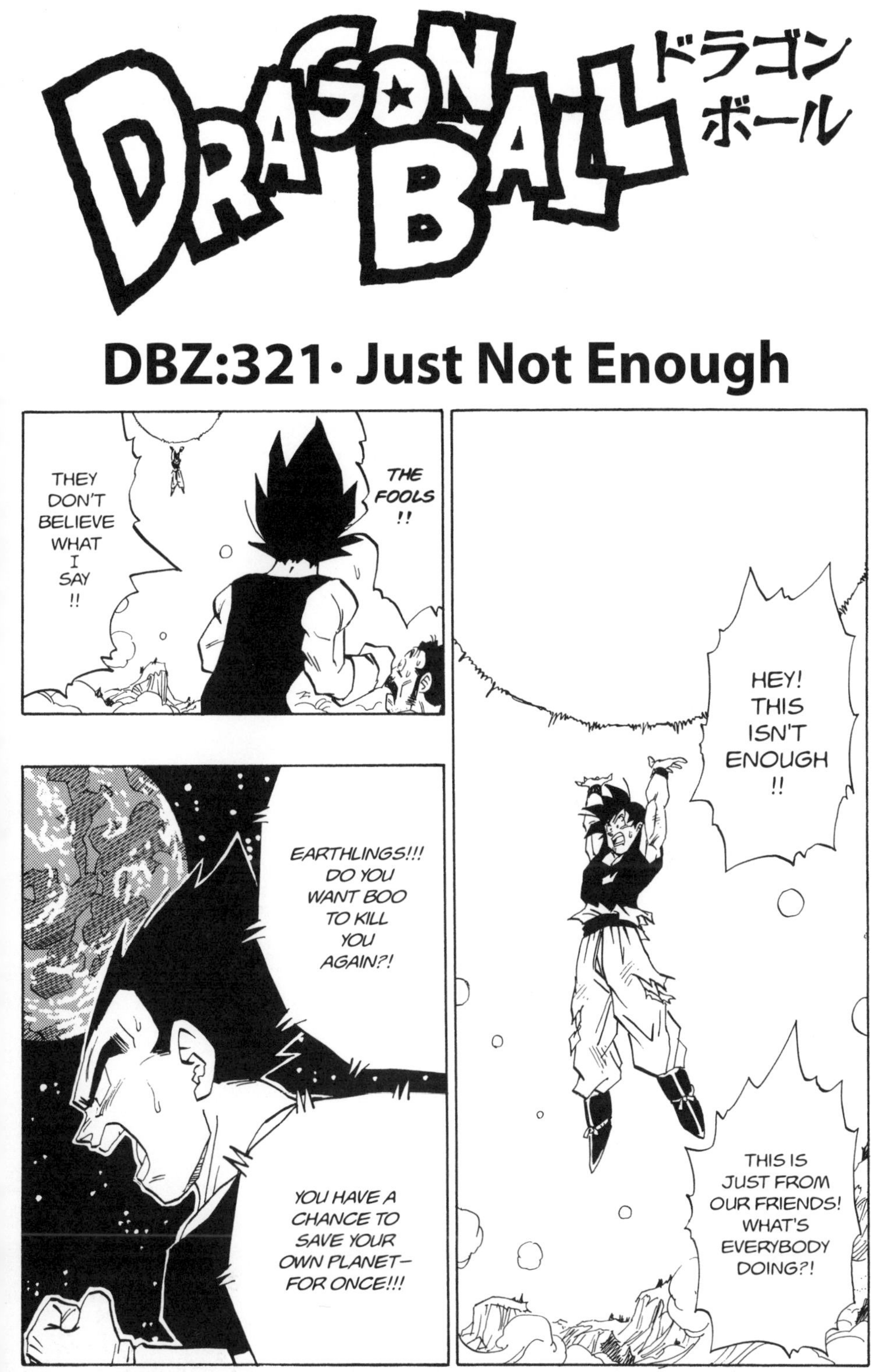

HEY! THIS ISN'T ENOUGH !!
THIS IS JUST FROM OUR FRIENDS! WHAT'S EVERYBODY DOING?!
THE FOOLS !!
THEY DON'T BELIEVE WHAT I SAY !!
EARTHLINGS!!! DO YOU WANT BOO TO KILL YOU AGAIN?!
YOU HAVE A CHANCE TO SAVE YOUR OWN PLANET— FOR ONCE!!!

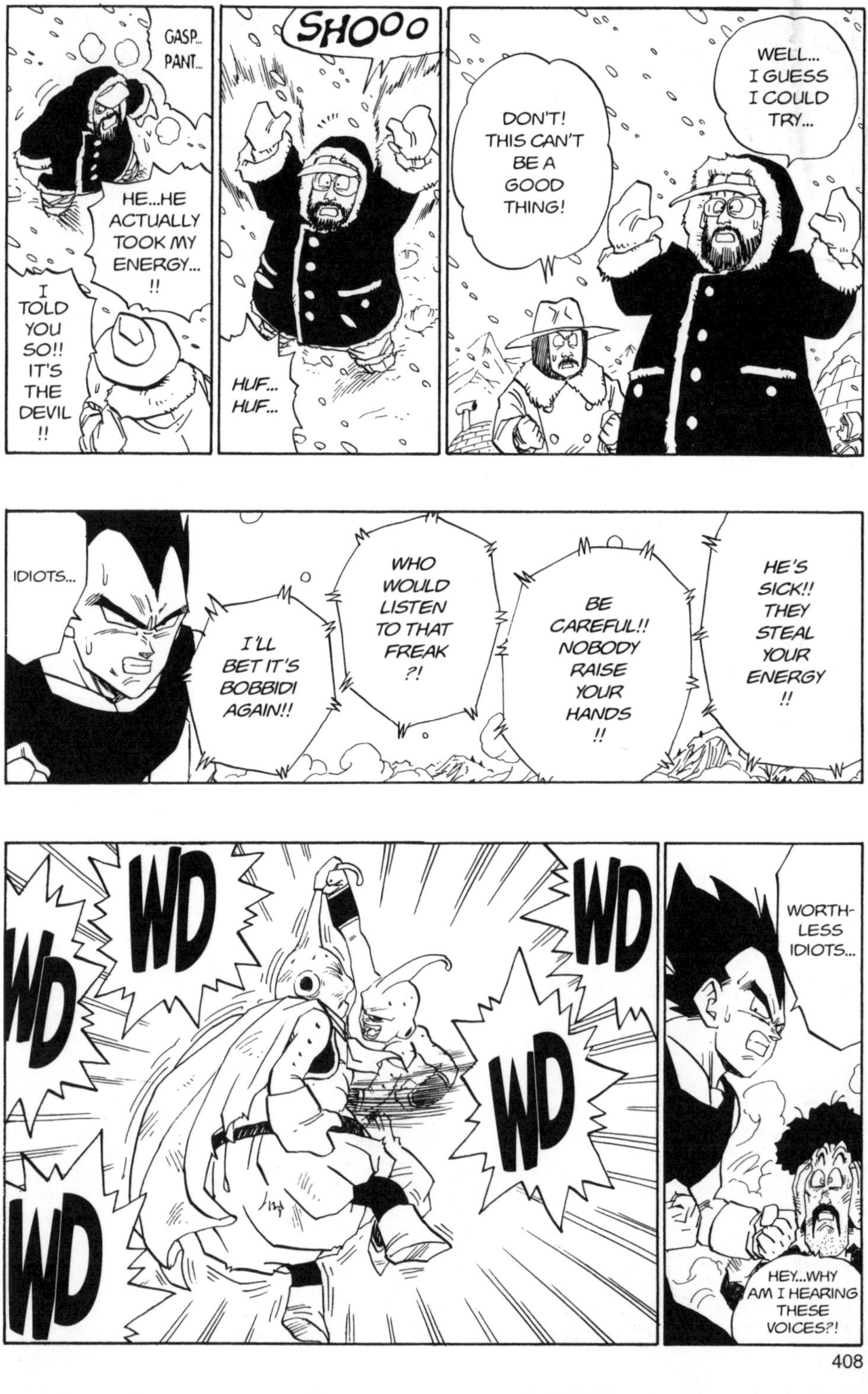
WELL... I GUESS I COULD TRY...
DON'T! THIS CAN'T BE A GOOD THING!
SHOOoo
HUF... HUF...
GASP... PANT...
HE...HE ACTUALLY TOOK MY ENERGY... !!
I TOLD YOU SO!! IT'S THE DEVIL !!
HE'S SICK!! THEY STEAL YOUR ENERGY !!
BE CAREFUL!! NOBODY RAISE YOUR HANDS !!
WHO WOULD LISTEN TO THAT FREAK ?!
I'LL BET IT'S BOBBIDI AGAIN!!
IDIOTS...
WORTHLESS IDIOTS...
HEY...WHY AM I HEARING THESE VOICES?!
WD
WD
WD
WD
WD

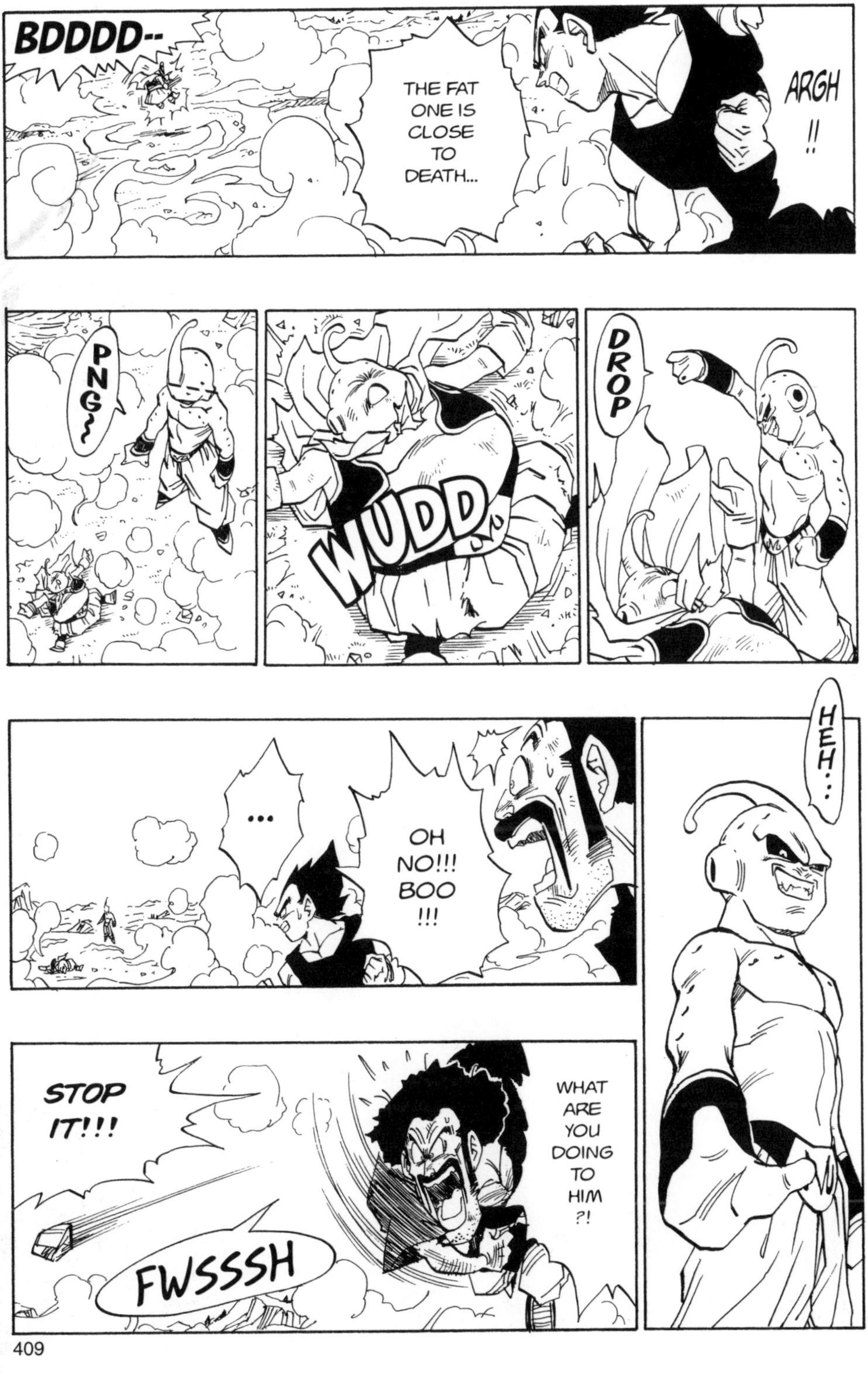

ARGH !!
THE FAT ONE IS CLOSE TO DEATH...
BDDDD--
DROP
WUDD
PNG~
HEH...
OH NO!!! BOO !!!
...
WHAT ARE YOU DOING TO HIM ?!
STOP IT!!!
FWSSSH

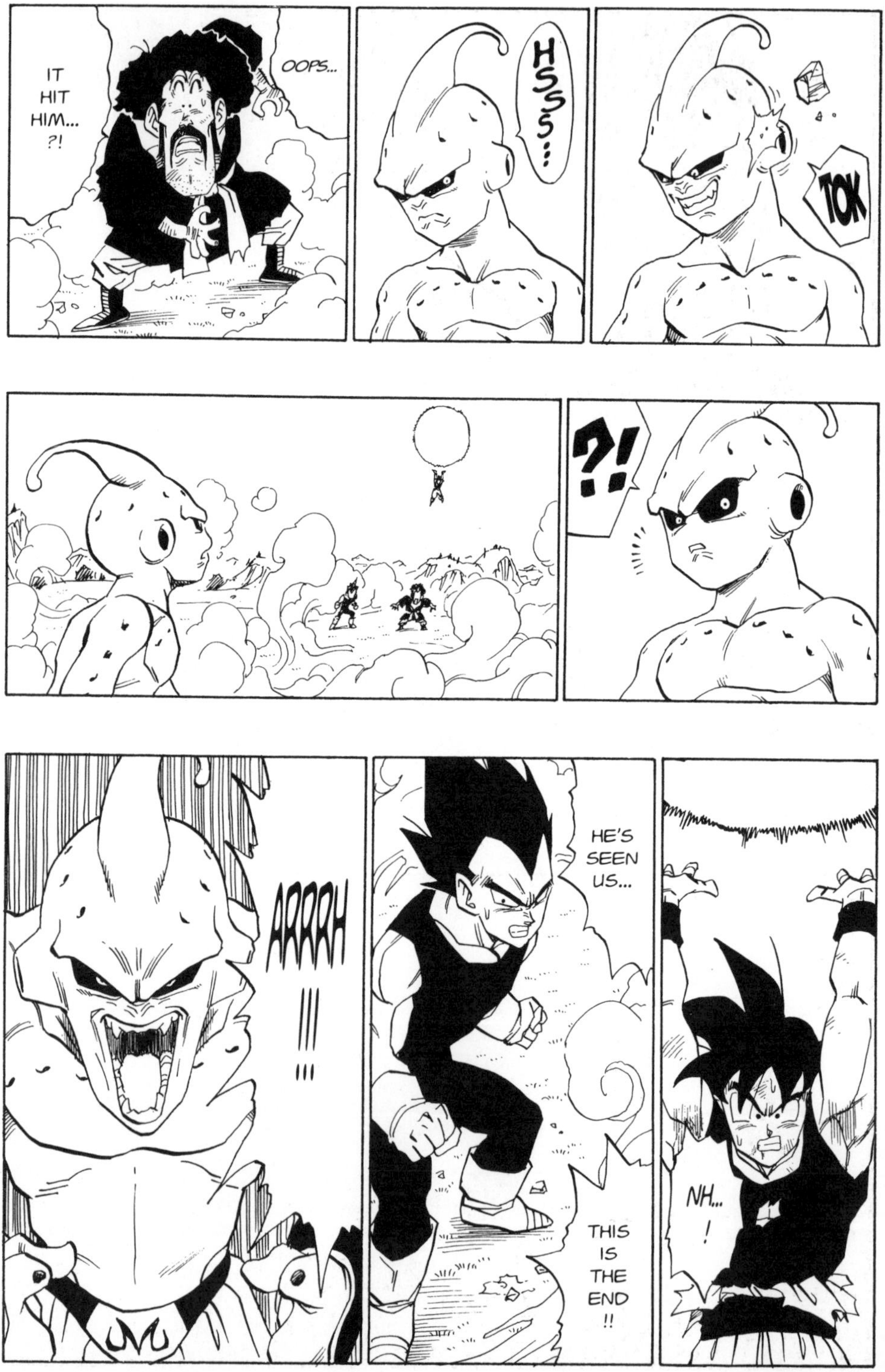
TOK
HSSS..!!
OOPS...
IT HIT HIM... ?!
?!
NH... !
HE'S SEEN US...
THIS IS THE END !!
ARRRH !!!!!!

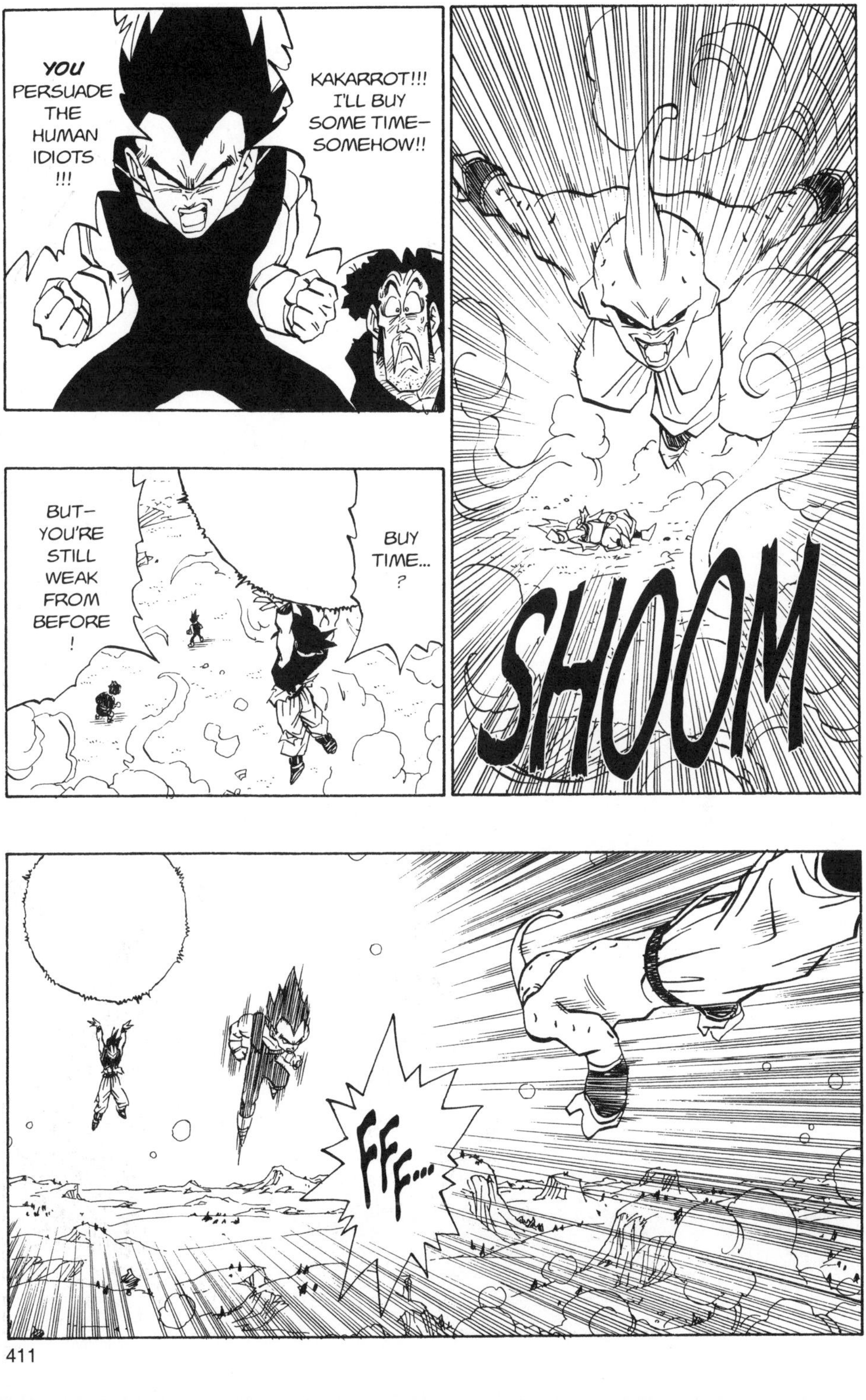
SHOOM
KAKARROT!!! I'LL BUY SOME TIME— SOMEHOW!!
YOU PERSUADE THE HUMAN IDIOTS!!!
BUY TIME...?
BUT— YOU'RE STILL WEAK FROM BEFORE!
FFF...

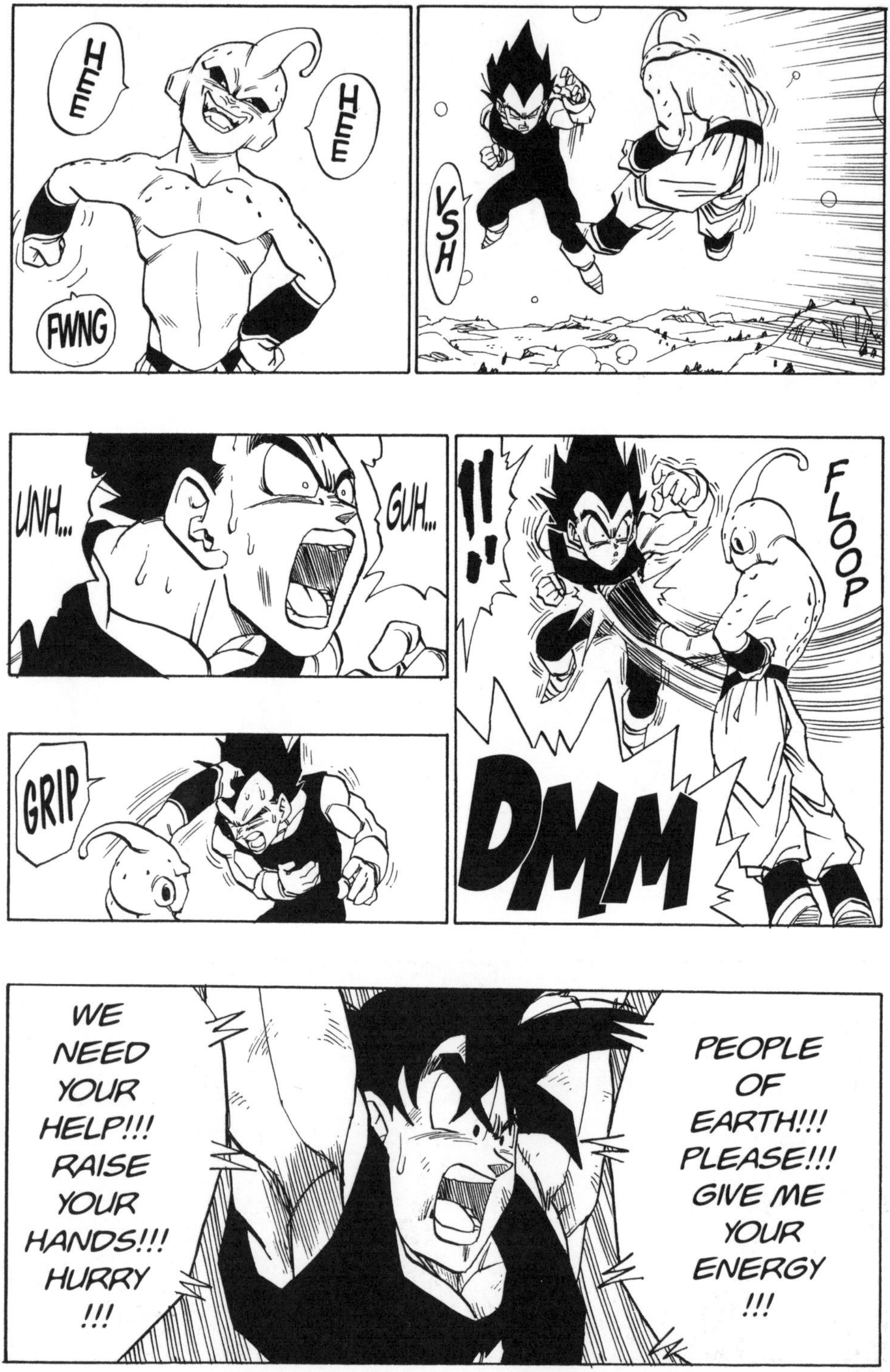
VSH
HEE
HEE
FWNG
FLOOP
!!
DMM
GUH...
UNH...
GRIP
PEOPLE OF EARTH!!! PLEASE!!! GIVE ME YOUR ENERGY !!!
WE NEED YOUR HELP!!! RAISE YOUR HANDS!!! HURRY !!!

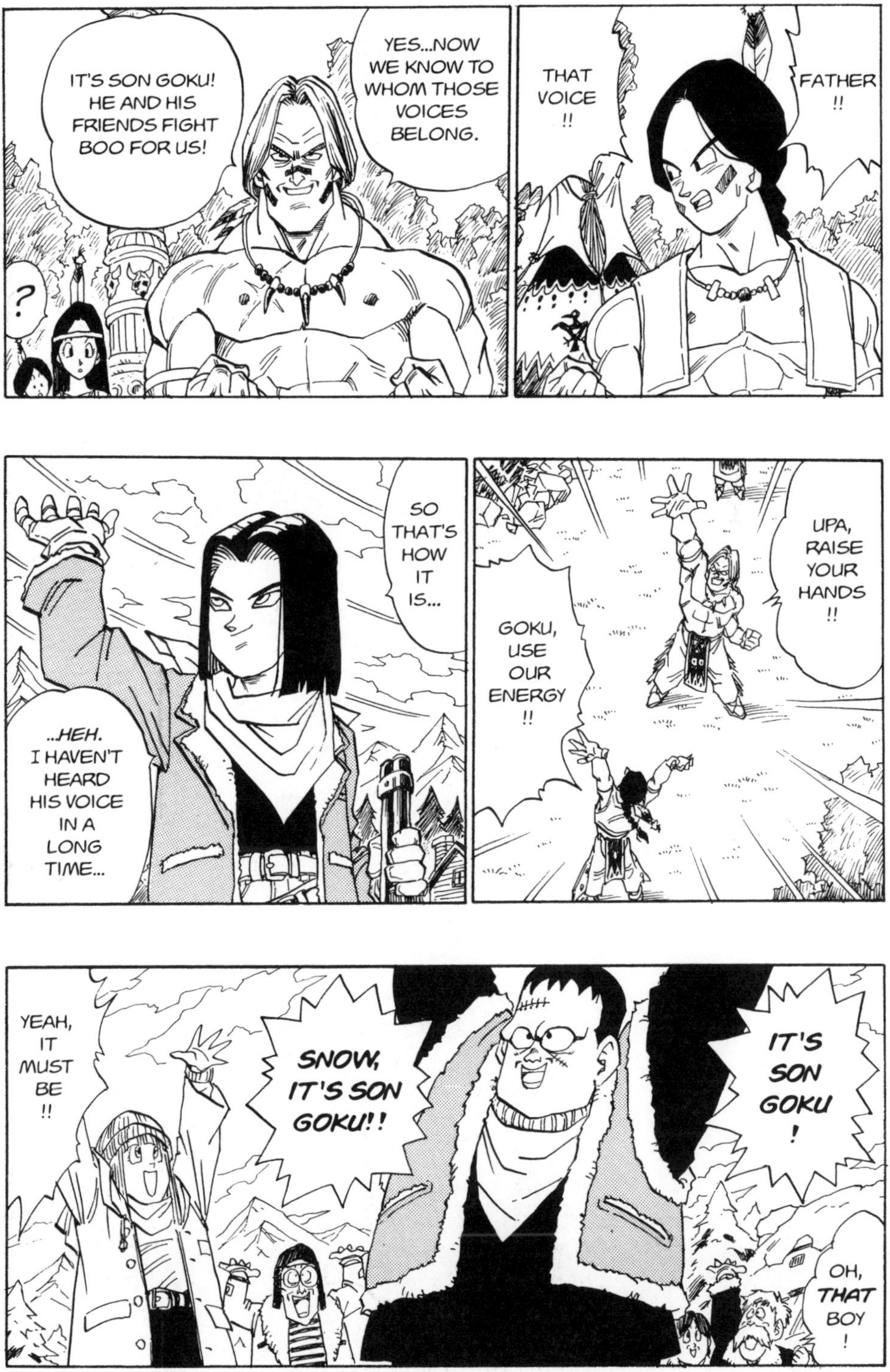
FATHER !!
THAT VOICE !!
YES...NOW WE KNOW TO WHOM THOSE VOICES BELONG.
IT'S SON GOKU! HE AND HIS FRIENDS FIGHT BOO FOR US!
?
UPA, RAISE YOUR HANDS !!
GOKU, USE OUR ENERGY !!
SO THAT'S HOW IT IS...
...HEH. I HAVEN'T HEARD HIS VOICE IN A LONG TIME...
IT'S SON GOKU !
SNOW, IT'S SON GOKU!!
YEAH, IT MUST BE !!
OH, THAT BOY !

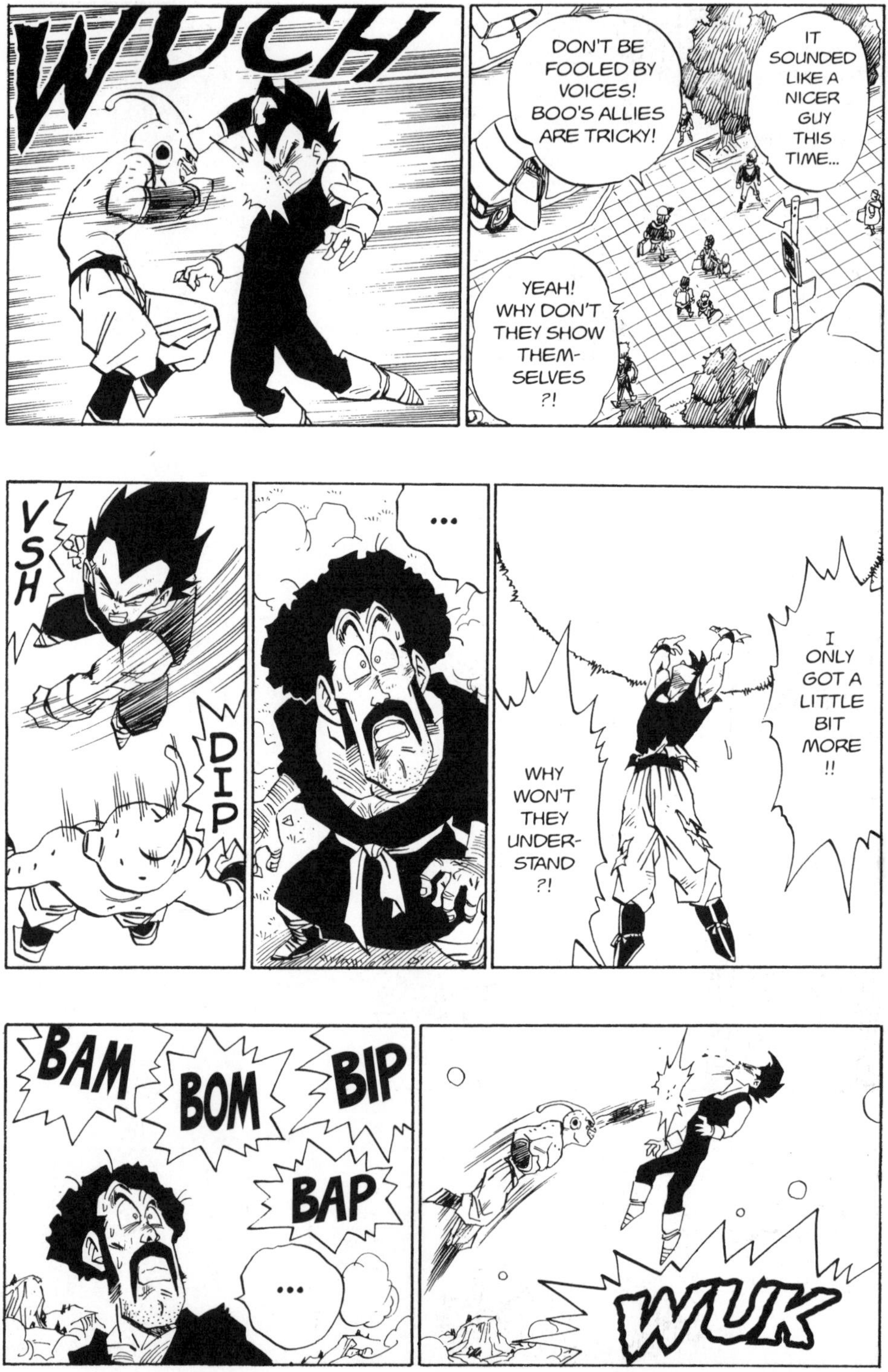
IT SOUNDED LIKE A NICER GUY THIS TIME...
DON'T BE FOOLED BY VOICES! BOO'S ALLIES ARE TRICKY!
YEAH! WHY DON'T THEY SHOW THEM-SELVES ?!
WUCH
I ONLY GOT A LITTLE BIT MORE !!
WHY WON'T THEY UNDER-STAND ?!
...
VSH
DIP
WUK
BAM
BOM
BIP
BAP
...

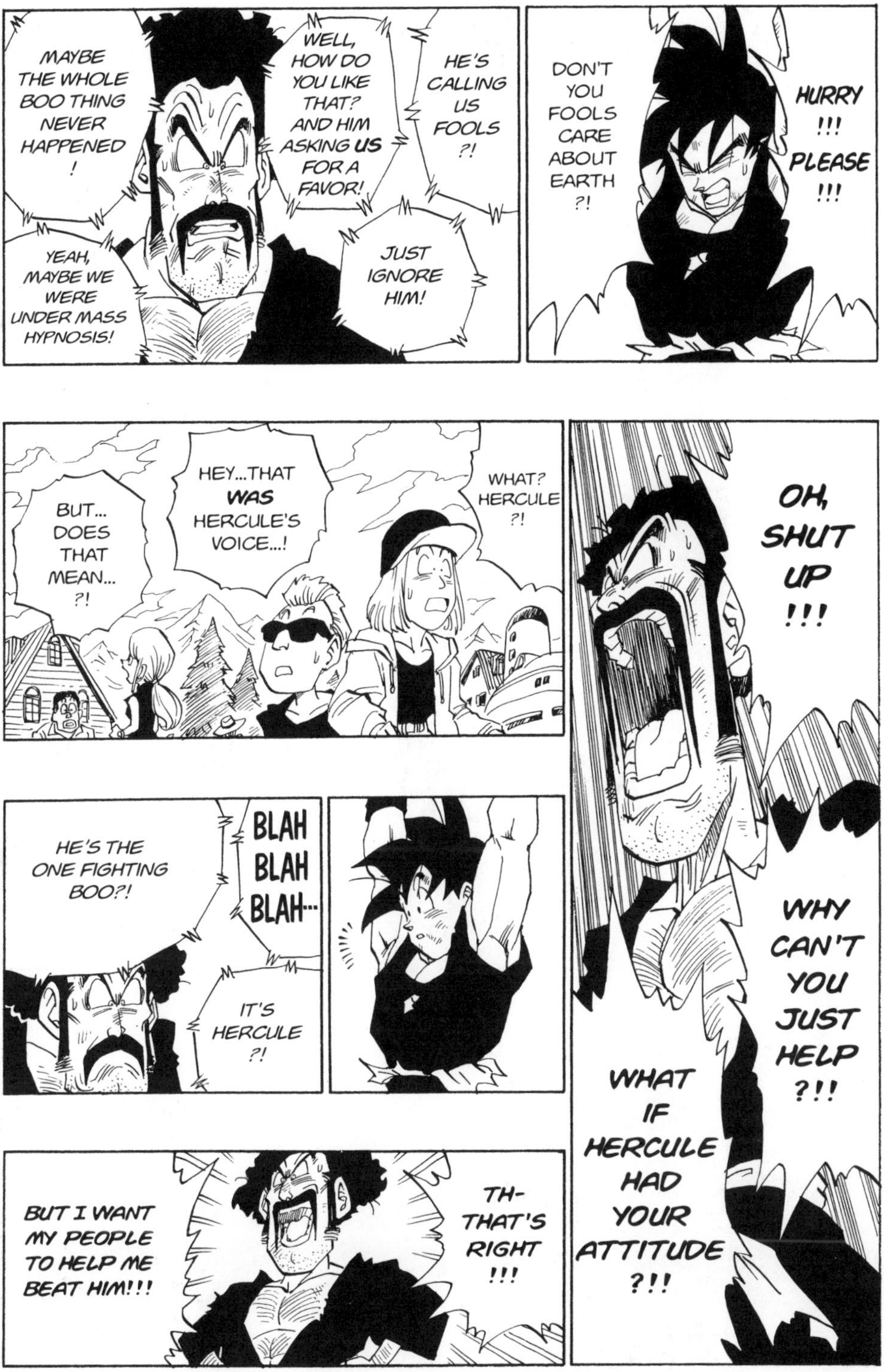
HURRY!!! PLEASE!!!
DON'T YOU FOOLS CARE ABOUT EARTH?!
HE'S CALLING US FOOLS?!
WELL, HOW DO YOU LIKE THAT? AND HIM ASKING **US** FOR A FAVOR!
MAYBE THE WHOLE BOO THING NEVER HAPPENED!
JUST IGNORE HIM!
YEAH, MAYBE WE WERE UNDER MASS HYPNOSIS!
OH, SHUT UP!!!
WHY CAN'T YOU JUST HELP?!!
WHAT IF HERCULE HAD YOUR ATTITUDE?!!
WHAT? HERCULE?!
HEY...THAT **WAS** HERCULE'S VOICE...!
BUT... DOES THAT MEAN...?!
BLAH BLAH BLAH...
HE'S THE ONE FIGHTING BOO?!
IT'S HERCULE?!
TH-THAT'S RIGHT!!!
BUT I WANT MY PEOPLE TO HELP ME BEAT HIM!!!

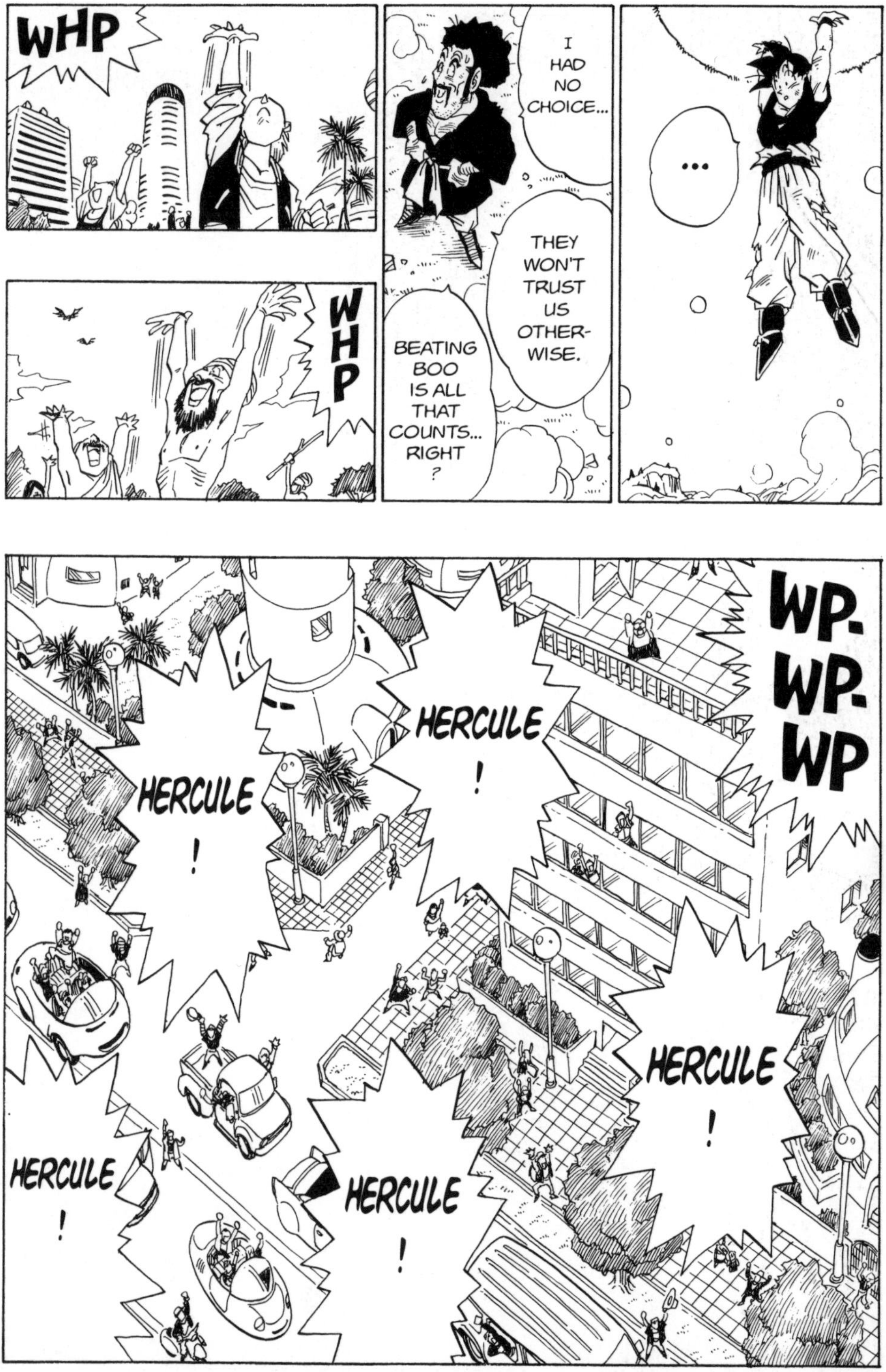
...
I HAD NO CHOICE...
THEY WON'T TRUST US OTHERWISE.
BEATING BOO IS ALL THAT COUNTS... RIGHT?
WHP
WHP
WP-WP-WP
HERCULE!
HERCULE!
HERCULE!
HERCULE!
HERCULE!

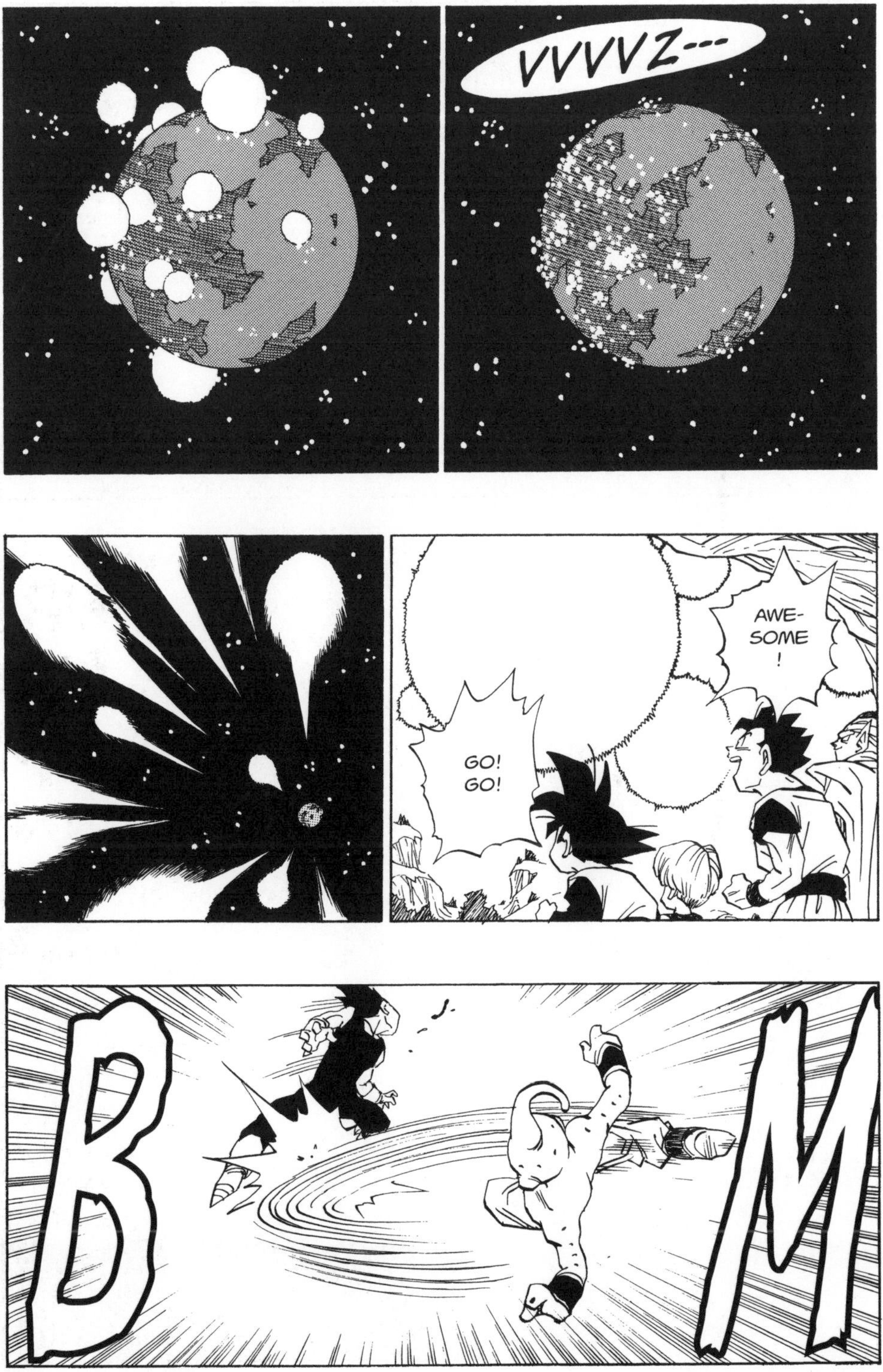
VVVVZ---
AWE-SOME!
GO! GO!
B
M

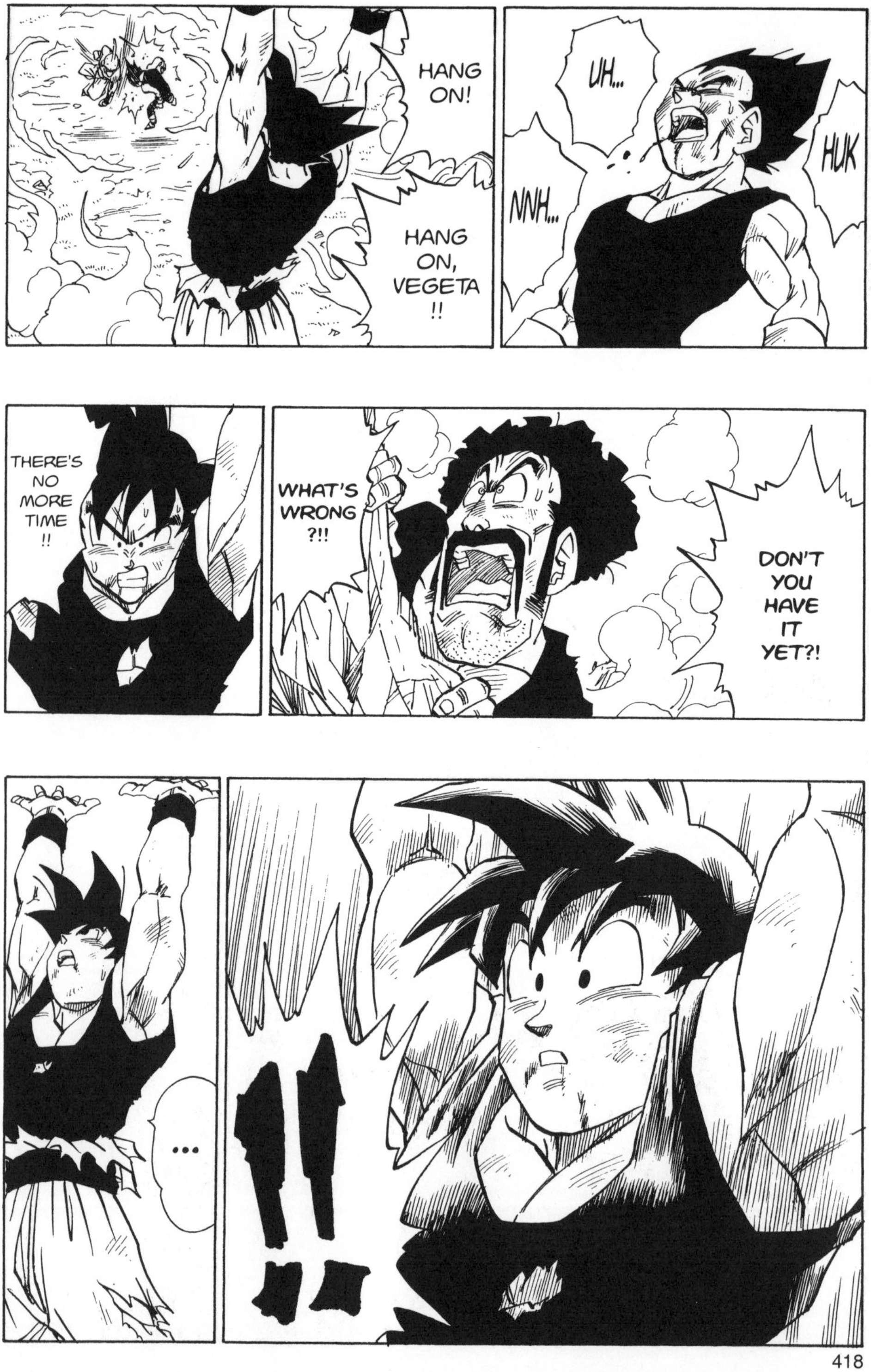
HUK
UH...
NNH...
HANG ON!
HANG ON, VEGETA!!
DON'T YOU HAVE IT YET?!
WHAT'S WRONG?!!
THERE'S NO MORE TIME!!
!!
...

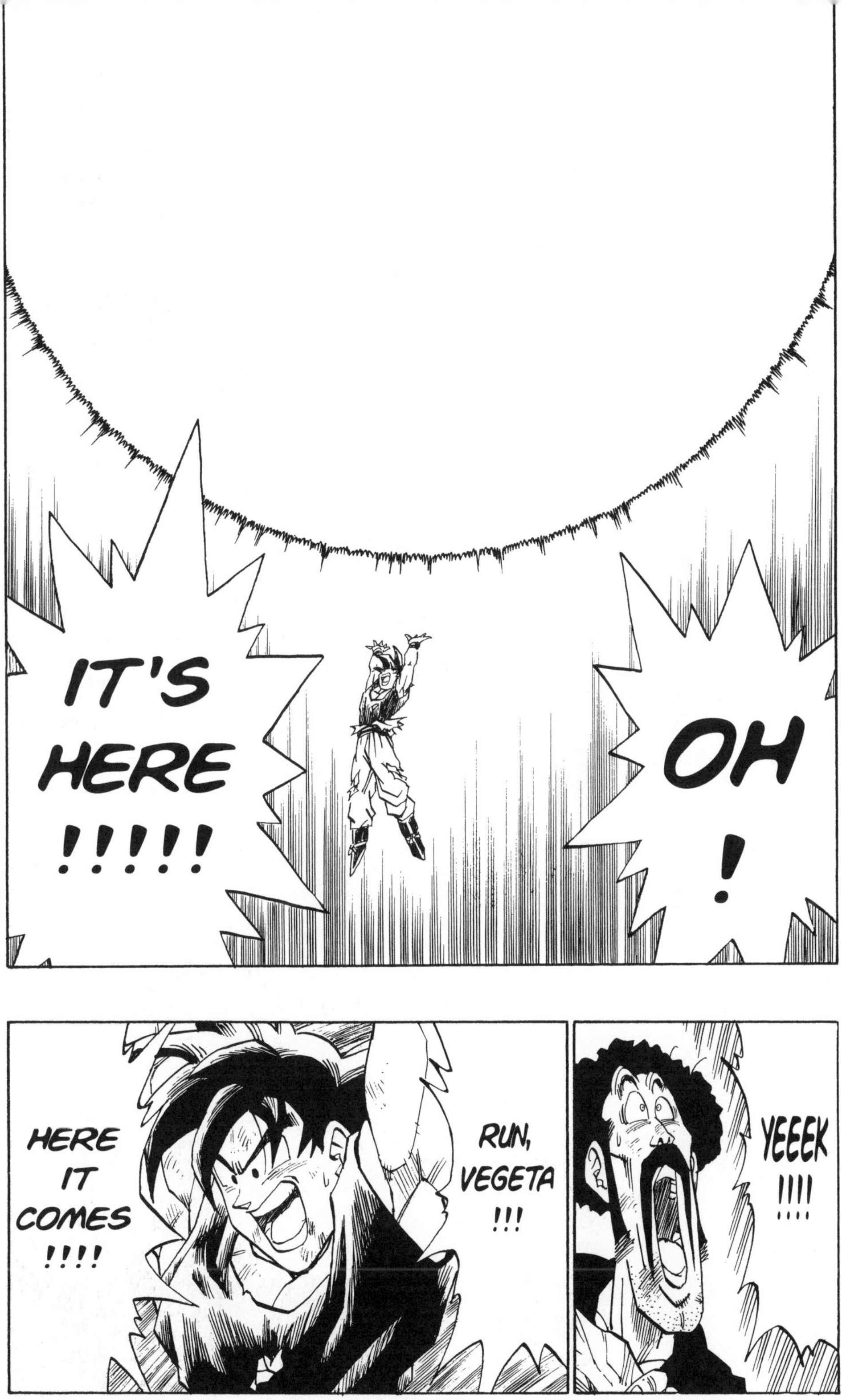
OH !
IT'S HERE !!!!!
YEEEK !!!!
RUN, VEGETA !!!
HERE IT COMES !!!!

DRAGON BALL ドラゴンボール

DBZ:322 • Battle's End

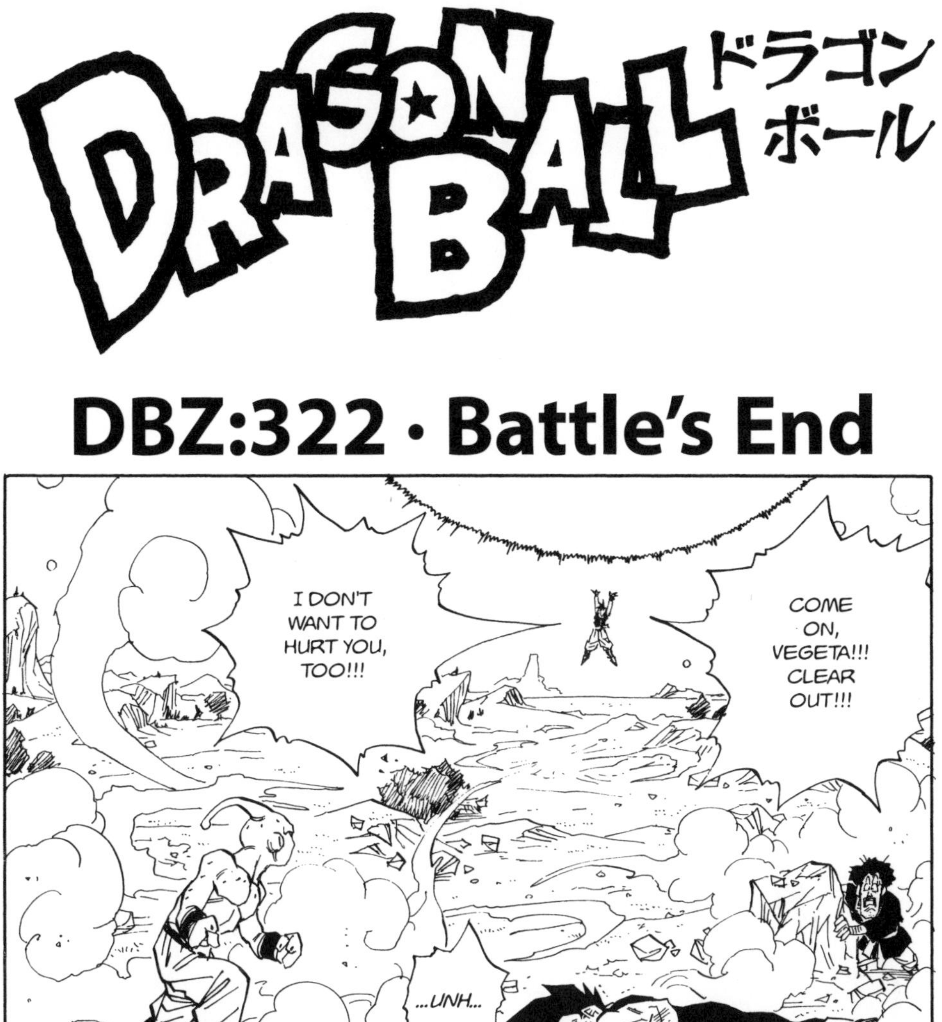
COME ON, VEGETA!!! CLEAR OUT!!!
I DON'T WANT TO HURT YOU, TOO!!!
...UNH...

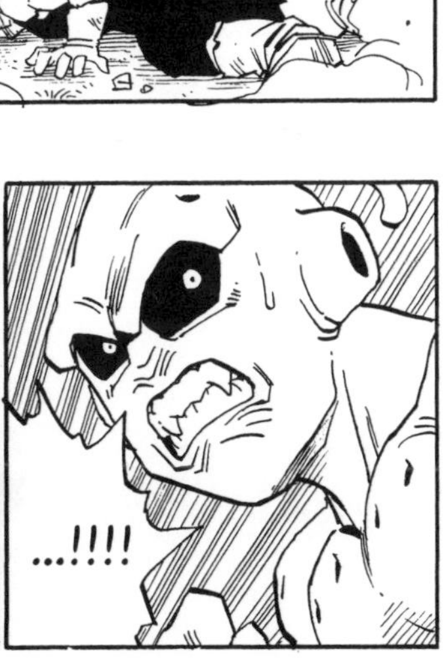
...!!!!

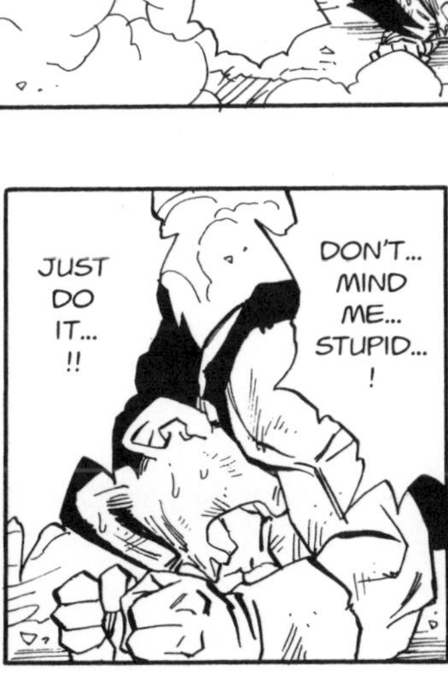
DON'T... MIND ME... STUPID...!
JUST DO IT...!!

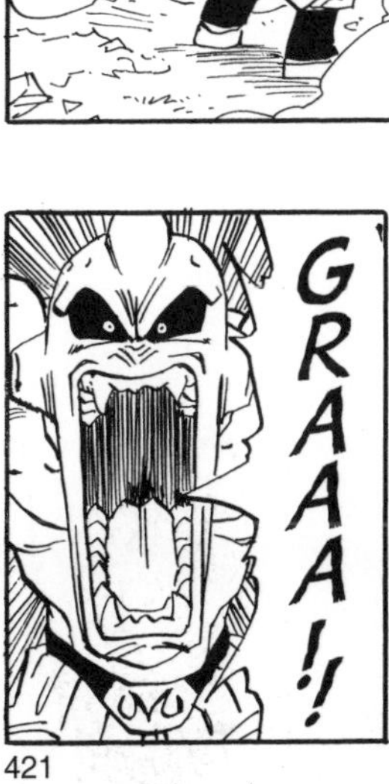
GRAAA!!

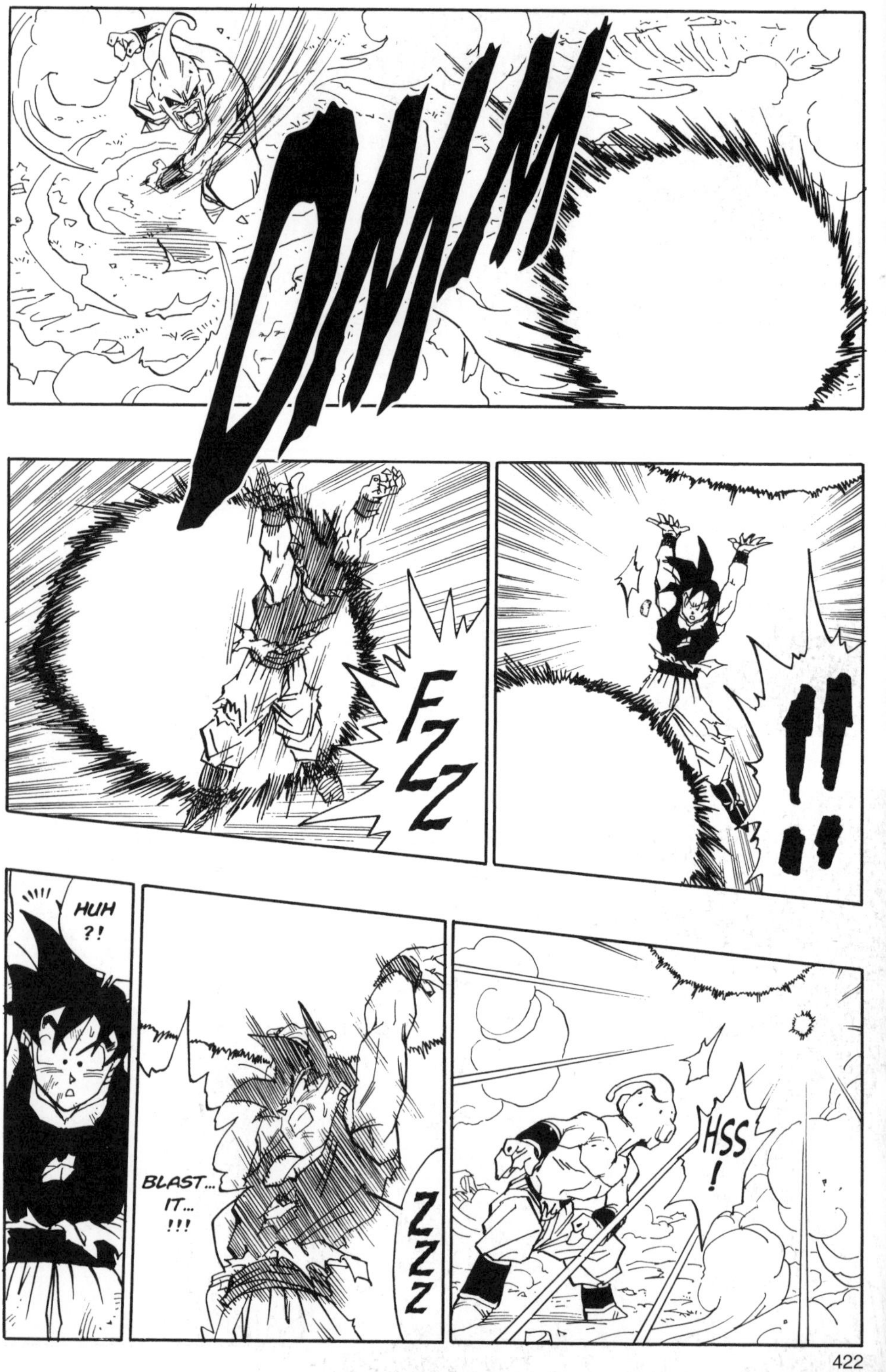
DMM
!!
!!
FZZ
HSS
!
ZZZ
BLAST... IT... !!!
HUH ?!

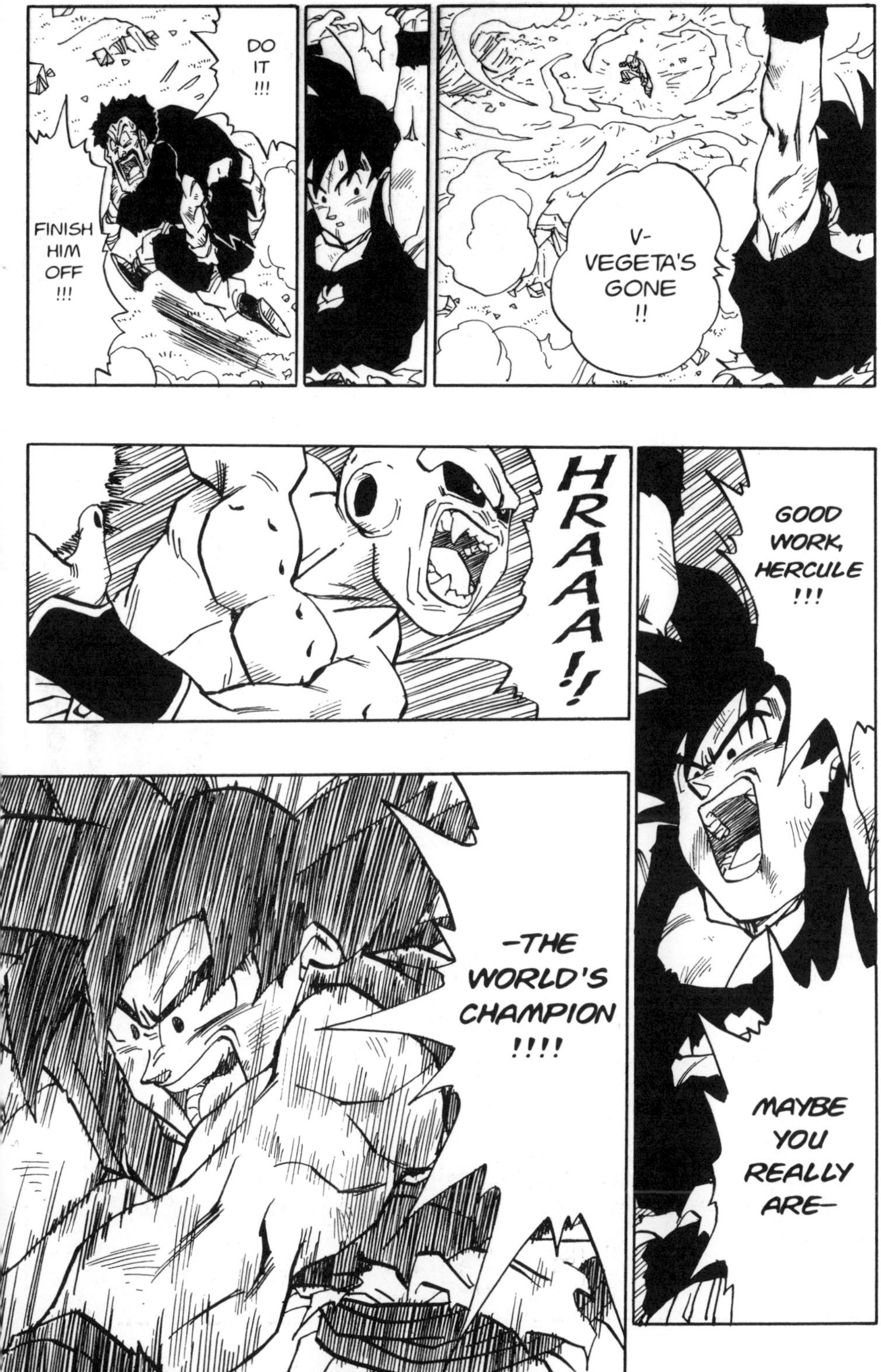
V-VEGETA'S GONE !!
DO IT !!!
FINISH HIM OFF !!!
GOOD WORK, HERCULE !!!
MAYBE YOU REALLY ARE—
HRAAAA!!
—THE WORLD'S CHAMPION !!!!

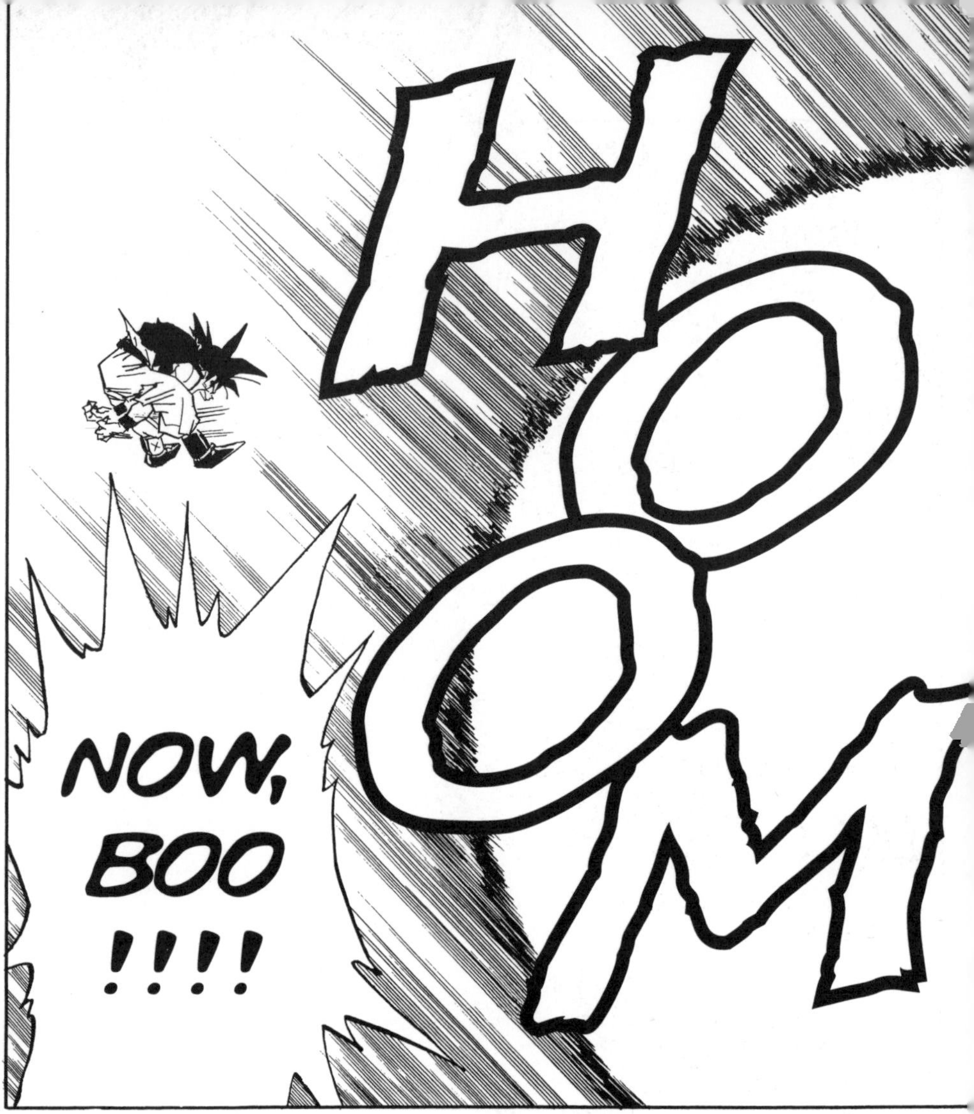
HOOM
NOW, BOO !!!!

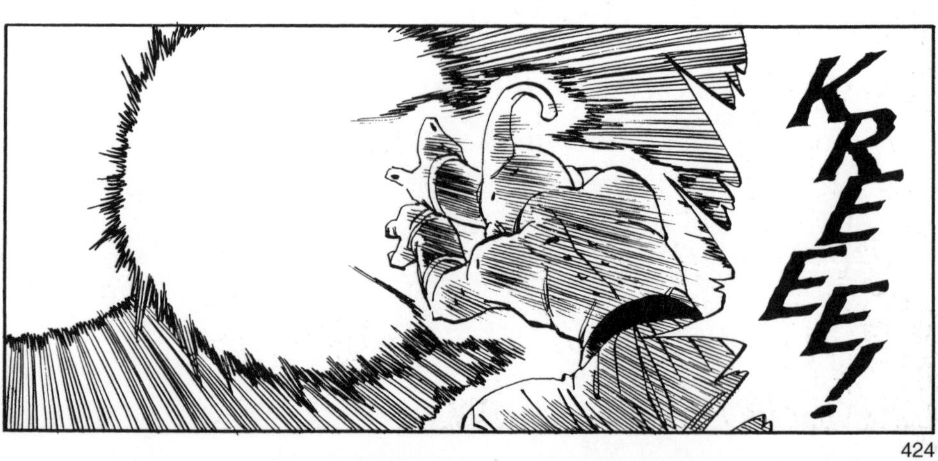
KREEE!

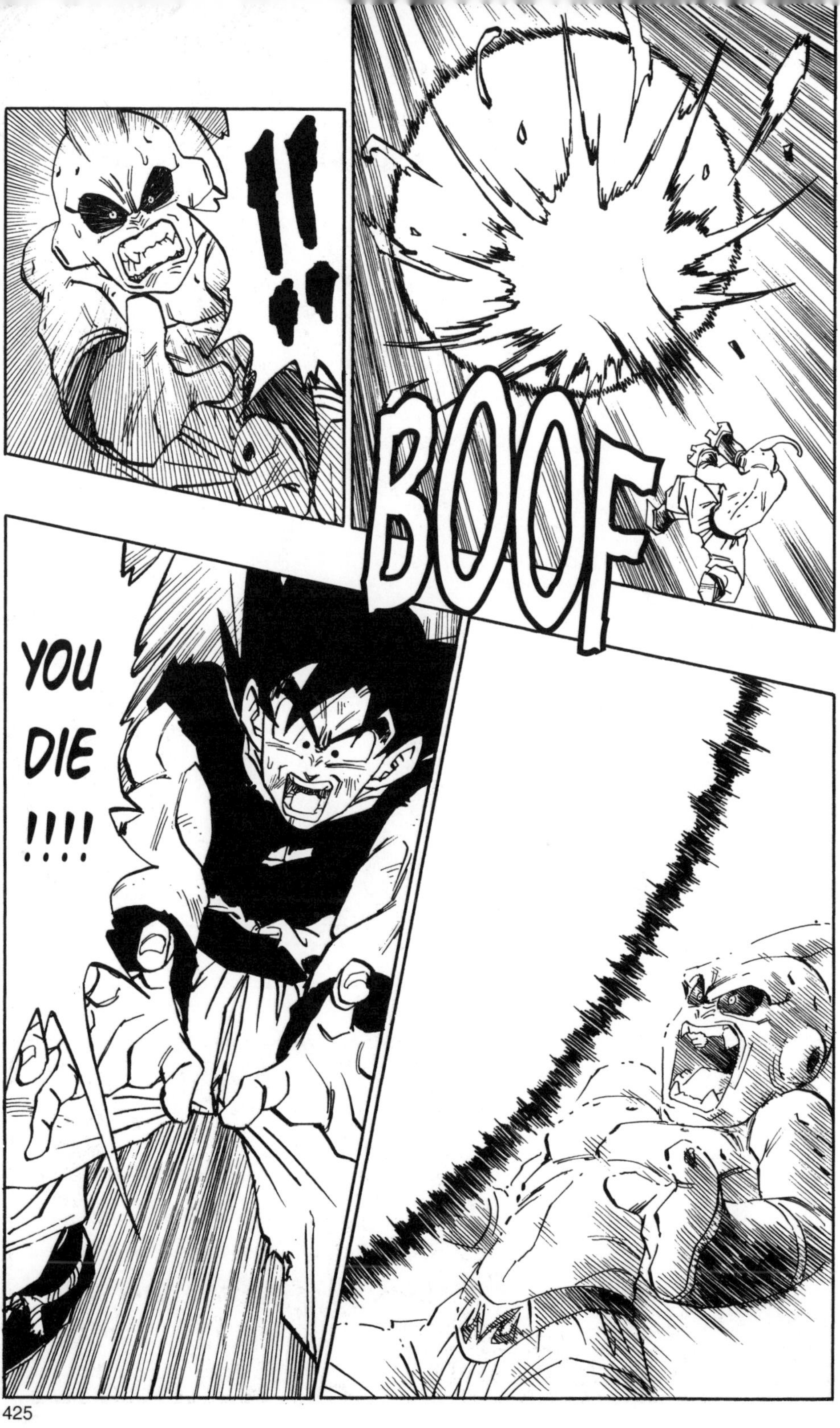
BOOF
!!
YOU DIE !!!!

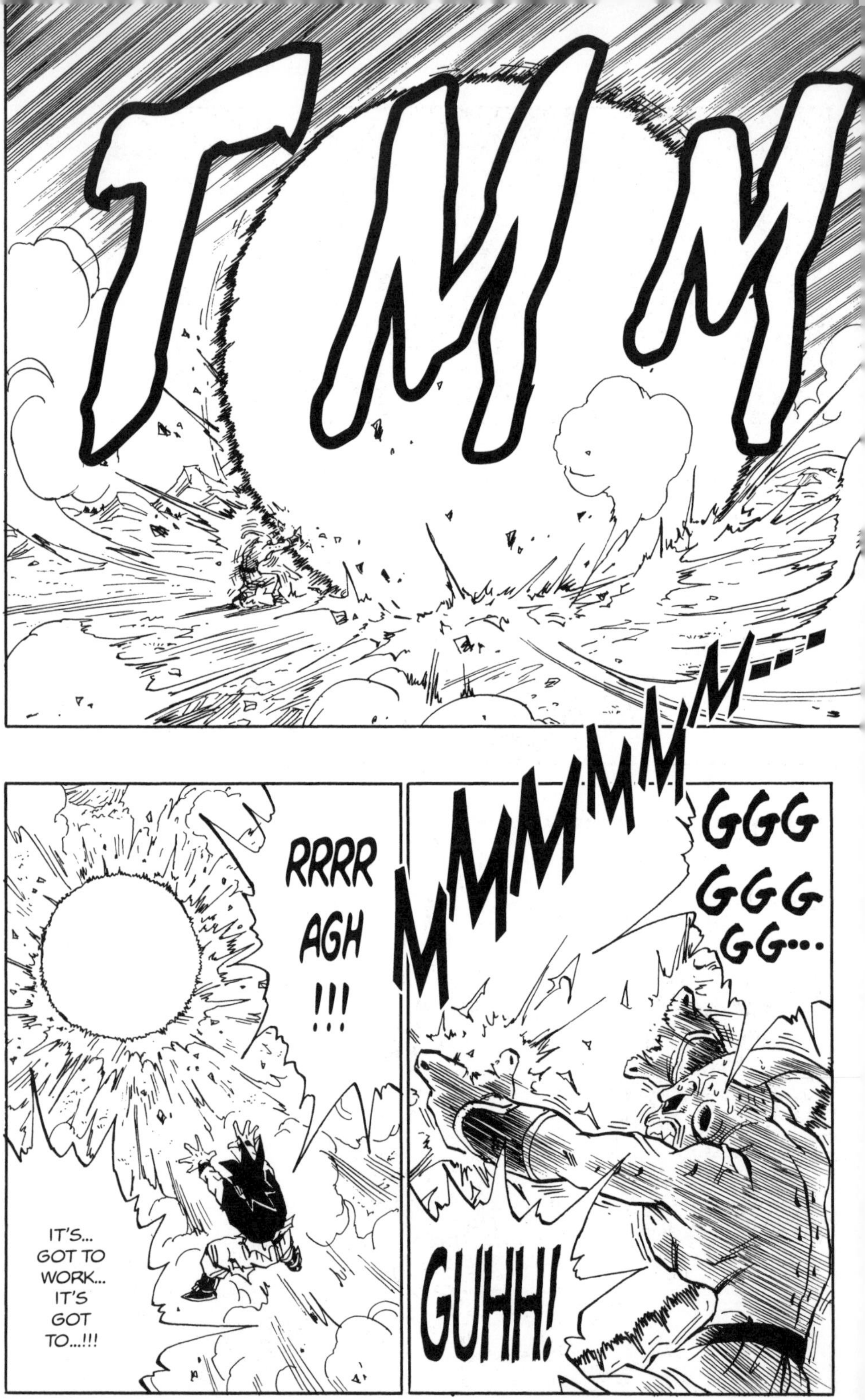
TMM
MMMMMMMM-...
GGG GGG GG...
GUHH!
RRRR AGH !!!
IT'S... GOT TO WORK... IT'S GOT TO...!!!

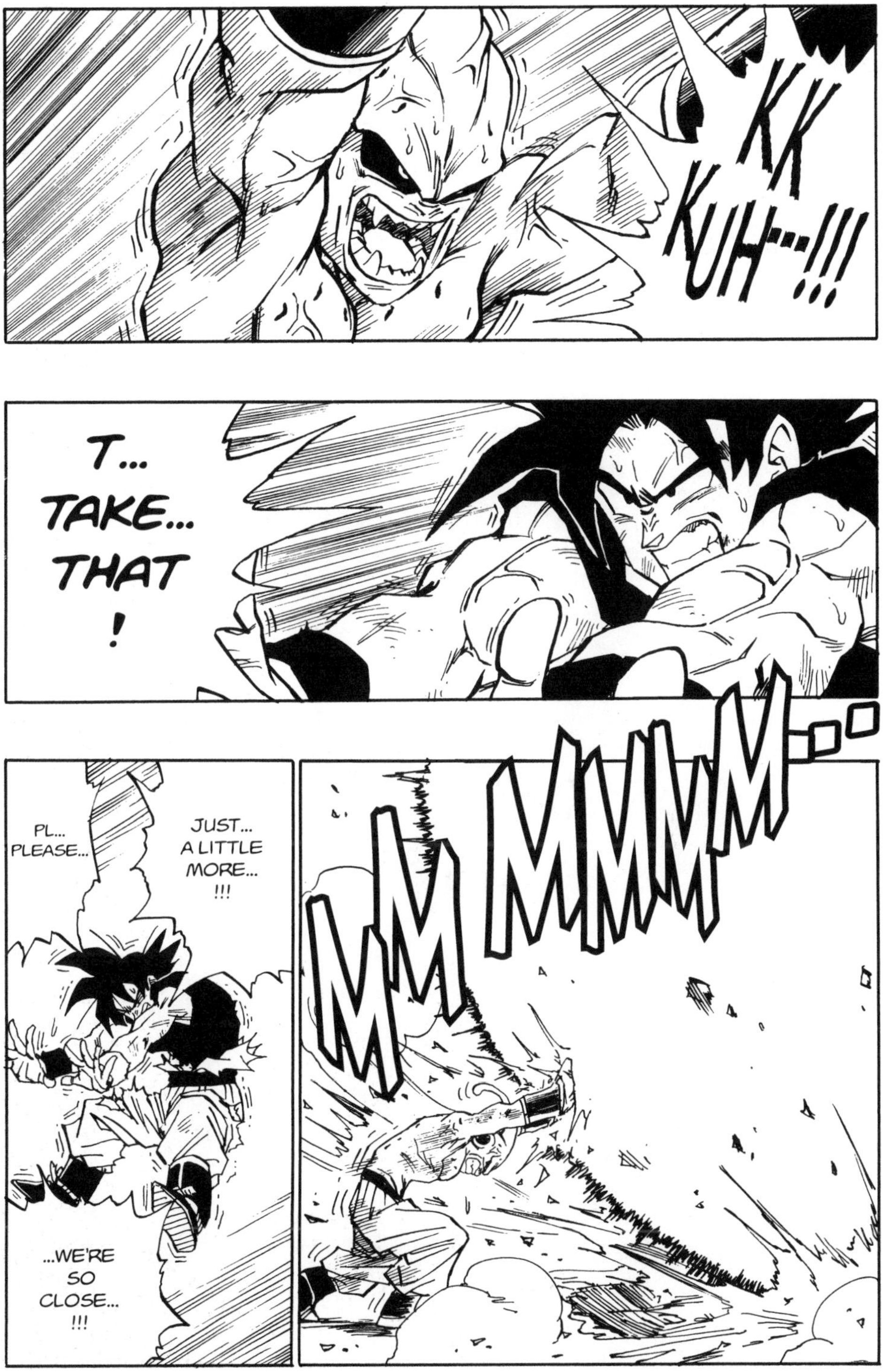
KK KUH...!!!
T... TAKE... THAT!
MM MMMM...
JUST... A LITTLE MORE...!!!
PL... PLEASE...
...WE'RE SO CLOSE...!!!

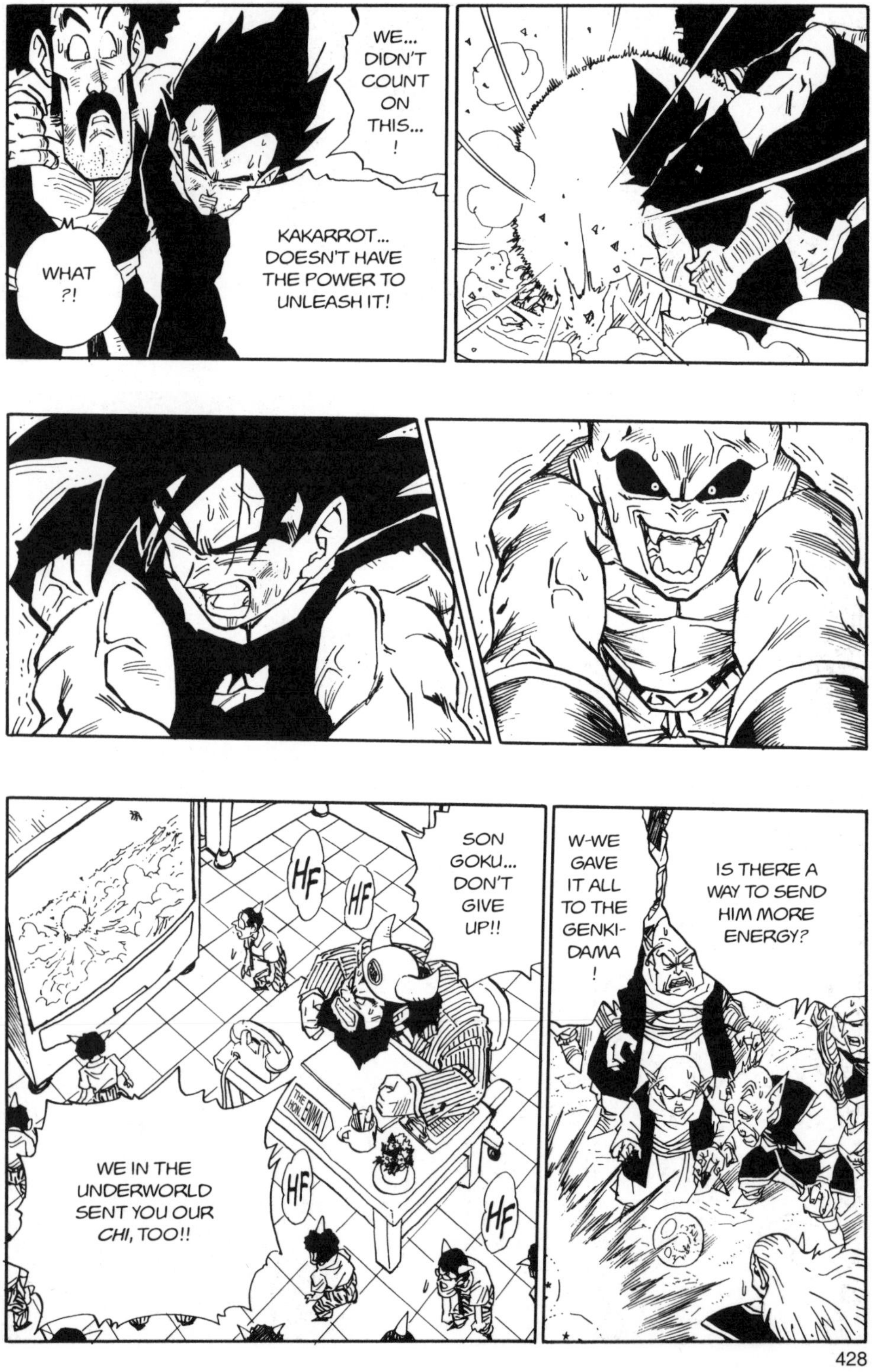
WE... DIDN'T COUNT ON THIS... !
KAKARROT... DOESN'T HAVE THE POWER TO UNLEASH IT!
WHAT ?!
IS THERE A WAY TO SEND HIM MORE ENERGY?
W-WE GAVE IT ALL TO THE GENKI-DAMA !
SON GOKU... DON'T GIVE UP!!
HF
HF
THE HON. ENMA
HF
HF
WE IN THE UNDERWORLD SENT YOU OUR *CHI*, TOO!!

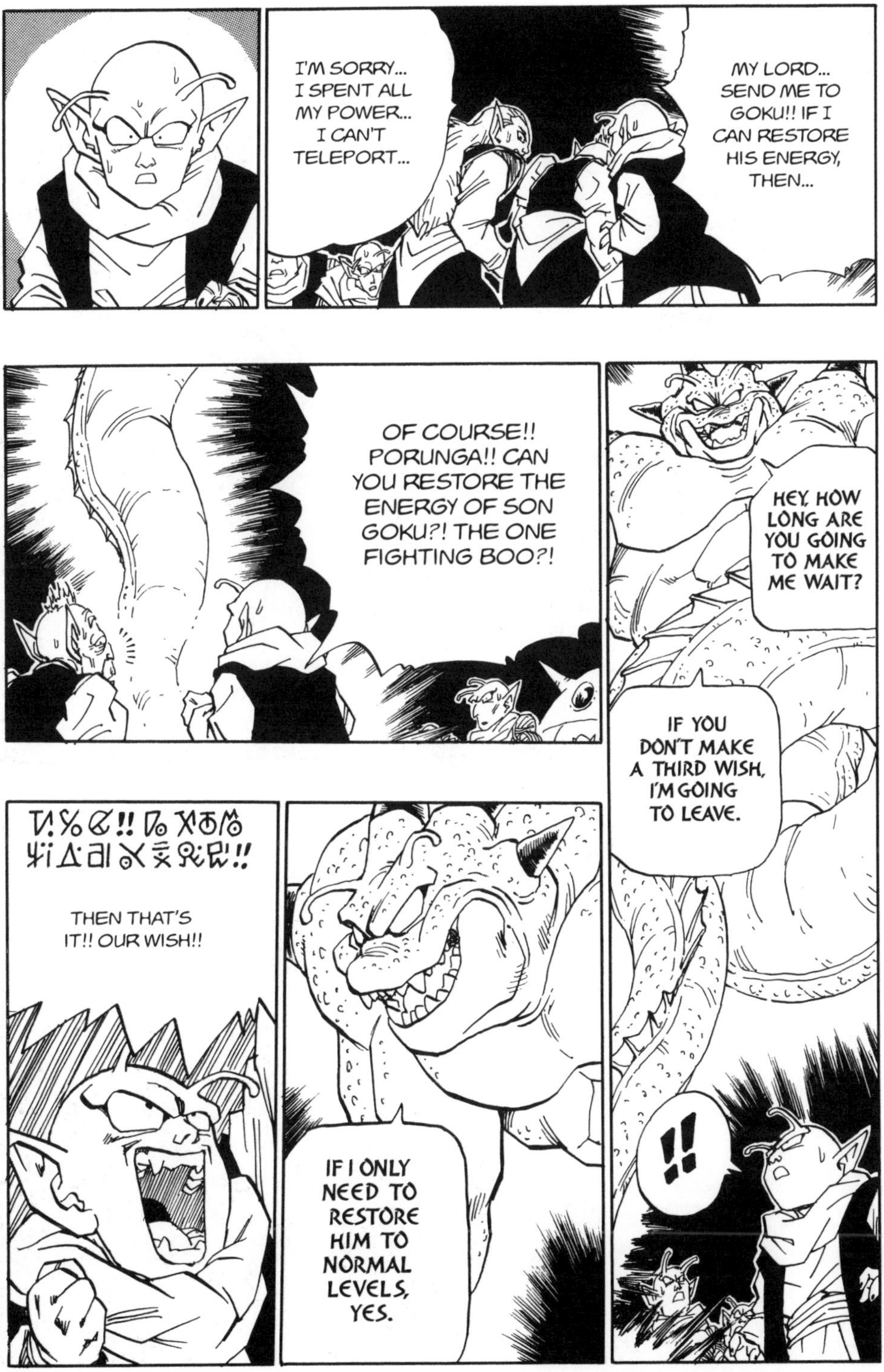
MY LORD... SEND ME TO GOKU!! IF I CAN RESTORE HIS ENERGY, THEN...
I'M SORRY... I SPENT ALL MY POWER... I CAN'T TELEPORT...
HEY, HOW LONG ARE YOU GOING TO MAKE ME WAIT?
IF YOU DON'T MAKE A THIRD WISH, I'M GOING TO LEAVE.
!!
OF COURSE!! PORUNGA!! CAN YOU RESTORE THE ENERGY OF SON GOKU?! THE ONE FIGHTING BOO?!
IF I ONLY NEED TO RESTORE HIM TO NORMAL LEVELS, YES.
THEN THAT'S IT!! OUR WISH!!

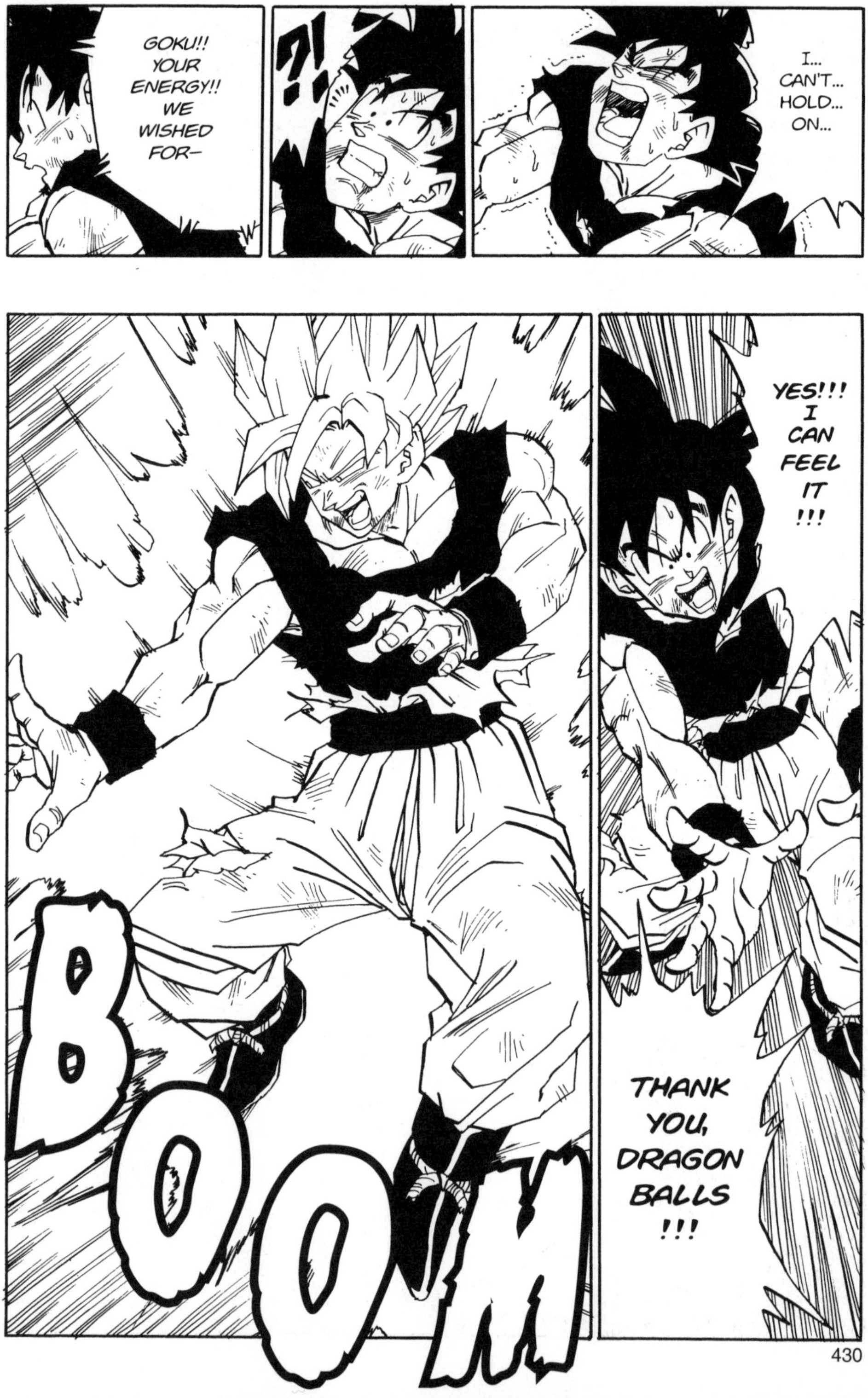
I... CAN'T... HOLD... ON...
?!
GOKU!! YOUR ENERGY!! WE WISHED FOR–
YES!!! I CAN FEEL IT !!!
THANK YOU, DRAGON BALLS !!!
BOOM

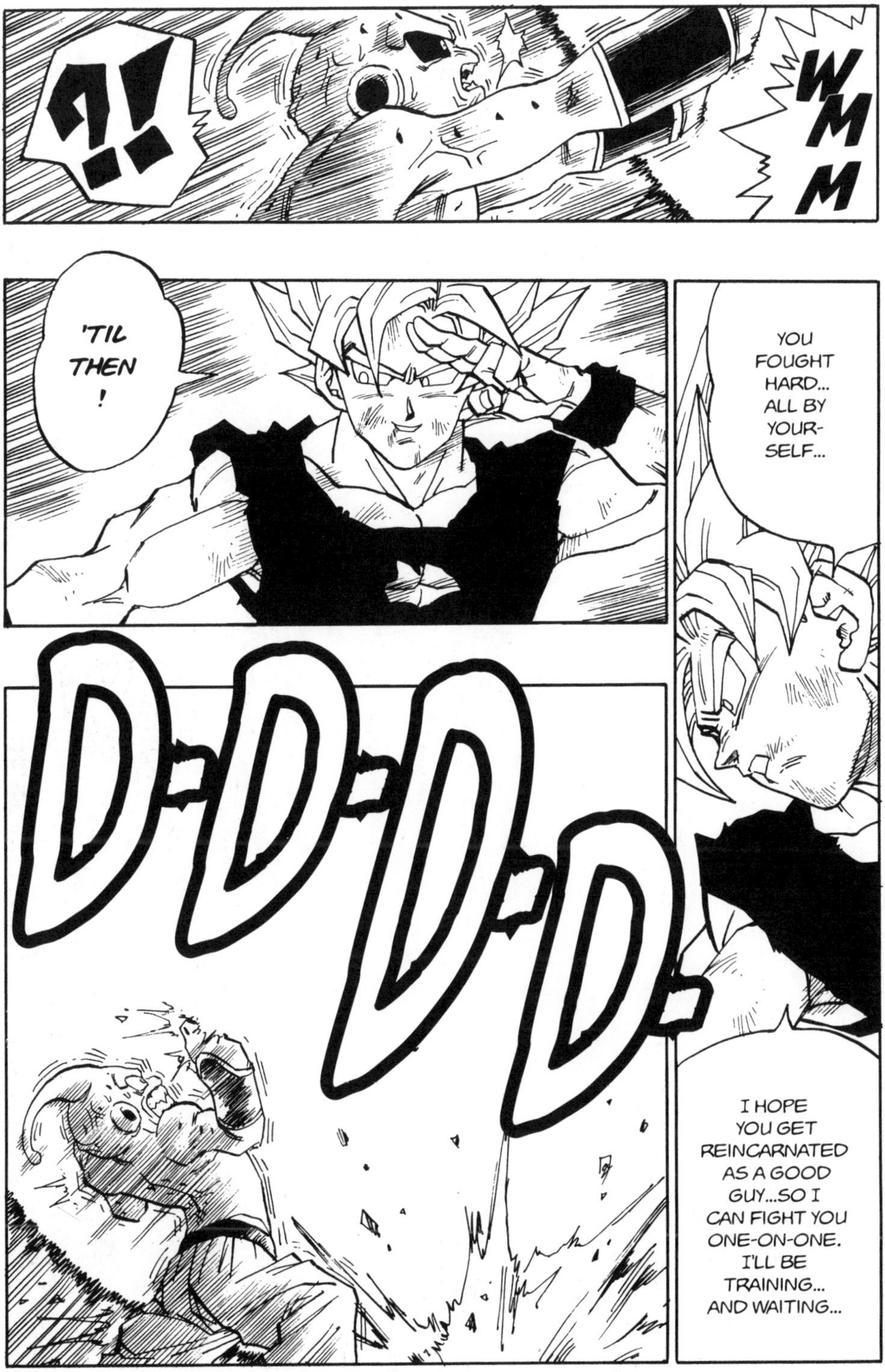
WMM
?!
YOU FOUGHT HARD... ALL BY YOURSELF...
I HOPE YOU GET REINCARNATED AS A GOOD GUY...SO I CAN FIGHT YOU ONE-ON-ONE. I'LL BE TRAINING... AND WAITING...
'TIL THEN!
D-D-D-D

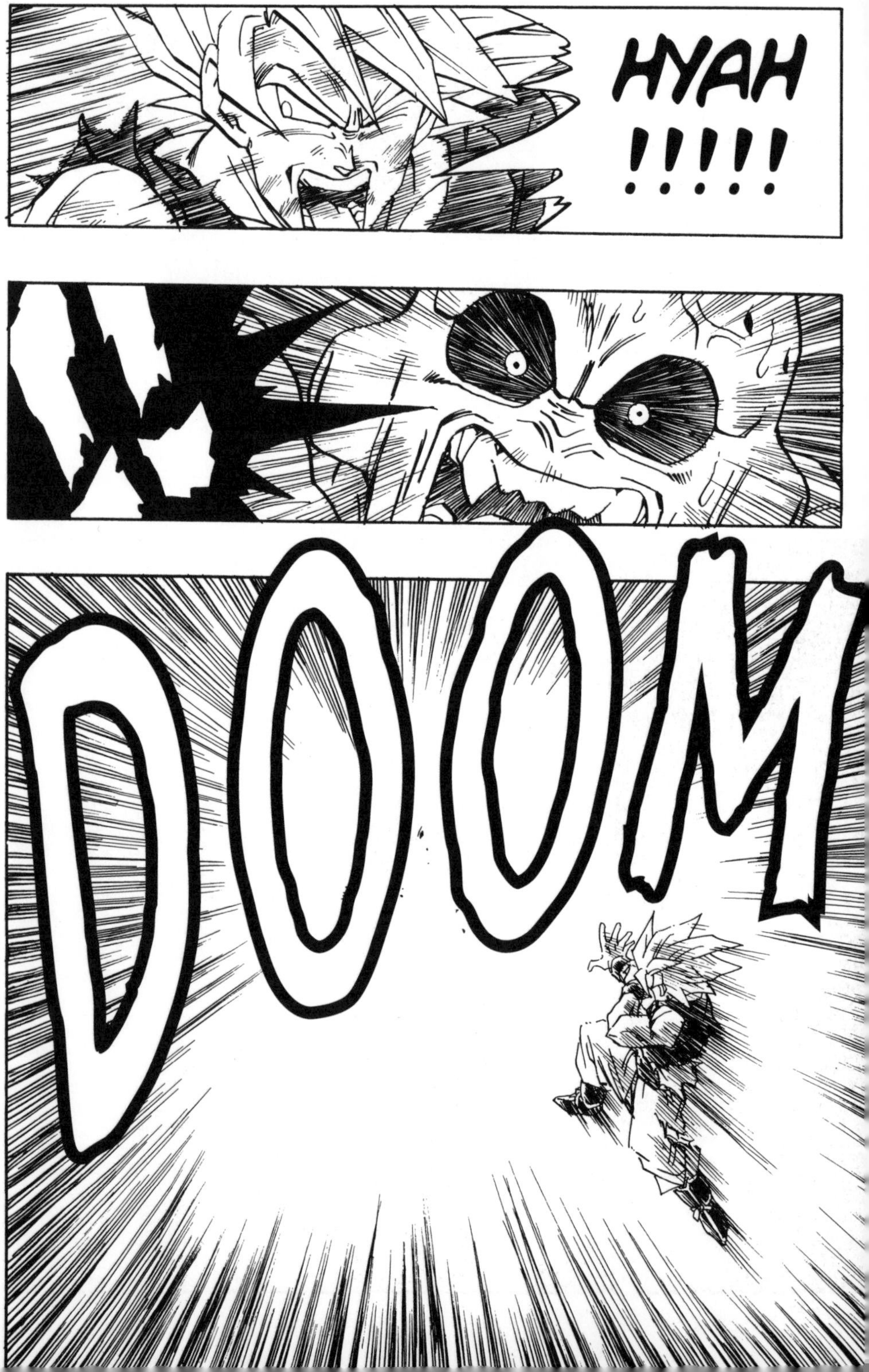
HYAH !!!!!
DOOM

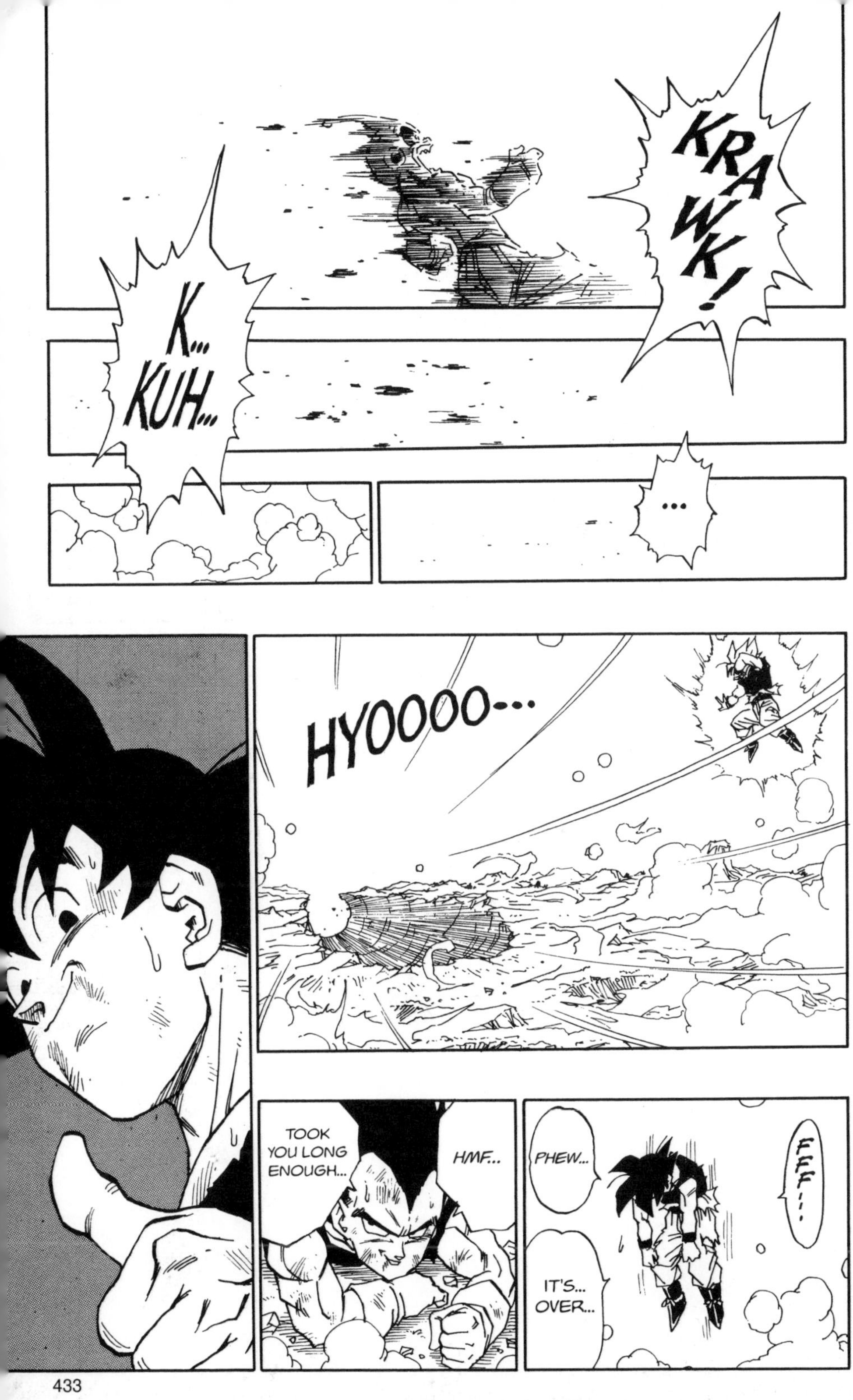
KRAWK!
K... KUH...
...
HYOOOO...
FFF...
PHEW...
IT'S... OVER...
HMF...
TOOK YOU LONG ENOUGH...

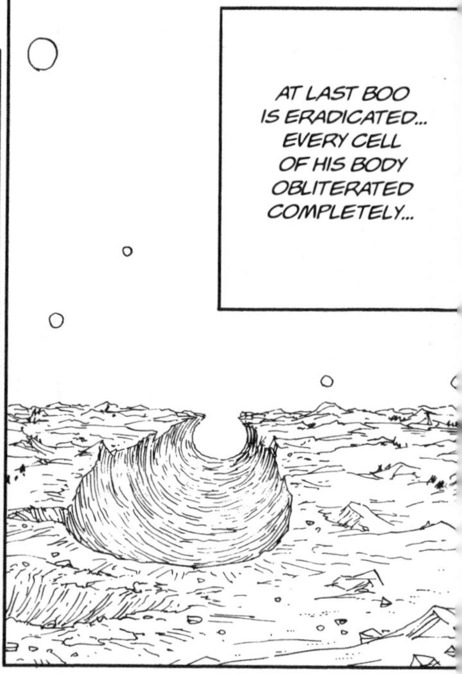
AT LAST BOO IS ERADICATED... EVERY CELL OF HIS BODY OBLITERATED COMPLETELY...

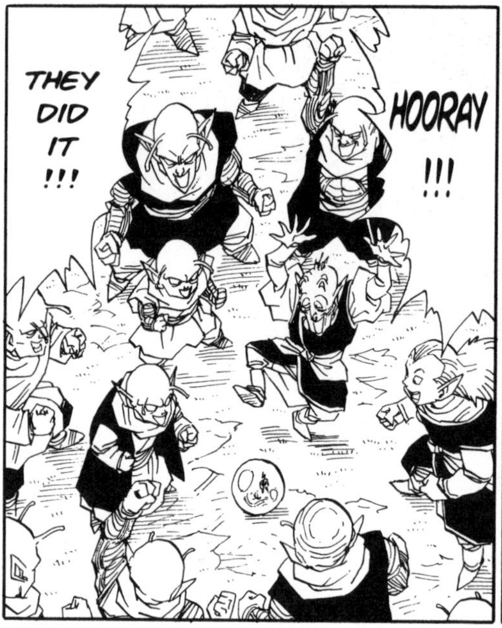
HOORAY !!!
THEY DID IT !!!

DBZ:323 • A Happy Ending...and Then...

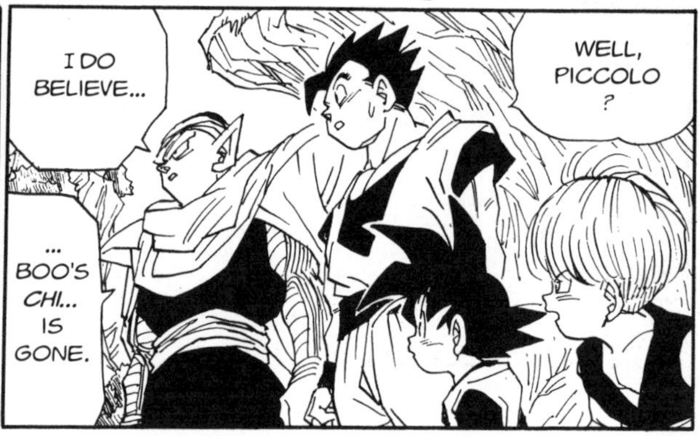
WELL, PICCOLO ?
I DO BELIEVE...
... BOO'S CHI... IS GONE.

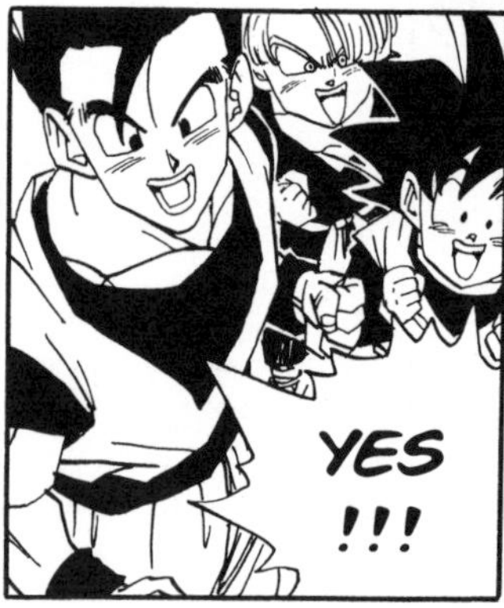
YES !!!

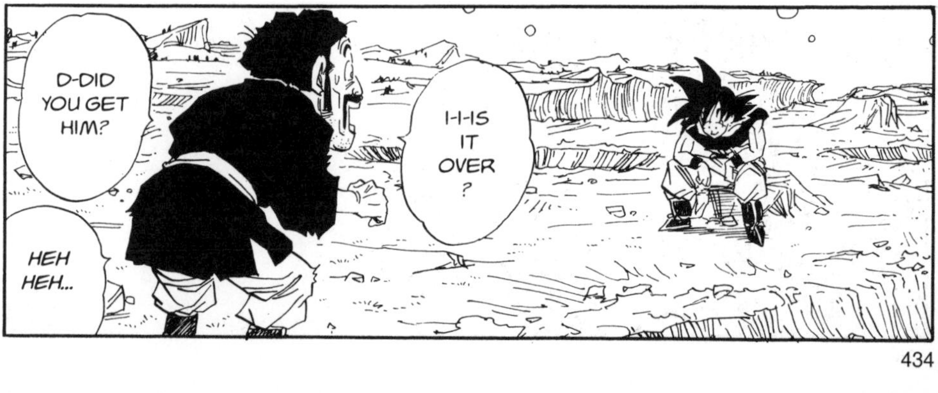
I-I-IS IT OVER ?
D-DID YOU GET HIM?
HEH HEH...

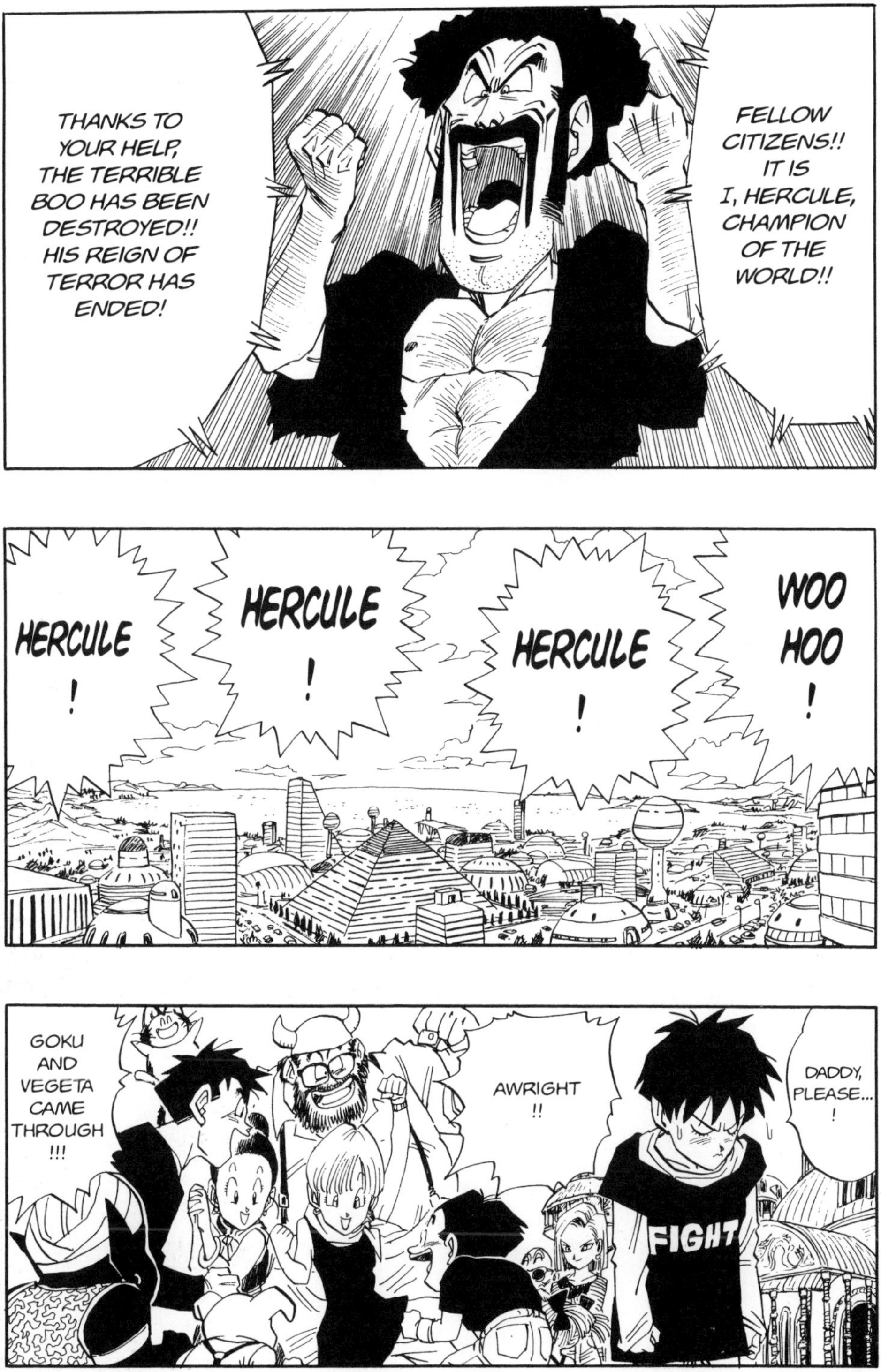
FELLOW CITIZENS!! IT IS I, HERCULE, CHAMPION OF THE WORLD!!
THANKS TO YOUR HELP, THE TERRIBLE BOO HAS BEEN DESTROYED!! HIS REIGN OF TERROR HAS ENDED!
WOO HOO!
HERCULE!
HERCULE!
HERCULE!
DADDY, PLEASE...!
AWRIGHT!!
GOKU AND VEGETA CAME THROUGH!!!

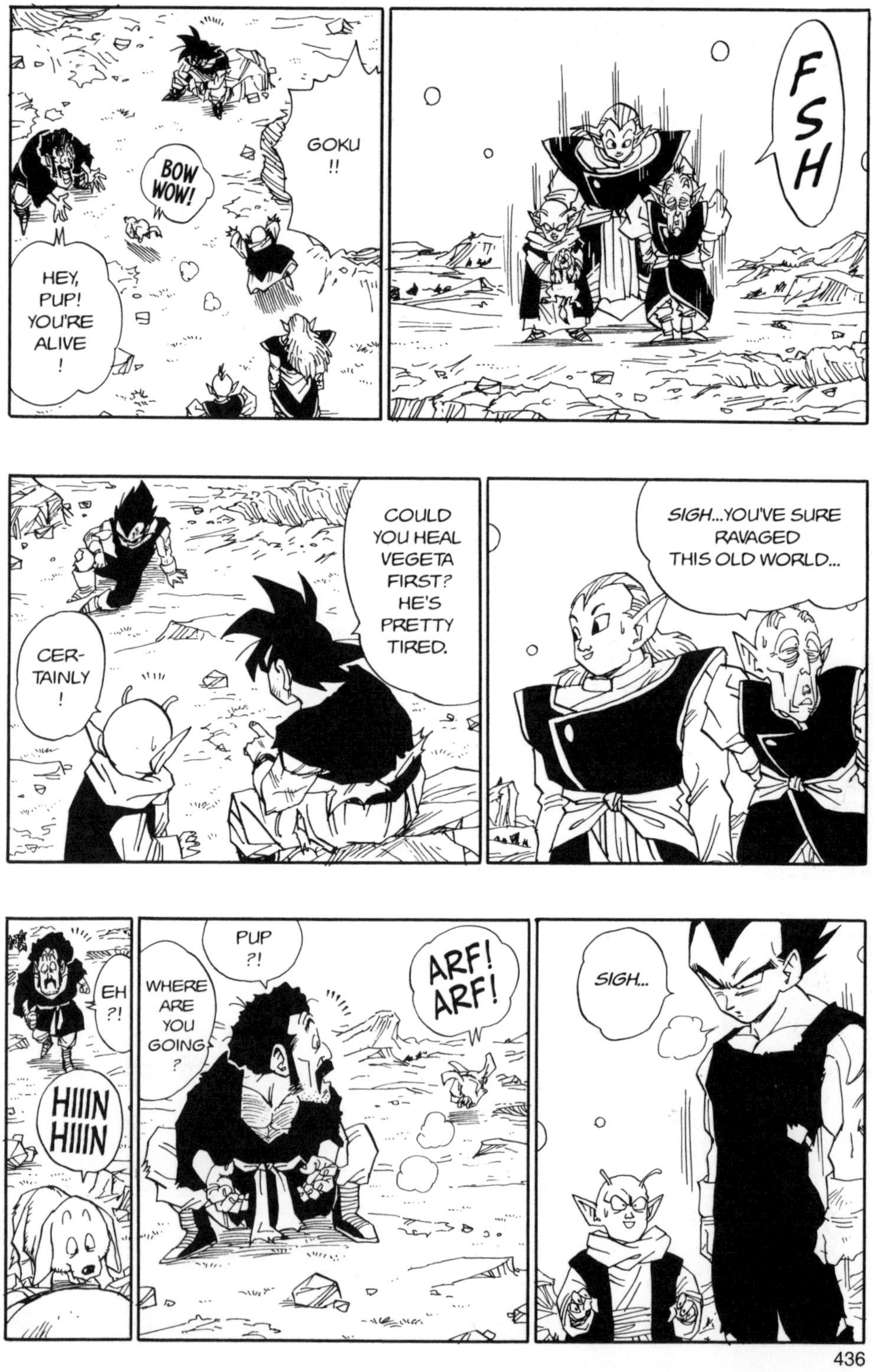
FSH
GOKU !!
BOW WOW!
HEY, PUP! YOU'RE ALIVE!
SIGH...YOU'VE SURE RAVAGED THIS OLD WORLD...
COULD YOU HEAL VEGETA FIRST? HE'S PRETTY TIRED.
CER-TAINLY!
SIGH...
ARF! ARF!
PUP ?!
WHERE ARE YOU GOING?
EH ?!
HIIIN HIIIN

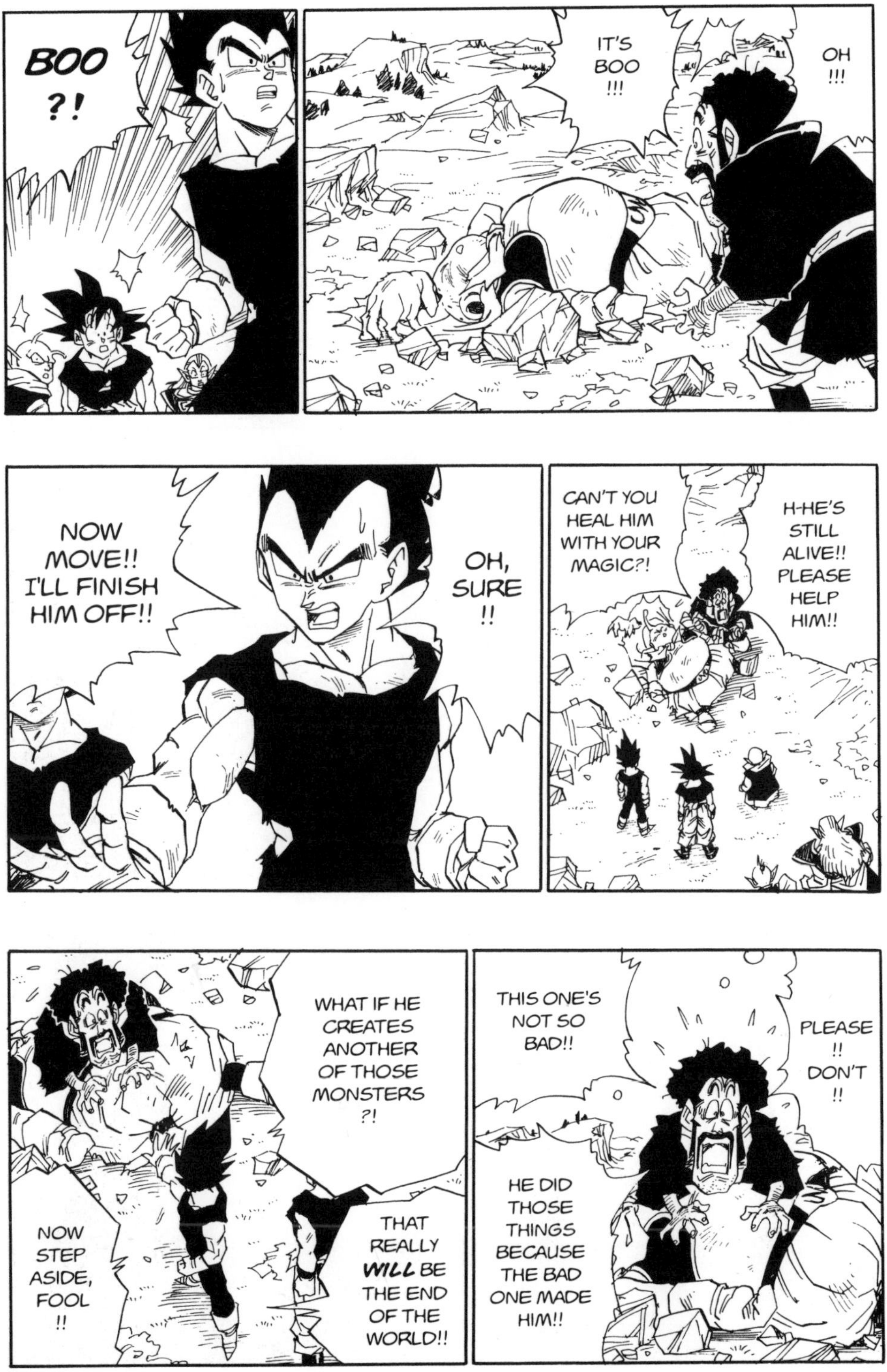
OH !!!
IT'S BOO !!!
BOO ?!
H-HE'S STILL ALIVE!! PLEASE HELP HIM!!
CAN'T YOU HEAL HIM WITH YOUR MAGIC?!
OH, SURE !!
NOW MOVE!! I'LL FINISH HIM OFF!!
PLEASE !! DON'T !!
THIS ONE'S NOT SO BAD!!
HE DID THOSE THINGS BECAUSE THE BAD ONE MADE HIM!!
WHAT IF HE CREATES ANOTHER OF THOSE MONSTERS ?!
THAT REALLY **WILL** BE THE END OF THE WORLD!!
NOW STEP ASIDE, FOOL !!

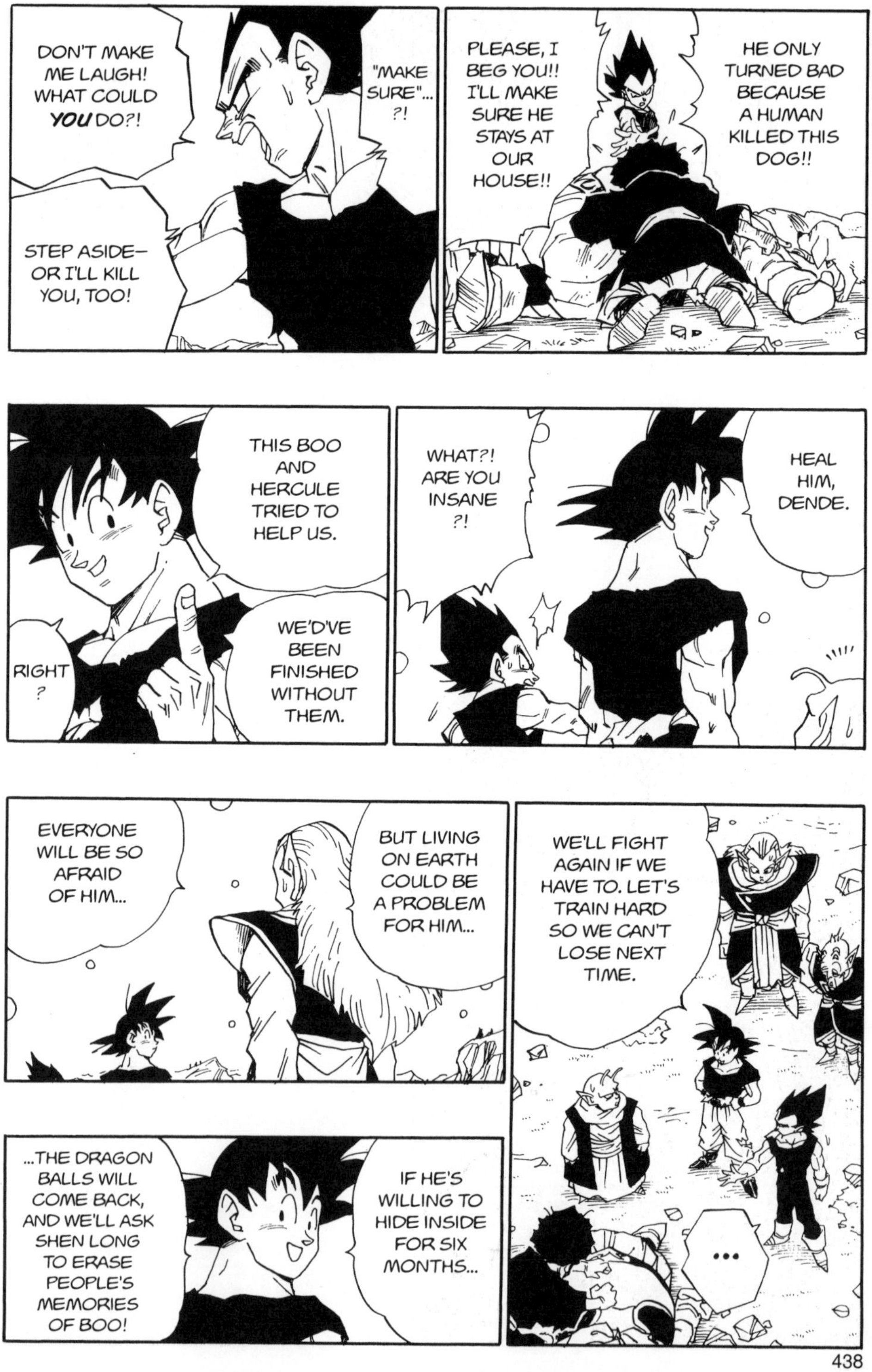
HE ONLY TURNED BAD BECAUSE A HUMAN KILLED THIS DOG!!
PLEASE, I BEG YOU!! I'LL MAKE SURE HE STAYS AT OUR HOUSE!!
"MAKE SURE"... ?!
DON'T MAKE ME LAUGH! WHAT COULD ***YOU*** DO?!
STEP ASIDE— OR I'LL KILL YOU, TOO!
HEAL HIM, DENDE.
WHAT?! ARE YOU INSANE ?!
THIS BOO AND HERCULE TRIED TO HELP US.
WE'D'VE BEEN FINISHED WITHOUT THEM.
RIGHT ?
WE'LL FIGHT AGAIN IF WE HAVE TO. LET'S TRAIN HARD SO WE CAN'T LOSE NEXT TIME.
...
BUT LIVING ON EARTH COULD BE A PROBLEM FOR HIM...
EVERYONE WILL BE SO AFRAID OF HIM...
IF HE'S WILLING TO HIDE INSIDE FOR SIX MONTHS...
...THE DRAGON BALLS WILL COME BACK, AND WE'LL ASK SHEN LONG TO ERASE PEOPLE'S MEMORIES OF BOO!

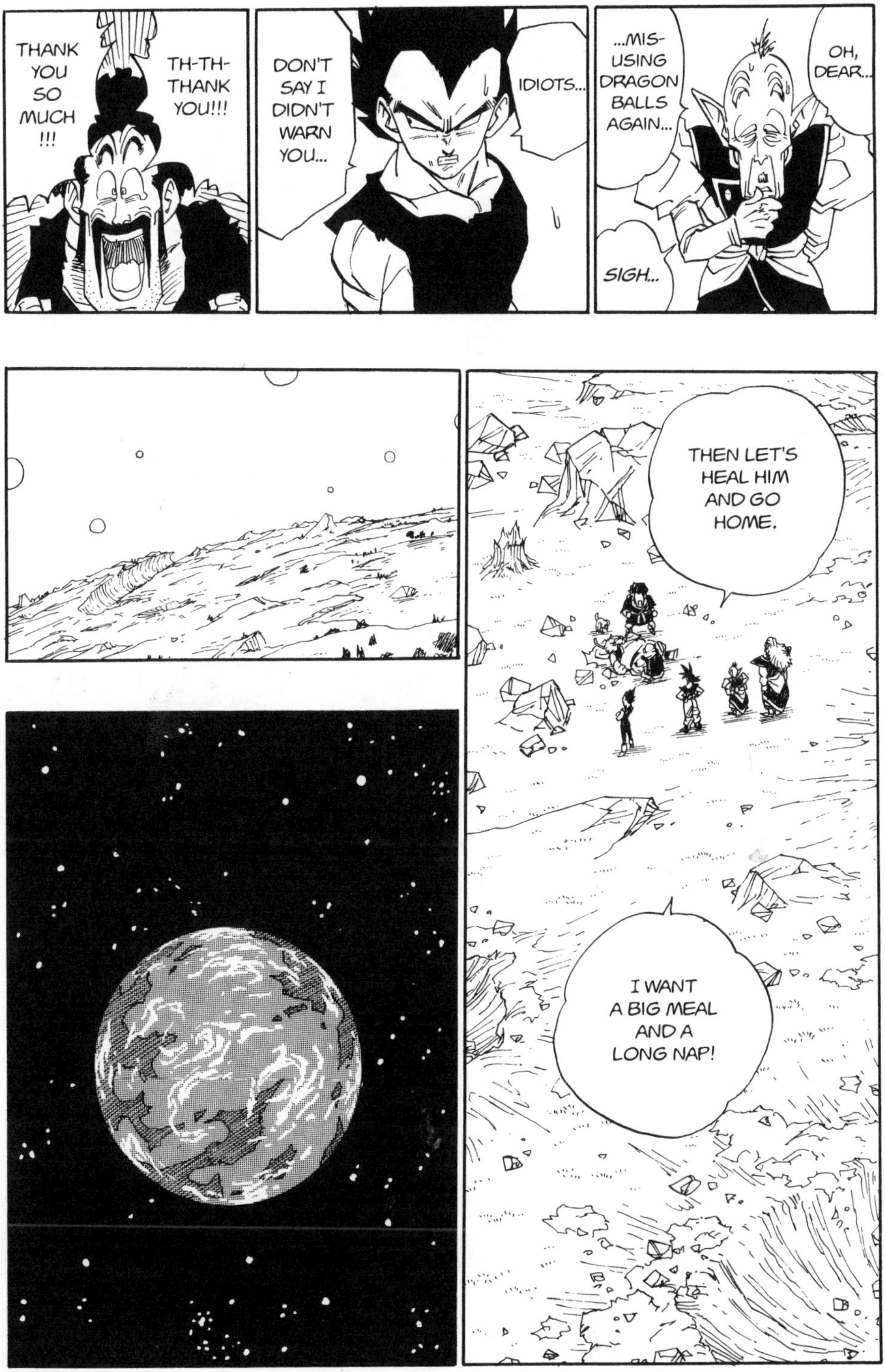
OH, DEAR...
...MIS-USING DRAGON BALLS AGAIN...
SIGH...
IDIOTS...
DON'T SAY I DIDN'T WARN YOU...
TH-TH-THANK YOU!!!
THANK YOU SO MUCH!!!
THEN LET'S HEAL HIM AND GO HOME.
I WANT A BIG MEAL AND A LONG NAP!

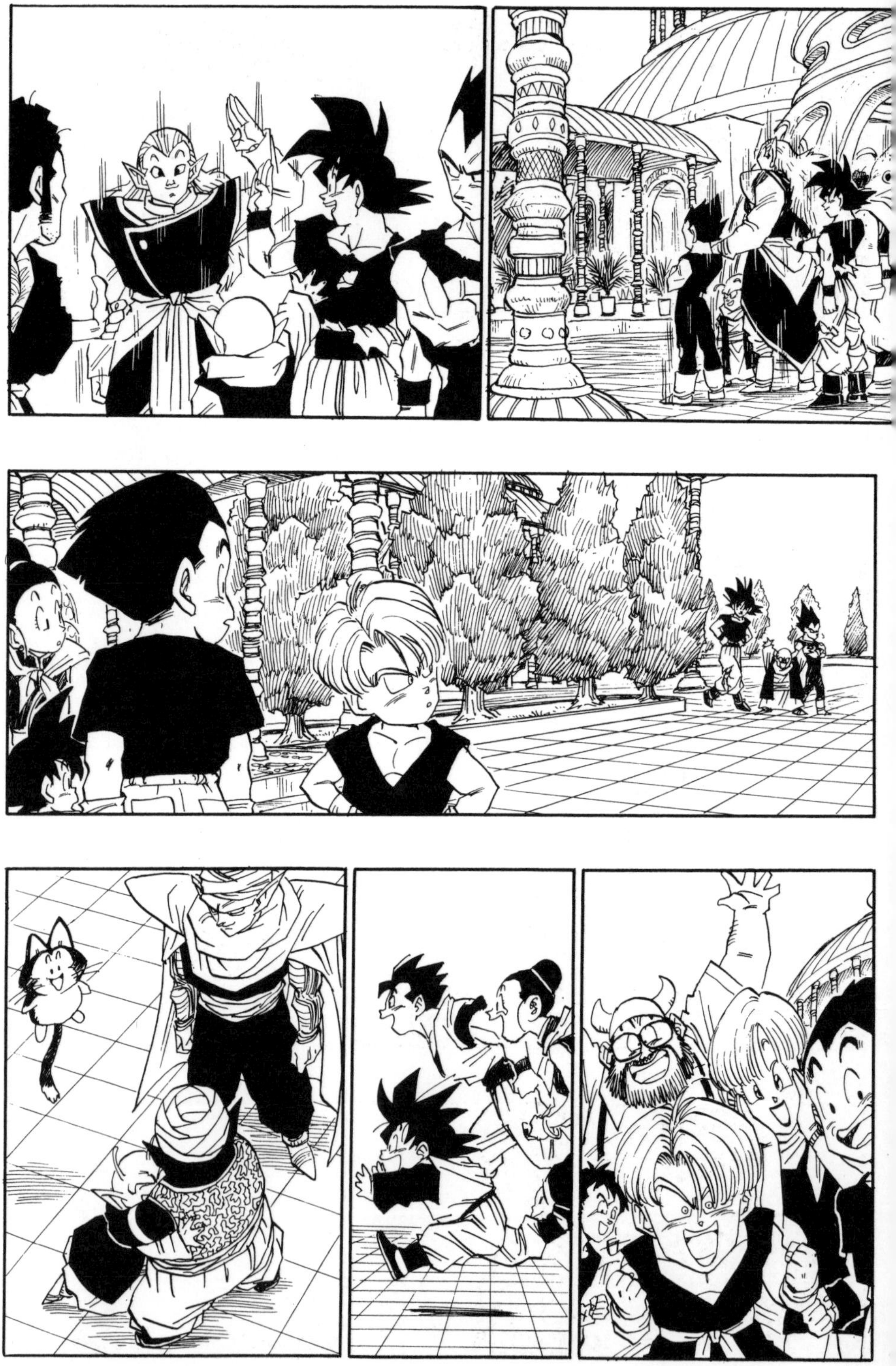

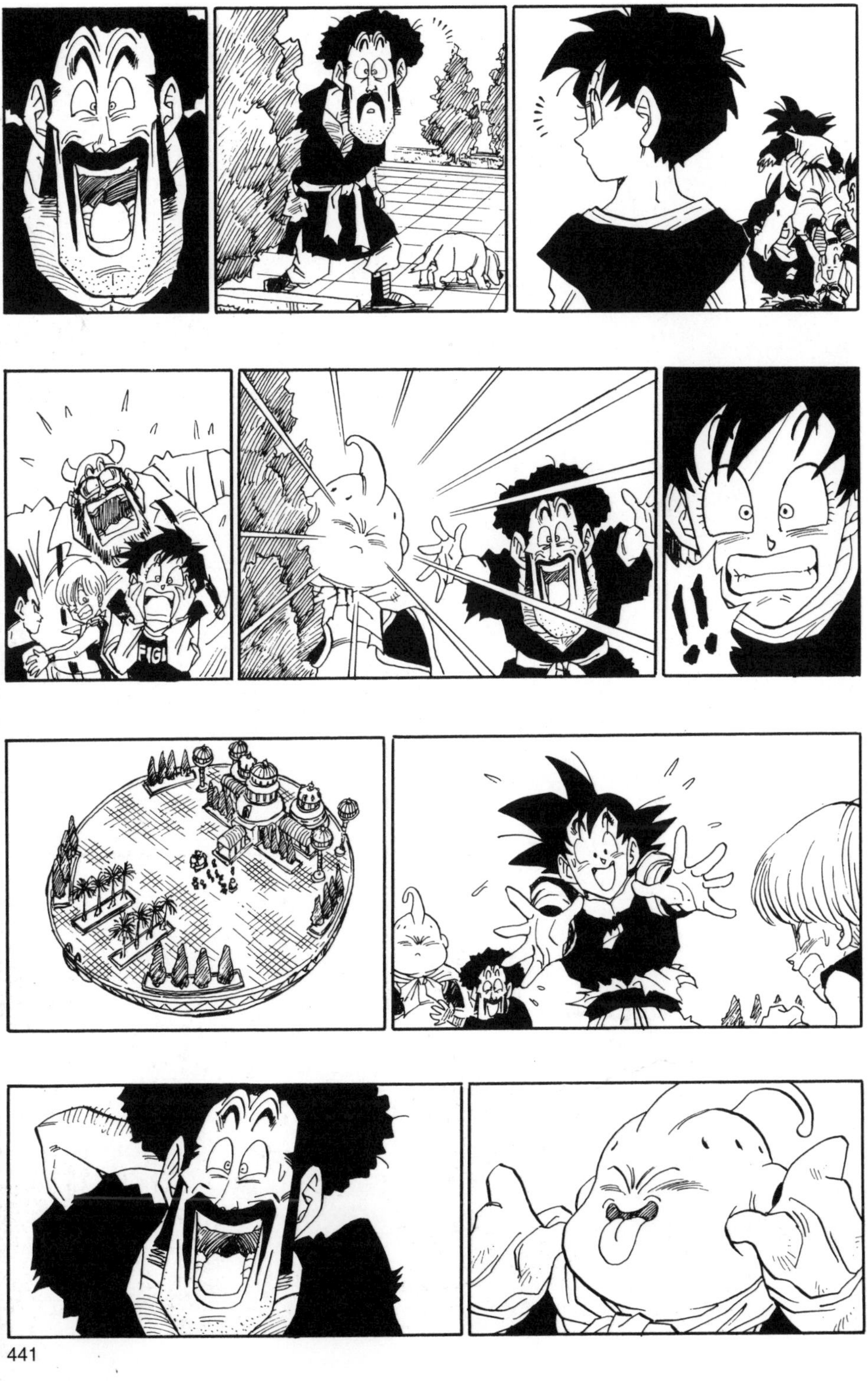

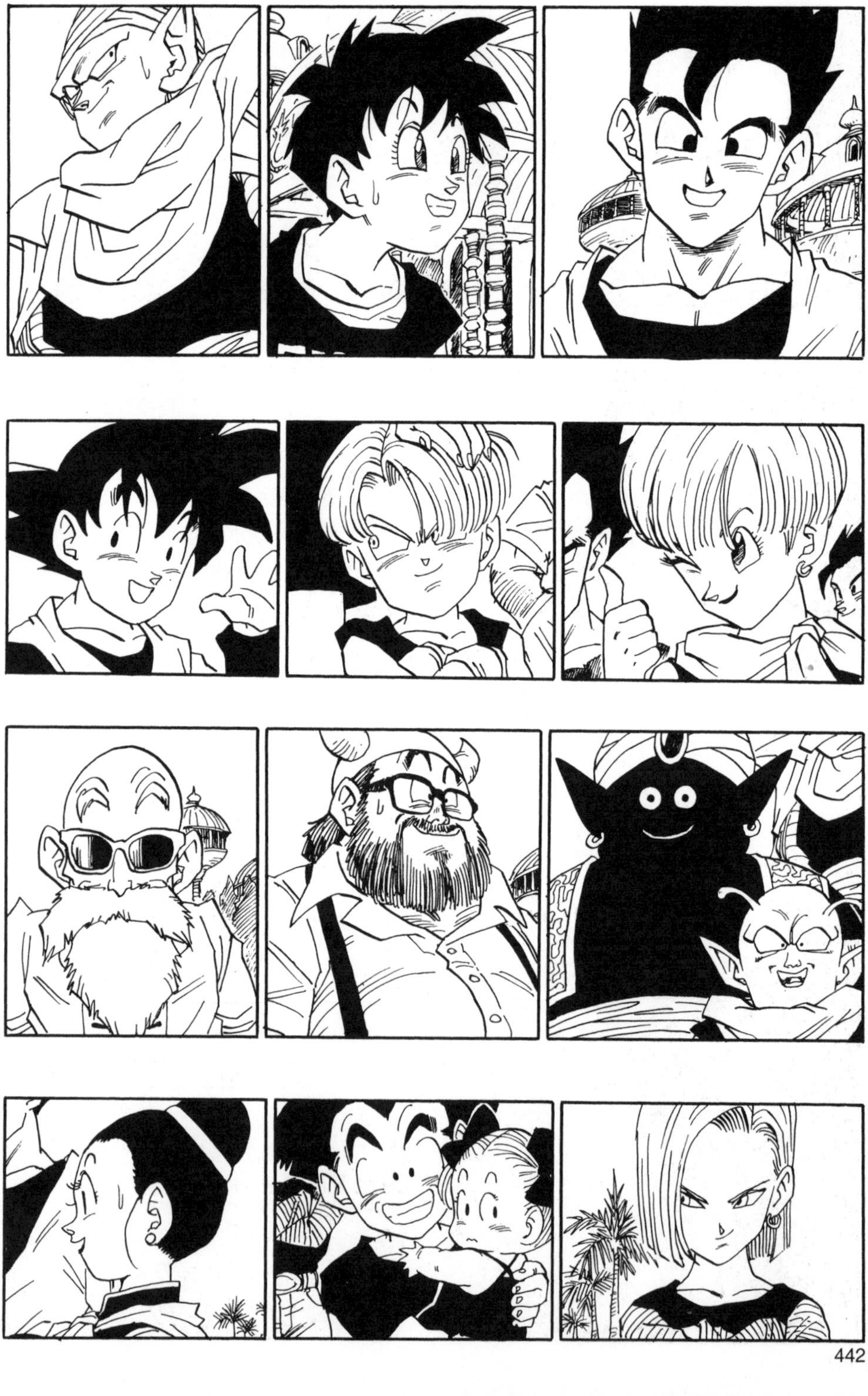

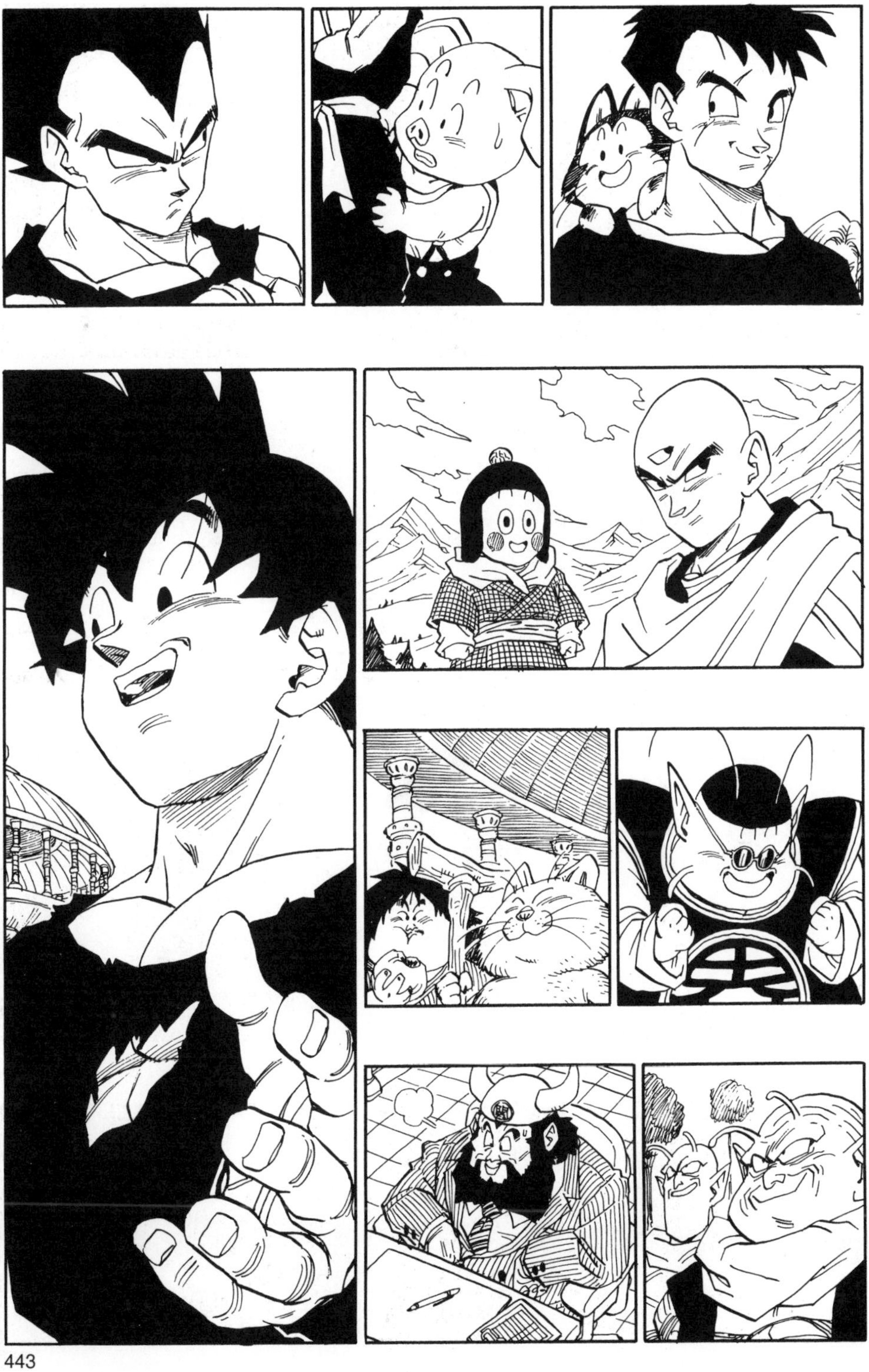

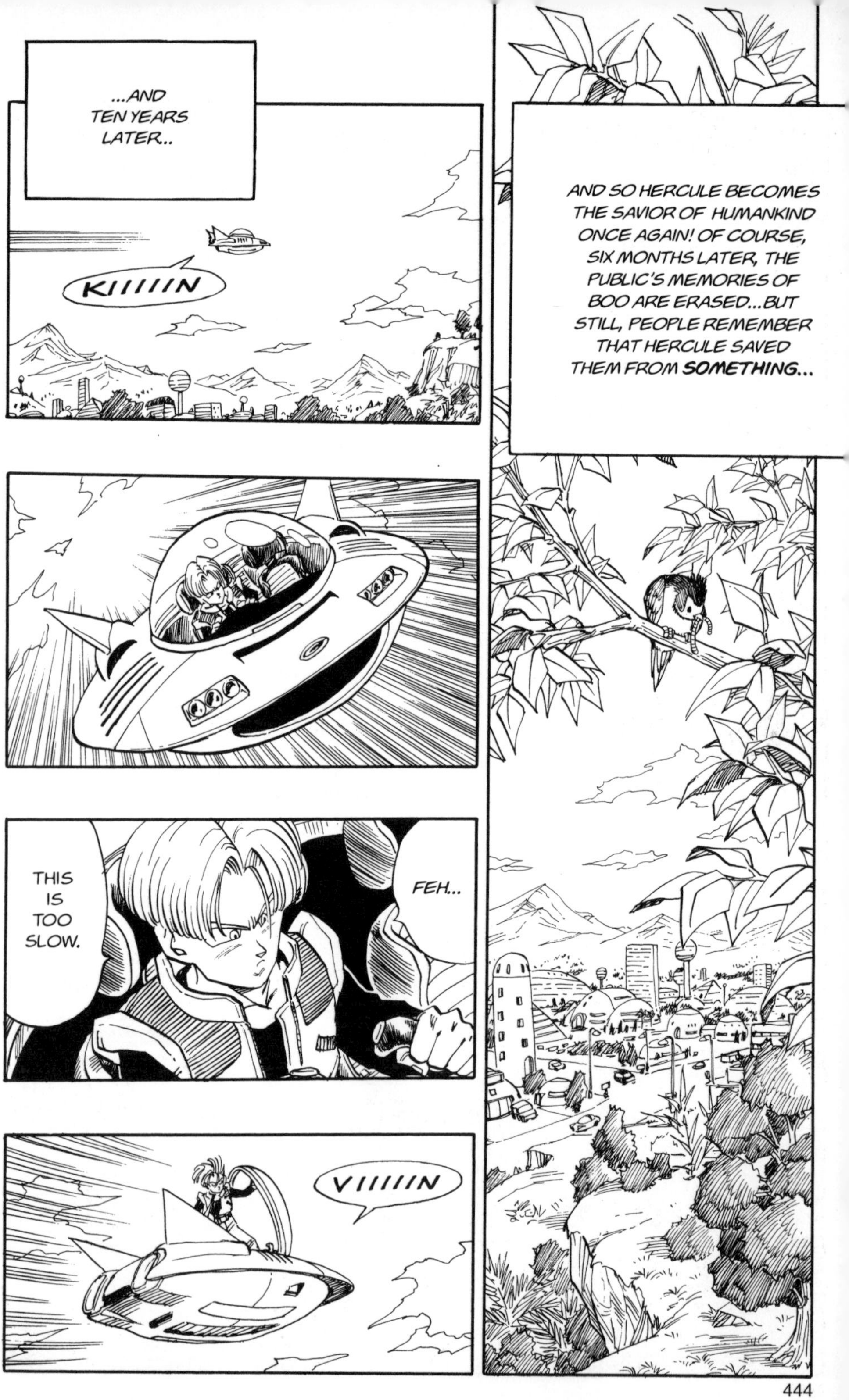
AND SO HERCULE BECOMES THE SAVIOR OF HUMANKIND ONCE AGAIN! OF COURSE, SIX MONTHS LATER, THE PUBLIC'S MEMORIES OF BOO ARE ERASED...BUT STILL, PEOPLE REMEMBER THAT HERCULE SAVED THEM FROM **SOMETHING...**
...AND TEN YEARS LATER...
KIIIIIN
FEH...
THIS IS TOO SLOW.
VIIIIIN

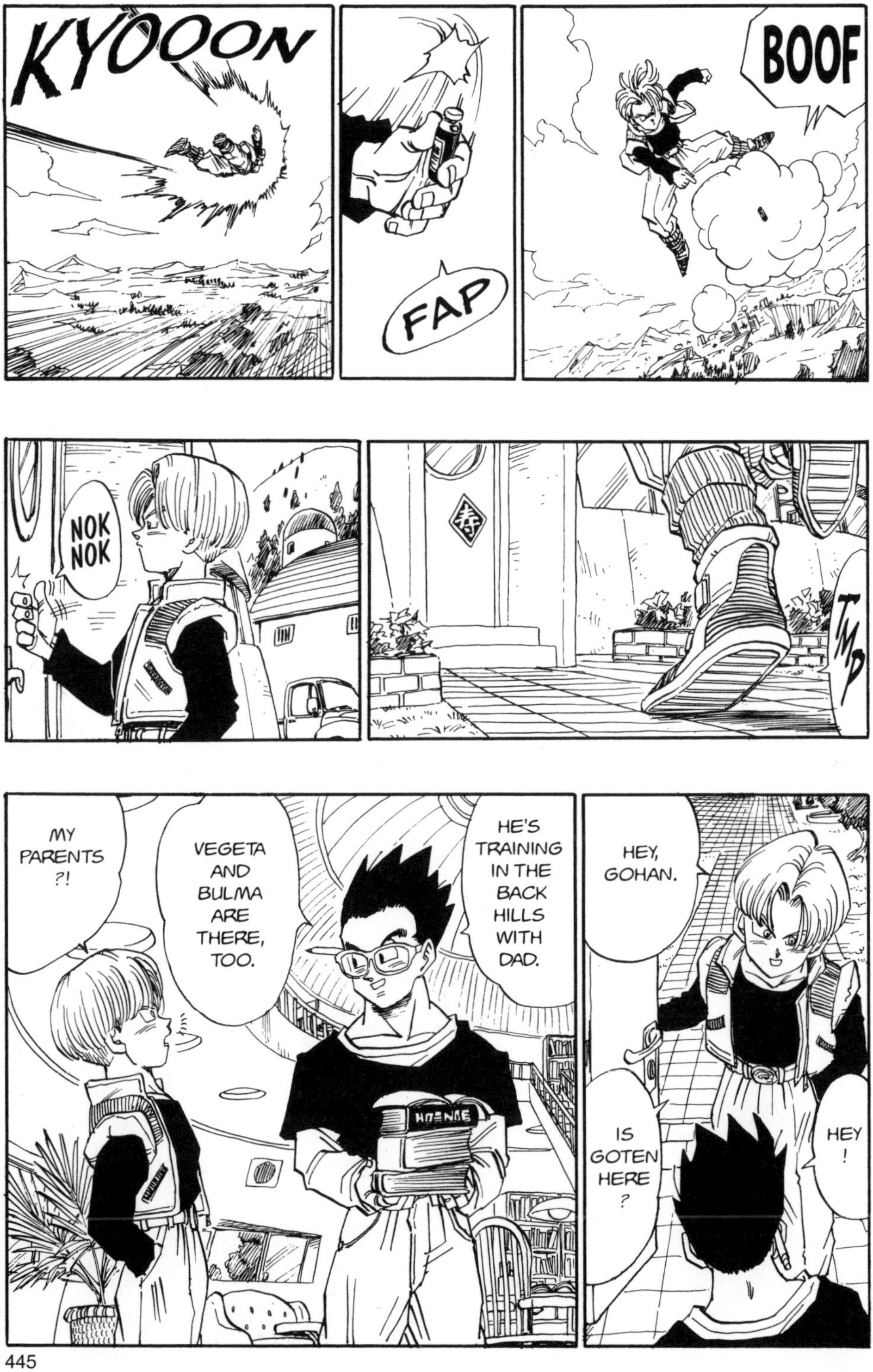
BOOF
FAP
KYOOON
TMP
NOK NOK
HEY, GOHAN.
HEY!
IS GOTEN HERE?
HE'S TRAINING IN THE BACK HILLS WITH DAD.
VEGETA AND BULMA ARE THERE, TOO.
MY PARENTS ?!

DRAGON BALL ドラゴンボール

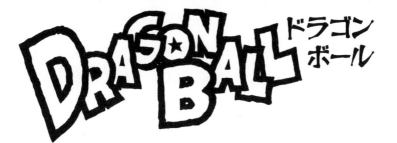

DBZ:324 • Ten Years After

★ The Cast—Ten Years Older ★

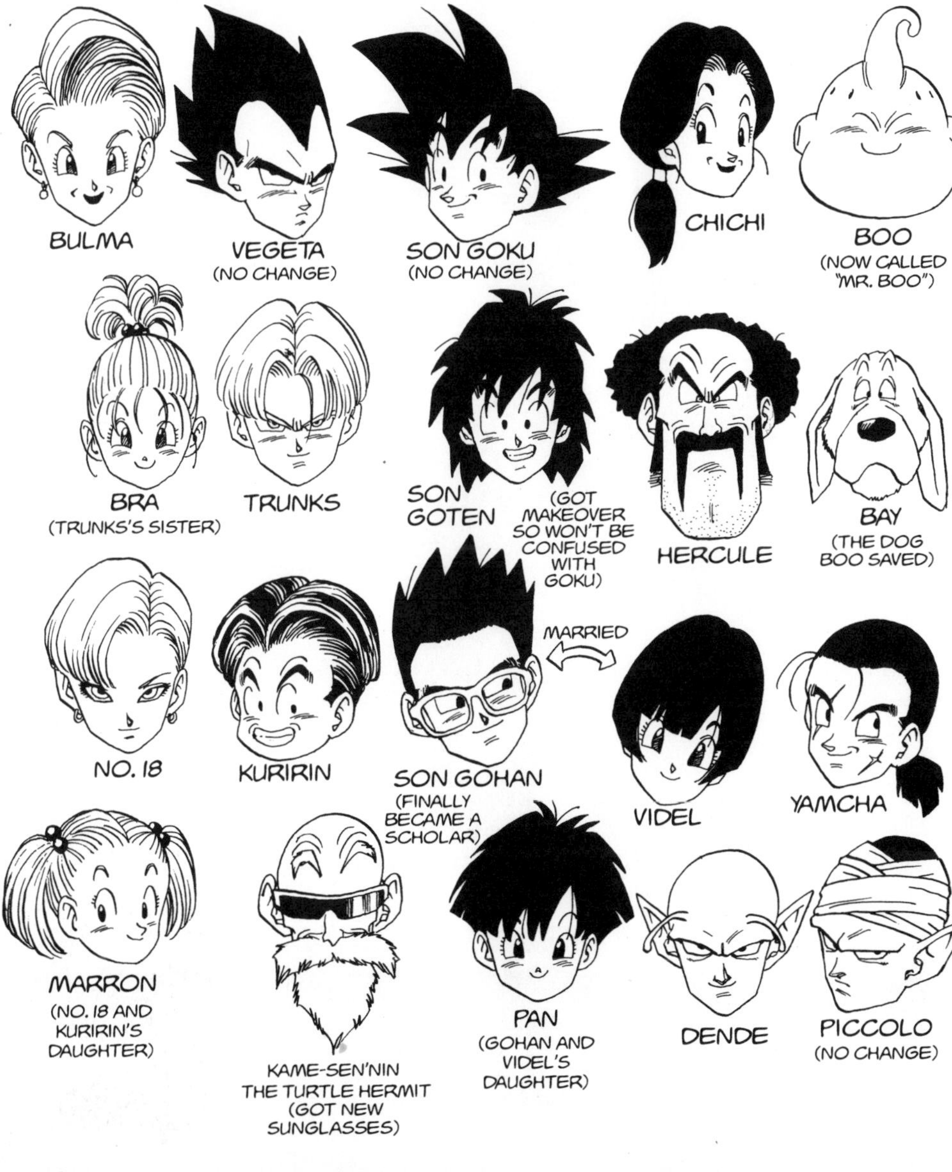
BULMA
VEGETA
(NO CHANGE)
SON GOKU
(NO CHANGE)
CHICHI
BOO
(NOW CALLED "MR. BOO")
BRA
(TRUNKS'S SISTER)
TRUNKS
SON GOTEN
(GOT MAKEOVER SO WON'T BE CONFUSED WITH GOKU)
HERCULE
BAY
(THE DOG BOO SAVED)
NO. 18
KURIRIN
SON GOHAN
(FINALLY BECAME A SCHOLAR)
MARRIED
VIDEL
YAMCHA
MARRON
(NO. 18 AND KURIRIN'S DAUGHTER)
KAME-SEN'NIN
THE TURTLE HERMIT
(GOT NEW SUNGLASSES)
PAN
(GOHAN AND VIDEL'S DAUGHTER)
DENDE
PICCOLO
(NO CHANGE)

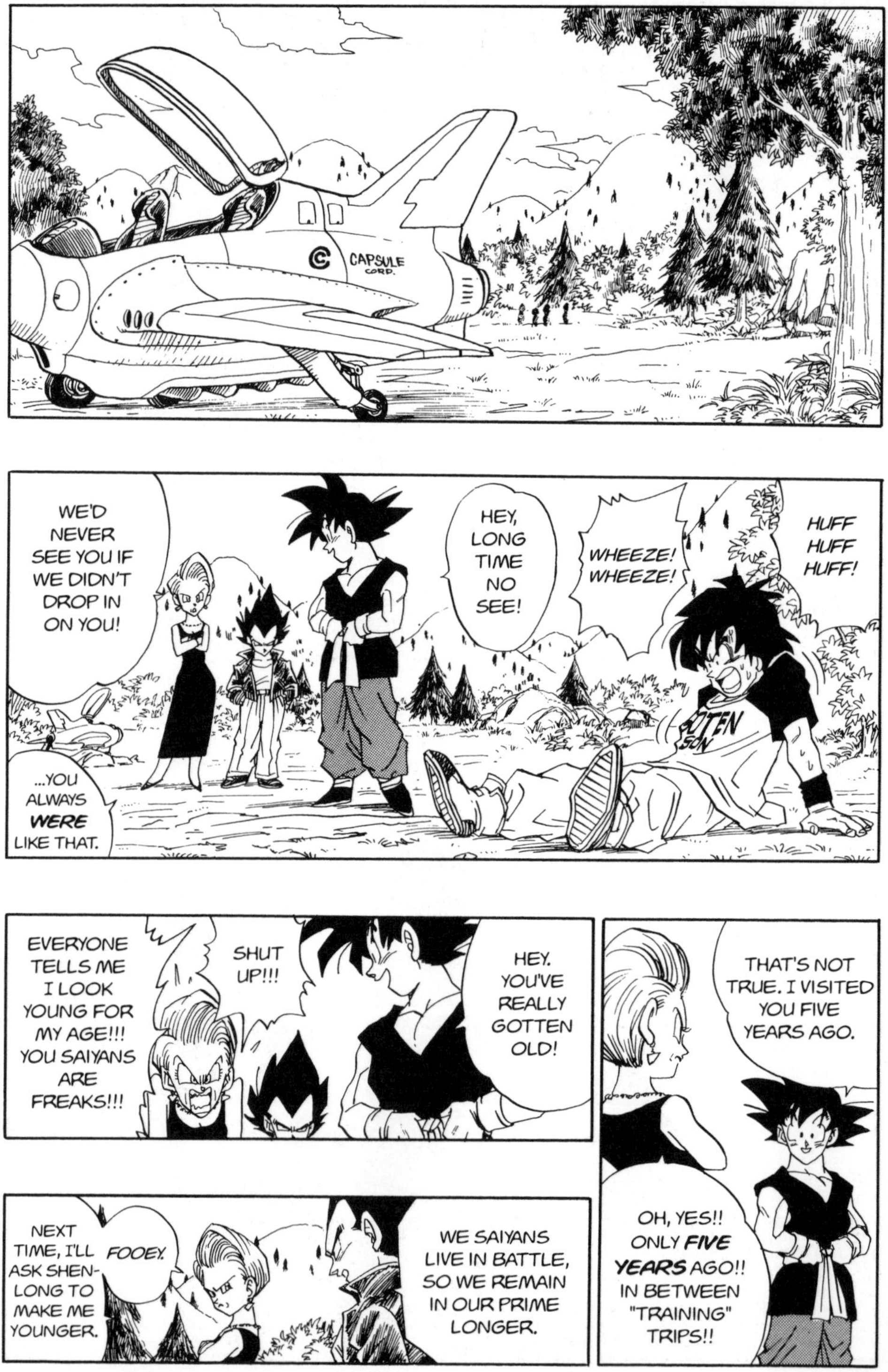
HUFF HUFF HUFF!
WHEEZE! WHEEZE!
HEY, LONG TIME NO SEE!
WE'D NEVER SEE YOU IF WE DIDN'T DROP IN ON YOU!
...YOU ALWAYS **WERE** LIKE THAT.
GOTEN SON
THAT'S NOT TRUE. I VISITED YOU FIVE YEARS AGO.
OH, YES!! ONLY **FIVE YEARS** AGO!! IN BETWEEN "TRAINING" TRIPS!!
HEY. YOU'VE REALLY GOTTEN OLD!
SHUT UP!!!
EVERYONE TELLS ME I LOOK YOUNG FOR MY AGE!!! YOU SAIYANS ARE FREAKS!!!
WE SAIYANS LIVE IN BATTLE, SO WE REMAIN IN OUR PRIME LONGER.
FOOEY.
NEXT TIME, I'LL ASK SHEN-LONG TO MAKE ME YOUNGER.

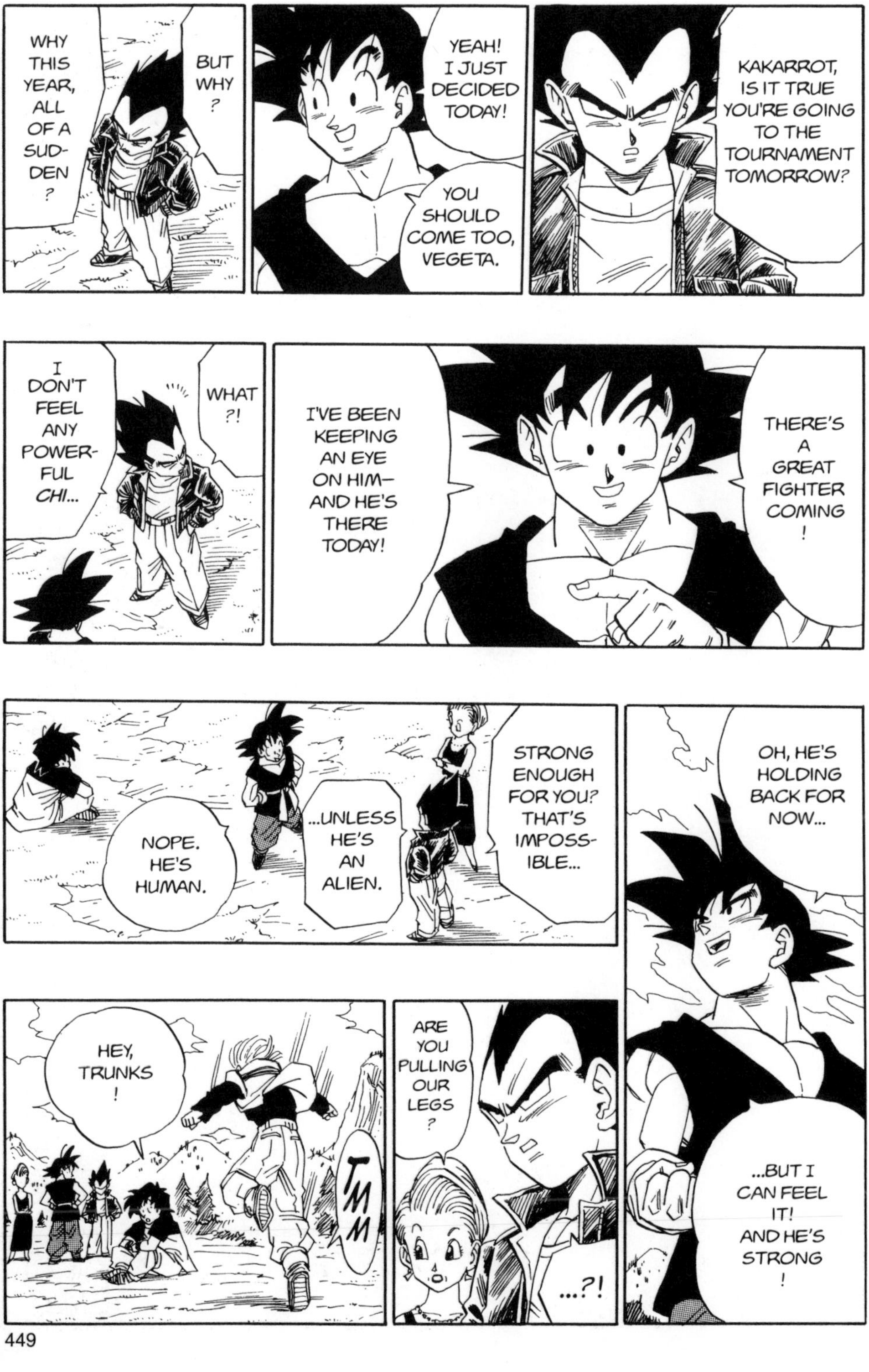
KAKARROT, IS IT TRUE YOU'RE GOING TO THE TOURNAMENT TOMORROW?
YEAH! I JUST DECIDED TODAY!
YOU SHOULD COME TOO, VEGETA.
BUT WHY?
WHY THIS YEAR, ALL OF A SUDDEN?
THERE'S A GREAT FIGHTER COMING!
I'VE BEEN KEEPING AN EYE ON HIM—AND HE'S THERE TODAY!
WHAT?!
I DON'T FEEL ANY POWERFUL CHI...
OH, HE'S HOLDING BACK FOR NOW...
...BUT I CAN FEEL IT! AND HE'S STRONG!
STRONG ENOUGH FOR YOU? THAT'S IMPOSSIBLE...
...UNLESS HE'S AN ALIEN.
NOPE. HE'S HUMAN.
ARE YOU PULLING OUR LEGS?
...?!
TMM
HEY, TRUNKS!

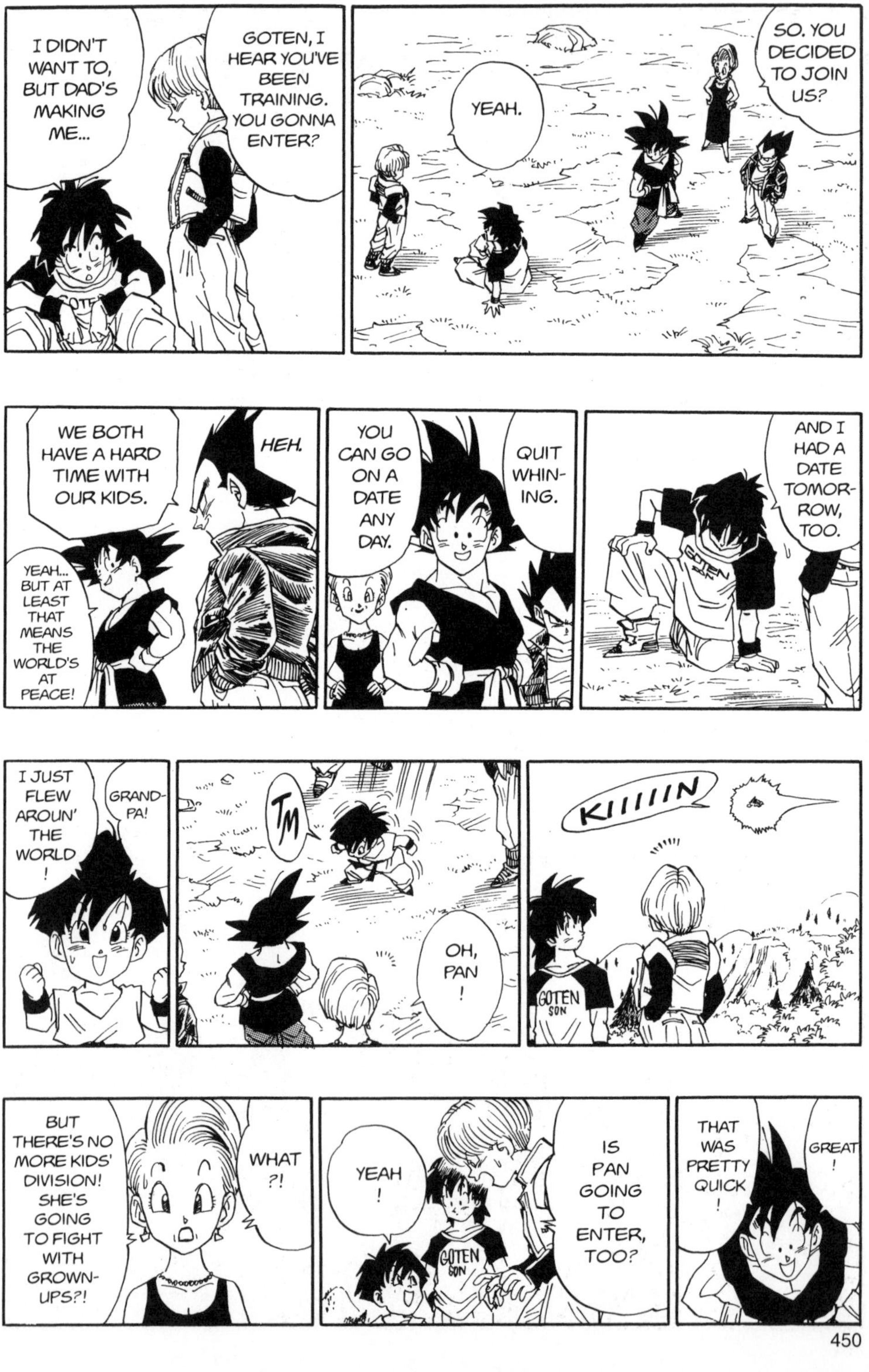
SO. YOU DECIDED TO JOIN US?
YEAH.
GOTEN, I HEAR YOU'VE BEEN TRAINING. YOU GONNA ENTER?
I DIDN'T WANT TO, BUT DAD'S MAKING ME...
AND I HAD A DATE TOMORROW, TOO.
QUIT WHINING.
YOU CAN GO ON A DATE ANY DAY.
HEH.
WE BOTH HAVE A HARD TIME WITH OUR KIDS.
YEAH... BUT AT LEAST THAT MEANS THE WORLD'S AT PEACE!
KIIIIIN
TM
OH, PAN!
GRANDPA!
I JUST FLEW AROUN' THE WORLD!
GREAT!
THAT WAS PRETTY QUICK!
IS PAN GOING TO ENTER, TOO?
YEAH!
WHAT?!
BUT THERE'S NO MORE KIDS' DIVISION! SHE'S GOING TO FIGHT WITH GROWN-UPS?!

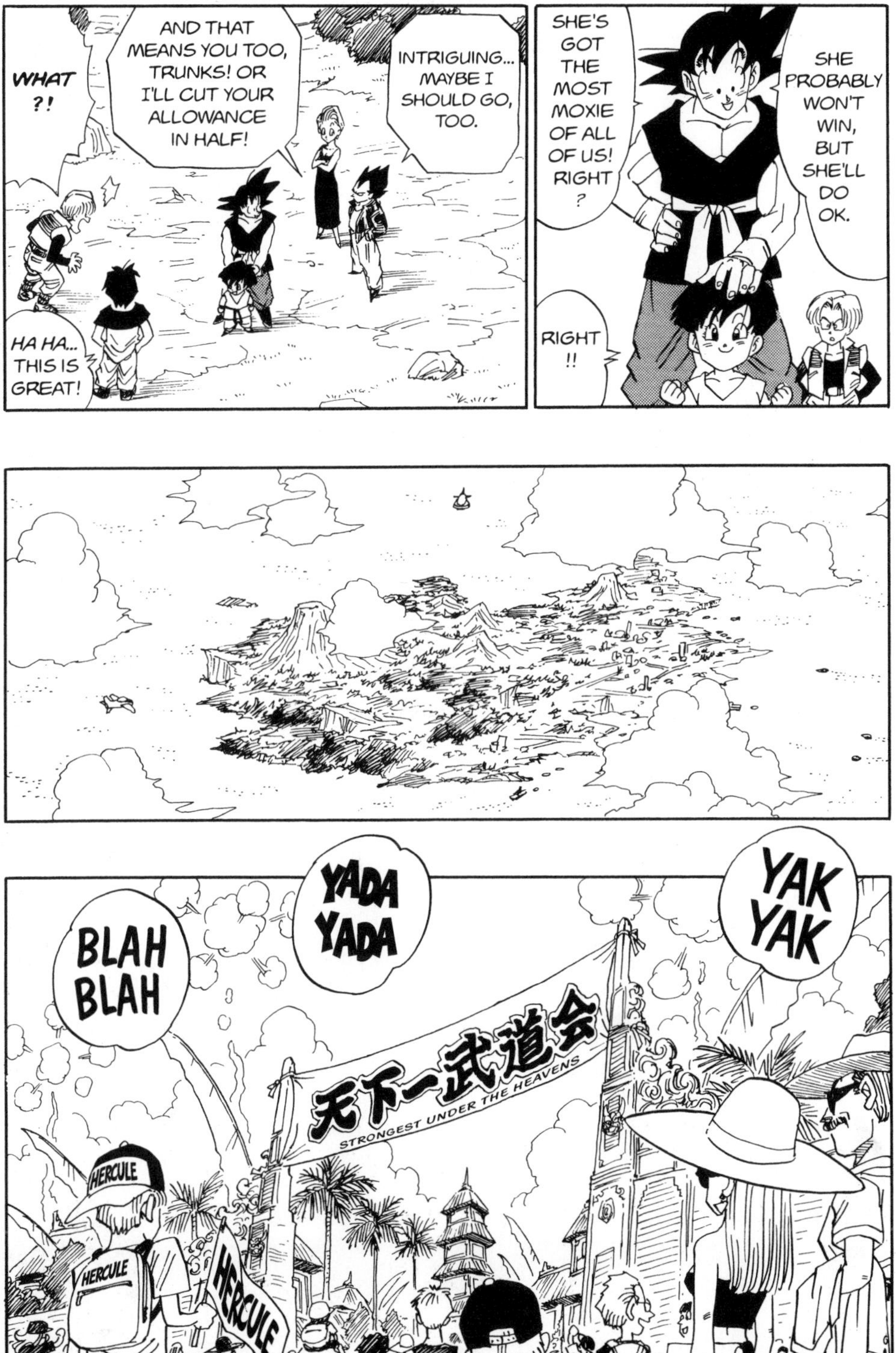
SHE PROBABLY WON'T WIN, BUT SHE'LL DO OK.
SHE'S GOT THE MOST MOXIE OF ALL OF US! RIGHT?
RIGHT!!
AND THAT MEANS YOU TOO, TRUNKS! OR I'LL CUT YOUR ALLOWANCE IN HALF!
INTRIGUING... MAYBE I SHOULD GO, TOO.
WHAT?!
HA HA... THIS IS GREAT!
YAK YAK
YADA YADA
BLAH BLAH
天下一武道会
STRONGEST UNDER THE HEAVENS
HERCULE
HERCULE
HERCULE

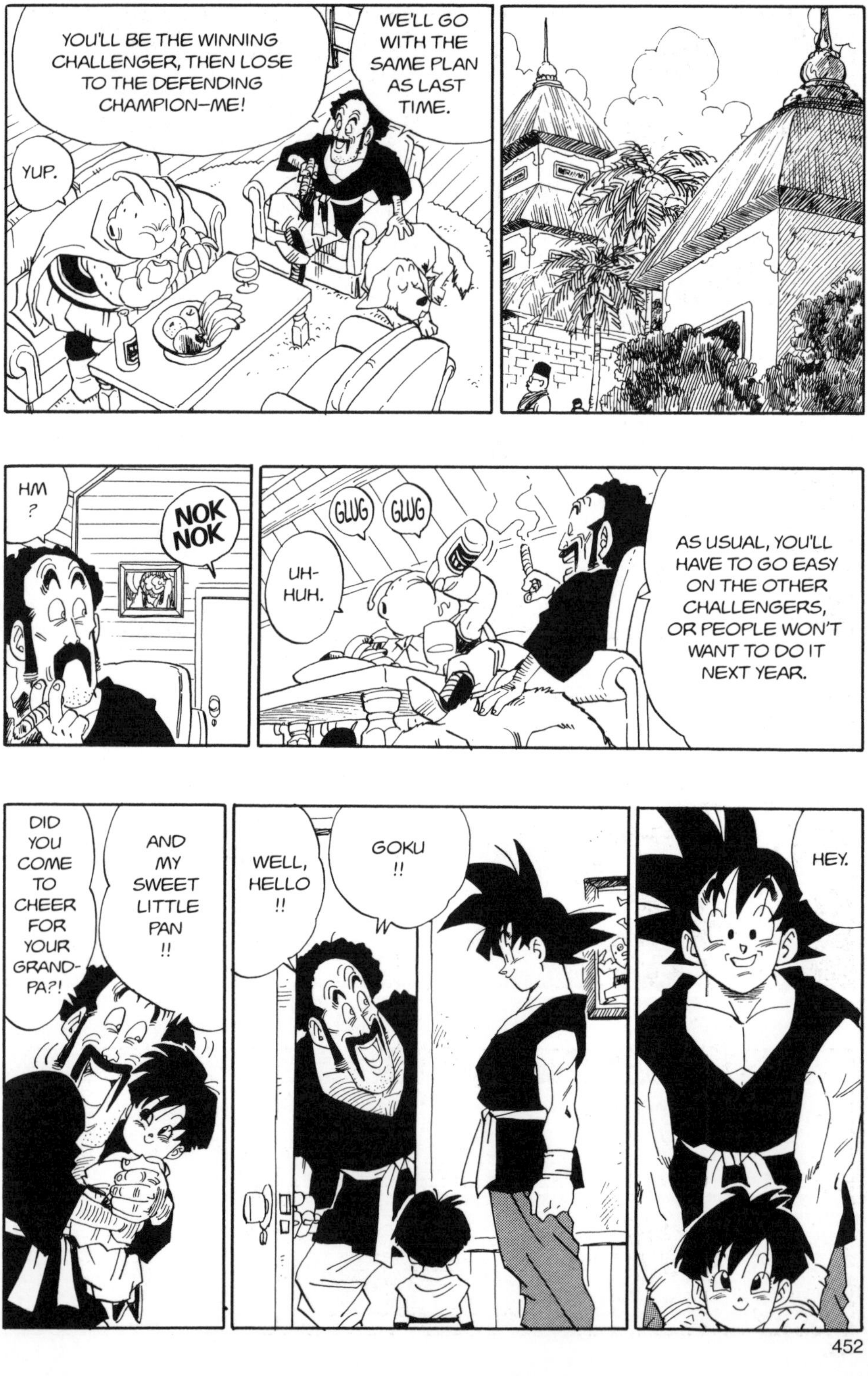
WE'LL GO WITH THE SAME PLAN AS LAST TIME.
YOU'LL BE THE WINNING CHALLENGER, THEN LOSE TO THE DEFENDING CHAMPION—ME!
YUP.
AS USUAL, YOU'LL HAVE TO GO EASY ON THE OTHER CHALLENGERS, OR PEOPLE WON'T WANT TO DO IT NEXT YEAR.
GLUG
GLUG
UH-HUH.
NOK NOK
HM ?
HEY.
GOKU !!
WELL, HELLO !!
AND MY SWEET LITTLE PAN !!
DID YOU COME TO CHEER FOR YOUR GRANDPA?!

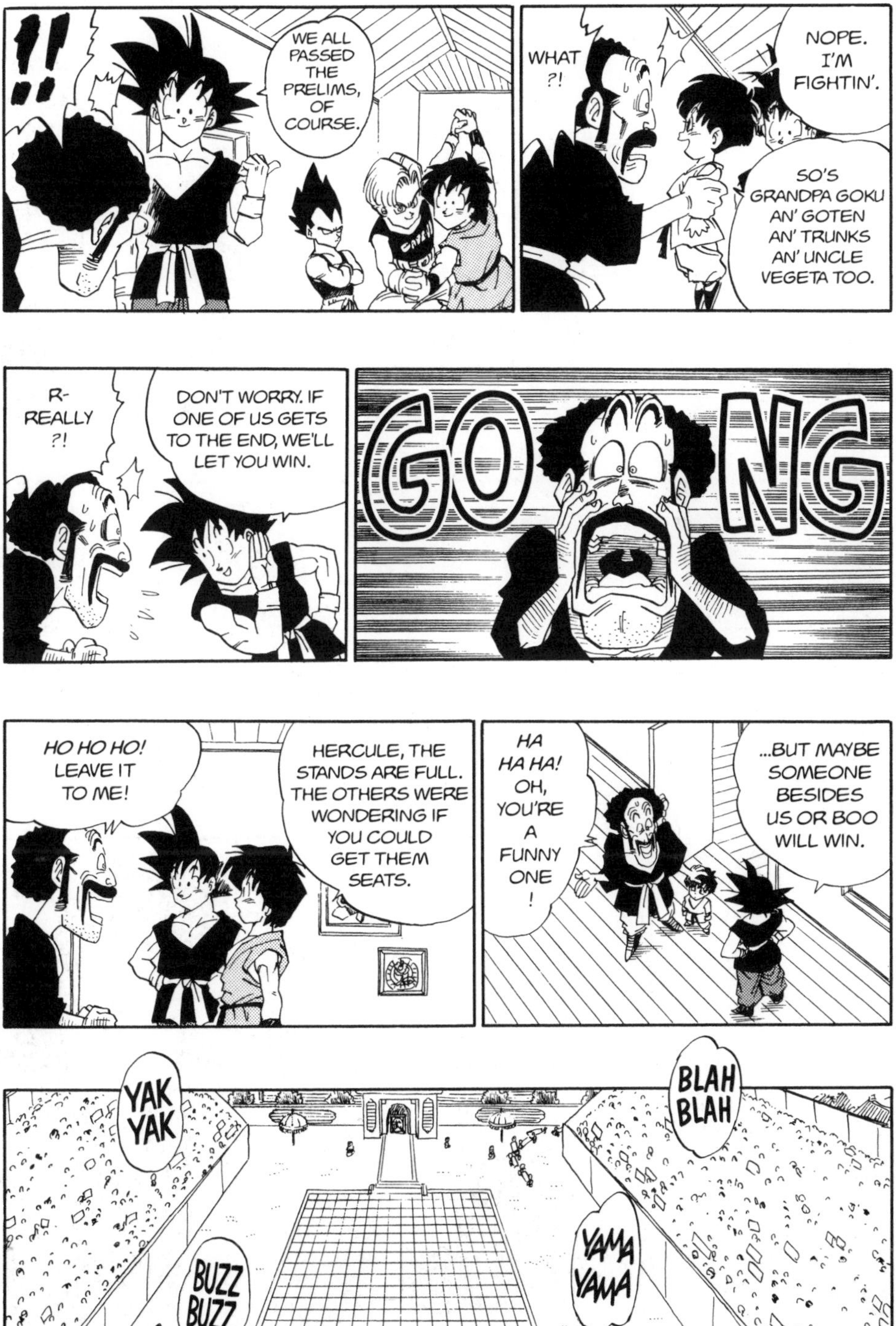
NOPE. I'M FIGHTIN'.
SO'S GRANDPA GOKU AN' GOTEN AN' TRUNKS AN' UNCLE VEGETA TOO.
WHAT ?!
WE ALL PASSED THE PRELIMS, OF COURSE.
!!
GONG
DON'T WORRY. IF ONE OF US GETS TO THE END, WE'LL LET YOU WIN.
R-REALLY ?!
...BUT MAYBE SOMEONE BESIDES US OR BOO WILL WIN.
HA HA HA! OH, YOU'RE A FUNNY ONE !
HERCULE, THE STANDS ARE FULL. THE OTHERS WERE WONDERING IF YOU COULD GET THEM SEATS.
HO HO HO! LEAVE IT TO ME!
BLAH BLAH
YAMA YAMA
YAK YAK
BUZZ BUZZ

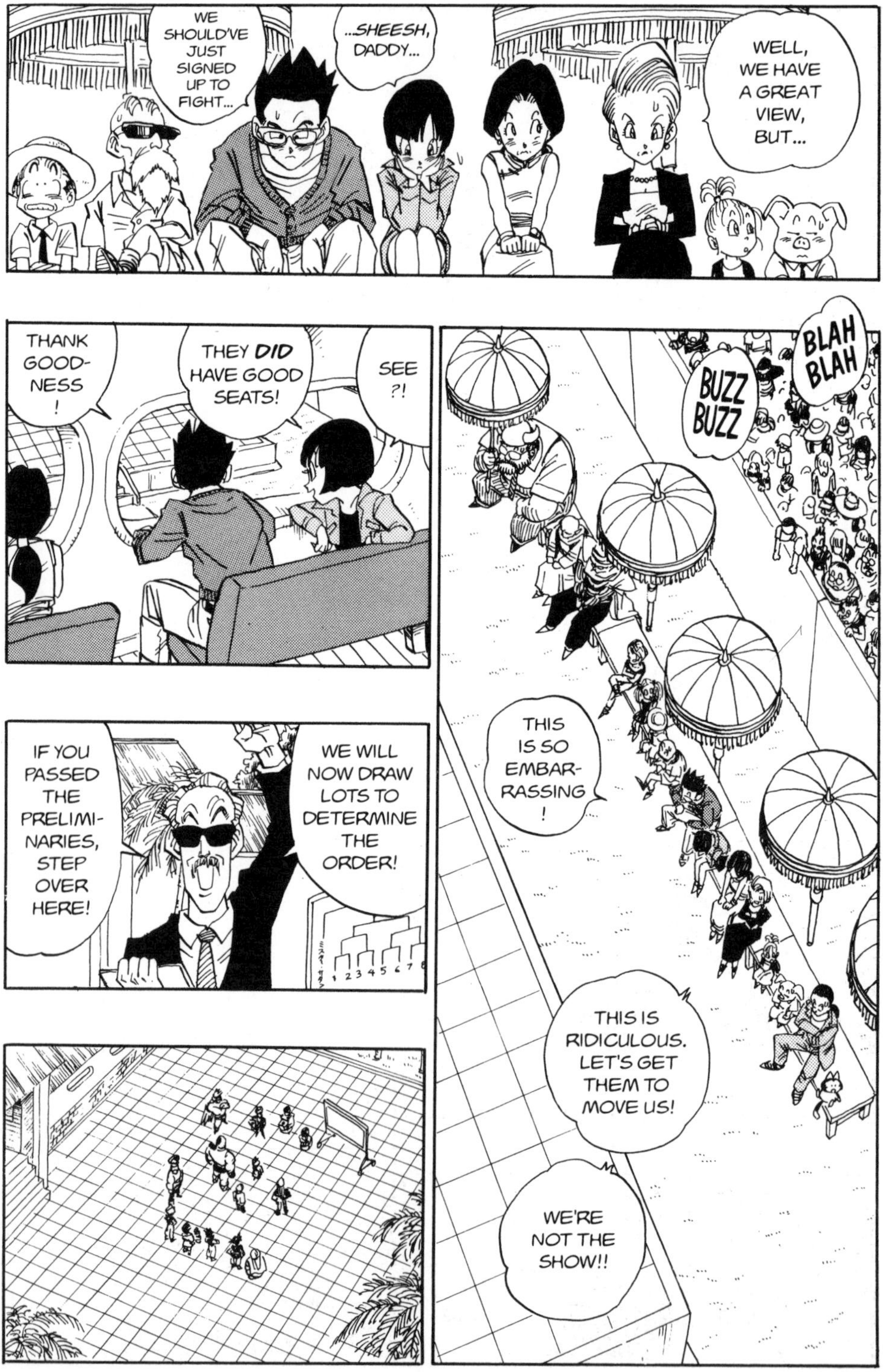
WELL, WE HAVE A GREAT VIEW, BUT...
...SHEESH, DADDY...
WE SHOULD'VE JUST SIGNED UP TO FIGHT...
BLAH BLAH
BUZZ BUZZ
THIS IS SO EMBARRASSING!
THIS IS RIDICULOUS. LET'S GET THEM TO MOVE US!
WE'RE NOT THE SHOW!!
SEE?!
THEY **DID** HAVE GOOD SEATS!
THANK GOODNESS!
WE WILL NOW DRAW LOTS TO DETERMINE THE ORDER!
IF YOU PASSED THE PRELIMINARIES, STEP OVER HERE!

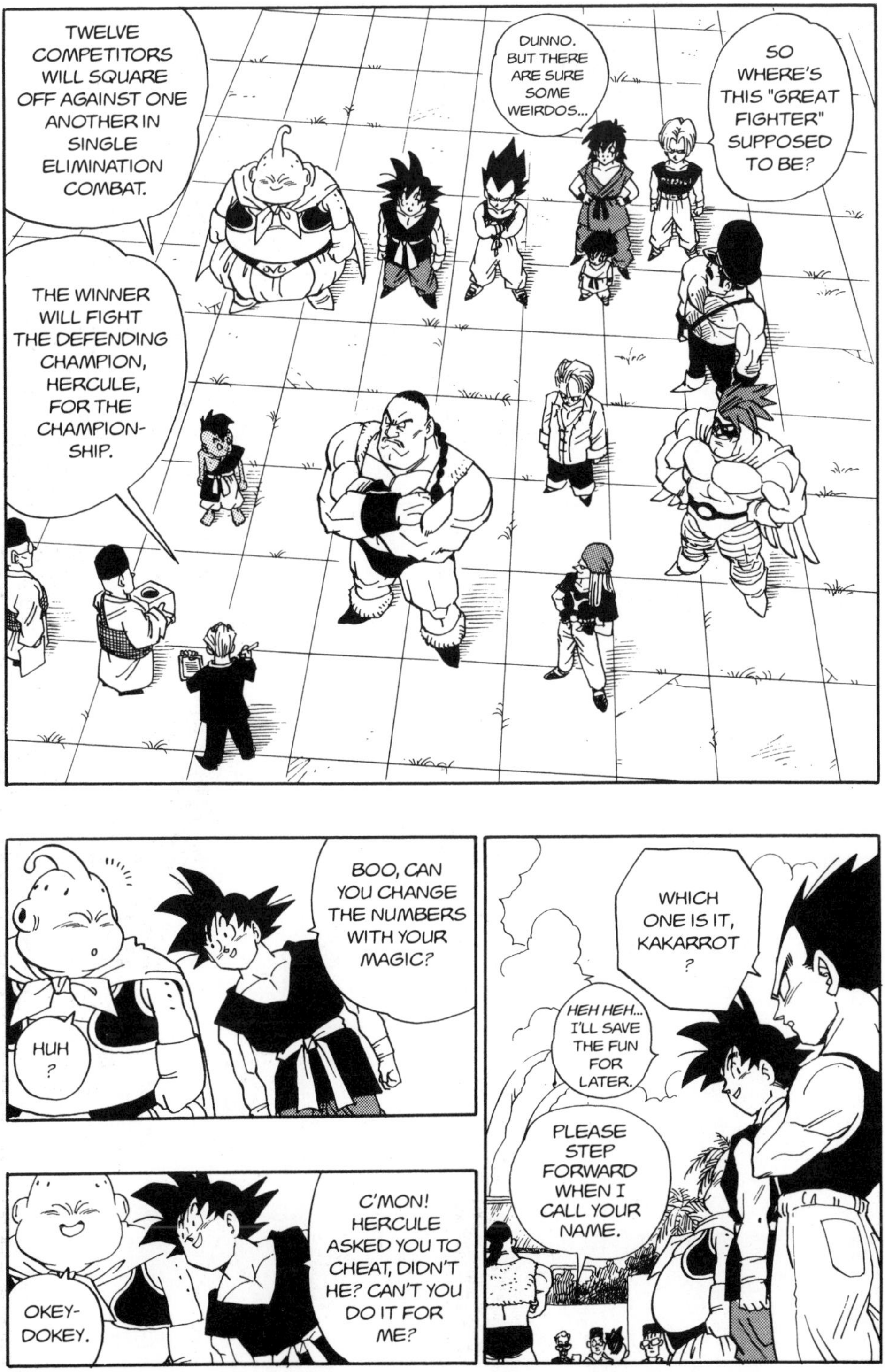
SO WHERE'S THIS "GREAT FIGHTER" SUPPOSED TO BE?
DUNNO. BUT THERE ARE SURE SOME WEIRDOS...
TWELVE COMPETITORS WILL SQUARE OFF AGAINST ONE ANOTHER IN SINGLE ELIMINATION COMBAT.
THE WINNER WILL FIGHT THE DEFENDING CHAMPION, HERCULE, FOR THE CHAMPIONSHIP.
WHICH ONE IS IT, KAKARROT?
HEH HEH... I'LL SAVE THE FUN FOR LATER.
PLEASE STEP FORWARD WHEN I CALL YOUR NAME.
BOO, CAN YOU CHANGE THE NUMBERS WITH YOUR MAGIC?
HUH?
C'MON! HERCULE ASKED YOU TO CHEAT, DIDN'T HE? CAN'T YOU DO IT FOR ME?
OKEY-DOKEY.

THE FINALISTS

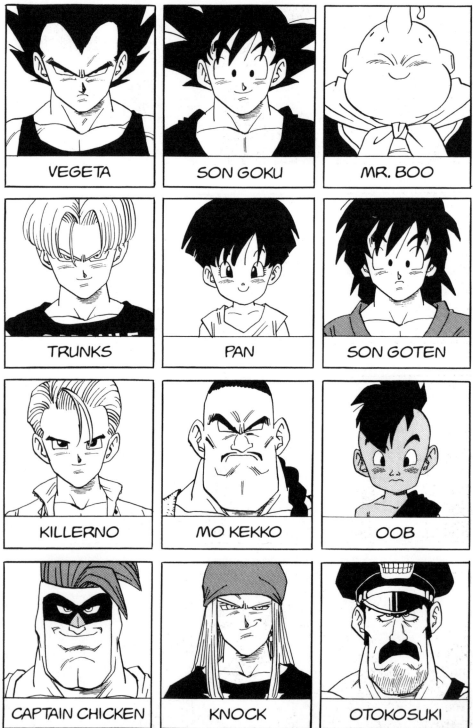

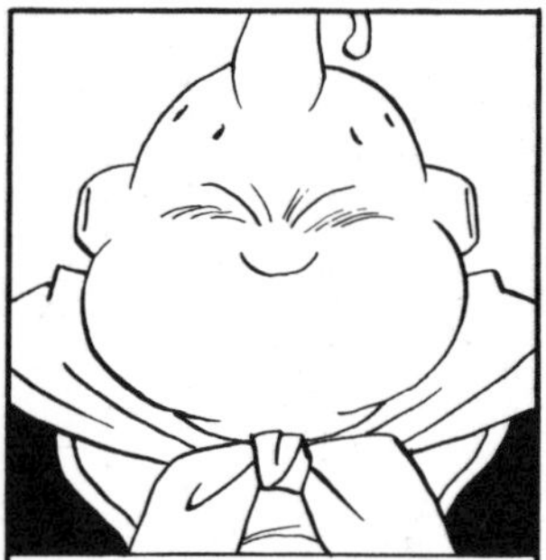
MR. BOO

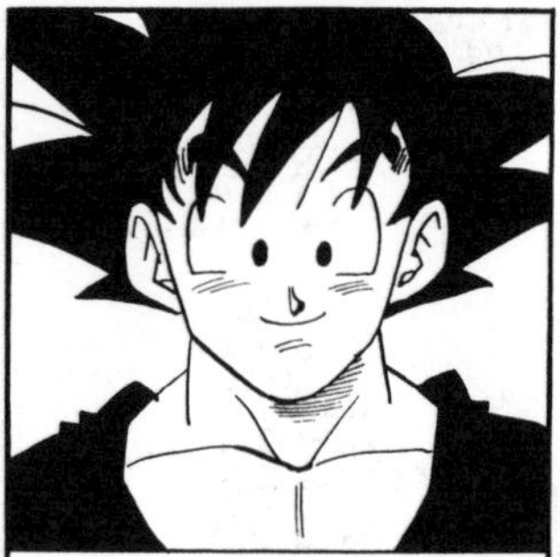
SON GOKU

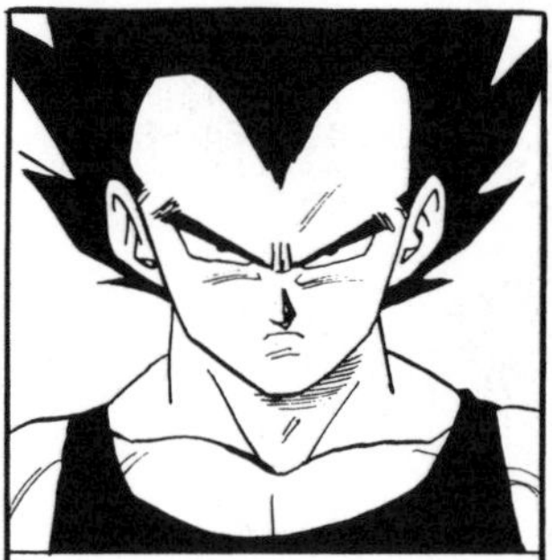
VEGETA

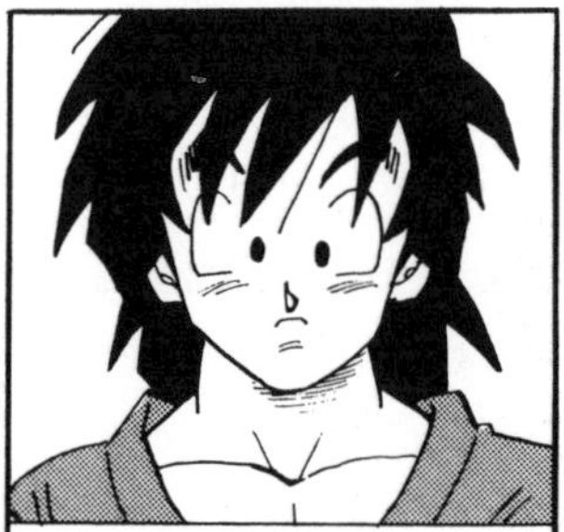
SON GOTEN

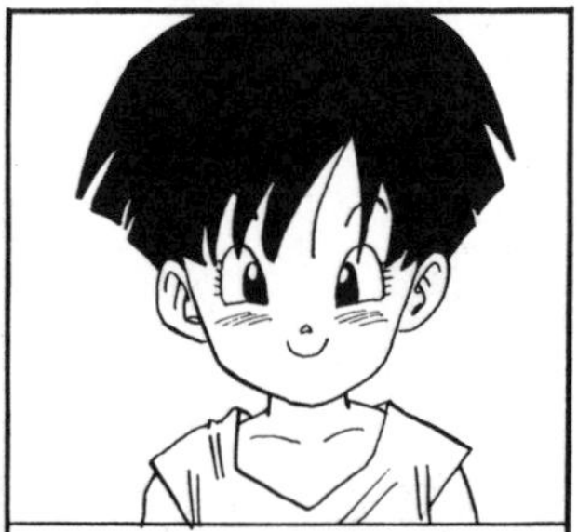
PAN

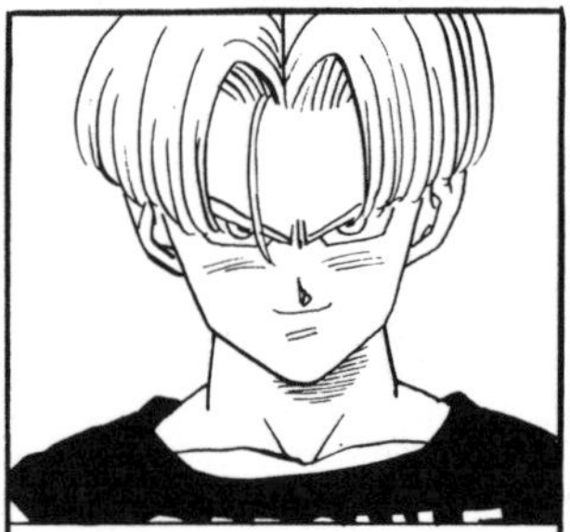
TRUNKS

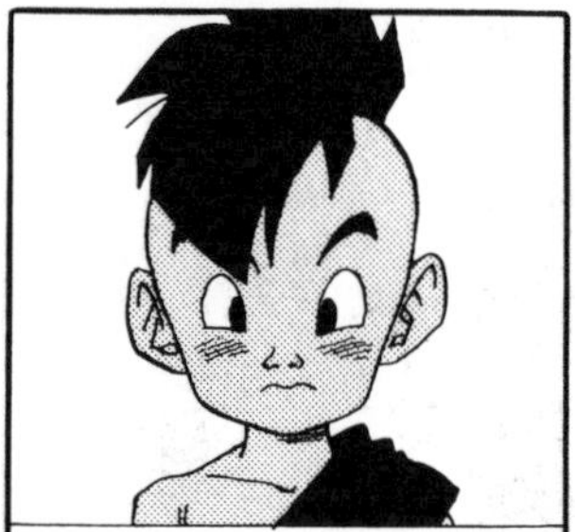
OOB

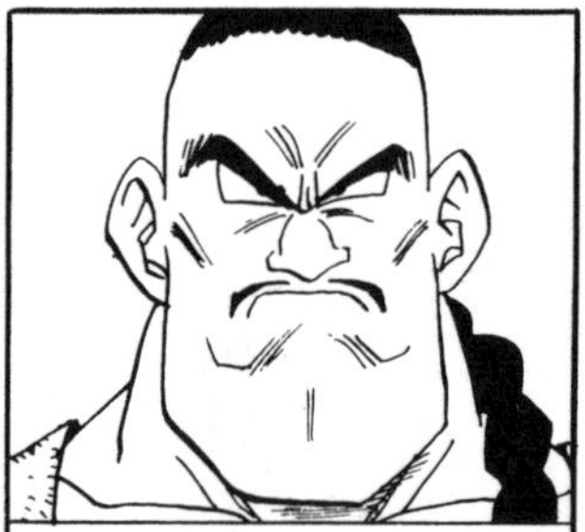
MO KEKKO

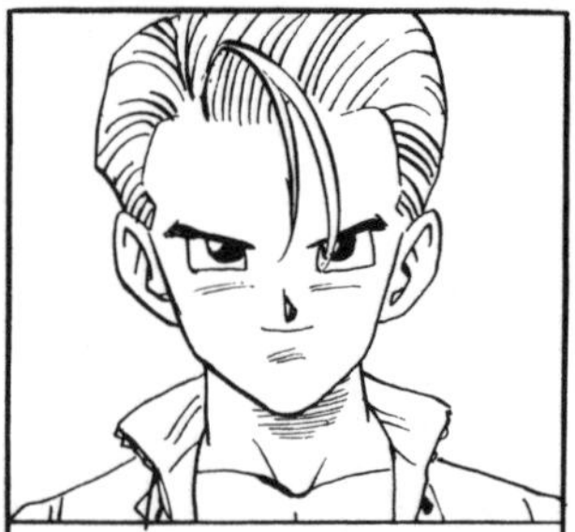
KILLERNO

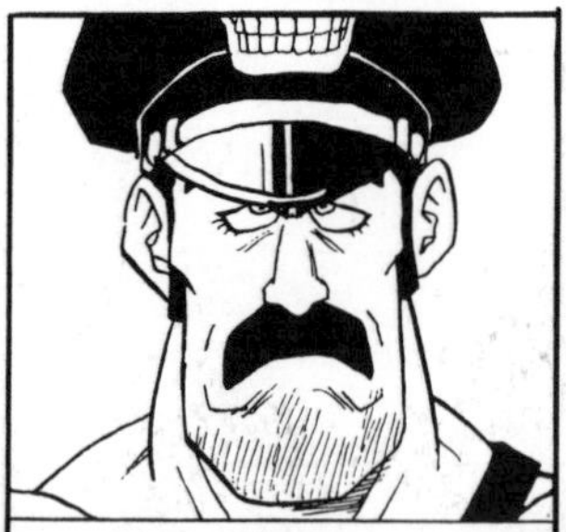
OTOKOSUKI

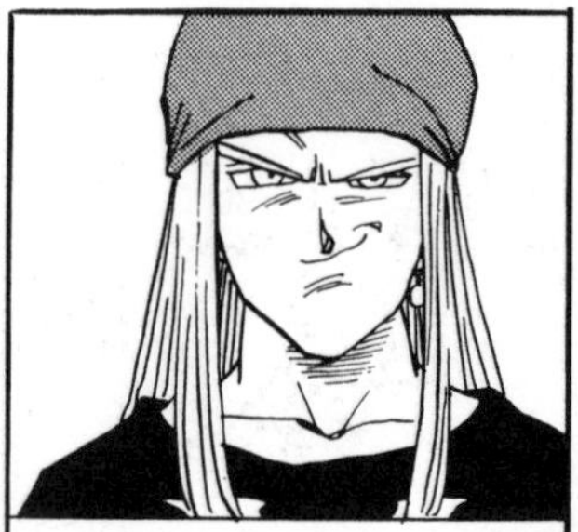
KNOCK

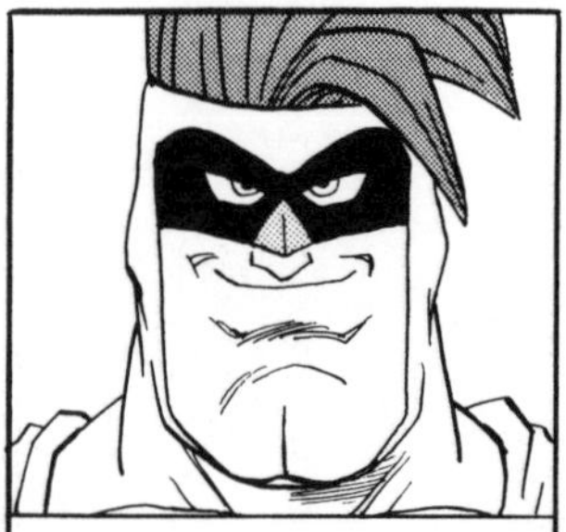
CAPTAIN CHICKEN

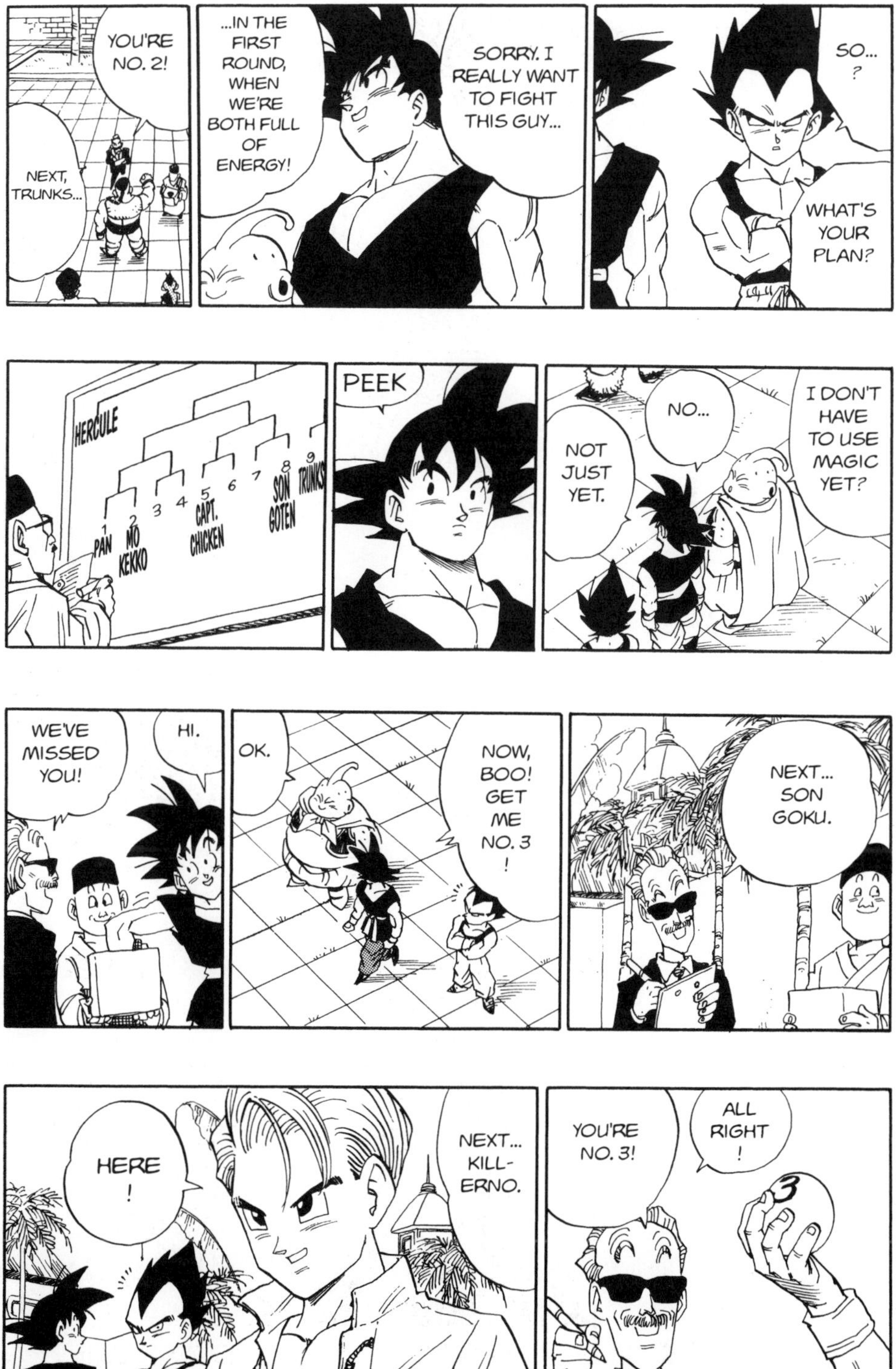
SO... ?
WHAT'S YOUR PLAN?
SORRY. I REALLY WANT TO FIGHT THIS GUY...
...IN THE FIRST ROUND, WHEN WE'RE BOTH FULL OF ENERGY!
YOU'RE NO. 2!
NEXT, TRUNKS...
I DON'T HAVE TO USE MAGIC YET?
NO...
NOT JUST YET.
PEEK
HERCULE
1 PAN
2 MO KEKKO
3
4
5 CAPT. CHICKEN
6
7
8 SON GOTEN
9 TRUNKS
NEXT... SON GOKU.
NOW, BOO! GET ME NO. 3!
OK.
HI.
WE'VE MISSED YOU!
ALL RIGHT!
YOU'RE NO. 3!
NEXT... KILL-ERNO.
HERE!

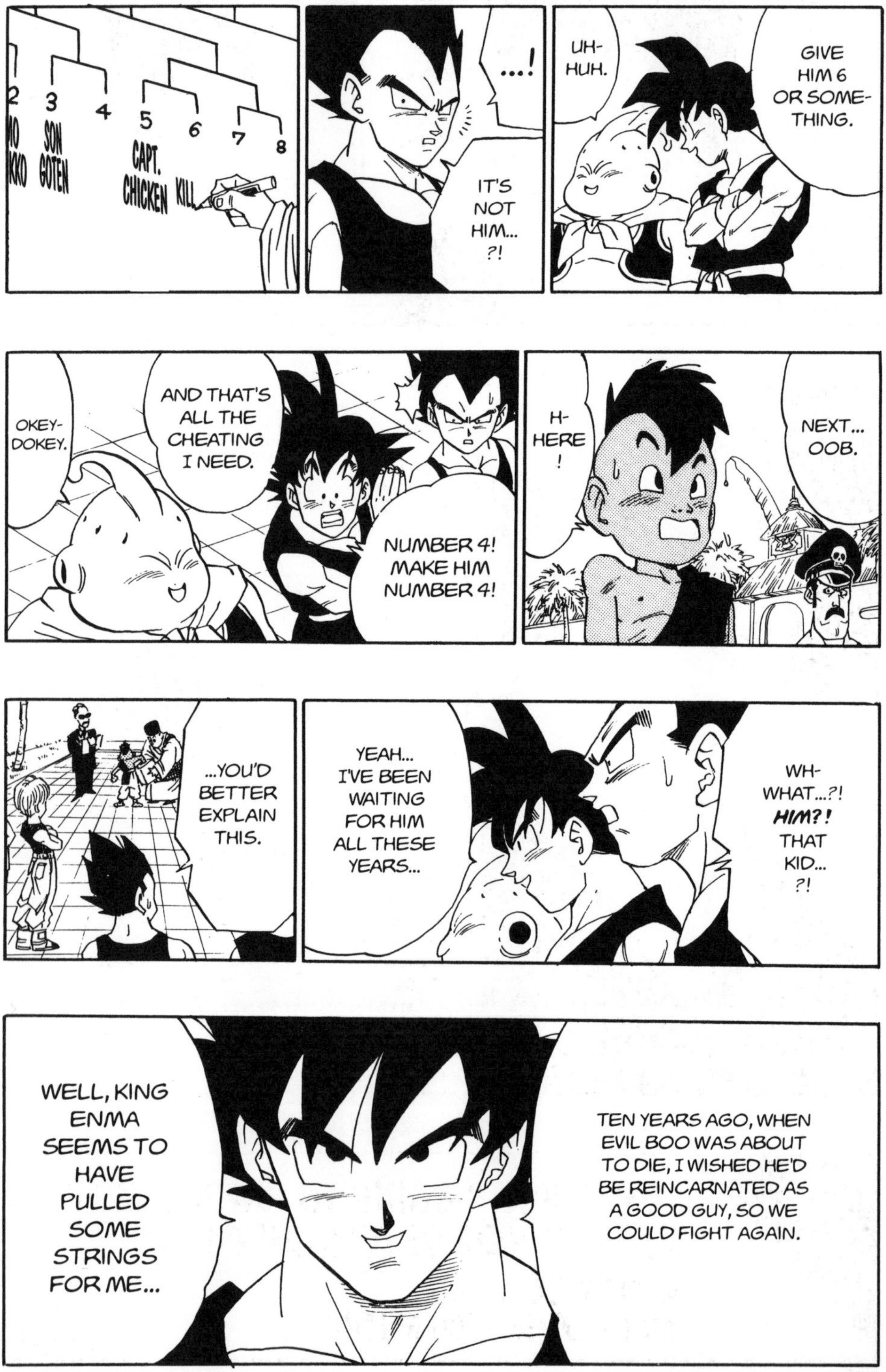
GIVE HIM 6 OR SOME-THING.
UH-HUH.
...!
IT'S NOT HIM...?!
2 3 4 5 6 7 8
SON GOTEN
CAPT. CHICKEN
KILL
NEXT... OOB.
H-HERE!
AND THAT'S ALL THE CHEATING I NEED.
OKEY-DOKEY.
NUMBER 4! MAKE HIM NUMBER 4!
WH-WHAT...?! HIM?! THAT KID...?!
YEAH... I'VE BEEN WAITING FOR HIM ALL THESE YEARS...
...YOU'D BETTER EXPLAIN THIS.
TEN YEARS AGO, WHEN EVIL BOO WAS ABOUT TO DIE, I WISHED HE'D BE REINCARNATED AS A GOOD GUY, SO WE COULD FIGHT AGAIN.
WELL, KING ENMA SEEMS TO HAVE PULLED SOME STRINGS FOR ME...

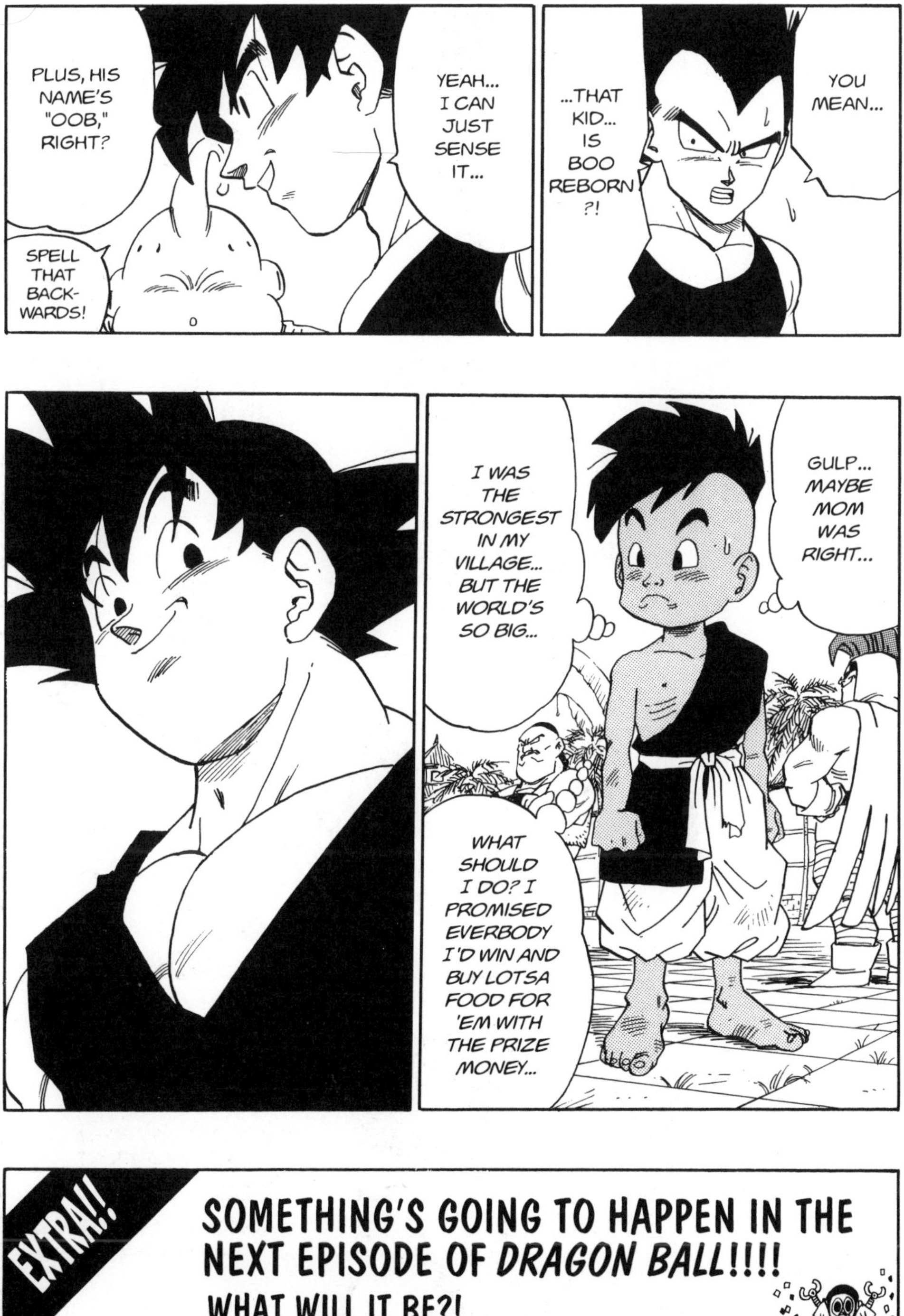
YOU MEAN...
...THAT KID... IS BOO REBORN?!
YEAH... I CAN JUST SENSE IT...
PLUS, HIS NAME'S "OOB," RIGHT?
SPELL THAT BACKWARDS!
GULP... MAYBE MOM WAS RIGHT...
I WAS THE STRONGEST IN MY VILLAGE... BUT THE WORLD'S SO BIG...
WHAT SHOULD I DO? I PROMISED EVERBODY I'D WIN AND BUY LOTSA FOOD FOR 'EM WITH THE PRIZE MONEY...
EXTRA!!
SOMETHING'S GOING TO HAPPEN IN THE NEXT EPISODE OF *DRAGON BALL*!!!!
WHAT WILL IT BE?!
DON'T EXPECT TOO MUCH!!
TORI

DRAGON BALL

DBZ:325 •
Farewell, Dragon
World!

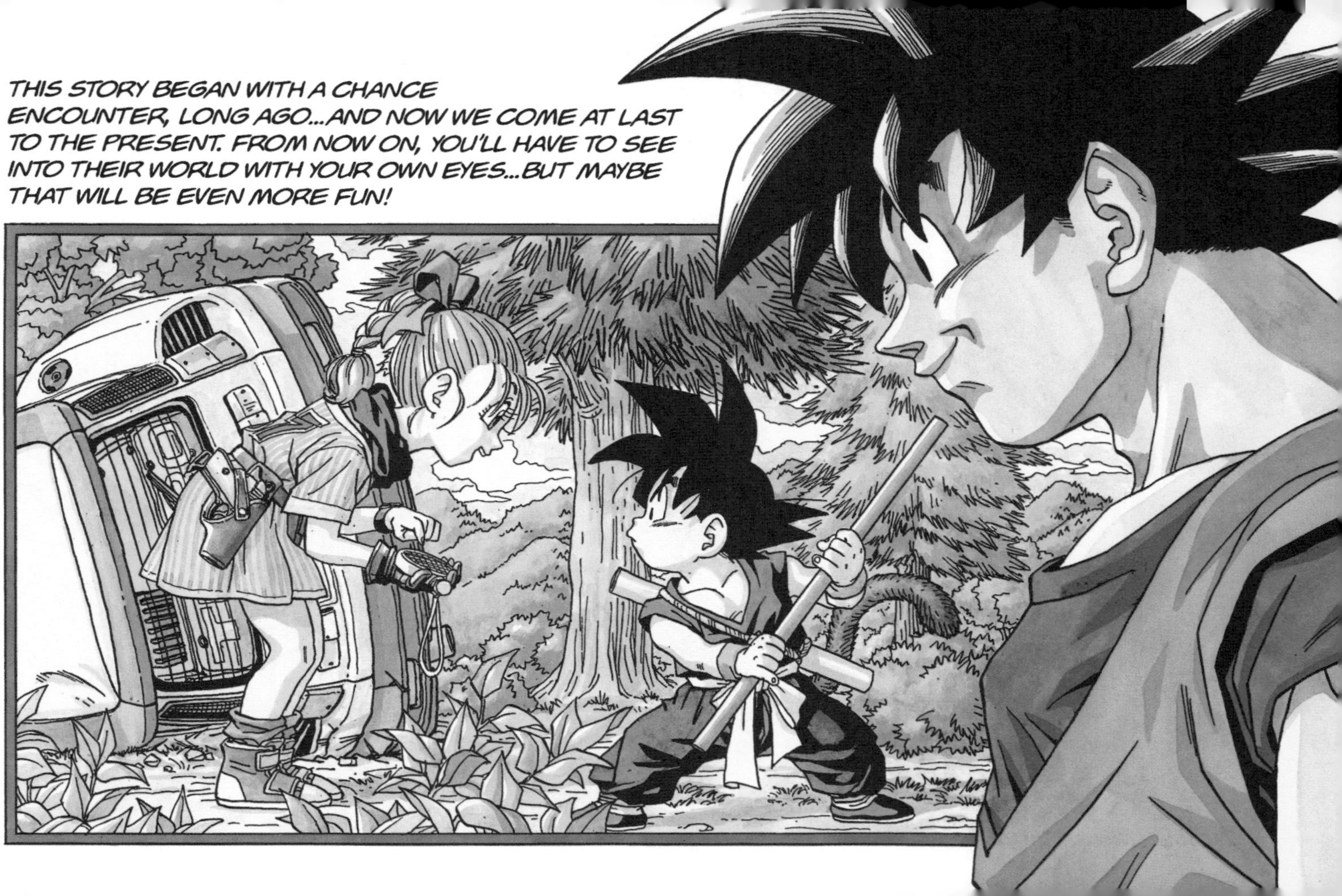
THIS STORY BEGAN WITH A CHANCE ENCOUNTER, LONG AGO...AND NOW WE COME AT LAST TO THE PRESENT. FROM NOW ON, YOU'LL HAVE TO SEE INTO THEIR WORLD WITH YOUR OWN EYES...BUT MAYBE THAT WILL BE EVEN MORE FUN!

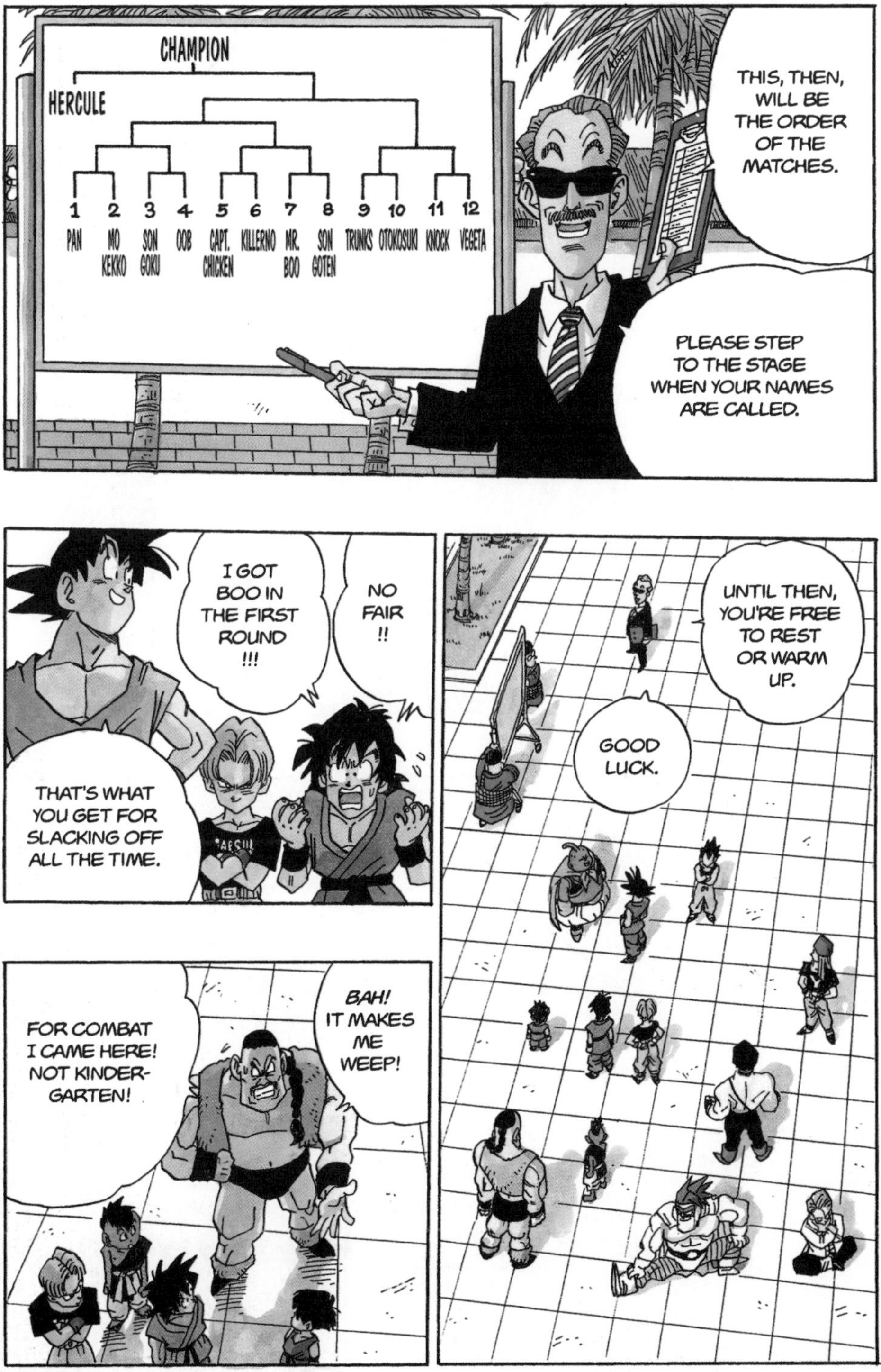
THIS, THEN, WILL BE THE ORDER OF THE MATCHES.
PLEASE STEP TO THE STAGE WHEN YOUR NAMES ARE CALLED.
CHAMPION
HERCULE
1 PAN
2 MO KEKKO
3 SON GOKU
4 OOB
5 CAPT. CHICKEN
6 KILLERNO
7 MR. BOO
8 SON GOTEN
9 TRUNKS
10 OTOKOSUKI
11 KNOCK
12 VEGETA
UNTIL THEN, YOU'RE FREE TO REST OR WARM UP.
GOOD LUCK.
NO FAIR !!
I GOT BOO IN THE FIRST ROUND !!!
THAT'S WHAT YOU GET FOR SLACKING OFF ALL THE TIME.
BAH! IT MAKES ME WEEP!
FOR COMBAT I CAME HERE! NOT KINDER-GARTEN!

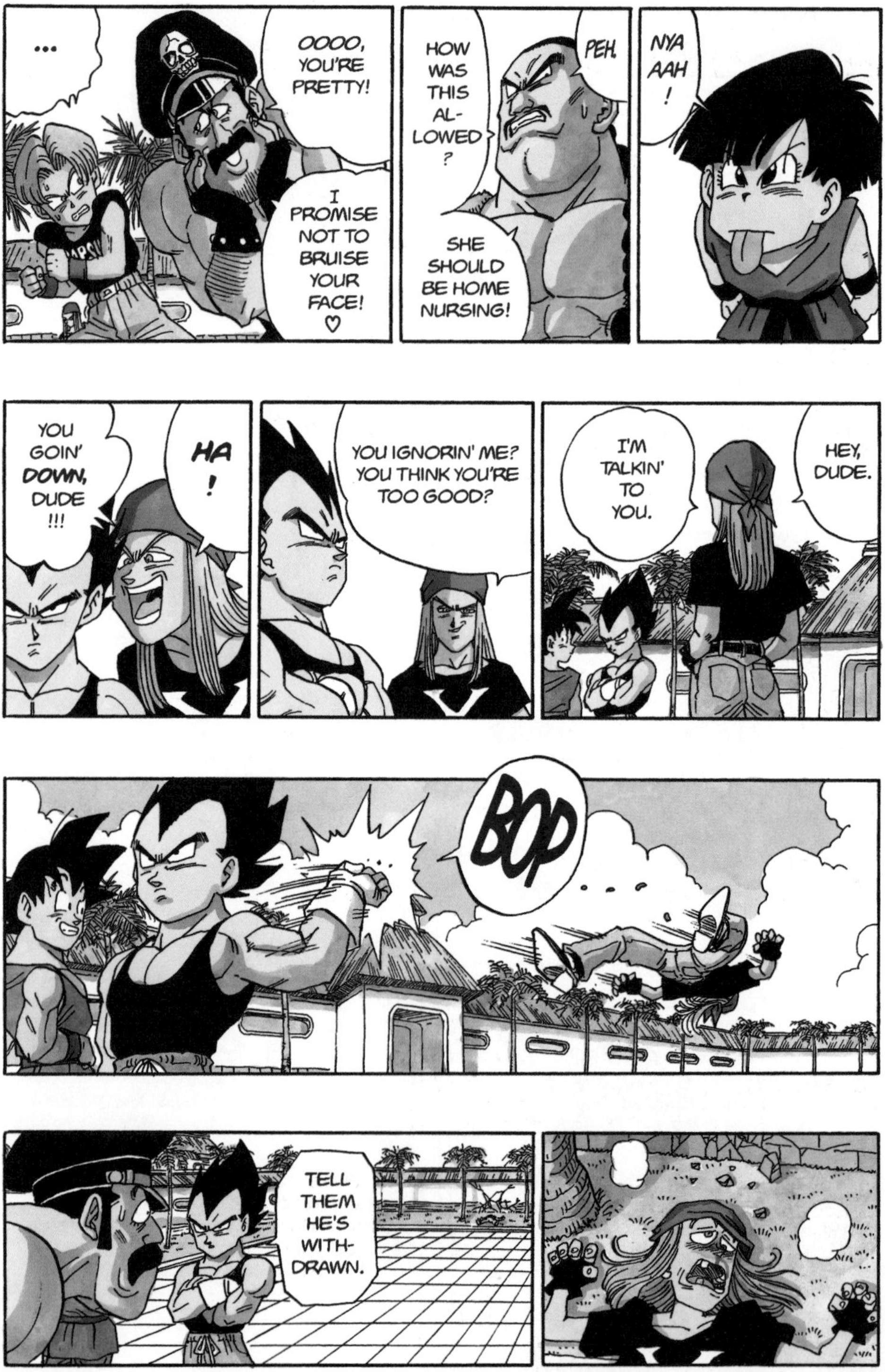
NYA AAH!
PEH.
HOW WAS THIS AL-LOWED?
SHE SHOULD BE HOME NURSING!
OOOO, YOU'RE PRETTY!
I PROMISE NOT TO BRUISE YOUR FACE! ♡
...
HEY, DUDE.
I'M TALKIN' TO YOU.
YOU IGNORIN' ME? YOU THINK YOU'RE TOO GOOD?
HA!
YOU GOIN' **DOWN,** DUDE!!!
BOP
...
TELL THEM HE'S WITH-DRAWN.

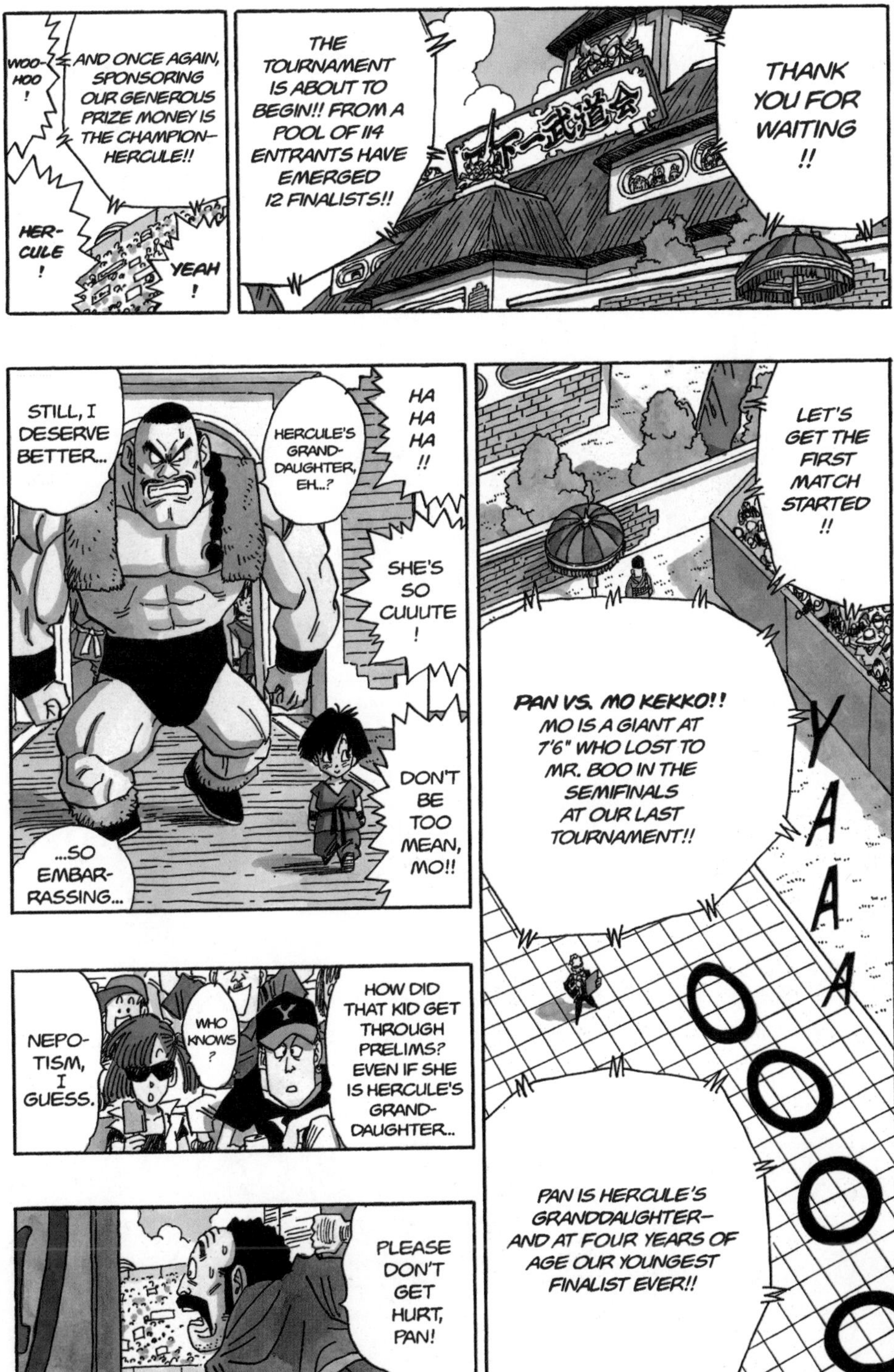
THANK YOU FOR WAITING!!
THE TOURNAMENT IS ABOUT TO BEGIN!! FROM A POOL OF 114 ENTRANTS HAVE EMERGED 12 FINALISTS!!
AND ONCE AGAIN, SPONSORING OUR GENEROUS PRIZE MONEY IS THE CHAMPION—HERCULE!!
WOO-HOO!
HER-CULE!
YEAH!
LET'S GET THE FIRST MATCH STARTED!!
PAN VS. MO KEKKO!! MO IS A GIANT AT 7'6" WHO LOST TO MR. BOO IN THE SEMIFINALS AT OUR LAST TOURNAMENT!!
YAAA
OOOOO
PAN IS HERCULE'S GRANDDAUGHTER—AND AT FOUR YEARS OF AGE OUR YOUNGEST FINALIST EVER!!
HA HA HA!!
HERCULE'S GRAND-DAUGHTER, EH...?
STILL, I DESERVE BETTER...
SHE'S SO CUUUTE!
DON'T BE TOO MEAN, MO!!
...SO EMBAR-RASSING...
HOW DID THAT KID GET THROUGH PRELIMS? EVEN IF SHE IS HERCULE'S GRAND-DAUGHTER...
WHO KNOWS?
NEPO-TISM, I GUESS.
PLEASE DON'T GET HURT, PAN!

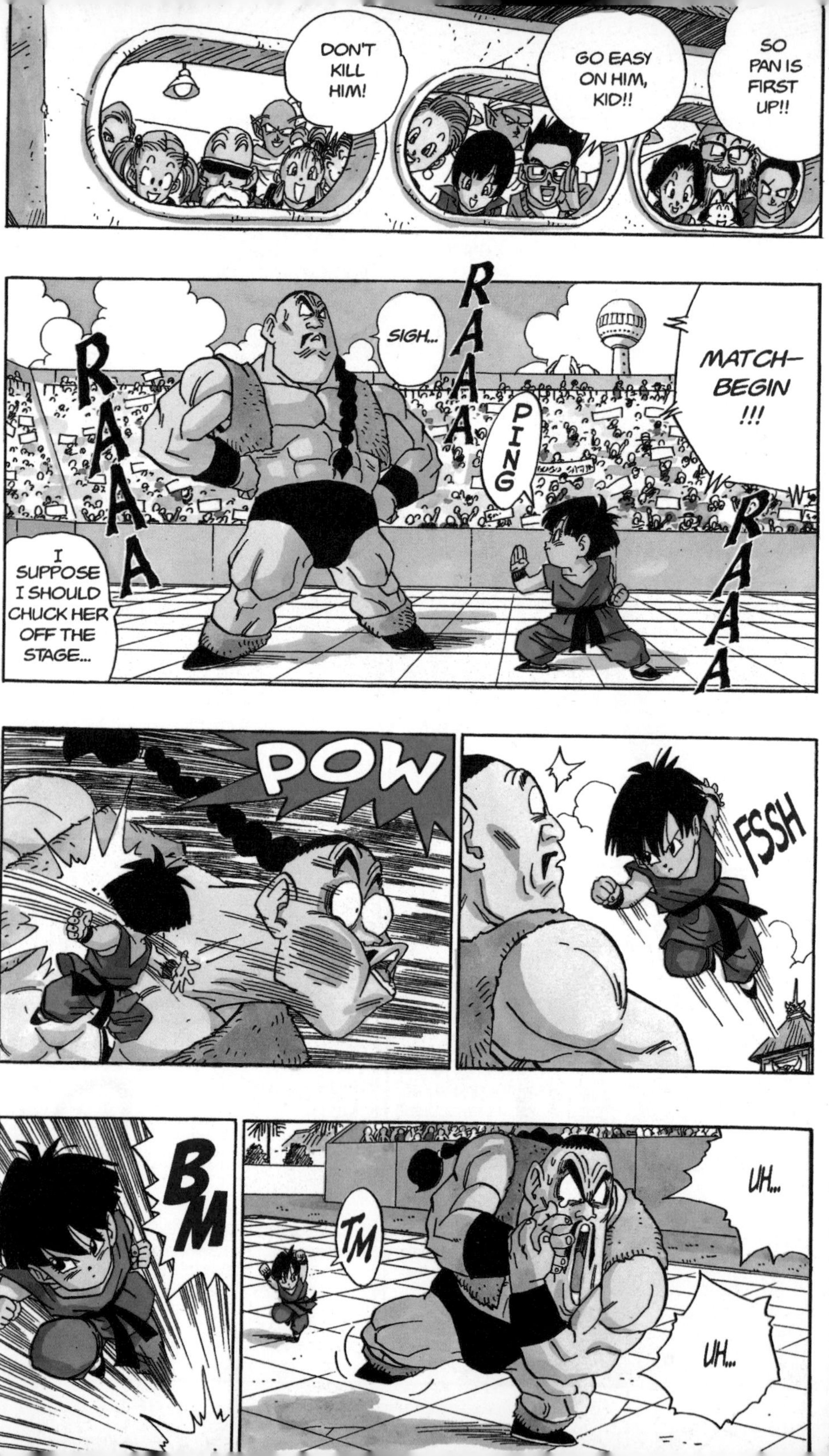
SO PAN IS FIRST UP!!
GO EASY ON HIM, KID!!
DON'T KILL HIM!
MATCH-BEGIN!!!
RAAAA
PING
RAAA
SIGH...
RAAAA
I SUPPOSE I SHOULD CHUCK HER OFF THE STAGE...
FSSH
POW
UH...
UH...
TM
BM

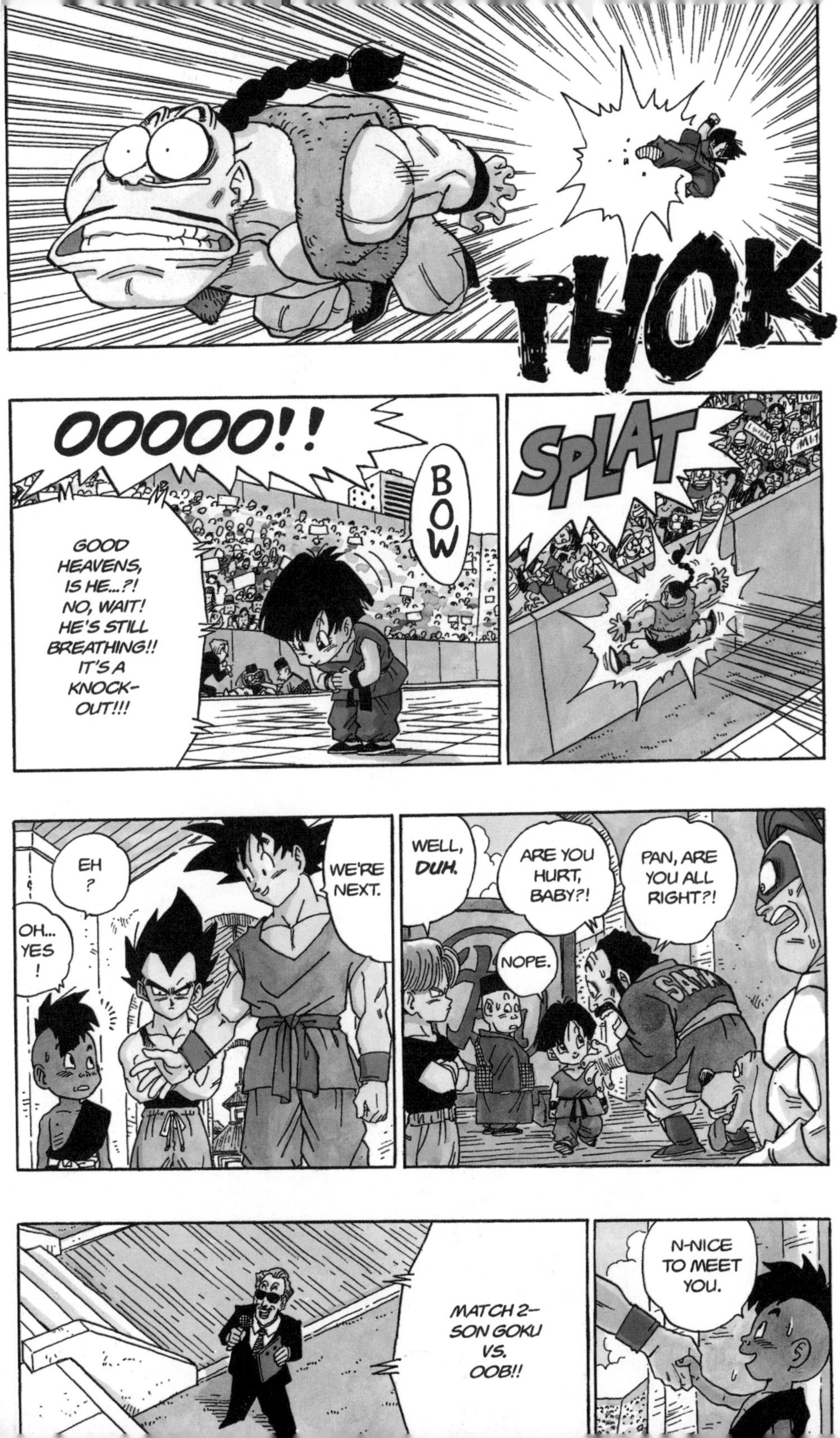
THOK
SPLAT
OOOOO!!
BOW
GOOD HEAVENS, IS HE...?! NO, WAIT! HE'S STILL BREATHING!! IT'S A KNOCK-OUT!!!
PAN, ARE YOU ALL RIGHT?!
ARE YOU HURT, BABY?!
WELL, DUH.
NOPE.
WE'RE NEXT.
EH ?
OH... YES !
N-NICE TO MEET YOU.
MATCH 2— SON GOKU VS. OOB!!

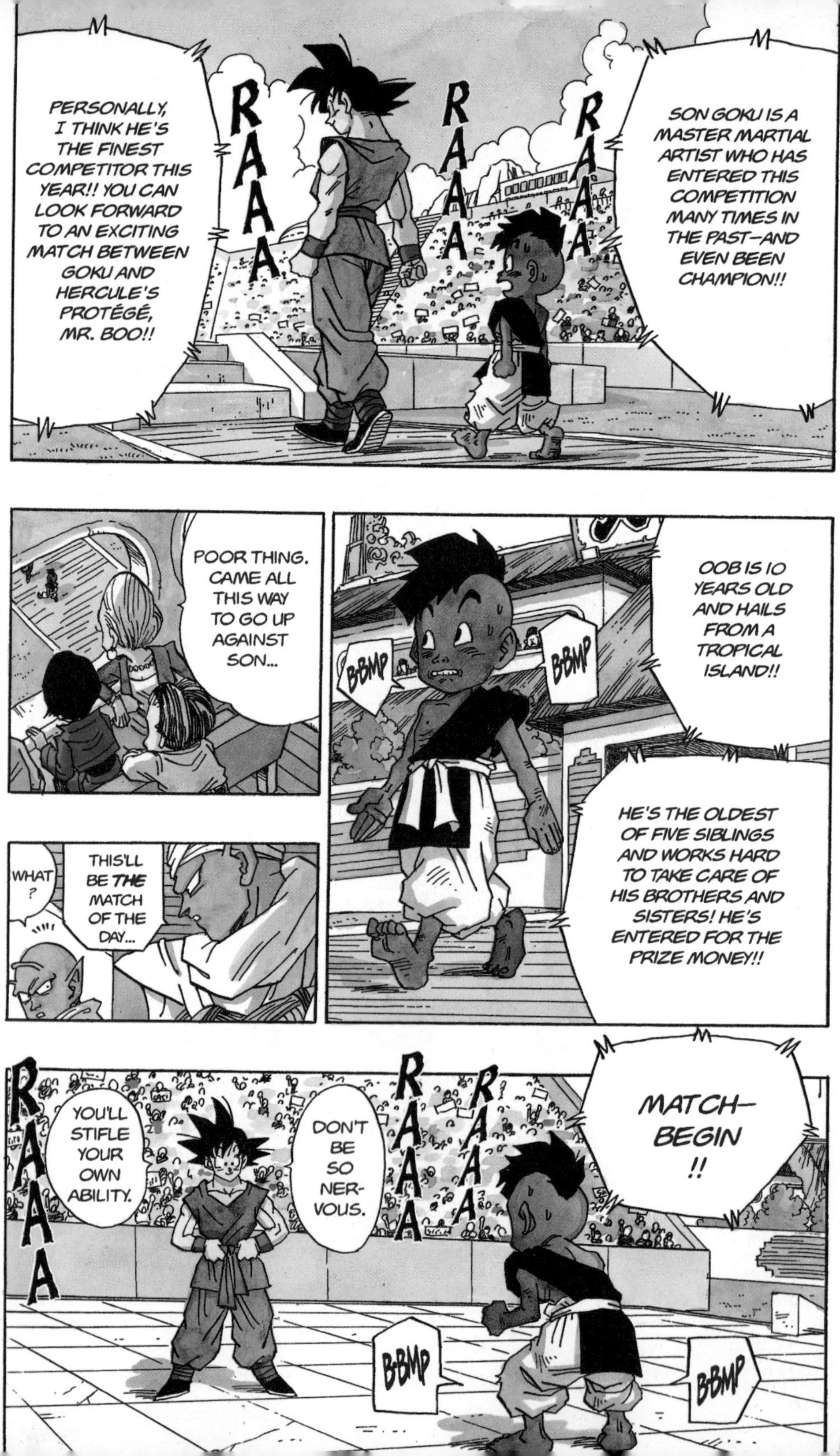
SON GOKU IS A MASTER MARTIAL ARTIST WHO HAS ENTERED THIS COMPETITION MANY TIMES IN THE PAST—AND EVEN BEEN CHAMPION!!
RAAA
RAAA
RAAA
PERSONALLY, I THINK HE'S THE FINEST COMPETITOR THIS YEAR!! YOU CAN LOOK FORWARD TO AN EXCITING MATCH BETWEEN GOKU AND HERCULE'S PROTÉGÉ, MR. BOO!!
OOB IS 10 YEARS OLD AND HAILS FROM A TROPICAL ISLAND!!
B-BMP
B-BMP
HE'S THE OLDEST OF FIVE SIBLINGS AND WORKS HARD TO TAKE CARE OF HIS BROTHERS AND SISTERS! HE'S ENTERED FOR THE PRIZE MONEY!!
POOR THING. CAME ALL THIS WAY TO GO UP AGAINST SON...
THIS'LL BE ***THE*** MATCH OF THE DAY...
WHAT?
MATCH—BEGIN!!
RAAA
RAAA
DON'T BE SO NER-VOUS.
YOU'LL STIFLE YOUR OWN ABILITY.
RAAA
B-BMP
B-BMP

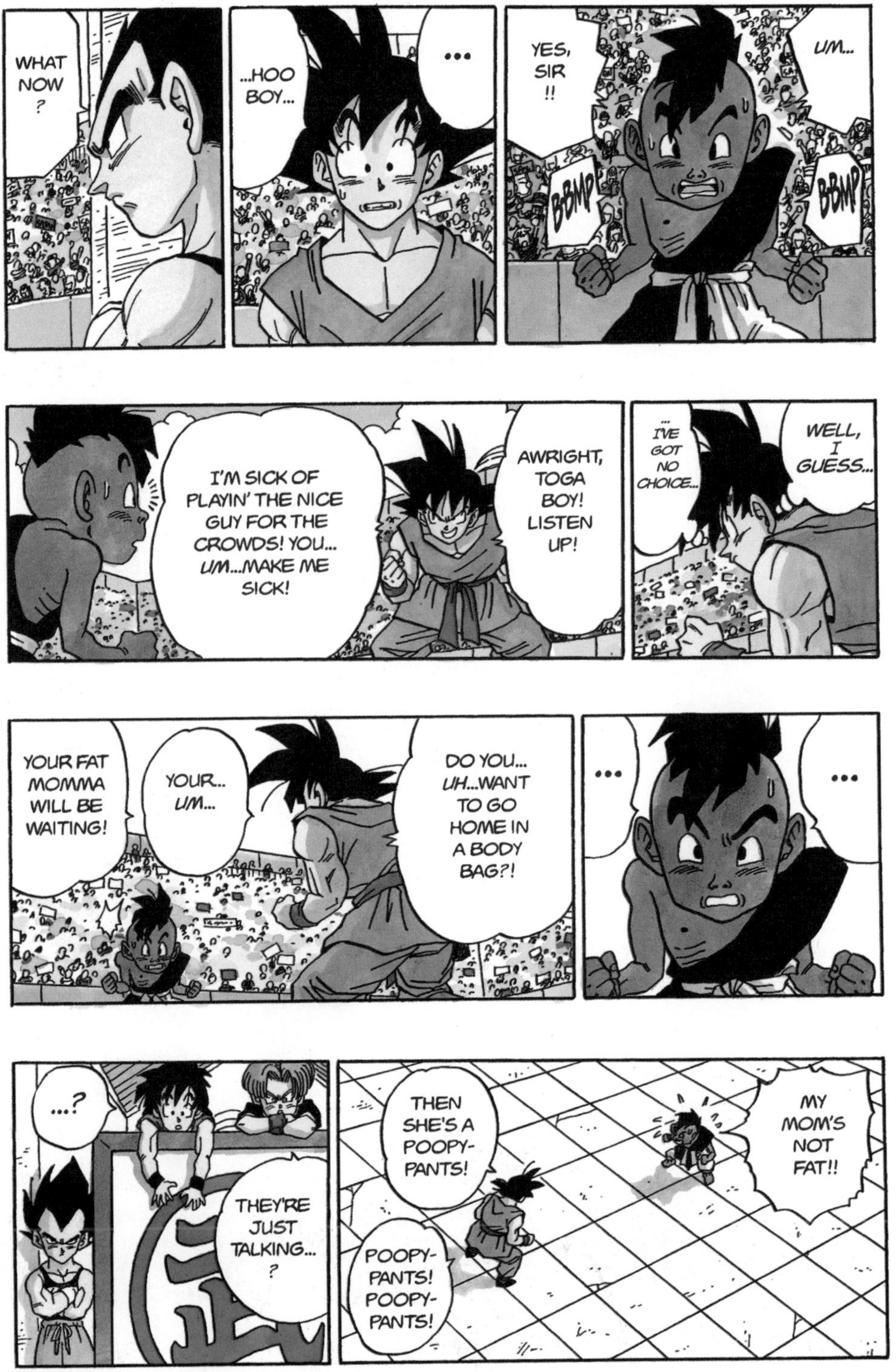
UM...
YES, SIR !!
BBMP
BBMP
...
...HOO BOY...
WHAT NOW ?
WELL, I GUESS...
... I'VE GOT NO CHOICE...
AWRIGHT, TOGA BOY! LISTEN UP!
I'M SICK OF PLAYIN' THE NICE GUY FOR THE CROWDS! YOU... UM...MAKE ME SICK!
...
...
DO YOU... UH...WANT TO GO HOME IN A BODY BAG?!
YOUR.. UM...
YOUR FAT MOMMA WILL BE WAITING!
MY MOM'S NOT FAT!!
THEN SHE'S A POOPY-PANTS!
POOPY-PANTS! POOPY-PANTS!
...?
THEY'RE JUST TALKING... ?

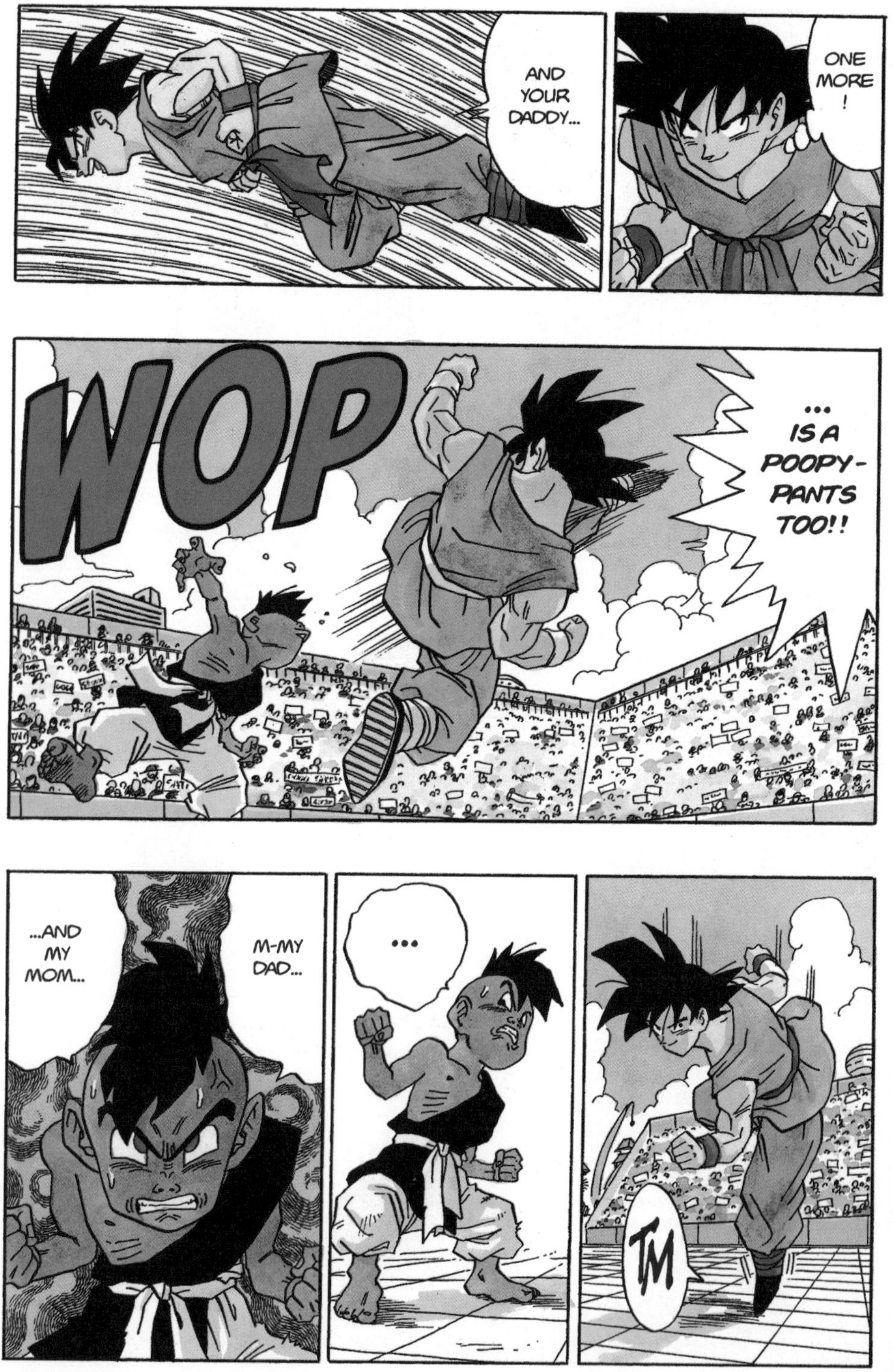
ONE MORE !
AND YOUR DADDY...
... IS A POOPY-PANTS TOO!!
WOP
TM
...
M-MY DAD...
...AND MY MOM...

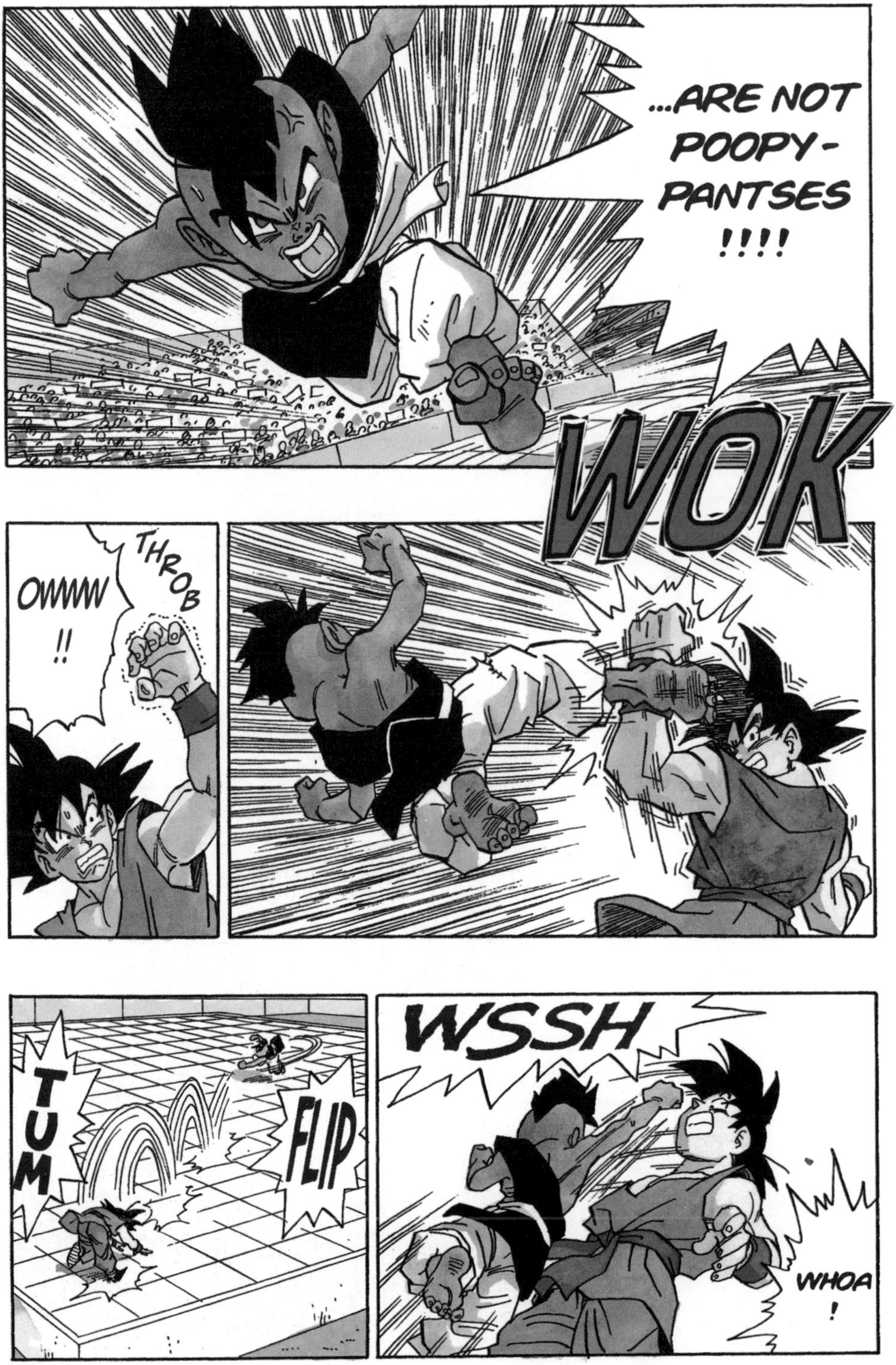
...ARE NOT POOPY-PANTSES !!!!
WOK
THROB
OWWW !!
WSSH
WHOA !
FLIP
TUM

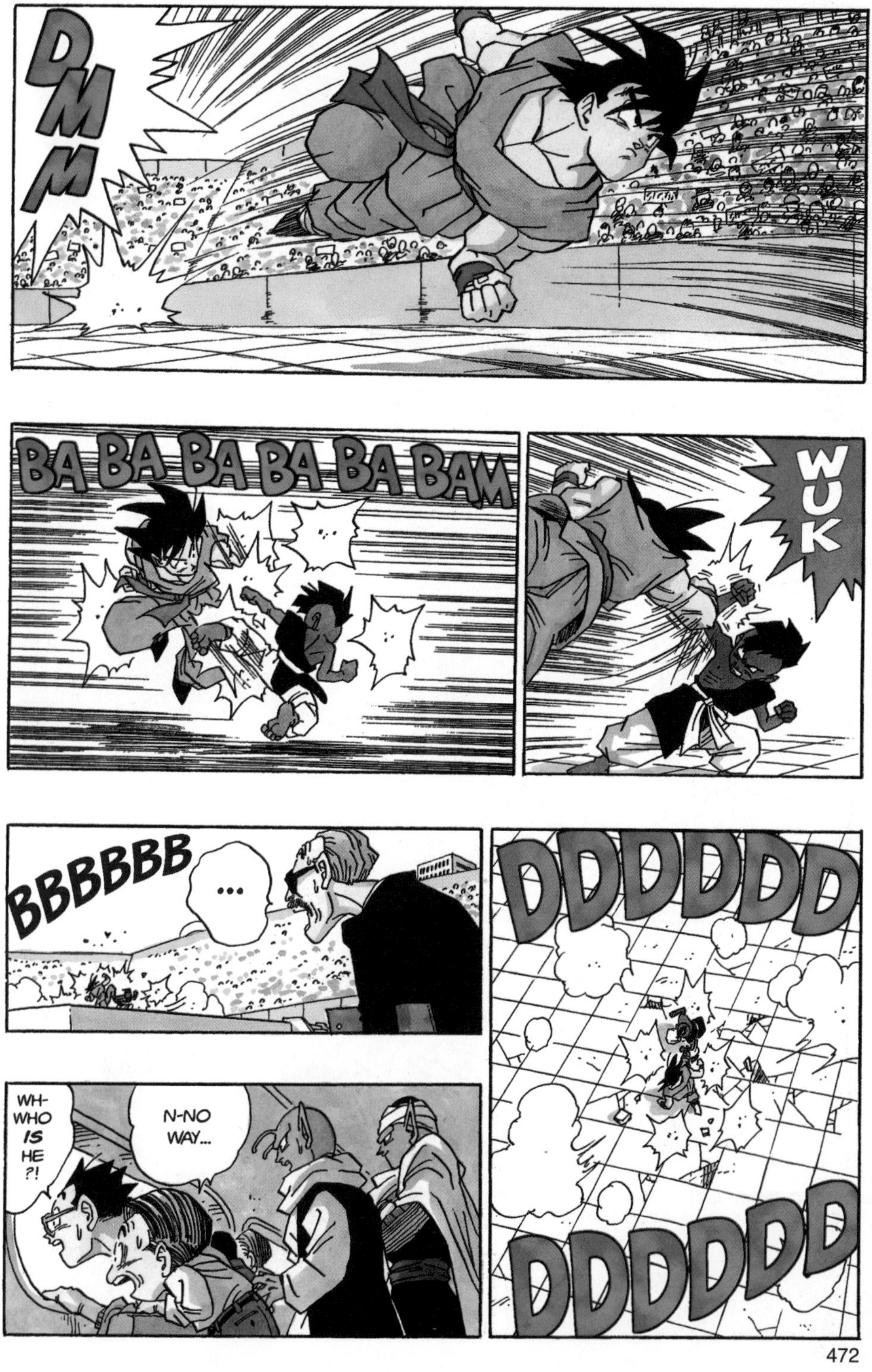
DMM
WUK
BA BA BA BA BA BAM
DDDDDD
DDDDDD
BBBBBB
...
N-NO WAY...
WH-WHO IS HE ?!

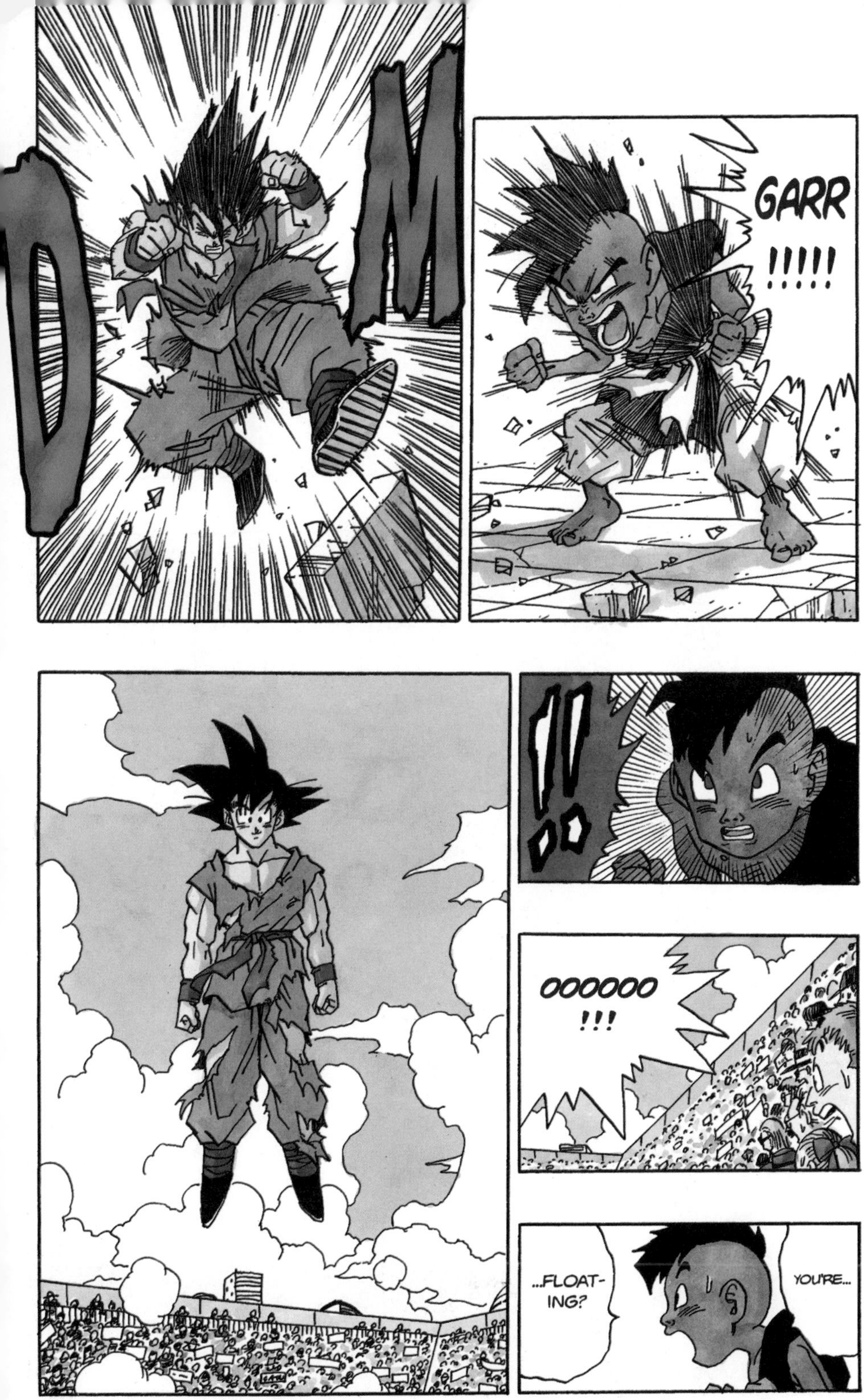
GARR
!!!!!
!!
OOOOOO
!!!
YOU'RE...
...FLOAT-
ING?

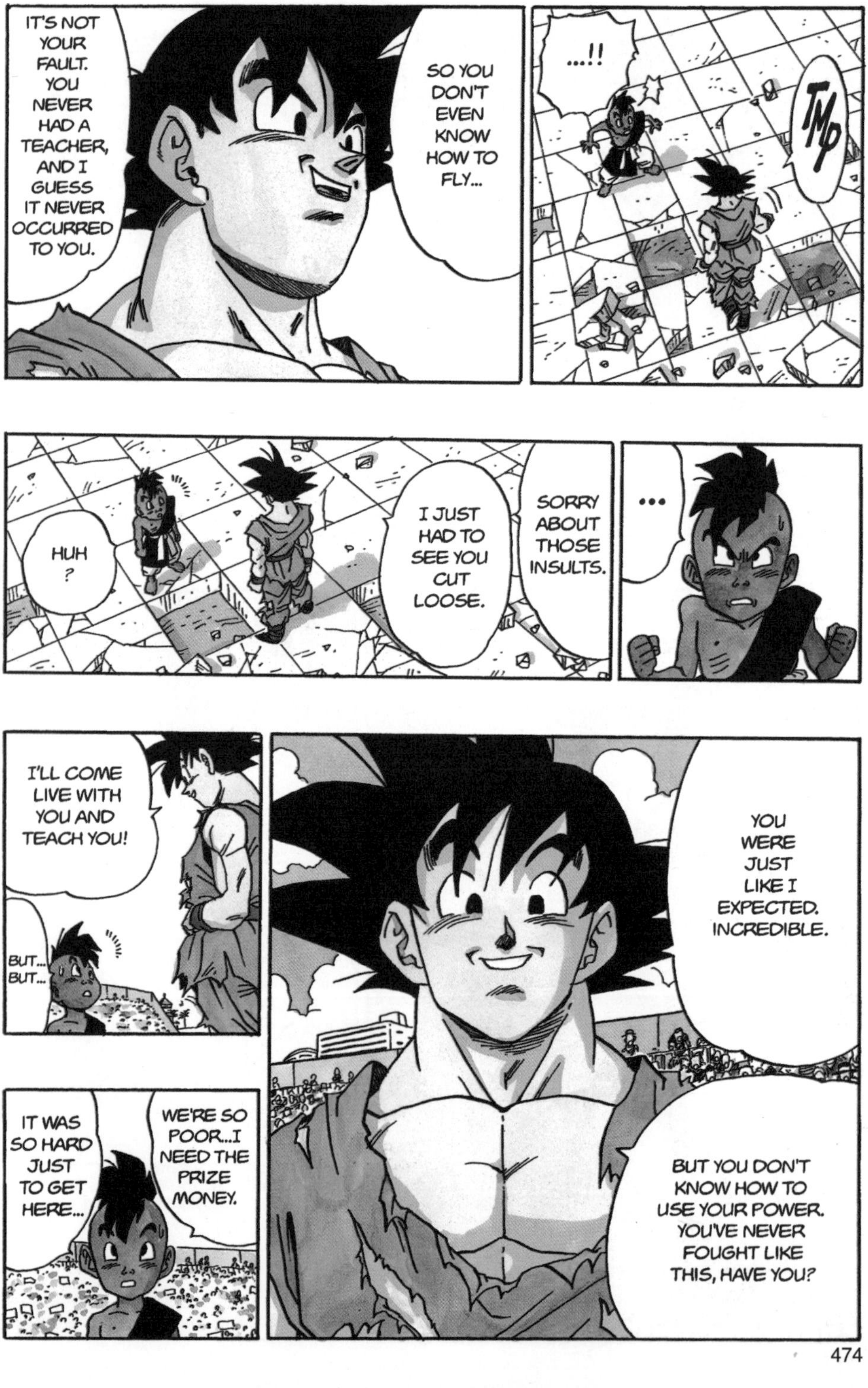
...!!
TMP
SO YOU DON'T EVEN KNOW HOW TO FLY...
IT'S NOT YOUR FAULT. YOU NEVER HAD A TEACHER, AND I GUESS IT NEVER OCCURRED TO YOU.
...
SORRY ABOUT THOSE INSULTS.
I JUST HAD TO SEE YOU CUT LOOSE.
HUH?
YOU WERE JUST LIKE I EXPECTED. INCREDIBLE.
BUT YOU DON'T KNOW HOW TO USE YOUR POWER. YOU'VE NEVER FOUGHT LIKE THIS, HAVE YOU?
I'LL COME LIVE WITH YOU AND TEACH YOU!
BUT... BUT...
WE'RE SO POOR...I NEED THE PRIZE MONEY.
IT WAS SO HARD JUST TO GET HERE...

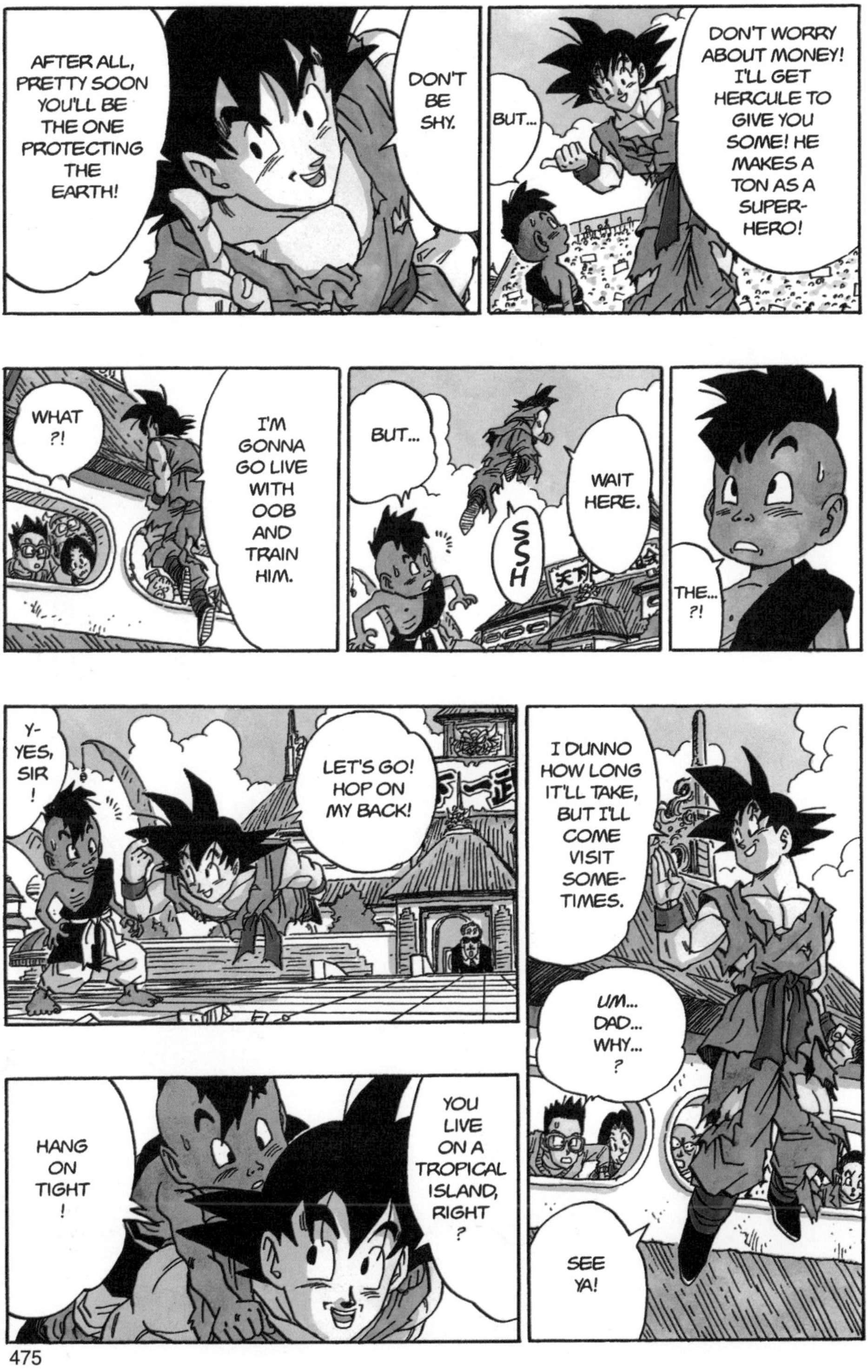
DON'T WORRY ABOUT MONEY! I'LL GET HERCULE TO GIVE YOU SOME! HE MAKES A TON AS A SUPER-HERO!
BUT...
DON'T BE SHY.
AFTER ALL, PRETTY SOON YOU'LL BE THE ONE PROTECTING THE EARTH!
THE...?!
WAIT HERE.
SSH
BUT...
I'M GONNA GO LIVE WITH OOB AND TRAIN HIM.
WHAT?!
I DUNNO HOW LONG IT'LL TAKE, BUT I'LL COME VISIT SOME-TIMES.
UM... DAD... WHY...?
SEE YA!
LET'S GO! HOP ON MY BACK!
Y-YES, SIR!
YOU LIVE ON A TROPICAL ISLAND, RIGHT?
HANG ON TIGHT!

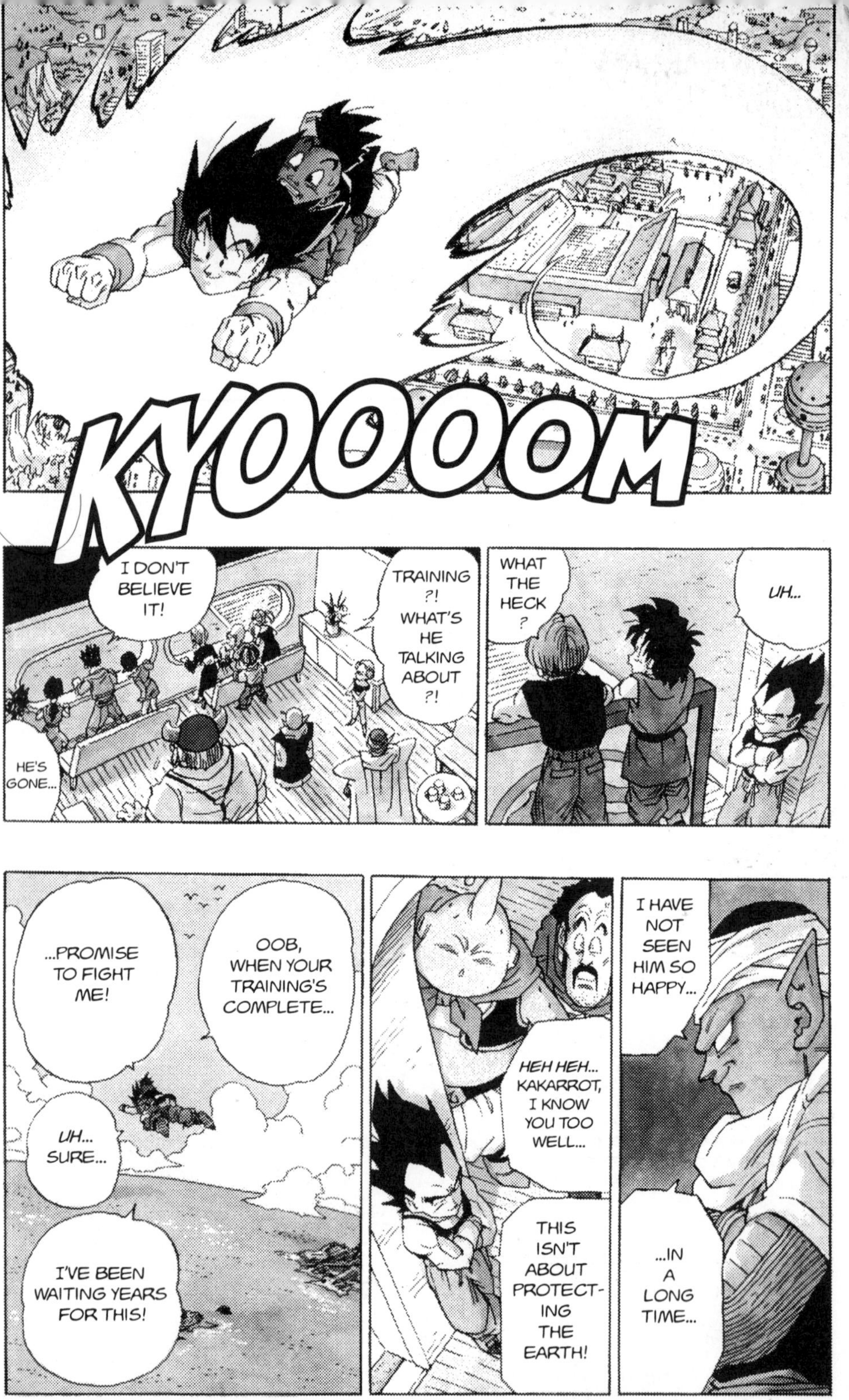
KYOOOOM
UH...
WHAT THE HECK?
TRAINING?! WHAT'S HE TALKING ABOUT?!
I DON'T BELIEVE IT!
HE'S GONE...
I HAVE NOT SEEN HIM SO HAPPY...
...IN A LONG TIME...
HEH HEH... KAKARROT, I KNOW YOU TOO WELL...
THIS ISN'T ABOUT PROTECT-ING THE EARTH!
OOB, WHEN YOUR TRAINING'S COMPLETE...
...PROMISE TO FIGHT ME!
UH... SURE...
I'VE BEEN WAITING YEARS FOR THIS!

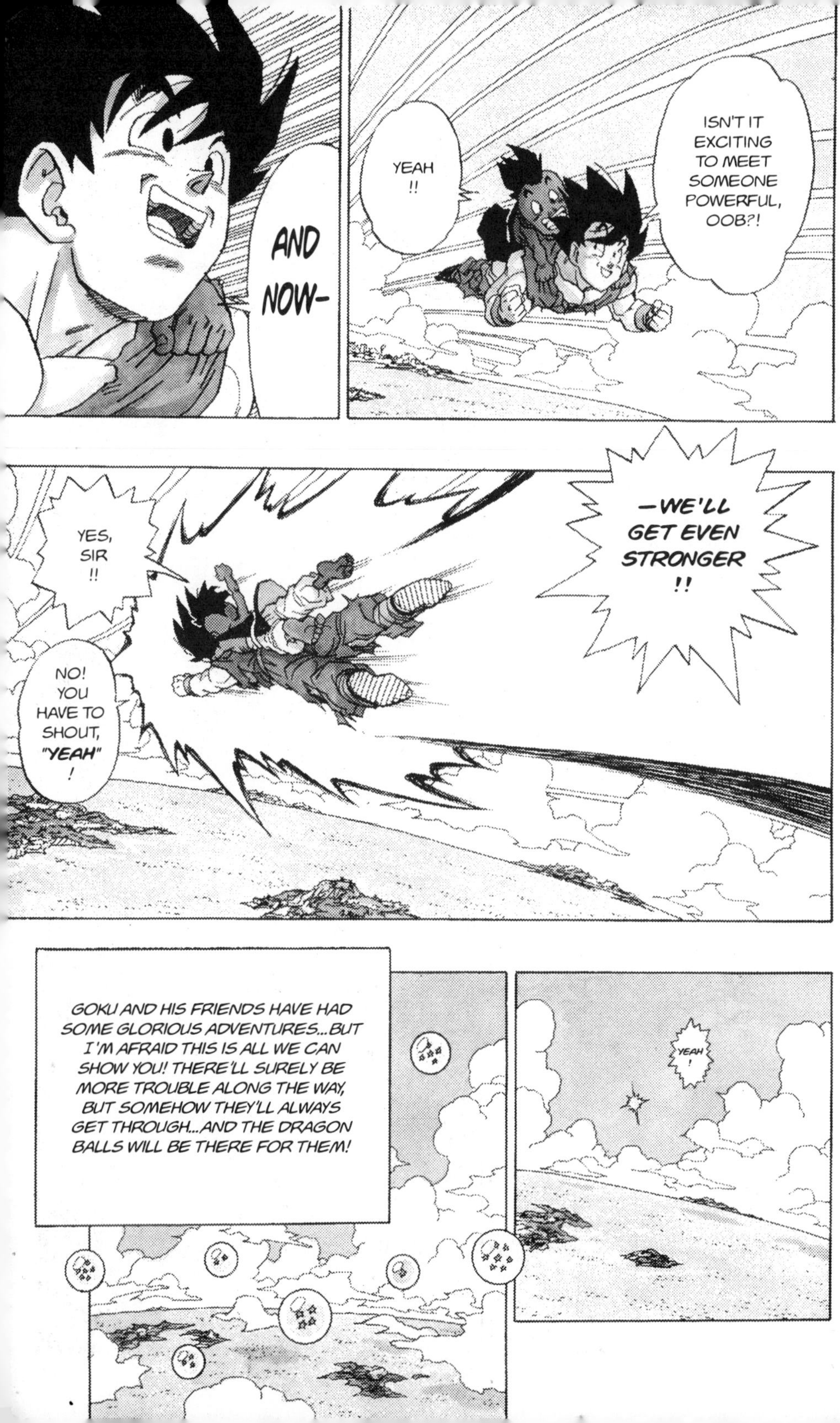
ISN'T IT EXCITING TO MEET SOMEONE POWERFUL, OOB?!
YEAH !!
AND NOW-
—WE'LL GET EVEN STRONGER !!
YES, SIR !!
NO! YOU HAVE TO SHOUT, "YEAH" !
YEAH !
GOKU AND HIS FRIENDS HAVE HAD SOME GLORIOUS ADVENTURES...BUT I'M AFRAID THIS IS ALL WE CAN SHOW YOU! THERE'LL SURELY BE MORE TROUBLE ALONG THE WAY, BUT SOMEHOW THEY'LL ALWAYS GET THROUGH...AND THE DRAGON BALLS WILL BE THERE FOR THEM!

THANK YOU!! AND GOODBYE!!

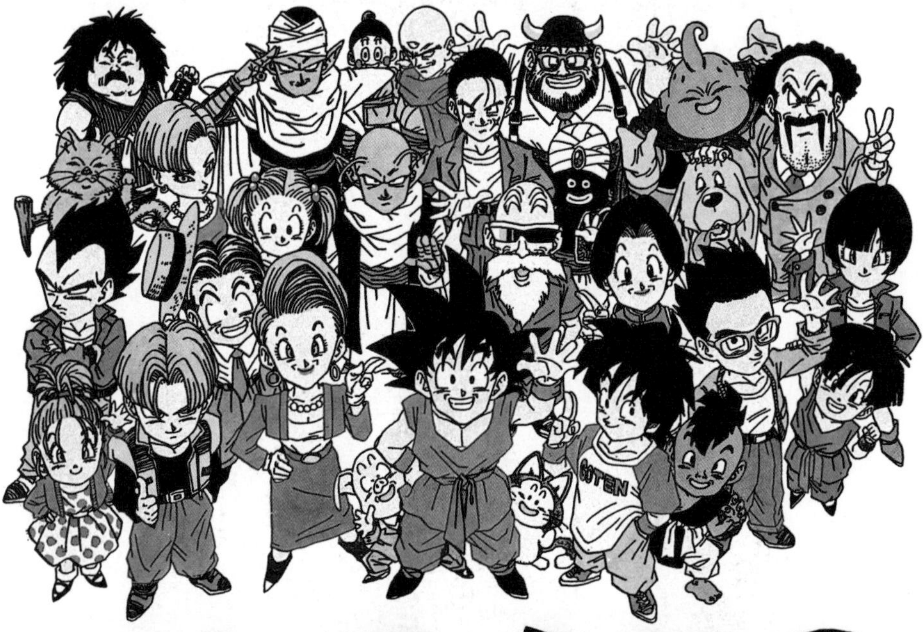

THE END

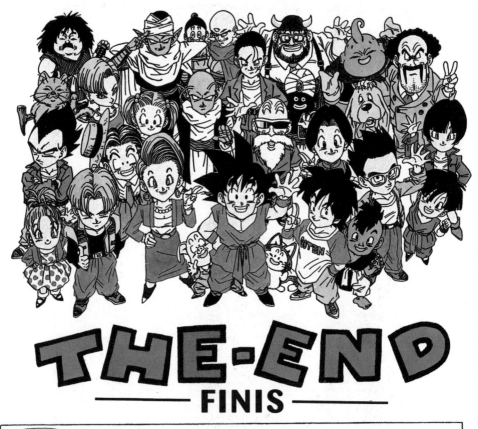

FINIS

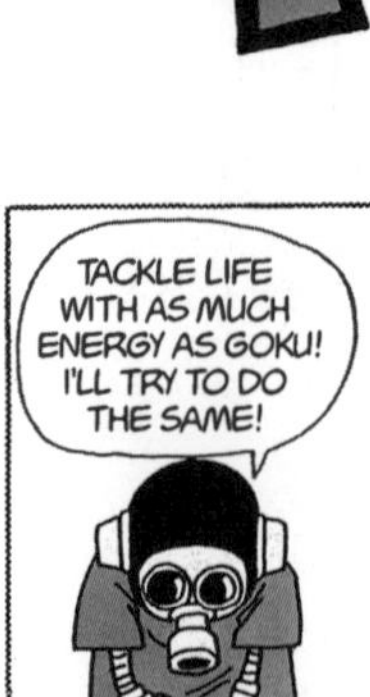
TACKLE LIFE WITH AS MUCH ENERGY AS GOKU! I'LL TRY TO DO THE SAME!

Thank you so much for reading **Dragon Ball** for all these years. I'm grateful for all the support you've shown me, right to the finish line! I've been planning this end for quite a while–I'm sorry that it had to be announced so suddenly. My editors have agreed to let me end this manga so I can take some new steps in life. It's time to take a break–although I may draw some one-shots here and there. I'm sure you'll see me again, and I'm sure it'll be fun (or at least, I hope so), so stay tuned! Until we meet again–so long!

–Akira Toriyama
May 1995

DRAGON BALL Z: THE END

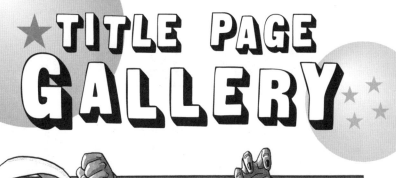

TITLE PAGE GALLERY

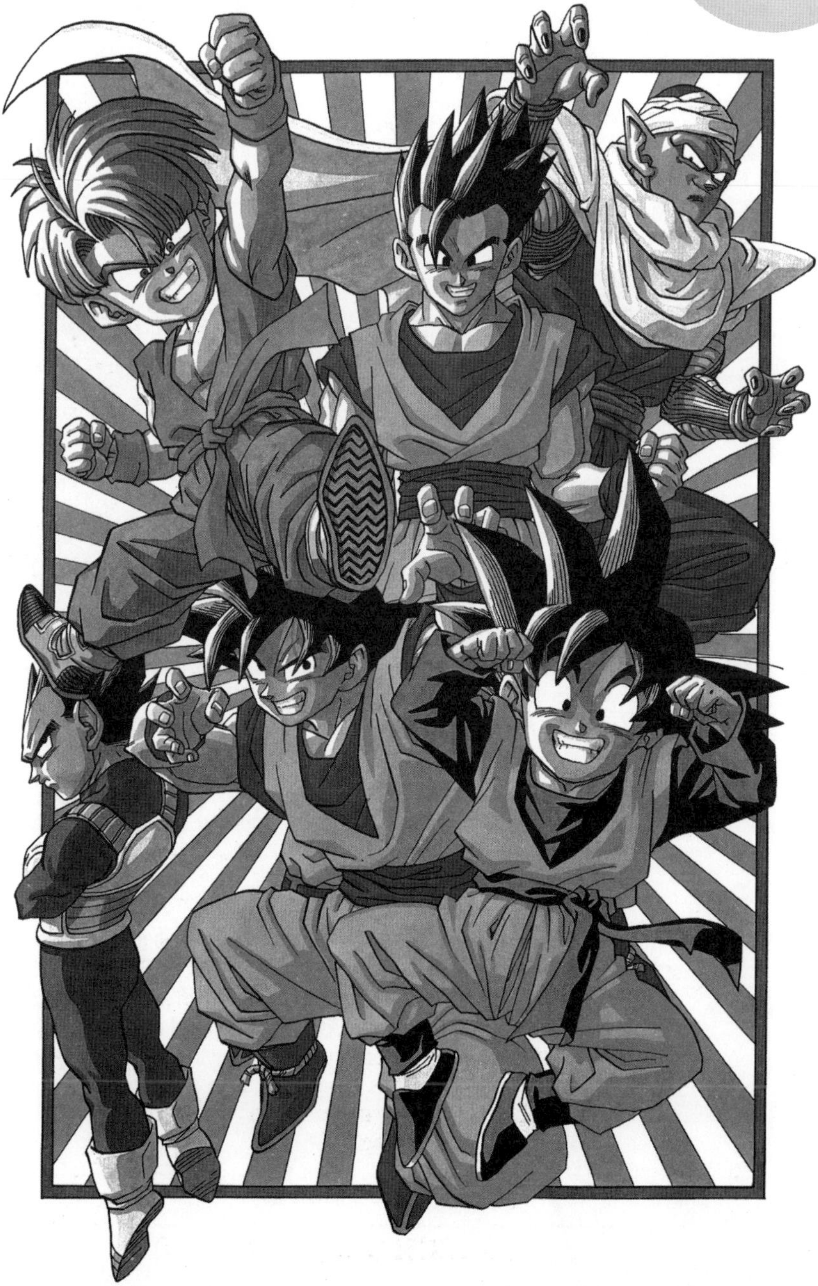

DRAGON BALL

DBZ:292
The New, Terrible Boo

DRAGON BALL ドラゴンボール

DBZ:295 · The Confidence Of Gotenks!!

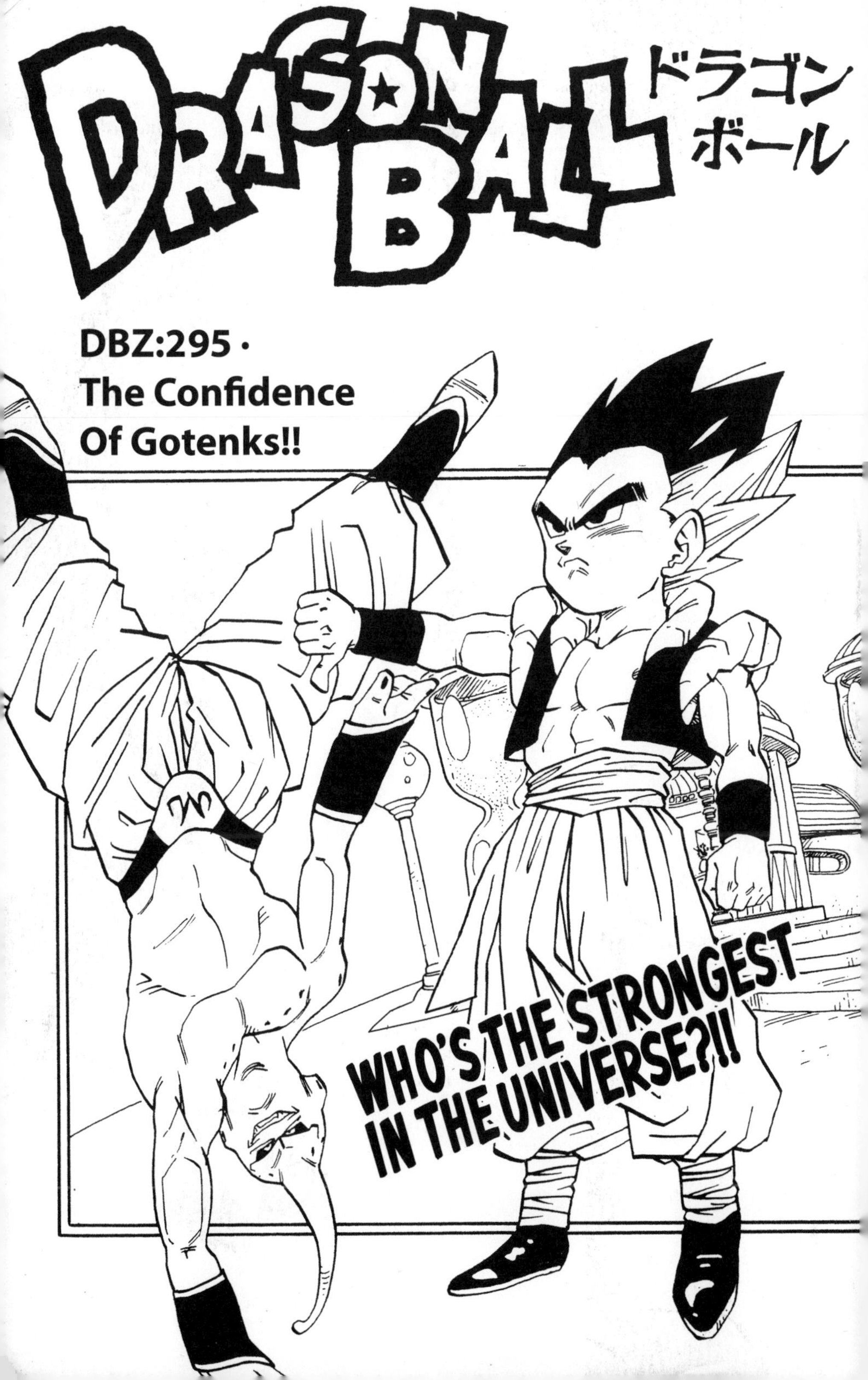
WHO'S THE STRONGEST IN THE UNIVERSE?!!

DRAGON BALL

ドラゴンボール

**DBZ:300 ·
Super Gotenks!**

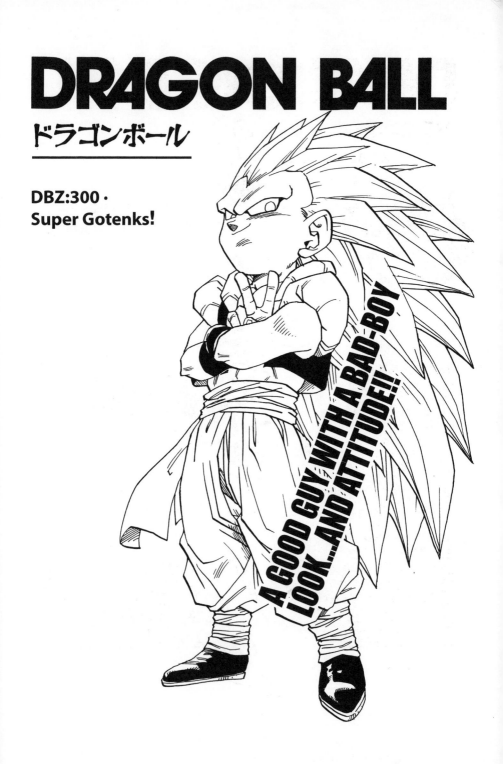

A GOOD GUY WITH A BAD-BOY LOOK...AND ATTITUDE!!

DRAGON BALL

ドラゴンボール

DBZ:303 · Gohan's Counterattack!

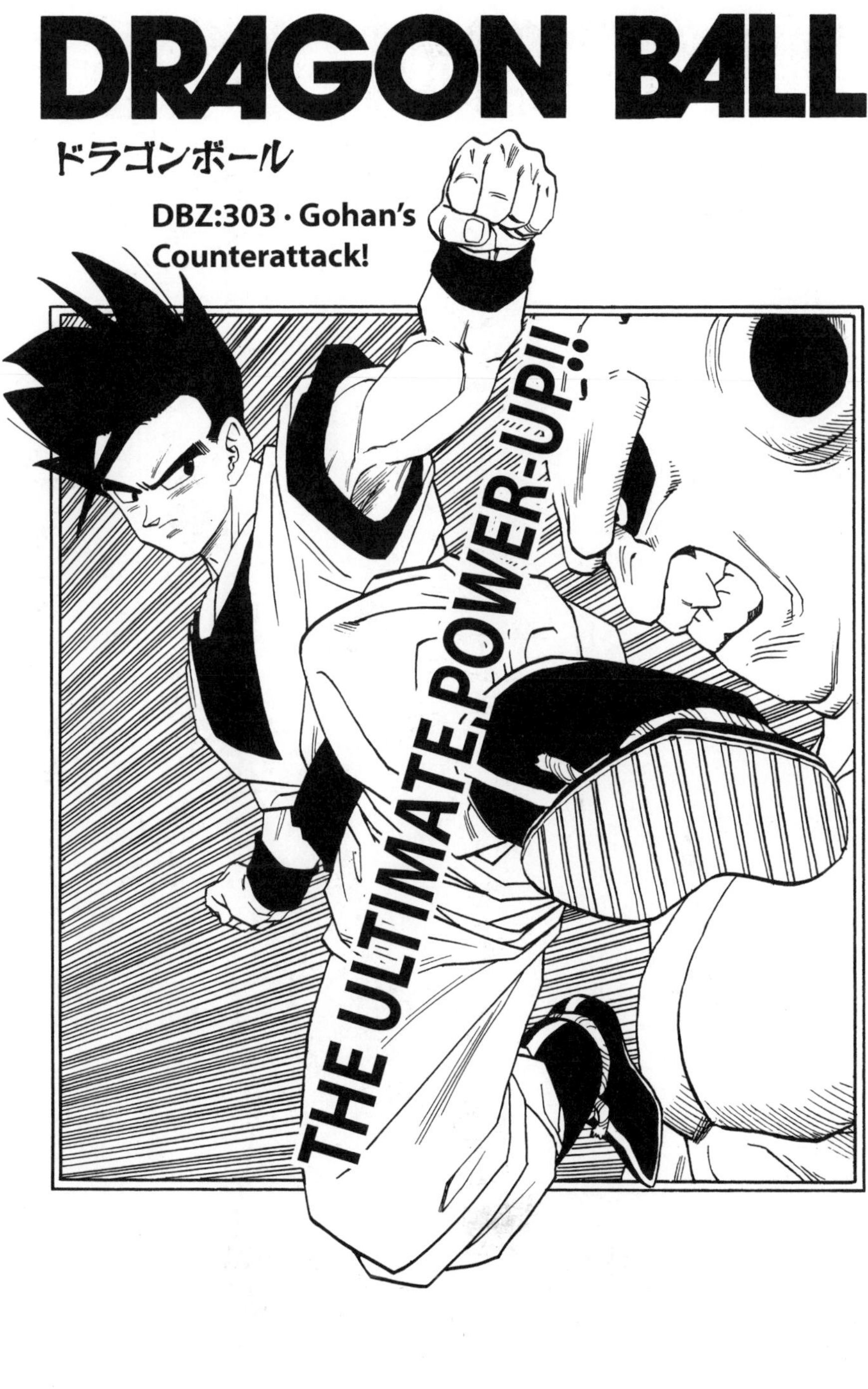
THE ULTIMATE POWER-UP!!

DRAGON BALL

ドラゴンボール

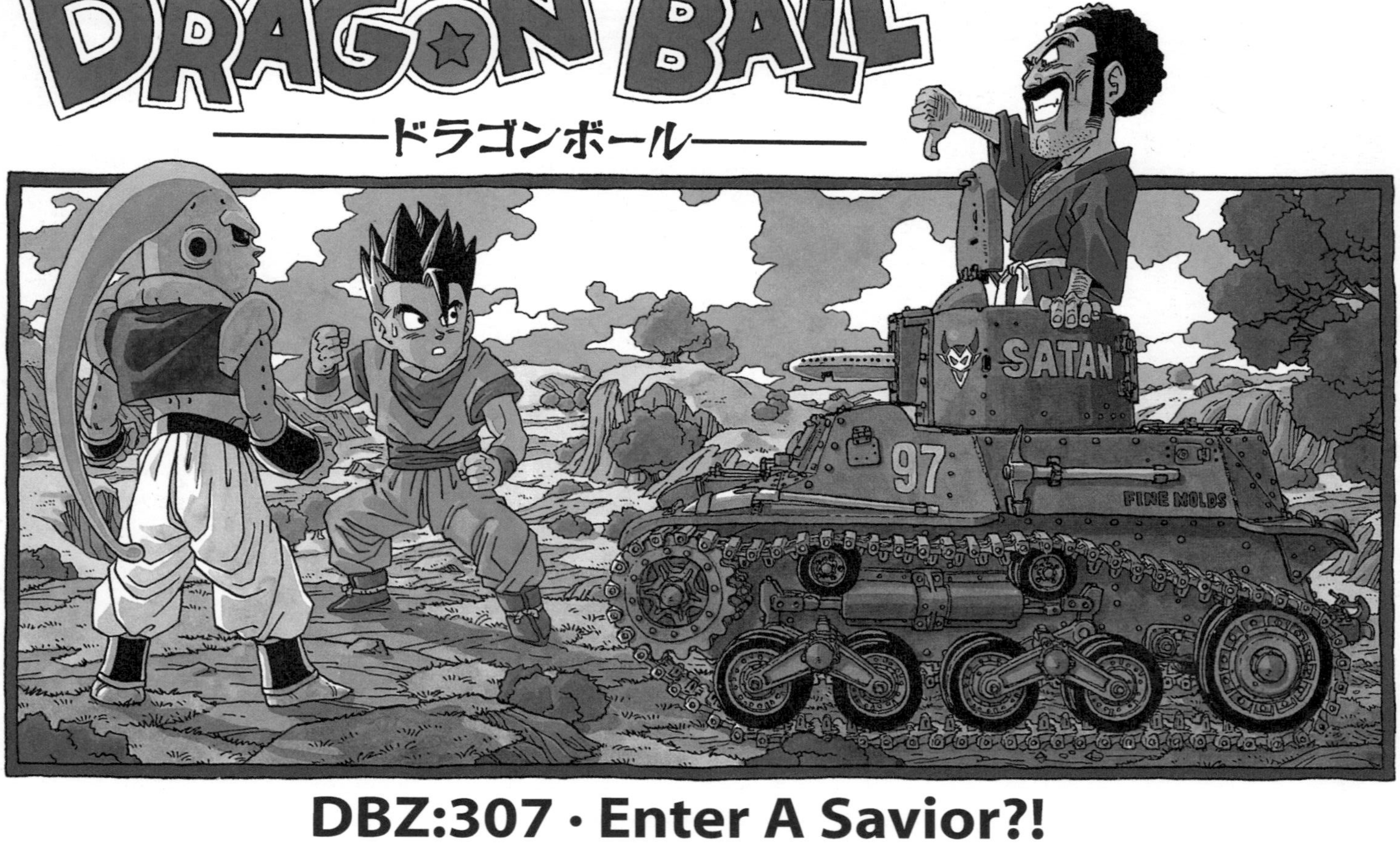
SATAN
97
FINE MOLDS

DBZ:307 · Enter A Savior?!

COLOR ART ILLUSTRATIONS

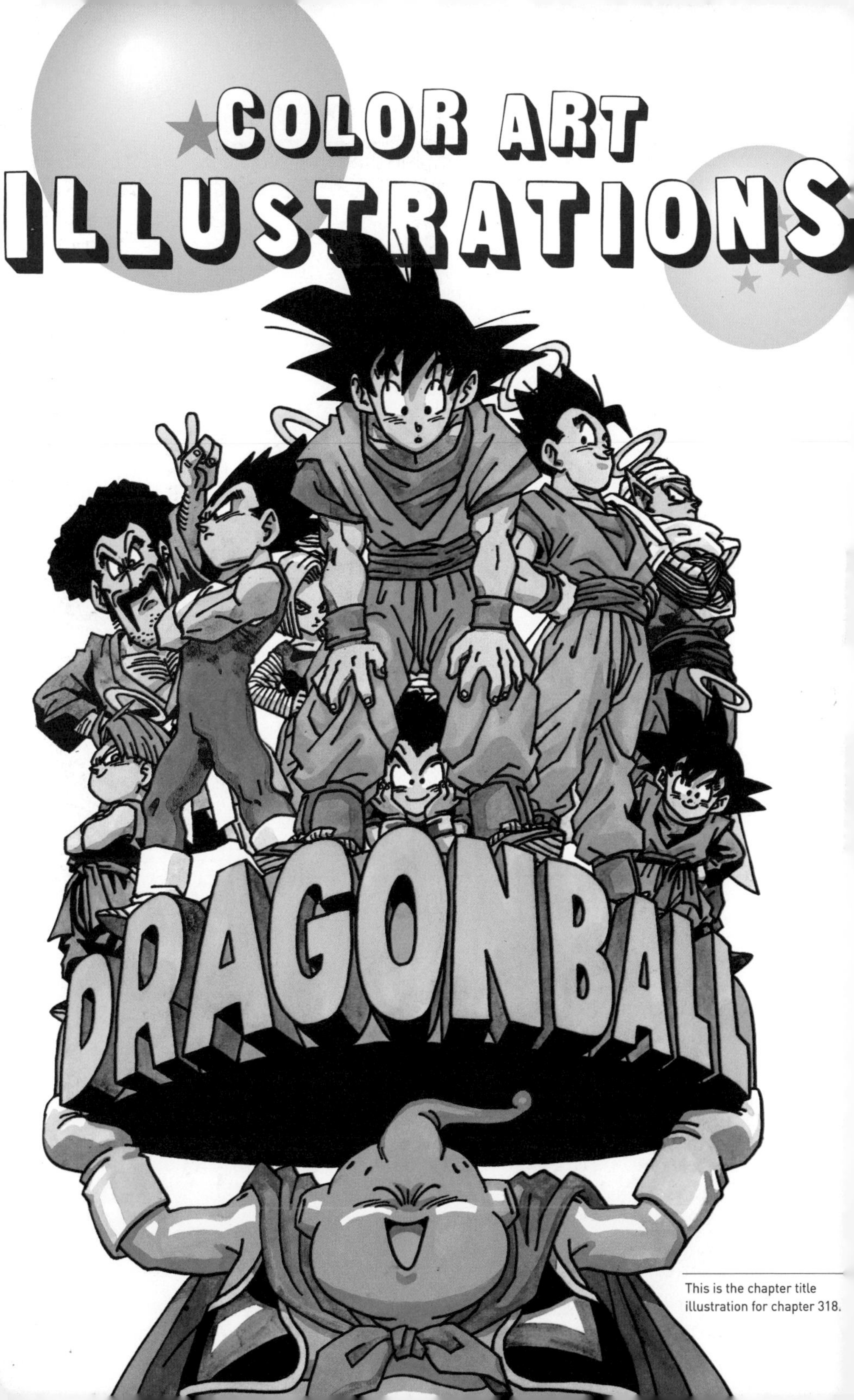
DRAGONBALL

This is the chapter title illustration for chapter 318.

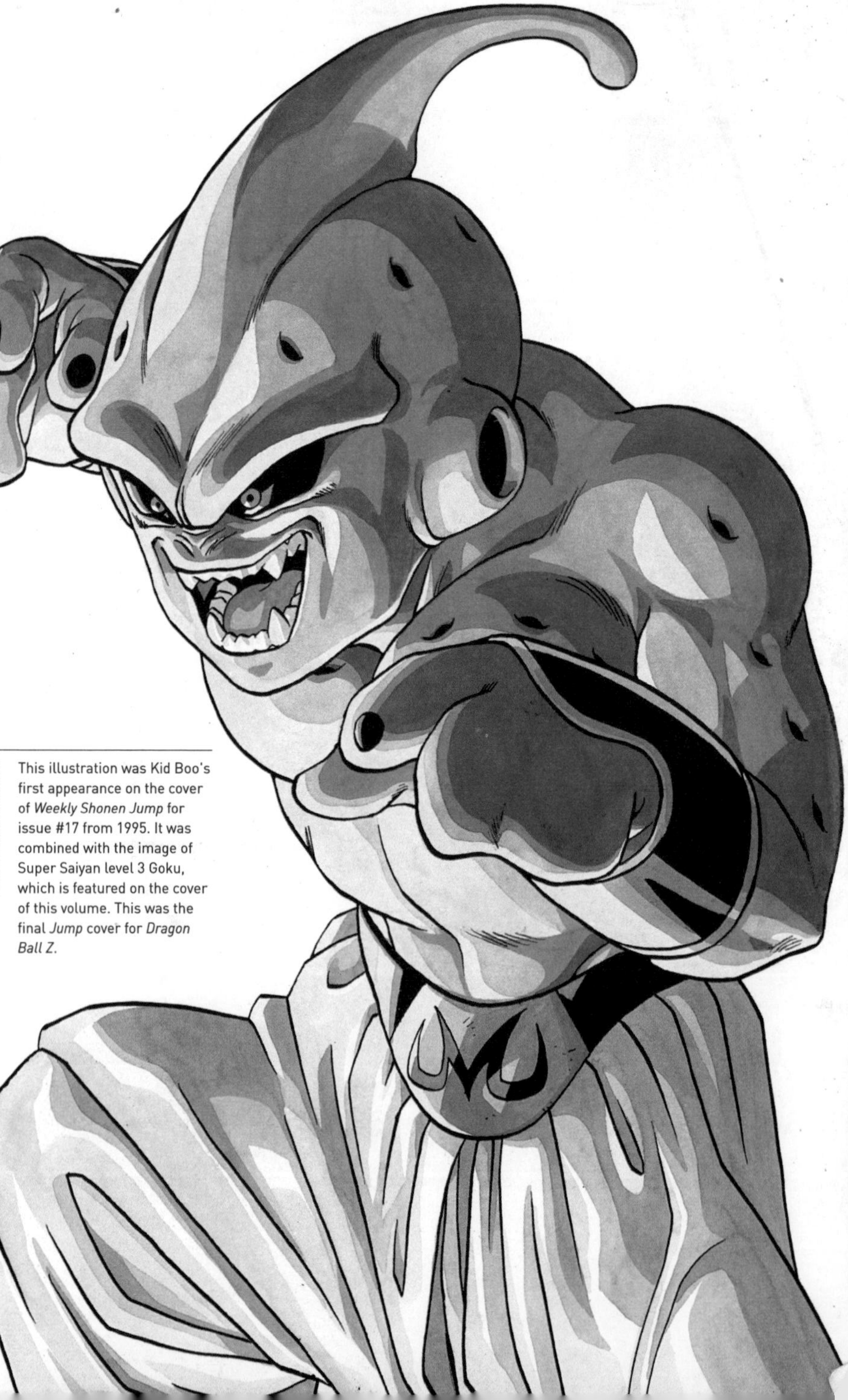

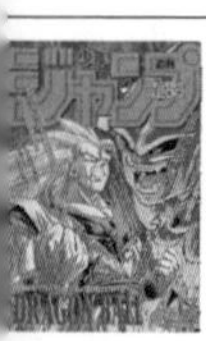

This illustration was Kid Boo's first appearance on the cover of *Weekly Shonen Jump* for issue #17 from 1995. It was combined with the image of Super Saiyan level 3 Goku, which is featured on the cover of this volume. This was the final *Jump* cover for *Dragon Ball Z*.

AUTHOR NOTES

1994

VOLUME 25

As of writing this, I have only three more chapters to do before *Dragon Ball Z* comes to its conclusion. It looks like it'll end on a high note thanks to all the fan support. Thank you!! I'm sorry it has come to an end, but I've wanted to take things easier for a while and draw new manga at a pace I find more comfortable. The series will end with volume 26, and the last volume with be extra thick—just like this one. Enjoy!

VOLUME 26

It's our final volume! I tried to keep the end low-key, almost as if the story might keep going. What do you think of it? Thanks to all of you who stuck with me through 42 volumes [counting from the beginning of *Dragon Ball*—Ed.] and to everyone who sent fan mail and presents. I'm sorry I haven't been able to reply. Thank you from the bottom of my heart!! Goodbye.

1995

THE END

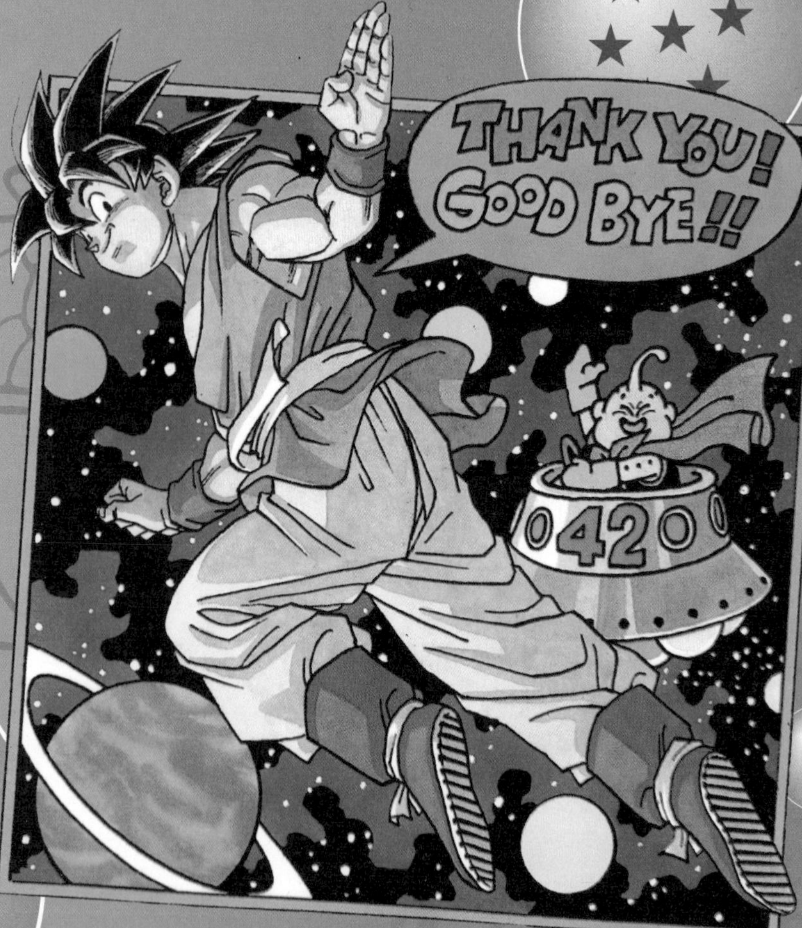
THANK YOU! GOOD BYE!!

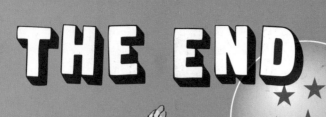

Thanks for reading *Dragon Ball Z* VIZBIG!
Now go tackle other manga with the same
enthusiasm as Goku. That's what I'm gonna do!